Social Work Practice

Method I & II

Dean Hepworth | Ronald Rooney | Glenda Dewberry Rooney | Kimberly Stron-Gottfried | Edward Neukrig | Alan Schwitzer | Karen Kirst-Ashman | Grafton Hull

CENGAGE Learning·

Australia • Brazil • Japan • Korea • Mexico • Singapore • Spain • United Kingdom • United States

Social Work Practice
Method I & II

Senior Manager, Student Engagement:
  Linda deStefano
  Janey Moeller

Manager, Student Engagement:
  Julie Dierig

Marketing Manager:
  Rachael Kloos

Manager, Production Editorial:
  Kim Fry

Manager, Intellectual Property Project Manager:
  Brian Methe

Senior Manager, Production and Manufacturing:
  Donna M. Brown

Manager, Production:
  Terri Daley

Direct Social Work Practice: Theory and Skills, Ninth Edition
Hepworth / Rooney / Dewberry Rooney / Strom-Gotfried
© 2013, 2010 Cengage Learning. All rights reserved.

Skills and Tools for Today's Counselors and Psychotherapists: From
Natural Helping to Professional Counseling
Neukrug / Schwitzer
© 2006 Cengage Learning. All rights reserved.

Understanding Generalist Practice, Seventh Edition
Kirst-Ashman / Hull
© 2015, 2012 Cengage Learning. All rights reserved.

For product information and technology assistance, contact us at
Cengage Learning Customer & Sales Support, 1-800-354-9706

For permission to use material from this text or product,
submit all requests online at **cengage.com/permissions**
Further permissions questions can be emailed to
permissionrequest@cengage.com

This book contains select works from existing Cengage Learning resources and
was produced by Cengage Learning Custom Solutions for collegiate use. As such,
those adopting and/or contributing to this work are responsible for editorial
content accuracy, continuity and completeness.

Compilation © 2014 Cengage Learning

ISBN-13: 978-1-305-01605-7
ISBN-10: 1-305-01605-X

WCN: 01-100-101

Cengage Learning
5191 Natorp Boulevard
Mason, Ohio 45040
USA

Cengage Learning is a leading provider of customized learning solutions with
office locations around the globe, including Singapore, the United Kingdom,
Australia, Mexico, Brazil, and Japan. Locate your local office at:
international.cengage.com/region.

Cengage Learning products are represented in Canada by Nelson Education, Ltd.
For your lifelong learning solutions, visit **www.cengage.com/custom.**
Visit our corporate website at **www.cengage.com.**

Printed in the United States of America

Brief Contents

CHAPTER 1

The Challenges of Social Work

CHAPTER OVERVIEW

This chapter presents a context and philosophy for direct practice, definitions of direct and clinical practice and descriptions of the varied roles played by direct social work practitioners. After completing this chapter, you will be able to:

- introduces the mission of social work and the purposes of social work services
- illustrates the roles played by social workers within the organizational context for such services
- identifies the value perspectives that guide social workers
- introduces systems and ecological concepts for understanding the interaction of individuals and families with their environments
- introduces competencies that you will be expected to achieve in your academic career
- introduces our perspective on diversity that will guide how we present issues related to diversity

EPAS COMPETENCIES IN THE 1ST CHAPTER

This chapter will give you the information needed to meet the following practice competencies:

2.1.1 Social workers Identify as professionals and conduct themselves accordingly

2.1.2 Social workers apply social work ethical principles to guide professional practice.

2.1.2a Social workers recognize and manage personal values in a way that allows professional values to guide practice

2.1.2b Social workers make ethical decisions by applying standards of the National Association of Social Workers Code of Ethics and, as applicable, of the International Federation of Social Workers/International Association of Schools of Social Work Ethics in Social Work, Statement of Principles

2.1.3 Social workers apply critical thinking to inform and communicate professional judgments.

2.1.3b Social workers analyze models of assessment, prevention, intervention, and evaluation

2.1.4 Social workers engage diversity and difference in practice

2.1.5b Social workers advocate for human rights and social and economic justice.

2.1.5c Social workers engage in practices that engage in social and economic justice.

2.1.6 Social workers engage in research-informed practice and practice-informed research.

2.1.7 Social workers apply knowledge of human behavior and the social environment.

2.1.8 Social workers engage in policy practice to advance social and economic well-being and to deliver effective social work services

2.1.9 Social workers respond to contexts that shape practice.

2.1.10 Social workers engage, assess, intervene, and evaluate with individuals, families, groups, organizations and communities.

2.1.10a Social workers substantively and affectively prepare for action with individuals, families, groups, organizations, and communities

2.1.10b Social workers use empathy and other interpersonal skills.

2.1.10c Social workers develop a mutually agreed-on focus of work and desired outcomes with clients.

2.1.10d Social workers collect, organize, and interpret client data to inform practice

2.1.10e Social workers assess client strengths and limitations.

B 2.2 Social workers carry out generalist practice.

M 2.2 Social workers carry out advanced practice.

This chapter begins with a case example that will provide the context for concepts to be introduced in the chapter.

This case example highlights several aspects of social work practice. As a profession, we are committed to the pursuit of social justice for poor, disadvantaged, disenfranchised, and oppressed people (Marsh, 2005; Finn & Jacobson, 2003a; Pelton, 2003; Van Wormer, 2002; Carniol, 1992). In this case, in addition to seeing Mrs. Ramirez as a parent struggling with school attendance issues, Tobias also saw her as a client experiencing challenges possibly related to the ambivalence and unresolved issues in the United States surrounding immigrants without documentation (Cleaveland, 2010; Padilla et al., 2008). A law passed by the U.S. House of Representatives in 2005, but not in the Senate, would have made it a crime for service providers to assist undocumented immigrants. However, according to the National Association of Social Workers' (NASW) Immigration

EP 2.1.5b & c

IDEAS IN ACTION

Marta Ramirez was referred to child welfare services because her two elementary school-aged children had more than seven days of unexcused absences from school during the semester, the standard for educational neglect in her state. When Tobias, a child welfare social worker, met with Mrs. Ramirez, he found that the children had missed similar amounts of time when they had previously lived in another state, as well as earlier, before they had emigrated without documents from Mexico. There had not been earlier investigations, however, as legal standards for educational neglect were different in the previous state. Mrs. Ramirez noted that her children had been frequently ill with "flu and asthma." She said that the children did not feel comfortable at the school. They felt that the teachers were mean to them because they were Hispanic. In addition, Mrs. Ramirez had sustained a back injury on her job that limited her ability to get out of bed some mornings. As an immigrant without documents, Mrs. Ramirez was ineligible for the surgery she needed. Finally, she acknowledged experiencing depression and anxiety.

Tobias shared with Mrs. Ramirez the reason for the referral under statute and asked for her perspective on school attendance. He explained that child welfare workers are called on to assist families in having their children educated. He also asked about how things were going for Mrs. Ramirez and her family in

their community. In so doing, Tobias explained his dual roles of responding to the law violation by statute and helping families address issues of concern to them.

Many social workers practice in settings, such as schools, where they perform dual roles, protecting both the community at large and vulnerable individuals, in addition to playing other supportive roles (Trotter, 2006). No matter where they are employed, social workers are influenced by the social work value of self-determination for their clients. For this reason, in addition to exploring school attendance issues with Mrs. Ramirez and her children, Tobias addressed Mrs. Ramirez's other concerns.

Mrs. Ramirez acknowledged that her children's school attendance had been sporadic. She attributed this to their illnesses, their feeling uncomfortable and unwelcome in the school, and her own health difficulties that inhibited her in getting the children ready for school.

Tobias asked Mrs. Ramirez if she would like to receive assistance in problem solving, both about how to get the children to school and how to help them to have a better educational experience there. In addition, while health issues were not served directly by his child welfare agency, Tobias offered to explore linkages with the medical field to address Mrs. Ramirez's health and depression concerns.

Toolkit (NASW, 2006, p. 4), "the plight of refugees and immigrants must be considered on the basis of human values and needs rather than on the basis of an ideological struggle related to foreign policy." The contrast between these two positions suggests that social workers grapple with issues of social justice in their everyday practice. As a social worker, Tobias could not personally resolve the uncertain situation of undocumented immigrants. However, he could work with Mrs. Ramirez and local health institutions to explore possible solutions. Social workers are not the only helping professionals who provide direct services to clients in need. We have a special interest, however, in helping empower members of oppressed groups (Parsons, 2002).

Social workers work in quite diverse settings—governmental agencies, schools, health care centers, family and child welfare agencies, mental health centers, business and industry, correctional settings, and private practices. Social workers work with people of all ages, races, ethnic groups, socioeconomic levels, religions, sexual orientations, and abilities. Social workers themselves variously describe their work as rewarding, frustrating, satisfying, discouraging, stressful, and, most of all, challenging.

In the case example, Mrs. Ramirez did not seek assistance. Instead, she was *referred* by school staff because of her children's poor class attendance, although she acknowledged problems in getting the children to school, as well as her health and depression concerns. Those who *apply* for services are most clearly *voluntary clients*. Many potential clients, including Mrs. Ramirez become more voluntary if their own concerns are explicitly addressed. Social workers practice with clients whose level of voluntarism ranges from *applicants* who seek a service to *legally mandated clients* who receive services under the threat of a court order. Many potential clients fall between these two extremes, as they are neither legally coerced nor seeking a service (Trotter, 2006). These potential clients who experience non legal pressures from family members, teachers, and referral sources are known as *nonvoluntary clients* (Rooney, R.H. 2009).

With each type of client (voluntary, legally mandated, and nonvoluntary), social work assessments include three facets:

EP 2.1.7 & 2.1.10e

1. Exploration of multiple concerns expressed by potential clients
2. Circumstances that might involve legally mandated intervention or concerns about health or safety
3. Other potential problems that emerge from the assessment

Such assessments also include strengths and potential resources. For example, Mrs. Ramirez's potential strengths and resources include her determination that her children have a better life than their parents and other community and spiritual support systems, both locally and in Mexico. Those potential resources must be assessed in the context of challenges, both internal and external, such as the lack of a health care safety net of undocumented immigrants and Mrs. Ramirez's own medical and psychological concerns.

The Mission of Social Work

The perspectives taken by social workers in their professional roles will influence how Mrs. Ramirez's concerns are conceptualized and addressed. According to the NASW, "the primary mission of the social work profession is to enhance human well-being and help meet the basic human needs of all people with particular attention to the needs and empowerment of people who are vulnerable, oppressed, and living in poverty" (NASW, 2008a). The International Federation of Social Workers defines the purpose of social work as including the promotion of social change and the empowerment and liberation of people to enhance well-being (IFSW, 2000, p. 1). Comparisons of the mission of social work in the United States to the international definition note the shared focus on marginalized peoples and empowerment, but add an emphasis on global and cultural sensitivity (Bidgood, Holosko, & Taylor, 2003).

In this book, we will delineate the core elements that lie at the heart of social work wherever it is practiced. These core elements can be classified into two dimensions: purposes of the profession and core competencies, where core competencies include characteristic knowledge, values, and practice behaviors (CSWE, 2008, p. 1). Chapter 1 presents the purposes of social work and the first nine core competencies. The tenth competency, which is to "engage, assess, intervene, and evaluate with individuals, families, groups, organizations, and communities" (EPAS, 2.1.10) will be reviewed in Chapter 3 and will become the foundation of the remaining chapters.

Purposes of Social Work

Social work practitioners help clients move toward specific objectives. The means of accomplishing those objectives, however, varies based on the unique circumstances of each client. Even so, all social workers share common goals that constitute the purpose and objectives of the profession. These goals unify the profession and help members avoid developing narrow perspectives that are limited to particular practice settings. To best serve their clients, social workers must be willing to assume responsibilities and engage in actions that expand upon the functions of specific social agencies and their designated individual roles as staff members. For example, the child welfare social worker who met with Mrs. Ramirez assessed her issues and concerns and went beyond the child protection mission of the child welfare setting.

EP 2.1.5

According to CSWE, the purpose of the social work profession is to "promote human and community well-being." Furthermore, that purpose "is actualized through its quest for social and economic justice, the prevention of conditions that limit human rights, the elimination of poverty, and the enhancement of the quality of life for all persons" (CSWE, 2008, p. 1). The pursuit of social and economic justice is central to social work's purpose. Social justice refers to the creation of social institutions that support the welfare of individuals and groups (Center for Economic and Social Justice, www.cesj.org/thirdway/economicjustice-defined.htm). Economic justice, then, refers to those aspects of social justice that relate to economic well-being, such as a livable wage, pay equity, job discrimination, and social security.

In 2007, the columnist George Will and a group of conservative scholars charged that the social work Code of Ethics, as well as the authors of the previous edition of this book, prescribed political orthodoxy in violation of freedom of speech and in opposition to critical thinking (Will, 2007; NAS, 2007). While support for social and economic justice as national priorities ebbs and flows in the political landscape of the United States, the social work profession supports those goals at all times as part of our core mission. It is not relevant to the profession whether the political majority in such times label themselves as liberal, conservative, green, independent, or otherwise. Social workers ally with those political groups that benefit the oppressed groups who form their core constituencies. Following this purpose, social workers seek to promote social and economic justice for both Americans and immigrants with or without documentation. The prevention of conditions that limit human rights and quality of life principle guides Tobias to take seriously the allegation that Mrs. Ramirez and her family have not been made to feel welcome at the school. Indeed, with national priorities of raising testing scores for reading and writing, attention to the needs of those who speak English as a second language may be in conflict with the goal of increasing test scores.

The purposes outlined also suggest that Tobias might assist Mrs. Ramirez and her family in a variety of ways to meet their needs. Those ways include the creation of policies to find solutions to the health needs of immigrants without documents. Social workers perform preventive, restorative, and remedial functions in pursuit of this purpose.

- *Prevention* involves the timely provision of services to vulnerable persons, promoting social functioning before problems develop. It includes programs and activities such as family planning, well-baby clinics, parent education, premarital and pre-retirement counseling, and marital enrichment programs.
- *Restoration* seeks to restore functioning that has been impaired by physical or mental difficulties. Included in this group of clients are persons with varying degrees of paralysis caused by severe spinal injury, individuals afflicted with chronic mental illness, persons with developmental disabilities, persons with deficient educational backgrounds, and individuals with many other types of disability.
- *Remediation* entails the elimination or amelioration of existing social problems. Many potential clients in this category are similar to Mrs. Ramirez in that they are referred by others such as the school system, family members, neighbors, and doctors who have perceived a need.

The Educational Policy and Accreditation Standards (EPAS) affirms the commitment of social programs to the core values of the profession: service, social justice, dignity and worth of the person, importance of human relationships, integrity, competence, human rights, and scientific inquiry (NASW, 2008A; CSWE, 2008). The purpose of promoting human and community well-being is "guided by a person and environment construct, a global perspective, respect for human diversity, and knowledge based on scientific inquiry" (CSWE, 2008, p. 1). "Guided by a person and environment construct" suggests that social workers always examine individual behavior in its context, reflecting on how that behavior is both a response to and, in turn, influences the individual's environment. Adopting a global perspective suggests that the profession look beyond national borders in assessing needs. A "global perspective" also suggests that Tobias and his agency be aware of the significance of Mrs. Ramirez's migration from Mexico as part of the context of her current circumstances related to school attendance and health care.

Social Work Values

EP 2.1.2b

All professions have value preferences that give purpose and direction to their practitioners. Indeed, the purpose and objectives of social work and other professions come from their respective value systems. Professional values, however, are not separate from societal values. Rather, professions espouse selected societal values. Society, in turn, sanctions the activities of professions through supportive legislation, funding, delegation of responsibility for certain societal functions, and mechanisms for ensuring that those functions are adequately discharged. Because a profession is linked to certain societal values, it tends to serve as society's conscience with respect to those particular values.

Values represent strongly held beliefs about how the world should be, about how people should normally behave, and about what the preferred conditions of life are. Broad societal values in the United States are reflected in the Declaration of Independence, the Constitution, and the laws of the land, which declare and ensure certain rights of the people. In addition, societal values are reflected in governmental entities and programs designed to safeguard the rights of people and to promote the common good. Interpretations of values and rights, however, are not always uniform. Consider, for example, the heated national debates over the right of women to have abortions; the controversy over the rights of gays, lesbians, and bisexuals to enjoy the benefits of marriage; and conflicts between advocates of gun control and those espousing individual rights.

The values of the social work profession also reflect strongly held beliefs about the rights of people to free choice and opportunity. They recognize the preferred conditions of life that enhance people's welfare, ways that members of the profession should view and treat people, preferred goals for people, and ways in which those goals should be reached. We next consider five values and purposes that guide social work education. These five values are italicized, and the content that follows each is our commentary.

1. *Social workers' professional relationships are built on regard for individual worth and dignity, and are advanced by mutual participation, acceptance, confidentiality, honesty, and responsible handling of conflict* (CSWE, 2008). This value is also reflected in several parts of the Code of Ethics. The first value of the code is simple: "Social workers' primary goal is to serve" (NASW, 2008a). That is, service to others is elevated above self-interest and social workers should use their knowledge, values, and skills to help people in need and to address social problems. The second value states that they serve others in a fashion such that "social workers respect the inherent dignity and worth of the person." Every person is unique and has inherent worth; therefore, social workers' interactions with people as they pursue and utilize resources should enhance their dignity and individuality, enlarge their competence, and increase their problem-solving and coping abilities.

   People who receive social work services are often overwhelmed by their difficult circumstances and have exhausted their coping resources. Many feel stressed by a multitude of problems. In addition to helping clients reduce their stress level, practitioners aid clients in many other ways: They help them view their difficulties from a fresh perspective, consider various remedial alternatives, foster awareness of strengths, mobilize both active and latent coping resources, enhance self-awareness, and teach problem-solving strategies and interpersonal skills.

   Social workers perform these functions while recognizing "the central importance of human relationships" (NASW, 2008a). This principle suggests that social workers engage clients as partners in purposeful efforts to promote, restore, maintain, and enhance the clients' well-being. This value is reflected in yet another Code of Ethics principle: "Social workers behave in a trustworthy manner" (p. 6). This principle suggests that social workers practice consistently with the profession's mission, values, and ethical standards, and that they promote ethical practices in the organizations with which they are affiliated (p. 6).

2. *Social workers respect the individual's right to make independent decisions and to participate actively in the helping process.* People have a right to freedom as long as they do not infringe on the rights of others. Therefore, transactions with people who are seeking and utilizing resources should enhance their independence and self-determination. Too often in the past, social workers and other helping professionals have focused on "deficit, disease, and dysfunction" (Cowger, 1992). The attention currently devoted to empowerment and strengths behooves social workers to assist clients in increasing their personal potential and political power such that clients can improve their life situation (Finn & Jacobson, 2003; Parsons, 2002; Saleebey, 1997). Consistent with this value, this book incorporates an empowerment and strength-oriented perspective for working with clients. Chapter 13

focuses on skills designed to enhance empowerments and enhance their capacity for independent action.

3. *Social workers are committed to assisting client systems to obtain needed resources.* People should have access to the resources they need to meet life's challenges and difficulties as well as access to opportunities to realize their potential throughout their lives. Our commitment to client self-determination and empowerment is hollow if clients lack access to the resources necessary to achieve their goals (Hartman, 1993). Because people such as Mrs. Ramirez from the case example often know little about available resources, social workers must act as brokers by referring people to resource systems such as public legal services, health care agencies, child welfare divisions, mental health centers, centers for elderly persons, and family counseling agencies. Some individual clients or families may require goods and services from many different providers and may lack the language facility, physical or mental capacity, experience, or skills needed to avail themselves of essential goods and services. Practitioners then may assume the role of case manager; that is, they may not only provide direct services but also assume responsibility for linking the client to diverse resources and ensuring that the client receives needed services in a timely fashion.

Clients sometimes need resource systems that are not available. In these cases, practitioners must act as program developers by creating and organizing new resource systems. Examples of such efforts include the following: working with citizens and public officials to arrange transportation to health care agencies for the elderly, persons with disabilities, and indigent people; developing neighborhood organizations to campaign for better educational and recreational programs; organizing tenants to assert their rights to landlords and housing authorities for improved housing and sanitation; and organizing support groups, skill development groups, and self-help groups to assist people in coping with difficult problems of living.

Social workers also frequently pursue this goal by facilitating access to resources. They perform the role of facilitator or enabler in carrying out the following functions: enhancing communication among family members; coordinating efforts of teachers, school counselors, and social workers in assisting troubled students; helping groups provide maximal support to their members; opening channels of communication between coworkers; including patients or inmates in the governance of institutions; facilitating teamwork among members of different disciplines in hospitals and mental health centers; and providing for consumer input into agency policy-making boards.

4. *Social workers strive to make social institutions more humane and responsive to human needs.* Although direct practitioners work primarily in providing direct service, they also have a responsibility to work toward improving clients' quality of life by promoting policies and legislation that enhance physical and social environments. The problems of individuals, families, groups, and neighborhoods can often be prevented (or at least ameliorated) by implementing laws and policies that prohibit contamination of the physical environment and enrich both physical and social environments. Therefore, direct social workers should not limit themselves to remedial activities, but rather should seek out environmental causes of problems and sponsor or support efforts aimed at improving their clients' environments.

Social workers also demonstrate this value when they assume the role of expediter or troubleshooter by scrutinizing the policies and procedures of their own and other organizations to determine whether their clients have ready access to resources and whether services are delivered in ways that enhance their clients' dignity. Complex application procedures, needless delays in providing resources and services, discriminatory policies, inaccessible agency sites, inconvenient service delivery hours, dehumanizing procedures or staff behaviors, and other factors may deter clients from utilizing resources or subject them to demeaning experiences.

Systematically obtaining input from consumers is one method of monitoring an organization's responsiveness to clients. Advocacy actions in conjunction with and on behalf of clients are sometimes required to secure the services and resources to which clients are entitled. Social workers may support this value by performing the roles of coordinator, mediator, or disseminator of information. For example, as a case manager, a social worker may coordinate the medical, educational, mental health, and rehabilitative services provided to a given family by multiple resource systems. A mediator may be required to resolve conflicts between agencies, minority and majority groups, and neighborhood groups. The social worker may disseminate information regarding legislation or new funding sources that could potentially affect the relationships between public and private agencies by strengthening interactions between these resource systems.

Social workers must also collaborate with key organizations to facilitate mutual awareness of changes in policies and procedures that affect ongoing relationships and the availability of resources.

EP 2.1.4

5. *Social workers demonstrate respect for and acceptance of the unique characteristics of diverse populations.* Social workers perform their services with populations that are characterized by great diversity, including the intersection of dimensions such as "age, class, culture, disability, ethnicity, gender, gender identity and expression, immigration status, political ideology, race, religion, sex and sexual orientation, religion, physical or mental ability, age, and national origin" (CSWE, 2008, p. 5). Similarly, NASW's Code of Ethics requires social workers to understand cultures, recognize strengths in cultures, have a knowledge base of their clients' cultures, and deliver services that are sensitive to those cultures (NASW, 2008a). This value suggests that social workers must be informed about and respectful of differences. They must educate themselves over time as a part of lifelong learning—unfortunately, there is no "how-to" manual that will guide the practitioner in understanding all aspects of diversity. To demonstrate this value, the practitioner must continually update his or her knowledge about the strengths and resources associated with individuals from diverse groups to increase the sensitivity and effectiveness of the services provided to those clients.

An increasing number of social workers are themselves members of these diverse populations. They face the challenge of working effectively with both clients and agency staff from the majority culture as well as persons from their own groups.

Values and Ethics

EP 2.1.2a

Turning the five values just described into reality should be the mutual responsibility of individual citizens and of society. Society should foster conditions and provide opportunities for citizens to participate in policy-making processes. Citizens, in turn, should fulfill their responsibilities to society by actively participating in those processes.

Considered individually, these five values and the profession's mission are not unique to social work. Their unique combination, however, differentiates social work from other professions. Considered in their entirety, these ingredients make it clear that social work's identity derives from its connection with the institution of social welfare. According to Gilbert (1977), social welfare represents a special helping mechanism devised to aid those who suffer from the variety of ills found in industrial society: "Whenever other major institutions, be they familial, religious, economic, or educational in nature, fall short in their helping and resource providing functions, social welfare spans the gap" (p. 402).

These five values represent the prized ideals of the profession and, as such, are stated at high levels of abstraction. As Siporin (1975) and Levy (1973) have noted, however, different levels of professional values exist. At an intermediate level, values pertain to various segments of society—for example, characteristics of a strong community. At a third level, values are more operational, referring to preferred behaviors.

For example, the ideal social work practitioner is a warm, caring, open, and responsible person who safeguards the confidentiality of information disclosed by clients. Because you, the reader, have chosen to enter the field of social work, most of your personal values probably coincide with the cardinal values espoused by the majority of social work practitioners. By contrast, at the intermediate and third levels of values, your views may not always be in harmony with the specific value positions taken by the majority of social workers.

Self-determination refers to the right of people to exercise freedom of choice when making decisions. Issues such as those described may pose value dilemmas for individual practitioners because of conflicts between personal and professional values. In addition, conflicts between two professional values or principles are common. Public positions taken by the profession that emanate from its values also sometimes stand in opposition to the attitudes of a large segment of society. Recently, professional support for universal health coverage coincided with efforts to achieve some measure of this during the Obama administration.

We suggest that social workers should be sufficiently flexible to listen to many differing value positions on most moral and political issues. Different value positions do not necessarily reflect divergence among social workers on the five core values of the social work profession. Rather, they reflect the existence of many means of achieving given ends. Indeed, rigid assumptions about preferred means to ends often crumble when put to the test of hard experience. Consistent with our preference for flexibility, we reaffirm our commitment to the value that social workers, whatever their beliefs, should assert them in a forum of professional organizations such as NASW. We maintain further that social workers should accord colleagues who differ on certain value positions the same respect, dignity, and right to self-determination that would be accorded clients. Differences on issues may be frankly expressed. Those issues can be clarified and cohesiveness among professionals can be fostered by debate conducted in a climate of openness and mutual respect.

Conflicts between personal and/or professional values and the personal values of a client or group sometimes arise. Not infrequently, students (and even seasoned social workers) experience conflicts over value laden, problematic situations such as incest, infidelity, rape, child neglect or abuse, spousal abuse, and criminal behavior. Because direct practitioners encounter these and other problems typically viewed by the public as appalling, and because personal values inevitably shape the social worker's attitudes, perceptions, feelings, and responses to clients, it is vital that you remain flexible and nonjudgmental in your work. It is equally vital that you be aware of your own values, recognize how they fit with the profession's values, and assess how they may affect clients whose values differ from your own or whose behavior offends you.

Social Work's Code of Ethics

EP 2.1.2b

An essential attribute of legitimate professions is a code of ethics consisting of principles that define expectations of each profession's members. A code of ethics specifies rules of conduct to which members must adhere so as to remain in good standing within a professional organization. It thus defines expected responsibilities and behaviors as well as prescribed behaviors. Central to the purpose of a code of ethics is its function as a formalized expression of accountability of (1) the profession to the society that gives it sanction, (2) constituent practitioners to consumers who utilize their services, and (3) practitioners to their profession. By promoting accountability, a code of ethics serves additional vital purposes, including the following:

1. It safeguards the reputation of a professional by providing explicit criteria that can be employed to regulate the behavior of members.
2. It furthers competent and responsible practice by its members.

3. It protects the public from exploitation by unscrupulous or incompetent practitioners.

Most states now have licensing boards that certify social workers for practice and review allegations of unethical conduct (Bibus & Boutte Queen, 2011; Land, 1988; DeAngelis, 2000). Similarly, local and state chapters of the NASW establish professional review committees to investigate alleged violations of the profession's Code of Ethics, and national committees provide consultation to local committees and consider appeals of decisions made by local chapters. We have blended the values in the code of ethics in our presentation of the five values stated by CSWE. These values are prescribed to underlie the social work curriculum and support the profession's commitment to respect for all people and quest for social and economic justice (CSWE, 2008, p. 2).

EPAS Competencies

The Education Policy and Accreditation standards of CSWE are based on a competency-based education format that prescribes attention to outcome performance (CSWE, 2008, p. 2). These competencies are based on knowledge, values, and skills with emphasis on integrating into practice with individuals, families, groups, and communities. We will state these competencies in terms of what a competent social work graduate should be able to do when they have completed their courses of study. We hope that you do not feel apprehensive about whether you are capable of performing these competencies now. It will be your task and that of your educational program to prepare you to reach these competencies by the time that you graduate. While each of these competencies will be covered in greater detail in later chapters, the main points of each competency are summarized in the following.

EPAS Competency 2.1

specifies that students identify themselves as professional social workers and conduct themselves accordingly. In order to meet this competency, social workers should be knowledgeable about the profession's history and commit to the enhancement of the profession and their own professional conduct and growth. A social worker meeting this competency will ensure client access to services; engage in self-reflection, self-monitoring, and correction; attend to professional roles and boundaries; demonstrate professional demeanor in behavior, appearance, and communication; engage in career-long learning; and use supervision and consultation (CSWE, 2008, p. 3).

EPAS Competency 2.1.2

This competency requires you to apply social work ethical principles to guide your professional practice. You should be knowledgeable about the profession's value base, ethical standards, and relevant laws. In meeting this competency, social workers recognize and manage their personal values such that professional values guide practice. For example, if Tobias had any personal values that might impede his work with Mrs. Ramirez and her children, he would take care that his professional values supersede those personal values. Social workers also make ethical decisions in applying standards such as the NASW Code of Ethics, tolerate ambiguity in resolving ethical conflicts, and apply strategies of ethical reasoning to arrive at principled decisions (CSWE, 2008, p. 4).

EPAS Competency 2.1.3

This competency requires you to apply critical thinking to inform and communicate professional judgments. Despite George Will and the National Association of Scholars' (2007) allegation that the social work profession emphasizes political orthodoxy over critical thinking, in fact this competency specifically requires us to use critical thinking in the professional setting. In carrying out this competency, you demonstrate that you are knowledgeable about the principles of logic, scientific inquiry, and discernment. Critical thinking requires the synthesis of relevant information augmented by creativity and curiosity. Applying this competency, social workers distinguish, appraise, and integrate multiple sources of information, including the use of research-based knowledge and empirical wisdom, analysis of assessment models, and creativity to synthesize meanings (CSWE, 2008, p. 4). Following this competency, Tobias would consult research-based knowledge and integrate it with empirical wisdom to guide his practice. Pursuit of this competency requires the social worker to consult multiple sources of information in making decisions.

EPAS Competency 2.1.4

Social workers are guided in this competency to recognize and engage diversity in social work practice. Specifically, this means recognizing the relation between cultural structures and values in alienating, creating, or enhancing privilege and power (EPAS, 2.1.4a). This

suggests that social work practitioners are responsible for assessing the role of privilege in how they perform their roles. They are expected to gain self-awareness to eliminate the influence of personal biases and values in work with diverse groups (EPAS 2.1.4b). While an admirable aspiration, we take the position that eliminating personal biases and values is probably not a feasible goal. Rather, social workers might better be expected to be aware of personal biases and reduce their negative impact on work with clients. For example, early on in working with Mrs. Ramirez, Tobias wrote in his case notes that he suspected that, in part, her children were not attending school because she and other undocumented immigrants did not value education as much as their fellow students and families in their new community in the United States. In fact, there is evidence to suggest that Mexican immigrants value education highly (Valencia and Black, 2002). This statement by Tobias might be seen as a belief, a hypothesis, or a possible bias that could have profound implications for his work with Mrs. Ramirez. If he acted on his belief that her children were not attending primarily because she and other Mexican immigrants were not motivated about education, he might not explore other community- or school-based barriers to their attendance, such as their perception that the children were not welcome. Holding members of oppressed groups personally responsible for all aspects of their condition is an unfortunate value predicated on the Horatio Alger myth that all successful people lifted themselves up by their own bootstraps. This competency requires sensitivity to structures that may act to oppress (p. 5).

Social workers are expected to "recognize and communicate their understanding of the importance of difference in shaping life experience" (EPAS 2.1.4c). Finally, social workers are expected to "view themselves as learners and engage those with whom they work as informants" (EPAS 2.1.4d.).

We also consider the importance of our commitment to diversity as we consider the Eurocentric assumptions that undergird many of our practice models (Sue & Sue, 2003). We take the position that some factors are universal. For example, pathology occurs across cultures although the forms may vary (Sue & Sue, 2003). On the other hand, much of social work practice relates to specific cultural manifestations of both difficulties and solutions.

We do not believe that cultural competence is attained as a satisfactory level of knowledge and skill that does not require continual upgrading over the course of your career. Just as your clinical or direct practice skills should continue to grow, so should your level of cultural competence. To do this, you will need to engage in continual education about the culture and experiences of client groups with whom you work. That also means that you must approach each client as a person whose experience is in many ways unique. That is, clients bear unique combinations of personality characteristics, family dynamics, experiences with acculturation and assimilation. You need to learn as much as you can about the cultural frames that are significant for the person before you can be open to learning the uniqueness of that person (Dean, 2001; Johnson and Munch, 2009). Hence, when we report some cultural characteristics as commonly represented in some groups, it is shared in the sense of background information that must be assessed with the person before you. For example, while some Asian American clients may expect the social worker to take an expert role and advise them, many will not according to their own individual experiences and personalities (Fong, 2007). Further, Asian American as a category can subsume great variation including Pacific Islanders and mainland Asians whose cultural heritages are very distinct from each other.

 VIDEO CASE EXAMPLE

In the interview "Working with Yanping," Kim Strom-Gottfried interviews an exchange student from the Republic of China. She cannot assume that there are shared assumptions about help seeking, so Kim carefully explores expectations and explains what she can offer. In this way, she guards against applying stereotypic assumptions about how the client views her concerns and what is possible in seeking help. They explore possibilities including goals and ways of working as well as whether a referral to a social worker more familiar with Yan Ping's culture could be helpful.

EPAS Competency 2.1.5

This competency requires you to advance human rights and social justice and asserts that each person in society has basic human rights such as freedom, safety, privacy, an adequate standard of living, health care, and education (CSWE, 2008, p. 5). This competency is also reflected in the second value in the social work Code of Ethics: "Social workers challenge social injustice" (NASW, 2008a). This value encourages social

workers to pursue social change on behalf of vulnerable or oppressed people who are subject to poverty, discrimination, and other forms of injustice. The focus of efforts geared toward populations at risk should increase the power of these individuals to influence their own lives. While the profession supports critical thinking about the means to achieve these goals, social work education is fully committed to human rights and social justice. If resources and opportunities are to be available to all members of society, then laws, governmental policies, and social programs must assure equal access of citizens to those resources and opportunities. Social workers promote social justice by advocating for clients who have been denied services, resources, or goods to which they are entitled. They also work to develop new resources to meet emerging needs.

To meet this competency, you should be aware of the global implications of oppression; be knowledgeable about theories of justice and strategies to promote human and civil rights; and strive to incorporate social justice practices into organizations, institutions, and society. You should also understand the mechanisms of oppression and discrimination in society and advocate for and engage in practices that advance human rights and social and economic justice. George Will and the National Association of Scholars reported that there were instances in which social work students were required by instructors to advocate for groups in conflict with their own religious beliefs (Will, 2007; NAS, 2007). For example, some students were required to advocate for gay and lesbian people to be able to adopt children. In many states, competency to adopt is not based on sexual orientation. There is room for debate whether it is ethical to require students to advocate for specific oppressed groups; however, this competency clearly specifies that advocating for human rights and social and economic justice is a professional expectation.

Following this competency, Tobias would attempt to understand the issue of children's school attendance in a broader framework of understanding why Mrs. Ramirez and her children had moved to his locality. Awareness of the economic incentive of seeking a better income as an influence on immigration would be appropriate. For example, in addition to working with Mrs. Ramirez alone, Tobias or other social workers might approach the circumstance of undocumented immigrants in their community from the standpoint of community organization and advocacy, working on the interests of the group rather than solely on those of the individual. While this book focuses primarily on direct social work intervention, other courses in your program and other texts will provide additional sources of information for pursuit of this goal.

EPAS Competency 2.1.6

This competency requires you to engage in research-informed practice and practice-informed research. To fulfill this competency, you use your practice experience to inform research, employ evidence-based interventions, evaluate your own practice, and use research findings to improve practice, policy, and social service delivery (p. 5). You will be knowledgeable about quantitative and qualitative research and understand scientific and ethical approaches to building knowledge. As a social worker, you will use your practice experience to inform scientific inquiry and use research evidence to inform practice (p. 5).

Some proponents suggest that employing evidence-based intervention entails being able to explain an evidence-based approach to clients, creating a useful, realistic evaluation format, refining such intervention and evaluation formats based on knowledge of the client, understanding the relevant elements of evidence-based techniques, incorporating evidence from use of the intervention, and being critical consumers of evidence in practice situations (Pollio, 2006, p. 224). Others suggest that knowledge of the context must also be employed in formulating such interventions, as well as considering the theoretical base in selecting interventions (Walsh, 2006; Payne, 2005; Adams, Matto & Le Croy, 2009). Given the range of evidence available in different fields of practice, we agree that evidence-based practice should be a highly valued source of information in the context of planning an intervention. Following this principle, Tobias and his agency would be advised to be mindful of evidence-based interventions that assist families with the problem of low school attendance. He and his agency would become familiar with programs that promote personal relationships between school personnel and families around attendance issues (Anderson et al, 2004). They would also need to integrate that knowledge with information about the environmental context and relevant interventions. For example, assisting Mrs. Ramirez in getting the children ready for transportation to school might be one part of the intervention, as well as working with the school to construct a more welcoming environment for the children. Part of this context is Mrs. Ramirez's physical and emotional health. She may be more likely to have her children ready for school if she is linked to health care providers who can assist her with her need for surgery and her depression.

EPAS Competency 2.1.7

This competency requires that you apply knowledge of human behavior and the social environment. To meet this competency, you should be knowledgeable about human behavior across the lifespan. You should also be knowledgeable about the social systems in which people live and how those systems promote or hinder people in maintaining or achieving health and well-being. You will apply theories and knowledge from the liberal arts to understand biological, social, cultural, psychological, and spiritual development (CSWE, 2008, p. 6). You will use those conceptual frameworks to guide the processes of assessment intervention and you will critique and apply that knowledge to understand the person and their environment (p. 6). In your academic program, you are likely to encounter other course work related to human behavior and the social environment to augment the knowledge available from this book.

EPAS Competency 2.1.8

This competency requires that you engage in policy practice to advance social and economic well-being and to deliver effective social work services (CSWE, 2008, p. 6). One of the distinguishing features of social work as a helping profession is the understanding that all direct practice occurs in a policy context. Hence, social workers need to know about the history of and current structures for policies and services. In pursuit of this competency, social workers analyze, formulate, and advocate for policies that advance the social well-being of clients (p. 6). They also collaborate with colleagues and clients for effective policy action. While some social workers provide direct services to clients, others act indirectly to influence the environments supporting clients, thereby developing and maintaining the social infrastructure that assists clients in meeting their needs. Many social work programs will contain one or more required courses in policy and practice as well as an advanced practice curriculum in this area. Tobias' interaction with Mrs. Ramirez must be considered in the context of policies related to school attendance and policies related to health care access.

EPAS Competency 2.1.9

This competency requires that you respond to and shape an ever-changing professional context. As described previously, social work as a helping profession is characterized by its sensitivity not only to the policy context of practice but also a broader professional context related to organizations, communities, and society. In pursuit of this competency, you should be informed, resourceful, and proactive in responding to the evolving organizations, community, and societal context at all levels of practice. You will discover, appraise, and attend to changing locales, populations, scientific and technological developments, and emerging societal trends in order to provide relevant services. Social workers also participate in providing leadership to promote sustainable changes in service delivery and practice to improve the quality of social services (CSWE, 2008, p. 6). Tobias would be acting in fulfillment of this competency if he had or gained knowledge of the circumstances of Hispanic speaking children in the elementary school that Mrs. Ramirez's children attended. As noted, pressures to increase reading scores for children may indirectly create pressure on children for whom English is a second language.

EPAS 2.1.10

This competency focuses on engaging with, assessing, intervening with, and evaluating individuals, families, groups, organizations, and communities (CSWE, 2008, p. 7). These competencies get at the heart of social work intervention and reflect the knowledge and skills that this book is designed to address.

EPAS Competency 2.1.10a

This competency focuses on engagement. In order to meet this competency, social workers prepare for action with individuals, families, groups, organizations and communities both substantively and emotionally (CSWE, 2008, p. 7). They do this by using empathy and other interpersonal skills and developing a mutually agreed-upon focus of work and identifying desired outcomes (p. 7). Utilizing these skills, Tobias would attempt to personally engage Mrs. Ramirez and her family. We recognize that the success of such engagement efforts depends in part on sensitivity to cultural norms and hence also include attention to Competency 2.1.3 on diversity.

EPAS Competency 2.1.10b

This competency focuses on assessment and refers to knowledge and skills required to collect, organize, and interpret client data. In this context, social workers must have skills in assessing both a client system's strengths and limitations. They must be able to develop mutually agreed-upon intervention goals and objectives and be able to select appropriate intervention strategies (CSWE, 2008, p. 7).

EPAS Competency 2.1.10c

This competency refers to knowledge and skills associated with intervention. Included here are knowledge and skills associated with prevention strategies designed to enhance client capacities; assist clients in resolving problems; negotiate, mediate, and advocate for client systems; and facilitate transitions and endings.

EPAS Competency 2.1.10d

This competency requires knowledge and skills in evaluation. To meet this competency, social workers must be able to critically analyze, monitor, and evaluate interventions (CSWE, 2008, p. 7). Following this competency, Tobias would establish goals with Mrs. Ramirez and regularly assess progress with her.

EPAS Competency B 2.2

This competency refers to knowledge and skills related to generalist practice. A generalist practitioner is grounded in the liberal arts and the personal and environmental constructs required to promote human and social well-being (CSWE, 2008, p. 8). The generalist practitioner uses a range of prevention and intervention methods to work with individuals, families, groups, organizations, and communities. This competency refers to the fact that many social work practitioners operate in agencies that provide varied services at many levels. Generalist practitioners identify with the social work profession and apply ethical principles and critical thinking in practice (p. 8). They incorporate diversity into their practice and are expected to advocate for human rights and social justice. They do so while building upon the strengths and resiliency of human beings. Finally, they engage in research-informed practice and are proactive in responding to an ever-changing professional context. Social work educations incorporate two practice degrees, BSW and MSW. This competency refers to what is expected of BSW practitioners and incorporates the first year of an MSW curriculum. As Tobias was a BSW practitioner, he was expected to use the range of skills and knowledge required of generalist practice.

EPAS Competency M 2.2

This competency refers to knowledge and skills required for advanced practice. Advanced practitioners are expected to be able to assess, intervene, and evaluate in order to promote human and social well-being in ways that are differentiated, discriminating, and self-critical (CSWE, 2008, p. 8). Advanced practitioners are expected to synthesize and apply a broad range of inter-disciplinary and multi-disciplinary knowledge and skills. Such practitioners are expected to refine and advance the quality of social work practice and the larger social work profession. They incorporate the core competencies augmented by knowledge and skills specific to a specialized concentration. (CSWE, 2008, p. 8). Advanced practice in social work means completion of a concentration as defined by their program. Such concentrations are often divided into those that specialize in some forms of micro, mezzo, and macro practice.

- *Micro-level practice.* At this level, the population served by practitioners includes a variety of client systems, including individuals, couples, and families. Practice at the micro-level is designated as direct practice because practitioners deliver services directly to clients in face-to-face contact. Direct practice, however, is by no means limited to such face-to-face contact,
- *Mezzo-level practice.* The second level is defined as "interpersonal relations that are less intimate than those associated with family life; more meaningful than among organizational and institutional representatives; [including] relationships between individuals in a self-help or therapy group, among peers at school or work or among neighbors" (Sheafor, Horejsi, & Horejsi, 1994, pp. 9–10). Mezzo events are "the interface where the individual and those most immediate and important to him/her meet" (Zastrow & Kirst-Ashman, 1990, p. 11). Mezzo intervention is hence designed to change the systems that directly affect clients, such as the family, peer group, or classroom.
- *Macro-level practice.* Still further removed from face-to-face delivery of services, macro practice involves the processes of social planning and community organization. On this level, social workers serve as professional change agents who assist community action systems composed of individuals, groups, or organizations in dealing with social problems. For example, social workers may work with citizen groups or with private, public, or governmental organizations. Activities of practitioners at this level include the following: (1) development of and work with community groups and organizations; (2) program planning and development; and

(3) implementation, administration, and evaluation of programs (Meenaghan, 1987).

Effective practice requires knowledge related to all three levels of practice. Nevertheless, schools of social work often offer "concentrations" in either micro or macro practice and require less preparation in the other methods. Concentrations are often designated around an area of direct practice in particular populations or settings such as adult mental health, child welfare, family practice, group work, school social work, aging, and work with children and adolescents. Such concentrations may emphasize micro practice or incorporate mezzo and macro practice. Some schools have generalist practice curricula, which require students to achieve balanced preparation in all three levels of practice. Undergraduate programs and the first year of graduate programs typically feature generalist practice curricula, which aim to prepare students for working with all levels of client systems.

Macro concentrations often refer to practice in community organization, planning, management, and advocacy. Administration entails playing a leadership role in human service organizations that seek to effectively deliver services in accordance with the values and laws of society. It includes the processes involved in policy formulation and subsequent translation of that policy into operational goals, program design and implementation, funding and resource allocation, management of internal and interorganizational operation, personnel direction and supervision, organizational representation and public relations, community education, monitoring, evaluation, and innovation to improve organizational productivity (Sarri, 1987, pp. 29–30). Direct practitioners are necessarily involved to some degree in administrative activities. In addition, many direct practitioners who hold master's degrees become supervisors or administrators later in their professional careers. Knowledge of administration, therefore, is vital to direct practitioners at the master's degree level, and courses in administration are frequently part of the required master's degree curriculum in social work. Although many direct practitioners engage in little or no macro-level practice, those who work in rural areas where practitioners are few and specialists in social planning are not available may work in concert with concerned citizens and community leaders in planning and developing resources to prevent or combat social problems.

EPAS Competency 2.1

This competency refers to the signature pedagogy of social work: field education. Signature pedagogy refers to the forms of instruction and learning by which the social work profession socializes students to perform the role of practitioner. Different professions have varied ways by which they train professionals to connect and integrate theory and practice. That is done in social work through field education. Field education is designed to connect the theoretical and conceptual contributions of classrooms with the practice setting (CSWE, 2008, p. 8). In social work, classroom and field are considered equally important in developing competent social work practice. It is designed, supervised, coordinated and evaluated in such a way that students can demonstrate achievement of program competencies. This text and practice workbook includes many exercises that are designed to be completed in field placements.

Orienting Frameworks to Achieve Competencies

Practitioners and beginning students need orienting frameworks to ground their work in achieving the competencies just described. There is ever increasing information from the social sciences, social work, and allied disciplines that point to specific interventions for specific problem situations. Successful use of such interventions represents formidable challenges because available knowledge is often fragmented. Further, since social work often takes place in agency settings with clients whose concerns cut across psychological and environmental needs, an orienting perspective is needed to address these levels of concerns and activities. The ecological systems model is useful in providing an orienting perspective (Germain, 1979, 1981; Meyer, 1983; Pincus & Minahan, 1973; Siporin, 1980). A system is a set of orderly elements that are related to make a whole. Systems theory emphasizes the interactions between these elements (Kirst-Ashman & Hull, 2012)

Ecological Systems Model

EP 2.1.3b

Adaptations of this model, originating in biology, make a close conceptual fit with the "person-in-environment" perspective that dominated social work until the mid-1970s. Although that perspective recognized the influence of environmental factors on human functioning, internal factors had received an inordinate emphasis in assessing human problems. In addition, a perception of the environment as constraining the individual did not sufficiently acknowledge the individual's ability to affect the environment.

This heavy emphasis, which resulted from the prominence and wide acceptance of Freud's theories in the 1920s and 1930s, reached its zenith in the 1940s and 1950s. With the emergence of ego psychology, systems theory, theories of family therapy, expanded awareness of the importance of ethnocultural factors, and emphasis on ecological factors in the 1960s and 1970s, increasing importance was accorded to environmental factors and to understanding the ways in which people interact with their environments. While systems models were first created in the natural sciences and ecological theory developed from the environmental movement in biology, ecological systems theory in social work adapted concepts from both systems and ecological theories.

Two concepts of ecological theory that are especially relevant to social workers are habitat and niche. *Habitat* refers to the places where organisms live and, in the case of humans, consists of the physical and social settings within particular cultural contexts. When habitats are rich in the resources required for growth and development, people tend to thrive. When habitats are deficient in vital resources, physical, social, and emotional development and ongoing functioning may be adversely affected. For example, a substantial body of research indicates that supportive social networks of friends, relatives, neighbors, work and church associates, and pets mitigate the damaging effects of painful life stresses. By contrast, people with deficient social networks may respond to life stresses by becoming severely depressed, resorting to abuse of drugs or alcohol, engaging in violent behavior, or coping in other dysfunctional ways.

Niche refers to the statuses or roles occupied by members of the community. One of the tasks in the course of human maturation is to find one's niche in society, which is essential to achieving self-respect and a stable sense of identity. Being able to locate one's niche, however, presumes that opportunities congruent with human needs exist in society. That presumption may not be valid for members of society who lack equal opportunities because of race, ethnicity, gender, poverty, age, disability, sexual identity, or other factors.

An objective of social work, as noted earlier, is to promote social justice so as to expand opportunities for people to create appropriate niches for themselves. Ecological systems theory posits that individuals constantly engage in transactions with other humans and with other systems in the environment, and that these individuals and systems reciprocally influence each other.

Each system is unique, varying in its characteristics and ways of interacting (e.g., no two individuals, families, groups, or neighborhoods are the same). As a consequence, people do not merely react to environmental forces. Rather, they act on their environments, thereby shaping the responses of other people, groups, institutions, and even the physical environment. For example, people make choices about where to live, whether to upgrade or to neglect their living arrangements, and whether to initiate or support policies that combat urban decay, safeguard the quality of air and water, and provide adequate housing for the elderly who are poor.

Adequate assessments of human problems and plans of interventions, therefore, must consider how people and environmental systems influence one another. The importance of considering this reciprocal interaction when formulating assessments has been reflected in changing views of certain human problems over the past decade. Disability, for example, is now defined in psychosocial terms rather than in medical or economic terms. As Roth (1987) has clarified, "What is significant can be revealed only by the ecological framework in which the disabled person exists, by the interactions through which society engages a disability, by the attitudes others hold, and by the architecture, means of transportation, and social organization constructed by the able bodied" (p. 434). Disability is thus minimized by maximizing the goodness of fit between the needs of people with physical or mental limitations and the environmental resources that correspond to their special needs (e.g., rehabilitation programs, special physical accommodations, education, and social support systems).

It is clear from the ecological systems perspective that the satisfaction of human needs and mastery of developmental tasks require adequate resources in the environment and positive transactions between people and their environments. For example, effective learning by a student requires adequate schools, competent teachers, parental support, adequate perception and intellectual ability, motivation to learn, and positive relationships between teachers and students. Any gaps in the environmental resources, limitations of individuals who need or utilize these resources, or dysfunctional transactions between individuals and environmental systems threaten to block the fulfillment of human needs and lead to stress or impaired functioning. To reduce or remove this stress requires coping efforts aimed at gratifying the needs—that is, achieving adaptive fit between person and environment. People, however, often do not have access to adequate resources or may lack effective coping methods. Social work involves helping such people meet their needs by linking them with or developing essential resources. It could also include enhancing clients' capacities to utilize resources or cope with environmental forces.

Assessment from an ecological systems perspective obviously requires knowledge of the diverse systems involved in interactions between people and their environments:

- *Subsystems of the individual (biophysical, cognitive, emotional, behavioral, motivational).*
- *Interpersonal systems (parent–child, marital, family, kin, friends, neighbors, cultural reference groups, spiritual belief systems, and other members of social networks).*
- *Organizations, institutions, and communities.*
- *The physical environment (housing, neighborhood environment, buildings, other artificial creations, water, and weather and climate).*

A major advantage of the ecological systems model is its broad scope. Typical human problems involving health care, family relations, inadequate income, mental health difficulties, conflicts with law enforcement agencies, unemployment, educational difficulties, and so on can all be subsumed under this model, enabling the practitioner to analyze the complex variables involved in such problems.

Assessing the sources of problems and determining the foci of interventions are the first steps in applying the ecological systems model. Assessment tools have been developed which can engage clients in gathering information to assist in discovering the strengths, resources, and challenges of the systems surrounding individuals and families. For example, ecomaps can depict a family context (Hartman, 1994). A solid line connecting systems to individuals and families can depict a strong relationship, a dotted line can depict a tenuous relationship, and hatch marks can depict a stressful relationship (Cournoyer, 2011; Mattaini, 1995). The ecomap depicted in Figure 1-1 follows suggests that Marta experiences her relationship with her spiritual community as sustaining while her relationships with the school system, health care system, and work are stressful. Those relationships are influenced by her work related injury and lack of access to health care as an undocumented person, and contribute to her symptoms of depression and oversleeping. Creation of an ecomap can then form the basis of a plan for utilizing available resources such as seeking assistance from her spiritual community and others.

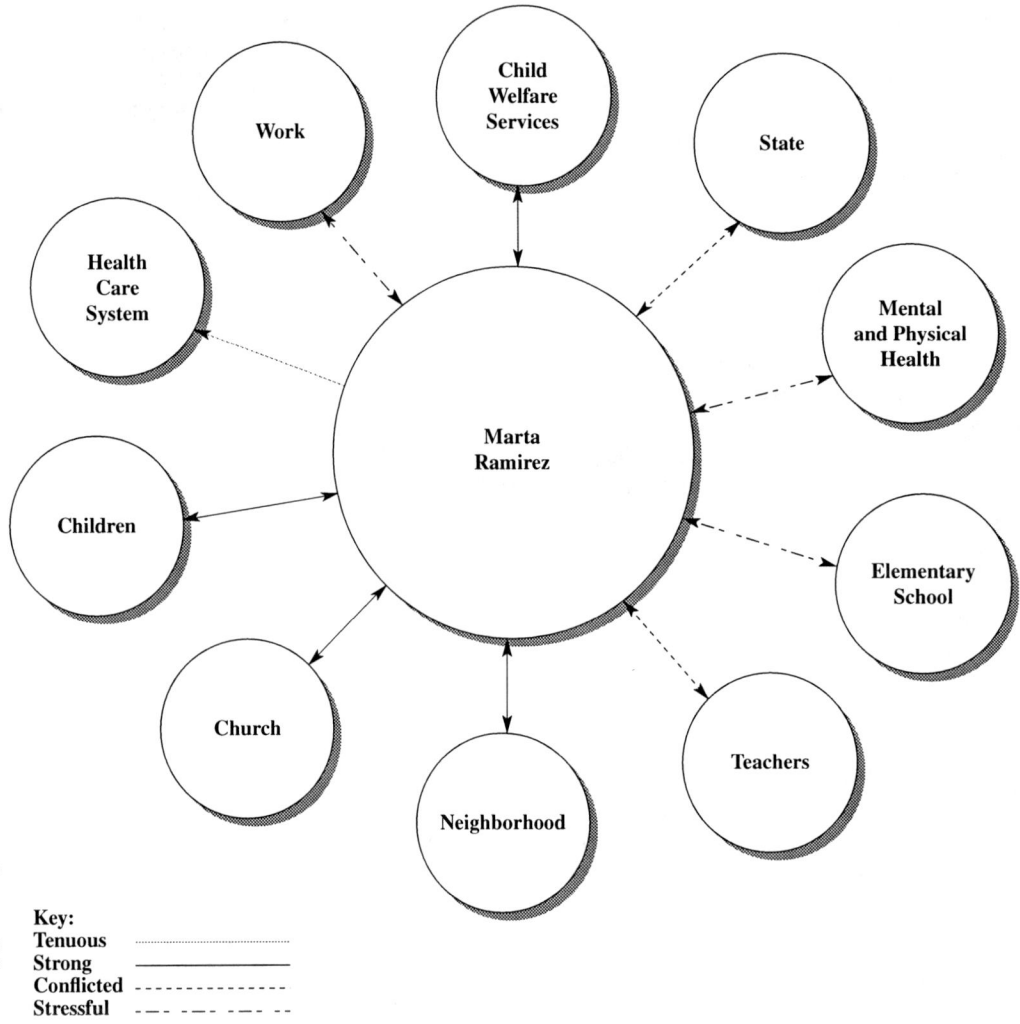

Key:
Tenuous ....
Strong ————————
Conflicted - - - - - - - -
Stressful — - — - — - —

FIG-1-1 Ecomap

Pincus and Minahan adapted systems models to social work practice, suggesting that a *client system* includes those persons who are requesting a change, sanction it, are expected to benefit from it, and contract to receive it (Pincus & Minahan, 1973; Compton, Galaway, & Cournoyer, 2005). Potential clients who request a change are described as *applicants*. Many clients reach social workers not through their own choice but rather through referral from others. *Referrals* are persons who do not seek services on their own, but do so at the behest of other professionals and family members. Meanwhile, *contacted persons* are approached through an outreach effort (Compton & Galaway, 2005). Some referred and contacted individuals may not experience pressure from that contact. As noted earlier, some individuals do experience pressure and social workers should consider them to be "potential clients"

and to be aware of the route that brought them to the social worker and their response to that contact. For example, Mrs. Ramirez could be considered a potential client as she was approached by child welfare services as part of a possible educational neglect assessment.

The next step is to determine what should be done related to the pertinent systems involved in the problem situation. In this step, the practitioner surveys the broad spectrum of available practice theories and interventions. To be maximally effective, interventions must be directed to all systems that are critical in a given problem system.

The *target system* refers to the focus of change efforts. With a voluntary client, it will typically encompass the concerns that brought the individual to seek services. With nonvoluntary clients, it may include illegal or dangerous behaviors that the person does

FIG-1-2 Target System

FIG-1-4 Action System

not acknowledge (see Figure 1-2). The *client system* consists of those persons who request or are expected to benefit from services. Note that this definition includes both voluntary clients (applicants) and nonvoluntary clients (see Figure 1-3).

When a client desires assistance on a personal problem, the target and client systems overlap. Frequently, however, clients request assistance with a problem outside themselves. In such instances, that problem could become the center of a target system. For example, Mrs. Ramirez acknowledges psychological and physical health concerns as well as concerns about how welcome her children feel in school. Meanwhile, Tobias must carry out a legally defined educational neglect assessment. These problem areas may merge as a contract is developed to address several concerns. It is important that target problems focus on a target concern rather than on the entire person as the target. Focusing on a person as the target system objectifies that individual and diminishes the respect for individuality to which each person is entitled. Hence, concerns with school attendance can be the target system rather than Mrs. Ramirez and her children.

The *action system* refers to those formal and informal resources and persons that the social worker needs to cooperate with to accomplish a purpose. It often

includes family, friends, and other resources as well as more formal resources. For example, an action system for school attendance might include school attendance officers, teachers, relatives, neighbors, spiritual resources or transportation providers, according to the plan agreed upon by Mrs. Ramirez and Tobias (see Figure 1-4).

The *agency system* is a special subset of an action system that includes the practitioners and formal service systems involved in work on the target problems (Compton & Galaway, 2005). In this case, the agency system primarily includes the elementary school and the child welfare agency (see Figure 1-5).

Social systems also vary in the degree to which they are open and closed to new information or feedback. Closed systems have relatively rigid boundaries that prevent the input or export of information. Open systems have relatively permeable boundaries permitting a more free exchange. Families may vary from being predominantly closed to new information to being excessively open. In fact, all families and human systems exhibit a tension between trying to maintain stability

FIG-1-3 Client System

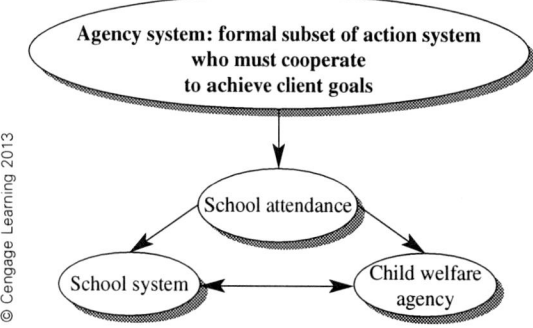

FIG-1-5 Agency System

and boundaries in some areas while seeking and responding to change in others. Systems theorists also suggest that change in one part of a system often affects other parts of the system. For example, Mrs. Ramirez's emotional and physical health may greatly influence her capacity to prepare her children for school. Hence, facilitating a referral for her may have a significant impact on the school attendance issue.

The principle of *equifinality* suggests that the same outcome can be achieved even with different starting points. For example, your classmates have come from different places both geographically and in terms of life experience. Despite their different origins, they have all ended up in the same program of study. The principle of *multifinality* suggests that beginning from the same starting points may end in different outcomes. Just as you and your classmates are engaged in the same course of study, you are likely to end in diverse settings and locales for your own practice experience.

Nonlinear Applications of Systems Theory

Traditional systems theory suggests that systems or organizations are characterized by order, rationality, and stability (Warren, Franklin, & Streeter, 1998). Hence, the emphasis in such stable systems is on concepts such as boundaries, homeostasis, and equilibrium. In addition to ordered circumstances, systems theory can be useful for consideration of nonlinear systems. Systems in the process of change can be very sensitive to initial events and feedback to those events. For example, a nonlinear change would be the circumstance in which an adolescent's voice changes by 1 decibel of loudness resulting in a change of 10 decibels in an adult (Warren et al., 1998). Minor incidents in the past can reverberate throughout a system. Some have suggested that this proliferation supports the notion that family systems can make significant changes as a result of a key intervention that reverberates and is reinforced in a system.

Such nonlinear circumstances emphasize the concept of multifinality—that is, the same initial conditions can lead to quite varied outcomes. Among the implications of multifinality are the possibility of considering chaos not as a lack of order but rather as an opportunity for flexibility and change.

Limitations of Systems Theories

While systems models often provide useful concepts for describing person–situation interactions, they may have limitations in suggesting specific intervention prescriptions (Whittaker & Tracy, 1989). Similarly, Wakefield

(1996a, 1996b) has argued that systems concepts do not add much to domain-specific knowledge. Others claim that, however faulty or inadequate, systems theory provides useful metaphors for conceptualizing the relations between complex organizations.

Perhaps we should not place such high expectations on the theory (Gitterman, 1996). We take the view that systems theory provides useful metaphors for conceptualizing the varied levels of phenomena social workers must recognize. By themselves, those metaphors are insufficient to guide practice. Concepts such as equifinality and multifinality cannot be rigidly applied in all human and social systems.

Deciding on and Carrying Out Interventions

EP 2.1.6

How do social workers decide on what interventions they will carry out to assist client systems in reaching their goals? Throughout our professional history, social workers have drawn selectively on theories to help understand circumstances and guide intervention. Psychodynamic theory was an important early source of explanations to guide social work interventions through adaptations such as the functional approach, the psychosocial approach, and the problem-solving approach (Hollis and Woods, 1981; Perlman, 1957; Taft, 1937). In each of these approaches, ego psychology was a particularly valuable source in explaining how individuals coped with their environments. While psychodynamic theory provided a broad-ranging explanatory framework, it was less useful as a source for specific interventions, and the level of abstraction required in the approach did not lend itself well to the evaluation of its effectiveness.

Concerns about the effectiveness of social work services led to an emphasis on employing methods that could be expected to be successful based on proven effectiveness (Fischer, 1973). Rather than seeking single approaches to direct practice in all circumstances, social workers were guided to find the approach that made the best fit for the particular client circumstance and problem (Fischer, 1978). Eclectic practice is designed to meet this goal, but carries its own concerns. For example, selecting techniques employed in particular approaches is best done based on knowledge of the approach the techniques come from and an assessment of the strengths and weaknesses of that approach (Coady and Lehmann, 2008; Marsh, 2004).

Berlin and Marsh suggest that there are legitimate roles for many influences on practice decision making. Those include clear conceptual frameworks to guide the social worker in what to look for, commitments and values, intuitive hunches, spontaneous improvisation, empathic understanding, and empirically derived data (Berlin and Marsh, 1993, p. 230) (see Figure 1-6).

Empirically derived data as a source has a prominent role in determining, together with clients, how to proceed. Empirically based practice refers to promoting models of practice based on scientific evidence (Barker, 2003). In such an approach, problems and outcomes are conceived in measurable terms, and data is gathered to monitor interventions and evaluate effectiveness. Interventions are selected based on their scientific support and effectiveness as systematically measured and evaluated (Cournoyer, 2004; Petr & Walter, 2005). The term "evidence-based practice" has been suggested as broader than "empirically based practice," since external research findings are considered in the context of fit to particular situations, which in turn are considered within the context of informed consent and client values and expectations (Gambrill, 2004; Petr & Walter, 2005, p. 252).

Evidence-based practice began in medicine as an attempt to make conscientiously identify best practices for client care, assess the quality of evidence available, and present that evidence to clients and patients so that they could share in decision making (Adams & Drake, 2006; Scheyett, 2006). More recently, two forms of evidence-based practice have become prominent.

The first form, the *process model,* is consistent with the medical definition of evidence-based practice cited previously and focuses on the practices of the individual practitioner. Specifically, the individual practitioner learns how to formulate a question that is answerable with data about his or her work with a client (Rubin, 2007). Based on that question, the practitioner gains access to appropriate empirical literature. The practitioner must have access to appropriate literature through computerized access to online journals and studies. The practitioner does not need to review all the relevant literature from all of the available studies but may seek secondary reviews and meta-analyses of an intervention that summarize the state of knowledge about that intervention. For example, the evidence about stages of change in a child welfare context has been summarized by Littell and Girvin (2004). In assessing studies of interventions, a hierarchy of levels has been developed to assess the reliability of an intervention measure. For example, multiple randomized studies are considered to provide potentially strong support for an intervention. With some social problems and settings such as child welfare, such studies are rare; however, studies with other adequate controls may be available (Thomlison, 2005; Whiting Blome, & Steib, 2004; Kessler, Gira, & Poertner, 2005). Whatever the range of studies available, the practitioner needs to have the skills to assess the level of support for the intervention. Based on this assessment of data, the social worker can share that evidence with his or her client in order to better make an informed decision together about what to do. After making this joint decision, the practitioner and client can implement the intervention with fidelity and assess how well it works. This has been characterized as a bottom-up model because the questions raised and interventions selected are assumed to be defined by the people closest to the intervention: the practitioner and client (Rubin, 2007).

There are several assumptions about the process model as presented in this form that must be assessed. It assumes that the practitioner is free to select an intervention and the client is free to accept or reject it. In fact, agency-level practice has many influences that determine which interventions can be utilized (Payne, 2005). Some interventions are supported by the agency and supervisor based on policies, laws, prior training, and accepted practices. Practitioners utilizing the process model hope that such interventions are supported by a review of the research evidence. Recognizing this issue and that the choice of intervention may not be fully in the control of the practitioner, some proponents have suggested that one solution is for teams to study

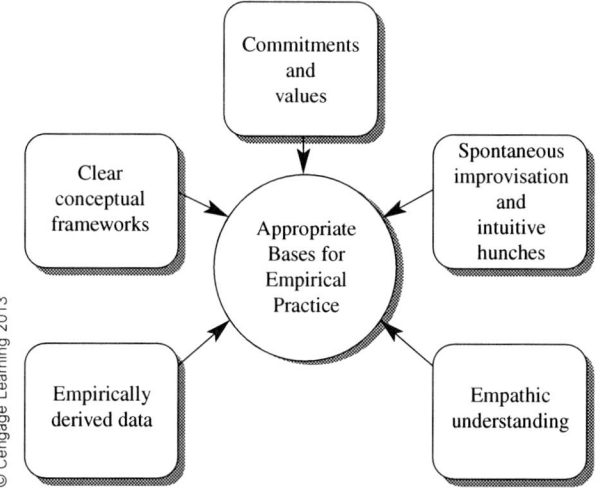

FIG-1-6 Appropriate Bases for Empirical Practice
Source: Adapted from Berlin and Marsh, 1993, p. 230.

evidence about particular problems and interventions and make recommendations about practices to be used by the team (Proctor, 2007). In partnership with schools of social work, agency teams can identify problems and secure administrative support while the schools provide training in evidence-based practices. Secondly, when clients are not entirely voluntary, practitioners and agencies may and should make evidence-based decisions; but involuntary clients may not feel empowered to reject them (Scheyett, 2006; Kessler et al, 2005). In such cases, however, clients are entitled through informed consent to know the rationale for the intervention and its evidence of effectiveness. This model also assumes that the practitioner has sufficient time to access the appropriate literature and appropriate resources. Finally, it assumes that the practitioner has the skill, training, and supervision to carry out the evidence-based intervention effectively (Rubin, 2007).

Partly in response to the difficulties associated with the process model, another version of evidence-based practice refers to training in these practices. In this approach, the emphasis is on identifying models of practice that have demonstrated efficacy for particular problems and populations, learning about them, and learning how to implement them. An advantage of this approach, according to proponents, is the fact that it focuses on not just knowing about the intervention but acquiring the skills necessary to carry it out effectively (Rubin, 2007). Critics suggest that this approach carries its own dangers. For one, students often experience anxiety in learning how to become effective practitioners and, having learned one evidence-based practice, might be inclined to generalize it beyond its original effectiveness, thus replicating in part the problem mentioned earlier of students trained in a theory or model and carrying it out without evidence of effectiveness and without having an alternative: If your only tool is a hammer, all problems may appear to be nails (Scheyett, 2006). Secondly, evidence-based practices have their own limited shelf life, with new studies supporting some methods and qualifying the support for others. Hence, the fact that you learn one evidence-based approach does not preclude and should not preclude learning others. In fact, we believe that becoming effective practitioners is a career-long proposition, not limited by the completion of your academic program. Finally, behavioral and cognitive-behavioral approaches are well-represented among evidence-based practices. Some have suggested that such approaches have some advantage because practice of the approach fits research protocols, and therefore that other approaches have been under-represented

(Coady & Lehmann, 2008; Walsh, 2006). It becomes a challenge to other approaches to enhance their effectiveness base rather than question the value of research protocols or representativeness of the model. There is growing evidence that some emerging approaches, such as the solution-focused approach are in fact increasing their effectiveness base (Kim, 2008).

Advocates suggest that there is room for both such approaches in social work education; that all students should learn how to carry out the process model of evidence-based practice and that all students should become proficient in at least one evidence-based practice modality (Rubin, 2007). These proponents also suggest that this kind of practice may require specialization in certain methods and may not be consistent with those programs that include an advanced generalist curriculum (Howard, Allen-Meares, & Ruffolo, 2007). We do not take sides on this issue, recognizing that programs that have developed advanced generalist curricula have done so mindful of the context and expectations for practitioners in their area, and that generalist practice remains the standard for BSW programs and the first year of MSW programs.

Guidelines Influencing Intervention Selection

We recommend the following guidelines to assist you in deciding when and how to intervene with clients in social work practice.

1. *Social workers value maximum feasible self-determination, empowerment, and enhancing strengths to increase the client's voice in decision making.* Thus, manualized approaches that imply that all major decisions are in the hands of and controlled by the social work practitioner are alien to these values. Following these values, we seek to include clients to the extent possible in access to information that would assist them in making decisions (Coady & Lehmann, 2008).

2. *Social workers assess circumstances from a systems perspective, mindful of the person in the situation, the setting, the community, and the organization.* We assess for the level of the problem and the appropriate level of interventions (Allen-Meares & Garvin, 2000). We recognize that resources are often needed at multiple levels and attempt to avoid a narrow clinical focus on the practitioner and client. Hence our use of data and perspectives to guide us must be governed in part by the multiple roles we play, including systems linkage as well as

direct practice or clinical interventions (Richey & Roffman, 1999).

3. *Social workers are sensitive to diversity in considering interventions.* We avoid assumptions that interventions tested with one population will necessarily generalize to another. In so doing, we are particularly sensitive to the clients' own perspectives about what is appropriate for them (Allen-Meares & Garvin, 2000).

4. *Social workers draw on evidence-based practices at both process and intervention levels as sources in determining, together with the client, how to proceed.* We expect social work practitioners to have access to evidence about efficacious interventions for the problem at hand. Such evidence may occur through individual study, through organizational priorities, or through collaboration with university teams to construct guidelines for practice in critical areas. Because our code of ethics requires us to act within our level of competence and supervision, knowledge of what interventions are efficacious does not mean that we can carry out those interventions. It may be a useful goal to learn how to carry out two or more evidence-based approaches as part of your education program. The goal of this book is, however, to equip you with the basic skills to carry out practice at the beginning level. We are influenced by the process model of evidence-based practice, and we seek to give you useful tools by modeling ways that questions can be asked and that data can be consulted in making decisions with clients. Further, in our chapters on intervention models we will be influenced by evidence-based practice models. It is not realistic at this level to attempt to teach evidence-based practice approaches such that you would be able to implement them right away. We can introduce you to them, but further training and supervision are required.

5. *Social workers think critically about practice, checking out assumptions and examining alternatives.* We try to avoid early social work patterns of applying theories more widely than data suggests by being open to examining alternatives (Briggs & Rzepnicki, 2004; Gambrill, 2004). One danger of following a single approach is that data that does not fit the preferences of the approach is discounted (Maguire, 2002). Conversely, this danger can also apply to selecting an approach based on its label as evidence-based, for example, without assessing fit with client and circumstances (Scheyett, 2006).

Summary

This chapter introduced social work as a profession marked by a specific mission and well-established values. As social workers and their clients operate in many different kinds and levels of environments, ecological and systems concepts are useful metaphors for conceptualizing what social workers and clients must deal with. Chapter 2 will delve deeper into specifying direct practice and the roles that social workers play.

Competency Notes

EP 2.1.1 Social workers identify as professionals and conduct themselves accordingly (p. 10).

EP 2.1.2 Social workers apply social Work Ethical Principles to Guide Professional Practice (p. 11).

EP 2.1.2a Social workers recognize and manage personal values in a way that allows professional values to guide practice (p. 9).

EP 2.1.2b Social workers make ethical decisions by applying standards of the National Association of Social Workers Code of Ethics and, as applicable, of the International Federation of Social Workers/International Association of Schools of Social Work Ethics in Social Work, Statement of Principles (pp. 7, 10).

EP 2.1.3 Social workers apply critical thinking to inform and communicate professional judgments (p. 11).

EP 2.1.3b Social workers analyze models of assessment, prevention, intervention, and evaluation (p. 16).

EP 2.1.4 Social workers engage diversity and difference in practice (pp. 9, 11).

EP 2.1.5 Social workers advance human rights and social and economic justice (p. 6).

EP 2.1.5b Social workers advocate for human rights and social and economic justice (pp. 4, 6, 12).

EP 2.1.5c Social workers engage in practices that engage in social and economic justice (pp. 4, 6, 12).

EP 2.1.6 Social workers engage in research-informed practice and practice-informed research (pp. 13, 20).

EP 2.1.7 Social workers apply knowledge of human behavior and the social environment (pp. 5, 13).

EP 2.1.8 Social workers engage in policy practice to advance social and economic well-being and to deliver effective social work services (p. 13).

EP 2.1.9 Social workers respond to contexts that shape practice (pp. 13, 14).

EP 2.1.10 Social workers engage, assess, intervene, and evaluate with individuals, families, groups, organizations and communities (p. 14).

EP 2.1.10a Social workers substantively and affectively prepare for action with individuals, families, groups, organizations, and communities (p. 14).

EP 2.1.10b Social workers use empathy and other interpersonal skills (p. 14).

EP 2.1.10c Social workers develop a mutually agreed-on focus of work and desired outcomes with clients. (p. 14)

EP 2.1.10d Social workers collect, organize, and interpret client data to inform practice (p. 14).

EP 2.1.10e Social workers assess client strengths and limitations (p. 5).

B 2.2 Social workers carry out generalist practice (pp. 14, 15).

M 2.2 Social workers carry out advanced practice (p. 14).

CourseMate

Access an integrated eBook and chapter-specific learning tools including glossary terms, chapter outlines, relevant web links, videos, and practice quizzes. Go to **www.cengagebrain.com**.

CHAPTER 4

Operationalizing the Cardinal Social Work Values

CHAPTER OVERVIEW

Social work practice is guided by knowledge, skills, and values. This chapter addresses the last of those three areas, introducing the cardinal values of the profession and the ethical obligations that arise from those values. Because, in practice, values can clash and ethical principles may conflict with each other, the chapter also describes some of these dilemmas and offers guidance about resolving them. As you read this chapter, you will have opportunities to place yourself in complex situations that will challenge you to analyze your personal values and to assess their compatibility with social work values. As a result of reading this chapter you will:

- Understand the core social work values and how they play out in practice

- Develop self-awareness and professional competence by examining the tensions that can occur when personal values intersect with professional values

- Learn the role that the NASW Code of Ethics plays in guiding professional practice

- Be familiar with four core ethical issues: self-determination, informed consent, professional boundaries, and confidentiality

- Know the steps for resolving ethical dilemmas and the ways in which these apply to a case

- Understand the complexities in applying ethical standards to clients who are minors.

EPAS COMPETENCIES IN THE 4TH CHAPTER

This chapter will give you the information needed to meet the following practice competencies:

2.1.1b Practice personal reflection and self-correction to assure continual professional development

2.1.1c Attend to professional roles and boundaries

2.1.1d Demonstrate professional demeanor in behavior, appearance, and communication

2.1.1f Use supervision and consultation

2.1.2a Recognize and manage personal values in a way that allows professional values to guide practice

2.1.2b Make ethical decisions by applying standards of the National Association of Social Workers Code of Ethics and, as applicable, of the International Federation of Social Workers/International Association of Schools of Social Work Ethics in Social Work, Statement of Principles

2.1.2c Tolerate ambiguity in resolving ethical conflicts

2.1.2d Apply strategies of ethical reasoning to arrive at principled decisions

2.1.10a Substantively and affectively prepare for action with individuals, families, groups, organizations, and communities

The Interaction Between Personal and Professional Values

Values are "preferred conceptions," or beliefs about how things ought to be. All of us have values: our beliefs about what things are important or proper that then guide our actions and decisions. The profession of social work has values, too. They indicate what is important to social workers

EP 2.1.10a

and guide the practice of the profession. Social workers must be attuned to their personal values and be aware of when those values mesh or clash with those espoused by the profession as a whole. They must recognize that their clients also have personal values that shape their beliefs and behaviors, and these may conflict with the social worker's own values or with those of the profession. Further, the larger society has values that are articulated through cultural norms, policies, laws, and public opinion. These can also diverge from social workers' beliefs, their clients' values, or the profession's values.

Self-awareness is the first step in sorting out these potential areas of conflict. The following sections describe the core values of the profession, provide opportunities to become aware of personal values, and describe the difficulties that can occur when social workers impose their own beliefs on clients.

The Cardinal Values of Social Work

The Code of Ethics developed by the National Association of Social Workers (NASW, 2008) and the professional literature articulate the core values of the profession and the ethical principles that represent those values. They can be summarized as follows:

- *All human beings deserve access to the resources they need to deal with life's problems and to develop their full potential. The value of service is embodied in this principle, in that social workers are expected to elevate service to others above their own self-interest. In particular, the professions' values place a premium on working for social justice. Social workers' "change efforts are focused primarily on issues of poverty, unemployment, discrimination, and other forms of social injustice. These activities seek to promote sensitivity to and knowledge about oppression and cultural and ethnic diversity. Social workers strive to ensure access to needed information, services, and resources; equality of opportunity; and meaningful participation in decision making for all people" (NASW, 2008, p. 5).*
- *The value that social workers place on the dignity and worth of the person is demonstrated through respect for the inherent dignity of the persons with whom they work and in efforts to examine prejudicial attitudes that may diminish their ability to embrace each client's individuality.*
- *Social workers view interpersonal relationships as essential for well-being and as "an important vehicle*

for change" (NASW, 2008, p. 5). The value placed on human relationships affects the way social workers relate to their clients and the efforts that social workers make to improve the quality of the relationships in their clients' lives.
- *The value of integrity means that professional social workers behave in a trustworthy manner. They treat their clients and colleagues in a fair and respectful fashion; they are honest and promote responsible and ethical practices in others.*
- *The value of competence requires that social workers practice only within their areas of ability and continually develop and enhance their professional expertise. As professionals, social workers must take responsibility for assuring that their competence is not diminished by personal problems, by substance abuse, or by other difficulties. Similarly, they should take action to address incompetent, unethical, or impaired practice by other professionals.*

What do these values mean? What difficulties can arise in putting them into practice? How can they conflict with social workers', clients', and society's values? The following sections describe these values and situations in which challenges can occur. Skill-building exercises at the end of the chapter and in the *Practice Behaviors Workbook* will assist you in identifying and working through value conflicts.

EP 2.1.1b

1. *All human beings deserve access to the resources they need to deal with life's problems and to develop to their fullest potential.* A historic and defining feature of social work is the profession's focus on individual well-being in a social context. Attending to the environmental forces that "create, contribute to, and address problems in living" is a fundamental part of social work theory and practice (NASW, 2008, p. 1).

Implementing this value means believing that people have the right to resources. It also means that as a social worker you are committed to helping secure those resources for your clients and to developing policies and implementing programs to fill unmet needs. While this value seems an easy choice to embrace, certain cases can bring out conflicting beliefs and personal biases that challenge the social worker in upholding it. To enhance your awareness of situations in which you might experience such difficulties, imagine yourself in interviews with the clients in each of the following scenarios. Take note of your feelings and of possible discomfort or conflict. Next, contemplate whether your response is consistent with the social work value in question. If the client has not requested a resource but the need for one is apparent, consider what resource might be developed and how you might go about developing it.

Situation 1 You are a practitioner in a public assistance agency that has limited special funds available to assist clients to purchase essential devices such as eyeglasses, dentures, hearing aids, and other prosthetic items. Your client, Mr. Y, lives in a large apartment complex for single persons and is disabled by a chronic psychiatric disorder. He requests special aid in purchasing new glasses. He says he accidentally dropped his old glasses and they were stepped on by a passerby. However, you know from talking to his landlord and his previous worker that, due to his confusion, Mr. Y regularly loses his glasses and has received emergency funds for glasses several times in the last year alone.

▣ VIDEO CASE EXAMPLE

Situation 2 In one of the videos accompanying this text, Yanping, a Chinese student studying in the U.S., has decided she wants to major in history, while her parents insist that she study business so that she can eventually take over the family company. The American social worker values Yanping's autonomy but understands the risk her client faces in defying parental authority and tradition. The Chinese social worker values family harmony, and probes Yanping's insistence on choosing a major at odds with her parents' wishes.

Situation 3 During a routine visit to an elderly couple who are recipients of public assistance, you discover that the roof on their home leaks. The couple has had small repairs on several occasions, but the roof is old and worn out. They have gathered bids for re-roofing, and the lowest bid was more than $3,500. They ask whether your agency can assist them with funding. State policies permit expenditures for such repairs under exceptional circumstances, but much red tape is involved, including securing special approval from the county director of social services, the county advisory board, and the state director of social services.

Situation 4 Mr. M sustained a severe heart attack 3 months ago and took a medical leave from his job as a furniture mover. His medical report indicates that he must limit his future physical activities to light work. Mr. M has given up looking for new work and is asking you to pursue worker's compensation and other resources that would help support his family. You are concerned that while Mr. M might be entitled to these supports, they may reduce his motivation to

pursue rehabilitation and work that he can reasonably do given his physical condition.

Situation 5 A military mental health provider is treating a client with mild trauma symptoms. The client wants to be sent home from the deployment, though his/her unit needs him/her to continue in combat. Is the client genuinely traumatized or malingering? Is going home ultimately more harmful for the person's mental health than staying and fulfilling his/her commitments to the unit, the mission, and fellow personnel? Since fear is common in combat, should everyone who is traumatized be allowed to go home? How should the client's self-determination be honored when he/she knew upon enlisting what the job would entail? (Simmons & Rycraft, 2010).

The preceding vignettes depict situations in which people need resources or opportunities to develop their skills or potential or to ensure their safety and quality of life. Possible obstacles to responding positively to these needs, according to the sequence of the vignettes, are as follows:

1. A judgmental attitude by the worker
2. A clash of values among the client, workers, and the client's family system.
3. Failure to offer options because of the effort involved or the pressure of other responsibilities
4. Skepticism that services will be effective in helping the client and apprehension that they may have unintended effects

Perhaps, as you read the vignettes, you experienced some of these reactions or additional ones. This discomfort is not uncommon, but such reactions indicate a need for expanded self-examination and additional experience to embrace the social work value in challenging situations. The next section describes some strategies for addressing these types of conflicting reactions.

2. Social workers respect the inherent dignity and worth of the person. Social workers recognize the central importance of human relationships (NASW, 2008, p. 5). These values mean that social workers believe that all people have intrinsic importance, whatever their past or present behaviors, beliefs, way of life, or social status, and that understanding these qualities is essential in involving clients as partners in change. These values embody several related concepts, sometimes referred to as "unconditional positive regard," "nonpossessive warmth," "acceptance," and "affirmation."

These values also recognize that respect is an essential element of the helping relationship. Before people will risk sharing personal problems and expressing deep emotions, they must first feel fully accepted and have trust in the goodwill and helpful intent of their service providers. This may be especially difficult when people feel ashamed or inadequate in requesting assistance. When clients are seeking services involuntarily, or when they have violated social norms by engaging in interpersonal violence, criminal behavior, or other infractions, they will be especially alert to perceived judgments or condemnation on the part of the social worker. Your role is not to judge whether clients are to blame for their problems or to determine whether they are good or bad, evil or worthy, guilty or innocent. Rather, your role is to seek to understand them, with all of their difficulties and assets, and assist them in searching for solutions to their problems.

Intertwined with acceptance and a nonjudgmental attitude is the equally important value of stating that every person is unique and that social workers should affirm the individuality of all the people they serve. People are, of course, endowed with widely differing physical and mental characteristics; moreover, their life experiences are infinitely diverse. People differ in terms of their appearance, beliefs, physiological functioning, interests, talents, motivation, goals, values, emotional and behavioral patterns, and many other factors. To affirm the uniqueness of another person, you must be committed to entering that individual's world, endeavoring to understand how that person experiences life. Only by attempting to walk in his or her shoes can you gain a full appreciation of the rich and complex individuality of another person. These recommendations are exemplified in the insights gained by social work students serving as volunteers in a camp for burn-injured children (Williams & Reeves, 2004). Not only did the students overcome feelings of fear, self-consciousness, pity, and horror at the campers' conditions, but they overcame stereotypes and animosity regarding their fellow volunteers (firefighters) who held different values and approaches than the social workers. Through respect, communication, attention to the other (versus oneself), appreciation for individuality over stereotypes, and a focus on shared purpose, all of the volunteers were able to create a successful community in which the campers could experience joy and healing.

Affirming each person's individuality, of course, goes far beyond gaining an appreciation of that person's perspectives on life. You must be able to convey awareness of what your client is experiencing moment by moment and affirm the validity of that experience. This affirmation does not mean agreeing with or condoning all of that person's views and feelings. Part of your role as a social worker entails helping people

disentangle their confusing, conflicting thoughts and feelings; align their perceptions with reality; mobilize their particular strengths, and differentiate rational reactions from irrational ones. To fulfill this role, you must retain your own separateness and individuality. Otherwise, you may over-identify with clients, thereby losing your ability to provide fresh input. Affirming the experiences of another person means validating those experiences, thus fostering that person's sense of personal identity and self-esteem.

Our opportunities for affirming individuality and sense of self-worth are lost when unexamined prejudices and stereotypes (either positive or negative) blind us to the uniqueness of each individual client. Labels—such as "gang banger," "sorority girl," "old people," or "psychiatric patient"—perpetuate damaging stereotypes because they obscure the individual characteristics of the people assigned to those labels. Whether the preconceptions are positive or negative, professionals who hold them may fail to effectively engage with the person behind the label; they may overlook needs or capacities and, as a result, their assessments, goals, and interventions will be distorted.

The consequences of such practices are troubling. Imagine an elderly client whose reversible health problems (associated with inadequate nutrition or need for medication) are dismissed as merely symptomatic of advanced age. Also consider the client with developmental disabilities who is interested in learning about sexuality and contraceptives, but whose social worker fails to address those issues, considering them irrelevant for members of this population. Perhaps the sorority member will fail to disclose symptoms of a learning disorder or suicidal ideation to the social worker who presumes she "has everything going for her." What about the man with schizophrenia who is more concerned about his aging parents than he is about his illness and symptom management? Clearly, avoiding assumptions and prejudices is central to effective social work practice.

Sometimes, the ability to embrace these first two sets of values comes with increased experience and exposure to a range of clients. Veteran practitioners have learned that acceptance comes through understanding the life experience of others, not by criticizing or judging their actions. As you work with service recipients, you should try to view them as persons in distress and avoid perceiving them based on labels such as "lazy," "borderline," "irresponsible," "delinquent," "dysfunctional," or "promiscuous." As you learn more about your clients, you will find that many of them have suffered various forms of deprivation and have themselves been victims of abusive, rejecting, or exploitative behavior. Remember also that all people have abilities and assets that may not be apparent to you. Consistent respect and acceptance on your part are vital in helping them gain self-esteem and mobilize capacities that are essential to change and to well-being.

However, withholding judgments does not mean condoning or approving of illegal, immoral, abusive, exploitative, or irresponsible behavior. It is often our responsibility to help people live, not according to our particular values and moral codes, but according to the norms and laws of society. In doing so, social workers, without blaming, must assist clients in taking responsibility for the part they play in their difficulties. Indeed, change is possible in many instances only when individuals gain awareness of the effects of their decisions and seek to modify their behavior accordingly. The difference between "blaming" and "defining ownership of responsibilities" lies in the fact that the former tends to be punitive, whereas the latter flows from the social worker's positive intentions to be helpful and to assist clients in change. As a professional, you will inevitably confront the challenge of maintaining your own values without imposing them on your clients (Doherty, 1995). A first step toward resolving this issue is addressing your own judgmental tendencies.

EP 2.1.1b

The value clarification exercises that follow will help you to identify your own particular areas of vulnerability. In each situation, imagine yourself in an interview or group session with the client(s). If appropriate, you can role-play the situation with a fellow student, changing roles so that you can benefit by playing the client's role as well. As you imagine or role-play the situation, be aware of your feelings, attitudes, and behavior. After each situation, contemplate or discuss the following questions:

1. What feelings and attitudes did you experience? Were they based on what actually occurred or did they emanate from preconceived beliefs about such situations or individuals?
2. Were you comfortable or uneasy with the client? How did your classmate perceive your attitudes toward the "client"? What cues alerted him or her to your values and reactions?
3. Did any of the situations disturb you more than others? What values were reflected in your feelings, attitudes, and behavior?
4. What assumptions did you make about the needs of the client(s) in each vignette?

5. What actions would you take (or what information would you seek) to move beyond stereotypes in understanding your client(s)?

Situation 6 Your client is a 35-year-old married male who was sentenced by the court to a secure mental health facility following his arrest for peering in the windows of a women's dormitory at your college. He appears uncomfortable and blushes as you introduce yourself.

Situation 7 You are assigned to do a home study for a family interested in adoption. When you arrive at the home for the first interview, you realize that the couple interested in the adoption consists of two male partners.

Situation 8 You are a child protection worker and your client is a 36-year-old man whose 13-year-old stepdaughter ran away from home after he had sexual intercourse with her on several occasions during the past 2 months. In your first meeting, he states that he "doesn't know what the big deal is ... it's not like we're related or anything."

Situation 9 Your 68-year-old client has been receiving chemotherapy for terminal cancer at your hospital for the past month. Appearing drawn and dramatically more emaciated than she was last month, the client reports that she has been increasingly suffering with pain and believes her best course of action is to take an overdose of sleeping pills.

Situation 10 You are a probation officer. The judge has ordered you to complete a pre-sentencing investigation of a woman who was arrested for befriending elderly and disabled individuals, then stealing their monthly disability checks.

Situation 11 You have been working for 8 weeks with a 10-year-old boy who has experienced behavioral difficulties at school. During play therapy he demonstrates with toys how he has set fire to several cats and dogs in his neighborhood.

Situation 12 Your client, Mrs. O, was admitted to a domestic violence shelter following an attack by her husband, in which she sustained a broken collarbone and arm injuries. This occasion is the eighth time she has contacted the shelter. Each previous time she has returned home or allowed her husband to move back into the home with her.

Situation 13 A low-income family with whom you have been working recently received a substantial check as part of a settlement with their former landlord. During a visit in which you plan to help the family budget the funds to pay their past due bills, you find the settlement money is gone—spent on a large television and gambling at a local casino.

Situation 14 You are a Latino outreach worker. One Caucasian client has expressed appreciation for the help you have provided, yet tells you repeatedly that she is angry at her difficulty finding a job, blaming it on "all these illegals."

Situation 15 You are working with a high school senior, the eldest girl in a large family from a strict religious background. Your client wants desperately to attend college but has been told by her parents that she is needed to care for her younger siblings and assist in her family's ministry.

If you experienced uneasy or negative feelings as you read or role-played any of the preceding situations, your reactions were not unusual. While social workers take many situations in stride, each of us may be tripped up by a scenario that is new to us, challenges our embedded beliefs, or triggers value conflicts. It can be challenging to look beyond differences, our comfort zones, or distressing behaviors to see clients as individuals in need. However, by focusing selectively on the person rather than on the behavior, you can gradually overcome initial reactions and learn to see them in full perspective.

EP 2.1.2a

How does this acceptance play out in practice? Acceptance is conveyed by listening attentively; by responding sensitively to the client's feelings; by using facial expressions, voice intonations, and gestures that convey interest and concern; and by extending courtesies and attending to the client's comfort.

If you are unable to be open and accepting of people whose behavior runs counter to your values, your effectiveness in helping them will be diminished, because it is difficult—if not impossible—to conceal negative feelings toward others. Even if you can mask your negative feelings toward certain clients, you are likely to be unsuccessful in helping them, as people quickly detect insincerity. To expand your capacity for openness and acceptance, it may be helpful to view association with others whose beliefs, backgrounds, and behaviors differ strikingly from your own as an opportunity to enrich yourself as you experience their uniqueness. Truly open people relish such opportunities, viewing differences as refreshing and stimulating and seeing these interactions as a chance to better understand the forces that motivate people. By prizing the opportunity to relate to all types of people and by seeking to understand them, you will gain a deeper appreciation of the diversity and

complexity of human beings. In so doing, you will be less likely to pass judgment and will achieve personal growth in the process. You might also find it helpful to talk with other social workers who have been in the field for some time. How do they manage value conflicts? How do they develop cultural competence? Are they able to treat others with respect, even if they disdain their actions?

3. *The value of integrity means that social work professionals behave in a trustworthy manner.* As an ethical principle, integrity means that social workers act honestly, encourage ethical practices in their agencies, and take responsibility for their own ethical conduct (Reamer, 1998). In practice, it means that social workers present themselves and their credentials accurately, avoid other forms of misrepresentation (e.g., in billing practices or in presentation of research findings), and do not participate in fraud and deception. Integrity also refers to the ways that social workers treat their colleagues. Professionals are expected to treat one another with respect, avoid involving clients or others in professional disputes, and be forthright in their dealings with fellow professionals. These expectations are important not only for our individual trustworthiness, but also because each of us serves as a representative of the larger profession and we should act in ways that do not dishonor it.

This may seem to be a relatively straightforward expectation. However, challenges can arise when pressures from other colleagues or employing organizations create ethical dilemmas. In those cases, the challenge is not what is right, but rather how to do it. Following are two examples of such dilemmas involving the principle of integrity. What strategies might you pursue to resolve these dilemmas and act with honesty and professionalism?

Situation 16 Your agency recently received a large federal grant to implement a "Return to Work" program as part of welfare reform. Although the evaluation protocol is very clear about what constitutes "work," the agency is pressuring you and your coworkers (none of whom are social workers) to count clients' volunteer efforts and other nonpaying jobs as "work" in an effort to ensure that this valuable program will continue. The agency maintains that paying jobs are difficult to find, so clients who are actively working—even in noncompensated jobs—"fit the spirit, if not the letter of the law."

Situation 17 Your supervisor wants to assess your effectiveness in conducting family sessions. Because he fears that client behaviors will change and his findings will be distorted if clients know they are being taped, he has told you to tape these sessions without their knowledge. The supervisor feels that because he discusses your cases with you anyway, the taping without explicit client permission should be acceptable.

EP 2.1.1f

4. *The value of competence requires that social workers practice only within their scope of knowledge and ability, and that they enhance and develop their professional expertise.* As with the value of integrity, this principle places the burden for self-awareness and self-regulation on the social worker. An expectation of practice as a professional is that the individual will take responsibility for knowing his or her own limits and seek out the knowledge and experience needed to develop further expertise throughout the span of his or her career. This principle means that social workers will decline cases where they lack sufficient expertise, and that they will seek out opportunities for continuous self-examination and professional development. The commitment to utilizing evidence-based practices means that professionals must be lifelong learners, staying abreast of practice-related research findings, discarding ineffective or harmful practices, and tailoring interventions to the client's unique circumstances (Gambrill, 2007). Each of these elements speaks to developing and maintaining professional competence. The NASW Code of Ethics also includes cultural competence among its expectations for social workers, requiring an understanding of various groups, their strengths, the effects of oppression, and the provision of culturally sensitive services (NASW, 2008).

EP 2.1.1b

Self-regulation also requires the social worker to be alert to events or problems that affect his or her professional competence. For example, is a health or mental health problem hindering the social worker's service to clients? Are personal reactions to the client (such as anger, partiality, or sexual attraction) impairing the social worker's judgment in a particular case? Are family problems or other stressors detracting from their capacity to respond to clients' needs? *Countertransference* refers broadly to the ways that a worker's experiences and emotional reactions influence his or her perceptions of and interactions with a client. Later in this book you will learn more about the ways that countertransference can be a constructive or destructive factor in the helping process. It is important to be alert to such reactions and use supervisory sessions to examine and address their impact.

Supervision is an essential element in professional development and ongoing competence. In the helping professions, a supervisor is not someone looking over the worker's shoulder to catch and correct mistakes. More typically, supervisors can be thought of as mentors, teachers, coaches, and counselors all wrapped up into one role (Haynes, Corey, & Moulton, 2003). Successful use of supervision requires you to be honest and self-aware in seeking guidance, raising issues for discussion, sharing your challenges and successes, and being open to feedback, praise, critiques, and change. Effective supervisors will help you develop skills to look clearly at yourself, so that you understand your strengths and weaknesses, preferences and prejudices, and become able to manage these for the benefit of your clients.

EP 2.1.1f

Developing and maintaining competence is a career-long responsibility, yet it can be challenging to uphold. Consider the following scenarios:

Situation 18 You are a new employee at a small, financially strapped counseling center. The director of your agency just received a contract to do outreach, assessments, and case management for frail elders. Although you took a human behavior course as a social work student, you have never studied or worked with older adults, especially those at risk. The director has asked you to lead this new program and has emphasized how important the new funding is for the agency's survival.

Situation 19 For the past few weeks, you've found yourself attracted to one of your clients, thinking about him or her often and wondering what the client is doing at different times of the day. You wonder if this attraction could affect your objectivity on the case but are reluctant to discuss the situation with your supervisor because it might affect his or her evaluation of you later this year.

Situation 20 Your internship is at a busy metropolitan hospital. In one morning alone you encounter a woman from Somalia whose dialect you are unfamiliar with, a Muslim woman reluctant to disrobe for the physical exam, and a Korean family at odds over the placement of their teenager's baby. You are called in to assist the medical team, but wonder how to effectively address all of the cultural and individual differences in these cases within the pressure-packed schedule of the hospital workday.

What is competence? Do social workers ever feel totally competent? What is impairment? And how can we tell when it applies to us and our practice?

Self-evaluation requires self-knowledge and introspection. Measuring one's competence requires honest self-examination and the pursuit of input from colleagues and supervisors. Professional development requires actively seeking out opportunities to hone existing skills and develop new ones, whether through reading, continuing education, course work, or case conferences. It means knowing what we do not know and being willing to acknowledge our shortcomings. It means being aware of the learning curve in developing new skills or testing new interventions and using staff development and supervision to assure that clients are receiving high quality services (NASW, 2008). It also means that when we lack the skills, abilities, or capacity demanded by a client's situation that we make proper referrals, thereby elevating the clients' needs above our own.

IDEAS IN ACTION

EP 2.1.1b

One way that social workers can assess and enhance competence is through the review of case recordings. These may be pen-and-paper process recordings of the dialogue in a client session or audio or video tapes of individual, family, or group meetings (Murphy & Dillon, 2008). Many social workers resist taping sessions on the premise that it makes clients uncomfortable, though the greater likelihood is that the client will forget the tape is there; it may be the worker him or herself that is distressed at its presence and at having to look at his or her performance at a later point. Ethical practice, however, requires facing this discomfort for the greater good of evaluating strengths and weaknesses and, ultimately, assuring competent practice. Ali, the worker interviewing Irwin and Angela Corning in the videos that accompany this text (Problem Solving with the Corning Family), received an array of insights as a result of reviewing the tapes of her sessions. Among her findings are the following:

At the outset of the first session, Irwin clearly stated his frustration with attending the meeting. His comment set the tone for our working relationship, which was strained at first. I remember thinking that exploring his frustration at that time would be a difficult conversation, and I did not want to get off to a bad start. The alternative was hardly any easier to work with. By ignoring his comment, though it was really his tone that got my attention, I communicated to both clients that I was not willing or ready to meet them where they were emotionally. The space between us was muddled for the remainder of the session. I could sense that Irwin was getting tense. I am thankful that rather than explode or walk out, he interjected himself into the conversation to explain his brusque demeanor and negative emotions.

Because I did not address Irwin's frustration, he remained distant, and the business of the meeting was conducted with Angela. For a majority of the first session, my legs were crossed in front of me and I was turned toward Angela. At times, I crossed my arms in front of me over the notepad. You can see by my posture that I was uncomfortable with the tension in the room.

I noticed that my nerves were showing in other ways as well. Occasionally during the interview I explored the details of personal situations with the couple. As I asked these sensitive questions, my voice trailed off, so much so that it is hard to hear the entire question on the recording. In contrast, a calm and even tone would normalize these difficult inquiries and the information they elicit.

It is amazing to hear how many times I said, "You know," and, "So." I never realized it before, but I use these phrases as a pause in my sentences. I have been trying to pay attention to it lately and make sure that when I am working with clients all of my words help to convey a point or information. I also say "you guys" a lot, which seems too casual and potentially disrespectful.

I also noticed that as I got more anxious, I talked a lot and fumbled around. Much of the time in the first session was spent sorting through what exactly I could provide the couple. Looking at it on tape, I can see why Angela and Irwin were so frustrated and uncomfortable. I eventually gave them a plan, to provide them with contact information for affordable apartment complexes and employment placement services, but I could have been clearer in how I conveyed the information. It just got more confusing when I sought the couple's corroboration in a partnership that they knew little about. This is a point in the interview where I could have checked in with the clients to be sure that we were all on the same page.

In the second session, my hesitancy to engage Irwin persisted. At that appointment, Irwin discovered for the first time that he and Angela were carrying a $2,000 balance on their credit card account. The couple exchanged words back and forth, which I remember was a poignant moment in my work with them. As I watched the tape, I was struck by this opportunity to explore the couple's money management methods. Instead of having that discussion, I got into the activity of listing all of the other barriers that the couple would face in attaining a new apartment. My personal goal was to be prepared in the second session. I wanted to be sure to get all of the items on my list, one of which was a discussion of the barriers to attaining the couple's stated goals.

Processing the disclosure of the credit card in the moment with the couple not only would have yielded information and helped the couple to share household financial tasks more effectively, but would have also engaged the clients and may have fostered rapport between Irwin and me. Because I did not address the issue, and it was a surprise and disappointment to Irwin, he was unable to follow the thread about barriers. When I checked in with him to see if he wanted to add anything, he revealed that he was consumed with thoughts of the debt discovery over the past several minutes rather than following the discussion.

I did a good job of seeking out which areas the clients wanted to address in their goals. The clients reported that they were happy with the outcomes of our work together and that they became more comfortable with the process as the relationship grew. At the same time, we could have been more detailed in making the task lists. While I was speaking with Irwin about his objectives for employment and career advancement he indicated that in the future he would like to see himself admitted to, or already enrolled in, a masonry apprentice program. This could have been thoughtfully broken down into task steps that Irwin would have control over. Should Irwin meet his objectives, but not attain the goal

because of factors out of his control, he would see documentation of his accomplishments and the efficacy of setting objectives and goals. (Unfortunately, we only had enough time to give this goal cursory treatment at the end of the interview.)

Near the end of our time together, Irwin and Angela had made considerable gains in the realms of housing, employment, and communicating with the school and I was feeling more confident in my work with them. I was glad to have the opportunity to go over the Eco-Map with them to illustrate how much they had done to change their lives. Watching the tape, I realized that I did not emphasize their success and efforts enough. I sense that this was a missed opportunity for offering congratulations and praise.

In the final session, I evaluated the work with Irwin and Angela. At one point I ask, "I didn't seem too nosy, did I?" Watching it, I realize that the wording of the question suggests a need for validation rather than feedback. Actually, one of my focal points for career development is to learn to encourage and foster self-determination as opposed to *doing for* the client. It is important to me that the clients I work with see the relationship as collaborative, with us all on equal ground. I really wanted to know if I seemed too pushy or bossy. I can see how rephrasing my question could allow Irwin and Angela to give more honest feedback. I could have asked, "Did you feel respected in our work together?" (or, "Did you feel disrespected in our work together?"). Did I respond to your needs and concerns?"

All in all I was glad to see the series of tapes, because I saw steady improvement in my skills and comfort over time. It is good that my supervisor reviewed them too, as she was able to identify strengths of mine that I can build on, as well as areas for change.

Challenges in Embracing the Profession's Values

EP 2.1.2a

In this section's presentation of the social work profession's cardinal values, numerous situations and cases have highlighted the potential for value conflicts. Self-awareness, openness to new persons and events, and increasing practice experience are all crucial elements in overcoming value conflicts. But what if you have made these efforts and your values continue to conflict with others' values?

Social workers occasionally encounter situations in which they cannot conform to the profession's values or in which a client's behaviors or goals evoke such negative reactions that a positive helping relationship cannot be established. For example, practitioners who have personal experience with child abuse or who are intensely opposed to abortions may find it difficult to accept a pedophile as a client or to offer help to a woman experiencing an unintended pregnancy. In such instances, it is important to acknowledge these feelings and to explore them through supervision or therapy. It may be feasible to help the worker overcome these difficulties in order to be more fully available as a helping person. If this is not possible, however, or if the situation is exceptional, the social worker and his or her supervisor should explore the possibility of transferring the case to another practitioner who can accept both the client and the goals. In such circumstances, it is vital to clarify for clients that the reason for the transfer is not personal rejection of them but rather a recognition that they deserve the best service possible and that the particular social worker cannot provide that service. It is not usually necessary to go into detail about the social worker's challenges. A general explanation conveys goodwill and safeguards clients' well-being. When a transfer is not possible, the social worker is responsible for seeking intensive assistance to ensure that services are provided properly and that ethical and professional responsibilities are upheld. Practitioners who are consistently unable to accept clients' differences or carry out their roles in a professional manner owe it to themselves and to future clients to reflect seriously on their suitability for the social work field.

EP 2.1.1d

Cross-cultural and cross-national social work offer further challenges in the application of professional values (Healy, 2007). Are values such as justice, service, and acceptance universally recognized guidelines for behavior, or should their application become tempered by cultural norms? Some have suggested that NASW and other social work codes of ethics place too great a value on individual rights over the collective good and emphasize independence over interdependence (Jessop, 1998; Silwawe, 1995). As such, they may reflect a Western bias and give insufficient attention to the values of other cultures. This is not merely a philosophical dispute. It creates significant challenges for practitioners working with individuals or groups with vastly different values. How can workers reconcile their responsibility to advocate for justice and equality while simultaneously demonstrating respect for cultural practices such as female circumcision, corporal punishment of children, arranged marriages, or differential rights based on social class, gender, skin tone, or sexual orientation? Cultural values shift and evolve over time, and social workers' systems change efforts may appropriately target stances that harm or disenfranchise certain groups. But how can social workers ensure that their efforts are proper and congruent with the desires of the particular cultural group and not a misguided effort borne of paternalism and ethnocentrism?

Healy (2007) recommends a stance of "moderate universalism" (p. 24), where the human rights of equality and protection are promoted along with the importance of cultural diversity and community ties. Ultimately, striking this balance means that social workers, individually and collectively, must be aware of their values and those of their colleagues and clients and engage in ongoing education and conversation in reconciling these value tensions. Congruent with cultural humility (Hunt, 2001), this approach encourages the professional to adopt a "learner" perspective, in order to determine where the ethical tensions reside and how much of an impediment they are for the helping process.

Ethics

Codes of ethics are the embodiment of a profession's values. They set forth principles and standards for behavior of members of that profession. In social work, the primary Code of Ethics is promulgated by the NASW. It addresses a range of responsibilities that social workers have as professionals, to their clients, to their colleagues, to their employers, to their profession, and to society as a whole. This section addresses four primary areas of ethical responsibility for social workers: self-determination, informed consent, maintenance of client-social worker boundaries, and confidentiality. First, however, it details how ethics are related to legal responsibilities and malpractice risks. The section concludes by summarizing the resources and processes available for resolving ethical dilemmas.

The Intersection of Laws and Ethics

The practice of social work is governed by a vast array of policies, laws, and regulations. Whether established by court cases, the U.S. Congress, state legislatures, licensure boards, or regulatory agencies, these rules affect social workers' decisions and actions. For example, state mandatory reporting laws require social workers to report cases where child abuse is suspected. The Health Insurance Portability and Accountability Act (HIPAA) regulates the storage and sharing of patient records (U.S. Department of Health and Human Services, 2003). Some states' health department rules may require social workers to divulge the names of HIV-positive clients to public health authorities; in other states, rules may forbid the sharing of patients' names or HIV status. Licensure board regulations may forbid social work

EP 2.1.10a

practice by persons with felony convictions. Federal court cases may extend evidential privilege to communications with social workers (Reamer, 1999). Federal, state or local laws may prohibit the provision of certain benefits to undocumented immigrants. Good social work practice requires workers to be aware of the laws and regulations that govern the profession and apply to their area of practice and the populations they serve. But knowing the laws is not enough. Consider the following case.

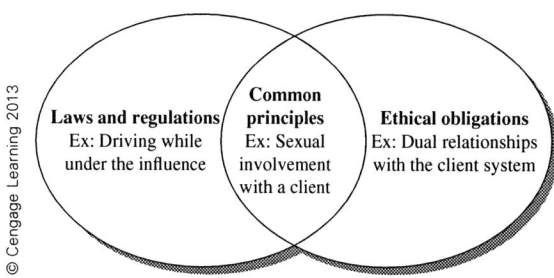

FIG-4-1 The Relationship of Law and Ethics

CASE EXAMPLE

Alice is a 38-year-old woman who has presented for treatment, filled with guilt as the result of a brief extramarital affair. In her third session, she discloses that she is HIV-positive but is unwilling to tell her husband of her status because then the affair would be revealed, and she fears losing him and her two young daughters. You are concerned about the danger to her husband's health and press her to tell him or to allow you to do so. Alice responds that if you do, you will be breaking your promise of confidentiality and violating her privacy. She implies that she would sue you or report you to your licensing board and to your profession's ethics committee.

This case neatly captures the clash of ethics, laws, and regulations and illustrates the stakes for workers who make the "wrong" decision. In a scenario such as this one, the social worker just wants a clear answer from a lawyer or supervisor who will tell him or her exactly what to do. Unfortunately, matters are not that simple. Good practice requires knowledge of both the applicable ethical principles and the relevant laws. Even with this knowledge, dilemmas may persist. In this case example, the ethical principles of self-determination and confidentiality are pitted against the principle to protect others from harm, which itself is derived from a court case (Cohen & Cohen, 1999; Reamer, 1995). The particular state or setting where the case takes place may have laws or regulations that govern the social worker's actions. Finally, the threat of civil litigation for malpractice looms large, even when the social worker's actions are thoughtful, careful, ethical, and legal.

When you think about the intersection of laws and ethics, it may be helpful to think of a Venn diagram with two ovals overlapping (see Figure 4-1). In the center are areas common to both ethics and laws; within each oval are items that are exclusive to laws and ethics, respectively. Some standards contained in the NASW Code of Ethics are not addressed by laws and regulations (such as the prohibition of sexual relationships with supervisees or standards on treating colleagues with respect). Similarly, some areas of the law are not covered by the Code of Ethics. For example, it is illegal to drive while intoxicated, but the Code of Ethics lacks a standard related to that act. Where the two realms intersect, there can be areas of agreement as well as areas of discord. As the Code of Ethics notes:

Social workers' primary responsibility is to promote the well-being of clients. In general, clients' interests are primary. However, social workers' responsibility to the larger society or specific legal obligations may on limited occasions supersede the loyalty owed clients, and clients should be so advised (NASW, 2008, p. 7).

Also:

Instances may arise when social workers' ethical obligations conflict with agency policies or relevant laws or regulations. When such conflicts occur, social workers must make a responsible effort to resolve the conflict in a manner that is consistent with the values, principles, and standards expressed in this Code. If a reasonable resolution of the conflict does not appear possible, social workers should seek proper consultation before making a decision (NASW, 2008, pp. 3–4).

The processes for ethical decision making are addressed later in this chapter. For now, it is important to acknowledge that social workers must know both the law and ethical principles to practice effectively. Workers must also recognize that sometimes conflicts will occur between and among ethical and legal imperatives. For example, state laws may prohibit the provision of services or resources to undocumented immigrants, but ethics would expect social workers to fill basic human needs. Thoughtful examination, consultation, and skillful application of the principles will serve as guides when laws and ethics collide.

Key Ethical Principles

The NASW Code of Ethics contains 155 standards, addressing a variety of ethical issues (such as conflicts of interest, competence, or confidentiality) for social workers in a range of roles (such as supervisor, teacher, direct practitioner, or administrator). In this section, we examine four key areas of immediate relevance to direct practitioners: self-determination, informed consent, professional boundaries and confidentiality.

Self-Determination

Biestek (1957) has defined self-determination as "the practical recognition of the right and need of clients to freedom in making their own choices and decisions" (p. 103). Self-determination is central to the social worker's ethical responsibility to clients:

> Social workers respect and promote the right of clients to self-determination and assist clients in their efforts to identify and clarify their goals. Social workers may limit clients' right to self-determination when, in their professional judgment, clients' actions or potential actions pose a serious, foreseeable, and imminent risk to themselves or others (NASW, 2008, p. 7).

This value also embodies the beliefs that individuals have the capacity to grow and change and to develop solutions to their difficulties, as well as the right and capacity to exercise free choice responsibly. These values are magnified when practitioners adopt a strengths-oriented perspective, looking for positive qualities and undeveloped potential rather than pointing out limitations and past mistakes (Cowger, 1994; Saleebey, 1997). Such a positive perspective engenders hope and courage on the client's part and nurtures self-efficacy. These factors, in turn, enhance the client's motivation, which is indispensable to achieving a successful outcome.

The extent to which you affirm an individual's right to self-determination rests in large measure on your perceptions of the helping role and of the helping process. If you consider your major role to be that of providing solutions or dispensing advice freely, you may foster dependency, demean clients by failing to recognize and affirm their strengths, and relegate them to a position of passive cooperation (or passive resistance, a frequent response under such circumstances). Such domineering behavior is counterproductive. Not only does it discourage open communication, but, equally important, it denies people the opportunity to gain strength and self-respect as they actively wrestle with their difficulties. Fostering dependency generally leaves people weaker rather than stronger and is a disservice to them.

The type of relationship that affirms self-determination and supports growth is a partnership wherein the practitioner and the client (whether an individual, a couple, or a group) are joined in a mutual effort to search for solutions to problems or to promote growth. As enablers of change, social workers facilitate clients in their quest to view their problems realistically, to consider various solutions and their consequences, to implement change-oriented strategies, to understand themselves and others more fully, to gain awareness of previously unrecognized strengths and opportunities for growth, and to tackle obstacles to change and growth. As helpful as these steps are, ultimately the responsibility for pursuing these options rests with the client.

Just as fostering self-determination enhances client autonomy, exhibiting paternalism (i.e., preventing self-determination based on a judgment of the client's own good) infringes on autonomy. Linzer (1999) refers to paternalism as "the overriding of a person's wishes or actions through coercion, deception or nondisclosure of information, or for the welfare of others" (p. 137). A similar concept is paternalistic beneficence, wherein the social worker implements protective interventions to enhance the client's quality of life, sometimes despite the client's objections (Abramson, 1985; Murdach, 1996).

Under what conditions might it be acceptable for a social worker to override a client's autonomy? Paternalism may be acceptable when a client is young or judged to be incompetent, when an irreversible act such as suicide can be prevented, or when the interference with the client's decisions or actions ensures other freedoms or liberties, such as preventing a serious crime (Abramson, 1985; Reamer, 1989). Murdach suggests three gradations of beneficent actions, which vary in their level of intrusiveness depending on the degree of risk and the client's decision-making capacity. Even under these circumstances, social workers must weigh the basis for their decisions against the potential outcomes of their actions.

For example, if a psychiatric patient refuses medication, some would argue that the client lacks competence to make such a decision, and that forcing him or her to take the medication would be "for the client's own good." Yet diagnosis or placement is not a sufficient basis for overriding a person's autonomy. For this reason, states have developed elaborate administrative and judicial processes that must be traversed before an individual can be involuntarily hospitalized or medicated.

Even when clients have reduced capacity for exercising self-determination, social workers should act to ensure that they exercise their capacities to the fullest feasible extent. For example, self-determination can be extended to individuals who are terminally ill by educating them about their options and encouraging them to articulate their desires through advance directives that provide instructions to health care personnel regarding which medical interventions are acceptable. These directives become operative when the patient's condition precludes decision-making capacity. Advance directives can take the form of living wills or authorizing an individual to act with durable power of attorney. The latter procedure is broader in scope and more powerful than a living will. The person designated to have durable power of attorney or medical power of attorney is authorized to make decisions as if he or she were the patient when grave illness or accident has obliterated the patient's autonomy.

Operationalizing clients' rights to self-determination can sometimes pose perplexing challenges. Adding to the complexity is the reality that in certain instances, higher-order principles such as safety supersede the right to self-determination. To challenge your thinking about how you might affirm the value of self-determination in practical situations, we have provided exercises that consist of problematic situations actually encountered by the authors or colleagues. As you read each scenario, analyze the alternative courses of action that are available and think of the laws, policies, and resources that you might consult as part of your decision making. Consider how you would work with the client to maximize self-determination, taking care also to promote his or her best interests.

EP 2.1.1c

Situation 21 In your work for the state welfare department, you oversee the care of numerous group home residents whose services are paid for by the state. Two of your clients, both in their twenties, reside in the same home and have told you that they are eager to get married. The administrator of the home strenuously protests that "those two are retarded" and, if they marry, "they might produce a child they could not properly care for." Further, she has stressed that she has no private room for a couple and that if they insist on marrying, they will have to leave the group home.

Situation 22 A 15-year-old runaway who is 4 months pregnant has contacted you several times in regard to planning for her child. During her last visit, she confided that she is habituated to heroin. You have expressed your concern that the drug may damage her unborn child, but she does not seem worried, nor does she want to give up use of the drug. You also know that she obtains money for heroin through prostitution and is living on the street.

Situation 23 While making a visit to Mr. and Mrs. F, an elderly couple living in their home on their own savings, you discover that they have hired several home health aides who have stolen from them and provided such poor care that their health and nutrition are endangered. When you discuss with them your concern about the adequacy of their care, they firmly state that they can handle their own problems and "do not want to be put in a nursing home!"

Situation 24 As a rehabilitation worker, you have arranged for a young woman to receive training as a beautician in a local technical college, a vocation in which she expressed intense interest. Although initially enthusiastic, she now tells you that she wants to discontinue the program and go into nursing. According to your client, her supervisor at the college is highly critical of her work and the other trainees tease her and talk about her behind her back. You are torn about what to do, because you know that your client tends to antagonize other people with her quick and barbed remarks. You wonder if, rather than change programs, your client needs to learn more appropriate ways of communicating and relating to her supervisor and coworkers.

Situation 25 A middle-aged woman with cancer was so debilitated by her latest round of chemotherapy that she has decided to refuse further treatment. Her physician states that her age, general health, and stage of cancer all argue for continuing her treatments, given the likelihood of a successful outcome. Her family is upset at seeing the woman in pain and supports her decision.

Providing Informed Consent

Six principles in the NASW Code of Ethics address facets of informed consent. At its essence, informed consent requires that social workers "use clear

EP 2.1.2b

and understandable language to inform clients of the purpose of the services, risks related to the services, limits to services because of the requirements of a third-party payer, relevant costs, reasonable alternatives, clients' right to refuse or withdraw consent, and the time frame covered by the consent. Social workers should provide clients with an opportunity to ask questions" (NASW, 2008, pp. 7–8). The Code of Ethics also indicates that clients should be informed when their services are being provided by a student. Timely and understandable informed consent sets the stage for social work services by acquainting the client with expectations for the process. For example, a common element of informed consent involves the limits on client privacy. Social workers explicitly state that in situations involving concerns about the client's danger to him or herself or others, the worker reserves the right to break confidentiality to seek appropriate help. Mandatory reporting requirements (for child and elder abuse and other circumstances, such as communicable diseases) are typically also covered at this time. In addition to respectfully educating the client about his or her rights and responsibilities, informed consent lays the groundwork for future actions the worker might need to take. In the earlier case about the woman who refused to let her husband know about her HIV-positive status, informed consent would have alerted the client at the outset to the worker's responsibility to protect others from harm and her duty to notify public health or other authorities about the risk created by the client's unprotected sexual activity.

Some workers view informed consent as a formality to be disposed of at the first interview or as a legalistic form to have clients sign and then file away. In fact, informed consent should be an active and ongoing part of the helping process. Given the tension and uncertainty that can accompany a first session, clients may not realize the significance of the information you are providing. In addition, new issues may emerge that require discussion of the client's risks, benefits, and options (Strom-Gottfried, 1998b). Therefore, it makes sense to revisit the parameters of service and invite questions throughout the helping process. Having a "fact sheet" that describes relevant policies and answers commonly asked questions can also help clients by giving them something to refer to between meetings, should questions arise (Houston-Vega, Nuehring, & Daguio, 1997; Zuckerman, 2008).

To facilitate informed consent for persons with hearing, literacy, or language difficulties, social workers should utilize interpreters and multiple communication methods as appropriate. When clients are temporarily or permanently incapable of providing informed consent, "social workers should protect clients' interests by seeking permission from an appropriate third party, informing clients consistent with the client's level of understanding" and "seek to ensure that the third party acts in a manner consistent with the client's wishes and interests" (NASW, 2008, p. 8). Even clients who are receiving services involuntarily are entitled to know the nature of the services they will be receiving and to understand their right to refuse service.

IDEAS IN ACTION

What elements of informed consent were covered in the initial moments of the videotaped interview with Anna and Jackie in "Home for the Holidays?"

- The expectation of confidentiality by the worker and by the two clients in regard to what each shared in the session.
- The limits of confidentiality: risk to self or others.
- Should either partner see the worker in an individual session, the information discussed or revealed there will not be held in confidence during conjoint sessions.
- The amount of time that the worker has set aside for the session (40 minutes).
- The purpose of the first session. The worker tells the clients that this is the time for them to tell her about themselves both as individuals and as a

couple and to share their concerns and struggles with her.
- The nature of couples' work. The worker informs the couple that she will not take sides or take the role of a referee. She explains to the couple that her clinical focus is on their interactions, and that she considers her client to be their relationship rather than either person individually.
- Although the relationship will be the therapeutic focus of the work, at times the worker will push and challenge one of the partners in particular. She explains that this is sometimes necessary to learn more about how the partners interact and to gain clarity about how the relationship works.

What else could have been covered as part of informed consent?

- The worker's experience with couples, specifically her previous work with same-sex partners.
- The worker's preferred theoretical framework for couple's therapy.

- Alternatives to pursuing couple's therapy with the worker (e.g., couple's education groups, group therapy, bibliotherapy).
- Fee schedule and terms of insurance coverage.
- The clients' right to withdraw consent and to cease therapy with the worker.

Preserving Professional Boundaries

EP 2.1.1c

Boundaries refer to clear lines of difference that are maintained between the social worker and the client in an effort to preserve the working relationship. They are intended to help prevent conflicts of interest, making the client's interests the primary focus and avoiding situations in which the worker's professional practice is compromised. In part, boundaries help clarify that the client-social worker relationship is not a social one. Also, even though it may involve a high degree of trust and client disclosure, the relationship is not an intimate one, such as might be experienced with a friend, partner, or family member. When clients can trust that boundaries exist and will be maintained by the social worker, they are more able to focus on the issues for which they are seeking help. They can freely share of themselves and trust that the social worker's reactions and statements—whether of support, confrontation, or empathy—are artifacts of the working relationship, not social or sexual overtures or personal reactions such as might arise when friends agree or disagree.

EP 2.1.1d

Sometimes social workers and other helping professionals have a difficult time with the notion of boundaries, perceiving that they establish a hierarchical relationship in which the client is deemed "less worthy" than the social worker. Some professionals may also feel that establishing such boundaries is a cold and clinical move, treating the client as an object instead of a fellow human deserving of warmth and compassion (Lazarus, 1994). Our viewpoint is that the two positions are not mutually exclusive. Social workers can have relationships with clients that are characterized by collaborative problem solving and mutuality, and they can react to clients authentically and kindly without blurring the boundaries of their relationship or obscuring the purpose of their work.

The NASW Code of Ethics addresses boundaries through six provisions:

EP 2.1.2b & 2.1.1c

1. "Social workers should not take unfair advantage of any professional relationship or exploit others to further their personal, religious, political, or business interests" (NASW, 2008, p. 9).
2. "Social workers should not engage in dual or multiple relationships with clients or former clients in which there is a risk of exploitation or potential harm to the client. In instances when dual or multiple relationships are unavoidable, social workers should take steps to protect clients and are responsible for setting clear, appropriate, and culturally sensitive boundaries. (Dual or multiple relationships occur when social workers relate to clients in more than one relationship, whether professional, social, or business. Dual or multiple relationships can occur simultaneously or consecutively.)" (NASW, 2008, pp. 9–10).
3. "Social workers should not engage in physical contact with clients when there is a possibility of psychological harm to the client as a result of the contact (such as cradling or caressing clients) ..." (NASW, 2008, p. 13).
4. "Social workers should under no circumstances engage in sexual activities or sexual contact with current clients, whether such contact is consensual or forced" (NASW, 2008, p. 13).
5. "Social workers should not engage in sexual activities or sexual contact with clients' relatives or other individuals with whom clients maintain a close personal relationship when there is a risk of exploitation or potential harm to the client. Sexual activity or sexual contact with clients' relatives or other individuals with whom clients maintain a personal relationship has the potential to be harmful to the client and may make it difficult for the

social worker and client to maintain appropriate professional boundaries. Social workers—not their clients, their clients' relatives, or other individuals with whom the client maintains a personal relationship—assume the full burden for setting clear, appropriate, and culturally sensitive boundaries" (NASW, 2008, p. 13).

6. "Social workers should not engage in sexual activities or sexual contact with former clients because of the potential for harm to the client" (NASW, 2008, p. 13).

Although these standards of practice may seem self-evident, they represent an area fraught with difficulty within social work and other helping professions. Research on ethics complaints indicates that in NASW-adjudicated cases, boundary violations accounted for more than half of all cases in which violations occurred (Strom-Gottfried, 1999a). Similarly, in research on the frequency of malpractice claims against social workers for the period 1961–1990, Reamer (1995) found that sexual violations were the second most common area of claim, and the most expensive in terms of money paid out. Most social workers cannot imagine developing sexual relationships with their clients; yet, this outcome is often the culmination of a "slippery slope" of boundary problems that may include excessive self-disclosure on the part of the worker, the exchange of personal gifts, socializing or meeting for meals outside the office, and arranging for the client to perform office and household chores or other favors (Borys & Pope, 1989; Epstein, Simon, & Kay, 1992; Gabbard, 1996; Gartrell, 1992).

It is not uncommon to experience feelings of attraction, even sexual attraction, for clients. When such feelings arise, however, it is crucial to raise them with faculty or supervisors so they can be acknowledged and examined. Such discussion normalizes and neutralizes these feelings and decreases the likelihood that the worker will act on the attraction (Pope, Keith-Spiegel, & Tabachnick, 1986). These issues will be explored further in Chapter 18 as we discuss relational reactions and their effects on the helping process.

Other boundary issues can be both subtle and complex. For example, you may meet a neighbor in the agency waiting room or run into a consumer while doing your grocery shopping. A client may ask to "friend" you on Facebook or visit his or her "Caring Bridge" website. You may

decide to buy a car and find that the salesperson is a former client. You may visit a relative in the hospital and discover that her roommate is a current or former client. Friends in need of social work services may ask to be assigned to your caseload because you already know them so well. A client may ask you to attend a "family" event, such as a graduation or wedding. You may resonate with a particular client and think what a great friend he or she could be. You may have experienced a problem similar to the client's and wish to tell the client how you handled it. You may sympathize with a particular client's job search plight and consider referring him to a friend who is currently hiring new workers.

Not all encounters with clients outside the helping relationship are unethical. Contacts with clients that are unplanned, manageable, temporary, and transparent may simply be boundary crossings rather than boundary violations (Reamer, 2001). Certain settings (such as rural practice) and types of work (such as home-based care and community-based interventions) may create special opportunities for boundary confusion (Strom-Gottfried, 2005; Strom-Gottfried, 2009). The possibilities for boundary complication are endless, and addressing them involves nuanced application of the standards on boundary setting and other ethical principles, such as maintaining confidentiality and avoiding conflicts of interest. Therefore, setting "clear, appropriate, and culturally sensitive boundaries" (NASW, 2008, pp. 9–10) might mean different things in different settings. Many social workers routinely discuss the possibility of public contact with clients during the first session, explaining, for example, that in deference to privacy, they will not acknowledge the client unless spoken to first. A social worker invited to "friend" a client on a social networking site (or join the client in an in-person social activity) can sensitively explain the importance of not blurring the working relationship with other kinds of contact. Buying a car (or some other product or service with variable pricing) from a client or former client could be exploitive of the client or the worker, and could complicate the working relationship if the product or service is flawed. In such a case, boundary setting may mean ending the commercial relationship or the helping relationship if the two cannot be successfully merged. If neither choice is a possibility, consultation and intercession of a supervisor would be recommended to assure that neither the client nor worker is disadvantaged by the transaction. An invitation to a client's graduation or marriage ceremony should be processed with the client to explore the meaning of the offer. Ethical boundary setting might variously involve declining the invitation, accepting it, or attending the public portion of the event rather than the more private elements, such as a reception. The desire to disclose personal experiences with a client may be a form of authenticity (discussed further in Chapter 5) or an upsetting derailment where attention is switched from the client's experiences and needs to the worker's. Social workers should always be mindful of what they are trying to accomplish in making a personal self-disclosure and consider alternate ways of achieving the same objective. For example, rather than the worker saying, "When I have that kind of conflict with my mother, I do X," the worker could simply state, "Sometimes, people in conflict with their parents find that X is helpful."

Later in this chapter, we discuss strategies for more thoroughly examining and resolving ethical dilemmas. The key in managing boundaries is to be alert to dual relationships, to discuss troubling situations with colleagues and supervisors, and to take care that the primacy of the helping relationship is preserved in questionable boundary situations (Brownlee, 1996; Erickson, 2001; Reamer, 2001). Consultation helps social workers determine whether dual relationships are avoidable or not and whether they are problematic or not. It is incumbent on the social worker to ensure that clients are not taken advantage of and that their services are not obscured or affected detrimentally when boundaries must be crossed.

Safeguarding Confidentiality

From a practical standpoint, confidentiality is a *sine qua non* of the helping process. Without the assurance of confidentiality, it is unlikely that clients would risk disclosing private aspects of their lives that, if revealed, could cause shame or damage to their reputations. This is especially true when clients' problems involve infidelity, deviant practices, illicit activities, child abuse, and the like. Implied in confidentiality is an assurance that the practitioner will never reveal such personal matters to others.

EP 2.1.2b

Social workers are bound by the NASW Code of Ethics to safeguard their clients' confidentiality. While numerous standards operationalize this principle, in essence, social workers are expected to respect clients' privacy, to gather information only for the purpose of providing

effective services, and to disclose information only with clients' consent. Disclosure of information without clients' permission should be done only for compelling reasons, and even then there are limits on what information can be shared and with whom. These exceptions to confidentially will be addressed later in this section.

An unjustified breach of confidentiality is a violation of justice and is tantamount to theft of a secret with which one has been entrusted (Biestek, 1957). Maintaining strict confidentiality requires a strong commitment and constant vigilance because clients sometimes reveal information that is shocking, humorous, bizarre, or titillating. To fulfill your responsibility in maintaining privacy, you must guard against disclosing information in inappropriate situations. Examples include discussing details of your work with family and friends, having gossip sessions with colleagues, dictating within the listening range of others, discussing client situations within earshot of other staff, and making remarks about cases in elevators or other public places.

The emergence of technology that permits the electronic collection, transfer, and storage of information raises new complexities for maintaining client privacy (Gelman, Pollack, & Weiner, 1999). When you leave a voice mail for a client, are you certain that only the client will receive the message? Will you agree to accept and send text messages to clients? When a colleague sends you a fax on a case, can you be sure that others will not see that information before you retrieve the document? Further complexities arise in the electronic provision of services through text messages, websites, online groups, etc. There are many advantages to such interventions: they are commonly used methods of modern communication, they can efficiently offer reminders of appointments or tips for relapse prevention, assist with symptom management and increase service access for homebound individuals and those who need access to services on a 24/7 basis (Shapiro, Bauer, Andrews, Pisetsky, Bulik-Sullivan, Hamer & Bulik, 2009; Kessler, et al, 2009). However, electronic media present challenges for confidentiality, informed consent, and professional liability (Santhiveeran, 2009; Manhal-Baugus, 2001).

Beyond ethical standards, the Health Insurance Portability and Accountability Act of 1996 (HIPAA) established federal standards to protect the privacy of personal health information. HIPAA regulations affect pharmacies, health care settings, and insurance plans as well as individual health and mental health providers. The rules affect identifiable client information in all forms, including paper records, electronic data and communications, and verbal communications. There are several important provisions for social workers in HIPAA (HIPAA Medical Privacy Rule, 2003; Protecting the Privacy of Patients' Health Information, 2003; U.S. Department of Health and Human Services, 2007; Zuckerman, 2008).

- *Psychotherapy notes have a particular protection under HIPAA. The release of those notes requires special, separate authorization. Psychotherapy notes must be kept separately in client files and must meet other criteria in order to be considered protected.*
- *A general principle of the Privacy Rule is that if a person has the right to make a health care decision then that person has a right to the **information** associated with that decision.*
- *While clients should be provided access to their records, and have the opportunity to seek corrections if they identify errors or mistakes, client access to psychotherapy notes is restricted.*
- *Clients must be given information on the organization's privacy policies and they must sign a form or otherwise indicate that they have received the information.*
- *Client records or data should be protected from nonmedical uses, such as marketing, unless the client gives specific permission otherwise.*
- *Clients should understand their rights to request other reasonable efforts to protect confidentiality, such as requesting to be contacted only at certain times or numbers.*
- *Organizations and the individuals who work in them (in clinical, clerical, administrative and other roles) must take care to ensure that security standards are in place and that they are reinforced through staff development and agency policies.*
- *When state laws are more stringent than the provisions in HIPAA (when they offer greater protections for clients), those laws take precedence over HIPAA.*
- *HIPAA recognizes the validity of professional standards, such as those contained in the NASW Code of Ethics, and in some cases, those provisions may be more stringent than HIPAA's.*
- *In the case of minors, parents are generally considered the "personal representatives" for their children and as such can have access to personal health information as well as make health care decisions on behalf of their children. Some exceptions are: 1) when State law does not require parental consent for a minor to receive treatment, 2) when a court has appointed someone other than the parent as the*

child's guardian, and 3) if the parent agrees to a confidential relationship between the health care provider and their child.
- *The health care provider does not have to disclose information to the parent of a minor if 1) the provider has reasonable belief of abuse or neglect or that the information to be provided may endanger the child, or 2) using personal judgment, the provider decides that it is not in the minor client's best interest to treat the parent as the minor's individual representative.*

What Are the Limits on Confidentiality?

While social workers are expected to safeguard the information they collect in the course of their professional duties, there are several situations in which helping professionals are allowed or compelled to share case information. These include: when seeking supervision or consultation, when the client waives confidentiality, when the client presents a danger to self or others, when reporting suspicions of child or elder maltreatment, and when presented with a subpoena or court order.

Supervision and Consultation

EP 2.1.1f

The right to confidentiality is not absolute, because case situations are frequently discussed with supervisors and consultants and may be presented at staff conferences. Disclosing information in these instances, however, is for the purpose of enhancing service to clients. Clients will generally consent to these uses when their purposes are clarified. The client has a right to be informed that such disclosures may occur, and practitioners seeking supervision have a responsibility to conceal the identity of the client to the fullest extent possible and to reveal no more personal information than is absolutely necessary to get assistance on the case.

Other personnel such as administrators, volunteers, clerical staff, consultants, board members, researchers, legal counsel, and outside persons who may review records for purposes of quality assurance, peer review, or accreditation may have access to files or case information. This access to information should be for the purposes of better serving the client, and these individuals should sign binding agreements not to misuse confidential information. Further, it is essential that social workers promote policies and norms that protect confidentiality and assure that case information is treated carefully and respectfully.

Client Waivers of Confidentiality

Social workers are often asked by other professionals or agencies to provide confidential information about the nature of their client's difficulties or the services provided. Sometimes, these requests can be made with such authority that the recipient is caught off guard, inadvertently acknowledging a particular person as a client or providing the information requested about the case. In these instances, it is important that such data be provided only with the written, informed consent of clients, as this releases the practitioner and agency from liability in disclosing the requested information. Even when informed consent is obtained, it is important to reveal information selectively based on the essential needs of the other party.

In some exceptional circumstances, information can be revealed without informed consent, such as a bona fide emergency in which a client's life appears to be at stake or when the social worker is legally compelled to do so, as in the reporting of child or elder abuse. In other instances, it is prudent to obtain supervisory and legal input before disclosing confidential information without the client's written consent for release of information.

A final example of the client's waiver of confidentiality occurs if the client files a malpractice claim against the social worker. Such an action would "terminate the patient or client privilege" (Dickson, 1998, p. 48), freeing the practitioner to share publicly such information as is necessary to mount a defense against the lawsuit.

Danger to Self or Others

In certain instances, the client's right to confidentiality may be less compelling than the rights of other people who could be severely harmed or damaged by actions planned by the client and confided to the practitioner. For example, if the client plans to commit kidnapping, injury, or murder, the practitioner is obligated to disclose these intentions to the intended victim and to law enforcement officials so that timely preventive action can be taken. Indeed, if practitioners fail to make appropriate disclosures under these circumstances, they may be liable to civil prosecution for negligence. The fundamental case in this area is the Tarasoff case (Reamer, 1994). In it, a young man seeing a psychologist at a university health service threatened his girlfriend, Tatiana Tarasoff. The therapist notified university police; after interviewing the young man, they determined that he did not pose a danger to his girlfriend. Some weeks later the young man murdered Tarasoff, and her family filed a lawsuit alleging that she should have been warned. Ultimately, the court ruled that mental health professionals have an obligation to protect their clients' intended victims.

This court decision has led to varying interpretations in subsequent cases and in resulting state laws, but two principles have consistently resulted from it (Dickson, 1998; Houston-Vega, Nuehring, & Daguio, 1997): If the worker perceives a serious, foreseeable and imminent threat to an identifiable potential victim, the social worker should (1) act to warn that victim or (2) take other precautions (such as notifying police or placing the client in a secure facility) to protect others from harm.

Another application of the duty to protect personal safety involves intervening to prevent a client's suicide. Typically, lawsuits that cite a breach of confidentiality undertaken to protect suicidal clients have not been successful (VandeCreek, Knapp, & Herzog, 1988). Conversely, "liability for wrongful death can be established if appropriate and sufficient action to prevent suicide is not taken" (Houston-Vega, Nuehring, & Daguio, 1997, p. 105). Knowing when the risk is sufficient to warrant breaking a client's confidence is both a clinical decision and an ethical matter. Chapter 9 offers guidelines to use for determining the risk of lethality in suicidal threats or in client aggression.

Suspicion of Child or Elder Abuse

The rights of others also take precedence over the client's right to confidentiality in instances of child abuse or neglect. In fact, all 50 states have statutes making it mandatory for professionals to report suspected or known child abuse. Moreover, statutes governing the mandatory reporting of child abuse may contain criminal clauses related to the failure to report. States have established similar provisions for reporting the suspected abuse of the elderly or other vulnerable adults (Corey, Corey, & Callanan, 2007; Dickson, 1998; Donovan & Regehr, 2010). The mandate to report suspicions of abuse does not empower the worker to breach confidentiality in other ways. That is, even though the worker is a mandated reporter, he or she should still use caution in the amount of unrelated case information he or she shares with child welfare authorities. Furthermore, the requirement is to report suspicions to specific protective agencies, not to disclose information to the client's family members, teachers, or other parties.

Although afforded immunity from prosecution for reporting, practitioners must still confront the difficult challenge of preserving the helping relationship after having breached the client's confidentiality. One way of managing this tension is through informed consent.

As noted earlier, clients should know at the outset of service what the "ground rules" for service are and what limits exist on what the social worker can keep private. When clients understand that the social worker must report suspected child abuse, such a report may not be as damaging to the helping relationship. Similarly, the Code of Ethics states, "Social workers should inform clients, to the extent possible, about the disclosure of confidential information and the potential consequences, when feasible before the disclosure is made" (NASW, 2008, p. 10). With a trusting relationship, informed consent, and careful processing of the decision to file a child abuse report, feelings of betrayal can be diminished and the working alliance preserved.

Subpoenas and Privileged Communication

Yet another constraint on the client's right to confidentiality is the fact that this right does not necessarily extend into courts of law. Unless social workers are practicing in states that recognize the concept of privileged communication, they may be compelled by courts to reveal confidential information and to produce confidential records. "Privileged communication" refers to communications made within a "legally protected relationship," which "cannot be introduced into court without the consent of the person making the communication," typically the patient or client (Dickson, 1998, p. 32). Statutes that recognize privileged communication exempt certain professions from being legally compelled to reveal content disclosed in the context of a confidential relationship.

EP 2.1.2c

Determining the presence and applicability of privilege can be complicated, however. As Dickson notes, "Privilege laws can vary with the profession of the individual receiving the communication, the material communicated, the purpose of the communication, whether the proceeding is criminal or civil, and whether the professional is employed by the state or is in private practice, among other factors" (1998, p. 33). At the federal level, the U.S. Supreme Court in *Jaffee v. Redmond* upheld client communications as privileged and specifically extended "that privilege to licensed social workers" (Social Workers and Psychotherapist-Patient Privilege: *Jaffee v. Redmond* Revisited, 2005).

Laws recognizing privileged communication are created for the protection of the client; thus the privilege belongs to the client and not to the professional (Schwartz, 1989). In other words, if the practitioner were called to take the witness stand, the attorney for the client could invoke the privilege to prohibit the practitioner's testimony (Bernstein, 1977). Conversely, the client's attorney could waive this privilege, in which case the practitioner would be obligated to disclose information as requested by the court.

Another important factor regarding privileged communication is that the client's right is not absolute (Levick, 1981). If, in a court's judgment, disclosure of confidential information would produce benefits that outweigh the injury that might be incurred by revealing that information, the presiding judge may waive the privilege. Occasionally, the privilege is waived in instances of legitimate criminal investigations because the need for information is deemed more compelling than the need to safeguard confidentiality (Schwartz, 1989). In the final analysis, courts make decisions on privilege-related issues on a case-by-case basis.

Because subpoenas, whether for records or testimony, are orders of the court, social workers cannot ignore them. Of course, subpoenas may sometimes be issued for irrelevant or immaterial information. Therefore, social workers should be wary about submitting privileged materials. Careful review of the subpoena, consultation with the client, and consultation with a supervisor and agency attorney can help you determine how to respond. The following sources provide helpful information for social workers contending with subpoenas: Austin, Moline, and Williams (1990); Barsky and Gould (2004); Bernstein and Hartsell (2005); Houston-Vega, Nuehring, and Daguio (1997); Polowy and Gilbertson (1997); Sarnoff (2004); and NASW (2008b) of the NASW.

Confidentiality in Various Types of Recording

Accreditation standards, funding sources, state and federal laws—all may dictate how agencies maintain record-keeping systems. Because case records can be subpoenaed and because clients and other personnel have access to them, it is essential that practitioners develop and implement policies and practices that provide maximal confidentiality. To this end, social workers should adhere to the following guidelines (Kagle & Kopels, 2008; Reamer, 2005; Moline, Williams, & Austin, 1998; Zuckerman, 2008):

1. Record no more than is essential to the services being provided. Identify observed facts and distinguish them from opinions. Use descriptive terms rather than professional jargon, and avoid using psychiatric and medical diagnoses that have not been verified.

2. Unconfirmed reports about a third party by the client, the personal judgments, opinions, or clinical hypotheses of the clinician, and sensitive information that is not relevant to treatment should be omitted from documentation.

3. Do not include verbatim or process recordings in case files.

4. Maintain and update records to assure their accuracy, relevance, timeliness, and completeness.

5. Employ private and soundproof dictation facilities.

6. Keep case records in locked files, and issue keys only to those personnel who require frequent access to the files. Take similar privacy precautions to protect electronically stored data.

7. Do not remove case files from the agency except under extraordinary circumstances and with special authorization.

8. Do not leave case files on desks where others might gain access to them or keep case information on computer screens where it may be observed by others.

9. Take precautions, whenever possible, to ensure that information transmitted through the use of computers, electronic mail, facsimile machines, voice mail and other technology is secure. Be sure it is sent to the correct party and that identifying information is not conveyed.

10. Use in-service training sessions to stress confidentiality and to monitor adherence to agency policies and practices instituted to safeguard clients' confidentiality.

11. Inform clients of the agency's authority to gather information, the conditions under which that information may be disclosed, the principal uses of the information, and the effects, if any, of limiting what is shared with the agency.

EP 2.1.2b

The NASW Code of Ethics reflects most of these provisions, stating that "social workers should provide clients with reasonable access to records concerning the clients" (NASW, 2008, p. 12). It further notes that the social worker should provide "assistance in interpreting the records and consultation with the client" (p. 12) in situations where the worker is concerned about misunderstandings or harm arising from seeing the records. Access to records should be limited "only in exceptional circumstances when there is compelling evidence that such access would cause serious harm to the client" (p. 12). In our opinion, the trend toward greater client access to records has enhanced the rights of clients by avoiding misuse of records and has compelled practitioners to be more prudent, rigorous, and circumspect in keeping case records.

Social workers sometimes tape record live interviews or group sessions so that they can analyze interactional patterns or group process at a later time, or scrutinize their own performance with a view toward improving their skills and techniques. Recording is also used extensively for instructional sessions between students and practicum instructors. Yet another use of recordings is to provide firsthand feedback to clients by having them listen to or view their actual behavior in live sessions.

Before tape recording sessions for any of the preceding purposes, social workers should obtain written consent from clients on a form that explicitly specifies how the recording will be used, who will listen to or view the recording, and when it will be erased. A recording should never be made without the client's knowledge and consent. Clients vary widely in their receptivity to having sessions recorded; if they indicate reluctance, their wishes should be respected. The chances of gaining their consent are enhanced by discussing the matter openly and honestly, taking care to explain the client's right to decline. If approached properly, the majority of clients will consent to taping.

Social workers who record sessions assume a heavy burden of responsibility in safeguarding confidentiality because live sessions can prove extremely revealing. Such recordings should be guarded to ensure that copies cannot be made and that unauthorized persons do not have access to them. When they have served their designated purpose, they should be promptly erased. Failure to heed these guidelines may constitute a breach of professional ethics.

The Ethics of Practice with Minors

**EP 2.1.2c
& 2.1.2d**

A particular challenge in social work practice is interpreting ethical standards as they apply to clients under the age of 18 (Strom-Gottfried, 2008). While minor clients have the right to confidentiality, informed consent, self-determination, and the protection of other ethical principles, their rights are limited by laws and policies, by differences in maturity and decision-making capacity, and by their very dependence on adults as their caretakers. As such, parents may retain the right to review a child's treatment record and to be kept informed of issues the child raises in therapy. A 15-year-old teen parent has the right to make decisions about her baby's health care that she cannot legally make about her own. Child welfare experts and other authorities are empowered to decide where to place children and when to move them based on their appraisal of the best interests of the child. A 10-year-old may resist medication or treatment but lacks the ability to withhold consent in light of his age and cognitive capacities. As such, his parents or guardians can compel him to comply, even against his expressed wishes.

Minors' rights are also affected by the particular service setting and by their presenting problems. For example, a youth seeking substance-abuse services would have privacy protections under federal regulations that assure confidentiality (42-CFR) even if his parents insisted on service information (Strom-Gottfried, 2008). Similarly, a minor in need of prenatal care or treatment for sexually transmitted diseases could offer her own consent for services and be assured of confidentiality. Emergency services may be provided for a minor if delaying for parental consent could jeopardize the minor's well-being. School districts that accept "abstinence only" funding for health care will limit the information that social workers and nurses can share with students about contraception and HIV prevention.

As you can see, practice with minors is a complex tangle of legal, developmental, ethical, and social issues. Unsnarling this web requires a thorough understanding of child development and the physical, emotional, and cognitive capacities that emerge over the first two decades of the life span. It also requires an understanding of ethical standards, so that the worker appreciates the areas in which tensions might arise between legal and developmental limits to a minor's rights and the expectations of the profession for honoring clients' prerogatives, irrespective of age. Professionals in child-serving settings should be familiar with the policies and practices that govern services for their clientele. Through supervision, staff consultation, and careful decision making, social workers must consider various factors on a case-by-case basis in order to ensure that minors' rights are maximized, even amid constraints on those rights.

IDEAS IN ACTION

In the "Hanging with Hailey" videos, several examples arise about ethical service to mature minors.

- In light of Hailey's age and the policies at the school, the social worker (Emily) wasn't required to get parental permission for service; Hailey could consent to her own treatment.
- The social worker carefully describes the parameters of confidentiality during the first session. During this segment, Hailey interjects, "I guess, but I still don't know why I'm here." While Emily is careful to acknowledge the statement, she continues with her explanation and checks to make sure Hailey understands the limits of privacy.
- Perhaps because of Hailey's age, Emily fails to include possible abuse as a reason for breaking

confidentiality; thorough informed consent would have also included letting Hailey know that if her safety was at risk, that information would need to be divulged.
- In the second session, when Hailey describes smoking "weed" and having suicidal ideations, Emily continues her assessment and concludes that the situation is not serious enough to necessitate informing Hailey's mother. This assessment has both clinical and ethical dimensions, weighing risk, the client's capacity for decision making, agency policies, parental rights, client self-determination, and safety. Changes in any of these factors might shift the balance, leading a worker to notify parents or guardians of risky behaviors, or to work with the client to do so.

Understanding and Resolving Ethical Dilemmas

EP 2.1.2c

Social workers sometimes experience quandaries in deciding which of two values or ethical principles should take precedence when a conflict exists. In the foregoing discussions of self-determination and confidentiality, for example, we cited examples of how these rights of clients and ethical obligations of social workers are sometimes superseded by higher-order values (e.g., the right to life, safety, and well-being). Thus, clients' right to confidentiality takes second place when they confide that they have physically or sexually abused a child, or when they reveal imminent and serious plans for harmful acts that would jeopardize the health or safety of other people. Dilemmas can also arise if you find that certain policies or practices of your employing agency seem detrimental to clients. You may be conflicted about your ethical obligations to advocate for changes, because doing so may jeopardize your employment or pose a threat to your relationships with certain staff members.

EP 2.1.2d

Situations such as these present social workers with agonizingly difficult choices. Reamer (1989) has developed general guidelines that can assist you in making these decisions. Here we present our versions of some of these guidelines and illustrate instances of their application.

1. *The right to life, health, well-being, and necessities of life takes precedence over rights to confidentiality and opportunities for additive "goods" such as wealth, education, and recreation.* We have previously alluded to the application of this principle in instances of child or elder abuse or threats of harm to another person. In such circumstances, the rights of both children and adults to health and well-being take precedence over clients' rights to confidentiality.

2. *An individual's basic right to well-being takes precedence over another person's right to privacy, freedom, or self-determination.* As stated in the language of the courts (which have consistently upheld this principle), "The protective privilege ends where the public peril begins" (Reamer, 1994, p. 31). For example, the rights and needs of infants and children to receive medical treatments supersede parents' rights to withhold medical treatment because of their religious beliefs.

3. *A person's right to self-determination takes precedence over his or her right to basic well-being.* This principle maintains that people are entitled to act in ways that may appear contrary to their best interests, provided they are competent to make an informed and voluntary decision with consideration of relevant knowledge, and as long as the consequences of their decisions do not threaten the well-being of others. For example, if an adult chooses to live under a highway overpass, we may find that lifestyle unwise or unhealthy, but we have no power to constrain that choice. This principle affirms the cherished value of freedom to choose and protects the rights of people to make mistakes and to fail. As noted earlier, this principle must yield when an individual's decision might result in either his or her death or in severe and impeding damage to his or her physical or mental health.

4. *A person's rights to well-being may override laws, policies, and arrangements of organizations.* Ordinarily, social workers are obligated to comply with the laws, policies, and procedures of social work agencies, other organizations, and voluntary associations. When a policy is unjust or otherwise harms the well-being of clients or social workers, however, violation of the laws, policies, or procedures may be justified. Examples of this principle include policies or practices that discriminate against or exploit certain persons or groups. An agency, for example, cannot screen clients to select only those who are most healthy or well-to-do (a practice known as "creaming" or "cherry-picking") and then refuse services to those individuals in dire conditions. In situations such as these, the well-being of affected groups takes precedence over compliance with the laws, policies, and arrangements at issue.

Ethical social work includes advocacy for changes in laws and policies that are discriminatory, unfair, or unethical. For example, in regard to the ethical challenges posed by managed care, Sunley (1997) suggests engaging in both "case advocacy" and "cause advocacy" to help both individual clients and groups of clients who may be disadvantaged by particular policies or practices. Resources such as Brager and Holloway (1983), Corey, Corey, and Callanan (2007), and Frey (1990) provide helpful guidance for acting as an effective agent of change within troubled systems.

Although Reamer's guidelines serve as a valuable resource in resolving value dilemmas, applying them to the myriad situations that social workers encounter inevitably involves uncertainties and ambiguities, a reality that practitioners must accept. What should you do when you find yourself confronted with an ethical dilemma? Ethical decision-making models are as yet untested for their capacity to yield high-quality outcomes. Nevertheless, a list of recommended steps can be used to ensure thoughtful and thorough examination of options (Corey, Corey, & Callanan, 2007; Reamer, 2006; Strom-Gottfried, 2007, 2008):

1. Identify the problem or dilemma, gathering as much information about the situation from as many perspectives as possible, including that of the client.
2. Determine the core principles and the competing issues.
3. Review the relevant codes of ethics.
4. Review the applicable laws and regulations.
5. Consult with colleagues, supervisors, or legal experts.
6. Consider the possible and probable courses of action and examine the consequences of various options.
7. Decide on a particular course of action, weighing the information you have and the impact of your other choices.
8. Develop a strategy for effectively implementing your decision.
9. Evaluate the process and results to determine whether the intended outcome was achieved and consider modifications for future decisions.

These procedures need not be followed in the order listed. For example, consultation can prove useful in revealing options, identifying pros and cons, and rehearsing strategies for implementing the decision. Laws, ethical standards, and values can be examined after options are developed. Even decisions that must be made on the spot with little planning or consultation can be evaluated using this model, so that critical thinking is brought to bear for future dilemmas and actions. The key is to go beyond mere intuition or reactionary decision making to mindful, informed, critically examined choices.

Beyond these steps, you should be sure to document carefully the input and considerations taken into account at each phase of the decision-making process. This documentation may be in the client's formal record, your informal notes, or in the notes from supervisory sessions.

To apply this model, let's use the case of Alice from earlier in the chapter. As you may recall, she is a 38-year-old woman who refuses to notify her husband of her HIV-positive (HIV+) status due to fears that it will lead to the revelation of her extramarital affair.

EP 2.1.2d

The dilemma for the social worker in the case arises from Alice's disclosure about her HIV+ status and her refusal to tell her husband, which places him at risk for infection. The worker has a loyalty to Alice's needs and wishes, but also a responsibility to prevent her from harming another person, namely, her husband. If the worker reveals the truth, he or she may save the husband's health (and ultimately his life), but in so doing is violating Alice's trust and right to privacy and potentially putting the marriage at risk by exposing the affair. On the other hand, maintaining the secret, although protecting Alice's privacy, could put the unwitting husband at significant risk for contracting a life-limiting or life-ending disease. The worker may also worry about legal liability for actions or inaction in the case. In fact, either party who is disgruntled or damaged in the case could seek to hold the worker accountable: Alice for the breach of privacy, or the husband for negligence in failing to protect him from harm.

Several provisions in the NASW code of ethics (2008) speak to this dilemma:

EP 2.1.2b

Social workers should protect the confidentiality of all information obtained in the course of professional service, except for compelling professional reasons. The general expectation that social workers will keep information confidential does not apply when disclosure is necessary to prevent serious, foreseeable, and imminent harm to a client or other identifiable person or when laws or regulations require disclosure without a client's consent. In all instances, social workers should disclose the least amount of confidential information necessary to achieve the desired purpose; only information that is directly relevant to the purpose for which the disclosure is made should be revealed (1.07c).

Social workers should inform clients, to the extent possible, about the disclosure of confidential information and the potential consequences, when feasible before the disclosure is made. This applies whether social workers disclose confidential information on the basis of a legal requirement or client consent (1.07d).

Social workers should discuss with clients and other interested parties the nature of confidentiality and limitations of clients' right to confidentiality. Social workers should review with clients circumstances where confidential information may be requested and where disclosure of confidential information may be legally required. This discussion should occur as soon as possible in the social worker-client relationship and as needed throughout the course of the relationship (1.07e).

Embedded in these provisions are important ethical concepts—the respect for client self-determination, the importance of informed consent, and the significance of discretion around private information. It would be helpful to know how the social worker handled informed consent with Alice at the outset of services. Did Alice understand the worker's responsibilities should she prove to be a danger to herself or someone else? If so, the question of notifying her husband should not come as a surprise or betrayal, but rather a natural consequence based on the conditions of service and the established limits of confidentiality.

Beyond ethical standards, social workers must be familiar with the laws, regulations, practices, and policies that apply in their jurisdictions and practice settings. The disclosure of HIV+ status is one example where laws and policies vary widely across states. Some states explicitly shield health professionals from liability for making disclosures to protect the health of another, as long as they do so following established procedures. Other states view partner notification as a public health responsibility and require professionals to alert health departments in cases such as Alice's so that health authorities can undertake necessary disclosures. Preferably, the agency where Alice sought services was already apprised of the laws and incorporated them into policies and informed consent procedures for all clients prior to the outset of service. The social worker should also consider how Alice knows she is HIV+ and the partner notification policies in the jurisdiction where she was diagnosed. Depending on where and how she was diagnosed, Alice's condition may have already been processed by medical personnel to initiate notification of her husband, her paramour, and any other individuals who may be at risk by contact with her.

EP 2.1.1f

Supervisory guidance is essential in this case. Alice's social worker needs help thinking through the implications (for Alice, her husband, the worker, the helping relationship, and the agency).

The worker should use supervision to help identify her alternatives of action and the various pros and cons involved, anticipate reactions and prepare to address them, and think through ways to improve her practices in the future. Beyond talking with her supervisor, the worker may get specific consultation from legal and medical experts to address particular questions about her choices, her legal liability, or best practices in working with clients with infectious diseases. In these conversations, the worker should protect the identity of her client, focusing on the issues that gave rise to her dilemma rather than details of the client's case.

As a result of these discussions, the social worker may identify at least five options that can be employed singly or in combination:

- *Honor Alice's wishes and keep the secret.*
- *Work with Alice to institute safe sex practices and other control procedures to limit her husband's exposure to her disease.*
- *Encourage Alice to tell her husband about her HIV+ status by educating her about the implications of her silence.*
- *Offer to assist Alice in telling her husband and processing the information.*
- *Offer Alice the chance to tell her husband and let her know that if she does not, the social worker will.*
- *Make an anonymous report to the public health authorities about the risk to Alice's husband.*

Regardless of what option the worker pursues, she should make sure that Alice understands the nature of her disease, is getting proper care, and is taking precautionary steps to protect others from contracting HIV. This is congruent with the ethics of putting the client's needs first, and has the pragmatic effect of mitigating damage resulting from Alice's secrecy about her illness.

The question, however, remains: to tell or not to tell? The options that ultimately involve alerting Alice's husband will protect his health and well-being, clearly an advantage of these choices. These options comply with ethical standards, principles, and policies that require social workers to protect others from significant, foreseeable harm. Alerting the husband will probably make the worker feel more comfortable if she is worried about her complicity and her liability should she keep Alice's secret and he contracts AIDS as a result.

The downsides of telling include violating Alice's expressed desire for privacy, rupturing the trust that is central to the helping relationship, and possibly putting Alice's marriage at risk if the secret of her affair is revealed. Alice may make good on a threat to file a regulatory board complaint or lawsuit against the worker or agency for breach of confidentiality. The options in which the worker encourages Alice to tell may take time to employ, but they have the advantage of empowering her to take control of the situation and face her dilemma head on. Her ability to rely on the worker is essential in this process. The worker can help her look at the long-term effects of deception, in contrast to the short-term effects of revealing her condition and how she contracted HIV. The worker can help Alice anticipate and plan for that very difficult conversation with her husband and family and can be a support to her after the fact, whatever the husband's reactions are. All of the advantages of working *with* the client on this challenging problem are lost if the worker decides to abruptly override Alice's wishes and notify the husband.

Honoring Alice's demands for secrecy without considering the husband's needs and interests fits with the principle of client self-determination, but may be at odds with laws and policies about protecting the safety of others. It may also be at odds with Alice's own best interests. Social workers must often navigate between clients' wishes and the steps needed to adequately address their problems. Alice's desire to avoid telling her husband in the short run will not spare anyone pain or harm in the long run. In fact, her insistence on silence now may keep her stuck while her health and family relationships suffer. The worker who can empathize with her and help her forthrightly address her fears and problems will be carrying out both ethical responsibilities and professional responsibilities. Should this process fail, the worker may resort to notification against Alice's will. Given the greater expertise and experience of public health authorities in the area of notifications, the worker should probably refer the case to them for assistance.

EP 2.1.1b

Self-awareness and self-evaluation are important elements of competent, ethical, and professional practice. Throughout this process, Alice's social worker should examine her own motivations, decisions, and actions. Supervision is also an important element in self-evaluation. An adept and involved supervisor can help the worker identify strengths and weaknesses in the decision-making process, positive and problematic outcomes, and areas for improvement and skill development. Did the decision adequately resolve the dilemma? If it created unplanned or problematic results, what can be done to remedy them? For example, if the worker's efforts to get Alice to inform her husband of her illness results in Alice's withdrawal from treatment, evaluation will help the worker to determine next steps as well as assess her past actions.

Summary

This chapter introduced the ethics and values that support the social work profession. It provided guidelines for supporting self-determination, respecting confidentiality, obtaining informed consent, maintaining boundaries, and resolving ethical dilemmas. The chapter suggested steps to aid in resolving ethical dilemmas and it applied these steps to a case in which self-determination and client confidentiality conflicted with another's safety. In the following chapters we will move toward putting these professional values into action as you learn beginning skills for effective communication with and on behalf of clients.

Competency Notes

EP 2.1.1b Practice personal reflection and self-correction to assure continual professional development: Social workers must be attuned to their intentions, feelings, and values so that these are used constructively and purposefully in helping relationships. Self-awareness and self-regulation are essential for enacting this practice behavior (pp. 58, 61, 63–64).

EP 2.1.1c Attend to professional roles and boundaries: Boundaries assure that the helping relationship and the client's interests are accorded the highest priority in social work practice. Social workers are careful not to mix roles (friend/worker). They are alert to actions that may create conflicts of interest or otherwise blur boundaries with clients (physical contact, nonprofessional communications, friending on Facebook, etc.) (pp. 69, 71).

EP 2.1.1d Demonstrate professional demeanor in behavior, appearance, and communication: Social workers strive for recognition on par with other professionals such as nurses, lawyers and psychologists. Professionalism involves adopting the roles, values, and norms of a particular discipline and consistently upholding high standards of conduct (pp. 66, 71).

EP 2.1.1f Use supervision and consultation: Social work practice is complex. Even experienced professionals require the expertise, feedback, and wisdom of supervisors and consultants. Through supportive conversation, practitioners can look at themselves and their cases to improve service, increase competence, and grow professionally (pp. 63, 72, 74, 81).

EP 2.1.2a Recognize and manage personal values in a way that allows professional values to guide practice: Our choices in life are guided by our values. In accepting the role as a professional social worker, the individual must also consider the values of the profession, society, and the clients served. Self-awareness and wise supervision are essential to ensure that personal values, experiences, and emotions don't negatively impinge on the helping process (pp. 62, 65).

EP 2.1.2b Make ethical decisions by applying standards of the National Association of Social Workers Code of Ethics and, as applicable, of the International Federation of Social Workers/International Association of Schools of Social Work Ethics in Social Work, Statement of Principles: Knowing the ethical standards for social work is a key step in making sound decisions and avoiding errors of omission and commission (pp. 68–69, 71, 73, 77, 80).

EP 2.1.2c Tolerate ambiguity in resolving ethical conflicts: Ethical dilemmas arise out of competing goods. The choice of which path to take is rarely clear cut. Helping professionals must be able to weigh a variety of factors to decide which decision is best in a given situation (pp. 72, 76, 78–79).

EP 2.1.2d Apply strategies of ethical reasoning to arrive at principled decisions: Using a thoughtful, stepwise process helps practitioners to weigh the various alternatives in ethical dilemmas; examine policies, principles, and standards involved; and select sound choices (pp. 68, 78–80).

EP 2.1.10a Substantively and affectively prepare for action with individuals, families, groups, organizations, and communities (pp. 57, 66).

Skill Development Exercises in Operationalizing Cardinal Values

To assist you in developing skill in operationalizing the cardinal values in specific practice situations, we have provided a number of exercises with modeled responses. As you read each one, note which values are germane to the situation. To refresh your memory, the values are as follows:

1. Social workers value service to others and a commitment to social justice in helping clients get deserved and needed resources.

2. Social workers value the inherent dignity and worth of others.
3. Social workers value the primacy of human relationships.
4. Social workers behave with integrity.
5. Social workers are responsible for practicing with competence.

Next, assume you are the client's service provider and formulate a response that implements the relevant social work value. After completing each exercise, compare your response with the modeled response that follows the exercises. Bearing in mind that the modeled response is only one of many possible acceptable responses, analyze it and compare it with your own. Also, remember that *vocal tone* is an essential component of effective, congruent communications. Imagine the modeled responses that follow spoken with different verbal and emotional tones: sensitivity, tentativeness, anger, impatience, pity, kindness, conceit. Which feel genuine to you? Which will help achieve your objectives with the client? Which are congruent with professional values of respect and support for client dignity? By carefully completing these exercises, you will improve your competence in putting values into action in the varied and challenging situations encountered in direct social work practice.

Client Statements

1. *Group member [in first group session]:* Before I really open up and talk about myself, I need to be sure what I say isn't spread around to other people. [*Turning to social worker.*] How can I be sure that won't happen?
2. *Adolescent in correctional institution [after social worker introduces him/herself]:* So you want to help me, huh? I'll tell you how you can help. You can get me out of this damn place—that's how!
3. *Female client, age 21 [to mental health practitioner]:* Yeah, I know that kicking the habit was a victory of sorts. But I look at my life and I wonder what's there to live for. I've turned my family against me. I've sold my body to more rotten guys than I can count—just to get a fix. I've had three STDs. What do I have to offer anyone? I feel like my life has been one big cesspool.
4. *Teenage male [in a group session in a correctional setting]:* [*Takes off shoes and sprawls in his chair. His feet give off a foul odor; other members hold noses and make derisive comments. He responds*

defensively.] Hey, get off my back, you creeps. What's the big deal about taking off my shoes?

5. *Female [initial interview in family counseling center]:* Before I talk about my marital problems, I need to let you know I'm a Seventh Day Adventist. Do you know anything about my church? I'm asking because a lot of our problems involve my religion.

6. *Female client [sixth interview]:* Maybe it sounds crazy, but I've been thinking this last week that you're not really interested in me as a person. I have the feeling I'm just someone for you to analyze or to write about.

7. *Teenage female [caught with contraband in her possession by a supervisor-counselor in a residential treatment center]:* Please don't report this, Mrs. Wilson. I've been doing better lately, and I've learned my lesson. You won't need to worry about me. I won't mess with drugs anymore.

8. *Client [observing social worker taking notes during initial interview]:* I'm dying to know what you're writing down about me. Maybe you think I'm a nut. Can I take a copy of your notes with me when we're done?

9. *Male parolee, age 27, who has a reputation as a con artist [in a mandatory weekly visit to his parole officer]:* Man, you've really got it made. Your office is really fine. But then you deserve what you've got. You've probably got a terrific wife and kids, too. Is that their picture over there?

10. *Female client, age 34 [in third interview]:* I'm really uptight right now. I've got this tight feeling I get in my chest when I'm nervous. [*Pause.*] Well, I guess I'll have to tell you if I expect to get anything out of this. [*Hesitant.*] You know the marital problems we've talked about? Well, Jack doesn't know this, but I'm attracted to other women. [*Blushes.*] I've tried—I've really tried, but Jack doesn't turn me on. I can't even tolerate sex unless I'm thinking about other women. Jack thinks something's wrong with him, but it's not his fault. [*Chin quivers.*]

11. *Black male probationer [to white therapist]:* You're so damn smug. You say you want to help me, but I don't buy that crap. You don't know the first thing about black people. Man, I grew up where it's an accomplishment just to survive. What do you know about life in my world?

Modeled Responses

1. "Ginny raises a good point that concerns all of you. So that you can feel more comfortable about sharing personal feelings and experiences with the group, we need an understanding that each of you will keep what is shared in the strictest confidence. What are your thoughts about Ginny's concern?"

2. "I guess that's what I'd want if I were in your situation. As a matter of fact, that's what I want for you, too. But we both know the review board won't release you until they feel you're prepared to make it on the outside. I can't get you out, but with your cooperation I can help you to make changes that will get you ready for release."

3. "I can hear that you're down on yourself. Even though you've done a lot that you feel bad about, I'm impressed at what it's taken to get and stay clean. That's a giant step in the right direction. How can we keep your misgivings about the past from sabotaging the path you're on now?"

4. "I think we need to look as a group at how we can give Jim some helpful feedback rather than making fun of him. Let's talk about what just happened. Maybe you could begin, Jim, by sharing with the group what you're feeling just now."

5. "I have to confess I know only a little bit about your religion, which may make you wonder if I can appreciate your problems. I can assure you I'll do my best to understand if you're willing to help me with that. The most important thing, though, is your comfort about it. How do you feel about sharing your problems with me under these circumstances?"

6. "That sounds like a painful feeling—that I'm not personally concerned with you as an individual. I'd like to explore that with you further because that's not at all how I feel about you. Let's talk a bit about how I've come across to you and how you've reached that conclusion."

7. "I'm sorry you're still involved with drugs, Joy, because of the difficulties it's caused you. I don't like to see you get into trouble but I have no choice. I have to report this. If I didn't, I'd be breaking a rule myself by not reporting you. That wouldn't help you in the long run. Frankly, I'm going to keep worrying about you until I'm satisfied you're really sticking to the rules."

8. "It's not nutty at all to wonder what I'm thinking and writing. I'm writing down what we talk about. What you tell me is important, and notes help to refresh my memory. You're welcome to look at them if you like. Actually, I would be interested in hearing a little more about your concerns regarding what I might think of you."

9. "As a matter of fact it is, and I think they're pretty terrific. But we're here to talk about you, Rex. I'd like to hear how your job interview went."

10. "Keeping this secret has been very painful for you. I gather you've been afraid I'd condemn you, but I'm pleased you brought it up so that we can work on it together. It took some real courage on your part, and I respect you for that."

11. "I'd be phony if I said I understood all about being black and living in your neighborhood … and I'm sorry if it seems I'm being smug. I am interested in you, and I'd like to understand more about your life."

Skill Development Exercises in Managing Ethical Dilemmas

The following exercises will give you practice in applying ethics concepts and ethical decision making to specific practice situations. These situations include some of the most difficult ones that we and our colleagues have encountered in practice. Note that the appropriate response or course of action is rarely cut and dry. After reading each situation, consider the following questions:

1. What conflicting principles and feelings are in play in the case?
2. What are the pros and cons of the various courses of action?
3. What guidelines are applicable in resolving this dilemma?
4. What resources could you consult to help you decide on an ethical course of action?

Ethics Case 1 A classmate has told you that she is Googling clients from her field agency as well as looking them up on Facebook. She states that the information is public, so there is no confidentiality involved, and the more she learns about them the better she can help them.

Ethics Case 2 You are forming a youth group in a state correctional facility. From past experience, you know that youths sometimes make references in the group to previous offenses that they have committed without being apprehended. You also know that they may talk about plans to escape from the institution or about indiscretions or misdemeanors they (or others) may have committed or plan to commit within the institution, such as smoking marijuana or stealing institutional supplies or property from peers or staff. Are you required to share all of the information you learn in the group? How can you encourage trust and sharing if there are limits to confidentiality?

Ethics Case 3 In conducting an intake interview with a young woman in a family agency, you observe that both of her young children are withdrawn. One of the children is also badly bruised; the other, an infant, appears malnourished. Throughout the interview, the client seems defensive and suspicious and appears ambivalent about having come for the interview. At one point, she states that she feels overwhelmed with her parenting responsibilities and is having difficulty in coping with her children. She also alludes to her fear that she may hurt them but then abruptly changes the subject. As you encourage her to return to the discussion of her problems with the children, your client says that she has changed her mind about wanting help, takes her children in hand, and hastily leaves the office.

Ethics Case 4 You have seen a husband and wife and their adolescent daughter twice regarding relationship problems between the parents and the girl. The parents are both extremely negative and blaming in their attitudes toward their daughter, stating that their troubles would disappear if she would just "shape up." Today, during an individual interview with the girl, she breaks into tears and tells you that she is pregnant and plans to "go somewhere" with her boyfriend this weekend to get an abortion. She pleads with you not to tell her parents; she feels they would be extremely angry if they knew.

Ethics Case 5 In a mental health agency, you have been working with a middle aged male who has a history, when angered, of becoming violent and physically abusive. He has been under extreme psychological pressure lately because of problems relating to a recent separation from his wife. In an interview today, he is extremely angry, clenching his fists as he tells you that he has heard that his wife has initiated divorce proceedings and plans to move to another state. "If this is true," he loudly protests, "she is doing it to take the kids away from me, and I'll kill her rather than let her do that."

CourseMate

Access an integrated eBook and chapter-specific learning tools including glossary terms, chapter outlines, relevant web links, videos, and practice quizzes. Go to **www.cengagebrain.com**.

CHAPTER 5

Building Blocks of Communication: Conveying Empathy and Authenticity

CHAPTER OVERVIEW

Social workers practice in a variety of environments, influenced by professional and organizational demands (Cameron & Keeran, 2010). Part of that context is an emphasis on exploring the use of evidence-based knowledge where possible to influence intervention. Whatever intervention and theory selected, there are underlying common factors that account for as much as 70 percent, of the success of interventions (Drisko, 2004; Lambert & Ogles, 2004; Norcross & Lambert, 2006; Wampold, 2001, p. 207). Research on treatment outcomes describes four factors as associated with much of the positive change in client outcomes: client or extra-therapeutic factors (40%); relationship factors (30%); placebo, hope, and expectancy factors (15%); and model/technique factors (15%) (Duncan & Miller, 2000; Hubble, Duncan, & Miller, 1999; Adams et al., 2008). Consequently, nearly half of the outcome relies on fundamental skills and abilities that social workers need to learn, apart from the type of treatment offered.

Social work relationships develop in a context. Chapter 5 will help you develop micro direct practice skills and apply them in a context to help your clients. Interviews follow a structure that reflects predictable elements of contact between a potential client, a social worker, and the setting that the social worker represents. In other words, interviews have beginnings that focus on settling into roles, reviewing legal and ethical limits and boundaries, and attempting to establish rapport. From this point, the social worker engages the client in assessing what has brought the client into contact with the setting or agency. Based on this joint exploration, the social worker and the client then discuss creating a contract or agreement about what they will attempt to do together to address the client's concerns and developing goals to guide the social worker's practice in the case. If contact will last beyond one session, the session ends with the development of tasks or concrete plans about what

the social worker and the client will do prior to the next session to advance their common work. This interview structure is held together with practice skills that are designed to help the social worker connect with clients by communicating empathically, assertively, and authentically.

As a result of reading this chapter, learning and applying skills, you will be able to:

- **Develop an empathic response**
- **Explain client rights and limits to confidentiality**
- **Explain social worker and client roles**
- **Act assertively**
- **Appropriately self-disclose**
- **Identify surface and deeper feelings**
- **Increase your ability to convey accurate empathy**
- **Convey positive feedback**
- **Make a firm request**
- **Confront in an empathic context**

EPAS COMPETENCIES IN THE 5TH CHAPTER

This chapter will give you the information needed to meet the following practice competencies:

2.1.1b Practice self-reflection and self-correction to assure continual professional development

2.1.1c Attend to professional roles and boundaries

2.1.10a A social worker substantively and affectively prepare for action with individuals, families, groups, organizations, and communities

2.1.10b in which a social worker uses empathy and other interpersonal skills

2.1.10e A social worker assesses client strengths and limitatons

2.1.10i A social worker implements preventive services to enhance client capacities

Roles of the Participants

EP 2.1.10a

Clients often have an unclear idea about what to expect from contact with a social worker and those ideas may differ from the social worker's expectations (Kadushin & Kadushin, 1997). This is most evident when the client has been referred or mandated for service. Clarifying expectations becomes a key intervention in work with clients who have not chosen to see a social worker (Rooney, et al., 2009; Trotter, 2006).

The following guidelines will assist you to achieve similar positive results in role clarification.

Determine your clients' expectations. The varied expectations that clients bring to initial sessions include lectures, magical solutions, advice giving, changing other family members, and so on. With clients who are members of ethnic minority groups or inexperienced with professional helping relationships, sensitively exploring expectations and modifying the social worker's role when necessary are critical.

EP 2.1.1c

Clients sometimes explicitly state their expectations without prompting from a social worker. For example, after reciting the difficulties created by her son, a mother declared, "We were hoping you could talk with him and help him understand how much he is hurting us." Notice that the mother's "hope" involved a request for specific action by the social worker. When clients express their expectations spontaneously in this way, you have the opportunity to deal with unrealistic goals. Frequently, however, clients do not openly express their expectations, and you will need to elicit them.

It is important not to probe too far into expectations until you have established rapport, however, because the client's request often turns out to be a most intimate revelation. For this reason, seeking disclosure too soon may put a client on the defensive. The social worker should therefore try to weave exploration of the client's expectations into the natural flow of the session sometime after the client has had ample opportunity to report his or her difficulties and to discern the sensitive understanding and goodwill of the social worker.

If voluntary clients have not spontaneously revealed their requests and the timing appears right, you can elicit their requests by asking a question similar to one of the following:

- *"How do you hope (or wish) I (or the agency) can assist (or help) you?"*
- *"When you thought about coming here, what were your ideas about the kind of help you wanted?"*

For potential clients who were referred or mandated to receive service, practitioners often find it necessary to describe the parameters of what accepting an offer of service might entail since potential clients did not seek the service.

▣ VIDEO CASE EXAMPLE

In the video "Getting Back to Shakopee," Dorothy, a practitioner in a private child and family service agency, finds that Valerie, a Native American client referred by her employer for job performance issues, has many concerns about confidentiality that need to be addressed before she will consider whether she will accept an offer of service.

It can be useful in circumstances like these, where the client did not seek service, to elicit client concerns in the following way:

1. *"We have explored the reasons why you were referred/ required to seek our service. But I would like to know what you hope to gain from this process."* In this way the social worker signals from the beginning that he or she is working with the potential client, not acting as the agent of the referring source.

2. *Briefly explain the nature of the helping process, and define the client-social worker relationship as partners seeking a solution to the client's difficulties.* Clients often hope that social workers will give them advice that they can implement immediately, thereby quickly remedying their problems. They will give up these unrealistic expectations with less disappointment in favor of a more realistic understanding if you clarify how you can actually be of help and why it would be less useful to approach their problems with this kind of "magic potion" strategy. It is very important to convey

your intention to help clients find the best possible solution and to clarify that offering advice prematurely would likely be a disservice to them. In the absence of such an explanation, clients may erroneously conclude that you are unwilling to meet their expectations because you are not concerned about them.. Taking the time to explore expectations and to clarify how you can help prevents clients from drawing unwarranted negative conclusions that may result in premature termination of the contact.

EP 2.1.1c

Note that we are not arguing against the value of giving advice to clients. Rather, our point is that to be effective, advice must be based on adequate knowledge of the dynamics of a problem and of the participants involved. This level of understanding is unlikely to be achieved in an initial session.

You can assist many clients to modify their unrealistic expectations and clarify your respective roles by delivering a message similar to the following.

- *"I can sense the urgency you feel in wanting to solve your problems. I wish I could give advice that would lead to an easy solution. You've probably already had plenty of advice, because most people offer advice freely. It has been my experience, though, that what works for one person (couple or family) may not work at all for another."*
- *"As I see it, our task is to work together in considering a number of options so that you can decide which solution best fits you and your situation. In the long run, that's what will work best for you. But finding the right solution takes some time and a lot of thought."*

The preceding role clarification embodies the following essential elements mentioned earlier: (1) acknowledging and empathizing with the client's unrealistic expectation and sense of urgency; (2) expressing the social worker's helpful intent; (3) explaining why the client's unrealistic expectation cannot be fulfilled; and (4) as part of the social worker's expertise, clarifying the helping process and defining a working partnership that places responsibility on the client for actively participating and ultimately making choices as to the courses of action to be taken.

EP 2.1.1c

When couples seek help for relationship problems, they commonly view the partner as the source of difficulties and have the unrealistic expectation that the couple's counselor will influence the partner to shape up. Because this expectation is so pervasive, we often elicit partners' expectations early in the initial session (individual or conjoint) and clarify the social worker's helping role, thereby setting the stage for more productive use of the exploration to follow. Clarifying the helping process early in the session tends to diminish the partners' tendency toward mutual blaming and competition. Moreover, partners are less likely to respond defensively when the social worker refuses to be drawn into the "blame game" and focuses instead on assisting each person to become aware of his or her part in the difficulties.

▣ VIDEO CASE EXAMPLE

The following excerpt of the video labeled "Home for the Holidays Part 1" (HFH1) demonstrates how the social worker can establish ground rules.

Social worker: Let me suggest some ground rules for how couples sessions may be useful to you. I want this to be a safe place, so anything said here will be private unless something is shared that would seriously harm someone else, such as possible suicide or transmission of AIDS. I won't take sides in your concerns but will act more like a referee to help you express your concerns.

Implied in the preceding excerpt is another aspect of the client's role—to be open in sharing feelings, thoughts, and events. By explaining the rationale for openness and by expressing your intent to communicate openly, you enhance clients' receptiveness to this factor. To focus on this aspect of the client's role, consider making the following points:

Social worker: For you to receive the greatest benefit, you need to be as open as possible with me. That means not holding back troubling feelings, thoughts, or events that are important. I can understand you and your difficulties only if you're open and honest with me. Only you know what you think and feel; I can know only as much as you share with me.

Sometimes it's painful to share certain thoughts and feelings, but often those are the very feelings that trouble us the most. If you do hold back, remind yourself that you may be letting yourself down. If you're finding it difficult to share certain things, let me know. Discussing what's happening inside you—why it's difficult—may make it easier to discuss those painful things. I'll be open and honest with you, too. If you have any questions or would like to know more about me, please ask. I'll be frank with you. I may not answer every question, but I'll explain why if I don't.

To enhance clients' participation in the helping process, it is also important to emphasize that they can accelerate their progress by working on their difficulties between appointments. Some people mistakenly believe that change will result largely from what occurs in sessions. In actuality, the content of sessions is far less significant than how they apply the information gained from them. The following message clarifies this aspect of a client's responsibility:

Social worker: We'll want to make progress toward your goals as rapidly as possible. One way you can accelerate your progress is by working hard between our sessions. That means carrying out tasks you've agreed to, applying what we talk about in your daily life, and making mental notes or actually writing down thoughts, feelings, and events that relate to your problems so we can consider them in your next session. Actually, what you do between sessions is more important in accomplishing your goals than the session itself. We'll be together only a brief time each week. The rest of the week you have opportunities to apply what we talk about and plan together.

Yet another aspect of the client's role involves keeping appointments. This factor is obvious, but discussing it emphasizes clients' responsibilities and prepares them to cope constructively with obstacles that may cause them to fail or to cancel appointments. The following message clarifies this aspect of the client's role:

Social worker: As we work together, it will be critical for you to keep your appointments. Unforeseen things such as illness happen occasionally, of course, and we can change appointments if such problems arise. At other times, however, you may find yourself feeling discouraged or doubting whether coming here really helps. You may also feel upset over something I've said or done and find yourself not wanting to see me. I won't knowingly say or do anything to offend you, but you may have some troubling feelings toward me anyway. The important thing is that you not miss your appointment, because when you're discouraged or upset, we need to talk about it. I know

that may not be easy, but it will help you to work out your problematic feelings. If you miss your appointment, you may find it even harder to return.

For example, conversely, when clients are referred, practitioners should not assume that potential clients plan to return for another session.

🖥 VIDEO CASE EXAMPLE

For example, the practitioner, Dorothy, in the "Getting Back to Shakopee" video, suggests near the end of the session: "If you decide to come back for another session, next time we would break down all of the concerns you are facing and try to address them one at a time, starting with the ones you consider most important."

A final task for the social worker is to emphasize that difficulties are inherent in the process of making changes. Clarifying this reality further prepares clients for the mixed feelings that they will inevitably experience. When these difficulties are highlighted early in the helping process, clients can conceive of such feelings and experiences as natural obstacles that must be surmounted, rather than yield to them or feel defeated. An explanation about these predictable difficulties similar to the following clarifies the vicissitudes of the change process:

Social worker: We've talked about goals you want to achieve. Accomplishing them won't be easy. Making changes is seldom possible without a difficult and sometimes painful struggle. People usually have ups and downs as they seek to make changes. If you understand this, you won't be disappointed. I don't want to discourage you. I am optimistic about the prospects of you attaining your goals.

Over the years, numerous clients have reported retrospectively that they appreciated receiving these kinds of explanations during the initial session. When the going became rough and they began to waver in pursuing their goals, they recalled that such discouragement was natural and, rather than discontinuing the contact, mustered up the determination to persevere.

In addition to clarifying the client's role, it is vital to clarify your own role. Stress that you will be a partner in helping clients to understand their difficulties more fully. Because you have an outside vantage point, you may be able to help them see their difficulties from a new perspective and to consider solutions that they may have overlooked. We recommend that you clarify further that, although you will be an active partner in considering possible remedial actions, the final decisions rest with the clients themselves. You will help them to weigh alternatives, but your desire is to see clients develop their strengths and exercise their capacities for independent action to the fullest extent possible. In addition, emphasize that you plan to assist clients in focusing on their strengths and any incremental growth they achieve. Stress that although you will actively perform this function in the initial stage of the helping process, at the same time, you will be encouraging your clients to learn to recognize their own strengths and grow independently.

> ### ▣ VIDEO CASE EXAMPLE
>
> In the "Serving the Squeaky Wheel" video, the social worker, Ron Rooney, is replacing another social worker who has been abruptly transferred. The client, Molly, has a serious and persistent mental illness. Much of the session is devoted to beginning to develop trust that has been jeopardized by the loss of the previous worker. Such circumstances are not ideal but occur frequently enough that it is important to have models for dealing with it. The social worker describes his role as helping Molly make a plan in which she will be supported to live safely in a community of her choosing.

Another aspect of the helping role that you should clarify for clients is your intention to assist them in anticipating obstacles they will encounter in striving to attain their goals and your willingness to help them formulate strategies to surmount these obstacles. Clarifying this facet of your role further reinforces the reality that change is difficult but you will be with and behind your clients at all times, offering support and direction. You might share that each family faces its own unique situation and has its own set of values, noting that it will be your job to get to know these values and situations from the clients' point of view. Only then will you attempt to help the clients plan what makes sense for them to do.

Some special hurdles must be overcome to develop productive working relationships between social workers and clients in mandated settings, because the mandated client did not seek the contact and often perceives it as being contrary to his or her interests. In the following dialogue, notice how the social worker begins to develop expectations about a collaborative relationship.

Client: I didn't like the earlier workers because they came into my house telling me what I can and can't do. One thing I don't like is someone telling me what I can do with my kids and what I can't.

Social worker: It sounds like you had a negative experience with earlier workers.

Client: Yeah, I did. I did not like it at all because they were telling me what I should do.

Social worker: I'm going to take a different approach with you because I don't feel that I know it all; you know best about the situation occurring in your own family and in your own life. I will want you to tell me about the problems you are concerned about and how we can best resolve those together.

Client: Okay.

Social worker: My job will be to develop a case plan with you. I won't be the one to say, "This is what you need to do." I want you to have input in that decision and to say, "Well, I feel I can do this." I will be willing to share ideas with you as we decide what to work on and how to do it. I will need to include any court-mandated requirements, such as our need to be meeting together, in the agreement. However, I want you to have a lot of say in determining what we work on and how.

The social worker interprets the client's comment about previous workers as pertinent to exploring what their own working relationship might be like. She describes her own role and clarifies what the client can do in a clear and tangible way to work on goals important to her.

Communicating about Informed Consent, Confidentiality, and Agency Policies

The encounter between the social worker and the client exists within a context of limits, possibilities, and rights. In this regard, the social worker must share the rights and limits to communication discussed in Chapter 4: discuss confidentiality and its limits, obtain informed consent, and share agency policies and legal limits.

EP 2.1.1c

In "Getting Back to Shakopee," the social worker, Dorothy, and her Native American client, Valerie, discuss limits to confidentiality for the first several minutes of the video. Valerie is concerned about what material from the session will get back to the supervisor who referred her for service. In addition, she has concerns about Dorothy's mandated reporter responsibilities related to child welfare because her teenaged daughter supervises younger children in the summer. This video demonstrates how discussion of confidentiality issues can be vital with clients who are referred by others in less than voluntary circumstances.

Dorothy, the social worker in the video example, might have shared these limits, possibilities, and rights in the following fashion:

Social worker: What you say to me is private in most circumstances. I will share what we have discussed with my supervisor. In certain circumstances, however, I might have to share what we have discussed with others. For example, if you threatened to seriously harm another person, I would have a duty to warn that would mean that I could not keep that information private. For example, if your children were in danger, I am a mandated reporter, and I would have to share that information. Similarly, if you were to seriously consider harming yourself, I would have to share that information. If a judge were to subpoena my records, he or she could gain access to a general summary of what we have done together. Do you have any questions about this?

It is important that this section of the initial interview be presented in language that the client readily understands so that the discussion embodies the spirit of informed consent. The exact content of this discussion will vary with the setting in which you work. It is important that you carry out this duty in a genuine fashion, rather than presenting it as a ritualistic sharing of written forms that has the appearance of obtaining informed consent but ignores its intent. In hurried agency practice, sometimes this principle is violated. Discuss with your supervisor what information needs to be shared with clients and how that is done in ways that are useful to those clients.

Facilitative Conditions

The social worker uses communication skills as building blocks to help develop a productive working relationship with clients. This chapter focuses on two of the three skills embodied in what have been called the facilitative conditions or core conditions in helping relationships. These conditions or skills were originally denoted by Carl Rogers (1957) as empathy, unconditional positive regard, and congruence. Other terms have since evolved, and we shall refer to the conditions as empathy, respect or nonpossessive warmth, and authenticity or genuineness. Because we addressed nonpossessive warmth or respect at length in Chapter 4, we limit our focus here to empathy and authenticity.

Research has supported the correlation of empathy with positive outcomes (Bohart and Greenburg, 1997). In addition, a study by a social worker (Nugent, 1992) found that these facilitative conditions were effective in fostering positive helping relationships. The conditions are often thought to be the foundation level skills that undergird many treatment models and help create a positive relationship; Hill and Nakayama, 2000; (Mason, 2009). For example, there is a particularly close relationship between techniques designed to enhance empathy that come from the Rogerian nondirective approach and motivational interviewing (Mason, 2009). Efforts in the latter are often intended to facilitate client change particularly related to problematical behavior. While social workers are often engaged in activities designed to influence such behavior, they are not always aimed at changing behavior and are guided by professional values supporting self-determination. Hence, these chapters will present techniques designed to enhance empathy as valuable in their own right. In some instances, social workers will also attempt to influence behavior.

These skills are particularly useful in treatment situations with voluntary clients. However, we will also describe ways that the facilitative conditions can serve as building blocks in both involuntary relationships and other situations that do not have therapy as the primary focus (Bennett, Legon, & Zilberfein, 1989).

Empathic Communication

EP 2.1.10b

Empathic communication involves the ability of the social worker to perceive accurately and sensitively the inner feelings of the client and to communicate his or her understanding of these feelings in language attuned to the client's experiencing of the moment. The first dimension of empathy, empathic recognition, is a precondition of the second dimension, demonstrating through accurate reflection of feelings that the social worker comprehends the client's inner experiencing. For social workers, it is not enough to grasp what the client is feeling and experiencing and reflect that understanding back. Social workers are also called on by our code of ethics to take empathic action (Gerdes & Segal, 2009). Beyond reflecting the conflict and pain clients may be experiencing, we are called on to consider ways they might alleviate their situation. Similarly, on a macro level, it is not enough for social workers to notice and document a deleterious condition plaguing a neighborhood. Social workers are called on to utilize social empathy to act with others to address social and economic justice concerns.

Empathic communication plays a vital role in nurturing and sustaining the helping relationship and in providing the vehicle through which the social worker becomes emotionally significant and influential in the client's life. In mandated circumstances in which involuntary clients are not seeking a helping relationship, conveying empathic understanding reduces the level of threat perceived by the client and mitigates his or her defensiveness, conveys interest and helpful intent, and creates an atmosphere conducive to behavior change.

In responding to clients' feelings, social workers must avoid being misled by the conventional facades used to conceal emotions. As a consequence, the empathic communicator responds to the feelings that underlie such flippant messages as "Oh, no, it doesn't really matter" or "I don't care what he does!" These messages often mask disappointment or hurt, as do messages such as "I don't need anyone" when the client is experiencing painful loneliness, or "I don't let anyone hurt me" when the client is finding rejection hard to bear. To enter the client's private world of practical experience, the social worker must also avoid making personal interpretations and judgments of the client's

private logic and feelings that, in superficial contacts, might appear weak, foolish, or undesirable.

Being empathically attuned involves not only grasping the client's immediately evident feelings, but also, in a mutually shared, exploratory process, identifying the client's underlying emotions and discovering the meaning and personal significance of the client's feelings and behavior. In getting in touch with these camouflaged feelings and meanings, the social worker must tune in not only to verbal messages but also to more subtle cues, including facial expressions, tone of voice, tempo of speech, and postural cues and gestures that amplify and sometimes contradict verbal meanings. Such nonverbal cues as blushing, crying, pausing, stammering, changing voice intonation, clenching jaws or fists, pursing the lips, lowering the head, or shifting the posture often reveal the presence of distressing feelings and thoughts.

Empathic communication involves "stepping into the shoes of another," in the sense that the social worker attempts to perceive the client's world and experiences. When the client feels pressure from an involuntary referral, the empathic social worker understands and is aware of that pressure and how it feels. At the same time, the social worker must remain outside of the client's world and avoid being overwhelmed by his or her fears, anger, joys, and hurts, even as the social worker deeply senses the meaning and significance of these feelings for the client. "Being with" the client means that the social worker focuses intensely on the client's affective state without losing perspective or taking on the emotions experienced by the client.

A person who experiences feelings in common with another person and is similarly affected by whatever the other person is experiencing usually responds sympathetically rather than empathically. Sympathetic responding, which depends on achieving emotional and intellectual accord, involves supporting and condoning the other person's feelings (e.g., "I'd feel the same way if I were in your position" or "I think you're right"). In contrast, empathic responding involves understanding the other person's feelings and circumstances without taking that person's side (e.g., "I sense you're feeling …" or "You seem to be saying …").

When social workers support their clients' feelings, the clients may feel no need to examine their behavior or circumstances and may not engage in the process of self-exploration that is vital to growth and change.

Instead, clients tend to look to the social worker to change the behavior of other persons who play significant roles in their problems. Retaining separateness and objectivity thus is a critical dimension in the helping process. Clearly, when social workers assume their clients' feelings and positions, they lose not only the vital perspective that comes from being an outsider but also the ability to be helpful.

Of course, being empathic entails more than just recognizing clients' feelings. Social workers must also respond verbally and nonverbally in ways that affirm their understanding of clients' inner experiencing. It is not unusual for a person to experience empathic feelings for another individual without conveying those feelings in any way to the second party. Exhibiting high-level empathy requires skill in verbally and nonverbally demonstrating understanding. A common mistake made by social workers is to tell clients, "I understand how you feel." Rather than producing a sense of being understood, such a response often creates doubts in the client's mind about the social worker's perceptiveness, because any specific demonstration of understanding is lacking. Indeed, use of this response may mean that the social worker has not explored the client's feelings sufficiently enough to fully grasp the significance of the problematic situation. Social workers attempt to share emotion and get on the inside without losing awareness of who they are.

Later in this chapter, we present theory and exercises for developing skill in empathic responding. Initially, we provide a list of affective words and phrases intended to expand your vocabulary so that you can meet the challenge of responding to the wide range of emotions experienced by clients. We also provide exercises to help you to refine your ability to perceive the feelings of others—a prerequisite to the mastery of empathic communication. To assist you to discern levels of empathy, we include a rating scale for empathic responding, accompanied by examples of social worker responses and exercises. These exercises will help you to gain mastery of empathic communication at an effective working level.

Developing Perceptiveness to Feelings

Feelings or emotions exert a powerful influence on behavior and often play a central role in the problems of clients. Applicants or voluntary clients often enter into the helping relationship with openness and hope that they will explore both their concerns and their related feelings. Conversely, involuntary clients experience strong feelings but have not actively sought out a helping relationship for dealing with them (Cingolani, 1984). Hence, use of the skills sometimes takes a slightly different course with these clients, as one of the social worker's goals is to express empathy with the *situation* the involuntary client experiences and the feelings related to those situations and experiences.

To respond to the broad spectrum of emotions and feeling states presented by clients, the social worker must be fully aware of the diversity of human emotion. Further, the social worker needs a rich vocabulary of words and expressions that not only reflect clients' feelings accurately but also capture the intensity of those feelings. For example, dozens of descriptive feeling words may be used to express anger, including furious, aggravated, vexed, provoked, put out, irritated, and impatient—all of which express different shades and intensities of this feeling.

When used judiciously, such words serve to give sharp and exact focus to clients' feelings. Possessing and utilizing a rich vocabulary of affective words and phrases that accurately reflect these feelings is a skill that often is not developed by even experienced social workers. It is important to realize that high-level empathic responding takes place in two phases: (1) a thinking process and (2) a responding process. A deficient vocabulary for describing feelings limits social workers' ability to conceptualize and hence to reflect the full intensity and range of feelings experienced by clients.

It has been our experience that beginning social workers typically have a limited range of feeling words from which to draw in conveying empathy. Although many words may be used to capture feelings, learners often limit themselves to, and use to excess, a few terms, such as "upset" or "frustrated," losing much of the richness of client messages in the process.

The accompanying lists illustrate the wide range of expressions available for social workers' use in responding to clients' feelings. Note, however, that using feeling words in a discriminating fashion is not merely important in empathic responding but is indispensable in relating authentically as well. Becoming a competent professional requires passing through a maturing process whereby social workers develop not only the capacity to deeply share the inner experiencing of others, but also a way to express their own personal feelings constructively. Please consult the following comprehensive list of affective words and phrases.

Affective Words and Phrases

Competence/Strength

convinced you can	confident
sense of mastery	powerful
potent	courageous
resolute	determined
strong	influential
brave	impressive
forceful	inspired
successful	secure
in charge	in control
well equipped	committed
sense of accomplishment	daring
undaunted	effective
sure	sense of conviction
trust in yourself	self-reliant
sharp	able
adequate	firm
capable	on top of it
can cope	important
up to it	ready
equal to it	skillful

Happiness/Satisfaction

elated	superb
ecstatic	on cloud nine
on top of the world	organized
fantastic	splendid
exhilarated	jubilant
terrific	euphoric
delighted	marvelous
excited	enthusiastic
thrilled	great
super	in high spirits
joyful	cheerful
elevated	happy
light-hearted	wonderful
glowing	jolly
neat	glad
fine	pleased
good	contented
hopeful	mellow
satisfied	gratified
fulfilled	tranquil
serene	calm
at ease	awesome

Caring/Love

adore	loving
infatuated	enamored
cherish	idolize
worship	attached to
devoted to	tenderness toward
affection for	hold dear
prize	caring
fond of	regard
respect	admire
concern for	taken with
turned on	trust
close	esteem
hit it off	value
warm toward	friendly
like	positive toward
accept	enchanted by

Depression/Discouragement

anguished	in despair
dreadful	miserable
dejected	disheartened
rotten	awful
horrible	terrible
hopeless	gloomy
dismal	bleak
depressed	despondent
grieved	grim
broken hearted	forlorn
distressed	downcast
sorrowful	demoralized
pessimistic	tearful
weepy	down in the dumps
deflated	blue
lost	melancholy
in the doldrums	lousy
kaput	unhappy
down	low
bad	blah
disappointed	sad
below par	unnerved

Inadequacy/Helplessness

worthless	depleted
good for nothing	washed up
powerless	helpless
impotent	crippled
inferior	emasculated
useless	finished
like a failure	impaired
inadequate	whipped
defeated	stupid
incompetent	puny
inept	clumsy
overwhelmed	ineffective
like a klutz	lacking
awkward	deficient
unable	incapable
small	insignificant
like a wimp	unimportant
over the hill	incomplete
immobilized	like a puppet
at the mercy of	inhibited
insecure	lacking confidence
unsure of self	uncertain
weak	inefficient
unfit	feeble

Anxiety/Tension

terrified	frightened
intimidated	horrified
desperate	panicky
terror-stricken	paralyzed
frantic	stunned
shocked	threatened
afraid	scared
stage fright	dread
vulnerable	fearful
apprehensive	jumpy
shaky	distrustful
butterflies	awkward
defensive	uptight
tied in knots	rattled
tense	fidgety
jittery	on edge
nervous	anxious
unsure	hesitant
timid	shy
worried	uneasy
bashful	embarrassed
ill at ease	doubtful
uncomfortable	self-conscious
insecure	alarmed
restless	

Confusion/Troubledness	
bewildered	puzzled
tormented by	baffled
perplexed	overwhelmed
trapped	confounded
in a dilemma	befuddled
in a quandary	at loose ends
going around in	mixed-up
circles	
disorganized	in a fog
troubled	adrift
lost	disconcerted
frustrated	floored
flustered	in a bind
torn	ambivalent
disturbed	conflicted
stumped	feeling pulled apart
mixed feelings	uncertain
about	
unsure	uncomfortable
bothered	uneasy
undecided	overwhelmed

Rejection/Offensive	
crushed	destroyed
ruined	pained
wounded	devastated
tortured	cast off
betrayed	discarded
knifed in the back	hurt
belittled	abused
depreciated	criticized
censured	discredited
disparaged	laughed at
maligned	mistreated
ridiculed	devalued
scorned	mocked
scoffed at	used
exploited	debased
slammed	slandered
impugned	cheapened
mistreated	put down
slighted	neglected
overlooked	minimized
let down	disappointed
unappreciated	taken for granted
taken lightly	underestimated
degraded	discounted
shot down	disrespected

Anger/Resentment	
furious	enraged
livid	seething
could chew nails	fighting mad
burned up	hateful
bitter	galled
vengeful	resentful
indignant	irritated
hostile	pissed off
have hackles up	had it with
upset with	bent out of shape
agitated	annoyed
got dander up	bristle
dismayed	uptight
disgusted	bugged
turned off	put out
miffed	ruffled
irked	perturbed
ticked off	teed off
chagrined	griped
cross	impatient
infuriated	violent

Loneliness	
all alone in the	isolated
universe	
abandoned	totally alone
forsaken	forlorn
lonely	alienated
estranged	rejected
remote	alone
apart from others	shut out
left out	excluded
lonesome	distant
aloof	cut off

Guilt/Embarrassment	
sick at heart	unforgivable
humiliated	disgraced
degraded	horrible
mortified	exposed
branded	could crawl in a hole
like two cents	ashamed
guilty	remorseful
crummy	really rotten
lost face	demeaned
foolish	ridiculous
silly	stupid
egg on face	regretful
wrong	embarrassed
at fault	in error
responsible for	goofed
lament	blew it

Use of the Lists of Affective Words and Phrases

The lists of affective words and phrases may be used with the exercises at the end of the chapter and in the *Practice Behaviors Workbook* to formulate responses that capture the nature of feelings expressed by clients. Note that potential clients referred by others and involuntary clients may be more likely to initially experience the emotions of anger, resentment, guilt, embarrassment, rejection, confusion, tension, inadequacy, helplessness, depression, and discouragement. In Chapter 7, we will explore barriers to effective communication. One of those barriers can be the social worker's inability to achieve empathy with such involuntary clients, as the social worker may believe that they have brought on these negative feelings as a result of their own irresponsible actions. That is, some social workers feel that perhaps involuntary clients deserve these feelings because they have not fully accepted responsibility for their part in the difficulties they have experienced. As noted in Chapter 4, the social work value of acceptance of worth suggests that we can empathize with feelings of despair and powerlessness even if clients have not yet taken responsibility for the consequences of their actions. In fact, involuntary and referred clients often express anger and frustration about even being in an introductory session with a social worker. You may note how this occurs in the video "Serving the Squeaky Wheel." Notice how the social worker attempts to reflect this anger and frustration and reframe it more constructively toward action they could take together to alleviate those feelings.

After you have initially practiced responding to messages in which clients convey feelings, check the lists to determine whether some other words and phrases might more accurately capture the client's feelings. Also, scan the lists to see whether the client's message involves feelings in addition to those you identified. The lists may similarly assist you in checking out the accuracy of your reflective responses as you review taped sessions.

The lists of affective words and phrases are offered for the purpose of helping you communicate more empathically with your clients. However, words can have different connotations within the same language based on age, region, ethnic group, and social class. We suggest that you sit down with your coworkers and fellow students to compile your own more specialized list of feeling words for specific groups that you routinely encounter. For example, formulating a list of terms commonly used by adolescents in various socioeconomic and ethnic groupings could be useful. Issues may also arise when you try to use an unfamiliar slang vernacular, thus defeating the purpose of empathizing. However, making the effort to clarify words that accurately describe what the client is feeling often conveys your genuine interest.

Acquisition of a broader emotional vocabulary is a step toward expressing greater empathy for clients. It allows you to more effectively convey your understanding and compassion for what they are experiencing. Because many clients want to change their situations as well as their feelings about it, conveying empathy is the first step toward helping them work on those concerns.

Although the lists of affective words and phrases presented in this chapter are not exhaustive, they encompass many of the feelings and emotions frequently encountered in the helping process. Feeling words are subsumed under 11 categories, running the gamut of emotions from intense anguish and pain (e.g., *grieved, terrified, bewildered, enraged,* and *powerless*) to positive feeling states (e.g., *joy, elation, ecstasy, bliss,* and *pride in accomplishment*). Given our emphasis on clients' strengths, we have taken care to include a grouping of

terms to assist social workers in capturing clients' feelings related to growth, strengths, and competence.

Feeling words in each category are roughly graduated by intensity, with words conveying strong intensity grouped toward the beginning of each category and words of moderate to mild intensity appearing toward the end. In responding to client messages, the social worker should choose feeling words that accurately match the intensity of the feelings the client is experiencing.

To illustrate, consider that you are working with an African American client in a drug aftercare program who has returned to work as a meter reader. He reports that when he knocked on the door in a largely white suburb intending to read the meter, the elderly white woman would not let him in, despite his wearing his picture identification name tag on his uniform: "I was so low down and depressed. What can you do? I am doing my thing to keep straight, and I can't even do my job because I'm black." Such a response appropriately calls for an intense response by the social worker: "Sounds like you felt demeaned and humiliated that you couldn't do your job because of this woman's fear of black people. And yet you did not let that carry you back to drug use—you kept straight, and were not stopped by other people's perceptions."

In addition to using words that accurately reflect the intensity of the client's feelings, it is important to respond with a tone of voice and nonverbal gestures and expressions that similarly reflect the intensity of feelings conveyed by the verbal response. The proper intensity of affect may also be conveyed by using appropriate qualifying words—for example, "You feel (somewhat) (quite) (very) (extremely) discouraged by your low performance on the entrance test."

Clients' messages may also contain multiple feelings. Consider the following client message: "I don't know what to do about my teenage daughter. I know that she's on drugs, but she shuts me out and won't talk to me. All she wants is to be out with her friends, to be left alone. There are times when I think she really dislikes me." Feeling words that would capture the various facets of this message include *confused, bewildered, alarmed, troubled, overwhelmed, lost, desperate, worried, frightened, alienated, rejected,* and *hurt.* A response that included all of these feeling words would be extremely lengthy and overwhelming to the client. However, a well-rounded empathic response should embody at least several of the surface feelings, such as *worried* and *confused,* and be delivered with appropriate timing. The social worker might also bring deeper-level feelings into focus, as explained in the following paragraphs.

Notice in the preceding client message that many feelings were implied but not explicitly stated. Some of these emotions would likely be just beyond the client's level of awareness but could easily be recognized if they were drawn to the client's attention. For example, the client might emphatically confirm a social worker response that sensitively identifies the hurt, rejection, and even anger inherent in the client's message. Without the social worker's assistance, the client might not develop full awareness of those deeper-level feelings.

In responding to client messages, you must be able to distinguish between readily apparent feelings and probable deeper feelings. In the early phase of the helping process, the social worker's objectives of developing a working relationship and creating a climate of understanding are best accomplished by using a reciprocal level of empathy—that is, by focusing on the client's immediately evident feelings. As the client perceives your genuine effort and commitment to understand his or her situation, that experience of being "empathically received" gradually yields a low-threat environment that obviates the need for self-protection.

Note that clients from oppressed groups, such as the African American client in the earlier example, may rightly feel better understood by the social worker yet continue to feel disillusioned by an alien environment. It is important to acknowledge those feelings about the environment. Trust may be gained by actions taken outside the session that indicate that the social worker is trustworthy and has the client's best interest at heart, as well as by verbal conveyance of empathy during the session. Similarly, Ivanoff, Blythe, and Tripodi suggest that too much emphasis on empathy can feel manipulative to involuntary clients (1994). With voluntary clients, the resultant climate of trust sets the stage for self-exploration, a prerequisite to self-understanding, which in turn facilitates behavior change. This positive ambience prepares the way for the use of "additive" or "expanded" levels of empathy to reach for underlying feelings as well as to uncover hidden meanings and goals of behavior.

Conversely, attempting to explore underlying feelings during the early phase of the helping process is counterproductive. Uncovering feelings beyond the client's awareness before a working relationship is firmly established tends to mobilize opposition and may precipitate premature termination of the contact. Involuntary clients in a negotiated relationship may never desire such uncovering of deeper feelings and may find exploration of them to be intrusive (Ivanoff, Blythe, and Tripodi, 1994, p. 21).

Exercises in Identifying Surface and Underlying Feelings

In the following exercise, identify both the apparent surface feelings and the probable underlying feelings embodied in the client's message. Remember that most of the feelings in the messages are merely implied, as people often do not use feeling words. As you complete the exercise, read each message and write down the feelings involved. Next, scan the lists of affective words and phrases to see whether you might improve your response. After you have responded to all four messages, check the feeling words and phrases you identified with those given at the end of the chapter. If the feelings you identified were similar in meaning to those identified in the answers, consider your responses to be accurate. If they were not, review the client messages for clues about the client's feelings that you overlooked.

Client Statements

1. *Elderly client:* I know my children have busy lives. It is hard for them to have time to call me.

   Apparent feelings:
   Probable deeper feelings:

2. *Lesbian client referring to partner who has recently come out to her family*: When I was at your brother's wedding, and they wanted to take family pictures, nobody wanted me in the pictures. In fact nobody wanted to talk to me.

   Note: This is a quote from a client in the "Home for the Holidays" video connected to this chapter.

   Apparent feelings:
   Probable deeper feelings:

3. *Client:* When I was a teenager, I thought that when I was married and had my own children, I would never yell at them like my mother yelled at me. Yet, here I am doing the same things with Sonny.

   [Tearful]
   Apparent feelings:
   Probable deeper feelings:

4. *African American client in child welfare system:* The system is against people like me. People think that we drink, beat our kids, lay up on welfare, and take drugs.

   Apparent feelings:
   Probable deeper feelings:

Exercises at the end of this chapter for formulating reciprocal empathic responses will also assist you in increasing your perceptiveness to feelings.

Accurately Conveying Empathy

Empathic responding is a fundamental, yet complex skill that requires systematic practice and extensive effort to achieve competency. Skill in empathic communication has no limit or ceiling; rather, this skill is always in the process of "becoming." In listening to their taped sessions, even highly skilled professionals discover feelings they overlooked. Many social workers, however, do not fully utilize empathic responding. They fail to grasp the versatility of this skill and its potency in influencing clients and fostering growth in moment-by-moment transactions.

In fact, some social workers dismiss the need for training in empathic responding, mistakenly believing themselves to already be empathic in their contacts with clients. Few people are inherently helpful in the sense of relating naturally with high levels of empathy or any of the other core conditions. Although people achieve varying degrees of empathy, respect, and genuineness through their life experiences, attaining high levels of these skills requires rigorous training. Research scales that operationalize empathy conditions have been developed and validated in extensive research studies (Duan & Hill, 1996; Truax & Carkhuff, 1967). These scales, which specify levels of empathy along a continuum ranging from high- to low-level skills, represented a major breakthrough not only in operationalizing essential social worker skills but also in establishing a relationship between these skills and successful outcomes in practice.

The empathic communication scale has been employed to help students distinguish between high- and low-level empathic responses and has been used by peers and instructors in group training to assess levels of students' responses. Students then receive guidance in reformulating low-level responses to bring them to higher levels.

The Carkhuff (1969) empathy scale, which consists of nine levels, has been widely used in training and research. Although we have found nine-point scales valuable as training aids, they have proven somewhat confusing to students, who often have difficulty in making such fine distinctions between levels. For this reason, we have adapted the nine-level scale described by Hammond, Hepworth, and Smith (1977) by collapsing it to the five-level scale presented here.

Empathic Communication Scale
Level 1: Low Level of Empathic Responding
At level 1, the social worker communicates little or no awareness or understanding of even the most conspicuous of the client's feelings; the social worker's responses are irrelevant and often abrasive, hindering rather than facilitating communication. Operating from a personal frame of reference, the social worker changes the subject, argues, gives advice prematurely, lectures, or uses other ineffective styles that block communication, often diverting clients from their problems and fragmenting the helping process. Furthermore, the social worker's nonverbal responses are not appropriate to the mood and content of the client's statement.

When social workers relate at this low level, clients often become confused or defensive. They may react by discussing superficialities, arguing, disagreeing, changing the subject, or withdrawing into silence. Thus, the client's energies are diverted from exploration and/or work on problems.

Unfortunately, level one responses occur with some frequency in settings in which clients are involuntary, stigmatized, or considered deviant. Such responses may provoke client anger but pose few consequences for the social worker unless there are norms that clients must be treated respectfully in all circumstances. These responses are shared not for the purpose of modeling them, but rather to alert you that if you see them occurring, or it occurs to you, it signals problems with the social worker or the setting. It could just be a social worker on a bad day; but worse if it has become a standard of practice that passes unnoticed. Consider the following example of a mother in the child welfare system who has recently completed a drug treatment program.

Client: I want to go into an aftercare treatment program near my home that is culturally sensitive and allows me to keep my job.

BELOW Level 1 response: You should not be thinking about what is convenient for you but rather what might ultimately benefit your child by your being a safe parent for her. Your thinking here is symptomatic of the problem of why your child is in custody, and your chances of regaining custody are limited.

This response is beneath the lowest levels of acceptable empathy. It is the opposite of empathy because it is actively judgmental and inappropriately confrontational. It is possible that the social worker might have valid reasons for wishing the client to consider a variety of options. Making the judgmental statement only makes the circumstances worse and makes it unlikely that the client will consider the worker's opinion. Social workers' frustration with clients who endanger others is understandable. Statements like the one above, however, greatly hinder further efforts to work with them in a collaborative fashion.

Level 1 response: "I see that you want to find a program near your home."

This response is minimally facilitative but at least avoids the judgmental statements of the previous example.

African American male: [to child welfare worker]: I don't trust you people. You do everything you can to keep me from getting back my son. I have done everything I am supposed to do, and you people always come up with something else.

Level 1 Responses

- *"Just carry out the case plan and you are likely to succeed."* (Giving advice.)
- *"Just think what would have happened if you had devoted more energy in the last year to carrying out your case plan: You would have been further along."* (Persuading with logical argument; negatively evaluating client's actions.)
- *"How did you get along with your last social worker?"* (Changing the subject.)
- *"Don't you think it will all work out in time?"* (Leading question, untimely reassurance.)
- *"Why, that's kind of an exaggeration. If you just work along with me, before you know it things will be better."* (Reassuring, consoling, giving advice.)

> ### ⬛ VIDEO CASE EXAMPLE
>
> You can see two versions of the same situation in the video "Domestic Violence and the Probation Officer." Note the client response to level 1 or below empathic responses in version one. Note also how the situation looks different when the practitioner employs higher levels of empathy in version two.

The preceding examples illustrate ineffective styles of communication used at this low level. Notice that messages reflect the social worker's own formulations concerning the client's problem; they do not capture the client's inner experiencing. Such responses stymie

clients, blocking their flow of thought and producing negative feelings toward the social worker.

Level 2: Moderately Low Level of Empathic Responding

At level 2, the social worker responds to the surface message of the client but erroneously omits feelings or factual aspects of the message. The social worker may also inappropriately qualify feelings (e.g., "somewhat," "a little bit," "kind of") or may inaccurately interpret feelings (e.g., "angry" for "hurt," "tense" for "scared"). Responses may also emanate from the social worker's own conceptual formulations, which may be diagnostically accurate but not empathically attuned to the client's expressions. Although level 2 responses are only partially accurate, they do convey an effort to understand and, for this reason, do not completely block the client's communication or work on problems.

Level 2 Responses

- **We provide here level 2 responses to the previous example of the African American male:** *[to child welfare worker]:* I don't trust you people. You do everything you can to keep me from getting back my son. I have done everything I am supposed to do, and you people always come up with something else.
- *"You'll just have to be patient. I can see you're upset."* The word upset defines the client's feelings only vaguely, whereas feeling words such as *angry, furious,* and *discounted* more accurately reflect the client's inner experiencing.
- *"You feel angry because your case plan has not been more successful to date. Maybe you are expecting too much too soon; there is a lot of time yet."* The listener begins to accurately capture the client's feelings but then moves to an evaluative interpretation ("you expect too much too soon") and inappropriate reassurance.
- *"You aren't pleased with your progress so far?"* This response focuses on external, factual circumstances to the exclusion of the client's feelings or perceptions regarding the event in question.
- *"You feel like things aren't going too well."* This response contains no reference to the client's immediately apparent feelings. Beginning social workers often use the lead-in phrase "You feel like ..." without noticing that, in employing it, they have not captured the client's feelings.

- *"You're disappointed because you haven't gotten your son back?"* This response, although partially accurate, fails to capture the client's anger and distrust of the system, wondering whether any of his efforts are likely to succeed.
- *"I can see you are angry and disappointed because your efforts haven't been more successful so far, but I think you may be expecting the system to work too quickly."* Although the message has a strong beginning, the empathic nature of the response is negated by the listener's explanation of the reason for the client's difficulties. This response represents a form of taking sides—that is, justifying the actions of the child welfare system by suggesting that too much is expected of it.

VIDEO CASE EXAMPLE

In the video "Getting Back to Shakopee," the social worker, Dorothy, heard an account of uncomfortable relations with co-workers on the job. She summarizes and adds a level 2 empathic comment: "So just that I understand what you are talking about, you were working on your own project and Mary came over and added hers to yours and asked you to finish it for her? What did that do for you?" The empathy is implied in the social worker's question, but it could have been more explicit. For example, Dorothy might have asked "did you feel as if she did not have the right to do this, that she was acting disrespectfully toward you?"

The preceding responses illustrate many of the common errors made by social workers in responding empathically to client messages. Although some part of the messages may be accurate or helpful, all the responses in some way ignore or subtract from what the client is experiencing.

Level 3: Interchangeable or Reciprocal Level of Empathic Responding

The social worker's verbal and nonverbal responses at level 3 convey understanding and are essentially interchangeable with the client's obvious expressions, accurately reflecting factual aspects of the client's messages and surface feelings or state of being. Reciprocal responses do not appreciably add affect or reach beyond the surface feelings, nor do they subtract from the feeling and tone expressed.

Acknowledging the factual content of the client's message, although desirable, is not required; if included, this aspect of the message must be accurate. Level 3 responses facilitate further exploratory and problem-focused responses by the client. The beginning social worker does well in achieving skill in reciprocal empathic responding, which is an effective working level.

Level 3 Responses

- *"You're really angry about the slow progress in your case and are wondering whether your efforts are likely to succeed."*
- *"I can tell you feel very let down and are asking yourself, 'Will I ever get my son back?'"*

VIDEO CASE EXAMPLE

The video "Serving the Squeaky Wheel" contains a lengthy exchange in which the client, Molly, expresses her suspicion about what is written about her in the social worker's case records. The social worker responds, "I am hearing that it is a real sore point with you about what I write and think and what goes into the records about you." This response deals directly with her concern.

Essentially interchangeable, level 3 responses express accurately the immediately apparent emotions in the client's message. The content of the responses is also accurate, but deeper feelings and meanings are not added. The second response also illustrates a technique for conveying empathy that involves changing the reflection from the third to the first person, and speaking as if the social worker were the client.

Level 4: Moderately High Level of Empathic Responding

Responses at level 4 are somewhat additive, accurately identifying the client's implicit underlying feelings and/or aspects of the problem. The social worker's response illuminates subtle or veiled facets of the client's message, enabling the client to get in touch with somewhat deeper feelings and unexplored meanings and purposes of behavior. Level 4 responses thus are aimed at enhancing self-awareness.

Level 4 Responses

- *"You feel very frustrated with the lack of progress in getting your son back. You wonder whether there is any hope in working with a new worker and this system, which you feel hasn't been helping you."*

 VIDEO CASE EXAMPLE

In the "Serving the Squeaky Wheel" video, the client, Molly, says that other people's conceptions of mental illness do not include her. The social worker responds, "Let me see if I understand what you are saying: some people may think because you have a car and you speak up for yourself, that you are a very competent person who doesn't need any resources [Client: "There you go."] and if you ask for them [Client: "I am screwing the system."] that you are trying to take things that you are not entitled to. But your view is that you can have a car and speak up for yourself and still have other needs." This response not only conveys immediately apparent feelings and content but also is noticeably additive in reflecting the client's deeper feelings. In this case, the client's immediate response—finishing the practitioner's sentences—indicates that the empathic response is perceived as accurate.

Level 5: High Level of Empathic Responding

Reflecting each emotional nuance, and using voice and intensity of expressions finely attuned to the client's moment-by-moment experiencing, the social worker accurately responds to the full range and intensity of both surface and underlying feelings and meanings at level 5. The social worker may connect current feelings and experiencing to previously expressed experiences or feelings, or may accurately identify implicit patterns, themes, or purposes. Responses may also identify implicit goals embodied in the client's message, which point out a promising direction for personal growth and pave the way for action. Responding empathically at this high level facilitates the client's exploration of feelings and problems in much greater breadth and depth than responding at lower levels. Conveying this level of empathy occurs rarely with inexperienced interviewers and only somewhat more often with highly experienced interviewers. The opportunity to respond at such depth is more likely to occur near the end of an interview and with clients who have become more voluntary.

Level 5 Responses

 VIDEO CASE EXAMPLE

In the video "Serving the Squeaky Wheel," a developing theme is that Molly, a client with serious and persistent mental illness, acts, as she puts it, as a "greasy wheel," always advocating for herself and acting assertively, as she has been trained to do in many education programs. And yet those skills act as a "two- or three-edged sword" in that sometimes she is punished for this assertiveness. Reflecting these themes and Molly's language, the social worker, Ron Rooney, says, "You just seem to be courageous in fighting battles, and you have learned some skills in assertiveness, and as you say, that can be a two-edged or three-edged sword. Sometimes your assertiveness gets you what you want and sometimes your assertiveness causes some people to look at you as the squeaky wheel that has squeaked too much."

Exercises in Discriminating Levels of Empathic Responding

The following exercises ask you to rate responses for their level of empathy and are designed to assist you in refining your ability to determine the helpfulness of responses. These exercises will prepare you for subsequent practice in formulating your own empathic messages. Three client statements are given, followed by several possible responses. Using the empathic scale, rate each response. Rating messages will be less difficult if, using the list of affective words and phrases, you first identify the feelings contained in the client's message. After you have rated each response, compare your rating with those given at the end of the chapter. Referring to the rating scale, analyze the responses you rated inaccurately, trying to pinpoint the reason for the authors' ratings. Additional exercises are available in the *Practice Behaviors Workbook*.

Client Statements

1. *Single woman, age 80 [to social worker concerning her request to move to an independent living complex provided for ambulatory elderly persons]:* Goodness, the more I think of moving, the more scared I get. I have neighbors here who look after me, and I won't know a soul there. I'm afraid I'll be all alone.

Level Responses

1. "It's pretty scary to you, leaving your neighbors and familiar surroundings. But there will be a lot of friendly people there and things to do. Besides, they fix one hot meal for you every day."
2. "Don't worry, you'll make friends in no time, and you'll wish you'd moved sooner."
3. "Did you sign those application papers I left with you a few days ago?"
4. "Just thinking about moving worries you because you'll be leaving your own neighborhood and friends. Even though your life would be much easier, you're unsure you'll be better off in other ways."
5. "So I gather in some ways you'd rather stay right where you are rather than gamble on a change."
6. "Lots of other people in the new apartments were just as scared as you before they moved, but I don't know a single one who's sorry now."
7. "It sounds as though you have some pretty mixed feelings about moving. Part of you wants to go because you could live more comfortably, but another part of you is afraid you'll feel alone and lost and wants to cling to people you know care about you."
8. "Are you saying we just ought to forget the whole thing?"

2. *Male, age 16* [*in weekly visit to social work probation officer*]: I don't see the sense in having to come here every lousy week. I haven't been in any trouble now since I went to court a month ago. You should know by now you can trust me.

Level Responses

1. "A month isn't very long, you know. And how can I be sure you're staying out of trouble?"
2. "I gather you'd rather not have to see me. I can understand that, but the judge ordered it and you'd be in trouble with him if you didn't meet the conditions of your probation."
3. "Has it been a month since you went to court? I didn't think that it had been that long."
4. "You'd prefer not coming here and feel you've earned my trust."
5. "Having to come here each week gripes you, and I gather you're irritated with me for encouraging you to follow the judge's order."
6. "Look, you got yourself into this mess so don't complain to me if you don't like it. Maybe you'd like to talk the judge into changing his mind."
7. "It irritates you to have to come here each week. You'd like to get me off your back."

8. "You're confused about why you have to come here and wish you didn't have to."

3. *Group member* [in hesitant, quiet voice]: It's really hard for me to say what I want to say in this group. When I do start to talk, I get tongue-tied, and my heart starts beating faster and faster. I feel like some of you are critical of me.

Level Responses
(By Group Members or Group Leader)

1. "Yeah, I feel that same way sometimes, too."
2. "It is frightening to you to try to share your feelings with the group. Sounds like you find yourself at a loss for words and wonder what others are thinking of you."
3. "I know you're timid, but I think it's important that you make more of an effort to talk in the group, just like you're doing now. It's actually one of the responsibilities of being a group member."
4. "You get scared when you try to talk in the group."
5. "I sense that you're probably feeling pretty tense and tied up inside right now as you talk about the fear you've had in expressing yourself."
6. "Although you've been frightened of exposing yourself, I gather there's a part of you that wants to overcome that fear and become more actively involved with the rest of the group."
7. "What makes you think we're critical of you? You come across as a bit self-conscious, but that's no big deal."
8. "You remind me of the way I felt the first time I was in a group. I was so scared, I just looked at the floor most of the time."
9. "I wonder if we've done anything that came across as being critical of you."

4. A homeless client who has been referred to a housing program is completing an intake with the social worker when he is asked about what led to his losing his job. He responds, "Budget cuts, lays offs, and I did not have seniority."

Level Responses

1. "How did you feel about that?"
2. "So several things, including cuts, lay offs, and low seniority, contributed to your losing your job and contributed to your homelessness."
3. "How long have you been homeless?"
4. "Don't you think you have some responsibility for losing your job?"

Responding with Reciprocal Empathy

EP 2.1.10b

Reciprocal or interchangeable empathic responding (level 3) is a basic skill used throughout the helping process to acknowledge client messages and to encourage exploration of problems. In the initial phase, empathic responding serves a vital purpose in individual, conjoint, and group sessions: It facilitates the development of a working relationship and fosters the climate of understanding necessary to promote communication and self-disclosure. In this way, it sets the stage for deeper exploration of feelings during subsequent phases of the helping process.

Note that the benefits of making additive empathic responses at levels 4 and 5 are not contingent on the frequency of their usage. In fact, making one such response in a first or second interview may be helpful and appropriate. More frequent attempts presume a depth of relationship that has not yet developed. Additive empathic responses often exceed the level of feelings and meanings expressed by clients during early sessions and are thus reserved, in large part, for the later phases of the helping process.

Because reciprocal responding is an essential skill used frequently to meet the objectives of the first phase of the helping process, we recommend that you first aim to achieve beginning mastery of responding at level 3. Extended practice of this skill should significantly increase your effectiveness in establishing viable helping relationships, interviewing, and gathering data. The remainder of this chapter provides guidelines and practice exercises that will help you in mastering reciprocal responding. Although responding at additive levels represents an extension of the skill of reciprocal responding, it is an advanced skill that can be used in a variety of ways to achieve specific objectives. For this reason, it has been grouped with other change-oriented or "action" skills presented in Part 3 of the book.

Constructing Reciprocal Responses

To reach level 3 on the empathic scale, you must be able to formulate responses that accurately capture the content and the surface feelings in the client message. It is also important to frame the message so that you do not merely restate the client's message.

The following paradigm, which identifies the elements of an empathic or reflective message, has proven useful for conceptualizing and mastering the skill of empathic responding:

You feel _____ about _____ because _____.

Accurately identifies or describes feelings

The response focuses exclusively on the client's message and does not reflect the social worker's conceptualizations.

The following excerpt from a session involving a social worker and a 17-year-old female illustrates the use of the preceding paradigm in constructing an empathic response:

Client: I can't talk to my father without feeling scared and crying. I'd like to be able to express myself and to disagree with him, but I just can't.

Social worker: It sounds as though you just feel panicky when you try to talk to your father. You feel down on yourself, because at this point you can't say what you want without falling apart.

This message conveys a reflection with a twist which we will explore more in the following chapter (Miller, Rollnick & Conforti, 2002). That is, it reflects the client's current feeling but implies that it could change at another point when she acquires more confidence and skill (Greene, Lee & Hoffpauir, 2005). Many times, client messages contain conflicting or contrasting emotions, such as the following: "I like taking drugs, but sometimes I worry about what they might do to me." In such cases, each contrasting feeling should be highlighted:

- *You feel _____ yet you also feel _____.*
- *I sense that you feel torn because while you find taking drugs enjoyable, you have nagging thoughts that they might be harmful to you.*[1]

Remember that to respond empathically at a reciprocal level, you must use language that your clients will readily understand. Abstract, intellectualized language and professional jargon create barriers to communication and should be avoided. It is also important to vary the language you use in responding. Many professionals tend to respond with stereotyped, repetitive speech patterns, commonly using a limited variety of communication leads to begin their empathic responses. Such leads as "You feel …" and "I hear you saying …" repeated over and over not only distract the client but also seem phony and contrived. This kind of stereotyped responding draws more attention to the social worker's technique than to his or her message. One of the many advantages to audio or video recording your own work is that these habitual responses that can be so instinctive you don't notice them as they occur, will become readily apparent to you.

The list of varied introductory phrases will help you expand your repertoire of possible responses. We encourage you to read the list aloud several times and to review it frequently while practicing the empathic communication training exercises in this chapter and in Chapter 17, which covers additive empathic responding. The reciprocal empathic response format ("You feel _____ because _____") is merely a training aid to assist you in focusing on the affect and content of client messages. The leads list will help you respond more naturally.

Exercises designed to help you to develop level 3 reciprocal empathic responses appear at the end of the chapter and in the *Practice Behaviors Workbook*. Included in the exercises are a variety of client statements taken from actual work with individuals, groups, couples, and families in diverse settings.

In addition to completing the skill development exercises, we recommend that you record the number of empathic responses you employ in sessions over several weeks to determine the extent to which you are applying this skill. We also suggest that either you or a knowledgeable associate rate your responses and determine the mean level of empathic responding for each session. If you find (as most beginning social workers do) that you are underutilizing empathic responses or responding at low levels, you may wish to set a goal to improve your skill.

Leads for Empathic Responses

Could it be that …

I wonder if …

What I guess I'm hearing is …

Correct me if I'm wrong, but I'm sensing …

Perhaps you're feeling …

Sometimes you think …

Maybe this is a long shot, but …

You're feeling …

I'm not sure if I'm with you but …

You appear to be feeling …

It appears you feel …

Maybe you feel …

Do you feel …

I'm not sure that I'm with you; do you mean …

It seems that you …

Is that what you mean?

I'm not certain I understand; you're feeling …

As I hear it, you …

Is that the way you feel?

The message I'm getting is that

Let me see if I'm with you; you …

If I'm hearing you correctly …

So, you're feeling …

You feel …

It sounds as though you are saying …

I hear you saying …

So, from where you sit …

I sense that you're feeling …

Your message seems to be …

I gather you're feeling …

If I'm catching what you say …

What you're saying comes across to me as …

What I think I'm hearing is …

I get the impression that …

As I get it, you felt that …

To me it's almost like you are saying …

So, as you see it …

I'm picking up that you …

I wonder if you're saying …

So, it seems to you …

Right now you're feeling …

You must have felt …

Listening to you, it seems as if …

You convey a sense of …

As I think about what you say, it occurs to me you're feeling …

From what you say …

I gather you're feeling …

Employing Empathic Responding

In early sessions with the client, empathic responding should be used frequently as a method of developing rapport and "staying in touch" with the client. Responses should be couched in a tentative manner to allow for inaccuracies in the social worker's perception. Checking out the accuracy of responses with appropriate lead-in phrases such as "Let me see if I understand …" or "Did I hear you right?" is helpful in communicating a desire to understand and a willingness to correct misperceptions.

In initially using empathic responses, learners are often leery of the flood of emotions that sometimes occurs as the client, experiencing none of the usual barriers to communication, releases feelings that may have been pent up for months or years. It is important to understand that empathic responses have not "caused" such feelings but rather have facilitated their expression, thus clearing the way for the client to explore and to consider such feelings more rationally and objectively.

You may worry, as do many beginning social workers, about whether you will "damage" the client or disrupt the helping relationship if your empathic responses do not always accurately reflect the client's feelings. Perhaps even more important than accuracy, however, is the commitment to understand conveyed by your genuine efforts to perceive the client's experience. If you consistently demonstrate your goodwill and intent to help through attentive verbal and nonverbal responding, an occasional lack of understanding or faulty timing will not damage the client–social worker relationship. In fact, your efforts to clarify the client's message will usually enhance rather than detract from the helping process, particularly if you respond to corrective feedback in an open, nondefensive, and empathic manner.

Multiple Uses of Empathic Communication

Earlier in the chapter, we referred to the versatility of empathic communication. In this section, we delineate a number of ways in which you can employ reciprocal empathic responding.

Establishing Relationships with Clients in Initial Sessions

As discussed previously, the use of empathic responding actively demonstrates the social worker's keen awareness of clients' feelings and creates an atmosphere in which clients feel safe enough to risk exploring their personal thoughts and feelings.

Although empathic communication is important in bridging cultural gaps, at times it can be used to excess. We must be careful with generalizations to ethnic groups because there is variation within each group related to individual differences, family experiences, education, interaction with other groups (Dean, 2001). Classification systems can tend to stereotype members of ethnic groups and in fact create distance (Johnson & Munch, 2010). Social workers have to be prepared to be learners, operating from a "not knowing" stance, which may however be influenced by hypotheses which they explore rather than act on as realities. With this caveat, some members of Asian American and Native American groups may tend to be lower in emotional expressiveness than members of other client groups, and they may react with discomfort and confusion if a social worker relies too heavily on empathic communication. Nevertheless, it is important to "read between the lines" and to sensitively respond to troubling emotions that these clients do not usually express directly. Like other clients, they are likely to appreciate a social worker's sensitive awareness to the painful emotions associated with their difficulties.

This can lead to assuming a more directive, active, and structured stance in situations such as crises where immediate action is required. This can also apply to some Asian American clients. As Tsui and Schultz (1985) have clarified, "A purely empathetic, passive, nondirective approach serves only to confuse and alienate the [Asian] client" (p. 568). The same can be said of many Native American clients, based on their levels of acculturation and experience with other groups.

IDEAS IN ACTION

In the videotape "Getting Back to Shakopee," the social worker, Dorothy, is working with a Native American client, Valerie, who appears guarded and apprehensive about contact with a social worker after referral by her employer. She appears worried that seeing a social worker might lead to a child welfare investigation. Her guarded stance appears to be associated with a belief based on her experience that social workers are more likely to remove children than act as her agent toward her own goals. In this case,

these beliefs are not so much cultural beliefs as "folk wisdom" about the experience of her group with public child welfare. Dorothy makes many efforts to establish empathic and cultural linkages. A turning point appears to occur when Valerie discovers that Dorothy knows about an upcoming powwow and plans to attend. Taking a not knowing, learner stance, leads Dorothy to find out about the particular employment, stress, sobriety and family responsibility pressures that Valerie experiences.

Staying in Touch with Clients

EP 2.1.10b

Reciprocal empathic responding operationalizes the social work principle of "starting where the client is" and keeps social workers attuned to their clients' current feelings. Although he or she inevitably employs many other skills and techniques, the social worker constantly returns to empathic responding to keep in touch with the client. In that sense, empathic communication is a fundamental intervention and a prerequisite to the use of other interventions. Gendlin (1974) used the analogy of driving a car to illuminate the vital role of empathy in keeping in touch with clients. Driving involves much more than watching the road. A driver does many things, including steering, braking, signaling, and watching signs. One may glance at the scenery, visit with others, and think private thoughts, but watching the road must be accorded the highest priority.

When visibility becomes limited or hazards appear, all other activities must cease and the driver must attend exclusively to observing the road and potentially dangerous conditions. Just as some drivers fail to pay proper attention to their surroundings and become involved in accidents, so some social workers also fail to attend sufficiently to cultural differences and changes in clients' moods and reactions, mistakenly assuming they know their clients' frame of mind. As a consequence, social workers may fail to discern important feelings, and their clients may perceive them as disinterested or insensitive and subsequently disengage from the helping process. Indeed, it is often true with beginners that so much of their own processing is focused on preparing the next thing they will say that they often miss what the client says. It takes time and experience to stay focused on what the client is expressing and trust that you will be able to respond adequately. Part of this is reframing your expectations of yourself. Instead of aspiring to be the social worker who can quickly assess and resolve client concerns, you can aspire to be a social worker who is able to accurately reflect what the client is saying and feeling and, in that process, be useful to them as they consider how to deal with their concerns.

EP 2.1.10b

Accurately Assessing Client Problems

The levels of empathy offered by social workers are likely to correlate with their clients' levels of self-exploration. That is,

high-level empathic responding should increase clients' exploration of self and problems. As the social worker moves "with" clients by frequently using empathic responses in initial sessions, clients will begin to lay out their problems and to reveal events and relevant data. Figuratively speaking, clients then take social workers where they need to go by providing information crucial to making an accurate assessment. Such an approach contrasts sharply with sessions that emphasize history-taking and in which social workers, following their own agendas rather than the clients', spend unnecessary time asking hit-or-miss questions and gathering extraneous information.

Responding to Clients' Nonverbal Messages

Through their facial features, gestures, and body postures, clients often hint at feelings that they do not express verbally. In the course of a session, for instance, a client may become pensive, or he or she may show puzzlement, pain, or discomfort. In such instances, the social worker may convey understanding of the client's feeling state and verbalize the feeling explicitly through a reflective response that attends to the emotion suggested in the client's nonverbal expressions. For instance, in response to a client who has been sitting dejectedly with her head down for several minutes after having reported some bad grades, a social worker might say, "At this moment you seem to be feeling very sad and discouraged, perhaps even defeated." In group or conjoint sessions, the social worker might reflect the nonverbal messages of several, or all, of the members. For example, the social worker might say, "I sense some restlessness today, and we're having a hard time staying on our topic. I'm wondering if you're saying, 'We're not sure we want to deal with this problem today.' Am I reading the group correctly?"

Children are likely to communicate more nonverbally with unfamiliar adults such as social workers than they communicate in verbal ways. It can be useful to ask about such nonverbals and what they might mean. A child interacting with a toy, making limited eye contact, and making one-word replies to questions about how things are going at home may be communicating some things about how uncomfortable or unfamiliar he or she is with the process. Rather than force the child to explain what is happening in words, play therapy techniques have permitted children to tell a story, through actions, of what is occurring to them (Lukas, 1993). A social worker working with a child who was having difficulties at school made a home visit. The child was particularly interested in a toy piano, playing little melodies on it. The social worker, attempting to tune in to the child client, sat beside him and played a little melody and sang a little song "how was your day?" The child sat for a moment then repeated the melody, singing "pretty good." The social worker responded with a variation of the melody "what was good about it?" and the child responded.

Empathic responses that accurately tune into clients' nonverbal experiencing will usually prompt clients to begin exploring feelings they have been experiencing.

Making Confrontations More Palatable

EP 2.1.10i

Confrontation is employed in the change-oriented phase to expand clients' awareness and to motivate them to action. It is most appropriate when clients are contemplating actions that are unlawful or that are dangerous to themselves or others. Confrontation is also appropriate when such actions conflict with the goals and values a client has chosen for himself or herself.

Of course, even well-timed confrontations may meet with varying degrees of receptiveness. Both concerns for the client's welfare and prudence dictate that the social worker determine the impact of a potential confrontation upon the client and implement a process for making such an intervention more palatable. This may be accomplished by employing empathic responses attuned to the client's reaction immediately following a confrontation. As social workers listen attentively and sensitively to their clients' expressions, the clients' defensiveness may abate. Indeed, clients often begin to process new information and think through and test the validity of their ideas, embracing those that fit and rejecting others that seem inapplicable. Guidelines for this important skill are presented in Chapter 17.

Blending confrontation and empathic responses is a particularly potent technique for managing group processes when the social worker must deal with a controversial issue or distractive behavior that is interfering with the work of the group.

Handling Obstacles Presented by Clients

Client opposition to what is happening in a session is sometimes healthy. What is often interpreted as unconscious resistance may, in fact, be a negative reaction to poor interviewing and intervention techniques used by the social worker or to client confusion, misunderstanding,

or even inertia. For these reasons, it is important to carefully monitor clients' reactions and to deal directly and sensitively with their related feelings. Clients' verbal or nonverbal actions may comment indirectly on what is occurring in the helping process. For instance, a client may look at her watch and ask how long the session will last, shift her body position away from the social worker, begin tapping a foot, or stare out the window. When it appears that the client is disengaging from the session in this way, an empathic response that reflects the client's verbal and/or nonverbal message may effectively initiate discussion of what is occurring.

Social workers sometimes practice with highly verbal clients who talk rapidly and jump quickly from one topic to another. Overly verbal clients present a particular challenge to beginning social workers, who must often overcome the misconception that interrupting clients is rude. Because of this misconception, novice interviewers sometimes spend most of an initial session listening passively to highly verbal clients without providing any form or direction to the helping process. They may also allow clients to talk incessantly because they mistakenly view this as constructive work on problems. Quite the contrary, excess verbosity often keeps the session on a superficial level and interferes with problem identification and exploration. It may also indicate a more serious affective mental health problem.

It is important that social workers provide structure and direction to each session, thereby conveying an expectation that specific topics will be considered in depth. Much more will be said about this in later chapters. For now, we simply underscore the necessity of using empathic responses with highly verbal clients as a preliminary strategy to slow the process and to provide some depth to the discussion.

For example, a social worker might interject or intervene with "I'd like to interrupt to check whether I'm understanding what you mean. As I get it, you're feeling ..." or "Before you talk about that topic, I would like to make sure I'm with you. You seem to be saying ..." or "Could we hold off discussing that for just a minute? I'd like to be sure I understand what you mean. Would you expand on the point you were just making?"

Managing Anger and Patterns of Violence

During individual or group sessions, clients (especially those who were not self-referred and may be involuntary clients) often experience surges of intense and conflicting feelings, such as anger, hurt, or disappointment. In such instances, empathic responding is a key tool for assisting them to work through those feelings. As empathic responses facilitate expanded expression of these feelings, clients engage in a process of venting, clarifying, and experiencing different feelings. Over time, they may achieve a mellowing of emotions and a more rational and thoughtful state of being.

When it is employed to focus sharply on clients' feelings, empathic responding efficiently manages and modifies strong emotions that represent obstacles to progress. As the social worker successfully handles such moments and clients experience increased self-awareness and cathartic benefits, the helping relationship is strengthened.

Empathic responding is particularly helpful in dealing with hostile clients and is indispensable when clients become angry with the social worker, as illustrated in the following client statement: "What you're doing to help me with my problems doesn't seem to be doing me any good. I don't know why I keep coming." At such moments, the social worker must resist the temptation to react defensively, because such a response will further antagonize the client and exacerbate the situation. Responding by challenging the client's perception, for instance, would damage the helping relationship. The social worker's responses should represent a genuine effort to understand the client's experiencing and feelings and to engage the client in fully exploring those feelings.

Involuntary clients sometimes become frustrated with the seemingly slow pace of progress toward goals and may feel that policies and individuals in the system are acting to thwart them. Empathizing with this anger is necessary before the social worker and client can collaborate productively and figure out how to make the system work toward client goals (Rooney & Chovanec, 2004).

Keeping this idea in mind, consider the impact of the following reciprocal empathic response: "You're very disappointed that things aren't better and are irritated with me, feeling that I should have been more helpful to you." This response accurately and nondefensively acknowledges the client's frustration with the situation and with the social worker. By itself, it would not be sufficient to calm the client's ire and to free the client to consider the problem more fully and rationally.

Carefully following the client's feelings and remaining sensitively attuned to the client's experiencing by employing empathic responses for several minutes usually assists both the social worker and the client to understand more clearly the strong feelings that prompted the client's outburst and to adequately assess the source of those feelings. Attending to the emotions expressed does not mean that the content is discounted. The social worker might, for example, follow the empathic response above by saying, "I'd like to explore more fully with you which parts of our work have not felt worthwhile to you."

When faced with angry clients in group and conjoint sessions, it is critical that the social worker empathically not only reflect the negative feelings and positions of the clients who are displaying the anger, but also reach for and reflect the feelings or observations of members who may be experiencing the situation differently. Utilizing empathic responses in this manner assists the social worker in gathering information that will elucidate the problem, helping angry members air and examine their feelings, and bringing out other points of view for the group's consideration. In addition, employing empathic responding at such moments encourages a more rational discussion of the issues involved in the problem and thus sets the stage for possible problem solving. For example, a group leader might emphasize with members' frustration at having chosen to be part of an involuntary group such as one addressing alternatives to violence rather than risking prosecution. Having made a limited choice to be part of the group, members can then be encouraged to take part in establishing content areas which they would like to have covered in the group.

The principles just discussed also apply to clients who are prone to violent behavior. Such clients often come to the attention of social workers because they have abused their children and/or partners. People who engage in violence often do so because they have underlying feelings of helplessness and frustration and because they lack skills and experience in coping with troubling situations in more constructive ways. Some have short fuses and weak emotional controls, and many come from backgrounds in which they vicariously learned violence as a mechanism of coping. Using empathy to defuse their intense anger and to tune into the exceptions when they have been more successful in managing it can be an important first step in working with such clients (Lee, Uken & Sebold, 2004). Other clients may have difficulties with anger and express this emotion only when under the influence of alcohol or other substances. Helping them experience and ventilate anger when sober and in control is a major approach employed to assist such clients to learn constructive ways of coping with anger (Potter-Efron & Potter-Efron, 1992).

VIDEO CASE EXAMPLE

Several parts of the "Serving the Squeaky Wheel" video deal with the client, Molly, expressing anger and frustration and the practitioner, Ron Rooney, attempting to respond empathically to that anger. In particular, Molly is frustrated with an abrupt replacement of her previous case worker by Rooney and insists on his proving his identity as a social worker. Note how this challenge is met. At other points, Molly scales her level of trust at below zero and attributes this to a history of distrust of social workers.

Utilizing Empathic Responses to Facilitate Group Discussions

EP 2.1.10i

Social workers may facilitate discussion of specific issues in conjoint or group sessions by first identifying a particular topic and then using empathic responses to reflect the observations of various group members in relation to that topic. The social worker may also actively seek responses from members who have not contributed and then employ empathic responses (or paraphrases) to acknowledge their observations. Utilized frequently in this manner, empathic responding encourages (and reinforces) clients' participation in group discussions.

Teaching Clients to Respond Empathically

Clients often experience difficulties in their relationships because their styles of communication include many barriers that prevent them from accurately hearing messages or conveying understanding to others. An important task for the social worker involves teaching clients to respond empathically. This task is accomplished in part by modeling, which is generally recognized as a potent technique for promoting client change and growth. People who distort or ignore others' messages (e.g., in marital, family, and other close relationships) may benefit vicariously by observing the social worker listen effectively and respond empathically. Moreover, clients who are hard to reach or who have difficulties in expressing themselves may gradually learn to recognize their own emotions and to express themselves more fully as a result of the social worker's empathic responding.

Teaching empathic communication skills to clients also can entail assuming an educational role. Several approaches to assisting partners who are having serious conflicts rely on teaching both parties to gain and express empathy for each other. Social workers' roles as educators require them to intervene actively at opportune moments to enable their clients to respond empathically, particularly when they have ignored, discounted, or attacked the contributions of others in a session. With respect to this role, we suggest that social workers consider taking the following actions:

1. Teach clients the paradigm for empathic responding introduced in this chapter. If appropriate, ask them to engage briefly in a paired practice exercise similar to the one recommended for beginning social workers at the end of the chapter. Utilizing topics neutral to the relationship, have each person carefully listen to the other party for several minutes, and then reverse roles. Afterward, evaluate with participants the impact of the exercise on them.

2. Introduce clients to the list of affective words and phrases and to the leads list provided in this chapter. If appropriate, you may wish to have clients assume tasks during the week to broaden their feeling vocabulary similar to the tasks recommended for beginning social workers.

3. Intervene in sessions when clients ignore or fail to validate messages—a situation that occurs frequently during direct social work with couples, families, and groups. At those moments, interrupt the process in a facilitative fashion to ask the sender to repeat the message and the receiver to paraphrase or capture the essence of the former's message with fresh words, as illustrated in the following example:

16-year-old daughter: I don't like going to school. The teachers are a bunch of dweebs, and most of the kids laugh and make fun of me.

Mother: But you've got to go. If you'd just buckle down and study, school wouldn't be half so hard for you. I think …

Social worker: [interrupting and speaking to mother]: I can see that you have some real concerns about Janet's not going to school, but for a moment, I'm going to ask you to show that you heard what she said to you by repeating it back to her.

Mother: [looking at social worker]: She said she doesn't like school.

Social worker: That's close, but turn and talk to Janet. See if you can identify what she's feeling.

Mother: [turning to daughter]: I guess it's pretty painful for you to go to school. And you don't like your teachers and you feel shut out and ridiculed by the kids.

Janet: *[tearfully]:* Yeah, that's it … it's really hard.

Notice that the mother did not respond empathically to her daughter's feelings until the social worker intervened and coached her. This example illustrates the importance of persevering in teaching clients to "hear" the messages of others, a point we cannot overemphasize. People often have considerable trouble mastering listening skills because habitual responses are difficult to discard. This is true even when clients are highly motivated to communicate more effectively and when social workers actively intervene to assist them.

4. Give positive feedback when you observe clients listening to each other or, as in the preceding example, when they respond to your coaching. In the example, the social worker might have praised the mother as follows: "I liked the way you responded, because your message accurately reflected what your daughter was experiencing. I think she felt you really understood what she was trying to say." It is also helpful to ask participants to discuss what they experienced during the exchange and to highlight positive feelings and observations.

Authenticity

Although many theorists agree that empathy and respect are vital to developing effective working relationships, they do not agree about the amount of openness or self-disclosure practitioners should offer. *Self-disclosure* refers to the sharing with the client of opinions, thoughts, feelings, reactions to the client, and personal experiences of the practitioner (Deal, 1999). Decisions about whether or when to self-disclose must be guided by a perception of benefit to the client, not the social worker's need to share. As one client said, "My case worker wanted to tell me all about his weekend and his girlfriend and so on. And I said, 'TMI: too much information. I don't need to know this, and I don't want to know this.' I don't want to share this kind of information with him and don't want to know it from him." Clearly, this client did not perceive the benefit of this kind of personal sharing. Deal reports that although beginning social workers frequently report engaging in self-disclosure, they seem less clear about the conditions under which it is appropriate to do so.

With respect to empirical evidence, numerous research studies cited by Truax and Mitchell (1971) and Gurman (1977) indicated that empathy, respect, and genuineness are correlated with positive outcomes. Critical analyses of these studies and conflicting findings from other research studies, however, have led experts to question these early findings and to conclude that "a more complex association exists between outcome and therapist 'skills' than originally hypothesized" (Parloff, Waskow, & Wolfe, 1978, p. 251). Research needs to distinguish between intellectual empathy and empathic emotions and identify whether they are identifying therapist or client experience of empathy (Duan and Hill, 1996). That is, conveying understanding of the client's perception of the situation (intellectual empathy) is not the same as conveying feeling the same emotions (empathic empathy). Both are useful but they may have independent effects.

Nevertheless, authenticity (also called genuineness) and the other facilitative conditions are still viewed as central to the helping process. *Authenticity* is defined as the sharing of self by relating in a natural, sincere, spontaneous, open, and genuine manner. Being authentic, or genuine, involves relating personally so that expressions are spontaneous rather than contrived. In addition, it means that social workers' verbalizations are congruent with their actual feelings and thoughts. Authentic social workers relate as real people, expressing their feelings and assuming responsibility for them rather than denying the feelings or blaming the client for causing them. Authenticity also involves being nondefensive and human enough to admit one's errors to clients. Realizing that they expect clients to lower their defenses and to relate openly (thereby increasing their vulnerability), social workers themselves must model humanness and openness and avoid hiding behind a mask of "professionalism."

Relating authentically does not mean that social workers indiscriminately disclose their feelings. Indeed, authentic expressions can be abrasive and destructive. Social workers should thus relate authentically only when doing so is likely to further the therapeutic objectives. This qualification provides considerable latitude and is merely intended to constrain social workers from (1) relating abrasively (even though they may be expressing genuine feelings) and (2) meeting their own needs by focusing on their personal experiences and feelings rather than those of the client.

With respect to the first constraint, social workers must avoid misconstruing authenticity as granting free license to do whatever they wish, especially with

EP 2.1.1.b

respect to expressing hostility. The second constraint reiterates the importance of social workers responding to clients' needs rather than their own. Moreover, when social workers share their feelings or experiences for a therapeutic purpose, they should immediately shift the focus back on the clients. Keep in mind that the purpose of relating authentically—whether with individuals, families, or groups—is to facilitate growth of clients, not to demonstrate one's own honesty or authenticity.

Types of Self-Disclosure

EP 2.1.1b

The aspect of authenticity denoted as self-disclosure has been variously defined by different authors (Chelune, 1979). For our discussion here, we define self-disclosure as the conscious and intentional revelation of information about oneself through both verbal expressions and nonverbal behaviors (e.g., smiling, grimacing, or shaking one's head in disbelief). Viewed from a therapeutic perspective, self-disclosure encourages clients to reciprocate with trust and openness.

Danish, D'Augelli, and Hauer (1980) have identified two types of self-disclosure, *self-involving statements* and *personal self-disclosing*. The former type includes messages that express the social worker's personal reaction to the client during the course of a session. Examples of self-involving statements follow:

- *"I'm impressed with the progress you've made this past week. You applied what we discussed last week and have made another step toward learning to control angry feelings."*
- *"I want to share my reaction to what you just said. I found myself feeling sad for you because you put yourself down unmercifully. I see you so differently from how you see yourself and find myself wishing I could somehow spare you the torment you inflict on yourself."*
- *"You know, as I think about the losses you've experienced this past year, I marvel you've done as well as you have. I'm not at all sure I'd have held together as well as you have."*

Personal self-disclosure messages, by contrast, center on struggles or problems the social worker is currently experiencing or has experienced that are similar to the client's problems. The following are examples of this type of self-disclosure:

- [To couple] *"As you talk about your problems with your children, it reminds me of similar difficulties I had with mine when they were that same age."* (The social worker goes on to relate his experience.)
- [To individual client] *"I think all of us struggle with that same fear to some degree. Earlier this week I ..."* (The social worker goes on to relate events in which she experienced similar fears.)

Research findings comparing the effects of different types of self-disclosure have been mixed (Farber, 2006). Given the inconclusive findings, social workers should use personal self-disclosure judiciously. They should also recognize cultural variations that may suggest that some relatively low-level self-disclosure may be necessary early in the helping process. Rosenthal-Gelman (2004) has reported in a study that Hispanic practitioners are more likely to engage in some self-disclosure at the beginning of contact with Hispanic clients, honoring the cultural norm of establishing a more personal contact. Logic suggests that self-disclosures of current problems may undermine the confidence of clients, who may well wonder how social workers can presume to help others when they haven't successfully resolved their own problems. Moreover, focusing on the social worker's problems diverts attention from the client, who may conclude that the social worker prefers to focus on his or her own problems. Self-involving disclosures, by contrast, appear to be of low risk and are relevant to the helping process.

> ### VIDEO CASE EXAMPLE
>
> As noted in the "Getting Back to Shakopee" video, self-disclosure of cultural experiences by the practitioner, Dorothy, appears essential in beginning to develop trust and rapport with her client.

Timing and Intensity of Self-Disclosure

Yet another aspect of self-disclosure focuses on the timing and level of intensity of the social worker's sharing, ranging from superficial to highly personal statements. Social workers should avoid sharing personal feelings and experiences until they have established rapport and trust with their clients and the clients have, in turn, demonstrated readiness to engage on a more personal level. The danger in premature self-disclosure is that such responses can threaten clients and lead to emotional retreat at the very time when it is vital to reduce threat and defensiveness.

The danger is especially great with clients from cultures where relating on an intense personal basis might be less common. Tsui and Schultz (1985) have suggested that self-disclosure by social workers may facilitate the development of rapport with some Asian clients. The logic of this recommendation is that given the generally low level of emotional expressiveness in some Asian families, the social worker is, in effect, acting as a role model for the client, thereby showing the client how the appropriate expression of emotion facilitates the treatment process (Tsui & Schultz, 1985, p. 568). Members of Asian American families, of course, are not homogenous, as their members differ in terms of their level of acculturation and familiarity with values such as self-disclosure. Hence, assessing their cultural experience can be part of determining whether self-disclosure might be useful.

As clients experience trust, social workers can appropriately relate with increased openness and spontaneity, assuming that their authentic responses are relevant to their clients' needs and do not shift the focus from the client for more than brief periods. Even when trust is strong, social workers should exercise only moderate self-disclosure—beyond a certain level, even authentic responses no longer facilitate the helping process (Truax & Carkhuff, 1964).

A Paradigm for Responding Authentically

Beginning social workers (and clients) may learn the skill of relating authentically more readily if they have a paradigm for formulating effective messages. This paradigm includes the four elements of an authentic message:

(1)"I"( )	*About*	*Because*
(2) Specific feeling or wants	(3) Neutral description of event	(4) Impact of situation upon sender or others

The following example (Larsen, 1980), involving a social work student intern's response to a message from an institutionalized youth, illustrates the use of this paradigm. The student describes the situation: "Don and I had a hard time together last week. I entered the living unit only to find that he was angry with me for some reason, and he proceeded to abuse me verbally all night long. This week, Don approached me to apologize."

Don: I'm really sorry about what happened the other night. I didn't mean to dis you.

Student: Well, you know, Don, I'm sorry it happened, too. I was hurt and puzzled that night because I didn't understand where all your anger was coming from. You wouldn't talk to me about it, so I felt frustrated, and I didn't quite know what to do or make of it. One of my real fears that night was that this was going to get in the way of our getting to know each other. I really didn't want to see that happen.

Note that the student uses all of the elements of the paradigm: identifying specific feelings (hurt, puzzlement, frustration, fear); describing the events that occurred in a neutral, nonblaming manner; and identifying the impact she feared these events might have upon the client-social worker relationship.

As you consider the paradigm, note that we are not recommending that you use it in a mechanistic and un-deviating "I-feel-this-way-about …" response pattern. Rather, we suggest that you learn and combine the elements of the paradigm in a variety of ways as you practice constructing authentic messages. Later, as you incorporate authentic relating into your natural conversational repertoire, you will no longer need to refer to the paradigm.

Note that this paradigm is also applicable in teaching clients to respond authentically. We suggest that you present the paradigm to clients and guide them through several practice messages, assisting them to include all of the elements of the paradigm in their responses. For example:

Specific "I" Feelings	Description of Event	Impact
I get frustrated	when you keep reading the paper while I'm speaking	because I feel very unimportant to you.

It is important to stress with clients the need to use conversational language when they express authentic messages. Also emphasize, however, that they should talk about their own feelings and opinions rather than slip into accusatory forms of communication.

Guidelines for Responding Authentically

As you practice authentic responding and teach clients to respond authentically in their encounters with others, we suggest you keep in mind the following guidelines related to the four elements of an authentic message

1. *Personalize messages by using the pronoun "I."* When attempting to respond authentically, both social workers and clients commonly make the mistake of starting

their statements with "You." This introduction tends to focus a response on the other person rather than on the sender's experiencing. In contrast, beginning messages with "I" encourages senders to own responsibility for their feelings and to personalize their statements.

Efforts by social workers to employ "I" statements when responding can profoundly affect the quality of group processes, increasing both the specificity of communications and the frequency with which their clients use "I" statements. As a general rule, groups (including couples and families) are likely to follow a social worker's communication style.

Just as groups tend to follow suit when social workers frequently use "I" messages, they may also imitate counterproductive behaviors of the social worker. That includes communicating in broad generalities, focusing on issues external to the individual, or relating to the group in an interrogative or confrontational manner.

Social workers must be careful to model the skills they wish clients to acquire. They should master relating authentically to the extent that they automatically personalize their messages and constructively share their inner experiencing with clients. To facilitate personalizing messages, social workers can negotiate an agreement with individuals or groups specifying that clients will endeavor to incorporate the use of "I" statements in their conversational repertories. Thereafter, it is critical to intervene consistently to assist clients to personalize their messages when they have not done so.

2. *Share feelings that lie at varying depths.* Social workers must reach for those feelings that underlie their immediate experiencing. Doing so is particularly vital when social workers experience strong negative feelings (e.g., dislike, anger, repulsion, disgust, boredom) toward a client, because an examination of the deeper aspects of feelings often discloses more positive feelings toward the client. Social workers need to be in tune with their feelings, positive and negative, and learn when and how sharing such emotions appropriately can be useful to clients. Expressing these feelings preserves the client's self-esteem, whereas expressing superficial negative feelings often poses a threat to the client, creating defensiveness and anger.

EP 2.1.1b

For example, in experiencing feelings of anger (and perhaps disappointment) toward a client who is chronically late for appointments, the social worker may first connect his feelings of anger to feeling inconvenienced. In reaching for his deeper feelings, however, the social worker may

discover that the annoyance derives from a concern that the client may not find the sessions useful. At an even deeper level may lie hurt in not being more important to the client. Further introspection may also uncover a concern that the client is exhibiting similar behavior in other areas of life that could adversely affect his or her relationships with others. The fact of the matter is that the social worker does not know why the client is late for appointments and overt exploration of the obstacles can lead the social worker and client into a more productive discussion on how to resolve the issue.

The social worker may discover multiple (and sometimes conflicting) feelings that may be beneficially shared with the client, as illustrated in the following message:

Social worker [To client]: I would like to check some things out with you. You apologized for being late for the session, and I appreciate that. However, this has occurred before so I wanted to check out with you how things are going for you about our sessions. You lead a busy life, balancing many commitments. I am not sure what part these sessions are playing for you in addressing the issues you brought in. I would also like to know what you're feeling just now about what I said.

Like prospective social workers, clients are prone to focus on one aspect of their experiencing to the exclusion of deeper and more complex emotions. Clients often have difficulty, in fact, pinpointing any feelings they are experiencing. In either case, social workers should persevere to help clients broaden their awareness of their emotions and to express them openly, as illustrated in the following exchange:

Social worker: When you told your wife you didn't want to take her to a movie, and she said you were a "bump on a log"—that you never seemed to want to do anything with her—what feelings did you experience?[2]

Husband: I decided that if that's what she thought of me, that's what I'd be.

Social worker: Can you get in touch with what you were feeling? You told me a little bit about what you thought, but what's happening inside? Try to use feeling words to describe what you're experiencing.

Husband [pause]: I felt that if she was going to get on my back …

Social worker [gently interrupting]: Can you use a feeling word like "bad," or "hurt," or "put down"? What did you feel?

Husband: Okay. I felt annoyed.

Social worker: So you experienced a sense of irritation. Good. I'm pleased you could get in touch with that feeling. Now see if you can get to an even more basic feeling. Remember, as we've talked about before, anger is usually a surface feeling that camouflages other feelings. What was under your annoyance?

Husband: Uh, I'd say frustrated. I just didn't want to sit there and listen to her harp at me. She never quits.

Social worker: I would like to check out something with you. Right now, as you're talking about this, it seems you're experiencing a real sense of discouragement and perhaps even hopelessness about things ever changing. It's as though you've given up. Maybe that's part of what you were feeling Saturday.

Husband: Yeah, I just turn myself off. There doesn't seem to be anything I can do to make her happy.

Social worker: I'm glad that you can recognize the sense of despair you're feeling. I also appreciate your hanging in there with me for a minute to get in touch with some of your feelings. You seem to be a person whose feelings run deep, and sometimes expressing them may come hard for you. I'm wondering how you view yourself in that regard.

In the preceding excerpt, the social worker engaged in extensive coaching to assist the client in discovering his underlying feelings. Deeper than the feelings of annoyance and frustration the client identified lay the more basic emotions related to feeling hurt and being unimportant to his wife. By providing other spontaneous "training sessions," the social worker can help this client to identify his feelings more readily, to find the feeling words to express them, and to begin formulating "I" statements.

3. *Describe the situation or targeted behavior in neutral or descriptive terms.* In their messages, clients often omit references or make only vague references to the situations that prompted their responses. Moreover, they may convey their messages in a blaming manner, engendering defensiveness that overshadows other aspects of their self-disclosure. In either event, self-disclosure is minimal and respondents do not receive information that could otherwise be of considerable value.

Consider, for example, the low yield of information in the following messages:

- "You're a nice person."
- "You should be more conscientious."

- "You're progressing well in your work."
- "You have a bad attitude."

All of these messages lack supporting information that respondents need to identify specific aspects of their behavior that are competent and warrant recognition or are substandard. Social workers should assist parents, spouses, or others to provide higher-yield feedback by including behavioral references. Examples of such messages follow (they involve a parent talking to a 6-year-old girl):

- "I've really appreciated all that you've done tonight by yourself. You picked up your toys, washed your hands before dinner, and ate dinner without dawdling. I'm so pleased."
- "I'm very disappointed with your behavior right now. You didn't change your clothes when you came home from school; you didn't feed the dog; and you haven't started your homework."

Note in the last example that the parent sent an "I" message and owned the feelings of disappointment rather than attacking the child for being undependable.

When responding authentically, social workers should carefully describe specific events that prompted their responses, particularly when they wish to draw clients' attention to some aspect of their behavior or to a situation of which they may not be fully aware. The following social worker's message illustrates this point:

Social worker: I need to share something with you that concerns me. Just a moment ago, I gave you feedback regarding the positive way I thought you handled a situation with your husband. *[Refers to specific behaviors manifested by client]* When I did that, you seemed to discount my response by *[mentions specific behaviors].* Actually, this is not the first time I have seen this happen. It appears to me that it is difficult for you to give yourself credit for the positive things you do and the progress you are making.

Social workers constantly need to assess the specificity of their responses to ensure that they give clients the benefit of behaviorally specific feedback and provide positive modeling experiences for them. It is also vital to coach clients in giving specific feedback whenever they make sweeping generalizations and do not document the relationship between their responses and specific situations.

4. *Identify the specific impact of the problem situation or behavior on others.* Authentic messages often stop short of identifying the specific effects of the situation on the

sender or on others, even though such information would be very appropriate and helpful. This element of an "I" message also increases the likelihood that the receiver will adjust or make changes, particularly if the sender demonstrates that the receiver's behavior is having a tangible effect on him or her.

Consider a social worker's authentic response to a male member of an adult group:

Social worker: "Sometimes I sense some impatience on your part to move on to other topics. *[Describes situation that just occurred, documenting specific messages and behavior.]* At times I find myself torn between responding to your urging us "to get on with it" or staying with a discussion that seems beneficial to the group. It may be that others in the group are experiencing similar mixed feelings and some of the pressure I feel.

Here the social worker first clarifies the tangible effects of the client's behavior on himself and then suggests that others may experience the behavior similarly. Given the social worker's approach, others in the group may be willing to give feedback as well. The client is then free to draw his own conclusions about the cause-and-effect relationship between his behaviors and the reactions of others and to decide whether he wishes to alter his way of relating in the group.

Social workers can identify how specific client behaviors negatively impact not only the social worker but also the clients themselves (e.g., "I'm concerned about *[specific behavior]* because it keeps you from achieving your goal"). Further, they may document how a client's behavior affects others (e.g., his wife) or the relationship between the client and another person (e.g., "It appears that your behavior creates distance between you and your son").

People often have difficulty in identifying the impact of others' behavior on themselves. For example, a mother's message to her child, "I want you to play someplace else," establishes no reason for the request, nor does it specify the negative impact of the behavior on her. If the mother responds in an authentic manner, however, she clearly identifies the tangible effect of her child's behavior: "I'm having a hard time getting through the hallway because I keep stumbling over toys and having to go around you. I've almost fallen several times, and others might, too. I'm worried that someone might get hurt, so I'm asking you to move your toys to your room."

The preceding illustration underscores the point that when clients clarify how a situation affects them, their requests do not appear arbitrary and are more persuasive; hence, others are likely to make appropriate accommodations. We suspect that an important reason why many clients have not changed certain self-defeating behaviors before entering the helping process is that others have previously attacked or pressured them to change, rather than authentically and unabrasively imparting information that highlights how the clients' behavior strikes them. Others may have also attempted to prescribe behavioral changes that appear to be self-serving (e.g., "Come on, stop that sulking") instead of relating their feelings (e.g., "I'm concerned that you're down and unhappy; I'd like to help but I'm not sure how"). Such statements do not strike a responsive chord in clients, who may equate making changes with putting themselves under the control of others (by following their directives), thereby losing their freedom to make their own decisions.

In the following exchange, note how the social worker assists Carolyn, a group member, to personalize her statements and to clarify her reaction to the behavior of another member who has remained consistently silent throughout the first two sessions:

Carolyn: We've talked about needing to add new guidelines for the group as we go along. I think we ought to have a guideline that everyone should talk in the group. *[Observe that Carolyn has not personalized her message but has proposed a solution to meet a need she has not identified.]*

Social worker [to Carolyn]: The group may want to consider this guideline, but for a minute, can you get in touch with what you're experiencing and put it in the form of an "I" statement?

Carolyn: Well, all right. Janet hasn't talked at all for two solid weeks, and it's beginning to really irritate me.

Social worker: I'm wondering what else you may be experiencing besides irritation? *[Assists Carolyn to identify her feelings besides mild anger.]*

Carolyn: I guess I'm a little uneasy because I don't know where Janet stands. Maybe I'm afraid she's sitting in judgment of us—I mean, me. And I guess I feel cheated because I'd like to get to know her better, and right now I feel shut out by her.

Social worker: That response helps us to begin to get to the heart of the matter. Would you now express yourself directly to Janet? Tell her what you are experiencing and, particularly, how her silence is affecting you.

Carolyn [to Janet]: I did wonder what you thought about me since I really opened up last week. And

I do want to get to know you better. But, underneath all this, I'm concerned about you. You seem unhappy and alone, and that makes me uncomfortable—I don't like to think of your feeling that way. Frankly, I'd like to know how you feel about being in this group, and if you're uneasy about it, as you seem to be, I'd like to help you feel better somehow.

In the preceding example, the social worker assisted Carolyn to experience a broader range of feelings and to identify her reaction to Janet's silence. In response to the social worker's intervention, Carolyn also expressed more positive feelings than were evident in her initial message—a not infrequent occurrence when social workers encourage people to explore deeper-level emotions.

Engaging one member in identifying specific reactions to the behavior of others provides a learning experience for the entire group, and members often expand their conversational repertoires to incorporate such facilitative responding. In fact, the extent to which social workers assist clients to acquire specific skills is correlated with the extent to which clients acquire those same skills.

Cues for Authentic Responding

The impetus for social workers to respond authentically may emanate from (1) clients' messages that request self-disclosure or (2) social workers' decisions to share perceptions and reactions they believe will be helpful. Next, we consider authentic responding that emanates from these two sources.

Authentic Responding Stimulated by Clients' Messages

Requests from Clients for Personal Information. Clients often confront students and social workers with questions aimed at soliciting personal information, such as "How old are you?", "Do you have any children?", "What is your religion?", "Are you married?", and "Are you a student?" It is natural for clients to be curious and to ask questions about a social worker in whom they are confiding, especially when their well-being and future are at stake.

Self-disclosing responses may or may not be appropriate, depending on the social worker's assessment of the client's motivation for asking a particular question. When questions appear to be prompted by an attempt to be sociable, such responses are often very appropriate. For example, it is appropriate for clients to want to know whether you are likely to be helpful to them and hence whether talking to you is a good use of their time

and energy. They often want to know "are you any good at what you do?" Their way of assessing this may take the form of asking about your personal experience with the topic at hand, whether it be drug use or raising children. Consider the following exchange from an initial session involving a 23-year-old student social worker and a 43-year-old woman who requested help in dealing with her marital problems:

Client: Are you married?

Student social worker: No, but I am engaged. Why do you ask?

Client: Oh, I don't know. I just wondered.

Given the context of an older adult with a much younger student, the client's question was likely motivated by a concern that the student might lack life experience essential to understanding her marital difficulties or the competence needed to assist her in resolving them. In this instance, immediate authentic disclosure by the student was inappropriate because it did not facilitate exploration of the feelings underlying the client's inquiry.

Conversely, such an exchange may yield information vital to the helping process if the social worker avoids premature self-disclosure. It is sometimes very difficult to distinguish whether the questions of clients are motivated by a natural desire for information or by hidden concerns or feelings. As a rule of thumb, when you have questions about clients' motivation for making personal inquiries, precede disclosures of views or feelings with either open-ended or empathic responses. Responding in this manner significantly increases the probability that clients will reveal their underlying concerns. Notice what happens when the social worker utilizes an empathic response before responding authentically:

Client: Are you married?

Student social worker: Is that an important consideration for you whether you have a social worker who is married?

Client: Well, I guess I was thinking that someone who is married could understand my situation. I hope it doesn't offend you.

Student social worker: Not at all, in fact I appreciate your frankness. It's natural that you want to know whether your social worker might be able to help you. I know there's a lot at stake for you. Tell me more about your concerns.

Here the student responded to the probable concern of the client and struck pay dirt. Such astuteness tends to foster confidence in clients and greatly facilitates the establishment of a therapeutic partnership. The fact that the student "leans into" the situation by inviting further exploration rather than skirting the issue may also be read by the client as an indicator of the student's own confidence in his or her ability to help. After fully exploring the client's concerns, the student can respond with an authentic response identifying personal qualifications:

Student social worker: I do want you to know that I believe I can be helpful to you. I have worked with other clients whose difficulties were similar to your own. I also consult with my supervisor regularly.

   Of course, the final judgment of my competence will rest with you. It will be important for us to discuss any feelings you may still have at the end of the interview as you make a decision about returning for future sessions.

Questions That Solicit the Social Worker's Perceptions.

Clients may also pose questions that solicit the social worker's opinions, views, or feelings. Typical questions include "How do I compare to your other clients?", "Do you think I need help?", "Am I crazy?", and "Do you think there's any hope for me?" Such questions can pose a challenge for social workers, who must consider the motivation behind the question and judge whether to disclose their views or feelings immediately or to employ either an empathic or an open-ended response.

   When social workers do disclose their perceptions, however, their responses must be congruent with their inner experiencing. In response to the question "Do you think there's any hope for me?" the social worker may congruently respond with a message that blends elements of empathy and authenticity:

Social worker: Your question tells me you're probably afraid that you're beyond help. Although you do have some difficult problems, I'm optimistic that if we work hard together things can improve. You've shown a number of strengths that should help you make changes.

   It is not necessary to answer all questions of clients in the service of authenticity. If you feel uncomfortable about answering a personal question or deem it inadvisable to do so, you should feel free to decline answering. When doing so, it is important to explain your reason for not answering directly, again utilizing

an authentic response. If a teenage client, for example, asks whether the social worker had sexual relations before she married, the social worker may respond as follows:

Social worker: I would rather not reveal that information to you, because it is a very private part of my life. Asking me took some risk on your part. I have an idea that your question probably has to do with a struggle you're having, although I could be wrong. I would appreciate your sharing your thoughts about what sparked your question.

The social worker should then utilize empathic responding and open-ended questions to explore the client's reaction and motivation for asking her question.

Authentic Responding Initiated by Social Workers

Authentic responding initiated by social workers may take several forms, which are considered next.

Disclosing Past Experiences. As previously indicated, self-disclosure should be sparingly used, brief, relevant to the client's concerns, and well timed. In relating to a particular client's struggle, a social worker might indicate, "I remember I felt very much like that when I was struggling with …" In so doing, they must be careful to check out whether the client considers this experience comparable.…" A fundamental guideline that applies to such situations is that social workers should be certain they are focusing on themselves to meet the therapeutic needs of their clients.

Sharing Perceptions, Ideas, Reactions, and Formulations. A key role of the social worker in the change-oriented phase of the helping process is to act as a "candid feedback system" by revealing personal thoughts and perceptions relevant to client problems (Hammond et al., 1977). Such responding is intended to further the change process in one or more of the following ways:

1. To heighten clients' awareness of dynamics that may play an important part in problems
2. To offer a different perspective regarding issues and events
3. To aid clients in conceptualizing the purposes of their behavior and feelings
4. To enlighten clients on how they affect others (including the social worker)
5. To bring clients' attention to cognitive and behavioral patterns (both functional and dysfunctional) that operate at either an individual or a group level

6. To share the social worker's here-and-now affective and physical reactions to clients' behavior or to processes that occur in the helping relationship

7. To share positive feedback concerning clients' strengths and growth

After responding authentically to achieve any of these purposes, it is vital to invite clients to express their own views and draw their own conclusions. Sharing perceptions with clients does involve some risk. In particular, clients may misinterpret the social worker's motives and feel criticized, put down, or rebuked. Clarifying the social worker's helpful intent before responding diminishes this risk somewhat. Nevertheless, it is critical to watch for clients' reactions that may indicate a response has struck an exposed nerve.

To avoid damaging the relationship (or to repair it), the social worker should be empathically attuned to the client's reaction to candid feedback, shifting the focus back to the client to determine the impact of the self-disclosure. If the client appears to have been emotionally wounded by the social worker's authentic response, the social worker can use empathic skills to elicit troubled feelings and to guide subsequent responses aimed at restoring the relationship's equilibrium. Expressions of concern and clarification of the goodwill intended by the social worker are also usually facilitative:

Social worker: I can see that what I shared with you hit you pretty hard—and that you're feeling put down right now. *[Client nods but avoids eye contact]* I feel bad about that, because the last thing I'd want is to hurt you. Please tell me what you're feeling.

Openly (and Tactfully) Sharing Reactions When Put on the Spot.

Clients sometimes create situations that put social workers under considerable pressure to respond to messages that bear directly on the relationship, such as when they accuse a social worker of being uninterested, unfeeling, irritated, displeased, critical, inappropriate, or incompetent. Clients may also ask pointed questions (sometimes before the relationship has been firmly established) that require immediate responses.

The first statement of one female client in an initial interview, for example, was "I'm gay. Does that make any difference to you?" In the opening moments of another session, a pregnant client asked the social worker, "How do you feel about abortion?" Over the years, students have reported numerous such situations that sorely tested their ability to respond in an appropriate fashion. In one instance, a male member of a group asked a female student leader for her photograph. In another case, an adolescent boy kept taking his shoes off and putting his feet (which smelled very bad) on the social worker's desk. In reflecting on your practice experience, you can undoubtedly cite instances in which the behavior of clients caused you to squirm or produced butterflies in your stomach.

Experiencing Discomfort in Sessions. Sometimes intense discomfort may indicate that something in the session is going awry and needs to be addressed. It is important to reflect on your discomfort, seeking to identify events that seem to be causing or exacerbating it (e.g., "I'm feeling very uneasy because I don't know how to respond when my client says things like 'You seem to be too busy to see me' or 'I'm not sure I'm worth your trouble'"). After privately exploring the reason for the discomfort, the social worker might respond as follows:

Social worker: I'd like to share some impressions about several things you've said in the last two sessions. *[Identifies client's statements.]* I sense you're feeling pretty unimportant—as though you don't count for much—and that perhaps you're imposing on me just by being here. I want you to know that I'm pleased you had the courage to seek help in the face of all the opposition from your family. It's also important to me that you know that I want to be helpful to you. I am concerned, however, that you feel you're imposing on me. Could you share more what contributes to that feeling for you?

Notice how the social worker specifically identifies the self-defeating thoughts and feelings and blends elements of empathy and authenticity in the response.

Other situations that put social workers on the spot include clients' angry attacks, as we discuss later in this chapter. Social workers must learn to respond authentically in such scenarios. Consider a situation in which an adolescent attacks a social worker in an initial interview, protesting, "I don't want to be here. You social workers are all assholes." In such instances, social workers should share their reactions, as illustrated in the following response:

Social worker: It sounds as though you're really angry about having to see me and that your previous experiences with social workers haven't been good. I respect your feelings and don't want to pressure you to work with me. I want you to know that I am interested in you and that I would like to know what you're up against.

Intertwining empathic and authentic responses in this manner often defuses clients' anger and encourages them to think more rationally about a situation.

Sharing Feelings When Clients' Behavior Is Unreasonable or Distressing.   Although social workers should be able to take most client behaviors in stride, sometimes they may experience justifiable feelings of frustration, anger, or even hurt. In one case, a client acquired a social worker's home phone number from another source and began calling frequently about daily crisis situations, although discussions of these events could easily have waited until the next session. In another instance, an intoxicated client called the social worker in the middle of the night "just to talk." In yet another case, an adolescent client let the air out of a social worker's automobile tires.

In such situations, social workers should share their feelings with clients—*if they believe they can do so constructively.* In the following case example, note that the student social worker interweaves authentic and empathic responses in confronting a Latino youth in a correctional institution who had maintained he was innocent of hiding drugs that staff had found in his room. Believing the youth's story, the student went to bat for him, only to find out later that the client had lied. Somewhat uneasy at her first real confrontation, the student tries to formulate an authentic response.

In an interesting twist, the youth helps her to be "up-front" with him:

Student social worker: There's something I wanted to talk to you about, Randy … *[Stops to search for the right words.]*

Randy: Well, come out with it, then. Just lay it on me.

Student social worker: Well, remember last week when you got that incident report? You know, I really believed you were innocent. I was ready to go to the hearing and tell staff I was sure you were innocent and that the charge should be dropped. I guess I'm feeling kind of bad because when I talked to you, you told me you were innocent, and, well, that's not exactly the way it turned out.

Randy: You mean I lied to you. Go ahead and say it.

Student social worker: Well, yes, I guess I felt kind of hurt because I was hoping that maybe you had more trust in me than that.

Randy: Well, Susan, let me tell you something. Where I come from, that's not lying—that's what we call survival. Personally, I don't consider myself a liar. I just do what I need to do to get by. That's an old trick, but it just didn't work.

Student social worker: I hear you, Randy. I guess you're saying we're from two different worlds, and maybe we both define the same thing in different ways. I guess that with me being Anglo, you can't really expect me to understand what life has been like for you.

Several minutes later in the session, after the student has further explored the client's feelings, the following interchange occurs:

Student social worker: Randy, I want you to know a couple of things. The first thing is that when social workers work with clients, they must honor what they call confidentiality, so I can't share what we talk about without your permission in most cases. An exception to this relates to rule or law violations. I can't keep that confidential. The second thing is that I don't expect you to share everything with me. I know there are certain things you don't want to tell me, so rather than lying about something that I ask you about, maybe you can just tell me you don't want to tell me. Would you consider that?

Randy: Yeah, that's okay. *[Pause.]* Listen, Susan, I don't want you to go around thinking I'm a liar now. I'll tell you this, and you can take it for what it's worth, but this is the truth. That's the first time I've ever lied to you. But you may not believe that.

Student social worker: I do believe you, Randy. *[He seems a little relieved and there is a silence.]*

Randy: Well, Susan, that's a deal, then. I won't lie to you again, but if there's something I don't want to say, I'll tell you I don't want to say it.

Student social worker: Sounds good to me. *[Both start walking away.]* You know, Randy, I really want to see you get through this program and get out as fast as you can. I know it's hard starting over because of the incident with the drugs, but I think we can get you through. *[This seemed to have more impact on Randy than anything the social worker had said to him in a long time. The pleasure was visible on his face, and he broke into a big smile.]*

Noteworthy in this exchange is that the social worker relied almost exclusively on the skills of authenticity and empathy to bring the incident to a positive conclusion. Ignoring her feelings would have impaired the student's ability to relate facilitatively to the client and would have been destructive to the relationship. In contrast, focusing on the situation proved beneficial for both.

Sharing Feelings When Clients Give Positive Feedback.
Social workers sometimes have difficulty responding receptively to clients' positive feedback about their own attributes and/or performance. We suggest that social workers model the same receptivity to positive feedback that they ask clients to demonstrate in their own lives, as illustrated in the following exchange:

Client: I don't know what I would have done without you. I'm just not sure I would have made it if you hadn't been there when I needed you. You've made such a difference in my life.

Social worker: I'm touched by your gratitude and pleased you are feeling so much more capable of coping with your situation. I want you to know, too, that even though I was there to help, your efforts have been the deciding factor in your growth.

Positive Feedback: A Form of Authentic Responding

Because positive feedback plays such a vital role in the change process, we have allocated a separate section in our attempt to do justice to this topic. Social workers often employ (or should employ) this skill in supplying information to clients about positive attributes or specific areas in which they demonstrate strengths, effective coping mechanisms, and incremental growth. In so doing, social workers enhance their clients' motivation to change and foster hope for the future.

Many opportune moments occur in the helping process when social workers experience warm or positive feelings toward clients because of the latter's actions or progress. When appropriate, social workers should share such feelings spontaneously with clients, as illustrated in the following messages:

- *"You have what I consider exceptional ability to 'self-observe your own behavior and to analyze the part you play in relationships. I think this strength will serve you well in solving the problems you have identified."*
- *"I've been touched several times in the group when I've noticed that, despite your grief over the loss of your husband, you've reached out to other members who needed support."*

- *[To newly formed group]: "In contrast to our first session, I've noticed that this week we haven't had trouble getting down to business and staying on task. I've been pleased as I've watched you develop group guidelines for the past 20 minutes with minimal assistance from me. I had the thought, 'This group is really moving.'"*

The first two messages acknowledge strengths of individuals. The third lauds a behavioral change the social worker has observed in a group process. Both types of messages sharply focus clients' attention on specific behaviors that facilitate the change process, ultimately increasing the frequency of such behaviors. When sent consistently, positive messages also have the long-range effect of helping people who have low self-esteem to develop a more positive self-image. When positive feedback is employed to document the cause-and-effect relationship between their efforts and positive outcomes, individuals also experience a sense of satisfaction, accomplishment, and control over their situation.

Positive feedback can have the additional effect of increasing clients' confidence in their own coping ability. We have occasionally had experiences with clients who were on the verge of falling apart when they came to a session but left feeling able to manage their problems for a while longer. We attribute their increased ability to function in part to authentic responses that documented and highlighted areas in which they were coping and successfully managing problems.

Taped sessions of students and social workers often reveal relatively few authentic responses that underscore clients' strengths or incremental growth. This lack of positive feedback is unfortunate because, in our experience, clients' rates of change often correlate with the extent to which social workers focus on these two vital areas. If social workers consistently focus on their clients' assets and the subtle positive changes that often occur in early sessions, clients will typically invest more effort in the change process. As the rate of change accelerates, social workers can in turn focus more extensively on clients' successes, identifying and reinforcing their strengths and functional coping behaviors.

Social workers face several challenges in accrediting clients' strengths and growth, including improving their own ability to recognize and express fleeting positive feelings when clients manifest strengths or progress. Social workers

EP 2.1.10e

must also learn to document events so that they can provide information about specific positive behaviors. Another challenge and responsibility is to teach clients to give positive feedback to one another.

To increase your ability to discern client strengths, we recommend that you and your clients construct a profile of their resources. This task may be completed with individuals, couples, families, or groups, and preferably occurs early in the helping process. In individual sessions, the social worker should ask the client to identify and list all the strengths she or he can think of. The social worker also shares observations of the client's strengths, adding them to the list, which is kept for ongoing review to add further strengths as they are discovered.

With families, couples, or groups, social workers may follow a similar procedure in assessing the strengths of individual members, but they should ask other group members to share their perceptions of strengths with each member. The social worker might also ask couples, families, or groups to identify the strengths and incremental growth of the group periodically throughout the helping process. After clients have identified their personal strengths or the strengths of the group, the social worker should elicit observations regarding their reactions to the experience. Often they may mutually conclude that clients have many more strengths than they have realized. The social worker should also explore any discomfort experienced by clients as they identify strengths, with the goal of having them acknowledge more comfortably their positive attributes and personal resources.

We further suggest that you carefully observe processes early on in sessions. Note the subtle manifestations of strengths and positive behavioral changes, systematically recording these in your progress records. Record not only the strengths and incremental growth of clients, but also whether you (or group members) focused on those changes. Keep in mind that changes often occur very subtly within a single session. For instance, clients may begin to discuss problems more openly during a later part of a session, tentatively commit to work on problems they had refused to tackle earlier, show growing trust in the social worker by confiding high-risk information about themselves, or own responsibility for the first time regarding their part in their problems. Groups and families may likewise experience growth within short periods of time. It is vital to keep your antenna finely tuned to such changes so that you do not overlook clients' progress.

Relating Assertively to Clients

Another aspect of relating authentically entails relating assertively to clients when a situation warrants such behavior. There are myriad reasons for relating assertively. To inspire confidence and influence clients to follow their lead,

EP 2.1.10b

social workers must relate in a manner that projects competence. This is especially important in the initial phase of the helping process. Clients often covertly test or check out social workers to determine whether they can understand their problems and appear competent to help them.

In conjoint or group sessions, clients may question whether the social worker is strong enough to protect them from destructive interactional processes that may occur in sessions. Indeed, family or group members generally will not fully share, risk, or commit to the helping process until they have answered this question affirmatively through consistent observation of assertive actions by the social worker.

If social workers are relaxed and demonstrate through decisive behavior that they are fully capable of handling clients' problems and providing the necessary protection and structure to control potentially chaotic or volatile processes, clients will typically relax, muster hope, and begin to work on problems. If the social worker fails to curtail dysfunctional processes that render clients vulnerable, clients will have justifiable doubts about whether they should be willing to place themselves in jeopardy and, consequently, may disengage from the helping process.

In this section, we identify guidelines that can help you to intervene assertively with clients.

Making Requests and Giving Directives

To assist clients to relate more easily and work constructively to solve their problems, social workers frequently must make requests of them. Some of these requests may involve relating in new ways during sessions. For example, social workers may ask clients to do any of the following:

1. Speak directly to each other rather than through the social worker.
2. Give feedback to others in the session.
3. Respond by checking out the meanings of others' messages, take a listening stance, or personalize messages.
4. Change the arrangement of chairs.

5. Role-play.
6. Make requests of others.
7. Take responsibility for responding in specified ways during sessions.
8. Agree to carry out defined tasks during the week.
9. Identify strengths or incremental growth for themselves or others in the group or family.

When making requests, it is important to express them firmly and decisively and to deliver them with assertive nonverbal behavior. Social workers often err by couching their requests in tentative language, thus conveying doubt to clients about whether they must comply with the requests. The contrast between messages delivered in tentative language and those phrased in firm language can be observed in the exchanges given in Table 5-1.

Many times social workers' requests of clients are actually *directives,* as are those under the column "Firm Requests" in Table 5-1. In essence, directives are declarative statements that place the burden on clients to object if they are uncomfortable, as the following message illustrates:

Social worker: Before you answer that question, please turn your chair toward your wife. *[Social worker leans over and helps client to adjust chair. Social worker speaks to wife.]* Will you please turn your chair, also, so that you can speak directly to your husband? Thank you. It's important that you be in full contact with each other while we talk.

If the social worker had given these clients a choice (e.g., "Would you like to change your chairs?"), they might not have responded affirmatively. We suggest that when you want clients to behave differently in sessions, you simply state what you would like them to do. If clients verbally object to directives or display nonverbal behavior that may indicate that they have reservations about complying with a request, it is vital to respond empathically and to explore the basis of their opposition. Such exploration often resolves fears or misgivings, freeing clients to engage in requested behavior.

Maintaining Focus and Managing Interruptions

Maintaining focus is a vital task that takes considerable skill and assertiveness on the social worker's part. It is often essential to intervene verbally to focus or refocus processes when interruptions or distractions occur. Sometimes, social workers may also respond assertively on a nonverbal level to prevent members from interrupting important processes that may need to be brought to positive conclusion, as illustrated in the following excerpt from a family session:

Kim, age 14 [in tears, talking angrily to her mother]: You hardly ever listen. At home, you just always yell at us and go to your bedroom.

Mrs. R: I thought I was doing better than that …

Mr. R [interrupting his wife to speak to social worker]: I think it's hard for my wife because …

Social worker [holds up hand to father in a "halt" position, while continuing to maintain eye contact with mother and daughter; speaks to Kim]: I would like to stay with your statement for a moment. Kim, please tell your mother what you're experiencing right now.

Interrupting Problematic Processes

Unseasoned social workers often permit problematic processes to continue for long periods either because they lack knowledge of how to intervene or because they think they should wait until clients have completed a series of exchanges. In such instances, social workers fail to fulfill one of their major responsibilities—that is, to *guide and direct* processes and to influence participants to interact in more facilitative ways. Remember that clients often seek help because they cannot manage their problematic interactional processes. Thus, permitting them to engage at length in their usual patterns of arguing, cajoling, threatening, blaming, criticizing, and labeling each other merely exacerbates their problems. The social worker should intervene in such circumstances, teaching the clients more facilitative behaviors

TABLE-5-1 TENTATIVE VERSUS FIRM REQUESTS	
TENTATIVE REQUESTS	**FIRM REQUESTS**
Would you mind if I interrupted …	I would like to pause for a moment …
Is it okay if we role-play?	I'd like you to role-play with me for a moment.
Excuse me, but don't you think you are getting off track?	I think we are getting off track. I'd like to return to the subject we were discussing just a minute ago.
Could we talk about something Kathy just said?	Let's go back to something Kathy just said. I think it is very important.

and guiding them to implement such behaviors in subsequent interactions.

If you decide to interrupt ongoing processes, do so decisively so that clients will listen to you or heed your directive. If you intervene unassertively, your potential to influence clients (particularly aggressive clients) will suffer, because being able to interrupt a discussion successfully demonstrates your power or influence in the relationship. If you permit clients to ignore or to circumvent your interventions to arrest problematic processes, you yield control and assume a "one-down" position in terms of the relationship to the client.

With respect to interrupting or intervening in processes, we advocate using assertive—not aggressive—behavior. You must be sensitive to the vested interests of clients, because even though you may regard certain processes as unproductive or destructive, clients may not. The timing of interruptions is therefore vital. If it is not critical to draw clients' attention to what is happening immediately, you can wait for a natural pause. If such a pause does not occur shortly, you should interrupt. You should *not* delay interrupting destructive interactional processes, however, as illustrated in the following excerpt:

Wife [to social worker]: I feel the children need to mind me, but every time I ask them to do something, he [husband] says they don't have to do it. I think we're just ruining our kids, and it's mostly his fault.

Husband: Oh—well—that shows how dumb you are.

Social worker: I'm going to interrupt you because finding fault with each other is not likely to help us resolve these issues.

In this exchange, the social worker intervenes to refocus the discussion after just two dysfunctional responses on the clients' part. If participants do not disengage immediately, the social worker will need to use body movements that interfere with communication pathways or, in extreme instances, an exclamation such as "Time out!" to interrupt behavior. When social workers have demonstrated their intent to intervene quickly and decisively, clients will usually comply immediately when asked to disengage.

"Leaning Into" Clients' Anger

We cannot overstate the importance of openly addressing clients' anger and complaints. It is not unusual to feel defensive and threatened when such anger arises. Many social workers, especially those who are working with involuntary clients who are alleged to have harmed others, are inclined to retaliate, conveying the message, "You have no right to your anger. You have brought this on yourself. Do it my way or suffer the consequences." Responding assertively to a person's anger does not mean that you become a doormat, accepting that anger passively and submissively. Unless social workers can handle themselves assertively and competently in the face of such anger, they will lose the respect of most clients and thus their ability to help them. Further, clients may use their anger to influence and intimidate social workers just as they have done with others.

To help you respond assertively in managing clients' anger, we offer the following suggestions:

- *Respond empathically to reflect clients' anger and, if possible, other underlying feelings (e.g., "I sense you're angry at me for _____ and perhaps disappointed about _____").*

- *Continue to explore the situation and the feelings of participants until you understand the nature of the events that inspired the angry feelings. During this exploration, you may find that the anger toward you dissipates and that clients begin to focus on themselves, assuming appropriate responsibility for their part in the situation at hand. The "real problem," as often happens, may not directly involve you.*

- *As you explore clients' anger, authentically express your feelings and reactions if it appears appropriate (e.g., "I didn't know you felt that way … "I want to hear how I might have contributed to this situation." "There may be some adjustments I'll want to make in my style of relating" … "I'm pleased that you shared your feelings with me.").*

- *Apply a problem-solving approach (if appropriate) so that all concerned make adjustments to avoid similar occurrences or situations in the future.*

- *If a particular client expresses anger frequently and in a dysfunctional manner, you may also focus on the client's style of expressing anger, identify problems that this communicative approach may cause him or her in relationships with others, and negotiate a goal of modifying this response pattern.*

- *In addition to empathizing with client anger, you can model assertive setting of personal limits and boundaries. For example, you might say, "I think that I have a good idea about how you are feeling about this situation and what you would like to have be different about it. But I can't readily talk with you when you are so upset. Do you have a way of calming yourself down, or should we plan to meet again when you feel more in control of your emotions?"* Alternatively, you might say, *"I have pledged to do my part to listen to and respond to the issues you have raised. I am not willing to continue to be verbally abused, however."*

Saying No and Setting Limits

Many tasks that social workers perform on behalf of their clients are quite appropriate. For example, negotiating for clients and conferring with other parties and potential resources to supplement and facilitate client action are tasks that are rightly handled by social workers (Epstein, 1992, p. 208). In contracting with clients, however, social workers must occasionally decline requests or set limits. This step is sometimes difficult for beginning social workers to take, as they typically want to demonstrate their willingness to help others. Commitment to helping others is a desirable quality, but it must be tempered with judgment as to when acceding to clients' requests is in the best interests of both social worker and client.

Some clients may have had past experiences that led them to believe that social workers will do most of the work required out of sessions. However, clients are often more likely to experience empowerment by increasing the scope of their actions than by having social workers perform tasks on their behalf that they can learn to do for themselves. Consequently, if social workers unthinkingly agree to take on responsibilities that clients can perform now or could perform in the future, they may reinforce passive client behavior.

Setting limits has special implications when social workers work with involuntary clients. Cingolani (1984) has noted that social workers engage in negotiated relationships with such clients. In negotiated relationships, social workers assume the roles of compromiser, mediator, and enforcer in addition to the more comfortable role of counselor. For example, when an involuntary client requests a "break" related to performance of a court order, the social worker must be clear about the client's choices and consequences of making those choices. He or she must also clarify what the client should expect from the social worker.

Rory [member of domestic violence group]: I don't think that it is fair that you report that I didn't meet for eight of the ten group sessions. I could not get off work for some of those sessions. I did all I could do.

Social worker: You did attend seven of the sessions, Rory, and made efforts to attend others. However, the contract you signed, which was presented in court, stated that you must complete eight sessions to be certified as completing the group. I do not have the power to change that court order. Should you decide to comply with the court order, I am willing to speak with your employer to urge him to work with you to arrange your schedule so that you can meet the court order.

In his response, the social worker made it clear that he would not evade the court order. At the same time, he assured Rory that if he chose to comply with the court order, the social worker would be willing to act as a mediator to assist him with difficulties in scheduling with the employer.

Being tactfully assertive is no easier for social workers with excessive needs to please others than it is for other persons. These social workers have difficulty declining requests or setting limits when doing so is in the best interests of clients. To remedy this, such social workers may benefit by setting tasks for themselves related to increasing their assertiveness. Participating in an assertiveness training group and delving into the popular literature on assertiveness may be highly beneficial as well. Dietz and Thompson (2004) have suggested that social work has given too much emphasis to distance between clients and social workers for fear of abuse of power. In so doing, these authors suggest that social workers may abrogate possibilities of special help that powerless clients may need. We suggest that you consult with your supervisor about requests that pose special questions. In some cases, this can lead to problem solving around where else a client might be assisted to find a resource, rather than dwelling only on whether it is appropriate to get that resource from the social worker. The following are a few of the many situations in which you may need to decline requests of clients:

1. When clients invite you to participate with them socially
2. When clients ask you to grant them preferential status (e.g., set lower fees than are specified by policy)
3. When clients request physical intimacy
4. When clients ask you to intercede in a situation they should handle themselves
5. When clients request a special appointment after having broken a regular appointment for an invalid reason

6. When clients ask to borrow money
7. When clients request that you conceal information about violations of probation, parole, or institutional policy
8. When spouses request that you withhold information from their partners
9. When clients disclose plans to commit crimes or acts of violence against others
10. When clients ask you to report false information to an employer or other party

In addition to declining requests, you may need to set limits with clients in situations such as the following:

1. When clients make excessive telephone calls or text messages to you at home or the office
2. When clients cancel appointments without giving advance notice
3. When clients express emotions in abusive or violent ways
4. When clients habitually seek to go beyond designated ending points of sessions
5. When clients consistently fail to abide by contracts (e.g., not paying fees or missing numerous appointments)
6. When clients make sexual overtures toward you or other staff members
7. When clients come to sessions while intoxicated

Part of maturing professionally means learning to decline requests, set limits, and feel comfortable in doing so. As you gain experience, you will realize that you help clients as much by ensuring that they have reasonable expectations as you do by providing a concrete action for them. Modeled responses for refusing requests and for saying no to clients are found in the answers to the exercises below designed to assist social workers to relate authentically and assertively.

Of course, social workers must also assert themselves effectively with other social workers and with members of other professions. Lacking experience and sometimes confidence, beginning social workers tend to be in awe of physicians, lawyers, psychologists, and more experienced social workers. Consequently, they may relate passively or may acquiesce in plans or demands that appear unsound or unreasonable. Although it is critical to remain open to the ideas of other professionals, beginning social workers should nevertheless risk expressing their own views and asserting their own rights. Otherwise, they may know more about a given client than other professionals but fail to contribute valuable information in joint case planning.

Beginning social workers should also set limits and assert their rights by refusing to accept unreasonable referrals and inappropriate assignments. Likewise, assertiveness may be required when other professionals deny resources to which clients are entitled, refer to clients with demeaning labels, or engage in unethical conduct. In fact, being assertive is critical when you act as a client advocate, a role discussed at length in Chapter 14.

Summary

This chapter should help you communicate with clients and other persons on behalf of clients with appropriate empathy, authenticity, assertiveness, and self-disclosure. Chapter 6 will build on these skills by developing your abilities in listening, focusing, and exploring. First, however, you should practice your new skills by completing the exercises in this chapter.

Competency Notes

EP 2.1.1b Practice self-reflection and self-correction to assure continual professional development (pp. 114, 116).

EP 2.1.1c Attend to professional roles and boundaries pages (pp. 90, 91).

EP 2.1.10a Substantively and affectively prepare for action with individuals, families, groups, organizations, and communities (p. 90).

EP 2.1.10b Use empathy and other interpersonal skills. Social workers use empathy and other interpersonal skills such as authenticity (pp. 95, 106, 109, 124).

EP 2.1.10e A social worker assesses client strengths and limitatons (p. 123).

EP 2.1.10i A social worker implements preventive services to enhance client capacities (pp. 110, 112).

Exercises in Responding Authentically and Assertively

The following exercises will assist you in gaining skill in responding authentically and assertively. Read each situation and client message, and then formulate a written response as though you were the social worker in the situation presented. Compare your written responses with the modeled responses, keeping in mind that these models represent just a few of the many possible responses that would be appropriate.

You will find additional exercises that require authentic and assertive responding in Chapter 17 (in the confrontation exercises) and in Chapter 18 (in the exercises concerned with managing relational reactions and resistance).

Statements and Situations

1. **Marital partner** *[in third conjoint marital therapy session]:* It must be really nice being a marriage counselor—knowing just what to do and not having problems like ours.

2. **Female client, age 23** *[in first session]:* Some of my problems are related to my church's stand on birth control. Tell me, are you a Catholic?

3. **Client** *[fifth session]:* You look like you're having trouble staying awake. *[Social worker is drowsy from having taken an antihistamine for an allergy.]*

4. **Adult group member** *[to social worker in second session; group members have been struggling to determine the agenda for the session]:* I wish you'd tell us what we should talk about. Isn't that your job? We're just getting nowhere.

5. **Male client** *[sixth session]:* Say, my wife and I are having a fund-raiser next Wednesday. We'd like to have you and your wife come.

6. **Client** *[calls 3 hours before scheduled appointment]:* I've had the flu the past couple of days, but I feel like I'm getting over it. Do you think I should come today?

7. **Client** *[scheduled time for ending appointment has arrived, and social worker has already moved to end session; in previous sessions, client has tended to stay beyond designated ending time]:* What we were talking about reminded me of something I wanted to discuss today but forgot. I'd like to discuss it briefly, if you don't mind.

8. **Client** *[has just completed behavioral rehearsal involving talking with employer and played role beyond expectations of social worker].*

9. **Female client** *[tenth interview]:* I've really felt irritated with you during the week. When I brought up taking the correspondence course in art, all you could talk about was how some correspondence courses are rip-offs and that I could take courses at a college for less money. I knew that, but I've checked into this correspondence course, and it's well worth the money. You put me down, and I've resented it.

10. **Client** *[seventh session]:* You seem uptight today. Is something bothering you? *[Social worker has been under strain associated with recent death of a parent and assisting surviving parent, who has been distraught.]*

Modeled Responses

1. *[Smiling.]* "Well, I must admit it's helpful. But I want you to know that marriage is not easy for marriage counselors either. We have our rough spots, too. I have to work like everyone else to keep my marriage alive and growing."

2. "I gather you're wondering what my stand is and whether I can understand and accept your feelings. I've worked with many Catholics and have been able to understand their problems. Would it trouble you if I weren't Catholic?"

3. "You're very observant. I have been sleepy these past few minutes, and I apologize for that. I had to take an antihistamine before lunch, and a side effect of the drug is I can get drowsy. My sleepiness has nothing to do with you. If I move around a little, the drowsiness passes."

4. "I can sense your frustration and your desire to firm up an agenda. If I made the decision, though, it might not fit for many of you and I'd be taking over the group's power to make its own decisions. Perhaps it would be helpful if the group followed the decision-by-consensus approach we discussed in our first session."

5. "Thank you for the invitation. I'm flattered that you'd ask me. I appreciate your asking, but, I must decline your invitation. If I were to socialize with you while you're seeing me professionally, it would conflict with my role, and I couldn't be as helpful to you. I hope you can understand my not accepting."

6. "I appreciate your calling to let me know. I think it would be better to change our appointment until you're sure you've recovered. Quite frankly, I don't want to risk being exposed to the flu, which I hope you can understand. I have a time open on the day after tomorrow. I'll set it aside for you, if you'd like, in the event you're fully recovered by then."

7. "I'm sorry I don't have the time to discuss the matter today. Let's save it for next week, and I'll make a note that you wanted to explore this issue. We'll have to stop here today because I'm scheduled for another appointment."

8. "I want to share with you how impressed I was with how you asserted yourself and came across so positively. If you'd been with your boss, he'd have been impressed, too."

9. "I'm glad you shared those feelings with me. I can see I owe you an apology. You're right, I didn't explore whether you'd checked into the program, and I made some incorrect assumptions. I guess I was overly concerned about your not being ripped off because I know others who have been by taking correspondence courses. But I can see I made a mistake because you had already looked into the course."

10. "Thank you for asking. Yes, I have been under some strain this past week. My mother died suddenly, which was a shock, and my father is taking it very hard. It's created a lot of pressure for me, but I think I can keep it from spilling over into our session. If I'm not able to focus on you, I will stop the session. Or if you don't feel that I'm fully with you, please let me know. I don't want to short-change you."

Skill Development Exercises in Empathic Communication

The following exercises, which include a wide variety of actual client messages, will assist you in gaining mastery of reciprocal empathic responding (level 3). Read the client message and compose on paper an empathic response that captures the client's surface feelings. You may wish to use the paradigm, "You feel _____ about (or because) _____," in organizing your response before phrasing it in typical conversation language. Strive to make your responses fresh, varied, and spontaneous. To expand your repertoire of responses, we strongly encourage you to continue using the lists of affective words and phrases.

After formulating your response, compare it with the modeled response provided at the end of the exercises. Analyze the differences, paying particular attention to the various forms of responding and the elements that enhance the effectiveness of your own responses and the modeled responses.

Because this exercise includes 20 different client statements, we recommend that you not attempt to complete the entire exercise in one sitting, but rather work through it in several sessions. Consistent practice and careful scrutiny of your responses are essential in gaining mastery of this vital skill.

Client Statements

1. *Father of developmentally disabled child, age 14 [who is becoming difficult to manage]:* We just don't know what to do with Henry. We've always wanted to take care of him, but we've reached the point where we're not sure it's doing any good for him or for us. Henry has grown so strong—we just can't restrain him anymore. He hit my wife last week when she wouldn't take him to the store late at night—I was out of town—and she's still bruised. She's afraid of him now, and I have to admit I'm getting that way, too.

2. *Latino [living in urban barrio]:* Our children do better in school if they teach Spanish, not just English. We're afraid our children are behind because they don't understand English so good. And we don't know how to help them. Our people have been trying to get a bilingual program, but the school board pays no attention to us.

3. *Female client, age 31:* Since my husband left town with another woman, I get lonely and depressed a lot of the time. I find myself wondering whether something is wrong with me or whether men just can't be trusted.

4. *Mother [to child welfare protective services worker on doorstep during initial home visit]:* Who'd want to make trouble for me by accusing me of not taking care of my kids? [Tearfully.] Maybe I'm not the best mother in the world, but I try. There are a lot of kids around here that aren't cared for as well as mine.

5. *Male ninth-grade student [to school social worker]:* I feel like I'm a real dweeb. In sports I am no good. When they choose up sides, I'm always the last one chosen. A couple of times they've actually got into a fight over who doesn't have to choose me.

6. *Member of abused women's group:* That last month I was living in mortal fear of Art. He'd get that hateful look in his eyes, and I'd know he was going to let me have it. The last time I was afraid he was going to kill me—and he might have, if his brother hadn't dropped in. I'm afraid to go back to him. But what do I do? I can't stay here much longer!

7. *Male, age 34 [to marital therapist]:* Just once I'd like to show my wife I can accomplish something without her prodding me. That's why I haven't told her I'm coming to see you. If she knew it, she'd try to take charge and call all the shots.

8. *African American man [in a group session]:* All I want is to be accepted as a person. When I get hired, I want it to be for what I'm capable of

doing—not just because of my skin color. That's as phony and degrading as not being hired because of my skin color. I just want to be accepted for who I am.

9. *Client in a state prison [to rehabilitation worker]:* They treat you like an animal in here—herd you around like a damn cow. I know I've got to do my time, but sometimes I feel like I can't stand it any longer—like something's building up in me that's going to explode.

10. *Client [to mental health worker]:* I don't have any pleasant memories of my childhood. It seems like just so much empty space. I can remember my father watching television and staring at me with a blank look—as though I didn't exist.

11. *Patient in hospital [to medical social worker]:* I know Dr. Brown is a skilled surgeon, and he tells me not to worry—that there's very little risk in this surgery. I know I should feel reassured, but to tell you the truth, I'm just plain panic-stricken.

12. *Female member, age 29 [in marital therapy group]:* I'd like to know what it's like with the rest of you. Hugh and I get into nasty fights because I feel he doesn't help me when I really need help. He tells me there's no way he's going to do women's work! That really irritates me. I start feeling like I'm just supposed to be his slave.

13. *Male college student, age 21*: Francine says she's going to call me, but she never does—I have to do all the texting, or I probably wouldn't hear from her at all. It seems so one-sided. If I didn't need her so much I'd ask her what kind of game she's playing. I wonder if she isn't pretty selfish.

14. *White student, age 14 [to school social worker]:* To be really honest, I don't like the black kids in our school. They pretty much stay to themselves, and they aren't friendly to whites. I don't know what to expect or how to act around them. I'm antsy when they're around and—well, to be honest—I'm scared I'll do something they won't like, and they'll jump me.

15. *Single female, age 27 [to mental health worker]:* I've been taking this class on the joys of womanhood. Last time the subject was how to catch a man. I can see I've been doing a lot of things wrong. But I won't lower myself to playing games with men. If that's what it takes, I guess I'll always be single.

16. *Married male, age 29 [to marital therapist]:* Sexually, I'm unfulfilled in my marriage. At times I've even had thoughts of trying sex with men. That idea kind of intrigues me. My wife and I can talk about sex all right, but it doesn't get better.

17. *Married female, age 32 [to family social worker]:* I love my husband and children, and I don't know what I'd do without them. Yet on days like last Thursday, I feel I could just climb the walls. I want to run away from all of them and never come back.

18. *Blind female [to other blind group members]:* You know, it really offends me when people praise me or make a fuss over me for doing something routine that anyone else could do. It makes me feel like I'm on exhibition. I want to be recognized for being competent—not for being blind.

19. *Male teacher [to mental health social worker]:* I have this thing about not being able to accept compliments. A friend told me about how much of a positive impact I've had on several students over the years. I couldn't accept that and feel good. My thought was, "You must be mistaken. I've never had that kind of effect on anyone."

20. *Lesbian, age 26 [to private social worker]:* The girls at the office were talking about lesbians the other day and about how repulsive the very thought of lesbianism was to them. How do you think I felt?

Modeled Responses

1. "So you're really in a difficult situation. You've wanted to keep Henry at home, but in light of his recent aggression and his increasing strength, you're becoming really frightened and wonder if other arrangements wouldn't be better for both you and him."

2. "I can see you're worried about how your children are doing in school and believe they need a bilingual program."

3. "It's been a real blow—your husband leaving you for another woman—and you've just felt so alone. And you find yourself dwelling on the painful question, 'Is something wrong with me, or is it that you just can't trust men?'"

4. "This is very upsetting for you. You seem to be saying that it's not fair being turned in when you believe you take care of your children. Please understand I'm not accusing you of neglecting your children. But I do have to investigate complaints. It may be that I'll be able to turn in a

positive report. I hope so. But I do need to talk with you further. May I come in?"

5. "It's humiliating to you to feel so left out and be the last guy chosen."

6. "It sounds as though you lived in terror that last month and literally feared for your life. You were wise to remove yourself when you did. A number of other women in the group have had similar experiences and are facing the same dilemma about what to do now. As group members, each of us can be helpful to other group members in thinking through what's the best course of action. In the meantime, you have a safe place to stay and some time to plan."

7. "Sounds like you get pretty annoyed, thinking about your wife's prodding and trying to take charge. It seems important right now that you prove to her and to yourself you can do something on your own."

8. "I gather you're fed up with having people relate to you because of your race instead of being accepted as an individual—as yourself."

9. "If I understand you, you feel degraded by the way you're treated—as though you're less than a human being. And that really gets to you."

10. "From what you say, I get a picture of you just feeling so all alone as you were growing up—as though you didn't feel very important to anyone, especially your father."

11. "So intellectually, you tell yourself not to worry, that you're in good hands. Still, on another level you have to admit you're terrified of that operation. *[Brief pause.]* Your fear is pretty natural, though. Most people who are honest with themselves experience fear."

12. "So the two of you get into some real struggles over differences in your views about what is reasonable of you to expect from Hugh. You seem to be saying you very much resent his refusal to pitch in—that it's not fair to have to carry the burden alone. Hugh, I'd be interested in hearing your views. Then we can hear how other members deal with this kind of situation."

13. "Sounds like part of you is saying that you have a right to expect more from Francine—that you don't feel good about always having to be the one to take the initiative. You also seem to feel you'd like to confront her with what she's doing, but you're uneasy about doing that because you don't want to risk losing her."

14. "So, you're uncomfortable around your black class-mates and just don't know how to read them. I gather you kind of walk on eggshells when they're around for fear you'll blow it."

15. "There is a lot of conflicting advice around these days about how men and women should relate to one another, and it is hard to figure out what to believe. You know you don't want to play games, yet that is what the class is telling you to do if you don't want to be single."

16. "Things don't get better despite your talks, and you get pretty discouraged. Sometimes you find yourself wondering if you'd get sexual fulfillment with men, and that appeals to you in some ways."

17. "So even though you care deeply for your family, there are days when you just feel so overwhelmed you'd like to buy a one-way ticket out of all the responsibility."

18. "Are you saying that you feel singled out and demeaned when people flatter you for doing things anyone could do? It bothers you, and you wish people would recognize you for being competent?

19. "In a way, you seem to be saying that you don't feel comfortable with compliments because you feel you don't really deserve them. It's like you feel you don't do anything worthy of a compliment."

20. "You must have felt extremely uncomfortable believing that they would condemn you if they knew. It must have been most painful for you."

Answers to Exercise in Identifying Surface and Underlying Feelings

1. *Apparent feelings:* unimportant, neglected, disappointed, hurt. *Probable deeper feelings:* rejected, abandoned, forsaken, deprived, lonely, depressed.

2. *Apparent feelings:* unloved, insecure, confused, embarrassed, left out or excluded. *Probable deeper feelings:* hurt, resentful, unvalued, rejected, taken for granted, degraded, doubting own desirability.

3. *Apparent feelings:* chagrined, disappointed in self, discouraged, letting children down, perplexed. *Probable deeper feelings:* guilty, inadequate, crummy, sense of failure, out of control, fear of damaging children.

4. *Apparent feelings:* frustrated, angry, bitter. *Probable deeper feelings:* depressed, discouraged, hopeless.

Answers to Exercises to Discriminate Levels of Empathic Responding

CLIENT STATEMENT

Client 1	
Response	Level
1.	2
2.	1
3.	1
4.	3
5.	2
6.	2
7.	4
8.	1

CLIENT STATEMENT

Client 2		Client 3	
Response	Level	Response	Level
1.	1	2	1
2.	3	1	4
3.	1	1	2
4.	2	3	2
5.	4	2	5
6.	1	2	1
7.	3	4	2
8.	2	1	2

Notes

1. Such highlighting of opposing feelings is a key technique for assisting clients in assessing their readiness for change in the motivational interviewing method (Miller & Rollnick, 2002).

2. In categorizing her husband as a "bump on a log," the wife makes a sweeping generalization that fits her husband's behavior into a mold. Although the social worker chose to keep the focus momentarily on the husband, it is important that he helps the couple to avoid labeling each other. Strategies for intervening when clients use labels are delineated in a later chapter.

CourseMate

Access an integrated eBook and chapter-specific learning tools including glossary terms, chapter outlines, relevant web links, videos, and practice quizzes. Go to **www.cengagebrain.com.**

CHAPTER **6**

Verbal Following, Exploring, and Focusing Skills

CHAPTER OVERVIEW

Chapter 6 introduces verbal following skills and their uses in exploring client concerns and focusing. This chapter includes skills for accurately following and reflecting what clients are expressing and feeling about their situation. It also introduces skills for helping clients to consider taking action on concerns about which they have been ambivalent. These skills are the building blocks for social workers' efforts to communicate empathically with clients. In addition to being helpful in work with clients in micro practice, such skills are useful at the meso level in work on behalf of clients, through advocacy, and in work with colleagues and other professionals. This chapter also includes references to videos accompanying the text.

As a result of reading this chapter you will be able to:

- **Construct an appropriate paraphrase and know when to use it**

- **Construct reflective responses including simple reflections and double sided reflections**

- **Construct furthering responses and know when to use them**

- **Construct open-ended questions and know when to use them**

- **Construct closed-ended questions and know when to use them**

- **Know how to seek concreteness**

- **Know how to provide and maintain focus**

- **Know how to summarize and when to do so**

EPAS COMPETENCIES IN THE 6TH CHAPTER

This chapter will give you the information needed to meet the following practice competencies:

2.1.1d A social worker demonstrates professional demeanor in behavior, appearance, and communication.

2.1.4c Recognize and communicate their understanding of the importance of difference in shaping life experiences

2.1.4d View themselves as learners and engage those with whom they work as informants

2.1.10a Substantively and affectively prepare for action with individuals, families, groups, organizations, and communities

2.1.10b Use empathy and other interpersonal skills

2.1.10d Collect organize and interpret data

2.1.10.g Select appropriate intervention strategies

2.1.10m Critically analyze monitor and evaluate interventions

Maintaining Psychological Contact with Clients and Exploring Their Problems

Verbal following involves the use and sometimes blending of discrete skills that enable social workers to maintain psychological contact with clients on a moment-by-moment basis and to covey accurate understanding of their messages. Moreover, verbal following behavior takes into account two performance variables that are essential to satisfaction and continuance on the part of the client:

1. *Stimulus-response congruence.* The extent to which social workers' responses provide feedback to clients that their messages are accurately received.

EP 2.1.10a

135

2. *Content relevance.* The extent to which the content of social workers' responses is perceived by clients as relevant to their substantive concerns.

Skills in following have been related to client continuance (Rosen, 1972). Further, incongruent responses to clients have been more associated with discontinuance (Duehn & Proctor, 1977). Continued use of questions and other responses that are not associated with previous client messages and that do not relate to the client's substantive concerns contribute to consistent client dissatisfaction. One study of the outcome of working with persons with drinking problems found that two-thirds of the variance of outcomes after six months was predicted by the degree of empathy demonstrated by the counselors (Miller, 1980). Effective use of attending behaviors and demonstrated empathy should enhance motivational congruence (the fit between client motivation and social worker goals), a factor that is associated with better outcomes in social work effectiveness studies (Reid & Hanrahan, 1982). Employing responses that directly relate to client messages and concerns thus enhances client satisfaction, fosters continuance, and greatly contributes to the establishment of a viable working relationship. Studies of practice by social work students of the skills taught in this book have shown that while most of the practice skills of second-year students were not significantly more advanced than those of first-year students, the second-year students were better able to focus on tasks and goals, an objective of this chapter, compared with first-year students (Deal & Brintzenhofe-Szok, 2004).

EP 2.1.4c

Clients do not always perceive social worker questions about concerns as helpful. While noting the differences within Asian and Pacific Islander groups, including those with immigrant and resident status, Fong (2007) notes that some Asian clients (as well as members of other groups) may express emotional conflicts in a somatized form. In such cases, the social worker must be respectful of the client's experience with the physical concern as well as explain the rationale for asking questions about factors such as family background that are not directly related to the physical complaint (Cormier & Nurius, 2003.) The linkage of these issues to their current symptoms is not clear to many clients. Some Asian clients conceive of mental distress as the result of a physiological disorder or character flaws. This issue must be dealt with sensitively before any useful therapeutic work can occur (Fong, 2007). Similarly, clients who are members of historically oppressed groups may perceive questions as interrogations not designed to help

them with their own concerns, but rather as ways to explore whether they have broken the law or endangered their children. That is, they may not readily assume that the social worker is acting as their agent or advocate, but rather as an agent of the state or majority community and hence a potential danger to their family (Sue, 2006).

> ### 🖥 VIDEO CASE EXAMPLE
>
> In the video "Getting Back to Shakopee, GBS," the potential client, Val has been referred to an employee assistance program by her employer. She asks many questions about who will gain access to the information shared in their sessions. These questions reflect a concern that her answers about child care and adult supervision could result in a child welfare investigation.

In addition to enabling social workers to maintain close psychological contact with clients, verbal following skills serve two other important functions in the helping process. First, they yield rich personal information, allowing social workers to explore clients' problems in depth. Second, they enable social workers to focus selectively on components of the clients' experiences and on dynamics in the helping process that facilitate positive client change.

EP 2.1.4d

The following pages introduce a variety of skills for verbally following and exploring clients' problems. Some of these skills are easily mastered. Others require more effort to acquire. The exercises in the body of the chapter will assist you in acquiring proficiency in these important skills. Although empathic responding is the most vital skill for verbally following clients' messages, we have not included it in this chapter because it was discussed in detail in Chapter 5. Later, we discuss the blending of empathic responses with other verbal following skills to bolster your ability to focus on and fully explore relevant client problems.

EP 2.1.10g

Verbal Following Skills

The discrete skills highlighted in this chapter include eight types of responses:

1. Furthering
2. Paraphrasing
3. Reflection
4. Closed-ended responses

EP 2.1.10b

5. Open-ended responses
6. Seeking concreteness
7. Providing and maintaining focus
8. Summarizing

Furthering Responses

Furthering responses indicate social workers are listening attentively and encourage the client to verbalize. There are two types of furthering responses: minimal prompts and accent responses.

Minimal Prompts

Minimal prompts signal the social worker's attentiveness and encourage the client to continue verbalizing. They can be either nonverbal or verbal.

Nonverbal minimal prompts consist of nodding the head, using facial expressions, or employing gestures that convey receptivity, interest, and commitment to understanding. They implicitly convey the message, "I am with you; please continue."

Verbal minimal prompts consist of brief messages that convey interest and encourage or request expanded verbalizations along the lines of the previous expressions by the client. These messages include "Yes," "I see," "But?", "Mm-mmm" "Tell me more," "And then what happened?", "And?", "Please go on," "Tell me more, please," and other similar brief messages that affirm the appropriateness of what the client has been saying and prompt him or her to continue.

Accent Responses

Accent responses (Hackney & Cormier, 2005) involve repeating, in a questioning tone of voice or with emphasis, a word or a short phrase. Suppose a client says, "I've really had it with the way my supervisor at work is treating me." The social worker might reply, "Had it?" This short response is intended to prompt further elaboration by the client.

Paraphrasing Responses

Paraphrasing involves using fresh words to restate the client's message concisely. Paraphrasing responses focus on the cognitive aspects of client messages (i.e., emphasize situations, ideas, objects, or persons) (Hackney & Cormier, 2005). Note that paraphrasing a client's or other person's comments does not mean that you agree with or condone those thoughts.

Four examples of paraphrasing follow.

Example 1

Elder client: I don't want to get into a living situation in which I will not be able to make choices on my own.

Social worker: So independence is a very important issue for you.

Example 2

Client: I went to the doctor today for a final checkup, and she said that I was doing fine.

Social worker: She gave you a clean bill of health, then.

Example 3

Native American Client (from "GBS" video): The idea of a promotion makes me feel good; I could earn more money, the supervisor in that department is real nice, she respects me, we get along really good.

Social worker: So you feel that you would get more support for you at work and for your family?

Example 4

Managed care utilization reviewer: We don't think that your patient's condition justifies the level of service that you recommend.

Social worker: So you feel that my documentation does not justify the need that I have recommended according to the approval guidelines you are working from.

Note that in Example 4, paraphrasing is used as part of the communication with a person whose opinion is important because it relates to delivering client

---

VIDEO CASE EXAMPLE

In the video "Elder Grief Assessment" (EGA) the social worker asks a senior recently widowed client what she would like to see occur at the end of their work together. The client replies: "I would like to feel better myself, the house looking better, the yard looking better, I would like to go grocery shopping when I want to, get to the doctor without calling someone." The social worker, Kathy, paraphrases the content by saying, "You would like to remain independent."

services—the health insurance care manager (Strom-Gottfried, 1998a). When employed sparingly, paraphrasing may be interspersed with other facilitative responses to prompt client expression. Used to excess, however, paraphrasing produces a mimicking effect. Paraphrasing is helpful when social workers want to bring focus to an idea or a situation for client consideration.

Exercises in Paraphrasing

In the following exercises, formulate written responses that paraphrase the cognitive messages of clients and other persons. Modeled responses for these exercises appear at the end of the chapter.

Client/Colleague Statements

1. **Client:** I can't talk to people. I just completely freeze up in a group.
2. **Wife:** I think that in the last few weeks I've been able to listen much more often to my husband and children.
3. **Elder client:** It wasn't so difficult to adjust to this place because the people who run it are helpful and friendly and I am able to make contacts easily—I've always been a people person.
4. **Mother** [speaking about daughter]: When it comes right down to it, I think I'm to blame for a lot of her problems.
5. **Member of treatment team:** I just don't see how putting more services into this family makes sense. The mother is not motivated, and the kids are better off away from her. This family has been messed up forever.

Reflection

While paraphrasing focuses on the content of a message, reflection responses focus attention on the affective part of the communication (Cormier, Nurius & Osborn, 2009).[1] In a reflection, social workers relate with responses that accurately capture clients' affect and assist them to reflect on and sort through their feelings. Sometimes social workers may choose to direct the discussion away from feelings for therapeutic purposes. For instance, a social worker might believe that a chronically depressed client who habitually expresses discouragement and disillusionment would benefit by focusing less on feelings and more on actions to alleviate the distress. When the social worker chooses to deemphasize

feelings, paraphrases that reflect content are helpful and appropriate.

Simple reflections, which identify the emotions expressed by the client, are a heritage from nondirective, client-centered counseling. That is, they simply identify the emotion. They do not take a stand or attempt to help the client deal with the emotion. They do not go beyond what the client has said or directly implied (Moyers, Martin, Manual, Miller & Ernst, 2003).

VIDEO CASE EXAMPLE

In the video "How Can I Help?" (HCH), Peter Dimock uses the Motivational Interviewing (MI) approach to work with Julie, a client who is recovering from drug use and is involved with the child welfare system. When Julie shares her frustration about all the things she has to do on her case plan, Peter responds with a simple reflection that stays closely with her message of being overwhelmed.

Julie: "Well it's just really hard getting around with baby and I just, you know I've got a lot of stuff that I'm supposed to be doing for my case plan and I just am having a really hard time getting to all the places on time."

Peter: "Well you've been pretty stressed, it sounds like. Having to do all these things and get around and make it to all of your appointments, it's pretty overwhelming."

Complex reflections go beyond what the client has directly stated or implied, adding substantial meaning or emphasis to convey a more complex picture. For example, they may *add content*, which focuses on meanings or feelings that the client did not directly express (ibid.). For example, when a teenaged client said "My mother really expects a lot from me," a social worker made a response that added implied content by saying "She has high expectations for you; she thinks that you have a lot of ability." *Verbalizing an unspoken emotion* is a form of reflection that names an emotion that the client has implied but not stated. When a teenaged client reflects on what it feels like to be new to her school by saying, "I am new here. I don't know anyone. I just try to stick to myself and stay out of trouble," the social worker could verbalize "that sounds to me as if it could be a little lonely," to tune in to the unspoken emotion of sadness.

A **reframe** is another form of adding content. Here, the social worker puts the client's response in a different light beyond what the client had considered (Moyers et al., 2003). For example, when a client reported on earlier drug treatment experience, he emphasized failure, saying, "I have gone through treatment three or four times. Maybe one of these times, I will get it right." The social worker chose not to agree with the failure message, but rather reframes to say "it sounds as if you have persisted, trying treatment again after earlier disappointments; you haven't given up on yourself."

Sometimes, the reflection can use a *metaphor* or *simile* to paint a picture of what the client has stated. For example, when a client commented about his job "I just do the same thing every day, nothing ever changes or ever gets better, always the same," the social worker responded, "It sounds like a rat in a maze" (ibid.). Sometimes the reflection might focus on *amplification*, either strengthening or weakening the intensity of client expression (ibid.). For example, a client shared "I am disappointed with how long this has taken," and the social worker chose to emphasize the strength of the implied feeling by saying "you are really frustrated and exhausted by all the time you have put into this with little to show for it." On the other hand, when a client expressed doubts about her abilities, saying, "I never get anything right," the social worker chose to agree but weaken its intensity "sometimes you doubt whether you can succeed."

Sometimes clients express indecision and conflict between several alternatives. In such circumstances, it is possible to present a *double-sided reflection* that captures both sides of the dilemma that is fostering ambivalence about acting (Miller & Rollnick, 2002). For example, a teen parent had expressed that she wanted to succeed in school and as a parent and one day become a probation officer or social worker. On the other hand, in their discussion she had reported frequent instances of verbal and physical altercations at school and gang involvement. She described members of the gang as members of her family. In a double-sided reflection, the social worker tried to identify the conflicting factors that make consistent decision making difficult. The social worker responded, "Rhonda, it sounds as if part of you is doing your best to succeed in school and act as a responsible parent and plan for the future. Another part of you is conflicted about wanting to be true to your friends and, as you describe them, family members, who are members of the gang."

▣ VIDEO CASE EXAMPLE

At a later point in the video "How Can I Help?" (HCH), Julie is commenting on how she is torn about returning to school to get a GED, seeing both advantages and disadvantages. She says "I don't know, I guess it would be a good accomplishment, but I just, I don't know, I just don't think, I don't just think I can do it, like, it's just hard. I don't know." Peter reflects the two sides of her feelings by saying "So it's important to you on one hand, and then on the other hand, you don't feel confident in your ability to do it. Is that true?"

Another version of reflection is the *reflection with a twist* (Miller & Rollnick, 2002) in which the social worker agrees in essence with the dilemma expressed by the client but changes the emphasis, perhaps to indicate that the dilemma is not unsolvable, but rather that the client has not at this time solved it. For example, in the previous situation with Rhonda, the social worker might add, "it sounds, Rhonda, as if at this point in time you don't feel that you can make a decision about what you are going to do about interacting with your friends in the gang."

These variations on reflections come from the Motivational Interviewing approach (MI) (Miller & Rollnick, 2002). They are useful in circumstances in which clients or potential clients are considering taking an action but have not decided on what to do. Rather than labeling such behavior as resistance, MI considers ambivalence as an important and useful step in deciding whether to address a situation. From the stages of change approach, such circumstances are described as being either in a state of **precontemplation**, in which a person has not decided whether an issue exists or whether they wish to address it, or **contemplation**, in which they are aware of an issue but have not decided whether to take action (De Clemente & Velasquez, 2002). These circumstances occur frequently in social work practice, but not always. Hence, the skills are presented here as important and useful adjuncts to reflection skills that can be applied when, in the course of exploration, potential ambivalence about considering an issue or taking action on it emerges. The spirit of MI is consistent with social work values of self-determination at this point in presenting the role of the helper as addressing ambivalence and helping the client consider whether he or she wishes to take action without exerting pressure on that decision (Miller & Rollnick, 2002).

Exercises with Reflections

In the following exercises, formulate written responses that reflect the affective state of clients. Modeled responses for these exercises appear at the end of the chapter.

Client/Colleague Statements

1. *Client:* Whenever I get into an argument with my mother, I always end up losing. I guess I'm still afraid of her.

2. *Mother [participating in welfare-to-work program]:* I don't know how they can expect me to be a good mother and make school appointments, supervise my kids, and put in all these work hours.

3. *Terminally ill cancer patient:* Some days I am really angry because I'm only 46-years-old and there are so many more things I wanted to do. Other days, I feel kind of defeated, like this is what I get for smoking two packs of cigarettes a day for 25 years.

4. *Elementary school student:* Kids pick on me at school. They are mean. If they try to hurt me then I try to hurt them back.

5. *Husband:* I just can't decide what to do. If I go ahead with the divorce, I'll probably lose custody of the kids—and I won't be able to see them very much. If I don't, though, I'll have to put up with the same old thing. I don't think my wife is going to change.

Closed- and Open-Ended Responses

Generally used to elicit specific information, **closed-ended questions** define a topic and restrict the client's response to a few words or a simple yes or no answer. Typical examples of closed-ended questions follow:

EP 2.1.10g

- *"When did you obtain your divorce?"*
- *"Do you have any sexual difficulties in your marriage?"*
- *"When did you last have a physical examination?"*
- *"Is your health insurance Medicare?"*

Although closed-ended questions restrict the client and elicit limited information, in many instances these responses are both appropriate and helpful. Later in this chapter, we discuss how and when to use this type of response effectively.

In contrast to closed-ended responses, which circumscribe client messages, **open-ended questions** and statements invite expanded expression and leave the client free to express what seems most relevant and important. For example:

Social worker: You've mentioned your daughter. Tell me how she enters into your problem.

Client: I don't know what to do. Sometimes I think she is just pushing me so that she can go live with her father. When I ask her to help around the house, she won't, and says that she doesn't owe me anything. When I try to insist on her helping, it just ends up in an ugly scene without anything being accomplished. It makes me feel so helpless.

In this example, the social worker's open-ended question prompted the client to expand on the details of the problems with her daughter, including a description of her daughter's behavior, her own efforts to cope, and her present sense of defeat. The information contained in the message is typical of the richness of data obtained through open-ended responding.

In circumstances like the example of a telephone conversation with a managed care utilization reviewer, the social worker can use an open-ended question to attempt to explore common ground that can lead to a mutually beneficial resolution.

Social worker [to managed care utilization reviewer]: Can you clarify for me how appropriate coverage is determined for situations such as the one I have described?

Some open-ended responses are unstructured, leaving the topic to the client's choosing (e.g., "Tell me what you would like to discuss today" or "What else can you tell me about the problems that you're experiencing?"). Other open-ended responses are structured such that the social worker defines the topic to be discussed but leaves the client free to respond in any way that he or she wishes (e.g., "You've mentioned feeling ashamed about the incident that occurred between you and your son. I'd be interested in hearing more about that."). Still other open-ended responses fall along a continuum between structured and unstructured, because they give the client leeway to answer with a few words or to elaborate with more information (e.g., "How willing are you to do this?").

Social workers may formulate open-ended responses either by asking a question or by giving a polite command. Suppose a terminally ill cancer patient said, "The doctor thinks I could live about six or seven months now. It could be less; it could be more. It's just an educated guess, he told me." The social worker could respond by asking, "How are you feeling about that prognosis?" or "Would you tell me how you are feeling about that prognosis?" Polite commands have the same effect as direct questions in requesting information but are less forceful and involve greater finesse. Similar in nature are embedded questions that do not take the form of a question but embody a request for information.

Examples of embedded questions include "I'm curious about…," "I'm wondering if …," and "I'm interested in knowing …." Open-ended questions often start with "what" or "how." "Why" questions are often unproductive because they may ask for reasons, motives, or causes that are either obvious, obscure, or unknown to the client. Asking how ("How did that happen?") rather than why ("Why did that happen?") often elicits far richer information regarding client behavior and patterns.

◼ VIDEO CASE EXAMPLE

In the video "Home for the Holidays, Part 1" (HFH), the practitioner, Kim Strom-Gottfried, asks one partner about the experience of when she came out to her parents as a lesbian: "Let me ask a bit about the coming out conversation. Sounds like it was not an easy one, yet one you were able to have. Can you tell me a little bit more about that?"

Exercises in Identifying Closed- and Open-Ended Responses

The following exercises will assist you to differentiate between closed- and open-ended messages. Identify each statement with either a C for a closed-ended question or O for an open-ended question. Turn to the end of the chapter to check your answers.

1. "Did your mother ask you to see me because of the problem you had with the principal?"
2. "When John says that to you, what do you experience inside?"

3. "You said you're feeling fed up and you're just not sure that pursuing a reconciliation is worth your trouble. Could you elaborate?"
4. "When is your court date?"

Now read the following client messages and respond by writing open-ended responses to them. Avoid using *why* questions. Examples of open-ended responses to these messages appear at the end of the chapter.

Client Statements

1. *Client:* Whenever I'm in a group with Ralph, I find myself saying something that will let him know that I am smart, too.
2. *Client:* I always have had my parents telephone for me about appointments and other things I might mess up.
3. *Teenager [speaking of a previous probation counselor]:* He sure let me down. And I really trusted him. He knows a lot about me because I spilled my guts.
4. *Group nursing home administrator:* I think that we are going to have to move Gladys to another, more suitable kind of living arrangement. We aren't able to provide the kind of care that she needs.

The next sections of the book explain how you can blend open-ended, paraphrases and reflective responses to keep a discussion focused on a specific topic. In preparation for that, respond to the next two client messages by formulating a paraphrase or reflection followed by an open-ended question that encourages the client to elaborate on the same topic.

5. *Unwed teenage girl seeking abortion [brought in by her mother, who wishes to discuss birth alternatives]:* I feel like you are all tied up with my mother, trying to talk me out of what I have decided to do.
6. *Client:* Life is such a hassle, and it doesn't seem to have any meaning or make sense. I just don't know whether I want to try figuring it out any longer.

The difference between closed-ended and open-ended responses may seem obvious to you, particularly if you completed the preceding exercises. It has been our experience, however, that social workers have difficulty in actual sessions in determining whether their responses are open- or closed-ended, in observing the differential effect of these two types of responses in yielding rich and relevant data, and in deciding which of the two types of responses is appropriate at a given moment. We recommend, therefore, that as you converse with your associates, you practice drawing them out by employing open-ended responses and noting how they respond. We also recommend that you use the form provided at the end of the chapter to assess both the frequency and the appropriateness of your closed- and open-ended responses in several taped client sessions.

Discriminant Use of Closed- and Open-Ended Responses

Beginning social workers typically ask an excessive number of closed-ended questions, many of which block communication or are inefficient or irrelevant to the helping process. When this occurs, the session tends to take on the flavor of an interrogation, with the social worker bombarding the client with questions and taking responsibility for maintaining verbalization. Notice what happens in the following excerpt from a recording of a social worker interviewing an institutionalized youth.

Social worker: I met your mother yesterday. Did she come all the way from Colorado to see you?

Client: Yeah.

Social worker: It seems to me that she must really care about you to take the bus and make the trip up here to see you. Don't you think so?

Client: I suppose so.

Social worker: Did the visit with her go all right?

Client: Fine. We had a good time.

Social worker: You had said you were going to talk to her about a possible home visit. Did you do that?

Client: Yes.

When closed-ended responses are used to elicit information in lieu of open-ended responses, as in the preceding example, many more discrete interchanges will occur. However, the client's responses will be brief and the information yield will be markedly lower.

Open-ended responses often elicit the same data as closed-ended questions but draw out much more information and elaboration of the problem from the client. The following two examples contrast open-ended and closed-ended responses that address the same topic with a given client. To appreciate the differences in the richness of information yielded by these contrasting responses, compare the likely client responses elicited by such questions to the closed-ended questions used from the previous section.

Example 1

Closed-ended: "Did she come all the way from Colorado to see you?"

Open-ended: "Tell me about your visit with your mother."

Example 2

Closed-ended: "Did you talk with her about a possible home visit?"

Open-ended: "How did your mother respond when you talked about a possible home visit?"

Occasionally, beginning social workers use closed-ended questions to explore feelings, but responses from clients typically involve minimal self-disclosure, as might be expected. Rather than encourage expanded expression of feelings, closed-ended questions limit responses, as illustrated in the following example:

Social worker: Did you feel rejected when she turned down your invitation?

Client: Yeah.

Social worker: Have there been other times when you've felt rejected that way?

Client: Oh, yeah. Lots of times.

Social worker: When was the first time?

Client: Gee, that's hard to say.

Here, the social worker was leading the client rather than finding out how she perceived the situation. Had the social worker employed empathic and open-ended responses to explore the feelings and thoughts associated with being rejected, the client would likely have revealed much more.

Because open-ended responses elicit more information than closed-ended ones, frequent use of the former technique increases the efficiency of data gathering. In fact, the richness of information revealed by the client is directly proportional to the frequency with which open-ended responses are employed. Frequent use of open-ended responses also fosters a smoothly flowing session; consistently asking closed-ended questions, by contrast, may result in a fragmented, discontinuous process.

Closed-ended questions are used chiefly to elicit essential factual information. Skillful social workers use closed-ended questions sparingly, because clients usually reveal extensive factual information spontaneously as they unfold their stories, aided by the social worker's open-ended and furthering responses. Although they are typically employed little during the first part of a session, closed questions are used more extensively later to elicit data that may have been omitted by clients, such as names and ages of children, place of employment, date of marriage, medical facts, and data regarding family or origin.

In obtaining this kind of factual data, the social worker can unobtrusively weave into the discussion closed-ended questions that directly pertain to the topic. For example, a client may relate certain marital problems that have existed for many years, and the social worker might ask parenthetically, "And you've been married for how many years?" Similarly, a parent may explain that a child began to have irregular attendance at school when the parent started to work 6 months ago, to which the social worker might respond, "I see. Incidentally, what type of work do you do?" It is vital, of course, to shift the focus back to the problem. If necessary, the social worker can easily maintain focus by using an open-ended response to pick up the thread of the discussion. For example, the social worker might comment, "You mentioned that Ernie began missing school when you started to work. I'd like to hear more about what was happening in your family at that time."

Because open-ended responses generally yield rich information, they are used throughout initial sessions. They are used most heavily, however, in the first portion of sessions to open up lines of communication and to invite clients to reveal problematic aspects of their lives. The following open-ended polite command is a typical opening message: "Could you tell me what you wish to discuss, and we can think about it together." Such responses convey interest in clients as well as respect for clients' abilities to relate their problems in their own way; as a consequence, they also contribute to the development of a working relationship.

As clients disclose certain problem areas, open-ended responses are extensively employed to elicit additional relevant information. Clients, for example, may reveal difficulties at work or in relationships with other family members. Open-ended responses like the following will elicit clarifying information:

- *"Tell me more about your problems at work."*
- *"I'd like to hear more about the circumstances when you were mugged coming home with the groceries."*

Open-ended responses can be used to enhance communication with collaterals, colleagues, and other professionals. For example, Strom-Gottfried suggests using effective communication skills in negotiation and communication between care providers and utilization reviewers. When a client has not been approved for a kind of service that the social worker has recommended, the social worker can attempt to join with the reviewer in identifying goals that both parties would embrace and request information in an open-ended fashion.

> *"I appreciate your concern that she gets the best available services and that her condition does not get worse. We are concerned with safety, as we know you are. Could you tell me more about how this protocol can help us assure her safety?"* (Strom-Gottfried, 1998a, p. 398)

It may sometimes be necessary to employ closed-ended questions extensively to draw out information if the client is unresponsive and withholds information or has limited conceptual and mental abilities. However, in the former case, it is vital to explore the client's immediate feelings about being in the session, which often are negative and impede verbal expression. Focusing on and resolving negative feelings (discussed at length in Chapter 12) may pave the way to using open-ended responses to good advantage.

When you incorporate open-ended responses into your repertoire, you will experience a dramatic positive change in your interviewing style and confidence level. To assist you to develop skill in blending and balancing open-ended and closed-ended responses, we have provided a recording form to help you examine your own interviewing style (see Figure 6-1). Using this form, analyze several recorded individual, conjoint, or group sessions over a period of time to determine changes you are making in employing these two types of responses. The recording form will assist you in determining the extent to which you have used open- and closed-ended responses.

In addition, you may wish to review your work for the following purposes:

1. To determine when relevant data are missing and whether the information might have been more appropriately obtained through an open- or closed-ended response
2. To determine when your use of closed-ended questions was irrelevant or ineffective, or distracted from the data-gathering process
3. To practice formulating open-ended responses you might use instead of closed-ended responses, to increase client participation and elicit richer data.

SOCIAL WORKER'S RESPONSES	OPEN-ENDED RESPONSES	CLOSED-ENDED RESPONSES
1.		
2.		
3.		
4.		
5.		
6.		
7.		

© Cengage Learning 2013

Directions: Record your discrete open- and closed-ended responses and place a check in the appropriate column. Agency time constraints will dictate how often you can practice it.

FIG-6-1 Recording Form for Open- and Closed-Ended Responding Seeking Concreteness

Seeking Concreteness

Many of us are inclined to think and talk in generalities and to use words that lack precision when speaking of our experiences ("How was your weekend?" "It was awesome."). To communicate one's feelings and experiences so that they are fully understood, however, a person must be able to respond concretely—that is, with specificity. Responding concretely means using words that describe in explicit terms specific experiences, behaviors, and feelings. As an example, in the following message, an intern supervisor provides feedback in vague and general terms: "I thought you had a good interview." Alternatively, he might have described his experience in more precise language: "During your interview, I was impressed with the way you blended open-ended with closed-ended questions in a relaxed fashion."

You should consider seeking concreteness when the client uses language that suggests to you that you may not understand their terms in the way they intend. This can be particularly true when interviewing children or adolescents whose colloquial expressions may not be entirely clear to the interviewer. Similarly, non native speakers may be conveying ideas that do not readily translate into the language you are speaking. In summary, seeking concreteness can be useful to:

1. Check out perceptions
2. Clarify the meaning of vague or unfamiliar terms
3. Explore the basis of conclusions drawn by clients
4. Assist clients to personalize their statements
5. Elicit specific feelings

6. Focus on the here and now, rather than on the distant past
7. Elicit details related to clients' experiences
8. Elicit details related to interactional behavior
9. Clarify details of timelines, expectations

To test your comprehension of the concept of concreteness, assess which of the following messages give descriptive information concerning what a client experiences:

1. "I have had a couple of accidents that would not have happened if I had full control of my hands. The results weren't that serious, but they could be."
2. "I'm uneasy right now because I don't know what to expect from counseling, and I'm afraid you might think that I really don't need it."
3. "You are a good girl, Susie."
4. "People don't seem to care whether other people have problems."
5. "My last social worker did not answer my calls."
6. "I really wonder if I'll be able to keep from crying and to find the words to tell my husband that it's all over—that I want a divorce."
7. "You did a good job."

You could probably readily identify which messages contained language that increased the specificity of the information conveyed by the client.

In developing competency as a social worker, one of your challenges is to consistently recognize clients' messages expressed in abstract and general terms and to assist them to reveal highly specific information related to feelings and experiences. Such information will assist you to make accurate assessments and, in turn, to plan interventions accordingly. A second challenge is to help clients learn how to respond more concretely in their relationships with others—a task you will not be able to accomplish unless you are able to model the dimension of concreteness yourself. A third challenge is to describe your own experience in language that is precise and descriptive. It is not enough to recognize concrete messages; in addition, you must familiarize yourself with and practice responding concretely to the extent that it becomes a natural style of speaking and relating to others.

The remainder of our discussion on the skill of seeking concreteness is devoted to assisting you in meeting these three challenges.

Types of Responses That Facilitate Specificity of Expression by Clients

Social workers who fail to move beyond general and abstract messages often have little grasp of the specificity and meaning of a client's problem. Eliciting highly specific information that minimizes errors or misinterpretations, however, represents a formidable challenge. People typically present impressions, views, conclusions, and opinions that, despite efforts to be objective, are inevitably biased and distorted to some extent. As previously mentioned, it is common for many of us to speak in generalities and to respond with imprecise language. As a consequence, those messages may be understood differently by different people.

To help you to conceptualize the various ways you may assist clients to respond more concretely, the following sections examine different facets of responses that seek concreteness:

In addition to discussing these aspects, this section includes 10 skill development exercises, which are designed to bring your comprehension of concreteness from the general and abstract to the specific and concrete.

Checking Out Perceptions

Responses that assist social workers to clarify and "check out" whether they have accurately heard clients' messages (e.g., "Do you mean …" or "Are you saying …") are vital in building rapport with clients and in communicating the desire to understand their problems. Such responses also minimize misperceptions or projections in the helping process. Clients benefit from social workers' efforts to understand, because clarifying responses assist clients in sharpening and reformulating their thinking about their own feelings and other concerns, thereby encouraging self-awareness and growth.

Sometimes, perception checking becomes necessary because clients' messages are incomplete, ambiguous, or complex. Occasionally, social workers may encounter clients who repetitively communicate in highly abstract or metaphorical styles, or clients whose thinking is scattered and whose messages just do not "track" or make sense. In such instances, social workers must spend considerable time sorting through clients' messages and clarifying perceptions.

At other times, the need for clarification arises not because the client has conveyed confusing, faulty, or incomplete messages, but rather because the social worker has not fully attended to the client's message or comprehended its meaning. Fully attending throughout each moment of a session requires intense concentration. Of course, it is impossible to fully focus on and comprehend the essence of every message delivered in group and family meetings, where myriad transactions occur and competing communications bid for the social worker's attention.

It is important that you develop skill in using clarifying responses to elicit ongoing feedback regarding your perceptions and to acknowledge freely your need for clarification when you are confused or uncertain. Rather than reflecting personal or professional inadequacy, your efforts to accurately grasp the client's meaning and feelings will most likely be perceived as signs of your genuineness and your commitment to understand.

To check your perceptions, try asking simple questions that seek clarification or combining your request for clarification with a paraphrase or empathic response that reflects your perception of the client's message (e.g., "I think you were saying _____. Is that right?"). Examples of clarifying messages include the following:

- *"You seem to be really irritated, not only because he didn't respond when you asked him to help, but because he seemed to be deliberately trying to hurt you. Is that accurate?"*
- *"I'm not sure I'm following you. Let me see if I understand the order of the events you described …"*
- *"Would you expand on what you are saying so that I can be sure that I understand what you mean?"*
- *"Could you go over that again, and perhaps give an illustration that might help me to understand?"*
- *"I'm confused. Let me try to restate what I think you're saying."*
- *"As a group, you seem to be divided in your approach to this matter. I'd like to summarize what I'm hearing, and I would then appreciate some input regarding whether I understand the various positions that have been expressed."*

VIDEO CASE EXAMPLE

In the video "Serving the Squeaky Wheel" (SSW), the social worker, Ron Rooney, asks Molly, a client with a diagnosed serious and persistent mental illness (SPMI), "So you feel that other people's ideas about what mental illness means is not the same as yours?"

In addition to clarifying their own perceptions, social workers need to assist clients in conjoint or group sessions to clarify their perceptions of the messages of others who are present. This may be accomplished in any of the following ways:

- By modeling clarifying responses, which occur naturally as social workers seek to check out their own perceptions of clients' messages.
- By directing clients to ask for clarification. Consider, for example, the following response by a social worker in a conjoint session: "You [mother] had a confused look on your face, and I'm not sure that you understood your daughter's point. Would you repeat back to her what you heard and then ask her if you understood correctly?"
- By teaching clients how to clarify perceptions and by reinforcing their efforts to "check out" the messages of others, as illustrated in the following responses:

[To group]: "One of the reasons families have communication problems is that members don't hear accurately what others are trying to say and, therefore, they often respond or react on the basis of incorrect or inadequate information. I would like to encourage all of you to frequently use what I call 'checking out' responses, such as 'I'm not sure what you meant. Were you saying...?' to clarify statements of others. As we go along, I'll point out instances in which I notice any of you using this kind of response."

[To family]: "I'm wondering if you all noticed Jim 'checking out' what his dad said.... As you may recall, we talked about the importance of these kinds of responses earlier. [To father] I'm wondering, Bob, what you experienced when Jim did that?"

Clarifying the Meaning of Vague or Unfamiliar Terms

In expressing themselves, clients often employ terms that have multiple meanings or use terms in idiosyncratic ways. For example, in the message, "The kids in this school are mean," the word *mean* may have different meanings to the social worker and the client. If the social worker does not identify what this term means to a particular client, he or she cannot be certain whether the client is referring to behavior that is violent, unfriendly, threatening, or something else. The precise meaning can be clarified by employing one of the following responses:

- "Tell me about the way that some kids are mean in this school."
- "I am not sure I know what is happening when you say that some kids act in a mean way. Could you clarify that for me?"
- "Can you give me an example of something mean that has happened at this school?"

Many other words also lack precision, so it is important to avoid assuming that the client means the same thing you mean when you employ a given term. For example, "codependent," "irresponsible," "selfish," and "careless" conjure up meanings that vary according to the reference points of different persons. Exact meanings are best determined by asking for clarification or for examples of events in which the behavior alluded to actually occurred.

Exploring the Basis of Conclusions Drawn by Clients

Clients often present views or conclusions as though they are established facts. For example, the messages "I'm losing my mind" and "My partner doesn't love me anymore" include views or conclusions that the client has drawn. To accurately assess the client's difficulties, the social worker must elicit the information on which these views or conclusions are based. This information helps the social worker assess the thinking patterns of the client, which are powerful determinants of emotions and behavior. For example, a person who believes he or she is no longer loved will behave as though this belief represents reality. The social worker's role, of course, is to reveal distortions and to challenge erroneous conclusions in a facilitative manner.

The following responses would elicit clarification of the information that serves as the basis of the views and conclusions embodied in the messages cited earlier:

- "How do you mean, losing your mind?"
- "How have you concluded that you're losing your mind?"

- *"What leads you to believe your partner no longer loves you?"*

Note that entire groups may hold in common fixed beliefs that may not be helpful to them in attempting to better their situations. In such instances, the social worker faces the challenging task of assisting members to reflect upon and to analyze their views. For example, the social worker may need to help group members to assess conclusions or distortions like the following:

- *"We can't do anything about our problems. We are helpless and others are in control of our lives."*
- *"People in authority are out to get us."*
- *"Someone else is responsible for our problems."*
- *"They (members of another race, religion, group, etc.) are no good."*

In Chapter 13, we discuss the social worker's role in challenging distortions and erroneous conclusions and identify relevant techniques that may be used for this purpose.

Assisting Clients to Personalize Their Statements

The relative concreteness of a specific client message is related in part to the focus or subject of that message. Client messages fall into several different classes of topic focus (Cormier, Nurius & Osborn, 2009), each of which emphasizes different information and leads into very different areas of discussion:

- Focus on self, *indicated by the subject "I" (e.g., "I'm disappointed that I wasn't able to keep the appointment.")*
- Focus on others, *indicated by subjects such as "they," "people," "someone," or names of specific persons (e.g., "They haven't fulfilled their part of the bargain.")*
- Focus on the group or mutual relationship between self and others, *indicated by the subject "we" (e.g., "We would like to do that.")*
- Focus on content, *indicated by such subjects as events, institutions, situations, ideas (e.g., "School wasn't easy for me.")*

People are more prone to focus on others or on content, or to speak of themselves as a part of a group rather than to personalize their statements by using "I" or other self-referent pronouns. This tendency is illustrated in the following messages: "Things just don't seem to be going right for me," "They don't like me," and "It's not easy for people to talk about their problems." In the last example, the client means

that it is not easy for *her* to talk about *her* problems, yet she uses the term *people,* thereby generalizing the problem and obscuring her personal struggle.

In assisting clients to personalize statements, social workers have a three-part task:

1. Social workers must model, teach, and coach clients to use self-referent pronouns *(I, me)* in talking about their concerns and their own emotional response to those concerns. For example, in response to a vague client message that focuses on content rather than self ("Everything at home seems to be deteriorating"), the social worker might gently ask the client to reframe the message by starting the response with "I" and giving specific information about what she is experiencing. It is also helpful to teach clients the difference between messages that focus on self ("I think …," "I feel …," "I want …") and messages that are *other-related* ("It …," "Someone …").

2. Social workers must teach the difference between self-referent messages and subject-related messages (i.e., those dealing with objects, things, ideas, or situations). Although teaching clients to use self-referent pronouns when talking about their concerns is a substantive task, clients derive major benefits from it. Indeed, not owning or taking responsibility for feelings and speaking about problems in generalities and abstractions are among the most prevalent causes of problems in communicating.

3. Social workers must focus frequently on the client and use the client's name or the pronoun *you.* Beginning social workers are apt to attend to client talk about other people, distant situations, the group at large, various escapades, or other events or content that give little information about self and the relationship between self and situations or people. In the following illustration, the social worker's response focuses on the situation rather than on the client:

Client: My kids want to shut me up in a nursing home.

Social worker: What makes you think that?

In contrast, the following message personalizes the client's concern and explicitly identifies the feelings she is experiencing:

Social worker: You worry that your children might be considering a nursing home for you. You want to be part of any decision about what would be a safe environment for you.

A social worker may employ various techniques to assist clients to personalize messages. In the preceding example, the social worker utilized an empathic response. In this instance, this skill is invaluable to the social worker in helping the client to focus on self. Recall that personalizing feelings is an inherent aspect of the paradigm for responding empathetically ("You feel _____ about/because _____"). Thus, clients can make statements that omit self-referent pronouns, and by utilizing empathic responding, social workers may assist clients to "own" their feelings.

Eliciting Specific Feelings

Even when clients personalize their messages and express their feelings, social workers often need to elicit additional information to clarify what they are experiencing, because certain "feeling words" denote general feeling states rather than specific feelings. For example, in the message, "I'm really *upset* that I didn't get a raise," the word "upset" helps to clarify the client's general frame of mind but fails to specify the precise feeling. In this instance, "upset" may refer to feeling disappointed, discouraged, unappreciated, devalued, angry, resentful, or even incompetent or inadequate due to the failure to receive a raise. Until the social worker has elicited additional information, he or she cannot be sure of how the client actually experiences being "upset."

Other feeling words that lack specificity include *frustrated, uneasy, uncomfortable, troubled,* and *bothered.* When clients employ such words, you can pinpoint their feelings by using responses such as the following:

- *"How do you mean, 'upset'?"*
- *"I'd like to understand more about that feeling. Could you clarify what you mean by 'frustrated'?"*
- *"Can you say more about in what way you feel bothered?"*

Focusing on the Here and Now

Another aspect of concreteness takes the form of responses that shift the focus from the past to the present, the here and now. Messages that relate to the immediate present are high in concreteness, whereas those that center on the past are low in concreteness. Many of us are prone to dwell on past feelings and events. Unfortunately, precious opportunities for promoting growth and understanding may slip through the fingers of social workers who fail to focus on emotions and experiences that unfold in the immediacy of the interview. Focusing on feelings as they occur will enable you to observe reactions and behavior firsthand, eliminating any bias and error caused by reporting feelings and experiences after the fact. Furthermore, the helpfulness of your feedback is greatly enhanced when this feedback relates to the client's immediate experience.

The following exchange demonstrates how to achieve concreteness in such situations:

Client [choking up]: When she told me it was all over, that she was in love with another man—well, I just felt—it's happened again. I felt totally alone, like there just wasn't anyone.

Social worker: That must have been terribly painful. *[Client nods; tears well up.]* I wonder if you're not having the same feeling just now—at this moment. *[Client nods agreement.]*

Not only do such instances provide direct access to the client's inner experience, but they also may produce lasting benefits as the client shares deep and painful emotions in the context of a warm, accepting, and supportive relationship. Here-and-now experiencing that involves emotions toward the social worker (e.g., anger, hurt, disappointment, affectional desires, fears) is known as *relational immediacy.* Skills pertinent to relational immediacy warrant separate consideration and are dealt with in Chapter 18.

Focusing on here-and-now experiencing with groups, couples, and families is a particularly potent technique for assisting members of these systems to clear the air of pent-up feelings. Moreover, interventions that focus on the immediacy of feelings bring buried issues to the surface, paving the way for the social worker to assist members of these systems to clearly identify and explore their difficulties and (if appropriate) to engage in problem solving.

Eliciting Details Related to Clients' Experiences

As previously mentioned, one reason why concrete responses are essential is that clients often offer up vague statements regarding their experiences—for example, "Some people in this group don't want to change bad enough to put forth any effort." Compare this with the following concrete statement, in which the client assumes ownership of the problem and fills in details that clarify its nature:

Client: I'm concerned because I want to do something to work on my problems in this group, but when I do try to talk about them, you, John, make some sarcastic remark. It seems that then several of you *[gives names]* just laugh about it and someone changes the subject. I really feel ignored then and just go off into my own world.

Aside from assisting clients to personalize their messages and to "own" their feelings and problems, social workers must ask questions that elicit illuminating information concerning the client's experiencing, such as that illustrated in the preceding message. Questions that start with "how" or "what" are often helpful in assisting the client to give concrete data. For example, to the client message, "Some people in this group don't want to change bad enough to put forth any effort," the social worker might respond, "What have you seen happening in the group that leads you to this conclusion?"

Eliciting Details Related to Interactional Behavior

Concrete responses are also vital in accurately assessing interactional behavior. Such responses pinpoint what actually occurs in interactional events—that is, what circumstances preceded the events, what the participants said and did, what specific thoughts and feelings the client experienced, and what consequences followed the event. In other words, the social worker elicits details of what happened, rather than settling for clients' views and conclusions.

An example of a concrete response to a client message follows:

High school student: My teacher really lost it yesterday. She totally dissed me, and I hadn't done one thing to deserve it.

Social worker: That must have been aggravating. Can you lay out for me the sequence of events—what led up to this situation, and what each of you said and did? To understand better what went wrong, I'd like to get the details as though I had been there and observed what happened.

In such cases, it is important to keep clients on topic by continuing to assist them to relate the events in question, using responses such as "Then what happened?", "What did you do next?", or "Then who said what?" If dysfunctional patterns become evident after exploring numerous events, social workers have a responsibility to share their observations with clients, to assist them to evaluate the effects of the patterned behavior, and to assess their motivation to change it.

Specificity of Expression by Social Workers

Seeking concreteness applies to the communication of both clients and social workers. In this role, you will frequently explain, clarify and give feedback, to clients. As a social worker who has recently begun a formal professional educational program, you may be prone to speak with the vagueness and generality that characterize much of the communication of the lay public. When such vagueness occurs, clients and others may understandably misinterpret, draw erroneous conclusions, or experience confusion about the meaning of your messages.

Consider the lack of specificity in the following messages actually delivered by social workers:

- *"You seem to have a lot of pent-up hostility."*
- *"You really handled yourself well in the group today."*
- *"I think a lot of your difficulties stem from your self-image."*

Vague terms such as *hostility, handled yourself well,* and *self-image* may leave the client in a quandary as to what the social worker actually means. Moreover, in this style of communication, conclusions are presented without supporting information. As a result, the client must either accept them at face value, reject them as invalid, or speculate on the basis of the conclusions. Fortunately, some people are sufficiently perceptive, inquisitive, and assertive to request greater specificity—but many others are not.

Contrast the preceding messages with how the social worker responds to the same situations with messages that have a high degree of specificity:

- *"I've noticed that you've become easily angered and frustrated several times as we've talked about ways you might work out child custody arrangements with your wife. This appears to be a very painful area for you. "I noticed that you responded several times in the group tonight, and I thought you offered some very helpful insight to Marjorie when you said…. I also noticed you seemed to be more at ease than in previous sessions."*
- *"We've talked about your tendency to feel inferior to other members of your family and to discount your own feelings and opinions in your contacts with them. I think that observation applies to the problem you're having with your sister that you just described. You've said you didn't want to go on the trip with her and her husband because they fight all the time, yet you feel you have to go because she is putting pressure on you. As in other instances, you appear to be drawing the conclusion that how you feel about the matter isn't important."*

In the video "HFH, Part 1," the practitioner, Kim Strom-Gottfried, makes a specific observation that simultaneously provides feedback and suggests the meaning for a behavior (something we will explore further in Chapter 17): "There is a dynamic here that is going on at many levels between the two of you as you sort out this holiday problem. And yet it sounds like it is part of a larger issue, in terms of conversations of how you put together this relationship with your family relationships."

When social workers speak with specificity, clarify meanings, personalize statements, and document the sources of their conclusions, clients are much less likely to misinterpret or project their own feelings or thoughts. Clients like to be clear about what is expected of them and how they are perceived, as well as how and why social workers think and feel as they do about matters discussed in their sessions. Clients also learn vicariously to speak with greater specificity as social workers model sending concrete messages.

Both beginning and experienced social workers face the additional challenge of avoiding inappropriate use of jargon. Unfortunately, jargon has pervaded professional discourse and runs rampant in social work literature and case records. Its use confuses, rather than clarifies, meanings for clients. The careless use of jargon with colleagues also fosters stereotypical thinking and is therefore antithetical to the cardinal value of individualizing the client. Furthermore, labels tend to conjure up images of clients that vary from one social worker to another, thereby injecting a significant source of error into communication. Consider the lack of specificity in the following messages that are rich in jargon:

- "Mrs. N manifests strong passive-aggressive tendencies."
- "Sean displayed adequate impulse control in the group and tested the leader's authority in a positive manner."
- "Hal needs assistance in gaining greater self-control."
- "The client shows some borderline characteristics."
- "The group members were able to respond to appropriate limits."
- "Ruth appears to be emotionally immature for an eighth-grader."

To accurately convey information about clients to your colleagues, you must explicitly describe their behavior and document the sources of your conclusions. For example, with the vague message, "Ruth appears to be emotionally immature for an eighth-grader," consider how much more accurately another social worker would perceive your client if you conveyed information in the form of a concrete response: "The teacher says Ruth is quiet and stays to herself in school. She doesn't answer any questions in class unless directly called upon, and she often doesn't complete her assignments. She spends considerable time daydreaming or playing with objects." By describing behavior in this way, you avoid biasing your colleague's perceptions of clients by conveying either vague impressions or erroneous conclusions.

EP 2.1.1d

It has been our experience that mastery of the skill of communicating with specificity is gained only through extended and determined effort. The task becomes more complicated if you are not aware that your communication is vague. We recommend that you carefully and consistently monitor your recorded sessions and your everyday conversations with a view toward identifying instances in which you did or did not communicate with specificity. This kind of monitoring will enable you to set relevant goals for yourself and to chart your progress. We also recommend that you enlist your practicum instructor to provide feedback about your performance level on this vital skill.

Exercises in Seeking Concreteness

In the following exercises, you should formulate written responses that will elicit concrete data regarding clients' problems. You may wish to combine your responses with either an empathic response or a paraphrase. Reviewing the eight guidelines for seeking concreteness as you complete the exercise will assist you in developing effective responses and help you to clearly conceptualize the various dimensions of this skill as well. After you have finished the exercises, compare your responses with the modeled responses.

Client Statements

1. **Adolescent** [speaking of his recent recommitment to a correctional institution]: It really seems weird to be back here.
2. **Client:** You can't depend on friends; they'll stab you in the back every time.
3. **Client:** He's got a terrible temper—that's the way he is, and he'll never change.

4. *Client:* My supervisor is so insensitive, you can't believe it. All she thinks about are reports and deadlines.

5. *Client:* I was upset after I left your office last week. I felt you really didn't understand what I was saying and didn't care how I felt.

6. *Client:* My dad's 58 years old now, but I swear he still hasn't grown up. He always has a chip on his shoulder.

7. *Elder client:* My rheumatoid arthritis has affected my hands a lot. It gets to be kind of tricky when I'm handling pots and pans in the kitchen.

8. *Client:* I just have this uneasy feeling about going to the doctor. I guess I've really got a hang-up about it.

9. *African American student [to African American social worker]:* You ask why I don't talk to my teacher about why I'm late for school. I'll tell you why. Because she's white, that's why. She's got it in for us black students, and there's just no point talking to her. That's just the way it is.

10. *Client:* John doesn't give a damn about me. I could kick the bucket, and he wouldn't lose a wink of sleep.

Modeled Responses

1. "Can you tell me how it feels weird to you?"

2. "I gather you feel that your friends have let you down in the past. Could you give me a recent example in which this has happened?"

3. "Could you tell me more about what happens when he loses his temper with you?" or "You sound like you don't have much hope that he'll ever get control of his temper. How have you concluded he will never change?" *[A social worker might explore each aspect of the message separately.]*

4. "Could you give me some examples of how she is insensitive to you?"

5. "Sounds like you've been feeling hurt and disappointed over my reaction last week. I can sense you're struggling with those same feelings right now. "It sounds as if you feel that your dad's way of communicating with you is unusual for someone his age. Could you recall some recent examples of times you've had difficulties with how he communicates with you?"

6. "It sounds as if the arthritis pain is aggravating and blocking what you normally do. When you say that handling the pots and pans is kind of tricky, can

you tell me about recent examples of what has happened when you are cooking?"

7. "Think of going to the doctor just now. Let your feelings flow naturally. *[Pause.]* What goes on inside you—your thoughts and feelings?"

8. "So you see it as pretty hopeless. You feel pretty strongly about Ms. Wright. I'd be interested in hearing what's happened that has led you to the conclusion she's got it in for black students."

9. "So you feel as if you're nothing in his eyes. I'm wondering how you've reached that conclusion?"

Focusing: A Complex Skill

Skills in focusing are critical to your practice for several reasons. Because your time with clients is limited, it is critical to make the best use of each session by honing in on key topics. You are also responsible for guiding

EP 2.1.10b

the helping process and avoiding wandering. Helping relationships should be characterized by purposeful focus and continuity, unlike normal social relations. As social workers, we perform a valuable role by assisting clients to focus on their problems in greater depth and to maintain focus until they accomplish desired changes.

In addition, families and groups sometimes experience interactional difficulties that prevent them from focusing effectively on their problems. To enhance family and group functioning, social workers must be able to refocus the discussion whenever dysfunctional interactional processes cause families and groups to prematurely drift away from the topic at hand.

To assist you in learning how to focus effectively, we consider the three functions of focusing skills:

1. Selecting topics for exploration
2. Exploring topics in depth
3. Maintaining focus and keeping on topic

Knowledge of these functions will enable you to focus sharply on relevant topics and elicit sufficient data to formulate an accurate problem assessment—a prerequisite for competent practice.

Selecting Topics for Exploration

Areas relevant for exploration vary from situation to situation. However, clients who have contact with social workers in the same setting, such as in nursing homes, group homes, or child welfare agencies, may share many common concerns.

Before meeting with clients whose concerns differ from client populations with which you are familiar, you can prepare yourself to conduct an effective exploration by developing (in consultation with your practicum instructor or field supervisor) a list of relevant and promising problem areas to be explored. This preparation will help you avoid a mistake commonly made by some beginning social workers—namely, focusing on areas irrelevant to clients' problems and eliciting reams of information of questionable utility.

EP 2.1.10d

In your initial interview with an institutionalized youth, for example, you could more effectively select questions and responses if you knew in advance that you might explore the following areas:

1. Client's own perceptions of the concerns at hand
2. Client's perceived strengths and resources
3. Reasons for being institutionalized and brief history of past problems related to legal authority and to use of drugs and alcohol
4. Details regarding the client's relationships with individual family members, both as concerns and sources of support
5. Brief family history
6. School adjustment, including information about grades, problem subjects, areas of interest, and relationships with various teachers
7. Adjustment to institutional life, including relationships with peers and supervisors
8. Peer relationships outside the institution
9. Life goals and more short-term goals
10. Reaction to previous experiences with helpers
11. Attitude toward engaging in a working relationship to address concerns

Because the institutionalized youth is an involuntary client, part of this exploration would include the youth's understanding of which parts of his work are nonnegotiable requirements, and which parts could be negotiated or free choices (Rooney, R. H., 2009).

Similarly, if you plan to interview a self-referred middle-aged woman whose major complaint is depression, the following topical areas could assist you in conducting an initial interview:

1. Concerns as she sees them, including the nature of depressive symptoms such as sleep patterns and appetite changes

2. Client's perceived strengths and resources
3. Health status, date of last physical examination, and medications being taken
4. Onset and duration of depression, previous depressive or manic episodes
5. Life events associated with onset of depression (especially losses)
6. Possible suicidal thoughts, intentions, or plans
7. Problematic thought patterns (e.g., self-devaluation, self-recrimination, guilt, worthlessness, helplessness, hopelessness)
8. Previous coping efforts, previous treatment
9. Quality of interpersonal relationships (e.g., interpersonal skills and deficiencies, conflicts and supports in marital and parent–child relationships)
10. Reactions of significant others to her depression
11. Support systems (adequacy and availability)
12. Daily activities
13. Sense of mastery versus feelings of inadequacy
14. Family history of depression or manic behavior

Because she is self-referred, this client is likely to be more voluntary than the institutionalized youth. You should therefore pay more attention to identifying the specific concerns that have led her to seek help at this point in time.

As noted previously, problem areas vary, and outlines of probable topical areas likewise vary accordingly. Thus, a list of areas for exploration in an initial session with a couple seeking marriage counseling or with a group of alcoholics will include a number of items that differ from those in the first list (i.e., the areas identified for the institutionalized youth). Note, however, that items 1, 2, and 8–11 would likely be included in all exploratory interviews with individual clients and would be equally applicable to preparatory interviews with prospective group members.

In using an outline, you should avoid following it rigidly or using it as a crutch; otherwise, you could potentially destroy the spontaneity of sessions and block clients from relating their stories in their own way. Instead, encourage your clients to discuss their problems freely while you play a facilitative role in exploring in greater depth any problems that emerge. In particular, you must use outlines flexibly—reordering the sequence of topics; modifying, adding, or deleting topics; or abandoning the outline altogether if using it hinders communication. You need to be alert to pacing related to appropriate depth and breadth given the time available.

Of course, you cannot always anticipate fruitful topical areas. After all, although clients from the same population may share many commonalities, their problems inevitably have unique aspects. For this reason, it is important to review tapes of sessions with your practicum instructor or a field supervisor for the purpose of identifying other topical areas you should explore in future sessions.

Exploring Topics in Depth

A major facet of focusing is centering discussions on relevant topics to assure that exploration moves from generality and superficiality to greater depth and meaning. Social workers must have the skills needed to explore problems thoroughly, because their success in the helping process depends on their ability to obtain clear and accurate definitions of problems.

EP 2.1.10d

Selectively attending to specific topics is challenging for beginning social workers, who often wander in individual or group sessions, repeatedly skipping across the surface of vital areas of content and feelings, and eliciting largely superficial and sometimes distorted information. This tendency is illustrated in the following excerpt from a first session with an adolescent in a school setting:

Social worker: Tell me about your family.

Client: My father is ill and my mother is dead, so we live with my sister.

Social worker: How are things with you and your sister?

Client: Good. We get along fine. She treats me pretty good.

Social worker: How about your father?

Client: We get along pretty well. We have our problems, but most of the time things are okay. I don't really see him very much.

Social worker: Tell me about school. How are you getting along here?

Client: Well, I don't like it very well, but my grades are good enough to get me by.

Social worker: I notice you're new to our school this year. How did you do in the last school you attended?

By focusing superficially on the topics of family and school, this social worker misses opportunities to explore potential problem areas in the depth necessary to illuminate the client's situation. Not surprisingly, this exploration yielded little information of value, in large part because the social worker failed to employ responses that focused in depth on topical areas. In the next sections, we further delineate the skills that will considerably enhance a social worker's ability to maintain focus on specific areas.

Open-Ended Responses

Social workers may employ open-ended responses throughout individual, conjoint, and group sessions to focus unobtrusively on desired topics. Earlier we noted that some open-ended responses leave clients free to choose their own topics, whereas others focus on a topic but encourage clients to respond freely to that topic. The following examples, taken from an initial session with a mother of eight children who has depression, illustrate how social workers can employ open-ended responses to define topical areas that may yield a rich trove of information vital to grasping the dynamics of the client's problems.[2]

- *"What have you thought that you might like to accomplish in our work together?"*
- *"You've discussed many topics in the last few minutes. Could you pick the most important one and tell me more about it?"*
- *"You've mentioned that your oldest son doesn't come home after school as he did before and help you with the younger children. I would like to hear more about that."*
- *"Several times as you've mentioned your concern that your husband may leave you, your voice has trembled. I wonder if you could share what you are feeling."*
- *"You've indicated that your partner doesn't help you enough with the children. You also seem to be saying that you feel overwhelmed and inadequate in managing the children by yourself. Tell me what happens as you try to manage your children."*
- *"You indicate that you have more problems with your 14-year-old daughter than with the other children. Tell me more about Janet and your problems with her."*

In the preceding examples, the social worker's open-ended questions and responses progressively moved the exploration from the general to the specific. Note also that each response or question defined a new topic for exploration.

To encourage in-depth exploration of the topics defined in this way, the social worker must blend open-ended questions with other facilitative verbal following responses that focus on and elicit expanded client expressions. After having defined a topical area by employing an open-ended response, for instance, the social worker might deepen the exploration by weaving other open-ended responses into the discussion. If the open-ended responses shift the focus to another area, however, the exploration suffers a setback. Note in the following exchange how the social worker's second open-ended response shifts the focus away from the client's message, which involves expression of intense feelings:

Social worker: You've said you're worried about retiring. I'd appreciate you sharing more about your concern. *[Open-ended response.]*

Client: I can't imagine not going to work every day. I feel at loose ends already, and I haven't even quit work. I'm afraid I just won't know what to do with myself.

Social worker: How do you imagine spending your time after retiring? *[Open-ended response.]*

Even though open-ended responses may draw out new information about clients' problems, they may not facilitate the helping process if they prematurely lead the client in a different direction. If social workers utilize open-ended or other types of responses that frequently change the topic, they will obtain information that is disjointed and fragmented. As a result, assessments will suffer from large gaps in the social worker's knowledge concerning clients' problems. As social workers formulate open-ended responses, they must be acutely aware of the direction that responses will take.

Seeking Concreteness

Earlier we discussed and illustrated the various facets of seeking concreteness. Because seeking concreteness enables social workers to move from the general to the specific and to explore topics in depth, it is a key focusing technique. We illustrate this ability in an excerpt from a session involving a client with a serious and persistent mental illness:

Client: I just don't have energy to do anything. This medicine really knocks me out.

Social worker: It sounds as if the side effects of your medication are of concern. Can you tell me specifically what those side effects have been?

By focusing in depth on topical areas, social workers are able to discern—and to assist clients to discern—problematic thoughts, behavior, and interaction. Subsequent sections consider how social workers can effectively focus on topical areas in exploratory sessions

by blending concreteness with other focusing skills. In actuality, the majority of responses that social workers typically employ to establish and maintain focus are blends of various types of discrete responses.

Empathic Responding

Empathic responding serves a critical function by enabling social workers to focus in depth on troubling feelings, as illustrated in the next example:

Client: I can't imagine not going to work every day. I feel at loose ends already, and I haven't even quit work. I'm afraid I just won't know what to do with myself.

Social worker: You seem to be saying, "Even now, I'm apprehensive about retiring. I'm giving up something that has been very important to me, and I don't seem to have anything to replace it." I gather that feeling at loose ends, as you do, you worry that when you retire, you'll feel useless.

Client: I guess that's a large part of my problem. Sometimes I feel useless now. I just didn't take time over the years to develop any hobbies or to pursue any interests. I guess I don't think that I can do anything else.

Social worker: It sounds as if part of you feels hopeless about the future, as if you have done everything you can do. And yet I wonder if another part of you might think that it isn't too late to look into some new interests.

Client: I do dread moping around home with time on my hands. I can just see it now. My wife will want to keep me busy doing things around the house for her all the time. I've never liked to do that kind of thing. I suppose it is never too late to look into other interests. I have always wanted to write some things for fun, not just for work. You know, the memory goes at my age, but I have thought about just writing down some of the family stories.

Note how the client's problem continued to unfold as the social worker utilized empathic responding, revealing rich information in the process. The social worker also raises the possibility of new solutions, not just dwelling in the feelings of uselessness.

Blending Open-Ended, Empathic, and Concrete Responses to Maintain Focus

After employing open-ended responses to focus on a selected topic, social workers should use other responses to maintain focus on that topic. In the following excerpt, observe how the social worker employs both open-ended and empathic responses to explore problems in depth, thereby enabling the client to move to the heart of her struggle. Notice also the richness of the client's responses elicited by the blended messages.

Social worker: As you were speaking about your son, I sensed some pain and reluctance on your part to talk about him. I'd like to understand more about what you're feeling. Could you share with me how it is for you to be talking about him? *[Blended empathic and open-ended response that seeks concreteness.]*

Client: I guess I haven't felt too good about coming this morning. I almost called and canceled. I feel I should be able to handle these problems with Jim [son] myself. Coming here is like having to admit I'm no longer capable of coping with him.

Social worker: So you've had reservations about coming *[paraphrase]*—you feel you're admitting defeat and that perhaps you've failed or that you're inadequate—and that hurts. *[Empathic response.]*

Client: Well, yes, although I know that I need some help. It's just hard to admit it, I think. My biggest problem in this regard, however, is my husband. He feels much more strongly than I do that we should manage this problem ourselves, and he really disapproves of my coming in.

Social worker: So even though it's painful for you, you're convinced you need some assistance with Jim, but you're torn about coming here because of your husband's attitude. I'd be interested in hearing more about that. *[Blended empathic and open-ended response.]*

In the preceding example, the social worker initiated discussion of the client's here-and-now experiences through a blended open-ended and empathic response, following it with other empathic and blended responses to explore the client's feelings further. With the last response, the social worker narrowed the focus to a potential obstacle to the helping process (the husband's attitude toward therapy), which could also be explored in a similar manner.

Open-ended and empathic responses may also be blended to facilitate and encourage discussion from group members about a defined topic. For instance, after using an open-ended response to solicit group feedback regarding a specified topic ("I'm wondering how you feel about …"), the social worker can employ empathic or other facilitative responses to acknowledge

the contribution of members who respond to the invitation to comment.

By utilizing open-ended responses, the social worker can successively reach for comments of individual members who have not contributed ("What do you think about …, Ray?").

In the next example, the social worker blends empathic and concrete responses to facilitate in-depth exploration. Notice how these blended responses yield behavioral referents of the problem. The empathic messages convey the social worker's sensitive awareness and concern for the client's distress. The open-ended and concrete responses focus on details of a recent event and yield valuable clues that the client's rejections by women may be associated with insensitive and inappropriate social behavior. Awareness of this behavior is a prelude to formulating relevant goals. Goals formulated in this way are highly relevant to the client.

Single male client, age 20: There has to be something wrong with me, or women wouldn't treat me like a leper. Sometimes I feel like I'm doomed to be alone the rest of my life. I'm not even sure why I came to see you. I think I'm beyond help.

Social worker: You sound like you've given up on yourself—as though you're utterly hopeless. At the same time, it seems like part of you still clings to hope and wants to try. *[Empathic response.]*

Client: What else can I do? I can't go on like this, but I don't know how many more times I can get knocked down and get back up.

Social worker: I sense you feel deeply hurt and discouraged at those times. Could you give me a recent example of when you felt you were being knocked down? *[Blended empathic and concrete response.]*

Client: Well, a guy I work with got me a blind date for a dance. I took her, and it was a total disaster. I figured that she would at least let me take her home. After we got to the dance, she ignored me the whole night and danced with other guys. Then, to add insult to injury, she went home with one of them and didn't even have the decency to tell me. There I was, wondering what had happened to her.

Social worker: Besides feeling rejected, you must have been very mad. When did you first feel you weren't hitting it off with her? *[Blended empathic and concrete response.]*

Client: I guess it was when she lit up a cigarette while we were driving to the dance. I kidded her about how she was asking for lung cancer.

Social worker: I see. What was it about her reaction, then, that led you to believe you might not be in her good graces? *[Concrete response.]*

Client: Well, she didn't say anything. She just smoked her cigarette. I guess I really knew then that she was upset at me.

Social worker: As you look back at it now, what do you think you might have said to repair things at that point? *[Stimulating reflection about problem solving.]*

In the next example, observe how the social worker blends empathic and concrete responses to elicit details of interaction in an initial conjoint session. Such blending is a potent technique for eliciting specific and abundant information that bears directly on clients' problems. Responses that seek concreteness elicit details. In contrast, empathic responses enable social workers to stay attuned to clients' moment-by-moment experiencing, thereby focusing on feelings that may present obstacles to the exploration.

Social worker: You mentioned having difficulties communicating. I'd like you to give me an example of a time when you felt you weren't communicating effectively, and let's go through it step by step to see if we can understand more clearly what is happening.

Wife: Well, weekends are an example. Usually I want to go out and do something fun with the kids, but John just wants to stay home. He starts criticizing me for wanting to go, go, go.

Social worker: Could you give me a specific example? *[Seeking concreteness.]*

Wife: Okay. Last Saturday I wanted all of us to go out to eat and then to a movie, but John wanted to stay home and watch TV.

Social worker: Before we get into what John did, let's stay with you for a moment. There you are, really wanting to go to a movie—tell me exactly what you did. *[Seeking concreteness.]*

Wife: I think I said, "John, let's take the kids out to dinner and a movie."

Social worker: Okay. That's what you said. How did you say it? *[Seeking concreteness.]*

Wife: I expected him to say no, so I might not have said it the way I just did.

Social worker: Turn to John, and say it the way you may have said it then. *[Seeking concreteness.]*

Wife: Okay. *[Turning to husband.]* Couldn't we go out to a movie?

Social worker: There seems to be some doubt in your voice as to whether John wants to go out. *[Focusing observation.]*

Wife *[interrupting]:* I knew he wouldn't want to.

Social worker: So you assumed he wouldn't want to go. It's as though you already knew the answer. *[To husband.]* Does the way your wife asked the question check out with the way you remembered it? *[Husband nods.]*

Social worker: After your wife asked you about going to the movie, what did you do? *[Seeking concreteness.]*

Husband: I said, nope! I wanted to stay home and relax Saturday, and I felt we could do things at home.

Social worker: So your answer was short. Apparently you didn't give her information about why you didn't want to go but just said no. Is that right? *[Focusing observation.]*

Husband: That's right. I didn't think she wanted to go anyway—the way she asked.

Social worker: What were you experiencing when you said no? *[Seeking concreteness.]*

Husband: I guess I was just really tired. I have a lot of pressures from work, and I just need some time to relax. She doesn't understand that.

Social worker: You're saying, then, "I just needed some time to get away from it all," but I take it you had your doubts as to whether she could appreciate your feelings. *[Husband nods.]* *[Turning to wife.]* Now, after your husband said no, what did you do? *[Blended empathic and concrete response.]*

Wife: I think that I started talking to him about the way he just sits around the house.

Social worker: I sense that you felt hurt and somewhat discounted because John didn't respond the way you would have liked. *[Empathic response.]*

Wife *[nods]:* I didn't think he even cared what I wanted to do.

Social worker: Is it fair to conclude, then, that the way in which you handled your feelings was to criticize John rather than to say, "This is what is happening to me?" *[Wife nods.]* *[Seeking concreteness.]*

Social worker *[to husband]:* Back, then, to our example. What did you do when your wife criticized you? *[Seeking concreteness.]*

Husband: I guess I criticized her back. I told her she needed to stay home once in a while and get some work done.

In this series of exchanges, the social worker asked questions that enabled the couple to describe the sequence of their interaction in a way that elicited key details and provided insight into unspoken assumptions and messages.

Managing Obstacles to Focusing

EP 2.1.10m

Occasionally you may find that your efforts to focus selectively and to explore topical areas in depth do not yield pertinent information. Although you have a responsibility in such instances to assess the effectiveness of your own interviewing style, you should also analyze clients' styles of communicating to determine to what extent their behaviors are interfering with your focusing efforts. Many clients seek help because they have—but are not aware of—patterns of communications or behaviors that create difficulties in relationships. In addition, involuntary clients who do not yet perceive the relationship as helping may be inclined to avoid focusing. The following list highlights common types of client communications that may challenge your efforts to focus in individual, family, and group sessions:

- *Responding with "I don't know"*
- *Changing the subject or avoiding sensitive areas*
- *Rambling from topic to topic*
- *Intellectualizing or using abstract or general terms*
- *Diverting focus from the present to the past*
- *Responding to questions with questions*
- *Interrupting excessively*
- *Failing to express opinions when asked*
- *Producing excessive verbal output*
- *Using humor or sarcasm to evade topics or issues*
- *Verbally dominating the discussion*

You can easily see how individuals who did not seek help from a social worker and want to avoid focusing might use these kinds of methods to protect their privacy. With such involuntary clients, such behaviors are likely to indicate a low level of trust and a skepticism that contact with a social worker can be helpful. You can counter repetitive behaviors and communications that divert the focus from exploring problems by tactfully drawing them to clients' attention and by assisting clients to adopt behaviors that are compatible with practice objectives. In groups, social workers must assist group members to modify behaviors that repeatedly disrupt effective focusing and communication;

otherwise, the groups will not move to the phase of group development in which most of the work related to solving problems is accomplished. Children as clients often respond at first contact in a limited, passive, nonexpressive style. This might be interpreted as noncommunicative behavior. In fact, such behavior is often what the children expect to be appropriate in interactions with strange authority figures (Evans, 2004; Hersen & Thomas, 2007; Lamb & Brown, 2006; Powell, Thomson, & Dietze, 1997).

VIDEO CASE EXAMPLE

In the video "Hanging with Hailey" (HWH), the adolescent client Hailey is apprehensive about having to see a social worker and insisting that she has done nothing wrong, has not gotten into trouble. The social worker Emily clarifies that Hailey can choose whether she wants to see a social worker, that she had not done anything wrong, but that teachers who knew her to be a good student had become concerned that something might have changed in her life to affect her school performance. By emphasizing her choice, Emily is able to allow Hailey to relax enough to share some of what is going on in her life currently.

Social workers may use many different techniques for managing and modifying client obstacles. These techniques include asking clients to communicate or behave differently; teaching, modeling for, and coaching clients to assume more effective communication styles; reinforcing facilitative responses; and selectively attending to functional behaviors.

Intervening to Help Clients Focus or Refocus

Communications that occur in group or conjoint sessions are not only complex, but may also be distractive or irrelevant. Consequently, the social worker's task of assisting members to explore the defined topics fully, rather than meander from subject to subject, is a challenging one. Related techniques that social workers can employ include highlighting or clarifying issues and bringing clients' attention to a comment or matter that has been overlooked. In such instances, the objective is not necessarily to explore the topic (although an exploration may subsequently occur), but rather to stress or elucidate important content. The social worker focuses clients' attention on communications and/or events that occurred earlier in the session or immediately preceded the social worker's focusing response. This technique is used in the following messages:

- [To son in session with parents]: *"Ray, you made an important point a moment ago that I'm not sure your parents heard. Would you please repeat your comment?"*
- [To individual]: *"I would like to return to a remark made several moments ago when you said _____. I didn't want to interrupt then. I think perhaps the remark was important enough that we should return to it now."*
- [To family]: *"Something happened just a minute ago as we were talking. [Describes event.] We were involved in another discussion then, but I made a mental note of it because of how deeply it seemed to affect all of you at the time. I think we should consider what happened for just a moment."*
- [To group member]: *"John, as you were talking a moment ago, I wasn't sure what you meant by _____. Could you clarify that for me and for others in the group?"*
- [To group]: *"A few minutes ago, we were engrossed in a discussion about _____, yet we have moved away from that discussion to one that doesn't really seem to relate to our purpose for being here. I'm concerned about leaving the other subject hanging because you were working hard to find some solutions and appeared to be close to a breakthrough."*

Because of the complexity of communications in group and family sessions, some inefficiency in the focusing process is inescapable. Nevertheless, the social worker can sharpen the group's efforts to focus and encourage more efficient use of its time by teaching effective focusing behavior. We suggest that social workers actually explain the focusing role of the group and identify desirable focusing behaviors, such as attending, active listening, and asking open-ended questions. During this discussion, it is important to emphasize that by utilizing these skills, members will facilitate exploration of problems.

Social workers can encourage greater use of these skills by giving positive feedback to group or family members when they have adequately focused on a problem, thus reinforcing their efforts. Indeed, given the difficulties in encouraging some clients to speak even minimally, some social workers can be so relieved to have a verbal client that they neglect use of their focusing

skills that might the session most valuable and useful to the client. Although group members usually experience some difficulty in learning how to focus, they should be able to delve deeply into problems by the third or fourth session, given sufficient guidance and education by social workers. Such efforts by social workers tend to accelerate movement of groups toward maturity, a phase in which members achieve maximum therapeutic benefits. A characteristic of a group in this phase, in fact, is that members explore issues in considerable depth rather than skim the surface of many topics.

Summarizing Responses

The technique of summarization embodies four distinct and yet related facets:

1. Highlighting key aspects of discussions of specific problems before changing the focus of the discussion
2. Making connections between relevant aspects of lengthy client messages
3. Reviewing major focal points of a session and tasks that clients plan to work on before the next session
4. Recapitulating the highlights of a previous session and reviewing clients' progress on tasks during the week for the purpose of providing focus and continuity between sessions

Although employed at different times and in different ways, each of these facets of summarization serves the common purpose of tying together functionally related elements that occur at different points in the helping process. They are considered in detail in the following sections.

Highlighting Key Aspects of Problems

During the phase of an initial session in which problems are explored in moderate depth, summarization can be effectively employed to tie together and highlight essential aspects of a problem before proceeding to explore additional problems. For example, the social worker might describe how the problem appears to be produced by the interplay of several factors, including external pressures, overt behavioral patterns, unfulfilled needs and wants, and covert thoughts and feelings. Connecting these key elements assists clients in gaining a more accurate and complete perspective of their circumstances.

Employed in this fashion, summarization involves fitting pieces of the problem together to form a coherent whole. Seeing the situation in a fresh and more accurate perspective often proves beneficial, because it expands clients' awareness and can generate hope and enthusiasm for tackling an issue that has hitherto seemed insurmountable.

Summarization that highlights problems is generally employed at a natural point in the session when the social worker believes that relevant aspects of the problem have been adequately explored and clients appear satisfied in having had the opportunity to express their concerns. The following example illustrates this type of summarization. In this case, the client, an 80-year-old widow, has been referred to a Services to Seniors program for exploration of alternative living arrangements because of her failing health, isolation, and recent falls. As the two have worked together to explore alternative living arrangements, the pair have identified several characteristics that would be important for the client in an improved living situation. Highlighting the salient factors, the social worker summarizes the results to this point:

Social worker: It sounds as if you are looking for a situation in which there is social interaction but your privacy is also important to you: You want to maintain your independence. You also want to have someone available to help in emergencies and some assistance with cooking and cleaning.

Summarizing responses of this type serve as a prelude to the process of formulating goals, as goals flow naturally from problem formulations. Moreover, highlighting various dimensions of the problem facilitates the subsequent identifications of subgoals and tasks that must be accomplished to achieve the overall goal. In the preceding example, to explore an improved living situation, the social worker would help the client analyze the specific form of privacy (whether living alone or with someone else) and the type of social interaction (how much and what kind of contact with others) she desires.

Summarizing salient aspects of problems is a valuable technique in sessions with groups, couples, and families. It enables the social worker to stop at timely moments and highlight the difficulties experienced by each participant. In a family session with a pregnant adolescent and her mother, for example, the social worker might make the following statements:

• [To pregnant adolescent]: *"You feel as if deciding what to do about this baby is your decision—it's your body and you have decided that an abortion is the best solution for you. You know that you have the legal right to make this decision and want to be supported in making it. You feel as if your mother wants to help but can't tell you what decision to make."*

• [To mother]: *"As you spoke, you seemed saddened and very anxious about this decision your daughter is making. You are saying 'I care about my daughter, but I don't think she is mature enough to make this decision on her own.' As you have noted, women in your family have had a hard time conceiving, and you wish that she would consider other options besides abortion. So you feel a responsibility to your daughter, but also to this unborn baby and the family history of conceiving children."*

Such responses synthesize in concise and neutral language the needs, concerns, and problems of each participant for all other members of the session to hear. This type of summarization underscores the fact that all participants are struggling with and have responsibility for problems that are occurring, thus counteracting the tendency of families to view one person as the exclusive cause of family problems.

Summarizing Lengthy Messages

Clients' messages range from one word or one sentence to lengthy and sometimes rambling monologues. Although the meaning and significance of brief messages are often readily discernible, lengthy messages challenge the social worker to encapsulate and tie together diverse and complex elements. Linking the elements together often highlights and expands the significance and meaning of the client's message. For this reason, such messages represent one form of additive empathy, a skill discussed in Chapter 17.

Because lengthy client messages typically include emotions, thoughts, and descriptive content, you will need to determine how these dimensions relate to the focal point of the discussion. To illustrate, consider the following message of a mildly brain-damaged and socially withdrawn 16-year-old female—an only child who is extremely dependent on her overprotective but subtly rejecting mother:

Client: Mother tells me she loves me, but I find that hard to believe. Nothing I do ever pleases her; she yells at me when I refuse to wash my hair alone. But I can't do it right without her help. "When are you going to grow up?" she'll say. And she goes out with her friends and leaves me alone in that old house. She knows how scared I get when I have to stay home alone. But she says, "Nancy, I can't just babysit you all the time. I've got to do something for myself. Why don't you make some friends or watch TV or play your guitar? You've just got to quit pitying yourself all the time." Does that sound like someone who loves you? I get so mad at her when she yells at me; it's all I can do to keep from killing her.

Embodied in the client's message are the following elements:

1. Wanting to be loved by her mother, yet feeling insecure and rejected at times
2. Feeling inadequate about performing certain tasks, such as washing her hair
3. Feeling extremely dependent upon her mother for certain services and companionship
4. Feeling afraid when her mother leaves her alone
5. Feeling hurt (implied) and resentful when her mother criticizes her or leaves her alone
6. Feeling intense anger and wanting to lash out when her mother yells at her

The following summarizing response ties these elements together:

Social worker: So you find your feelings toward your mother pulling you in different directions. You want her to love you, but you feel unloved and resent it when she criticizes you or leaves you alone. And you feel really torn because you depend on her in so many ways. Yet at times, you feel so angry you want to hurt her back for yelling at you. You'd like to have a smoother relationship without the strain.

In conjoint interviews or group sessions, summarization can also be used effectively to highlight and to tie together key elements and dynamics embodied in transactions, as illustrated in the following transaction and summarizing responses of a social worker:

VIDEO CASE EXAMPLE

In the conjoint interview entitled "HFH, Part 1," partners who come to family treatment are in conflict about how open to be about their relationship to their families. Jackie comes from a family in which there is open communication. She is frustrated with the reticence to deal openly with feelings that is reflected in Anna's family. Kim, the social worker, makes the following summarizing statement: "Often when we are forming new families and new couples we are torn between the families we come from and the new family we are creating. This can play out in logistical decisions about the holidays."

Occasionally, client messages may ramble to the extent that they contain numerous unrelated elements that cannot all be tied together. In such instances, your task is to extract and focus on those elements of the message that are most relevant to the thrust of the session at that point. When employed in this manner, summarization provides focus and direction to the session and averts aimless wandering. With clients whose thinking is loose or who ramble to avoid having to focus on unpleasant matters, you may need to interrupt to assure some semblance of focus and continuity. Otherwise, the interview will be disjointed and unproductive. Skills in maintaining focus and continuity are discussed later in this chapter and in Chapter 13.

Reviewing Focal Points of a Session

During the course of an individual, conjoint, or group session, it is common to focus on more than one problem and to discuss numerous factors associated with each problem. Toward the end of the first or second session, depending on the length of the initial exploration, summarization is employed to review key concerns that have been discussed and to highlight themes and patterns related to these problems. Summarizing themes and patterns expands each client's awareness of concerns and tunes them in to promising avenues for addressing those concerns, awareness of opportunities and potential resources.

In fact, through summarizing responses, social workers can review themes and patterns that have emerged in their sessions and test clients' readiness to consider goals aimed at modifying these problematic patterns.

VIDEO CASE EXAMPLE

In the video "GBS" Dorothy, the social worker, summarizes: "You have had a lot of stress at work with a poor performance review and anxiety that your co-workers are being rude to you over the possibility that you might get promoted. At home, you are dealing with your mother, who is living with you; your son and his girlfriend not working outside of the home and their baby; your daughter who helps take care of the little ones. All of the work of keeping up the household comes back to you. You are not eating, not sleeping very well, and have lost interest in some things you used to like to do."

Providing Focus and Continuity

The social worker can also use summarization at the beginning of an individual, group, or conjoint session to review work that clients have accomplished in the last session(s) and to set the stage for work in the present session. At the same time, the social worker may decide to identify a promising topic for discussion or to refresh clients' minds concerning work they wish to accomplish in that session. In addition, summarization can be employed periodically to synthesize salient points at the conclusion of a discussion or used at the end of the session to review the major focal points. In so doing, the social worker will need to place what was accomplished in the session within the broad perspective of the clients' goals. The social worker tries to consider how the salient content and movement manifested in each session fit into the larger whole. Only then are the social worker and clients likely to maintain a sense of direction and avoid needless delays caused by wandering and detours—problems that commonly occur when continuity within or between sessions is weak.

Used as a "wrap-up" when the allotted time for a session is nearly gone, summarization assists the social worker to draw a session to a natural conclusion. In addition to highlighting and linking together the key points of the session, the social worker reviews clients' plans for performing tasks before the next session. When the session ends with such a summarization, all participants should be clear about where they have been and where they are going in relation to the goals toward which their mutual efforts are directed.

Analyzing Your Verbal Following Skills

After taking frequency counts over a period of time of some of the major verbal following skills (accents, reflections, paraphrases, concreteness, open-ended and closed-ended responses), you are ready to assess the extent to which you employ, blend, and balance these skills in relation to each other. On the form for recording verbal following (Figure 6-2), categorize each of your responses from a recorded session. As you analyze your relative use and blending of responses alone or with your practicum instructor, determine whether certain types of responses were used either too frequently or too sparingly. Think of steps that you might take to correct any imbalances in your utilization of skills for future sessions.

CLIENT MESSAGE	OPEN-ENDED RESPONSES	CLOSE-ENDED RESPONSES	EMPATHIC RESPONSES	LEVEL OF EMPATHY	CONCRETE RESPONSES	SUMMA-RIZING RESPONSES	OTHER TYPES OF RESPONSES
1.							
2.							
3.							
4.							
5.							
6.							
7.							

Directions: Categorize each of your responses from a recorded session. Where responses involve more than one category (blended responses), record them as a single response, but also check each category embodied in the response. Excluding the responses checked as "Other Type of Responses," analyze whether certain types of responses were utilized too frequently or too sparingly. Define tasks for yourself to correct imbalances in future sessions. Retain a copy of the form so that you can monitor your progress in mastering verbal following skills over an extended period of time.

FIG-6-2 Recording Form for Verbal Following Skills

Summary

This chapter has helped you learn how to explore, paraphrase, and appropriately use closed- and open-ended responses as a means of better focusing, following, and summarizing in your social work practice. These skills may be applied both with clients and with other persons and colleagues, on behalf of clients. In Chapter 7, we will explore some common difficulties experienced by beginning social workers and some ways to overcome them.

Competency Notes

EP 2.1.1d A social worker demonstrates professional demeanor in behavior, appearance and communication (p. 150).

EP 2.1.4c Social workers recognize and communicate their understanding of the importance of difference in shaping life experiences (p. 136).

EP 2.1.4d Social workers view themselves as learners and engage those with whom they work as informants (p. 1).

EP 2.1.10a Substantively and affectively prepare for action with individuals, families, groups, organizations, and communities (p. 135).

EP 2.1.10b Use empathy and other interpersonal skills. Social workers use verbal following skills such as furthering, paraphrasing, reflecting, summarizing, open and closed ended questions (p. 136).

EP 2.1.10d Collect organize and interpret data (pp. 152, 153).

EP 2.1.10g Select appropriate intervention strategies (pp. 136, 140).

EP 2.1.10m Critically analyze monitor and evaluate interventions (p. 157).

Modeled Responses to Exercise in Paraphrasing

1. "You just get so uptight in a group you don't function."
2. "So you've made some real progress in tuning in to your husband and children."
3. "So people's helpfulness here and your own skills in meeting people have helped your adjustment here."
4. "So you see yourself as having contributed to many of her problems."

5. "It sounds as if your experience causes you to doubt whether more services would be helpful. Could you tell me about your feeling that the mother is not motivated?"

Modeled Responses to Exercise in Reflection

1. "Because your fears really block you when you argue with your mother, you seem to feel anxious and frustrated." (simple reflection)
2. "So you feel caught by competing parenting and work responsibilities; if you meet all your work hours, you are concerned about how it affects your parenting. If you do what you think you should as a parent, it can conflict with work requirements." (double-sided reflection)
3. "So sometimes you feel cheated by life and at other times that your illness is a consequence for your smoking history." (double-sided reflection)
4. "So it sounds as if it has not been easy for you to relax and have friends in this school; when they have acted in a way that feels mean to you, you have felt a need to act to protect yourself." (simple reflection)
5. "You're really torn and wonder if not seeing the children very often is too high a price to pay for a divorce. On the other hand, you fear that if you stay with her, there won't be any improvement. Right now you don't see a way out of this dilemma." (reflection with a twist)

Answers to Exercise in Identifying Closed- and Open-Ended Responses

Statement	Response
1	C
2	O
3	O
4	C

Modeled Open-Ended Responses

1. "Could you tell me more about your wanting to impress Ralph?"
2. "What are you afraid you'd do wrong?"

3. "Given your experience with that probation officer, how would you like your relationship with me to be?"

4. "So you feel that your facility cannot provide what Gladys needs. Can you describe the kind of care you believe she needs?"

5. "So you don't trust that I want to try to help you make what you feel will be the best decision. Can you tell me what I have done that has caused you to think that your mother and I are allies?"

6. "You sound as if you are at a pretty hopeless point right now. When you say you don't know if you want to keep trying to figure it out, can you tell me more about what you are thinking about doing?"

Notes

1. In the Motivational Interviewing approach, reflection refers to the process of using new words to describe either the content of a message or emotions entailed. We have chosen to follow Hackney and Cormier's (2005) description of paraphrasing as the use of new words to describe the content of a message. We have reserved the term reflection to refer to the use of fresh words to express an emotion.

2. Note that several of these messages could also be categorized as seeking concreteness. Messages that seek concreteness and open-ended messages are not mutually exclusive; indeed, they often overlap to a considerable extent

CourseMate

Access an integrated eBook and chapter-specific learning tools including glossary terms, chapter outlines, relevant web links, videos, and practice quizzes. Go to **www.cengagebrain.com**.

Developing Resources, Organizing, Planning, and Advocacy as Intervention Strategies

CHAPTER OVERVIEW

Chapter 14 transitions from direct practice intervention to macro-level change strategies. In this chapter you will become familiar with macro-level problem-solving activities where the change effort is directed toward systems rather than towards the individual. The chapter concludes with a discussion of general guidelines for evaluating macro practice outcomes.

As a result of reading this chapter you will acquire knowledge that will enable you to:

- **Understand macro practice intervention strategies**
- **Understand the connection between micro problems and macro practice**
- **Use the social justice perspective to analyze social problems and conditions**
- **Become familiar with skills used for social action, advocacy, and community organizing**
- **Understand your role as a change agent**
- **Apply social work ethical principles and standards to macro practice**
- **Evaluate macro practice activities**

EPAS COMPETENCIES IN THE 14TH CHAPTER

This chapter provides information that you will need to meet the following practice competencies:

2.1.1a Advocate for client access to services

2.1.1d Demonstrate professional demeanor in behavior, appearance, and communication

2.1.4b Gain sufficient self-awareness to eliminate the influence of personal biases and values in working with diverse groups

2.1.4a Recognize the extent to which culture's structures and values alienate, create, or enhance power and privilege

2.1.4d View themselves as learners and engage those with whom they work as key informants

2.1.5a Understand forms and mechanisms of oppression and discrimination

2.1.5b Advocate for human rights and social and economic justice

2.1.5c Engage in practices that engage in social and economic justice

2.1.6b Use research evidence to inform practice

2.1.8a Analyze, formulate, and advocate for policies that advance social well-being

2.1.9a Continuously discover, appraise, and attend to changing locales, populations, scientific and technological developments, and emerging societal trends to provide relevant services

2.1.9b Provide leadership in promoting sustainable changes in service delivery and practice to improve the quality of social services

2.1.10a Substantively and effectively prepare for action with individuals, families, groups, and communities

2.1.10b Use empathy and other interpersonal skills

2.1.10c Develop mutually agreed-upon focus of work and desired outcomes

2.1.10d Collect and organize client data

2.1.10e Assess client strengths and limitations

2.1.10g Select appropriate intervention strategy

2.1.10h Initiate action to achieve organizational goals

2.1.2d Apply strategies of ethical reasoning skills to arrive at principled decisions

Social Work's Commitment

Brueggemann (2006) and Schneider and Lester (2001) trace the historical commitment of the profession of social work to the ideal of improving the human condition through social reform, social justice, and equality. These longstanding ideals are practice principles that are reflected in the National Association of Social Workers (NASW) Code of Ethics and the Council of Social Work Education (CSWE) Educational Policy Accreditation Standards (EPAS) for the professional educational preparation of social workers. Guided by the ethical principles of NASW, professional social workers are obligated to enhance the welfare of individuals and improve social conditions by developing resources, planning, and engaging in social action (NASW, 1996). Promoting social and economic justice and improving social conditions to include populations at risk are overarching principles articulated in EPAS. These principles underscore the profession's commitment "to advance human rights and social and economic justice" and to ensure that social workers are prepared to "engage in policy practice to advance social and economic well-being, and to deliver effective social work services" (CSWE, 2008, pp. 5–6).

Global standards that frame the core purpose of international social work also emphasize social action, political action, and advocacy, "to facilitate the inclusion of marginalized, socially excluded, dispossessed, and vulnerable at-risk groups of people" (Global Standards for Social Work Education and Training, 2004, p. 3). Fundamental among the principles of international social work are respect for diverse beliefs, traditions, and cultures as well as regard for human rights and social justice. Similarly, these principles are articulated in the NASW Standards for Cultural Competence in Social Work Practice (NASW, 2001).

The ethical standards and educational policy statements of the national professional organizations regarding economic and social justice and equality are hardly the exclusive domains of social work as a profession. There are organizations, including faith communities, that articulate similar principles and that engage in social action and advocacy. The profession of social work, however, has embraced these principles as organizing values. Urging the profession to go a step further in its social justice agenda, Hodge (2007) points to the need of the profession to advocate for a *Universal Declaration of Human Rights*, in particular, for religious freedom and to work toward ending religious persecution on a national and global level. Like Hodge, McKinnon (2008) advocates for expanding the ecological focus in the profession to include the challenges of the physical environment and its impact on people.

Defining Macro Practice

By definition, macro practice involves professionally guided interventions in which the targets are social problems and conditions. As summarized by Brueggemann (2006, p. 7), macro social work is the "practice of helping people solve social problems and make social change at the community, organizational, societal and global levels." In essence, a distinctive feature of macro-level interventions is that seeing the whole picture and intervening can ultimately change and improve the lives of people (Burghardt, 2011; Parsons, Jorgensen, & Hernandez, 1988, 1994; Long, Tice, & Morrison, 2006). In the course of examining the whole picture, you are able to determine the impact on human behavior (Alexander, 2010; McKinnon, 2008; Saleeby, 2004).

Historically, the profession's capacity to see a relationship between people and their environment can be traced to the belief system that guided the work of the Settlement House Movement. Settlement House workers believed that improving social conditions and changing the social and economic environment through advocacy, community organizing, and social action, would ultimately improve the functioning of the individual and the community. Reminiscent of this movement, Breton (2006) asserts "there is a dialectical relationship between social change and personal change" (p. 34). Recall the case of Angela and Irwin Corning. The loss of Irwin's job and the subsequent loss of their home typify the plight of millions of Americans, as well as citizens in other countries. In helping the couple to regain a sense of equilibrium in their lives, it would be important for you to be aware of the broader economic context in which their problems occurred and were sustained over time.

Linking Micro and Macro Practice

EP 2.1.10d

It is not unusual for you as a direct service practitioner to observe patterns in the prevalence of certain problems and conditions throughout your caseload. In your work with individuals and families, you are in an opportune position to make the connection between micro concerns, which may require macro strategies to remedy. There may be days in which you feel that with each individual client you are working at the edge of a much larger problem, one person at a time. You may however question your ability to act, given your role in your organization. Nonetheless, your observations of the experience of individual clients, as illustrated in Figure 14-1, can become an important linkage from micro to macro practice.

Essentially, the figure illustrates how micro level observations can inform social workers of common problems and conditions that are experienced by individuals, groups, and communities. For example, let's say that you have observed the frequency of a certain presenting problem among the people with whom you have contact. As a beginning to your inquiry as to whether your observation is in fact true, or emblematic of a large system change opportunity, you might ask yourself: *To what extent is the individual's problem pervasive among the larger group experience to which they belong?* This question enables you to obtain a snapshot of the whole picture, which leads to a macro-level assessment of a problem (Breton, 2006; Burghardt, 2011; White & Epston, 1990). Because of the dual and interlocking connection between the public and the private, there are times when a two-prong approach (specifically

a combination of micro and macro) is required to respond to needs and conditions (Long, Tice & Morrison, 2006). In essence, you bridge micro- and macro-practice strategies by addressing the individual's situation, as well as the external social and economic conditions that perpetuate their problems (Parson, Jorgenson & Hernandez, 1994; Vodde & Gallant, 2002; White & Epston, 1990)

Macro Practice Intervention Strategies

EP 2.1.10b

Targets of change at the macro-level may focus on policy analysis, organizations, communities, or groups. Irrespective of their focus, a collective, large scale intervention to effect change is a common distinctive feature of macro strategies (Burghardt, 2011). As you read this chapter, you will appreciate that knowledge and skills you learned in earlier chapters are also instrumental in macro practice. Austin, Coombs, and Barr (2005) note the uniformity in the skills of micro and macro practice. For instance, you will use both structural and interpersonal skills in macro practice as in micro practice. Structural skills include assessment, developing and planning measurable strategic goals, and monitoring and evaluating outcomes. On an interpersonal level, you will utilize oral and written communication skills, and facilitative and relationship building skills such as empathy, authenticity, genuineness, and self-awareness. Roles are also similar (e.g., educator, mediator, advocate, resource developer), although professional titles may differ. Netting, Kettner, and McMurtry (2004) have identified the professional titles associated with these roles such as supervisor, manager, program coordinator, planner, policy analyst, and community organizer.

Many different types of interventions are used to change conditions, improve environments, and respond to needs found within organizations, groups, or communities. A full discussion of the various macro-level strategies is beyond the scope of this practice foundation of this text. Instead, we will focus our discussion on selected methods and strategies associated with the following macro-level interventions:

- *Developing and mobilizing resources*
- *Advocacy and social action*
- *Community organization*
- *Improving organizational environments*
- *Organizational change*

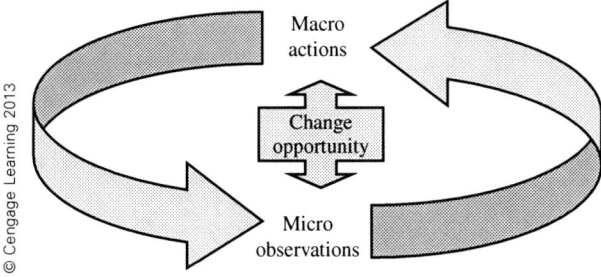

© Cengage Learning 2013

FIG-14-1 Linking Micro and Macro Practice

Before discussing each of these macro-level interventions, we will address empowerment, strengths, and social problem analysis, as relevant factors in macro practice.

Empowerment and Strengths

EP 2.1.10a

Empowerment means that groups or communities can act to prevent problems, gain or regain the capacity to interact with the social environment, and expand the resources available to meet their needs (Gutierrez, GlenMaye & Delois, 1995; Long, Tice, & Morrison, 2006; Weil, 1996). As a process, empowerment actively engages people in decisions about their well-being, potential, life satisfaction, and the outcome of realizing control over their lives to the extent possible. Empowerment also promotes social and economic justice when communities and groups are able to secure resources that have a positive influence on their lives (Long, Trice, & Morrison, 2006).

EP 2.1.10e

Why the focus on empowerment and strength? All people at various times in their lives experience limited power. But, constituents of social work, however, may include groups and entire communities who lack the power because of their minimized status in the larger social environment. Indeed, the powerless are more likely to have government agencies and public policies exert significant authority over their lives. The empowerment perspective assumes that power and powerlessness are inextricably linked to the experience of inequality. Furthermore, the lack of power is a common experience, particularly in racial and ethnic minority and poor communities.

When working with certain vulnerable groups who may have a limited sense of individual and collective efficacy, you may have the tendency to think of empowerment as giving them power. Even in these circumstances, empowerment means that you tap into and mobilize people's power by working in collaboration with them to develop their competence to alter or improve their situation (Carter, 2000; White & Epston, 1990). In essence, empowerment is a process in which you work to develop the capacity of people to change their situations (Gutierrez & Ortega, 1991). Whether you are involved in creating more favorable conditions for a group or community, for example, in developing resources or advocacy, you should be careful that your actions are not disempowering to those whom you are attempting to help. To this end, it is vital that you

observe and respect their values and beliefs and that your actions are consistent with the ethical principles of the profession.

As social workers, we respond to the needs and interests identified by groups or communities in ways that build on their strengths and that will assist them to realize their hopes, dreams, and aspirations. Recognizing strengths at the macro-level sees people as resourceful and resilient, is respectful of their stories, and works in collaboration with them to achieve a range of human and community capital goals based on their viewpoint. In your entry into a community or group, valuing their definitions of problems is vital to forging a collaborative helping relationship (Gutierrez, 1994; Gutierrez & Lewis, 1999; Long, Tice, & Morrison, 2006; Saleebey, 2004; Van Voorhis & Hostetter, 2006). Combined strengths and empowerment are critical to assisting communities and groups to develop, own, and govern their self-efficacy. In this way, the shape and influence of the change effort is directed by active community leadership (Weil, 1996; Van Voorhis & Hostetter, 2006).

Analyzing Social Problems and Conditions

Policy analysis involves understanding conditions and solving macro-level problems, which includes evaluating social justice and inequality (Barusch. 2009; Finn & Jacobson, 2003). In the traditional sense, policy analysis is a process that begins with defining the problem, gathering information, and setting strategic goals and outcomes (Bardach, 2009). The following discussion is a slight departure from policy analysis, and instead focuses on analyzing social problems and conditions using a social justice perspective as a primary lens. As social workers who are regularly in contact with people whose lives are affected by social problems and conditions and the impact of policy decision, our analysis provides us with data that can be used to inform policymakers of the realities of the lives of clients. In this way, we meet the obligation of the profession to advance clients' collective well-being.

Social justice questions that may be posed to analyze social conditions and problems are adapted from the work of Finn and Jacobson (2003b) and Segal (2010).

EP 2.1.8a

- *What are the social justice issues affecting the people with whom I work?*
- *What are the particular values expressed for groups and communities when resources are distributed in our society?*

In addition to these questions, a social justice perspective would also examine the following:

- *Who is affected by policy decisions and in what way?*
- *Does social policy have a disparate impact on a particular segment of the population?*

To these questions, we add a core question from the FrameWorks Institute:

- *Who and what is responsible for the problem?*

The FrameWorks Institute is a nonprofit organization that provides training for professionals and other advocates in "thinking strategically" about social problems and reframing issues that appeal to basic societal values when communicating with policymakers or the public.

Social Justice Issues

EP 2.1.4a

All people are born into different economic, cultural, or social circumstances. Not all people are equal in their abilities. These are facets of our society and the global community. It is, however, unacceptable by virtue of one's birth that some people are relegated to lives in which inequality and oppression are distinctive factors that diminish opportunities for some, resulting in a sustained experience of social problems or impoverished conditions. In general, there is stratification in our society in which privilege places some individuals and groups at the top, and others at a lower level (Alexander, 2010). Using social justice as a lens to examine social problems and conditions gives rise to the question of whether people at the lower stratification level have equal access to resources and to opportunities that promote their well-being, dignity, and worth; or whether they are stigmatized and marginalized because of who they are. Social justice also includes examining the nexus between the problems that people have, the conditions in which they live, and the social policies that in affect determine them, and the extent to which policy decisions adversely impact individuals, groups, and communities. For practitioners, self-evaluation requires examining the extent to which their practice with people in need supports the basic tenets of the profession regarding equality and the primacy of clients' rights, including human and civil rights. The questions posed are by no means exclusive, but rather, serve as a frame of reference by which you can use for analyzing the social problems and conditions and whether the policy decisions intended to alter social problems and conditions adversely impact groups and communities.

Values and the Distribution of Resources

EP 2.1.5b

To a large extent, social welfare services continue to be directed primarily toward individual change (Breton, 2006; Brueggemann, 2006; Long, Tice, & Morrison, 2006). Over the past several decades, this focus has been reinforced by the emphasis on personal responsibility at the expense of social justice (Linhorst, 2002). As noted by Breton (2006), the funding entities upon which social welfare organizations depend are rarely interested in collective social action. Adherence to the notion of individual change or responsibility tends to emphasize goals and values that for the most part are acceptable to society. What is acceptable to society can shift because of conflicting political and societal ideologies. For example, individual autonomy has influenced the ideological notion of personal responsibility that can be observed in social policies that are intended to respond to a range of social problems and conditions. Conversely, social responsibility, a collective ideological view point, emphasizes that social conditions and problems are beyond the individual's ability to resolve and, as such, calls for a more comprehensive policy response (Breton, 2006; Segal, 2010). From a social justice perspective, you might question whether personal or social responsibility contributes to the rights and well-being of people, in particular those without power and resources.

Who Is Affected by Policy Decisions and in What Way?

EP 2.1.8a

The Personal Responsibility and Work Opportunity Reconciliation Act of 1996 (PRWORA)—which reformed the system of public welfare—and the Adoption and Safe Family Act of 1997 (ASFA) are examples of policy decisions that affected large segments of social work constituents. The Personal Responsibility and Work Opportunity Reconciliation Act, which mainly affected poor, single women, ended a 60-year-old entitlement to cash aid, and was replaced by 60-month lifetime and work requirements. In addition, states were given discretion in the requirements that they could develop as a means to dissuade people from applying for assistance. At the same time, the Adoption and Safe Family Act emphasized greater scrutiny of the ability of poor families to care for their children, but did not take into account the removal of some of the safeguards by the PRWORA.

Undoubtedly, there was a need to reexamine both the public welfare and the child welfare systems, but the competing and conflicting demands of these two concurrent pieces of legislation resulted in many families experiencing long-term system-level difficulties in meeting requirements and timelines. Ultimately, the burden of the corrective action undertaken in both welfare reform and child-welfare reform fell on individuals. An assumption inherent in child welfare policy was that neglectful parents and their lack of parental responsibility were the primary culprits affecting their ability to meet the reunification and permanency timelines. However, the review of the delays in permanency and reunification failed to consider the possibility that the excess time that a child remained in care resulted from an overloaded, underfunded, and fragmented system. In much the same manner, a core belief driving welfare reform was the idea that people receiving public assistance lacked motivation to work. In reality, the policy in effect at the time disallowed those receiving benefits from being employed. There is research evidence that suggests a relationship between welfare reform and a significant increase in reports of child maltreatment and neglect (Courtney, 1999; Hutson, 2001).

Disparate Impact and Social Justice

EP 2.1.5b

Implementation of both the welfare assistance and child welfare policies had an uneven impact on segments of the population, and in particular on minority communities, which raised questions about justice and inequality. In both instances, the implementation of these policies affected women as heads of household in single-parent families and communities of color. As social workers, we are in contact with individuals and families who are affected by policy decisions. Therefore, we have access to a wealth of information that can be used to inform policymakers of the realities of our clients' lives. To this point, consider the following discussion of policies related to PWORA and AFSA and their long-term implications for social and economic well-being. Also, think about your role as a social worker in responding to the issues presented.

Leaving welfare, as many recipients did, and not returning was not as easy as the policymakers imagined. The ability of welfare leavers to gain employment and sustained financial self-sufficiency was hampered by the very real presence of structural and economic barriers, such as unstable low-wage jobs, the high concentration of recipients in large urban areas, and limited supportive services (Anderson, Halter, & Gryzlak, 2004; Banerjee, 2002). Findings from studies by

Banerjee (2002) and Anderson and colleagues (2004) countered the popular image of the unmotivated, self-satisfied welfare recipient. Instead, they show women who were dissatisfied with their economic situation and the stigma attached to being on welfare, and whose aspirations were not dissimilar from mainstream society. In addition, under the new federal tax and spending decisions, states could decide how to distribute supportive resources and what services to provide; for example, whether or not to provide funds for child care, and if provided, for how long (Abramovitz, 2005; Linhorst, 2002). Ultimately these decisions had an impact on the level of services available to welfare leavers through nonprofit organizations and both county and state programs.

Given the reality of the structural and economic barriers faced by welfare leavers that influenced the availability of jobs and limited supportive services (for example, the recession), are the sanctions and penalties against those who are unable to achieve work just?

Disparate impact on clients can also be measured in what a policy requires of practitioners in so far as it intrudes on their ability to engage in practice that is consistent with the standards and principals of the social work profession. For

EP 2.1.4a

example, at issue for many social workers is the fact that their work has little to do with professional practice, such as developing or helping clients find resources. Because of federal and state compliance mandates and performance benchmarks for agencies and client compliance, social workers likened their role to that of a compliance officer or investigator, rather than that of a professional helper, raising ethical dilemmas (Abramovitz, 2005; Withorn, 1998).

While Withorn (1998) questioned the ethics and justice of welfare reform, a study by Abramovitz (2005) highlighted the ethical tensions experienced by social workers and agency administrators as they attempted to balance policy compliance with mandates for clients and ethical practice. A particular area of concern related to protecting client's rights and autonomy, while also responding to performance-based agency contracts that ignored their choices. For example, the "work first mandate" meant that participants were required to find employment rather than pursuing or continuing educational opportunities (Banerjee, 2002). These ethical tensions are also intertwined with just practice. Specifically, do policy mandates, penalties, and performance-based evaluation further disenfranchise and marginalize people by constraining their choices and forcing them to make decisions that are not in their best or long-term interest?

EP 2.1.8a

As another example of the disparate impact of a policy, consider the Adoption and Safe Family Act (AFSA, 1997). This public policy was intended to move children to permanent homes. Specific timelines were enacted to ensure that children did not languish within the child welfare system. For instance, parents were given 12 months to rectify the circumstances that prompted a child's placement in foster care and to achieve reunification. During this time period, a permanency alternative for the child or children would be pursued. Because of the number of children in foster care who remained in limbo for lengthy periods of time, the goal of permanency was an overdue initiative. But, the wisdom of the abbreviated time period is called into question as a matter of justice in light of concurrent planning. Concurrent planning involves the simultaneous planning for both reunification and adoption as permanent outcomes for children who are placed outside of their home (Curtis and Denby, 2004). A specific justice concern centered on the fact that resources were available to potential foster/adoptive parents but not uniformly so for biological parents. Moreover, the restrictive timelines and limited services led to an increase in the termination of parental rights of poor and minority parents.

The implementation of this law disproportionately affected specific segments of communities, mainly those who were poor and minority. The impact on poor African American communities was particularly difficult because the majority of the children placed out of their homes are African Americans (Hill, 2005; Curtis & Denby, 2004; Morton, 1999). Roberts (2002) likened the child welfare system to apartheid, the effects of which constitute "group harm" because entire communities experience the impact. In fact, in large urban communities, the intervention of child welfare and child protection services may be traced to specific ZIP codes where the residents are largely poor and minority families.

EP 2.1.4a

Pervasive poverty, including homelessness, is one reason that a majority of African American and other children of color are placed out of the home. Such pervasive poverty is a cause to examine justice and disparate impact; specifically, whether poor families should lose their children because of their economic circumstances, or whether there is a need for greater economic supports for poor families. A key question to be considered in placement decisions raised by Wulczyn and Lery (2007) is whether poor parents have the resources to protect children, and, if not, what resources are needed. In large part, according to Chipungu and Bent-Goodley (2003), the child welfare system has become a "safety net for poor children" funded by Title IV-E, rather than a system that provides the services and resources that would support and sustain the family system.

Inequality and justice issues can also be considered on two other levels. In the current child welfare child protection system, there is little distinction made between child neglect and child abuse, in particular egregious harm. Hence, poverty-related neglect, a primary reason that families of color have contact with child protective services, is treated in the same criminalized and stigmatized fashion as the harm associated with child abuse. Involvement with child protection has far reaching effects on parents. An allegation of neglect, whether substantiated or not, can influence a parent's ability to obtain housing and employment. Therefore, is it just that poor families of color, who are already marginalized in many cases by pervasive poverty and other structural barriers, be further stigmatized as criminals simply because they lack the resources to care for their children?

Secondly, and perhaps foremost, is the concern related to the uncertain outcomes of out-of-home placement for children of color when measured against established and long-term expectations related to health and well-being standards. For example, funding to states is based on the number of placements, and once placement has occurred, there is little or no follow-up to determine child well-being (Munroe, 2004). It is the perception of many advocates in minority communities that out-of-home placement is a first step in the disruption of a minor's life, and a precursor to the juvenile justice system, eventually leading to a transition to adult corrections or becoming homeless. You might question the social justice of this negative trajectory of outcomes. As noted by a child welfare administrator, "In spite of the fact that everyone in the [child welfare] system wants to do the right thing, there is still an unwillingness to look critically at whether what we are doing makes a difference in a concrete way" (Robinson, 2000).

Who and What Is Responsible for the Problem?

The question of who or what is responsible for the problem is perhaps the most difficult to answer as often a multiplicity of factors are involved, including values.

EP 2.1.8a

Values frame almost all of public and private discussions about remedies to social problems. Lens (2005), noting that every "social problem has its own value constellation" emphasized the differences between a theme of compassion in discussions about universal health and welfare-to-work requirements catered to values related to independence and responsibility. Of course, responsibility assumes that all citizens have equal standing and opportunity. Inherent in the previously discussed social problems and policies is the notion of personal responsibility as opposed to that of society's responsibility to ensure equality and the well-being of all citizens. On balance, the question of *"who"* in particular is responsible appears to have overshadowed the questions of *"what"* is responsible, and, in consequence, societal obligation to resolve social problems and conditions is diminished.

Perhaps a confirming conclusion about who and what is responsible for the problem is not possible. Nonetheless, an examination of social problems and conditions is worthwhile. You should understand that the distribution of resources, limited power and representation, and structural and economic inequality are factors that negatively impact segments of the population. We know, for example, that poverty is connected to other human needs and problems. Poverty and the related stressors influence child development and education level, family stability, health, and mental health status. Poor families, and even entire communities, experience chronic stressors in their everyday lives because they lack the minimum resources required to meet their basic needs (Tolan & Gorman-Smith, 1997). In the article "Enough to Make You Sick," Epstein (2003) vividly described life in "America's rundown urban neighborhoods," noting that illnesses normally associated with old age are showing up in young, inner-city residents. A parent interviewed for the article described her life as "you wake up stressed, you go to sleep stressed." Who and what is responsible for the problem when such conditions as described relegate certain people to live under these conditions?

On balance, let's return to the values dichotomy related to personal or societal responsibility and the consequences of the values that influence policy decisions about this matter. Are people poor because they lack aspirations or because of the realities of structural barriers and social policies that have failed to adequately address this longstanding social problem? This question is worth considering because poverty has long-term implications for quality of life over the lifespan (Brooks-Gunn, 1997; Rank & Hirschl, 1999).

Findings from a study that examined the relationship between poverty and psychopathology (specifically, behavioral symptoms identified in *DSM-IV*) are encouraging. Results of this study emphasized that improved family income had a "major effect on children's psychiatric disorders" (Costello, Compton, Keeler, & Angold 2003, p. 2023). Similarly, behavioral symptoms such as oppositional defiant behavior (a common diagnosis of children in poor families) significantly decreased when family income improved.

EP 2.1.9b

Analyzing problems, conditions, and social policies provides an opportunity for you as a social worker to give voice to the powerless by framing issues so that the public becomes invested in the problem, irrespective of their values. Does the public, for example, appreciate a costly child welfare system that has uncertain or poor outcomes? What would be the public response if people had an understanding of the sanctions and penalties applied to welfare recipients for failing to comply with the 60-month lifetime limits on support without regard to their circumstances, for example, having a disabled parent or child, or the state of the economy being poor?

Breton (2006) asserts that social workers need not become revolutionaries in order to affect change. Justice work demands, however, that we as social workers articulate the consequences of social problem and conditions as well as evaluate and monitor the impact of policies on those problems or conditions. Acting on behalf of or with client groups by taking an active role and documenting the impact, outcome, and effectiveness of policies and their implementation is justice work (Breton, 2006; Jansson, 2003; Linhorst, 2002).

Different Perspectives of Social Justice

EP 2.1.4a

Many of the shortcomings in social policies and services can be traced to the social distance between those in need and those who make policy. This distance contributes to a lack of *social empathy* (Segal, 2007), the results of which are mandates and procedural requirements that are by nature punitive. For example, the prevailing thought behind curtailing support for the needs of children in single-parent families was that it contributed to family dissolution, out-of-wedlock births, and long-term dependency (Ozawa & Yoon, 2005).

You should be aware of the fact there can be a distance between how the term "social justice," as articulated by the social work profession, is understood by social workers and policymakers. Specifically, promoting economic and social equality and defending the rights of disenfranchised and oppressed people are not universal viewpoints. Barusch (2002) argues that social justice can be defined differently depending on the philosophical orientation of the audience, public opinion, and the framers of social policy. For example, presented with the idea that the mandate and compliance requirement for welfare recipients is unjust, libertarian values, according to Barusch, would perhaps stress the "distribution of benefits on the basis of production." Conversely, liberals tend to be utilitarian in their thinking (e.g., the greatest good for the greatest number of people) and therefore, place emphasis on "economic liberty and political equality for all" (p. 15). Differing viewpoints, however, can find common ground on particular issues, and political labels should not prevent you from exploring opportunities for involving certain individuals or building coalitions. Recognition of this fact might lead you, as suggested by one of the strategic frame questions, to explore how opinions about a particular issue were influenced. Presenting information about a particular problem to the public and policymakers is a means by which you can lessen the distance between them and those who are affected by the policy. Also, consider that people's thinking is complex and their perspectives can range from liberal to moderate to centrist to conservative, depending on the issue at hand. Understanding the basis of different perspectives is essential. The knowledge of the ideological, political, and values context in which social problems and policies are framed can inform your analysis of the forces that may promote or inhibit change.

In this next section of the chapter, we focus on the selected macro–level methods and strategies that can be used to address social problems and conditions.

Developing and Mobilizing Resources

EP 2.1.9a

In some instances, resource needs in response to social problems or conditions are obvious. For example, working families in all economic strata are in need of affordable child care, and some need financial assistance to meet all of the costs of daily living. Resource needs can change over time. While a resource was appropriate at one particular point in time, shifts in the needs of people may require that new resources are developed or

existing ones expanded. For instance, food banks, primarily developed to serve the urban poor, have expanded as a result of the current economic climate, high unemployment, and state cuts to cash assistance programs. Increases in the demand for this resource, from a range of income levels and geographical areas, have, in some cases, overtaxed food banks.

Needs for resources vary according to specific concerns and they can differ substantially from one community or population to another. For example, the resource needs of aging gay and lesbian individuals in rural areas tend to be different from the needs of their urban peers. In examining the landscape for resource needs, the rural–urban or urban–suburban configuration may be applicable to addressing almost any need within a population. In some instances, existing resources may be inadequate for the level of need, in which case resources may need to be supplemented or expanded. In some scenarios, you may find that certain values and beliefs about people and stigmatization of groups may result in reinforcing oppression and a denial of access to needed resources. These and other regional and global demographic trends will continue to shape the ways that services are designed and delivered.

Both demand and normative resource needs are likely to change because of our changing demographic landscape—a landscape in which the number of older people is growing faster than the young—and the increasing immigrant population. In the beginning of the year 2011, the first group of the post World War II generation referred to as the "Baby Boomers" in the United States will turn 65 years of age. Aging, specifically the number of people over the age of 65, is a global trend. An aging population will have a profound effect on the types of resources that are needed, ranging from ways to keep this population healthy and to ensure economic and family stability to the ways in which business is conducted. Aging needs will, of course, vary and will be influenced by such factors as income, health status, geographical residence, gender, sexual orientation, and race. Data from the 2010 U.S. Census Survey provides a portrait of a changing and more diverse population, adding to the diversity that already exists in this country. Increasingly, immigrants—who will account for a larger percentage of population growth in the United States—can be expected to have a range of resource needs. In addition, more immigrants will follow jobs and settle in suburban and rural communities, resulting in a change in the homogeneity of these communities, both in terms of people and resource needs. The aging and growing immigrant populations are among the demographic trends that can be expected to result in shifting resource needs and, therefore, the development of resources.

Social workers must develop resources when it is apparent that a significant number of people within a given ecological boundary have needs that are not met or for which matching resources are not available. Regular, meaningful contact with individuals, families, and groups places you in a strategic position to identify resource needs. Resource development may include educating policymakers, civic or community groups, and administrators of social welfare organizations about social conditions for which responsive resources are needed.

EP 2.1.6b

Whether the goal is to develop resources, deliver useful services, or influence a social policy, a starting point is gaining an understanding of and documenting the nature and the extent of resource needs. Questions that can be useful to guide the need for resource development and guide which data should be gathered include:

- *What are the resource needs of a particular group?*
- *How would a group or community describe their resource needs?*
- *Are there unmet needs, gaps, or underutilized existing resources?*
- *How prevalent are the needs across the population and in various subgroups?*
- *Are there barriers to the utilization of existing resources?*
- *Are the current resources an effective response?*

Numerous tools are available for understanding and documenting resource needs include mapping, specifically using organizational or government statistical data and needs assessment. Also, inviting and involving client groups to identify their resource needs can be accomplished by group interviews or dialogue, using critical or participatory action research models (DePoy, Hartman, & Haslett, 1999; Reese, Ahern, Nair, O'Faire, & Warren, 1999). Descriptive examples of the implementation of each of these methods are described here.

- Mapping *involves utilizing geographical information systems to track problems of interest (Hillier, 2007). Accessing geographical data about homeless youth in an area of Los Angeles, for example, led to the development of a new resource intervention*

strategy *that focused on service-related needs, employment training, and mental health resources (Ferguson, 2007).*

- Needs Assessment *gathers information in order to identify unmet resource needs. You must first determine whether the resource is intended to respond to a normative or a demand need (Rubin & Babbie, 2005). Normative needs are compared to a specific community's experience with the normal experience of other communities. Demand needs, conversely, relate to the needs of a particular community and address a particular concern. As sources of information, you can utilize group interviews, standardized self-administered questionnaires, community forums with key informants, or a targeted group. Whichever method that you use, the information that you are seeking should focus on discovering needs that are unmet or undeclared, otherwise in talking to people you gather information about a wider range of issues (Homan, 2008). Noting that all communities have resource capabilities, the overall intent of the needs assessment is to assist the community to determine if there is a need for action in order to address a resource need (Homan, 2008, Lewis, Lewis, Packard, & Souflee, 2001). One such example is the Homeless Against Homelessness Project, in which homeless individuals worked with a social worker to determine the resource needs of other homeless individuals. The social worker combined facets of the critical action research framework with needs assessment. Participatory action research involves the governance, composition, and active participation of stakeholders throughout the project (Depoy, Hartman, & Haslett, 1999). In this case, the active stakeholders were the homeless individuals who actually designed the project and conducted the assessment interviews. As key informants, they were essential to the development of interview questions that were relevant to the population and which could easily be administered on the street. The findings from this project were presented to the county commission on homelessness.*

- Dialogue Groups and Interviews *are qualitative methods that can be used to gather pertinent information on the unmet needs and needed resources for specific segments of the population. Butler and Hope (1999) conducted group interviews with older lesbian women living in metropolitan and rural communities in order to better understand their current and future resource needs. Dialogue groups proved to be an effective method to understand and subsequently educate service providers to the particular issues and concerns of older gays and lesbians in a community (Anetzberger, Ishles, Mostade, & Blair, 2004). Observing the low participation of ethnic and racial minorities in using hospice services as a resource, Reese, Ahern, Nair, O'Faire, and Warren (1999) relied on a group of African American ministers as key informants to identify cultural and institutional barriers that prevented African Americans from using hospice care.*

These examples represent ways in which you can identify and document resource needs in the aggregate. You should also be aware of the wealth on information available in your agency's case records. For example, a review of case records can inform you as to whether needs were satisfied at intake and whether the same needs remained a concern at termination. Whichever method that you use to document resource needs, the results may lead to advocacy for social action involving a coalition of agencies and professionals in order to influence a desired outcome.

Developing Resources with Diverse Groups

EP 2.1.4b

You need not feel intimidated when documenting a need for diverse groups so that a resource can be developed. You should, however, be aware of the fact that a group may identify resource needs that are different from your own ideas and that can be observed within group differences (Sue, 2006; Green, 1999). For instance, the needs of immigrants or refugees can be dependent on their length of stay and their extent of acculturation, and may ultimately influence the types and appropriateness of resources. Therefore, whether you are looking to develop resources in response to the needs of old or newly arrived diverse groups, it is critical for you to familiarize yourself with their cultural nuances, values, norms, and social and political structures. Beyond your effort to assess and document a resource need, entry into a situation that is unfamiliar to you requires interpersonal skills such as respectful preparation and engagement, building trust and relationship resources, and facilitating empowerment. In addition, unfamiliar situations call for you to engage in self-reflection, so that you are aware of your bias and any predetermined notions you might have of a particular group.

Most of the previously discussed questions and data collection methods can be used to identify and document the resource needs of a diverse group. Mapping, for example, can show you whether a group is clustered in a particular geographical area. From this point, you can assess the resources available in a community and whether there are resource gaps. Your ultimate aim, however, is that of *discovery* (Green, 1999) and *humility* (Tervalon & Murray-Garcia 1998), both of which can guide your action. In essence, discovery and humility prompt you to rely on the group or community as key informants and as cultural interpreters in educating yourself about their resource needs.

EP 2.1.4d

Mobilizing Community Resources

Mobilizing existing resources can address concrete needs, but available resources can vary depending on the community and the situation. There are certain situations, nonetheless, that arouse an emotional and altruistic response in people, irrespective of where they live. Nowhere has this been more evident than in the community responses during the aftermath of national and global disastrous events.

EP 2.1.10a

Homan (2008, p. 187), citing the Pew Partnership for Civic Change (2001) report, asserts that people are the most valuable resource and that a majority are willing to become and remain involved when asked. The results of the report showed that 90 percent of Americans "believe that working with others is the way to solve community problems." Primary factors were, "knowing what to do," "having a linkage to the community," and "a strong cultural or ethnic identity." In mobilizing community resources, Homan provides four steps for eliciting and encouraging the involvement of people (p. 188):

1. *Contact people.*
2. *Give them a reason to join.*
3. *Ask them to join.*
4. *Maintain their involvement.*

An appeal from Project Homeless Connect, a coordinated partnership effort to mobilize resources, is illustrative of Homan's steps. The success of the project depended on volunteers who were recruited through book clubs, fraternal and civic groups, and faith and professional communities. During the course of the two-day event, homeless persons were able to take showers, see health and mental health professionals,

IDEAS IN ACTION

Project Homeless Connect

Greetings! We Need Your Help!

Ending Homelessness, one person at a time. Project Homeless Connect is a one-stop model for delivering services to people experiencing homelessness. Hennepin County and the City of Minneapolis partner with service providers, businesses, citizens, and faith communities to bring multiple resources to one location where people can find the help they need. These services include: housing providers, employment specialists, medical and mental health care, eye care, haircuts, transportation assistance, food, and clothing.

December Success

Thanks to the wonderful work of 500 volunteers and 100 service providers, and over 1200 men, women, and children. The last event was a great success:

- *1500 meals were served*
- *221 people received immediate medical care*
- *42 received dental care*
- *443 were given vouchers for shoes*
- *62 new voice mail numbers were established so that people could receive messages about work and housing*
- *300 were able to have free haircuts*

- *473 received employment referrals*
- *157 housing applications were submitted, with 6 people placed in housing on the day of the event, and 12 more in the following days*
- *36 veteran contacts were made*

700 Volunteers Needed

The reason for this communication is that we are asking you to help at the upcoming event. With even more participation expected this year, we need at least 700 volunteers to make this another success. The Convention Center will be set up with tables, rooms and areas for the various services available, and volunteers will assist guests in connecting with the assistance that they need or request. Volunteers must be 18 years of age or older.

Sign Up to Volunteer

To volunteer, click below on the Click here to Volunteer box. Please also choose a training date. Share this e-mail with anyone who is interested in helping us reach our goal. You may go directly to our Web site to volunteer to help to end homelessness.

We are counting on you. Won't you connect? Thank you.

---

meet with housing and benefit specialists, and receive concrete goods, for example, backpacks, toothbrushes, and clothing. The announcement that volunteers received can be seen in the above Ideas in Action box.

Overall, the communication had a strong appeal, beginning with the first sentence, "We need your help." It effectively engaged volunteers as active stakeholders in responding to the needs of the homeless population in their community. Direct appeals, such as this one, have the potential to engage the altruistic instincts and basic values of potential volunteers, many of whom desire equality and dignity for the disenfranchised, but are unaware of how to achieve it.

In describing the event as a one-day opportunity, new volunteers are alerted to the time that they are being asked to participate. Former volunteers were encouraged to remain involved by documenting and personalizing their contributions to the success of the previous event, which would also be attractive to new recruits. This information also appealed to

new volunteers and provided them with concrete reasons to participate. Options other than direct involvement, such as the donation of cash or services, were also available. For those who might have been reluctant to volunteer, training was available as an incentive.

As you develop, tap into, or mobilize existing resources, the capacity of the community should be considered, and the appeal need not be on a large scale basis like Project Connect. The capacity to help others in times of need can be found

EP 2.1.9a

in most communities. Community-level resources can be inspired when people become aware of a particular situation for which help is needed. McRoy (2003), for instance, worked collaboratively with congregations to respond to the need for adoptive homes for children. This faith-based initiative called "Saving a Generation," resulted in the adoption of more than 50 African American children.

Within communities, kin, informal networks, and natural support systems can be mobilized in much the same manner. For instance, kinship care as a resource in child welfare is among the practices that organizations have adopted as an alternative to foster care placement (Testa, 2002; Gibson, 1999; Haight, 1998; Tracy & Whittaker, 1990; Jackson, 1998; Brookins, Peterson & Brooks, 1997). Kinship studies (e.g., the placement of children with kin) found that this resource lasted longer and was more supportive of the child's stability, familial connections, and cultural, racial, or ethnic identity (Hegar, 1999; Danzy & Jackson, 1997). Mobilizing the resources can make use of natural support systems within communities. For example, training women in a community as nutritional counselors proved to be an effective means to teach healthy eating habits to inner-city women who were at risk for diabetes. Because the women were interconnected through their community, they were more receptive when the information about diabetes was provided by peers, neighbors, or friends (Mays, 2003). Using barbershops as natural gathering places, the Montgomery County, Maryland, Health and Human Services Department tapped in to this resource to educate men about cancer and to address some of the barriers that prevented the men from seeking oncology screening (Mallory, 2004).

Advocacy and Social Action

EP 2.1.9a

The social work profession has a long and proud tradition of advocacy and social action leading to social reform. Indeed, Stuart (1999) characterizes the "linking of clients and social policy as a distinctive contribution of the social work profession" (p. 335). Haynes and Mickelson (2000) trace the involvement of social workers during the development of some of the more enlightened and humane social policies in both the nineteenth and twentieth centuries. In some instances, in particular communities, practice with individuals involves advocacy and social action that focused on the "private troubles of individuals and the larger policy issues that affected them" (Carlton-LaNey, 1999). Diverse individuals and groups of social workers have been devoted activists and advocates, often acting in concert with grassroots or minority civic groups. For example, social workers supported the United Farm Workers, the Equal Rights Amendment, the National Welfare Rights Organization, and the Civil Rights Movement by either joining in the activities of these groups directly or providing expert testimony.

Case and Cause Advocacy

After reading the analysis of the Personal Work Opportunity and Personal Responsibility Act and the Adoption and Safe Family Act, seeing their disparate impact on poor families, and thinking about related social justice concerns, you might

EP 2.1.4a

wonder, "*What can I do?*" Perhaps you have acted as a case advocate, working on behalf of a client to ensure that he or she receives those benefits and services to which he or she is entitled and to ensure that his or her dignity is safeguarded. This aspect of advocacy closely corresponds to a dictionary definition of an *advocate* as one who acts on behalf of another person. Because advocacy and social action include this key element, confronting the effects of legislation and policies cannot rely on the efforts of a single practitioner. Indeed, the profession is actively involved in addressing many of these issues (Marsh, 2005). The shift in policymaking from the federal to the state level is an opportunity for you to join in collaborative policy advocacy to influence policy at the state level on behalf of clients (Jackson-Elmore, 2005; Hoefer, 2005; Lens, 2005; Rice, 1998; Sherraden, Slosar, & Shrerraden, 2002). Other opportunities for you to join advocacy efforts include the National Association of Social Workers' collaboration with social work programs' "Social Work Day at the Capital," and National Association of Social Workers' PACE Committee.

Advocacy and Social Action Defined

Proposing a new definition of advocacy, Schneider and Lester (2001) define social work advocacy as the "exclusive and mutual representation of a client(s) or cause in a forum, attempting to systematically influence decision making in an unfair and unresponsive system." Barker (1996) defined social action as "a coordinated effort to achieve institutional change to meet a need, solve a social problem, correct any injustices or enhance the quality of human life" (p. 350). Both advocacy and social action are inherently political. Hyde (1996), referring to a major tenet of feminist organizing and advocacy, suggests that the "the personal is political."

By integrating advocacy and social action, we have adapted elements from each to form a unified definition, because there are often instances in which advocacy and social action are combined to achieve the desired results. Together,

EP 2.1.10a

they represent a process of affecting or initiating change either with or on behalf of client groups to:

- *Obtain services or resources that would not otherwise be provided*
- *Modify or influence policies or practices that adversely affect groups or communities*
- *Promote legislation or policies that will result in the provision of requisite resources or services*

Models of advocacy are defined and discussed by Haynes and Mickelson (2000) and Freddolino, Moxley, and Hyduk (2004). These authors stress that using particular models are important because they guide the intervention and the strategies used. We refer you to these informative resources as guides.

Indications for Advocacy or Social Action

EP 2.1.1a

Advocacy and social action may be appropriate when there are conditions or problems that affect a group or community, including the following:

1. When services or benefits to which people are entitled are denied to a group or community.
2. When services or practices are dehumanizing, confrontational, or coercive.
3. When discriminatory practices or policies occur because of race, gender, sexual orientation, religion, culture, family form, or other factors.
4. When gaps in services or benefits cause undue hardship or contribute to dysfunction.
5. When people lack representation or participation in decisions that affect their lives.
6. When governmental or agency policies and procedures or community or workplace practices adversely affect or target groups of people.
7. When a significant group of people have common needs for which resources are unavailable.
8. When clients are denied basic civil or legal rights.

Other circumstances for which advocacy or social action may be necessary include situations in which a group or community is unable to act effectively on its own behalf, such as persons who are institutionalized, people who have a need for immediate services or benefits because of a crisis situation, or people who cannot act as self-advocates because of their legal status.

Competence and Skills for Macro Practice and Social Action

EP 2.1.10a

Skills that are used in direct practice easily translate to advocacy and social action (Breton, 2006). But, Schneider and Lester (2001, p. 71) emphasize that advocacy is not problem solving in the tradition of direct practice problem-solving models. In contrast to the problem-solving process, "advocacy requires particular actions, such are representation, influencing and the use of a forum" to bring about specific change.

Specific skills required in advocacy or social action include:

- *Policy analysis*
- *Group facilitation*
- *Oral and written communication skills*
- *Negotiation and mediation*
- *Analysis of multidimensional and systematic information.*

EP 2.1.10d

Let's say, for example, that you are approached to represent and act on behalf of a group of mothers who believe that the placement of their children was unjust. Undoubtedly, you posses the characteristics of an advocate, that is, you are action-oriented and opposed to injustice. For you, after hearing their stories, inaction on your part, in your opinion, is not an option (Schneider & Lester, 2001). Nonetheless, before acting, you are advised to document the circumstances of each individual's situation and educate yourself about and analyze the relevant state and federal policies. These situations, in which injustice—real or perceived—arouses emotions, can incite anger in those affected and in the advocate. However, an analysis will help you and the group that you intend to represent avoid making assumptions and premature or erroneous conclusions that may lead to undesired or embarrassing consequences. The strategies for documenting and quantifying needs (discussed earlier in this chapter) will be essential at this stage.

Assuming that the situation indicates that advocacy or social action is necessary, a decision would be made as to how the group wants to proceed. To gather support for an intended action you would compile information that documents the problem, the population affected, and in what way that population is affected. Then you would present this information to others who are interested in the problem. In essence, you are building a coalition of interested parties. In building a coalition, group facilitation, negotiation, consensus building, and interpersonal skills are critical.

Advocacy and Ethical Principles

EP 2.1.2d & 2.1.10c

Both advocacy and social action assume a wide range of social work roles and skills, each of which observes the values and ethics of the profession as guiding principles. Advocacy and social action embody values and ethical principles that the social work profession has embraced, such as dignity and worth, self-determination, and giving a voice to the powerless (Schneider & Lester, 2001). Advocacy and social action may, at times, constitute a delicate balance between self-determination and beneficence. Ezell (2001) calls attention to this dilemma, citing the conflict that can occur in deciding "whether to empower clients to advocate for themselves or to represent them" (p. 45). Schneider and Lester (2001) provide guidance with respect to ethical behavior in their definition of advocacy. They emphasize that the relationship between the social worker and the client group is mutual, which means observing their interdependence and reciprocity in collaborative decision-making and planning. In other words, you are working with the group in your representation of their concerns. Furthermore, Schneider & Lester (2001) caution that advocates do not "dominate or set the agenda." A potential dilemma that you might face with respect to self-determination is that a group or community may not wish to assert this right if they feel that they will face formidable opposition or backlash. Should a group make such a decision, you are ethically bound to respect their decision. In essence, the advocacy or social action effort should go no further than the client group wishes it to go.

Ethics are also indicated in informing groups about the risks and limitations associated with advocacy and social action. Rothman (1999) cautions community practitioners about the potential for opposition and obstacles to social action and organizing activities, including "institutions that block needed improvements in education, housing, employment and law enforcement." He further states that "change advocates have to keep in mind that elites will lash out when they perceive that their interests are challenged." To deal with this resistance, advocates should "calculate" their ability and that of their client group to maintain a sustained focus, as well as be able to defend themselves against counterattacks (p. 10). You have a responsibility to discuss potential barriers and the possible adversarial or negative consequences of advocacy and social action with the client group. Implementing advocacy and social action typically creates a certain amount of strain and tension; moreover, a positive outcome cannot always be assured. For example, what if a landlord under pressure from a resident action group ignored building code violations that caused the complex to be condemned, resulting in the residents being displaced? Discussing possible consequences or barriers not only allows for the planning of alternative strategies, but also ensures that those with whom you work are informed about the pros and cons of an intended action, leaving the final decision in their hands.

Techniques and Steps of Advocacy and Social Action

EP 2.1.9b

Targets of advocacy or social action may be individuals (e.g., a landlord or public official), organizations, or divisions of government (e.g., on behalf of or with groups or communities). Approaches to situations vary considerably according to the target system, but all require a thorough understanding of how organizations or communities are structured and function, how the legislative and rule-making processes work, and an appreciation of the influence of organizational politics (Alexander, 2003; Homan, 2008; Roberts, 2000; Rothman, 1991).

Advocacy can involve different levels of assertive intensity, ranging from discussion and education to a high level of social action such as organizing, protests, boycotts, or social media campaigns. Sosin and Callum (1983) developed a useful typology of advocacy to assist practitioners to plan strategic advocacy actions. Along with the models discussed by Haynes and Mickelson (2000) and Freddolino, Moxley, and Hyduk (2004), Sosin and Callum's (1983) typology can help determine the opportunities that exist, the techniques or strategies to be used, and at what level these techniques and strategies should be implemented. As a general rule, you should rely on the techniques that have the greatest promise of achieving a given objective. Deciding which technique to use depends on the nature and analysis of the problem, the wishes of the group or community, the nature of the action, and the political climate. For instance, although militant action may be desirable, militancy should be utilized with great discretion, because the short-term gains may not outweigh the long-term negative images, the response from the public, and the potential for fractured relationships.

EP 2.1.10a

Effective social action and advocacy require a rational, planned approach incorporating the following steps:

1. Analyze the problem or condition.
2. Systematically gather information and complete an analysis of the people, structure, system, or policy to be changed.
3. Assess both the driving forces that may promote change and the forces that may conceivably resist or inhibit change.
4. Identify specific goals, eliciting a broad range of viewpoints from within the client group.
5. Carefully match techniques or strategies to the desired outcome.
6. Make a feasible schedule for implementing the plan of action.
7. Incorporate in the plan a feedback process for evaluating the changes that the action stimulates.

In addition to the steps and the skill competencies, other factors that are vital to effective social action and advocacy include: a *genuine* concern for the cause, the ability to keep the cause in *focus, tenacity*, and *stamina*. Successful advocates have a thorough understanding of how their government and systems are organized and changed. Blind emotion may work a few times, but maintaining a successful, sustained advocacy and action requires know-how. In many instances, class advocacy and social action are best described as a marathon rather than a race. Finally, the manner in which an issue is presented may make a substantial difference.

The FrameWorks Institute suggests translating messages about what can be done to address social problems into language that engages ordinary people and advances their interest in policy and program solutions. Questions that facilitate formulating the institute's "strategic frame analysis" are illustrated in the following examples:

- *What shapes public opinion about a particular social condition or problem, for example, issues that affect children, families, and poor people?*
- *What role do [can] the media play?*
- *How do policymakers gauge public opinion?*

Answers to these questions can facilitate the direction of advocacy or social action. Further, the questions may assist you to sharpen your message to a specific group about a specific problem, and to effectively communicate about social conditions framed by the tenets of social justice.

Community Organization

EP 2.1.10a

Social transformation is a primary goal of community organizing (Hardina, 2004). Similar to advocacy and social action, community organizing is action-oriented on a larger scale and intended to effect social change in which "neighborhood organizations, associations and faith communities join together to address social problems in their community" (Brueggemann, 2006, p. 204). Further, it is an arena in which participants "develop their own solutions, advance their own needs or build capacity" in partnership with private or governmental organizations (Bruggemann, 2006; Weil & Gamble, 1995).

Communities are social systems that have distinct characteristics in the manner in which they are organized, their collective sense of connectivity, identity and power, and the issues about which they have concerns, which is some instances may be confined to a particular geographic location. Organizing communities requires that you have an understanding of what matters to them, their needs and strengths, and the context of the person [community] in environment relationship.

Models and Strategies of Community Intervention

EP 2.1.10g

Models of community organizing and intervention and their basic means of influence are described by Rothman, Erlich, and Tropman (2001) and Carter (2000). The most frequently referred to methods or strategies for organizing communities are summarized in Table 14-1.

Locality development seeks to build relationships within the community and enhance community integration and capacity thorough broad participation. Locality development supports empowerment in that the community is actively involved in defining its problem and determining goals (Cnaan & Rothman, 1986). In Quebec, Canada, for example, locality development utilized natural helping networks and lay citizens in

TABLE-14-1 STRATEGIES AND METHODS OF COMMUNITY INTERVENTION
Locality Development
Social Action
Social Planning
Capacity Building

© Cengage Learning 2013

analyzing problems and planning remedial measures (Gulati & Guest, 1990). Users of services were considered to be partners as opposed to client–consumers. They facilitated the integration and coordination of programs and services and prevention efforts in their community. The flexibility in organizational structure and decentralized administration enabled the local communities to develop programs that responded to their unique needs.

Social Action as a community organization strategy is similar to our discussion of advocacy in its approach. It is the action on the part of communities to advocate so that institutions and decision makers address unfairness in resource distribution (e.g., the relocation of bus routes that disadvantaged a specific population), remedy the imbalance of power through neighborhood associations or concerned citizens (e.g., the coordinated efforts of seniors, relatives, and senior citizen advocates), and solve problems or conditions identified by the community.

Social Planning as a strategy tends to be expert-driven, relying on consultants and technical assistance for solving problems (Rothman & Tropman, 1987). These professionals generally work with community leaders and the focus of their work is to expand, develop, and coordinate social policies and social services (Carter, 2000). Unlike locality development, participation by the larger community may be limited.

Capacity building increases the ability of a community to act on its own behalf, make decisions, and directs its own actions as its main focus (Hannah, 2006). This approach takes exception to the assumption that expert or governmental interventions are a primary means to achieve a solution to a community problem. Instead, the community develops its own agenda and the work to be completed is directed "from the inside out" (Rivera & Erlich, 1998, p. 68). Organizing efforts under the auspices of Communities United to Rebuild Neighborhoods (CURN) in Chicago is an example of residents working together to resolve their community concerns. They focused on their collective community strengths and individual talents at all age levels, believing that these attributes were central to the change effort, and therefore should be identified, energized, and deployed.

Within each of the first two methods, activities may support coalition building and evolve into political and social action or social movements capable of influencing social planning. In some instances, they may overlap or be employed simultaneously (Carter, 2000; Hyde, 1996: Rothman, 1995, 2008). Carter (2000), for example, documents how a coalition evolved into effective political and social action in response to the

inaction on the part of the Department of Justice to incidents of arson in southern U.S. African American churches in isolated rural communities in 1996. By challenging the inaction of the agents and that of the United States Justice Department about the cause of the fires, communities realized their self-efficacy as a group, bolstering their coming together and taking action as an effective organizing coalition. Hannah (2006) notes that community capacity initiatives must be able to gain and maintain involvement of the community, which is possible if the initiative has community support.

Relying on a specific model or strategy is useful for directing the organizing effort. Burghardt (2011) proposes three strategic development levels of community intervention that can facilitate decisions about which model would be most

EP 2.1.10g

useful. *Entry*, the first strategic level, emphasizes capacity building and empowerment among community members, growing their sense of their power, responsibilities, and skills. During this process, issues and long term goals are identified. Burghardt refers to the second strategic level as the *Coalition Strategy Formation*. In this process, the organizer seeks to understand and make use of the various actors that may contribute to or distract from the problem to be addressed. For example, the extent to which there is a commonality of concerns should be identified among the various individuals, groups, or other organizations in the community that could form a unified coalition issue. The *Transformational Strategy Formation* is able to make use of strategies from various models. Specifically, at this level, building coalitions or individual and community capacity can be implemented to bring about a planned change. Some advantages of the three strategic levels are that they provide a means to understand the position of a community relative to an issue, where development may be needed, and the fact that they build upon each other. For instance, in the entry strategic level, building capacity within a community can be a precursor to developing a coalition. Whether you begin with a specific model or make use of Burghardt's (2011) developmental strategies in advance of a model decision, maintaining focus is important. As Homan (1999, p.160) points out, you should keep in mind that organizing to promote change "involves more than just fixing a specific problem." Further, in advancing the empowering capacity of a community, productive organizing includes the goal of increasing the capability of people to effectively respond meaningfully in the face of future challenges.

Steps and Skills of Community Intervention

EP 2.1.10a

Theorists conceptualize community organizing in different ways, outlining different stages that vary according to the levels of elaboration of relevant tasks. Rothman, Erlich, and Tropman, (1995) and Rothman (1999) use a six-phase process to address community concerns:

1. Identification of need, condition, or problem as framed by the community
2. Definition and clarification of the need, condition, or problem
3. Systematic process of obtaining information
4. Analysis of the information
5. Development and implementation of a plan of action
6. Terminal actions and evaluation of outcome or effects

This process may not be entirely linear, because new information can require alternative action, including making a new start or reframing strategies and tactics and a mix of intervention models (Rothman, 2008; Rothman, Erlich, & Tropman, 1999).

Organizing Skills

EP 2.1.10b

When working with communities, implementing organizing strategies requires a set of behaviors and skills that are observable and measurable. For example, you should gauge your ability to establish rapport with and be sensitive to diverse groups, the extent to which you demonstrate genuineness and empathy, and the effectiveness of your communication skills. Because organizing involves groups or communities, skills in group facilitation, fostering interpersonal relationships, and managing group dynamics

are also critical. Homan (2008) adds to the skill base, emphasizing a balance between the objective and subjective, self-awareness, patience, focus, and timing. Other skills and competencies include those embodied in policy analysis, research methods, and the management of data.

Organizing and Planning with Diverse Groups

EP 2.1.10g

Rivera and Erlich (1998), in analyzing models of community development or organizing, challenge the assumption that prevailing models (i.e., locality development, social planning, and social action) are color-blind and therefore applicable in any community. They conclude that there are additional factors to be considered in working with communities of color:

- *Racial, ethnic, and cultural aspects of the community*
- *Implications of this uniqueness in particular communities*
- *The empowerment process and the development of a critical consciousness*

Rivera and Erlich's work is intended to guide our thinking in planning and organizing and, in fact, represents a significant contribution to organizing strategies. Heretofore, methods had an implicit assumption that good intentions sufficed in community interventions and that, unlike direct practice, considerations of the race, ethnicity, and culture in this work were secondary. The three levels of contact for entry into communities, as conceptualized by Rivera and Erlich (1998), facilitate a greater understanding of work with diverse groups and of the roles beyond those traditionally considered in social work. Table 14-2 outlines the three levels.

TABLE-14-2 LEVELS OF COMMUNITY CONTACT

ENTRY LEVEL	CHARACTERISTICS
Primary	Requires that an individual has the same racial, cultural, and linguistic background as the community. The community is open to and respects this individual.
Secondary	The individual need not be a member of the same racial, ethnic, or cultural group, but should be closely aligned and sensitive to community needs. He or she may serve as a liaison to the broader community, and facilitate contact with institutions outside the community.
Tertiary	The individual is an "outsider," yet shares the community's concerns. The practitioner's skills and access to power—rather than his or her ethnic, racial, or cultural identity—are valued assets.

SOURCE: Adapted from Rivera and Erlich (1998).

Ethical Issues in Community Organizing

EP 2.1.2d

It is the groups or associations within communities that are best able to identify their needs and plan solutions. As social workers, we can become involved in their efforts as advocates, change agents, and planners, using our skills, knowledge, and values grounded in principles of social justice and empowerment to help groups and communities to achieve their goals. A question discussed earlier for advocates is equally applicable to organizers. Specifically, when should organizers act on behalf of the community and when is it advisable for representatives to speak for their community to represent themselves (Ezell, 2001)?

Hardina (2004) points out that community organizing and its methods address issues that are not directly covered in the social work Code of Ethics. For example, the Code does not address dual relationships (situations in which two or more distinct relationships involve the same person) between the organizer and community residents. Nor does the Code address the choice of tactics that an organizer might use. To the first point, specifically in regard to dual relationships, you are a member of the community as well as an organizer at entry level one of the Rivera and Erlich (1998) schema. Because you are a part of the community, there may have been numerous occasions in which you have interacted with other residents socially and politically. In community practice, for instance, you may have relationships with people as friends, relatives, or as a member of a sports team. Your memberships in the community provide you with a familiarity to the community, the people, their values, and concerns. As a member, your involvement can lessen mistrust, and in effect, lessen the time needed to build relationships and bonds. However, in the strict sense of the Code, being involved in boundary spanning relationships may be perceived as an ethical violation.

EP 2.1.2d

Ethical behavior requires that community organizing observe self-determination and that a community is informed of and consent to the tactics to be used, as well as understands the risks and benefits. Hardina (2004) suggests that if the ethical principle and subsequent dilemma is not obvious, the organizer should use the Ethical Rule Screen proposed by Loewenburg, Dolgoff, and Harrington (1996, 2005). For example, "protection of life" or "privacy and confidentiality" must be

weighed when considering a forceful tactic that may place people at risk. An *Ethical Decision-Making Framework by* Reisch and Lowe (2002), as discussed by Hardina (2004, p. 600), also provides a series of steps that are useful for community organizers:

- *Identify the ethical principles that apply to the situation at hand.*
- *Collect additional information necessary to examine the ethical dilemma in question.*
- *Identify the relevant ethical values and/or rules that apply to the ethical problem.*
- *Identify any potential conflicts of interest and the people who are likely to benefit from such conflict.*
- *Identify ethical rules and rank them in terms of importance.*
- *Determine the consequences of applying different ethical rules or ranking these rules differently.*

Although the Code may be limited with respect to specific macro-level strategies, in most instances it, along with the principle beliefs of the profession, can guide ethical practice. For example, the code and principle beliefs of the profession can be helpful in considering questions of the primacy of clients' rights, the uniqueness and worth of people, as well as the social justice focus on economic and social equality.

Social Media as a Resource of Social Advocacy and Community Organizing

In today's world of instant messaging, e-mail, social networks, social media, and other forms of digital communications, the capacity to reach, engage, and organize people about a particular issue is infinite. The use of these resources may be generational in that their appeal can vary by age. Specifically, it may be easier for young people to access and respond to this form of communication than it is for some older people. Irrespective of age, utilization can also depend on the access ability of an individual or community. Nonetheless, because these resources provide for connective relationship opportunities between people, you should evaluate their benefit.

Improving Institutional Environments

Social welfare organizations are organized to provide a service, information, benefits, or goods. They are formal social systems with multiple constituents and dynamic arenas in which client eligibility for services is determined and the resources vital to the organization's existence are distributed. The culture of organizations includes core values and purposes as portrayed in mission statements, leadership styles, and assumptions and rituals. Schein (1985) describes organizational culture as follows:

> *A pattern of basic assumptions-invented, discovered, or developed by a given group as it learns to cope with its problems of external adaptation and internal integration, that has worked well enough to be considered valid and therefore to be taught to new members as the correct way to perceive, think and feel in relation to those problems. (p. 9)*

Improving Organizational Environments

Organizational environments, in particular the culture of an organization, are influenced by their leadership, staff, resource environment, and public policy. The resource environment (e.g., the state of the economy) and public policy can require changes or modifications to decisions with respect to how the organization functions, its leadership, the allocation of resources, and the strategies that are implemented to achieve the organization's goals or mission (Condrey, Facer, & Hamilton, 2005; Proehl, 2001). Welfare reform (PWORA), for example, had a significant impact on both public and private organizations, their internal operations, staff functions, job satisfaction, goals, and resources (Abramovitz, 2005; Condrey, Facer & Hamilton, 2005; Proehl, 2001; Reisch & Sommerfeld, 2003). In effect, federal requirements set forth specific performance standards, which included the monitoring and reporting of the work-related activities of recipients. Many nonprofit organizations and some social workers have struggled with the mandated goals of welfare reform. At issue for many were requirements which were counter to their mission and the values of the social work profession. At the same time, the leadership and culture of the organization enabled some organizations to respond to these pressures in ways that were less disruptive and more beneficial to the organization (Condrey, Faces, & Hamilton, 2005; Reisch & Sommerfeld, 2003).

EP 2.1.10h

The quality of the organizational environment and the values of the organization, as experienced by clients, are important aspects of service delivery. In this section, ways in which the organizational environment can be improved are considered. Three major aspects of an organizational

environment are discussed; specifically staff, organizational policies and practices, and programs.

Staff

In spite of the impact that external influences have on an organization's environment, the organization's staff forms the heart of the environment. The staffing mix of an organization includes professionals who have regular contact with clients, support personnel, and administrative personnel. Administrative personnel, specifically managers and supervisors, direct, monitor, coordinate, evaluate, and bear the responsibility for the oversight of overall organizational operations. In the organization's highly interdependent environment, each position is critical to achieving its mission. To a large extent, staff behavior is governed by a mix of factors that are internal and external to the organization. Internal factors include things like organizational philosophy, goals, and mission. Professional orientations, ethical codes and standards, union contracts, funding sources, the media, public policy, and licensing or regulatory boards are external factors.

When an organization has staff who are dedicated, caring, and responsive to clients' needs, as well as congenial with one another, the climate in the organization's environment tends to be conducive to the growth and well-being of all concerned. To be optimally effective, an organization's culture (and hence its climate) should promote staff empowerment and a commitment to deliver high-quality client services. Characteristics of a healthy organizational culture and climate involve such factors as open communications, a willingness to deal with conflict, a balance between flexibility and risk taking, a sense of interdependence and cohesiveness, and respect for boundaries. Although the creation of an organization's environment is within the domain of organizational leadership, it is the responsibility of all staffing levels.

Hackman and Oldham (1976, 1980) have conceptualized the most elaborate and widely accepted theories of job design and motivation as contributing to the overall psychological states of meaningfulness, staff responses, morale, and job satisfaction of staff. They have identified the following core characteristics as being instrumental in advancing toward an organizational environment in which staff are productive:

- *Task identity*
- *Task significance*
- *Skill variety*
- *Job feedback*
- *Autonomy*

Task identity, task significance, and skill variety add to the feeling that work is meaningful. Feedback with regard to one's job performance provides information about the results achieved, thereby acting as both a developmental and a motivating factor. Autonomy inspires a sense of responsibility for one's own work, the outcomes of this work, and the work of the team. Empowerment, which is implicit in autonomy, works in much the same way as self-determination does for clients. Just as clients may terminate social work contact when their interests and needs are ignored, a lack of staff empowerment can affect job performance, reduce productivity, and contribute to rapid turnover. Lack of attention to these dynamics can have a spill-over affect on staff-client interactions and create situations in which staff treat clients in ways that are counterproductive to the goals and purpose of the organization.

From this discussion, you can observe the contributions of staff to the overall environment of an organization. For instance, when staff behavior is guided by a lack of autonomy or significance in their work, they may perceive the organization's environment as a "psyche prison"—a construction of reality and conformity to a preferred way of thinking and doing (Morgan, 1997). The extent to which staff are empowered and able to participate in work-related decisions makes a significant difference in the extent to which they feel valued. Likewise, the five characteristics identified by Hackman and Oldham (1976, 1980) can influence the extent to which staff engages in prosocial or extra-role behavior within the organization, specifically a willingness to go beyond what is generally required of an individual's position.

Organizational Policies and Practices

EP 2.1.10d

Whether your role in an organization is that of a direct service practitioner or an administrator, a key part of your responsibility is to evaluate the impact of organizational policies, procedures, and practices on service delivery. When certain organizational practices or policies impede service delivery or block the agency from fulfilling its mission in an optimal fashion, it is up to you to identify those barriers and propose a change or modification. In this role, you would function as organizational diagnostician/facilitator, mediator, expediter, and advocate. In this section, the focus highlights three areas in which organizational policies and practices act as barriers to service delivery:

- *Policies or practices and staff behavior that fail to promote client dignity and worth*

- *Institutionalized racism and discrimination*
- *A lack of cultural competence at the organizational level*

Institutional programs

Before beginning the discussion of these main areas, information in the following section can assist you in critiquing policies and practices in your organization.

Examining Organizational Policies and Practices

EP 2.1.10d

The extent to which organizational policies and practices promote social justice, support client self-determination, and adhere to the principles of empowerment and strengths are lenses through which you can examine agency policies and practices. G.D. Rooney (2000) has developed an exercise for students designed to examine the values and ethics reflected in organizational policy decisions and practice. Policies or practices that lend themselves to a review include criteria for determining eligibility for services, rules that govern clients' behavior in residential or institutional settings, policies related to access to services, and procedures for developing treatment plans. Rooney (2000) has outlined the following key points to consider when assessing organizational policies or practices:

1. What are the origins, ideology, and values that appear to have influenced the policy?
2. What are the intended and unintended consequences of the policy's application?
3. To what extent are the policy and its expectations of clients influenced by societal ideology (e.g., the worthy and unworthy poor), social control, or compliance?
4. What is the image of clients and practitioners portrayed by the policy?
5. What does the policy or practice demand of clients and practitioners?
6. How do clients react to the practice or policy?
7. To what extent do the policy and its procedures support or constrain social work values, ethics, and social justice concerns?

Unfortunately, some organizations may have practices or policies that create barriers to delivering services fully and effectively. The implementation of such policies may deny people the resources to which they are entitled and result in others receiving services that are of lesser quality. In responding to their resource environment, organizational practice can be influenced by rules, policies and procedures, and in some instances the language that communicates a certain ideology and image of people who need services (Abramovitz, 2005; Lens, 2005; Riesch, 2002).

The series of questions for assessing organizational policies and practices developed by Rooney is intended to provide social workers with guidelines with which to critique the effects of policy on clients and service delivery. Many students who have completed this assessment provided the following insightful questions:

- *In working with involuntary clients, does the policy or practice require clients to be compliant, such that the social worker's role becomes that of an enforcer?*
- *How do you reconcile unintended consequences of the implementation of policies or rules?*
- *When clients have a strong reaction to a policy or practice, are there mechanisms in place so that the organization can respond to their concerns?*
- *Do policies and practices provide an image of clients that promotes dignity and worth, and acknowledges strengths as well as problems?*
- *How does the policy or practice ensure equal access to and equality of services? In particular, does the policy or practice provide differential treatment for one client group at the expense of another group?*

Many times, policies and practices are intended to help organizations manage limited resources and to ensure their distribution to those in need. For example, rules limiting the number of times people are able to access a food bank are critical to preserving resources, thereby ensuring that help will be available to the greatest number possible. At the same time, from an individual's perspective, these limits can convey the idea that they are taking advantage of this resource. Policies may be considered to be counterproductive when they intend to ensure compliance but unduly burden clients, and when procedures are implemented such that the potential for cheating takes precedence over service provisions.

Promoting Dignity and Worth

EP 2.1.10h

Social welfare organizations have the best of intentions when it comes to serving clients. Yet, in many ways, service delivery in ways that retains a person's dignity remains a challenge. These difficulties may be related to the images portrayed of those in need, the residual nature of assistance, the media, or funding resources; public policy or organizational practices; and the behavior of individual professionals. In some cases, organizations may strip service recipients of their dignity by requiring them to go to unreasonable lengths, for example, to establish eligibility for concrete aid or services. A vignette entitled "Four Pennies to My Name" is a powerful illustration of one client's perspective of this experience as she attempted to comply with the eligibility requirements for financial assistance (Compton & Galaway, 1994). In the vignette, a woman recounts her experience, which includes feeling humiliated and treated as just another number. Using social justice as an organizing perspective, Reisch (2002) proposes criteria for how people are to be treated, beginning with belonging, a notion articulated by Bertha Reynold's (1951) where people are "treated as human beings, not as problem to be solved" (p. 350). Further, Reisch (2002) states, the provision of services should observe people's humanity and be compassionate without regard to the ends sought by the profession or society.

Routine practices to which we may have become accustomed can compromise dignity, for example, inadequate privacy in the physical space where client interview or calls take place, within the earshot of others. Angry clients, concerns for safety, and threats of violence have prompted both public and private organizations to install metal detectors to screen visitors. Another practice involves the use of private guards or off-duty police. While you as an administrator or staff may regard these practices as essential for managing risks and ensuring a safe work environment, you should also be aware of the message it sends to clients and the power it affords to ancillary individuals (e.g. security guards) who are not associated with the mission and goals of the organization. Safety measures, although responding to very real concerns, nonetheless convey an image to service recipients and influence how they experience the organization. Legal questions have been raised about the legitimacy and authority of private security personnel in human services organizations. Although some view their presence as another form of oppression and social control, this practice is unlikely to go away. When practices such as this result in clients being treated in an indiscriminate manner, without regard for their dignity, as a social worker you are obligated to call attention to these issues and advocate for change.

Influence of Public Policy

EP 2.1.5c

As discussed earlier, public policy can have a positive or negative effect on an organization's environment. Furthermore, public policy (an external factor) can influence the organizational culture and the ethics of the organization's service delivery. Recall the discussion of the impact that welfare reform had on the ethical practice of social workers, and ultimately the way clients were treated. In the highly charged and often emotional response to child abuse and neglect, the dignity and worth of the parents involved takes a back seat to the demands of a rigid and legalized protocol inherent in the response system.

Parents involved in the child protection intervention report the experience as one in which there is a power imbalance, and they feel judged, fearful, and hopeless as a result of the uncaring, less than empathetic response by social workers who seem more interested in punishing them than understanding their situation (Fazilo, Lawson, & Hardiman, 2009; Dumbrill, 2006, 2003; Maiter, Palmer, Manji, 2006; Albert, 2000; Van Najnatten, 2005; Holland, 2000; Diorio, 1992).

In a system where contact with people begins with an allegation of guilt, the inherent assumption is that the parents are not concerned about their child or children's well-being and therefore their worth is questionable. Such interventions as *Signs of Safety* (Turnnell, 2004, 2006; Turnell & Edwards, 1999, 1997) and *Family Group Conferencing* (Waites, MacGowan, Pennell, Carlton-LaNey, & Weil, 2004) provide for a response to parents that honors their dignity and worth in spite of the dictates of public policy. *Signs of Safety* is an approach to child protection in which the professional builds a partnership with parents to ensure child safety and well-being. The partner relationship, like the assessment, is where the parent and the professional work together to determine safety and resources needs. This way, the professional's view does not overshadow the voice of the parent and is vastly different from the often-times contentious investigative process in which parents feel powerless. Instead, when there has been an allegation of abuse or neglect, the primary focus is on identifying safety and potential danger signals and a plan is developed on this basis. Family Group Conferencing, also referred to as *Family Group Decision-Making*, brings together family members as resources who are actively involved in ensuring child safety and well-being. Both practices can be instrumental in improving the organizations environment in that they

diminish the role of staff as enforcers, which overtime can have an adverse affect on their functioning, including burnout. For clients, the experience is more empowering, and it is consistent with the profession's standards holding that the uniqueness, dignity, worth, and rights of the individual are primary considerations.

Staff

EP 2.1.1d

Positive staff behaviors and attitudes are essential to maintaining an organizational environment in which client dignity and worth are integral to operations and service delivery. In their encounters with an organization people should be able to expect common courtesies, such as promptness of response, respect, and nonjudgmental attitudes as a part of the organizational culture. It is unfortunate when staff persons may be either openly or subtly judgmental of clients, making remarks about their morality, veracity, character, or worthiness. Also troubling are incidents when staff members are brusque or rude, act in a way that humiliates or demeans clients, breach confidentiality, or intrude unjustifiably into deeply personal aspects of clients' lives, needlessly subjecting them to embarrassment and humiliation.

EP 2.1.2d

You may encounter a situation that leads you to question a colleague's competence and to consider whether this behavior with clients is a result of his or her impairment. These ongoing behaviors or actions can evolve from bad professional behavior into an organizational issue when supervisors or managers and staff allow them to go unchallenged. Moreover, such behaviors are an inhumane and unethical practice (e.g., NASW Code, 2000, Standards, 2.09, 2.10, and 2.11). Speaking with the colleague is a first step, and further discussion may involve the organization's administration. If necessary, you can pursue filing a complaint with the appropriate licensing board and professional organization. You may be thinking to yourself that these are dramatic or extreme measures. Further, you may question the benefits or risks associated with becoming involved. *Whistle blowing*, as discussed by Greene and Latting (2004), is a form of advocacy to be implemented when client's rights are ignored or in situations that represent a serious threat to their well-being and dignity. A primary reason most people are reluctant to report wrongful acts or behaviors is that the act of whistle blowing can have negative individual and organizational consequences. Whistleblowers may also question perceptions or motives and fear losing status and relationships with colleagues and the organization. These are legitimate concerns. Greene and Latting (2004, pp. 220–221) have identified factors, with integrity at their core, that you can use to assess your potential action. Whistleblowers are:

- *Motivated by their altruism, and their actions are to the benefit of those being wronged*
- *Utilitarian, with a high level of moral development, and are driven by their sense of integrity and social [professional] responsibility to speak out, even under symbolic or literal pressures to keep silent*
- *Seemingly uninterested in tailoring their behavior to conform to particular situations and behave consistently across situations*
- *Allowing their own attitudes and beliefs to guide them and they refuse to lie or cover up*
- *Well-educated, hold professional or managerial positions, and keep well-documented records of what they perceive to be abuse or waste*

Staff behavior is a critical facet of organizational culture. The organization's stance on ethical behavior is vital to ensuring ethical conduct, and, ultimately, the manner in which people are perceived and served.

Institutionalized Racism and Discrimination

EP 2.1.5a

Racism and discrimination are embedded in the fabric of our society to such a pervasive extent that many people fail to recognize their many manifestations. Institutional racism often affects service delivery and availability of resources and opportunities in subtle ways. Therefore, it is vital that you, irrespective of your role in the organization, are sensitized to its manifestations, especially in treatment, allocation of resources, and client experience.

Racism and discrimination, whether direct, indirect, or subtle, are in reality facets of educational, legal, economic, and political institutions, all of which influence how people are perceived and treated and the services that they receive (Abramovitz, 2005; Rodenborg, 2004; Chipungu & Bent-Goodley, 2003; Hill, 2005; Savner, 2000; Morton, 1999; Williams, 1990). At times, discrimination can lead to organizational practices resulting in disparate treatment of clients. At other times, discrimination can collude with the professional bias of theoretical perspectives and the personal bias of the professional. Ample evidence of professional bias shows that persons of color in their encounters with systems are much more likely to be perceived as pathological without regard to their ecological circumstances or needs (Barnes, 2008; Feldman, 2008; Richman, Kohn-Woods, & Williams, 2007; Allen, 2007; Whaley, 1998; Wolf, 1991).

The NASW Code (e.g., 4.02) speaks directly to the social worker's responsibility with regard to discrimination. Social workers have an ethical responsibility to work toward (1) obliterating institutional racism in organizational policies and practices and (2) enhancing cultural competence. These are worthy goals, but they also represent formidable challenges. The first step toward meeting these challenges is developing an awareness of possible traces of racist attitudes and bias within oneself and its influence on your practice.

Cultural Competence: A Macro Perspective

As discussed in Chapter 1, social workers, guided by the Educational Policy and Accreditation Standards (EPAS), are expected to recognize and engage diversity in their practice (Council on Social Work Education, 2008). To refresh your memory, this means you understand that social

EP 2.1.4b & 2.1.4d

structures enhance and create power and privilege in your work with diverse clients. Further, social work practitioners are expected to be aware of the way in which their interactions with diverse clients are influenced by their personal biases and values. Finally, achieving cultural competence is a process by which social workers position themselves and become open to those with whom they work as key informants in their competence journey. Cultural competence is focused primarily on the interaction between the professional and the client. While professionals are ethically obligated to engage in the process of becoming competent to work with diverse groups, the organization's leadership is equally responsible. Achieving organizational cultural competence requires the commitment to competence, and the achievement of competence is the domain of the organization's leadership.

Organizational Cultural Competence

Achieving organizational cultural competence should not be limited to supporting the sensitivity and awareness of staff, the assignment of staff to work with their respective racial or cultural group, providing printed materials, or the use of inter-

EP 2.1.10h

preters. These measures are nonetheless worthy beginnings in an ongoing process of achieving competence.

Both public and private organizations have attempted to accommodate diverse populations by hiring professionals or community staff who represent a target group. Public agencies have also developed purchase-of-service (POS) contracts with ethnic or race-specific community-based agencies. Cultural or racial matching, in same-race or same-culture individuals and agencies, would more likely result in professionals identifying with their respective clients and, as a result, they would have a greater understanding of the group experience. However, research about the effectiveness of racial or cultural matching and its benefits to clients is inconclusive (James, 2008; Karlsson, 2005; Malgady & Zayas, 2001; Neville, Spanierman & Doan, 2006).

The practice of racial or cultural matching in organizations evolved out of a very real need to have a diversity of color, language, and understanding in organizations where the majority of staff members were white. While this practice is useful on one level, it is a beginning rather than an end. In effect, it creates an agency within an agency and is, at best, an interim solution. As such, it is inadequate as a means to achieve organizational cultural competence. Although it can enhance the organization's standing, the practice of matching raises other concerns for consideration:

- *In essence, the ethnic or racial representative is solely responsible for clients with whom they share demographic characteristics, and therefore may rarely have the opportunity to work with other clients.*
- *When representative staff provide services only to one client group, other staff may ignore and are limited in their exposure to clients who are different, further perpetuating racial inequality.*
- *The practice limits the organization's ability to expose all clients to diverse professionals.*
- *Representative staff assigned on the basis of their race, culture, or sexual orientation are often overwhelmed by the volume of work, which can include responding to the demands of representing their community.*

The NASW Standard for Cultural Competence in Social Work Practice speaks to the issue of overload, asserting that the "special skills and knowledge that bicultural and bilingual staff bring to the profession" should be compensated rather than exploited (2001, p. 26). This issue should be addressed at the organizational level, because it has implications related to workload, morale, and unintentional forms of discrimination.

EP 2.1.10h To be effective, organizations must embrace cultural sensitivity and competence and demonstrate their commitment through their policies and practices (Chesler, 1994a; Chesler, 1994b; Fong &

Gibbs, 1995; Nybell & Grey, 2004; Rogers & Potocky, 1997). Achieving organizational cultural competence at the organizational level as discussed by Nybell and & Gray (2004), requires the organization's leadership to take deliberate steps such as:

- *Reviewing organizational policies and practice*
- *Assessing the organization's standing in communities of color*
- *Evaluating the equity in resource allocation, in particular the programs or services that consist of a disproportionate number of poor clients and clients of color*
- *Assessing staffing patterns, with a specific focus on who is hired, what positions are held by whom, and who is promoted or terminated*
- *Examining the distribution of power, focusing on who benefits and who is excluded*
- *Examining the narrative structures that inform agency practices, public relations, fundraisers, and board members*
- *Analyzing the decision-making process, specifically who is involved (including clients) in such matters as agency location, allocation of resources, and who has access to this process*

Additional resources exist for organizations to utilize to analyze their competence. The Child Welfare League of America (1990), for example, has developed a Cultural Competence Self-Assessment Instrument, which provides guidance to organizations in assessing and developing cultural competence at all levels of the organization. In addition, Strom-Gottfried and Morrissey (2000), and Cross, Bazron, Dennis, and Issacs (1989) have developed organizational audits for agency policies and practice and for assessing organizational strengths and effectiveness with respect to diversity.

Public Policy. A culturally competent social worker or organization cannot always ensure that clients are immune from direct or unintentional bias in public policy. In fact, in the face of public policy, the competence of organizations

EP 2.1.8a

and social workers are often at a disadvantage, irrespective of the level of cultural competence they have attained. To this end, we recommend analyzing cultural competence of public policy. What is the basis for this recommendation? Bias is inherent in most policies, even though their intent is to be neutral with respect to race, class, culture, and gender. Public policy, for instance, has tended to have a narrow view of the culturally or racially determined dynamics that influence how people function. Further, seldom does public policy reflect a recognition of how family networks and relationships are defined within diverse groups. For example, services for the elderly, mental health services, and child welfare services are structured around the Western concept of the nuclear family, rather than broad informal or kinship networks. Informal kinship arrangements, such as those found in many diverse communities, tend to be unrecognized in public policy. In child welfare, for example, relatives as well as nonrelatives have often assumed responsibility for children; nevertheless, these individuals are unable to access resources unless they formally adopt the children. The concept of formally adopting a relative, while it has certain legal safeguards, is perceived differently in minority communities. In light of this discussion, you might conclude that the impact of public policy is not neutral.

Van Souest and Garcia (2003) suggest that cultural competence at the public policy level is an issue of social justice. As such, administrators and social workers, acting as advocates, are required to confront aspects of policies and practices that are inherently biased and that have disparate and oppressive effects on various segments of the population. As Weaver (2004) asserts, "the social justice aspect of cultural competence is often obscured by cultural competence conceptualized and highly focused on individual interaction." Because of the emphasis on the cultural competence of the practitioners, the cultural relevance of public policy can be ignored. Conclusions drawn by Voss, Douville, Little Soldier, and Twiss (1999), speaking to policies related to Native Americans, are relevant in this context. Specifically, these authors claim that when "social policies and interventions are not inclusive of cultural dynamics," they "rigidly enforce a kind of clinical colonialism" (p. 233). Therefore, another dimension to cultural competence for the organization and the social worker involves an analysis of public policy.

Given that laws and public policy influence service provisions, particularly who is served and how, a stronger focus on an analysis of public policy is crucial to the cultural competence of organizational practices and social worker-client interaction. This analysis should examine the effects of public policy as well as the extent to which public policies and laws are culturally relevant or incompetent, leading to different treatment of different groups or to discrimination. In their implementation of public policy, organizations should proactively examine their influence on their constituent groups to ensure that they are not, in fact, acting as a party to social injustice. Finally,

procedural justice demands that leaders of organizations position themselves with and/or on behalf of their constituents so that the needs of diverse groups are articulated to policymakers, thereby ensuring that public policy is indeed culturally relevant. Distributive justice, the aspect of justice in which agencies are most often engaged, is compromised without an articulation of the needs, values, and interests of diverse groups.

Cultural competence is a three-pronged effort revolving around the competence of practitioners, committed leadership, and an analysis of public policy in so far as it acknowledges and respects diversity and the equality of service delivery.

Institutional Programs

EP 2.1.5b

Programs are the final facet to be addressed in improving the organizational environment of institutions. A positive, nurturing environment of institutional programs that serve people in residential settings is crucial to the functioning of its clients. Out of necessity, organizations as social systems establish policies and rules that govern the behavior of clients and staff. Rules and policies maintain the equilibrium of the organization so that it is able to operate in a predictable manner. Stimulating, constructive, and growth-promoting programs enhance client functioning, whereas custodial care (which tends to diminish clients involvement in decisions about their lives) can be disempowering, foster apathy, and create reactance, in some instances. Moreover, institutional environments, where even the most routine resident behavior is governed by rules, can be unproductive in that they often inspire challenges to the rules, potentially resulting in a cycle of punishing the behavior of offenders.

An important aspect of institutional programming is the extent to which residents are able to exercise choice and control over their daily living and participate in their treatment plans. To enhance choice and foster participation, you should advocate for democratic participation in the institution's governance and individual rights and choices about how they spend their time and use their resources. When this is not the case, both residents and staff may experience the residual effects of discord. For example, an adult group home resident, referred to the social work case manager because he was "acting out," complained that he did not like having cigarettes and money rationed to him by staff; he felt that this practice suggested he was incapable of making his own decisions. A common complaint you may have heard in adolescent group homes or from other institutional residents is their dislike of the point system in which they lose points or privileges for failing to comply with rules (e.g., failing to comply with "lights out" orders, or exhibiting independent behaviors). Many perceive these systems as further limiting their already limited choices. Often, failure to respond to complaints of this nature escalates in the form of more assertive or aggressive behaviors by residents, which in turn leads to disciplinary action.

Prisons are institutions in which rules are strictly enforced and the residents can feel isolated by their confinement. Aspects of programs within these environments can become more humane through such practices as using volunteers and special visitation days for minors whose parents are incarcerated (Ardittti, 2008). These efforts effectively link the incarcerated to the outside world. Volunteers are invaluable resources in that they teach skills from which those in prison can achieve a sense of mastery and connectedness. Special visitation days for minors help them maintain their parental attachment, but the physical space provided and the location of the prison can be a factor in the family's ability to visit (Christian, 2005; Enos, 2008; From, 2008; Genty, 2008). With an increase in the number of women in prisons, advocates are calling for more family-friendly policies, citing the impact on minors as punishing when they lose contact with their mothers or fathers because of incarceration.

Although there are organizational and legal constraints in residential settings, the principles of social work and advocacy for basic human rights are no less important. Empowerment and self-efficacy are realized when residents are able to exercise control over their lives and their environment to the best of their capacity, given organizational constraints. A sense of power is closely linked to competence, self-esteem, and the belief that individual actions or actions in concert with and supported by other systems can lead to improvements in one's life situation. These attributes or factors, in turn, are reciprocally influenced by the quality of the environment.

Organizational Change

EP 2.1.10a

Change within organizations requires an understanding and analysis of organizational structure, function, culture, and resource environment. Martin and O'Connor (1989) analyzed the social welfare organization using systems theory as a conceptual framework. Analyzing an organization would also include analyzing the organization's relationship with its resource environment (funding sources, the organization's internal structure and processes, and social, cultural, and political-economic environment). Change efforts, according to Netting, Kettner, and McMurtry (2004), can occur in an organization on two levels:

- *Improving resources provided to clients*
- *Enhancing the organization's working environment so that personnel can perform more efficiently and effectively, thus improving services to clients*

Similarly, organizational change as conceptualized by Brager and Holloway (1978) can focus on three areas: people-focused change, technological change, and structural change, which may take the form of a new policy, modifications to an existing policy, the development of a program, the initiation of a project in which the results can be used to inform service delivery, or by the organization positioning itself as a learning organization (Kettner, Daley, & Nichols, 1985; Senge, 1990, 1994).

Organizational Learning and Learning Organizations

Organizational learning and the learning organizations are approaches to affect organizational change. A *learning organization* is a process that enables members of the organization to periodically review performance and make adjustments to

EP 2.1.10h

improve it. It is also considered to be a relevant factor in the quality of staff work life with respect to job design and performance awards (Lewis, Lewis, Packard, & Souflee, 2001; Morgan, 1997). A learning organization positions itself so that it can continuously review and revise its operations, purposes, and objectives so as to ensure the quality of the organizational experience for clients and staff. Questions that might be posed include: How is work done? What are the outcomes of this work? Through this process the organization has an opportunity to reflect on its strengths and limitations, so that it can develop strategies that enhance the former and address the latter. *Organizational learning* emphasizes a set of activities pertinent to the organization's internal operations and the interdependence among its various units.

Organizational learning and the learning organization are often discussed as a single concept. A *learning organization*, as defined by Senge (1990, 1994) and Morgan (1997), essentially speaks to the ecology of the organization. That is, it refers to a particular type of organization and its ability to scan, anticipate, and respond to environmental changes. The learning organization develops capacities that empower members to question and challenge operating norms and assumptions, thereby ensuring its stability and promoting its evolution through strategic responses and direction (Morgan, 1997).

Both approaches require a supportive environment in which the organization's culture fosters dialogue, open communication and feedback. For example, a county human health and human services administrator initiated a series of "community dialogues" among staff to position itself as a learning organization and a shared vision to facilitate organizational change. For example, how well did the various units serving families coordinate and work together? Lewis et al. (2001) encourage the adoption of the learning organization as a way to create opportunities for growth in human service organizations.

Staff as Agents of Change

EP 2.1.10a

Although most social workers are adept in advocating for their clients or developing resources or support networks, many may be reticent or feel unable to influence or propose changes within their own organizations. In some instances, they may identify organizational concerns in a hierarchical fashion, and therefore conclude that the impetus for change or resolutions resides in the management domain. In some instances, and with certain problems, this view may be valid. Nonetheless, because of the interactions between staff and clients, managers and administrators need to be able to rely on you and other staff at the street-level of service delivery to alert them to the need for change in a program or policy or the development of a new resource. In initiating changes at the organizational level, you are acting as a diagnostician and facilitator/expediter. Assuming responsibility for and participating in change is the essence of staff empowerment, and participation in change efforts is consistent with the ethical obligation to your employment organization.

To be an effective organizational change agent, you must be aware of the benefits and risks of a proposed change. In your benefit-risk analysis, it is essential that you document and clarify the need for change. If service delivery is a concern, will your proposal, for example, improve the situation (Brager & Holloway, 1978; Netting, Kettner & McMurtry, 2004)? In addition, what is the form that the proposed change should take? For

example, if service delivery is the target, would you recommend a change in a policy or a program? Furthermore, what are the expected outcomes of the proposed change?

Risks, Benefits, and Opposition

EP 2.1.9b

Promoting change in organizations is a complex process, and opposition is perhaps as common as that found in families, individuals, and groups. Organizations are systems that seek to maintain equilibrium; therefore, you may encounter opposition to proposals for change. Opposition may arise in response to proposals that challenge or exceed the capacity of the organization to implement proposals due to resource constraints or ideological differences. Likewise, proposals that would significantly change the purpose, mission, and goals of the organization may spur resistance. Extending an agency's operating hours may be considered to be a peripheral change and have little or no effect on organizational goals or mission. In contrast, programmatic changes, which alter a program's objectives, have greater effects on organizational depth.

Frey (1990) has developed a useful framework with which you can assess organizational opposition. In assessing the potential benefits and to minimize opposition to a proposal, it is important to obtain the input of four groups:

- *Clients, including the extent to which the proposed change offers direct benefits to this group and will effectively alter and enhance the services they receive*
- *Administrators, who ultimately have legitimate authority for accepting the proposal and providing the resources for implementation*
- *Supervisors or staff, who will have responsibility for planning and/or overseeing implementation*
- *Staff persons, who ultimately carry out the change or are affected by it, once it is implemented*

By considering the impact of the potential change on each group, you can weigh benefits against potential detrimental effects and plan strategies to counter reactions and resistance when the former (i.e., the benefits) clearly and substantially outweigh the latter.

Frey (1990) also suggests that you weigh risk, benefits, and opposition by assessing whether your proposal is "high risk" as characterized by the following:

- *Substantial costs to the organization, for example, purchasing expensive equipment or creating new units*

- *Actions that must be adopted in their entirety rather than implemented in stages*
- *Radical ideas that are in conflict with the dominant values of the organization, its members, or the public*

The following example describes a successful low-risk proposal initiated by a social worker; in particular, the proposal was in tandem with the goals of the organization and it did not involve costly changes. The aim of the proposal was consistent with Netting and colleagues' (2004) change strategy of "enhancing the organization's working environment so that personnel can perform more efficiently and effectively, thus improving services to clients."

CASE EXAMPLE

The primary client group was made up of individuals and families for whom English was their second language (ESL population). The agency provided counseling, educational programs, and assistance to clients in applying for financial benefits. However, a majority of clients had difficulty in completing the applications, despite the fact that they had been translated into several different languages. The particular problem documented by the social worker was the amount of staff time required (which far exceeded the contact hours allowed) to assist individuals or families in completing the forms. Incomplete applications resulted in the need for additional appointments and delays in establishing clients' eligibility and required additional staff time.

To remedy the situation, the social worker proposed using instructional groups, to be scheduled at different times during the week, instead of individual appointments. The groups would be led by staff or volunteers. She envisioned that groups would have two benefits: First, group meetings would address staff concerns related to scheduling, rescheduling, and excessive contact hours. Second, volunteers, specifically other clients who had successfully completed the applications, would help clients, especially new arrivals, become connected to a social network.

The success of this proposal was attributed to the fact that the change did not require substantial organizational expenditures. Nor did it radically compromise the organization's goals and mission. In fact, rather than taxing organizational resources, it redeployed resources in a more efficient manner. By using a group approach and utilizing volunteers, the social worker's proposal augmented the agency's ability to serve the ESL population. Staff responded favorably, as it effectively addressed their frustrations about the time they spent in assisting individuals and families to complete the financial forms.

In general, proposals that fit with an organization's ideology, resource capacity, and potential are likely to win the support of a significant number of members and, therefore, are likely to succeed. Of course, irrespective of its nature, change is often met with skepticism and resistance. Indeed, the social worker's proposal encountered some opposition. In response, the social worker documented the cost-benefit ratio to the organization (which satisfied administrators) and clarified the benefits for staff (their time would be freed so that they could accomplish other tasks). To build support for her proposal, the social worker spoke with co-workers, especially those who were most affected by the need to reschedule appointments for the purpose of completing the eligibility forms. The social worker met with other staff even though they were not directly involved in the ESL program; she recognized that their support would facilitate acceptance. A final point illustrated in the case example is that individual staff were favorable to the proposal because they perceived it as either benign or a benefit to their position and function.

Macro Practice Evaluation

Each of the macro-level strategies discussed in this chapter lends themselves to a variety of procedures for which intermediate and final outcomes can be assessed. Evaluation seeks to assess the extent to which the change effort and the strategies

EP 2.1.6b

employed were successful and can include collecting quantitatively, qualitatively, or a combination to methods. For example, after completing an assessment that documented a need and the subsequent development of a resource, you would want to measure the level in which the resource was responsive. You might also wish to determine the perceptions and opinions of individuals for whom the resource was developed.

Empowerment, whether through organizing, social action, or improving institutional environments, is a consistent theme in macro-level practice. In keeping with the empowerment theme, the evaluation process should include client groups. They should be involved in establishing success indicators and outcomes of the change effort, as well as their perceived level of empowerment (Gutierrez, Parsons, & Cox, 1998; Lum, 2004; Secret, Jordan, & Ford, 1999). Because evaluation is a process, another facet involves examining how the outcome was achieved. For example, determining which of the strategies that were implemented to mobilize resources engaged the general public or public officials, organized a community, and resulted in the most effective response. Should your change effort enlist the help of volunteers and solicit feedback from them, for example, asking them to rate the appeal of specific recruitment literature or presentations? It may be necessary to target your evaluation to a specific group. For instance, did congregations respond more favorably to a presentation during worship service when compared with an announcement in the church bulletin or email newsletter? Collecting this information helps to determine which strategies were the most effective, under what conditions, and with which populations.

Measures of success used by organizations tend to be reported in aggregated client statistical data; therefore, evaluating the effectiveness of macro-level practice can be a challenge. In evaluating the outcomes of a program objective, for example, an organization's questions might be the number of "homeless families with children that found affordable housing." Further analysis might involve examining a change in status of the families who obtained housing. Here, the evaluation focuses on the overall outcome.

A pre- and post-intervention rating scale measuring the change may be applied in situations involving social action and advocacy (e.g., Single Subject Design, scales). Change can be measured on an incremental basis, after a particular action technique, and at the end of the project. You may also decide to collect qualitative information along with statistical data. For example, in an interview format, groups and communities provide descriptive information regarding improved relationships between the police and a community. The evaluation may be implemented as a summative or formative process and include both qualitative and quantitative data (Weiss, 1998). For example, in conducting a needs assessment, you might question the extent that needs were being met or that new resources are required, by using a survey and also group interviews.

Several innovative approaches hold promise for enhancing the effectiveness of developing and planning community programs. The first approach utilizes the methodology of developmental or intervention research (Comer, Meier, & Galinsky, 2004; Rothman & Thomas, 1994; Thomas, 1989). Developmental research is a rigorous, systematic,

and distinctive methodology consisting of techniques and methods taken from other fields and disciplines. Its methodology relies on social research and model development and is sufficiently flexible to accommodate the unpredictable and uncontrolled conditions in most practice settings (Comer, Meier, & Galinsky, 2004). Using this approach allows for strategies and change efforts in the form of programs to be tested and then modified based on the results.

To see how this process works, let's say for example that your agency developed a program for youth who had repeated stays in the shelter system. The primary goal was to reunite them with their families and a secondary goal was permanency. This approach was a significant departure from the way in which the shelter system functioned, thus the system was the target of change. Home visits, while the youth were still in the residential phase of the program, were identified as critical factors in moving them toward reunification. After a period of time, you would collect both qualitative and quantitative data so that you could determine the effectiveness of home visits and the resources required. Gathering this information would enable the agency to direct its resources toward achieving the second goal of the program. Evaluation, irrespective of the method, requires clearly specified goals and clearly articulated objectives in measurable terms. In general, evaluation is an ongoing process for which it is important to establish indicators at the beginning of the intervention. The process involves continuous, systematic monitoring of the intervention's impact, and this requires development and implementation of techniques of data management. Systematic analysis of data allows you to determine, for example, if the program activity or intervention is being implemented as planned and whether it is accomplishing the stated program goals (Gardner, 2000; Lewis, Lewis, Packard, & Souflee, 2001). Conducting evaluation requires skills in selecting an appropriate research design, techniques of measurement, and analysis of data. The specific details of the various methods are beyond the scope of this book. The requisite knowledge needed to implement the evaluation process is commonly discussed in research courses. Keep in mind that your ultimate aim is to track the impact of a change effort with regard to the desired outcomes.

Summary

This chapter discussed macro-level intervention strategies for which the target of change is a system. Today's social, economic, demographic, and political trends present numerous opportunities for action and intervention at the macro practice level. In talking to social workers in preparation for writing this chapter, we were impressed with the breadth and depth of macro practice strategies they used, and the ease with which they understood the need to bridge micro and macro. The social workers saw their practice as holistic and were comfortable employing a range of strategies to help people resolve problems or change social conditions. As one social worker stated, "It would be difficult to ask people to change without also addressing the circumstances and conditions that contribute to their situations." The person and environment focus reflected in this statement, in essence, frames the fundamental tenets and foundation of macro practice.

Competency Notes

EP 2.1.1a Advocate for client access to services. Social workers pay attention to the needs of groups and communities and, when necessary, engage in advocacy to obtain resources to address needs (p. 452).

EP 2.1.1d Demonstrate professional demeanor in behavior, appearance, and communication. Professional practice requires that social workers interact with people in ways that demonstrate the principles and ethics of the profession (p. 462).

EP 2.1.4a Recognize the ways in which culture's structures and values alienate, create, or enhance power and privilege. People vary in their ability, identity, and social and economic status. Structural barriers can determine the extent to which differences are valued or problematic. It is important that social workers recognize such barriers as they work with clients to achieve well-being (pp. 443–446, 451).

EP 2.1.4b Gain sufficient self-awareness to eliminate the influence of personal biases and values in working with diverse groups. The social and cultural identity of clients is diverse and may be unfamiliar. In situations in which a social worker encounters the unfamiliar, an evaluation and awareness of self, beliefs, and values can be critical so that personal preferences do not influence the work to be completed with clients (pp. 449–462).

EP 2.1.4d View themselves as learners and engage those with whom they work as key informants. Understanding diverse groups and communities is an ongoing process. Social workers use diverse interactions as an opportunity to learn from the people with whom they are involved (pp. 449, 462).

EP 2.1.5a Understand forms and mechanisms of oppression and discrimination. Social workers analyze policies and practices that may discriminate and contribute to the unequal or disparate treatment of clients that reinforce their marginalized status (p. 462).

EP 2.1.5b Advocate for human rights and social and economic justice. As advocates, social workers critique social policies and agency practices to ensure that clients rights are observed and that clients are not disadvantaged by structural barriers that influence their ability to achieve social and economic justice (pp. 443–444, 464).

EP 2.1.5c Engage in practices that engage in social and economic justice. Social workers make use of evidence and best practices so that their practice promotes social and economic justice (p. 461).

EP 2.1.6b Use research evidence to inform practice. Social workers use research methods to obtain data needed in such practice activities as developing resources and evaluating the outcome of an intervention (pp. 448, 467).

EP 2.1.8a Analyze, formulate, and advocate for policies that advance social well-being. Social workers analyze social policies and agency practices to determine if advocacy is needed (pp. 442–443, 445, 463).

EP 2.1.9a Continuously discover, appraise, and attend to changing locales, populations, scientific and technological developments, and emerging social trends to provide relevant services. Population changes and demographic shifts will require different or new resources to meet needs. Also, resources exist within communities. Understanding resource needs so that they are relevant to a particular group requires social workers to continually review research and statistical information, as well as evaluate resources within a demographic community (pp. 447, 450–451).

EP 2.1.9b Provide leadership in promoting sustainable changes in service delivery and practice to improve the quality of social services. Social workers act as change agents in organizations, as advocates for groups and communities, and by influencing policies and legislation (pp. 446, 453, 466).

EP 2.1.10a Substantively and effectively prepare for action with individuals, families, groups, and communities. Advocacy, social action, and community organizing requires interpersonal skills and skills in problem analysis, the development of strategic goals, and the evaluation of outcomes (pp. 442, 449, 451–452, 454, 456, 465–466).

EP 2.1.10b Use empathy and other interpersonal skills. In engaging and working with communities and groups, social workers use interpersonal skills, such empathy, as well as a range of communication skills (pp. 441, 456).

EP 2.1.10c Develop mutually agreed-upon focus of work and desired outcomes. Working with groups and communities should be collaborative. In this way, the focus of the social worker's involvement is determined by the client's needs, interests, and values (p. 453).

EP 2.1.10d Collect and organize client data. It is important for social workers to collect and review information to inform advocacy, social action, resource development, and organizations analysis so that their work is focused on client's needs and to improve service delivery (pp. 441, 452, 459).

EP 2.1.10e Assess client strengths and limitations. Assessing clients' strengths and empowerment are core principles of social work practice (p. 442).

EP 2.1.10g Select appropriate intervention strategy. In working with communities, social workers select strategies that are best suited to the needs and interest of the community (pp. 454–456).

EP 2.1.10h Initiate actions to achieve organizational goals. Social workers assist organizations to improve and maintain a service delivery system in which staff are active participants, the environment is inclusive, and clients rights and dignity is fundamental (pp. 458, 460, 462–463, 465).

EP 2.1.2d Apply strategies of ethical reasoning skills to arrive at principled decisions. In situations in which the CODE may not provide clear guidance or there are competing ethical obligations, social workers should rely on an ethical decision-making framework to guide their decisions (pp. 453, 457, 461).

Skill Development Exercises

1. Assess the organizational policies or practices using the questions identified by Rooney.
2. Using Figure 14-1, think of the potential benefit of linking an individual client situation that you have worked with to a change effort at the macro-level.
3. Choose a public policy or social problem. How would you describe your position on either one or both? Would you describe yourself as a liberal (conservative, moderate, or radical) a conservative (fiscal, religious, or social) or a centrist? Think about how your identified position influences your thinking about the policy or problem.
4. Describe how client dignity and worth is fostered in your agency.
5. Think about the potential ways in which social work practice is influenced by public policy.
6. Rate your current position of each of Hackman and Oldham's core characteristics of job design and motivation.
7. Identify a change that you would like to make in your agency. Identify the risks, benefits, and potential opposition to your change proposal.
8. Using Rivera and Erlich's Level of Community Contact, what steps would you take in working with a community at each level? What are potential ethical issues at each level?
9. Reflect upon the organizational cultural competence factors discussed by Nybell and Gray (2004). How would you measure your agency using these factors?

CourseMate

Access an integrated eBook and chapter specific learning tools including glossary terms, chapter outlines, relevant web links, videos, and practice quizzes. Go to **www.cengagebrain.com**.

Understanding the Nature of the Helping Relationship

The three chapters of Part I provide you with an overview of the text and offer you a sense of why the clinical skills and clinical tools that you will read and learn about in Parts II and III are so critical. In addition, you are introduced to the notion that being a professional counselor is a planned and deliberate process that entails the learning of a number of counseling skills and tools. This is contrasted with the qualities of the natural helper whose intentions are good but whose actions are not always conducive to a positive helping relationship.

Chapter 1 is entitled "From Natural Helper to Professional Counselor" and begins by reviewing the research on whether or not counseling and psychotherapy are effective. After establishing that counseling is effective, the chapter introduces you to the notion that clinical work with clients is a planned process and that you must learn a number of critical skills and tools to be effective at it. This leads into a discussion of eight core areas of knowledge and skills one should master to become a proficient, professional counselor, including (a) ethical, professional, and cross-cultural issues, (b) helper attitudes, (c) techniques, (d) diagnosis, (e) case conceptualization, (f) treatment planning, (g) case management, and (h) theory.

Chapter 2 introduces the relative importance of each of the core areas to the following stages of the counseling relationship: the preinterview, rapport and trust-building, problem identification, goal-setting, work, closure, and the postinterview. As we discuss the stages, we offer a case example to show how a client and a clinician work as they move through the stages of the counseling relationship, and we note that this case example (and others) will appear again in Part III of the text. The goals of the stages and how the core areas emerge as a function of the stages are summarized in the Chapter 2 Appendix, and these tables are also useful as a guide to the rest of the text. The chapter concludes with a discussion of the importance of continually trying to master the core areas throughout our careers and of remaining open to embracing changes in the core areas as we continue on our professional journey.

Chapter 3 is entitled "Ethical, Professional, and Cross-Cultural Issues." It starts by defining ethics and distinguishing between ethics and morality. Next, there is a discussion of the development and importance of professional ethical codes, and we highlight some codes of ethics and ethical hot spots in the helping professions. This is followed by a review of some critical ethical and legal issues, including breach of confidentiality, confidentiality of records, privileged communication, and confinement against one's will. As we continue, we offer three models of ethical decision making: decision-making models, moral models, and developmental models.

The next section of Chapter 3 examines a number of critical professional issues that impact the work of the clinician, including managed care, accountability, use of medication, and matching client problem with intervention strategy. The chapter continues with an examination of cross-cultural issues, where we specifically address the fact that counseling, as it is practiced today, often is not effective for many people of color. We next present some models of cross-cultural counseling and offer suggestions on how to work with a number of diverse groups. The chapter concludes by noting that improving our ability to work with cross-cultural clients, and indeed, with all clients, is a never-ending process; that is, we should always be fine-tuning our skills and learning how to be more effective with all of the clients with whom we work.

From Natural Helper to Professional Counselor

Do counseling and psychotherapy work? That is the first critical question this chapter explores. And after presenting research that answers this question with a resounding "yes," we examine why counseling and therapy work and then distinguish what we call "natural helping" from professional counseling. This leads to a discussion of eight core areas of knowledge and skills needed if one is to become a professional counselor, including (a) ethical, professional, and cross-cultural issues, (b) helper attitudes, (c) techniques, (d) diagnosis, (e) case conceptualization, (f) treatment planning, (g) case management, and (h) theory. These essential core areas will be extensively discussed throughout this book. But let's start with the most basic question: Do counseling and psychotherapy work?

Do Counseling and Psychotherapy Work?

> *How well counselors perform, what they do, and what they will become is a complex interaction of credentialing requirements, expectations of the settings in which they are employed, personal characteristics, and the quality and content of their preparation as counselors.* (Herr, 1985, p. 33)

In 1952, Eysenck looked at 24 uncontrolled studies that examined the effectiveness of psychotherapy and found that "roughly two-thirds of a group of neurotic patients will recover or improve to a marked extent within about two years of the onset of their illness, *whether they are treated by means of psychotherapy or not*" (p. 322, italics added). Eysenck's research sent tremors through the professional community, and a debate ensued concerning the effectiveness of counseling. Although Eysenck's research was shown to be flawed, it did lead to debate concerning the effectiveness of counseling and resulted in hundreds of studies that examined counseling effectiveness. The results of this massive amount of research showed the following:

> *The evidence accumulated over the last 40 years is relatively clear: Counseling is a process from which most clients who remain involved for at least a few*

sessions benefit. When counseling effectiveness is calculated by determining the number of clients who improved, the results are amazingly similar across various studies. On the basis of both client and counselor ratings, approximately 22% of clients made significant gains, 43% made moderate changes, while 27% made some improvement. . . . (Sexton, 1993, p. 82)

Sexton goes on to say that "counseling outcome research findings are so compelling that the debate regarding whether counseling is effective is no longer a major issue" (p. 84) (also see Sexton, 1999). Despite being assured that counseling works for a large majority of clients, questions concerning how it works and for whom it works best are still debated. For instance, a number of questions remained largely unanswered, including: Does counseling work for all types of problems? Does counseling work equally well for all cultural groups? Does counseling work equally well for all problems when conducted under all types of therapies? Are the effects of counseling long term? Does the personality style of the therapist have a differential effect on client outcomes? In an attempt to answer some of these questions, Lambert and Cattani-Thompson (1996) and Lambert and Ogles (2004) have reviewed the research on the effectiveness of counseling and found the following:

1. The vast majority of clients do better at the time of treatment termination.
2. For as many as 50% of clients, counseling can be effective in as few as 5 to 10 sessions.
3. Although 20% to 30% of clients will require treatment that is longer term, most of these will see improvements with counseling.
4. For the majority of clients, gains made in counseling seem to last long term.
5. As one might expect, less defensive, motivated clients who accept personal responsibility and do not have severe chronic problems do better in counseling.
6. Some techniques work better with specific problems, and clinicians should try to match techniques to problems.
7. Some clients will get worse in counseling, and clinicians should make every attempt to monitor client progress and make changes in technique or refer as quickly as possible.
8. The counselor–client relationship, or how the clinician brings himself or herself into the helping relationship, seems to be the best predictor of success in counseling.

As evidenced by the research, it is now clear that counseling is effective. It follows that clinicians should have the knowledge and skills that have been found to make it so. But how exactly does one gain such knowledge? That question is critical if we are to understand the nature of the effective counseling relationship.

Natural Helping Versus Professional Counseling

Have you ever listened to the radio talk-show host Dr. Laura or TV personality Dr. Phil? They certainly are heavy on the advice giving. It's not our style of doing counseling, and some have criticized them for being unprofessional, but they clearly are following their natural inclination to give advice. However, is following one's natural inclination or style the most effective way to do counseling? We would argue that it is not. In fact, the professional counseling relationship is quite different from the more familiar experience of natural everyday helping. Natural helpers, such as friends, relatives, and supportive others, rely on intuition, familiarity, natural responsiveness, and personal opinions as they spontaneously listen, support, encourage, challenge, analyze, make hopeful suggestions, and offer whatever advice they find most sensible. In contrast, the professional clinician attempts to purposely direct the counseling relationship by applying a broad range of critical skills in a systematic fashion.

HIGHLIGHT 1.1 **Counseling Does Work and Provides a Deliberate Mechanism to Help Clients**

In addition to the research that shows the efficacy of counseling, literally hundreds of publications have provided various mechanisms for how to do counseling. One manuscript by Daniels (2003) lists approximately 450 citations that speak to various skills important in the training of counseling.

Typically, we have found new students in clinical training describe themselves as natural "listeners," "analyzers," "problem solvers," or "challengers." And although such students have their hearts in the right place, they often have little knowledge of how to apply critical professional skills. For instance, those who define themselves as "natural listeners" tend to be caring, good listeners and focus on client self-expression and self-growth. These students might be heard saying the following:

1. "Counseling has to do with listening to another person's pain."
2. "I really want to show my clients I care about them—they are people!"
3. "I know I can help my client find out more about herself by listening intensely to her."

These new counselors are emphasizing active listening, empathic understanding, and rapport and trust building—skills that are most salient in the early stages of the counseling relationship. In their experience as natural helpers, they primarily have been "listening ears" who effectively offer support, help the person in need express himself or herself, and facilitate the client's understanding of his or her thoughts and feelings. However, they tend to be more reactive to clients, rarely guide or lead, and are usually less comfortable with case conceptualization, diagnosis, and treatment planning—skills that are critical in today's world. For them, the helping skills of listening, reflection, and empathic understanding, which we will study in Chapter 5, come naturally and will be strong assets early in their professional education and development.

In contrast to the listener, there are "analyzers," or students who mainly define counseling by assessing and analyzing client concerns and by focusing on gaining a better understanding of the issues. These students might be heard saying the following:

1. "I like to help people by analyzing and interpreting their problems for them."

2. "I love investigating the lives of clients—their past, present, and future. I think this helps clients understand the reasons for their feelings and problems and is a good basis for developing goals."
3. "Counseling is like a puzzle. I help the client put it together by probing and exploring parts of the client's psyche."

These new counselors are emphasizing case conceptualization, diagnosis, and treatment planning—skills that are most salient in the early to middle stages of the counseling relationship. In their experience as natural helpers, they primarily explore and probe and offer critical analyses of the problem's root causes and the factors that sustain or exacerbate the current situation. Usually, they are most comfortable deriving an intellectual understanding of client problems and less accustomed to soliciting expressions of emotion or listening empathically. They will enjoy learning about the skills of diagnosis, case conceptualization, and treatment planning (Chapters 8, 9, and 10) and will feel at home with the information-gathering skills we will discuss in Chapter 6. However, they might have a more difficult time with building relationships and using some of the foundational skills found in Chapter 5.

Then there are students who see themselves as "problem solvers." Here are some possible descriptions problem solvers might give of the counseling relationship:

1. "Counseling has to do with giving advice or direction."
2. "Why spend so much time analyzing or probing when you can get right down to the solution?"
3. "I love to offer guidance to a client. I think I can help a client, in a relatively short amount of time, solve his or her problem."

These students are emphasizing the work stage of the counseling relationship. In their experience as natural helpers, they primarily have been "problem solvers" and "action takers." They like to identify problems and tend to be more directive, attempting to mobilize the person in need to make decisions, take action, or decisively change behavior. Usually, they are most comfortable moving steadfastly toward problem resolution but are uncomfortable with listening, empathy, and case conceptualization. They tend to prefer the solution-focused skills of offering advice, offering alternatives, and giving feedback, which we will examine in Chapter 7, and they will also like the treatment-planning process described in Chapter 10. They may bring to the relationship an emphasis on brief counseling, solution-focused approaches, or guidance.

Finally, there are the "challengers." These students like to confront their clients, and you might find them saying the following about the counseling relationship:

1. "Why spend all that time listening to thoughts and feelings when you can directly ask a client why they feel a certain way?"
2. "Counseling has to do with pushing clients to understand how they created their current situation and challenging them to find ways of improving it."

PROFESSIONAL PERSPECTIVES 1.1
Pushing a Client Too Far

As a therapist at a mental health center, I (Ed Neukrug) worked with a psychiatrist who was the director of an inpatient unit. This psychiatrist was known for verbally confronting his clients in what some considered an abusive manner. Many a client (and therapist) were intimidated by him. One day, he chose the wrong client to confront, for as he berated this client for not following his treatment plan, the client lifted him in the air, held him against the wall, and told him, "Nobody tells me what to do." Many of the other clients (and quite a few therapists) could be heard quietly cheering on this client.

This example is an important reminder to the natural challenger that the manner in which a client is challenged is an artful skill that needs to be done carefully and appropriately and that other skills, such as listening, analysis, and problem solving, also need to be used if the natural challenger is to be effective.

3. "The counselor's role is to point out discrepancies between clients' actions, feelings, and behaviors."

The challenger likes to confront the manner in which the client views the world. This student cares little for understanding the stages of the helping relationship and has little patience for the natural rhythm of the helping relationship—concepts we examine in Chapter 2. In fact, this student often thinks that he or she can quickly push the client into seeing the world in a different manner and will often confront clients through the use of questions, particularly "why" questions, as we will discuss in Chapter 6. This student is not particularly comfortable with empathy, as he or she believes there is no reason to take a lot of time indirectly getting to the problem when you can ask the client directly what's going on. Similarly, case conceptualization is not seen as a particularly important skill by these students because it relies on having a complex cognitive understanding of the client's predicament and on understanding theory and is not, on the surface, goal oriented. However, he or she may feel comfortable challenging a client and telling the client his or her diagnosis while assisting the client in creating a treatment plan—concepts we will examine in Chapters 7 and 10, respectively (see Professional Perspectives 1.1).

As suggested in the examples given, each new trainee has a natural inclination toward a style of being with a client. And it should be stressed that each style has a unique and important perspective to offer to the counseling relationship. However, often trainees know little about how to apply their style in the most effective manner, how to apply their style in a timely fashion, or how knowledge and skills in other core areas will increase the probability that he or she will work effectively with clients. Although you might find that you have more of an affinity for one style of helping over the others (see Exercise 1.1), we believe that if you are to be an effective clinician, you must be well-rounded and deliberate; that is, you will need to learn a wide range of core knowledge and skills and be able to apply them in a manner that can be most helpful to the client. Thus, one purpose of this text is to move you from your natural helping style toward a professional counseling approach in which you have at your disposal a large repertoire of knowledge and skills.

EXERCISE 1.1 **Natural Styles of Helping**

Using the scale shown, give yourself a rating for each style of natural helping listed. Then, rank order the style and write its corresponding score. See the example below. As you read through the text, identify those skills that most coincide with your natural style.

These are the skills you will likely be particularly good at, and you probably will have a more difficult time learning the skills associated with your secondary styles.

1	2	3	4	5	6	7	8	9	10
Not at All Important				Moderately Important			Critically Important		
Possibly Harmful							Probably Very Helpful		

STYLE

___ Listener: Likes to understand another's point of view by listening and showing empathy. Has feelings for another.

___ Analytical: Likes to explore, probe, and offer a critical analysis of a situation. Involved in the intellectual process of understanding a client's predicament.

___ Problem Solver: Likes to define the problem, set goals, and take action to reach a solution.

___ Challenger: Likes to push and confront a client into viewing the world differently.

EXAMPLE

	Rank	Score
1.	Listener	10
2.	Analyzer	8
3.	Problem Solver	3
4.	Challenger	2

YOUR SCORE AND RANK

	Rank	Score
1.	_____	____
2.	_____	____
4.	_____	____
5.	_____	____

Core Areas of Knowledge and Skills

As noted earlier, becoming a professional counselor means that you have mastered the knowledge and skills in a number of core areas, such as the eight that we have identified. In this text, each core area, with the exception of theory, has one or more chapters dedicated to it. Theory is mentioned briefly throughout the text, and you will likely have a separate course devoted to it.

PART I:
UNDERSTANDING THE NATURE OF THE HELPING RELATIONSHIP
All Core Areas: Chapter 1
All Core Areas: Chapter 2
Core Area 1:   Ethical, Professional, and Cross-Cultural Issues (Chapter 3)

PART II:

CLINICAL SKILLS: ATTITUDES AND TECHNIQUES FOR EFFECTIVE
COUNSELING

Core Area 2:   Helper Attitudes (Chapter 4)
Core Area 3:   Techniques (Chapters 4–7)

PART III:

CLINICAL TOOLS: MANAGING THE CHANGE PROCESS
Core Area 4:   Diagnosis (Chapter 8)
Core Area 5:   Case Conceptualization (Chapter 9)
Core Area 6:   Treatment Planning (Chapter 10)
Core Area 7:   Case Management (Chapter 11)
Core Area 8:   Theory (briefly mentioned in Chapters 1, 2, 9,
and 10)

PART IV:

PROFESSIONAL TOOLBOXES

Expands on core areas of knowledge and skills presented in text and DVD.

What follows are brief descriptions of these core areas. As you read through the text, you will have an opportunity to delve further into each of them.

Ethical, Professional, and Cross-Cultural Issues

The natural helper has not learned, and likely has little interest in learning, the broad array of professional and ethical issues that can impact on a helping relationship. These issues are critical to the relationship because they affect the manner in which the clinician works with his or her client. For instance, understanding the limits of our ability as a therapist, how we describe our work to our clients (e.g., professional disclosure statements), knowing the limits of confidentiality, assuring that we have the necessary knowledge of cross-cultural differences in our application of helping skills, understanding the importance of the boundaries of the helping relationship, knowing what to do when a client is in danger of harming himself or herself or another, and knowing when to refer a client to another therapist are just a few of the myriad ethical concerns that might be faced by the professional counselor and are addressed in ethical codes (see Toolbox A for Web sites of the ethical codes of select mental health professional associations). Ethical, professional, and cross-cultural issues will be discussed at length in Chapter 3 and highlighted at other times throughout the text.

Helper Attitudes

The natural helper relies on his or her intuitive sense of what attitudes and behaviors should be applied in the informal helping relationship. In contrast, the professional counselor has adopted personality characteristics that have been theoretically or empirically shown to be critical to the effective helping relationship. It is essential that the professional counselor learns how to let go of behaviors and attitudes that would be detrimental to the helping relationship and purposefully and actively adopt new behaviors and attitudes that will facilitate client growth. Research on effectiveness of counseling has pinpointed some attitudes that seem to be more critical than others. Some of these include being empathic, genuine, accepting, and open-minded. Others include cognitive complexity, being adjusted psychologically, being able to build a relationship with your client, and being competent (see Neukrug, 2003, 2004). These characteristics will be examined in Chapter 4.

Techniques

Natural helpers tend to randomly apply a hodgepodge of techniques when helping an individual. Unfortunately, their techniques have often been shown not to be theoretically or empirically sound. Professional counselors, on the other hand, have at their disposal a wide range of helping skills that have been shown to be effective in assisting clients through the stages of the helping relationship. A number of chapters in this text are dedicated to understanding these skills, including Chapter 5, which covers the foundational skills of silence and pause time, listening, paraphrasing, and empathy; Chapter 6, which examines the information-gathering skills of asking questions, conducting a structured interview, and administering assessment procedures; and Chapter 7, which examines the commonly used skills of affirmation-giving, encouragement, modeling, self-disclosure, collaboration, and confrontation, as well as the commonly used solution-focused skills of offering alternatives, information-giving, and advice-giving.

Diagnosis

Studies have shown that a large percentage of Americans have or will experience an emotional disorder (Hersen & Van Hasselt, 2001). Thus, regardless of where a counselor is employed, he or she will be working with clients who have serious emotional problems, and often, these clients will be given a diagnosis based on their symptoms (see Davison & Neale, 2004). Whereas the natural helper will not apply a formal diagnosis, he or she may come up with a nonresearched diagnosis from popular literature. On the other hand, the professional counselor will rely on a systematic mechanism of making a diagnosis that relies on professional sources, such as the *Diagnostics and Statistical Manual-IV, Text Revision* (American Psychiatric Association, 2000). Making an accurate diagnosis is critical for treatment planning because it helps determine the kinds of goals and techniques to be used. Recognizing this, most training programs now include in their curriculum a focus on psychopathology and diagnosis (Hinkle, 1994a; Hohenshil, 1993, 1994).

Controversy still exists about the use of diagnosis and includes such issues as (a) Is diagnosis a social construction? (b) Why are minorities misdiagnosed at higher rates than Whites? and (c) Is associating a person with a diagnostic "label" in the long run harmful to how the client views himself or herself and how others view the client? Despite this controversy, it is clear that all clinicians today must be familiar with how to make a diagnosis and with the purposes diagnoses serve (Fong, 1995; Hinkle, 1994a, 1994b; Hohenshil, 1994). Thus, how to diagnosis clients' symptoms will be discussed in detail in Chapter 8.

Case Conceptualization

Case conceptualization, the next logical step after making a preliminary diagnosis, is the process that allows the clinician to understand, through his or her unique theoretical perspective, a client's presenting problems and subsequently apply appropriate counseling skills and treatment strategies. Whereas experienced counselors develop their own systematic method of conceptualizing client problems, natural helpers do not have a mechanism for understanding clients. If not given a method for case conceptualization, beginning counselors and therapists, who are often still struggling with their theoretical orientation, will have a difficult time conceptualizing client problems. This leaves students floundering, often relying on their intuition, falling back on basic counseling skills, and, much like natural helpers, randomly attempting a hodgepodge of techniques (Martin, Slemon, Hiebert, Hallberg, & Cummings, 1989). Thus, we believe it is critical that every student have a model of case conceptualization. One model of case conceptualization that we will discuss in this text is Schwitzer's (1996, 1997) inverted pyramid heuristic (IPH). How to conceptualize client problems will be discussed in detail in Chapter 9.

Treatment Planning

Whereas natural helpers rarely, if ever, develop a planned mechanism for working with clients, the professional counselor and therapist has the knowledge and professional responsibility to provide a client with a treatment plan that will address presenting issues. A treatment plan is based on one's conceptualization of client problems and on the diagnosis of the client. It establishes the process that will be used to address identified problems and can include such elements as the length of treatment, intervention skills, and possible medication that might be used. Treatment planning is critical in the accountability process because it defines a method of treatment that can later be used to evaluate progress. Treatment planning will be addressed in Chapter 10.

Case Management

Case management has been viewed as the overall process involved in maintaining the optimal functioning of clients (Sullivan, Wolk, & Hartmann, 1992; Woodside & McClam, 2003). Thus, case management involves a broad array of activities including (a) documentation, (b) consultation, supervision, and collaboration, (c) communicating with stakeholders, (d) business-related activities, and (e) caseload management. Whereas the natural helper has rarely even considered the vast majority of the case management issues just listed, the professional counselor sees case management as a critical piece of his or her work with the client. And with a greater emphasis on accountability in the mental health professions, these issues have become increasingly important. Thus, case management will be examined in detail in Chapter 11.

Theory

Generally, natural helpers have not thought through their understanding of human nature, which is basic to one's theoretical orientation. In contrast, professional counselors should be able to clearly identify their view of human nature and the subsequent theory of change that is derived from it. Theories, and the view of human nature that they are based on, typically take into account the effects of biology, genetics, and environment (e.g., family, neighborhood, social situation) on the personality development of the individual. Theories are heuristic; that is, they are researchable and testable and ultimately allow us to discard those aspects shown to be ineffective. Having a counseling theory is the clinician's template for conceptualizing client problems, applying techniques, and predicting change (Brammer & MacDonald, 2003; Brammer, Shostrom, & Abrego, 1993). To "function without theory is to operate without placing events in some order and thus to function meaninglessly" (Hansen, Rossberg, & Cramer, 1994, p. 9). Today, there are dozens of counseling theories, although only a handful are practiced by the majority of clinicians (Neukrug, Milliken, & Shoemaker, 2001; Neukrug & Williams, 1993). Although it is not the purview of this text to focus in depth on theory, theory is mentioned throughout the text and is critical to understanding the case conceptualization process described in Chapter 9.

LEARNING TO BE A COUNSELOR: An Ongoing Process

You are about to take the journey from natural helper to professional counselor. However, whether you have never been a counselor, have 50 years of counseling experience and are first obtaining your degree, or are a master therapist recognized around the world, you have something in common—you still have a lot to learn. During that learning process, we hope you spend time examining and delving deeper into each of the core areas identified in this book.

As you continue on your journey, and as years pass, you will find that the core knowledge and skills identified in this book will evolve. As they transform, we believe that each of us has the responsibility to remain knowledgeable about how the core areas have changed and how other new core areas may arise. Stay informed, keep practicing, and remember that the best clinicians are those who have a solid foundation but also recognize advances in the field and are willing to judiciously change with the times.

 At this point, we recommend that you pause reading the text, turn to the DVD, and view the section entitled:

Introduction

Chapter Summary

This chapter began by examining the research on the effectiveness of counseling and psychotherapy. We first presented Eysenck's (1952) study, which suggested that professional counseling might not be effective. However, due to the furor this study created, and the fact that the study was found to have serious methodological flaws, a vast amount of follow-up research was conducted that showed the efficacy of counseling and psychotherapy. We concluded that the vast majority of clients do better as a result of counseling, with most of them making gains within 10 sessions. We also noted that the reason counseling works seems to be a mixture of counselor attitudes and the techniques used.

As the chapter continued, we distinguished the natural helper from the professional counselor. We suggested that many beginning counselors enter training with one of four natural orientations to working with clients: listeners, analyzers, problem solvers, or challengers. We also suggested that each of these styles works best at different stages of the helping relationship and that the effective helper is well-rounded and deliberate; that is, he or she has learned a wide range of core knowledge and skills and can apply them in a manner that can be most helpful to the client. Thus, we proposed that the purpose of this text is to move you from your natural helping style toward a professional counseling approach in which you have at your disposal a large repertoire of knowledge and skills.

Based on the literature, we next went on to identify eight core areas of knowledge and skills we deemed critical if one is to be an effective clinician, including: (a) ethical, professional, and cross-cultural issues, (b) helper attitudes, (c) techniques, (d) diagnosis, (e) case conceptualization, (f) treatment planning, (g) case management, and (h) theory. We noted that each core area cited, with the exception of theory, has one or more chapters dedicated to it.

The chapter concluded with a discussion of the importance of continually trying to master the core areas of knowledge and skills throughout our careers and the importance of remaining open to embracing changes in the core areas and, ultimately, in the skills and tools we use.

The Stages of the Counseling Relationship

In contrast to natural helpers, who do not tend to view the helping relationship as a process, professional counselors understand that the relationship has a natural progression that begins with the building of a therapeutic alliance, leads toward the identification of problems, moves forward toward working on those problems, and has a clear ending based on the attainment of goals. Each stage in this helping relationship is seen as an important building block in the overall helping process and carries with it a unique primary goal. In this chapter, we identify the primary goal of each stage of the helping relationship. Then, we show how each of the core areas of knowledge and skills identified in Chapter 1 are critical in varying ways during every stage of the counseling relationship. The chapter concludes with three tables that summarize the stages and the critical knowledge and skills areas that are needed in each stage.

 If you have not done so already, we recommend that you pause reading the text, turn to the DVD, and view the section entitled:

Introduction

Understanding the Stages of the Counseling Relationship

If clinicians are to be successful, they must understand the natural unfolding progression of the helping relationship and how to apply the core areas of knowledge and skills, identified in Chapter 1, at an opportune moment. Thus, this chapter describes the stages of the helping relationship, notes the primary goal of the stage, and then details which core areas of knowledge and skills are associated with each stage. The core areas of knowledge and skills are described under three general headings: Clinical Skills, where attitudes and techniques are discussed; Clinical Tools, where diagnosis, case conceptualization, treatment planning, case management, and theory are covered; and Ethical, Professional, and Cross-Cultural Issues. Each of these core areas are covered in the subsequent chapters of this text. The stages include the preinterview, rapport and trust building, problem identification, goal setting, work, closure, and the postrelationship (Neukrug, 2002).

The Preinterview (Preparatory) Stage

The preinterview process consist of the counselor's preparation for the first meeting as well as the client's experiences prior to that meeting, including making the decision to seek help and taking the first steps inside the agency walls. The primary goal at the preinterview stage is to prepare for an optimal first professional encounter with the client (see Chapter 2 Appendix for a summary of this stage).

Clinical Skill

ATTITUDES During the preinterview stage, it is the clinician's responsibility to take a self-inventory of his or her attitudes to assure that he or she is psychologically ready to work with clients throughout all of the stages. Although each attitude is critical throughout all of the stages, some emerge as more important than others as a function of stage. *Being open-minded and accepting, being psychologically adjusted,* and *cognitive complexity* deserve special mention at the preparatory stage. Although at times it is natural for clinicians to have difficulty being nonjudgmental, it is critical to begin each new counseling relationship with an open-minded, accepting attitude and an inviting manner. Also, because clients come to counseling for a myriad of reasons, the counselor must have the psychological preparedness to handle whatever emotionally charged or value-laden issues the client presents. In addition, the clinician must have the cognitive complexity to understand that any information obtained in the early stages likely gives only a glimpse of the whole client picture. Thus, the clinician should not try to jump to premature conclusions about the client, and the clinician should be psychologically able to deal with whatever issues the client brings to therapy.

Clinical Tool

CASE MANAGEMENT If the relationship is to begin on a positive note, good case management is needed even before meeting the client for the first time (Neukrug, 2002, 2004). For instance, the counselor should assure an appointment time is made and be punctual for the interview. Also, he or she should assure that all related paperwork and agency files are in order and review any advance information such as reports from previous clinicians, assessment results, or other clinical material. Preparatory case management also requires that the counselor and administrative staff handle all preinterview phone contacts, scheduling matters, waiting room situations, and so forth in a professional and courteous manner that gives a positive impression to the soon-to-be client.

Ethical, Professional, and Cross-Cultural Issues

COMPETENCE AND PROFESSIONAL LIMITATIONS   Prior to the helping relationship beginning, the clinician should determine if the client's concerns and dynamics are within the counselor's range of competencies and whether the agency or setting is appropriate for the presenting problem. Knowing one's professional limits is important if the clinician is to make thoughtful and wise decisions about whether to counsel the client, seek consultation and/or supervision, or refer the client to another professional.

OFFICE DECOR   Professional counselors are intentional about the image they want their office to convey. In general, professional items and neutral decor are preferable, although some personal items like family photos are acceptable. Although items reflecting personal values, such as political flyers and religious books, are usually avoided, this is not always the case. For instance, the clinician who works in a religiously based counseling center or one who works in a counseling center for gays and lesbians might be more apt to have materials that are biased toward the values of his or her clients. Ultimately, the clinician should make purposeful, wise decisions about office decor, taking into account its impact on clients.

KNOWLEDGE OF AND SKILLS TO USE WITH DIVERSE CLIENTS   As the ethnic/cultural background of the client is determined, the clinician needs to consider whether he or she has the knowledge and skills necessary to be effective with the client. If not, the clinician should do the preparatory work to gain the needed knowledge and skills or refer the client to someone who is more familiar with the client's culture.

ATTITUDES TOWARD DIVERSE CLIENTS   Prior to meeting with the client, the clinician needs to take a self-inventory to assure that he or she does not hold biases toward the client's culture. Because biases can be unconscious, such a self-inventory must be taken very seriously.

CASE ILLUSTRATION 2.1   Preinterview (Preparatory) Stage

The following case example is provided in installments throughout this chapter to highlight the clinical responsibilities associated with each stage of the counseling relationship. (Please note that we will return to this case in Part III of the text.)

Sienna, a 23 year old, African American, second-year college female, calls the student counseling center presenting moderate, persistent depression. Sienna comes from an intact family, now lives on campus with an assigned roommate, and is involved with a White male college student.

PREINTERVIEW CLIENT DYNAMICS
Sienna's self-referred main concerns were low mood and feelings of depression lasting for several months. Prior to seeking counseling, Sienna had tried to cope by using an old coping mechanism of "just trying to be happy," distracting herself with social activities, working out, and concentrating on school. When her

problems continued, she tried new ways of coping, including discussing her problems with her resident assistant and seeking support from her best friend and from her boyfriend. Finally, when none of these helped change her mood, she began downsliding—that is, feeling worse, having less energy, performing poorly academically, and having growing, distressing self-doubts about her ability to handle adult life.

PREINTERVIEW CLINICAL DYNAMICS
When she contacted the center, basic information was gathered from Sienna and she was given an initial appointment (case management). The counselor was a clinician experienced with college student mood problems but also was prepared to refer Sienna to a consulting psychiatrist to evaluate her for medication or hospitalization if needed (competence). Based on the limited information the counselor had received about the client prior to intake, she prepared herself for tearfulness, presentations of sadness, and perhaps pessimistic thoughts of leaving school or even suicide but also tried to remain open to whatever issues may arise (openness). She also made a mental note of the importance of being accepting and nonjudgmental regarding Sienna's problem and the fact that the limited amount of information that she had might not be a full indication of the extent of Sienna's problem (cognitive complexity). In addition, the counselor, who is White, completed a self-inventory to assure she was not holding biases and reflected on the literature she had read concerning working with female, African American young adults.

EXERCISE 2.1 **Reflections on the Preinterview**

In small groups, consider the following issues that clinicians often face during the preinterview stage of the counseling relationship.

1. RESOLVING ISSUES AND EXPECTATIONS OF COUNSELING: Think of a time when you were confronted with the emergence of a new stressor, longstanding unresolved developmental concern, or growing entrenched problem in your own life. How did you resolve the concern? How might you have felt seeking counseling for the first time about your problem? What expectations would you have about the counselor?

2. MAINTAINING A NONJUDGMENTAL ATTITUDE: It is natural for clinicians to face difficulties being nonjudgmental at times. Which clients, or what counseling issues, do you believe will be most challenging for you as you attempt to remain nonjudgmental? How will you manage this when confronted by a new client with the characteristics or issues you identified?

Stage 1: Rapport and Trust Building

Stage 1 begins with the actual interview, and the primary goal of this stage is to gather initial information about the client and establish a trusting, facilitative therapeutic alliance. Although Stage 1 begins with the first interview, it can last from one to many sessions depending on the client and the nature of the problem (see Chapter 2 Appendix for a summary of this stage).

Clinical Skills

ATTITUDES Having *empathy* and showing *acceptance* are two attitudes that assist in building a strong alliance early in the clinical relationship. These attitudes help the client feel safe, encourage self-disclosure, and set the tone for the helping relationship. Unlike natural helpers who are often uncomfortable with the strong emotions of helpees, as client self-disclosure occurs, the professional counselor has the ability to listen and be accepting of the expression of deep emotions, such as sobs of depression, rage, or feelings of guilt and shame. This ability is the result of the clinician's work on his or her own psychological adjustment.

The beginning of the helping relationship is critical to successful outcomes, and clinicians must have embraced the notion that if they do not have the *competence* to work with a particular client, they will seek consultation or supervision, or refer the client to a clinician who can be effective with the client.

TECHNIQUES The major goal of this stage is to build trust and rapport, and the foundational skills of *silence* and *pause time, listening, paraphrasing,* and *empathic understanding* are critical to this process. *Information gathering* is important at this early stage because it helps the clinician understand the totality of the client's situation. In addition, in this age of accountability, information is needed quickly to form diagnostic impressions and to develop treatment plans, which often are required by funding sources and insurance companies. Thus, *conducting a structured interview* and gently probing and *asking questions* are often used during this early part of the helping relationship and continued in Stage 2. One of the challenges faced by the counselor during this stage is to build a strong therapeutic alliance through the use of foundational skills and also to conduct the information gathering that needs to take place, which often requires skills that are not as conducive to relationship building. As the clinician readies to move on to the next stage, *collaboration* is important because the clinician wants to assure that his or her expectations match those of the client.

Clinical Tools

CASE CONCEPTUALIZATION Although the case conceptualization process has barely begun in this stage, clinicians do begin to make some tentative hypotheses about client issues and possible ancillary concerns that will be used later in the case conceptualization process.

DIAGNOSIS As the client begins to identify issues, the clinician will very tentatively consider diagnoses. However, it is critical that the clinician wait until more information is gathered in Stage 2 before making a firm diagnosis of symptoms.

CASE MANAGEMENT Extensive case management early in the helping relationship is usually needed to ensure that all related paperwork and intake assessment materials are completed, billing and other business matters are attended to, necessary correspondence with other professionals is conducted, and agency records have been addressed.

Ethical, Professional, and Cross-Cultural Issues

PROFESSIONAL COMPETENCE During Stage 1, the clinician should confirm that the client's concerns and dynamics are within the counselor's range of competencies and that the agency or setting is appropriate for the presenting problem. Thus, the clinician should make thoughtful decisions about whether counseling can be productive for the client's presenting problem, whether to make an effective referral, or whether to consult with another professional.

CROSS-CULTURAL COMPETENCE As the clinician gets to know the client, he or she should become acutely aware of gaps in knowledge and skills that exist relative to the client's ethnic/cultural background (Arredondo, 1999). In addition, competent cross-cultural clinicians should be cognizant of any biased attitudes they might have toward a client. When gaps in knowledge or skills cannot be appropriately dealt with to assure positive client outcomes, or when counselors have biased attitudes that cannot be overcome, the client should be referred to another clinician.

COUNSELOR SELF-DISCLOSURE Professional counselors are planful about self-disclosure, and they make purposeful decisions concerning what, if any, personal information will be shared with clients. Self-disclosure should only be done when it is expected to benefit the client. Some clinicians share very little personal information to keep the focus squarely on the client, but other counselors use more self-disclosure. Regardless of how much sharing the clinician believes will be helpful, a general rule during Stage 1 is to focus almost completely on the client and then to gradually allow more counselor self-disclosure later in the process.

ESTABLISHING BOUNDARIES Another way professional counseling is different from natural helping is that the relationship has built-in limits. During Stage 1, clients should obtain a clear picture of how often and for how long sessions will take place, what they can expect and should not expect from the counselor during the relationship, and how to reach the counselor for emergency as well as nonemergency matters (e.g., suicidal thoughts, billing, cancellations, rescheduling, etc.).

ASSESSING FOR HARM TO SELF OR OTHERS Although more formally done in Stage Two (see the subsection on Assessing for Psychopathology and Breaking Confidentiality), it is critical that clinicians are aware of any signs that the client might be potentially harmful to self or others. Clinicians should know how to ask questions to assess for such lethality and when it is ethically and legally critical to break confidentiality.

PROFESSIONAL DISCLOSURE STATEMENT AND INFORMED CONSENT To help orient clients and to assure there are no misunderstandings, it is often wise for the helper to provide a verbal or written professional disclosure statement that describes such counseling-related issues as the helper's theoretical orientation, credentials held, the purpose of the interview, relevant agency rules, limits to confidentiality, legal issues, fees for service, and so forth (American Mental Health Counselors Association [AMHCA], 1987; Corey, Corey, & Callanan, 2003). After reviewing the professional disclosure statement, the helper should obtain the client's informed consent for the helping process to proceed. Such consent involves the client giving his or her verbal or written permission to participate in the helping interview. (Professional disclosure statements and informed consent will be discussed in more detail in Chapter 6.)

CASE ILLUSTRATION 2.2   Stage 1: Rapport and Trust Building

During Sienna's initial interview, she starts to sob profusely and states that she does not understand why she is so depressed. She reports having fleeting thoughts of wanting to kill herself, but states that she does not have a plan and believes that suicide would be an "easy way out." She quickly identifies a number of issues in her life that seem important, but she is not sure that they are particularly "causing" her current state of depression. The issues in her life include being sad about moving away from home, being confused about dating a person who is from a different culture, finding school more work than she had imagined, and having difficulties with her roommate. She notes that she has felt depressed in the past, "but these feelings are much more intense," and she is concerned that she will not be able to concentrate on her schoolwork.

CLIENT DYNAMICS

As with most clients, making it to the first session took some amount of courage. Although nervous about meeting with her counselor for their first time, Sienna was also relieved, and the counselor quickly helped her feel more at ease by allowing her a few moments to look around the office. Sienna also felt more comfortable after the counselor offered her a professional disclosure statement that highlighted the nature of the counseling relationship and the limits of confidentiality. Sienna was now relatively comfortable sharing her thoughts about what brought her to the session and responding to the counselor's inquiries. Sienna was only vaguely aware of the counselor's mix of inquiry and empathic listening skills.

CLINICAL ISSUES

The counselor realized the importance of sharing the professional disclosure statement and explaining the limits of confidentiality, although it was a little awkward taking care of these issues prior to Sienna talking about why she had come to the counseling center. After signing the informed consent statement, the counselor asked Sienna to discuss what brought her to the interview. This was followed by the counselor gathering information. At the same time, the counselor tried to make sure she listened empathically to Sienna in an effort to understand the client at deeper levels and to assist in building rapport. This balance between inquiry and empathy at times felt awkward to the counselor. However, to gather information so as to understand the full context of the client's difficulties, and in an effort to build rapport, both were deemed important skills during this first session.

Although the counselor had experienced some moderate depression herself a few years back, she chose not to self-disclose at all during the session because it would seem to give the wrong message as to the nature of the counseling relationship and the kinds of boundaries that would exist. During the session, the counselor had little difficulty handling Sienna's sometimes strong affect and did not attempt to "rescue" her from these strong feelings. Although she was supportive of Sienna, she also knew it was important to set boundaries by explaining the center's appointment schedule and emergency on-call contacts. Due to the level of depression Sienna was exhibiting and her inability to concentrate on school, the counselor also considered a referral for Sienna to be evaluated for possible antidepressant medication. In addition, a second appointment later in the week was set up for Sienna to see the counselor.

EXERCISE 2.2   **Reflections on Rapport and Trust Building**

In small groups, consider the following questions that clinicians often face during the rapport and trust building stage of the counseling relationship.

1. OFFICE DECOR: Describe what you believe is appropriate decor in a counseling office, how you might prepare the physical environment of your own office, and what messages you would want to convey by your selections.

2. SELF-DISCLOSURE: When, if ever, do you believe it would be appropriate or necessary to self-disclose in a helping relationship?

3. CLIENT AFFECT: Which client emotions do you believe will be most challenging for you when working with a client? How might you respond when confronted by a client expressing the feelings you described?

4. BUILDING THE RELATIONSHIP AND GATHERING INFORMATION: How comfortable might you feel trying to balance the foundational skills needed to build a relationship (e.g., empathic understanding) with the information-gathering skills needed to gain a deeper understanding of the client (e.g., questions, structured interview)?

Stage 2: Problem Identification

The primary goal of Stage 2 is to identify, describe, and understand the client's concerns (Schwitzer, 1996, 1997). Although problems begin to emerge in Stage 1, they are fully identified in Stage 2, and the stage is set to establish goals in Stage 3. This often takes a few sessions (see Chapter 2 Appendix for a summary of this stage).

Clinical Skills

ATTITUDES Whereas natural helpers tend to jump into problem solving prior to fully understanding an individual's concerns, professional counselors methodically collect and make sense of all the key information and then design a careful plan for change. Such a methodical, planful process requires *cognitive complexity* (Duys & Hedstrom, 2000). Thus, it is not surprising that new counselors tend to experience more ambiguity, more confusion, and less confidence, and they delay treatment planning more than seasoned practitioners (Hill & Ridley, 2001; Ladany, Marotta, & Muse-Burke, 2001; Martin, Slemon, Hiebert, Hallberg, & Cummings, 1989). Of course, *competence,* or having a thirst for continually seeking the most effective ways of working with a client, is critical at this stage.

TECHNIQUES During this stage, the clinician uses his or her *foundational skills* to follow the client's story and to gently guide the storytelling so that all the important information is covered. In addition, *empathic understanding* can allow the client to delve deeper into a problem and is critical if rapport and trust are to be maintained. During this stage, clinicians must also be skilled at in-depth *information gathering* to identify client needs and issues (Seligman, 2004). Information gathering, begun in Stage 1, assures that enough information can be collected to make a good decision about the treatment that will follow. To facilitate the gathering of information, a number of techniques are used, including *asking questions* and the use of a *structured interview.* Other kinds of information-gathering tools include having clients complete intake forms, problem checklists, informal rating scales, and personality measures. As clinicians leave this stage and get ready for goal setting and treatment planning, they use *collaboration* to assure that they are in sync with the client regarding what issues are to be addressed.

Clinical Tools

CASE CONCEPTUALIZATION In Stage 2, the case conceptualization process begins by identifying client needs from among the presenting concerns. The clinician then examines whether associated features, or additional concerns that accompany the client's central reason for seeking counseling, are present. Next, the clinician explores whether unrecognized or undetected problems might also be present. Finally, the clinician attempts to identify etiological factors, which are the roots, origins, or causes of the client's difficulties, and sustaining factors, which are the circumstances or forces currently keeping the problem going. Ultimately, the clinician's theoretical orientation will influence how the clinician views the information gathered and how those problems will be addressed (Stage 3).

DIAGNOSIS Although very tentatively begun in Stage 1, a diagnosis is formally made during this stage. Professional counselors and psychotherapists must be skilled using the *DSM-IV-TR* (American Psychiatric Association [APA], 2000) to make clinical diagnoses (Seligman, 1998, 2004). Diagnoses are used to describe client problems, lend direction in treatment planning, and communicate about client concerns with other clinicians.

CASE MANAGEMENT During this stage, the clinician should take accurate case notes, check on business-related issues, and attend to any progress reports that may be required for supervisors, insurance companies, and funding agencies.

Ethical and Professional Issues

ASSESSING FOR PSYCHOPATHOLOGY AND BREAKING CONFIDENTIALITY Today's professional counselor encounters a wide range of client functioning (Seligman, 2004). As the clinician delves further into the client's issues, significant clinical concerns may arise. For instance, the therapist may be faced with a client who is suicidal, shows potential for harming others, or is evidencing other signs of psychopathology. It is the clinician's responsibility to know when to break confidentiality due to an assessment of probable client harm toward self or others. If psychopathology is missed or not diagnosed accurately, the clinician may be working on inappropriate goals, inadvertently damaging the client, or be responsible for harm caused to others by not acting quickly enough.

REFERRAL As problems are identified during this stage, referrals to other resources are sometimes needed. Thus, clinicians must recognize when to refer a client (a) for a physical examination to rule out a medical problem, (b) for testing to better identify a diagnosis, (c) for a psychiatric evaluation for medication, or (d) to another counselor because the identified problem appears beyond one's area of competence.

CONSULTATION AND SUPERVISION As clients reveal deeper parts of themselves, they will sometimes present issues with which the clinician has little experience or will tap into unfinished issues in the clinician's life. Thus, it is always prudent for a clinician to have a supervisor with whom he or she can consult. Supervision allows the clinician to understand how his or her issues may interfere with effective treatment, offers different perspectives on understanding client problems, and is a mentoring process that can gradually assist the clinician in improving his or her skills (Bernard & Goodyear, 2004).

CASE ILLUSTRATION 2.3   Stage 2: Problem Identification

After Sienna's first session, she was asked and readily agreed to complete a number of assessment instruments to help fully understand some of the issues underlying her presenting problem. During the next session, she finds herself feeling increasingly comfortable in the helping relationship and begins to identify additional issues important to her, including feelings of enmeshment with her parents, dependence on her boyfriend, and lack of clarity about her values. She also realizes that many of her symptoms, such as problems sleeping, lack of concentration, lethargy, and poor appetite, are related to her depression.

CLIENT DYNAMICS

As Sienna continues in counseling, she begins to feel more trusting of her counselor. She soon feels comfortable sharing additional information about herself and even finds that she gets in touch with issues of which she was not aware. In addition, she now feels comfortable when the clinician gently probes into her life and feels safe enough to answer her probes as fully as possible. She is realizing that sharing the deepest parts of herself will eventually lead to her feeling better, and ideally, to having a more fulfilling life.

Through counseling, Sienna comes to understand that she was experiencing many unrecognized associated features of depression, such as lethargy, trouble getting up in the morning for classes, trouble sleeping, poor appetite, and trouble concentrating on schoolwork. Sienna also recognizes an undetected concern that seems to be both an etiological and sustaining factor—her emotional dependence on her parents before going to college and on her boyfriend and others since coming to college.

Sienna soon sees a connection between her depression and feelings of enmeshment with her parents. She notes that her parents had always tried to keep her "close to home," and now that she is at college, she feels a freedom that had never existed before. However, her new found freedom is connected to feelings of

(continued)

(continued)

guilt and shame. On the one hand, she tries to be free from her parents, and on the other hand, she experiences guilt and shame about behaving in a manner in which her parents would not approve. She also realizes that although she feels a strong sense of love for her boyfriend, she is increasingly feeling dependent on him. She begins to wonder if she always needs to be emotionally tied to someone—first her parents, now her boyfriend. Despite her sense of caring for him, she also wonders if seeing someone from another culture could be an act of rebellion toward her parents. She soon realizes that despite her freedom from her parents, she finds that she espouses many of her parents' values and is beginning to wonder if these values are ones she would want as her own. She is increasingly gaining clarity on the many issues she has to work on.

CLINICAL ISSUES

Although the clinician initially accepts the presenting problems as potential issues for Sienna to work on, she also realizes that there may be other underlying concerns. Although she does not initially share these thoughts with Sienna, through the building of trust and later through probing, Sienna eventually comes to realize this also. In addition, the interpretation of assessment instruments helps the client gain new insights about herself.

Sienna had described depression as one reason for coming to the counseling center, and her test results were consistent with moderate depression and emotional dependence. However, as the clinician uses foundational skills to build rapport, and as the clinician also gathers additional information, a number of potential issues to work on come to the forefront, including (a) depression, which is sometimes debilitating, (b) problems with her roommate, (c) inability to concentrate and study, (d) emotional dependence on others, and (e) confusion about her values.

As the clinician works with Sienna and gets to know her on deeper levels, she begins to formulate a possible diagnosis for Sienna's problems. Such a diagnosis will assist in treatment planning and in any possible referrals that may need to be made. In this case, the clinician tentatively diagnoses Sienna as having an adjustment disorder with depressed mood and, for now, rules out diagnoses of dysthymia or a major depressive disorder.

EXERCISE 2.3   **Reflections on Problem Identification**

In small groups, consider the following questions that clinicians often face during the problem identification stage of the counseling relationship.

1. IDENTIFYING CLIENT CONCERNS AND MAINTAINING SUPPORT: With the main goal of Stage 2 being to identify, describe, and understand the client's concerns, describe how you might balance the continual probing that is critical in this stage with the need to maintain a supportive trusting relationship.

2. POTENTIAL FOR HARM: What might your response be to a client who presents with suicidal thoughts; self-harm, such as cutting oneself; threats of harm to someone else; or severe psychopathology, such as delusions or hallucinations?

Stage 3: Goal Setting and Treatment Planning

The primary goal of Stage 3 is to specify expected outcomes of the counseling process. At this stage, goals that will lead to a plan of therapeutic action are determined (Jongsma & Peterson, 2003) (see Chapter 2 Appendix for a summary of this stage).

Clinical Skills

ATTITUDES In contrast to natural helpers, professional counselors and psychotherapists collaborate with their clients to set specific goals for change. Based on these goals, treatment plans are devised that can vary according to the client's interests and needs, the counselor's theoretical orientation, and the counseling agency's mission. The development of a treatment plan requires *cognitive complexity* and clinical *competence* because it is an involved process that requires clinicians to consider alternative ways of reaching goals and necessitates that the clinician has a repertoire of clinical skills.

TECHNIQUES Professional counselors must be skilled at setting reasonable, measurable goals. Treatment plans focused on such goals can prevent the onset of problems, improve normal psychosocial development and adjustment, and/or therapeutically resolve more distressing, disruptive problems that are firmly entrenched (Drum & Lawler, 1988). A number of skills can assist in setting goals and treatment plans that are achievable. For instance, *offering alternatives* and *giving information* can offer new directions for the client when setting goals, and, if done carefully, *advice giving* can be critical in helping to reach one's goals. Whichever techniques are used, it is imperative that goals and treatment plans are developed *collaboratively* so that the client feels a sense of ownership and empowerment in his or her own therapeutic process.

Clinical Tools

CASE CONCEPTUALIZATION The case conceptualization process, which began in Stage 2, continues in Stage 3 as goals are developed and a treatment plan is put in place. The treatment plan is based on the clinician's unique view of the world, which is a function of his or her theoretical orientation.

DIAGNOSIS Although already made, the competent and reflective clinician always reconsiders the accuracy of the original diagnosis and is open to changing it if necessary.

TREATMENT PLANNING The goals, which are an outgrowth of case conceptualization, become a critical element in the treatment planning process. Treatment plans are individualized to meet client needs and include measurable milestones for charting the client's progress (Jongsma & Peterson, 2003). A good treatment plan requires a clinician who has extensive knowledge of intervention skills that can be matched to the goals that have been set. Skillful treatment planning is a road map that sets the stage for the work to follow.

CASE MANAGEMENT During goal setting and treatment planning, the clinician should take accurate case notes, check on business-related issues, and attend to any progress reports that may be required for supervisors, insurance companies, and funding agencies.

Ethical, Professional, and Cross-Cultural Issues

LIMITATIONS OF THE SETTING In recent years, an increasing number of constraints have been placed on the counseling relationship, including limitations on the number of sessions, the amount of reimbursement for clients from healthcare agencies, and time restraints due to large caseloads (Ackley, 1997; Seligman, 2004). With such constraints, clinicians have a professional responsibility to set goals that are reasonable for the number of contacts, amount of time the client is seen, and professional attention the clinician is able to devote to the client. When client needs cannot be met due to existing constraints, the clinician is obligated to help the client find a more amenable setting in which to achieve his or her counseling goals.

CASE ILLUSTRATION 2.4   Stage 3: Goal Setting

Sienna has identified a number of important issues in her life and now voices some concern over what to do next. As she does so, the clinician assures her that the two of them will work collaboratively on identified goals based on the issues noted earlier. Realizing that it is now the end of the third session, and the center only allows for twelve sessions, Sienna is faced with some important decisions about which issues to focus on. With the help of her counselor, she develops a hierarchy of the problems she would like to tackle. Based on this hierarchy, Sienna decides to do the following:

1. Seek psychiatric consultation for possible medication to address her depressive symptoms. Medication, if taken, could also help with a number of the associated symptoms such as lack of appetite, sleep disturbance, and inability to concentrate.
2. Hold off on dealing with her roommate problems. Sienna sees this as the least of her concerns and hopes that once she is feeling better, the problem will dissipate and/or she will have the strength to talk with her roommate directly.
3. Learn study skills and design a time management log with her counselor to help her study.
4. Spend the rest of her sessions discussing her feelings of emotional dependence and her confusion over her values. Sienna hopes this will help her understand herself more clearly and lead to greater decision-making skills.
5. Reevaluate her goals after eight sessions to see if they are realistic.

CLIENT DYNAMICS

Sienna feels a sense of accomplishment related to her ability to identify issues and delve more deeply into herself. She also has an underlying sense that she must soon work on identified problems. She begins to seek direction from her counselor, who helps her identify which problems to focus on. She is beginning to feel a sense of collaboration—almost teamwork—as the two of them begin to develop a treatment plan. She is both apprehensive and excited about working on her issues.

CLINICAL ISSUES

The counselor felt good about progress made during the session. She was able to help Sienna identify a broader range of issues than she had originally come in with and has now offered her a mechanism to work on these issues. The main service constraint for Sienna and the counselor was a 12-session-per-school-year limit employed by the counseling center. In consultation with the counselor, Sienna had come up with what the counselor thought was a reasonable treatment plan for the limited number of sessions. It was critical that the counselor have a good referral base for possible medication, and her diagnosis of adjustment disorder with depression will be helpful to the psychiatrist to whom she refers. To work with Sienna, the counselor must be well read about effective treatments of depression and its related symptoms. In addition, the counselor should know how to teach study skills or refer to others who can do so, and the counselor should be able to develop a time management log. Finally, the counselor should understand the developmental issues that many late adolescents and young adults face—autonomy and value identification.

EXERCISE 2.4 **Reflections on Goal Setting and Treatment Planning**

In small groups, consider the following questions that clinicians often face during the goal setting and treatment planning stage of the counseling relationship.

1. SERVICE LIMITATIONS: What are your attitudes about the following service limitations: (a) session limits, (b) client ability to pay, (c) caseload size? Discuss how you might raise and discuss these topics with a client. Role-play these issues with a fellow student.

2. GOALS AND FOCUS: Consider how the goals of counseling will change as a function of whether one is focusing on prevention, normal developmental issues, or in-depth psychotherapy work. What professional settings are a good match for the type of counseling goals with which you would prefer to work?

3. CASE MANAGEMENT: In this age of accountability, case management issues have become paramount. What case management concerns would you have at this stage in the counseling relationship and how comfortable do you feel spending a fair amount of time doing the necessary paperwork?

Stage 4: Work

Perhaps it is misleading to wait until the fourth stage to say that "work" has begun, since in many ways work starts the moment the client contacts the counseling setting. However, it is during Stage 4 that the "work" of facilitating progress toward specified treatment goals formally begins (see Chapter 2 Appendix for a summary of this stage).

Clinical Skills

ATTITUDES In Stage 4, both the client and counselor work. The counselor works by applying his or her advanced skills and intervention strategies. Thus, the counselor shows *competence* and mastery of a number of skills that will assist the client toward reaching his or her goals. Becoming a competent clinician begins with mastery of the skills covered in this textbook, is reinforced and strengthened with advanced coursework and extensive supervised practical experience, and continues after one's professional training is completed by keeping up with the literature and being involved with professional workshops and conferences. Competence is more than just learning the skills—it is a desire and thirst for knowledge. It is an attitude that says, "learning never ends."

TECHNIQUES Some universal helping skills are commonly used during the work stage. For instance, it is not unusual during this stage to find clinicians using *affirmation giving,* as the client reaches goals; modeling of new behaviors by the counselor for the client; selective *self-disclosure* on the part of the counselor as an example of ways to reach goals and to affirm the client in his or her goal-seeking behavior; and *confronting* the client in an effort to encourage new ways of understanding the problem while encouraging change.

Also during the work stage, the clinician must be skilled in applying theory to practice in an effort to reach identified goals set in the previous stage. Sometimes called *theory-driven skills,* today's professional counselors employ one of three different approaches to clinical work: (a) a purist adherence to a single theoretical orientation, (b) eclecticism, or (c) an integrative approach. Purists consistently use the same formal model of doing therapy (e.g., person-centered, cognitive-behavioral, psychodynamic, reality therapy, existential, gender-aware approach, family systems, or another approach). Eclectic counselors form different treatment combinations for each client on the basis of their clinical experience, counseling knowledge base, or other professional preferences. Clinicians with an integrative framework use one dominant model as their main basis for viewing clinical work and also planfully borrow techniques and concepts into their main model to tailor fit the approach to client needs. Although this text will not go into depth about the various theoretical orientations to which one could adhere, effective clinicians should be able to apply their theoretical approach to a wide range of client goals.

Clinical Tools

CASE CONCEPTUALIZATION AND TREATMENT PLANNING The issues the client works on is an outgrowth of the case conceptualization process that started during the problem identification stage, continued into the goal setting and treatment planning stage, and is now focused on in the work stage. It therefore makes sense that one's treatment plan will be based on the case conceptualization process; that is, the course of treatment is based on which problems were identified, the goals set, and how the counselor's theory will be used to reach those goals. In essence, a road map is formed earlier in the relationship that guides the use of advanced skills and theory-driven skills during the work stage. For instance, Sienna's goal of working on her dependence needs were identified earlier in the helping relationship and led toward a treatment plan. How this goal is now attained, during the work stage, may differ quite a bit depending on the clinician's theoretical orientation.

DIAGNOSIS AND TREATMENT PLAN RECYCLING As the client begins to work on his or her issues, it may become evident that the goals chosen and the treatment plan devised may not be meeting the client's needs and therefore should be revised. Clinicians should be open to revising the goals and treatment plans based on progress made during this stage.

CASE MANAGEMENT During the work stage, the clinician should continue to take accurate case notes, check on business-related issues, and attend to any required progress reports that may be required for supervisors, insurance companies, and funding agencies.

Ethical and Professional Issues

PROFESSIONAL COMPETENCE Whereas natural helpers offer temporary support, professionals take on the ethical and legal responsibility for assisting the client in need. Thus, throughout the counseling relationship, the clinician must keep an eye on whether the client's concerns and dynamics are within the counselor's range of competencies. During the work stage, the clinician must adequately apply his or her theoretical orientation to client goals; modify goals and treatment plans when necessary; suggest additional assessment; seek peer consultation or clinical supervision; make decisions about alternative treatment modes, such as group or family counseling or inpatient hospitalization; and know when to help the client move on to a clinician with different competencies better suited to the client's needs. Being competent, then, is a professional responsibility and carries with it an attitude that assumes vigilance on the part of the clinician to assure that the best clinical work is being practiced.

CASE ILLUSTRATION 2.5   Stage 4: Work

Sienna enters the work stage of the counseling relationship realizing that change is within reach and that she must actively work on her goals to make this happen. She focuses on each of the identified issues and begins to tackle them one at a time. She is given a referral to a psychiatrist, who defers prescribing antidepressant medication until it is seen whether counseling can produce enough improvement in mood. She also receives a referral to a study skills group. In addition, the counselor helps Sienna create a log for managing her time. Finally, Sienna begins to discuss her relationship with her parents and the kinds of values that were instilled in her. She begins to sort through the values that seem most important to her.

(continued)

(continued)

CLIENT DYNAMICS

Now that goals have been agreed on, Sienna realizes that she has work to do in the helping relationship. Although she seeks guidance from the clinician, she realizes that much of the work is in her hands; that is, she must actively take steps to change her life. She feels both apprehensive and eager about the work she has to do. With some well-appreciated help from her therapist, she finds a psychiatrist with whom to consult about medication, finds a study skills groups, and develops a time management log. Now she feels ready to work on what she perceives to be the most difficult part of counseling—her relationship with her parents and how that defines who she is.

CLINICAL ISSUES

The counselor employs an integrative approach in her work with Sienna. Although her main grounding was humanistic, she has incorporated into her approach a number of techniques from other theories, including brief counseling, psychodynamic theory, systems theory, developmental theory, and cognitive/behaviorism. As she works with Sienna, she (a) sets goals to be reached in a limited number of sessions (brief), (b) develops a time management log and reinforces Sienna's adherence to it (behavioral), (c) refers to a study skills group to learn about new behaviors (behavioral), (d) discusses family issues from a systemic and psychodynamic perspective, and (e) explains life stage developmental issues to Sienna (psychoeducational).

EXERCISE 2.5 **Reflections on Work**

In small groups, consider the following questions that clinicians often face during the work stage of the counseling relationship.

1. APPROACHES TO CLINICAL WORK: What do you think are the advantages and disadvantages of the purist, eclectic, and integrative approaches to professional counseling? At this point in your development, which one of these seems the best fit for you?

2. BRIEF OR LONG-TERM TREATMENT: At this point in your development, which seems the best fit with your own natural helping style: (a) a brief approach that deals directly with symptom relief or (b) a longer term, indirect approach that focuses on underlying causes?

3. COMPETENCE THROUGHOUT ONE'S CAREER: In what ways can you challenge yourself to broaden your theoretical viewpoint through future learning and practice?

Stage 5: Closure

Stage 5, the closure stage, is sometimes referred to as the termination phase of treatment, and its primary goals are to summarize, review, and make the transition out of counseling as smooth as possible (see Chapter 2 Appendix for a summary of this stage).

Clinical Skills

ATTITUDES During the closure stage, the therapist helps the client review and summarize the changes achieved and goals attained; outlines areas for the client to continue working on after termination; and discusses the experience of the counseling relationship, particularly feelings about the relationship coming to an end. Within professional boundaries, the clinician may share some of his or her experiences of the relationship and feelings about termination.

Helping clients process their thoughts and feelings during this stage facilitates movement from the dependence they often feel during the relationship to the independence needed once counseling ends. *Empathy* and *acceptance* are two key attitudes that help the client review progress made and deal with current feelings about closure and autonomy, while *genuineness* is critical if the clinician is to be real regarding his or her feelings about the relationship coming to an end.

As the relationship closes, clinicians are often faced with a wide range of feelings, some of which may be uncomfortable to acknowledge. For instance, they may feel a sense of accomplishment; they might second-guess the work done; and they can grow alert to feelings toward the client they developed in earlier stages but did not act on, such as need for approval, frustration, anger, or sexual attraction. Most often, these are common, passing feelings. However, to remain helpful to the client during closure, the clinician must manage his or her own reactions to termination. Dealing with these reactions is a part of the professional's work duties, and developing the emotional capacity to handle them requires the counselor to be *adjusted psychologically.*

TECHNIQUES During closure, the clinician must be skilled at bringing the relationship to a productive conclusion. The foundational skills associated with *listening* and *empathy,* and the commonly used skills of *affirmation giving, modeling,* and *self-disclosure,* are used to help the client discuss his or her thoughts and feeling about the relationship and to assist in saying good-bye. For instance, effective clinicians can listen and understand the strong feelings some clients have about ending. Good clinicians are able to model genuineness by self-disclosing appropriate feelings when saying good-bye. Seasoned professionals can affirm client progress and the positive changes that have been made, while also *challenging* the client to continue to move on in his or her life. At the end of this stage, the clinician *collaborates* with the client to assure that expectations about follow-up are similar and to make sure that there is no unfinished business.

Clinical Tools

CASE MANAGEMENT Extensive case management usually is needed at the end of the counseling relationship to ensure that all related paperwork and billing issues are up-to-date, correspondence with other professionals is handled, and any after-planning and follow-up have been arranged.

Ethical and Professional Issues

AFTER-PLANNING At closure, it is the clinician's responsibility to help the client plan for needs following termination. For instance, when necessary, concrete arrangements should be made for follow-up visits, referral to another professional such as a psychiatrist or school counselor, or transition to another treatment mode, like group or family counseling. Specific suggestions for self-guided after-work should be made when needed, such as reading assignments or a self-help program for continued behavior change. Overall, the client should leave with a good sense of how to keep up the progress already made, a mechanism to continue to work independently toward unreached goals, and a road map to tackle any challenges or obstacles that might be encountered.

CASE ILLUSTRATION 2.6   Stage 5: Closure

Although told at the beginning of the helping relationship that there was a maximum of twelve sessions at the counseling center, Sienna is somewhat surprised when the counselor notes, during the tenth session, that there are only two sessions left. Although initially feeling apprehensive, Sienna begins to mentally review what she has done in counseling. She is relieved when the counselor also begins to review the course of the helping relationship and summarizes the gains that have been made. In addition, the counselor begins to focus on how Sienna will follow up with the psychiatrist to reevaluate whether to prescribe a low dose of an antidepressant, maintain her time management log, continue with her study skills group, and integrate the knowledge she has gained about herself relative to her family and developmental stage. Sienna is also relieved when the counselor suggests that she join an 8-week self-esteem group for college students. Although a little apprehensive, when the last session ends, Sienna thanks her counselor and feels ready to move on.

CLIENT DYNAMICS

Sienna is actually a little panic stricken when she realizes that the counseling relationship will be ending. However, she does not show the full extent of her panic to the counselor and realizes that one of her issues has been emotional dependence on others. Sienna begins to think that she can function on her own and be healthy without the counselor, and she decides to discuss this notion with her counselor during the sessions that are left. She sees this as a large step for herself. Sienna also realizes that she is in charge of her life and that she is capable of continuing the changes she has made. She is going to miss her counselor a lot but knows that she can contact her if there is an emergency. She is also looking forward to her new group experience.

CLINICAL ISSUES

Due to Sienna's dependence issues, the counselor is prepared for a negative reaction from Sienna when she tells Sienna that they have only two sessions left. She knows that it will be important to structure the next couple of sessions in a manner that will relieve anxiety as they move out of the helping relationship. In the eleventh and final twelfth sessions, the counselor structures the discussion to help Sienna summarize the changes she has experienced, talk out loud about how the counseling experience had been for her, and talk about continuing work on her own. They also discuss how she will maintain contact with the psychiatrist, continue her time management log, and continue with her study skills group. She also purposefully tells Sienna about the self-esteem counseling group in an effort to ease her out of the individual counseling relationship. She believes the group will be a good transition from individual counseling to independent functioning.

During the last session, the counselor and Sienna discuss how Sienna would handle things if she felt herself "losing ground" or if some of her mood problems reemerged every now and then. In addition, the counselor expresses her positive feelings and admiration for the work Sienna has accomplished. Finally, the counselor feels it is especially important to reach a clear termination so Sienna can practice her newly developing emotional independence with a successful closure rather than allowing the sessions to continue too long.

EXERCISE 2.6 **Reflections on Closure**

In small groups, consider the following questions that clinicians often face during the closure stage of the counseling relationship.

1. COUNSELOR'S REACTIONS: People differ in how they experience relationship endings and in how they go about saying good-bye. What have your experiences been with relationship endings? What are your attitudes regarding counseling as a temporary relationship that will ultimately come to an end?

2. CHANGES IN FOCUS AND OVEREXTENDED COUNSELING: The counseling relationship may extend beyond the predetermined closure point because important new issues arise that must be addressed due to client dependence or as a result of counselor ambivalence about termination. When you find a counseling relationship continuing past expectations, how will you decide the cause? How will you determine what is appropriate? How might you deal with an overextended counseling relationship?

Stage 6: Postinterview

We believe that patients [and clients] can and should return as needed.
(Budman & Gurman, 1988, p. 20)

Closure of the relationship may not be the ultimate conclusion of the counselor's contact with the client, and it is not unusual for some clients to return to the same counselor or seek another professional sometime in the future (Neukrug, Milliken, & Shoemaker, 2001; Neukrug & Williams, 1993). Clients may need to revisit old concerns, return with new problems, or come back during life transitions to explore adjustment and development. Thus, the primary goal of the postinterview is to maintain appropriate availability (see Chapter 2 Appendix for a summary of this stage).

Clinical Skills

ATTITUDES Clinicians should continue to maintain a professional stance in their relationships with clients, even after counseling has ended. This allows the client to foster his or her independence yet leaves the door open for the client to seek the same clinician again for counseling. The *competent* clinician has the desire to follow up with clients and has the ability, due to his or her own *psychological adjustment,* to maintain appropriate boundaries despite the end of the clinical relationship.

Clinical Tools

CASE MANAGEMENT Case management continues beyond the end of the counseling relationship. At the postinterview stage, case management is needed to store and protect files and records, conduct any needed monitoring or follow-up contacts, conduct follow-up assessment when it is used, finalize any billing or business matters, and respond to requests for information from referral resources and possible future clinicians the clients might see.

Ethical and Professional Issues

MAINTAINING BOUNDARIES Clinicians should continue to maintain a professional stance in their relationships with clients even after counseling has ended, and ethical codes support this view (see American Counseling Association [ACA],1995; National Association of Social Workers [NASW], 1999; also see list of ethical code Web sites in Toolbox A), Thus, most clinicians try to avoid any close relationships with clients after termination. This includes dating and romantic relationships, friendships, positions of power like clinical supervisor or dissertation adviser, and other relationships that are too familiar.

ETHICS OF FOLLOW-UP ASSESSMENT Follow-up contacts such as letters, surveys, questionnaires, and phone calls can help measure client satisfaction and goal attainment. This type of information helps the counselor evaluate which approaches have been most successful (Hutchins & Cole, 1997; Kleinke, 1994) and provides a brief chance to reinforce the client's progress (Neukrug, 2002, 2004). It is also an opportunity for the client to request additional counseling if needed. Although many clients appreciate and benefit from follow-up, others prefer no interaction once closure is reached. Therefore, clinicians should be sensitive to these differing reactions when conducting follow-up. One or two attempts can be made, usually within a few weeks to 6 months after closure, but a clinician should avoid multiple, relentless attempts to contact clients.

CASE ILLUSTRATION 2.7   Stage 6: The Postinterview

At termination, Sienna was asked to complete closure paperwork and measures of change. Her assessment instruments showed significant improvement in most areas, and she reported substantial goal accomplishment.

After counseling had ended, Sienna followed up with her group counseling experience and her appointment with the psychiatrist, who felt that progress had been made and no further appointments would be necessary. Over time, she stopped using her time management log but continued with her study skills group until it had ended. After 2 months, as agreed on during the last session, the counselor made a follow-up phone call to Sienna. Sienna noted that she was doing well, despite some moments of depression. She stated that she had broken up with her boyfriend but at times missed him terribly. She noted that her relationship with her parents was more distant than in the past but that it seemed to have a new, "healthier" quality. She stated that she was happy to hear from the counselor and no longer felt counseling to be necessary. The counselor noted that she had sent a client satisfaction survey and encouraged Sienna to complete it fully and honestly. She noted that she would not see the survey directly but that her supervisor reviewed all of the returned surveys and, once a year, gave her feedback while maintaining the anonymity of clients.

CLIENT DYNAMICS

Sienna feels good when counseling ends and, despite some momentary setbacks, continues with progress in all areas of her life. She reflects back on her counseling experience with a sense of accomplishment and satisfaction. Although not wanting to go back into counseling, she is not opposed to it should other significant issues develop in her life. In quiet, alone moments, she realizes that her view of herself and of life in general has significantly changed.

CLINICAL ISSUES

Results from counseling are often longlasting, although clients sometimes lose track of how much has changed for them. Sienna's case is an example of how change is self-perpetuating. She now sees herself differently, understands her relationship with her parents in a new way, and has a new outlook on her future. The clinician can feel a sense of accomplishment with the progress Sienna made but should also reflect on other ways she could have assisted Sienna with her goals.

Exercise 2.7 **Reflections on the Postinterview**

In small groups, consider the following questions that often face clinicians during the postinterview stage of the counseling relationship.

1. PROFESSIONAL BOUNDARIES: Over the years, the kinds of boundaries a counselor should have relative to his or her relationship with former clients have been debated. What are your beliefs about this? For example, should the counselor have any personal-social contact after termination of counseling? Would it make a difference if the client initiated the contact? Are friendships allowable after a specified amount of time? What about intimate or romantic relationships? What about professional relationships such as instructor, clinical supervisor, or colleague?

2. ETHICAL GUIDELINES AND PROFESSIONAL BOUNDARIES: What do the most common professional ethical guidelines, such as those of the ACA, APA, and NASW, say about postcounseling relationships between clinicians and counselors? Find out and discuss. (See list of Web sites of code of ethics of professional associations in Toolbox A.)

LEARNING TO BE A COUNSELOR: An Ongoing Process

Understanding the natural progression of the counseling relationship is critical to your success at being a clinician. But understanding it isn't enough. One has to live it. And as you live it, you realize that each counseling relationship has a rhythm of its own that unravels naturally if we allow it to. This means that each of us has to have patience to allow for the unfolding of this relationship: patience so we don't push our clients too fast; patience so we can enjoy our work and "go with the flow" of this critical relationship; and patience so we can give our "patients" time to heal from whatever pain they have to deal with in life—and then move on.

Sometimes having patience will not be easy, especially when you are beginning this journey and want so badly to watch your clients get better quickly. However, if you can allow yourself the freedom to let clients heal in their own time, your clients will get better more quickly than if you tried to push them along, and you will enjoy the journey more.

 If you like, you can skip ahead in the DVD and view the sections entitled:

Clinical Tools and Intake Interview Introduction

Intake Interview

Working Stage Interview

and

Termination Interview

You will also be prompted to view these sections of the DVD later in the text.

Chapter Summary

This chapter identified seven stages of the helping relationship, which included: (a) the preinterview stage, (b) the rapport and trust building stage, (c) the problem identification stage, (d) the goal setting stage, (e) the work stage, (f) the closure stage, and (g) the postrelationship stage. For each of these stages, we identified its primary goal and discussed how each of the eight core areas of knowledge and skills emerge as a function of stage. These goals and the core areas of knowledge and skills are summarized in the Chapter 2 Appendix. As we discussed the stages, we offered a case example, Sienna, to show how a client and a clinician work as they move through the stages of counseling, and we noted that this example (and others) will be discussed again in Part III of the text.

The chapter concluded with a discussion concerning the importance of clinicians allowing the progression of the helping relationship to unravel naturally. It was suggested that patience is a critical factor in this process and that sometimes such patience comes with experience.

Summarizing the Stages

As you can see throughout the chapter, there are a myriad of counseling skills, clinical tools, and professional and ethical issues to which a clinician must attend throughout the counseling relationship. The following tables in the Chapter 2 Appendix help summarize the stages and the important core areas associated with them.

CHAPTER 2 APPENDIX: Stages and Associated Core Areas of Knowledge and Skills

TABLE 2.1

Attitudes and Skills throughout the Helping Relationship

STAGE	GOAL	CRITICAL ATTITUDES	CRITICAL TECHNIQUES
Preinterview	Preparation for optimal first encounter	• Acceptance: Ready self to accept client's issues and feelings. • Open-Mindedness: Ready self to not jump to conclusions about client. • Cognitive Complexity: Information gained is just one small piece of whole. • Psychological Adjustment: Take self-inventory to assure emotional readiness to work with client and to deal with any issue the client might touch upon.	• None. Client hasn't met with clinician.
Stage 1: Rapport and Trust Building	Establish a trusting, facilitative, therapeutic relationship	• Empathy: So client will feel heard, to build the alliance, and to encourage client self-disclosure. • Acceptance: So client will feel welcomed and safe. • Relationship Building: Most critical factor to successful client outcomes. Make sure one builds an alliance. • Psychological Adjustment: Being able to handle client's emotions and emotions of self toward client. • Competence: If clinician does not have competence to work with client, he or she will seek consultation, supervision, or refer client.	• Foundational Skills: Silence and pause time, listening, paraphrasing, and empathic understanding to build relationship and understand client fully. • Information Gathering: Asking questions and use of structured interview to probe and gather information to understand extent of client situation and to begin the process of developing a diagnosis and forming a treatment plan. • Commonly Used Skill: Collaboration to assure client and counselor expectations regarding treatment match.

Stage 2: Problem Identification	Identification, description, and understanding of client concerns	• Cognitive Complexity: Important for making sense of client situation after gathering information. • Being Competent: Is facile at using necessary skills to build relationship and gather information to identify client needs.	• Foundational Skills: To follow and guide story and maintain rapport. In particular, empathic understanding for delving deeper into problems and obtaining broader view of client's situation. • Information Gathering: To identify needs to develop goals in next stage. Use of questions, structured interview, intake forms, checklists, ratings scales, personality tests. • Commonly Used Skill: Collaboration to assure client and counselor identification of problem areas match.
Stage 3: Goal Setting and Treatment Planning	Specification of expected outcomes	• Cognitive Complexity: Clinician should have alternative ways of reaching goals that are based on client's expressed needs. • Being Competent: Clinician should be able to accurately identify problems and set achievable goals and treatment plan by having a repertoire of skills.	• Goal Setting Skills: Giving advice, offering alternatives, and giving information can all be critical when collaboratively setting goals. • Commonly Used Skill: Collaboration when setting goals and developing treatment plans to assure that goals and intervention strategies match.
Stage 4: Work	Facilitate progress toward specified outcomes	• Being Competent: Competence and mastery of a number of skills that will assist the client toward reaching his or her goals. "Learning never ends."	• Theory-Driven Skills: Used to work on goals from clinician's theoretical orientation (e.g., single orientation, eclecticism, integrative). • Commonly Used Skills: Affirmations, encouragement modeling, self-disclosure, confronting client to view problem in new ways while encouraging change.

(continued)

TABLE 2.1 *(continued)*

STAGE	GOAL	CRITICAL ATTITUDES	CRITICAL TECHNIQUES
Stage 5: Closure	Summarize, review, and resolve client experience	• Being Empathic, Accepting, and Genuine: Helpful in understanding and accepting client's feelings and thoughts about the ending of the therapeutic relationship. • Psychological Adjustment: Important for counselor's sometimes ambivalent feelings about closure and feelings toward client.	• Foundational Skills: Listening and being empathic are used to summarize progress, hear client's feelings about ending, and highlight significance of relationship. • Commonly Used Skills: Affirmation giving to affirm client progress. Modeling to show client how to say good-bye. Self-disclosure to express clinician's feelings concerning end of helping relationship. Collaboration to assure no unfinished business, to assist in saying good-bye, and to assure similar expectations regarding follow-up.
Stage 6: Postinterview	Maintain appropriate availability	• Competence: Assures for proper follow-up. • Psychological Adjustment: Important for maintenance of postrelationship boundaries.	None: Client no longer in therapeutic relationship.

TABLE 2.2
Clinical Tools throughout the Helping Relationship

STAGE	PRIMARY GOAL	CASE CONCEPTUALIZATION	DIAGNOSIS	TREATMENT PLANNING	CASE MANAGEMENT
Preinterview	Preparation for optimal first encounter	None: Haven't yet met client.	None: Haven't yet met client.	None: Haven't yet met client.	• Attend to appointment times, paperwork, files, advance information (e.g., previous reports, assessment results), preinterview contacts, etc.
Stage 1: Rapport and Trust Building	Establish a trusting, facilitative, therapeutic relationship	• Very early hypotheses made about client concerns and ancillary issues.	• Very tentative diagnosis may begin, but clinician is open to changing diagnosis in Stage 2.	None: Too early in relationship.	• Attend to paperwork, intake issues, billing, business matters, correspondence with other professionals, and agency records.
Stage 2: Problem Identification	Identification, description, and understanding of client concerns	• Begins with problem identification and examines possible undetected features, associated features, etiological factors, and sustaining factors.	• Diagnosis is formally made. Used to describe client problems, communicate client concerns with other professionals, and in treatment planning.	None: Too early in relationship.	• Write case notes, check on business-related issues, attend to required progress reports for supervisors, insurance companies, and funding agencies.
Stage 3: Goal Setting and Treatment Planning	Specification of expected outcomes	• Process continues as clinician develops goals and treatment plans. Conceptualization and resulting treatment plan are based on clinician's theoretical orientation.	• Competent and reflective clinician always reconsiders accuracy of original diagnosis and is open to changing it if necessary.	• Based on previously identified goals. Outgrowth of case conceptualization. Road map for work stage.	• Write case notes, check on business-related issues, attend to required progress reports for supervisors, insurance companies, and funding agencies.

(continued)

TABLE 2.2 (continued)

STAGE	PRIMARY GOAL	CASE CONCEPTUALIZATION	DIAGNOSIS	TREATMENT PLANNING	CASE MANAGEMENT
Stage 4: Work	Facilitate progress toward specified outcomes	• Client's work is an outgrowth of case conceptualization process.	• Recycling: Revisit diagnosis if client is not meeting goals.	• Treatment plan is an outgrowth of case conceptualization process that tentatively started in Stage 2, continued into the Stage 3, and is now focused on in this stage. • Recycling: Revisit treatment plan if client is not meeting goals.	• Write case notes, check on business-related issues, attend to required progress reports for supervisors, insurance companies, and funding agencies.
Stage 5: Closure	Summarize, review, and resolve client experience	None: Counseling coming to an end.	None: Counseling coming to an end.	None: Counseling coming to an end.	• Extensive near end of helping relationship: ending paperwork, billing issues, correspondence with other professionals, after-planning.
Stage 6: Postinterview	Maintain appropriate availability	None: Counseling is finished.	None: Counseling is finished.	None: Counseling is finished.	• Protect files and records, conduct monitoring, conduct follow-up contact and assessment, finalize business matters, respond to requests from referral sources.

TABLE 2.3
Ethical and Professional Issues throughout the Helping Relationship

STAGE	PRIMARY GOAL	ETHICAL, PROFESSIONAL, AND CROSS-CULTURAL ISSUES
Preinterview	Preparation for optimal first encounter	• Competence and Professional Limitations: Client's concerns should be within counselor's competencies. Make thoughtful and wise decisions about whether one needs to consult, seek supervision, and refer. • Office Decor: Consider what might be offensive to clients. Be intentional about how you decorate your office. • Knowledge of, and Skills to Use with, Diverse Clients: Assure you have the knowledge and skills. • Attitudes toward Diverse Clients: Take a self-inventory to assure no biases.
Stage 1: Rapport and Trust Building	Establish a trusting, facilitative, therapeutic relationship	• Professional Competence: Assure client's concerns within range of competence. • Assess for Cultural Competence: Assure that you are aware of the knowledge, skills, and attitudes necessary to work effectively with clients from diverse backgrounds. • Self-Disclosure: Should be planful, purposeful, and limited during this stage. • Establishing Boundaries: Client should understand the boundaries of a counseling relationship (e.g., length of sessions, expectations of relationship, emergency and nonemergency ways of contacting clinic). • Assessing for Harm to Self or Others: Know what questions to ask and when it is ethically and legally important to break confidentiality. • Professional Disclosure Statement: Given to client. • Informed Consent: Received from client.
Stage 2: Problem Identification	Identification, description, and understanding of client concerns	• Assessing Potential for Harm and Psychopathology: As client issues emerge, clinician should know how to assess for psychopathology and when to break confidentiality. • Referral: Know when to refer for physical problems, testing, evaluation for medication, or referral to another clinician. • Consultation and Supervision: Disclosure of deeper issues by client may tap into clinician's unfinished business. Be open to consultation and supervision to work through these issues.

(continued)

TABLE 2.3   (*continued*)

STAGE	PRIMARY GOAL	PROFESSIONAL, ETHICAL, AND CROSS-CULTURAL ISSUES
Stage 3: Goal Setting and Treatment Planning	Specification of expected outcomes	• Limitations of Setting: Take into account limits settings place on number of sessions, client's ability to pay, size of caseload, and other factors.
Stage 4: Work	Facilitate progress toward specified outcomes	• Professional Competence: Myriad issues face the competent professional during the work stage, including adequately applying theory, modifying goals when necessary, seeking consultation and supervision, deciding on alternative treatment modes, referring to another clinician. Be up on best practices in field.
Stage 5: Closure	Summarize, review, and resolve client experience	• After-Planning: When necessary, arrange for follow-up, referrals to others, transition to other treatment modes, specific suggestions for self-guided after-work, etc.
Stage 6: Postinterview	Maintain appropriate availability	• Maintaining Boundaries: Avoid nonprofessional contact after relationship. • Ethics of Follow-Up: Evaluate self by measuring client satisfaction and goal attainment. Follow-up can also reinforce progress by client. Offer opportunity to seek counseling again if needed. Avoid relentless contacts for clients not interested in follow-up.

Introducing Generalist Practice: The Generalist Intervention Model

Image Source/Digital Vision/Getty Images

Learning Objectives (LOs)   *This chapter will help prepare students to:*

LO 1-1 Employ a unique approach to helping in the field of social work.

LO 1-2 Define the process of generalist practice by describing its inherent concepts.

LO 1-3 Acquire and apply an eclectic knowledge base to practice.

LO 1-4 Apply the systems theory conceptual framework to practice.

LO 1-5 Apply the ecological conceptual framework to practice.

LO 1-6 Acquire professional values and apply professional ethics to practice.

LO 1-7 Recognize a wide range of practice skills to work with individuals, families, groups, organizations, and communities.

LO 1-8 Emphasize principles involving values that underlie generalist practice.

LO 1-9 Appreciate and stress the importance of human diversity.

LO 1-10 Advocate for human rights, and pursue social and economic justice.

LO 1-11 Demonstrate a wide range of professional roles.

LO 1-12 Define critical thinking skills and apply them to practice.

LO 1-13 Incorporate research-informed practice.

LO 1-14 Follow a planned change process.

LO 1-15 Employ the Generalist Intervention Model (GIM), which uses a seven-step planned change focus.

DACEY, AGE 26, IS THE MOTHER OF THREE CHILDREN. She hasn't seen or heard from the children's father for over a year. To make ends meet, she works as a waitress and bartender for as many shifts as she can get. She only has a 10th-grade education and is struggling to keep her family fed, clothed, and housed. Often she's forced to leave Danny, her eldest at age 8, in charge when she can't find or afford a babysitter. When she gets home, she's beat and finds it's easy to get cranky and impatient with the kids. Although she hasn't given them specific rules for behavior, she expects them to "be good" and not add to her already heavy burden of problems. She fluctuates from being really strict to being overly indulgent, allowing the kids to do almost whatever they want. Sometimes, she "loses it" and takes a belt to them to get them to behave. For example, Rudy, her 6-year-old, got caught shoplifting a bag of his favorite candy, Mega Warheads. Dacey subsequently beat him severely enough that he couldn't go to school the next day. School personnel had noted bruises on the two oldest children several times. As a result, Dacey had become involved with Child Protective Services. She loves her kids and doesn't want to lose them. However, she clearly understands it can be done, as she herself was removed from her parents' home and placed in foster care.[1]

Frederika, age 86, lives by herself in a small urban apartment with 17 cats. She has been living there for the past 13 years since her husband died. She has no living relatives except an older sister living across the country and a niece a state away. Frederika has always considered herself a strong, independent woman and had worked outside of the home much of her younger life. However, now she is forced to admit to herself that she's getting weaker. Everything seems harder to do than it used to. She is also starting to forget things. For example, she sometimes forgets to cook and eat. To compensate for this forgetfulness, Frederika keeps writing herself little notes on Post-its and leaving them everywhere to remind her to do things. The apartment is getting messier. She deeply loves her cats, but it is getting more and more difficult to keep their litter boxes clean. The landlord has been up three times to complain about the mess and tell her she must clean it up. She does not want to leave her home. She is terrified of losing her dignity and independence.

A family of four—the fifth generation to live on the family farm—is dispossessed. They had several years of crop failures and were unable to pay back the loans they so desperately needed to survive at the time. They're living in their '02 Chevy van now. They can't find any housing they can possibly afford even though both parents, Leah and Robert, work full-time, minimum-wage jobs. Fall is almost here. They dread the winter when it gets much colder. Leah is striving to keep the kids, ages 9 and 11, fed. They're supposed to go to school soon. She also worries about Robert, who is getting seriously depressed about losing the farm and not providing adequately for his family. They just don't know where to turn.

Introducing Generalist Practice

EP B2.2

The previous situations confront generalist social work practitioners daily. Social workers do not pick and choose which problems and issues they would like to address. They see a problem, even a difficult problem, and try to help people solve it.

Social workers are generalists (Council on Social Work Education [CSWE], 2008). That is, they need a wide array of skills at their disposal. They are prepared to help people with individualized personal issues and with very broad problems that affect whole communities.

This book is about generalist practice and what social workers do to help people with problems in virtually any setting. There are many ways to describe what social workers do. They work with individuals, families, groups, organizations, and communities. Their work is based on a body of knowledge, practice skills, and professional values. They work in settings that focus on children and families, health, justice, education, and economic status.

Social workers and social work educators have seriously debated the definition of generalist practice for decades (Hernandez, 2008; Landon, 1995). Currently, at least five concepts are generally accepted as underpinnings for generalist practice (CSWE, 2008; Hernandez, 2008). First, a theoretical approach is assumed in which individuals, families, groups, organizations, and communities are viewed as systems within their environments. (Systems terms and concepts are explained and discussed later in the chapter.) Second,

---

1. This vignette is loosely based on one presented by R. M. DeMaria (1999) entitled Family Therapy and Child Welfare in C. W. LeCroy (Ed.), *Case Studies in Social Work Practice* (2nd ed., pp. 59–63). Pacific Grove, CA: Brooks Cole.

generalist practitioners use a problem-solving, planned change approach to resolve issues encountered by any of these systems. In other words, generalist social workers follow a designated plan or procedure for getting things done. Third, ethical principles and social work values are exceptionally significant in all aspects of generalist practice. These include a focus on human well-being, human rights, and social and economic justice, as well as an appreciation of human diversity. Fourth, practitioners assume a wide range of roles to achieve their goals. A professional social work *role* is behavior and activity involved in performing some designated function that is part of professional practice. Fifth, it is essential that generalist social workers select the most effective intervention strategies possible, carefully evaluate the results of their work, and be competent. In effect, generalist social workers must have infinite flexibility, a solid knowledge base about many things, and a wide range of skills at their disposal.

Proposed here is a model of planned change based on a specific definition of generalist practice. It views practice from a systems perspective. The intent is to clarify in a practical manner what occurs in generalist social work practice. The model addresses the qualities that make social work unique and special. It demonstrates how a social work planned change approach can be applied virtually to any situation, no matter how difficult or complex. Finally, the model integrates an orientation to advocacy and a focus on more than just an individual as the target of the change efforts. Social work intervention may involve work with families, groups, organizations, or communities.

The terms *micro, mezzo,* and *macro* will periodically be used throughout the book to refer to their respective systems. Practice with individuals is considered as *micro* practice, practice with families as *micro/mezzo* practice, practice with groups as *mezzo* practice, and practice with larger systems, including organizations and communities, as *macro* practice. Note that families are designated with the term *micro/mezzo*. Families are groups, yet have distinctive status because of their intimate nature. Therefore, we will treat them as a special system on a continuum between micro and mezzo practice.

Generalist practice skills are integrally linked. They are built upon each other in a progression from micro to mezzo to macro levels. Relating to individuals in groups (mezzo practice) requires basic micro skills for working with individuals. Likewise, macro practice requires mastery of both micro and mezzo skills for relating to and working with individuals and groups of individuals in organizational and community (macro) settings. As an introduction to generalist prac-

tice, this book establishes a framework for analyzing issues and problems from a generalist perspective. It then describes and discusses the micro skills necessary to formulate the foundation for the ongoing development of mezzo and macro skills. Linkages with mezzo and macro practice are emphasized throughout.

LO 1-1* Employ a Unique Approach to Helping in the Field of Social Work

The purpose of social work is "to (1) enhance the problem solving and coping capacities of people, (2) link people with systems that provide them with resources, services, and opportunities, (3) promote the effective and humane operation of these systems, and (4) contribute to the development and improvement of social policy" (Pincus & Minahan, 1973, p. 8). In other words, the purpose of social work is to help people in need by using any ethical means possible. However, specifying a cookbook recipe for social work practice is impossible because of the variety of problems encountered and the methods employed. Flexibility and creativity are key qualities for generalist social work practitioners.

Other fields also perform some of the same functions as social work. For instance, mental health clinicians in psychology, psychiatry, and counseling use interviewing skills. Some use a planned change approach. Figure 1.1 illustrates how social work overlaps to some extent with other helping professions. All, for example, have a common core of interviewing and counseling skills.

However, social work is much more than having a clinician sit down in his or her office with an individual, group, or family and focus on solving mental health problems. (We don't want to imply that this is all that other helping professions do. Their own unique thrusts and emphases are beyond the scope of what can be included here.) Social work has at least six major aspects that make it unique.

FOCUS ON ANY PROBLEM

The first unique aspect of social work involves how practitioners may focus attention on *any problem* or cluster of problems, even those that are very complex and difficult. Social workers do not refuse to work with clients or refer them elsewhere because those clients have unappealing characteristics. There may be a family where sexual abuse is occurring. That abuse must stop. Likewise,

---

*Note that content headings in chapters throughout the book are tagged with learning objectives [e.g., LO 1-1, LO 1-4]. These indicate what content relates to which learning objective.

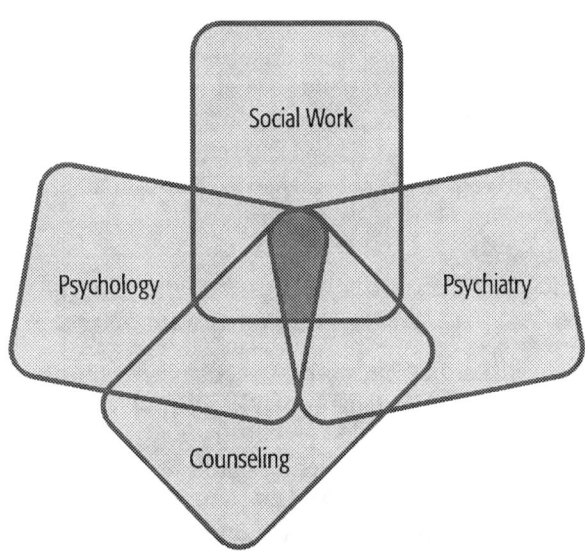

The darkened area reflects a common core of interviewing and counseling skills used by the helping professions.

FIGURE 1.1 Social Work and Other Helping Professions

© Cengage Learning

there may be a community where the juvenile crime rate is skyrocketing. Something needs to be done.

Generalist practice does not imply that every problem can be solved, although it does mean that some of them can be solved or at least alleviated. Generalist practitioners are equipped with a repertoire of skills to help them identify and examine problems. They then make choices about where their efforts can be best directed.

TARGETING THE EXTERNAL ENVIRONMENT FOR CHANGE

The second aspect that makes social work unique involves *targeting the environment* for change. The system that social workers need "to change or influence in order to accomplish (their) goals" is called the *target system* or *target of change* (Hepworth, Rooney, Rooney, & Strom-Gottfried, 2013; Pincus & Minahan, 1973, p. 58). Targets of change are not limited to individuals or families. Sometimes, services are unavailable or excessively difficult to obtain, social policies are unfair, or people are oppressed by other people. Administrators and people in power do not always have the motivation or insight to initiate needed change. Social workers must look at where change is essential outside the individual and work with the environment to effect that change.

For example, consider a large northern city where homelessness has become a major problem. Loss of

industry to other locations where production is cheaper, unemployment, and lack of low-income housing have caused the homelessness problem to escalate. Many people have run out of resources and have few options. They have been forced into homelessness. A social worker concerned about this issue might strive to identify other individuals in the community, such as professionals, politicians, and other community leaders, who are also concerned about this problem. Such people might include public social services administrators, social workers in other agencies, leaders of charitable organizations and churches, and faculty and students in the social work departments of area universities. The social worker initiating change could identify these individuals, contact them, and call a meeting to discuss plans. Established goals might then include improving "community awareness and acceptance of the problem of homelessness," establishment of "emergency shelter space for homeless people," exploration of the possibility of developing "long-term…transitional and low-priced housing arrangements for homeless families," and enhanced "coordination of existing services for homeless people" (Alexander, 2004, p. 135). Here the community would be the target of change on the behalf of people in need, namely, the homeless population.

ADVOCACY

The third aspect that makes social work unique is related to targeting the environment. Namely, social workers often find the need to *advocate* for their clients. Advocacy involves actively intervening in order to help clients get what they need. Most frequently, this intervention focuses on "the relationship between the client and an unresponsive 'system'" (Epstein, 1981, p. 8). Clients have specified needs. Social agencies, organizations, or communities may not be meeting these needs. These unresponsive systems must be pressured to make changes so needs can be met. Specific techniques of advocacy will be addressed in much greater detail later in Chapter 14.

PROFESSIONAL VALUES AND ETHICS

The fourth aspect that makes social work unique is its emphasis on and adherence to a *core of professional values*. The *Code of Ethics* of the National Association of Social Workers (NASW) is available on the Web at http://www.naswdc.org/pubs/code/code.asp. This code focuses on the right of the individual to make free choices and to have a good quality of life.

PARTNERSHIPS WITH CLIENTS

The fifth aspect making social work unique is related to the core of social work values and how important it is for clients to make their own decisions. Social workers do not lead people into specific ways of thinking or acting. Rather, they practice in a *partnership* with clients, making and implementing plans together. Most other professions emphasize the authority and expertise of the professional, on the one hand, and the subordinate status of the client as recipient of services, on the other.

ADHERENCE TO PROFESSIONAL STANDARDS

A sixth aspect that makes social work unique involves how social work education is held accountable regarding specifically what makes social workers competent in their practice. Highlight 1.1 discusses the relationships among social work, social work education, and the *Educational Policy and Accreditation Standards* that govern what is taught in social work programs. Highlight 1.1 also explains how content in this book relates to educational standards and how "helping hands" icons placed throughout this book identify such content.

LO 1-2 Define the Process of Generalist Practice by Describing Its Inherent Concepts

Generalist social work practice may involve almost any helping situation. A generalist practitioner may be called upon to help a homeless family, a physically abused child, a pregnant teenager, a sick older adult unable to care for him- or herself any longer, an alcoholic parent, a community that is trying to address its drug abuse problem, or a public assistance agency struggling to amend its policies to conform to new federal regulations. Therefore, generalist practitioners must be well prepared to address many kinds of difficult situations.

The social work profession has struggled with the idea of generalist practice for many years. In the past, new practitioners were educated in primarily one skill area (e.g., work with individuals, groups, or communities) or one area of practice (e.g., children and families, or policy and administration). A generalist practitioner needs competency in a wide variety of areas instead of being limited to a single track.

THE DEFINITION

For our purposes, the definition of generalist practice involves 12 key concepts. We will define generalist practice as the application of an *eclectic knowledge base*,[2] *professional values and ethics*, and a *wide range of skills* to *target systems of any size* for change. Generalist practice is then guided by *three primary principles involving values*. It occurs within the *context* of an organizational structure. Finally, it employs *four major processes* (CSWE, 2008, Educational Policy [EP] 2.1).[3] (Highlight 1.2 identifies each of these 12 major concepts characterizing generalist practice and outlines major notions related to them. Each concept is described more thoroughly later in this chapter and in subsequent chapters.)

In summary, the core of generalist practice, then, rests on a solid *foundation of knowledge, values, and skills*. Knowledge includes a range of conceptual frameworks and information about understanding and practicing social work *(concept 1 in the definition of generalist practice)*. Values are based on professional ethics and the ability to distinguish between personal and professional values *(concept 2)*. Skills include those for working with individuals, families, groups, organizations, and communities *(concept 3)*. Necessary skills include those directed at initiating and implementing changes in any of these systems *(concept 4)*.

Three Principles Involving Values That Characterize Generalist Practice

Three primary principles involving values characterize generalist practice. The first of these principles involving values entails an emphasis on client *empowerment, strengths,* and *resiliency (concept 5 in the definition of generalist practice)*.

- *Empowerment* is "the process of increasing personal, interpersonal, or political power so that individuals can take action to improve their life situations" (Gutierrez, 2001, p. 210). It concerns ensuring that others have the right to power, ability, and authority to achieve *self-determination* (each individual's right to make his or her own decisions).
- *Strengths* include any "capacities, resources, and assets" that can be accessed to increase empowerment (Saleebey, 2013, p. 102).

---

2. The term *eclectic* refers to selecting concepts, theories, and ideas from a wide range of perspectives and practice approaches.

3. Most of these concepts are taken directly from the *Educational Policy and Accreditation Standards* (EPAS) developed by the Council on Social Work Education (CSWE, 2008, EP 2.1). Acquiring knowledge begins to prepare students for competent practice. Linking content to the EPAS ultimately is intended to assist in a social work program's accreditation process.

HIGHLIGHT 1.1

Social Work, Social Work Education, and Educational Policy

Students require knowledge in order to develop skills and become competent. In social work, the words *competence* and *practice behavior* have a unique meaning beyond the typical dictionary definitions. "Competence" in the usual sense means that a person possesses suitable skills and abilities to do a specific task. Competent baseball players must move quickly, catch, throw, and play as part of a team. They also have to think quickly, understand the rules of the game, and be knowledgeable of their environment. In the same way, competent social workers should be able to do a number of job-related duties, think critically, and understand the context of their work. For example, social workers must develop and use interviewing, assessment, intervention, and evaluation skills with their clients. The Council on Social Work Education (CSWE), social work's formal accrediting organization, has defined specific Core Competency areas for all social work students, and their corresponding practice behaviors. (*Accreditation* is the official authorization that a social work program has fulfilled and maintains the required standards to achieve this credential.) Professional social work education programs teach content and skills that comply with these *Educational Policy and Accreditation Standards* (EPAS).

The EPAS articulates what a professional social worker should be competent to do. This answers the question, "What should a social worker be capable of and proficient at accomplishing?" Note that the EPAS also contains standards governing other aspects of social work programs, such as "Program Mission and Goals" and "The Learning Environment" (CSWE, 2008, pp. 2, 10).

What Is Competent Social Work Practice?

The EPAS specifies 10 competencies that are operationalized by 41 practice behaviors. *Competencies* are basic capabilities involving social work knowledge, skills, and values that can be demonstrated and measured by practice behaviors. Competencies reflect more general expectations for proficient social workers. *Practice behaviors*, on the other hand, are measurable actions that demonstrate the application of social work knowledge, skills, and values for effective social work practice. Practice behaviors are more specific and are used to measure competency. Note that each of the

10 competencies is preceded by "EP 2.1.", which refers to the more general category of "Core Competencies" and distinguishes its location in the more extensive EPAS accreditation standards that also address other programmatic matters. Practice behaviors are alphabetized under each competency. The EPAS competencies and practice behaviors are as follows:

2.1.1: Identify as a Professional Social Worker and Conduct Oneself Accordingly

a. Advocate for client access to the services of social work
b. Practice personal reflection and self-correction to assure continual professional development
c. Attend to professional roles and boundaries
d. Demonstrate professional demeanor in behavior, appearance, and communication
e. Engage in career-long learning
f. Use supervision and consultation

2.1.2: Apply Social Work Ethical Principles to Guide Professional Practice

a. Recognize and manage personal values in a way that allows professional values to guide practice
b. Make ethical decisions by applying standards of the National Association of Social Workers *Code of Ethics* and, as applicable, of the International Federation of Social Workers/International Association of Schools of Social Work *Ethics in Social Work, Statement of Principles*
c. Tolerate ambiguity in resolving ethical conflicts
d. Apply strategies of ethical reasoning to arrive at principled decisions

2.1.3: Apply Critical Thinking to Inform and Communicate Professional Judgments

a. Distinguish, appraise, and integrate multiple sources of knowledge, including research-based knowledge and practice wisdom
b. Analyze models of assessment, prevention, intervention, and evaluation
c. Demonstrate effective oral and written communication in working with individuals, families, groups, organizations, communities, and colleagues

2.1.4: Engage Diversity and Difference in Practice

a. Recognize the extent to which a culture's structures and values may oppress, marginalize,

alienate, or create or enhance privilege and power
b. Gain sufficient self-awareness to eliminate the influence of personal biases and values in working with diverse groups
c. Recognize and communicate their understanding of the importance of difference in shaping life experiences
d. View themselves as learners and engage those with whom they work as informants

2.1.5: Advance Human Rights and Social and Economic Justice
a. Understand the forms and mechanisms of oppression and discrimination
b. Advocate for human rights and social and economic justice
c. Engage in practices that advance social and economic justice

2.1.6: Engage in Research-Informed Practice and Practice-Informed Research
a. Use practice experience to inform scientific inquiry
b. Use research evidence to inform practice

2.1.7: Apply Knowledge of Human Behavior and the Social Environment
a. Utilize conceptual frameworks to guide the processes of assessment, intervention, and evaluation
b. Critique and apply knowledge to understand person and environment

2.1.8: Engage in Policy Practice to Advance Social and Economic Well-Being and to Deliver Effective Social Work Services
a. Analyze, formulate, and advocate for policies that advance social well-being
b. Collaborate with colleagues and clients for effective policy action

2.1.9: Respond to Contexts That Shape Practice
a. Continuously discover, appraise, and attend to changing locales, populations, scientific and technological developments, and emerging societal trends to provide relevant services
b. Provide leadership in promoting sustainable changes in service delivery and practice to improve the quality of social services

2.1.10: Engage, Assess, Intervene, and Evaluate with Individuals, Families, Groups, Organizations, and Communities

a. Substantively and affectively prepare for action with individuals, families, groups, organizations, and communities
b. Use empathy and other interpersonal skills
c. Develop a mutually agreed-on focus of work and desired outcomes
d. Collect, organize, and interpret client data
e. Assess client strengths and limitations
f. Develop mutually agreed-on intervention goals and objectives
g. Select appropriate intervention strategies
h. Initiate actions to achieve organizational goals
i. Implement prevention interventions that enhance client capacities
j. Help clients resolve problems
k. Negotiate, mediate, and advocate for clients
l. Facilitate transitions and endings
m. Critically analyze, monitor, and evaluate interventions

The concepts and terminology used in the competencies will be defined and explained in subsequent sections of this book. The competencies, practice behaviors, and chapters in which they are addressed are noted in a chart on the inside covers of this book.

Competencies, Practice Behaviors, and Content in This Book

 We have established that future social workers require knowledge in order to develop skills and become competent. This book relates how designated content is linked to the development of specific competencies and practice behaviors. This is done by the placement of a **"helping hands" icon** (a figure with two hands embracing a flourishing tree, such as that illustrated in this paragraph) next to relevant content throughout the book. The "helping hands" icons located in the text are then labeled with the competencies or practice behaviors associated with that section's content. For example, an icon might be labeled "EP 2.1.1e" or "EP 2.1.7a."

"Competency Notes" are provided at the end of each chapter that explain how EPAS competencies and practice behaviors are related to designated content in the chapter. These are listed in the same order in which they occur in the EPAS document. Page numbers regarding where the icons appear in the chapter are furnished for easy reference.

HIGHLIGHT 1.2

Concepts in the Definition of Generalist Practice

1. *Acquisition of an eclectic knowledge base*
   A. Fields of practice
   B. Systems theories
   C. The ecological perspective
   D. Human behavior and the social environment
   E. Social welfare policy and policy practice
   F. Social work practice
   G. Research-informed practice and practice-informed research
   H. Values and principles that guide practice
2. *Acquisition of professional values and application of professional ethics*
   A. National Association of Social Workers *Code of Ethics*
   B. International Federation of Social Workers/International Association of Schools of Social Work *Ethics in Social Work, Statement of Principles*
   C. Awareness of personal values
   D. Management of ethical dilemmas
3. *Use of a wide range of practice skills*
   A. Skills for working with individuals and families (micro skills)
   B. Skills for working with families and groups (mezzo skills)
   C. Skills for working with organizations and communities (macro skills)
4. *Orientation to target systems of any size*
   A. Micro
   B. Mezzo
   C. Macro

5. *Primary value principle:* Emphasis on client empowerment, strengths, and resiliency
6. *Primary value principle:* The importance of human diversity
7. *Primary value principle:* Advocacy for human rights, and the pursuit of social and economic justice
8. *Context:* Work within an organizational structure
9. *Process:* Assumption of a wide range of professional roles
   A. Counselor
   B. Educator
   C. Broker
   D. Case manager
   E. Mobilizer
   F. Mediator
   G. Facilitator
   H. Integrator/Coordinator
   I. Manager
   J. Initiator
   K. Negotiator
   L. Spokesperson
   M. Organizer
   N. Consultant
   O. Advocate
10. *Process:* Application of critical thinking skills
11. *Process:* Incorporation of research-informed practice
12. *Process:* Use of planned change

• *Resiliency* is the ability of an individual, family, group, community, or organization to recover from adversity and resume functioning even when suffering serious trouble, confusion, or hardship (Clark, 2013; Glicken, 2006).

The second principle involving values that is emphasized in generalist practice is the importance of "understand[ing] how *[human] diversity* characterizes and shapes the human experience and is critical to the formation of identity" (emphasis added) (CSWE, 2008, EP 2.1.4) *(concept 6)*. Human diversity entails multiple factors, including "age, class, color, culture, disability, ethnicity, gender, gender identity and expression,

immigration status, political ideology, race, religion, sex, and sexual orientation" (CSWE, 2008, EP 2.1.4).

The third principle involving values that is accentuated in generalist practice concerns *advocacy for human rights, and the pursuit of social and economic justice* (CSWE, 2008, EP 2.1.5) *(concept 7)*.

The Context for Generalist Practice

Another concept significant to generalist practice is its *context (concept 8 in the definition of generalist practice)*. Most social workers are employed by an organization. They work in an agency environment complete with policies, management, and a designated clientele.

Thus, generalist practice occurs within the *context of an organizational structure.*

Four Processes That Characterize Generalist Practice

Four processes characterize generalist practice. First, generalist practice requires the assumption of a wide range of *professional roles (concept 9 in the definition of generalist practice).* Second, it requires the application of *critical thinking skills* throughout the course of intervention *(concept 10).* Third, generalist practice incorporates *research-informed practice* to determine the most effective ways to help people and serve clients *(concept 11).* Fourth, practitioners follow a seven-step *planned change* process to achieve intervention goals *(concept 12).*

How Concepts Fit Together

We have indicated that this chapter will address in greater detail the 12 key concepts inherent in the definition of generalist practice (summarized in Highlight 1.2). The order in which they are presented does not imply that one concept is more important than another. Each is significant. Figure 1.2 illustrates how the various concepts fit together. The large square labeled *Organizational Structure* represents the organization (or agency) that employs you to do a social work job. Organizational structure involves the operation of lines of authority and communication within an agency, how the administration runs the organization, and what the agency environment is like. As a generalist practitioner, you will work in this environment with all its constraints, requirements, and rules. Thus, Figure 1.2 pictures you, the generalist practitioner, as a rectangle within this large square. In that same square you see the concepts *Knowledge, Values,* and *Skills.* These illustrate that you bring to your job a broad knowledge base, professional values, and a wide range of skills.

The concentric circles at the bottom of Figure 1.2 illustrate your potential *target systems.* As we have established, generalist practitioners may choose to work with an individual (micro system), a family (micro/mezzo system),[4] a group (mezzo system), or an organization or community (macro systems) as the target of their change efforts. These systems are positioned in concentric circles according to their respective sizes.

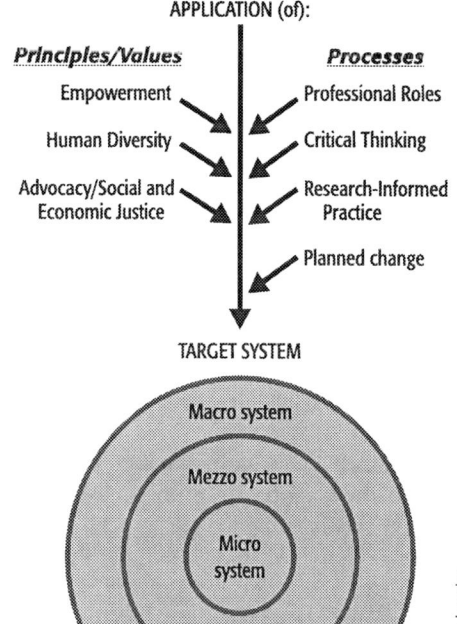

FIGURE 1.2 Definition of Generalist Practice

An arrow flows from the Organizational Structure square down to the Target System circles. This indicates that you, as a generalist practitioner, will apply your knowledge, skills, and values to help change a micro, mezzo, or macro system.

Other arrows point from concepts on the right and left to the central "application" arrow. This means that generalist practitioners apply the concepts represented by the arrows as they undertake generalist practice. "Principles/values" concepts, portrayed on the left, include empowerment, human diversity, advocacy for human rights, and the pursuit of social and economic justice. Social workers also apply the "processes" inherent in generalist practice. These, depicted on the right,

---

4. As already indicated, families, by their intimate and special nature, lie on a continuum between micro and mezzo systems.

consist of the assumption of various professional roles, use of critical thinking skills, incorporation of research-informed practice, and the undertaking of the planned change process.

Note that terms can sometimes be confusing. This book focuses on generalist practice and assumes that social workers are generalists. Therefore, the terms *generalist social worker, worker, generalist practitioner,* and *practitioner* will be used interchangeably throughout this book to refer to professionals undertaking generalist social work practice.

LO 1-3 Acquire and Apply an Eclectic Knowledge Base to Practice

 Acquisition of an eclectic knowledge base is the 1st concept involved in the definition of generalist practice. Social work has a growing and progressive knowledge base. More and more is being researched and written about how social workers can become increasingly effective in helping people solve problems. Additionally, the field has borrowed much knowledge from other fields such as psychology and sociology. Social work then applies this knowledge to practice situations.

Knowledge involves understanding the dynamics of people's situations and recognizing the skills that work best in specific situations. We have emphasized that generalist social workers need a broad knowledge base because they are called upon to help people solve such a wide variety of problems. One important content area in the knowledge base that is discussed here involves fields of practice. A second important content area concerns the "conceptual frameworks" of systems theory and the ecological perspective (CSWE, 2008, EP 2.1.7a). These two conceptual frameworks are intended "to guide the processes of assessment, intervention, and evaluation" (CSWE, 2008, EP 2.1.7a). In addition, the social work profession considers it necessary that you assimilate knowledge and develop competencies related to the following content areas: human behavior and the social environment; social welfare policy and policy practice; social work practice; research; and values and principles guiding generalist practice (CSWE, 2008). A *competency* is the proven ability to demonstrate the acquisition of sufficient knowledge, skills, and values in a designated area in order to practice effective social work.

AN ECLECTIC KNOWLEDGE BASE: FIELDS OF PRACTICE

There are a number of ways to classify the kinds of knowledge generalist social workers need. One is by *fields of practice,* broad areas in social work that address certain types of populations and needs. Each field of practice is a labyrinth of typical human problems and the services attempting to address them. Some fields of practice currently characterizing the profession include families and children, mental health, schools, aging, and substance abuse (Gibelman, 1995). Other fields of practice are occupational social work (focusing on work in employee assistance programs or directed toward organizational change), rural social work (addressing the unique problems of people living in rural areas), police social work (emphasizing work within police, courthouse, and jail settings to provide services to crime victims), and forensic social work (dealing with the law, educating lawyers, and serving as expert witnesses) (Barker, 2003).

Generalist social workers require information about people who need help in each of these areas. Workers also must be knowledgeable about the services available to meet needs and the major issues related to each area. On one hand, a social worker may be called upon to work with a problem that clearly falls within one field of practice. On the other hand, a problem may involve several of these fields.

For example, the Steno family comes to a social worker's attention when a neighbor reports that Ben, a 5-year-old child, is frequently seen with odd-looking bruises on his arms and legs. The neighbor suspects child abuse. Upon investigation, the social worker finds that the parents are indeed abusive. They often grab the child violently by a limb and throw him against the wall. This problem initially falls under the umbrella of family and children's services.

However, the social worker also finds a number of other problems operating within the family. The mother, Natasia Steno, is seriously depressed and frequently suicidal. She needs mental health services. Additionally, the father, Eric Steno, is struggling with a drinking problem that is beginning to affect his performance at work. A program is available at his place of employment where an occupational social worker helps employees deal with such problems. Thus, occupational social work may also be involved.

There is a maternal grandmother, Emma, living in the home with the Steno family, whose physical health is failing. She is also overweight and finds moving around by herself increasingly difficult. As a result, she is demanding more and more physical help and support from Natasia, who has back problems herself and finds helping her mother increasingly burdensome. Although she dreads the idea of nursing home placement, Natasia knows the issue must be addressed. Finally, Vernite, the 12-year-old daughter in the family, is falling behind in school. Truancy is becoming a major problem. This last issue falls under the school's umbrella.

Most of the problems that social workers face are complex. They may involve a variety of practice fields all at one time. In order to understand clients' needs, social workers must know something about a wide range of problems and services.

LO 1-4 Apply the Systems Theory Conceptual Framework to Practice

EP 2.1.7
EP 2.1.7a
EP 2.1.10

Systems theory provides social workers with a conceptual framework that can guide how they view the world. Generalist practitioners must be knowledgeable about "the range of social systems in which people live" and "the ways social systems promote or deter people in maintaining or achieving health and well-being" (CSWE, 2008, EP 2.1.7). Social work focuses on the interactions of various systems in the environment including "individuals, families, groups, organizations, and communities" (CSWE, 2008, EP 2.1.10). A *system* is a set of elements that are orderly and interrelated to make a functional whole. A person, your class, your family, and your college or university are all systems. Each involves many components that work together in order to function.

Understanding systems theory is especially important because, as we have established, generalist practice targets systems of virtually any size for change. Regardless of your field of practice, having a sound knowledge base in systems theory is helpful. As a generalist, you will evaluate any confronting problem from multiple perspectives. You will determine whether change is best pursued by individual, family, group, organizational, or community avenues. You might decide that any of these systems should be the target of your planned change efforts.

In order to understand how a systems model can provide the framework for intervention, one must understand some of the major terms involved. These terms include *system, dynamic, interact, input, output,*

homeostasis, and *equifinality* (Zastrow & Kirst-Ashman, 2013).

We defined a *system* as a set of elements that forms an orderly, interrelated, and functional whole. Several aspects of this definition are important. The idea that a system is a "set of elements" means that a system can be composed of any type of things as long as these things have some relationship to each other. Things may be people or they may be mathematical symbols. Regardless, the set of elements must be orderly and arranged in some pattern that is not simply random.

The set of elements must also be interrelated. They must have some kind of mutual relationship or connection with each other. Additionally, the set of elements must be functional. Together, they must be able to perform some regular task, activity, or function and fulfill some purpose. Finally, the set of elements must form a whole, a single entity. Examples of systems include a large nation, a public social services department, a Girl Scout troop, and a newly married couple.

The conception of a system helps a social worker focus on a target for intervention. The system may be an individual or a state government. The fact that the target is conceptualized as a system means that an understanding of the whole system and how its many elements work together is necessary. Consider, for example, an individual named Bill as a functioning system. Bill says he is depressed. The psychological aspects are only one facet of the entire functioning system; physical and social aspects are among numerous other system characteristics. A worker who looks at the person as a total system would inquire further about the individual's health and social circumstances. The worker finds that Bill is suffering both from a viral flu infection that has been "hanging on" for the past 3 weeks and from a chronic blood disease. Both of these elements affect his psychological state. Additionally, the worker discovers that Bill has recently been divorced and, because he has only partial custody, misses his three children desperately. These aspects, too, relate directly to Bill's depression.

Thus, a systems approach guides social workers to look beyond a seemingly simplistic presenting problem. Workers view problems as being interrelated with all other aspects of the system. Many aspects work together to affect the functioning of the whole person.

A systems perspective also guides workers to view systems as dynamic—that is, having constant dynamic movement because problems and issues are forever changing. This perspective provides workers with an outlook that must be flexible. They must be ready to address new problems and apply new intervention strategies. For instance, a worker's assessment of the situation and intervention strategies would probably change if Bill, described previously, was fired from his current job or was reunited with his ex-wife.

Systems constantly *interact* with each other. A system can be an individual, a group, or a large organization. A systems focus provides the worker with a framework that extends far beyond that of the individual as the sole target of intervention. A systems perspective diverts the attention from the individual to the interaction between that individual and the environment (Hartman, 1970). There is a constant flow of input and output among systems. *Input* is the energy, information, or communication flow received from other systems; *output* is the same flow emitted from a system to the environment or to other systems.

Reconsider Bill, the depressed man. His relationship with his ex-wife and children is seriously affecting not only him, but also his interactions at work. Coworkers who were once his friends are tired of hearing him complain about how hard life is. They no longer like to associate with him. Bill feels that he is in a dead-end, low-level, white-collar job that requires a minimal level of skill. Even worse, his boss has cut back his hours so he no longer can work any overtime. Now he can barely scrape by financially. The courts have mandated support payments for his children, which he has not been able to make for 3 months. His ex-wife is threatening not to let him see his kids if he does not get some money to her soon.

Of course, one should note that Bill's ex-wife Shirley views the situation from a totally different perspective. She attributes the divorce to the fact that Bill had a long series of affairs throughout their marriage. She had sacrificed her own employment and career in order to remain the primary caretaker of home and children. She just could not stand the infidelity any longer and filed for divorce. Her serious financial situation is magnified by the fact that she has neither an employment nor credit history of her own. She remains extremely angry at Bill and feels demanding support payments is her right.

Bill, on the other hand, is expending much energy to hold his life together. This situation is his output. However, he is receiving little input in return. As a result, he is unable to maintain his *homeostasis*, which refers to the tendency for a system to maintain a relatively stable, constant state of equilibrium or balance.

A systems perspective takes these many aspects of Bill's life into account. It focuses on his input, output,

and homeostasis with respect to the many systems with which he is interacting. Sitting in an office with this man for 50 minutes each week and trying to get him to talk his way out of his depression will not suffice in generalist practice. His interactions with his family and impinging mezzo systems (e.g., his coworkers) and macro systems (e.g., the large company he works for and the state that mandates his support payments) provide potential targets of intervention and change. Can visits with his children and his support payment schedule be renegotiated? Can reconciliation with Shirley be pursued? Are the policies mandating his support payments and controlling his visitation rights fair? Are there any support groups available that he could join whose members had similar situations to his own and from whom he could gain support? Is there any potential for job retraining or perhaps a job change?

Equifinality refers to the fact that there are many different means to the same end. In other words, there are many ways of viewing a problem and, thus, many potential means of solving it. Bill's interaction with friends, family, coworkers, governmental offices, and health care systems all affect his psychological state. Therefore, targets of intervention may involve change or interaction with any of these other systems.

Conceptualizing Workers and Clients as Systems

A helpful orientation for practice is to conceptualize yourself and your clients in terms of systems. We have already established that a target system or target of change is the system that social workers need "to change or influence in order to accomplish [their] goals" (Pincus & Minahan, 1973, p. 58). Targets of change may be individual clients, families, formal groups, administrators, or policymakers, depending on what you need to change. At the micro level, a 5-year-old child with behavior problems might be the target of change, the goal being to improve behavior. At the mezzo level, a support group of people with eating disorders might be the target of change, aiming to control their eating behavior. Finally, at the macro level, an agency director might be the target of change if your aim is to improve some agency policy and she is the primary decision maker capable of implementing that change.

Three other systems critical to the planned change process are the client, target, and action systems (Hepworth et al., 2013; Pincus & Minahan, 1973). A *client system* is any individual, family, group, organization, or community that will ultimately benefit from generalist social work intervention. Your individual clients are client systems. The *change agent system* is the individual who initiates the planned change process. This book assumes you will function as the change agent system while helping your client systems.

You might gain the support of and join in coalitions with others who also believe in the proposed change, especially when you work for changes at the macro level. Then you as a single change agent might become part of a larger system. Whether you undertake macro change by yourself or join together with others, you are or are part of an *action system*. The action system then includes those people who agree and are committed to work together in order to attain the proposed change. An action system might undertake the planned change process to change an agency policy, develop a new program, or institute some project such as evaluating intervention methodology or setting up agency in-service training sessions.

LO 1-5 Apply the Ecological Conceptual Framework to Practice

EP 2.1.7a

The ecological perspective is another relevant part of social work's knowledge base. Like systems theory, it provides a useful conceptual framework for generalist practice. This text assumes a systems theory approach; however, it takes and utilizes selected terms from the ecological perspective that are exceptionally useful in describing human interaction with other systems. For instance, the term *social environment* is grounded in the ecological perspective. Generalist practitioners work with clients within the context of their social environments.

There exists some debate regarding the relationship between systems theory and the ecological perspective. That is, to what extent are the theoretical approaches similar and dissimilar? The ecological approach assumes a person-in-environment focus. Each perspective has, at various times, been described as being a theory, model, or a theoretical underpinning. A number of the major terms involved in the ecological perspective will be explained. Subsequently, some similarities and differences will be discussed. Finally, the question of which approach is best will be addressed.

Ecological Terms

We have already reviewed some of the major terms in systems theory. We will now discuss some of the primary terms in the ecological perspective, including *social environment, person-in-environment, transactions,*

energy, input, output, interface, adaptation, coping, and *interdependence.*

The *social environment* involves the conditions, circumstances, and human interactions that encompass human beings. Persons are dependent on effective interactions with this environment in order to survive and thrive. The social environment includes the types of homes people live in, the types of work they do, the amount of money available, and the laws and social rules they live by. The social environment also includes all the individuals, groups, organizations, and systems with which a person comes into contact.

A *person-in-environment* focus sees people as constantly interacting with various systems around them. These systems include the family, friends, work, social services, politics, religion, goods and services, and educational systems. The person is portrayed as being dynamically involved with each. Social work practice then is directed at improving the interactions among the person and the various systems. This focus is referred to as improving person-in-environment fit.

People communicate and interact with others in their environments. Each of these interactions or *transactions* (i.e., something is communicated or exchanged) is active and dynamic. However, they may be positive or negative. A positive transaction may be the revelation that the one you dearly love loves you in return. A negative transaction may involve being fired from a job you have held for 15 years.

Energy is the natural power of active involvement among people and their environments. Energy can take the form of input or output. *Input* is a form of energy coming into a person's life and adding to that life (e.g., an older adult in failing health may need substantial physical assistance and emotional support in order to continue performing necessary daily tasks) or output. *Output*, on the other hand, is a form of energy going out of a person's life or taking something away from it. For instance, a person may volunteer time and effort to work on a political campaign.

The *interface* is the exact point at which the interaction between an individual and the environment takes place. During an assessment of a person-in-environment situation, the interface must be clearly in focus in order to target the appropriate interactions for change. For example, a couple entering marriage counseling may first state that their problem concerns disagreements about how to raise the children. On further exploration, however, their inability to communicate their real feelings to each other surfaces. The actual problem—the inability to communicate—is the interface at which one individual affects the other. Each person is part of the other's social environment. If the interface is inaccurately targeted, much time and energy will be wasted before getting at the real problem.

Adaptation is the capacity to adjust to surrounding environmental conditions. It implies change. A person must change or adapt to new conditions and circumstances in order to continue functioning effectively. As people are constantly exposed to changes and stressful life events, they need to be flexible and capable of adaptation. Social workers frequently help people in this process of adaptation. A person may have to adapt to a new significant other, a new job, or a new neighborhood. Adaptation usually requires energy in the form of effort. Social workers often help direct people's energies so that they are most productive.

People are affected by their environments and vice versa. People can and do change their environments in order to adapt successfully. For instance, a person would find surviving a Montana winter in the natural environment challenging without shelter. Therefore, those who live in Montana change and manipulate their environment by clearing land and constructing heated buildings. They change their environment so they are better able to adapt to it. Therefore, adaptation often implies a two-way process involving both the individual and the environment.

Coping is a form of human adaptation and implies a struggle to overcome problems. Although adaptation may involve responses to new positive or negative conditions, coping refers to the way we deal with the problems we experience. For example, a person might have to cope with the sudden death of a parent or the birth of a baby.

Interdependence is the mutual reliance of each person on each other person. Individuals are interdependent as they rely on other individuals and groups of individuals in the social environment. Likewise, these other individuals are interdependent on one another for input, energy, services, and consistency. People cannot exist without each other. The business executive needs the farmer to produce food and customers to purchase goods. Likewise, the farmer must sell food products to the executive in order to get money to buy seeds, tools, and other essentials. People—especially in a highly industrialized society—are interdependent and need each other in order to survive.

Similarities Between Systems Theory and the Ecological Perspective

Some basic similarities exist between systems theory and the ecological perspective. Both emphasize systems and focus on the dynamic interaction among many levels of systems. Some of the terms (especially *input* and *output*) are similar. Additionally, each provides social workers a framework with which to view the world. Finally, both perspectives emphasize external interactions instead of internal functioning. In other words, from a social work point of view, both emphasize helping people improve their interactions with other systems. As a result, these two perspectives are different from a focus on fixing or curing the individual. Highlight 1.3 summarizes some of the key terms in both.

HIGHLIGHT 1.3

Summary of Some of the Major Terms in Systems Theory and the Ecological Perspective

Some Major Terms in Systems Theory	Similar Terms in Both	Some Major Terms in the Ecological Perspective
System	Input	Social environment
Dynamic	Output	Person-in-environment focus
Interact		Transactions
Homeostasis		Energy
Equifinality		Interface
		Adaptation
		Coping
		Interdependence

Differences Between Systems Theory and the Ecological Perspective

In the simplest sense, there are two major differences between systems theory and the ecological perspective. First, the ecological approach refers to living, dynamic interactions. The emphasis is on active participation. People, for example, have dynamic transactions with each other and with their environments. Systems theory, on the other hand, assumes a broader perspective. It can be used to refer to inanimate, mechanical operations such as a mechanized assembly line in a pea-canning plant. It can also be used to describe the functioning of a human family.

A second difference between the ecological perspective and systems theory is based on the emphasizing of different terms. For example, the ecological approach focuses on transactions between individuals and the environment at the interface or point at which the individual and environment meet. Systems theory, on the other hand, addresses boundaries of subsystems within a system and the maintenance of homeostasis or equilibrium within a system. Some theoreticians might posit that the ecological model is an offshoot or interpretation of systems theory, as it is a bit more limited in scope and application.

Which Perspective Is Best?

Both systems theory and the ecological perspective provide major tools for conceptualizing social work (Kondrat, 2008). The important thing is that both emphasize interactions with the environment. Depending on the circumstance, one perspective might be more helpful to employ than the other. For example, systems theory might be more helpful when addressing problems within a family. Using notions like subsystems and boundaries helps social workers understand the ongoing dynamics. Likewise, analysis of a particular family system using these notions provides cues for how to proceed to improve family functioning.

On the other hand, an ecological perspective can also be useful. The notion of transactions with the social environment helps provide focus when a homeless family is not getting the resources it needs. A focus on the interface between family and environment leads a social worker to emphasize getting the family the services and support it requires to survive.

EP 2.1.7
EP 2.1.7b

AN ECLECTIC KNOWLEDGE BASE: ASSESS HUMAN BEHAVIOR IN THE CONTEXT OF THE SOCIAL ENVIRONMENT

Knowledge about human behavior and the social environment (HBSE) is an essential foundation on which to build practice skills. Accurate assessment of the person, problem, and situation is a critical step in effective intervention. The environment is vitally important in the analysis and understanding of human behavior. As social work has a person-in-environment focus, the interactions between individuals, systems, and the environment are critical. Such a conceptual perspective provides social workers with a symbolic representation of how to interpret the world. It provides ideas for how to assess clients' situations and identify their alternatives.

People are constantly and dynamically involved in social transactions. There is ongoing activity, communication, and change. Social work assessment seeks to answer the question: "What is it in any particular situation that causes a problem to continue despite the client's expressed wish to change it?" A person-in-environment perspective allows social workers to assess many aspects of a situation. Assessment may involve not only individual, personal characteristics and experiences, but also interaction with people in the immediate environment. These experiences often concern relationships with peer, social, and work groups.

Assessments also often involve family situations. Because of the intimacy and intensity of family relationships and the importance of the family context to individuals, we have established that families deserve special status and attention.

Assessment may also relate to people's transactions with large organizations and systems around the individual in the macro social environment. The *macro social environment* involves the organizations[5] and communities[6] (including neighborhood, local, state, national, and global) with which people are engaged and the social,[7] economic,[8] and political[9] forces that affect these individuals. An individual's place within the total scheme of things can be analyzed.

---

5. *Organizations* are "(1) social entities that (2) are goal-directed, (3) are designed as deliberately structured and coordinated activity systems, and (4) are linked to the external environment" (Daft, 2013, p. 12).

6. A *community* is "a number of people with something in common that connects them in some way and that distinguishes them from others" (Homan, 2011, p. 8).

7. *Social forces* are values and beliefs held by people in the social environment that are strong enough to influence people's activities, including how government is structured or restricted.

8. *Economic forces* are the resources that are available, how they are distributed, and how they are spent.

9. *Political forces* are the current governmental structures, the laws to which people are subject, and the overall distribution of power among the population.

Conditions in the macro environment may include poverty, discrimination, social pressures, and the effects of social policies. Such circumstances mean that clients' problems are not viewed solely as each client's own fault. The forces surrounding the client frequently cause or contribute to problems. Thus, social workers must focus their assessment on many levels. How the client and the problem fit into the larger picture is critically important.

For instance, consider Kevin, a 15-year-old inner-city gang member. The gang is involved in drug dealing, which, of course, is illegal. However, when assessing the situation and what might be done about it, a broader perspective is necessary. Looking at how the environment encourages and even supports the illegal activity is critical in understanding how to solve the problem. Kevin's father is no longer involved with Kevin's family. Now only Kevin, his mother, and three younger brothers remain. Kevin's mother works a 6-day-per-week, 9-hour-per-day second shift job at Boogie's Burger Bungalow, a local all-night diner where she slings burgers. Although she loves her children dearly, she can barely make ends meet. She has little time for their supervision, especially Kevin's, as he is the oldest.

All of the neighborhood kids seem to belong to one gang or another. This gives them a sense of identity and importance and provides social support. In many instances, such support is almost completely lacking elsewhere. Easy access to drugs offers a readily available chance to escape from impoverished, depressing, and apparently hopeless conditions. Finally, gang membership gives these young people a source of income. In fact, they can get relatively large amounts of money in a hurry.

The gang members' alternatives appear grim. There are few, if any, positive role models to show them other ways of existence. They do not see their peers or adults close to them becoming corporate lawyers, brain surgeons, nuclear physicists, or editors. In fact, they do not see anyone who is going or has gone to college. Finishing high school is considered quite a feat. Neighborhood unemployment runs at more than 50 percent. A few part-time, minimum-wage jobs are available— cleaning washrooms at Burger King or hauling heavy packages off trucks at Pick 'n' Save. These options are unappealing alternatives to the immediate sources of gratification provided by gang membership and drug dealing. Even if another minimal source of income could be found, the other rewarding aspects of gang membership would be lost. Also, there is the all-consuming problem of having no positive prospects to look forward to. The future looks pretty bleak, so the excitement of the present remains seductive.

This situation is not meant to imply that joining vicious gangs and participating in illegal activities is right for people such as Kevin. Nor does it mean that Kevin's plight is hopeless. Going beyond a focus on the individual to assess the many environmental impacts and interactions gives the social worker a better understanding of the whole situation. The answer might not be to send Kevin to the state juvenile correctional facility for a year or two and then put him back in the same community with the same friends and same problems. That focuses on the individual in a limited manner.

A generalist social work practitioner views Kevin as a person who's acting as part of a family and a community. Kevin is affected, influenced, supported, and limited by his immediate environment. Continuing along this line of thought, other questions can be raised. For example, how might Kevin's environment be changed? What other alternatives are available to him?

Many potential alternatives would involve major changes in the larger systems around him. Neighborhood youth centers with staff serving as positive role models could be developed as an alternative to gang membership. Kevin's school system could be evaluated. Does it have enough resources to give Kevin a good education? Is there a teacher who could single Kevin out and serve as his mentor and enthusiastic supporter? Can a mentor system be established within the school? Are scholarships and loans available to offer Kevin a viable alternative of college or trade school? Can positive role models demonstrate to Kevin and his peers that alternative ways of life may be open to them? Where might the resources for implementation of any of these ideas come from?

Concerning Kevin's family environment, can additional resources be provided? These resources might include food and housing assistance, good day care for his younger brothers, and even educational opportunities for Kevin's mother so that she, too, could see a brighter future. Is there a Big Brother organization to provide support for Kevin and his siblings? Can the neighborhood be made a better place to live? Can crime be curbed and housing conditions improved?

There obviously are no easy answers. Scarcity of resources remains a fundamental problem. However, this illustration is intended to show how a generalist social work practitioner would look at a variety of options and targets of change—not just at Kevin.

Critical Thinking Questions 1.1

- How would you evaluate Kevin's situation?
- What changes in Kevin's environment and his support system do you think would be most helpful to him?
- From where might resources to support change come?

(Critical thinking is explained and examined later in this chapter. Critical thinking questions like this will be interspersed throughout the text. Chapter 11 examines in greater depth ethical dilemmas such as Kevin's situation.)

AN ECLECTIC KNOWLEDGE BASE: ENGAGE SOCIAL WELFARE POLICY THROUGH POLICY PRACTICE

Social workers must be knowledgeable about social welfare policy in order to be competent practitioners. Policy, in its simplest portrayal, might be thought of as *rules*. Our lives and those of our clients are governed by rules. There are rules about how we drive our cars, when we must go to school, and how we talk or write sentences.

Policies, in essence, are rules that tell us which actions among a multitude of actions we may and may not take. Policies guide our work and our decisions. In its broad sense, *social welfare policy* includes the laws and regulations that determine how resources are distributed and what opportunities are made available so that people may lead fruitful and fulfilling lives; this includes numerous dimensions ranging from how taxes are levied to how the educational system is structured (Herrick, 2008). Social welfare policies also govern which social programs exist, what categories of clients are served, and who qualifies for a given program. Such policies set standards regarding the type of services to be provided and the qualifications of the service provider.

Basically, social welfare policies dictate how money can be spent to help people and how these people will be treated. There are policies that determine who is and who is not eligible for public assistance. Likewise, policies specify what social workers can and cannot do for sexually abused children.

Generalist practitioners must be well versed in social welfare policy. Social workers must know what is available for a client and how to get it. In order to get what is needed, they must understand the rules or policies for getting it. For example, Adam, a social worker for a county social services department, has a young client with three small children who has just been evicted from her apartment. Although the rent was relatively low and the apartment small (one bedroom), she had been unable to pay the rent for the past 3 months. All her money had gone to clothing and feeding her children.

Adam needs to know what other resources, if any, are available for this client and whether or not she is eligible to receive these resources. Policies determine the answers to these questions. Will the client qualify for some temporary additional public assistance in order to help her relocate? Is there a local shelter for the homeless available whose policies will allow the client and her children admission? If so, what is the shelter's policy for how long she and her children can stay? Is there any low-rent housing available? If so, what does its policy designate as the criteria and procedure for admittance? Such questions may continue on and on.

In addition to broader social welfare policies, there are agency policies concerning social service delivery. A *social services agency* is an organization providing social services that typically employs a range of helping professionals including social workers in addition to office staff, paraprofessionals (persons trained to assist professionals), and, on occasion, volunteers (Barker, 2003). Social agencies generally serve some designated client population experiencing some defined need. Examples of social services agencies include a family service agency, a Department of Human Services, and a nursing home.

Agency policies are those standards adopted that govern how the organization is structured, the qualifications of supervisors and workers, the services that are provided, and what staff including social workers may or may not do. For example, an agency providing services to families might have an agency policy concerning the proper procedures for practitioners to follow when conducting a family assessment.

The point here is that knowledge about policy is vitally important. An organization's policy can dictate how much vacation an employee can have and how raises are earned. An adoption agency's policy can determine who is and is not eligible to adopt a child. A social services agency's policies determine who receives and does not receive needed services and resources.

Iatridis (2008) stresses that social workers must become actively involved in establishing and changing policies on multiple levels, including social welfare and agency policy, for the benefit of their clients. Sometimes, resources are unavailable or inadequate to meet clients' needs. Social workers should be able to "analyze, formulate, and advocate for policies that advance social well-being" (CSWE, 2008, EP 2.1.8a).

At times, for whatever reason, policies are unfair or oppressive to clients. Sometimes, a social worker will decide that a policy is ethically or morally intolerable. In those events, the worker may decide to advocate on the behalf of clients to try to change the policy.

Generalist practitioners require the ability to analyze policy and undertake change when it is needed. In other words, they have responsibility for undertaking policy practice. *Policy practice* involves "efforts to change policies in legislative, agency, and community settings, whether by establishing new policies, improving existing ones, or defeating the policy initiatives of other people" (Jansson, 2011, p. 14). Policy practice may also concern advocacy on behalf of "relatively powerless groups, such as women, children, poor people, African Americans, Asian Americans, Latinos, Native Americans, gay men and lesbians, and people with disabilities, [to] improve their resources and opportunities" (Jansson, 2011, p. 15). Later chapters will say more about advocacy and making changes in larger systems and their policies.

Additionally, generalist practitioners need a sound foundation of knowledge concerning social services. This includes a historical perspective about how services have been developed and an analytical perspective concerning how well services "advance social well-being" for those in need (CSWE, 2008, EP 2.1.8).

AN ECLECTIC KNOWLEDGE BASE: ENGAGE IN SOCIAL WORK PRACTICE

 Social work practice is what this book is all about. It is the *doing* of social work. It involves how to form relationships with clients, help them to share information with you, define issues and problems, identify strengths, collect and assess information, identify and evaluate numerous alternatives for action, make specific plans, implement these plans, evaluate progress, terminate your client–worker relationship, and do follow-up to make certain intervention is no longer necessary.

Practice involves working with individuals, families, groups, organizations (both large and small), and large social and governmental structures. The acquisition of practice skills is what makes social work useful and

practical. Skills provide the muscle to make social work practice effective.

The social work knowledge base includes knowledge about skills in addition to knowledge of problems and services. A social worker must know which skills will be most effective in which situation.

Consider a family whose home suddenly burns to the ground. Its members need immediate shelter. The social worker decides that using brokering skills is necessary, that is, skills for seeking out and connecting people with the resources they need. The immediate crisis must be resolved by finding a place for the family to stay. In this situation, brokering skills take precedence over other skills. For instance, using less directive counseling techniques to explore the relationship between the spouses is inappropriate at this time. There is no current evidence of need. Such intervention may be necessary in the future, but only after the immediate crisis has been resolved.

There are multitudes of practice techniques and theories about these techniques from which social workers can choose. Social workers' skills are truly eclectic. Knowledge about the effectiveness of techniques is critical in order to select those that can accomplish the most in any specific situation. Regardless of techniques chosen and used, emphasis is currently placed on client strengths and empowerment, appreciation of diversity, and the use of practice approaches that empirical evidence has proven effective (Corcoran, 2008; Parsons, 2008).

AN ECLECTIC KNOWLEDGE BASE: INCORPORATE RESEARCH-INFORMED PRACTICE AND PRACTICE-INFORMED RESEARCH

 Research accompanies HBSE, social policy and policy practice, and social work practice as necessary components of the knowledge base for generalist practice. Knowledge about social work research is important for at least three basic reasons (Tripodi & Lalayants, 2008). First, it provides a scientific orientation to identifying, evaluating, and choosing intervention approaches that are effective. *Research-informed practice* is social work practice based on empirical evidence. (Highlight 1.4 discusses a related term—evidence-based practice.) Framing social work interventions so that they can be evaluated through research imparts information about which specific techniques work best with which specific problems. *Practice-informed research* refers to scientific investigation designed to attain results related to successful social work practice.

Evidence-Based Practice

A term related to research-informed practice is *evidence-based practice.* Rubin and Babbie (2011) explain:

> *Evidence-based practice (EBP) is a process in which practitioners make practice decisions in light of the best research evidence available. But rather than rigidly constrict practitioner options, the EPB model encourages practitioners to integrate scientific evidence with their practice expertise and knowledge of the idiosyncratic circumstances bearing on specific practice decisions. . . .*
>
> *Evidence-based practice also involves evaluating the outcomes of their decisions. Although evidence-based practice is most commonly discussed in regard to decisions about what interventions to provide clients, it also applies to decisions about how best to assess the practice problems and decisions practitioners make at other levels of practice—such as decisions about social policies, communities, and so on. For example, a clinical practitioner following the EPB model with a newly referred client will attempt to find and use the most scientifically*

> *validated diagnostic tools in assessing client problems and treatment needs and then develop a treatment plan in light of the best research evidence available as to what interventions are most likely to be effective in light of that assessment, the practitioner's clinical expertise regarding the client, and the client's idiosyncratic attributes and circumstances. At the level of social policy, evidence-based practitioners will attempt to formulate and advocate policies that the best research available suggests are most likely to achieve their desired aims. Likewise, evidence-based practitioners working at the community level will make practice decisions at that level in light of community-level practice research. Moreover, evidence-based practitioners at each level will utilize research methods to evaluate the outcomes of their practice decisions to see if the chosen course of action is achieving its desired aim. If it is not, then the evidence-based practitioner will choose an alternative course of action—again in light of the best research evidence available and again evaluating its outcome. (p. 26)*

The second reason research is important is that, with this scientific perspective, it can guide social workers to become more effective in their practice. It can help them get better and clearer results. When work with a client is clearly evaluated, social workers can determine whether they are really helping a client with his or her problem. Additionally, practitioners can monitor their progress during the actual implementation process. Similarly, whole agencies can use research to evaluate their programs' effectiveness.

The third reason is that accumulated research helps to build an effective knowledge base for the social work profession. This helps to define social work practice, increase the effectiveness of interventions, and enhance the profession's accountability. Research forms the basis for the development of whole programs and policies that affect large numbers of people. Such knowledge can also be used to generate new theories and ideas to further enhance the effectiveness of social work.

Each social worker must master three dimensions of basic research skills. First, social workers need research skills to evaluate effectively the work they do with

clients on all levels. (Evaluation is the fifth step of the planned change process emphasized in this book. It involves determining whether what you do as a practitioner is effective or not. On a micro level, are your clients' needs being met? Are they generally attaining their goals? On a mezzo level, is the group you are running effective? Are individual members and the entire group as a whole accomplishing their respective goals?)

The second dimension of basic research skills necessary for generalist practice involves the evaluation of macro system effectiveness. On a macro level, is your agency generally effective in its provision of services? Are clients really getting what they need? Practitioners, thus, need research competence in evaluating the effectiveness of service provision at all three levels of practice.

A third dimension is the ability to understand, analyze, and critically evaluate social work literature and research. Wide varieties of competing intervention approaches and techniques are available. Practitioners require research competence to make effective choices in their own generalist practice. How much faith can you place in some specific research findings, considering the research methodology used? How useful is the research for your particular client population? How relevant are the findings for your own generalist practice?

AN ECLECTIC KNOWLEDGE BASE: VALUES AND PRINCIPLES THAT GUIDE GENERALIST PRACTICE

Knowledge, skills, and values in social work have many overlaps. For example, consider the values and principles that guide generalist practice. These include the broad category of professional values and ethics in addition to the principles of client empowerment, understanding and appreciation of human diversity, and advocacy for human rights along with the pursuit of social and economic justice. There is much vital information in the eclectic *knowledge* base concerning each of these areas that is necessary for competent social work practice. Such knowledge should be applied via *skills* during implementation of planned change. However, each concept is an important component in the definition of generalist practice. Therefore, subsequent sections involving primary *values* and principles in generalist social work will address each concept more thoroughly in its own right.

LO 1-6 Acquire Professional Values and Apply Professional Ethics to Practice

EP 2.1.2

Not only must generalist practitioners have substantial and diverse knowledge at their disposal, but they must also have assimilated professional values and ethical principles, the 2nd concept in the definition of generalist practice. *Values* are principles, qualities, and practices that a designated group, individual, or culture deems inherently desirable. Values, then, give direction concerning what is considered right and wrong. Subsequently, values provide guidelines for behavior. Ideally, one should behave in accordance with the values one holds.

Ethics are standards based on a set of values that serve to guide one's behavior. Values reflect what you consider to be right and wrong; ethics involves how you behave based on these values. Generalist practitioners must have a sound basis for making ethical decisions that are in accord with social work values. Highlight 1.5 introduces several aspects of professional values and ethics critical for social workers to address.

Social work values focus on "a commitment to human welfare, social justice, and individual dignity" (Reamer, 1987, p. 801). This focus frames the perspective with which social workers view their work with people. In other words, the well-being of people is more important than making the largest business profit or becoming the most famous actor. Social workers care about other people and spend their time helping people improve the conditions of their lives.

Social work values address individual needs and concerns, those of communities, and those of society in general. Professional values are interwoven throughout the micro, mezzo, and macro levels of practice. The individual well-being of a person with a severe physical disability is critical, as is the way public services and laws generally treat such persons.

Superficially, this situation appears simple. The profession provides ethical guidelines for how to help people. Theoretically, then, all you should have to do is closely adhere to those guidelines, and ethical practice should be easy. You are simply supposed to look out for the well-being of your clients, right?

To say that people are complicated, as is life in general, is a cliché. However, one can also say that the application of ethics to actual decision making is often tremendously complicated. Many times, the monster of ethical conflict will raise its hoary head: Adherence to one aspect of ethics will effectively contradict adherence to another aspect of ethical conduct.

For example, the NASW *Code of Ethics* states that "social workers should respect clients' right to privacy" and "should protect the confidentiality of all information obtained in the course of professional service" (NASW, 2008, §§1.07a, 1.07c). However, the *Code* goes on to state that confidentiality should be protected, "except for compelling professional reasons" or "when disclosure is necessary to prevent serious, foreseeable, and imminent harm to a client or other identifiable person" (NASW, 2008, §1.07c).

Consider the situation in which a client, Bob, reveals that he has recently been given the diagnosis that he is HIV-positive. This condition can be fatal in the long run, and the social worker, Mia, knows that the client has been having unprotected sexual relations with several people over the past months. During their meetings, Bob has specifically named these people. After discussing options, he refuses to tell his sexual partners about his diagnosis. Additionally, for a variety of reasons, Mia doubts that Bob will begin to use precautions against spreading the disease. Agency policy mandates that social workers may not violate clients'

HIGHLIGHT 1.5

Achieve Competency in Ethical Practice by Applying Ethical Standards

EP 2.1.2a–d

Aspects of professional values and ethics for generalist practice include the National Association of Social Workers (NASW) *Code of Ethics*; the International Federation of Social Workers/International Association of Schools of Social Work *Ethics in Social Work, Statement of Principles;* awareness of personal values; and management of ethical dilemmas. Chapter 11 will discuss each in much greater detail.

National Association of Social Workers (NASW) Code of Ethics

Social work has a clearly delineated set of professional values reflected in the NASW *Code of Ethics* (2008). The *Code's* mission "is to enhance human well-being and help meet the basic human needs of all people, with particular attention to the needs and empowerment of people who are vulnerable, oppressed, and living in poverty" (NASW, 2008, Preamble). The *Code of Ethics* addresses six aspects of professional responsibility: social workers' ethical responsibilities "to clients," "to colleagues," "in practice settings," "as professionals," "to the social work profession," and "to the broader society" (NASW, 2008). The *Code* has the following six core values that reflect ethical principles, which social workers should seek to follow:

1. *Service:* Social workers should provide help, resources, and benefits so that people may achieve their maximum potential.
2. *Social justice:* Social workers should pursue social justice, the idea that in a perfect world all citizens would possess equal fundamental "rights, protection, opportunities, obligations, and social benefits," regardless of their backgrounds and membership in diverse groups (Barker, 2003, pp. 404–405).
3. *Dignity and worth of the person:* Social workers should hold people in high esteem and appreciate individual value.
4. *Importance of human relationships:* Social workers should value supportive interpersonal interaction, effective communication, and collaboration to achieve positive changes with clients and enhance the well-being of individuals, families, groups, organizations, and communities.

5. *Integrity:* Social workers should be responsible, honest, and reliable.
6. *Competence:* Social workers should possess the necessary skills and abilities to perform work with clients effectively.

International Federation of Social Workers/ International Association of Schools of Social Work Ethics in Social Work, Statement of Principles

Although the NASW *Code of Ethics* is the primary code followed by social workers in the United States, note that other ethical codes also are available in other nations and on an international basis. The International Federation of Social Workers (IFSW) and the International Association of Schools of Social Work (IASSW) have developed an *Ethics in Social Work, Statement of Principles*. The *Statement* focuses on international and global issues concerning human rights. Additionally, it stresses the need for social workers around the world to work together on a global basis.

Develop Awareness of Personal Values

Before you are able to prevent personal values from interfering with ethical professional practice, you must clearly identify those personal values. This proposition stems directly from the fourth NASW *Code of Ethics* core value cited earlier concerning "valuing human relationships" (NASW, 2008, Preamble). Valuing the client–worker relationship means keeping it clear of personal opinions. You certainly have the right to maintain personal values and opinions. However, a generalist practitioner is professionally obligated to prevent personal values that conflict with professional values from interfering with practice.

Tolerate Ambiguity, Address Ethical Dilemmas, and Make Principled Decisions

An *ethical dilemma* is a problematic situation in which ethical standards are in conflict. In other words, sometimes it is not possible to make a perfect choice and abide by all ethical guidelines. For example, consider a client who tells you he plans to murder his girlfriend, yet forbids you to tell anybody. You cannot maintain

(continued)

HIGHLIGHT 1.5 (continued)

the primary ethical standard of protecting human life (namely, your client's girlfriend) and confidentiality at the same time. (*Confidentiality* is the ethical principle that workers should not share information provided by or about a client unless that worker has the client's explicit permission to do so.) You are in the midst of an ethical quandary. Generalist practitioners must be vigilant and prepared to address such ethical dilemmas, because they occur regularly. Often, potential answers are unclear, confusing, and ambiguous.

Generalist practitioners must be able to tolerate imperfect alternatives to arrive at the most effective solution. Each dilemma is unique. Social workers must learn to work through such situations and "apply strategies of ethical reasoning to arrive at principled decisions" (CSWE, 2008, EP 2.1.2d). Chapter 11 addresses a wide range of ethical dilemmas occurring in generalist practice and discusses how practitioners might make strategic decisions about what to do in such situations.

---

confidentiality, which means that according to policy a social worker may not tell anyone about the HIV-positive diagnosis without Bob's clearly expressed written permission. Mia worries that, among other things, prior sexual partners unaware of the HIV diagnosis and their potential exposure may continue to spread the disease.

Which ethical conceptions are more important: respect for Bob's privacy, compliance with agency policy, or the general welfare of society and the well-being of other people? The worker cannot fulfill all of her responsibilities. However, in this case the *Code* provides some guidance by directing Mia to determine whether or not the situation is "compelling" or involves "imminent harm." If so, confidentiality takes a back-seat. Another section of the *Code* states that "workers generally should adhere to commitments made to employers and employing organizations" (NASW, 2008, §3.09a). It continues that "social workers should not allow an employing organization's policies, procedures, regulations, or administrative orders to interfere with their ethical practice of social work" (NASW, 2008, §3.09d). Therefore, the *Code* directs Mia to use her own best ethical judgment.

Ethical dilemmas are numerous. For instance, the law may dictate a lengthy procedure for removing the perpetrator in a case of alleged sexual abuse. However, what about the immediate, critical safety needs of the victim? For instance, a public assistance agency may require that applicants maintain residency for a specified time period before they become eligible for help. The single parent of a family of five comes in and says her children are starving. She has not lived in the area long enough to satisfy the residency requirement. What should the social worker do? Should the family be

allowed to starve? Highlight 1.6 provides an exercise that addresses an ethical dilemma.

The potential variety of ethical dilemmas is endless. Professional values and ethics do provide some basic guidelines. However, many times, a social worker will have to make choices about what is more ethical or more critical to do. Chapter 11 will further address the issue of making ethical decisions by evaluating problems, breaking down potential solutions, and prioritizing ethical principles.

Critical Thinking Question 1.2

EP 2.1.3

- As a social worker, what would you do if you were working with a client who made choices that were clearly bad for him or her (e.g., abusing alcohol or other drugs or refusing to leave a violent, physically harmful relationship)?

LO 1-7 Recognize a Wide Range of Practice Skills to Work with Individuals, Families, Groups, Organizations, and Communities

EP 2.1.10

We have reviewed the knowledge base practitioners need as part of their foundation for generalist practice and emphasized the significance of social work values and ethics. The 3rd and 4th concepts in the definition of generalist practice are the *wide range of skills* needed to implement the planned change process and the use of these skills to target and work with a *system of any size*. These two concepts are so intertwined that we will address them together.

HIGHLIGHT 1.6

Learn to Make Difficult Ethical Decisions

EP 2.1.2c

One of the ethical dilemmas commonly faced by social workers is deciding who is to get help when there are limited resources. In many instances, there is a given amount of money, and a social worker must choose regarding who will and will not receive help. Answers can be vague and ambiguous. No perfect solution may exist.

The following is an exercise designed to help you understand how difficult ethical dilemmas can be. (Later, Chapter 11 will help you work through some of the dilemmas social workers commonly face. It will also provide suggested structures for making difficult decisions.)

The Exercise

You have $60,000 to spend. You must choose one situation where it will be spent from 10 possibilities. Each situation requires the full amount of $60,000 in order to do any good. Dividing the money up would be useless and would help no one. You must decide where to spend the money.

Which of the following persons should have the $60,000 made available to help them?

1. A premature infant (born 3 months early) who needs to be maintained in an incubator and receive medical benefits

2. A 52-year-old man who needs a heart transplant in order to survive

3. Your 52-year-old father who needs a heart transplant to survive

4. A 5-year-old child who has a rare genetic disease that requires extremely expensive medication and therapy

5. You, who recently graduated and have been out of work for 6 months

6. A divorced single mother with three children, a 10th-grade education, and nothing but the clothes on her back

7. A person who has an intellectual disability (formerly referred to as mental retardation) who needs the money to live in a group home with others who have similar disabilities

8. A 14-year-old runaway, addicted to cocaine and alcohol, who has been prostituting herself to survive and needs the money to enter a drug treatment program

9. A man convicted of child sexual abuse who was himself sexually abused as a child and seeks rehabilitation

10. A dispossessed urban family—a couple in their late 20s with three small children

There are no easy answers.

Historically, social work skills were clustered into three major categories. First, *casework* primarily involved direct interaction with individual clients. This is analogous in many ways to the micro level of practice. Second, *group work* involved organizing and running a wide variety of groups (e.g., therapeutic groups or task groups). The mezzo level of practice might be said to comprise this cluster of skills. Third, *community organization* involved working with organizations and communities. This skill is analogous to the macro level of social work practice.

Under this old model of practice, social workers considered themselves experts in basically only one approach. They were either caseworkers, group workers, or community organizers. They did not see themselves as having a sound basis of skills in all areas for working with individuals, families, groups, organizations and communities as generalist practitioners do.

GENERALIST PRACTICE SKILLS FOR WORKING WITH INDIVIDUALS (MICRO SKILLS)

Those skills used in working with individuals provide the foundation for work with larger groups, organizations, and communities. They involve basic interpersonal skills including good communication and interviewing skills.

Endless scenarios come to mind that illustrate the use of micro skills. Social workers counsel people addicted to alcohol or other drugs. They try to find places to live and other resources for homeless families. They manage service provision for older adults who are ill or for people who have developmental disabilities (e.g., intellectual disabilities, cerebral palsy, hearing impairment, visual impairment, or autism spectrum disorders) and require numerous resources. They investigate potential child abuse situations. They help displaced homemakers and their families who are survivors of domestic violence. Chapter 2 focuses on micro-level skills.

GENERALIST PRACTICE SKILLS FOR WORKING WITH GROUPS (MEZZO SKILLS)

Generalist practitioners learn and use skills to work with small groups. We propose that working with families involves the use of both mezzo skills because the family is a group and micro skills because of a family's intimate nature. Social workers use mezzo skills with a wide range of groups. They run support groups for people who have been diagnosed with cancer. They run treatment conferences to evaluate progress and establish treatment recommendations for young people with serious emotional and behavioral problems living in group homes and residential treatment centers. They participate in educational groups in schools to talk about birth control. They facilitate activity groups in nursing homes for older adults. They run agency meetings aimed at developing new treatment programs or a new policy manual. Building upon the basic interpersonal skills established in Chapter 2, Chapter 3 examines skills for working with groups in greater detail.

GENERALIST PRACTICE SKILLS FOR WORKING WITH FAMILIES (MICRO/MEZZO SKILLS)

Because of the special and intimate nature of families, skills for working with them include both skills for working with individuals and skills for working with groups. Chapters 9 and 10 explore understanding and working with families in greater detail.

GENERALIST PRACTICE SKILLS FOR WORKING IN AND WITH ORGANIZATIONS AND COMMUNITIES (MACRO SKILLS)

Building upon the mastery of skills for working with both individuals and groups, *macro skills* are those used to work with large systems, including organizations and communities. Working with macro-level problems requires working with other individuals and groups of individuals. Chapter 4 discusses macro skills and the types of situations social workers frequently encounter in working with organizational and community systems.

Macro practice most frequently involves issues concerning a number of people or a specific group of people. For example, illegal drug use might be identified as a major difficulty in an urban neighborhood. Violence over drug sales is escalating. More and more people, including teens, are being shot as dealers and users squabble. The incidence of persons diagnosed as HIV-positive is abruptly increasing as addicts share needles and contaminate each other. Child neglect and abuse in the community are skyrocketing. Truancy rates are soaring. Parents on a "high" fail to attend to their young children. Parents' anger at themselves, at unsatisfied needs, and at the world in general is taken out on the easiest scapegoats: their children.

Approaches to solving these problems may reach far beyond helping an individual break a drug habit. Drug rehabilitation programs may be needed. Policies regarding the treatment of dealers may need to be addressed. Alternatives to a drug-related lifestyle may need to be pursued and developed for community residents. A youth center may be needed as a place for younger people to socialize, participate in activities, and have fun. Community residents may need job training and help in finding adequate employment.

The list of needs and possibilities is endless. A social worker involved in the community needs skills for organizing residents to come together and plan solutions. Skills in approaching community leaders and policymakers are important so that they may be persuaded to support and help finance needed services. Highlight 1.7 illustrates some case scenarios where macro practice skills may be useful.

LO 1-8 Emphasize Principles Involving Values That Underlie Generalist Practice

An emphasis on empowerment, strengths, and resiliency is the 5th concept in the definition of generalist practice and a primary value inherent in practice. We have defined *empowerment* as "the process of increasing personal, interpersonal, or political power so that individuals can take action to improve their life situations" (Gutierrez, 2001, p. 210). Empowerment means emphasizing, developing, and nurturing strengths and positive attributes. It aims at enhancing individuals', groups', families', and communities' power and control over their destinies.

THE STRENGTHS PERSPECTIVE

EP 2.1.10e

Cowger maintains that social work historically has focused on dysfunction, pathology, and "individual inadequacies" (1994, p. 262). He states that "if assessment focuses on deficits, it is likely that deficits will remain the focus of both the worker and the client during remaining contacts. Concentrating on deficits ... can lead to self-fulfilling prophecies" (1994, p. 264). However, concentrating on strengths

HIGHLIGHT 1.7

The Macro-Level Approach

It's very easy for social workers, especially when they are just beginning in practice, to focus on changing the individual. Using interviewing and planned change techniques with an individual in a practice situation is exciting. Figuring out how an individual client thinks and functions is fascinating. Additionally, the individual is right in front of you. The other systems with which the individual client is involved are much more abstract. Their interactions and effects may seem vague and distant. Because of the complexity of outside systems, pinpointing targets of change often seems more difficult.

However, generalist social work practitioners must also think in terms of needed changes beyond the individual client system. The individual is only one focus for potential change.

Macro-system changes are seldom easy. They often involve influencing large numbers of people or key decision makers. Sometimes conflict is necessary. However, focusing on large system change is a unique aspect of social work that may open up multitudes of new planned change alternatives.

The following three scenarios put you in various situations. For each one, think in terms of how the problem might be solved through macro-level changes. For this exercise, do not change or move the individual. Think in terms of what major organizations or community groups can do to effect change. What policies might be changed? What community services might be developed? What strategies might achieve these changes? Remember, do not change the individual—focus only on macro-system change.

What Might You Do When:

1. You are a public social services worker in a rural county. Your job includes doing everything from helping older adults obtain their Social Security payments to investigating alleged child abuse. Within the past 6 months, six farm families in the county have filed for bankruptcy. Government farm subsidies that used to be available have been withdrawn, and the past 2 years have been hard on crops. Now the banks are threatening to foreclose on the farm mortgages. Thus, the six families will literally be put out in the cold with no money and no place to go. What do you do?

2. You are a social worker for Pinocchio County Social Services. It is a rural county with a few towns and no large cities. Your job as intake worker is to do family assessments when people call up with problems (anything from domestic violence to coping with serious illnesses). Your next task is to make referrals to the appropriate services.

   You have been hearing about a number of sexual assaults in the area. Women are expressing fear for their safety. People who have been assaulted do not know where to turn. The nearest large cities are over 80 miles away. You have always been interested in women's issues and advocacy for women. Now what do you do?

3. You have a 70-year-old client named Harriett who lives in an old inner-city neighborhood in a large city. Since her husband died 7 years ago, she has been living alone. She has no children, is still in good health, and likes to be independent.

   The problem is that her house has been condemned for new highway construction. The plans are to tear it down within 6 months. There is no public housing available for older adults within five miles of where she lives. She would like to stay in the area because she has a lot of older adult friends there. Now what? (Remember, do not move Harriett.)

A Commentary

The preceding scenarios are difficult to solve. They are not designed to frustrate you but rather to encourage you to think about interventions beyond the micro and mezzo levels. Sometimes, macro-system service provision is inadequate, ineffective, or simply wrong. The generalist practitioner's unique perspective is one of potential system change at all levels.

This text is designed to help you clarify that perspective and assimilate a wide variety of practice skills. The dimension of macro skills focuses on targeting the environment, not the person in the environment, for change.

---

can provide "structure and content for an examination of realizable alternatives, for the mobilization of competencies that can make things different, and for the building of self-confidence that stimulates hope" (1994, p. 265).

Focusing on strengths in this way is sometimes referred to as the *strengths perspective*, an orientation focusing on client resources, capabilities, knowledge, abilities, motivations, experience, intelligence, and other positive qualities that can be put to use to solve problems and pursue positive changes (Blundo, 2008; CSWE, 2008, EP B2.2; Kim, 2008; Sheafor & Horejsi, 2012). This perspective can provide a sound basis for empowerment. Saleebey (2013) proposes that the following principles are among those underlying the strengths perspective:

1. "Every individual, group, family, and community has strengths."
2. "Trauma and abuse, illness, and struggle may be injurious but they may also be sources of challenge and opportunity."
3. "Assume that you do not know the upper limits of the capacity to grow and change and take individual, group, and community aspirations seriously."
4. "We best serve clients by collaborating with them."
5. "Every environment is full of resources." (pp. 17–20)

RESILIENCY: SEEKING STRENGTH AMID ADVERSITY

We have established that a notion related to the strengths perspective and empowerment is *resiliency*, the ability of an individual, family, group, community, or organization to recover from adversity and resume functioning even when suffering serious trouble, confusion, or hardship (Clark, 2013; CSWE, 2008, EP B2.2; Greene & Conrad, 2012). For example, Norman (2000) provides an illustration of this notion:

> When a pitched baseball hits a window, the glass usually shatters. When that same ball meets a baseball bat, the bat is rarely damaged. When a hammer strikes a ceramic vase, it too usually shatters. But when that same hammer hits a rubber automobile tire, the tire quickly returns to its original shape. The baseball bat and the automobile tire both demonstrate resiliency. (p. 3)

Resiliency involves two dimensions—"risk factors" and "protective factors" (Greene & Conrad, 2012; Norman, 2000, p. 3). In this context, *risk factors* involve "stressful life events or adverse environmental conditions that increase the *vulnerability* [defenselessness or helplessness] of individuals" or other systems (Norman, 2000, p. 3). *Protective factors*, on the other hand, concern those factors that "buffer, moderate, and protect against those vulnerabilities" (p. 3).

The following situation provides a poignant example of resiliency at the micro level:

> For 16-year-old Kameka, the turning point from risk to resilience occurred when she exclaimed to a school counselor, "Look, I'm not going home. I'll kill myself

first." That comment signaled an important shift in her road to healing from a life filled with violence and victimization: sexual and physical abuse, severe neglect, extreme poverty, and subsequent self-abuse. Raised in a crime-ridden, inner-city environment by her drug-addicted mother, she adopted self-injurious behaviors as her way of coping, including multiple suicide attempts and self-mutilation. At the point that she recognized that her options had run out and that her only other choice was to return to a life she perceived as deadly, she found the inner resources to reach out for help. By 21 years of age, just 5 years later, Kameka was attending college and passionately committed to starting an art school for low-income African American youths. Especially noteworthy was her readiness to accept healing relationships in her life, such as intimate relationships with males. Articulate and insightful, she emphasized feeling grateful for what she had learned from all her previous life challenges (Williams, Lindsey, Kurtz, & Jarvis, 2001).

> How was this young woman able to transcend her early life of victimization and violence to access the inner strength necessary to adopt a seemingly positive life direction? In a qualitative study of former runaway and homeless youths, researchers explored pivotal factors that enabled young people who endured significant trauma over time to reclaim their personal power as survivors rather than as victims (Williams et al., 2001). Among the factors were determination, taking care of self, accepting help, and finding meaning in the person's experience, including a spiritual relationship with a benevolent, higher power. In the case of Kameka, it also appeared that she possessed innate qualities of intelligence as well as a solid sense of self-efficacy through her achievements that contributed significantly to her ability to shift her life trajectory. [Self-efficacy, which involves self-confidence and self-worth, is a person's perception that he or she is capable of successfully completing tasks, achieving goals, and dealing with life's challenges.] Kameka's symptoms and (mal)adaptive behaviors reflected the substantive risk factors to which she had been exposed: poverty, sexual abuse, severe physical and emotional neglect, wounding at the attachment level, and lack of family resources. However, throughout her hospitalizations and self-destructive behaviors, she apparently was gathering her inner strength to change directions. . . . Many of the evolving behaviors that Kameka eventually harnessed— determination, thrust for independence, learning of new skills, and especially the readiness to take

advantage of the availability of professional helpers—allowed her to emerge from her traumatic experiences stronger and wiser. This is the essence of the strengths-based approach. (Williams, 2002, pp. 199–200)

In summary, Kameka's strengths became protective factors shielding her from the risk factors threatening to ruin her life. Instead, her strengths allowed her to thrive and build a foundation for a fruitful life.

Resiliency can also characterize larger systems. An example at the organizational level is a public university experiencing budget cuts of several million dollars. That university is resilient to the extent that it responds to the risk of loss, protects its most important functions, makes plans to adapt to the shortfall of resources, and continues providing students with a quality education. Resiliency involves focusing on strengths to maintain basic functioning.

Resiliency in a community is illustrated by a group of urban neighborhoods that address an increasing crime and drug use problem. These troubles put the community at risk of disorganization and destruction. Community strengths include availability of organizations that provide resources, residents' expectations for appropriate, positive behavior, and opportunities for "neighborhood youths to constructively participate in the community" (Greene & Livingston, 2002, p. 78). A resilient community might use its concerned citizens to form neighborhood organizations that oversee community conditions and upkeep, work with public services to improve conditions, and advocate for increased resources (Homan, 2011). Neighborhood Watch programs may be formed where neighborhood residents volunteer to keep careful watch upon each other's premises to prevent and combat crime. Community residents might work with local police and schools to establish drug education and prevention programs for young people. They might also advocate for more police to increase surveillance and apprehension of drug dealers. A resilient community uses its strengths to address the risks threatening it and protect its residents.

LO 1-9 Appreciate and Stress the Importance of Human Diversity

 EP 2.1.4

Human diversity refers to the vast range of differences among people. Such variations may involve "the intersectionality of multiple factors including age, class, color, culture, disability, ethnicity, gender, gender

identity and expression, immigration status, political ideology, race, religion, sex, and sexual orientation" (CSWE, 2008, EP 2.1.4). (Highlight 1.8 defines each of these groups.) The importance of human diversity is the 6th concept and a major value inherent in the definition of generalist practice. Social work by nature addresses virtually any type of issue posed by any type of person from any type of background. Practitioners must be open-minded, nonjudgmental, knowledgeable, and skilled in order to work with and help any client.

INTERSECTIONALITY OF DIVERSE FACTORS

The concept of *intersectionality* involves the idea that people are complex and can belong to multiple, overlapping diverse groups. "The intersectional perspective acknowledges the breadth of human experiences, instead of conceptualizing social relations and identities separately in terms of either race *or* class *or* gender *or* age *or* sexual orientation"; rather, an intersectional approach focuses on the "interactional affects" of belonging to multiple groups (Murphy, Hunt, Zajicek, Norris, & Hamilton, 2009, p. 2). People may experience injustice from a combination of reasons. The concept of intersectionality "underscores the complex nature of cultural and personal identities and human experiences that cannot be defined simply by one dimension of inequality or difference—either race or gender or sexual orientation or ability. The social worker, who is involved in working with individuals, families, groups, and communities belonging to diverse groups, must develop the cultural competence to work with people at the intersections of the multiple dimensions of diversity" (Murphy et al., 2009, p. 42).

Murphy and her colleagues (2009) provide the following case example demonstrating the complexity of intersectionality:

The Vue family emigrated from Laos six months ago. They were happy to find a small apartment that is convenient to a grocery store and meat-packing plant where Mr. Vue works long hours. They have three daughters, aged five years, four years, and six months. Shortly after they moved in, a neighbor called the local Department of Human Services (DHS). The neighbor, Mrs. Smith, had spotted one of the girls sitting alone in front of the apartment door one afternoon. Mrs. Smith was surprised to see the front door open, the younger girl on the couch, and the infant sleeping. The police arrived on the scene about the same time Mrs. Vue returned home, carrying grocery bags. She was taken aback to see the police in her apartment. Mrs. Vue said she had left

Dimensions of Diversity

Age: Some period of time during a person's lifespan. Age is often considered an important aspect of human diversity for older adults as they experience *ageism*, discrimination based on preconceived notions about older people, regardless of their individual qualities and capabilities.

Class (or social class): People's status or ranking in society with respect to such standards as "relative wealth, power, prestige, educational level, or family background" (Barker, 2003, p. 402).

Culture: "A way of life including widespread values (about what is good and bad), beliefs (about what is true), and behavior (what people do every day)" (italics deleted) (Macionis, 2013, p. 5).

Disability: "Any physical or mental impairment [or ongoing health or mental health condition] that substantially limits one or more major life activities"; these activities include "seeing, hearing, speaking, walking, breathing, performing manual tasks, learning, caring for oneself, and working" (U.S. Equal Employment Opportunity Commission, 2008, p. 1).

Ethnicity: The affiliation with a large group of people who have "common racial, national, tribal, religious, linguistic, or cultural origin or background" (Mish, 2008, p. 429).

Gender: The behavioral, social, and psychological traits and characteristics generally associated with being female or male.

Gender expression: The manners in which we express ourselves to others in ways related to gender that include both behavior and personality.

Gender identity: A person's internal psychological self-concept of being either a male or a female, or, possibly, some combination of both (Gilbert, 2008).

Immigration status: A person's position in terms of legal rights and residency when entering and residing in a country that is not that person's legal country of origin.

(People of) color: "A collective term that refers to the major groups of African, Latino and Asian Americans, and First Nations People [Native Americans] who have been distinguished from the dominant society by color" (Lum, 2011, p. 129).

Political ideology: The "relatively coherent system of ideas (beliefs, traditions, principles, and myths) about human nature, institutional arrangements, and social processes" that indicate how a government should be run and what principles that government should support (Abramovitz, 2010, p. 131).

Race: The category of people who share a common descent and genetic origin that may be distinguished by "certain physical traits," or "interests, habits, or characteristics" (Mish, 2008, p.1024).

Religion: People's spiritual beliefs concerning the origin of, character of, and reason for being, usually based on the existence of some higher power or powers, that often involves designated rituals and provides direction for what is considered moral or right.

Sex: The biological designation of being either female or male that usually is based on sexual anatomy including reproductive organs and chromosomal makeup.

Sexual orientation: Sexual and romantic attraction to persons of one or both genders.

the children for thirty minutes to buy milk. The children were taken into DHS custody, and Mr. and Mrs. Vue were told that they would have to appear in court three days later.

The Vue family will be assigned a case worker who is responsible for understanding how race, ethnicity, and class affect this family. Moving from a small village in Laos, could this family have understood the new dangers and expectations that come with parenting in the United States? How does their economic position affect their ability to find appropriate child care? What other factors affect their needs as a family? (p. 42)

THE POTENTIAL FOR DISCRIMINATION AND OPPRESSION

Membership in groups that differ from the young white male heterosexual mainstream can place people at increased risk of discrimination and oppression. *Discrimination* is the act of treating people differently based on the fact that they belong to some group instead of judging them on their own merits. *Oppression* involves putting extreme limitations and constraints on the members of some identified group. Discrimination and oppression often result from *stereotypes*, fixed mental images of members belonging to a group based on assumed attributes that portray an overly simplified opinion about that group. Stereotypes neither consider nor appreciate individual differences.

One might envision a number of scenarios concerning potential discrimination and oppression based on stereotypes. For instance, think of an African-American family moving into a virtually all-white small midwestern town. Picture a 55-year-old woman applying for a job in a software production center where all employees are under age 30, or consider a gay couple expressing affection in a primarily heterosexual bar.

Membership in any diverse group provides a different set of environmental circumstances. A wealthy Asian-American middle-aged man who just immigrated to Los Angeles from Tokyo experiences a very different world from an older adult woman of Scandinavian heritage living in Michigan's economically depressed Upper Peninsula.

ACHIEVE CULTURAL COMPETENCY

Another critical notion related to human diversity is *cultural competency* or *cultural competence*, "the set of knowledge and skills that a social worker must develop in order to be effective with multicultural clients" (Lum, 1999, p. 3). Highlight 1.8 defines *culture* as "a way of life including widespread values (about what is good and bad), beliefs (about what is true), and behavior (what people do every day)" (italics deleted) (Macionis, 2010, p. 2). It includes language, religious beliefs, art, music, rules about appropriate behavior, and expectations for interpersonal relationships. Aspects of culture are often related to people's ethnic, racial, and spiritual heritage. People from different cultural backgrounds may be at risk of discrimination and oppression from other dominating groups.

Cultural competency for practitioners, strongly supported by the NASW *Code of Ethics*, involves at least the following six dimensions (Lum, 2011; NASW, 2008, 1.05):

1. Development of an awareness of personal values, assumptions, and biases (practitioners should seek to eliminate those that interfere with culturally competent practice)
2. Recognition that cultural values and differences directly shape life experiences
3. Understanding that stereotypes, discrimination, and oppression may have direct negative effects on various diverse groups

4. Commitment to ongoing learning about clients' cultures on a career-long basis
5. Establishment of an appreciation of other cultures, recognition of their strengths, and nurturance of attitudes that respect difference
6. Acquisition of effective skills for working with people from other cultures

LO 1-10 Advocate for Human Rights, and Pursue Social and Economic Justice

EP 2.1.5b-c

Advocacy for human rights and the pursuit of social and economic justice is the 7th concept and basic value inherent in generalist practice. A number of related terms are integrated under this general heading. *Advocacy* is the act of representing, championing, or defending the rights of others. *Human rights* involve the premise that all people, regardless of characteristics or circumstances (including those of race, culture, nationality, class, orientation, age, gender, ability, religion, or beliefs), are entitled to basic rights and fair, humane treatment. We define and describe *social justice* as the idea that in a perfect world all citizens would possess equal fundamental "rights, protection, opportunities, obligations, and social benefits" (Barker, 2003, pp. 404–405). Similarly, *economic justice* concerns the distribution of resources in a fair and equitable manner.

In real life, both social and economic justice are hard goals to attain. Rarely are rights and resources fairly and equitably distributed. Even the definitions of *fair* and *equitable* are widely debated. What does *fair* mean? Does it mean that all people should receive the same income regardless of what work they do or even whether or not they have jobs at all? The point is that social workers must be vigilantly aware of the existence of injustice. It is our ethical responsibility to combat injustice whenever it is necessary and possible to do so.

When we speak of ethical responsibility, we are really referring to the application of professional values. In addition to knowledge about the promotion of social and economic justice, generalist practitioners must understand that such promotion is a basic professional value. We as social workers must make practice decisions with this value in mind. Likewise, we must learn practice skills so that we might apply the values and knowledge to advocate for human rights, and advance social and economic justice. Chapter 14 explores advocacy in much greater depth.

Defining Generalist Practice: Work Within an Organizational Structure

As a social work practitioner, you are most likely to *work within an organizational structure* (or agency context). This is the 8th concept in the definition for generalist practice. It is also the *context* for practice. *Organizational structure* is the formal and informal manner in which tasks and responsibilities, lines of authority, channels of communication, and dimensions of power are established and coordinated within an organization. Understanding organizational structure involves knowing how decisions are made and what chain of command is followed, what procedures regulate service provision to clients, and how your own job expectations fit into the larger scheme of things.

Tasks and responsibilities, of course, involve what you and other staff are supposed to accomplish during your workday. *Lines of authority* concern who supervises whom. You might think of them as the chain of command. For example, who has the responsibility for overseeing your work performance? *Channels of communication* entail who communicates with whom and how. *Dimensions of power* delineate whose opinions carry the most weight in agency decision making. Who captivates other staff members' attention during meetings and who bores them to tears? Who has the most control over agency policy?

In addition to understanding formal and informal agency operations, there are other aspects of agency life about which you should be heedfully aware. One involves the importance of developing and demonstrating a professional identity and demeanor. How should a "professional" act? What does a "professional" look like?

Another important facet of effective work within an organizational structure concerns using supervision and consultation appropriately. What does this mean? *Supervision* is the process of overseeing, directing, coordinating, enhancing, and evaluating the "on-the-job performance" of workers for whom the supervisor is responsible (Kadushin & Harkness, 2002, p. 23). *Consultation*, the act of seeking help from someone with expertise in a subject to devise a plan or solve a problem, should involve only a colleague, administrator, or

other who has the appropriate competence or experience. Supervision is generally an ongoing process by someone designated as a supervisor over a supervisee. Consultation, on the other hand, is sought out when needed from someone (who may not be a supervisor and may even be from outside your agency) who has specific experience or expertise.

LO 1-11 Demonstrate a Wide Range of Professional Roles

Assuming a wide range of professional roles is the 9th concept in the definition of generalist practice. It is also an important part of the process of practice. We have emphasized that generalist practitioners can tackle a wide range of problems by using many different methods. Another way of making this point is that you will assume many roles. A *role* is a culturally expected behavior pattern for a person having a specified status or being involved in a designated social relationship. For example, people have certain expectations regarding how social workers are supposed to act and what functions they should perform. We have established that a professional role is behavior and activity involved in performing some designated function. Generalist practitioner roles may involve practice with individuals, families, groups, organizations, or communities. Some of the roles characterizing generalist practitioners are briefly summarized. These include counselor, educator, broker, case manager, mobilizer, mediator, facilitator, integrator/coordinator, manager, initiator, negotiator, spokesperson, organizer, consultant, and advocate:

- *Counselor:* One who provides guidance to clients and assists them in a planned change or problem-solving process. For example, a worker might help a teenager decide which form of contraception is best for her.
- *Educator:* One who gives information and teaches skills to others (Kirst-Ashman & Hull, 2012; Yessian & Broskowski, 1983). For instance, a practitioner might teach parents child management skills.
- *Broker:* One who links client systems to needed resources (Connaway & Gentry, 1988; Kirst-Ashman & Hull, 2012). For example, a worker might refer a client to a substance abuse treatment center for inpatient treatment.

- *Case manager:* A practitioner who, on the behalf of a specific client, coordinates needed services provided by any number of agencies, organizations, or facilities. For instance, a worker might coordinate the many services needed by a quadriplegic living in a group home.
- *Mobilizer:* One who identifies and convenes community people and resources to identify "unmet community needs" and "effect changes for the better in their community" (Halley, Kopp, & Austin, 1998, p. 179). For example, a practitioner might encourage community residents to band together and start a drug education program for residents' children.
- *Mediator:* One who resolves arguments or disagreements among individuals, families, groups, organizations, or communities in conflict (Kirst-Ashman & Hull, 2012; Yessian & Broskowski, 1983). For instance, a worker might serve as a go-between to establish an agreement between an agency wanting to start a group home for people with developmental disabilities and neighborhood residents who violently oppose having the facility in their neighborhood.
- *Facilitator:* One who guides a group experience. For instance, a practitioner might run a support group for young women with bulimia.[10]
- *Integrator/Coordinator:* One who integrates or coordinates people by bringing them together and organizing their performance (Kirst-Ashman & Hull, 2012). *Integration* is the process of assembling different elements to form a cohesive whole. *Coordination* involves bringing components together in some kind of organized manner. For example, an integrator/coordinator might coordinate community residents as they pursue the goal of cleaning up and developing a local park.
- *Manager:* One who assumes some level of administrative responsibility for a social services agency or other organizational system (Brody, 2005; Kirst-Ashman & Hull, 2012).
- *Initiator:* One who calls attention to an issue. For instance, a social worker may recognize that a policy has the potential to create problems for particular clients and bring this to the attention of her supervisor.
- *Negotiator:* One who represents an organization or group trying to wrestle something from another group.
- *Spokesperson:* One who is authorized to speak on behalf of others.
- *Organizer:* One who coordinates individuals or groups to pursue some designated function(s).
- *Consultant:* One who provides advice, suggestions, or ideas to another person, group, or organization.
- *Advocate:* One who steps forward and speaks out on the behalf of clients in order to promote fair and equitable treatment or gain needed resources. For example, a worker might meet with an administrator on the behalf of a client to change an agency policy on that client's behalf.

LO 1-12 Define Critical Thinking Skills and Apply Them to Practice

EP 2.1.3

Not only does the process of generalist practice involve *working within an organizational structure* and *assuming a wide range of roles,* but also using *critical thinking skills.* The 10th concept in the definition of generalist practice involves the process of using critical thinking skills. Because critical thinking questions are interspersed throughout this book, we will spend considerable time discussing the concept here.

Critical thinking is: (1) the careful scrutiny of what is stated as true or what appears to be true and the resulting expression of an opinion or conclusion based on that scrutiny and (2) the creative formulation of an opinion or conclusion when presented with a question, problem, or issue (Kirst-Ashman, 2013). Critical thinking concentrates on "the process of reasoning" (Gambrill & Gibbs, 2009, p. 3). It stresses *how* individuals think about the truth inherent in a situation or statement or *how* they analyze an issue to formulate their own conclusions. As Gambrill and Gibbs (2009) so aptly state, "Critical thinkers question what others take for granted" (p. 19). In generalist practice, critical thinking involves seriously thinking about a client system's problems, issues, and macro environment in order to determine how to proceed in the helping process.

Two facets included in the definition of critical thinking are significant. First, critical thinking focuses

---

10. *Bulimia* is an eating disorder occurring primarily in females and characterized by uncontrolled overeating followed by purging activities such as self-initiated vomiting and the use of diuretics and laxatives in addition to excessive guilt and shame over the compulsive behavior.

on the questioning of beliefs, statements, assumptions, lines of reasoning, actions, and experiences. This means that social workers must be able to critique arguments, statements, and experiences for inconsistencies. They must also be able to distinguish between assertion and fact, observation, and impression. When social workers meet with clients, what thoughts go through their heads? What assumptions do they automatically make? How valid are these thoughts and assumptions? Another component of critical thinking is recognizing what one does not know. In other words, what information is missing?

The second facet of the definition of critical thinking is the creative formulation of an opinion or conclusion when presented with a question, problem, or issue. What do *you* think is the answer to a question or solution to a problem? For example, you as a generalist practitioner would use critical thinking to determine the most effective approach to help solve a particular client's problem. You would choose techniques not on hearsay, but rather on such variables as their track record of effectiveness with that specific client population. Workers should carefully examine any statements or claims made as facts by evaluating arguments on both sides of an issue (Gibbs et al., 1994).

For instance, Carlene, a colleague, tells you that the most effective child management technique ever is to "bonk the misbehaving child on the nose with a flyswatter." She swears that it immediately and permanently curbs obnoxious behaviors such as swearing, hitting other children, or sticking fingers into various facial orifices. Critical thinking would lead you not to accept Carlene's proclamation as fact. Rather, it encourages you to ask some serious questions about the validity of Carlene's assertion. What are the theoretical underpinnings of the flyswatter approach to behavior management? How has it been proven effective, with whom, and under what conditions? What are some potential negative consequences of this technique?

Of course, we are being facetious when talking about the flyswatter approach to child management. The point is that critical thinking concerns not automatically accepting situations or stories as being accurate and true.

In generalist practice, the goal of critical thinking is to evaluate the accuracy of impressions, assess diverse aspects of a situation, and develop creative approaches to finding solutions and making plans. One basic method for critical thinking involves the following Triple A approach (Kirst-Ashman, 2013):

1. *Ask* questions.
2. *Assess* the established facts and issues involved.
3. *Assert* a concluding opinion.

For example, the parents of a 16-year-old named Jorge bring him to a public social services agency. They explain to the intake worker that they feel Jorge has withdrawn from his old friends, is frequently truant from school, and does not listen to what they tell him, and they suspect him of using drugs. (*Intake* is the initial process that introduces a client to an agency, provides clients with information about service provision, and gathers relevant initial assessment information from clients to determine how to proceed.) The intake worker refers Jorge to Yolanda, a social worker in the agency who serves as a youth mentor. Her job involves work with young people who have "a history of truancy, disorderly conduct, or an unstable family life"; her role is "to help guide youth toward more positive activities and help them attain better decision-making skills" (Lad Lake, 2007).

Yolanda begins meeting with Jorge. She might initially focus on Jorge's potential for depression as a medical condition that may require a referral to a therapist and medication to control it. At first, she may think of Jorge as an isolated adolescent with a terrible self-concept who avoids school to shun peer contact and uses drugs to escape from his distasteful reality. However, using critical thinking means going beyond superficial appearances and *asking questions* about what is really going on. Jorge may indeed fit the depressed profile she has in her mind. However, that may be off track entirely.

Yolanda begins establishing a worker/client relationship with Jorge through the process of engagement. Trust begins to take hold, and Jorge reveals to Yolanda what is really going on in his life.[11] After long periods of silence, he expresses some relief that he finally has found someone he can talk to about his problems.

Jorge sees himself as a quiet person. He feels his parents never really understood that dynamic energy

---

11. Note that in reality the process of a client gaining trust in a social worker may not be easy. Many variables are involved. Revealing one's most private thoughts and issues can make a person feel very vulnerable. It may take some time before trust develops. The worker may need to convey a combination of "patience, encouragement," and skills in problem solving to help the client develop trust (Egan, 2014, p. 200).

and an outgoing style were not part of his personality, despite their own expectations. He tells Yolanda that his girlfriend Juliette, about whom his parents know little, is 3 months pregnant. He, of course, has not told his parents, whom he feels would be horrified. He has been very worried about what to do. Neither he nor Juliette believes in abortion. He has been skipping school both to spend time with her and to work a part-time job about which his parents also know nothing. He thinks he and Juliette might need money in the future. At this point, he indicates that he has neither time for nor interest in doing drugs.

By using critical thinking and asking questions, Yolanda helps Jorge *assess* his situation. Together, they identify Jorge's alternatives and assess the pros and cons of each. They discuss Jorge's relationship with his parents and the fact that they will eventually find out about the pregnancy. They talk about whether, how, and when he might talk to his parents. What about soliciting their help? Would their horror at the pregnancy really supersede their love and caring for their son? What strengths does Jorge possess that will help him deal with the issues facing him? How will the pregnancy and birth affect Jorge and Juliette's relationship? Would they be able to continue in school? Meanwhile, who would care for the baby? Is adoption a possibility?

As a generalist practitioner, Yolanda also considers Jorge's macro environment and what supports are available for him there. Practitioners who use critical thinking should be predisposed to ask questions about how their clients are served and treated by other systems. Is there a program in Jorge's school to provide emotional and educational support to pregnant adolescents and their partners? If not, why not? How does the school handle truancy issues? Can a school social worker become involved to help Jorge develop a plan to keep up with his studies? Are there other programs available in the community to support teenagers in similar situations? If they exist, are Jorge and Juliette eligible to receive services from them?

Much more input from Juliette, her parents, and Jorge's parents is necessary before a concluding plan of action can be developed and *asserted*. Jorge may have impressions about what the other involved parties think. However, assumptions cannot be made about what other people feel is right or wrong without their direct input. Yolanda must use critical thinking skills to investigate people's perceptions and help Jorge determine what choices he has available and which would bring him the most positive consequences.

"FACTS" MAY NOT BE TRUE

There are infinite situations in which generalist practitioners can use critical thinking. Social work practitioners should regularly use "scientific reasoning" to analyze arguments, keeping their eyes open for inconsistencies and deviations from the truth (Gambrill & Gibbs, 2009, p. 33). In other words, do not believe everything you hear. Rather, the first task is to critically evaluate for yourself whether what you hear is true or not. Perhaps you read a "fact" in a book or hear about it from a friend, instructor, or colleague. Critical thinking focuses on *not* taking this "fact" at face value. Rather it entails seriously examining and evaluating its validity by using the Triple A or a similar approach. Practitioners must be able to compare and contrast new information with existing valid information and with professional or generally accepted standards.

The following applies the Triple A approach to another example concerning the selection of effective practice techniques. Someone might tell you "the best treatment approach for a social worker is to let clients do most of the talking to find out as much as possible about them." To what extent is this statement really true? To find out, first you could *ask* questions about what the statement is really saying. What does "best" mean? Is there one "best treatment approach" to work with all clients with their vast range of issues and problems? Should you just let clients talk about whatever they want? How will you find out the information you need to make plans to help them? What does "most of the talking" mean? If one believes this statement, then how much participation should the worker have in the client/worker interaction? What experiences has the person who made this statement had in the past that led him or her to such a conclusion?

Your second task would be to *assess* the established facts and issues involved by seeking out information to answer the questions. Is there any established data to indicate this is an effective treatment approach? Generalist practitioners should be inquisitive about how interventions are supposed to work and whether or not they are truly effective. To what extent does it make sense that one treatment approach is effective with all clients? With which clients, if any, has it been proven effective?

The third task is to *assert* a concluding opinion. To what extent do you agree with the person's statement that the best way for a social work practitioner to work with clients is to let the clients do most of the talking? Do you have other ideas and data about what constitutes effective social work practice with designated client populations? Under what conditions is it appropriate and effective for clients to talk, and under what conditions should the worker provide input?

THE WIDESPREAD APPLICATION OF CRITICAL THINKING

Critical thinking can be applied to virtually any belief, statement, assumption, line of reasoning, action, or experience proposed as being true. Consider the following statements that someone might maintain as "facts":

- *Rich people are selfish.*
- *Politicians are crooks.*
- *A crocodile cannot stick its tongue out.*
- *A shrimp's heart is in its head.*
- *Most lipstick contains fish scales.[12]*

These statements are silly (although some may be true), but the point is that critical thinking can be applied to an infinite array of thoughts and ideas. For each of the preceding statements: (1) what questions would you *ask*; (2) how would you *assess* the established facts and issues involved; and (3) what concluding opinion would you finally *assert*?

Critical thinking in generalist practice also involves the creative formulation of an opinion or conclusion when presented with a question, problem, or issue that concerns the macro social environment. How would you answer the following questions?

- *Should immigrants who have entered the country illegally and worked here for years be granted citizenship?*
- *Should military spending be increased or decreased?*
- *What is the best way to eliminate poverty in this nation?*

Consider answering the last question. First, what questions about it would you *ask*? What are the reasons for poverty in a rich industrialized country? What social welfare programs are currently available to address poverty? What innovative new ideas for programs might be tried? Where might funding for such programs be found? How much money would it take to eliminate poverty, and who would pay for it?

Second, what facts and issues would you seek to address and *assess*? You probably would first seek to define poverty—what makes a person or family considered "poor"? What income level or lack of income is involved? You then might research statistics, costs, and

studies concerning effectiveness of various programs intending to reduce poverty. You might also investigate innovative ideas. Perhaps there are proposals for programs that you feel look promising. You might explore what various programs cost and how they are funded. Note that these suggestions only scratch the surface of how you might examine the issue.

Third, *assert* your opinion or conclusion. To what extent do you think it is possible to eliminate poverty? What kinds of resources and programs do you think it would take? What do you feel citizens and their government should do about poverty?

Because of the importance of critical thinking in generalist social work practice, a wide range of critical thinking questions will be posed throughout this book.

Highlight 1.9 identifies an array of traps that can trick you into believing potential falsehoods and avoiding critical thinking.

Critical Thinking Questions 1.3

- Do you consider yourself a critical thinker?
- To what extent do you feel you use critical thinking skills in your daily life?

LO 1-13 Incorporate Research-Informed Practice

The 11th important concept of generalist practice involves the use of research (discussed earlier as part of generalist practice's eclectic knowledge base). We have established that social work students must be knowledgeable about various approaches to research for a number of reasons. Subsequently, as generalist practitioners, they must demonstrate competency in *research-informed practice*. This means social workers should use the approaches and interventions in their practice that research has determined are effective. Social workers should employ research findings to improve their effectiveness in solving various kinds of problems, improving social policies to enhance people's health and well-being, and enhancing the service delivery process.

LO 1-14 Follow a Planned Change Process

The 12th concept inherent in the definition of generalist practice is planned change. *Planned change* is the

---

12. The last three statements were received in an e-mail from Keith McClory.

Pitfalls to Critical Thinking

Critical thinking is not necessarily easy. It entails expending mental energy and effort to analyze issues and solve problems. Critical thinking enhances self-awareness and the ability to detect various modes of distorted thinking, ploys, and traps that can trick people into believing potentially false convictions (Gambrill & Gibbs, 2009). The following are among the many traps to avoid by using critical thinking (Ruscio, 2006, pp. 6–10):

1. *Outward appearance of science.* A supposed "fact" may superficially be cited in the context of scientific proof. How many times have you seen some well-groomed individual wearing a doctor's lab coat appear in a television commercial and state that this weight loss supplement's effectiveness has been scientifically proven many times over? What questions might you ask about this? What tests were run to prove this effectiveness? Was the supplement taken by people who were at the same time also implementing other weight loss approaches including exercise and diet restrictions? Is the professional-looking person on television telling the truth or being paid to read from a script? A related issue involves dietary supplements of all kinds that are supposed to do miraculous things for your health. Current federal standards allow "for anyone to sell almost any drug to the public, as long as he or she refers to the drug as a dietary supplement and does not make specific health claims about its effects. . . . Unproven remedies . . . are now officially tolerated under the guise of dietary supplements. . . . Vague wording and the sheer number of people who routinely violate . . . [legislative] provisions . . . have resulted in insufficient enforcement of even these weak standards" (Ruscio, 2006, p. 65). Hence, we really do not know the extent to which various supplements are helpful—or harmful.

2. *Absence of skeptical peer review.* Has the fact been evaluated by credible professionals who support its validity? There is an almost infinite number of Web sites on the Internet addressing almost any topic you could think of and claiming almost any "fact" to be true or practice approach to be valid. A scary thing is that it is almost

impossible to tell which sites have well-established validity and credibility and which do not. Usually, Web sites ending in *.edu* or *.gov* enhance credibility potential because they are supposed to be initiated by formal educational or governmental organizations. But, how do you know for sure?

3. *Reliance on personal experience and testimonials.* A woman enthusiastically proclaims, "This exercise equipment gave me awesome abs and made me look 20 years younger!" Because an approach worked for one person does not mean it will work for all. Perhaps that woman worked out with the equipment 3 hours a day for the past year. How has diet and stress management contributed to her youthful appearance? How old is she anyway, and can she prove it? Is she telling the truth? What scientific evidence is available to document the effectiveness of the equipment? One major aspect of critical thinking is the ability to recognize emotional aspects that are influencing new information. In other words, simply because someone is excited about a new intervention does not make it valid or effective. If you find yourself getting caught up in the emotion of a situation that calls for a careful judgment, this is a warning sign.

4. *Wishful thinking* (p. 43). Hoping that something is so can provide a powerful incentive to believe in it. For example, consider the idea that "putting magnets on your head can cure headaches." It would be nice to find an automatic cure for headaches that did not involve imbibing some substance. However, Ruscio (2006) explains:

   What about the alleged healing power of magnets as they interact with our bodies? The suggestion for how a magnetic field might be useful in curing disease is that it increases the flow of blood (which contains iron) to a targeted area, thereby bringing extra nutrients and carrying away the waste products of our metabolism. This theory, too, is directly contradicted by known facts. Blood, as with other bodily tissue and fluids, consists primarily of water. Thus, the fact that water is slightly repelled by a magnetic field is

(continued)

especially relevant. Why? Because the primary constituent of the human body—including not only our blood but also, as in most forms of life, all of our tissues and fluids—is water. We are therefore weakly repelled by magnetic fields. In principle, a strong enough magnet [placed on the ground] could be used to levitate a person, as has been done with drops of water, flowers, grasshoppers, and frogs. The small amounts of iron in our blood's hemoglobin do not exist in sufficiently dense quantities to offset the repulsive effect of the much larger amount of water. Therefore, to the extent that magnets have any influence on our blood—and this influence is minimal— they will drive blood away from the targeted areas. (pp. 82–83)

5. *The "ancient wisdom" fallacy* (Ruscio, 2006, p. 59). "That must be the right way to do it because we've always done it that way." "This type of argument can have dangerous consequences, however. If beliefs are granted truth owing merely to their age, this would provide justification for sexism, racism, anti-Semitism, and a host of other repellent notions that have been widely held throughout human history" (Ruscio, 2006, p. 59).

6. *The popularity fallacy* (p. 59). "Everybody else is doing it, so it must be right." I once had a classmate, age 26 no less, who said in an election year that he was going to vote for the current president because that president had already been elected, and all those people who voted for him surely could not be wrong. I stared at him in total disbelief. How could he be so naïve? How could he not think for himself? At his age? He obviously believed in the popularity fallacy.

---

development and implementation of a strategy for improving or altering "some specified condition, pattern of behavior, or set of circumstances in an effort to improve a client's social functioning or well-being" (Sheafor & Horejsi, 2012, p. 88). Planned change is a process whereby social workers engage a client; assess issues, strengths, and problems; and establish a plan of action, implement the plan, evaluate its effects, terminate the process, and do subsequent follow-up to monitor the client's ongoing status. The Generalist Intervention Model proposed in the next section of this chapter explores this process much more thoroughly.

Note that another term often used to describe what generalist practitioners do is *problem solving*, initially introduced by social work pioneer Helen Harris Perlman in 1957. Essentially, problem solving refers to the same process as planned change, although many debate the nuances of difference. Social work's more recent emphasis on client strengths may be at odds with the more negative connotations of the word *problem*. The term *change* may have more positive connotations, despite the fact that most social work intervention deals with problem situations.

LO 1-15 Employ the Generalist Intervention Model (GIM), Which Uses a Seven-Step Planned Change Focus

Our definition of generalist practice provides the foundation for the Generalist Intervention Model (GIM). GIM is a practice model providing step-by-step direction concerning how to undertake the planned change process, which is generally directed at addressing problems.

Social workers help people deal with problems ranging from personal relationships to lack of resources to blatant discrimination. A social worker may need to address the problem of a battered woman who is economically and emotionally dependent on her abusive husband and who also has three children to protect. In another instance, a social worker might have an adolescent client who has committed a number of serious crimes and is heavily involved with an urban gang. At yet another time, a social worker may need to advocate and fight for change in a public assistance policy—one that discriminates against people who speak little to no English and are unable to follow an intricate, exasperating application process in order to receive benefits. Regardless of what problem is addressed, the planned change effort follows the same course of action.

Three major features characterize GIM. First, GIM assumes that workers acquire an eclectic knowledge base, a wide range of skills to target systems of any size, and a professional values base, all emphasized in our definition of generalist practice. GIM's second major feature is its core seven-step planned change process (illustrated in Figure 1.3) that emphasizes the assessment and use of client strengths. The third key feature is its generalist approach, which means virtually any problem may be analyzed and addressed from multiple levels of intervention. GIM is oriented toward addressing problems and issues that involve not only individuals, but also groups, organizations, communities, and even major social policies. In other words, the model involves individuals, families, groups, organizations, or communities as targets of change. Figure 1.4 illustrates this approach.

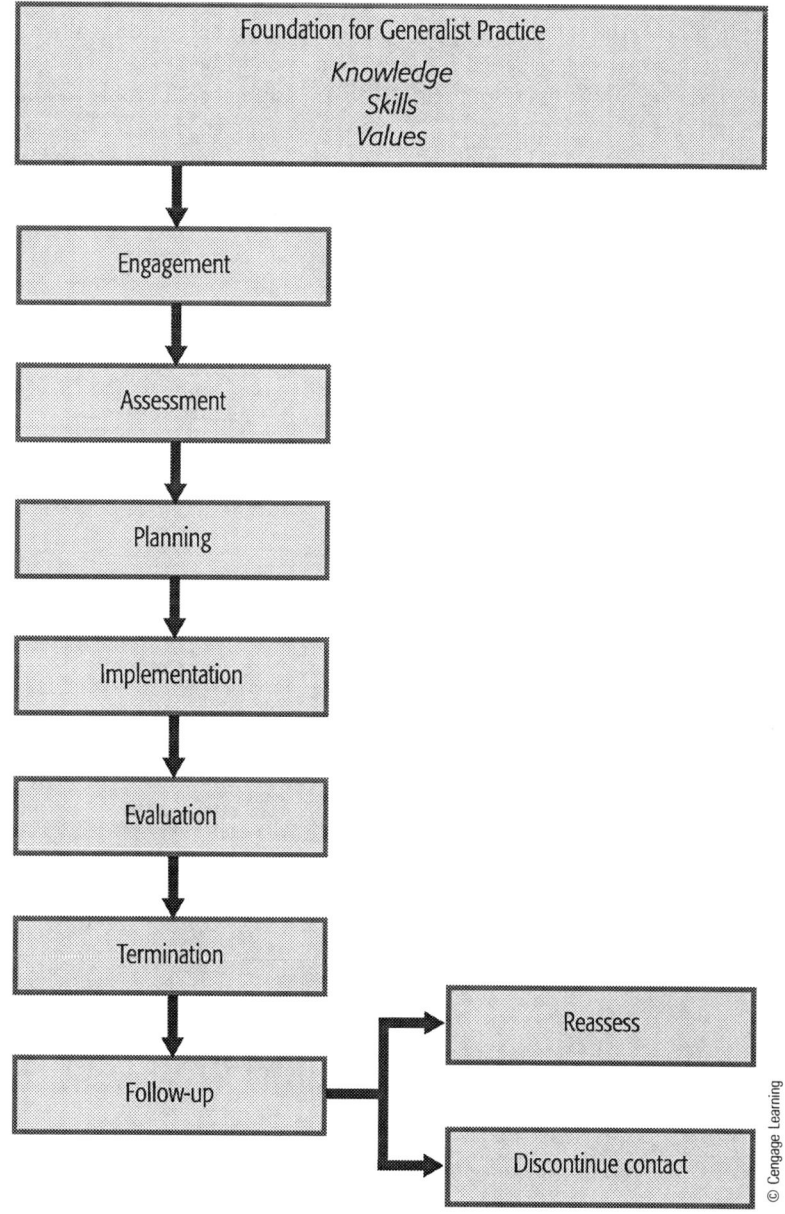

© Cengage Learning

FIGURE 1.3 Planned Change Steps in the Generalist Intervention Model (GIM)

For example, suppose you are a school social worker in a large, urban community that serves primarily a low-income population. In your role you may be called upon to work with students with behavioral problems, "to help collect data on the student's behaviors, to recommend behavioral intervention strategies, to teach social skills and strategies to the student, and/or to provide support for the student as part of the behavior intervention plan" (Atkins-Burnett, 2010, p. 180). You participate with other professionals (e.g., speech therapists, psychologists, teachers) on multidisciplinary teams to determine treatment plans. Often, you serve as a case manager who coordinates the treatment efforts. The school is legally responsible for providing supportive and remedial services to students who experience difficulties in their learning environment.

You receive a new case referral, Takashi, a 5-year-old boy who has severe speech and behavioral problems. He stutters and has difficulty enunciating words and formulating sentences. He frequently refuses to obey his parents at home, often lashing out in violent temper tantrums. At school he has poor communication and relationship-building skills with his peers. He is unable to play with peers without acting out aggressively, such as hitting them in the stomach or poking them in the eye. Such behavior causes serious problems for him with his kindergarten teacher.

As a generalist practitioner, you can assess and proceed with this case on several levels, considering the possibility of intervention with the individual, family, groups, organizations, or communities that are involved (as indicated in Figure 1.4). First, on an individual level, Takashi requires speech and behavioral assessments to determine a treatment plan. To what extent are his speech difficulties physiologically based? What speech therapy goals might be established? How do Takashi's speech problems affect his ability to interact with others? How are his parents and other family members reacting to and handling his speech and behavior problems?

On a family level, Takashi is having difficulty interacting with family members. Takashi's parents may require family counseling and education about behavior management techniques. Takashi is also having

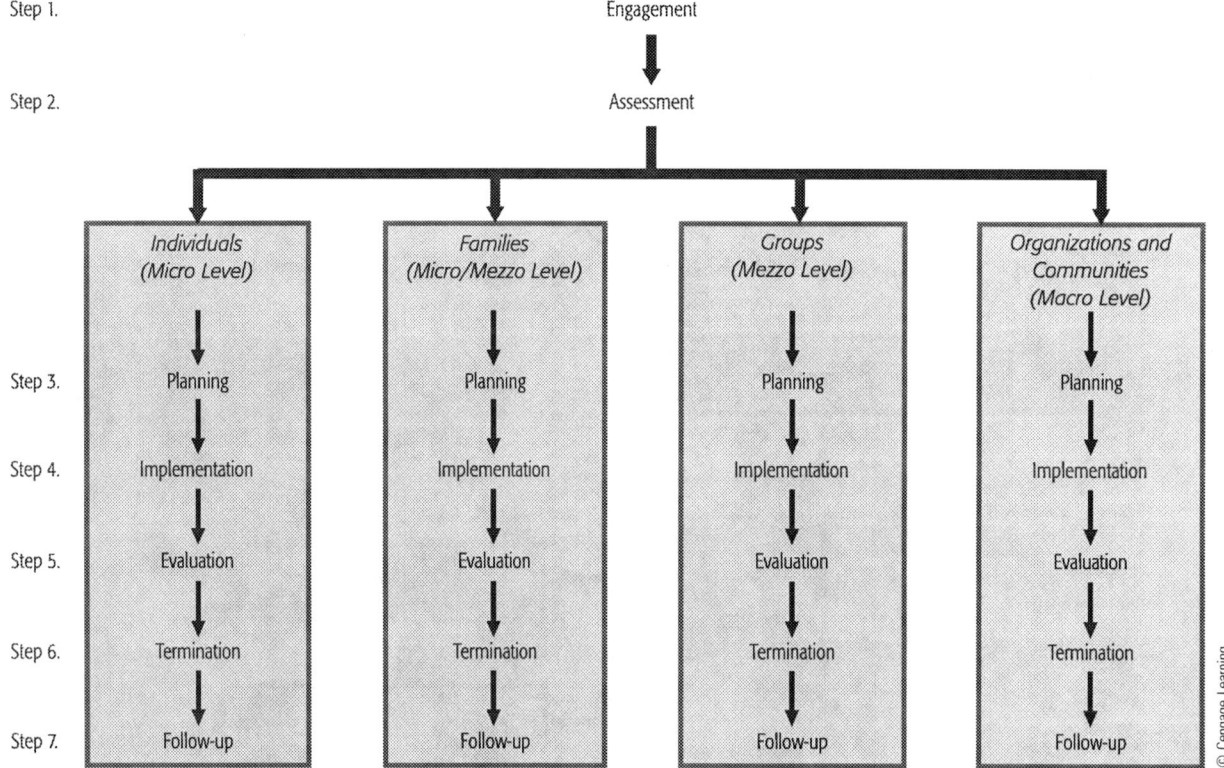

FIGURE 1.4 Initiating Change with Individuals, Families, Groups, Organizations, and Communities during Assessment

difficulty with peers and other adults. Group-level intervention also may address Takashi's peer relationships. His teacher may need consultation regarding behavioral control in the classroom. Takashi might benefit from membership in a treatment group with other children experiencing similar difficulties. Group involvement might include discussing feelings and behavior, providing role models for improved behavior, and encouraging positive interaction among group members.

Intervention focusing on organizations and the community investigates and promotes changes in the broader macro environment. The school (as an organization) is only responsible for providing services directly related to improving students' performance in school. Takashi and his parents may need additional help. School social workers also "serve as trained mediators, ... lead parent education and informational groups, ... and facilitate the development of relationships that link the services of the school with those found in the community. ... [T]o function in the public school ... a social worker must stay informed about legislation and litigation that affect the school and other service providers' responsibility to this group as well as their roles and those of others. Social workers will need to be advocates for many of the children and their families" (Atkins-Burnett, 2010, pp. 187–188).

Follow the Planned Change Steps in the GIM

EP 2.1.10

Regardless of what kind of problem is addressed, the planned change process presented here involves seven major steps. We will define each step briefly now; later chapters will provide more extensive elaboration. The planned change steps are engagement, assessment, planning, implementation, evaluation, termination, and follow-up.

STEP 1: ENGAGEMENT: ENGAGE THE CLIENT SYSTEM

EP 2.1.10a

Engagement, the first step in the GIM, is the initial period where you as a practitioner orient yourself to the problem at hand and begin to establish communication and a relationship with the client and others also addressing the problem. Regardless of whether you pursue micro, mezzo, or macro change, you must establish rapport or a harmonious relationship with clients and target systems in order to communicate and get things done. Engagement is based on the acquisition of a range

of skills for working with individuals. Both the words you speak (verbal communication) and your coinciding actions and expressions (nonverbal communication) can act to engage others in the helping process. Nonverbal communication conveys information in ways other than spoken words (e.g., eye contact, facial expressions, body positioning).

Many other dimensions are involved in engagement. Your overall demeanor, including your ability to convey warmth, empathy, and genuineness, can enhance engagement.[13] Likewise, how you introduce yourself and arrange an initial meeting's setting affects the engagement process. Other engagement skills include alleviating initial client anxiety and introducing your purpose and role. Chapter 5 describes more thoroughly engagement and how it relates to practice skills with individuals.

STEP 2: ASSESSMENT: ASSESS THE CLIENT AND SITUATION

According to Siporin, assessment is the "differential, individualized, and accurate identification and evaluation of problems, people, and situations and of their interrelations, to serve as a sound basis for differential helping intervention" (1975, p. 224). Meyer defines assessment simply as "knowing, understanding, evaluating, individualizing, or figuring out" (1995, p. 260). For our purposes, *assessment*, the second step in GIM, is the investigation and determination of variables affecting an identified problem or issue as viewed from micro, mezzo, or macro perspectives. (Assessment is discussed more thoroughly in Chapter 5.) In the first place, assessment refers to gathering relevant information about a problem so that decisions can be made about what to do to solve it. Second, assessment can involve preparation for intervention at any level of practice. As Figure 1.5 indicates, assessment includes the following four substeps:

1. Identify your client.
2. Assess the client-in-situation from micro, mezzo, macro, and diversity perspectives.
3. Cite information about client problems and needs.
4. Identify client strengths.

---

13. *Conveying warmth* involves enhancing the positive feelings of one person toward another by promoting a sense of comfort and well-being in that other person. *Empathy* involves not only *being in tune* with how a client feels, but also *conveying to that client* that you understand how the client feels. This process involves sharing your ideas and feelings in an open, authentic manner. *Genuineness* simply means that you continue to be yourself, despite the fact that you are working to accomplish goals in your professional role. Chapter 2 discusses these qualities more thoroughly.

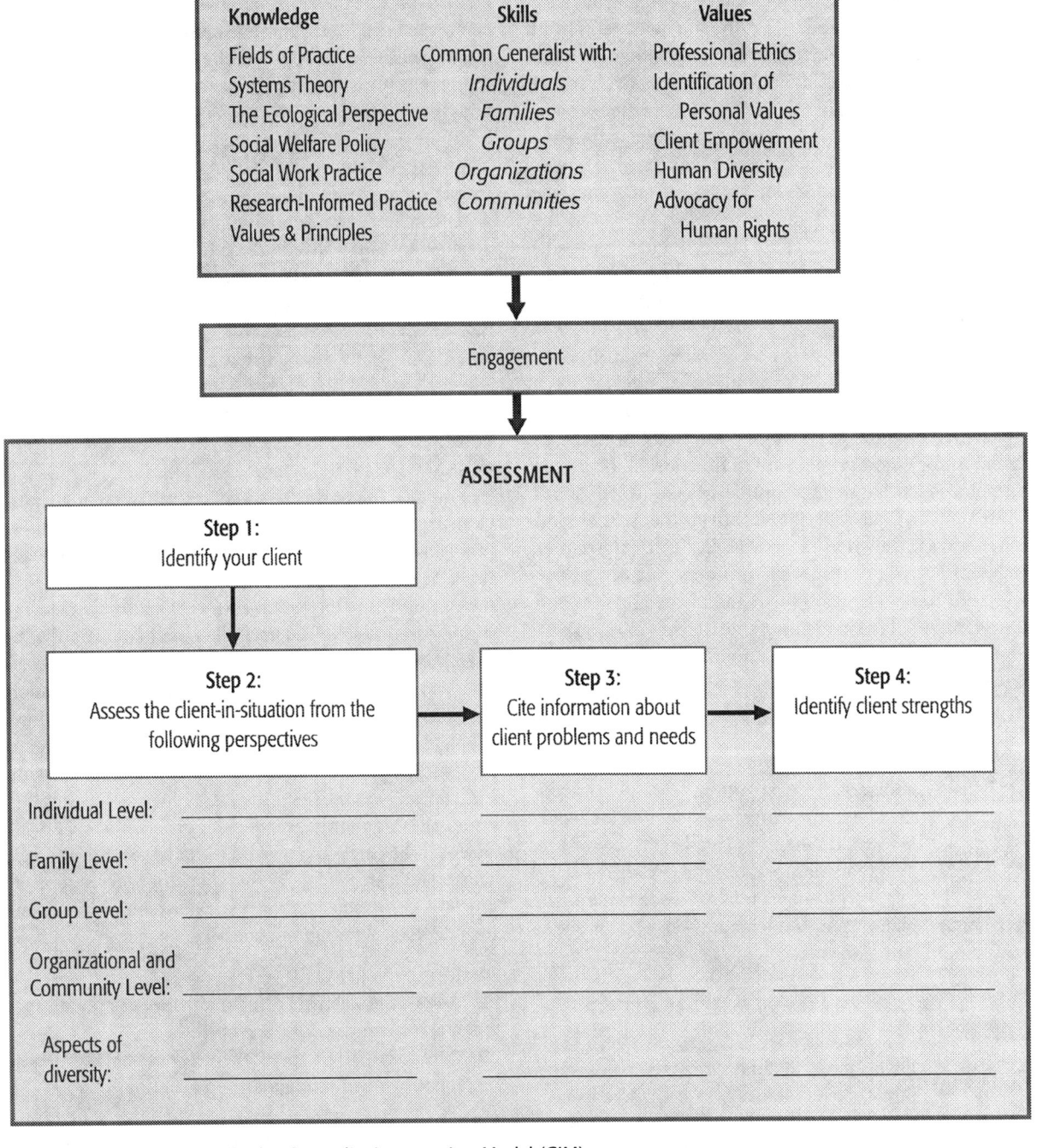

FIGURE 1.5 Assessment in the Generalist Intervention Model (GIM)

Identify Your Client

Substep 1 in assessment is to determine who your client is. At first glance, this method may sound overly simplistic. To say your clients are those people cited on your client list (i.e., your caseload)

seems logical. However, we have already established that people, their lives, and their problems are often complicated. The designation of who is really your client and who is not may become blurred and vague.

For example, say you are a probation officer. Justin, age 15, is a client on your caseload. He was adjudicated delinquent because he had stolen over a dozen cars. Because Justin is clearly listed on your caseload, he is your client, right?

However, you determine that Justin needs support and guidance from his parents. He currently lives at home with them, and both parents are currently using illegal drugs. Both also have conviction records for drug dealing. Additionally, Justin has three younger siblings also living in the home. You worry that they are likely to follow in Justin's footsteps and become involved in theft and other illegal activities.

Who is your client? Whom do you need to help? Is it just Justin? Is his entire family your client? Is your client really the community that employs you to monitor lawbreakers and help them fit into the community more appropriately?

To answer these questions, thinking in terms of a *client system* is helpful. Who is your client system? Who will benefit from the planned change process?

The probation officer may decide that Justin alone is the client system or that Justin and his entire family will become the client system. Whoever is identified as "those who have sanctioned (or asked for) his services, are expected to be beneficiaries of the change efforts, and have entered into a working agreement or contract" with the social worker becomes the client system (Pincus & Minahan, 1973, p. 57). One should note, however, that clients may be voluntary or involuntary. Justin surely did not choose to have a personal probation officer. His family may not be thrilled with the idea either. Rather, society forced the probation situation upon Justin and his family in response to the boy's behavior. Nonetheless, in this case Justin and his family are intended to receive the benefits of the intervention effort. Additionally, the probation office will make agreements with whoever is identified as part of the client system by establishing a contract with them. This situation fits the definition of client system that was provided earlier.

Assess the Client-in-Situation, Cite Information About Client Problems and Needs, and Identify Strengths

After the client system is established, a generalist practitioner will continue with the assessment. Substeps 2 through 4 in assessment concerns examining clients in their situation, identifying relevant issues, and emphasizing strengths. This process of gathering information is tied directly to what the social worker does about the problem. How social workers intervene is based on the information they have and on the judgments they have made about that information. Assessment in generalist practice focuses on understanding the many aspects of a problem. Information is needed about the client and about those aspects of the client's environment that the worker feels are significant.

For example, a social services worker in a rural county receives a call about Hilda from Hilda's neighbor. Hilda, 84, lives in an old farmhouse in the country where she has lived for most of her life. Hilda's health is deteriorating; as a result, she is falling more and more frequently, and her eyesight is failing. The neighbor worries that Hilda may fall, break something, and lie helpless and alone for days.

The worker visits Hilda and does an assessment of her and her situation. The worker needs information to make decisions about what he and Hilda can do. Hilda may need some supportive services or even health care center placement.

The information needed falls into five major categories. These include looking at elements related to the individual, family, group, organizational, and community contexts in addition to consideration of elements of human diversity. At each level, problems must be defined and strengths identified.

Individual Aspects. The first category of elements the worker must explore concerns aspects of the situation concerning the individual involved. What are Hilda's most critical problems? What things about Hilda contribute to her problems? On the other hand, what are Hilda's strengths? What does she do well? What aspects of her life does she consider important?

The worker explores both biological and psychological aspects of Hilda's situation. In Hilda's case, the biological aspects primarily involve her current health problems. Yes, Hilda admits she falls occasionally, but she thinks that a cane might help. Her failing sight is especially difficult for her. She talks of how she is not eating very well lately because she cannot see well enough to cook.

Also, from the individual perspective the worker explores Hilda's psychological situation. How does Hilda feel about herself and her situation? The worker discovers that Hilda, too, finds taking care of herself increasingly difficult. She loves her home and expresses the strong desire to remain in it. However, she feels she could use some help, especially with food purchase and preparation. The worker finds that Hilda expresses herself well. Although Hilda is somewhat discouraged about her eyesight, she appears to be emotionally stable.

Family Aspects. The second category of elements explored by the worker concerns the family. Because of a family's special and intimate nature, this involves using skills for working with both individuals and groups. The worker asks Hilda about her family. Does Hilda have any relatives in the immediate vicinity? Does she have children who are available to help out? What are her relationships with relatives who might be accessible?

The worker discovers that Hilda has three children in the area. They call and visit frequently but haphazardly. They occasionally take her shopping or to visit their homes.

Group Aspects. The third category of elements the worker then pursues relates to group involvement. The worker poses questions about groups with which Hilda might be involved. Does Hilda have friends she can talk to? Do people visit her? How often? Does she have opportunities to get out of the house at all?

The worker establishes that Hilda has a number of friends in the area. However, she rarely sees them because of the transportation difficulties for both her and them. She is, however, affiliated with a church and participates in church activities as frequently as she can. Spirituality can provide a beneficial means of support.

Organizational and Community Aspects. The fourth category of elements the worker explores concerns the macro aspects of the situation. These elements involve organizations and the community. What services might be available to help Hilda with her identified problems? Is there a Meals-on-Wheels program available? Meals-on-Wheels provides regular delivery of hot meals to older adults throughout a designated area. Is there a Visiting Friends program through which paraprofessionals regularly visit older adult residents in their homes and help them with shopping, paying bills, making medical appointments, and so on? Note that the organizational and community aspects of assessment are often integrally involved with each other. For instance, what organizations and services are available in and supported by the community? Organizations are fundamental components of communities. Additionally organizational policies and legislation are integrally involved in the operation and control of organizations and communities. Therefore, we will often use the word *macro* to refer to the broader integrated context of the social environment and to generalist practice within that environment.

The worker determines that no such services are readily available at this time. He decides that the community is not prepared to meet Hilda's needs or the needs of other older adults in similar positions.

Aspects of Diversity. The fifth category of elements the worker needs to consider while assessing Hilda and her situation concerns aspects of diversity. Are there any significant facets involving the effects of human diversity? The worker finds that Hilda is of German heritage. This aspect of ethnic and cultural diversity is relevant. Hilda also feels strongly about her membership in a local Lutheran church that many other older adults of similar heritage also attend. For many reasons, Hilda's church involvement is important to her.

Another aspect of diversity is Hilda's age. Is Hilda being treated differently or in a discriminatory manner because of ageism? *Ageism* refers to discrimination based on predisposed notions about older people, regardless of their individual qualities and capabilities. The worker closely evaluates his own attitudes. For instance, is he tempted to make assumptions about Hilda's mental capability because of the stereotype that older people can no longer think as clearly as they could when they were younger?

Likewise, the worker must be aware of any sexist biases he might harbor. *Sexism* refers to predisposed notions about a person based on that person's gender. For instance, does the worker feel that Hilda is a dependent person who needs to be taken care of simply because she is a woman? Such a bias fails to take into account the client as a unique individual with particular strengths and weaknesses.

Assessment and Planning. After reassessing the client and her situation (the five categories of elements just described), the worker and Hilda together establish the following plan. First, regarding intervention at the individual level, Hilda needs a cane. Hilda also needs some supportive care related to family, in addition to organizational and community interventions. The worker and Hilda decide to meet with Hilda's children and their families to work out a schedule for visitation and assistance. In this way, her relatives can regularly check to make certain Hilda is all right. Hilda feels strongly about remaining in her home as long as possible. The worker, Hilda, and Hilda's family agree that until her health deteriorates further, they will try to maintain her in her own home.

The macro intervention in Hilda's case involves the lack of supportive services available to her. The worker and his supervisor bring Hilda's situation to the attention of the social services department's administration. On further investigation, a substantial number of other older adults are found to be in positions similar to Hilda's. Thus, the change process is initiated to pursue funding for new resources to help older adults.

Hilda's example provides only a brief summary of the social service worker's assessment. However, it does highlight the basic categories of information needed in virtually every assessment. As Figure 1.5 indicates, five general categories of information should be considered: *information concerning the individual,* which includes both biological and psychological aspects; *family information,* which involves the individual's interaction with and support of family; *group information,* which involves immediate groups with which clients have interaction; *organizational and community information,* which concerns the impact of the broader social environment, organization, laws, and policies upon the client(s); and finally, *aspects of diversity,* which focus on special qualities or characteristics that may place clients in a designated group. Concerning the last category, the potential for discrimination must also be considered.

The crucial task of generalist practice is to look beyond the individual and examine other factors that impinge on the client's environment. In any individual case, the emphasis upon one or the other assessment categories may vary. However, each category must still be reviewed and considered for its potential contribution to the problem.

For instance, a couple may come to a social worker for help in their marital relationship. Thus, assessment of the family aspects or relationship issues of the situation would be emphasized. However, a generalist practitioner would also consider both the individual perspectives—such as the strengths, needs, and issues of each partner—and the macro aspects impinging upon their situation. Macro aspects might involve the fact that both spouses have been laid off from their jobs at the local Mega Turbo tractor factory. They have held these jobs for over 10 years, and the layoff was due to a serious depression in farm prices. In this case, the social worker might not be able to do much about the current economy, but the economic impact on the couple is vital in an assessment of the current marital conflict.

Chapter 5 discusses assessment more thoroughly.

STEP 3: PLANNING: FORMULATE A PLAN FOR THE INTERVENTION PROCESS

The third step in the GIM involves planning what to do. Planning follows assessment in the problem-solving process. Assessment sets the stage for the intervention, whereas planning specifies what should be done.

(Chapter 6 discusses planning more thoroughly.) As shown in Figure 1.6, planning involves the following eight substeps:

1. Work with the client.
2. Prioritize problems.
3. Translate problems into needs.
4. Evaluate levels of intervention for each need.
5. Establish goals.
6. Specify objectives.
7. Specify action steps.
8. Formalize a contract.

Substep 1: Work with the Client

The generalist practitioner follows eight substeps in the planning process. Substep 1 in the planning process concerns working *with* the client, not *at* the client. Earlier on, we established that generalist practice stresses how workers and clients proceed in a partnership to address issues and problems. The client must be involved in problem definition and must agree as to which problems merit attention. Additionally, the planning process should take advantage of the client's strengths.

Substep 2: Prioritize Problems

Substep 2 in the planning process is to prioritize the problems. Again, the client must be a partner in this process. Many times, what the worker feels is important differs drastically from what the client thinks is most significant. For example, a social worker may be most concerned about Carol's potential for abusing her small children and about her alcohol consumption. Carol, on the other hand, may be most interested in solving her financial problems. Her work schedule has been cut back in terms of hours, so she now works only part-time. Meanwhile, her rent is rising astronomically, she owes growing debts on her credit cards, and she sees herself as a failure because she cannot take adequate care of her family. Part of the worker's job is to examine the various aspects of the problems at hand and to focus on problems and issues considered significant by the client and the worker.

Substep 3: Translate Problems into Needs

Substep 3 in the planning process involves translating problems into needs. Clients come to you because they are suffering from problems. The way you can help them is to establish what they *need* to solve the problem. This relatively simple step in planning helps to restructure how you look at the situation so that it is easier to decide on solutions.

Foundation for Generalist Practice

Knowledge
Skills
Values

↓

Engagement

↓

Assessment

↓

PLANNING

	Problem
Step 1:	Work with the client.
Step 2:	Prioritize problems.
Step 3:	Translate problems into needs.

Problem box:
Problem
1.
2.
3. etc.

Step 3 detail:
Problem ⟶ Need
1. ⟶ 1.
2. ⟶ 2.
3. ⟶ 3.

Step 4: Evaluate levels of intervention for each need.

Need #1: _____ etc.

a. Identify alternatives: ⟶ b. Propose solutions: ⟶ c. Evaluate:

		Pros	Cons	Client strengths
Individual				
Family				
Group				
Organizational and Community				

Step 5: Establish goals.

Step 6: Specify objectives.

Step 7: Specify action steps.

	Who?	Will do what?	By when?	How will you measure success?
1.				
2.				
3.				

Step 8: Formalize a contract.

© Cengage Learning

FIGURE 1.6 Planning in the Generalist Intervention Model (GIM)

Substep 4: Evaluate Levels of Intervention (Individual, Family, Group, Organizational, and Community Levels)

Substep 4 in the planning process involves first focusing on one client need at a time, beginning with those of highest priority. Possible alternative solutions should be discussed with the client.

Alternative solutions may focus on the individual, family, group, organizational, or community levels of change. The proposed alternative thus may involve what the individual can do at the micro level. For instance, one alternative solution aims at having Carol change her own behavior. She might enter an alcohol and other substance abuse treatment program. Another tack might be to help her find a new, more suitable job.

Perhaps the worker and client might address the problem at a group level. Carol could join a support group for people dealing with similar issues. Still another option may involve proposed change at the macro level. The worker might advocate to get Carol into low-rent housing. Another strategy might be to develop a plan for instituting rent control in the community. This last idea would make life more affordable for people facing financial conditions similar to Carol's.

Each proposed alternative solution should be evaluated regarding its pros and cons. How feasible or doable is it? What are the chances of success? How long will it take? Client strengths should be constantly kept in mind and involved in the solutions whenever possible. One result should be the selection of an alternative plan of action.

Substep 5: Establish Goals

Substep 5 in the planning process is to establish goals that are mutually agreed upon with the client. *Goals* are proposed ending attainments that provide you and your client with general direction regarding how to proceed with the intervention. What do you really want to accomplish? How can your client's major needs be met? What are your primary and necessary end results?

Substep 6: Specify Objectives

Substep 6 in the planning process concerns specifying objectives. Goals are often not very specific. In fact, many times clients identify goals that are vague or unclear and that do not let us know when they have or have not been attained. At the same time, clients' initial goals give an important sense of the problems and needs they are experiencing. For example, think of the following client-stated goals: "I want to improve communication with my husband" or "I need to find housing." By themselves, these goals are not specific enough to do anything more than state a general direction for our work with the client. They do not give you a clue regarding *how* to achieve them or where you would go to meet these needs. It is the worker's task to help move vague goal statements into more explicit ends or objectives.

Think of *objectives* as clearly stated goals that help identify what steps we must take to proceed. Using the preceding goals, our objectives might look like this: "Reduce the number of arguments I have with my husband" or "locate affordable and clean housing that has at least three bedrooms." Each of these objectives is specific and measurable and allows us to know whether we succeeded in its attainment. As such, they are important for evaluating our work with clients. It is entirely possible that one broad goal might generate several objectives. For example, Ms. Schultz might also like to spend 1 hour with her husband each week, talking over their activities and experiences. This would then be a second objective under the goal of improving communication with her husband. However, objectives do not tell us who will do what nor do they necessarily contain a time frame in which activities should be accomplished. Further, they do not really tell us how things will get done. This is the role of *action steps*.

Substep 7: Specify Action Steps

Substep 7 in the planning process involves specifying action steps to achieve the objectives. *Action steps* are detailed listings that specify *who* will do *what* by *when*, and *how* that individual should do it. They represent tasks that must be completed in order to move toward achieving the objective and ultimately the client's goals. For example, "Ms. Schultz will maintain a chart listing each of the arguments she had with her husband this week and bring it to our next session." Another example would be "I will contact the housing authority Monday and get a list of three-bedroom apartments or houses." Each objective might have multiple action steps, each specifying how things are going to get done. Action steps allow us to monitor our work with clients. For example, if Ms. Schultz fails to maintain a chart, quits midweek, or does not bring it to the session, we must reassess whether our action steps are appropriate. Perhaps other means are needed to help move toward her objective of reducing arguments with her husband. Similarly, if you do not get a list from the housing authority, you and the client cannot move forward with locating housing. Failure to complete important action steps can lead to failure to attain objectives. Needless to say, if we do not achieve our objectives, we also will not reach the client's goals.

Substep 8: Formalize a Contract with the Client
Finally, substep 8 in the planning process involves formalizing a contract with the client. A *contract* is a working agreement between a social worker and client system that specifies the expectations of each, roles, responsibilities, goals, and time frames that structure the intervention process (Rothman, 2009). The contract is the final substep in the planning process. It can be used to specify the many ways in which the worker and client are going to work together toward their goals. A contract formalizes the agreement between client and worker. It also clarifies their expectations.

A wide variety of items can be included in a contract. These items include specific aspects of the plan—such as who will do what by when, fees or financial responsibility, meeting times, types of services provided, and virtually any other condition involved in the intervention. As in other aspects of the planned change process, the client system must be an active participant in contract development. The worker must make certain that the client understands all of the specific words used in the contract. Technical jargon (or "psychobabble," as a business major friend once labeled it) must be clearly explained to the client or paraphrased in words the client readily understands.

Contracts are flexible agreements. In this manner, they are strikingly different from legal contracts, which require that all parties concur with their terms. This latter type of contract cannot be easily altered. Contracts with clients must be formal enough to clarify expectations but informal enough to let the worker respond flexibly to the client's changing needs or conditions.

STEP 4: IMPLEMENTATION: PUT THE PLAN INTO ACTION

The fourth step in the GIM involves implementation of the intervention, the actual *doing* of the plan (discussed in Chapter 7). Client and worker follow their plan to achieve their goals. Progress during implementation must be constantly monitored and assessed. Sometimes, new issues, situations, and conditions require that the plan be changed (see Figure 1.7).

For example, consider a case in which the intervention plan involves the goal of determining custody and

---

Foundation for Generalist Practice
Knowledge
Skills
Values

↓

Engagement

↓

Assessment

↓

Planning

↓

IMPLEMENTATION
Levels of implementation

	Individual	Family	Group	Organization and Community
Follow plan				
Monitor progress				
Revise plan (when necessary)				
Complete plan (to the greatest extent possible)				

© Cengage Learning

FIGURE 1.7 Implementation in the Generalist Intervention Model (GIM)

visitation rights following a divorce. The couple suddenly decides to stay together. Determining custody rights is no longer relevant. However, new goals might need to be developed concerning more effective behavioral management of the children to prevent family feuding and future disruptions of the marital relationship.

STEP 5: EVALUATION: EVALUATE RESULTS AND EFFECTIVENESS

Evaluation of implementation, the fifth step in the GIM, is critical for accountability. Social workers must be accountable. That is, they must prove that their interventions have been effective. Each goal is evaluated in terms of the extent to which it has been achieved. The decision then must be made about whether the case should be terminated or reassessed to establish new goals (see Figure 1.8).

Evaluation techniques are becoming increasingly more effective. They involve the application of research principles to generalist practice. Chapter 8 explores evaluation both for direct-service practitioners and for whole programs.

STEP 6: TERMINATION: CONCLUDE THE PLANNED CHANGE INTERVENTION PROCESS

The sixth step in the GIM concerns termination (discussed in Chapter 8). The worker–client relationship must eventually come to an end. To get up one day and, out of the clear blue sky, say "well, good-bye" is not a good ending for a worker. Termination in generalist practice involves specific skills and techniques. This fact is true regardless of the level of intervention (see Figure 1.3).

There are various ways the planned change process may be terminated (Ballan & Mera, 2008). It might be a planned ending when major goals have been achieved. Unanticipated circumstances might occur, such as a worker gets another job or funding for the agency's program is lost. For any number of reasons, clients may drop out of the treatment process and simply do not come back. Clients may feel the intervention is not working, or they no longer feel the discomfort initially causing them to seek help. The family moves. The client is no longer motivated to return. Other aspects of a client's life take precedence over the problem he or she came to the social worker to solve.

The most effective terminations, regardless of client system, follow a planned, steady progression. Social workers need to acknowledge that endings are near before they abruptly occur. They must encourage clients to share feelings about the termination and in turn

share their own. Additionally, practitioners must clearly identify whatever progress has been made. This process increases the chance that the client will use what has been learned during this intervention to help solve other problems in the future.

STEP 7: FOLLOW-UP: REEXAMINE THE SITUATION AND PROGRESS MADE

Follow-up is the seventh and final step in the GIM. *Follow-up*, also discussed in Chapter 8, is the reexamination of a client's situation at some point after the intervention is completed (Eaton & Roberts, 2009; Knox & Roberts, 2009). Its purpose is to monitor the ongoing effects of treatment. Many times, this step is the most difficult to follow. Caseloads may be too heavy and too filled with crises. The worker may be distracted by other issues and demands. Follow-up information might be hard to get.

Follow-up is an important step in the intervention process. It involves checking to find out whether clients have maintained progress and are still functioning well on their own. Does a client need to be reassessed for another intervention?

Other Practical Generalist Skills: A Perspective on the Rest of the Text

This text introduces a generalist perspective to social work practice, one that is directed at practitioners working primarily in micro settings. It emphasizes a wide range of micro-skills acquisition and relates the use of these skills to the mezzo and macro levels of practice.

Chapter 2 emphasizes the acquisition of skills for working with individuals. Following Chapter 2 are chapters focusing on the relevance of skills for working with groups and with organizations and communities. Chapters 5 through 8 explain the seven steps in the planned change process.

Remaining chapters address a range of skills and issues pertinent to direct-service practitioners. They involve knowledge and skills for use throughout the GIM's planned change process. These include:

- *understanding families;*
- *working with families;*
- *values, ethics, and resolution of ethical dilemmas;*
- *ethnically and racially sensitive social work practice;*
- *gender-sensitive social work practice;*
- *advocacy;*
- *brokering and case management; and*
- *recording skills.*

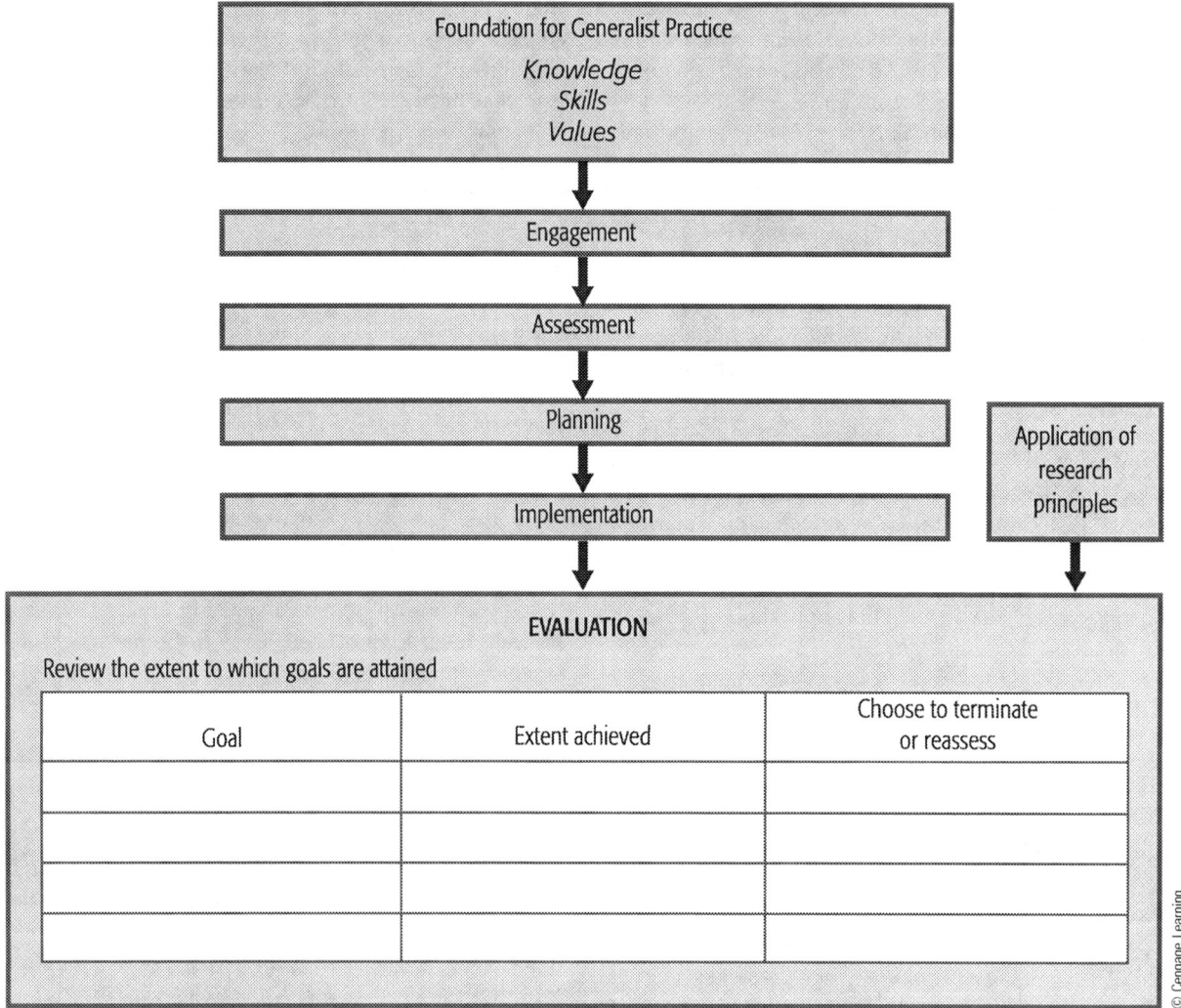

FIGURE 1.8 Evaluation in the Generalist Intervention Model (GIM)

Chapter Summary

The following summarizes this chapter's content as it relates to each learning objective (LO) presented at the beginning of the chapter. Chapter content helps prepare students to:

LO 1-1 Employ a unique approach to helping in the field of social work.

Social work is unique in that it focuses its attention on any problem or cluster of problems, often targets the environment for change, stresses advocacy on clients' behalf, emphasizes adherence to a core of professional values, and is held accountable by educational policy to educate competent practitioners.

LO 1-2 Define the process of generalist practice by describing its inherent concepts.

Generalist practice is the application of an eclectic knowledge base, professional values and ethics, and a wide range of skills to target systems of any size for change. It is characterized by 12 primary concepts. The core of generalist practice rests on a solid foundation of an eclectic knowledge base (concept 1), acquisition of professional values (concept 2), and use of a wide range of practice skills (concept 3) that can be used to change individuals, families, groups, organizations, or communities (concept 4).

Three more concepts vital to generalist practice relate to adopting professional values. These values involve: an emphasis on client empowerment, strengths, and resiliency (concept 5); the importance of diversity (concept 6); and advocacy for human rights, and the pursuit of social and economic justice (concept 7). The context of generalist practice is work within an organizational structure (concept 8).

Four final concepts inherent to generalist practice concern its process. Generalists assume a wide range of professional roles (concept 9), apply critical thinking skills (concept 10), incorporate research-informed practice (concept 11), and use a planned change process (concept 12).

LO 1-3   Acquire and apply an eclectic knowledge base to practice.

Areas of knowledge related to competent practice include fields of practice, systems and ecological conceptual frameworks, human behavior and the social environment, social welfare policy and policy practice, social work practice, research-informed practice and practice-informed research, and values and principles that guide generalist practice.

LO 1-4   Apply the systems theory conceptual framework to practice.

The systems conceptual framework can be readily applied to generalist practice and provides a useful way of viewing the interactions of various systems within the environment. These systems include individuals, families, groups, organizations, and communities. Systems terms include *system, dynamic, interact, input, output, homeostasis,* and *equifinality.*

LO 1-5   Apply the ecological conceptual framework to practice.

An ecological conceptual framework offers a helpful perspective for understanding generalist practice. Ecological terms include *social environment, person-in-environment, transactions, energy, input, output, interface, adaptation, coping,* and *interdependence.*

LO 1-6   Acquire professional values and apply professional ethics to practice.

Values are principles, qualities, and practices that a designated group, individual, or culture deems inherently desirable. Ethics are standards based on a set of values that guide one's behavior. Aspects of professional values and ethics for generalist practice include the National Association of Social Workers (NASW) *Code of Ethics;* the International Federation of Social Workers/International Association of Schools of Social Work *Ethics in Social Work, Statement of Principles;* awareness of personal values; and management of ethical dilemmas.

LO 1-7   Recognize a wide range of practice skills to work with individuals, families, groups, organizations, and communities.

The wide range of skills used in generalist practice is introduced. Skills include those for working with individuals, families, groups, organizations, and communities. Micro skills are those used for working with individuals. Mezzo skills are those used to work with small groups. Because of a family's special nature, working with a family involves the use of both micro and mezzo skills. Macro skills are those used to work with large systems, including organizations and communities.

LO 1-8   Emphasize principles involving values that underlie generalist practice.

Empowerment is "the process of increasing personal, interpersonal, or political power so that individuals can take action to improve their life situations" (Gutierrez, 2001, p. 210). *Strengths* include any "capacities, resources, and assets" that can be accessed to increase empowerment (Saleebey, 2013, p. 102). *Resiliency* is the ability of an individual, family, group, community, or organization to recover from adversity and resume functioning even when suffering serious trouble, confusion, or hardship (Glicken, 2006).

LO 1-9   Appreciate and stress the importance of human diversity.

The importance of understanding and appreciating human diversity is stressed. Dimensions of human diversity include age, social class, race, ethnicity, color, culture, disability, gender, gender identity, gender expression, sex, sexual orientation, immigration status, political ideology, and religion.

LO 1-10   Advocate for human rights, and pursue social and economic justice.

Advocacy is the act of representing, championing, or defending the rights of others. Human rights involve the premise that all people, regardless of characteristics or circumstances, are entitled to basic rights and fair, humane treatment. Social justice is the idea that in a perfect world all citizens would possess equal fundamental "rights, protection, opportunities, obligations, and social benefits" (Barker, 2003, pp. 404–405).

Economic justice concerns the distribution of resources in a fair and equitable manner.

LO 1-11 Demonstrate a wide range of professional roles.

A professional role is behavior and activity involved in performing some designated function in generalist practice. Professional roles that can be assumed in generalist practice include counselor, educator, broker, case manager, mobilize, mediator, facilitator, integrator/coordinator, manager, initiator, negotiator, spokesperson, organizer, consultant, and advocate.

LO 1-12 Define critical thinking skills and apply them to practice.

Critical thinking is: (1) the careful scrutiny of what is stated as true or what appears to be true and the resulting expression of an opinion or conclusion based on that scrutiny and (2) the creative formulation of an opinion or conclusion when presented with a question, problem, or issue. The Triple A approach to critical thinking involves the following steps: (1) ask questions; (2) assess the established facts and issues involved; and (3) assert a concluding opinion. In generalist practice, critical thinking can be applied to virtually any belief, statement, assumption, line of reasoning, action, or experience proposed as being true. Fallacies in critical thinking may include (Ruscio, 2006, pp. 6–10) the outward appearance of science, the absence of skeptical peer review, reliance on personal experience and testimonials, wishful thinking (Ruscio, 2006, p. 43), the "ancient wisdom" fallacy (Ruscio, 2006, p. 59), and the popularity fallacy (Ruscio, 2006, p. 59).

LO 1-13 Incorporate research-informed practice.

Generalist practitioners must demonstrate competency in *research-informed practice,* where they use the approaches and interventions in their practice that research has determined are effective. Such practice may include solving problems, improving social policies, and enhancing service delivery.

LO 1-14 Follow a planned change process.

Planned change is the development and implementation of a strategy for improving or altering "some specified condition, pattern of behavior, or set of circumstances in an effort to improve a client's social functioning or well-being" (Sheafor & Horejsi, 2012, p. 88).

LO 1-15 Employ the Generalist Intervention Model (GIM), which uses a seven-step planned change focus.

The steps involved in the Generalist Intervention Model are: (1) engagement, (2) assessment, (3) planning, (4) implementation, (5) evaluation, (6) termination, and (7) follow-up. Assessment, planning, implementation, and evaluation each have a series of substeps.

Competency Notes

This section relates chapter content to the Council on Social Work Education's (CSWE) *Educational Policy and Accreditation Standards* (EPAS; CSWE, 2008). One major goal of social work education is to facilitate students' attainment of the EPAS-designated 10 core competencies and their 41 related practice behaviors so that students develop into competent practitioners.

Students require knowledge in order to develop skills and become competent. Our intent here is to specify what chapter content and knowledge coincides with the development of specific competencies and practice behaviors. (This ultimately is intended to assist in the accreditation process.) Therefore, the following listing first cites the various Educational Policy (EP) core competencies and their related practice behaviors that are relevant to chapter content. Note that the listing follows the order that competencies and practice behaviors are cited in the EPAS.

We have established that "helping hands" icons are interspersed throughout the chapter to indicate where relevant accompanying content is located. The page numbers noted indicate where icons are placed in the chapter. Following the icon's page number is a brief explanation of how the content accompanying the icon relates to the specified competency or practice behavior.

The following identifies where Educational Policy (EP) competencies and practice behaviors are discussed in the chapter.

EP 2.1 **Core Competencies:** *(p. 5):* The definition of generalist practice proposed here takes most of its concepts directly from the EPAS, including the concepts of strengths; diversity; advocacy for human rights, and the pursuit of social and economic justice; ethical principles; professional roles; critical thinking; research-informed practice; and engagement, assessment, intervention, and evaluation with individuals, families, groups, organizations, and communities, among others.

EP 2.1.1 Identify as a professional social worker and conduct oneself accordingly. *(p. 30):* Professional identification and conduct are part of being involved effectively in an organizational setting.

EP 2.1.1c Attend to professional roles and boundaries. *(p. 30):* Social workers must be knowledgeable about and prepared to assume a wide range of professional roles.

EP 2.1.1e Engage in career-long learning. *(p. 29):* Cultural competency involves career-long learning about clients' cultures.

EP 2.1.1f Use supervision and consultation. *(p. 30):* Effective work within an organizational structure involves using supervision and consultation effectively.

EP 2.1.2 Apply social work ethical principles to guide professional practice. *(p. 20):* Ethics consists of standards that guide professional behavior.

EP 2.1.2a Recognize and manage personal values in a way that allows professional values to guide practice. *(p. 21):* Practitioners must become aware of personal values so that these don't interfere with professional values and conduct.

EP 2.1.2b Make ethical decisions by applying standards of the National Association of Social Workers [NASW] *Code of Ethics* **and, as applicable, of the International Federation of Social Workers [IFSW]/International Association of Schools of Social Work [IASSW]** *Ethics in Social Work, Statement of Principles.* *(p. 21):* The NASW *Code of Ethics* and the IFSW/IASSW *Ethics in Social Work, Statement of Principles* are introduced.

EP 2.1.2c Tolerate ambiguity in resolving ethical conflicts. *(p. 21):* Practitioners often face unclear and imperfect situations and ethical dilemmas where they must determine the most effective and ethical plan of action. *(p. 23):* An exercise is proposed to help students tolerate ambiguity as they struggle to make ethical decisions.

EP 2.1.2d Apply strategies of ethical reasoning to arrive at principled decisions. *(p. 21):* The notion of using ethical principles to make decisions is introduced.

EP 2.1.3 Apply critical thinking to inform and communicate professional judgments. *(pp. 17, 22, 34):*

Critical thinking questions are posed. *(p. 31):* Critical thinking involves careful evaluation of what is truth and what is assumption. It requires formulating thoughtful conclusions about how to proceed in practice.

EP 2.1.4 Engage diversity and difference in practice. *(p. 27):* Human diversity refers to many differences among people, including those identified in Highlight 1.8.

EP 2.1.4a Recognize the extent to which a culture's structures and values may oppress, marginalize, alienate, or create or enhance privilege and power. *(p. 29):* Cultural competency involves awareness that cultural values may cause oppression for some diverse groups.

EP 2.1.4b Gain sufficient self-awareness to eliminate the influence of personal biases and values in working with diverse groups. *(p. 29):* Cultural competency involves increased self-awareness of personal cultural values and biases.

EP 2.1.4c Recognize and communicate their understanding of the importance of difference in shaping life experiences. *(p. 29):* Cultural competency concerns understanding the importance of difference in shaping life experiences.

EP 2.1.4d View themselves as learners and engage those with whom they work as informants. *(p. 29):* Cultural competency involves learning about other cultures on an ongoing basis.

EP 2.1.5b Advocate for human rights and social and economic justice. *(p. 29):* Championing for human rights, social justice, and economic justice is a core value of generalist practice.

EP 2.1.5c Engage in practices that advance social and economic justice. *(p. 29):* The idea that social workers should engage in practices that advance social and economic is stressed.

EP 2.1.6 Engage in research-informed practice and practice-informed research. *(p. 18):* Empirical evidence should guide the intervention process to maximize effectiveness.

EP 2.1.6b Use research evidence to inform practice. *(p. 34):* Social workers should use the approaches and interventions in their practice that research has determined are effective.

EP 2.1.7 Apply knowledge of human behavior and the social environment. *(p. 11):* Generalist practice involves systems of all sizes. *(p. 15):* The acquisition of knowledge about human behavior and the social environment is essential to guide the planned change intervention process. A person-in-environment perspective is essential for understanding human behavior.

EP 2.1.7a Utilize conceptual frameworks to guide the processes of assessment, intervention, and evaluation. *(p. 10):* Generalist practice requires the acquisition of a wide range of conceptual frameworks to guide the planned change intervention process. *(p. 11):* Systems theory provides a useful conceptual framework for guiding the intervention process *(p. 13):* The ecological perspective is a useful conceptual framework to guide the intervention process.

EP 2.1.7b Critique and apply knowledge to understand person and environment. *(p. 15):* Generalist practitioners must have a sound knowledge base about human behavior in the social environment to be effective.

EP 2.1.8 Engage in policy practice to advance social and economic well-being and to deliver effective social work services. *(p. 17):* Understanding social welfare policy is essential before undertaking policy practice and advocating for policy change.

EP 2.1.8a Analyze, formulate, and advocate for policies that advance social well-being. *(p. 17):* Policy practice involves "efforts to change policies in legislative, agency, and community settings" to advance social well-being, especially on behalf of oppressed populations (Jansson, 2011, p. 14).

EP 2.1.10 Engage, assess, intervene, and evaluate with individuals, families, groups, organizations, and communities. *(p. 11):* Understanding systems theory helps prepare social workers to practice with systems of all sizes. *(p. 18):* Understanding of the process of social work practice is a basic part of the social work knowledge base. *(p. 22):* Practitioners must possess a wide range of skills to work with systems of all sizes. *(p. 36):* Generalist social work practice involves planned change intervention with systems of all sizes. *(p. 39):* The Generalist Intervention Model incorporates engagement, assessment, implementation, and evaluation as aspects of the intervention process. *(p. 46):* Implementation of the intervention is a basic part of the intervention process.

EP 2.1.10a Substantively and affectively prepare for action with individuals, families, groups, organizations, and communities. *(p. 39):* Generalist practitioners should view practice situations from a macro perspective in addition to micro and mezzo standpoints. *(p. 25):* Engagement is part of preparing for action with client systems.

EP 2.1.10e Assess clients' strengths and limitations. *(p. 24):* Practitioners should assess and build on clients' strengths in the intervention process.

EP 2.1.10f Develop mutually agreed-on intervention goals and objectives. *(p. 45):* Practitioners should always work with the client to establish intervention goals.

EP 2.1.10l Facilitate transitions and endings. *(p. 47):* Effective termination involves a planned, steady progression.

EP 2.1.10m Social workers critically analyze, monitor, and evaluate interventions. *(p. 47):* Practitioners are responsible for evaluating the effectiveness of their practice interventions.

EP B2.2 Generalist Practice. *(p. 2):* Generalist practice is the foundation of social work practice.

On the Internet

Visit the *Understanding Generalist Practice* CourseMate at **www.cengagebrain.com** for resources such as quizzes, glossaries and videos.

Practice Skills for Working with Individuals

© Rob Marmion/Shutterstock.com

Learning Objectives   *This chapter will help prepare students to:*

LO 2-1   Use interviewing skills to engage, assess, intervene, and evaluate with individuals in the planned change process.

LO 2-2   Demonstrate effective nonverbal behavior when working with clients.

LO 2-3   Use empathy and other interpersonal skills when working with clients.

LO 2-4   Maintain a commitment to client self-determination and empowerment.

LO 2-5   Prepare for action with individuals and families by effectively starting the interview.

LO 2-6   Demonstrate effective oral communication while conducting the interview.

LO 2-7   Enhance cultural competence through the use of ethnographic interviewing.

LO 2-8   Stress clients' strengths.

LO 2-9   Apply critical thinking to address challenges in interviewing.

LO 2-10   Develop cross-cultural awareness in interviewing.

LO 2-11   Address spirituality as an aspect of diversity.

LO 2-12   Terminate the interview.

LO 2-13   Employ multiple roles when working with clients.

HOW CAN YOU GET PEOPLE to open up and tell you about their problems?

- Do you have to have an answer to every question?
- What if you do not know how to solve someone's problem?
- How do you work with a client who does not want to be there?
- What if the client will not say anything?
- How do you handle a hostile or angry client?
- What should you do if a client starts to cry?
- How much should you tell a client about your personal life?
- What if a client wants to be friends with you?
- What should you do if you think a client is not listening to what you are saying?

These and many other questions arise in the interpersonal relationship between a social worker and a client and are especially important for beginning practitioners. Being able to work with individuals is the first step in learning how to practice generalist social work. You must understand interpersonal dynamics and have interviewing skills before being able to work with groups of people and larger systems.

Introduction

The Generalist Intervention Model (GIM) follows a seven-step planned change process consisting of engagement, assessment, planning, implementation, evaluation, termination, and follow-up. Chapters 5 through 8 elaborate on what occurs during each of these phases. The worker needs to direct and control each worker–client interview during all of these stages. Interviewing provides a major means for gathering data during the assessment phase of a problem situation. There are a number of specific interviewing techniques that help workers to gather data, and this chapter will focus largely on those basic skills.

Sometimes, interviewing is broken up into beginning, middle, and ending phases. Most of the techniques described here are useful at almost any point of the interviewing process. However, some—such as how to introduce yourself to a client—are more oriented toward a particular interviewing phase.

This chapter focuses on the techniques necessary for communicating with individuals and addresses numerous questions like those listed at the chapter's beginning. Later chapters discuss how these techniques are useful throughout the intervention process. Also, keep in mind that these techniques form the foundation for learning and applying mezzo skills (working with groups) and macro skills (working with agencies, organizations, communities, and social systems). Learning how to communicate well and to work with individuals is a necessity for any type of social work practice.

Skills for Working with Individuals and the Generalist Intervention Model (GIM)

Skills for working with individuals (micro-practice skills) involve relationship building, the effective use of verbal and nonverbal behavior, and proficiency in interviewing. They focus on your ability to relate to other individuals and communicate effectively. The planned change process entails ongoing interaction and communication with many individuals in your work environment, including clients, colleagues, administrators, and other decision makers.

We have established that skills for working with individuals form the basis for working with groups and with larger systems such as organizations and communities. You must effectively interact with individuals in the context of groups, organizations, and communities in order to get anything done. Skills for working with individuals are used throughout each phase of the planned change process—engagement, assessment, planning, implementation, evaluation, and follow-up—whether you are pursuing micro, mezzo, or macro change.

Engagement requires establishing an initial relationship with an individual or each person in a group of individuals, regardless of what type of change you seek. During this phase, you use verbal and nonverbal skills to establish rapport and introduce your purpose and role. For example, a practitioner working at Planned Parenthood must establish an initial rapport with a client who may be feeling embarrassed or frightened. The client may be seeking some form of contraception or be distressed by an unwanted pregnancy. The worker must use micro skills to make the client feel comfortable enough to communicate her concerns and to begin looking at alternatives. The initial use of effective micro skills is critical if the worker eventually decides to focus on the client's individual plans (micro intervention), suggest an educational group (mezzo intervention), or pursue a statewide policy change concerning contraception or abortion on the behalf of this client and others like her (macro intervention). The worker who eventually pursues mezzo or macro intervention must use micro skills to establish rapport with individuals in those settings in order to achieve mezzo or macro change.

Assessment, likewise, involves interaction and communication with other individuals regardless of whether the planned change process involves individuals, families, groups, organizations, or communities. Through it, you strive to solicit enough information about the issue or problem involved to initiate positive change. You must talk with and relate to other individuals effectively in order to accomplish this task. For example, consider a social worker at the AIDS Support Network (an agency aimed at providing a range of services to people who are HIV-positive). The worker must gain information about each client's health, social, financial, and emotional conditions before the worker and client can plan together what to do. Assessment proceeds after the initial engagement has been successfully completed. The client must feel comfortable and safe with the worker. Micro skills are necessary whether pursuing individual counseling with the client (micro intervention), working with the client's family or involving the client in a support network (mezzo intervention), or advocating for greater resources on behalf of this client and others in similar situations (macro intervention). Change at any level concerns interacting and communicating effectively with the individuals involved.

Similarly, the remaining steps in the GIM—planning, implementation, evaluation, termination, and follow-up—all require interaction and communication with other individuals. *Planning* involves working integrally with the client to establish a plan of action. *Implementation* entails working with targeted others in the environment to achieve the plan's goals. For example, a plan might entail seeking financial support for an older adult with failing health. This plan necessitates working directly with other individuals who control the distribution of such support.

Evaluation concerns determining whether or not a plan has been effective. This often entails using micro skills to communicate with the client and others involved in the change process to procure information and validate accomplishments. *Termination* involves using micro skills to bring the worker–client relationship and change process to an end in a considerate, planned, positive manner. Finally, practitioners use micro skills during *follow-up* to solicit information regarding how planned change goals have been maintained.

LO 2-1 Use Interviewing Skills to Engage, Assess, Intervene, and Evaluate with Individuals in the Planned Change Process

 Communication with clients is obviously necessary to work with and help them. Interviewing provides a primary means for such communication and is a core skill in micro practice. Practitioners can use interviewing skills "to engage, assess, intervene, and evaluate with individuals" in the planned change process (Council on Social Work Education [CSWE] 2008, Educational Policy 2.1.10). "The simplest definition of an interview is 'a person-to-person interaction that has a definite and deliberate purpose that is recognized and accepted by both participants.' An interview resembles a conversation in many significant ways. Both involve verbal and nonverbal communication between people, during which they exchange ideas, attitudes, and feelings. Both are usually face-to-face interactions" (Kadushin & Kadushin, 2013, p. 6).

In generalist social work practice, interviews are more than pleasant conversations because they have a specified purpose. This purpose is to "exchange information systematically, with a view toward illuminating and solving problems, promoting growth, or planning strategies or actions aimed at improving the quality of life for people" (Hepworth, Rooney, Rooney, & Strom-Gottfried, 2013, p. 47). For example, you usually meet with a client to find a solution to some problem or to pursue some necessary change.

In addition to a designated purpose, an interview has two other characteristics, a prescribed structure in terms of purpose and roles, and a process. The structure involves meeting for a predetermined purpose. This also entails time constraints, appointment times, and location (often the worker's office). Roles concern how you assume the position of worker and professional helper, whereas the client, who is the focus of attention, requires assistance. The interview's process in terms of what transpires resembles the GIM's steps of engagement, assessment, planning, implementation, and termination. Later, we will address some techniques commonly used in the beginning, middle, and closing portions of the interview.

A place to start when learning how to interview and work with individual clients is to examine the skills of how to establish a good worker–client relationship. These skills form the foundation for engagement, the

GIM's first step. Because they are important throughout the intervention process and are among the bases for micro practice, we will elaborate upon them here.

Beginning the Worker–Client Relationship

EP 2.1.1b

When learning how to work with clients, examining how to establish a good worker–client relationship is useful. Some people are naturally popular, others are not. There are some basic behaviors and characteristics that make a person more appealing to others. Similarly, in worker–client situations, certain behavior and personal qualities tend to nurture interpersonal relationships. When manifested by the worker, these traits and deeds tend to put clients at ease and make them feel important and cared about. This chapter begins by discussing how verbal and nonverbal behavior can enhance worker–client relationships.

LO 2-2 Demonstrate Effective Nonverbal Behavior When Working with Clients

At the most basic level, human interaction and communication involve both verbal and nonverbal behavior. *Verbal behavior* is what is being said. Various techniques for enhancing verbal behavior are addressed in a subsequent section of this chapter. *Nonverbal behavior* is communication in ways other than spoken words. People communicate by facial expressions, hand movements, eye contact, the manner in which they sit, and how close they stand to you. Any aspect of a person's presence that conveys ideas or information without being spoken is nonverbal communication.

An example is a student who is 10 minutes late for a statistics exam (she was up until 4:30 that morning "cramming" in a panic, and for whatever reason, her alarm did not go off). She runs into her academic advisor, a talkative individual who starts to chat about next semester's registration. The student does not want to offend the advisor by dashing off. However, she needs to get to her exam right away. She fidgets, looks repeatedly at her watch, frequently glances in the direction she needs to go, and starts edging away step by step. Without actually using words, she is trying to nonverbally tell the advisor, "I don't want to be rude, and I appreciate the time you're taking to talk to me, but please stop talking and let me sprint to my stats exam." The advisor finally gets the nonverbal hint

and asks, "Oh, are you in a hurry?" It probably would have been much more efficient, thoughtful, and straightforward for the student to have verbally stated those words to the advisor in the first place. Assertiveness is addressed in Chapter 13.

There are many aspects of nonverbal behavior. Here we will focus on four of them: eye contact, attentive listening, facial expressions, and body positioning.

EYE CONTACT

Eye contact is important when establishing rapport with clients. However, the appropriate type and amount of eye contact varies depending upon the client's cultural background. From the European–North American middle-class perspective, holding your head straight and facing clients during interviews conveys to them that they are important and that you are listening to what they are saying.

You must know people who have difficulty looking you in the eye. This inability to make eye contact often conveys that they are afraid or insecure. It might also imply disinterest or dishonesty. On the other hand, maintaining continuous eye contact can make a person uncomfortable. Additionally, it can also be tedious, as if you were in a who-can-hold-out-and-not-blink-the-longest contest. Eye contact is a complex nonverbal behavior. Moderate eye contact, somewhere between no eye contact and constant eye contact, seems most likely to put people at ease (Cormier & Hackney, 2008). Thus, direct eye contact with an occasional glance away at your hands, a bookcase, or simply into nowhere is probably most appropriate in many circumstances.

Remember that cultural differences in eye contact expectations are important. For example, Chinese people speaking together "use much less eye contact, especially when it is with a person of the opposite sex"; thus, a male interviewer's direct eye contact with a Chinese woman might be "considered rude or seductive in Chinese culture" (Ivey, Ivey, & Zalaquett, 2012, p. 66; Zhang, 2012, p. 66). Similarly, Ivey and his colleagues (2012) reflect:

Among some Native American and Latin groups, eye contact by the young is a sign of disrespect. Imagine the problems this may cause when the [interviewer] . . . contradicts basic cultural values by saying, "Look at me!" Some traditional Native American, Inuit, or Aboriginal Australian groups generally avoid eye contact, especially when talking about serious subjects. Cultural differences in eye contact abound, but we must recall that individual differences are often even greater and avoid stereotyping any client or group with so-called "normative" patterns. (p. 63)

Appreciating and responding to various aspects of cultural diversity is a continuous learning process. Chapter 12 addresses such issues more thoroughly.

ATTENTIVE LISTENING

Of course, you are supposed to listen to what a client is saying, right? In reality, listening is not so simple. First, the distinction must be made between *hearing* and *listening*. Listening implies more than just audio reception of words that are said. It focuses on comprehending the meaning of what is said.

There are a number of barriers to attentive listening. They involve three aspects of communication. First, the person sends a message with some *intent* of what needs

to be conveyed (what the sender hopes the receiver will hear). Second, the receiver of the message tries to decipher the meaning of what has been said. Thus, the message has some *impact* on the receiver (which refers to what the receiver thinks the sender said). What the receiver actually hears may or may not be what the sender intended the receiver to hear. Third, there may be environmental barriers impeding communication of the message (see Figure 2.1).

The first cluster of communication barriers mentioned involves the sender, in this case the client. The client might not be using words, phrases, or concepts that are clear to you. The client may say something vague. The sender's *intent* may not be the same as the *impact* on the receiver.

Perhaps the client may view things from a different cultural perspective where the same words have

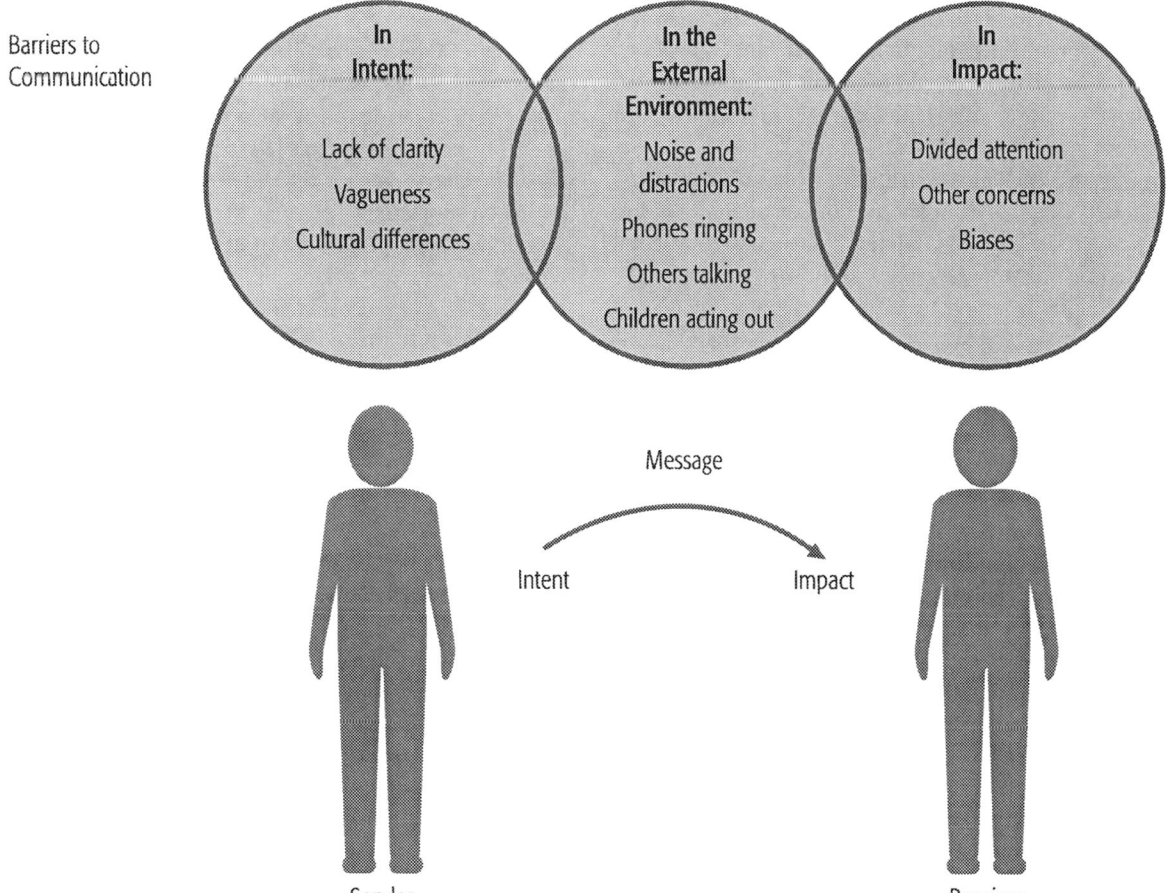

Barriers to Communication

In Intent:
Lack of clarity
Vagueness
Cultural differences

In the External Environment:
Noise and distractions
Phones ringing
Others talking
Children acting out

In Impact:
Divided attention
Other concerns
Biases

Message

Intent   Impact

Sender   Receiver

© Cengage Learning

FIGURE 2.1 Barriers to Attentive Listening
Source: The concepts of *intent* and *impact* were taken from the film *Behavioral Interviewing with Couples* available from Research Press, Dept. 98, P.O. Box 7886, Champaign, IL 61826.

different meanings. For instance, a Chicano father says, "The problem is that my daughter disobeys me and goes out with boys." A white middle-class social worker may interpret this statement to mean that the daughter is seeing a number of men. Sexual activity and related issues such as pregnancy and sexually transmitted infections may enter the worker's thinking. Finally, the possibility that the father is overly domineering may be a concern. However, what the Chicano father really means is that his daughter thinks she is in love with a boy and is sneaking out to see him. In their traditional Chicano culture, such behavior is inappropriate if a couple is not engaged to be married, and in any case, a chaperone is still needed to supervise them.

The second type of communication barrier involves the receiver, in this case, the social worker. The worker's attention may be divided between what the client is saying and what the worker is going to say next. Likewise, the worker may be focusing on what direction the interview should go in the future. Paying full attention to the client and listening to all that is said is not easy.

The third cluster of communication barriers to attentive listening involves the external environment and potential noise and distractions. For example, a social worker visits a client's home. The television is blaring, and four young children are running through the house with toy rifles playing "GI Joe." Such environmental distractions make organizing one's own thoughts difficult, let alone listening to what the client is saying.

In summary, listening is not easy. It demands concentration, perceptiveness, and the use of a range of interviewing skills. A number of these skills are described in this chapter.

FACIAL EXPRESSIONS

Facial movements and expressions provide an excellent means of communicating. A furrowed brow may convey intense concentration, uncertainty, or concern. A casual smile may indicate pleasure and even warmth. Raising the eyebrows can indicate surprise or sudden interest. In contrast, a blank expression conveys little or no information about what you mean or think.

Facial expressions can be used to reinforce what is said verbally and corroborate the fact that you mean what you say. However, two aspects about using facial expressions should be noted. First, being aware of your facial responses so that you know how you are communicating is important. Second, make certain that your facial expressions correspond with both your other types of nonverbal behavior and with what you are saying verbally. Giving a client a mixed message by

saying one thing, while *looking like you mean* another, is not helpful. Such action can convey doubt that you are being truthful. For instance, if you say, "Oh, I'm so glad to see you," with an ugly scowl on your face, you communicate inconsistent messages.

BODY POSITIONING

Body movement and positioning also provide information to others. The tense/relaxed and formal/informal continuums are especially important.

Body tension involves how rigid or tense our muscles appear as we position ourselves and most frequently coincides with emotional tension. If we look uptight, we probably feel uptight inside. Such tension can be demonstrated by sitting perfectly straight and allowing minimal movement of extremities. Tension is also apparent when a person makes quick, nervous gestures, such as continuously tapping a foot or finger or jingling loose change in his or her pocket.

The opposite of a tense stance is a relaxed one. Relaxation can be portrayed by slow, loose movements and a decidedly casual, informal presentation of self. The most extreme form of a relaxed stance would probably be to lie down. The term *laid back* is often used to refer to such a relaxed approach.

When working with a client, being aware of how you nonverbally present yourself is important. Extreme tension may convey lack of confidence or excessive nervousness. It may put distance between you and your clients and make feeling comfortable and trusting you difficult for them.

On the other hand, an extremely relaxed stance may convey to a client that you do not care much about what happens. It may also damage your professional credibility.

Ideally, presenting yourself somewhere in between the two extremes is best. To some extent, body positioning is a matter of personal style. You need to appear genuine, that is, that you are reflecting aspects of your true individual personality to the client. Being aware of your body positioning and how it affects your interaction with clients is crucial.

The second continuum, formal/informal, relates to some extent with the tense/relaxed continuum. Being more rigid and tense reflects formality, while being relaxed is associated with informality. Formality implies greater structure and less warmth. To the extent that you are more formal with a client, you are less personal. You allow less of your true personality to show through the professional facade. On the other hand, complete informality or lack of structure impedes getting anything done. A worker–client relationship is not a friendship; it exists for the purpose of solving a problem or attaining a goal. This fact implies some degree of formality and structure.

As with the tense/relaxed continuum, the extent of formality often relates to personal style. The best approach lies somewhere between being extremely formal and extremely informal. The important thing is to be aware of how you are presenting yourself, how you feel most comfortable, and how the client reacts and relates to you.

A student once asked an instructor a question before undertaking her very first interview (which happened to be a relatively simple, very structured social history). She wondered if, while doing the interview, she should act like a "social worker" or act like herself. The instructor thought to herself, "Hmmmm, what does a social worker act like?" The answer is to use the techniques and planned change focus inherent in generalist social work practice (which the rest of this book is all about), yet to do so as yourself. Ask questions in the manner and tone of voice with which you feel comfortable. Smile when you feel like smiling. Use the gestures and personal presentation that reflect your true personality.

Critical Thinking Questions 2.1

- When interacting with others, how do you perceive your own interpersonal style on the tense/relaxed and formal/informal continuums?
- How do you think others perceive you?
- What specific nonverbal behaviors do you tend to display to make this impression?

The use of personal space—the actual space or distance between you and the client—is another part of body positioning. The European–North American expectation for appropriate distancing during interviews is usually a few inches to a few feet beyond arm's length. This allows for comfortable discussion, yet provides an adequate degree of personal space so that a client does not feel threatened.

However, Ivey et al. (2012) reflect on the importance of recognizing different cultural expectations and explain that "the English prefer even greater distances. Many Latin people often prefer half that distance, and those from the Middle East may talk practically eyeball to eyeball" (p. 65). Therefore, it is important to be sensitive to clients' expectations.

"A natural relaxed body style is likely to be most effective, but be prepared to adapt and be flexible according to the individual client" (Ivey et al., 2012, p. 65).

Another aspect of body positioning and defining personal space involves where workers sit in their offices in relationship to where clients sit. Typically, an office has a desk, and you as a worker may have some flexibility regarding placement of that desk. Sitting behind the desk and talking to a client seated in front of the desk implies greater formality and difference in status and may be appropriate in some settings where the worker feels such formality is needed. For instance, a probation officer might find it useful to sit behind a desk in a more formal situation where the goal is to monitor a client's adherence to prescribed probationary conditions. However, in many other situations, having the desk's front side abutting the wall, sitting behind the desk, and being able to turn your chair in order to talk to a client can convey greater informality and warmth.

LO 2-3 Use Empathy and Other Interpersonal Skills When Working with Clients

In generalist social work practice, a variety of relationship-enhancing characteristics can be defined and learned. Demonstrating these characteristics involves employing the appropriate corresponding verbal and nonverbal behavior. Three specific relationship-enhancing traits are warmth, empathy, and genuineness. The social work literature suggests that these attributes are among the most basic and important in developing relationships with clients (Chang, Scott, & Decker, 2013; Collins, Jordan, & Coleman, 2013; Sheafor & Horejsi, 2012).

WARMTH

Displaying *warmth* involves conveying a feeling of interest, concern, well-being, and affection to another individual. Warmth is a vehicle for acceptance. "Respectful and valuing statements about the client are accompanied by a smile, appropriate touching, pleasant surprise, and enthusiasm for the client's rendition of personal experience" (Keefe & Maypole, 1983, p. 62). Showing acceptance of clients, warts and all, communicates warmth. Conveying warmth also involves enhancing the positive feelings of one person toward another. It promotes a sense of comfort and well-being in that other person.

Warmth can be communicated to a client both verbally and nonverbally. Such behaviors can be defined, practiced, and learned. The following are examples of verbally communicating warmth:

- "Hello. It's good to meet you."
- "I'm glad we have the chance to talk about this."
- "It's pleasant talking with you."
- "It's good to see you again."
- "Please sit down. Can I get you a cup of coffee?"

These are just a few of the many statements you can make to show that you respect the client and are glad he or she is there. These statements help to convey a sense of concern for the client and for the client's well-being. Similarly, there are many ways to communicate warmth to a client nonverbally. We have discussed how eye contact, attentive listening, body positioning, and tonal quality can be all used to a worker's advantage.

EMPATHY

Empathy is a second basic characteristic that has been found to enhance a worker–client relationship. *Empathy* is crucial for the helping process to be effective. Empathy involves not only *being in tune* with how a client feels, but also *conveying to that client* that you understand how he or she feels. It does not necessarily mean you think the client's feelings are positive or negative, nor does it mean that you are having the same feelings yourself. Empathy is purely acknowledgment that you understand the client's situation. For instance, consider the case of Ms. Wilson, who has been referred to a protective services worker for abusing her 2-year-old son, Tyrone. A neighbor reported Ms. Wilson after seeing odd, straplike, black bruises on her child's arms 2 weeks in a row. During the interview, Ms. Wilson says, "Tyrone never does what he's told. He runs away from me when I call him. He gets into all of my things and breaks them. Sometimes I get so angry I could kill him. I tie him up to the bed with old ties just so I can get some peace."

The worker empathetically responds, "Two-year-olds can be very difficult and trying. I understand how sometimes you feel like you're at your wits' end." This response conveys that the worker *understands* the situation and Ms. Wilson's feelings. However, it does not *condone* Ms. Wilson's behavior. Empathy can be used to demonstrate to clients that you are on their side. Clients who feel that you have listened to how they feel and that you are not against them are much more likely to be willing to work with you toward finding solutions to problems. Empathy communicates to a client that you are there to help solve the problem (see Highlight 2.1).

In this example, what do you think Ms. Wilson's reaction would have been if the worker had responded with her statement by saying, "How can you hurt your own child like that? What kind of mother are you? Don't you have any feelings?" The latter statement criticizes Ms. Wilson and communicates to her that the worker does not understand her feelings and her situation. It totally lacks empathy. Ms. Wilson could easily view the worker as "the enemy," someone to fight with or avoid.

Establishing initial rapport is only the first among a number of reasons for employing empathy, as there are a number of other uses. Empathy enables the worker to keep up with the client and the client's problems and concerns throughout the worker–client relationship.

Empathizing with positive emotions can also be helpful. For example, if a client appears exceptionally happy one day, an empathetic response may get at the reason. Maybe some problem has already been solved. Perhaps, a new client strength can be identified that can be used in the change process. Acknowledging positives may help in the maintenance of the worker–client relationship.

Additionally, empathic responding may elicit feelings and discussion about previously unmentioned issues. Empathy provides the worker with a means of getting at feelings that are not expressed verbally. For example, a worker can say, "When you frown like that, it looks like you're very worried about something." The client now has an opening to talk about what is on his or her mind, even though it has not been expressed verbally.

Yet another use of empathy involves making confrontations less hostile. For example, a client enters a worker's office and demands his financial assistance check right now instead of five days later when he is supposed to receive it. He is breathing fast, his face is red, and his vocal tone is loud, gruff, and hostile. The worker chooses not to respond initially to what the client said. The worker does *not* say something like, "You're here 5 days early, and you can't have the check until it's ready." Instead, the worker can make an empathic response by saying, "Mr. Carlton, you sound so angry. It seems like you desperately need the money right now." This latter response is much more likely to help Mr. Carlton calm down and talk about his problem. The worker may or may not be able to get Mr. Carlton his check. However, an empathic response will more likely convey to Mr. Carlton that the worker is on his side. He should be much more likely to settle

HIGHLIGHT 2.1

Practicing Empathic Responses

There are a number of leading phrases that you can use to begin an empathic statement. Here are some examples:

- "My impression is that. . . ."
- "It appears to me that. . . ."
- "Is what you're saying that. . . ?"
- "Do I understand you correctly that. . . ?"
- "I'm hearing you say that. . . ."
- "Do you mean that. . . ?"
- "Do you feel that. . . ?"
- "I feel that you. . . ."
- "I'm getting the message that. . . ."
- "You seem to be. . . ."
- "When you say that, I think you. . . ."
- "You look like you. . . ."
- "You sound so _____. Can we talk more about it?"
- "You look _____. What's been happening?"

The following are several vignettes about client situations. Formulate and practice your own empathic responses for each one. The first vignette provides an example.

Example

You are a social worker in foster care. You are visiting one of the foster homes on your caseload. The purpose is to talk with both foster parents and determine how things are going with their 9-year-old foster child, Katie. The couple has three children of their own, all of whom are in college. In the past, the foster couple has expressed interest in adopting Katie. When you arrive at the home, only the mother is present. After polite greetings, the foster mother says, "Katie certainly doesn't like to read very much like the rest of us. I think she gets bored when she's not doing something active. Many times I just don't know what to do with her."

Possible empathic responses include:

- "You sound like you're having some problems with Katie that you didn't expect. Can we talk more about it?"
- "It seems like you're somewhat frustrated with Katie these days."
- "I feel like you're telling me that Katie's more difficult to take care of than perhaps you thought."

Vignette 1

You are a social worker in a health care facility for older adults. Helen is a resident who has been living there for approximately 2 years. All rooms have two residents, which has consistently been a problem for Helen. Her current roommate is Emma, a quiet woman who rarely interacts with any of the other residents. Helen is very possessive of her things and wants no one else to touch them. Additionally, Helen does not like to share the bathroom, which is also used by the two residents in the next room. Helen, a strong, outspoken woman even at age 97, approaches you and says, "Emma keeps using my bathroom and moves my things around. I want her out of there right now! You do something immediately!"

You empathetically respond . . . (Remember that you *do not* have to solve the problem right now. You only need to let your client know that you understand how she feels.)

Vignette 2

You are a school social worker. Romy, age 16, was in the men's bathroom when several other students were caught using drugs. Romy insists the others are guilty and he is innocent; he just happened to be in the restroom at the same time. The teacher who found the boys could not distinguish who was guilty and who was not, so he put them all on "penalty," which means detention after school and exclusion from any sports for 2 weeks. Romy is furious. He comes up to you and says, "It's not fair! It's just not fair! I'm innocent, and I'm getting punished anyway. I should've used the drugs if I'm going to get the punishment."

You empathetically respond. . . .

Vignette 3

You are a social worker at a diagnostic and treatment center for children with multiple disabilities. Your primary function is to work with parents, helping them to cope with the pressures and connecting them with resources they need. A mother of a 5-year-old boy with severe cerebral palsy talks with you on a weekly basis. Her son has a severe disability and has very little muscular control. He cannot walk by himself or talk, although the other therapists feel he has normal intelligence. The boy's father belongs to a religion that

(continued)

HIGHLIGHT 2.1 *(continued)*

denies the existence of disease and physical impairment. Thus, he denies that his son has a disability. The burden of caregiving rests solely upon the mother. She loves her son dearly and is generally enthusiastic in doing what she can for him. She enters your office one day, says hello, and sits down. She immediately puts her hand to her eyes and breaks down in tears.

   You empathetically respond. . . .

Vignette 4

You are an intake worker at a social services agency in a rural area. Your job is to take telephone calls, assess problems, and refer clients to the most appropriate services. You receive a call from an adult male. After identifying who you are and asking what you can do for the caller, he responds, "I just lost my job. Nothing's going right. I feel like I want to kill myself."

   You empathetically respond. . . .

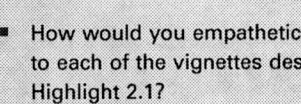

Critical Thinking Question 2.2

- How would you empathetically respond to each of the vignettes described in Highlight 2.1?

---

down, talk about what is wrong, and pursue possible alternative courses of action.

Nonverbal communication can also be used to enhance empathy. A worker's gestures can mirror how a client feels. For instance, furrowing the brow can convey a serious focusing of attention and reflect a client's grave concern over some issue. Nonverbal communication can also emphasize or enhance verbal empathic responses. For example, consider a client who appears happy. Smiling while making an empathic verbal response indicates more convincingly to the client that you really understand how the client feels.

GENUINENESS

The third quality found to enhance client–worker relationships is *genuineness*, the honest, natural, and open expression of yourself. Genuineness simply means that you continue to be yourself despite the fact that you are working to accomplish goals in your professional role.

Personality refers to the unique configuration of qualities and attributes that make you an individual. Some people have effervescent, outgoing personalities. Others have more subdued, quiet temperaments. Some people relate to others using a sense of humor, while others prefer to relate in a more serious manner. The point is that there is no one type of personality that is best for a professional role. Rather, it is more important that you be yourself and not pretend to be something or someone that you are not. Genuineness conveys a sense of honesty to clients and makes them feel that you are someone they can trust.

Two sisters, Karen, a social worker, and Susie, an occupational therapist, illustrate this point. Both women have worked with similar clients, primarily children and teenagers with behavioral problems. Karen is extremely outgoing, fast-moving, excitable, and tries to make jokes at every opportunity. Others have often labeled her "hyperactive" and frequently complain that she talks too fast. Susie, on the other hand, is calm, evenly paced, and sedate. Her manner has often been labeled "dignified." If Karen accidentally put her hand on a hot burner, she would utter a piercing scream, dash around frantically, and spew forth a stream of colorful obscenities. If Susie placed her hand on the same hot burner, she would calmly lift her hand, look at it, and quietly reflect, "Oh, I burned my hand." (One might note that Susie's husband has commented that if you put Karen and Susie into a giant blender together, mixed them up, and poured them into two equal portions, they would turn into two "normal" human beings.) The point is that despite extreme differences in personality and style, both sisters worked effectively with similar clients. Each was herself, while still performing her professional functions (although Karen did have to carefully monitor her tendency to utter obscenities).

Critical Thinking Questions 2.3

- What do you consider your primary strengths?
- What do you consider your primary weaknesses?
- What adjectives would you use to describe yourself?

LO 2-4 Maintain a Commitment to Client Self-Determination and Empowerment

In addition to demonstrating warmth, empathy, and genuineness, maintaining a commitment to client self-determination enhances a positive relationship between worker and client (Blundo, 2008; Hepworth et al., 2013). The *Code of Ethics* of the National Association of Social Workers (NASW) prescribes that "[s]ocial workers respect and promote the right of clients to self-determination and assist clients in their efforts to identify and clarify their goals" (2008, §1.02). *Self-determination* is each individual's right to make his or her own decisions.

An assumption about self-determination is that social workers have the responsibility to help clients make the best informed choices and decisions possible. This responsibility means practitioners must use their skills to provide clients with necessary information. Workers must also assist clients through the decision-making process by helping them identify the positive and negative consequences of their various alternatives.

For example, Marta is a single mother of three small children who applies for public assistance. In order to receive assistance, she must enter a 6-week work training program after which she must actively seek and gain employment in order to continue receiving assistance. Available programs involve instruction in basic work habits in addition to more specialized training in food preparation, building maintenance, reception, construction, day care, or initial secretarial work. Esi, Marta's assigned social worker, is responsible for providing Marta with enough information about each training program and helping her weigh the pros and cons of each so that Marta can decide which she should pursue.

The situation increases in complexity because Marta needs day care for her children. Marta has no available friends or relatives to help with child care. There are a few publicly subsidized day care programs available, but their reputations are fairly poor. Marta surely could not afford private day care.

Esi must help Marta review her training and day care options to establish a plan that Marta feels is best for her. With Esi's help in exploring and evaluating options, Marta decides to enter the day care training tract. Marta feels that she might then work in the same day care center that cares for her children and, thereby, observe and monitor their treatment.

Maximizing client self-determination to whatever extent possible is a practitioner's responsibility. Sometimes, this responsibility is more difficult, such as when a client is mentally incompetent or intends to hurt him- or herself or others. Chapter 11 discusses such instances and the dilemmas involved more thoroughly.

Self-determination is related to empowerment, a major concept in the definition of generalist practice. We have defined empowerment as the "process of increasing personal, interpersonal, or political power so that individuals can take action to improve their life situations" (Gutierrez, 2001, p. 210). In micro practice and during the interviewing process, clients' involvement, input, and participation are paramount to any intervention's effectiveness.

LO 2-5 Prepare for Action with Individuals and Families by Effectively Starting the Interview

The major goal of any interview is effective communication with the client. Interviews make use of communication with clients to solve problems, encourage positive change, and promote clients' well-being. We have talked about the importance of both verbal and nonverbal behavior in communication. We have also established that warmth, empathy, and genuineness are qualities that help foster professional relationships with clients. Now we will propose some specific suggestions for *starting* and, subsequently, *conducting* the interview. The emphasis is on planning and action. As a practitioner, you are there to help your client clearly identify what the problems are and what can be done to solve them. In this section, we will discuss typical interview settings, how to dress and prepare for interviews, initial introductions, alleviating clients' anxiety, conveying confidence and competence, and stating the interview's purpose. Skills for addressing these issues are absolutely necessary for the engagement step in the GIM's planned change process. Because most are basic micro skills that continue to be essential for later meetings and ongoing involvement, they will be discussed here rather than in Chapter 5 (which discusses engagement and assessment).

THE INTERVIEW SETTING

Interviews may occur in a variety of settings, depending on the field of practice and type of agency. Some interviews take place in hospitals or schools. Many occur in the worker's own office, which gives him or her more control over the environment. We have already discussed positioning the desk and chairs to enhance the client's comfort level. Offering the client a cup of coffee, whether it is accepted or not, is another way of displaying warmth.

Social workers need to be sensitive to the overall impression their office environment itself presents. There are no absolute guidelines for dictating office decor. Putting pictures you like on the walls and trinkets you enjoy on the shelves is appropriate. However, you need to be aware of their potential effect on clients. If you paint your office bright orange and put giant posters of your favorite rock stars or rap artists on the walls, you need to be aware that this environment may be unnerving to some clients. On the other hand, if your clients are primarily adolescents who like some of the same pop icons you do, such posters may provide a means of making a connection with your clients. (The orange walls, however, should probably go.)

Some interviews will take place in the client's own home, which provides the advantage of seeing where and how he or she lives. However, home visits may have the disadvantage of distractions such as children, pets, and television, which can make controlling the interview more difficult. Home visits often provide an excellent means of making assessments and are discussed more extensively in Chapter 5.

HOW TO DRESS FOR THE INTERVIEW AND FOR THE JOB

The main thing to remember when deciding how to dress for interviews with clients and for social work positions in general is that your appearance will make an impression. It is certainly to your advantage to make a good one. A basic rule is to start out dressing "nicely" and "relatively conservatively." What this rule means is up to individual interpretation. Noting how other workers in your agency dress is important because each agency has its own personality. Some agencies are formal, while others are informal.

Paying attention to clients' reactions to how you and the other workers in your agency dress is also important. If you are a woman who works in a corrections institution for delinquent youth, wearing three-inch-high heels and tight short skirts may be inappropriate. You may be expected to participate in recreational activities with clients or, in the event that they lose control, help to physically restrain them. More informal clothing then would be to your great advantage.

If you are a practitioner working in a protective services unit who must go out and interview families in poverty-stricken areas of the city, you may not want to flaunt wealth. In other words, wearing expensive three-piece gray flannel suits may not enhance clients' impressions of you or your relationship with them. On the other hand, it might. Some clients may perceive such efforts of formality as a demonstration of your professionalism and respect for them. Jeans and a T-shirt might have the opposite effect. Thus, carefully watching clients' reactions to you and dressing in a way that enhances your professional performance are important.

THINKING AHEAD ABOUT AN INTERVIEW WITH A CLIENT

Before the interview begins, the worker needs to think ahead about at least three variables. First, is there any specific information that will be needed, such as addresses and phone numbers of specific resources? Can you anticipate any questions the client might ask for which you should be prepared?

Second, the interview's time frame should be clearly specified. The time frame means when the interview is scheduled to begin and when it needs to end. The meeting should start punctually. Making the client wait beyond the scheduled starting time may imply that the client's time is not important and that you have better things to do. A timely start conveys common courtesy and respect for the client. In the event that you are late for whatever reason, an appropriate apology should be made.

The interview should have a timely ending, and the next client should not be kept waiting. One means of alerting the client that the interview is coming to a close is to make a statement such as, "Well, we only have another 10 minutes left, so perhaps we should talk a bit about our next meeting."

The third variable that needs consideration prior to the interview is the interview's purpose. Preparing for an interview includes clarifying the interview's intent, breaking down the intent into more precise topics that should be addressed, specifying questions to ask, and planning how the interview should progress from beginning to end. In other words, the worker should have some general idea about what he or she wants to accomplish by the end of the interview.

INITIAL INTRODUCTIONS

Initial introductions resemble those in other formal and informal interactions. Names are exchanged with typical pleasantries such as "It's nice to meet you."

Using surnames is usually in your best interest, since they imply greater respect. Handshakes are also often appropriate. However, you need to be aware of the client's levels of comfort and anxiety. If a client cringes as you extend your hand, nonchalantly take it back and continue with a verbal interchange.

Sometimes, ethnic or cultural differences require you to behave differently than you normally would. For instance, the Hmong, who migrated to the United States during the past few decades from Southeast Asia, initially abhor the type of physical contact involved in shaking hands. Immigrants who have been here for a while, on the other hand, have quickly adopted this traditional greeting. Working with clients from a variety of cultural backgrounds will be described more thoroughly in Chapter 12.

When beginning the interview, initiating brief, innocuous exchanges about some bland topic such as the weather may also be appropriate. For example, "I'm glad you made it here despite the heat (or the blizzard)." A short interchange can be used to soften the formal edge of the interview and make the situation warmer and more human.

ALLEVIATING THE CLIENT'S ANXIETY

"Starting where the client is" is a phrase social workers often use to describe how they begin an interview. The first important aspect of this concept is to think about how the client must feel coming into the initial interview with you. Put yourself into the client's shoes. You, too, would probably be anxious about approaching an unknown situation and would not feel in control. The client may wonder, "Will this 'professional' interrogate me under bright lights as if I were a foreign spy? Will this social worker criticize all the things I'm doing wrong? Will I be attacked for something I did or didn't do?"

Many clients will approach the interview with anxiety; others, however, may arrive with resentment or hostility. For instance, if clients are forced to see you for some reason, having negative feelings is logical for them. The important thing is for you to pay close attention to their verbal and nonverbal behavior. Empathy is essential to communicate and begin the problem-solving process. Specific suggestions for how to deal with difficult situations such as hostility are discussed later in this chapter.

Other conditions that may be affecting a client's perspective and attitude should also be considered. Is your office hard to find? Did the client have to wait a long time before the appointment? Was there a bad experience with your agency in the past? Did the client have a flat tire on the way in to see you? Being aware that these and many other variables may be affecting a client's feelings is important (see Highlight 2.2).

HIGHLIGHT 2.2

Using Direct and Indirect Questions

EP 2.1.3c

Questions can also be categorized as being either *direct* or *indirect*. Direct questions are those that clearly ask for information and usually end in a question mark. Examples are:

- "Did your mother ask you to see me?"
- "What do you see as the major problem areas?"
- "How did you arrange for your transportation here?"
- "When do you intend on completing that plan?"

Indirect questions ask questions without seeming to. They provide an excellent vehicle for gathering information. Examples include:

- "Many mothers would find having three children under the age of 5 difficult."

- "You seem like you're under a great deal of stress today."
- "Taking care of your brother after school each day must make it hard to find time to play with your friends."
- "I wonder how you manage to care for little Johnny and your aging mother at the same time."

In each of these indirect questions, the interviewer is asking the client to respond, but is not stating a direct question. Notice there are no question marks ending the sentences. This technique can be helpful in gathering information from clients without asking a tediously long list of direct questions.

PORTRAYING CONFIDENCE AND COMPETENCE

A common situation many new workers, especially those who are in their early and middle 20s, encounter is a client questioning their level of competence. A client might think, say, or both, "How can somebody your age possibly help me? I'm old enough to be your parent." In some cases, the last part of the statement is true.

A similar situation arises when a worker without children must work with clients who have problems with their children. Such clients may ask how a childless individual can possibly understand and help them.

There are at least five things a worker can do about these types of situations. First, when a client says something that is true (even if you do not want to make an issue of it), acknowledge that it is the truth. You can do this at least silently to yourself or make a statement to that effect. For example, you might say, "Yes, I am younger than you are," or, "No, I don't have any children." This statement gets the cards out on the table, so to speak, and prevents you from seeming defensive.

A second approach to addressing client concerns is to respond to the client with a question. You might say, "Is it important to you that I have children?" or, "Does my being younger pose a problem for you?" Again, this tactic gets the issue out on the table without making the worker appear defensive.

The third thing a worker can do is to follow up the true statement with another statement of truth. You might share examples of your competence. For instance, you could say, "I have a degree in social work and have been trained to help solve problems just like yours. Why don't you give me a chance to show you what I can do for you?"

The fourth thing a worker can do in a situation where his or her competence is questioned is simply to rely on the relationship-building skills that we have already discussed. Keep warmth, empathy, and genuineness in mind. Be assertive verbally and nonverbally. Speak calmly and look the client in the eye. As the client gains trust in you as a professional, the question of competence will cease to become an issue. The best way to convince a client of your competence is by your own behavior. When you actually help a client, that client will probably perceive you as competent.

The fifth thing you can do to demonstrate competence is to be knowledgeable. Planning the interview conveys to the client a sense of organization and purpose. Knowing your role and where to find information the client needs also reflects your competence.

BEGINNING STATEMENT OF PURPOSE AND ROLE

Not only must the purpose of the interview be clearly identified in the worker's own mind, it must also be clearly understood by the client. There are four major tasks that should be undertaken at the beginning of the interviewing process. The first, as we have already indicated, is to clearly explain the interview's purpose to the client. An example of this purpose involves a worker in an alcohol and other drug abuse (AODA) assessment unit in a large urban social services agency. The worker meets with her 27-year-old male client for the first time. After the initial introductions, the worker says, "I'm happy to talk with you today. I understand that you voluntarily came in for some help with controlling your drinking. What we need to do today is to find out more about you and your drinking, so I'd like to ask you a few questions."

In this example, the worker expressed warmth and concern. Without blaming the client, she indicated the need to work together. Finally, she explained in straightforward terms that her goal was to assess his drinking problem.

The second major task in an interview's beginning phase is to explain the worker's role to the client. We have discussed how clients often have significant apprehension about interviews for a variety of reasons. Explaining your role does not mean reciting a job description. However, it does mean describing in general terms to the client what you intend to do and talk about.

For example, let us return to our original example of the AODA assessment worker with the 27-year-old client. After clarifying the interview's purpose, the worker might say, "I will be asking a number of questions that are typically asked when people want to work on controlling their drinking. Some of the questions may seem odd to you. They ask about a lot of things from work to friends to family to personal interests to the drinking itself. These questions help me get to know you better and give me a better idea about where we can start in helping to change."

The third important task in the initial interviewing process concerns encouraging the client to share thoughts and feelings about the interview and what's being said. This encouragement means that the worker should ask how the client feels about the identified purpose. Actively involving the client from the beginning of the change process is necessary. Back to our AODA example, the worker might say, "I feel like I've done most of the talking so far. How do you feel about what I've said? Do the plans so far sound good to you? Is there something you'd like to change or add?"

The final task in the initial interview involves making a statement about the usefulness of the intervention process. In other words, the worker can convey to the client that there is hope to begin to solve his or her problems. For example, the worker might say, "When you talk about your drinking, I hear you say how worried you are. I think it is a serious problem. However, I give you lots of credit for having the courage to come in and talk to me about it. There are a number of excellent techniques we can use and alternatives we can look at. It's hard, but I think we have a good chance at helping you over the next few weeks and months."

These statements reflect only one combination of words and ideas for accomplishing the four tasks. In other words, there are many ways to define the purpose of the interview or to ask for feedback. The interview may indeed have any number of purposes. The intent may be to help a 15-year-old decide whether to have an abortion or to assist an 85-year-old in deciding where it would be best for her to live. The words used to define the purpose vary as dramatically as the actual intent of the interview. The important thing is for the client to understand why he or she is there and what you intend to do.

The discussion of the four tasks previously mentioned is oriented primarily toward one of the initial interviews with clients. Subsequent interviews with clients will not require such extensive, detailed explanations of purpose and other facets of the interviewing process. Clients already will have learned about your general intent. However, these tasks are good to keep in mind even with clients whom you have seen a number of times. In review, the four tasks include defining the interview's specific purpose, explaining what you will be doing, asking clients for feedback, and expressing hope that things can improve. All four help provide direction to interviews and enhance your positive interaction with clients.

LO 2-6 Demonstrate Effective Oral Communication While Conducting the Interview

EP 2.1.1d
EP 2.1.3c

Regardless of the specific purpose of the interview, its major function is communication with the client. Communication, of course, involves exchange of information. There is a variety of specific skills and techniques that can facilitate the exchange of information. Using these techniques

helps to maximize the chances that your *intent* matches your *impact* on the client and vice versa.

There is also a vast array of communication techniques for workers to use, such as ways of initiating communication with a client or responding to something a client says. We will define and explain a number of specific methods of responding to clients that place the focus of attention on the client. Next, we will examine a number of issues and difficulties frequently encountered in interviews.

Remember that the pursuit of cultural competency is an ongoing process for practitioners. Becoming familiar with client's cultural values, expectations, and issues should always be on a worker's mind. Highlight 2.3 introduces the concept of enhancing cultural competency through ethnographic interviewing.

VERBAL RESPONSES TO THE CLIENT

Some techniques that enhance worker–client communication are used to solicit information, while others encourage the client to enhance the worker–client relationship. The approaches include simple encouragement, rephrasing, reflective responding, clarification, interpretation, providing information, emphasizing clients' strengths, self-disclosure, summarization, and eliciting information.

Simple Encouragement

Encouragement is the act of prompting someone to continue, often by raising that person's level of self-confidence. Many times, a simple one-word response or nonverbal head nod, while maintaining eye contact, is enough to encourage a client to continue (Evans, Hearn, Uhlemann, & Ivey, 2008; Ivey et al., 2012). Vocal clues such as "mm-mm," "uh-huh," "I see," or "please go on" demonstrate to clients that you are listening to what they are saying. Such responses may also be used to keep a client on the right track in conjunction with the purpose of the interview.

Rephrasing

Rephrasing is stating what the client is saying, but using different words. Rephrasing has a variety of purposes. It can communicate to clients that you are really trying to listen to what they are saying. On the other hand, if you had not heard the client's real intent, it can give the client the opportunity to clarify his or her meaning. It can also help the client take time out and reflect on what was just said.

HIGHLIGHT 2.3

LO 2-7 Enhance Cultural Competence Through the Use of Ethnographic Interviewing

An ongoing quest of social work practitioners is to continue learning about and appreciating the infinite facets of human diversity. A critical part of "cultural awareness...centers on ethnographic interviewing" (Lum, 2007, p. 154). *Ethnographic interviewing* focuses on learning about a client's cultural world, including values, behavioral expectations, and language (Padgett, 2008; Rubin & Babbie, 2013; Thornton & Garrett, 1995). This is done by using conversation to gather "information in a nonthreatening manner" and working with the client to develop intervention plans that comply with both the client's right to self-determination and cultural perspective (Leigh, 1998, p. 12). Leigh (1998) explains:

> The ethnographic model...[emphasizes] that the expert on construction of meanings of any culture is a member of the culture, not the social worker.... Ethnographic interviewing is a method of cultural discovery that requires the social worker to move beyond professionally bound methods of conversation with those who request assistance in solving personal or social-generated problems. The person being interviewed becomes the social worker's cultural guide, and this notion has an impact on the professional relationship. In some aspects the person is a teacher guiding the social worker as a student through the intricacies of the contrasting culture. The social worker has to become a skilled listener. (p. 12)

Green (1999) emphasizes the special orientation of ethnographic interviewing:

> "Empathy" and "openness" as primary techniques are inadequate because they presume an ability to enter into the sensibilities of another without first learning the context from which those sensibilities arise. The real skill in cross-cultural social work, as in any kind of cross-cultural learning, is to comprehend what the client knows and how that information is used in the mundane traffic of daily activities. Stylized "caring responses" are not an effective way of doing that. Rather, it is what our clients tell us about themselves, and how they do the telling, that is crucial to genuine understanding and insight. (p. 129)

Three concepts relate to preparing for the ethnographic interview and initiating the engagement and assessment processes. Used sequentially in practice, they are *global questions, cover terms,* and *descriptors* (Green, 1999; Leigh, 1998).

Global Questions

Global questions are initial, general inquiries posed to solicit information about culturally relevant aspects of the client's life. Their purpose is to enhance a practitioner's ability to successfully initiate and undertake the intervention process. Such questions focus on areas with which you are unfamiliar and yet would enhance your understanding of the client's environment and situation. It's a good idea to "list topics of general interest, write questions, and arrange them in an order that seems to make sense" prior to the interview (Green, 1999, p. 134).

For instance, Green (1999) tells of a mental health worker newly assigned to an area of New York City with a large Puerto Rican population. The worker (whom we will arbitrarily call Brittany) is unfamiliar with the community and speaks no Spanish. She drives through the area noting her impressions and questions. A more seasoned colleague traveling with her talks about how housing is deteriorating, overcrowding is escalating, schools are underfunded, most jobs pay only minimum wage, and there is a swelling demand for public health services. Brittany watches residents of various age groups actively converse with each other as they participate in life and work on the streets. She observes that numerous Spanish posters announce festivals, community projects, and events. Despite the obvious poverty and related social problems, Brittany perceives that there is a strong sense of community, active resident interaction and participation in neighborhood activities, and a strong adherence to a Hispanic heritage.

Brittany observes that there are several publicly funded health centers and outpatient clinics in addition to private physicians' offices and pharmacies in the area. However, she also sees that "[t]here are *botanicas* or herb shops, and many *centros,* small storefront or basement 'churches'" where adherents of traditional spiritual beliefs both gather for worship and to receive "indigenous forms of mental health treatment, *consultas,* provided by specially trained folk healers" (Green, 1999, p. 135). Brittany carefully considers what she sees and thinks about how cultural beliefs and traditions might affect her ability to practice with this population. As a result, in the hope of enhancing her own ability to serve potential clients concerning their mental health needs, she identifies the following global questions to investigate with them:

1. *What are the various activities of the centros?*
2. *How is a healing session conducted?*
3. *What other persons assist the healer, and what do they do that is important?*
4. *How are healers trained, and what specific skills do they say they have?*
5. *What distinguishes problems that are physical, supernatural, or both in their origins?*
6. *What are some examples of diagnoses the healer makes?*
7. *What are the causes of the problems healers see in their practice? (p. 136)*

Note that such global questions are only starting points. Answers to each might only initiate numerous questions to clarify ideas and refine Brittany's understanding of the culture.

Cover Terms

Cover term is a word that covers a realm of concepts, ideas, and relationships within a cultural context and that has significant and special meaning to members of the cultural group. Cover terms often surface repeatedly as clients respond to global questions. Often, a worker unfamiliar with the cover term's depth of meaning initially will fail to understand the word's significance and relevance within the cultural context.

For example, the term *Issei* has immense implications for Japanese Americans (Green, 1999). Murase (1995) comments on the significance of this concept in terms of family values, cultural acceptance, and assimilation into the dominating culture:

> The traditional Japanese values and practices were most evident in the immigrant generation (the Issei). As succeeding generations of Japanese Americans have become acculturated, there has been a change in the family structure and behavior. The original patriarch, male-dominated family network has given way among the second generation (the Nisei) to an increasingly important role for women in family affairs. The devastating World War II experience of incarceration in concentration camps also took its toll. Many Nisei parents tried to dissociate themselves and their children from traditional Japanese culture and become

> model Americans in the Anglo-Saxon tradition, often at great psychological cost (Nagata, 1991). (p. 243)

Workers must pay close attention to what clients say in order to detect the presence and significance of important cover terms. Cover terms can initiate topics and open doors to greater understanding. However, they only scratch the surface. More detail is still needed in order to better comprehend a client's cultural world.

Descriptors

Descriptors are words solicited to explain cover words. In ethnographic interviewing a practitioner starts by thoughtfully preparing global questions, then identifies cover terms, and finally seeks out descriptors to fill in more of the cultural picture. For example, consider the words *extended family* within a cultural context (Green, 1999). A client might mention the words several times during a social work interview. The concept can serve as a cover term. But what does it really mean within a particular client's cultural context? The meaning probably is quite different "among immigrant Vietnamese from what it is among the Amish, Louisiana Cajuns, or *barrio* [neighborhood community] residents of East Los Angeles" (Green, 1999, p. 141). Depending on the cultural context, extended family might involve aunts, uncles, great-aunts and -uncles, cousins, second cousins, nieces, nephews, parents, grandparents and great-grandparents, other relatives who are much more distant, or even members of other families who are emotionally or economically close to the client's family.

Finding descriptors through ethnographic interviewing helps practitioners fill in gaps of information and more fully enhance understanding of clients' cultural views of their world. Other examples of cover words are infinite. For instance, consider a male adolescent who angrily states, "I got my ass kicked yesterday" (Leigh, 1998). What does "ass kicked" really mean for that young man in his own cultural environment? Does it mean that members of a neighborhood gang tied him up and beat him until he bled? Does it mean his father caught him doing something wrong and beat him with his fists, all the while lecturing him about how he should never do the bad thing again? Does it mean he lost $40 in a basketball bet?

Summary

In summary, global questions, cover words, and descriptors are just a few of the concepts inherent in ethnographic interviewing, one important means of developing cultural competency. Becoming culturally competent is an ongoing learning process.

One example of rephrasing is a client who says, "I feel really miserable today." The worker may respond, "You really don't feel well at all today." Rephrasing does not involve offering an interpretation of what the client has said. It simply repeats a statement by using other words.

Reflective Responding

Reflective responding is translating what you think the client is feeling into words. It is a means of displaying empathy. Such responding conveys that you understand what clients are going through and how they feel about it. A typical scenario involves a client who is *talking about* problems, but does not really articulate how he or she *feels about* them. Part of your job as the worker is to bring these feelings out into the open so the client knows they are there and can begin to work on them. Both verbal and nonverbal behavior can be used as cues for reflective responding. For example, a client comes to you with her shoulders slumped and her eyes downcast. She slumps into a chair and says, "Yep, he dumped me. He finally told me to get lost. He's been talking about it for months, but the old coot finally did it."

As a worker, you might respond, "You sound like you feel crushed and angry that your boyfriend left you. You also sound like you're a bit surprised even though he's been threatening for a long time."

Clarification

Clarification is making certain what the sender says is understood. Clarification is typically used in one of two ways. First, you can help clients articulate more clearly what they really mean by providing the words for it. The process is clarification for the clients' benefit. Second, you can use a clarifying statement to make what the client is saying clearer to yourself. This latter type of clarification is for your benefit. Many times clarification will benefit both worker and client. An example of this involves a client who comes to a worker and says, "I just lost my job. Everything's gone. What will I do? Where will I go?"

The worker may respond, "You mean you lost your income along with your job and you're wondering about how to pay the rent and other bills this month?" This example depicts the worker's attempt to clarify what the real issues are that must be addressed and to help the client proceed from the more global to the specific. Trying to solve the problem of losing "everything" is difficult. However, deter-

mining the exact amount needed to pay the rent and other bills or even finding an alternate residence are more concrete, doable goals. Helping clients to specify what they really mean makes a problem much more workable.

Clarification is used when there is a question about what clients mean. Restatement, on the other hand, involves understanding clients and simply paraphrasing what they have said. Finally, reflective responding adds the dimension of emotion and feeling to clients' statements.

Interpretation

Interpretation is seeking meaning beyond that of clarification by bringing to a conclusion, enlightening, or pursuing a greater depth of meaning than what has been stated. Interpretation helps lead clients to look deeper into themselves and their problems. It enhances clients' perceptions of their own situations.

For example, a client says, "I hate it when my mother tells me what to do. And, yet, if I don't do what she says, she makes me feel guilty. She makes me feel like I don't care about her anymore."

The worker might respond, "It seems like you have very ambivalent feelings toward your mother. You want to be independent, yet you don't want to hurt your mother's feelings. Perhaps, on some level, she realizes that, doesn't want to lose you, and is able to manipulate you."

To interpret means to take a statement a step beyond its basic meaning. In the preceding example, the worker went beyond the client's feelings of anger, guilt, and resentment. Instead, the worker focused in on both the client's and the mother's motivations for their behavior. The worker attempted to provide some insight into both of their feelings.

Providing Information

Sometimes, *providing information* to clients is appropriate. Providing information is educating clients by giving them the data they need. They may ask you frank questions. They may not know where to find resources or how a social services system works. They may not understand why they must provide certain information or follow some rule. Sometimes, they will be misinformed, and accurate information will need to be provided.

For example, a female teenager asks a worker, "My friends tell me you can't get pregnant the first time you do it. Is that true?" To this the worker might respond, "No, that's not true. You're just as likely to get pregnant the first time as any other time. There are some other things to consider, though, any time you choose to have sex. Would you like to talk about them?"

Note that sometimes, in addition to providing information, it's tempting to tell clients what you think they should do about some problem or situation. Giving specific direction should be undertaken *very* carefully, if at all. Highlight 2.4 discusses this issue more thoroughly.

HIGHLIGHT 2.4

Critical Thinking: Telling a Client What to Do

EP 2.1.3

Can you make suggestions to clients without interfering with their right to individual choice? Should you give a client advice? Should you urge clients to pursue an alternative when you are absolutely certain it is the best thing for them to do?

These are often difficult questions that may be encountered where critical thinking is very important. There is some controversy regarding the extent to which a worker can direct a client into taking some particular action. A major problem is that if you tell a client what to do, in a way you are taking responsibility for the result. In other words, if it turns out that the result of the action is bad for whatever reason, the client has you to blame.

Another problem involves the difficulty of putting yourself in another person's shoes. Can you really understand being that person and understand his or her values and ideas? Is it ethical for you to tell other people what route is best for them to take when you do not have to suffer any possible consequences yourself?

Helping a client identify the alternatives available to him or her is one thing. Directing the client as to which one is the best is another. An underlying theme in the planned change process is to help clients explore the pros and cons of the various alternatives available to them. As a worker, you can help them think through what each possible action really would mean to them.

Consider a teenager with an unwanted pregnancy. More than likely, each of us has a strong opinion about what the teenager *should* do or, rather, about what *we think we would do* in her situation. However, she has her own life situation with worries about her future, parents, friends, school, guilt, and religious ideas. The choice needs to be hers.

This is not to say that there are never times when encouraging a client to pursue the alternative he or she has chosen to be the best is appropriate. Sometimes, for a client to get going and move onward is difficult and scary. In those circumstances, a worker needs to use professional judgment regarding how forcefully to encourage the client to proceed. A helpful thought is to emphasize to the client that taking no action is indeed a decision to take one alternative. Making no decision has definite consequences. For example, if the pregnant teen decides not to make a decision and ignore her pregnancy, at five or six months' gestation, she has already narrowed the alternatives available to her. She has begun to make a decision by not making a decision.

There will be times when clients will pressure you to tell them what to do. For instance, I once worked with a woman who had a variety of crises in her life and in her marriage. She spoke about a married man with whom she once had an affair. She said that she still thought about him often, even though the affair had ended over 5 years ago. She had not seen him since then because he lived in another city. She asked me point-blank if I would call him if I were her. Bewildered, I replied, "I can't answer that because I'm not you." The woman never spoke to me again.

After much thought, there would have been a number of more effective replies. For instance, I could have said, "That's a difficult thing for me to answer. Help me think through how you feel about this man, your husband, and your marriage, so that I can better understand your situation." In this way, I could have gotten back on the track of helping her think through her own decision.

There are some instances where encouragement to take some action may need to be more forceful. One example of this approach is crisis intervention, which is discussed more thoroughly in Chapter 7. In a crisis situation, clients may need to be pushed out of their frozen, emotional, and perhaps illogical state. Once again, however, this is a matter of professional judgment.

There's one other thing to consider when thinking about telling a client what to do. Namely, how do *you* feel when someone tells you what you *should* do. Do you run right out and do it readily? Do you resent the intrusion and ignore the advice or even take off in the opposite direction?

Empowerment: Emphasizing Clients' Strengths

EP 2.1.10e

Social workers deal with the most difficult human problems. Their clients are often those people who are most oppressed and have the most obstacles to living healthy, happy lives. Many clients are so overwhelmed by their problems that focusing on anything but problems is difficult for them. They assume a tunnel vision, that is, they have difficulty focusing on anything but this long, dark entrapping tunnel of stressful life issues.

Sometimes, identifying clients' strengths will be quite difficult because their problems will seem so insurmountable. However, as we will discuss in later chapters that focus on the planned change process, emphasizing clients' strengths is critical throughout (Saleebey, 2013) and helps in several ways. First, it reinforces a client's sense of self-respect and self-value. Second, it provides rays of hope even in "tunnels of darkness." Third, it helps identify ways to solve problems by relying on the specified strengths.

Client strengths may be found in at least three major areas. The first involves behaviors and accomplishments. The second concerns personal qualities and characteristics. Finally, the third revolves around the client's material and social resources. Highlight 2.5 illustrates how to focus on client strengths.

Self-Disclosure

Self-disclosure is a worker's divulgence to a client of personal thoughts, information, feelings, values, or experiences. Many generalist practitioners, especially those new to the field, wonder to what extent they should disclose information about themselves.

What and how much about yourself should be disclosed during a professional interview has been, historically, a controversial issue (Okun & Suyemoto, 2013). On the one hand, some amount of self-disclosure can enhance relationships (Kadushin & Kadushin, 2013; Corey, 2013; Sheafor & Horejsi, 2012)—people are more apt to like others who reveal things about themselves. Similarly, the more you reveal to someone, the more likely that person will be to self-disclose to you. On the other hand, we all know people who seem to never stop talking about themselves. They are so interested in their own issues and activities that they never think of asking how you are. We also all know our reactions to people who behave this way: "Let me out of here!"

We have already established that warmth, empathy, and genuineness are important characteristics to demonstrate in professional worker–client relationships. To some extent, self-disclosure is necessary to give feedback to the client. Feedback involves providing input about how the client is functioning and how others perceive the client. This feedback is an important aspect of working through the planned change process.

Cormier and Hackney (2008) cite four major types of self-disclosure. The first three involve communicating something about the worker–client relationship and the ongoing interviewing process. These types of self-disclosures also frequently overlap with some of the other interviewing techniques mentioned earlier. They focus directly on the worker–client role and the purpose of the interview.

First, you can give information about *your professional role*. Second, you can share your feelings and impressions about the *client* and the client's behavior by giving feedback. Third, you can provide feedback about your perceptions concerning *your ongoing interaction and relationship with the client*. These latter two types of self-disclosure are especially useful when you cannot think of anything else to say during an interview. You can share your feelings about what is happening with the client inside or outside of the interview or self-disclose what you feel is happening in your relationship with the client at that point in the interview.

The fourth type of self-disclosure, however, differs significantly from the other three. It involves *relating aspects about your own life or problems* in some way to the client's feelings or situation. This approach can convey empathy to the client and indicate that you really understand. It can also provide a positive role model under some circumstances by showing the client that others have learned to live through similar problems.

The amount you choose to self-disclose about your own life is, ultimately, an individual decision. Some people are naturally more outgoing and self-disclosing than others. Regardless, when you as a worker choose to self-disclose, there are some basic guidelines.

The first guideline is to make certain that the self-disclosure is really for the client's benefit and not for your own. Friendships provide arenas for mutual self-disclosure and support, but professional worker–client relationships exist to benefit the client only (see Figure 2.2).

A second guideline is to make the self-disclosure relevant to the client, which involves demonstrating both "genuineness" and "timeliness" (Ivey et al., 2010, pp. 332–333). In other words, self-disclose for some

LO 2-8 Stress Clients' Strengths

Focusing on client strengths involves both seeking information out about them and emphasizing their importance. Saleebey (2013) cites the following five types of questions you might ask to explore client strengths:

> *Survival questions. Given all the challenges you have had to grapple with, how have you managed to survive (or thrive)? What is it that enables you to rise to the challenges put before you? . . . What have you learned about yourself and your world during your struggles? Have any of these difficulties given you special strength, insight, or skill? Which of these do you rely upon as you face the demands of daily life?*
>
> *Support questions. In times of difficulty what people or groups have given you special understanding, support, and guidance? Of the people in your life who do you see as exceptional and dependable? What is it that these people give you that is [special?] . . . How did you find them or how did they come to you? . . . What associations, organizations, or groups have been especially helpful to you in the past? . . .*
>
> *Exception questions. There are times in our lives when things were or are going more smoothly. What is different about those moments? In those moments when you felt that your life was better, more worthwhile, or more stable, what about the people and places in your world was distinct or different? What parts of your world and your being would you like to recapture, reinvent, or relive? What incidents in your life have given you special understanding, resilience, guidance, and hope?*
>
> *Possibility questions. At this moment, what now do you want out of life? How would you describe your hopes, visions, and aspirations? How far along are you toward achieving these? What people and/or personal qualities are helping you move in these directions? What do you like to do? What are your special talents and abilities? . . .*
>
> *Esteem questions. When people say good things about you, what are they likely to say? What things have you done in your life that give you real pride? When things are going well in your life? What is different? What events or people*

give you genuine pleasure? Do you or are you ready to believe that you might achieve some of the things you want in life? (pp. 107–108)

Once strengths have been identified, you can use your interviewing skills to stress their importance.

The following examples are statements workers might use to emphasize a client's strengths in three basic areas.

Client Behaviors and Accomplishments

- "You've done a nice job of following those suggestions. Look what you've accomplished."
- "Sometimes you emphasize all the things that have gone wrong, but look at all the things you've done well. You've kept your family together even when your husband left you and you lost a primary source of income. You've managed a tight budget and kept your children fed, housed, and in school. You're going back to school part-time. I think that's wonderful."

Personal Qualities

- "You're very bright and easy to talk to."
- "I think you're very motivated to work on this goal."
- "It's nice to work with you. You're so cooperative."
- "You have a very pleasant personality. I think you will do very well in the group."
- "You brighten up when you're happy. It makes people feel good to see your cheery smile."
- "You look very nice today."

Client's Resources

- "I know it's been hard, but you've found yourself a part-time job and have worked out a schedule for paying your bills. That's a great start."
- "It's really good that you have close friends (or a minister or a relative) to talk to. It helps."
- "Your family is very supportive. That's really good."
- "There are several resources available to you here at the agency that can get you off to a good start."

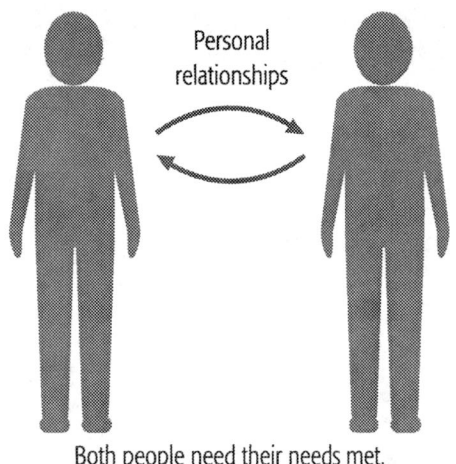

Personal relationships

Both people need their needs met.

Worker

Client

Professional relationships

The purpose is to meet the client's, not the worker's, needs.

© Cengage Learning

FIGURE 2.2 Personal versus Professional Relationships

definite purpose. For example, the client may need some reassurance that talking about a particular issue is all right, or at some specific point you can make an empathic self-disclosure about an issue related to that of the client and he or she will feel more comfortable.

The third guideline for making self-disclosures is that they should be short and simple. You want to share a small slice of your life, feelings, or experience for a specific purpose. Details are unimportant. Most likely you just want to convey to your client that, to some extent, you really do understand how he or she feels.

Sometimes, clients will initiate asking you uncomfortable personal questions such as, "Are you married?" "Are you going with anybody?" "Did you sleep with your spouse before you were married?" or "Did you ever drink when you were underage or try any drugs?"

Under such circumstances, you have two choices. First, you can answer honestly, briefly, and simply. Then you can say something like, "I think we'd better get back on track. The important thing we're here to work on is your problem and what to do about it."

Your second choice is to avoid answering the question by instantly focusing on something else, such as the client or the interviewing process. In other words, you can ignore the question and talk about how the client is participating in the interviewing process. For example, you might say any of the following:

- *"You seem really anxious to get off the topic today. What's on your mind?"*
- *"It seems as though you don't feel like talking about the problem right now. Is something bothering you?"*
- *"That really doesn't have much to do with what we're talking about here. We don't have that much time. Let's get back to the subject."*
- *"I feel as though you're trying to avoid my questions. What do you think are the reasons for that?"*

This second approach of avoiding the answer may or may not work. If it does not, you may have to simply and honestly say something like, "I really don't feel comfortable answering that. Let's get back to the matter at hand."

Self-disclosure requires judgment about when, what, and how much to share with a client. When you carefully and thoughtfully select the information you provide to the client, you are also engaging in what social workers call "professional use of self." You are using your knowledge, experience, and perceptions in the professional worker–client relationship in a conscientious and deliberate manner. In so doing, you may be modeling appropriate behavior for the client or demonstrating the willingness to deal nondefensively with difficult topics. In each case, you are monitoring what information you disclose and how it is used based upon what is needed at this point in time. Your sharing is not done because it feels good to you to get something off your chest. Rather, it is done to facilitate the relationship-building and planned changed efforts.

Self-disclosure may also be especially helpful when working with cultural groups suspicious of or uncomfortable with the worker. Sharing items of personal information may help the client feel a greater closeness or comfort with the worker. However, the focus should be shifted back to the client as soon as feasible. You do not want clients to think that you need more help than they do.

Summarization

Summarization is restating the main points of an interview or a portion of an interview in a brief and concise manner. Periodic summarization helps the client focus on the main points covered during a portion of the interaction and also helps keep the interview on track. It can help clients concentrate on one significant topic before addressing other issues. It can also serve as a means of transitioning from one subject to another by bringing the former issue to a close. Summarization is difficult in that the worker must carefully select and emphasize only the most important facts, issues, and themes.

Summarizing what has been accomplished during the entire interview is helpful when terminating the interview because it allows the client to leave on a positive note. Also, summarizing recommendations about who is to do what before the next meeting crystalizes the plans that have been made in both the client's and the worker's minds. Summarization as a major aspect of terminating the intervention process is also covered in Chapter 8.

Eliciting Information

As a part of the communication process, a worker must *encourage a client to reach for and share information.* One way of doing this is simply to ask questions. There are two basic types of questions, closed-ended and open-ended. Closed-ended questions include those that seek simple "yes" or "no" answers, such as:

- *"Are you coming tomorrow?"*
- *"Did you have a nice time?"*
- *"Is Harry here?"*
- *"Did Francesca take the dog out yet?"*
- *"Are you getting along better with your wife?"*

Closed-ended questions may also involve those where there are a number of clearly defined answers from which to choose. They do not encourage or even allow for an explanation of why the answer was chosen or for an elaboration of thoughts or feelings about the answer. For example, consider these questions:

- *"Are you male or female?"*
- *"Do you want chocolate, vanilla, or super-duper tutti-frutti ice cream?"*
- *"Are you working at Burger King, Mac's, or Heavenly Hash Heaven next summer?"*
- *"How many brothers do you have?"*
- *"What is your birthdate?"*

In each of these instances, a simple response is required. The choices for the response are established ahead of time and have a closed number of options. Your job is simply to choose one. Even the last two questions have a limited number of responses. The number of brothers must be from none to probably under 20. A birthdate is limited to specific days in the 12 months of the year.

"Machine-gunning" or bombarding the client with one closed-ended question after the other is easy, especially for beginning interviewers. Frequently, this situation occurs when a worker is anxious and trying to keep the interview going. Often, the worker wonders why the client is not saying much or initiating any discussion on his or her own.

The answer to this dilemma is to use the open-ended question. Instead of requiring simple, established answers from a predetermined selection, the open-ended question seeks out the client's thoughts, ideas, and explanations for answers. It encourages elaboration and specifics about answers unique to particular clients and situations. Consider the following examples:

- *"What are your reasons for wanting to leave home?"*
- *"How are you feeling about the situation?"*
- *"What do you plan on doing in the future?"*
- *"What are the people in your family like?"*
- *"How are you planning to accomplish this?"*

Each of these questions allows for a more detailed answer, unique to every individual and situation. For example, how you would describe your family members at any particular point in time would be different from the way anyone else would.

The Use of Why?

One thing to consider when formulating questions for clients is if and when to use the word *why*. This word can be threatening to clients because it is "intrusive" (Cormier & Hackney, 2008, p. 91) and often implies that the person to whom it is directed is at fault. For example, a student enters a classroom three minutes late. The instructor asks in front of the whole class, "Why are you late?" This question places a demand on the student to explain her reasons for doing something wrong by not being on time. The following are other examples:

- *"Why do you beat your children?"*
- *"Why do you drink so much?"*
- *"Why don't you get a job?"*
- *"Why don't you get straight A's?"*
- *"Why do you always nag me so much?"*

The word *why* also can put the burden of seeking out a solution on the individual to whom it is directed. The solution often involves reaching inside one's mind for facts, organizing one's thoughts and ideas, and presenting them in an understandable form right then and there. The following questions illustrate this:

- *"Why does it take at least 4 years to graduate from college?"*
- *"Why does the sun shine?"*
- *"Why don't I have enough money?"*
- *"Why do they have that rule?"*
- *"Why can't I do what I want to?"*

In summary, being cautious when using the word *why* is best.

Using Sensitivity and Tact

The verbal responses just discussed provide a range of ways to help clients through the planned change process. One other suggestion involves the use of sensitivity and tact. Especially, when addressing an exceptionally challenging situation, it's sometimes easy to respond to the information sender by blurting out an insensitive, trite response. The presenting problem may strike you as being too hard to solve. You might not have ready access to a more effective idea for how to respond. When unsure, you may become defensive. Regardless, it's important to avoid responses that are condescending, terse, or evasive. It shouldn't be a newsflash that no one is perfect and no one will say the most appropriate thing every time in every situation. Some statements that are clichés can turn a client off. The important thing is to learn effective techniques and do your best to communicate clearly and help the client solve problems and work through the planned change process.

Chang and her colleagues (2013) cite a number of insensitive responses and clichés that lack insight and that should never be said to clients; consider what your reaction would be if you approached someone with a problematic issue only to hear one of the following responses:

- *"Let me tell you how to fix your problem."*
- *"Something just like that happened to me and _____ is what I did to solve the problem."*
- *"Everything will be fine after a few days."*
- *"Everything happens for a reason."*
- *"You are never given more than you can handle."*
- *"Think of it as a growth opportunity."*
- *"There must be an important lesson in this for you."*

- *"I am sure it will all work out in time."* . . .
- *"I just read an article about that kind of a problem so I know that you should do ____."* (p. 101)

OVERLAP OF TECHNIQUES

Sometimes labeling a technique specifically as being a "clarification" or a "self-disclosure" is difficult. Some responses fulfill only one purpose and fit obviously into one category, while others combine two or more techniques if they fulfill two or more functions. The important thing is to master a variety of techniques and thereby become more flexible and effective.

Interviewing, Specific Techniques, and the Planned Change Process

You may be asking yourself at this point, "OK, how do these specific interviewing techniques work in real interviews? How will they fit into the planned change process with real clients?" The answers to these questions are in Chapters 5 through 8, which address each phase of the planned change process. The phases are engagement, assessment, planning, implementation, evaluation, termination, and follow-up. The first and most basic step before beginning the intervention process is mastering how to communicate with a wide range of clients.

LO 2-9 Apply Critical Thinking to Address Challenges in Interviewing

EP 2.1.3 A fascinating aspect about working with and helping people is that you never really know what to expect. Every person, problem, and situation is different. However, you must frequently deal with a number of issues in order to continue with the planned change approach, often posing dilemmas for workers about how to proceed. Among these issues are the development of cross-cultural awareness in interviewing, silence in the interview, confronting clients, involuntary clients, and suspicion of untruth. Often critical thinking is required.

LO 2-10 Develop Cross-Cultural Awareness in Interviewing

EP 2.1.1e
EP 2.1.4a b, c, & d

We have established that appreciation of diversity is one of the founding concepts of generalist practice. Understanding the client's "ethnic reality" is critical. This reality involves "a group's cultural values as embodied in its history, rituals, and religion..., a group's migration experience or other processes through which the encounter with mainstream culture took place..., [and] the way a group organizes its family systems" (Devore & Schlesinger, 1999, p. 55). These experiences affect the way designated groups function, thrive, or face oppression within the macro environment. Understanding the dynamics involved to empathize with clients and help them evaluate alternatives is essential for workers. Such learning is a career-long process. Working with clients who have diverse backgrounds in terms of culture, ethnicity, and race requires several dimensions of cross-cultural awareness.

The first dimension involves the fact that learning about people from other cultures is a continuous process. Social workers should view themselves as learners and their clients as informants. Cultural variations are almost endless. Not only are there multitudes of cultural and ethnic groups, but also cultures and values diverge significantly within groups. A wealthy person from northern India has different preferences, lifestyles, and even choices of cuisine than an impoverished person from southern India. People from Germany differ in language, cultural values, and lifestyle from people in Norway, despite the fact that they may be white Europeans. The important thing is to keep your mind open and seek out information about your clients' cultural groups, whatever they may be.

Green emphasizes that the first step in learning about another culture involves going through "the trouble to learn some of what members of a culture know, including their beliefs about their history, their values, and what they see as their relationship to the rest of the world" (1999, p. 86). You can accomplish this "by combining reading, listening, watching, and consulting with knowledgeable insiders" (1999, p. 86). For example, when working with Hispanic clients, major aspects involved in Latino ethnicity include language, country of origin, spirituality and religion, the importance of family, immigration or citizenship status, art, and cultural expression (Furman & Negi, 2010). Likewise, when working with Alaskan natives, important values include "respect for elders, love for children, respect for others, respect for nature, domestic skills, humility, sharing, cooperation, hard work, hunting skills, family roles, humor, spirituality, knowledge of language, knowledge of family tree, avoidance of conflict, and responsibility to clan or tribe" (Lally & Haynes, 1995, p. 198).

But learning is only the beginning. Cultural knowledge involves understanding people's values, actions, preferences, and expressions. This understanding includes observing "such overt activities as singing, dancing, arguing, playing, and working," in addition to "offhand comments, facial expressions, joking relationships, exchange of favors, and styles of demeanor" (Green, 1999, p. 86).

When working with people from other cultures and racial groups, remembering the concept of individualization is important. *Individualization* is the crucial social work value maintaining that every person is unique, with unique characteristics distinguished from those generally characterizing a cultural, ethnic, or racial group. Workers must remain vigilant to individual values, preferences, and choices that may not reflect those generally embraced by the client's particular ethnic or cultural heritage. It's very important to show respect; "go out of your way to express genuinely the understanding, honor, and esteem that you continually cultivate for the persons" from diverse cultures (Hogan, 2013, p. 65). Listening carefully to individual differences and appreciating personal values is one significant means of showing respect.

A second dimension of cross-cultural awareness involves national origin and understanding the extent to which clients are acculturated and assimilated into the mainstream culture. *Acculturation* refers to "the process wherein the ethnic values, behaviors, and rituals clients hold from their traditional culture change over time and integrate with the values, behaviors, and rituals of the majority or host culture" (Lum, 2007, p. 310). *Assimilation* is the process of being incorporated into and becoming part of the majority culture. *Full assimilation* is "the end product of those who have completely removed all aspects of their traditional culture and replaced them with those of the host culture. An ultimate gesture may be to even change their name, for example, from Martinez to Marten, in order to be viewed as fully American" (Lum, 2007, p. 310).

Attending to this measure of cross-cultural awareness requires great sensitivity and perceptiveness to communicate with clients as effectively as possible. For example, newly migrated Afghani immigrants probably are much more embedded in their native culture and its values than those who have lived in the United States for a decade or more. Residents gradually assimilate some values and customs.

Likewise, differences develop between Hmong who migrated here as adults and those who were born and grew up here. The values of Hmong adolescents who join gangs diverge significantly from those of their parents. The family is traditionally "the most important influence in the lives of Hmong people," members' major goals being to enhance "its dignity and well-being" (McInnis, 1990, p. 29). Discord swells when teenagers' loyalties to gang and family conflict. Devore and Schlesinger reflect that "[t]he sense of family cohesion often diminishes in the second and third generation of immigrants or migrants. The family as transmitter of old values, customs, and language is often seen as restrictive by members of the younger generation" (1999, p. 145).

A third dimension of cross-cultural awareness concerns attention to the stereotypes, prejudices, discrimination, and oppression negatively affecting people from various ethnic and racial groups. A *stereotype* is a fixed mental picture of members of some specified group based on some attribute or attributes that portray an overly simplified opinion about that group without considering and appreciating individual differences. *Prejudice* is an opinion or prejudgment about an individual, group, or issue that is not based on fact and is usually negative. *Discrimination* is unequal treatment of people based on prejudgment because they belong to some category, such as one involving race, ethnicity, gender, or religion. *Oppression* is the longer-term result of putting extreme limitations upon or discriminating against some designated group.

Prejudice based on stereotypes often results in discrimination and oppression. Alternatives are limited for the oppressed group, and behavior is restricted. Nurturing their awareness of these conditions is absolutely essential for practitioners in order to understand clients' positions and establish viable alternatives for action. For example, a school social worker must seriously consider the wisdom of referring a shy, withdrawn Native American boy to a local recreation center whose members are renowned for their racist attitudes. Similarly, a practitioner must be aware of the potential consequences of referring a Jewish woman to a support group composed of neo-Nazis wrought with anti-Semitism.

A fourth dimension of cross-cultural awareness involves the importance of self-awareness, one's own ethnic and cultural background, and how that background may affect a worker's ability to practice (Sisneros, Stakeman, Joyner, & Schmitz, 2008). Questions you might ask yourself include:

- *How do I view members of this cultural, ethnic, or racial group? What adjectives immediately come to mind?*
- *Do I have stereotypes and prejudged expectations about how these group members will behave? Do I*

have negative expectations not based on fact or that fail to take individualization into account?
- *How does my own cultural, ethnic, and racial background affect my view of various groups and of the world in general?*
- *How can I open my mind to cultural differences and view them with objectivity and appreciation?*
- *How can I nurture my ongoing learning about cultural differences? What can I do to learn more?*

Highlight 2.6 addresses another aspect of human diversity—spirituality.

SILENCE IN THE INTERVIEW

What if, try as you might, the client will not say much? Silence can operate within human interaction including interviews in a number of significant ways (Kadushin & Kadushin, 2013). First, "when people come together with the intent of talking to each other, silence generates social anxiety and is embarrassing. But the social worker feels a professional anxiety at the thought that continued silence signals a failing interview" (1997, p. 213). In other words, a worker may feel threatened, inadequate, boring, or out of control if long periods of silence occur during the interview. Silent times almost seem to demonstrate the uselessness or lack of substance of the interview. However, in reality, "something is happening all the time, even when the participants appear to be totally passive. Silence is a period filled with lack of speech, in which both interviewer and interviewee participate" (1997, p. 214). In other words, silence is meaningful and may occur for a number of reasons (Cormier, Nurius, & Osborn, 2013; Ivey et al., 2012).

Client-Initiated Silence

Silence in the interview is either client initiated or worker initiated. Client-initiated silence means that the client is taking responsibility for having the silent period happen. This silence occurs for different reasons. First, the client may be addressing an issue, then come to a point of uncertainty as to where to go, and need time to organize thoughts. Second, the client may be trying to pressure the worker to give some answer, response, or solution to a problem. A third use of silence is to offer resistance or to reject the worker's authority.

Negative Worker-Initiated Silence

The other type of silence in an interview is worker initiated —that is, the worker has been talking and feels

HIGHLIGHT 2.6

LO 2-11 Address Spirituality as an Aspect of Diversity

Religion and spirituality reflect yet another aspect of human diversity. *Religion* involves people's spiritual beliefs concerning the origin, character, and reason for being, usually based on the existence of some higher power or powers; these beliefs often include designated rituals and provide direction for what is considered moral or right. *Spirituality*, a related concept, is "the individual search for meaning, purpose, and values" that typically rises above everyday physical limitations and connects one to something greater than oneself (O'Neill, 1999, p. 3). Religion implies membership in a spiritual organization with customs, traditions, and structure. Spirituality may involve religion, or it may reflect a personal, internalized view of existence.

Gotterer (2001) explains the significance of spirituality and religion for social work practice:

> *Social workers, typically involved with vulnerable people in situations of pain or crisis, need a greater awareness of spiritual and religious issues. Tragedies such as the untimely death of a loved one force a person to confront the inexplicable. People nearing death often wonder whether there is an afterlife. Trying times may cause a person to question the meaning and purpose of life. Those subjected to serious disease or long-term oppression need some way to make sense of their experience. Spiritual concerns such as hope, meaning, inner strength, and doubt are relevant in many clients' lives. (p. 187)*

Here we will address the importance of workers not imposing their own personal spiritual beliefs on clients, some suggestions for approaching spiritual issues with clients, and the context of working in a faith-based organization.

Do Not Impose Personal Beliefs on Clients

A client's spirituality may be a great source of strength. However, workers must be exceedingly careful not to impose their own religious and spiritual views upon clients. The overriding principle of self-determination clearly affirms that "social workers should never try to impose their own beliefs on clients" (Derezotes, 2006; O'Neill, 1999, p. 3). Mattison, Jayaratne, and Croxton (2000) surveyed a random sample of 1,278 social workers regarding their personal spiritual beliefs and how these affected their practice. The researchers determined that it is very important for workers to fully understand their own spiritual and religious convictions in order to maintain clear boundaries between their beliefs and those of their clients.

On the one hand, workers should not seek to convert clients to the workers' own ways of thinking. On the other, "it is also problematic to ignore or fail to adequately address clients' religious and spiritual needs because they are viewed as unimportant or irrelevant" (Mattison et al., 2000, p. 54). Therefore, it is best to learn about clients' religious and spiritual beliefs from various sources including religious readings, spiritual leaders, or the clients themselves. "Social workers must develop sensitivity and competence in dealing with spiritual diversity, just as in dealing with cultural diversity" (Canda, 1997, p. 304; Carroll, 1997). This means that a social worker with Muslim beliefs who is working with Christian clients should help these clients focus on the strengths they can draw from their Christian faith. Likewise, a Christian worker should help Muslim clients utilize the strengths inherent in their Muslim faith. Frame (2003), however, warns that "[i]f clients are not open to religious or spiritual aspects of their difficulties, it is inappropriate to bring . . . [these issues] into counseling or to employ methods that are particularly based in religious or spiritual beliefs or practices" (p. 184).

How to Approach Spiritual Issues with Clients

Carroll (1997) makes five suggestions for exploring client empowerment through spirituality:

1. *be alert to the client's point of view and level of awareness of his or her spirituality [e.g., To what extent is spirituality vital or fundamental to the client's life?];*
2. *identify the role of spirituality in the client's life [e.g., How involved is the client in religious practices or a spiritual community?];*
3. *assess spiritual issues and spiritual components of the client's major concerns or difficulties [e.g., How does the client's spiritual perspective potentially affect the client's problems and life issues?];*
4. *provide opportunities for discussion by picking up on subtle openings and initiating inquiries*

(continued)

HIGHLIGHT 2.6 (continued)

[e.g., During a general discussion about a client's values, to what extent are religious beliefs part of the client's value system?]; and 5. be open to exploring spiritual modalities [e.g., What are some of the major components of the client's faith or spiritual belief system?]. (p. 31)

A number of questions can be asked to initiate discussion about spirituality:

- When did you first start thinking about spirituality and religion? What were your thoughts at that time?
- What, if any, significant experiences have you had in your life that started you thinking about spirituality or religion?
- "What [if any] strengths and supports do you gain from your spiritual/religious orientation? Be as specific as possible.
- [If appropriate] How could you draw on this resource when faced with life challenges?
- Could you give a specific example [if there is one] of how spirituality has helped you in the past?" (Ivey et al., 2012, p. 46)

Faith-Based Social Services

A common context in which social workers come in contact with issues in spirituality involves faith-based organizations. It is possible that you will either work in faith-based agencies or be working with them in some capacity.

Faith-based organizations may offer a broad assortment of services. These include "job-search, job-readiness, job-skills training programs; Literacy, General Education Development (GED) and English as a Second Language (ESL) programs; food, shelter, and clothing; social services and referral; child care and transportation; and counseling services among others" (Texas Workforce Commission, 2004).

Tangenberg (2005) identifies six basic organizational categories "based on the religious content of mission statements,[a] organizational histories, affiliations with external agencies, selection criteria for board [of directors][b] and staff members, financial and nonfinancial (volunteer) support from religious communities" (p. 201):

1. Faith-permeated organizations *have explicitly religious mission statements, were founded by*

religious groups or for religious purposes, are affiliated with external religious agencies, are explicitly religious in their selection of staff and board members, and refuse funding likely to compromise organizational religious mission or identity.

2. Faith-centered organizations *are similar to faith-permeated organizations, but are less adamant about the need for all staff members to share organizational beliefs and less likely to have policies refusing funding that could undermine religious mission or identity.*

3. Faith-affiliated organizations *have explicit or implicit religious mission statements, were founded by religious groups or for religious reasons, often are affiliated with external religious agencies, expect some degree of shared faith commitments among staff and board members, and often seek financial and volunteer support from religious communities.*

4. Faith-background organizations *may implicitly refer to religious values in their mission statement, have weaker connections to religious institutions, hold few, if any, expectations regarding the faith commitments of board and staff members, and vary in their pursuit of support from religious communities.*

5. *The religious content of* faith-secular partnership organizations *varies according to the characteristics of the faith partners. Secular [non-religious] partners provide administrative leadership, and secular staff members are expected to respect the religious beliefs of faith partners, from whom significant financial and volunteer support is sought.*

6. Secular organizations *have no religious content or affiliations with external religious organizations. No attention is given to the faith commitments of staff or board members, and requests for assistance are rarely made to religious communities. (pp. 201–202, numbers added)*

Many issues can surface when social workers enter the realm of spirituality in a faith-based setting. Questions can arise regarding how the worker's own sense of spirituality coincides or contrasts with the host agency's perspective, especially in faith-permeated or faith-centered organizations. There are no easy answers to such questions. A worker may struggle with personal views that are at odds with the agency's. A practitioner must always address such issues in an ethical and professional manner. If views between the agency and the worker are too incongruent, leaving the agency may be an appropriate solution.

Questions also can emerge regarding treatment of clients who have differing spiritual views from that of the host agency. Derezotes (2006) reflects upon social workers' own faith and their practice in faith-based agencies:

> When doing direct practice within a faith-based program, the spiritually oriented social worker respects the religious faith system that the client has, whether the client is a member of a major religion or has no religion at all. Regardless of the setting, the worker believes that clients should have an informed and free choice in whether they attend any program that has a particular religious bias. The social worker does not try to change or influence the client's religion in any publically supported program. (p. 261)

Case Example

Consider the following practice situation and the subsequent critical thinking questions (Roeder, 2002): "You are functioning in the role of a case manager[c] at a community based human services organization that strives to meet the needs of clients who are living with HIV. One of your frequent responsibilities is to discuss with each client the status of his or her advanced directives (health care power of attorney, financial power of attorney, and legal living will[d])."

Critical Thinking Questions 2.4

- In this context, what would prompt you to address spirituality?
- Conversely, why might you choose to purposely not address spirituality? (p. 11)

Notes

a. An organization's *mission statement* is a declaration of an organization's purpose and goals.
b. An organization's *board of directors* is a group of volunteers, usually recruited from the community on the basis of "their power, status, and influence in the community; their expertise; and their representation of particular interest groups and constituencies" (Toseland & Rivas, 2012, p. 38), who are "authorized to formulate the organization's mission, objectives, and policies and to oversee the organization's ongoing activities" (Kirst-Ashman, 2011, pp. 123–124).
c. Chapter 1 defined a *case manager* as a practitioner who, on the behalf of a specific client, coordinates needed services provided by any number of agencies, organizations, and facilities.
d. A *living will* is a formal document signed by an individual that provides instructions concerning what should be done if the individual becomes incapacitated and is unable to make decisions about his or her health care.

responsible for the silence. The first negative scenario involves a worker who demonstrates a quiet, noninvolved, nonassertive personality style. For this worker, working that hard at directing the interview is not natural. Such behavior is inappropriate and a "cop-out" for a professional. Professional skills must transcend individual personality styles.

The second negative type of worker-initiated silence occurs when the worker's mind becomes a blank and he or she cannot think of anything to say. This form of silence occurs more frequently with new workers who are anxious about their own performance.

Ivey and his colleagues (2012) reflect on how to handle this situation:

> For a beginning interviewer, silence can be frightening. After all, doesn't counseling mean talking about issues and solving problems verbally? When you feel uncomfortable with silence, look at your client. If the client appears comfortable, draw from her or his ease and join in the silence. If the client seems disquieted by the silence, rely on your attending skills. Ask a question or make a comment about something relevant, mentioned earlier in the session. (p. 67)

You might "acknowledge and explore with your client the meaning of the silence" when it occurs (Corey, 2013, p. 30). A subsequent section discusses how workers can use silence beneficially to enhance the interviewing and treatment process.

Focusing on the Client Instead of Yourself

When a social worker comes upon a new situation or new type of problem, becoming anxious is easy if you are not sure about what to do next. The answer to this dilemma is to tune in to your anxiety and do one of two things. First, you can allow yourself a brief period of silence in order to get your thoughts together. (This type of silence will be discussed further in the next section titled "Therapeutic Worker-Initiated Silence.") Second, you can think about what is happening in the interview and label it. For example, you might say, "It's pretty quiet in here. Where are your thoughts?" or "It seems like you're taking some time to think about the issue. That's all right. We can start again when you're ready."

Therapeutic Worker-Initiated Silence

Cormier and Hackney cite four ways that worker-initiated silence can be beneficial or therapeutic: "pacing the interview," "silent focusing," "responding to defenses," and "silent caring" (2008, pp. 60–61). Each type assumes that the worker initiates or is in control of the silent period.

Sometimes, conversations and information move rapidly during the interview, and there is not enough time for the client to keep up or to absorb all that is transpiring. *Pacing the interview* involves using small periods of silence to allow time to think about and assimilate what is occurring.

A second type of therapeutic silence involves *silent focusing*. This period of silence is a bit longer than those used to pace interviews and is only allowed to occur after some significant revelation has surfaced. Silent focusing enables the client to focus in on and think more intensively about an issue without having to rush right into something else.

The third type of therapeutic silence concerns the worker *responding to defenses* in the client. The silence occurs when a client has an emotional outburst directed toward the worker. Usually, the client is angry at something else (e.g., spouse, children, an agency that is denying benefits, landlord, in-laws, and so on). However, clients may vent their intense emotions at you the worker just because you are there. It may be tempting to become defensive yourself or immediately try to provide insight into the client's behavior. Nevertheless, a period of silence with congruent nonverbal behavior (e.g., maintenance of direct eye contact with the client and a somber facial expression) may give clients time to think about how and why they are acting the way they are.

Silent caring is the fourth type of therapeutic silence (Ivey et al., 2012). Sometimes, there will be a period of intense emotion during an interview, often involving profound sadness, grief, or regret. Many times, a client will cry during these moments. Culturally, we are often taught that crying implies weakness and is essentially bad. This view is a misconception, however, because crying allows for an honest expression of emotion and an opportunity to let pain out and experience it. Unless such poignant emotions are identified and allowed expression, people cannot work through them and get on with life. A period of silent empathy during an interview may best convey your caring and understanding. Incidentally, subtly offering the client a tissue or at least having a box of tissues readily available should a client need them may also be appropriate.

Finally, one should note that there are distinctive cultural differences regarding the treatment of silence in conversations and interviews. Being sensitive to these nuances and respectful of the client's values about silent communication is important.

CONFRONTING CLIENTS

Confrontation in almost any situation is difficult for many people. To confront means to disagree with another person and make a point of stating that disagreement. Confrontation also involves risking a negative or hostile reaction from the person you are confronting.

Nonetheless, confrontation is an important tool in the problem-solving process of generalist practice. *Confrontation* is a direct encounter where people come together with opposing opinions, perspectives, or ideas in order to scrutinize, compare, or refute them. Confrontations involve identifying and examining participants' issues, needs, and emotions. A confrontation in social work practice often involves pointing out to clients their incongruences or inconsistencies between what they say and what they do (Cormier & Hackney, 2008; Ivey et al., 2012). Any confrontation first involves clearly identifying the existing discrepancy and then working toward some resolution (Ivey & Ivey, 2008). In other words, confrontations are necessary to help clients face factors that block progress toward attaining goals and, thus, heighten their motivation to make positive changes.

Framing Discrepancies in Confrontation

Confrontation by definition involves addressing discrepancies. There are at least three types, two of which are internal (involving the client's verbal and nonverbal behavior) and one external (entailing the client's interactions with other people and situations) (Ivey et al., 2012).

The first internal discrepancy involves "incongruities between two verbal statements" (p. 164). For example, a client states, "I want to stay here and work on the problem. I really want to go home now."

A second internal discrepancy concerns those between what a person verbally says and how that person actually behaves. For instance, after having gone out the prior evening to "hang one on in a big way," a client says, "I don't drink anymore." Another illustration is a client who states, "I feel so at ease here talking to you," while chewing her fingernails, tapping her foot, and grimacing fervently. Still another example of this type of discrepancy is a client who verbally states she hates her mother, but nonverbally smiles broadly as she says it.

The third type of discrepancy, which is external, involves conflict between clients and other people or issues. Such conflicts may involve family, friends, or fellow workers. Clients may be in disagreement with others around them. An example of a discrepancy between people concerns parents who disagree about disciplining their children. One parent may say, "I am responsible for all the discipline of the children." The other parent replies, "You're all talk and no action. I'm the one who does all the disciplining around here."

External discrepancies may also concern such potentially difficult issues as where to attend college or whether to buy a house (Ivey et al., 2012). Clients may make choices that bring them negative consequences. For instance, they may choose to purchase an expensive SUV, which will escalate credit card debt, economic hardship, and stress.

Sometimes, confrontations are necessary when clients are trying to resist intervention for a certain reason. At other times, clients may not be certain whether or not they want to be helped and are hesitant to cooperate. Still other times, for reasons of their own, clients will not want to follow through on recommendations. Sometimes, clients will find making actual changes in their behavior too difficult. Clients may also make excuses for behavior that you feel are unacceptable. Finally, clients may be behaving in ways that are contrary to their own best interests.

Hepworth et al. (2013) postulate that identifying the discrepancy during confrontations involves four components. First, the worker should communicate caring about the client and interest in the client's well-being. Second, the worker should clearly express the client's stated goal within the problem-solving process. Third, the worker should illustrate exactly what the discrepancy is. Finally, the worker should indicate the realistic results of the discrepancy.

Figure 2.3 illustrates a formula you might use to structure a confrontation.[1]

For example, a supported employment worker for adults with intellectual disabilities might say to a client:

- *"I like you and I care about how you perform here"* (communication of caring).
- *"You've told me that you'd like to continue working here for a long time"* (client's stated goal).
- *"You say you like working here, but every half-hour of work you take a half-hour break"* (identification of the discrepancy).
- *"You know that everybody here is expected to work two hours straight, and then they get a half-hour break. You know that you and everyone else must follow these rules or you can't continue working here"* (realistic results of the discrepancy).

Suggestions for Using Confrontation

The following are suggestions for maximizing the use of confrontation:

1. As a worker, consider whether or not your relationship with the client is strong enough to withstand the potential stress caused by confrontation (Compton, Galaway, & Cournoyer, 2005; Cormier et al., 2013; Cournoyer, 2011). For instance, confronting a client within 10 minutes after the initial interview with the client has begun would probably be unwise.

2. Be aware of the client's emotional state. If a client is extremely upset, agitated, or anxious, a confrontation probably would have little value (Compton et al., 2005; Cournoyer, 2011). Clients who are preoccupied with other issues probably will have little energy left to respond positively and helpfully to confrontations.

3. Never confront a client to vent your own annoyance, antagonism, or frustration (Cormier et al., 2013; Egan, 2014). Shebib (2003) suggests that "[w]hen workers are not in control of their own feelings, clients are more likely to view them as aggressive and to feel their confrontation is unsupportive. The counseling relationship is formed to meet the needs of clients, and responsible workers will forego their own needs to this end. They should be self-aware to know their reasons for wanting to confront" (p. 205).

---

1. Figure 2.3 is roughly adapted from concepts presented by Hepworth et al., 2013, p. 546.

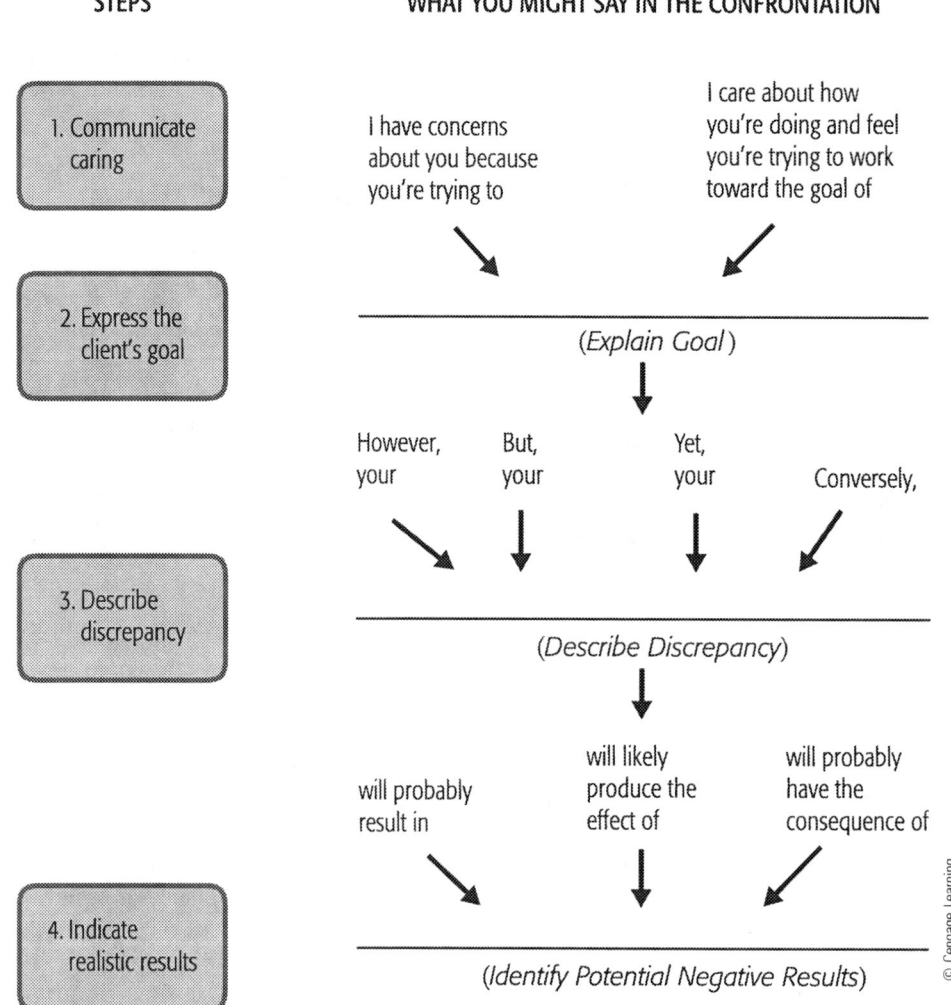

STEPS

WHAT YOU MIGHT SAY IN THE CONFRONTATION

1. Communicate caring

I have concerns about you because you're trying to

I care about how you're doing and feel you're trying to work toward the goal of

2. Express the client's goal

(Explain Goal)

However, your

But, your

Yet, your

Conversely,

3. Describe discrepancy

(Describe Discrepancy)

will probably result in

will likely produce the effect of

will probably have the consequence of

4. Indicate realistic results

(Identify Potential Negative Results)

© Cengage Learning

FIGURE 2.3 Framing a Discrepancy during a Confrontation

4. Use confrontations carefully and only when you determine that they will likely be effective (Compton et al., 2005; Cormier et al., 2013; Hepworth et al., 2013). Confrontations are often difficult and imply some risk to the relationship. If they are used as an integral part of a confrontational style, the client may feel downtrodden and terminate the worker–client relationship.

5. Continue to demonstrate respect for the client throughout the confrontation (Egan, 2014; Sheafor & Horejsi, 2012). This respect involves listening to what the client is saying whether or not you agree with it and also acknowledging the fact that the client ultimately has the right to choose his or her own course of action. Finally, respect concerns keeping in mind that, as the worker, you are there to help the client, not to get the client to do what you want done.

6. Remain empathic with the client throughout the confrontation and do not get overly involved in trying to get your own way. Continue to work on understanding how the client feels and views the problems from his or her own perspective.

7. Use "I" statements during the confrontation (Okun & Kantrowitz, 2008; Sheafor & Horejsi, 2012). Simply rephrasing your thoughts to include the word "I" enhances the quality of personal caring and empathy. This technique emphasizes the fact that you are giving feedback instead of criticizing or blaming. For example, a worker might say, "*I* would like to share with you some inconsistencies I've noticed between what you've been saying and what you've

actually been doing." This statement is far more personal and far less blaming than, "*You've* been saying one thing and doing another."

8. Make certain your feedback is very clear and behaviorally oriented. Clients must understand exactly what you are trying to say. Providing examples can be helpful. For instance, Cormier and Nurius (2003) explain: "A poor confrontation might be 'You want people to like you, but your personality turns them off.' In this case, the practitioner is making a general inference about the client's personality and also is implying that the client must undergo a major 'overhaul' in order to get along with others. A more helpful confrontation would be 'You want people to like you, and at the same time you make frequent remarks about yourself that seem to get in the way and turn people off'" (p. 160).

9. Have patience and allow the client some time to change (Hepworth et al., 2013; Johnson, 2009). Applying intense pressure for a client to change may be a turnoff because people are likely to resent being told what to do. Additionally, expecting instantaneous change is inappropriate. Clients need time to integrate new information, think things through, and make gradual changes in their lives and behavior.

INVOLUNTARY CLIENTS

Voluntary clients are those who willingly seek counseling and help in attaining their goals. For example, "spouses may voluntarily seek marital counseling from family service agencies; parents may ask for assistance in dealing with tensions to avoid abusing their children; and substance abusers may voluntarily participate in counseling to reduce the frequency of their undesirable behaviors" (Ivanoff, Blythe, & Tripodi, 1994, p. 5).

However, many social workers find themselves in the position of trying to help involuntary clients, those who are forced into involvement with social workers or other professionals but really do not want to be there. Involuntary clients may be either *mandated* or *nonmandated* (Ivanoff et al., 1994, pp. 5–6). Some involuntary clients are legally required or mandated to receive services. These include prisoners, people in institutions or residential treatment centers, and others under court order. "Other examples of involuntary services include counseling for alcoholics involved in automobile accidents, group therapy for wife batterers, and parenting skill training for neglectful parents" (Ivanoff et al., 1994, p. 5).

Nonmandated involuntary clients are those "who are pressured by important persons in their environment to seek assistance" (Ivanoff et al., 1994, p. 5). These clients include an employer urging an alcoholic employee to get help from the company's employee assistance program,[2] one spouse forcing the other into marriage counseling under threat of divorce, or staff and family pressuring an older adult in a nursing home to cooperate with treatment plans.

There is no question that working with people who do not want to work with you is difficult. However, there are a number of suggestions that can help the intervention process along even when clients are involuntary. (Note that Highlight 2.7 addresses an issue related to dealing with involuntary clients—handling client hostility.)

First, acknowledge to yourself that the client is indeed involuntary. Do not ignore the fact that the client does not want to be there. Rather, accept it. Instead of trying to force the client to like being there with you, start where the client is.

Second, try to put yourself in your client's shoes. We have already discussed some of the negative feelings with which clients may come to interviews. They may be wary and suspicious. They may have had bad experiences with your agency or others before. They might be trying desperately to maintain their own homeostasis and thus strongly resist any attempt to change. Just looking at the reality of the situation instead of trying to fight it is a good start (see Highlight 2.7).

The third suggestion for working with involuntary clients involves labeling and helping them express their negative feelings. If the client is resistant, bring that out into the open. For example, you might say, "I get the strong impression that you don't really want to be here. I'd like to know how you're feeling right now."

Identifying the reasons you suspect for the client's resistance is also helpful. For example, if appropriate, you might say, "I know it's been difficult for you to come in and see me. I realize that you're required to do this by the court." Once again, labeling the reality of the situation often both disperses anxiety and introduces opportunities for clients to get their real feelings out on the table.

---

2. *Employee assistance programs (EAPs)* "are services provided by organizations that focus on workers' mental health and on adjustment problems that interfere with their work performance" (Kirst-Ashman, 2013, p. 403).

HIGHLIGHT 2.7

Handling Hostility

Sometimes clients will be angry when they arrive for your interview. They may raise their voices and even scream, shake their fists, scowl, snarl, be sarcastic, or behave aggressively in other ways. Displaying hostility is one way a client has of dramatizing a conflict. Conflicts may involve disagreements, disappointments, or general displeasure. What is certain is that something is making the client mad.

Johnson (2009) points out that, although conflicts are generally viewed as being unpleasant incidents to be avoided, there are some positive aspects to conflict. For example, conflicts bring to the surface issues that are of serious concern to clients. Instead of hiding their negative feelings, clients may voice some hostility. A worker then knows what he or she is up against and can begin to address the issues involved. Additionally, conflict can provide motivating arenas for change. A client who is uncomfortable enough with a situation to voice hostility may be more motivated to work to resolve the problem causing the discomfort. Only then can the client revert to a calmer, more comfortable state.

In addition to the suggestions provided for working with involuntary clients, the following points propose ways for dealing with client hostility:

1. Do not get angry or defensive. Recognize your own reactions. Remember that this is a professional and not a personal issue.
2. Focus on the client's hostile *behavior* instead of labeling the client a hostile *person*. Label the hostile behavior and other dynamics as they occur.
3. Allow the client briefly to voice his or her anger. Be empathic. See the situation from the client's perspective.
4. Emphasize the client's personal strengths. Do not attack the client. You want to close, not widen, the rift in communication.
5. Know the facts regarding the client's situation. To help the client deal with reality, you must know what reality is.
6. Focus on the present and future. Avoid allowing the client to dwell on the past. Emphasize what can be done positively—not what has already happened negatively and cannot be changed.
7. Look at the various alternatives open to the client and their consequences. Help the client evaluate the pros and cons of each alternative.
8. Do not moralize. (It is helpful to remember the times someone has moralized to you about what you *should* do and how annoying it was.)
9. *Summarize* what has occurred during the interview and what *recommendations* have been made. Sometimes, this summarization helps the client to keep on track. You want to help the client deal objectively with his or her reality, not go off on tangents of emotional outbursts.
10. Establish short-term, initial goals with a hostile client. These might include calming the client down and establishing short-term goals, such as making a basic agreement to discuss a particular issue or to come to another appointment. These goals are quite different from addressing major problems as part of the intervention process.

A fourth suggestion involves clarifying your role for the client (Sheafor & Horejsi, 2012; Trotter, 2006). Trotter (2006) explains:

Clarification of role involves workers helping their clients to understand the nature of the direct practice process. It involves more than simply explaining the conditions of a court order or the mandate under which the worker operates. It is about exploring with clients the purpose of the intervention—what the worker and client each hope to achieve. (p. 65)

A fifth suggestion related to the fourth involves knowing the limits of your authority and, in effect, power over the client (Sheafor & Horejsi, 2012; Trotter, 2006). Giving the client the idea that you are the master and he or she must do what you say is usually a turnoff. However, you do want to clarify, at least in your own mind, the ultimate consequences of the client's involvement or lack of involvement with you. Depending on the circumstances, you may even want to state these consequences in the interview. Trotter (2006) emphasizes:

Involuntary clients should be clear about what is required of them, and what the likely consequences are if they do not comply with those requirements. They should be clear about whether these are legal requirements, organizational requirements or worker requirements.

For example, a child protection worker working with a family on a court order may have power to remove a child in certain circumstances. In what circumstances might this happen? Would a further incidence of physical assault automatically result in this occurring? Are there other "bottom lines" with which the parent must comply to keep the child? Can the parents use other forms of discipline with the child—for example, is any smacking acceptable? (pp. 69–70)

The sixth suggestion for work with involuntary clients concerns giving them as many choices as possible, including minor options (Cormier & Nurius, 2003; Sheafor & Horejsi, 2012). Having choices enhances people's self-respect, confidence, and sense of control over their lives. You might ask a client whether a meeting time at 1:00 p.m. or 4:00 p.m. better meets her schedule, or depending on the circumstances, you might ask a client what aspect of the treatment plan he would prefer to discuss for the next 10 minutes.

The seventh suggestion for involuntary client situations involves figuring out what the client would like you to do for him or her (Cormier & Nurius, 2003). This requires careful *listening* to what the client says. What is really important to the client? What can you do that will make the intervention worthwhile? Your usefulness is often best demonstrated to the client by providing some concrete service, benefit, or help the client needs (e.g., you might help set up a medical appointment, orchestrate transportation to work or an appointment, or make calls to arrange for child day care).

An eighth suggestion for working with involuntary clients concerns using "pro-social modeling and [positive] reinforcement in order to encourage and promote client pro-social values and behaviors" (Trotter, 2006, p. 87). *Modeling* is "the learning of behavior by observing another individual engaging in that behavior"; *positive reinforcement* includes "positive events or consequences that follow a behavior and strengthen it" (Zastrow & Kirst-Ashman, 2013, pp. 182, 185). The concept *pro-social* refers to "actions and values" that "support and care for others. Examples might include nonviolent interaction in domestic situations, equal personal relationships, caring for your children, trying to support yourself financially and not abusing drugs" (Trotter, 2006, p. 23). As a worker, you can

demonstrate socially appropriate, positive behaviors for an involuntary client and subsequently positively reinforce similar positive behavior when the client demonstrates it him- or herself. Workers should clearly identify "the values they wish to promote" and intentionally encourage "those values through the use of praise and other rewards" (Trotter, 2006, p. 67).

You can positively reinforce both clients' comments and behavior. Examples of pro-social comments are statements about the positive aspects of children's behavior or the desire to stop hitting a spouse. Examples of pro-social behaviors are: "using non-physical means to discipline children; undertaking a parenting skills course; arranging access with an estranged parent; talking to a child about feelings; showing interest in a child's schooling; attending an educational course; attending a case-planning meeting; or simply attending a meeting with the worker" (Trotter, 2006, p. 90).

Trotter (2006) discusses the use of positive reinforcement to encourage pro-social comments and behavior:

The most powerful reward or reinforcer available to the worker is praise. The pro-social approach involves the frequent use of praise for pro-social actions and comments. If, for example, a client attends a case-planning meeting, the social worker should make it clear that this is a good thing. . . .

[Another example of reinforcing pro-social behavior] relates to the place in which an interview is held. In deciding to conduct an interview in McDonald's, for example, rather than in the worker's office, the worker may be providing a reward to the client (particularly if the client also gets a free lunch). If the client is left to think that this is simply routine, then an opportunity is lost. Rather, using the pro-social approach, the worker would make it clear that the interview is being conducted away from the office because the client prefers this. The worker would point out that she is happy to put herself out in this way because the client has, for example, kept appointments regularly, followed up a referral to a parenting group and has openly discussed problems with the worker. The client in this instance gets a sense that doing the things that the worker wants will help to get what she (the client) wants. (pp. 91–92)

The ninth suggestion for working with involuntary clients involves allowing the client time to gain trust in you and in the intervention process (Hepworth et al., 2010). Expecting instant motivation is illogical. Allowing the client to get to know you as a competent professional while you establish a positive worker–client relationship is important.

The tenth suggestion for working with unwilling clients involves accepting the fact that, ultimately, the client has the right to choose whether or not to cooperate with you. After you have done your best, clients still may decide not to work with you. This choice is their right, and clients must live with the consequences of their decisions. You can help clients explore the negative and positive consequences of their decisions; however, they get to make the decision.

SUSPICION OF UNTRUTH

There may be times when a worker has a *gut reaction* that a client is not telling the truth. Gut reactions involve feelings that you get in reaction to situations where you feel in the back of your mind that something is occurring or something is wrong. Are details consistent? Are there gaps or inconsistencies in what the client is saying? Do some things not make sense to you? Becoming adept at identifying your gut reactions is useful because they often provide excellent clues about what is happening in any given situation.

Although we would probably prefer it otherwise, clients are not perfect. They may choose to lie for various reasons. Unfortunately, practitioners most often dislike addressing the issue of whether or not a client is telling the truth. Such confrontation often violates a worker's idea of "starting where the client is" and respecting the client. Confronting a possible lie is uncomfortable. For one thing, you may be wrong. The client may really be telling the truth.

Regardless, lying sometimes occurs. There are four suggestions regarding what to do if you think a client may be lying to you. First evaluate the situation logically. Do you have a feeling that something is not right? Are there discrepancies in facts? Does the client's story not have a realistic sense to it?

Consider a 3-year-old child with odd-looking, round burn marks on the tops of his hands. The parent explains that the burns are the result of accidentally spilling some hot water on his hands. Your gut reaction, however, is to question how such a hot water burn resulted in small circular burn marks instead of a large reddened area. Logically, you might think such burns are more likely to result from a lighted cigarette. Such a gut reaction may give you a clue that child abuse may be occurring. You then must pursue an investigation.

The second suggestion for dealing with possible lying is to examine the client's pattern of prior behavior. The examination, of course, can only be done if you have a history of interaction with the client or if you have access to records about how the client has behaved in the past. Has the client omitted facts or lied before? Have you suspected lying before? Is this the first time such behavior is suspected?

The third suggestion is that you may choose not to confront the client if this is the first time the possibility of lying has come up. You might give the client the benefit of the doubt.

The fourth suggestion about a client's lying is to evaluate the costs of believing or not believing your client. Is losing the client's trust more costly than you expressing disbelief? Is ignoring what you think is not true and risking possible severe consequences more costly? For example, if you strongly suspect that a pregnant mother is lying about abusing cocaine, can you afford to ignore the lie at the expense of the fetus's health?

LO 2-12 Terminate the Interview

EP 2.1.10l

Sometimes, bringing an interview to a close is difficult or uncomfortable. You may think the client is finally feeling comfortable with you. During the last five minutes of an interview, the client may raise strikingly significant issues. The client may express the strong need to continue talking.

Terminating the intervention process in general is addressed in Chapter 8. However, there are several points about how to end interviews and worker–client relationships that are relevant here.

First, before the actual interview termination (e.g., 5, 10, or even 15 minutes before), mention exactly how much time is left (Kadushin & Kadushin, 2013). You might say something like, "We're starting to get into some things you feel very strongly about. We've got another 10 minutes to talk about them today, and then we can continue them in our discussion next week." This reference to the time communicates that the ending is approaching. It acts as a guidepost for how much more the client will be able to pursue, and it also sets a time limit so that the client is not abruptly surprised when the interview draws to a close.

The second suggestion involves "sharing ending feelings" (Cournoyer, 2011, p. 429). You can tell the client about how you feel as the interview is coming to a close. Statements may include positive feelings you have toward the client and about what the client has accomplished. Of course, these statements must reflect genuine feelings. For example, you might say, "I've really enjoyed working with you. I think you've made great strides toward achieving your goals."

Social workers have many roles. The following diagrams illustrate some of the roles commonly assumed in micro practice. Circles are used to represent worker, client, and macro systems. Lines and arrows depict how systems relate to each other. Macro systems are usually organizations or communities. Client systems illustrated in these particular diagrams are individuals.

However, you should note how working on behalf of individuals often involves helping your clients deal with the many other systems with which they interact. The distinctions between micro, mezzo, and macro practice blur. Your goal as a professional social worker is to help your clients solve problems, obtain resources, and address issues by using the most effective means possible. These illustrations are what being a generalist practitioner is all about.

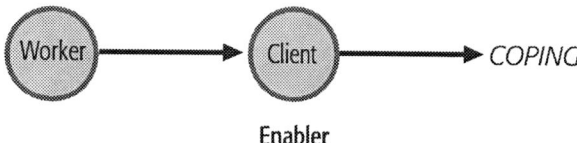
Enabler

The *enabler* role involves providing support, encouragement, and suggestions to a client system so that the client may proceed more easily and successfully in completing tasks or solving problems. The preceding diagram illustrates how workers can provide such support. An arrow pointing from the worker circle to the client-system circle depicts the worker's support. The desired result is that the client system will be better able to cope with problems and to pursue some course of action.

Broker

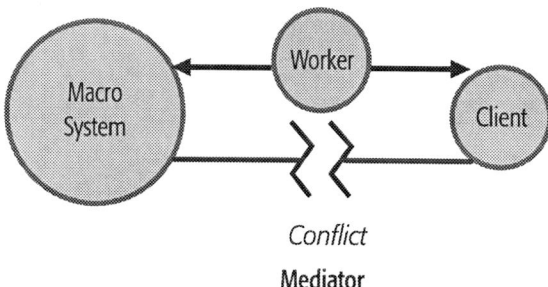
Conflict
Mediator

The *broker* role involves linking clients with needed resources. The line from the worker circle to the arrow in the preceding diagram portrays the worker's role. It illustrates the worker's active involvement in obtaining resources for the client. The arrow points from the macro-system circle, which provides resources, to the client-system circle, which receives them.

Mediators work to help conflicting parties settle disputes and agree on compromises. A mediator maintains a neutral stance between the involved parties, taking no one's side. In the preceding diagram, the broken line beneath the worker circle depicts the two parties' broken lines of communication and their inability to settle differences.

 Here the worker is mediating between a client system and a macro system. However, mediation can occur between systems of virtually any size, including between two macro systems or two micro systems. Consider, for instance, divorce mediation, where disputes are settled and agreements made between divorcing spouses.

FIGURE 2.4 Social Work Roles with Micro Systems

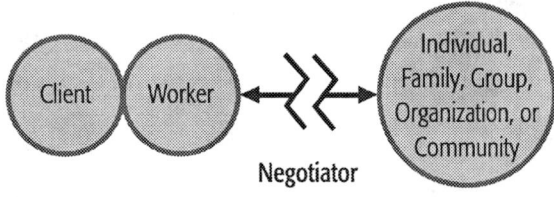

Negotiator

A *negotiator* is an intermediary who acts to settle disputes and/or resolve disagreements. However, unlike mediators, negotiators clearly take the side of one of the parties involved.

Here the client and the worker are located together represented by circles on the left side of the figure. This indicates that the worker is negotiating on behalf of the client. Two jagged lines with arrows pointing away from them in opposing directions characterize the conflict that has arisen. The circle on the right may represent an individual, family, group, organization, or community that is engulfed in conflict with the client and the worker/negotiator on the left. The worker/negotiator seeks to resolve the conflict, but does so on behalf of one side of the conflict, namely, the client.

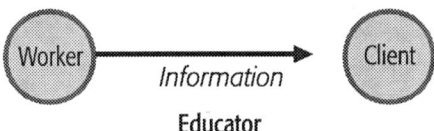

Educator

As an *educator*, a worker conveys information to a client. The arrow leading from the circle representing the worker on the left to the circle representing the client on the right illustrates that information is being communicated.

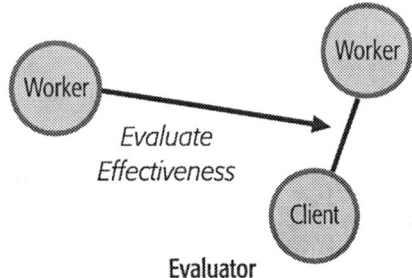

Evaluator

All practitioners need to assume the role of *evaluator* in terms of the effectiveness of their own practice. The arrow in the preceding diagram portrays the worker evaluating his or her own intervention with a client.

FIGURE 2.4 Continued

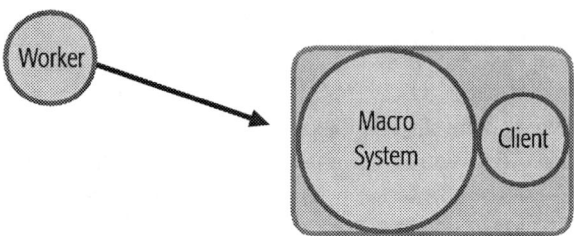

Case Manager/Coordinator

Many clients have multiple problems and are involved with many other systems. One role social workers often assume is that of *case manager* or *case coordinator*. This role involves seeking out resources, planning how they might be delivered, organizing service provision, and monitoring progress.

The box enclosing the macro and client systems represents the coordinated interactions between these two systems. The arrow pointing from the worker to the box depicts the worker's active involvement in coordinating all of the systems involved. Although the preceding diagram illustrates the coordination of one macro and one micro client system, such coordination can occur among any number of macro, mezzo, and micro systems.

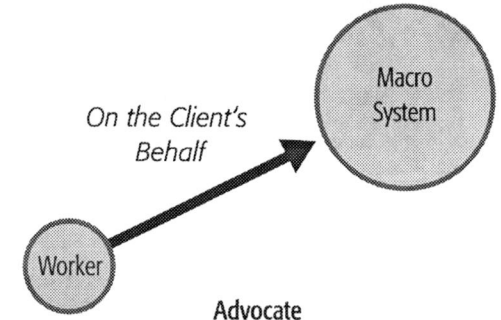

Advocate

EP 2.1.1a

Advocates champion the rights of others. They usually advocate with the goal of empowering their clients. The arrow in the preceding diagram, which leads from the worker to the macro system, is exceptionally thick. This line represents the significant amount of energy needed to have an impact on larger, more powerful systems. Advocacy is an extremely significant role in generalist social work practice.

© Cengage Learning

A third recommendation for terminating interviews concerns asking clients to summarize what they think they have learned and accomplished (Fortune, 1995; Shulman, 2012). As the intervention progresses, the client should become increasingly articulate about what goals have become established and attained. How to identify and monitor goals is discussed more thoroughly in Chapters 6 through 8. Summarization helps a client focus in on the core meaningfulness of the intervention. Additionally, clarifying exactly what has been learned so it can be used to address new problems and situations again in the future helps a client.

The final suggestion for terminating interviews involves encouraging clients to share their own feelings about the intervention process (Fortune, 1995). Not only can you as a worker share your feelings about the interview and intervention process, but you can also draw out your client's reactions. As we have discussed earlier, expressing feelings openly allows clients to deal with them and move on with their lives. For example, a worker might say, "You seem awfully anxious right now. We've been working together for quite awhile. Sometimes, it's scary to move on alone. How are you feeling?"

LO 2-13 Employ Multiple Roles When Working with Clients

This chapter reviewed a wide range of skills for working with individuals that can be used while fulfilling numerous roles. Figure 2.4 depicts seven such roles.

Chapter Summary

The following summarizes this chapter's content as it relates to each learning objective (LO) presented at the beginning of the chapter. Chapter content helps prepare students to:

LO 2-1   Use interviewing skills to engage, assess, intervene, and evaluate with individuals in the planned change process.

The interview can provide an effective mechanism for communicating and pursuing planned change with clients. Dimensions to consider include beginning the worker–client relationship, verbal and nonverbal behavior, relationship-enhancing characteristics, client self-determination and empowerment, starting the interview, conducting the interview, and using critical thinking skills to address difficult issues.

LO 2-2   Demonstrate effective nonverbal behavior when working with clients.

Important aspects of nonverbal behavior include eye contact, attentive listening, facial expressions, and body positioning.

LO 2-3   Use empathy and other interpersonal skills when working with clients.

Warmth involves conveying a feeling of interest, concern, well-being, and affection to another individual. Empathy concerns not only being in tune with how a client feels, but also conveying to that client that you understand how he or she feels. Genuineness is the honest, natural, and open expression of yourself.

LO 2-4   Maintain a commitment to client self-determination and empowerment.

Self-determination is each individual's right to make his or her own decisions. Self-determination is related to empowerment, a major concept in the definition of generalist practice. Empowerment is the "process of increasing personal, interpersonal, or political power so that individuals can take action to improve their life situations" (Gutierrez, 2001, p. 210).

LO 2-5   Prepare for action with individuals and families by effectively starting the interview.

Starting an interview involves a number of aspects to consider, including the interview setting, how to dress, planning ahead, initial introductions, alleviating the client's anxiety, portraying confidence and competence, and the beginning statement of purpose and role.

LO 2-6   Demonstrate effective oral communication while conducting the interview.

When interviewing, verbal techniques include simple encouragement, rephrasing, reflective responding, clarification, interpretation, providing information, emphasizing the client's strengths, appropriate self-disclosure, summarization, eliciting information, and the cautious use of the word *why*.

LO 2-7   Enhance cultural competence through the use of ethnographic interviewing.

One aspect of cultural competence involves the use of ethnographic interviewing. Ethnographic interviewing focuses on learning about a client's cultural world, including values, behavioral expectations, and language. This incorporates the understanding and use of global questions, cover terms, and descriptors.

LO 2-8 Stress clients' strengths.

Questions that stress and assess clients' strengths include those concerning client behaviors and accomplishments, clients' personal qualities, and clients' resources.

LO 2-9 Apply critical thinking to address challenges in interviewing.

Critical thinking should be involved when facing various challenges in interviewing. These include cross-cultural awareness, dealing with and using silence in the interview, confronting clients, working with involuntary clients, handling client hostility, and dealing with suspicion of untruth.

LO 2-10 Develop cross-cultural awareness in interviewing.

Learning about people from other cultures is an ongoing, continuous process. Practitioners should consider national origin and the extent to which clients are acculturated into the mainstream culture. Workers should also give special attention to the stereotypes, prejudices, discrimination, and oppression negatively affecting people from various ethnic and racial groups.

LO 2-11 Address spirituality as an aspect of diversity.

Religion involves people's spiritual beliefs concerning the origin of, character of, and reason for being, usually based on the existence of some high power or powers; these beliefs often include designated rituals and provide direction for what is considered moral or right. Spirituality is "the individual search for meaning, purpose, and values" that typically rises above everyday physical limitations and connects one to something greater than oneself (O'Neill, 1999, p. 3). Social workers should not impose their personal beliefs on clients. Rather, they should seek out clients' own beliefs and emphasize them as a source of strength. Faith-based social services range from "faith-permeated" to "faith-secular partnership organizations" (Tangenberg, 2005, p. 201).

LO 2-12 Terminate the interview.

Suggestions for terminating interviews include alerting clients to how much time remains, "sharing ending feelings" (Cournoyer 2011, p. 429), summarizing what has occurred, and encouraging clients to share their own feelings.

LO 2-13 Employ multiple roles when working with clients.

Professional roles in micro practice include broker, enabler, mediator, educator, evaluator, case manager/coordinator, and advocate.

Competency Notes

The following identifies where Educational Policy (EP) competencies and practice behaviors are discussed in the chapter.

EP 2.1.1a Advocate for client access to the services of social work. *(p. 89)*: Figure 2.4 describes the role of advocate. *(p. 91)*: The role of advocate described in this section may involve working with agency and community macro systems so that clients receive the social work services they need. It may also entail improving clients' access to such services. For example, a practitioner might advocate for a change in agency policy to expand clients' eligibility requirements. The result would be that a broader range of clients could receive the services they need.

EP 2.1.1b Practice personal reflection and self-correction to assure continual professional development. *(p. 56)*: Emphasizing self-awareness and improving both communication and relationship skills are continuous processes for social workers. The subsequent sections on nonverbal behavior, including warmth, empathy, and genuineness, and verbal communication explore some of the dimensions involved. *(p. 63)*: Preparing for and conducting each interview requires significant personal reflection about the impression you make and how you can be most effective. Each interview may require adjustments, depending on the clients and the situation.

EP 2.1.1c Attend to professional roles and boundaries. *(p. 89)*: Professional roles in practice with individuals and families include broker, enabler, mediator, negotiator, educator, evaluator, case manager/coordinator, and advocate.

EP 2.1.1d Demonstrate professional demeanor in behavior, appearance, and communication. *(p. 64)*: Professional social workers should dress appropriately and maintain a professional appearance. *(p. 67)*: Profession practitioners should demonstrate effective communication with clients.

EP 2.1.1e Engage in career-long learning. *(pp. 68, 76)*: Learning about people from other cultures is a continuous process.

EP 2.1.3 **Apply critical thinking to inform and communicate professional judgments.** *(pp. 59, 62, 81):* Critical thinking questions are posed. *(p. 71):* Highlight 2.4 discusses the professional judgment used in a case and provides suggestions for improvement. *(p. 76):* Challenges in interviewing often require critical thinking to make informed professional judgments.

EP 2.1.3c **Demonstrate effective oral and written communication in working with individuals, families, groups, organizations, communities, and colleagues.** *(p. 65):* Using direct and indirect questions appropriately demonstrates effective oral communication *(p. 67):* Effective oral communication when working with individuals may involve the range of techniques discussed here.

EP 2.1.4 **Engage diversity and difference in practice.** *(p. 68):* Dimensions of diversity include color (of skin), culture, and ethnicity. Ethnographic interviewing provides one means of enhancing cultural competence to understand how diversity characterizes and shapes the human experience. *(p. 79):* Religion and spirituality are other important aspects of diversity.

EP 2.1.4a **Recognize the extent to which a culture's structures and values may oppress, marginalize, alienate, or create or enhance privilege and power.** *(p. 76):* It's important to be aware of factors involved in oppressing diverse cultural groups.

EP 2.1.4b **Gain sufficient self-awareness to eliminate the influence of personal biases and values in working with diverse groups.** *(p. 76):* Social workers should strive to enhance their awareness of personal biases that might affect their work with clients from other cultures.

EP 2.1.4c **Recognize and communicate their understanding of the importance of difference in shaping life experiences.** *(p. 76):* Cultural values and practices affect people's choices and situations.

EP 2.1.4d **View themselves as learners and engage those with whom they work as informants.** *(p. 76):* Practitioners should learn from their clients about these clients' cultures.

EP 2.1.10 **Engage, assess, intervene, and evaluate with individuals, families, groups, organizations, and communities.** *(p. 55):* Interviews can be used to help implement various phases of planned change in generalist practice. Dimensions to consider addressed throughout this chapter include

beginning the worker–client relationship, verbal and nonverbal behavior, relationship-enhancing characteristics, client self-determination and empowerment, starting the interview, conducting the interview, and using critical thinking skills to address difficult issues.

EP 2.1.10a **Substantively and affectively prepare for action with individuals, families, groups, organizations, and communities.** *(p. 63):* Preparing for action with individuals entails a range of aspects involved in starting the interview. These include the interview setting, how to dress, planning ahead, initial introductions, alleviating the client's anxiety, portraying confidence and competence, and the beginning statement of purpose and role.

EP 2.1.10b **Use empathy and other interpersonal skills.** *(p. 59):* Warmth, empathy, and genuineness are interpersonal characteristics used to enhance the process of engagement with clients. Highlight 2.1 provides an opportunity to practice empathic responses.

EP 2.1.10c **Develop a mutually agreed-on focus of work and desired outcomes.** *(p. 63):* Because client self-determination is so important, the intervention should have a focus that is mutually agreed upon by the client and worker.

EP 2.1.10e **Assess client strengths and limitations.** *(p. 72):* Emphasizing and assessing client strengths is critical in assessment and other phases of planned change. Highlight 2.5 provides specific suggestions for assessing client strengths.

EP 2.1.10f **Develop mutually agreed-on intervention goals and objectives.** *(p. 63):* Client self-determination is a basic foundation of practice, so goals should be mutually agreed upon by the client and worker.

EP 2.1.10k **Negotiate, mediate, and advocate for clients.** *(p. 89):* Social work roles described in this section include mediator, negotiator, and advocate. *(p. 90):* The mediator role is portrayed.

EP 2.1.10l **Facilitate transitions and endings.** *(p. 88):* Means are presented to facilitate the ending or termination process.

On the Internet

Visit the *Understanding Generalist Practice* CourseMate at **www.cengagebrain.com** for resources such as quizzes, glossaries and videos.

Practice Skills for Working with Groups

© Monkey Business Images/Shutterstock.com

Learning Objectives   *This chapter will help prepare students to:*

LO 3-1	Articulate the benefits and functions of treatment and task groups.
LO 3-2	Attend to professional roles in groups.
LO 3-3	Utilize conceptual frameworks in group assessment, intervention, and evaluation.
LO 3-4	Select appropriate problem-solving and decision-making approaches with groups.
LO 3-5	Use empathy and other interpersonal skills with groups.

SIX YOUNG ADULTS sit around the room fidgeting nervously and avoiding each other's eyes. Each wonders what the others are thinking. All would describe themselves as shy, inadequate, and depressed. This is despite the fact that their individual personalities vary drastically. All had tried to kill themselves at least once, which is why they are gathered together in that room. The six are about to begin their involvement in a treatment group. The group's initial purpose is to help participants explore the reasons for their sadness and begin to build more fortified self-concepts and lives. The social worker enters the room. Group treatment is about to begin.

The group's chairperson is feeling increasingly anxious. She has already interrupted Mr. Fischer twice. Now he is rambling on again about irrelevant details. He simply will not stop talking and she has only 23 more minutes to bring the group to a consensus. This group was a task group trying to initiate a plan for publicizing a new child abuse prevention program. Finally, at her wit's end, she states loudly and assertively, "Excuse me, Mr. Fischer. I appreciate your ideas and input. Our time is very limited. We need to hear what the other group members have to say." The rest of the people in the room seem to breathe a simultaneous sigh of relief. The meeting proceeds.

Jimmy is a 9-year-old with cognitive disabilities who has lived with foster parents almost since birth. Jimmy has a number of serious developmental delays, including intellectual, language, social, and physical (both fine and gross motor). Even though he resides in foster care, he remains involved with his biological parents and his seven siblings still living with them. The biological family struggles with a multitude of problems, including poverty, truancy, illness, and the mother's own cognitive disability. The foster parents and the biological parents do not like each other much and quarrel regularly. Jimmy visits his biological family on a weekly basis.

A number of professionals sit around a large rectangular table discussing Jimmy and his situation. Each had evaluated his case and now will make professional recommendations. They comprise an interdisciplinary staffing team (i.e., a planning meeting involving a number of different professional disciplines). A social worker is the case coordinator. It is her job to run the meeting and help bring the team to conclusions regarding the best plan to help Jimmy. The speech, physical, and occupational therapists along with the nurse, physician, psychologist, and psychiatrist will all share their findings. Together they will formulate plans to help Jimmy, his foster family, and his biological family. As case coordinator, the social worker is responsible for pulling together a broad range of information so that it makes sense. Her task is to lead the group in formulating effective intervention plans.

LO 3-1 Articulate the Benefits and Functions of Treatment and Task Groups

EP 2.1.10a

The previous examples show the types of groups that social workers might lead. Much of social work occurs within, by, or for groups. A social worker, therefore, needs both group knowledge and skills. Increasingly, social workers use groups for a variety of purposes. A *group* is a collection of people with shared interests who come together to pursue individual, group, organization, and/or community goals. Groups help chemically dependent people and those trying to lose weight. Groups help children cope with the divorce of their parents, teach new foster parents about the effects of separation and placement on foster children, and help family members deal with many problem areas. They assist persons with psychiatric disabilities to live in their own communities through such mechanisms as peer-led recovery groups, advocacy groups, and family support groups (Farone, 2006; Mackelprang & Salsgiver, 2009).

Social workers also play a role in some self-help groups such as Parents Anonymous.

In addition, social workers use groups to gather information about clients and to help plan interventions. In many settings, social workers participate in staffings where colleagues from other disciplines share their knowledge about a particular client. Case conferences are common in medical settings and other types of agencies.

Most social workers will participate in agency staff meetings where the focus may be on new policies, in-service training, or agency problems. In some cases, social workers may be involved in using social groups such as those using Facebook. Regardless of the type, purpose, or location of the group, the social worker will need specific knowledge and skills to participate as an effective group member, leader, or facilitator.

Benefits of Groups

It is no accident that groups have become an important component of our lives. We are born into a group (family) and eventually become a member of multiple groups through our associations at work, church, and other venues. Humans are social animals and need to belong, to be accepted by others. Groups also provide a variety of benefits that go beyond those available in one-to-one relationships. These benefits include mutual assistance, connecting with others, testing new behaviors, goal achievement, and decision making. The advent of social networks underscores the importance of being connected with others. At the time of this writing, Facebook has at least 750 million subscribers or followers, Twitter has 250 million, and LinkedIn has 110 million, and there are at least a dozen other social networking sites also with millions of participants (EBiz/MBA, 2013). Some are focused on specific groups sharing common characteristics—such as Cafe-Mom, which caters to mothers, and Meetup, which focuses on getting neighbors together. In addition, there are multiple dating sites, many of which focus on a particular segment of the population, such as Christians, singles over 50, or members of specific ethnic groups. Clearly, the need to affiliate with other human beings is a significant factor in the growth of social networking.

MUTUAL ASSISTANCE

Groups offer the opportunity to give help to and receive help from others. This mutuality is the basis for our affiliations with many groups. The help given or used may include companionship, material assistance, emotional or spiritual support, access to resources, and others. Sometimes only a group can provide the array of assistance needed by the individual member.

CONNECTING WITH OTHERS

The ability to connect with other people helps reduce individual isolation and allows sharing of thoughts, feelings, and beliefs. By being connected, we feel less alone and are in a better position to test our reality against those of others. By talking with others, we can also place our problems in perspective. Groups give us a chance to identify with others who share our feelings and interests. This is a prime purpose of social networking sites.

TESTING NEW BEHAVIORS

Groups allow us to test out new behaviors in a safer environment than might ordinarily be available. Group members are in a position to provide feedback, suggestions, and support for the efforts of the individual to change.

GOAL ACHIEVEMENT

The combined ability of a group to accomplish things is typically greater than that of any random individual. Groups can generate ideas, solutions, and responses in greater numbers than is true for a single person. In addition, the combined resources of a group—which include such things as energy, expertise, and wisdom—offer a much greater likelihood that a problem can be solved.

DECISION MAKING

One additional benefit of groups is the capacity to bring the wisdom of many to the decision-making process. Different people looking at the same problem are likely to have varied opinions based on their own experiences, knowledge, and thinking skills. That groups often make better decisions than individuals is well recognized (Bonner, 2004). To get the best results from the varied abilities of group members requires that the potential contributions of each member are considered and that the opinions of those with special expertise receive attention. Not only will careful use of groups to make decisions likely produce better results, but also group members are more likely to accept and feel commitment to the decisions that are made. Buy-in by members is especially important when they will be expected to carry out decisions made in the group.

The benefits of group decision making also extend to family groups. Sheets et al. (2009) explored the use of family group decision making in Child Protective Services with Anglo, African-American, and Hispanic families and found several positive outcomes. These included a higher level of satisfaction among participants, an increased sense of empowerment, and faster exits from foster care.

Critical Thinking Questions 3.1

EP 2.1.3

- As the leader of a group responsible for making a decision, what would you do to encourage critical thinking in your group?
- What do you see as the pros and cons of using a group to make decisions?

Differentiating Types of Groups

There are different ways to categorize the types of groups with which social workers are frequently involved. Perhaps the most common approach is to divide groups into either *task groups* or *treatment groups.* Each of these two basic types can be further divided into more specific categories.

TASK GROUPS

As their name suggests, *task groups* exist to achieve a specific set of objectives or tasks. Concerted attention is paid to these tasks, and attainment of the desired ends assumes great importance. The objectives help determine how the group operates and the roles played by members. The following list is not exhaustive but provides examples of the types of task groups with which the social worker may come in contact. They include boards of directors, task forces, committees and commissions, legislative bodies, staff meetings, multidisciplinary teams, case conferences (staffings), and social action groups. The possible roles the social worker might play are described under each type.

EP 2.1.1a
EP 2.1.1c
EP 2.1.5b
EP 2.1.8
EP 2.1.10h

Boards of Directors

A *board of directors* is an administrative group charged with responsibility for setting the policy governing agency programs. The board is a legal entity established by the bylaws, organizational charter, or articles of incorporation. Normally, the board hires and supervises the agency director and determines policy within which the agency operates. Such policy has direct impact on what agency practitioners can and cannot do for clients. Boards often establish subgroups or committees responsible for such things as personnel policies, finance, and buildings.

Members of the board are not usually experts in the operation of the agency but are elected or selected based upon other contributions they may make. For instance, they are often prominent community citizens and may financially support the agency.

Social workers working with a board of directors for the first time may find it challenging. Board members know a great deal less about the agency than many staff members and must be kept well informed. As laypersons, they may not understand why a program exists and may not share all the values of agency staff. Because their position is one of authority (remember, they hire and fire the director who can hire or fire you and your supervisors), working with board members takes tact and finesse. Because they provide the agency with a strong connection to the community and are often instrumental in fundraising, board members are an irreplaceable asset for the agency.

Task Forces

Task forces are groups established for a special purpose and usually disbanded after completion of their task. They may be created by any of the other task groups mentioned in this section. For example, a board of directors might appoint a task force to explore new funding approaches for the 21st century. A United Way task force may be established to consider better ways of distributing funds to new agencies. Members of a task force usually are appointed because of their special expertise or interest in the topic under consideration. They are expected to study the idea or problem, consider alternatives, and prepare a report. After completion of the report, the task force usually goes out of existence.

Committees and Commissions

Committees are groups responsible for dealing with specific tasks or matters. They may be formed by people in virtually any agency or organization. Members of a committee may be appointed or elected, depending upon the type of committee. A board of directors may create a personnel committee to develop personnel policies for the agency and evaluate the agency director's performance. An agency may appoint a committee to plan the annual holiday party. Committees typically work in a particular area and are typically one of two types: standing or ad hoc. A standing committee is one that exists on a continuous basis. It may be provided for in an organization's bylaws (e.g., an executive committee or finance committee) or it may be established by agency administrators (e.g., a speakers' committee).

An *ad hoc committee,* like a task force, is set up for one purpose and expected to cease operation after completing its task. A committee to revise an organization's bylaws is a good example of an ad hoc committee. Much like task force members, committee members may be selected because they have a particular interest in the committee's task or because of their expertise.

Commissions are similar to committees in that they also are responsible for a particular task. They are usually ongoing in nature. Examples of commissions include the Council on Social Work Education's (CSWE) Commission on Accreditation and the National Association of Social Workers' (NASW) Commission on Inquiry. A community may have a city planning commission, a nondiscrimination and affirmative action commission, and a police and fire commission. These groups exist to help city officials with particular tasks. The planning commission may review all requests for new buildings or consider only those falling into a certain category. The nondiscrimination committee may investigate charges of discrimination in the application of city laws and regulations. The police and fire commission may help set policy for the police and fire departments. Commission members may be elected but usually are appointed by an administrator with approval of the governing board. Members of the CSWE's Commission on Accreditation are appointed by the president of the CSWE after consultation with the board of directors. Members of such groups are called commissioners.

Legislative Bodies

Legislative bodies include city councils, county boards of supervisors, state legislatures, and the U.S. Congress. Composed of elected representatives, these bodies have legal responsibility for establishing laws and appropriating funds for programs established by law. A social worker's interaction with these bodies can occur in many ways. Social workers currently serve as elected members of each of these bodies. They may also be called upon or choose to testify before legislative bodies on particular issues. Examples might include laws affecting clients, funding for social programs, family leave legislation, or Social Security policy. Sometimes, a social worker may serve on the staff of a legislative body, handling details such as scheduling, locating meeting sites, and ensuring that identified tasks are carried out. Social workers may also staff local offices of legislators handling constituent concerns. Because legislative bodies establish policies (laws) that affect which social programs are created and funded, being familiar with how these bodies operate is important for social workers. They also must be prepared to testify about the need for programs and to work with members of legislative bodies to achieve social work purposes. Such purposes might include licensing of social workers at all levels (BSW, MSW, and so on) and funding for social programs. Finally, social workers must be willing to serve as members of legislative bodies.

Staff Meetings

Staff meetings are meetings composed of agency staff members who assemble periodically for some identified purpose. Some agencies have meetings of all staff members on a regular basis. Others assemble only small groups regularly (such as all supervisors or all members of the foster care staff). Staff meetings occur for the purposes of explaining new policy, providing continuing education, keeping all participants informed about changes in the agency, or introducing new staff. Sometimes, the meetings have the social or emotional function of bringing all staff members together to enhance the sense of community or "we" feeling. Often, the agency director or other supervisory personnel preside over the staff meeting. Depending upon the type of agency (and preferences of the director), the meeting may consist of an administrator announcing new policies and everyone else listening, or it may be a discussion session where all members are equally free to contribute ideas and reactions.

Multidisciplinary Teams

Multidisciplinary teams, or *M teams,* are groups of professionals from various disciplines that meet to discuss specific clients with whom team members are working. In a state institution for patients with severe cognitive disabilities, a team may consist of a social worker, nurse, medical doctor, psychologist, and aide. In a hospital health works program, the M team may include a registered nurse, social worker, dietician, and psychologist. One member of the team often serves as the leader, but all members are responsible for their specific area of expertise. Typically, teams meet regularly.

Case Conferences and Staffings

Case conferences are agency or organizational meetings in which all professionals involved in a particular case (client) discuss such things as the client's identified problems, goals, and intervention plans. An example would be a child protection case conference involving parents, child protection social workers, and other professionals gathered to review a specific child who is considered at risk of neglect or abuse. Case conferences, also called *staffings*, are similar to multidisciplinary teams. One difference is that, unlike the M team, the members who compose the case conference may not be perceived as or see themselves as a team. They may meet on an as-needed basis instead of regularly. Depending upon the type of agency, members participating in the case conference or staffing may be from the same or different disciplines.

Sometimes an entire department will staff a client. Here, all members can contribute to the decision making. For example, one juvenile probation department staffs all cases where the probation officer's presentence investigation includes a recommendation for incarceration. Other probation officers look at the same evidence gathered by the investigating officer and consider whether or not the recommendation was appropriate. The purpose of a staffing is to bring the wisdom of others to bear on a particular situation and engage in critical thinking to arrive at the best solution or recommendation.

Social Action Groups

Social action involves efforts undertaken by individuals and groups to bring about solutions to social and economic problems. Although we often think of social action as involving social workers and their clients, the process may be initiated and conducted by professionals from various fields (e.g., economics, political science, religion) as well as by those directly affected by social or economic injustice. The goal is to cause change in some aspect of the environment. This can include social policies, physical conditions, or any other condition that is considered undesirable. Social action is being employed by environmentalists in the United States, Russia, and central Asia to bring about sustainable societies and stop global warming. It is also being employed by groups to empower youth in Zimbabwe, ensure the availability of sanitary water in Bangladesh, and collect clothes for the homeless in Washington, D.C. Beneficiaries of this change may be either members of the social action group or other nonmembers.

Goals might include getting the city to enforce health and building codes, changing the eligibility requirements for a specific social program, or modifying rules or laws that discriminate against a particular class of persons.

Highlight 3.1 describes the use of a specialized type of research called *Participatory Action Research (PAR)* to develop data that could be used to bring about change in a government program. Also called "critical action research" (Dudley, 2005, p. 29) or "empowerment evaluation" (Krysik & Finn, 2010, p. 356), PAR is based on the belief that it is important to work directly with those who are affected by a situation and involve them in the process of gathering data, analyzing the results, and translating the findings to decision makers. The model has been used to conduct needs assessments (Dudley & Stone, 2001), improve skills in older adults (Blair & Minkler, 2009), and address health inequities in a population (Chirewa, 2012), and has been employed with youth groups, clients with serious mental health challenges, indigenous populations, and other marginalized groups. The principle behind PAR is consistent with the social work emphasis on empowerment, capacity building, sustainability, and collaboration. By using their own talents and efforts, those affected by the research are fully involved in the end product.

HIGHLIGHT 3.1

Engaging in Research-Informed Practice: A Participatory Action Research Group

EP 2.1.6

The Disability Coalition, an advocacy group for people with disabilities, had been rebuffed several times as it tried to convince a legislative committee that the health needs of those with disabilities were not being adequately met. Lobbying for additional funds from the state was a frustrating and, ultimately, unsuccessful endeavor. Members of the Disability Coalition decided to gather data to underscore their arguments about unmet health care needs of those they served. Working with an advisor from a nearby college, they carefully thought about what kinds of data they would need, what methods they would employ to gather the data, and how the data would be reported once acquired. They met with both members of their own organization as well as with other individuals with disabilities to consider what questions to ask. They identified a set of survey questions, designed a needs assessment (described further in Chapter 4), trained those who would be asking the questions, and developed a protocol for analyzing their findings. They then used a snowball sample method in which each person interviewed was asked to identify another person with a disability whom the group might interview. By the end of the process, they had interviewed over 250 individuals with a disability and identified 12 common health needs that were unmet in this group. They convinced the local newspaper to write an article on their findings, which was published just prior to the start of the next legislative session, where the Disability Coalition was successful in getting additional state funding.

As another example, a social action group might be composed of social workers testifying before a legislative body requesting funds for drug and alcohol treatment programs. Yet another example would be citizens asking the city council to rezone their neighborhood to stop the conversion of existing homes into multifamily housing. The social worker may be a group member or serve as the group's leader. Another possible role is as a staff or resource person to the group. In this role, the worker might help arrange meetings, provide the names of contact persons within existing agencies and organizations, or assist the group in whatever ways are needed. Having the skill to help the group reach its goal, while ensuring sufficient stability of the group until completion of the task, is important for the worker (Toseland & Rivas, 2012). For example, the worker might help the group over rough spots such as early setbacks or failures by encouraging and supporting their efforts and then might follow up on all decisions to make certain that the group's wishes are carried out. Highlight 3.2 provides an example of a social action group.

As is evident, many task groups exist to help achieve organizational goals. Examples include boards of directors, committees, and staff meetings. Others may be created to advocate for client access to services, promote policies that advance social well-being, and advocate for human rights and social and economic justice (see Highlight 3.2).

TREATMENT GROUPS

Treatment groups' primary focus is on the emotional and social needs of their members. Six types of treatment groups will be discussed: growth, therapy, educational, socialization, self-help, and support (Toseland & Rivas, 2012). In each group, there is a presumption that the individual member of the group is going to benefit directly from the existence of the group. Usually, individual change occurs within group members, and that change is often the reason for the group's creation.

Growth Groups

As the name suggests, *growth groups* are designed to encourage and support the growth of the individual group member. The presumption is that this growth can be done by helping the member achieve insight or self-understanding. The group experience may consist of various activities designed to help participants reach their goals. One example would be a group focused on helping couples learn to communicate better. A series of exercises might be done emphasizing listening skills, values clarification, and sending clear messages. Another example is a group composed of women who have sought refuge in a domestic violence shelter. The group meets twice a week with a focus on helping the members explore what they want from their lives. Activities include a time for each person to talk about her immediate and long-term goals and didactic presentations on the pattern of violent relationships.

HIGHLIGHT 3.2

Advocating for Human Rights and Social Justice: Social Action

EP 2.1.5b

The staff members in the university counseling and health office were becoming increasingly concerned about policies and procedures being initiated by the program director. The policies and procedures did not seem directed toward helping students and appeared increasingly erratic. The director often threatened to fire staff who disagreed with him and implied that all his actions had the backing of his immediate supervisor. Although he possessed a nursing degree, the director was also making decisions beyond his level of training and competence. After several failed attempts to talk directly to the director, staff members met and decided that additional steps would be neces-

sary to change the situation and restore harmony within the program. Each staff member wrote to the vice president for Health and Counseling Services (the program director's supervisor) and identified individual concerns. A copy of each letter was sent to the director so that he was made aware of the staff's continuing concern. The letter also clearly stated that the staff had decided to follow the appropriate chain of command to create change. In other words, the staff was committed to take the issue up to the director's supervisor and even higher levels, if necessary. Following discussions between the vice president, the director, and members of the staff, the director chose to resign his position, and a search was conducted for a replacement.

The group also makes the women aware of alternatives open to them, such as court-imposed restraining orders and financial resources in the community, and supports them in their efforts to be free of abuse. Growth groups focus on helping individuals achieve their potential and building on their strengths. There is no presumption that members necessarily have a "problem."

In growth groups, the worker is a facilitator, helping the group members attain their goals. As with most groups, the worker's role involves a higher level of activity in early stages and less activity as the group develops.

Therapy Groups

Therapy groups help clients who have an identified goal of changing some aspect of their behavior or thinking. The term includes groups where the objective is recovering from problematic life experiences. Such groups include a hospital-sponsored group for clients 20 percent or more overweight, an inpatient group for chemically dependent patients, and a group for people who abuse their children. The focus is on correcting a perceived intrapersonal or interpersonal problem or learning better problem-solving and coping styles. For example, Brown, Reyes, Brown, and Gonzenbach (2012) demonstrated the effectiveness of groups for female adult incest survivors. Similarly, Duffany and Panos (2009) found that group treatment is an effective intervention for child victims of sexual abuse and results in fewer of these youth becoming perpetrators later in life. Long, Fulton, Dolley, and Hollin (2011) also found positive outcomes with group treatment of dual-diagnosed women in secure mental health facilities as did Morell and Myers (2009) in their review of group treatment effectiveness with substance abusers.

The worker role is one of higher visibility in this type of group. The worker may begin as a director, expert, or leader, depending upon the needs of the group, but probably will become more of a facilitator as the group progresses.

Educational Groups

Educational groups include a variety of groups designed to provide members with information about themselves or others. The purpose, as suggested by the name, is to educate or teach the group members about some issue or topic. This education may be done through didactic presentations, role playing, activities, and discussions. Examples include a group for prospective adoptive parents, natural childbirth groups, and practical parenting groups. Another example is a socialization group serving recent immigrants. The group offers an orientation to newcomers and provides information on housing, available social services, language instruction, and other items useful for surviving in a strange society. Educational groups are similar to growth groups in that there is no presumption that members have a "problem." Educational groups tend to have less interaction among leaders and members than growth or therapy groups.

As in the therapy group, the worker in an educational group is often a group leader who may be doing much of the presentation of new information and serving as the group expert. In a group focused on teaching parents new child nurturing skills, a BSW field student developed the curriculum after reviewing similar programs, put together the charts and exercises to be used by participants, and led the group through each session.

Socialization Groups

Socialization groups assist participants in acquiring skills necessary to become "socialized" into the community. The presumption is that the group members have a deficit of some sort in social skills. For example, a group might be developed for adolescents who have been involved in delinquent behavior. By their actions, they have demonstrated an inability to abide by society's norms. Socialization groups frequently make great use of structured experiences or activities as a medium for change, relying less on member-to-member discussion. In some cases, the activities become the primary or only intervention that occurs. Adventure-based or experiential counseling programs are one example. These adolescent programs include heavy emphasis on physical skill, testing one's courage, and building both teamwork and self-reliance. The programs increase the self-confidence of group members, improve their social skills, and redirect their energies into socially approved activities. In these programs, group members are challenged by a series of physical hurdles, including climbing over barriers, rappelling down a cliff, and crossing a stream on a rope.

A current events group at a nursing home is another example. In this case, group emphasis is on getting the residents to interact with one another by discussing current events. The group also has a goal of helping to keep the residents' minds active and oriented to the present.

The social worker role in socialization groups is often one of highest visibility. This visibility may include serving as director or expert, designing the program, and leading members through the process and exercises. As with other types of groups, that role may change as the group enters later stages of development.

The role of the social worker in each of these treatment groups has some similarities and some differences. To summarize, the leader will have the highest visibility in educational, therapy, and socialization groups. In each case, the worker may be a director, expert, or leader. In the growth group and some therapy groups, the leader may be more of a facilitator, simply helping the group members attain their goals. Commonly, the worker is more active in the early stages of all groups. Once a group becomes established, the worker's role often changes to that of a consultant, expert, and role model. Group needs usually determine the role to be played by the social worker. Therefore, social workers must be flexible and modify their type and level of involvement as needed. They also need to use a variety of skills, depending upon the group's stage of development, the skills of the members, and the type of group.

Self-Help Groups

As should be obvious at this point, many groups overlap in their purpose, with some engaging in socialization and education and others providing therapy and education. The same is true for *self-help groups*, which are "led by members who share the problem experienced by the other members of the group" (Toseland & Rivas, 2012, p. 27). It is not uncommon for a professional to play a role in self-help groups either advising or consulting with lay leaders or serving as co-leaders. Self-help groups exist to assist members with a variety of problems that can range from substance abuse (Alcoholics Anonymous, Narcotics Anonymous), child abuse (Parents Anonymous), overeating (Overeaters Anonymous), to any number of concerns. There are self-help groups for people with chronic health problems; parents whose children have specific disorders; adults suffering from serious mental health challenges, alone or in combination with substance abuse problems; for chronic gamblers and shoplifters; and for individual professions (e.g., Lawyers Concerned for Lawyers, Nurse Recovery Groups); sexaholics, hoarders; and more. Most states provide online information on such groups through state-operated clearinghouses.

Self-help group members may also be working directly with social workers and other helping professionals outside the group. This may occur when seeking additional intervention on the concern dealt with by the self-help group or on an unrelated issue or problem.

Support Groups

Support groups are groups of people sharing certain characteristics who get together to provide one another with emotional sustenance, encourage new coping mechanisms, and allow a strengths-based sharing of issues, concerns, and problems. They typically have a professional leader and may be formally or informally organized. Because they exist to accomplish a variety of goals, they may share some characteristics with the groups we have already discussed. For example, one support group is the La Leche League. This group is devoted to encouraging breast-feeding of infants and to helping parents better understand the advantages of this method over the use of baby formula. In some ways, this organization is similar to the educational group in that members are not presumed to have a "problem." Rather, they share the characteristic of being parents (or prospective parents) of infants. As might be expected, much of the activity in group meetings is educational in purpose.

Anderson-Butcher, Khairallah, and Race-Bigelow (2004) found that support groups were effective for long-term recipients of Temporary Assistance for Needy Families (TANF). Group members identified increased social support, lowered stress levels, and new social and problem-solving skills as some of the benefits of participating in the support groups. They also reported increased knowledge of community resources, greater self-esteem, and feelings of empowerment.

Another example is a support group offered by a domestic violence shelter. This program, aimed at older women, deals with topics such as medical insurance, money management, and age discrimination in the workplace. Meeting twice a month for one and a half hours, the group provides emotional support, fosters learning opportunities, and helps more mature women experiencing domestic violence recognize their unique strengths, problems, and options.

The importance of social support has been demonstrated repeatedly and appears to be effective with a variety of client situations. Lou and Zhang (2006) found it useful for working with Chinese type 2 diabetes patients and enhancing their quality of life. Similarly, Chien, Norman, and Thompson (2006) found support groups effective for Chinese family members providing care for patients with schizophrenia in Hong Kong, suggesting that social support may be an appropriate intervention in other cultures and countries. Strozier (2012) looked at the use of support groups for kinship caregivers, concluding that they showed good potential for effectiveness with this client group. Hurdle (2001) discusses how the use of support groups and other models can have a significant role in promoting health among women of all ages.

The term *support group* is sometimes used interchangeably with *self-help group,* as both share a goal of having members provide support to one another. Self-help groups, however, are less likely to have professional leadership. To further complicate matters, you will recognize that many different types of groups provide members with advice, emotional support, information, and other help. Examples include support groups for people with chemical dependency problems, educational groups for new foster parents, and treatment groups for men who batter. Thus, support might be considered a component of many different types of groups. As a result of this confusion, the term *support group* is less clearly delineated than the other types of groups previously discussed. What is most important to remember is that the term is frequently used in social work to refer to groups with a strong mutual support emphasis.

All of the group types identified earlier are merely examples of the range of groups used in social work. In practice, seeing two or more approaches used within the same group is common. For example, Berge, Law, Johnson, and Wells (2010) reported on the effectiveness of a psychoeducational parenting group that combined educational programs for both parent and child, along with discussion and support from therapists. Lefley (2010) found similar positive results by the combination of support and educational activities conducted in families where at least one member suffered from serious mental illness. Common elements used in these groups included values clarification, role playing, counseling, and educational programming. The name "psychoeducational" reflects the merging of educational and socioemotional approaches.

Mishna, F., Michalski, J., & Cummings, R. (2001) also point out how groups are used in camping programs to foster a variety of changes with children and adolescents. In particular, groups benefit participants by increasing social functioning within a peer context. The authors note that group camping experiences have been employed effectively with youth experiencing learning disabilities and other emotional problems.

Groups have been developed to work with some of the most severe mental disorders, particularly those that are resistant to many traditional approaches. For example, Hurdle (2001) describes how a combination of therapy, educational, and socialization groups was utilized to help clients with personality disorders. The author notes that such approaches are cost effective, efficient, and can be used in the current managed care environment.

As should be clear, treatment groups exist largely to help clients resolve problems, a major goal of social work practice. Both treatment and task groups tend to employ the processes of engagement, identifying desired outcomes, collecting, organizing, and interpreting client data, assessing strengths and limitations, agreeing on goals and objectives, carrying out interventions designed to achieve those ends, and monitoring and evaluating the interventions. Each of these processes is a component of the Generalist Intervention Model.

Social Networking Groups

Although *social networking groups* are not usually included in the category of task groups, the ability to use computer mediated communication has had a major impact on various kinds of working groups. Committees, boards of directors, and just about any other type of task group can employ video conferencing to conduct their business. It is relatively easy to hold meetings of people who are located hundreds or thousands of miles apart and the flexibility of the technology has been demonstrated for teaching purposes, conference presentations, and a host of other purposes. With the exception of occasional connection challenges, electronic meetings have been a means of cutting costs, travel time, and ensuring maximum participation by members. Of course, like many things in life, there are drawbacks. For example, Johnston, Bettenhausen, and Gibbons (2009) "found that team members who used computer-mediated communication more often experienced lower levels of positive affect while working with their teams and had lower levels of affective commitment to their teams" (p. 623). In addition, Marett and George (2013) found that group members using computer-mediated communication tend to lie more than is true in face-to-face groups.

The use of computer-mediated groups for treatment groups has been a bit slower in development, largely because of factors such as practitioner facility with the technology, clients' lack of access, and potential ethical concerns. Despite these challenges, use of computer-mediated groups has been growing (Toseland & Rivas, 2012). The terminology in use varies widely, with terms such as *e-therapy, computer-mediated intervention, online counseling, web-based therapy, e-interventions*, and *cybertherapy* commonly used to refer to the same activity (Barak, Klein, & Proudfoot, 2009). In areas such as mental and physical health, the value of using the Internet has been repeatedly demonstrated. Practitioners in myriad fields use these tools to maintain contact with clients, patients, and colleagues; monitor progress; and share information about issues facing the client. They also are used by clients to pose questions for practitioners and others with similar issues, share experiences, and assist others. Levesque, Ciavatta, Castle, Prochaska, and Prochaska (2012) found that the use of computer-administered sessions with domestic violence offenders was effective in reducing the incidence of subsequent interpersonal violence. Similar positive outcomes were found in the use of computer-delivered intervention with heavy drinkers (Hester, Delaney, & Campbell, 2012). Morrongiello, Schwebel, Bell, Stewart, and Davis (2012) have successfully used interactive computer gaming to teach fire safety information to children under age 6.

How the technology is used varies greatly. For example, e-mail is a frequent means of communicating with practitioners, and in many medical settings allows clients to review their own medical records. Listservs give people opportunity to send and receive information at times of their own choosing as well as discuss topics in real time.

Skype and similar software allows face-to-face video interactions as people sit in front of their video-camera-equipped smartphones, tablets, laptops, or desktop computers. Video groups provide advantages because such interaction makes it is easier to recognize and respond to nonverbal cues (Toseland & Rivas, 2012). Individuals limited by geographical location, physical infirmities, and travel-related challenges can benefit from video groups.

Dietrich, Shipherd, Gershgoren, Filho, and Basevitch (2012) used the social networking site Facebook to provide group consultation to members of two soccer teams. The services made available included "group and individual meetings, and instruction in sport psychology skills such as: imagery, self-talk, goal setting, arousal regulation, and time management. Additional short-term team building, group cohesion, communication, anger management, injury rehabilitation, mental toughness, commitment and leadership workshops were provided" (p. 323). To enhance confidentiality and security, a special Facebook page was created that was available only to the players and consultants. Interestingly, both the consultants and athletes were located

across the globe, underscoring that distance is not a barrier when this technology is used. Although generalist social workers likely won't be providing services to the same group of clients, it is clear that some of the activities and interventions carried out by the consultants are similar to those employed by social workers.

The Veterans Administration has been using virtual reality as a treatment for soldiers experiencing post-traumatic stress disorders and chronic pain, and Wood et al. (2010) have noted its success in helping with stroke rehabilitation. In virtual reality, a computer is used to create a three-dimensional world within which patients work on their most serious challenges.

In a study by Callahan and Inckle (2012), the authors found that despite the concerns many practitioners held about online counseling and emotional support, "online conversations are shown to span a greater variety of topics and focus on more sensitive issues than verbal sessions. Online services have potential for reaching clients in accessible and meaningful ways" (p. 261). However, they warned that practitioners need to be better trained and become more comfortable with these electronic forms of communication. Emmelkamp (2011) also found that Internet-based cognitive behavior therapy (CBT) has been proven effective in multiple studies, although there are still concerns about issues such as representativeness of samples, and questions about cost-effectiveness.

Other benefits of computer-mediated groups are noted by Martínez-Moreno Zornoza, González-Navarro, and Thompson (2012). Investigating face-to-face and virtual teamwork over time (2012), who found that task conflict was less likely to occur in these groups than in face-to-face groups. This is especially important because conflict over the task can also evolve into relationship conflict, harming the group's ability to perform. Bickel, Christensen, and Marsch (2011) argue, based on their review of the literature, that "new technologies appear to produce better or similar results in detecting, informing, and educating individuals with substance abuse disorders relative to traditional counselor-facilitated methods" (p. 7). Bragadóttir (2008) also confirmed the value of computer-mediated support groups for parents of children who had been diagnosed with cancer. She concluded by noting that parents experienced lower levels of anxiety and that such groups may be a "valuable addition to, or substitute for, a traditional face-to-face mutual support group and might suit both genders equally" (p. 32).

LO 3-2 Attend to Professional Roles in Groups

EP 2.1.1c

That social workers play multiple leadership roles in groups will be clear from the many examples in this chapter. This section briefly discusses some common social worker roles and describes how they are used in work with groups. The roles are broker, mediator, educator, and facilitator.

BROKER

Brokers help group members obtain needed resources by connecting them with community agencies. This process requires that the worker be familiar with community resources, have general knowledge about eligibility requirements, and be sensitive to client needs. A broker may help the client obtain emergency food or housing, legal aid, or other needed resources. A worker may act as a broker either in one-to-one situations or in a group.

Community resource books or interest-based directories can prove helpful to new and experienced workers. These books typically describe most services in a community, including eligibility requirements, contact persons, addresses, and telephone numbers. These resource directories are often available online and brokers can use such listings to augment those with which they are familiar. To be most helpful, the worker should attempt to aid the client through referral to specific staff members. Clients going to a new agency without having a contact person or much information about how to use the resource can have a bad experience and become discouraged from using the agency. A more detailed review of the broker role appears in Chapter 15.

MEDIATOR

EP 2.1.10k

Mediators help group members resolve conflicts or other dissension (Toseland & Rivas, 2012). To be most successful in this role, the worker must believe that different sides to a disagreement are legitimate and help each side recognize that the other side's views are valid. Avoiding win-lose situations (described later in this chapter) is an important task of the mediator. Therefore, the worker must help the parties identify their points of disagreement and of mutual interest. The worker then must focus on finding a solution that meets the needs of all. Finally, on another level, the worker may help group members negotiate with the environment and other systems. This negotiation is especially important when the client finds resource systems intimidating and impersonal. The worker can help bridge this gulf and build on the broker role described earlier.

EDUCATOR

As a teacher, the social worker provides group participants with new information, structures the presentation of that information, and uses modeling to help members learn new skills. This role is discussed later in the chapter.

FACILITATOR

The facilitator, as the name suggests, guides, eases, or expedites the way for others. This role is important whether the problem is between individuals and their environment or between members in the same group. In a task group, the facilitative role may involve helping the group stick to the agenda, creating a safe environment for open discussion, and encouraging all to participate and supporting their contributions. It also includes helping members test new skills and assume greater responsibility for the group (Corey, 2011).

Clearly, the social worker must play various roles depending upon the group's needs and the problems confronted. Conceiving of social work as being made up of a series of roles is consistent with the idea that generalist social workers have numerous responsibilities. It also helps the worker think more clearly about what a group needs at any given time in its developmental life.

LO 3-3 Utilize Conceptual Frameworks in Group Assessment, Intervention, and Evaluation

EP 2.1.7a

Social workers who have dealt with various types of groups frequently comment about how each group seems to develop a life of its own. Each group has its own unique configuration of varied individual personalities, as well as its own set of dynamics that affect what is said or done, the roles members play, and how the group relates to the leader. There have been repeated efforts to provide a framework for understanding group dynamics and to help those working with groups. Many frameworks attempt to explain group development through a single model. Each of these approaches has strengths and weaknesses. This section focuses on six broad areas: group development; group culture, norms, and power; group size and composition; group duration; group decision-making patterns; and group functions and roles.

GROUP DEVELOPMENT

Most groups proceed through an identifiable set of four steps or stages. This pattern of development has allowed group observers to describe the stages and to predict what may occur in each stage. In the first stage of development, most groups display *a strong reliance on the leader*. Members expect the leader to provide direction, and they tend to be more hesitant or reluctant to participate actively. The leader assists members in this stage by encouraging participation, supporting positive group norms (informal rules of behavior), and helping members rely more on one another. The first stage is often focused on trust issues as members learn whether they can trust others in the group. Group members are unsure about whether they will be accepted by other members or by the leader and are often seeking some sense that the group approves of them.

In the second stage, the group members begin to assert themselves more. During this time, *some level of conflict is common*. As members feel safer in the group, they begin to assert their autonomy and express their feelings more openly. The second stage is often characterized by some degree of tension and strain as both worker and members adjust to the changed atmosphere. Power and control issues arise more frequently as members become more comfortable with each other and take greater responsibility for what happens in the group. There may be disagreement over goals agreed upon in the previous stage and challenges to the leader that can be unsettling. That the leader encourages open discussion of the conflict so that the group will ultimately be responsible for its decision is important. Recognizing that conflict is expected, acceptable, and often even healthy is also important.

Once past the conflict stage, the group is ready to go ahead with the primary work facing it. Group productivity increases, and there is greater attention to achieving its goals. This level is stage 3, the *"working" phase* of the group. Members frequently feel positive about the group, may have developed affection or liking for it and its members, and are more willing to share their ideas and reactions. Trust has developed among members as roles become clearer and a group culture has developed. The role of the leader is likely to change during this phase. There is more need for a leader who can

serve as consultant, advisor, or resource to the group instead of a director.

Finally, there is usually a fourth phase, *separation*, where the group has reached its goals and members begin to separate emotionally from the group. In this phase, there are often feelings of loss when the group ends, but there also may be angry feelings. Again, the worker should expect and realize that members might need help to accept and discuss their feelings.

The group stage model (see Highlight 3.3) appears to apply well to growth or treatment groups (groups that focus on changing the individual group member) and to many task groups (committees, teams, social action groups). However, the ongoing nature of task groups (agency staff meetings, boards of directors, and so on) may complicate or mix up some stages. Because some staff groups do not have a separation phase where members prepare to leave, there is less likely to be the same kinds of reactions found in other groups with a defined ending period. Open-ended groups, such as Parents Anonymous, where members enter and leave the group at different times, may change how the group develops. The previous model fits most closely those groups where members join and leave the group together (closed groups), such as the teen group described in Highlight 3.3.

There may also be a difference in group development between formed groups and those that exist naturally. *Formed groups* are those where the members have been brought together by an outside agency, organization, or individual. Therapy groups created by the social worker are an example. *Natural groups* are those where the members have come together through bonds of friendship or kinship. One type of natural group, a family, already has an established pattern of interacting with one another, which may also be true of a gang. Formed groups composed of clients with similar problems or characteristics (e.g., substance-addicted or delinquent girls) are perhaps more likely to fit the model described. Thus, when these group members achieve their treatment or personal goals, the group will enter stage 4, where separation occurs.

Realizing that any development model for groups is only an abstraction is important. Individual groups may not proceed exactly as outlined earlier. Some groups will seem to skip a stage or move backward instead of forward from time to time. Remember, failure to proceed in the precise manner described earlier is neither an unhealthy sign nor necessarily problematic. The social worker must be flexible and adaptable when working with groups because they vary so drastically in purpose, composition, and dynamics.

HIGHLIGHT 3.3

Intervening with a Group: Stages in Teen Group Therapy

Stage 1 in a Teen Group: Reliance on the Leader

As she looked around the group of teenagers, Mary was reminded once again about the effect a group can have on its members. Mary had been assigned to work with this group because she had previously had some group experiences during her field placement. Having read the files on all of the members, Mary knew something about each of the girls present in the teen center meeting room. Jacque was quiet, which for her was unusual. She was always the most talkative person in any group. Belinda was whispering to Angel, and both were smiling knowingly. Cindy was looking down and flipping absentmindedly through her notebook. Alice stared out the window. When Mary got up to close the door, the room became as quiet as a tomb. Each girl looked up at Mary, expecting her to say something.

Stage 2 in a Teen Group: Addressing Conflict

Mary had asked the group to agree on the major activities they would pursue during the next 6 weeks. Although there had been ample time to decide, the group seemed hopelessly deadlocked. Jacque was arguing that the group should hold a party, and Cindy testily reminded her that they were in this group because they partied too much. Belinda asked if they could have a session focused on getting along better with parents. When Mary responded favorably to Belinda, Angel said she did not want to talk about her parents. After

10 more minutes, the group was no closer to a decision than when the meeting started.

Stage 3 in a Teen Group: Working

When Alice said she felt her parents did not care what happened to her and began to cry softly, Jacque reached over and put an arm around her. "Maybe they just don't know how to show they care," Cindy said. "I mean, we can't know what's in someone else's head." "That's right," said Belinda, "don't assume anything about parents." As the group meeting came to an end, Mary smiled and said quietly, "I'm very proud of how the group reached out to Alice and used the ideas we've been talking about the last few weeks. You've really supported one another."

Stage 4 in a Teen Group: Separation

For the last meeting, Mary had asked the girls what they wanted to do that would appropriately conclude their work together. They decided to write each other brief notes stating what good qualities they learned about one another during the past few weeks. This method of saying goodbye was encouraged by Mary, who had also arranged for soda and pizza for the meeting. The group had spent the last week talking about their feelings as the group ended and reviewing the various plans group members had for the summer. Mary told them she would miss their weekly meetings and encouraged them to stay in touch with her and with each other.

GROUP CULTURE, NORMS, AND POWER

All groups have an identifiable culture comprised of the traditions, customs, and values/beliefs shared by group members. Culture affects how members react to and interact with one another and the leader, typical coping styles used, how work is done, and how status and power are distributed. Sometimes, this culture exists prior to the worker's involvement, as with families or groups of friends. At other times, it occurs after group formation. *Norms* are unwritten expectations about how individuals will act in certain situations. Norms are part of the culture of all groups and can help or hinder the accomplishment of group goals. The worker has a role in helping to create norms that support attainment of these goals. For example, a norm of openness and a willingness to admit mistakes can be

encouraged by a worker who models these characteristics for group members. Evidence of a positive group culture includes free expression of ideas, open disagreement, and a safe atmosphere in which the contributions of members are respected and considered. The worker can help ensure development of such a culture by describing for members what is desired or expected in the group, modeling appropriate behavior, and supporting group members as they interact within the group.

Value differences among group members may contribute to difficulties within the group. For example, within a group of teens discussing sexual behavior, it is likely that some members will view sexual activity as a part of adolescence and others (because of religious or other values) may not want to talk about the topic.

The worker should encourage members to discuss the values they bring to the group and to listen carefully to the values of other members. When a climate of trust and safety exists, members are more likely to accept individual differences and allow fellow members to express their individuality. If members do not sense such a climate, they are less likely to be honest in expressing opinions and will be more guarded in what they say and do. This type of climate is less likely to lead to positive outcomes. The leader should help to establish a culture where members are free to talk and are supportive of each other. This permits the business of the group to be accomplished in an open and frank manner.

Power issues always exist within groups. In many groups, there is a period in which the group or individual members of the group vie with the leader for power. In most groups, individual members have different levels of status and power. Those accorded the highest status by other group members are more likely to be listened to. Subgroups may develop as two or more members find themselves holding similar views and feeling at odds with other group members. Struggles over decisions may occur, exacerbated by these divisions.

GROUP SIZE AND COMPOSITION

Sometimes both the size and composition of a group are established ahead of time, and the worker lacks control over these elements. For example, consider families and other preexisting groups. The size of the family is not within the control of the worker, nor is its composition. In other situations, the worker is responsible for making decisions about who will be included as members and how large the group will be. For instance, a worker leading a parent nurturing group may set the limit on members at seven or nine and not allow a larger group.

Group size has a definite impact on what occurs within a group. It affects both the level and type of interaction in addition to members' feelings about the group. Large groups tend to be less popular with members because of lessened opportunity for discussion and interaction. Members of larger groups are more likely to feel inhibited and will often participate less than members in smaller groups. Guidelines for group size tend to depend on the type of group. For example, groups that focus on the needs of individual members, such as therapy, support, or growth groups, might have anywhere from five to nine members. Groups with an educational focus can be of various sizes, from 5 up to as many as 15 members, depending in part on how the

information is being delivered and what learning methods are employed by the group leader. Many social work groups have as many as 10 members, and some groups are much larger. Larger groups may be more effective at handling difficult and involved problems because the number of possible contributors is greater. Thus, the task or objectives of the group may be a factor affecting group size. Although composition of a group may be beyond the control of the worker, many situations do allow the leader to select the members. Formed groups lend themselves nicely to this kind of selection, as the worker often chooses individual members.

The worker must decide the degree of heterogeneity and homogeneity appropriate for a given group. A heterogeneous group has members with different problems and personality characteristics. A homogeneous group has members with similar problems and personalities. Practically speaking, few groups are completely homogeneous because as human beings we all differ from one another in many ways. Workers must take these differences into consideration when selecting members for a group.

We must also remember that there may be real advantages in selecting people for a group who are alike in some ways and different in others. For example, selecting people who share similar problems (e.g., child abusers) but who have differing personalities might make sense. For another example, selecting seven nonverbal group members would not be wise. A healthy mix of talkers and listeners is likely to be more useful.

Age also may be a factor in composition. Different levels of development probably preclude starting a group composed of children ranging in age from 8 to 15. The difference in interests and attention spans could be especially problematic. Ultimately, the purpose of the group should be considered when deciding group size and composition.

Gender is also an important consideration. Gender similarity may be important in groups of children, but gender diversity is desirable among adolescents when the objective is helping group members develop socialization skills. Diversity is also helpful in terms of problem solving and decision making. A degree of heterogeneity in areas such as background, prior experiences, ability, ethnicity, and gender can allow members to bring fresh perspectives to a situation and improve overall group performance. A mix of members with such dissimilar behavioral characteristics as verbal ability, leadership skills, and level of assertiveness may also be useful. Members with differing life experiences and other characteristics can serve as models for other members. Social workers need to give this matter careful consideration when they are composing a group. In an ideal arrangement, groups would have a mixture of members that provide for group vitality as well as for stability. Finding this exact balance is not often easy, however, because predicting how well a particular group's members will function together is often impossible.

DURATION

Determining the duration of a group requires that the worker decide how many sessions will be held and how long each will last. Having groups meet for one and a half to two hours per session is common, which provides enough time to conduct the business of the meeting without becoming too drawn out. Specifying in advance the length and number of sessions helps members focus on the topic and discourages nonfunctional behavior such as wasting time on irrelevant topics. A group planning to meet for 6 sessions is more likely to stay on task than one meeting for 20 sessions. A general observation is that the closer to the ending point a group gets, the more likely it is that group members will attend to the task. This fact is a phenomenon familiar to many students who find that their interest in and efforts to write a class paper increase as the deadline approaches.

Flexibility is helpful in the matter of duration. If a preselected length of time proves counterproductive, the worker should feel free to suggest a change. The judgment of the worker and clients about what works best is as important as any set of guidelines.

LO 3-4 Select Appropriate Problem-Solving and Decision-Making Approaches with Groups

EP 2.1.7a

How groups, especially task groups, make decisions is important to understanding why some groups are more successful than others. Task groups, like committees, administrative groups such as boards of directors, delegate assemblies such as the NASW Delegate Assembly, teams, treatment conferences, and social action groups, must often make decisions. These task groups share some similarities, yet each is different from the others in some important ways, including how they interact and come to decisions. In this section, several common approaches to group decision making will be discussed: consensus decision making, compromise, de-

cision making by majority, rule by an individual, persuasion by a recognized expert, averaging of the opinions of individual group members, and persuasion by a minority of the group (see Highlight 3.4). In addition, we will review three special techniques to help groups make decisions and solve problems: nominal group technique, brainstorming, and parliamentary procedure.

Consensus Decision Making

An attractive, albeit time-consuming, approach to making decisions is through consensus. Consensus is a process used by groups to reach a general agreement about what they want and how they will get it. Consensus decision making is attractive because, when concluded, all members accept and support the decision even if they were not initially so inclined. To make decisions by consensus requires an atmosphere of openness in which all members have an opportunity to be heard and influence the final outcome. This approach presumes that members can present alternate ideas, that opposing views are solicited, and that creative solutions are encouraged. The emphasis is on finding the best solution instead of getting one's way. The real advantage of achieving consensus is that it increases the commitment of group members to the decision. In situations where this commitment is particularly important, there is no adequate substitute.

Compromise

Most of us have been involved in decision making by compromise. In these situations, the group attempts to reach a solution that most, if not all members, can support. In some cases, the compromise pleases no one entirely but is viewed as the best that can be done under the circumstances. Each side gives up something to reach an agreement with the other side. Groups that begin with an idea, amend it repeatedly to satisfy divergent points of view, and then approve the final product usually are making decisions by compromise. The degree of satisfaction with the compromise is often lower compared to decisions reached by consumers.

Decision Making by Majority

Most deliberative bodies (e.g., legislatures, boards of directors) make decisions by majority rule. In this model, a decision occurs when over one-half of the decision makers support (or vote for) an idea. Decisions made in this fashion typically are accepted by the winning side and disliked by the losing side. Losers do not necessarily feel as compelled to support the outcome of the group decision making as is true with

HIGHLIGHT 3.4

Conceptual Frameworks: Approaches to Decision Making

Consensus Decision Making

The Blackwell City Council was at an impasse. After a year of study, debate, and argument, the new library was no closer to fruition than when the council started discussing the idea. The primary issue that had stymied the group was the proposed location. The library board had proposed that the new building be located on an undeveloped site near Lake Prosper, a recommendation supported by two or three council members. Other members wanted the new library adjacent to the old library, a location that many felt was too small to meet future needs. After a lengthy debate, Greg Hanson, a social worker on the city council, suggested holding an advisory referendum on the location, allowing the residents of the city the opportunity to voice their opinion. Council members were all in agreement with this proposal, a consensus decision that was unusual for this body. At least temporarily, it got the issue off their agenda and offered hope of a clear mandate from the voters.

Compromise

"Finally, a package we can live with." Lenore was exhausted. As president of the social work union, she had been deeply involved in the negotiations for next year's contract. After an initial (and unacceptable) offer from the finance committee, the union representatives had been going through the usual process of making proposals and rejecting them. Finally, a package was agreed to. It contained salary increases agreeable to the union and gave management more flexibility to move workers within the agency. It was a compromise for both parties, since it did not give either side exactly what it would have liked. It was a classic labor agreement, something for everyone but less than each side had desired.

Decision Making by Majority

The five agency supervisors were in the second hour of what was supposed to be a one-hour meeting. The issue that had stymied efforts to conclude the meeting was a proposed reorganization of services and service units. Don was unhappy with the proposal because it would increase the workload of his unit slightly at a time when he felt his staff was already overloaded. Still, the proposal would give the agency an opportunity to

offer a very specialized service, which a previous needs assessment had determined was long overdue. Finally, the agency deputy director asked for a show of hands for those who supported the proposed change. All supervisors but Don voted in favor of the proposal. The deputy director said, "Don, I know you are not crazy about this idea, but it has the support of the others, and we're going to go with the majority this time. I will see, however, what I can do about getting another position assigned to your unit to help with the overload."

Rule by an Individual

The Millard School Rec Club was having difficulty choosing an activity to mark the end of the high school year. In past years, the group had held pizza parties, donated gifts to the school, and contributed their time to a neighborhood cleanup project. Mike, the captain of the baseball team and a respected student, argued forcefully that the club should donate money to the school to purchase a pitching machine. Other members of the group were reluctant to express their opinions for fear of appearing to oppose Mike's suggestion. When no one spoke up, Mike then said, "Well, then it's settled. I'll tell the principal and the coach." The group had just allowed one member to rule (make a decision) for the entire club.

Persuasion by a Recognized Expert

When it came time to discuss how the new social work program would be evaluated, everyone on the administrative staff looked to Gerry for guidance. He was considered the resident expert on program evaluation and was familiar with a variety of approaches that could be used in different situations. Although Jack had some reservations about a couple of Gerry's ideas, his opinions did not sway the staff group very much. Jack knew in advance that Gerry's recommendations would be accepted by the group based on his reputation and past experience. Sure enough, when the meeting was over, Gerry's ideas were approved, and his plan for evaluation was accepted.

Averaging of the Opinions of Individual Group Members

Mary had asked her foster care unit to evaluate her performance as a supervisor. Mary had only recently become a supervisor after several years as a line social worker. Most of the people in the foster care unit had been her friends before her promotion 6 months ago. Now she wanted to get their feedback on her work as their supervisor.

After much discussion, unit members decided to rate Mary on five different characteristics they considered important in a supervisor. When they were done, they decided to present Mary with a composite picture of how the unit felt about her leadership. Rather than give her their individual ratings, the unit members decided to average their individual ratings on each of the five characteristics and give her one set of ratings. This method eliminated extremes at both ends (e.g., very high or very low ratings) and gave a more "middle-of-the-road" view of her performance.

Persuasion by a Minority of the Group

The night was getting quite late as the Franklin Avenue Neighborhood Association neared the end of its agenda. The last item to discuss was what to do about the vacant house at the end of the block. The property had been abandoned by its owner and was attracting children and local teenagers who sought access through its broken windows and door. Since the house was really on the edge of the neighborhood, many members did not see it as a matter of great concern. There was even a question of whether the property was part of Franklin Avenue, since it faced a side street.

Quietly, but firmly, Mr. Alison and Mrs. Gonzales spoke of the dangers to the neighborhood children and the way the property detracted from the quality of the neighborhood. Ms. Washington, usually rather quiet, then spoke passionately about how this house was a danger to her small children. She angrily asked how the other members would feel if the house was next door to their homes. She demanded that the group take a position and ask the city to have the house torn down or renovated. The group decided to follow her recommendation, less out of commitment and more because of her ardent and outspoken position on a matter of relatively less concern to them.

consensus. Because majority rule is a less time-consuming method, large groups often use it. When a matter is of little consequence, majority rule may be a satisfactory method for making a decision. When the matter is complex or requires a high level of commitment from the group to the decision, this method is problematic. Losers may not support the decision and may passively undercut the proposal. In some cases, losers may be resentful and actively work to make the idea fail. Alternate methods of arriving at majority rule involve increasing the percent of votes required for passage (revisions of bylaws or constitutions of organizations frequently require a two-thirds majority) or developing a weighted system of voting. While these methods help increase the percent of members who support a decision, they do not truly overcome the disadvantages of this style of decision making.

One example of decision making by majority is the passage of the Affordable Care Act (Obamacare) by the U.S. Congress. The final passage in both the House and Senate occurred without a single member of the Republican Party voting in favor of the bill. The Democratic Party had a sufficient majority to approve the bill without minority (Republican) votes. At the same time, many of the changes or amendments to the bill were suggested and supported by Republican members of the House and Senate while the bill was being debated.

Rule by an Individual

Many groups make decisions by default and allow one individual to make choices that affect the entire group. This situation may occur because of the forcefulness of the speaker, members' fear of offending the decision maker, disinterest in the decision itself, or lack of assertiveness. Essentially, one member makes a decision, and the rest of the group acquiesces. Sometimes, there is discussion among the members about the options; at other times, there is none.

Persuasion by a Recognized Expert

Many groups have members with expertise in a certain area. For example, one member of an educational group may have had experience placing a loved one in a nursing home. Other group members typically listen to members who are perceived to be knowledgeable about a given subject. When a group comes to making a decision, it may accede to the recommendations of the "expert."

Averaging of the Opinions of Individual Group Members

In some groups, decisions are made by averaging the opinions of individual group members. This process is done most easily when the opinions are really able to be averaged. That is, the opinions may be in the form of numerical ratings that can be averaged using standard mathematical techniques. Unlike a compromise, there is really no giving in by individual members but rather an acceptance that one's opinion will be merged with those of the rest of the group. This technique has the advantage of not requiring people to give up their opinion or change it in response to group pressure.

Persuasion by a Minority of the Group

Persuasion by a minority often occurs when one or more members of a group feel strongly about a particular decision. It happens more frequently when a subgroup has intense attitudes and the rest of the group is less invested in the matter at stake. A vocal and persuasive group of individuals thus may be successful in swaying the opinions of a larger group.

Nominal Group Technique

One of the more interesting methods used to help groups make decisions is the nominal group technique. Its intent is to help group members arrive at a consensus with respect to a pending decision. It assists in getting group members to generate ideas and helps build commitment to a decision. This approach can be used by groups of various sizes. To begin, members receive a problem statement and list their ideas about the problem. Each member does this without consulting other members; once this process is completed, the leader goes around the group one by one, asking each member to provide one of the ideas from his or her list. This process continues until all items on each person's list have been exhausted. Members may choose to pass when they no longer have any ideas to contribute. They are also free to contribute additional ideas they thought of while listening to other members. The worker writes each idea on a board or flip chart visible to all members. No evaluation of ideas occurs during this round-robin procedure.

Once all the ideas are collected and listed for the members, the leader begins to go through each idea briefly. This process helps ensure clarity and allows each member to explain the merits of an idea. No lengthy discussion of any idea occurs at this point.

In the third stage, members review the ideas collected and list those they believe are the most impor-tant or have highest priority. They may be asked to select a specific number such as 5 or 15. The goal is to reduce the overall list by one-half to three-quarters. Once completed, the leader places a check mark by each idea supported by a member. This tabulation may be accomplished by the member listing the best ideas on a card and handing the card in or by going around in round-robin fashion again. When completed, the group has a list of those ideas that showed the most promise.

In the final stage, members rank the new list of ideas. Usually, the priority list will be small, with only five ideas permitted. These are listed on index cards, one idea per card. The cards are collected, and the leader tallies the results on the flip chart. The highest-priority idea receives a point value of five and on down to the lowest-priority item, which receives a one. A mean rank for each idea is computed by adding the numbers together and dividing by the number of members. Once completed, the idea or ideas that have the greatest support and group interest are usually clear.

The nominal group technique can produce a larger number of alternatives than most other approaches while being perceived as highly cooperative and effective by members (Graefe & Armstrong, 2011; Rietzschel, Nijstad, & Storebe, 2006). This approach is usually enjoyable for the participants. It is an effective technique for developing alternatives because it encourages participation of all members. It also allows all points of view to be expressed and discourages making decisions without adequate discussion.

Brainstorming

Brainstorming is a group technique used to encourage members to produce a variety of ideas about a specific topic. It is an efficient way to develop alternate solutions to a problem. Useful in both large and small groups, brainstorming begins with a problem to be solved. Each member presents one idea, and then another member has a turn. This process continues until the leader lists all ideas on the board or flip chart. No attempt is made to rate or evaluate the ideas. Members should be free to present ideas they thought of after hearing other members' contributions (piggybacking) and should raise their hands before participating. The leader should encourage all contributions and clarify any ideas that are not clear.

Unlike the nominal group approach, the evaluation phase does not closely follow the idea-generating phase. Ideas tend to be better if the problem is clearly and specifically defined. Brainstorming can produce large numbers of ideas and works best when the goal is generation of multiple alternatives. It does not work as well with complex situations or those in which there is only a single correct answer. There is, however, no clear evidence that brainstorming is more or less effective than the nominal group approach. Because both methods rely on an atmosphere of openness to new ideas, the worker should encourage this process and resist premature attempts to evaluate the ideas presented. In either case, ideas that receive immediate evaluation, especially a negative assessment, are less likely to be followed by other ideas. Members may feel threatened because someone ridiculed or challenged their idea and will be less likely to risk offering other ideas to the group.

DeRosa, Smith, and Hantula (2007), in a meta-analysis of previous research on the use of electronic brainstorming methods, found that conducting nominal groups online was also an effective alternative to face-to-face groups. It is also a method that has been used in many countries across the globe, including Great Britain, Netherlands, Malaysia, and China, suggesting that it is a cross-culturally effective method. Finally, it increases members' commitment to the outcome.

Parliamentary Procedure

Parliamentary procedure is a highly structured technique used by groups of various sizes to make decisions and conduct business. The model of parliamentary procedure described in *Robert's Rules of Order* (Robert & others, 2011) was devised over 100 years ago and remains the most common set of guidelines in use today. Groups agree in advance to use the rules, so that there is no last-minute disagreement about how decisions will be made. Most deliberative bodies (legislatures) and large task groups and many smaller task groups use *Robert's Rules* to facilitate their work. While parliamentary procedural rules are clear and designed to help the group, they are not always followed closely. Sometimes, the procedures called for in the rules become barriers to accomplishment of group goals. For example, smaller committees may decide to operate by consensus and dispense with voting on items where the group is in agreement. In this case, parliamentary procedure may be too time consuming and unwieldy. In legislative bodies a person can easily waste the body's time by endlessly speaking on a matter before the group. Called *filibustering,* this method may stymie a body and prevent it from conducting its normal business. In these situations, groups may decide to temporarily suspend some of the usual rules of parliamentary procedure, thus preventing filibustering.

In parliamentary procedure, the business of the group occurs in the form of *motions,* which are proposed actions that the group is asked to support. A member of the social work student organization may make a motion to buy paint to refurbish the child care center. The motion might be stated as follows: "I move we purchase three gallons of paint for the child care center." If anyone else supports this motion, the member would say, "I second the motion." The motion or proposal would then be open for debate or discussion by the members. Motions generally fall into two major categories, primary motions and secondary motions. *Primary motions* bring business to the group for consideration. The motion to purchase paint is an example of a primary motion. Primary motions include both main motions (example above) and incidental motions. *Incidental motions* are used for such purposes as adjourning the group and repealing an action already taken.

Secondary motions are those used to act upon the primary motion. They include motions to amend a main motion, to refer a matter to another body, or to defer action on a motion (postpone or table). They also are used to limit debate on a motion, to reconsider a motion, or to bring up for discussion an item that had been previously tabled. Last, secondary motions include motions to challenge improper actions and to request information (e.g., point of order or point of information). For example, a member who seeks clarification on why the body is dealing with a matter that seems to belong to another group would raise a hand and address the presiding officer by stating: *"Point of information."* The chair would then ask the member to state the point of information and would attempt to respond to the question the member has raised. Similarly, if a group strays in its debate and is now discussing a matter that is not related to the motion on the floor, a member might state: *"Point of order."* The member would then remind the group that they have not yet voted on the motion before them and have begun to debate some other matter. The chair would then rule on the member's point of order, ask if there is any additional debate on the motion on the floor, and then call for the vote.

Other motions do exist, but they are used too infrequently to mention in this chapter. *Robert's Rules of Order* should be consulted by those who frequently use parliamentary procedure.

The primary principle established by parliamentary procedure is that each person has a right to be heard without interruption. The person who makes a motion speaks first on a topic. All members must have an opportunity to speak if they so wish. Debate must be related to the motion on the floor and cannot be on superfluous matters. Once each person who wishes has had a chance to speak, the leader (chair) asks if there is any further debate. If there is none, the group will then vote on the proposal. Sometimes a member of the group will wish to stop debate and bring a matter to a vote. This is achieved by saying "I call the question." This motion is not debatable—it immediately halts discussion on a matter if supported by two-thirds of those present.

When the group is ready to vote, the chair will say "All those in favor of the motion, say aye." Restating the motion to be voted on or having the secretary read the motion may be best. At that point, all favoring the motion will respond "aye." Then the chair will call for all no (or nay) votes and then all abstentions. The chair will decide which side prevailed based on this voice vote and announce the results. Sometimes, members vote by raising their hands or by using paper ballots, especially when the vote appears to be close. Normally, a simple majority must approve a motion. If a tie occurs in the voting, the motion does not pass. Sometimes, however, the chair may vote to break a tie or to create a tie.

As mentioned earlier, a motion may be amended. This *amendment* means it may be changed by a member proposing to add or delete something in the original motion. To amend the previously mentioned motion, a member might say "I move to amend the motion to place a limit of 50 dollars on the amount to be spent for paint." This amendment also needs a second and would be voted on. If approved, the amendment would then become a part of the original main motion. After all amendments are considered and voted on, the main motion (as amended) would be voted on.

There are other rules governing parliamentary procedure. These include specification of a *quorum* (the minimum number of group members that must be present to conduct business) and use of an *agenda* (an ordered list of the topics to be covered in the meeting). Most groups have a leader or chairperson responsible for helping the group conduct its business. A secretary is charged with the task of keeping the minutes (official record of a group's actions). Other officers, such as a treasurer or vice chairperson, may be needed depending upon the type and size of the group.

In larger groups, there may be subgroups or committees to which certain business is sent for review. For example, to have both standing (ongoing) committees (such as a finance committee and a personnel committee) and special ad hoc committees set up to handle specific bits or categories of business is common. Committee members and the chairperson of the committee are appointed by the chair of the larger group. The smaller the committee, the less likely it is to use more formalized parliamentary procedures. A useful online resource is the official *Robert's Rules of Order* Web site: http://www.Robertsrules.com. A social worker skilled in the use of parliamentary procedure can be of enormous assistance to task groups. Knowing how to make and amend motions and otherwise properly handle the group's business can make the group's task go smoothly. Parliamentary procedure provides a set of rules to guide groups in their deliberations; it was never meant to serve as an obstacle. In the final analysis, the wishes of the group must prevail even if a violation of *Robert's Rules* occurs.

Critical Thinking and Groups

 Although groups can be effective decision makers, they can also fail to use critical thinking skills in their deliberations, sometimes with disastrous results. When group members do not critically evaluate ideas or options that are presented but simply go along with the rest of the group, they are abdicating their responsibility to themselves, the other members, and the group as a whole. Janis (1982) coined the term *groupthink* to describe situations where groups have the illusion of agreement but have really failed to carefully consider their decisions. It usually arises when group members seek decisions too quickly, feel that dissent is not welcome, or do not want to upset the camaraderie by expressing opposing opinions. Sometimes it occurs when members do not want to be seen disagreeing with the group leader. Groupthink has been identified as a factor in multiple situations ranging from decisions to go to war in Iraq, jury decisions, corporate governance, and health care. A critically thinking group will weigh alternatives carefully, consider both advantages and disadvantages of each option, and value the insights of all group members. Group leaders can help encourage critical thinking and reduce the tendency toward groupthink by encouraging members to present dissenting views, testing for consensus rather than assuming it exists, modeling independent thinking, and assigning a member to raise objections or present the worst-case scenario if a particular decision is carried out. Postmes, Spears, and Cihangir (2001) point out that critical group norms produced better decisions than groups that were focused on consensus building. They note that "the content of group norms is an important factor influencing the quality of group decision-making processes and that the content of group norms may be related to the group's proneness for groupthink" (p. 918). Further review of the research by Brownstein (2003) suggested that the homogeneous composition of a group tended to produce poor decision making and Sibony (2012) highlighted the importance of members having the courage to speak up.

Critical Thinking Questions 3.2

- Have you ever been part of a group where you chose not to voice your disagreement despite your misgivings about the idea being discussed?
- What motivated you to not share your objections?
- If you were the group leader, how would you have encouraged members to think critically about their decisions?

GROUP FUNCTIONS AND ROLES

Observers of most groups have concluded that there are two types of basic functions that each group must fulfill: task functions and maintenance functions. *Task functions* help to keep a group on task and working toward agreed-upon ends. *Maintenance functions*, on the other hand, ensure that the needs of group members receive attention. Both task and treatment (therapeutic) groups require members who attend to task and maintenance functions. In task groups, we are typically less concerned about the needs of the individual member and more focused on the group task. In contrast, within treatment or growth groups, the needs and interests of individual members receive more attention. Remembering that no group operates without attending to both functions is important. The emphasis placed on each function will vary depending upon the group.

In practice, the members of the group are the people who often carry out the various functions described earlier. This process occurs through one or more roles that members (and leaders) play in the group.

Task Roles

As mentioned previously, task roles are functional roles designed to help the group reach agreed-upon goals.

Members of a group engage in particular behaviors that help facilitate this process. One such role is *information seeking* from the leader or other members. In addition to seeking information, a member may solicit the opinions of group members to help determine how people perceive some topic. *Opinion seekers* often want this information before stating their own position. *Elaborators* expand on ideas proposed to the group and help to ensure that a complete explanation is provided for all ideas.

Other members may engage in teaching or *instructing* roles. These members often clarify and remind the other members about previous decisions they have made. Still other members will *evaluate* or make judgments about the wisdom or appropriateness of any particular idea or course of action.

Some members engage in an *energizing* role by showing excitement and enthusiasm for projects; by force of their interest, they bring other members along. Energizers are the spark plugs in any group.

Once a group has made a decision, some members will serve as *recorders,* or unelected secretaries, by keeping a log or record of decisions reached or actions taken. Some may actually jot down these items, while others maintain only a mental notebook. Recorders are sometimes assisted by other members who remind the group to follow some agreed-upon rules or procedures as they continue their deliberations. *Recorders* are helpful because they help the group stay on task and serve as the unofficial historian in a group. The *procedural technician* helps the group follow their own agreed-upon ways of making decisions.

Persons playing task roles are interested in the group completing its agreed-upon task and try to help this process. They tend to be more committed to the task and may be less concerned about the importance of group maintenance.

Maintenance Roles

Group maintenance is an important function needing attention in any group. Group maintenance roles are concerned with improving, enhancing, or increasing group functioning. Task groups often pay less attention to this facet than treatment groups do, but the function of group maintenance cannot be ignored. Group maintenance roles include harmonizer, compromiser, encourager, follower, tension reliever, and listener. The titles assigned to these different roles are less important than the behaviors that members perform to accomplish the group maintenance function. As suggested by the titles, group members focusing on group building and maintenance encourage other members to participate *(encourager),* and they listen carefully *(listener).* They also follow the directions of others *(follower),* emphasize harmony and compromise *(harmonizer* and *compromiser),* and relieve rough moments in the group, often through humor *(tension reliever).* The goal is to attend to the group's socioemotional climate and help the group maintain its "we" feeling.

Paying attention to the needs of individual members naturally occurs in most treatment groups. Members are selected for or join these groups with the expectation that their social and emotional needs will be given concerted attention. Task groups, on the other hand, often assume that members' personal needs are secondary to the group's purpose. A balance between meeting both types of needs, task and socioemotional, must occur in all groups. There almost always will be more attention to the task of the group and less to individual needs of the members in a board of directors or a multidisciplinary care conference in a hospital. Likewise, a group for men who abuse their spouses or a group for women surviving breast cancer will have a greater emphasis on individual needs and feelings of the members. Ultimately, all groups need members who attend to both functions. Task groups that ignore the feelings and needs of members are not likely to endure because members will drop out or otherwise avoid participating. Treatment groups without sufficient task focus will not reach their goals of changing individual behavior. Group members will become frustrated because they see no progress. Eventually, a therapeutic group that does not maintain a task focus will lose members, funding, or both.

Nonfunctional Roles

Both task and maintenance rolls are designed to help achieve the goals of the group. However, not all the behavior of group members can be classified into the two categories described previously. Some roles played by members simply meet only their own needs. These behaviors include aggressiveness, blocking, seeking recognition for self, dominating the group, seeking help, and confessing past errors. These roles do not further the progress of the group.

Aggressive members attack others and, by putting them down, attempt to raise themselves. Such members are likely to challenge the ideas and motives of others and soon become a problem for the group. *Blockers* are usually the ones to say "Yes, but . . ." to all the ideas or solutions proposed in the group. No matter what the

proposal, they will always have a reason why it will not succeed. *Recognition seekers* will engage in a variety of behaviors, all of which are designed to focus the group's attention on themselves. Like the people who dominate *(dominators)* the group by talking incessantly or people who seek help from the group for their own problems, those *seeking recognition* have personal needs that are not being met. That behavior indicates a need to which the group cannot respond. The person who confesses *(confessor)* past mistakes often embarrasses the group by inappropriately disclosing personal behavior. For example, at the first meeting of a group, when members take turns introducing themselves, one member remarks that she had an abortion once. This disclosure makes some members of the group uncomfortable and shows the member's insensitivity to the usual boundaries experienced within such groups. These roles are important because they indicate the needs of the individual member, but they often do not help the group toward its goals. A member who behaves in this fashion often risks rebuke from the group and slows the group in its achievement of objectives.

Other nonfunctional roles include the scapegoat, deviant member, defensive member, quiet member, and internal leader (Shulman, 2012). *Scapegoats* draw upon themselves the wrath of other members and serve as someone to blame when things are not going well. *Defensive members,* on the other hand, do not accept blame for anything and deny responsibility for their actions. *Deviant members* engage in behavior they know the group will oppose or find annoying, such as continuing to speak out of turn, interrupting others, or refusing to participate in group activities. *Quiet members* simply do not participate, and they make getting to know them impossible for anyone. Finally, the *internal leader* may vie for leadership of the group and attempt to wrestle control from the designated leader. Internal leaders are often members with significant natural leadership ability or influence over other members.

Groups need guidance and help from the leader to recognize and confront nonfunctional roles. At various times in the developmental history of a group (i.e., as a specific group develops and changes over time), different roles may be needed. The leader must be familiar with task and group-building or maintenance roles and skilled enough to model them for group members. Leaders also must be keenly aware of what the group needs at any time. They then must either address that need themselves or draw upon other group members who will play the proper role. Continued nonfunctional

TABLE 3.1 A Variety of Group Roles

Potentially Positive Roles

Information Seeker

Opinion Seeker

Elaborator

Instructor

Evaluator

Energizer

Recorder

Procedural Technician

Harmonizer

Compromiser

Encourager

Follower

Tension Reliever

Listener

Potentially Negative Roles

Aggressor

Blocker

Recognition Seeker

Dominator

Help Seeker

Confessor

Nonfunctional Roles

Scapegoat

Defensive Member

Deviant Member

Quiet Member

Internal Leader

© Cengage Learning

role playing by a group member usually suggests that the group itself is not functioning well. Such behavior should not be ignored or allowed to continue unabated. Table 3.1 summarizes the wide variety of potentially positive and negative group roles as well as those considered nonfunctional.

LO 3-5 Use Empathy and Other Interpersonal Skills with Groups

Chapter 2 discusses a variety of skills important for micro or one-on-one practice, such as relationship-building skills with clients (warmth, empathy, and genuineness) and attending skills (including eye contact, active listening, facial expressions, and body position). In addition, Chapter 2 describes a number of interviewing skills, including encouragement, reflective responding, rephrasing, clarification, interpretation, providing information, summarizing, and self-disclosure. As

might be expected, these skills are as applicable in groups as they are in one-on-one interviews. In therapeutic or growth-oriented groups, the worker is likely to use these skills and to encourage group members to do the same. Part of the worker's function, indeed, may be to teach these skills to members of the group. For example, members of a parenting skills group will benefit from learning how to listen actively to their children. Members of chemical dependency treatment groups will need to engage in self-disclosure and leaders may engage in modeling this behavior.

Task groups typically have less emphasis on such matters as self-disclosure because it is not usually related to the purpose of the group. Likewise, interpretation of behavior and reflective responding is used less often in a staffing for a nursing home patient. Listening skills and the ability to summarize, clarify, and provide information are, however, just as important in task groups as they are in one-on-one interviews and in treatment-oriented groups. Viewing the development of skills as a continuing process is important. Some skills essential for one-on-one situations must be used in small groups and when working with larger system levels such as an agency or large governmental organization. At the same time, a worker with a group must use additional skills that include playing task and group maintenance roles and using parliamentary procedure and nominal group and brainstorming techniques.

Groups and the Generalist Intervention Model (GIM)

EP 2.1.10

The ability to utilize the steps in the Generalist Intervention Model (GIM) is also important with groups. For example, the engagement step is important in treatment groups where the worker develops a professional relationship with group members and conveys warmth, empathy, and other indicators of interest toward all of them. In task groups, engagement is often seen in the behavior of the worker who introduces him- or herself and seeks introductions from other members. It is also evident in the listening skills used by the worker, whether as leader or member.

The assessment step occurs in both task and treatment groups as members seek to understand the purpose of the group, the needs and potential contributions of members, and their commitment to the group. Recognizing and acknowledging the strengths of each group member helps maintain the focus on growth and helps empower the group. Group members must identify issues or problems they will work on while considering the role that the larger environment plays in influencing the problem.

Planning also occurs in both treatment and task groups. The planning step identifies the actions that need to be taken to address the task of the group. It includes prioritizing the issues to be dealt with, including translating problems into needs. Consideration of alternative solutions is done by group members in both task and treatment groups. Selecting goals and objectives, which then suggest concrete steps that members or the group itself will take, is required in all types of groups. For example, a group for women experiencing domestic abuse might discuss alternatives available to a member considering whether or not to return to the abuser. A board of directors will review various possible ways to increase income and reduce expenses for the agency. Treatment groups often use a general working agreement (or contract) whereby members might commit themselves to meeting for six sessions to learn assertiveness skills.

The implementation phase of GIM is sometimes referred to as the working stage of the group. Individual members wrestle with the goals and objectives they have set for themselves. In task groups, the day-to-day discussion and decision making is what occurs. Groups follow (and sometimes revise) the plans made during the planning stage. Progress toward goals is monitored and acknowledged.

Evaluation is a critical activity in groups. Both task and treatment groups have goals and objectives that can be measured or otherwise assessed. Those struggling with substance abuse issues can tally the number of days away from drug use. Patients recovering from surgery can determine the extent to which they feel more in control of their lives and confident about the future. A multidisciplinary team can determine if the group devised a thorough set of recommendations for helping a particular client.

Critical Thinking Questions 3.3

Assume your class is asked to evaluate the effectiveness of a new course designed to help students become more assertive. If the class is not effective, it will be eliminated and the instructor terminated.

- What are some possible options to help evaluate the effectiveness of the assertiveness class?
- Of the options you identified, which one do you believe is most useful? Why?

- What would you say to a fellow student who was worried that a bad evaluation of the class would mean that an instructor would lose his or her job?

All groups reach a point of termination, which may occur, for example, when the six sessions for learning anger management techniques have ended or when the ad hoc committee has completed its set of recommendations. Both task and treatment groups are concerned about the need for follow-up. A task group that failed to come up with a proposal may be asked to continue or be replaced by another group. A treatment group where clients have ongoing individual needs may suggest an appropriate referral. The GIM is an important tool for workers involved with groups.

Intervention Skills for Task and Treatment Groups

Whether the social worker is leading a task group or facilitating a treatment group, several essential skills are likely to be needed. These skills include conflict resolution, modeling and coaching, team building, confrontation, consultation, coordination, and using structure.

CONFLICT RESOLUTION

Conflict is a fact of life. It occurs routinely within relationships and can have positive or negative consequences depending upon how it is handled. Conflict may arise from power or status differences, personality disagreements, or from opposing values or belief systems.

Conflict tends to be viewed as negative because too often it is not resolved or managed successfully. Conflict situations may be approached in a logical and step-by-step method that includes recognizing it, assessing the conflict, identifying an appropriate method of resolution, and implementing the resolution.

Recognizing Conflict

Recognizing potential or actual conflict is easy when people do not talk to one another or are openly hostile, unnecessarily polite, or outright rude. Ideas suggested by one side may be routinely rejected by the other. The conflict may be between individuals or groups. It may be created by jealousy and other personal reactions, confusion, or misunderstanding. The example in Highlight 3.5 suggests how even the best plans can create conflict.

HIGHLIGHT 3.5

The Family Treatment Program: Recognizing Conflict

The new specialized family treatment program was barely 6 months old when problems began to appear. It was designed to provide intensive in-home treatment by a team of family workers with low caseloads. The program had initially been greeted as a very positive approach to working with multi-barrier families. Within a few months, the team was beginning to prove the merits of the idea. At the same time, workers who were not part of the specialized unit began to complain. Soon, the source of the complaints became clear. With several workers attached to the special program, those

remaining were being asked to handle larger caseloads. Many saw the benefits of the new program but felt their extra work was unfair. Those with larger caseloads felt they were assuming too much of the burden and resented it.

When designed, the new program had no alternative plans to handle an increased caseload. Nor was any thought given to how removing workers from the regular family unit would affect the workload of those who remained. Clearly, the agency administration had a problem.

HIGHLIGHT 3.6

That Is Not What I Said: Assessing Conflict

John was in his second month as director of the Eastern Washington Service Center (EWSC). The agency had been wracked with scandal before John became director. Under a recent director, the agency had lost its entire building fund because of poor stock investments. John's task was to return the agency to a healthy financial footing and restore its reputation. In his first report to the board of directors, John explained recent changes in the agency and tried to highlight some of the accomplishments. To help improve staff morale

and productivity, he announced that he had recently bought some chairs. Almost immediately one board member at the other end of the room exclaimed angrily, "What?" John was momentarily perplexed. Surely purchasing a couple of office chairs was not a matter of major concern to a member of the board of directors. Then the board member asked, "Did you say you bought shares or chairs?" John quickly assured the board that he had indeed purchased desk chairs, not shares of stock, the cause of the earlier scandal.

Assessing Conflict

Assessing conflict usually requires talking directly to the parties involved. Often, the source becomes clear during this process. In the situation in Highlight 3.5, the source was readily identified. Sometimes, other problems mask the source, or the problem is the result of miscommunication. In the latter case, the problem can be more easily resolved. Highlight 3.6 gives a simple example.

Creating a problem does not take much effort. Undoubtedly, unclear messages between sender and listener cause their share of conflictual situations.

Choosing a Strategy and Intervening

Identifying the source of a conflict is an important step in resolving it. Once identified, appropriate strategies can be considered or devised. For example, if the

problem is simply between people, a variety of approaches can be used. These include bargaining or negotiating (discussed in Chapter 4) and other methods designed to separate those in conflict. When a structural problem (one related to agency design or organization) is causing the conflict, the solution must also be structural. For example, a disagreement over assignments may be resolved by modifying the assignment system or redistributing an unfair workload. Sometimes, an interpersonal problem can be resolved through structural means. Highlight 3.7 illustrates this point.

Although positive outcomes are not always possible and some conflicts cannot be managed, progress can usually be made. In some cases, the following strategies will prove effective.

Square Peg in a Round Hole: Choosing a Strategy

Both workers and clients complained about the treatment they received from Ann. With responsibility for the reception area, Ann was supposed to greet all clients and visitors, notify workers of their arrival, answer phone calls and direct them to other staff, and keep track of clients when the worker came to the front desk to meet them. Workers considered her rude to clients and felt she was impatient and irritable most of the time. She was likened to Charles Dickens's character Scrooge.

The agency administrative staff had discussed the situation before, and the supervisor had talked to Ann, all to no avail. Ann would try to improve, but things always seemed to end up the same. The administrative staff was working on a reorganization plan that would require assigning new responsibilities to one supervisor and reassigning an additional experienced clerical staff

member. After a brief discussion, the group decided to reassign Ann to new duties and move her from the reception desk to the reorganized unit. A new receptionist would be hired, and Ann would be working with day care providers and foster parents. She would handle financial details and report to a new supervisor. Within days of the administrative reorganization, Ann was hard at work on her new tasks. She stopped complaining, treated everyone with respect, and underwent a remarkable transformation. This change continued, and Ann was never again reported for abusive or rude behavior. The agency reorganization had not been designed to end the problem in the reception area but had the effect of doing so. Once away from the stress of being the receptionist, Ann developed into a highly valued member of the agency team.

Win-Lose and Win-Win Situations. One of the ways we can avoid becoming involved in conflict is to recognize when a win-lose conflict situation is developing. The nature of competition often produces a win-lose mentality. Much of our society is structured around the idea of winning or beating the competition. In group meetings, there are always clues to win-lose situations. When you feel yourself lining up on one side or the other, you are probably becoming involved in a win-lose incident. Sometimes our language gives us away. If we say or believe that our way is the only way or the best way, we are implicitly giving a message that the other person's point of view is wrong. Eventually, win-lose situations become lose-lose situations because neither side benefits. The side that loses feels bad and may be resentful. They often lose their sense of being part of the group and may even sabotage things if sufficiently upset. Losers stop listening to the other side and soon see additional areas where they disagree. Resolving win-lose situations requires that we first be aware of them. Once alerted, there are a number of skills and techniques that can be employed to defuse the situation. Some strategies that are often successful for resolving or avoiding win-lose situations in groups include:

1. Asking each person to listen actively to the other. Active listening requires that you demonstrate your understanding of what the other person has said by paraphrasing it.

2. Role playing for the parties to show how their communication looks to an outsider.
3. Asking both sides to list their areas of similarity and agreement.
4. Attempting to identify goals that transcend the differences between the parties and working for solutions that fulfill these goals.
5. Finding objective criteria or values that can be used to evaluate other solutions.
6. Seeking agreement from each side to make concessions that will meet the needs of the other.
7. Meeting with one or more members outside the group to try to find a solution to the conflict.

Once agreements appear to be reached, testing to make sure they are real is important. Asking both sides to describe explicitly their understanding of the agreed-upon solution is wise. Miscommunication that originally caused a problem can just as easily disrupt the solution. The ability to resolve conflict successfully or at least to manage it is an important skill for any social worker.

MODELING AND COACHING

Albert Bandura's (1986, 2004, 2006) work on modeling suggests the enormous importance that watching others has on our behavior. Social workers may find modeling helpful in a number of situations, including teaching new skills, showing clients alternative methods for resolving problems, and helping clients develop a repertoire of responses to problematic situations. An example of this is presented in Highlight 3.8. Bandura has identified conditions that enhance the likelihood that a model's behavior will be copied. These conditions include: (1) the observer's attention level or awareness of the model; (2) the observer's retention of the modeled behavior; (3) the observer's ability to perform modeled behavior; and (4) the observer's motivation to perform the behavior. Awareness of the factors that influence effective modeling allows the social worker to increase the likelihood that the modeled behavior will be performed by the observer. In groups, this modeling can be achieved by several methods, including:

1. Asking group members to pay special attention to the model's behavior
2. Describing for the group why the modeled behavior is important
3. Having members role play the modeled behavior to ensure that they understood and can perform it
4. Using praise both for the group members and the person who models the appropriate behavior
5. Giving members immediate corrective feedback when they attempt a new behavior

Coaching is a skill that includes giving the client specific information as well as corrective feedback. For example, a social worker may suggest a new way of approaching a difficult coworker, ask the client to role play it, and then provide feedback about ways to improve. In coaching, the worker may choose to intervene immediately after a client has engaged in a behavior. If the behavior to be changed includes verbal communication, the worker may wish to ignore the content and focus on the process. Describing the group member's behavior, instead of evaluating it, is always appropriate. Evaluative comments typically exacerbate problems instead of assisting communication skills. People often resent direct criticism.

One approach to coaching would be to ask a group member to speak directly to another member, rather than to the group as a whole or to the worker. This method is especially helpful if the group involves family members or others with whom the speaker frequently interacts. For example, in the couples group, Juan tells the social worker that he would like his wife to be more affectionate. The social worker asks Juan to turn directly to his wife and tell her specifically what he would like her to do. In this way, Juan must address his wife, who is ultimately the only person who can meet his need. This approach forces Juan to be more specific because "being more affectionate" has many meanings.

Coaching also involves encouraging members to try new behavior. A common barrier to behaving differently is fear that one will look stupid or perform poorly. The worker can help overcome this fear by

---

HIGHLIGHT 3.8

Teaching Disciplinary Techniques: Modeling and Coaching

The second meeting of the practical parenting group began with a review by the social worker, Marjorie, of what had been learned in the first session. Marjorie then discussed the program for the day. The major goal was to learn two new, nonpunitive techniques for disciplining children. The first technique was a time-out procedure. Marjorie told the group they would see a brief videotape of a mother using the time-out technique with her child. Group members were asked to watch the mother carefully and take notes on what she did. Marjorie emphasized the importance of this technique for managing certain kinds of situations that commonly arise between parent and child. She quickly summarized the research on this approach as well as her own experience with its use. Using this approach described, Marjorie was dem-

onstrating two of the guidelines for modeling: asking the observer to pay special attention to the model and describing why the modeled behavior was important.

After the videotape had been played twice, Marjorie asked one of the parents to volunteer to model the time-out technique with Marjorie playing the child's role. Then each parent took a turn playing the roles of parent and child. Marjorie praised good examples of the time-out technique and suggested improvements for group members who were having more difficulty.

In this last section, Marjorie used the remaining guidelines. She asked the group members to role play the desired behavior and used praise or corrective feedback, depending upon how well the person performed the desired behavior.

encouraging and supporting the member. This technique is especially effective if the behavior to be copied has already been modeled. Assertiveness training typically uses a combination of modeling and coaching to help group members develop and use new skills. When used by the worker in tandem, these skills can increase the likelihood that the members will adopt and continue the new behavior or communication patterns.

TEAM BUILDING

Team building is the process of creating a group of individuals with the expertise, dedication, and characteristics needed to achieve a specific purpose. It requires both careful consideration of those who will compose the team and attention to the conditions that will enhance the team's ability to perform. The importance of working as a team member should be clear by now. The use of multidisciplinary teams, staffings, and similar work groups is sufficiently common in social work that every worker can expect to become a member of one such team or another. Whether or not the team works effectively is often a result of the team-building efforts that have occurred. Johnson and Yanca (2010) and others have identified some of the problems that frequently interfere with the ability of a team to develop. Our emphasis here is on strategies to build a team, while overcoming common barriers.

Team building can best occur when there is strong organizational support for the team. An important way of supporting a team is by use of time. This process requires providing sufficient time for the team to meet independently of their case-handling responsibilities, so that team meetings will not be an additional burden competing with their regular job responsibilities. If the only time the team meets is around individual cases, there will likely be limited ability to develop the "we" feeling so important to effective functioning. Adequate time for team building also allows the team to agree on goals and roles and responsibilities ahead of time. These responsibilities include not only decision making processes, but also who will assume leadership responsibilities.

Leadership for the team can be handled in a variety of ways. The leader can be selected by the team members or appointed by an outside supervisor. That the leader be well qualified is crucial. That is, he or she should have experience working on teams and making decisions as part of a team. Although members bring varying levels of expertise to the team, all should be seen more or less as equal participants. Clear status differentials among members may impair group functioning. Some team building will occur as members become more familiar with their colleagues. This familiarity includes communication patterns, terminology, professional jargon, and interpersonal styles. Quite simply, it involves getting used to each other and how the team interacts. A well-functioning team will be composed of members who understand and respect one another's expertise, carry out agreed-upon tasks, and are cooperative. Individual members must be comfortable working in an interdisciplinary environment and not lose sight of their professional orientation. A social worker on an interdisciplinary team is still a social worker; no other professional is likely to bring an identical perspective to the team's deliberations. Social work is the only profession with a primary focus on the person within the environment and a concomitant obligation to work for change with both the client system and that environment.

The work of teams is achieved in the same planned change steps described earlier in this text. The team must define the problem, select appropriate goals, use their collective knowledge to consider alternatives, develop an intervention plan, and carry it out. Evaluation of the plan and process must follow the implementation phase. Team members should agree in advance how this process will occur. If this process is done and the other tasks mentioned earlier are performed, an effective team is likely to result.

CONFRONTATION

Confrontation within a group tends to be more discomforting than confronting individuals on a one-on-one basis. Yet, to be effective as a team player, group leader, or member, the worker must be able to use confrontation. Chapter 2 describes some of the situations where confrontation is appropriate. In this section, we will discuss briefly the importance of confrontation in groups.

Chapter 2 describes confronting discrepancies, primarily in relation to working with individuals. Discrepancies that occur within groups also require some level and type of confrontation. A worker in a treatment group who determines that a member has engaged in behavior warranting confrontation has a responsibility to follow through and confront that individual. There are, however, at least two ways to approach confrontation that can make it more palatable and effective. When workers choose to confront a client directly, for example, because of a discrepancy between verbal and other behavior, this situation provides a good opportunity to model appropriate confrontation for other members. The worker engages in a nonblaming type of confrontation by pointing out the discrepancy and how it affects the worker, for example, by using an "I" statement.

A second manner of confrontation involves having the worker in a group ask the entire group to take responsibility for problem solving. Thus, a worker might say, "Is anyone else bothered by Mike's assertion that he is going straight, after saying that he was arrested again last night?" This approach places responsibility for confronting Mike on the group instead of the worker, underscoring an important principle in treatment groups.

Confrontation in task groups is also essential. Members must be able to confront other members who do not carry out agreed-upon tasks or who engage in other behavior that threatens the group. For example, a team member represents himself to the public as having more authority and responsibility in the group than what he really had. In other words, he believes he does most of the work, and therefore wants most of the credit. In one example, group members charged with planning a conference took responsibility for telling the errant member that no single member is appointed as a conference coordinator and that the group reserves this role for itself. In their view, they all put in a lot of effort and deserve to share the credit accordingly.

Although there will usually be a brief moment of discomfort when confrontation is used, the costs of not being confrontational are too high to avoid this responsibility. As always, confrontation should be used judiciously and tactfully. One should have both empathy and respect for the sensitivities of the person being confronted.

CONSULTATION

As described throughout this chapter, the worker may serve as a consultant to the group. Consider a worker who provided consultation to a Parents Anonymous group. The group's goal was to provide a supportive experience for parents who abuse their children and to help these parents avoid such behavior in the future. The worker's role included providing consultation on available community services, strategies for successfully negotiating agency bureaucracies, and nonpunitive ideas for child management. The worker informed group members about local resources, shared his knowledge of agency eligibility requirements, and helped clients assess the appropriateness of the service

for meeting their needs. The consultant role is basically that of an advisor who provides information, suggestions, ideas, and feedback. A consultant lacks administrative power over the consultee but has special knowledge or expertise that is of value to the recipient. The consultee is free to accept, modify, or reject the advice.

Consultation may be either case consultation or program consultation, or it may include elements of both. In *case consultation,* the focus is on a specific client or situation, and the consultation may be provided to either social workers or nonsocial workers. An example would be consultation provided to a nursing home staff on a particular client.

Program consultation may occur when the consultant works with supervisory or administrative staff about ways to improve service. In this case, the focus may be on agency policies and practices instead of a specific client.

In one instance, a social worker was asked to serve as a consultant to a family planning agency. The agency director believed that the intercession of a consultant could help ameliorate problems occurring among volunteers serving the agency. The problems seemed to focus on disagreements between and among volunteer group members and the director. Volunteers appeared resistive to suggestions and direction provided by the agency director. The consultant met separately with the director and then jointly with the director and the volunteers. Several salient issues of concern to the volunteers were identified during this meeting. The primary issue involved a perception that the director was favoring one member of the volunteer group over the others. The consultant suggested that the director address this issue directly with the group. The director publicly announced his engagement to the "favored" volunteer and took pains from that point on to ensure that his interactions with the group did not show favoritism. The end result was improved service delivery to agency clients, increased openness on the part of the director, and a greater sense on the part of the volunteers that they were making a valued contribution to the agency.

Although no single model of social work consultation has emerged, consultation does involve a purpose, a problem, and a process. Ultimately, the success of the consultation depends upon the relationship between consultant and consultee. The expertise and capability of the consultant is only as effective as the relationship between the two allows. Once again, skills important for one-on-one interventions are just as useful when working with groups.

COORDINATION

Coordination "is the working together of two or more service providers in activity focused on a particular client or focused on persons in a particular category" (Yanca & Johnson, 2010, p. 436). Yanca and Johnson describe the coordinating function of social work as encompassing both collaboration and teamwork. To be successful, coordination requires that all parties have a common goal. The goal may relate to a particular client or include provision of services to a target population. There is an expectation that all parties believe that improvements will occur if coordination of services is accomplished.

Case management often involves coordination of services provided by a variety of professionals. The focus is on assuring that all services provided to a client are accomplished in a way that achieves common goals and meets client needs. Often the social worker is the person who has the case management responsibility and ensures that agreed-upon services are provided. (Case management is discussed further in Chapter 15.) Coordination is especially important when the service providers have different professional orientations or when both formal and informal resources must be used to help the client. To be most effective, the social worker providing coordination must value and believe in the competence of services provided by others. The worker must also ensure that all important information is communicated to all parties. That sufficient time be made available for building relationships among the participants, in addition to participants having support for their efforts, is important.

USING STRUCTURE

Structure describes "the use of planned, systematic, time-limited interventions and program activities" (Toseland & Rivas, 2012, p. 271). One of the facets of structure is the use of time. Group meetings should begin and end at an agreed-upon time. Material brought up at the last minute is best held for the next meeting.

Agendas help structure time, ensuring that topics or activities to be covered are known to all. This structuring places responsibility on all members to stay on task. Sometimes, the amount of time to be spent on each topic is specified, further structuring the use of time. In treatment groups, structure may include spending different amounts of time on each client's issues. In many groups, all members take turns sharing their progress since the previous meeting, with major focus on one member. This process is then followed in successive meetings so all members have opportunities to focus on their problems. The worker is largely responsible for enforcing time constraints and models this for the members. Frequently, the entire intervention is highly structured. Many educational groups are well-structured and include blocks of time allocated for specific topics, group activities designed to teach important concepts, and even role playing. The degree of structure needed may vary from one type of group to another. The worker will need to be flexible in planning and working with groups.

Chapter Summary

The following summarizes this chapter's content as it relates to each learning objective (LO) presented at the beginning of the chapter. Chapter content helps prepare students to:

LO 3-1 Articulate the benefits and functions of treatment and task groups.

Working with groups requires recognizing the benefits of groups, which include mutual assistance, connecting with others, testing out new behaviors, achieving individual and group goals, and decision making. It also involves awareness of the types of groups, both task and treatment, that are used in social work. Task groups include boards of directors, task forces, committees and commissions, legislative bodies, staff meetings, multidisciplinary teams, case conferences and staffing, and social action groups.

Treatment groups include growth, therapy, educational, socialization, and support groups. As the name suggests, these groups are focused on the individual needs of group members.

Social networking groups often are used in concert with both task and treatment groups, and social media may prove helpful for addressing certain client needs.

LO 3-2 Attend to professional roles in groups.

Workers play multiple roles in groups. Included roles are broker, mediator, educator, and facilitator. The roles played by social workers tend to depend on the needs of the group as well as the type of group that is being led.

LO 3-3 Utilize conceptual frameworks in group assessment, intervention, and evaluation.

An understanding of basic group dynamics is essential for leading or participating in both task and treatment groups. Factors of importance include the stages of group development, through which most groups evolve, and the group's culture, norms, and power structure, all of which will influence the behavior of individual members. Size is another factor in group dynamics, as it can impact on the effectiveness of the group's work. Too large a group may interfere with members' attraction to the body as well as their willingness to interact with each other.

The composition of the group is also an important dynamic. Characteristics such as members' age, gender, personalities, verbal ability, ethnicity, and others can affect the degree to which the group achieves its purpose. Although there is no hard and fast rule for deciding what factors are most important in every type of group, the social worker must pay attention to these characteristics when forming a group.

The duration or length of a group may also be an important consideration. Some groups are designed to be ongoing whereas others are expected to conclude after a finite number of sessions. The needs of the group members and the purpose of the group usually influence its duration.

LO 3-4 Select appropriate problem-solving and decision-making approaches with groups.

All groups must make some decisions, and this is particularly true of task groups. There are many avenues to decision making in groups, each with strengths and drawbacks. They include decision making by consensus, by compromise, by majority rule, by individual fiat, by persuasion by an expert, through averaging of individual members' opinions, and through persuasion by a minority. Decision making by consensus and compromise usually lead to more satisfaction among members, while decision making by majority is often used with larger groups and may satisfy only those in the majority.

Other methods of decision making and problem solving include the nominal group technique and brainstorming, both of which are designed to deeply involve individual members in the process. Parliamentary procedure, a highly structured decision-making technique, is often used by larger groups such as legislative bodies and involves procedures designed to allow minority voices to be heard and majority voices to make the final decision.

Social workers leading groups also must use a variety of knowledge and skills such as understanding how to ensure critical thinking in the decision-making process, recognizing both task and maintenance roles needed to help a group function, and being aware of nonfunctional roles that impede the group's progress.

Task roles include information and opinion seeking, elaborating, instructing, energizing, recording roles, and that of procedural technician.

Maintenance roles of members include encourager, listener, follower, harmonizer or compromiser, and tension reliever. Both task and maintenance roles can be played by group members as well as by the group leader.

Nonfunctional roles include aggressors, recognition seekers, dominators, confessors, scapegoats, defensive members, nonparticipators, and internal leaders.

LO 3-5 Use empathy and other interpersonal skills with groups.

As group leaders, social workers must be able to use many micro skills, including relationship building, empathy, warmth, genuineness, and attending skills such as eye contact, active listening, appropriate facial expressions, and body position. Other important skills are discussed in more depth in Chapter 2 of this text.

Workers need to be familiar with the Generalist Intervention Model as it applies to groups as well as specific skills needed in both task and treatment groups. These include conflict resolution strategies and steps, modeling and coaching group members, team building, confrontation, consultation, and coordination. They also must know how to use structure to help the group achieve its goals. Structure includes the use of time and the development of an agenda, or plan, for what is going to occur at a given meeting. The degree of structure needed may vary from one type of group to another.

Competency Notes

The following identifies where Educational Policy (EP) competencies and practice behaviors are discussed in the chapter.

EP 2.1.1a Advocate for client access to the services of social work. *(p. 97):* Task groups can serve many purposes, including advocating for client access to services.

EP 2.1.1c Attend to professional roles and boundaries. *(p. 97):* Task groups involve a variety of groups, including boards of directors, committees, and social action groups. Social workers are called upon to play different professional roles depending on the needs of the particular type of group. *(p. 105):* Common roles in social work include broker, mediator, educator, and facilitator.

EP 2.1.1f **Use supervision and consultation.** *(p. 123):* Social workers may engage in consultation with groups in order to assist them to reach their own goals.

EP 2.1.3 **Apply critical thinking to inform and communicate professional judgment.** *(p. 96):* Critical thinking is required when making decisions and involves considering the pros and cons of particular courses of action. *(p. 114):* Critical thinking is needed when helping a group make decisions. Failure to employ critical thinking can lead to groupthink and other poor decisions. *(p. 115):* Thinking critically about evaluation of practice helps produce better outcome assessments.

EP 2.1.5b **Advocate for human rights and social and economic justice.** *(p. 97):* Task groups involving social action goals are often aimed at advocating for human rights and social and economic justice. *(p. 100):* Social action groups can occur in almost any setting.

EP 2.1.6 **Engage in research-informed practice and practice-informed research.** *(p. 99):* Participatory Action Research (PAR) is a method of conducting research in a community to gather data about a particular problem. It is a method that uses research tools to inform practice and practice skills to enhance the quality of the research.

EP 2.1.7a **Utilize conceptual frameworks to guide the processes of assessment, intervention, and evaluation.** *(p. 105):* Various conceptual frameworks and models are needed to understand groups. These include such things as basic group dynamics. *(p. 109):* Decision-making models and patterns are often employed when working with groups. *(p. 110):* Concepts such as group functions and roles are important to consider when working with groups.

EP 2.1.8 **Engage in policy practice to advance social and economic well-being and to deliver effective social work services.** *(p. 97):* Task groups and committees are often created to more effectively pursue social and economic justice goals.

EP 2.1.10 **Engage, assess, intervene, and evaluate with individuals, families, groups, organizations, and communities.** *(pp. 101, 117):* Working with groups typically involves the processes of engagement; identifying desired outcomes; collecting, organizing, and interpreting client data; assessing strengths and limitations; agreeing on goals and objectives; carrying out the interventions; and monitoring and evaluating the intervention. These are essentially the same steps as in the Generalist Intervention Model (GIM) planned change process.

EP 2.1.10a **Substantively and affectively prepare for action with individuals, families, groups, organizations, and communities.** *(p. 95):* Social workers must understand, employ, and participate in groups as part of their professional responsibility. Groups represent another size of systems with which generalist social workers must engage. Working effectively with groups requires specific knowledge and skills.

EP 2.1.10h **Initiate actions to achieve organizational goals.** *(p. 97):* Groups such as boards of directors and agency committees often are created to serve organizational needs.

EP 2.1.10j **Help clients resolve problems.** *(p. 101):* Treatment groups are commonly used to help clients resolve problems.

EP 2.1.10k **Negotiate, mediate, and advocate for clients.** *(p. 105):* One possible role of the practitioner working with groups is to help members mediate disputes and negotiate with the environment or other systems.

On the Internet

Visit the *Understanding Generalist Practice* CourseMate at **www.cengagebrain.com** for resources such as quizzes, glossaries and videos.

Skills for Working with Organizations and Communities

National Archives and Records Administration

Learning Objectives   *This chapter will help prepare students to:*

LO 4-1 Utilize a conceptual framework for an organizational context of practice.

LO 4-2 Analyze, formulate, and advocate for interventions, including policy/planning, capacity development, and social advocacy.

LO 4-3 Use empathy, interpersonal skills, and group skills in macro practice.

LO 4-4 Utilize effective macro-practice skills, including evaluating results, fundraising, budgeting, negotiating, mediating, influencing decision makers, needs assessment, planning, and working with coalitions.

LO 4-5 Engage in professional roles, including initiator, negotiator, advocate, spokesperson, organizer, mediator, and consultant.

GEORGIANA HARRISON WAS DOG-TIRED. Her primary job was to license foster homes, make foster home placements, and oversee her agency's receiving homes for children. The receiving homes provided temporary shelter for up to 3 weeks, while other, more permanent arrangements could be made (e.g., foster care or a return to the child's own home). But this year had been an especially bad one for Janna, as her friends called her, as well as for the county human services agency for which she worked.

First, Janna had become aware that fewer people were applying to be foster parents. She did not know the reasons why, but the lack of homes was becoming serious.

Second, she recognized that her agency badly needed a group home for adolescent boys. The number of referrals for group-home care was increasing, and none of her traditional foster homes was designed to handle half-a-dozen delinquent boys.

Janna found that her colleagues were also confronting many problems. Too many sexually active young people had no access to family planning services. Many clients could not afford to see a physician.

Finally, her own agency seemed reluctant to provide clients with adequate resources unless administrators were legally pressured to do so. Past efforts to get the agency director to be more flexible were not particularly successful.

As a line social worker (i.e., not a supervisor or administrator), Janna did not think of herself as a community organizer or organizational change agent. However, in the next 3 years, Janna would be involved in all of the following macro-level change activities:

1. developing a family planning clinic for low-income clients (she later served as vice chair of its board of directors);

2. creating community education programs designed to increase the number of licensed foster homes (she prepared radio and newspaper ads and appeared on local talk-radio shows);

3. writing a grant to establish a group home for delinquent boys (she wrote the grant, defended it before a review panel, and supervised operation of the group home);

4. pressuring of her agency's director to recognize client rights and provide better service; and

5. creating a new program to provide part-time tutoring jobs for delinquent adolescents.

Engaging with Organizations and Communities

EP 2.1.2

Macro practice in generalist social work involves working on behalf of whole groups or populations of clients. It transcends working with individual clients, families, or small treatment groups. Macro practice involves questioning and sometimes confronting major social issues and global organizational policies. Sometimes, the services your clients need are not being provided; at other times, the policies under which you are expected to work are unfair or inhumane. At these times, you will need to consider whether or not to try to change the organization, policy, or system on behalf of your clients. You may need to assess the situation from a broad perspective, and you may have to evaluate what impact "the system" (whichever one may be involved) has on your clients.

Many, perhaps most, social workers, in their early practice, focus on working with individual clients or groups of clients. Thinking about changing "the system" is vague or overwhelming. The specific "system" that needs changing may be hard to define (e.g., "the system" may be the organization you work for, a county social services agency, your state government, or a federal bureaucracy). How one makes changes in "the system" may be unclear. The work necessary to implement changes is probably not in your written job description. You might be awed by the amount of effort such change demands.

Core value themes in social work include the fundamental rights of people to have their basic needs met, to make their own choices (assuming such choices harm neither others nor themselves), and to maintain their human dignity. A central theme of the empowerment tradition in social work practice is the emphasis on expanding client resources and choices, especially for groups denied social and economic justice (Gutiérrez, Parsons, & Cox, 2003; Simon, 1994). There will be times when you will find these value themes violated. You will see inequities and unfairness that you cannot ethically tolerate. These instances are most likely to be the times when you will call upon your macro-practice skills to implement changes outside the individual client or client group. Something in the environment, in some part of "the system," will need to be the target of your change effort.

This chapter focuses on the skills needed to work *with* and *within* the various systems enveloping us. Most macro-change efforts will be pursued within an agency context. Therefore, we will view macro practice primarily from an organizational perspective.

Defining Macro Practice

Macro practice is social work practice designed to improve or modify some aspect of society. Improvements or changes can be sought in organizational or societal policies and procedures that regulate distribution of resources to clients. These improvements might occur when clients are either not getting needed resources or when the resource is not provided as effectively or efficiently as possible.

Similarly, macro practice is concerned with developing new resources when what clients need is unavailable. Sometimes, new policies and procedures must be developed and implemented. At other times, whole new groups, agencies, or organizations must be established.

Another task common to macro practice is helping clients get their due rights. Changes need to be made in "the system" so that clients can exercise their rights. Change is needed whether for the benefit of one client or 10,000 clients.

Macro practice targets "the system" to determine where and how changes need to be made. Numerous systems make up our general society. They include political systems such as town, county, state, and federal governments. They also include legal systems involving the police, legislature, and courts. Additionally, they involve social-service-delivery systems such as county social service agencies, residential mental health facilities, and federal Veterans' Administration services.

Macro practice often requires the use of advocacy on behalf of clients. Advocacy involves intervening in order to help clients get what they need. Sometimes, it means going further and working much harder than the specifications of your job description. This element of social work is one that makes the profession special and distinct from other fields.

Finally, macro practice occurs frequently in an organizational context. In other words, most macro practice is carried out by those in agencies or organizations. Agencies have policies or constraints that often act to limit workers' behavior. This aspect differs from social workers who can act as independent agents, attack a problem, and do whatever they want. The following is a detailed exploration of this issue.

LO 4-1 Utilize a Conceptual Framework for an Organizational Context of Practice

EP 2.1.7a

Most social workers spend all, or part, of their professional careers within formal organizations. Similarly, all persons live and practice within a community (rural, urban, or suburban). The benefits of formal organizations include such tangible resources as office space, salary, clerical support, paper, telephone, and the like. They also provide less tangible benefits such as sanction for one's professional efforts.

Consider, for example, that the social worker in a child welfare agency must complete investigations following allegations of child abuse. She was hired for that job, supported by the agency in her performance, and is generally respected by the agency and community for her efforts to protect vulnerable children. In pursuing the mandate for child protection, the worker has an office, telephone, mileage allowance, secretarial support, salary, and fringe benefits. These are provided because the agency and community believe in the potential good to be accomplished by the worker. Clearly, such formal organizations as social and other human service agencies provide much of value to the social worker. In turn, the social worker pursues actions that are designed to achieve organizational goals such as responding to community problems or assisting various-size client systems.

With the benefits of belonging to or working for an organization, however, come drawbacks. These include policies, rules, and regulations that circumscribe behavior, and procedures that sometimes become a source of difficulty. The worker who has not found working within an organization sometimes troublesome or downright antithetical to professional obligations to the client is rare.

Moreover, changes in some practice settings have forced social workers to better understand and master new organizational challenges. For example, Gray and Coates (2013); Peckover, Vasquez, Van Housen, Saunders, and Allen (2013); and Bransford (2006) note the enormous changes affecting social work practice in a variety of settings. As hospitals and other facilities strive for greater efficiency and cost reductions, social workers have learned to participate in the change process while identifying ways that they can contribute to improvements in services. At the same time, involvement in organizational change can be stressful, confusing, and even demoralizing. Understanding how organizations confront change is an important facet of social work if practitioners are to function effectively in service agencies.

Highlight 4.1 illustrates how an agency can sometimes become part of the problem. Moreover, many social workers move into macro-level positions within a few years of graduation. This transition also confronts social workers with the challenge of making their own agencies responsive to the social and economic justice needs of clients. Keep in mind that on some community issues your agency will not believe it has a dog in the fight. In those cases, the agency will neither actively support nor oppose your efforts and you will need to work outside your organization to produce change (Corey, Corey, & Callanan, 2011).

RECOGNIZING PROFESSIONAL–ORGANIZATIONAL CONFLICTS

 Conflicts such as the one Glen experienced (see Highlight 4.1) are common for workers in most human service agencies. Frequently, the problem is even more serious than the one in our example. Social workers who feel a sense of professional identity with the social work profession and subscribe to the *Code of Ethics* of the National Association of Social Workers (NASW) may find serious conflicts arising between their professional role as change agents and their responsibilities to the employing agency. These naturally occurring conflicts reflect the reality of professional practice within formal organizations. All social

workers have an obligation to follow the policies of their agency, and most of the time this is not a problem. The conflict described in Highlight 4.1 was real, and the dilemma faced by the social worker was challenging. Formal organizations require rules and regulations (policies) to function effectively. Similarly, the profession of social work has established guides to professional behavior to ensure a minimum level of service to all clients. When these two obligations collide, the worker (and often the client) is frequently in the middle. Glen identified with the social work profession and sought to achieve its goals while conducting himself as a professional. How should he handle this situation?

Another area of potential conflict between your organization and your professional obligation could be the former's concern about your involvement in community change activities that fall outside your prescribed duties. Not all supervisors and administrators will understand your professional commitment to, and values that support, social and economic justice. They may fear your actions place the agency in a bad light or offend influential community members, and thus discourage your involvement. When you take public positions the organization may fear that others will believe you are speaking for the agency rather than representing others in the community. This represents just one more challenge facing those who seek to end oppression and injustice.

Recognizing Ethical Conflicts: When the Agency You Work for Is Part of the Problem

Glen had worked only a short time for the Manitou County Department of Human Services. As foster care coordinator, he was responsible for recruiting, screening, training, and licensing of foster homes. It was a job of which he was very proud. Glen put in many extra hours meeting prospective foster parents in the evening, so neither foster parent would have to take off from work to meet with Glen. During one of their regular supervisory conferences, Glen's supervisor, Peggy, said he was accumulating too much compensatory time and should stop the evening visits.

Glen liked Peggy and generally felt that she was supportive of his work. Peggy said that if people cared enough about becoming foster parents, most would come in during regular business hours. The new policy troubled Glen. In his view, foster parents were providing an important and irreplaceable service to the community and agency. Foster parents were always badly needed, and most of the couples interested in becoming foster parents had at least one parent working during the day. Most were in what some might call the lower-middle class, hardworking people with limited financial resources. Glen saw them in the evening because he was reluctant to ask parents to take time off from work and possibly lose income. Glen felt an obligation to the foster parents and a duty to follow the rules of his agency, and now these responsibilities seemed in conflict.

CONSIDERING LIMITATIONS AND RISK ASSESSMENT

When such a situation arises, the worker must decide how to handle it. The planned change process explained earlier in this text is applicable here. The worker must assess several items. Knowing, for example, whether Glen's view is correct, that foster parents should not have to take off from work to participate in the interviews, would be important. Glen's position, however, rests largely on his values and nothing stronger. Knowing if scheduling meetings during the day discourages foster parents from participating might be important. Learning why the supervisor felt the amount of compensatory time was excessive might also be helpful. Was there some agency rule that set the maximum amount that could be accrued? Was the supervisor just worried about how much evening work Glen was putting in? Glen needed to know where the problem lay in order to find a solution. Also, Glen was a new worker, albeit a valuable one. He felt challenging his supervisor would be difficult because of his newness.

Glen's reluctance illustrates the importance of assessing the risk inherent in trying to change any part of an organization. Glen was also aware of other rules that were equally problematic but seemed more intractable. Glen knew that there are limitations in how many, what type of, and how fast problems within an agency can be solved. A new worker who tries to change some part of an agency is in a vulnerable position. Before making efforts to change an organization, the worker must realistically assess the probability of success, the importance of securing this change, and the risks to him- or herself for pursuing such a change.

This last risk cannot be accurately assessed without considering the strategies Glen might undertake to challenge the rule. Some strategies carry increased risk to the worker. Angering a supervisor is risky. Getting fired is unappealing. The worker is more vulnerable at certain times. Many agencies, for example, place a new worker on probation for 6 months. During that time, the worker may be fired for almost any reason without recourse to the usual protections afforded more experienced workers (union contract, personnel policies, and so on).

Critical Thinking Questions 4.1

- If you were in Glen's situation, what would you do? Why?
- List some of the possible reasons Glen's supervisor may have had for objecting to the amount of compensatory time he was accumulating. Which do you consider the most persuasive reason? Why?

Utilizing a Conceptual Framework for Organizational and Community Change

EP 2.1.3
EP 2.1.7a

Typically, social workers identify several broad theoretical perspectives that underlie practice with large systems. These include systems theory, organizational theory and community theory. Systems theory is employed in most, if not all, areas of social work, whether we are working with individuals, groups, families or large entities. This theory was discussed in Chapter 1.

Organizations include any structures with staff, policies, and procedures, whose purpose in operating is to attain certain goals. For example, schools, public social welfare departments, and an agency operating four group homes for adults who have a developmental disability are all organizations. Organizational theory is concerned with how organizations function, what improves or impairs the ability of an organization to accomplish its mission, and what motivates people to work toward organizational goals. Some approaches to organizational theory have focused on management or leadership style, whereas others have dealt with such structural issues as organizational hierarchy, planning, staffing patterns, budgeting, policies, and procedures.

Early theorists believed that organizations shared certain characteristics that included an emphasis on making rational decisions, using rules and policies to ensure uniformity in decision making, assigning work to staff based on their specializations, and a reward system that encouraged compliance with rules (Netting, Kettner, McMurtry, & Thomas, 2012). Bureaucratic organizations, in particular, were considered to be one of the most efficient and effective mechanisms for producing goods, delivering services, and making decisions.

Subsequent studies of organizations (and the personal experiences of many who come into contact with them) left little doubt that bureaucracies had their own problems. Rigidity, fostered by unbending rules, frustrated both employees and customers/clients. Specialization often led to narrowness of interests and stifled the ability of employees to be creative. Reward structures often resulted in employees being promoted beyond their level of competence (the so-called Peter Principle). In addition, social relationships among employees often circumvented or limited the effectiveness of organizational policies. Peer pressure, for example, would encourage employees to produce products at slower rates than they were capable, despite financial incentives to work harder.

Over time, various theories have been developed about how best to achieve organizational goals. Most were based on beliefs about the characteristics of employees who were seen in some theories as lazy and needing close supervision, whereas other theories believed that they were self-directed and inherently creative. Clearly, the perceptions management has of its employees plays a role in how the workers see themselves. Other approaches to understanding organizations employed systems theory, often using the same concepts as were discussed in Chapter 1. Still others looked at the culture of organizations to learn why some bureaucracies are effective and others are not. Today it is not unusual to find different organizations employing a variety of theories ranging from traditional ones to those that emphasize employee empowerment, creativity, and communication. As you might surmise, understanding organizations is easier if the social worker recognizes the theories that operate within such systems.

Community theory has two primary components: the nature of communities and social work practice within communities. Warren and Warren, major scholars of communities, argue that a community is a "combination of social units and systems that perform the major social functions" important to the locality (1984, p. 28). The first major social function includes the production, distribution, and consumption of goods and services. According to their formulation, all community institutions (churches and businesses, professional and governmental organizations) provide a variety of goods and services.

The second function of a community is socialization, or the process by which knowledge, values, beliefs, and behaviors are taught to members of the community. Socialization is particularly important to children, as this is the way they learn the community's expectations for them. Families are one of the primary socialization units in the community.

The third function, social control, is the community's efforts to make sure members live within the norms of the community. Social control is exerted through laws, police powers, and the court systems.

Social participation, the fourth function, is the involvement of community members in various activities designed to enhance a sense of belonging. It is achieved through religious organizations such as churches, social clubs such as the Junior League, membership organizations such as the NASW, and friendship groups. In addition, many businesses and governmental agencies encourage social participation through organized events such as sporting activities.

The final community function is mutual support, which involves caring for the sick, helping the poor or homeless, and providing a variety of health and human services. Mutual support activities are carried out by individuals and families, social and religious organizations, and the government. Seeing how problems could occur in carrying out any of these functions is easy. One can also see the ways in which social workers might become involved in solving these problems.

Warren and Warren (1984) have also helped us conceptualize communities from multiple perspectives. For example, one may think of a community as having specific geographical boundaries, like a city, or as denoting a group with shared interests and beliefs, such as the social work community. The community may be seen as a target for change, as the problem, or as the context within which change occurs. The advantages of these perspectives become more apparent when assessing the problem, deciding among several possible interventions, and evaluating the outcome.

Social work practice in the community is the second component of community theory. Each of the following sections highlights a particular approach to social work practice in the community. As will be evident, however, some of the approaches, such as social action and advocacy (case and cause), can be employed to change organizations as well as communities. In both cases, the goal is change, but the nature and extent of change may vary dramatically.

LO 4-2 Analyze, Formulate, and Advocate for Interventions, Including Policy/Planning, Capacity Development, and Social Advocacy

POLICY/PLANNING

Policy/planning typically uses data to identify needs and plan a solution to community problems. It is often carried out by city and county planning agencies that focus on local issues such as city streets, parks, and recreational facilities. It may also be carried out at the state level through such considerations as location of new highways, prisons, and state parks. Sometimes it will be combined with other interventions such as capacity development or social advocacy. One example is a city that wanted to install a large park adjacent to a residential area. The park would have basketball and volleyball courts, soccer fields, and a running track, would serve hundreds of residents each day, and would be lighted and open until at least 10:00 p.m. The Parks Department recommended the size and attributes of the park and held a public hearing on the plan. Normally, this would have been a poorly attended hearing because the city was likely to adopt the Parks Department recommendation. However, dozens of residents from the residential area adjacent to the proposed park showed up to register their concerns. They protested keeping the park open late in the evening, complained that the new traffic would overburden the neighborhood streets, and argued that the park would encourage more traffic through their quiet subdivision and increase crime. In this case, the use of social advocacy by the neighbors countered the policy/planning activities of the city.

CAPACITY DEVELOPMENT

Capacity development involves building the competency of a group or community to undertake large-scale change. It includes such things as neighborhood associations, Peace Corp projects, and similar groups (Rothman, 2007). The focus is on empowerment of residents and other community dwellers to take actions that improve the quality of life in a community. In some cases it includes building a sense of solidarity across different groups on behalf of a goal from which all can benefit. Previously referred to as locality development, it can extend well beyond a geographical area and include those with specific needs or challenges, such as people with disabilities, women, or others.

SOCIAL ADVOCACY

As the term suggests, *social advocacy* is about using pressure to bring about changes that will ultimately benefit individuals and groups experiencing social and economic injustice. This can include the powerless, the poor, and any group that has been denied equal opportunity. The civil rights movements of the 1950s–1960s period falls in this category, as does the movement to permit gay marriage and overturn laws that discriminate against lesbian, gay, bisexual, and transgendered (LGBT) people. The target of the pressure may include any group or individual that hinders achievement of the goal. This can include legislators, administrators, politicians, and agencies that carry out policies viewed as problematic.

The basic concern of the social advocate is the development and improvement of social conditions. Early efforts at social advocacy included creation of kindergartens, recreational programs for children and adults, and educational programs for adults. Early social advocates fought large-scale problems related to immigration and the impact of urbanization. Social workers helped develop vocational education, hot lunch programs, neighborhood playgrounds, and community housing codes. These changes came about through the reformers' involvement in the political process.

Like their forebears, social workers today actively pursue a legislative agenda designed to improve client services and meet large-scale problems with large-scale programs. The social reformer's focus is on modifying the conditions of society that seriously threaten the well-being of citizens or prevent them from developing their potential. The social worker reformer today works to maintain and strengthen such programs as Head Start; the Special Supplemental Nutrition Program for Women, Infants, and Children (WIC) food program; and family planning. Social workers fight homelessness and drug abuse, and oppose changes in public assistance programs that will hurt or penalize the programs' recipients. In summary, social reform is more concerned with problems on a larger scale and focuses efforts in such legislative arenas as Congress, state legislatures, county boards of supervisors, and city councils.

Social advocacy is a term given to at least three different but related types of activity: (1) advocacy around specific populations and issues such as the homeless and food and hunger, (2) working in local and national elections to elect sympathetic representatives and to support new programs designed to combat large-scale problems, and (3) networking with other groups pursuing a similar agenda. The latter may include organizations of women or gays and lesbians who combine efforts to combat such problems as sexist or homophobia-induced rules. Clearly, overlap exists between the models and social workers may combine two or more of the models.

CAUSE ADVOCACY

Advocacy is directly representing or defending others. *Cause advocacy* is a term used to describe advocacy efforts by social workers on behalf of an issue of overriding importance to a *group* of clients. It assumes that the expected beneficiaries are likely to share certain common characteristics. Examples of causes for which advocacy might be appropriate include education for children with disabilities, expanded medical insurance coverage for the elderly, or both. These can be described as advocating for social and economic justice. Sometimes, the terms *cause advocacy* and *class advocacy* are used interchangeably. The latter term also suggests that one is advocating for all members of a particular class or group of persons (e.g., poor people, people with physical disabilities, or people of a particular ethnic group).

A good example of this is Ramona, a social worker practicing in a residential facility serving adolescent clients with serious emotional disabilities. Ramona worked with adolescent males on the open unit that provided a less restrictive milieu for nonsuicidal/nonviolent residents. The open unit was a transition unit, housing residents who were preparing themselves to go home. Only residents who had made significant progress while on the locked ward were placed on the open unit where they could be more autonomous. Open unit residents were expected to use their new skills in managing anger and depression and were able to go home on weekend passes. However, Ramona's agency had a policy that said all residents on either locked or open units must use their razors to shave only in the presence of staff. Ramona considered the policy problematic for several reasons. First, the residents were being treated as though they could not be trusted when the very purpose of the open unit was to demonstrate client strengths and progress and to encourage continued improvement. Second, the policy ignored the fact that residents went home on the weekends and used their razors without anyone monitoring them. Third, requiring staff members to monitor each resident while shaving took them away from more important chores.

Ramona discussed her concerns with other staff members and the unit manager. This led to a meeting between the staff members and the chief psychiatrist, who vetoed any change in policy. The staff members prepared a position paper reiterating their proposal and empowered clients to express their own views in the paper. After a couple of months of internal agency discussions, the policy on the open unit was changed. Shortly after, Ramona received a letter of commendation from the agency deputy director for her interest in the welfare of residents.

CASE ADVOCACY

Case advocacy, as the name implies, refers to activity on behalf of a single case: an individual, family, or small group. Case advocacy typically involves different strategies from those used to advocate for a cause. For example, the focus may be on the way a particular rule is preventing a client from receiving services to which he or she is otherwise entitled. The expectation is that this client will benefit from waiving the rule or interpreting it differently, but there is no general sense that a large group of clients will benefit in a similar fashion. Because of its significance to generalist social work practice, Chapter 14 is devoted to discussing advocacy in much greater depth.

These approaches share at least one characteristic: the desire to produce a change that will benefit an identified client or group of clients. For the purposes of this chapter, this commonality will be highlighted and the differences among the various concepts minimized. The key point is the obligation of the social worker to work for change that will benefit clients, not just because of the client, but also because of the worker's identification with the profession of social work.

Because of the similarities between organizations and communities, the problem-solving model discussed in Chapter 1 is clearly applicable. However, a problem need not exist for intervention to occur. A worker might, for instance, choose to intervene after identifying a potential problem, to prevent future difficulties, or simply to improve an already existing program or condition. The advantage of this approach is that it allows the social worker to be *proactive* instead of *reacting* to problems or issues. Thus, a social worker may recognize that a change in a particular program or policy might produce additional benefits or that greater efficiency could be achieved by modifying some aspect of the services provided.

An example of case advocacy is Selena, who worked with the local mental health agency providing services to clients with chronic mental illnesses. They were a difficult client group with which to work, but Selena loved the challenge. Responding to a recent situation reported in the local paper, the agency administration began to worry about issues related to physical contact between workers and clients. However, the agency had never experienced a problem of workers engaging in inappropriate physical contact with clients. Moreover, almost all of the staff members were BSW and MSW social workers who understood and respected the ethical boundaries between themselves and their clients.

Still, the agency administration decided to propose a blanket policy that forbade staff from touching clients in any way. This would eliminate such gestures as reaching out to touch a client on the arm to show support, hugging clients, or patting them on the back. Selena believed the proposed policy went too far and would eliminate an important tool for connecting with some of her clients. In particular, she knew that two of her clients always hugged her at the end of the session and that they would react badly if she suddenly rebuffed them. After thinking about what to do, she contacted one of her former social work professors and together they researched the issue of touching in client–worker relationships. After gathering examples of how touch can be beneficial to certain clients and the wisdom of leaving its use to the professional staff, Selena presented a position paper to the agency administrator. She also asked that the policy be discussed with agency supervisors to get additional input. Ultimately, Selena's advocacy on behalf of one or two clients worked. The agency director withdrew the proposal and allowed the staff members to use their own professional judgment about the use of touch with individual clients. Although Selena was advocating for a single case, the result was applied to all of the agency clients. This is one way that case advocacy can lead to cause advocacy.

LO 4-3 Use Empathy, Interpersonal Skills, and Group Skills in Macro Practice

EP 2.1.10b

Earlier chapters have explained some key skills necessary for intervention at all system levels. The intent of this chapter is to briefly summarize the ways in which these skills apply when working for organizational and community change. Chapter 2 identifies

warmth, empathy, and genuineness as important attributes for working with individuals. Much of the work of organizational or community change occurs in face-to-face interactions. These interventions might be worker to client, worker to administrator or supervisor, or worker to elected or appointed official. The capacity for genuineness and empathy are equally important in these situations. The worker mentioned in Highlight 4.2, who was attempting to modify local procedures, must be perceived as genuine and sensitive to the problems of decision makers. Most people respond better to warmth than to criticism. This fact applies to administrators or others in positions of power. There may be situations where the worker does not wish to be considered sensitive to the target's position or where clear adversarial strategies are most appropriate. These situations, however, are much less common.

Usually, positively reinforcing others and the ability to form relationships with people from vastly different backgrounds and orientations are essential for work in the community. Finally, the capacity to observe and understand verbal and nonverbal behavior and to interpret and summarize the words of others and the ability to portray oneself as confident and competent are important skills for organizational or community change.

HIGHLIGHT 4.2

Advancing Social Justice

EP 2.1.5c

The meeting room of the Algoma City Council was full, an unusual event, as hardly anyone ever attended the council's bimonthly meetings. Residents of the small community simply allowed the council the freedom to conduct business and rarely asked to address the body.

Tonight, the situation was different. Residents in the Knollwood subdivision were out in force to protest a business park proposed for property next to their residential neighborhood. Each resident spoke and shared misgivings about the potential effect this development might have on their property values. They also expressed anger at not being formally notified about the proposal. Council members stated their sensitivity to the plight of the residents and agreed to gather additional information before making a decision. They also promised that residents would have an opportunity to review any proposed building in the business park.

When a speaker said that many members had attended this meeting because their neighbor had seen the topic on the council agenda, another potential problem surfaced. If residents did not know about a proposed development, they could not voice their concerns. The present system relied mainly on word of mouth to inform people about issues pending before the council. Suspicion existed in such circumstances and prevented an impartial review of the proposal.

Finally, a social worker in the audience proposed a solution. A brief amendment to the zoning law would provide for residents within 300 feet of a proposed development to be notified about the changes under consideration. Most residents believed this would provide ample warning, allow citizens to voice concerns, and allay fears that some secret development would adversely affect their lives. The result would be better communication between the city government and citizens and prevention of the angry and disenfranchised feelings that emerged tonight. Over time, both sides would benefit from the change.

Employing Group Skills for Organizational and Community Change

Much of the work of social workers occurs on a one-on-one basis or through working in small task groups. These groups have several advantages. Groups are often better equipped to handle complex activities or to undertake projects beyond the ability of a single person. In addition, participants in the group are usually more committed to the outcome when they are involved in the decision-making process. Chapter 3 discusses groups in greater detail, and no attempt will be made here to recap that material. Instead, an example of a successful project involving a task group within a community is provided in Highlight 4.3.

As our example in Highlight 4.3 suggests, mezzo skills useful for organizational and community change include the following:

- *conflict resolution*
- *developing win-win outcomes*
- *team building*
- *public speaking*
- *consultation*

The final mezzo skill needed is coordination. In Highlight 4.3, several steps had to be achieved simultaneously, whereas others followed a sequence. The worker sought examples of other landmark ordinances that could be used as a model. He arranged meeting times and places for the group. He also helped plan a

---

HIGHLIGHT 4.3

Saving a Community: A Task Group at Work

Clearwater had once won an award for its beauty. The growth of the local university and the concomitant destruction of Victorian-era homes had left many in the town in a state of despair. Not only were the remaining homes being converted into student housing, but also the lovely elm trees lining the streets had died, leaving a denuded landscape.

At the request of local officials, the community development specialist called a meeting at which citizen concerns would be explored. Using techniques such as nominal group (a combination of brainstorming and prioritizing issues by the group), the worker helped the group identify three major problem areas. Three groups were formed, each in response to a particular problem. One group focused on trying to save the remaining historic homes, a second worked on community beautification, and a third looked at downtown business development. The worker met separately with each group to help them get started. Periodically, all three groups met together to discuss accomplishments and future tasks. The historic preservation task group studied the problem and considered the work of other cities with similar problems.

Eventually, this group wrote an ordinance protecting historic buildings from destruction or unsympathetic remodeling. They lobbied the city planning commission and the city council, organized mailings to council members, and spoke at various public meetings. Despite vigorous opposition from the most powerful property owner in town, the council adopted the ordinance and established a permanent landmark commission to enforce it.

Achieving this was not easy. Overcoming opposition and resolving areas of conflict were formidable tasks. Conflict resolution, described in Chapter 3, is equally important at both the organizational and community levels. The ability to diffuse potentially problematic situations, to find a satisfactory middle ground, is critical. Win-win outcomes, where all parties benefit, are desirable and should be the worker's goal whenever possible.

Similarly, the ability to use the disparate strengths of many individuals and to build an effective task group requires skill in team building. In this case, the worker assessed the strengths and weaknesses of each group member and helped the group accomplish its goal by building on the former and overcoming the latter. Thus, members who were more comfortable speaking in public presented the group's ideas to the city planning commission, the city council, and the chamber of commerce. Others wrote letters, telephoned people, and addressed envelopes.

After the historic preservation group became an effective body, the worker's role changed to that of a consultant, offering ideas and providing feedback to the group leaders. Skill in offering consultation is important because most workers will usually not continue indefinitely as leader. Yet they will want to provide for a certain degree of continuity or stabilization of the change effort.

lobbying campaign and assisted the group in each of its chores. Because some members of this task group were also members of other community groups, avoiding overlap in meeting times was essential. Ensuring that each member knew exactly whom to talk to regarding the ordinance was also important. Skill in coordinating the efforts of group members is essential to any organizational or community change effort.

LO 4-4 Utilize Effective Macro-Practice Skills, Including Evaluating Results, Fundraising, Budgeting, Negotiating, Mediating, Influencing Decision Makers, Needs Assessment, Planning, and Working with Coalitions

This chapter will address nine major skills important in macro practice: evaluating results, fundraising, budgeting, negotiating, mediating, influencing decision makers, needs assessment, planning, and working with coalitions.

EVALUATING RESULTS

Evaluating the outcome or results of one's practice has become increasingly important. Clients have a right to expect their social worker to be competent for the task at hand. Working to improve one's practice is also incumbent upon the social worker. Learning what does and does not work and in what situations is essential. The social worker should always operate under the dictum that governs medical doctors: "First, do no harm." Without a plan for evaluating interventions, we run the risk of inadvertently hurting the people and causes we are trying to help.

Chapter 8 takes a more concentrated look at types of evaluations available to the social worker. For purposes of this section, however, we will identify two major approaches: practice evaluation and program evaluation. *Practice evaluation* is evaluating the effectiveness or results of what individual social workers do. It may take the form of single-subject designs, task achievement scaling (Reid & Epstein, 1972), client satisfaction surveys, target problem ratings (Marlow, 2011), or goal attainment scaling (Weinbach, 2005), also called goal accomplishment (Timberlake, Faber, & Sabatino, 2002).

Program evaluation is evaluating the effectiveness and results of entire programs. Program evaluation techniques might include needs assessments, process evaluation, outcome analysis, and cost-effectiveness analysis

(Royce, Thyer, & Padgett, 2010). These approaches are discussed further in Chapter 8.

FUNDRAISING

For many people, asking for money is a difficult task. In the social work context, asking for money is called fundraising. Social programs usually cannot exist without financial support. Money is needed to pay staff, buy equipment, and rent space. It is also required for such consumables as paper, pens, and so on. Fundraising may be needed to purchase equipment for refurbishing a park in a low-income section of the city. Money may be required to support an AIDS awareness project being undertaken by a local social service agency. The shelter for survivors of domestic violence may undertake fundraising to pay staff or purchase groceries. Many social programs depend upon a combination of public funding and private donations to cover operating costs. In addition, political campaigns require money. Social workers may be called upon to raise funds and should be familiar with the basics of fundraising.

The fundraiser should keep multiple sources of funds in mind. These include individual donors, corporate donors, foundations, membership dues, and benefits/events. In addition, church organizations and service clubs often provide funding if the area to be supported falls within their sphere of interest. Foundations and corporations are most likely to have the resources to make major contributions to a cause or program. On the other hand, they are also the most difficult and time consuming to solicit. Individual donations are more easily acquired, but generally the amounts received are likely to be limited. Whereas individuals typically give once for a cause, corporations are often more willing to provide continuing funds. Foundations are also more likely to give matching funds if the program promises to raise an equal amount from other sources. This type of fundraising is often an effective way to start up a program but does not guarantee any long-term support. Service clubs and church groups often provide small donations for specific projects. For example, they may offer to purchase a piece of equipment or provide time and money to build a wheelchair ramp.

Membership dues are generally free of the restrictions that other kinds of donations carry. Because they depend upon membership, the size of the member pool becomes important. Membership dues are ongoing, but often the dollar amount raised is low when compared to other sources. Equally limiting are benefits or events. Most of us are familiar with benefits of one type: the bake sale or car wash. Although benefits can take this form, the most successful benefits in terms of money raised are those involving some activity in which the public can participate. A musical program, comedy show, raffle, dance, or some similar activity that will attract the public holds more promise than such things as bake sales. Held annually, benefits can be very successful and become a continuing source of funding.

All fundraising takes time, hard work, and dedication by the social worker. There is only one real secret to fundraising: You must ask for money. Asking others to donate is scary; it is a taboo subject with many people. Many groups start by selling a product, such as a sweatshirt or cookbook. The product is produced at minimal cost and sold at a good profit. Later, requesting money specifically for support of your cause may be possible. Some organizations sell memberships to the public, knowing that the purchaser will not likely attend any of the organization's meetings. Joining the organization allows one to give indirectly to support the group's goals.

In many situations, making the program's request through a formal presentation will be necessary for the fundraiser. The audience may be the entire membership, such as with a service organization, or a select group, such as a foundation's board of directors. In other scenarios, all fundraising may be achieved through mail solicitations. This scenario is not uncommon when raising money for political campaigns. In these situations, the fundraisers begin by listing those likely to support the cause. Next, they decide the best person to make the request. Direct person-to-person solicitation uses a similar process. If the contact is through a letter, making it clear why the potential donor should give to the cause is important. Making the request as relevant to the individual donor as possible is desirable. Some letters suggest an amount to be donated, whereas others leave this up to the donor. In fundraising drives dedicated to purchasing equipment, listing the cost of the items may be helpful. Some who receive the solicitation may choose to donate money for a specific item or to donate the equipment itself.

In more extensive solicitations, especially to foundations or corporations, a packet of materials about the program may be developed. Formal presentations may include visual aids or videotaped information and printed materials. Whatever the source of funding, providing a "thank you" is critical. This should include at least a note of appreciation, preferably handwritten, and perhaps a verbal "thank you" as well.

Finally, it is important to remember that people usually do not give to a cause without being asked.

The person doing the fundraising must believe in the cause and be willing to explain to potential donors why they should support the project. Once begun, the process of asking for money becomes easier, and even the novice fundraiser becomes more self-confident. Remember, if you want something, you have to ask for it.

Another potential source of funding is grant writing. Typically, an organization, government, or foundation will provide funding for short-term projects that help meet the entity's mission. For example, a government agency or political organization may provide funding to increase voter registration and actual voting. Funds for helping individuals become familiar with new health insurance laws and acquire coverage have been provided by both the federal government and private groups. A community foundation may have funds for projects that improve conditions within their identified target area.

Funding might be available if the target population is a minority group or one that is not receiving adequate service. Grants may be available to test out new approaches that involve disease prevention, offer the opportunity to tap into ongoing funding, or increase the sustainability of a service (Gitlin & Lyons, 2008). Projects that involve multiple disciplines working together to solve human or social problems are also considered by funding sources. For a fuller discussion of grant writing and funding sources, see Kirst-Ashman and Hull (2012) *Generalist Practice with Organizations and Communities*.

BUDGETING

Budgeting involves money, which is critically important to all agencies and organizations where social workers function. Budgeting is an important concept to understand. Most beginning generalist practitioners will not be responsible for actually making up a budget. However, the budget and the budgeting process will *always* affect them.

A budget is a statement of planned revenues, that is, all types of income and expenses during some time period. We all have budgets—specific allotments of money we can spend for rent or food or fun. The important thing about budgets is that they involve some predetermined and limited amount of money. If more money is spent on one thing, such as rent, there is less money to be spent on other things, such as food and fun.

The same principle applies to social agencies and organizations. Each has a budget regarding how much money it can spend and on what. When more money is spent on one item (e.g., equipment), then less money is available to spend on other items (e.g., social workers' salaries). The amount of money allotted to you (as salary and benefits) and to your clients (as services or resources) is critically important.

In effect, different parts and functions of an organization compete for the same money or portions of that money. When you work for an agency, there will be times when you strongly feel that clients have needs that are not being met at all or at least not satisfactorily. When advocating for these clients, you will need to understand budgets and this competition for funds.

For instance, a social worker at a private day treatment center for children and adolescents with behavior disorders was concerned about the "snacks" given to the children each morning when they arrived at the center. Day treatment provided troubled children with therapy and special education during the day. Yet, the children returned to their own homes each night. Many of the children came from severely impoverished homes with little, if any, food in the house. When they arrived at the center in the morning, they were hungry. The "snack" they received then was often the only nourishment they would get until the lunch the center provided at noon.

The day treatment program was owned by a private individual who sold the agency's services to surrounding counties that did not provide these services themselves (this is referred to as "purchase of service," in that public agencies buy some kind of service from someone else who provides it). All staff at the day treatment center, including social workers, received exceptionally high salaries. However, these salaries were at the expense of the other services. For instance, the offices and classrooms were poorly furnished, and the building was badly in need of repair.

Additionally, there was the problem of the "snacks." The owner of the agency apparently had gotten a "deal," whereby he had purchased a whole truckload of crumb cakes at little expense. After 3 weeks of crumb cakes every morning, the center's clients were becoming tired of them. Despite their hunger, the children began to refer to the cakes by a quite vile term. The teachers and social workers, also quite sick of the cakes, found reprimanding the children for their vocabulary difficult, as the staff members were beginning to feel the terms were almost appropriate.

The social worker we initially talked about was concerned over the lack of adequate nutrition provided, as these cakes were all most of the children were getting. She was also concerned about the sugar-initiated "high" the children experienced immediately after eating the cakes and the subsequent drop in energy level a while later. These children already had problems with being overly active, controlling their behavior, and attending to classroom tasks. Should the worker approach the higher-level administration about this problem? Was the issue important enough to do so? She did not want to seem as though she was the type of person who complained about everything.

She finally did approach the center's director (who was one level below the owner). His response was that having the crumb cakes at such a reduced rate helped to keep the agency within its budget. Was she willing to take a cut in salary to improve the quality of morning snacks?

How would you have responded to the director's question had you been this social worker? Would you have said, "Oh sure, I'll gladly take a cut in pay"? Would you have sheepishly backed away? Would you have countered the director's question with a statement suggesting that money could be redistributed from some other part of the budget?

The point is that budgeting is extremely important. The greater the depth of your understanding of your agency's budget and of the budgeting process, the more potential you will have to impact budgeting decisions.

The task of preparing and managing a budget for any enterprise is similar. Usually, one establishes the budget for a given period (such as a year). Three types of budgeting may be encountered: line item, program or functional, and incremental (Sheafor & Horejsi, 2012).

Line-Item Budgets

A line-item budget is a statement of expenditures for a designated period of time, usually a year, where each cost item is noted on a separate line. Items are then added to portray the total budget expenditure. A line-item budget depicts how money will be spent but tells little about services the agency offers. For example, one might have a category called personnel (further divided into salary, fringe benefits, and so on), another called equipment, and as many other categories as needed. An agency may operate multiple programs, such as protective services, foster care, and juvenile court services, but the costs of each program are not separated and identified. In effect, costs of these programs (and any new ones) may be invisible because everything is lumped together into one big budget.

Setting initial budgets or continuing budgets may represent something of a guess. In the former situation, there is no existing budget to use as a model. With continuing budgets, there is an existing budget, but the estimates for future years must be prepared before the current year has been completed. Many social agencies use this method of budgeting.

Program Budgets

Program budgets list expenditures broken down according to programs the agency provides. The program budget relates directly to how the agency spends its money in addition to the amount the agency spends. A program budget, also known as a functional budget, uses the same structure as line-item budgets. It also identifies functions such as the adoption program, delinquency project, or group home. This process allows the cost of each program to be identified and is useful in making decisions about spending priorities. Such a system is not perfect because it relies on estimates of certain items. For example, in one agency the secretary spends a portion of her time entering data for the adoption program and another portion doing bookkeeping for the group home. To assign her salary into the proper categories depends upon the accuracy of the estimates of the time she contributes to each program. This estimation is not always a simple chore. When accomplished, program budgets are helpful for accountability in that they indicate where money is actually being spent. They also allow some measure of cost-effectiveness. In short, they can help establish that money is being put to the best use.

Table 4.1 compares two budgets for the same agency. One is a line-item budget, and the other is a program budget. The line-item budget reflects the entire cost of running the agency but does not give detailed information on either of the two programs operated by Happy Daze Family Services. The program budget shows the relative expenses and income from the two programs. As is evident, the family counseling program actually brings in more income than it costs to operate. On the other hand, the international adoption program costs almost $100,000 more to operate than it brings in. The family counseling program subsidizes or helps pay for the adoption program, a fact that would not be evident without a program budget.

Line-item budgets and program budgets are common ways of describing existing budgets. In other words, they describe how the current budget is organized. Once a budget exists, the common system for dealing with requests for budgets for subsequent years is an incremental budget.

Incremental Budgets

An incremental budget is a system in which an agency's budget from last year is used as a starting point for this year's budget. Typically, one would plan for the next year's budget by starting with the existing budget and then acting according to assumptions. If one assumes, for example, that income and expenditures will rise at the same rate as inflation (e.g., 3 percent), then the existing budget will be increased by 3 percent for next year. If the rate increases differently across categories (e.g., personnel or equipment), these differences should be reflected in the increment used. If salaries are going up at the rate of 5 percent and equipment at 2 percent, one would raise the amount budgeted for both categories accordingly.

Similarly, a decrease in revenues would result in reductions of anticipated income and expenditures of a given amount. This method is a common form of budgeting.

One potential disadvantage of this budget model is that it does not force the agency to look at how the money is actually being spent or whether the current spending is consistent with agency needs. If we simply add 3 percent to the existing budget for next year, we are assuming no significant changes in services provided. We will continue to provide family counseling services and operate the money-losing international adoption program. However, over the past year, a flood of refugees from the Middle East has arrived in the community, few of whom speak English and most of whom escaped their countries with few or no resources. Rather than subsidize the international adoption program and provide it with a 3 percent increase, perhaps it would be prudent to consider whether this is the best use of limited funds. Might it make more sense to establish a program for families from the Middle East whose needs may be more pressing or life challenging than those of clients served by the international adoption program?

Critical Thinking Questions 4.2

EP 2.1.3

- If you were the agency director for Happy Daze Family Services, Inc., what would you do? Why?
- Are there any ethical considerations you might face?
- If you did decide to discontinue the adoption program, what might be the consequences?
- If you decided to offer a program for Middle Eastern families, what challenges would you face?

TABLE 4.1 Comparison of Line-Item and Program Budgets

2012 Line-Item Budget Happy Daze Family Services, Inc.		2012 Program Budget Happy Daze Family Services, Inc.	
		Family Counseling Program	
Expenses		*Expenses*	
Personnel		Personnel	
Professional Staff	$250,000	Professional Staff	$100,000
Support/Clerical Staff	50,000	Support/Clerical Staff	20,000
Travel	5,000	Travel	2,000
Rent	35,000	Rent (40% of total)	14,000
Maintenance/Cleaning	4,500	Maintenance/Cleaning	1,800
Utilities	34,750	Utilities	13,900
Phone	19,750	Phone	7,900
Total Expenses	$399,000	Total Expenses	$159,600
Income		*Income*	
Fees for Service	$150,000	Fees for Service	$25,000
Donations	10,000	Donations	500
United Way Allocation	75,000	United Way Allocation	75,000
State Contract	164,000	State Contract	164,000
Total Income	$399,000	Total Income	$264,500
		International Adoption Program *Expenses*	
		Personnel	
		Professional Staff	$150,000
		Support/Clerical Staff	30,000
		Travel	3,000
		Rent (60% of total)	21,000
		Maintenance/Cleaning	2,700
		Utilities	20,850
		Phone	11,850
		Total Expenses: *Income*	$239,400
		Fees for Service	$125,000
		Donations	9,500
		Total Income	$134,500
		Total Expenses: Both Programs	$399,000
		Total Income: Both Programs	$399,000

NEGOTIATING

EP 2.1.10k

Negotiating is a process in which at least two individuals participate in a face-to-face interaction in order to reach a mutually acceptable decision. Negotiations occur over any issue where people disagree or conflict with each other. Sometimes, disagreements are marginal. For example, you might think your client needs a clothing allowance of 100 dollars, and your supervisor thinks 50 dollars is sufficient. At other times, disagreements reflect opposite opinions. For instance, you think your client needs services; another worker thinks she does not.

Negotiating (sometimes called bargaining) can be problematic. When one side gains and the other side loses, bad feelings often result. Such outcomes contribute to a long list of problems and interfere with future working relationships. Homan (2011) and Rubin and Rubin (2008) and others identify some possible guidelines for effective negotiation.

First, separating the problem from the people involved is important. In practice, this separation means we cannot personalize the differences that exist. To do otherwise is to create an adversarial situation when a problem-solving approach would be more effective. Disliking the *ideas* or *demands* of others without disliking the *person* is possible. It is not uncommon for two lawyers representing opposing sides in a negotiation to get together for a drink later in the day. The ability to argue a position without denigrating your opponent personally is a strength. Remember that today's opponent may be your ally in some other matter or situation.

The second step is to direct attention to the mutual interests of both parties and not to the positions they are taking. Both sides have goals they value highly and others that they feel are less important. Negotiating based on this approach allows for creative problem solving and increases the likelihood that both sides will be pleased with the outcome.

The third step requires devising new options or choices that benefit both sides. The value of this approach is that it steers away from the tendency to think there is only one answer. Recall that one concept in systems theory is *equifinality,* or the fact that there are often multiple ways to do something. Negotiation is one of the areas where this concept is extremely important because it encourages the creation of alternatives that help meet the needs of both sides. Flexibility is important.

Consider saving the most difficult issues for last, raising them only after you have resolved less troublesome items. This approach builds on the success of earlier negotiation. This method works, however, only when all issues have been placed on the table at the beginning of the bargaining session. Obviously, if all the issues are not on the table to begin with, it would be impossible to determine which are likely to be more difficult. Consequently, piecemeal negotiation in which each topic is brought up in random order should be avoided, if possible.

If needed, you can have a third party suggest a compromise or agree to use some objective criteria to decide an issue. For example, some state child welfare agencies, in an effort to garner more funds from legislators, have used the Child Welfare League of America[1] standards as an outside arbiter to illustrate appropriate staffing and funding levels. The use of such external means for settling disagreements does require agreement on the part of both sides that the third party is fair and impartial.

"Be Prepared" is not just the motto of the Boy Scouts, but sound advice when entering negotiations. Get your facts straight and be prepared for your opponent's arguments and positions. Using a colleague as an opponent in a dry run can help you anticipate questions and practice your responses.

When negotiating, ask for more than you want or expect to get but keep it reasonable. Your position is weakened if the other side thinks you are not serious about negotiation and are just grandstanding.

Avoid putting the opposing side in a position where they perceive themselves as losing face and ending up embarrassed. Most people will go to great lengths to avoid this painful experience and will reject even reasonable proposals if it feels like they are being put down or losing everything.

Be certain that agreements and concessions that are negotiated are clear. Finding out later that one or both parties either did not understand what was agreed to or is using the vagueness of terms can be frustrating and perpetuate disagreements.

Negotiation allows both you and your opponent to win and makes the chance that each of you will be satisfied with the outcome more likely. Achieving this

---

1. The Child Welfare League of America is the best-known national organization promoting the interests of children in the United States. The organization establishes standards of practice and advocates for the needs of children.

goal is not always easy, but it will result in more positive feelings on both sides.

MEDIATING

Mediating is also a process used to resolve disputes between opposing parties. However, unlike negotiations, in mediation both parties meet with a third party who serves as an impartial referee or peacemaker. Mediation is becoming a more common approach to solving differences of agreement in many areas. Mediating is common in divorce situations where the husband and wife disagree over such things as custody arrangements, child support, and maintenance.

Mediation has grown as an approach used by social workers spurred by state legislation that permits alternative ways of resolving disputes. The result has been increased satisfaction for participants and a resultant empowerment for clients who actively participate in the process. Like other processes discussed in Chapter 3, mediation can lead to win-win solutions of conflicts between individuals and groups. Mediation settles disputes between neighbors, vendors and customers, and landlords and tenants (Emery, Sbarra, & Erover, 2005). It has also been used at the community level to lessen gun violence and gang conflicts (Whitehill, Webster, & Vernick, 2013). Studies by Emery et al. (2005) and Kelly (2006) suggest that mediation produces positive outcomes. Whenever possible, social workers should use interventions that have been shown to produce favorable results. Such studies are at the heart of evidence-based practice.

Mediators must be able to recognize the legitimate interests of both parties. As in negotiating, the goal of mediation is to work toward the common interests of each member, focusing on the specific areas of disagreement. The goal is to produce an outcome satisfactory to both sides. Social workers may be involved in mediating between clients and such institutions as schools, social agencies, and government agencies. The worker's task is to motivate and help each side reach out to the other.

For example, a school might object to the dress or hairstyle of a student and suspend her from school. As a mediator, you could work with the school and the student (and parents) to reach a compromise with which both could live. Of course, another approach to this particular situation is to serve as a negotiator on behalf of the student and her family. As a social worker, you may be involved in both negotiation and mediation at different times. In your role as negotiator,

you will represent yourself or another party and attempt to reach a settlement that satisfies you or the party for whom you are negotiating. Hopefully, it will also produce an agreement with which the other side can live. As a negotiator, you are clearly on one side of the issue or dispute. As a mediator, you are positioned right in the middle; you cannot be seen as favoring one side or the other, or you will lose your credibility with the other side. Thus, in mediation you are the third party to whom both sides can look for fairness and helpfulness. Your task is to motivate and help each side reach out to the other. Although both negotiation and mediation can result in each side feeling like they have achieved their goals, they are fundamentally different roles.

INFLUENCING DECISION MAKERS

Chapter 3 identifies several common ways that groups make decisions. Of course, not all decisions are made by groups. Some decisions are made by individuals acting alone or by only a couple of people acting together. In many instances, social workers want to influence those who make the final decision, especially when that decision has a major impact on our clients and the programs of which we are a part. In fact, influencing others is a common role for social workers. Sometimes, this influence is direct—as in the role of probation officer. At other times it is indirect—such as when one models behavior for a client. In many areas of social work practice and in one's life, there is a need to influence other people, particularly those with decision-making power such as supervisors, administrators, elected and appointed officials, and others in similar positions. The tactics one adopts often depend upon several factors: the target, the ability of the social worker, the likelihood of success, and the risk to both client and worker.

If the target is an individual, the tactics may differ from those used when dealing with an organization. We also must consider our own ability to bring about change, including such aspects as our ability to influence others, our power, and our resources. In addition, some approaches may be more or less likely to bring success in certain situations. For example, a letter-writing campaign may not be effective against entrenched individuals who do not care what others say or think.

Finally, all large system interventions carry some risk to both the client and worker. In many situations, the risks are minimal, entailing no more than perhaps a few ruffled feathers for a short time. Yet other cases may involve the risk of losing a job or position. In all cases, we must recognize that the decision to select a strategy is a serious one with a variety of components.

In the next section, we will discuss seven strategies for influencing decision makers, although each is not equally effective in all situations.

Petitioning

Petitioning is the collecting of signatures on a document asking an organization or person to act in a particular manner. Petitions have a section where supporters may sign their names as a show of support for the ideas presented. Petition signatures are somewhat easy to obtain and therefore not as effective as other methods. For example, it is not uncommon to sign a petition when asked by a friend, even when holding views opposite to those expressed in the petition. In a recent situation, a group opposed to an elected official gathered enough signatures to force a recall election. When the election occurred, the recalled candidate's opponent received fewer votes than there were signatures on the recall petition. In some situations, however, petitions can be effective. The example in Highlight 4.4 illustrates this point.

The use of computers and "smart" cell phones has opened up opportunities for electronic petitions (sometimes referred to as e-petitions). Electronic petitions can be operated from Web sites where a visitor would go to "sign" a petition stating a particular position. This method has been used by citizens wanting to force a revision in the ethics rules governing state legislators in Utah. Another option is an e-petition that is sent directly to you from another organization asking you to add your name to those favoring or opposing some issue. This method has been repeatedly employed in the political arena by national and state political organizations as well as by other advocacy groups. One

concern that has not yet been resolved is the legality of e-petitions under various state laws. For example, the attorney general of one state ruled that electronic petitions were not acceptable for placing an initiative on the ballot in his state. Other advocates challenge this interpretation, and the issue may well end up in court.

It is interesting to note that petitions are used in many countries and cultures as a means of demanding that institutions or decision makers engage in specific behaviors. This method of addressing grievances and requesting action appears to be commonplace across the globe. It is not just the disenfranchised who use petitioning as a change effort. Unions have used it to protest pay cuts, industries to oppose government regulation, and dog owners to object to rules that ban certain breeds. Social workers must respond to such new technologies and other changes that shape the environment and our practice.

Communication Skills: Working with the Media

Any type of media, including television, radio, and newspapers, can be employed with good results. Using the media is an effective way to bring attention to one's cause and to influence decision makers. For instance, you could use the media to help get transportation services to therapy sessions for children with physical disabilities when their parents cannot afford transportation costs. A newspaper article or a segment on television illustrating the plight of these children can gain public support. The public might subsequently pressure the city or county government to finance transportation services, whether they like it or not.

You can also use the media to inform the public and promote your own agency. For example, one large urban children's hospital sponsors a 5-mile run each year.

HIGHLIGHT 4.4

Petitioning Works

EP 2.1.3c

The Evergreen City Council was preparing to vote on whether or not to build a bypass highway around the city. Several members of the council had already stated their support for the bypass. They argued that it would reduce congestion on the city's main street and make crossing a dangerous street easier. Prior to the vote, Mrs. White, who owned a small antiques business on Main Street, presented the council with a petition signed by most of the businesses located on Main Street. The petition opposed building the bypass highway because it might negatively affect some businesses along the street. During balloting, not a single member of the council voted to build the bypass. Even stubborn council members who supported the bypass were influenced by a petition signed by so many business leaders.

The purpose is not only to raise funds, but also to publicize its services and increase public use and support.

The decision to use media often occurs when no other method has proven effective or will have the same degree of effectiveness. There are several general guides to using the media. First, reach out to the media. Contact them early before problems arise and provide ideas for stories regarding your agency (e.g., you can use both radio and newspapers to publicize a need for foster parents and television to promote the formation of a Parents Anonymous chapter).

Second, build contacts within the media. Just as we develop resources of other agencies to which a referral can be made, media contacts should also be nurtured. This can be newspaper, radio, television, blogs, or any other entity that has the public's attention.

Third, if you are speaking for an organization or agency, be certain you are authorized to do so. You don't want to be seen as someone who was doing an end run around your supervisor or to have agency representatives disavow your statements.

Fourth, provide ease of access for media representatives to contact you. Give them both home and office phone numbers and addresses and suggest the name of someone else they may contact if you are unavailable. If a news media reporter contacts you to get an opinion or quote on a topic, help them identify a resource. Although it may not be a topic in your area of expertise, it helps identify you as a potential resource.

Fifth, learn the timetables necessary for all media. Newspapers have deadlines, as do radio and television. Reporters appreciate timely notice of newsworthy events.

Sixth, do not play favorites. Give all forms of media the same opportunity to present your story, unless you are granting an exclusive interview. In these cases, no one else will have access to the story until it appears in the media.

Seventh, if the media make a mistake, consider your reactions with care. If a correction is necessary, be tactful and explain the reasons for your request. Usually, minor errors should be left alone. Recognize that error acknowledgements tend to be buried in newspapers and really do not undo the error.

Eighth, like everyone else, media representatives react to praise and support. If you thank them for the exposure and express satisfaction with the result, they are more likely to cooperate in the future.

Finally, if you gave your story, posed for pictures, and waited in vain for the article to appear, you are not alone. Many articles do not get printed or used because more important news supersedes the story. Reporters do not like this situation to happen, because it affects them as well, but they recognize it is an occupational hazard. Again, thank the reporter for the effort and express your willingness to work with him or her again.

Media Releases

In certain situations, you will have to prepare a media release. A media release is a public announcement that may acknowledge the opening of an agency, the creation of a new program, or a problem that needs attention from the community. A sample press release is shown in Figure 4.1.

Writing a press release requires a degree of careful planning. Remember that the media like news and fresh information for their viewers or readers. Just because you think something is interesting does not mean the media will consider it newsworthy. Rubin and Rubin (2008) and Homan (2011) provide some excellent suggestions for developing an effective news release. Think about what would make your information of interest to the general public. Identify the primary theme to be used in the release. It could be a compelling statistic on teen pregnancy or the unusually effective outcomes experienced by a particular program. Perhaps the release responds to an issue that has been in the headlines recently. Do not go overboard in the release. Provide factual information focusing on such possible items as an announcement of an event or activity, critical background information on an issue, human-interest topics, or follow-up on an important community event.

The first paragraph of the news release should include the most crucial information. Subsequent paragraphs should include (in priority order) those ideas that you believe elaborate on the first paragraph. Remember also that the media still tend to use the five W's—who, what, when, where, and why. Do not neglect any of these items. If the editor chooses not to print a specific piece of information, that is the paper's right. You, however, do not want to leave out critical information that is key to whether or not the news release gets the editor's attention. Following up a news release with a phone call solely as a matter of courtesy is permissible. The call will serve as a reminder to the editor and could lead to a request for further information, a news feature, or other, more extended coverage.

Working with the media requires the social worker to communicate in a professional manner and to

Rural Mental Health Clinic
12 East North Street
East North Overshoe, Vermont
(802) 658-0371

For Immediate Release:

Drug and Alcohol Program a First in State

EAST NORTH OVERSHOE, VT–June 28, 2013. The Rural Mental Health Clinic has added a drug and alcohol program to its new service center in East North Overshoe. According to the director, James Beam, the new program is the first in the state to offer both inpatient and outpatient service to individuals who are chemically addicted. The clinic has added three staff members and will be hosting an open house on Friday, July 12th, from 1:00 p.m.–3:00 p.m. The office for the program is located at 232 Spring Street in the recently renovated old brewery.

For further information, contact Margo Rhita (802) 658-0371 or 658-9981.

© Cengage Learning

FIGURE 4.1 Using the Media: An Example of a News Release

demonstrate effective oral and written communication. Whether the media is print based or audiovisual, the practitioner must be articulate and thoughtful in communicating ideas and opinions.

Of course, news releases need not be limited to announcement. Any topic can be of interest to the media and can be used to your cause's advantage. As a general rule, stories of interest to the media are likely to share several characteristics. For example, stories must be interesting to at least a major segment of the readership or viewership. Topics that interest only tiny segments of the population are less likely to be covered by the media. Items must be timely and, if not new, bring a new perspective on an old problem. Stories that involve conflict or scandal, well-known personalities, and are easier to explain are more likely to be picked up by the media. Topics with significant support in the community also are more likely to be covered (Rubin & Rubin, 2008).

Educating

Educating is providing information and teaching skills to others. Often, decision makers are not as familiar with every aspect of a situation as others may be. Thus, the circumstance may only take educating a decision maker about a situation to produce the desired outcome. This fact is often true with such public officials as legislators, who must represent many different points of view. For example, a legislator who does not believe there is a problem may not feel allocating resources to combat child abuse and neglect is important. As a social worker, you may need to inform or educate that legislator about how serious the problem is before she is convinced spending the necessary money is worthwhile.

In some situations, simply presenting the information in written form and/or in person will convince the decision maker of the validity of your position. In other situations, it will require repeated efforts. It is important to remember that people do not like to appear ignorant or to be treated as if they were. Avoid talking down to the decision maker but present the information as matter-of-factly as possible. Sometimes, sending a written position statement as background is helpful before proceeding to the point of an in-person interview. It allows the target to become familiar with your ideas and to have some basis for beginning a dialogue with you. Often, the educating function is an adjunct to the next skill, persuading.

Persuading

Persuading is the process of presenting your point of view with the intent of getting another person to concur. Persuading people or organizations to change may be easy or difficult, depending upon several variables. Persuasion is easiest when the target or decision makers share your values and perspectives. Persuasion is more difficult when the target shares similar values but does not perceive the problem in the same light. Persuasion is most difficult when the target neither shares similar values nor accepts your identification of the problem. These variables must be carefully considered when attempting to persuade. Chapter 14 provides a more detailed discussion of persuasion.

We are not suggesting workers persuade clients to adopt a position similar to their own. Client self-determination is still a cardinal value. Instead, we are recommending that this knowledge can be used on behalf of client systems, especially when the target for change is an agency or larger system. Persuasion is a positive alternative to the next skill to be discussed, confrontation.

Confrontation

Confrontation is the act of challenging another, usually in a face-to-face meeting. Few of us like confrontation. When asked why they decided to become social workers, many students reply, "Because I want to help people." Helping people and confronting people sometimes seem like opposing ideas. In actuality, much of social work practice involves confrontation. The clinician confronts a client about lying or confronts a patient who says one thing and does another. Confrontation is common in work with correctional clients and others who have in some way violated community standards. Confrontation requires certain assumptions concerning action and target systems. An *action system* is those people who agree and are committed to work together in order to obtain the proposed change. Included might be individuals and organizations or other community resources. An action system for an older adult who needs assistance to remain in her own home might include the local area agency on aging and private social agencies serving the aging populations, among others. A *target system,* on the other hand, is composed of those who we are trying to influence in order to attain a specific goal. The target system may be an individual, decision maker, elective body, community agency, or any other system that prevents achievement of social work goals. Confrontations may be appropriate under the following circumstances:

1. *Action system goals* and *target system goals* are in sharp contrast to one another.

2. The action system poses a credible threat to the target system. (This threat usually means that there is an availability of coercive power the action system can use against the target system.)
3. The target system resists change because of its investment in the status quo or fear of the outcome of the proposed change. It may also lack information about the economic costs of the change or be concerned about loss of support from groups that favor the existing system.

Confrontation can take many forms, but the two most difficult are legal action and public embarrassment. In taking legal action, the social worker is proceeding with the belief that the target has violated a law, code, or other regulation and that other methods have not borne fruit. Legal action may involve reporting a landlord for violating city building or health codes by failing to provide hot water or allowing vermin to exist within a building. It may include pressing charges against the target for violation of a criminal law, such as battery or violation of a court order. Another possibility is filing a civil suit against a person for violating one's rights. Examples include getting fired from a job because of one's race or gender. Pursuing the latter forms of legal action is potentially expensive, time consuming, and lengthy. The outcome is uncertain, and there is always some risk for the worker and client. Other strategies should be used whenever possible, as they provoke less emotion and are more likely to lead to win-win results.

Another form of confrontation is public embarrassment, which occurs when the worker makes the target system's shortcomings or errors public knowledge. An example of this situation is shown in Highlight 4.5.

Such tactics are dramatic and extreme and do not always succeed. Yet, in certain circumstances, they may be effective in forcing change in larger systems. Confrontation may not be an easy route to follow. However, the needs of clients and the worker's obligation to the client should take precedence over any initial discomfort about tactics.

Ultimately, client empowerment is heightened when the worker clearly communicates the risks involved with confrontation tactics. Client systems should know the possible outcomes and consequences of specific tactics and be directly involved in undertaking the change efforts. By this involvement, clients develop the political/social power and personal empowerment that is a goal of most social and economic justice interventions (Corey et al., 2011).

Confrontation is the approach most likely to raise potential ethical concerns for social workers. Hardina (2000) and Rabinowitz (2013) identified a variety of tactics that social workers felt raised ethical problems. These include "violence, deceit, and causing personal degradation or harm" (p. 13). Specific objectionable activities included destroying property, lying, and stealing, and other respondents felt that causing emotional harm by demonstrating at a target's home was unethical. Reisch and Lowe (2000) identify some additional ethical issues that affect social work practice in the community. These include conflicts between social workers' obligation to employers versus their responsibility to clients, concerns about how best to allocate scarce resources, and drawing a line between the public interest and the interests of individuals or groups we represent. In addition, the social worker may acquire information when working in the community that normally would be reported to the police or child welfare

---

HIGHLIGHT 4.5

Embarrassing a Landlord

Tenants in the Smith Apartments were angry. No matter how much they complained to the city and their landlord, their living conditions remained the same. The building in which they lived was in violation of many city ordinances, and the landlord refused to make any changes. The city did not follow through on its enforcement responsibilities, and the situation remained deadlocked. Finally, the tenants decided to try a different approach. Late one afternoon, they gathered in front of the landlord's home in an exclusive suburban neighborhood and picketed, their signs expressing anger with his neglect. The group called the news media, and television crews appeared at the site to record the event for the evening news. Both city officials, who had been lax in their enforcement of the building codes, and the landlord himself experienced enough embarrassment to undertake the changes demanded by the tenants.

services. What is the ethical thing to do in such situations and how do you balance your ethical obligations? Chapter 11 discusses ethical guidelines and dilemmas in more detail.

Critical Thinking Questions 4.3

Each of the following tactics has been employed in the context of confrontation. Which of the following do you consider ethical, and which do you believe to be unethical? Give your reasons for each choice.

- Organizing a boycott of a store that discriminates against non-English-speaking customers.
- Organizing a sit-in in the bathroom of a city swimming pool in order to get the city to expand its hours to better meet the needs of low-income families.
- Removing and destroying signs advertising a rally by the Ku Klux Klan.
- Going door-to-door talking to residents in the neighborhood of a grocer who raises his prices just prior to the arrival of welfare checks so that low-income clients pay more.
- Placing a sign in your car window stating that a city council member is a bigot because of statements she made about stopping the influx of immigrants who "were a danger to the well-being of society."
- Participating in a gay/lesbian rights parade on the weekend, although your supervisor is a very conservative individual who believes homosexuality is a sin.

Collaborating

Collaboration is the procedure in which two or more persons work together to serve a given client. If the target system is rational and will listen to new or challenging ideas and is acting with good faith, collaboration is the preferable route. The client may be an individual, family, group, or community. In collaboration, the focus is on three principles. The first is a focus on outcomes, the second on relationships among collaborators, and the third is building resilience. By a focus on outcomes, we mean that working together should result in identified results. We collaborate because we believe the outcome of these efforts will be positive and desirable. Collaboration is not simply for the sake of working with others. A focus on relationships suggests that working together will strengthen the relationships

between all parties to the collaboration. If working together is likely to result in bad feelings, trigger underlying problems, or otherwise worsen the situation, it is best not to choose this option. Finally, collaboration should increase the capacity of participants to work together in the future. The potential for all parties to the collaboration to tackle future problems together should be obvious. If collaboration cannot produce at least one of these three goals, it is less likely to be successful.

In some situations, a potential target for collaboration may resist participation because of legitimate concerns about the wisdom or achievability of a project or proposal. Strategies that may soften the opposition and increase a willingness to collaborate include all of the following:

1. Supplying facts about the actual problem assumes that the target does not know much about the existence of a particular problem.
2. Offering options for resolving the problem helps the target consider other solutions that the action system believes are or will be effective.
3. Asking permission to try a solution on a trial basis is often helpful because it does not commit the target to an open-ended agreement with unknown consequences.
4. Requesting permission to set up a committee to consider the problem and possible alternatives increases the target's involvement in the problem and expands the number of people aware of the situation. It is less threatening, as the only request is for a study committee.
5. Requesting increased opportunities for target and action (or client) systems to get together and share interests may be somewhat more threatening to the target, but it gets the two parties talking about their respective concerns.
6. Appealing to the values, ethics, or scruples of the target system assumes that the values or ethics of the target are consonant with those of the action system.
7. Convincing the target system through rational debate and discussion is most effective when the target and action system share certain values or when the data presented lead to a conclusion the target system can accept.
8. Identifying adverse outcomes that arise from continuation of the present situation can be effective if the negative outcomes are realistic or have a realistic probability of occurring. (Homan, 2011; Patti & Resnick, 1980)

Collaborative strategies should be attempted before using adversarial approaches to problem solving. Adversarial approaches run the risk of alienating both the target and those not directly involved in the situation, such as coworkers. Collaborative strategies are good faith efforts to change the target system based on positive assumptions about the target. Only when they fail should other approaches be used.

There may be times when collaborative and adversarial strategies work together or when a given tactic may be used differently than previously described. For example, the petition case described in Highlight 4.4 was not an adversarial tactic, as defined by Patti and Resnick, but a collaborative effort to let the target system (city council) know of a potential problem that could be caused by the decision to relocate the highway. Ultimately, the actual mechanisms used to cause change depend on many factors. These include the competence of the worker, the desires of the intended beneficiary, assumptions about the target system, and the risks of one strategy versus another.

Letter Writing

Letter writing is not always recognized as a strategy for influencing decision makers, yet it can be effective in certain situations. Elected officials frequently receive letters on topics and often keep a tally of how many letters arrive on a particular subject. Virtually any issue—from the need for alcohol and other drug abuse prevention programs to nuclear war—may be addressed. Sheafor and Horejsi (2012) provide suggestions for writing better letters, which are incorporated in Highlight 4.6. Letter writing, which is discussed more fully in Chapter 16, also requires the ability to communicate professionally.

HIGHLIGHT 4.6

Communication Skills: Letter-Writing Strategies

To be effective, letters should:

1. Be carefully planned, revised, polished, and proofread.
2. Include letterhead (with address), date, salutation (Dear___), body, complimentary close (Sincerely), and both typed and written signatures.
3. Be businesslike and pleasant, using appropriate titles.
4. Be brief (preferably one page) and discuss only one topic.
5. Open with a positive comment.
6. Be factual and simply written.
7. Request a response.
8. Never reveal confidential information.
9. Always keep a copy of any correspondence.

Letters that are less likely to be effective include those that appear identical, those copied out of newspaper advertisements, or clearly mass-produced letters (e.g., duplicated copies instead of originals). Letters attacking the reader are less likely to work and may backfire. Some people advocate handwritten letters, but the advantages of a clear, typed message outweigh those of handwritten communication.

If letters are to be mass-produced, as might be desired when a group is trying to sway many individ-

uals, vary the letters so that they do not appear identical. Written letters are helpful in certain situations and help create a record of communication with the decision maker. They should be used as an adjunct to, not instead of, other, more personal forms of contact. Person-to-person communication is still superior to written messages as a means of influencing people.

The use of e-mail communications can complicate the letter-writing process in several ways. First, e-mails don't usually contain letterhead information, making it critical that you clearly identify yourself and the organization (if any) you are representing. Protocols for saving copies of e-mail correspondence should be in place within the agency that give clear guidance about how and what is to be saved or archived. Because e-mails can be written and sent quickly, it is important to think carefully about what you are writing. Letting your emotions control your writing can lead to embarrassment after you calm down. If you are charged up about something, it is probably best to wait a bit before sending your e-mail. Keep in mind that emoticons and other accouterments (☺, :) LOL, etc.) to e-mail communications that are used to convey feelings should be left out of your professional communications.

NEEDS ASSESSMENT

EP 2.1.10d A needs assessments is both a product and a process that includes a systematic gathering of data designed to identify the extent and nature of a social problem or condition, the resources available to deal with the problem, and potential obstacles and solutions to an intervention. A needs assessment may include information gleaned from official records as well as active efforts to gather data from those affected by the social problem or condition. Needs assessments may be conducted to determine the number of homeless in a community, the unmet needs of immigrants or refugees from a particular area, or the extent of poverty in a specific neighborhood.

Needs assessments are used for various purposes, but their primary role is to estimate the extent of demand for a particular service or program.

There are a variety of ways to conduct a needs assessment. The five primary methods are the key informant approach, the community forum approach, the rates-under-treatment approach, the social indicators approach, and the field study. Each method is briefly described in the following list using the models explicated by Rubin and Babbie (2013) and Royce et al. (2010).

1. The *key informant* approach asks especially knowledgeable individuals about the needs of a given community. Examples include a county judge or other local officials. These individuals would be approached to seek their opinions about needs in a particular area.
2. The *community forum* approach assumes that the general public also has knowledge of a community's needs. A series of widely advertised meetings is held to bring in a cross section of the population.
3. The *rates-under-treatment* approach counts the people who seek and receive a given service (e.g., supportive home care) to estimate the actual need in a community.
4. The *social indicators* approach uses information in existing public records, such as the census, to estimate the actual need for a service.
5. A *field study* needs assessment relies on gathering actual data in the community through interviews and observation.

All but the last of these methods are relatively inexpensive and easy to use. When undertaking a needs assessment, thinking through the exact information that one wishes to gather is important. One must define goals and decide how the goals will be measured and what data should be collected. Sometimes those collecting the data will need special training or orientation. At other times, information will be readily available using the Internet as a resource. Census data, for example, are easy to access, as are a number of other federal government publications. Statistics are routinely available on such topics as homelessness, poverty, health issues, crime, and many others. A good starting point is http://www.firstgov.gov, a portal to various federal government agencies. Similarly, one can often acquire information about elected and appointed officials at every level of government. One starting point is a state or community's official Web site. For example, in Utah it is http://www.utah.gov, and in San Francisco it is http://www.ci.sf.ca.us. A little detective work on the Internet can provide a wealth of information about any level of government. A needs assessment is an effective method for determining unmet needs in a community and, sometimes, for determining the existence of an overlap of services. Each social worker should be able to conduct a needs assessment using one or more of the preceding approaches.

PLANNING

EP 2.1.10 Planning is a key step in social work practice. Planning with large systems, however, requires a higher level of skill than working with individual clients. Fortunately, several techniques exist that help the planner to identify all steps, establish a time frame, and assign specific tasks to responsible parties. One of the more useful approaches is the Program Evaluation and Review Technique (PERT). PERT assists the planning process for both business and social services (e.g., one author used this technique to plan a group home program and to prepare for accreditation of three social work programs at a university). In PERT, four steps must be undertaken: (1) identifying major tasks to be accomplished, (2) placing them in sequential order, (3) determining the probable time needed for completion of each step, and (4) identifying those responsible for completing each specific task.

Once these steps are completed, it is possible to map out the total project graphically, showing what will occur, when it will occur, and who is responsible. The sample PERT chart in Figure 4.2 uses planning for a party as the project.

The chart shows the tasks to be accomplished and the date by which each step is to be completed. If a

January 15	January 20	February 1	February 7	February 13	February 14
Decide date for party	Identify invitees	Mail invitations	Select refreshments	Clean house	Host party

Buy Valentine decorations

Decorate house

© Cengage Learning

FIGURE 4.2   A Sample Program Evaluation and Review Technique (PERT) Chart

committee planned this party, each task might be delegated to a particular subcommittee, and the chart would reflect this assignment. Assignments may be shown by coloring in the chart, a different color for each responsible party, or by placing initials in the lower corner of a square. Sometimes, two or more tasks occur simultaneously, and this would be reflected by a vertical line connecting the two boxes, with one box placed under the other, as shown in the figure. If the tasks are complex, a detailed work plan can be drawn up to show the activity, describe the steps within, identify those responsible, and specify the date for completion. The PERT system allows larger projects to be planned and allows for constant monitoring of tasks. It shows what will be accomplished and helps hold people responsible for their assignments. It is simple, easy to use, and can be applied to any number of tasks or projects.

Computer programs are available to help set up the steps in doing a PERT chart as well as other frequently used diagrams, such as organizational charts, GANTT charts, flow charts, floor plans, and calendars. Two of the most popular include Visio (Microsoft Corp.) and SmartDraw (Smartdraw.com).

WORKING WITH COALITIONS

EP 2.1.8b

Many tasks associated with changing large systems require the concerted efforts of more than one group. A coalition is a collection of different groups or organizations designed to work toward a common goal. The types of groups that form a coalition may be similar or diverse. For instance, well-to-do business owners as a group and single parents receiving public assistance might form a coalition to help their community combat

drug abuse. Environmentalists and area residents might work together to prevent locating a hazardous waste facility in or near a poor neighborhood. Social workers often must collaborate with coalitions of colleagues and clients to pursue effective policy action.

Toseland and Rivas (2012) note that coalitions may be effective because they combine resources of multiple groups or organizations. Having several groups with like interests work together to achieve ends that each group desires is quite common. For example, the efforts to create and strengthen licensing laws for social workers often involve coalitions between social work organizations, such as the NASW, and other groups, such as marriage and family therapist associations and nursing home social workers. The creating of coalitions occurs frequently because relatively few laws pass through the efforts of only one group. Coalitions are often essential when the task is large and requires a complex effort by several participants. Perhaps the primary advantage of working with coalitions is the increased strength that occurs when several groups combine forces.

Coalitions may be designed to be ongoing or developed to respond to a specific problem. Sometimes, a coalition created to respond to a particular problem may continue indefinitely as the groups or individuals involved recognize advantages of the new structure. Of course, any coalition may cease to exist after achieving the initial goal. Permanent alliances are difficult to maintain but are potentially effective in uniting diverse interests in a common cause.

Deciding which groups to include in a coalition is not difficult. One must be aware of the network of community groups already in existence. Knowing the primary goals of each group and assessing the compatibility of these goals with those of your organization is important. Knowing which groups are influential and attempting to align with them, if possible, is also important. Begin by listing organizations already working in a specific area. An organization focused on youth might determine that it shares interests with many other groups. Examples include groups focused on children with developmental disabilities, service clubs giving to youth causes, scouting organizations, teacher organizations, YMCAs or YWCAs, and so on. Arranging a meeting with the leadership of these groups to explore the possibility of working together to establish a drug education program is one example. If the leadership of several organizations can work together well, the process becomes easier to manage. Individual personalities or styles can be either a barrier or an asset to this collaboration.

After the coalition is created, the real work begins. Although there is enormous strength in coalitions, they also suffer from serious shortcomings. Sometimes a coalition can be broken apart by playing up the differences among or between organizations that form it. Opponents use this tactic to try to sidetrack or otherwise weaken the group.

Similarly, keeping every coalition member informed of what is happening is important. This is especially true where there is a history of organizations not working together or where there is an unequal power balance among the various subgroups.

If one group is clearly the strongest and has the most to gain from the effort to organize and use the coalition, having the leaders of the stronger group keep the others apprised of what is happening is essential. If the weaker partners fear being left out of significant decisions, there is greater likelihood that they will drop out.

The importance of shared leadership is obvious. Making certain that, all groups in the coalition are represented on some sort of coordinating board or steering committee helps them to feel they have a stake in the outcome.

The governing committee members must often take any plans developed by the governing body back to their respective groups for approval. This process is cumbersome, but it ensures that no group will be dragged into a project against the wishes of its members. For ongoing coalitions, the decision by one group to withdraw from a specific project is not likely to threaten the coalition. On the other hand, an ad hoc coalition formed to pursue a specific purpose is vulnerable to dissolution if one or more of the component groups withdraw.

Coalitions are most effective when the task is clear and the responsibilities are specified. Coalition members may continue to work on other projects, but individual goals must be sacrificed for the good of the coalition. This sacrifice means each organization in the coalition must agree that the primary goal is of sufficient importance and that achieving it supersedes the petty jealousies and difficulties that traditionally exist. A decision must also be made about the contributions to be provided by each group. In addition, assessing which group is more likely to be effective with which tasks is important. Just as in any other endeavor, assigning tasks to those most competent to carry them out makes sense. An effective coalition can multiply exponentially the capacity to achieve desired ends. Creating a coalition from existing groups is easier than building an individual membership organization with the same goal. In the end, the former is more likely to accomplish its goals, to shorten the time needed to achieve desired ends, and to build a reputation for effectiveness. Working with coalitions also increases the opportunity to collaborate with colleagues and clients to effectively bring about changes in policies and pursue social and economic justice goals.

LO 4-5 Engage in Professional Roles, Including Initiator, Negotiator, Advocate, Spokesperson, Organizer, Mediator, and Consultant

Identifying Professional Roles in Organizational and Community Change

Thinking of a practitioner's work as a series of roles is possible and sometimes helpful. This section will briefly describe several key roles assumed when working for change in organizations and communities: initiator, negotiator, advocate, spokesperson, organizer, mediator, and consultant. Some of these roles are also used at the micro and mezzo levels of generalist price.

INITIATOR

The initiator is the person or persons who call attention to an issue. The issue may be a problem existing in the community, a need, or simply a situation that can be improved. It is important to recognize that a problem need not exist before attention can be called to it. Often, preventing future problems or enhancing existing services is a satisfactory reason for creating a change. Thus, a social worker may recognize that a policy is creating problems for particular clients and bring this to the attention of the supervisor. For example, the agency's office hours may force clients to come at difficult times, resulting in lost pay and jeopardizing their jobs. A client may identify ways that service could be improved. In each case, the person is playing the role of initiator. Usually, this role must be followed up by other kinds of work because just pointing out that a problem exists is no guarantee that it will be fixed.

NEGOTIATOR

In some situations, the worker may play the role of negotiator, representing an organization or group trying to wrestle something from another group. For instance, a worker may negotiate better police protection for a neighborhood hit by a rash of drive-by shootings. As mentioned earlier, negotiators who can construct a win-win situation are more likely to be successful than those who adopt a win-lose approach. Successful negotiators also remain calm when others are more emotionally involved. Negotiators cannot personalize the attacks or comments of the other person or group with whom they are negotiating. The task is to find a middle ground that satisfies both sides. Negotiators need the skills of an advocate to push for achievement of organizational goals and those of a mediator to find a satisfactory compromise.

ADVOCATE

Advocates speak out and act on behalf of clients. Advocates help decide what their clients are entitled to and what problems are keeping clients from receiving what they need. The worker must also assess the adversary to figure out its strengths and weaknesses. Although some adversaries may quickly meet the requests (demands) of an advocate, it is more likely that additional work will be required. This work may include assessing the client's situation to determine if advocating for the client is likely to cause further problems. The client may be in a vulnerable situation, and the worker would not want to worsen things. Sometimes documenting a problem so that the adversary understands the reasons for the client's concerns is possible. In other situations, documentation alone will not suffice. As discussed earlier, an opponent who does not share your values or perception

of the problem is unlikely to accede to your wishes. Consider an agency director who is more concerned about saving money than serving needy clients. Documenting that many clients receive only a portion of the services they need is unlikely to sway the director who believes additional services will increase agency costs. In addition, very few people or organizations give up power willingly. Thus, the advocate must expect to use skills other than simply marshalling evidence. The worker may have to negotiate or bargain with the adversary or use pressure tactics to achieve desired ends. Advocacy is discussed in much greater depth in Chapter 14.

SPOKESPERSON

A spokesperson is someone authorized to speak on behalf of others. This role can be troublesome. Sometimes, the spokesperson begins to personalize the information provided until it reflects the spokesperson's ideas more than those of the organization. Spokespersons should seek to present the organization's views and positions without coloring them with their own views. This is not always easy. In addition, a special problem exists when you disagree with the position taken by your organization or group. The dilemma can be resolved in two ways. First, you can cease to speak for the group and give up the role as spokesperson. Second, you can reflect accurately the organization's position and submerge your own hesitation or disagreement. Doing anything else, such as presenting the organization's opinion in a way that satisfies your own beliefs, is violating the principle of representing the group.

Marshall Winston learned about this limitation the hard way. Marshall was the president of the West Bend Community Service League (CSL), a membership organization dedicated to improving the city of West Bend. The League's board of directors had recently decided not to undertake a community recreation project because a clear need had not been demonstrated. Marshall did not agree with the board's decision, which was final. When Sally Wombat asked Marshall—as CSL president—to speak at the next Rotary Club meeting about needs in the community, he presented the recreation project as critical for the community. In so doing, he went against the wishes of his own board of directors. At the next board meeting, several members raised concerns about Marshall's right to speak as the president of CSL when his comments clearly did not reflect the opinion of the organization.

ORGANIZER

An organizer is one who coordinates individuals or groups to pursue some designated function(s). The organizer may be organizing individuals or groups. As mentioned earlier, organizing existing groups is easier and usually more effective than creating groups from scratch. Organizers' tasks include developing the potential of others to serve as leaders, stimulating others to act, teaching others, identifying likely targets for change, serving as a staff member or facilitator, and linking the organization with others sharing similar interests (Rubin & Rubin, 2008). The tasks vary, depending on the nature of the problem and the strengths and limitations of the components to be organized. Where indigenous leadership already exists, the worker may serve as a consultant or advisor; where it is not present, the worker may become a mentor or teacher. In either case, organizing others is a formidable role. One example is Alicia Gunn, who organized a group of social workers all dealing with the juvenile court in Porter County. Membership in the group was composed of probation officers, social workers from protective services, foster care workers at the local family and children agencies, and adoption social workers from the State Department of Human Services. Alicia's goal was to improve the services to children and adolescents who ended up in the juvenile court system. She believed that if all of the agencies and workers dealing with children coming into the court system could sit down and talk about the situation, service improvements could result.

MEDIATOR

As Chapter 1 explains, mediators are neutral persons who resolve disagreements among various systems in conflict. Mediators can achieve several desired ends. Mediators may help two sides work out a compromise. They must understand the positions of both parties and attempt to find a suitable compromise. This compromise requires listening to each side and drawing out feelings and beliefs about the disagreement (Hepworth, Rooney, Rooney, & Strom-Gottfried, 2013). The worker as mediator can clarify positions, recognize miscommunication about differences, and help both parties present their ideas clearly. The mediator helps take the emotion out of the situation, allowing better problem solving. As discussed earlier in this chapter, mediation skills are becoming increasingly important in such situations as divorce and child custody disagreements.

CONSULTANT

A consultant is someone who provides advice, suggestions, or ideas to another person, group, or organization. Consultants advise cities on zoning laws, suggest better ways of structuring human service programs, and help groups become more effective. There are two requirements for consultants.

First, they must know more than the individual consultee. This knowledge may be specific on a particular topic, such as zoning laws, or of better ways of problem solving. Second, consultants must be able to see their advice ignored without becoming offended. A consultant does not have supervisory or administrative power over the consultee. If the consultee chooses to ignore the consultant's advice, no matter how good, the consultant must accept that the client has this right. The principle of self-determination is clearly operable in such situations. With accepting consultation comes the concomitant right to take or ignore the advice provided.

For example, the Central State Hospital for Developmental Disabilities invited in a team of social work practitioners, nurses, and physicians experienced in services to clients with developmental disabilities. The consultant team's role was to identify how the hospital could become more effective in serving its clients and recommend strategies to foster independence for residents. Although the recommendations were all well developed and documented, the hospital implemented only the suggestions that administrators felt would not increase costs.

Utilizing Conceptual Frameworks: Generalist Intervention Model (GIM) in Macro Practice

As we have seen in each of the preceding chapters, the Generalist Intervention Model (GIM) involves a series of steps used to create change. These steps are guidelines for planned change efforts with individuals, families, groups, organizations, and communities. Consider Manuel Gossett, a social worker with the La Casa social service agency. La Casa serves Hispanic clients in the community, providing bilingual counseling for individuals and families, outpatient treatment groups for chemical dependency, and a homeless shelter. Manuel's supervisor asked him to prepare a needs assessment to determine if the agency should consider establishing an inpatient program for clients with substance abuse. As part of his task, Manuel was to meet with directors of other agencies who were already serving clients with chemical dependency problems. Manuel followed each of the GIM steps in more or less the correct order. He decided to use a couple of different needs assessment approaches rather than to rely on any single model. Not only would he gather information from key informants, but he would also incorporate statistics from existing programs to document the need for additional programs.

Because Manuel did not know all of the agency directors beforehand, he realized that he would need to meet each of them and establish a relationship that would foster his goal of gathering information. Thus, he entered the first step—*engagement.* He used a number of micro skills, including conveying warmth and genuineness, attentive listening, and using rephrasing and clarification to ensure he understood the information being provided by each person he interviewed. He also planned ahead and developed a set of questions that he wanted to ask each director.

As he gathered his data from these interviews and other sources, he made a tentative *assessment* about the level of need for an inpatient chemical dependency program. He concluded there appeared to be considerable need for such a program. However, he also identified a number of potential concerns expressed by each of his key informants. He noted, for example, that several new group-home-like programs in the city had met with resistance from neighbors who did not want such programs in their backyards. He also noted that funding from various health insurance companies was getting reduced or restricted through various forms of managed care. Manuel decided that he needed to include these concerns in his report.

When he turned in his completed needs assessment, Manuel's supervisor was quite impressed, so impressed that he asked Manuel to proceed to the next step, which was to develop an agency plan for creating a new program. In the *planning* stage of the GIM, Manuel prioritized the problems he had identified in his report. He also developed appropriate solutions for each problem after thoroughly considering the pros and cons of each alternative. He noted, for example, that the neighborhood-related problems experienced by other residential programs probably would be much reduced in the Hispanic community served by his agency. He knew of at least two occasions where new group homes had been sited without anyone raising the kind of fuss mentioned by the other agency directors. He also drew up a plan for including neighborhood residents on an advisory board for the new facility.

As another part of the planning stage, Manuel also specified the goals and objectives of this effort, which included a tentative timetable and a list of tasks to be completed by La Casa staff. Implementation of the plan was more complicated. Because Manuel was not a supervisor or administrator, he decided that *implementation* would require a concerted effort by his superiors in the agency. He volunteered to monitor progress toward achieving the objectives and to suggest changes in the plan where needed. However, Manuel felt that details such as locating and renting space, hiring and training social workers, and dealing with health insurance companies needed more expertise than he possessed. This understanding was an appropriate assessment of his own level of competence and the mark of a good social worker. At the same time, he could certainly monitor whether a given step had been achieved or where plans were not being carried out.

Six months later Manuel prepared an *evaluation* report for his supervisor to take to La Casa's board of directors. The report noted that a final contract was being negotiated to rent a large two-story home about six blocks from the agency's main office. Advertising was being prepared to hire one more social worker. The agency had tentative agreements with 14 other agencies interested in referring clients to the substance abuse program. A small purchase-of-service contract was being presented to the county human service agency that would pay La Casa a set amount for each client admitted to the facility. (The county agency found it easier to pay other agencies to provide inpatient services than to start its own facility.) A local college social work program was helping to design an evaluation plan that could be used to determine the new program's effectiveness. Manuel included all of this information in his report. His supervisor, duly impressed with the fine work that went into this effort, told Manuel that he would use his talents again when such special projects were being considered. Manuel smiled and asked if this recognition would come with a salary increase. His supervisor was still laughing as Manuel headed down the hallway.

Chapter Summary

The following summarizes this chapter's content as it relates to each learning objective (LO) presented at the beginning of the chapter. Chapter content helps prepare students to:

LO 4-1 Utilize a conceptual framework for an organizational context of practice.

Macro practice involves questioning and sometimes confronting major social issues and global organizational policies. It is based on the fundamental rights of people to have their basic needs met, make their own choices, and maintain their human dignity. Macro practice assumes that most social workers spend all or part of their professional time within formal organizations and become aware of policies, rules, and regulations that undermine these fundamental rights and sometimes run counter to the social work profession's values. Tackling these situations is both an obligation for social workers as well as a professional challenge. Undertaking change in one's own organization carries a degree of risk, requiring the worker to thoroughly understand what those risks entail.

Two broad theoretical perspectives underlie practice with large systems: organizational theory and community theory. Organizational theory is concerned about how such entities function, what improves or impairs an organization's ability to accomplish its mission, and what motivates people toward organizational goals. Working within an organization requires an understanding of bureaucracy, a familiarity with management theories, and an awareness of an organization's culture.

Community theory is focused on both the nature of communities and the role that social work practice plays in the community. Communities serve several functions, including the production, distribution, and consumption of goods and services; socialization of members; social control; social participation; and mutual support. Social workers view the community as one or more of three things: a target for change, the problem itself, or the context in which change occurs.

LO 4-2 Analyze, formulate, and advocate for interventions, including policy/planning, capacity development, and social advocacy.

At least three types of interventions are involved in working with a community: policy/planning, capacity development, and social advocacy. Each may be employed individually or together depending on the situation. Policy/planning is focused on using data to identify needs and plan for a solution to community problems. Capacity development involves building the competency of a group or community to undertake large-scale community change. Social advocacy uses pressure to bring about changes that benefit individuals or groups experiencing social and economic injustice. Advocacy can involve both cause and case advocacy. The former focuses on issues that are important to groups or classes of people, such as availability of health care for the uninsured or education for children with disabilities. Case advocacy is concerned with a single case, such as helping an individual who has been discriminated against or denied due process. Sometimes a benefit obtained in the process of case advocacy ends up helping an entire group of people, but this is not the primary purpose of case advocacy.

LO 4-3 Use empathy, interpersonal skills, and group skills in macro practice.

Effective organizational and community practice requires many of the same skills as does work with individual and families. This includes such things as warmth, empathy, and genuineness because the ability to form relationships remains essential in the community. Sensitivity to others, the ability to work with those who are different from us in some way, observational skills, and being attuned to verbal and nonverbal behavior can be very useful when working with both allies and targets. Useful group skills include conflict resolution, developing win-win outcomes, team building, public speaking, consultation, and the ability to coordinate the work of the group.

LO 4-4 Utilize effective macro practice skills, including evaluating results, fundraising, budgeting, negotiating, mediating, influencing decision makers, needs assessment, planning, and working with coalitions.

In addition to using micro and mezzo skills, effective work to achieve organizational and community change requires specific abilities related to the special challenges of large system interventions. One such skill is the ability to evaluate program results. Another skill is fundraising designed to help acquire and maintain the resources needed to implement and operate a program. A related macro skill is budgeting, as all organizations and communities operate budgets designed to ensure their continued existence and provide needed programs. Three common models for budgeting are line-item budgets, program (functional) budgets, and incremental budgets.

Two important macro skills are negotiating and mediating. The former involves bargaining between different parties to arrive at an agreement that both can live with. Negotiating requires separating the problem from the people so that differences do not become personalized, identifying the shared interests of both parties, and devising new options that will benefit both sides. Typically, negotiators focus on the easiest issues first to set the stage for more difficult concerns that will be addressed later. Social workers engaged in negotiating are typically representing the interests of others and are trying to achieve an agreement that both sides can live with.

Mediating, on the other hand, involves playing the role of a third party to a disagreement with responsibility to neither side in the dispute. The goal is helping both sides reach an acceptable outcome, preferably a win-win result. Mediators must be fair and impartial, recognize the legitimate interests of both parties, and be dedicated to helping them achieve their goals.

Another major macro skill is influencing decision makers to advance human rights and achieve social and economic justice. This requires several subskills. The first, petitioning, involves collecting signatures on a document asking an organization or person to act in a particular manner. Petitions are relatively easy to construct, although there may be some legal requirements imposed if the petition involves requesting a ballot initiative. Working with the media requires the ability to use such things as radio, TV, newspapers, and similar means for spreading information about one's cause. It also requires the ability to produce press releases.

Another skill is the ability to educate others so that they will support your position or at least remain neutral. Persuading others is more involved because the goal is to get another person or group to concur with your position. Confrontation, on the other hand, is the act of challenging another individual or group and is more difficult. It is used when less threatening options have not worked, target and action system goals are sharply divergent, and the action system poses a credible threat to the target system.

Collaborating is a much more congenial approach in that it involves two or more entities working together to achieve a specific goal. Multiple collaborative strategies are available, including providing factual information to the target; offering options for problem resolution; engaging in experimental programs to test the effectiveness of an idea; requesting a study committee to further study an issue, requesting more time to work out differences; appealing to the values, ethics, or scruples of the target system; employing rational debate, and pointing out potential negative outcomes associated with continuing along the current path. Letter writing is another skill useful in the macro environment because it is often used as a means to influence decision makers.

Assessing the needs of an organization or community is another macro skill. Several methods are commonly used in this effort, including the key informant, community forum, rates-under-treatment, social indicators, and field study approaches. Each can be used alone or in combination to gather the information needed to accurately and adequately assess need.

Planning is another macro skill that can be helpful when working with larger systems. It involves identifying what has to be done, by when, and with whose help. Plans can be as simple as a list of tasks, time lines, and responsible parties. More complex plans can be developed using computer programs that produce more elaborate planning tools, such as PERT and GANTT charts.

The final skill addressed is working with coalitions, as it is often possible to accomplish more with multiple groups behind an issue. It enhances the resources available to bring about change and multiplies the potential impact beyond what any single group can produce. Like other skills, working with coalitions has both strengths and drawbacks that must be addressed as the process goes forward. Useful subskills are such things as keeping all parties informed, using shared leadership, and ensuring clarity of tasks and lines of responsibility.

LO 4-5 Engage in professional roles, including initiator, negotiator, advocate, spokesperson, organizer, mediator, and consultant.

Social workers in the macro environment pursue a number of professional roles designed to achieve change within large systems. These include that of initiator (the person who calls attention to an issue) and negotiator (the individual empowered to bargain on behalf of one group in a dispute). Social workers also act as advocates who work and speak on behalf of clients. Spokespersons are authorized to speak on behalf of others but only within the confines of the group's position on the topic. They are not free to state their own positions or to change the position of the group they represent.

Mediators, as mentioned earlier, are neutral parties who try to help two or more sides in a disagreement to reach a mutually acceptable agreement. Finally, a consultant role is generally limited to providing suggestions and advice designed to help a group or organization achieve its goals. Lacking administrative power, the consultant must leave the final decision to the group with whom he or she has been asked to consult.

Competency Notes

The following identifies where Educational Policy (EP) competencies and practice behaviors are discussed in the chapter.

EP 2.1.1 **Identify as a professional social worker and conduct oneself accordingly.** *(p. 130):* Identifying as a professional social worker sometimes requires social workers to balance obligations to both one's agency and one's clients. This challenge requires that the social worker use appropriate professional behavior to help resolve the situation.

EP 2.1.1a **Advocate for client access to the services of social work.** *(p. 154):* An advocate must expect to use skills that include but are not limited to documenting problems.

EP 2.1.1c **Attend to professional roles and boundaries.** *(p. 153):* Within the community, the social worker may be called upon to play the role of initiator, negotiator, advocate, spokesperson, organizer, mediator, and consultant.

EP 2.1.1d **Demonstrate professional demeanor in behavior, appearance, and communication.** *(p. 145):* Social workers must be able to effectively communicate both orally and in written form. Being articulate and thoughtful in communicating the ideas is an important part of effective communication.

EP 2.1.1f **If Use supervision and consultation.** *(p. 155):* Social workers may engage in consultation with organizations and other community entities.

EP 2.1.2 **Apply social work ethical principles to guide professional practice.** *(p.128):* Social workers may encounter conflicts between their ethical obligation to the clients and their obligations to the employer.

EP 2.1.2b **Make ethical decisions by applying standards of the NASW *Code of Ethics* and, as applicable, of the International Federation of Social Workers/International Association of Schools of Social Work *Ethics in Social Work Statement of Principles.* ** *(p. 130):* Ethical issues can and will arise in a variety of settings, including one's place of employment, and must be resolved.

EP 2.1.3 **Apply critical thinking to inform and communicate professional judgment.** *(p. 131):* Critical thinking is important when deciding how best to allocate agency resources. *(pp. 140, 149):* Social workers must carefully and critically examine the potential strategies they are considering when working with organizations and communities.

EP 2.1.3c **Demonstrate effective oral and written communication in working with individuals, families, groups, organizations, communities, and colleagues.** *(pp. 144, 145, 150):* Working with the media requires strong oral and written communication skills.

EP 2.1.5 **Advance human rights and social and economic justice.** *(p. 153):* Working with coalitions increases the opportunity to collaborate with colleagues and clients to achieve social and economic justice.

EP 2.1.5b **Advocate for human rights and social and economic justice.** *(p. 133):* Cause advocacy is typically concerned with seeking social and economic justice for oppressed groups and individuals. *(p. 154):* The opportunity to advocate for social and economic justice can occur both in one's employment as well as in the role of citizen.

EP 2.1.5c **Engage in practices that advance social and economic justice.** *(p. 135):* Working with coalitions is an effective approach to achieve social and economic justice, as it combines the strengths of multiple groups and individuals.

EP 2.1.7a **Utilize conceptual frameworks to guide the processes of assessment, intervention, and evaluation.** *(p. 129):* Various conceptual frameworks and models are needed to work with larger systems, including the organizational context of social work practice. *(p. 131):* Conceptual frameworks are important when undertaking organizational and community change. *(p. 155):* The Generalist Intervention Model (GIM) is a useful conceptual model for working with macro systems.

EP 2.1.8a **Analyze, formulate, and advocate for policies that advance social well-being.** *(p. 133):* Cause advocacy is designed to achieve policies that benefit clients or an identified group. It may also be employed to seek general well-being in society.

EP 2.1.8b **Collaborate with colleagues and clients for effective policy action.** *(pp. 152, 153):* Collaborating with clients and colleagues in various coalitions is an effective means to bring about changes in policies that support social work goals.

EP 2.1.9 **Respond to contexts that shape practice.** *(p. 143):* One of the ways that social workers respond to contexts that shape practice is by keeping abreast of the use of technology employed to achieve social work goals. In particular this means being aware of how computers, cell phones, and the Internet are being used by clients and citizens to bring about changes.

EP 2.1.9b **Provide leadership in promoting sustainable changes in service delivery to improve the quality of social services.** *(p. 155):* Serving in the professional role of organizer involves providing leadership to help others achieve changes that will enhance social service delivery and the quality of services available to clients.

EP 2.1.10 **Engage, assess, intervene, and evaluate with individuals, families, groups, organizations and communities.** *(p. 151):* Planning is an important step in social work practice that precedes intervention.

EP 2.1.10b **Use empathy and other interpersonal skills.** *(p. 135)* Many of the interpersonal skills needed for working with individuals and families are equally useful when dealing with large systems.

EP 2.1.10d **Collect, organize, and interpret client data.** *(p. 151):* Needs assessments are an effective means for collecting, organizing, and interpreting data about a community problem.

EP 2.1.10h **Initiate actions to achieve organizational goals.** *(p. 130):* Most social workers are employed in agencies to help achieve such organizational goals as responding to community problems and working with various-size systems.

EP 2.1.10k **Negotiate, mediate, and advocate for clients.** *(pp. 142, 143, 154, 155):* Negotiating and mediating skills are useful for a generalist social worker.

EP 2.1.10m **Critically analyze, monitor, and evaluate interventions.** *(p. 137):* Evaluating results is an important macro skill for organizational and community change.

On the Internet

Visit the *Understanding Generalist Practice* CourseMate at **www.cengagebrain.com** for resources such as quizzes, glossaries and videos.

Engagement and Assessment in Generalist Practice

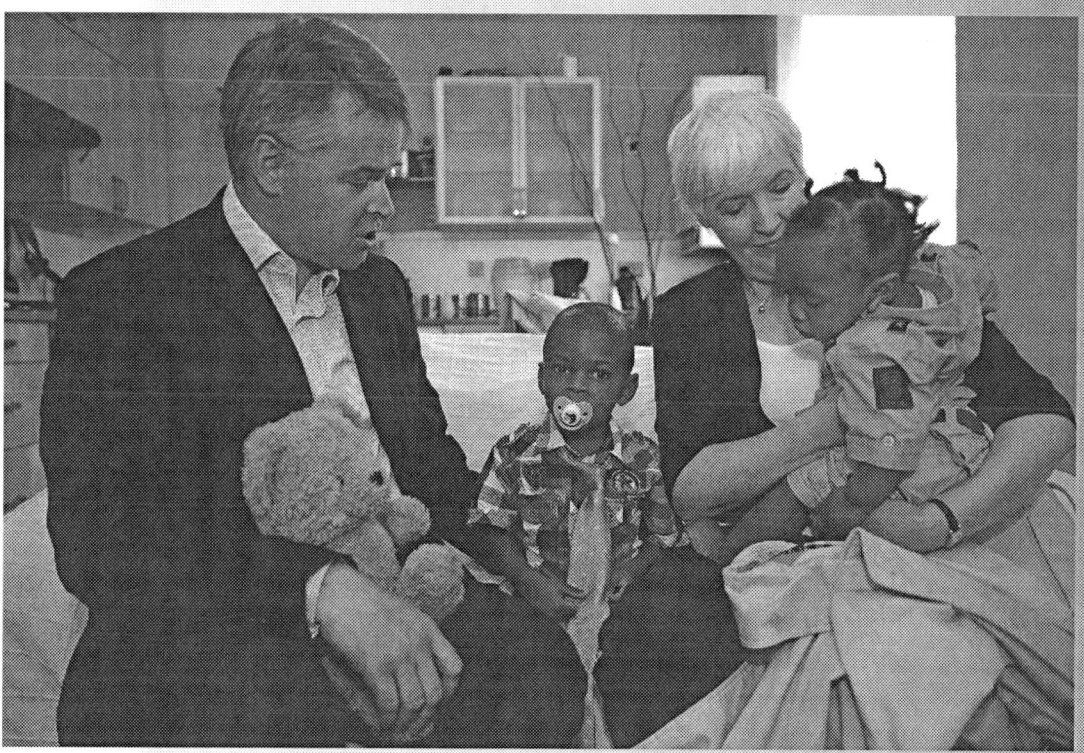

Chris Harris/WPA Pool/Getty Images

Learning Objectives   *This chapter will help prepare students to:*

LO 5-1   Employ activities and skills needed for engagement with various-size systems.

LO 5-2   Assess goals prior to intervention.

LO 5-3   Use practice behaviors such as defining and describing problems.

LO 5-4   Assess client strengths and limitations.

LO 5-5   Utilize micro-assessment tools such as the *Diagnostic and Statistical Manual (DSM-5)*, the Rathus Assertiveness Schedule, and an alcoholism test.

LO 5-6   Decide to work with families following assessment.

LO 5-7   Effectively use home visits as an assessment mechanism.

LO 5-8   Assess both task and treatment groups.

LO 5-9   Use assessment tools to determine community and neighborhood needs.

Elisha White, a protective services worker called in to assess a reported case of child abuse, looked around the room. An emaciated child, age 3 or 4, squatted in the corner, her long, dark hair snarled and greasy. Whimpering, she hid her eyes with her hands. Her skin was mottled with dirt and what appeared to be purplish bruises. The floor and walls were barren and smeared with dirt. Tattered drapes fluttered at the open windows. The autumn air was nippy with early morning frost. The archaic radiator in the corner emitted no heat.

A neighbor had called in reporting that the girl's mother was a "coke freak" who frequently left the little girl home alone. In her brief, initial assessment of the situation, Elisha noted the girl's apparent neglect (the lack of appropriate physical care, food, and heat) in addition to potential abuse (the bruises from some unidentified cause).

A number of thoughts went through Elisha's mind. They included the procedures for reporting this situation and removing the little girl from the premises. How was the little girl feeling inside? What emotional and physical damage had already been done to her? Elisha approached the tiny body slowly and spoke in a calm, soothing tone, trying to assure the child that everything would be "OK."

Other thoughts swept through Elisha's consciousness. Where was the mother? In what condition was she? How could she be contacted? What would the mother's chances be in a drug rehabilitation program, if drug abuse was indeed one of the woman's problems? Were there relatives available who could help?

If there was no one else, how fast could Elisha place the little girl in temporary foster care? What kind of care was available?

Sometimes, good foster placements were hard to find. What effects would placement have on the little girl?

Child abuse and neglect were massive problems in the large city where Elisha worked. Agency caseloads were large, and treatment services were too limited.

Elisha decided that something needed to be done. She herself knew of dozens of cases similar to this one. The needs of these children had to be publicized. The community needed to do more about this increasingly serious problem. Elisha decided to talk to her supervisor as soon as she returned to the agency. Her supervisor just might be receptive to setting up an agency task group to work on the problem. Maybe, if these children's needs could be more easily identified, people in the community would respond positively to supporting more services. Perhaps then the community and city leaders would listen and devote more resources to this problem. Even members of her church might respond to her pleas. She decided she would bring the topic up at the next church meeting.

Elisha was committed. First, she must attend to this small child's immediate needs. But the problem was much larger than this little girl. The entire community should be involved in confronting the problem and the issues. Next, she would set out to assess the problem on a macro basis. How extensive were child abuse and neglect? What services were already in place to combat the problem and provide intervention for the children and their families? How effective were these services? Were there other resources in the community that could be called upon for help?

LO 5-1 Employ Activities and Skills Needed for Engagement with Various-Size Systems

Engagement and assessment are the first two steps in the planned change process. Each is important to the eventual outcome of the helping relationship between the generalist social worker and the client system. Engagement is concerned with the process of establishing the client–worker relationship upon which subsequent steps depend. Assessment considers the process of gathering and organizing data and information in order to arrive at an accurate picture of the person-in-environment situation. This chapter will discuss engagement and assessment considering potential micro,

mezzo, and macro dimensions of each. However, because this text emphasizes micro skills in generalist practice, they will be the primary focus of this chapter.

Engagement

EP 2.1.10

Engagement, the first step in the planned change process, focuses on establishing a professional relationship between the worker and the client system. The profession of social work has long believed that this relationship is an absolute requisite for successful practice. Miley, O'Melia, and DuBois (2011) refer to building these relationships as forming partnerships with clients. Professional worker–client relationships are characterized by a clear purpose, a commitment to meeting client needs, ethical standards of practice, and worker emphasis on communicating warmth, genuineness, and empathy. As you can see, many of the skills identified in Chapter 2 are used in the engagement phase. Engagement is the point where the worker and client first meet and begin to identify client needs. It is also where the empowerment process begins.

Engagement begins with the first contact between worker and client. Sometimes referred to as "intake," this initial contact may be over the phone or in person. Either way it sets the stage for each of the following steps in the planned change process. Engagement occurs whether the client willingly initiates the contact or is required to meet with the worker. Involuntary contact with the worker may come about in situations such as those involving child abuse/neglect investigations or probation and parole work, among others. In either case, the generalist practitioner must understand the common activities and actions needed to successfully complete the engagement phase. These activities include.

- greeting clients in such a way as to encourage them to talk with you;
- demonstrating effective attending skills that communicate your interest in the client's situation;
- discussing agency services and client expectations;
- deciding whether the agency and worker can be of assistance;
- offering agency and worker services to the client;
- orienting the client to the helping relationship; and
- completing any required paperwork.

GREETING THE CLIENT

Building a solid relationship with a client begins with your first contact. Recommended behaviors include personally meeting the client in the waiting room and providing a face-to-face greeting. Eye contact and a handshake are common courtesies that should be extended to the client (Kadushin & Kadushin, 2013). Greeting the client is relatively simple. For example, you might say, "Ms. Bowen, I'm Annie Nervosa, the social worker here at The Elms Center." Offer your hand to the client and offer her a seat unless you have reason to believe this might be considered offensive because of the client's culture or religion. You might follow this offer with a question, "Would you prefer to be called Ms. Bowen or Jane? You may call me Annie." Be careful to use clients' full names rather than

automatically assuming they want to be addressed informally. Using more formal forms of address indicate respect for the client, a critical element when working with individuals or groups that have experienced discrimination and adverse treatment from others.

Small talk and initial socializing is not only acceptable, but may help break the ice. It often helps put individuals at ease and helps them in the transition to their new role as clients. It can also build rapport as the worker and client discover shared interests or experiences (Kadushin & Kadushin, 2013).

If you do not know the reason for the client's visit, follow your introduction with a comment such as, "I understand you wanted to talk with me about something." This statement then opens the discussion, allowing the client to elaborate on the reason for the interview. If you do know the reason for the initial contact, you might say, "I asked to see you because your son Frank came to school today with bruises all over his legs and buttocks." Or you might say, "In your phone call you said you wanted to discuss problems you're having with your mother." You will note that each of these worker responses was in the form of a statement to which the client could respond. You could also solicit the same information by asking the client directly, "What brings you to our agency today?" Or, "How can I help?" Both encourage the client to talk with you.

DEMONSTRATING EFFECTIVE ATTENDING SKILLS

Effective attending skills enable the worker to understand precisely what the client is saying, including both verbal and nonverbal communications. Attending skills have as their goal enhanced understanding between worker and client. Listening carefully is one attending skill. A common problem in novice workers is the tendency to be thinking about their next question rather than listening attentively to the client. Listening skills are learned. They require practice, focusing on both the client's words and meanings. For example, a worker might say, "Jean, you talked about Scotty's cutting class as a problem, but you also smiled as you talked." Jean then responds, "Well, I was just thinking that he reminds me so much of me at his age. I hated school and usually hung out with my friends." By pointing out a discrepancy between the client's verbal and nonverbal communication, the worker is demonstrating interest in the client's situation as well as evidencing effective attending skills. Moreover, she may have discovered a factor in why

Scotty skips school, namely tacit parental support or at least mixed communication.

Other attending skills include making eye contact with the client, leaning forward to communicate interest, and nodding or otherwise encouraging the client to continue. Of course, there is always the potential for attending behaviors to cause problems. For example, direct eye contact is considered rude by some cultures, and nodding may confuse clients into thinking you are agreeing with what they are saying. Common behaviors such as handshakes or touching of a female client by a male worker can be considered extremely rude and a violation of religious tenets by Muslims. The key is always to pay attention to see whether your responses and actions are facilitating or discouraging the client's communications.

Attending skills also allow focusing on both client thoughts and feelings. Sometimes, clients are unclear about what they are thinking and feeling. A worker may say something like, "You sound really angry about Hansel's behavior," and the client might respond with, "I think it's just terrible the way he acts." By listening carefully to what emotions are expressed or evident, the worker can help the client recognize these as well. Clients may even need help understanding the difference between what they are thinking and what feelings accompany those thoughts. The ultimate goal of this exchange is to communicate to clients your interest in them and your willingness to explore both feelings and thoughts.

Questions used during this phase should be open-ended, designed to offer clients an opportunity to discuss and expand upon their thoughts and feelings. This period is not the time to reach a decision but rather a time to understand the client. Ask, "How did that make you feel?" rather than, "Did that make you mad?" Try, "Describe what that was like," instead of, "That sounds awful." Let the client articulate the problem. Use closed-ended questions to gather data such as birth dates, ages, and addresses or when trying to pin down exactly what the client wants.

Use silence as necessary to allow the client time to think about your questions or comments. Although it may be uncomfortable at first, silence can be useful to help clients consider their thoughts and feelings without the worker needing to fish for these items.

Take notes of information you are unlikely to remember but always discuss this with the client. You might state, "I'd like to take a few notes while we talk. What you're telling me is important, and I want to be sure I get the key ideas down. Will that be OK?" Do not let the note-taking distract you or the client from the main task.

DISCUSSING AGENCY SERVICES AND CLIENT EXPECTATIONS

Sometimes, clients come to the worker with totally unrealistic ideas about what the agency or practitioner can or will do. Part of the purpose of the engagement phase is to help the client realistically assess whether the worker and agency can help. The worker should describe the services offered by the agency, any costs involved, and the possible length of such services. If the agency's services do not match client needs, helping the client find an appropriate agency or organization that can help is your responsibility. Making a referral may be the best outcome of an engagement phase when your agency cannot help. Chapter 15 discusses some basic guidelines for making appropriate referrals.

If you are asked a question about the agency you cannot answer, tell the client you do not know. Admitting ignorance is good role modeling. You can always get the information later. After all, you want to empower the client, and learning that the worker is just as capable of lapses in memory or knowledge can sometimes help.

DECIDING IF THE AGENCY AND WORKER CAN HELP

Your responsibility is to accurately convey the nature and extent of help available. Only when they are informed about what is available can clients' choices be exercised. Having a choice is critical to empowerment. Sometimes, the agency offers services that are related but not directly concerned with the client's problem. Perhaps you can advocate for change within your own agency to see that a given service is provided, which is especially important if numerous clients all need a service that is not currently available. You should answer clients' questions or get them the information they need. If the agency cannot be of service, offering to make a referral is appropriate. Again, the choice is up to the client. A client should never be in the situation of thinking a service is available only to find out later that it was not. The provision of correct information is key to this part of the engagement process.

OFFERING AGENCY AND WORKER SERVICES TO THE CLIENT

Once clients are well informed about the services available, they must decide if a continued relationship with you or your agency is desirable. Clients must feel free to make that decision without the worker's interference. There are exceptions to this rule, however. Involuntary clients may not have much freedom to reject an agency's services. A convicted child molester may be required to undergo treatment. An abusive husband may be ordered to participate in anger management sessions by a court or probation agency. In these situations, maximizing client freedom and sense of empowerment is still desirable. Although choice may be reduced to selecting the night of the week when sessions will be attended, having some choice is still preferable to none at all.

ORIENTING THE CLIENT TO THE HELPING PROCESS

If the engagement process is handled appropriately, the early stages of it should model the helping process. A willing and active listener coupled with a committed client should be a given. Sometimes, additional clarification is needed. A worker might ask a client, "Do you have any questions about what will go on during these group meetings?" The client can then respond by asking for information. If clients mistakenly assume that the worker will ask questions to better understand their problem and then will give them a magic answer, they will be disappointed and angry to discover how the helping process really works. If, on the other hand, the worker clearly indicates that the practitioner and client will share their respective expertise about the problem, this process makes a good beginning. After all, clients are already experts on their own difficulties as well as what resources they have employed. Part of the function of the helping relationship is to explore, locate, or build additional resources and to help the client draw upon these for problem resolution.

The clients also need to know the rules and conditions under which help is given. Laws, policies, and professional ethical standards may need to be discussed so that clients are apprised of their rights. Workers should never promise complete confidentiality unless the laws of the state and agency policy provide for it. Usually, clients should know that their communications with the worker may be shared with a supervisor, law enforcement agency, insurance company, or others as needed.

Finally, workers should negotiate with clients such matters as frequency of sessions, as well as time and place of meetings. They should also discuss the total number of sessions.

COMPLETING REQUIRED PAPERWORK

All agencies have paperwork. Sometimes, the generalist social worker seems to be buried in paper. Clients may need to sign contracts, insurance forms, release-of-information forms, and other documents needed for service. The worker should help in this process by explaining the forms, answering any questions, and indicating the degree of confidentiality in which these documents will be held. Agency records may be subpoenaed, and all forms in the record will be available for others to see; clients should know this fact. At the same time, the chances of being subpoenaed are relatively rare with any particular case. Clients should be aware of this rarity as well. The kinds of documentation that must be completed depend a great deal upon the agency and its policies. Many agencies maintain electronic systems for recording data about clients. These management information systems are critical, and one of the first things you will learn as a generalist social worker is what is required of you when recording client information. Chapter 16 on recording will help familiarize you with some of the paperwork records that are maintained by agencies. As demanding as the need to maintain records can be, it is part of your professional role as a social worker. It also demonstrates to your colleagues your effectiveness in written communications. The previous steps are generally common to all engagement processes no matter where they occur. The diverse nature of generalist practice, however, can affect where this engagement process actually occurs. Although the face-to-face meeting between worker and client located in an office setting is common, it is certainly not the only place where engagement may occur. Sometimes the first step in engagement happens over the phone when a client solicits help. Crisis phone services, for example, can be provided without face-to-face contact. Similarly, the initial client contact with a worker may involve a lengthy phone conversation where some elements of the engagement process are completed telephonically.

Additionally, many engagement processes occur during home visits. Here the courtesy and respect shown in the office are compounded because the meeting place is the client's home, no matter how poorly kept or sparsely furnished. Asking permission to sit and commenting positively about such things as family pictures, drawings, and other child-produced artwork is good practice. There is generally a good deal less privacy in the home than in the office, which you should anticipate. If concentrating is impossible because, for example, of a loud television, you may ask to have the volume lowered so that you can better hear the client. Remember that the situation you are in may be an accurate reflection of everyday life in this household; use this information as part of the assessment process described later in this chapter.

Finally, some interviews may occur in other settings. For example, you may interview a patient dying from an AIDS-related sickness in a hospice or hospital. Having an elderly nursing home client may mean that the engagement process takes place there. You might conduct the engagement process in a school, prison, or other institutional facility. It could occur on a downtown street or in a community center. The engagement process may be begun, conducted, and completed in any number of nonoffice or nonhome locations.

Many of the factors that clients consider successful in a helping relationship begin in the engagement phase of social work. For example, clients are more likely to view their working relationship with the practitioner as positive if the worker is seen as flexible, nonjudgmental, accessible, willing to go the extra mile, and treats the client as an equal (Kadushin & Kadushin, 2013). If the engagement phase is completed appropriately, both you and the client will be ready to take the next step: assessment.

LO 5-2 Assess Goals Prior to Intervention

EP 2.1.4a&b

Assessment is the second step in the planned change process. It involves defining the problem, identifying contributing factors, and recognizing what can be done to reduce or eliminate the problem. The generalist social worker evaluates problem situations within an environmental perspective (see Highlight 5.1). A problem involves not only individuals and families, but also the larger communities and systems in which these people live. From the onset of the planned change process, generalist practitioners focus on problems and issues from the macro and mezzo perspectives, in addition to the micro.

It is important to keep in mind that the assessment process begins at the moment we meet the client whether it is an individual, family, group, or larger system. In many ways, assessment is a largely internal process through which the social worker begins to put together the pieces of the puzzle with a goal of understanding the person in the environment (Kadushin & Kadushin, 2013). At various points along the way, workers will share with the client system their understanding and ask for reactions. This feedback helps further sharpen the assessment and begins to lead to a plan.

People are dramatically affected by the individuals, groups, and organizations around them. A young child may be devastated by a sharp scolding from a parent. The presence or lack of friends and social supports within an office environment may affect whether people love or hate their jobs. Which president is elected may affect the amount of taxes an individual is required to pay, the types of freedom a person can enjoy, and the absolute quality of life itself. Assessment can be considered from several perspectives. First, we can assess individuals and families, considering such factors as transactions between and among clients, family members, friends, and other systems in the immediate environment. We can look at the actual functioning of a family, its strengths, culture, and customs. Finally, we can look at the environment and its impact on the individual or family.

Hooyman and Kiyak (1999) suggest that people function best when their "environmental press" exceeds their capacity to adapt by a small margin. This small difference challenges the person to new accomplishments and builds his or her strengths for future events. However, challenges in the environment that overwhelm the client are often the basis for the client's involvement in the social service process. The overload produced by the client's environment effectively prevents him or her from being able to have a good quality of life (Byrnes, Lichtenberg, & Lysack, 2006). Family crises, for instance, may be so great that the client is no longer able to use the tools that previously worked well in problem situations. Loss of income from being unemployed may also overwhelm the capacity of the individual. On the other hand, environmental challenges that are well below the client's ability to adapt may produce boredom, dependence on others, and learned helplessness. For example, clients who are employed in jobs below their level of competence or education (underemployed) are also likely to be unhappy. Practitioners need to understand clearly the role that environmental stressors play in creating problems encountered by clients.

Second, focusing on functioning at different points in the life cycle is also possible. For example, the challenges of childhood and adolescence present different potential problems than does adulthood or the aging

The Difference Between Diagnosis and Assessment

Social work education in the early 1900s was very different from what it is today. From the 1920s to the 1960s, most social work programs used a medical model to understand human behavior and human problems.

The medical model views clients as *patients*. The social worker's first task is seen as making a *diagnosis* as to the causes of a patient's problems and then providing treatment. The diagnostic process is analogous to how physicians work. Namely, medical doctors will examine patients to identify problems. Problems are viewed as illnesses or diseases based inside the patient.

In the 1960s, social work began questioning the usefulness of the medical model. Environmental factors were shown to be *at least* as important in causing a client's problems as internal factors, if not more. During this time, social work shifted its attention from individual pathology (i.e., the idea that there is something wrong with the client) to problems in the client's environment. Social workers began to identify inequities and unfair treatment to which clients were subjected. The need to advocate for clients oppressed by systems and to try to change or reform these systems became paramount. Social workers began to assess problems by viewing clients in their situations instead of *diagnosing* what was wrong with the clients themselves.

Assessment differs from diagnosis in at least four major ways. First, environmental surroundings, which include the mezzo and macro aspects of the client's situation, are considered as important as the micro aspects when trying to understand any problem situation.

Second, because problems may exist outside of the client, outside systems can become targets of change.

In other words, organizational policies or public laws may be the source of the problem. Thus, social workers often focus their efforts on changing these laws rather than trying to "cure" clients.

The third major difference between diagnosis and assessment involves the client's involvement in the planned change process. Using the medical model, a client is diagnosed as having a problem. Then a social worker provides some kind of therapy to help cure the client. The client responds to therapy and thus expends some effort. However, the client is the target of change, rather than a partner in the change process. Assessment in generalist practice emphasizes that practitioners work *with*, not *on*, clients. The social worker and client work together in the change process. Both work to assess the problems, both inside and outside an individual client's life. Thus, both can work together to make changes and solve the problem.

The fourth primary difference between diagnosis and assessment concerns the approach to clients' strengths. Diagnosis focuses on pathology. What are the problems? What's wrong with the individual client? Assessment, on the other hand, targets not only the client's problems, but also the client's strengths. Emphasizing strengths allows the social worker to tap both clients' growth opportunities and their sense of competence.

In summary, social work's focus on assessment rather than diagnosis is one of the dimensions that makes social work unique. Assuming an approach that stresses analysis of mezzo and macro systems in addition to micro provides a very different view of the world and of how that world might be improved.

---

process. Whereas adolescents must deal with issues of peer pressure, sexual development, and independence, older adults are grappling with different concerns. For a large percentage of seniors, religion and spirituality issues are major themes in their lives as they face declining health, physical challenges, loss of loved ones, and their own impending death (Couture, 2012; Nelson-Becker, Nakashima, & Canda, 2003). Yet each stage in the human life cycle involves tasks, stresses, strengths, and resources that can be the focus of assessment.

Third, specific problems can be the focus of our assessment. These problems include disorders such as depression, substance abuse, and behavioral problems of children and adults. Different approaches and, perhaps, instruments are available to assist in assessing these areas. This chapter will describe one such instrument used with clients struggling with alcoholism.

The techniques and assessment methods used by social workers run the gamut from micro to mezzo to macro situations. Some assessment approaches require graduate education and are less appropriate for generalist practitioners. Of course, ethnic, racial, and cultural factors may play a role in assessment. For example, a worker may assume that a client or family will display a particular pattern of behavior because of ethnic background and allegiance. This assumption could lead to an inaccurate assessment. The fact that a client, family, or other group being assessed belongs to a particular ethnic group must be considered as an additional variable in assessment just as age and gender. Chapters 12 and 13 provide information that will assist in understanding the role these factors may play in assessment and practice.

APPROACHING ASSESSMENT

EP 2.1.10e

Accurate assessment of the person, problem, and situation is well documented as a critically important step in the social work process (Kadushin & Kadushin, 2013). Information about the problem or situation needs to be gathered, analyzed, and interpreted. Such situations may involve parents who have difficulty controlling the behavior of their children or families not receiving the public assistance they desperately need. Regardless of the type of situation, careful thought is necessary in order to make effective decisions about how to proceed.

Assessment in generalist practice should always involve four considerations. These include micro, mezzo, and macro dimensions of a client situation, in addition to aspects of human diversity. This chapter will focus primarily on the first three. Chapter 12 covers human diversity more thoroughly. Each dimension requires a focus on two broad categories of information. The first involves clients' problems and needs. The second is clients' strengths. Figure 5.1, originally proposed in Chapter 1 (the Generalist Intervention Model), illustrates this approach.

Before describing specific assessment techniques, five major points need to be made. First, *involvement of the client is absolutely essential.* To formulate in your own mind what you think the client's problems really are is tempting; however, these formulations may differ radically from what the client sees as the problems. For example, you might determine that the client has an alcohol addiction problem. The client, however, may feel that the real problem is abject poverty. To him, drinking provides an escape from his stark, cold reality. Thus, part of the art of social work intervention is to view any problem from a variety of perspectives and to develop a mutually agreed-upon plan.

A second major point is that social work *assessment always involves making judgments, sometimes with insufficient or incomplete information.* Life would probably be easier if there were a recipe book for problem solutions—you could look up some designated problem and follow a clearly specified, step-by-step process to reach a solution. However, we know that people, their lives, and their situations are complicated. Each configuration of strengths, weaknesses, and issues is different. You need to make decisions regarding what appears to you to be relevant and what does not. This decision making involves isolating certain aspects of a problem for assessment and intervention. It also involves prioritizing what you feel is important to pursue. On the one hand, this process is not always easy. On the other hand, it is one of the things that makes social work so interesting.

The third significant point to be made about assessment involves *strengths.* We have already established that highlighting strengths is one of the striking ways assessment differs from diagnosis. You have clients because they have problems. Therefore, concentrating on these problems is easy. One cannot emphasize enough how attending to strengths is as important, perhaps more so, than attending to problems. Strengths provide you with an already available means of finding solutions.

A fourth important point about assessment is that *a single, clear definition of the problem may not exist.* Later we will explore the complexity and variety of problems social workers address. Doing the best you can to identify, define, and prioritize problems is the task of a skilled social worker. Frequently, it is not an easy task as problems can be vague and multifaceted. Even problems are not perfect.

A fifth major point is that *assessment is a continuous activity.* We identify assessment as the second step in planned change, which it is. However, because problems, strengths, and issues can be vague and aspects of any situation can change over time, social workers must be vigilant. They must regularly fine-tune, modify, or even make major changes in their plans and interventions. They must continue to make judgments about what might be the most effective plan and intervention approach as time goes on. In other words, as a generalist practitioner, you may need to focus on and assess different aspects of a client's situation as your work with that client progresses. Social workers must be infinitely flexible.

Figure 5.2 illustrates assessment as an ongoing process. Arrows below each of the other planned change steps lead back to the assessment phase.

A single, pregnant teenager provides one example of the importance of assessment as an ongoing process. When the young woman initially discovers her unplanned pregnancy, you may need to help her evaluate

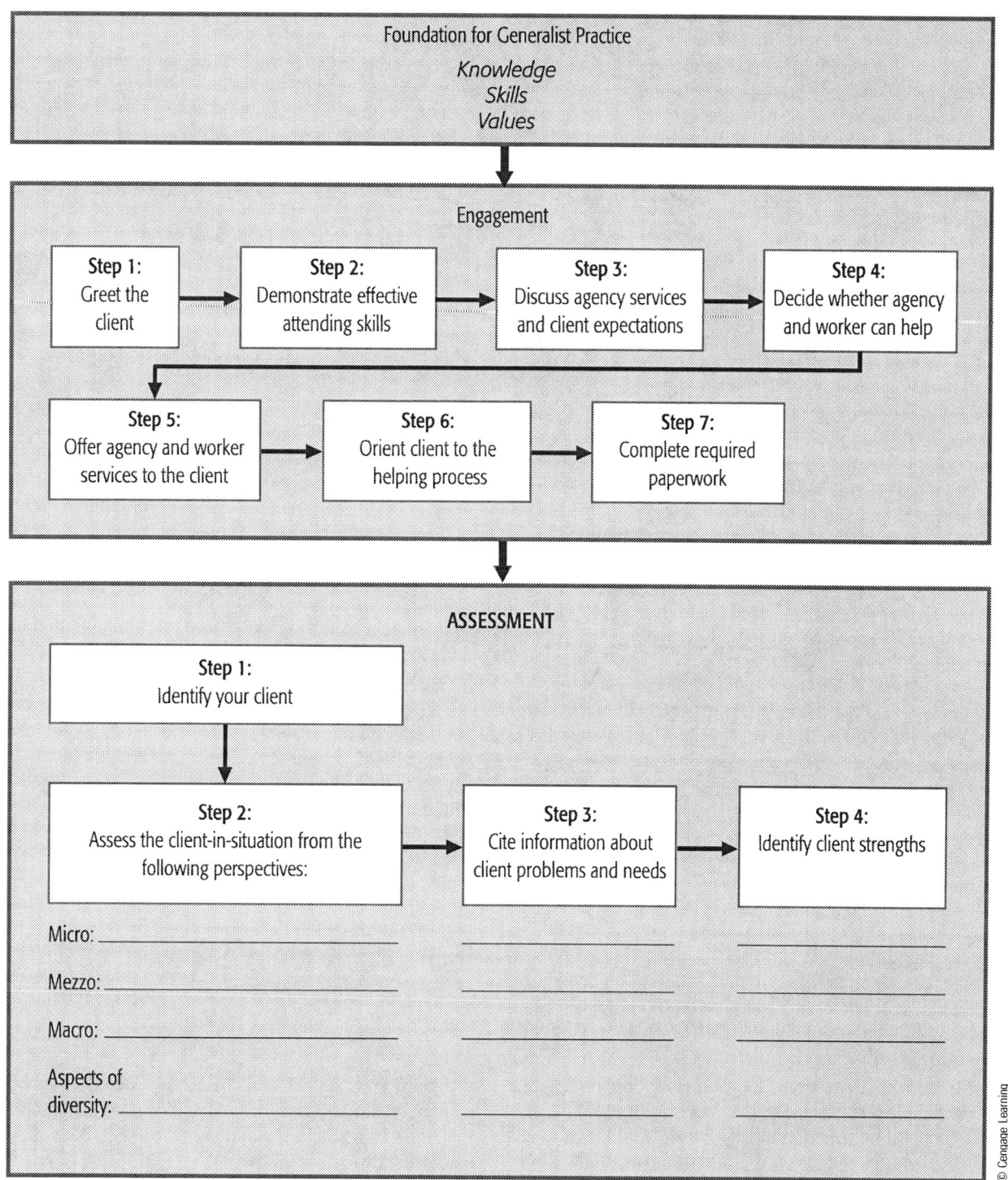

FIGURE 5.1 Assessment in the Generalist Intervention Model (GIM)

FIGURE 5.2 Assessment in Planned Change is an Ongoing Process

her various alternatives (abortion, adoption, or keeping the baby). If her decision is to have and keep the baby, your focus of attention changes. You would then likely decide to assess her current environment. From a micro perspective, this assessment would include health and nutritional status. You might also assess her family relationships and support systems. If you deem support lacking from a mezzo perspective, you might refer her to a support group of other single, pregnant teenagers. Finally, from a macro perspective, you might assess the programs and services available to her and other young women in similar circumstances. You may determine that they can function as strengths for her. You then would try to involve her with the appropriate services and resources. On the other hand, if you found resources lacking, you might turn your attention to assessing and improving these resources.

Assessment is a process that involves critical thinking skills and should reflect best practice in social work. This means that the social worker must employee assessment methods and tools that are valid and carefully evaluate information that is gathered about the client. It is important not to overstate the effectiveness of services provided by your agency and to inform the client about all options available. It is wrong to ignore possible adverse consequences that might occur if the client decides to employ your services. You can also invite clients to correct you when you say something that they feel is inaccurate or does not apply to them. These approaches will help ensure that your assessment will result in an accurate picture of the clients and their situations and that your work with them is consistent with best practice in the social work field.

Critical Thinking Questions 5.1

Consider the following scenario. You are a social worker at a social service agency responsible for doing intake interviews with new clients. A women in her late 20s has asked to see you about some problems she is having in her home. She tells you that she has been depressed since the birth of her child 6 months ago. In addition, her husband is out of work and is angry all of the time. She is afraid he will become violent toward the baby but also talks about how it would have been better if they had never had the child, given the family's current situation.

* Who is the client?
* Is this a case that requires an individual assessment, a family assessment, or both? Why?
* What strengths are evident in this scenario?

ACHIEVING THE GOALS OF ASSESSMENT

During any assessment, the generalist practitioner should aim to accomplish several goals. First is achieving a clear understanding of the need, problem, or situation that will be the focus of work with the client. For example, is the problem drug dependency, drug dealing, child abuse, marital interaction, truancy, or lack of resources? How the worker frames the problem provides direction for intervention.

Second, it is critical to recognize the strengths, assets, skills, and abilities that clients bring to the client–worker relationship. These may include persistence, spiritual resources, motivation, intelligence, and commitment to others, as well as a close experience dealing with the problem at hand, among many others. These strengths will be crucial during your work in the planned change process.

Third, it is important to formulate a clear description of the client system. This is true whether the client system is an individual, family, support group, social services agency, or a community. On whose behalf is the worker intervening? Does the delinquent child, parents, or the entire family compose the client system? Is the worker trying to get resources for a single family or an entire community?

Fourth, the generalist practitioner needs to understand the client system's interactions with other systems. Is the client system isolated or estranged from friends, family members, or significant others? Is the client system connected to any support networks? Has the community been deprived of adequate county, state, and social service support and resources?

Fifth, a practitioner must identify any missing information that is important for better understanding the situation. Missing information could range from psychological tests results, medical examination details, opinions or positions of significant others, and data available from community agencies to any other data that will help complete the assessment. The types of missing information sought will probably depend on whether the client system is an individual, family, group, organization, or community.

Finally, it is critical to put all of the information together. We assess client situations in order to formulate intervention plans. In turn, plans provide guidelines to help solve client problems. This process involves making a number of judgments and prioritizing different aspects of the situation. Likewise, the practitioner must decide whether intervention is best approached from a micro, mezzo, or macro perspective or some combination.

LO 5-3 Use Practice Behaviors Such as Defining and Describing Problems

ASSESSING FROM A MICRO PRACTICE PERSPECTIVE

This section will focus on assessment of individual client systems. First, how to define the problem will be described. A classification of common problem areas will then be identified, and a number of areas targeting potential client strengths will be recognized. Finally, a variety of assessment instruments for assessing individual characteristics will be discussed.

Defining Problems and Issues

To begin assessment, the client system must be clearly identified. Problem definition immediately follows.

First, the worker must recognize the client's unmet needs. What does the client lack that is causing a problem? Second, the worker must identify the barriers that prevent the client's needs from being fulfilled. Third, the worker must determine the capacities, strengths, resources, and motivations that are present in the client and/or environment. Problem definition is important because it provides direction for the worker for proceeding with planning and intervention. It is often helpful to look at the problem in terms of what needs are lacking. Thus, the problem for a homeless client is lack of shelter. The worker knows that one intervention goal will be to meet that client's unmet need of locating some kind of shelter.

Types of Problems

Being aware of the types of problems clients typically have is important for generalist practitioners. As a worker, you need to know what to look for and what areas to assess. Here, we will look at 10 categories of problems commonly confronting clients (Hepworth, Rooney, Rooney, & Strom-Gottfried, 2013; Karls & O'Keefe, 2009).

One should note that micro, mezzo, and macro aspects of practice are frequently intertwined. Therefore, identifying any particular category of problems with only one of these practice perspectives is not possible. For example, take a person addicted to cocaine. From the micro perspective, a worker would focus on the personal habits and impact on the individual. The mezzo perspective, on the other hand, would accentuate the addicted client's interactions with the people close to him or her. Additionally, it would address the impact the addiction was having on these people because family, friends, work groups, and neighbors might all be affected by the client's behavior. Finally, a macro perspective would direct attention to the major social problems in society that foster cocaine addiction, the ease with which cocaine can be purchased, and the treatment services available to the client.

Similarly, Olesen, Butterworth, Leach, Kelaher, and Pirkis (2013) have identified the impact that job loss has on one's mental health and relationships within families. They concluded that mental health is both a result of and a risk factor for unemployment. Such job losses often result from corporate downsizing or attempts by companies to wring increased profits from their operations. Although shifting a manufacturing plant from the United States to another country might make financial sense for the company, it can

have devastating impacts on the individual, family, and community. In both assessment and planning stages, the generalist practitioner must be acutely aware of how global or national trends at the macro level significantly affect the micro and mezzo levels.

Another example involves people with disabilities. Kim and Canda (2006) point out that focusing on the individual without attending to the macro level is approaching disability from a medical model of practice. It tends to identify problems as rooted in the fact that the client has a disability rather than looking more broadly at the situation. Social workers must use a holistic perspective that looks at the client within an environment that can oppress and prevent the client with an impairment from full participation in society. Assessment that recognizes and addresses systemic barriers encountered by the client with an impairment is consistent with the goal of empowerment.

Interpersonal Conflict. The first category of problems involves "interpersonal conflict" (Karls & O'Keefe, 2009, p. 373). These problems involve individuals having difficulty relating to each other. A delinquent teenager may be unable to form friendships with peers. A woman in a nursing home may refuse to cooperate with health care staff attempting to meet her serious health care needs. An adult with a developmental disability may get into frequent fights with his peers at a sheltered workshop because of his poorly developed social and communication skills. A married couple may be in almost constant verbal conflict.

Interpersonal conflicts may involve both communication and behavior. Problems may exist regarding how information is conveyed and received between two people. Likewise, problems may center on how people treat or act toward each other.

Dissatisfaction in Social Relations. Even when no overt conflict exists, people may identify unhappiness with their relationships with family and friends as a primary problem. One may feel unable to get as close to others as she would like. Another may feel that lack of assertiveness prevents his needs from being met the way he would prefer. Still another might feel unable to divorce himself from the guilt that he feels his mother imposes upon him.

Problems with Formal Organizations. Clients often report difficulties with the formal organizations with which they interact. Clients may not feel they are getting the resources they need. A Social Security check may be received late or be for an amount less than anticipated. Adequate health care services for pregnant teens may be unavailable. A client may feel that she is being treated rudely or abruptly when signing in to see her caseworker. The client may feel that she has been made to wait an inordinately long period of time to see a worker.

Difficulties in Role Performance. Sometimes, clients will face challenges in performing specific expected roles. A role is a culturally expected behavior pattern that characterizes people having a particular position and status in society. For example, people who assume the role of social worker are expected to behave in certain ways.

Most problems in role performance involve family-related roles including parent and spouse, as well as roles involving outside interactions. These might include problems functioning as an employee or in the role of student. A difficulty in role performance can best be distinguished from interpersonal conflict by the fact that role performance is more one-sided. An example is a father who is physically abusing his 5-year-old daughter because "she just won't behave." He is having difficulty fulfilling his role as parent. One intervention tactic would be to train him in more appropriate and effective child management techniques. He, not the daughter, would be the target of intervention.

Problems of Life Transition. Sometimes, clients will have problems making the normal transitions that occur in life (Hepworth et al., 2013). In other words, they will experience difficulty dealing with some major change in their lives. Such changes may include divorce, having a baby, moving to a new locale, adjusting to a new job, or coping with a loved one's death. Any of these may involve serious emotional upset and disruptions in clients' coping abilities.

Psychological and Behavioral Problems. Clients may experience mental health problems (Karls & O'Keefe, 2009). These involve a broad gamut of emotional upheavals and inappropriate, self-defeating, criminal, or uncontrollable behavior. A client may be seriously clinically depressed. Another may be struggling with anorexia nervosa, a serious eating disorder mainly affecting teens and women in their early 20s. A client may have uncontrollable *agoraphobia,* which involves a fear of being in places where escape might be difficult or problematic. This often may apply to using public transportation such as buses or subways, being in a crowd, waiting in long lines, and other scenarios (American Psychiatric Association, 2013). Individuals with this disorder often avoid situations that might cause them to panic and may be unable to venture out without someone accompanying them.

Many of these conditions affect both psychological state and behavior. Depressed people often isolate themselves emotionally and physically from others. Anorexics allow food, or the lack of it, to become the focus of their whole lives and behave accordingly. Agoraphobics experience both psychological terror and severely restricted behavior.

Inadequate Resources. Lack of adequate resources may reflect a number of deprivations of basic needs (Karls & O'Keefe, 2009). Many times, this problem is related to poverty. Without enough money, you may not be able to buy sufficient food, visit a physician when you are sick, or pay rent.

Inadequate resources may also refer to a lack of resources or services available to the client. On the other hand, the service may not exist. For example, a Native American community may have no health services available within a realistic distance, or the existing resources may not cover the need. Consider a family of six that needs a minimum of $700 each month to provide adequate nutrition. They receive only $500 in public assistance and food stamps. Thus, their need is not being met, and they are subject to inadequate resources.

Decision-Making Problems. Sometimes clients will find themselves in emotional dilemmas in which they experience serious difficulties in making important decisions (Hepworth et al., 2013). They may come upon life crises that create emotional turmoil and for which they see no positive solution. When under such duress, losing objectivity is easy. Emotional crises can blind people to their rational choices. Such emotion-laden decisions include an infinite number of scenarios: whether or not to have the baby in an unwanted pregnancy; whether or not to follow through on the divorce if the husband is unfaithful but the wife still loves him; or whether to place a person recently paralyzed in a car accident in his own home, a group home, or some other residential setting.

In any of these instances, generalist practitioners can help clients immobilized by emotion to identify the various alternatives available. Because of their training, workers can assist clients in evaluating the pros and cons of each realistic alternative and come to decisions.

Cultural and Religious Conflicts. "Cultural and religious conflicts" provide a final category of problems typically encountered by clients. Sometimes they involve discrimination and oppression by majority groups. For instance, urban African-American students may be denied access to similar educational benefits available to white suburban students. At other times, these conflicts concern difficulties in relating to and becoming acclimated into the larger society. For instance, consider the Hmong people who emigrated to the United States and Canada from Southeast Asia after the Vietnam War. They had to learn a new language and customs while still striving to maintain their own values and cultural integrity. Similarly, religious conflicts are at the heart of many problems, both in the United States and around the world. As a social worker, you may find it a challenge to work with clients who have vastly different belief systems that are anchored in their religious values. In addition, clients may feel themselves at odds with neighbors or a community that do not accept or understand their religion. This is evident in the Middle East, in Asia, and in different areas of the United States where clashes occur between Jewish and non-Jewish groups, Mormons and non-Mormons, Muslims and Christians. Recent violence in the United States aimed at different groups is one measure of the seriousness of such religious conflicts.

Prioritizing Problems. When working with actual clients, the number of potential problems may seem overwhelming. However, there are approaches for prioritizing which problem to work on first, second, and so on. Such prioritizing is part of the planning phase in the planned change process and thus will be discussed in the next chapter.

Some Final Notes. These categories of problems are intended to provide ideas about what aspects of clients' lives require assessment. They are not necessarily distinct from one another. An example is a two-parent family where the father is sexually abusing his two adolescent daughters. This situation involves at least the following: difficulties in role performance, dissatisfaction in social relationships, and psychological/behavior problems.

LO 5-4 Assess Client Strengths and Limitations

EP 2.1.10e

Saleebey (2013) and Bertolino (2010) emphasize the importance of identifying strengths in the assessment process. Strengths can include anything the client is good at, all those people in a client's life who can provide assistance, and any other identifiable resource. Strengths can be divided into the following seven categories:

1. family and friends;
2. education and employment background;
3. problem-solving and decision-making skills;
4. personal qualities and characteristics;
5. physical and financial resources;
6. attitudes and perspectives; and
7. miscellaneous other strengths.

Family and Friends. Does the client have family and friends, or both, available to provide support and resources? How motivated might these family members and friends be to help? Is their help potentially significant to assisting the client deal with the situation at hand?

For instance, consider Blake, a 9-year-old child with developmental disabilities living with his single, alcohol-addicted mother, Stephanie. Stephanie has been accused of neglecting Blake on four occasions. She has previously been told that unless she undergoes inpatient treatment for her addiction, Blake will be removed from her home. The court warns her that the removal may be permanent. Stephanie states that she loves Blake dearly and does not want to lose him. She just cannot stop her addiction on her own. She is finally willing to seek help.

The problem involves who will care for Blake while Stephanie is in treatment. Good foster homes, especially those equipped to care for children with special needs, are hard to find. Stephanie's worker explores potential support systems with Stephanie. The worker discovers that Stephanie's mother lives in the same city and has expressed willingness to care for Blake, even on a permanent basis. Additionally, Stephanie's sister Sabrina lives within several blocks of Stephanie's home. Both sister and mother are terribly concerned about Stephanie's addiction and have urged her to seek treatment many times. Although Sabrina has three children of her own in addition to a full-time job, she is willing to assist their mother in Blake's care. Both Sabrina and her mother can now serve as significant resources. In addition to taking care of Blake, they may be sources of significant emotional support as Stephanie seeks help.

Education and Employment Background. This information is especially significant in cases where unemployment or financial need is a major problem. Does the client have educational prerequisites, skills, or work experience that would qualify him or her for work with adequate or better compensation? Can skills formerly used in one setting now be transferred to and applied in a different setting?

Jennifer, age 54, provides an example. Her husband Brian died suddenly in a car crash. Not only was she emotionally distraught, but she also found herself in serious financial turmoil. Brian had handled the finances (at least she had thought he had) throughout their 21-year marriage. Upon his death, she abruptly discovered that they were deeply in debt, having lived way beyond their means for years. She suddenly needed to find a job, and fast.

Jennifer had not worked full-time since she married Brian. However, she did have a college degree in biology. For the past 3 years, she had been working for a small local hardware store. Her job was to do the ordering and keep the accounts. She had discovered that she was exceptionally good at such activities. In fact, she had revamped the store's entire accounting system. She also found she had a knack for working with computers. Such assessment of Jennifer's life experience thus established strengths including organization skills, dependability, and computer skills. These, in addition to her college degree and her mature, well-developed social skills, made her an attractive job candidate for a number of potential positions.

She initially found a job as an administrative assistant for a firm assisting companies in computer system installation. Although this was an entry-level job with relatively low pay, she soon worked her way up. Eventually, she became a consultant to companies all over the country.

The point here is that many times people have valuable skills and qualities that can be applied to jobs even when clients have never formally held those specific jobs. As the worker, you need to investigate specific qualities they have developed. Many times, people will be surprised that they do have valuable assets. You can help them clarify their strengths and the value of such strengths. Resulting enhanced self-esteem can help make clients stronger and better able to pursue their goals.

Problem-Solving and Decision-Making Skills. The extent to which clients have past experience solving difficult problems can also be useful. What means have they used to remedy similar situations before? Can this approach be used again? Assessing their handling of previous problems may provide significant clues regarding how they can proceed now.

Personal Qualities and Characteristics. Many strengths fall within the personal realm. For instance,

is your client articulate and pleasant? Intelligent? A good listener? Does the client keep appointments dependably and punctually?

Labeling and emphasizing positive qualities can educate the client about him- or herself and build self-confidence. Additionally, this information can provide clues about ways to proceed in the planned change process. For instance, will he be able to approach the landlord in a rational manner and request necessary repairs? Will she check back at the unemployment office regularly in search of work? Will his pleasant, caring manner toward others enhance his ability to make friends (despite his lack of self-esteem)? Is she well respected in her neighborhood and able to assume leadership responsibility?

Physical strengths can also be pertinent. For example, is she strong enough to accomplish a job requiring some degree of physical strength? Is the client attractive in appearance?

Health is also an important asset not to take for granted. Even for those with some physical disability, defining and emphasizing what people *can* do, instead of dwelling on what they *cannot* do, is important.

Physical and Financial Resources. Because clients most frequently stress their problems to social workers, overlooking strengths is easy. Does the client currently reside in adequate housing? What kinds of property does the client own? Does he have a car or other vehicle? Are there any savings upon which to rely? Does she have a source from which she could borrow money should the need arise? These things can provide a sense of security and continuity.

Attitudes and Perspectives. Does the client appear motivated to work on solving the problem? Has he indicated willingness to cooperate with the agency? Does she seem willing to talk and work with you? Motivation and positive attitudes toward change are critically valuable assets. Conversely, clients whose perspectives embrace a high degree of fatalism may be unmotivated to try to change, believing that they have little or no control over events in their lives. The extent to which they see themselves as victims of fate is likely to affect their motivation and belief that they can bring about change.

Religiosity and Spirituality. A client's religion and spirituality have often been overlooked during the assessment process, often reflecting the social worker's own unwillingness to broach the subject (Canda, 2006). Asking questions about these areas is just as important for the generalist practitioner as seeking information about ethnic identity, client feelings, and mental or physical health. Each is an important facet of understanding the client within the environment. Hodge (2005) promotes the use of a spiritual lifemap as a tool to help social workers better integrate aspects of spirituality into the assessment process.

Some clients maintain strong values, which sustain them during difficult times or motivate them to make changes. For instance, an extremely religious client may rely on her beliefs, minister, and fellow parishioners to help her cope with the death of her father. These avenues can provide her with strength. Likewise, parents who maintain a strong belief in the value of education can provide substantial support for a teenage son contemplating dropping out of school to join a neighborhood gang.

Clients may have spiritual beliefs that govern how they perceive negative experiences, sickness, or bad luck. They may have perspectives on what is right and wrong, responsibility for caring for oneself or others, or a basic philosophy about life in general. Ai, Evans-Campbell, Aisenberg, and Cascio (2006) found that reactions to the events of 9/11 such as turning to one's religion and faith and praying with other people were more common coping mechanisms than negative responses such as seeking revenge on the guilty or reducing Islamic immigration to the United States. Some clients may gain from working with faith-based organizations in which the added element of a religious connection augments more traditional interventions. Yoon (2006) noted that older adults who looked to God for strength or decision-making help reported greater levels of life satisfaction than those relying only on their families for social support. Harris-Robinson (2006) also reported that working-class African-American women frequently found spiritual-focused coping strategies effective in managing stress. Looking at spirituality and religious beliefs of clients during the assessment process is critical to recognizing strengths and identifying coping mechanisms that may be useful in other stages of the planned change process. Hodge (2005) identifies types of questions that you might ask clients to help better understand the role that spiritual and religious views play in their lives. These include:

- Has your relationship with God helped you understand this problem?
- How does your faith help you cope when negative things occur?
- To what extent does your church help you in difficult times?

- Are there portions of the scriptures that are particularly important to you?
- Are there individuals in your church who are supportive and helpful to you?

Miscellaneous Other Strengths. We know that each individual is unique. Thus, there are innumerable possibilities regarding strengths that may neither occur to you nor be readily apparent. Listening carefully to what clients say is important to them is invaluable. Sometimes strengths appear or develop during the course of the assessment and even during the intervention process.

For example, take Abe, age 15. He was in a special education and treatment program because of uncontrollable physical attacks on peers and some minor delinquent acts. As a child, he had been seriously physically abused by a stepfather. Thus, he was trying to cope with the awesome rage he felt within.

Abe moved in with his natural biological father upon entrance into the special program at age 13. Major therapeutic goals involved getting in touch with his feelings and in control of his temper. He became involved with Junior Achievement. There he made friends, gained confidence, and developed innovative projects. One of his other strengths was that he was exceptionally bright. By age 17, Abe returned to regular public school and later successfully graduated.

Other strengths may involve athletic ability, musical talent, acting ability, or special interests. Interests may range from collecting old beer cans to counted cross-stitch to deer hunting. Any of these may provide potential sources of satisfaction, motivation, and enhanced self-esteem.

Resistance in Assessment

Sometimes a client will indicate a degree of resistance to the results of assessment. For example, a person addicted to alcohol may object to an assessment that suggests he has a serious drinking problem, saying, "I can quit drinking anytime I choose" or "My drinking is really hurting no one." Resistance is a common occurrence among clients who are not yet sufficiently motivated to undertake change or are still coming to grips with the idea they have a problem. At other times resistance is simply a way of trying to retain control of one's life and denying anyone else the right to control one's behavior. Although resistance can be perceived as a problem, it also signifies that the person is strong enough to reject information that he deems as inapplicable to the situation. Rather than suggesting that the client is wrong in the self-assessment, the social worker can respond to the preceding statements by several methods. Simply acknowledging that the client has a different perspective on the problem is one method. You might say, "You don't see that your drinking has any effect on your life." Another response is to acknowledge, "It is certainly your choice about whether you change your drinking patterns." You might also tell the client that, "The fact that you came in to see me is a pretty good indication that you have some concerns that we might address. Rather than arguing over whether you have a drinking problem, let's start there." Becoming defensive or challenging the client about the problem is likely to be unsuccessful. It is also likely to result in a premature termination of the helping relationship if the client fears that the worker neither understands nor appreciates the client's point of view. Starting where the client is becomes an important concept in assessment.

Critical Thinking Questions 5.2

EP 2.1.3

Clients often display a degree of resistance in the process of engagement and assessment.

- In what ways might resistance be displayed by a client?
- What emotional or feeling reasons might lie behind a client's resistance?
- What emotional or feeling reactions might a social worker have to a client's display of resistance?

Which Problem Should You Work On?

EP 2.1.10 c&f

Many of your clients will have multiple problems on multiple levels. In view of the numerous categories of problems, how will you choose which to work on?

Generally speaking, problems chosen for the helping process should reflect three considerations. First, clients must recognize that the problem exists. Second, the problem should be clearly defined in understandable terms. Third, you and the client should realistically be able to do something to remedy the problem.

Deciding which problem constitutes the target problem is essential. The problem must be explicitly defined in behavioral terms so that both you and the client are clear about the scope and nature of the challenge. Additionally, the problem statement should include descriptions of behaviors that will later allow you to measure your progress and determine when you succeed in solving the problem. Chapter 6, which discusses planning and goal setting in generalist practice, elaborates further on the importance of behavior specificity.

Frequently, clients have such complex problems or so many problems that they are overwhelmed by them. Everything seems to be wrong. A helpful approach for the generalist is to use the skill of partialization. *Partialization* is breaking down a problem or a series of problems into manageable parts. The client who says his life is a mess is really describing an overall feeling he has about himself and his situation. Unfortunately, this statement does not help you much in your assessment. Knowing what specific areas of his life are going poorly is more important. Only then can you begin to gather important clues about what strengths and resources are needed to bring about a change. Thus, you might ask the client to tell you the three major areas where he feels things are not going well. You may discover that these also must be partialized into problems you can both understand and manage. Teaching clients how to use partialization as a general method for attacking their own problems can help them later when they are no longer receiving services (see Highlight 5.2).

Finally, problems should be ordered in terms of their priority to the client. This process alerts you to which problem you should address first. For example, a client may be concerned with the following problems in order of priority: paying the rent, her husband's drinking, her child's truancy, and an overweight condition that is resulting in a number of health problems. Paying the rent is probably the problem you should address first.

Ordering priorities is not as easy as it sounds. Frequently you will rank the client's problems differently than the client will. In these cases, exploring the problems with the client is up to you. You will need to establish a list of priorities satisfactory to you both. Once again, this process involves both good communication skills and making judgments.

Collecting, Organizing, and Interpreting Client Data

EP 2.1.10d

There are at least seven basic "sources of information" about your clients (Hepworth et al., 2013, p. 195). First, many agencies require clients to fill out forms to provide information. Client self-assessments can be mailed to the client prior to a scheduled appointment or completed in the office. Clients can provide

HIGHLIGHT 5.2

Examples of Questions You Can Ask during Assessment

The following are examples of the types of questions you can ask as you assess the client and his or her situation (Hepworth et al., 2013). Of course, each situation is unique. These questions are simply examples. They are merely intended to provide you with some direction regarding how an assessment interview may progress.

- "What do you feel are your major concerns at this time?"
- "How would you rate these concerns in terms of their severity?"
- "How are other people involved in this situation?"
- "Have you been involved with other agencies or received services before? If so, what were they?"
- "How do you think this particular problem affects you?"
- "In what situations is the problem most likely to take place?"
- "How often does the problem occur?"

- "How long does the problem usually last?"
- "How do you usually react when the problem occurs?"
- "How have you tried to solve the problem in the past?"
- "Has anything you've tried been at all helpful? If so, what?"
- "What do you think you need to solve the problem?"
- "What are your strengths (e.g., you work hard, have a good, supportive family, or you're easy to get along with)?"
- "Do you think any of these strengths can help to solve the problem?"
- "What kind of help or resources do you feel you need (e.g., financial, health care, legal, etc.)?"
- "What are you willing to do to solve the problem?"
- "What things about your situation are preventing you from solving the problem?"

such details as: childhood and current relationships with one's own parents, siblings, and peers; parenting expectations and behaviors; employment information; current family relationships with one's spouse, significant other, and children; sexual history information; and financial or legal data. The worker can then review the information and obtain greater detail than that which might be solicited during a standard interview.

Second, of course, as the worker you can obtain much information from clients' responses to questions during your interview. These questions are designed to elicit data that will help you in understanding what kinds of concerns the client has, gathering client interpretations of events or situations, teasing out unclear communications or messages, clarifying information, and seeking a better understanding of the situation.

The third means of gleaning information can also occur during the interview. Observe the client's nonverbal behavior. Is the client fidgeting? Does she avoid eye contact when approaching certain topics? Do nonverbal and verbal behaviors coincide? If not, this is an area of potential exploration. Nonverbal behaviors tend

to be the ones we take most seriously because they are often considered most valid. Conflicts between verbal and nonverbal communications often suggest problem areas or at least areas for concern.

Fourth, if you have the opportunity, you can observe the client's interactions with other people. Observing interaction with other family members can provide you with useful insights about the client.

Fifth, information is sometimes available from outside sources. These sources can include the client's family and friends, along with any professionals having knowledge of the client or situation. Referral sources may also be able to provide information, as will reports from other agencies that have worked with the client. With the client's permission, data from physicians, psychologists, psychiatrists, and other counselors should be sought if available.

Sixth, sometimes the client has gone through psychological and other testing. If so, what information does this provide about the client's emotional state and behavior? Later on in this chapter, we will discuss specific instruments, including the Rathus Assertiveness Scale (RAS) and an alcoholism test.

Finally, your seventh source of information is based on your own interactions with the client. Does the client react with hostility to your questions? Does he appear extremely needy or dependent? Is she speaking irrationally? Here, your own "gut reactions" may be useful. If you have certain types of reactions to or impressions of the client, the chances are likely that other people will have similar responses.

LO 5-5 Utilize Micro-Assessment Tools Such as the *Diagnostic and Statistical Manual (DSM-5)*, the Rathus Assertiveness Schedule, and an Alcoholism Test

EP 2.1.3

Multitudes of assessment instruments are available to evaluate various aspects of clients' lives. Mental health, suicide potential, assertiveness, spirituality, self-esteem, a child's need of protection from abuse, interaction between spouses, and availability of resources are among the many variables frequently assessed by generalist practitioners. Examples include the Child Behavior Checklist (http://www.aseba.org/products/cbcl6-18.html) and the Family Assessment Form from the California Children's Bureau (http://www.familyassessmentform.com/). Of course, the worker's field of practice will dictate which variables are most important to evaluate. For instance, a protective services worker must make assessments regarding the extent to which children are in danger of abuse. Likewise, a worker in public assistance must primarily assess the extent to which a client has access to financial resources.

Three assessment instruments have been selected for discussion here. They reflect the varied types of approaches to assessment available today and include some likely to be used in social work practice. The specific assessment approaches addressed here are the *Diagnostic and Statistical Manual,* the Rathus Assertiveness Schedule, and an alcoholism test.

Diagnostic and Statistical Manual (DSM-5). The *Diagnostic and Statistical Manual (DSM-5)* represents the American Psychiatric Association's (APA) official classification of mental disorders. Each disorder is labeled with a numerical code and criteria for distinguishing among various mental disorders. Mental disorders (another term for mental illness) involve impairment in cognition (thinking) or psychosocial functioning caused by one or more of a variety of factors, including physical (biological, chemical, or genetic), social, or psychological factors.

The APA originally published the manual in 1980 and periodically revises it to reflect new research and information.

As a generalist social work practitioner, you will not practice "therapy" in a private office with comfortable couches. Rather, you will intervene with clients *and* the multiple systems with which they are involved. You will probably not be called upon to make a formal assessment using the *DSM,* In other words, you will not have to figure out the specific numerical code that best reflects a client's mental status. However, you will be expected to work both with clients who have been diagnosed and with the system of other professionals working with those clients.

Mental health professionals use the *DSM-5* to assess individuals by considering specific criteria and descriptors that point to categories of disorders (APA, 2013). The goal is to clearly identify challenges facing clients as well as consider factors that help explain behavior.

The categories identified in the *DSM-5* are extensive and often are further divided into subcategories. There are 22 categories of disorders ranging from neurodevelopmental to schizophrenic disorders, anxiety to eating disorders, and sexual to personality disorders. There are also categories for problems such as substance abuse, sleep–wake disorders, trauma and stressor-related problems, to those that are caused by medication. Although the details of the *DSM-5* are too numerous and specific to be included in this text, the book remains a useful tool for understanding terminology and diagnoses used by other mental health professionals.

Together, these assessment dimensions can depict a relatively clear picture of an individual's behavior, life functioning, and emotional status. The *DSM* emphasizes characteristics of the various mental disorders without specifying causes; this process allows professionals to maintain their own theories regarding why such mental illnesses occur. It also includes information about the development and course of specific disorders.

There are several reasons why the *DSM* is relevant to social workers (Williams, 2009). First, it provides a means for a variety of professionals (e.g., nurses, psychiatrists, psychologists, and social workers) to communicate with each other about specific mental, emotional, and behavioral problems. Giving a client's problem a diagnosis makes it easier for each professional to know what others are talking about when they discuss that problem.

A second benefit of the *DSM* is its helpfulness in evaluating and treating clients with mental disorders. The manual focuses more on descriptions of the symptoms and behaviors of a particular disorder rather than on what causes that disorder. Therefore, defining the specific problem that requires intervention helps.

A third benefit is the manual's utility in teaching about mental disorders. Classifying a disorder by describing its symptoms enhances our understanding of that disorder.

Fourth, the *DSM* provides better opportunities to do research on mental disorders. For instance, it enables researchers to place people receiving treatment into specific categories. They can then investigate whether certain treatments or interventions are effective with specific disorders.

The fifth benefit of the *DSM* is the fact that it allows the gathering of statistics that can assist in planning for mental health services. If we know that depression among the elderly is growing, for example, it encourages a focus on this target population by local, state, and federal policymakers.

Generalist practitioners, however, should be critical thinkers about four factors when using the *DSM*. First, it only describes particular conditions. It does not provide intervention strategies and is only an assessment mechanism upon which specific interventions can be built.

Second, there can be some tendency to focus on the individual pathology or "mental illness" instead of on a client's interaction with the environment. The manual does avoid the use of the terms "client" or "patient" and incorporates content on cultural issues related to specific diagnoses. Earlier in the chapter, we discussed the difference between "diagnosis," a medical term focusing on individual pathology, and "assessment," which in generalist social work practice also stresses the environment's impact upon the client. Still, the manual targets individuals. There may be some tendency to "cure" the individual, rather than intervene in the systems intimately intertwined with the client. People using the manual as a formal assessment tool are primarily psychiatrists, psychologists, and "psychiatric social workers." The psychiatric tradition is rooted in the medical model. Thus, generalist practitioners must be cautious to maintain their orientation toward the environment and its profound impact on clients. As we know, this orientation is one of the dimensions that makes social work unique and special.

A third reason for wariness when using the *DSM* concerns imperfections in its categories. Professional discretion is involved in assigning diagnoses to individual clients. Individuals and their behaviors are complex and difficult to place in neat, compact categories. Questions can also be raised regarding the potential hazards of labeling people. How might such labels affect and bias expectations? Labels tend to interfere with the notion that each individual is unique, having a unique combination of strengths and weaknesses. Labels also can stigmatize clients, affecting their self-perceptions and the perceptions of others.

A fourth concern is that the latest *DSM-5* identifies some behaviors as disorders so broadly that it can result in people being diagnosed with a mental illness or disorder needlessly. This can lead to pathologizing behavior that most people would consider normal and contribute to labeling. It can also lead to overmedicating individuals who otherwise would not be considered as needing help.

Finally, the *DSM* is primarily focused on deficits. It is not a strength-based assessment tool and gives little help in identifying client resources.

Assessing Assertiveness. Assertiveness involves being able to state your thoughts, wants, and feelings straightforwardly and effectively. It concerns the ability to establish an appropriate stance between being too aggressive and too timid. Aggressiveness in this context implies taking only your needs into account. Essentially, you ignore the needs and rights of others. Timidity, on the other hand, concerns placing the needs and wishes of others far before your own. Assertiveness means striking a balance. The implication is that you take both your needs and the needs of others into account. You then try to make some objective judgment about what behavior, response, or plan of action is fair to you both.

It is important to point out that assertiveness is a valued quality in American society, but not necessarily in others. For example, in many Asian cultures, placing your own needs above those of your parents or family may be seen as rude or disrespectful. When assessing assertiveness, it is important to take into account the cultural values of the client. Teaching someone to be assertive in a way that ignores his or her cultural beliefs is probably unwise in many situations.

The Rathus Assertiveness Schedule (RAS) is an instrument composed of 30 items that measure an individual's assertiveness. It can be a useful tool to gauge clients' ability to determine how well they can speak on their own behalf assertively without aggression. The scale is illustrated in Figure 5.3.

Assessing Alcohol and Other Drug Abuse. Drug abuse involves improper use of some chemical substance in a manner that is harmful physically, emotionally, or socially. Alcohol abuse, of course, is a form of drug abuse. It can be detrimental to the user and to others. The National Institute on Alcohol Abuse and Alcoholism (2013, p. 1) reports that "each year, nearly 80,000 people die from alcohol-related causes, making it the third leading preventable cause of death in the United States. Alcohol problems cost the U.S. $225 billion each year, primarily from lost productivity, but also from health care and property damage costs." Related problems include family and social troubles, violence, aggression, and problems associated with law breaking. Alcoholism is also associated with increased risk for a variety of health problems, including stroke, hypertension, certain cancers, and mental disorders.

Directions: Indicate how characteristic or descriptive each of the following statements is of you by using the code given below.

+3   Very characteristic of me, extremely descriptive
+2   Rather characteristic of me, quite descriptive
+1   Somewhat characteristic of me, slightly descriptive
−1   Somewhat uncharacteristic of me, slightly nondescriptive
−2   Rather uncharacteristic of me, quite nondescriptive
−3   Very uncharacteristic of me, extremely nondescriptive

____   1.   Most people seem to be more aggressive and assertive than I am.
____   2.   I have hesitated to make or accept dates because of "shyness."
____   3.   When the food served at a restaurant is not done to my satisfaction, I complain about it to the waiter or waitress.
____   4.   I am careful to avoid hurting other people's feelings, even when I feel that I have been injured.
____   5.   If a salesman has gone to considerable trouble to show me merchandise which is not quite suitable, I have a difficult time in saying "no."
____   6.   When I am asked to do something, I insist upon knowing why.
____   7.   There are times when I look for a good and vigorous argument.
____   8.   I strive to get ahead as well as most people in my position.
____   9.   To be honest, people often take advantage of me.
____   10. I enjoy starting conversations with new acquaintances and strangers.
____   11. I often don't know what to say to attractive persons of the opposite sex.
____   12. I will hesitate to make phone calls to business establishments and institutions.
____   13. I would rather apply for a job or for admission to a college by writing letters than by going through personal interviews.
____   14. I find it embarrassing to return merchandise.
____   15. If a close and respected relative were annoying me, I would smother my feelings rather than express my annoyance.
____   16. I have avoided asking questions for fear of sounding stupid.
____   17. During an argument I am sometimes afraid that I will get so upset that I will shake all over.
____   18. If a famed and respected lecturer makes a statement which I think is incorrect, I will have the audience hear my point of view as well.
____   19. I avoid arguing over prices with clerks and salesmen.

continued

FIGURE 5.3 Rathus Assertiveness Schedule (RAS)

Source: D. B. Hull and J. H. Hull, "Rathus Assertiveness Schedule: Normative and Factor-Analytic Data." Behavior Therapy, 9 (1978), p. 673. Copyright ©1978 by the Association for Advancement of Behavior Therapy. Reprinted by permission of Elsevier

____ 20. When I have done something important or worthwhile, I manage to let others know about it.
____ 21. I am open and frank about my feelings.
____ 22. If someone has been spreading false and bad stories about me, I see him (her) as soon as possible to "have a talk" about it.
____ 23. I often have a hard time saying "no."
____ 24. I tend to bottle up my emotions rather than make a scene.
____ 25. I complain about poor service in a restaurant or elsewhere.
____ 26. When I am given a complaint, I sometimes just don't know what to say.
____ 27. If a couple near me in a theater or at a lecture were conversing rather loudly, I would ask them to be quiet or to take their conversation elsewhere.
____ 28. Anyone attempting to push ahead of me in a line is in for a good battle.
____ 29. I am quick to express my opinion.
____ 30. There are times when I just can't say anything.

To score:
1. Take the RAS.
2. Change the sign from positive (+) to negative (−) or negative (−) to positive (+) for your answers to the following questions: 2, 4, 5, 9, 11, 12, 13, 14, 15, 16, 17, 19, 23, 24, 26, 30.
3. Add up your total.
    a. A score of −90 to −20 means you're generally unassertive and probably too much so. The lower your score, the less assertive you are.
    b. A score of −20 to +60 indicates that you're within the realm of being appropriately assertive much of the time.
    c. A score of +60 to +90 means you're very assertive or possibly aggressive. This is a warning category.

−90	−20	+60	+90
Unassertive	Assertive	Very Assertive Maybe Aggressive	

© Cengage Learning

FIGURE 5.3 Continued

Because of the prevalence of alcohol and other drug abuse, assessing the extent to which it is a problem for a client is important for a generalist practitioner. There are numerous assessment instruments available. One is illustrated in Figure 5.4.

FAMILY ASSESSMENT

The family is a primary group sharing both a history and a future. Family members have obligations to each other and typically live in the same household. Family membership is intimate. Family members share tasks and responsibilities that contribute to the maintenance of the family's identity and functioning. On one hand, families are made up of unique individuals. On the other, each individual family member is a subsystem of the larger family system. Therefore, anything affecting an individual member also has repercussions for the entire family and all of its members.

Because of their unique qualities involving identity and intimacy, families are considered special types of groups. In one respect, families, as groups, are part of mezzo practice. In another, the importance of the family to individual clients often places family intervention within the realm of micro practice. For our purposes, we will consider work with families to lie somewhere on a continuum between micro and mezzo practice.

LO 5-6 Decide to Work with Families Following Assessment

 EP 2.1.10

Working with the family system is one of many intervention alternatives in the planned change process. A worker may choose during assessment (step 2 of the Generalist Intervention Model) to plan (step 3) and implement the plan (step 4) to address

Use the scale below to rate <u>HOW OFTEN</u> you have had any of the following problems over the past year <u>as a result of drinking alcoholic beverages.</u>

1. Feeling sad, blue, or depressed

   (1) Never   (2) Yes, but not in the past year   (3) 1–2 times
   (4) 3–5 times   (5) 6–9 times   (6) 10 or more times

2. Nervousness, irritability

   (1) Never   (2) Yes, but not in the past year   (3) 1–2 times
   (4) 3–5 times   (5) 6–9 times   (6) 10 or more times

3. Caused you to feel bad about yourself

   (1) Never   (2) Yes, but not in the past year   (3) 1–2 times
   (4) 3–5 times   (5) 6–9 times   (6) 10 or more times

4. Problems with appetite or sleeping

   (1) Never   (2) Yes, but not in the past year   (3) 1–2 times
   (4) 3–5 times   (5) 6–9 times   (6) 10 or more times

5. Engaged in unplanned sexual activity

   (1) Never   (2) Yes, but not in the past year   (3) 1–2 times
   (4) 3–5 times   (5) 6–9 times   (6) 10 or more times

6. Drove under the influence

   (1) Never   (2) Yes, but not in the past year   (3) 1–2 times
   (4) 3–5 times   (5) 6–9 times   (6) 10 or more times

7. Did not use protection when engaging in sex

   (1) Never   (2) Yes, but not in the past year   (3) 1–2 times
   (4) 3–5 times   (5) 6–9 times   (6) 10 or more times

8. Illegal activities associated with drug use

   (1) Never   (2) Yes, but not in the past year   (3) 1–2 times
   (4) 3–5 times   (5) 6–9 times   (6) 10 or more times

While this instrument is more useful for college-age adults, other instruments are designed for use with adolescents, women, and the elderly.

FIGURE 5.4 College Alcohol Problems Scale–Revised

the family as the primary target of attention. Of course, this brings up the question of when a generalist practitioner should choose to work with a family and when to work with either the individual alone or with some other external system.

There is no easy answer to this question. However, there are some variables to take into account when making an assessment and planning an intervention. First, you need to ask yourself to what extent the problem affects other family members. Second, do you have the time and resources to work with other family members?

Third, in terms of prioritizing problems, are those aspects of the problem involving other family members among the most critical to be addressed? Finally, to what extent do you think family intervention is likely to be successful?

Family Assessment Skills

EP 2.1.7a&b

We have established that the family is a special type of system. It has momentous significance concerning individual members' physical and emotional well-being. Assessing families also poses social challenges for the generalist practitioner. It is not unusual for family members to have different ideas about the nature, source, and extent of the problems they are experiencing. These differences are to be expected because each member experiences his or her familial environment differently. From these contrasting views you are to develop a real understanding of what being a member of that family is like. For example, that family members see one member as the primary "problem" or that individual members feel excluded from the family is common. Your task is to ensure that all perspectives are valued and that each member feels you are interested in his or her views. Because you have several family members, there are additional sets of strengths to consider. These include individual strengths as well as strengths that characterize the entire family. Working with the entire family, however constituted, requires you to communicate with all members, while avoiding the perception that you are "siding" with any individual or dyad in the family. Remember that you are not only assessing just the individual family members, but also the interactions among and between them. Of course, family assessments also run the risk of producing more data than you can handle, but this overabundance is inherent in the task. Working with families is a major dimension of generalist social work practice. Therefore, Chapter 9 is devoted to assessing families (additionally, Chapter 10 concentrates on skills for working with families). Only a brief summary of assessment concepts will be provided here. They include family communication, family structure, life-cycle adjustments, and the impacts of the social environment.

Family Communication. Family communication involves how well family members convey feelings and ideas to the other members. To what extent does each sender's *intent* match the *impact* on the receiver? The effectiveness of a family's internal communication is important, not only for assessment purposes, but also for planning and undertaking the intervention. Improving communication is frequently a core goal when working with families.

Family Structure. Family structure involves the organization of relationships and patterns of interaction within the family. Assessment of five dimensions of family structure is especially relevant. First, the family is *functioning as a system* that is intact with appropriate boundaries and subsystems. The second dimension involves *family norms,* the rules that specify the behavior within the family group. Third, there are *family roles* that concern both the status differential and

behavioral expectations the family has for each of its members. The fourth dimension involves the appropriate *balance of power* within the family and among its members. Finally, *intergenerational aspects* and the impact of family history upon current family functioning are vital. To help you understand and competently assess the family and its environment, it is important that you critically consider the conceptual frameworks and theories you have learned about families in past courses.

Life-Cycle Adjustments. Assessment of how the family adapts to various predictable phases of its life cycle is important. Births, deaths, marriages, and grown children's departures are included among the many events that call upon the family's coping abilities.

Impacts of the Social Environment. How good is the *family's fit* with its social environment? Does it have adequate social supports, or is it isolated? Is the family receiving satisfactory resources to survive and thrive? How well integrated is the family with its surrounding community? These and related questions are critical for assessing family functioning and planning interventions.

Key Areas of Family Conflict. Chapter 9 also examines four key areas of family conflict: marital difficulties, parent–child relationship difficulties, personal problems of individual family members, and external environmental stresses.

Family Relationships

Assessing family relationships involves understanding the entire family system. The amount of data involved in family assessments requires the use of some method for sorting out and organizing the information. Moreover, the family must be involved in this assessment and understand the potential meanings of the information. Two useful tools for gathering and helping families understand the data are the eco-map and genogram (Hartman, 1978). The eco-map provides a graphic representation of the family's ecological system. It depicts family membership and relationships and can help individuals and families recognize their own strengths and areas of weakness. Because eco-maps and genograms convey a view of the family at a particular point in time, they can also be used to monitor or evaluate changes over time. The breadth of systems reflected in the eco-map assists clients to visualize their situation from a different point of view, to suggest areas where change is needed or where resources appear to be absent, and to highlight areas of support within the broader community and environment.

Constructing an eco-map begins with a large circle at the center of a piece of paper. In that circle we place the individual members of a family. Males are identified by boxes and females by circles. Around the outside of the center circle are a series of other smaller circles representing other systems with which the family interacts. These systems might include extended family members, friends, schools, law enforcement, social welfare agencies, church, employment, and health systems. Once each significant system is entered, relationships among the various systems are depicted by a series of lines. For example, a straight solid line _____ is used for strong relationships. Weak or insignificant relationships are shown as a series of dashes. - - - - - Relationships characterized as stressful or strained are indicated by a zigzag line. Arrows along the lines indicate the direction in which energy or resources flow. Figure 5.5 shows the Ruth family eco-map. Several things are evident from this diagram. For example, the Ruth family has four children, two boys and two girls, and the Ruths themselves are middle-aged.

Anita is involved in a group for first time criminal offenders after an arrest for shoplifting last year. She says she enjoys the group, which is the family's only involvement in the criminal justice system. Anita has an IQ of 75 and works around the farm helping her dad. Mario, currently in graduate school, is a member of a gay and lesbian student organization on campus. He "came out" to his parents last year when the family was in crisis over Anita's arrest. His relationship with his dad is strained because of his sexual orientation. He does not have a partner at this time.

Mark is trying to make a living as a professional bowler. Sports are the only thing he is interested in, and he has tried his hand at baseball, football, and basketball. He hates farming, which affects his relationship with his father.

Tia just graduated from college with a degree in criminal justice. She has applied to be a police officer and is living with her parents in the meantime. Like the rest of her siblings, Tia is single.

Jan, like the rest of the family, is very much involved in the church, which provides a good deal of support. Even though she does not work outside of the home, she serves on several committees and participates in most church functions. She has a very stressful relationship with her father, as does the rest of the family. Her father engaged in sexual abuse with his daughters and now is experiencing Alzheimer's disease. He lives alone and probably will need a nursing home soon. Neither Jan nor her sister is interested in trying to help their dad. Their mother is deceased.

Jed is a farmer by occupation, but the family farming business has lost ground to agribusiness. Jed does not own enough land to make his farm profitable and figures he will eventually be forced to sell it. His single hobby is playing in an oldies-style rock band with a few of his school-days friends. Unfortunately, his hearing was damaged from years of working around loud farm machinery. Now he finds himself increasingly limited as a musician because he cannot hear some of the music the band plays, and because of his disability, he joins the band infrequently. Jed refuses to be tested for a hearing aid, claiming "they're for old folks." Jed's parents are very much involved in the family, providing emotional ties and financial help. They sold the family farm to Jed and still feel a great deal of attachment to the land.

Obviously, there are a number of relationship and resource problems facing this family. The father's reluctance to get a hearing aid is undermining one of his most important sources of support. His relationship with his two sons is problematic at this time, and he feels a great deal of stress over his failure to maintain the family farm. Jan does not work outside the home, and he worries about what changes will occur with Jan and Anita when the family has to leave the farm.

An eco-map can be helpful in displaying to families and individuals how their connections and resources actually look. It can also help remind them of the things that are or were truly important in their lives. Arrows showing a general flow of energy away from the family can help in understanding why they lack the emotional resources to deal with new crises. Changes in the eco-map over time can be used to help a family recognize the progress they are making. Whenever possible, clients should be involved in creating the eco-map because they can help the social worker organize information for an assessment.

A genogram is another useful tool for family assessment because it provides a means of depicting a family from one generation to the next. More specifically, it presents a chronological picture of the family noting such things as important events, additions and losses to the family, communication and relationship patterns, and occupational or work connections. Generally, a genogram denotes three or more generations in a family. Like an eco-map, genograms are best constructed by the social worker and family members working together. Also like eco-maps, genograms use boxes for males and circles for females. Triangles are used in the event that the sex of a person is not known. Marriage is shown as a line connecting male and female, usually with the wedding date noted. Divorces are evident by a line bisecting the marital line with the date shown. Children are listed

Male ▪ **Female** ●

—————— Connections between family and other systems

◀————— Direction of flow of energy and other resources

- - - - - - Stressful relationship

© Cengage Learning

FIGURE 5.5 Eco-Map

in chronological order from left to right. Deaths are noted by an "X" through the box, circle, or triangle, again with the date indicated. A dotted line is usually drawn around family members living in the same household. Figure 5.6 shows a typical genogram.

This genogram shows the Johnson family over two generations. Deaths of Jamal senior and granddaughter Meg are shown. Marriages and, in the case of Jamal and Gwen, divorce are evident. The pattern of giving children family names is also noticeable. From the dotted line we can see that Jared, Sheree, and Gwen are now living together in the same household. Like a family tree, a genogram can be used to record important connections between and among family members and

FIGURE 5.6 Genogram

generations. A pattern of divorces may be evident from one generation to the next as well as traditions having to do with family size. Because the information needed to construct the genogram must come from family members, the absence of information can pinpoint cutoffs between relatives. Additional information about the cause of family members' deaths may identify risk factors. Of course, a genogram can serve as a written record for all family members and may provide useful information for children to be placed for adoption (Hartman, 1978). Both the genogram and eco-map are useful tools for working with families and individuals.

Software is available to help in constructing both eco-maps and genograms. They include:

- Genopro (http://www.genopro.com/family-tree-software/)
- Relativity and Ecotivity (http://www.interpersonaluniverse.net/)

LO 5-7 Effectively Use Home Visits as an Assessment Mechanism

EP 2.1.4b

Home visits involve calling upon clients in their own homes in order to provide some type of professional service. This content is included here because of the significance home visits can have in assessing an individual family or environment. Striking information can

be gained during a home visit that is simply not available in the more sterile, agency interview situation.

One should note, however, that there are other reasons for making home visits than to do assessments. Some clients may have physical disabilities that prevent them from getting to an office setting. Perhaps the worker needs to see the client in the home situation, as often happens in child welfare situations. Home visits may be required to check up on older clients living alone or on clients with chronic mental illnesses. Sometimes, the home is simply a more comfortable place for the client who is in his or her own element. In addition, there may be times when home visits are needed to gather collateral information from members of the client's family. In some instances, social workers will be in the client's neighborhood as part of an effort to bring about social change in the environment or community. In the latter case, workers need to get involved in the community in order to gain community members' trust and commitment.

Workers' Reactions. One aspect of home visits that can be difficult for workers is the shocking nature of what people must endure as a result of their impoverished environments or their state of physical or mental health. Many social workers come from a middle-class background where there is a certain level of learned expectations regarding cleanliness and household organization. Of course, clients vary drastically regarding their values, just as any group of people varies. However,

© Cengage Learning

generalist social workers address and deal with the very worst of people's problems. Thus, there are times when workers must be prepared to look beyond extreme circumstances, remain objective, and try to see things from the client's point of view.

For instance, during her internship, one student confided in her faculty liaison about a serious problem she was having with one of her clients. Her placement involved providing supportive services to a caseload of older clients so that they might remain living in their own homes. The student would regularly visit clients and help them get groceries, pay their bills, see friends, visit physicians when needed, and complete other daily living tasks. The student described this particular client as living in an old trailer cluttered with cast-off clothing, broken furniture, and garbage. The sink was piled high with dishes filled with rotting remnants of food. Although the student found the environmental situation difficult to visit, this was not the major problem. She stated that she was horrified at how cockroaches seemed to be crawling everywhere throughout the trailer. She continued that the very last straw was seeing a cockroach crawl out of her client's ear, up the side of the woman's face, and across her forehead.

The faculty liaison acknowledged that this was an extremely difficult situation. Together with the student's agency field instructor, the student and liaison planned an evaluation of the client and her living conditions. Such evaluations were done frequently at the field placement agency. Together with the client, living conditions were assessed and decisions made. Some alternatives for this particular situation included providing the client with additional homemaker services, involving a visiting nurse to assess health conditions, considering removing the client from the trailer, and arranging for alternative living conditions. One of the things discovered was that the woman's intellectual functioning appeared to be deteriorating. This deterioration was magnified by her almost total isolation, except for the visits by people providing her with supportive services.

A major issue that the faculty liaison helped the student address involved the student's own perceptions and reactions to the cockroach situation. The student worked to shift her focus of attention from fear of the cockroaches to concern for the well-being of the client. This change in focus had to be done despite its difficulty. The client was the person who was suffering and in desperate need of help. The situation was alleviated, of course, once the cockroaches were exterminated.

Another example of a difficult home visit situation involved a 34-year-old single, extremely obese mother of four male children, ages 17, 12, 9, and 4. The 12-year-old son was currently in a day treatment center for children and adolescents with behavioral disorders. There he received therapy and special education, while residing in his own home. The 17-year-old son had spent several years in a residential treatment center for children with emotional disturbances. He currently resided in the state correctional facility for youth because, among other things, he had sexually abused his 2-year-old neighbor.

The purpose of the home visit was to assess the home situation and to talk to the mother about the 12-year-old's attendance at the treatment program. The worker functioned as the child's counselor at the program. Truancy was becoming an increasingly serious problem. After making an appointment with the mother, the worker came to the home for the interview. The mother answered the door and invited the worker inside. As in some of the other examples cited, filth was a problem.

Being behaviorally or descriptively specific regarding what is considered dirty and what is not is important. We all have different expectations concerning what level of dirt is tolerable. The worker in this situation was not renowned for her own housekeeping abilities. However, she based her observation that the house was filthy on a number of observable facts. The colors of the furniture and walls were barely discernible due to the covering of dirt. About a half-dozen odorous bags of garbage resided on the blackened kitchen floor. Dishes streaked with food remnants overflowed the kitchen sink and were scattered throughout the house. Finally, there were three or four piles of animal feces scattered about the living room floor.

The worker proceeded to discuss the truancy situation with the mother. Despite trying to use the skills she had learned, the worker was unable to establish with the client a workable plan of action. The worker then ended the interview and was escorted by the mother out of the door onto the outside porch. At this point, a small puppy standing on the porch lifted its leg and urinated directly onto the porch floor. As the worker was ending the meeting by making plans for another visit, she watched the puppy in amazement. The mother, who was also watching the puppy's behavior, looked up at the worker and said, "Well, at least he didn't do it inside the house." The worker then said good-bye and left.

This situation did indeed shock the worker, who found it hard to accept that a person could effect such little control over her own and her family's environment. This case was extremely difficult, as problems included abject poverty, depression, physical child abuse, sexual abuse, and alcoholism. Although doing a lengthy case analysis is beyond the scope of this book, this mother clearly felt she had little control over her environment. This situation was manifested by the dirty house and the urinating puppy. She felt she had little control over her children. Finally, she felt she had little control over herself. The whole point of this example is that focusing on the client and the client's problems rather than on their own uncomfortable reactions is important for generalist practitioners. This woman and her family desperately needed help.

Although dirt seems to be the emphasis in the prior examples, one must realize that many other things can be learned from a visit to the client's home environment. Two examples involve adolescent males.

The first case involves a 13-year-old. His primary problems involved his insensitivity to the feelings of others and his long history of delinquent behavior. The latter included shoplifting, battery, and theft. He was extremely bright and seemed to enjoy manipulating his peers so that they would get into trouble. For example, he would goad one peer whom he knew to be extremely impressionable into shooting a spit wad at another peer whom he knew would get angry, jump up, and try to punch the spitter. Meanwhile, he would sit back, watch, and enjoy the activity.

A home visit revealed some interesting information. He lived alone with his single mother and 17-year-old brother, the latter of whom was not very involved with the other two. His mother was very straightforward, terse, and sarcastic. She refused to answer most of the questions the worker asked. The interview was very short, due to the fact that after 15 minutes, the mother abruptly asked the worker to leave her home. The worker's impression was that she was a very cold, uncaring person who kept any emotions carefully in check. The interesting and striking observation of the home environment was that not only was each piece of furniture carefully covered with transparent plastic, but also so were the lampshades and the drapes. Additionally, there were plastic runners on the carpet over the major walkways. The rooms were spotless and covered in plastic. The worker noted that it was the coldest "home" she had ever been in.

Several implications of the home situation for the 13-year-old's treatment were established. A discovery was made that he had never had the chance to learn how to care about anyone but himself. Apparently, he had rarely, if ever, been the recipient of love, caring,

and warmth. How could he learn such feelings and behaviors if he had never experienced them? He almost seemed to lack a conscience. He made certain that he was taken care of but cared little or nothing about anyone else.

Another example of a home visit illustrated what can be learned about the family environment. This 16-year-old male client was significantly behind academically. He had also broken into several of his neighbors' garages to steal tools.

In school, he had much difficulty relating to peers but was very cooperative with staff. He never misbehaved and would volunteer for extra tasks.

A home visit revealed some interesting things about this client. He lived with his single mother and his 11-year-old sister who had Down syndrome. The family lived on the second story of an ancient house in one of the poorest areas of the inner city. The furniture was old and mismatched but neatly arranged. There was a pervasive aura of warmth throughout. For instance, crocheted doilies were carefully arranged under knickknacks and lamps. When the worker arrived, there was a pleasant aroma of something being fried in the kitchen. The walls were carefully spotted with paint designs made to look like wallpaper. Most of the other rooms had doors that led into the living room, so their walls could also be seen. Each room had similar painted designs, and each was painstakingly painted in a different color.

The mother, a short, frail-appearing woman, greeted the worker at the door with a wide smile. She proudly introduced her daughter, who had an observable developmental disability. The 16-year-old client was also in the room. When talking and answering questions, each, especially the mother and son, looked at each other, smiled at each other, and talked to each other about which answers would be most correct. At two points during the interview, the mother asked her son to get something for her. Each time he did so immediately and apparently willingly. The mother appeared to be concerned about both of her children and very willing to help.

The worker found out a lot about her 16-year-old client. Apparently, until about a year earlier, he had lived with his father somewhere in the rural Deep South. One day, for no determinable reason, his father purchased a Greyhound bus ticket for him and sent him to live with his mother in a northern urban city. It continued to be unclear how long he had initially lived with his mother before going to live with his father.

When he got to the city, he felt, frankly, like "a fish out of water," although he was African-American and lived in a primarily African-American neighborhood. He was totally unsophisticated regarding urban living. As a result, he hated school, had no friends, and resorted to stealing tools so that he would have something to do. He loved to tinker with wood and machines and seemed to have some talent in that area.

This home visit revealed much about this client. Apparently, he received much warmth and support from his mother. It also appeared he was in no way a discipline problem for her. Intervention implications for this client involved examining his interpersonal skills and interactions with his peers. Among other things, he needed to build his self-confidence. Other implications concerned improving his academic performance and looking at possible vocations involving skilled trades.

Scheduling Home Visits. Home visits should be at a time as convenient as possible for family members. Often this convenience is not during typical 9-to-5 office hours. Evenings or even weekends might be the only times family members are usually home. In such cases, having a job where such flexible scheduling is possible is helpful. Otherwise, you must work overtime or accept the fact that some home visits are impossible to make within your job specifications.

Home visits can be scheduled by phone. During the initial conversation, you should identify who you are and clearly state the purpose of the visit. For instance, you would like to talk about the Hamptons' son's progress in school.

Some clients will not have phones, which makes arranging for a visit more difficult. In this case, one possibility is to write to the family and schedule a time that you anticipate to be most convenient for them. Simply notify them that because you cannot contact them by phone, you would like to meet with them at a specific time and date in their home. You might then ask them to notify you if that time is bad for them. You also might ask them to suggest another time that they feel is better.

Sometimes, this suggestion will not work. For example, a social worker attempts to visit a family four times without success. Each time, he notifies them by mail as suggested earlier. Each time, he stops by their house and rings the doorbell to no avail. They are either not at home or are not answering the door. The bottom line is that they simply did not want to see him, for whatever reason. On this occasion, he has to accept the fact that he will be unable to make this particular visit.

Taking Care of Your Own Safety. Considering your safety when visiting various areas and neighborhoods is important. Some areas are simply rougher than others. You must weigh the extent to which you need or are required to make a home visit against the potential danger in which it will place you. For instance, a home visit in a gang-ridden, urban neighborhood at night is a bad idea.

You should also be aware of areas with high crime rates and take as many precautions as possible. Be aware of where you are and who is around you. If ethnic tensions are high and you are a minority person in that neighborhood, being aware of this fact is especially important.

Doing a risk assessment should be part of your thinking when you are working away from your office (Siberski, 2003). For example, risk can come in many forms. These might include environmental factors (snow, ice storms) that could threaten your getting to and from your appointment, as well as potential threats from other people. This could include clients with a history of violence, stalkers, people currently using drugs or alcohol, or those who experience mental illnesses that include psychotic behavior. Knowing something about one's client ahead of time is one way of assessing the risk involved. Clients that have used verbal threats in the past are likely to do so again. In fact, this is one of the most commonly reported situations faced by social workers and other helpers (Blank, 2005). Blank (2005) offers some suggestions for situations that become volatile:

- Remain outwardly calm regardless of how you feel inside. Do not show anger, anxiety, or fear.
- Remain respectful toward the individual who is threatening.
- Continue to face the aggressor and do not turn away from the person. Back up if needed to put some physical space between you and the other individual.
- Use a calm voice in talking with the individual. Avoid trying to outshout or screaming at the individual, as this can lead to further escalation.
- If the client is standing, ask him or her to sit down to talk with you. Sitting posture tends to be less threatening both to the aggressor and the one being threatened.
- Avoid defensiveness or taking the person's anger personally. It is not always about you.

- Be honest in what you say and do not try to promise something that you cannot deliver, such as immediate return of a child, avoidance of consequences for the client's behavior, and so forth.
- Use appropriate empathy toward the individual's feelings.
- If de-escalation is not working, ask the person to stop or remove yourself from the situation.

This warning is not meant to scare you. Neighborhoods, as we know, vary drastically regarding these safety issues. Being aware of facts and making rational decisions is vital. Highlight 5.3 provides an example of a potentially dangerous case, and Highlight 5.4 lists a number of safety tips.

LO 5-8 Assess Both Task and Treatment Groups

TASK AND TREATMENT GROUP ASSESSMENT

In the assessment process, a generalist practitioner identifies a need and then may determine that this need can best be met through formulating and working with a group of individuals. Needs can potentially involve almost any issue. A category of clients may have some kind of treatment need because of problems they

have (e.g., alcohol addiction, incest, or lack of assertiveness). There might be a need to structure a group within an agency to revise policies. There may be a need to formulate a group for lobbying a state legislature to provide more funds for day care.

In Chapter 3, we recognized the two major types of groups: task and treatment. Task groups, of course, are designed to accomplish some specified task or goal. Treatment groups, on the other hand, focus on goals targeting growth, remedying problems, providing education, or enhancing socialization (Toseland & Rivas, 2012).

Assessment in groups is an ongoing process carried out prior to the group's formation, throughout intervention, and after completion of the group (Toseland & Rivas, 2012). As we know, assessment and evaluation are two sides of the same coin. During the initial assessment phase, problems, strengths, and needs must be clearly established so that progress may later be evaluated. Regardless of the type of group, two dimensions must be the first focus of attention: potential sponsorship and potential membership.

Potential Sponsorship

Almost all practitioners function under position descriptions, summaries of the duties and responsibilities inherent in the particular worker's job. Working with task and treatment groups may or may not

---

HIGHLIGHT 5.3

Avoiding a Dangerous Situation

Anna Flactic was a child welfare social worker charged with locating, training, and licensing foster parents. She received an application to become foster parents from the Dodge family, who indicated they were interested in caring for school-age children and adolescents. Anna phoned the Dodges to schedule a home visit later that day. During the visit she would talk to the Dodges more fully about the responsibilities of being a foster parent, and ensure that the home met minimum standards, and had adequate room for a foster child.

One of the requirements to be a foster parent involved providing several references, which Anna would typically call before making a home visit. The Dodges listed three people to contact and Anna phoned each of them. The first two references said the Dodges would provide a good home for foster children, but it was the third refer-

ence that worried Anna. He mentioned in passing that Anna's agency already was familiar with the family but offered no more information. Anna could find no current record of the family receiving services and then remembered that the agency had stored older files in the basement. When she checked this source, she was shocked to learn that the family had been reported for child abuse several years before. When the protective service worker came to the house, Mr. Dodge met her at the door with a gun. Anna quickly realized that making a home visit to this family could place her at risk, especially because of the prior relationship between the Dodges and her agency. She talked it over with her supervisor and they decided to notify the Dodge family by letter that they would not be licensed as foster parents. Anna learned a lesson in taking care of her own safety.

HIGHLIGHT 5.4

Taking Care of Yourself

Social work by its very nature involves working with populations and in areas that engender some risk. Social workers have been killed, assaulted, or otherwise harmed while on the job. The risks tend to be higher when out of the office making home or collateral visits. Potential sources of harm can include clients, their family members or significant others, and complete strangers. While it is impossible to protect yourself from all danger you might encounter in social work, there are some steps you can take to lessen your risk. They require you to act sensibly, maintain awareness of your surroundings, and practice a degree of care. Since you will find yourself in many different situations both as a student and as a social worker, the steps you take must be sensitive to your surroundings. Areas of concern include using private and public transportation, walking, using elevators, and dealing with potentially threatening events.

Public Transportation

Most use of public transportation is relatively uneventful. Travel on subways and metro systems, buses, and taxis are generally safe but some caveats are in order:

- Know your exact stop without having to ask the driver or other passengers for directions.
- Whenever possible wait for public transportation in areas that are well-used and where lighting is provided.
- Move close to other passengers so that you do not stand out as being alone.
- In buses, try to sit near the front of the bus.
- Remain awake and hang on to your personal possessions such as briefcases, purses, or other items.
- Note whether riders make eye contact with each other and adopt a similar behavior.
- If someone is bothering you, tell them clearly and loudly to leave you alone.
- When departing public transportation, continue to walk with others to avoid appearing alone.

Driving

Driving is generally safe but there are things you can do to increase your level of safety:

- Know your route well enough to avoid having to ask directions of strangers.
- Use a GPS or navigation system to guide you to your destination but recognize that such devices are not foolproof.
- Be courteous to other drivers and avoid any situations that could lead to road rage.

- Keep your car doors locked both when inside your car and after parking it.
- Stay aware of your surroundings when entering or leaving your vehicle.
- If you feel uncomfortable or threatened, stay in your car or move to a different location.
- Close your car windows and avoid having valuable items sitting on the passenger seat where they may become a target for a smash-and-grab criminal.
- At stoplights and stop signs, be aware of anyone approaching your vehicle and take evasive action if you feel threatened.
- Make sure your car is properly maintained with sufficient fuel both to reach your destination and return to your starting point.
- In the event of car trouble, use your cell phone to call for assistance and remain in the vehicle.
- When parking your car, try to choose a location that is well-lit and will remain bright until you return. Park under street lights if you will be returning after dark.
- When approaching your vehicle, keep your key in your hand both to avoid fumbling for it in your pocket or purse and to use to protect yourself. If equipped, hit the panic button on your car remote to attract attention should you encounter a threat.
- When re-entering your vehicle, check to see if it is still secure, and check the backseat before getting in the driver's seat.
- If you feel another vehicle is following you, drive around the block to see if the vehicle follows. If it does, use your cell phone to notify police and drive to a place of safety.

Walking

Walking involves some degree of risk, depending on when and where you are. Protecting yourself can be as simple as:

- Plan your trip to minimize unnecessary walking, particularly in areas with which you are unfamiliar. Know where you are going.
- Whenever possible, protect your purse or briefcase by using a strap that goes over your shoulder and/or across your body. Hold firmly to any strap or handle.
- Wear sensible and comfortable clothing and shoes if you are walking in areas with which you are unfamiliar or that involve uneven pavement.

- Restrict the amount of money on your person and do not offer money to panhandlers.
- Keep your cell phone handy and do not wear ear buds or other devices that impair your ability to stay alert to your surroundings.
- Home visits are not the place to show off your new watch, expensive jewelry, or other valuables.
- Walk with others whenever possible to make yourself less of a potential target.
- Keep your distance from areas where others can be hiding. This can include corners of buildings, vegetation, and doorways. In the evenings, particularly, such areas often become temporary lodging for the homeless population.
- Stay out of alleys and similar locations.
- Pay attention to your surroundings by noting well-lighted areas and stores and businesses that are open and potentially safer than the street.
- Carry only the absolute minimum when walking. Avoid items that will impede your ability to move quickly or run should this become necessary.
- Walk as if you are in charge of the street. Be calm, stand up straight and carry yourself with a sense of purpose.
- Make brief eye contact with strangers but don't stare or look afraid.

Using Elevators

Most elevators pose little or no threat to riders. However, there are some general suggestions to increase your safety:

- Before entering an elevator, look inside to see if someone is still there.
- If you perceive another rider as worrisome or dangerous, do not enter the elevator.
- When entering an elevator, look for the buttons that can be used to summon help and stand next to button panel.
- Leave the elevator at the next opportunity if someone boards that you feel is a potential threat.
- If someone does attack you, push the alarm button and floor buttons to attract attention.

Demonstrating Street Smarts

Using city streets is usually a safe bet as a means of getting around, but there are some general guidelines to keep in mind:

- Remain alert wherever you are and save your daydreaming for the office.
- Know who or what is in front, beside, and ahead of you.
- Leave your headphones, ear buds, and any other potential distractors at home.

- Let others know where you are going, when you expect to return, and how to reach you while you are out of the office or home.
- Look at the case record before starting out to spot anything that would suggest the possibility of violence on the part of the client, family members, or in a specific neighborhood. Cases involving child welfare, domestic violence, mental health issues and criminal or juvenile justice problems increase the risks. Clients with a history of violence, problems with authority figures, fights, and use of drugs or weapons are increased risks.
- If you perceive a potential threat talk with your field instructor or supervisor about the case. You may need to cancel a visit, have a colleague join you or have a police officer accompany you, or schedule the meeting in a safe environment.
- Set up appointments in the early part of the day instead of toward evening, especially if you will be visiting a potentially dangerous area.
- When entering homes or buildings look for alternate exits in an emergency.

If Threatened

In the unlikely situation in which a real threat presents itself, there are some steps you can take to help reduce the danger:

- Maintain your sense of calm when threatened; now is not the time to panic.
- If entering a home or other location is clearly threatening, terminate the visit.
- De-escalate threatening situations and leave if possible.
- If an attacker simply wants your possessions, give them up. You are more important than any purse, jewelry, or money the thief takes.
- If you feel that it is safe to resist, use your voice. Yell anything that will draw attention: help, fire, no, etc.
- If it is possible to temporarily distract or incapacitate the threat so that you may escape, take this action. Jabbing the attacker in the eye, throat, or groin may provide that opportunity. Kicking the attacker in the knee may also allow you to escape.
- Report the attack as soon as possible, relating all you can recall about the individual including facial characteristics, size, dress, scars, gender, race or any other distinguishing characteristics. If a vehicle was involved, as might occur in a case of road rage or attempted abduction, try to note the license plate and vehicle description.
- Recognize that any such event is traumatic and talk with friends, family, colleagues, and if necessary another professional about the experience. Victim assistance programs often provide such services.

synchronize well with the worker's primary job responsibilities. The extent to which the job description incorporates working with groups has a direct impact on the ease with which a worker can run groups.

Consider the worker responsible for many duties, none of which directly covers formulating groups. Work with groups may be difficult or impossible for that worker to do. She may have no time flexibility in view of her other duties. Likewise, the agency may see working with groups as an activity of lower priority. On the other hand, a job description that includes the responsibility of teaching parenting skills to individuals and *groups* thereby includes group work as a natural part of the worker's expected activities. In such cases your work with groups is designed to achieve organizational goals and is appropriate.

The agency's sponsorship or support of group work is very important (Shulman, 2012). Before beginning work with groups, a worker must assess the extent to which this support exists. Toseland and Rivas explain, "Treatment groups rely on agency administrators and staff for sanctions, financial support, member referrals, and physical facilities. Similarly, task groups are intrinsically linked to the functioning of their sponsoring agencies and must continually refer to the agency's mission, bylaws, and policies for clarification of their task, charge, and mandate" (2012, p. 165).

Treatment groups may be incorporated into the goals of agencies geared to working with some category of clients' problems. Running such groups may then be part of the worker's normal routine. On the other hand, the agency administration may be oriented toward working with *individuals* on their specific problems. Strong resistance on the part of the administration makes the formulation of groups very difficult and sometimes impossible. When you consider forming a treatment group, assessing your agency's support is crucial. If support is seriously lacking, you should ask yourself if the time and effort it will take are worth the exertion.

Assessment regarding agency support of task groups is also important. If you determine that a task group is needed to accomplish a purpose or fulfill some need, you must first assess how open the agency is to evaluating issues and implementing changes in policy and practice. A number of questions may be appropriate: Do agency decision makers typically react positively to innovative suggestions? Does the agency usually adhere tightly to how things have been done in the past? Which decision makers might be most likely to provide support for a task group? What kinds of information

would be helpful to them? Are the chances of successfully formulating a task group worth the effort of persuading the administration to support it? In summary, the practitioner must assess the potential agency support, how that support might best be mustered, and, in the end, whether the endeavor is worth the effort.

Who Should Be Members of the Group?

Assessing agency support should be done early in the assessment process. Another early step concerns figuring out whom the group members should be. This decision involves clearly defining the proposed group's purpose and addressing a number of questions: What characteristics should group members have? How will their needs be met by the group's purpose? How motivated will they be?

Toseland and Rivas (2012) suggest that the practitioner collect information about potential group members. What are potential members' problems, needs, and strengths? Information can be gathered through interviewing, consultation with colleagues about the problem or issue, and reading any available information and documentation about the issue (e.g., see Highlight 5.5).

Selection Criteria for Treatment Group Membership

Unfortunately, there appears to be no clear-cut recipe for perfect group membership. Shulman (2012) reflects upon this by telling an entertaining story. He relates how he once led a group of five couples having marital problems. A group of students observed the counseling sessions on video in a nearby room. Following the first session (which had gone very well), students flooded him with a number of specific questions about how the group was formed.

First, the students asked how the group had been composed, as members of couples ranged in age from their 20s to their 70s. The students apparently wondered what kind of prescribed plan had led the group leader to compose the group so creatively and successfully. Shulman replied, "much to the disappointment of the students, that these were the only five couples referred for the group" (2012, p. 364).

One of the students then asked how the magic number of five couples was established, once again in view of the excellent and dynamic interaction observed during the first session. Shulman replied that the room available to them had space enough for only five couples.

Finally, the students asked how the group leader had arrived at such a specific plan, namely, that the group

HIGHLIGHT 5.5

Sociograms

A common technique for assessing children's interaction is referred to as *sociometry* (Toseland & Rivas, 2012). This assessment involves asking children questions about their relationships and feelings toward other people. After information is gathered, the relationships can be illustrated on a diagram called a *sociogram*. Sociograms can be extremely useful for assessing children's interactional patterns, such as for those who have low self-esteem and difficulty relating to peers. A sociogram can be useful for showing how children's behavior changes as a result of treatment or intervention.

Children in a group might be asked such questions as which three peers they like the best, which three they like the least, whom they most admire, whom they would like to sit next to, and whom they are most afraid of. Each child can be represented by a circle. Arrows can then be drawn to the people they indicate in answer to each question.

A sociogram of a special education class is depicted here. A sociogram can be created to illustrate the results of each question asked. Our example plots out two questions. Sociogram A reflects students' feelings about who they thought was the strongest leader in the group. Sociogram B illustrates which peer they most liked in the group.

Sociogram A clearly illustrates that Toby was thought to be the strongest leader in the group. He is bright, energetic, and very "street smart." However, Sociogram B clearly illustrates that he is not the most popular or best liked in the group. Both Tom and Gertie shine there. They are more mature than the other group members. They are assertive and fairly self-confident, yet they do not impose their will on the others. They are among the brightest in the group. Toby, on the other hand, is more feared than respected in the group. The others admire his apparent sophistication, yet they do not trust him. He does not let anyone get close to him emotionally or even spatially.

Vince's opinions differ radically from those of the other group members. Vince stays by himself most of the time. He loves to wander off whenever he can sneak away. He sees Dean as being both a strong and likable leader. Dean is a very active, verbal person who is always in the center of activity. He has some trouble controlling his behavior and tends to provoke the other students. Perhaps Vince admires Dean's involvement.

These two sociograms are examples of how a group's interaction can be assessed and visually pictured. Although they only begin to portray some of the complexities of the group's interaction, they do provide some interesting clues upon which later interventions can be planned.

Computer programs now allow for sociograms to be produced electronically rather than doing them by hand. Moreover, although sociometry can be used to produce sociograms to use in assessing group relationships, it has much broader possibilities. It has been employed, for example, to find the most ideal locations in which to resettle refugees and to help individuals in a new community form more satisfying personal relationships (Thomas, 2004). It has also been used to better understand the mating aspirations of men and women (Kavanagh, Robins, & Ellis, 2010).

Sociogram A

Sociogram B

© Cengage Learning

would be run for exactly 23 sessions and then terminate. One might imagine a complex algebraic formula filled with *x*'s and *y*'s and hieroglyphic-like symbols. The group leader responded that for administrative reasons they could not get started any earlier than they did, and there were only 23 weeks until the end of the semester—so much for concise scientific assessment and planning.

On a more serious note, the point is that most groups are formed and run while dealing with limited resources, infinite variation of individual characteristics, and agency or job constrictions. A precise formula involving exacting measurements is unrealistic and virtually impossible. However, there are a number of commonsense principles that can help to determine group composition. These include motivation, group purpose, common communication skills, and a generalized assessment of the potential advantages and disadvantages of the group.

Motivation. One of the most critical variables in including a particular member in a group is motivation. Little can be accomplished with individuals who are not committed to the group and not willing to work on behalf of themselves and the group.

However, often generalist practitioners will be in the situation of running treatment groups where members are wary or simply involuntary. For example, consider groups run in residential treatment centers or group homes for children with behavioral and emotional problems. Consider a deferred prosecution group where first-time offenders are given the choice of paying a large fine, going to jail for a while, or participating in a group (such a group might focus on increasing self-awareness, understanding one's motivation for committing the crime, and designing ways to avoid committing crimes in the future).

Making an accurate assessment of a client's motivation for participating in a group is important. Often, this assessment involves more than the decision of whether a member will or will not become a member of a group. It will also involve the extent to which the worker needs to work on enhancing the motivational level of an individual or that of the entire group.

Group Purpose. That people are assessed and selected for membership in a particular treatment group for some clearly specified reason makes sense. The reason might be to work on marital issues, as mentioned earlier. Likewise, any number of other reasons might be pertinent (a social skills improvement group, a child management group, or a support group for adult children whose parents are placed in a nursing home). The important thing is that group members are there to work together on some common problem or issue.

Common Communication Skills. Group treatment is based on communication. Whatever is accomplished in a group is done through this medium. Therefore, group members must be able to communicate effectively with each other, which implies that group members should have a similar ability to use language and express themselves. The important thing is for you to determine that group members will be able to communicate ideas and feelings to each other adequately.

Group Advantages versus Disadvantages. For each group member there are frequently benefits and limitations to participating in a given group. If the advantages exceed the less appealing aspects of the group, the member is more likely to be motivated to join and continue in a group. Rewards might include the potential for seeing improvement in the handling of the problem, decreased emotional pain, enjoyment of other group members, or an increase in self-confidence. Disadvantages, on the other hand, might include the time and effort it takes to participate, dislike of or lack of communication with other group members, or resentment about feeling forced to participate.

Toseland and Rivas (2012) suggest some approaches for dealing with resistance on the part of group members. These include staying alert to obvious and covert behaviors that suggest a lack of interest in the group's work, acknowledging the coercion members feel about being forced to participate, encouraging maximum member self-determination and feelings of control within the group, and reminding members that they can choose not to participate. The latter decision carries consequences for those mandated by the court or other agencies to attend, but the final decision always rests with the client.

Gathering Information about Potential Treatment Group Members

For treatment groups there are at least three primary assessment mechanisms. First, interviews with potential group members prior to beginning the group are helpful. Assessment regarding the clients' problems, communication skills, social interaction skills, prior experience with groups, attitudes toward such a group, and motivation to participate can all be assessed.

A second mechanism involves the use of self-assessments. There are many such highly developed and widely used instruments available. The appropriate instrument would be chosen, of course, in view of the problem to be addressed. For example, earlier in this chapter in a section on assessment in micro practice, several such instruments were mentioned, including the Rathus Assertiveness Schedule. Traditional psychological testing is another possible means of providing useful information about potential group members.

Third, those who referred a client to the group may also be able to provide useful information. This might include a health care practitioner, family member, professional colleague, employer, or another social agency. The client should give permission prior to the worker soliciting information from collateral contacts, although with some mandated group participants the degree of freedom in this regard may be limited.

Selection Criteria for Task Group Membership

Selection criteria for task groups are similar to those for treatment groups. Toseland and Rivas (2012) suggest a number of variables to consider, including each individual's interests and areas of expertise, homogeneity versus heterogeneity of group members, potential group members' prestige in the community, group members' relationship with the sponsoring agency, and group members' diversity and demographic characteristics.

Individual Interests. Assessing the extent to which a potential member is genuinely interested in the group and the group's task is essential for a group leader. This interest is directly related to motivation—a motivated individual is more likely to cooperate and work in the group. In assessing potential motivation, a worker might ask him- or herself a number of questions. For instance, what interest has the individual expressed in this or similar tasks before? How important will the potential member view the tasks? What direct or indirect benefits might the individual get out of the group (e.g., increased status, enjoyable or profitable interpersonal contacts, or greater visibility)?

Expertise. As discussed in Chapter 3, task groups often need a range of competencies or expertise to best accomplish their goals. For instance, a task group aimed at establishing a rape crisis center could benefit by inclusion of a physician concerning the medical implications, a police officer regarding legal aspects, and representatives from local women's groups regarding advocacy.

Homogeneity versus Heterogeneity. There are no clear guidelines regarding the extent to which a group should be homogeneous (composed of people with similar characteristics) or heterogeneous (consisting of people with dissimilar characteristics). On the one hand, group members need to be homogeneous enough to communicate and work with each other. On the other, members must be dissimilar enough to provide the necessary range of both skills and ideas. The group leader needs to attend to these issues, weigh the pros and cons of various alternatives, and make final decisions regarding what is potentially best for the group and its purpose.

Prestige in the Community. Many times, depending on the group's purpose, gaining outside public support in order to accomplish a task is important. This support can involve inviting important or well-respected community members to join the group.

An example involves a task group aimed at developing a stronger sex education program in a school district. Appropriate members might not only include such experts in sexuality education as teachers in that area, but also local religious leaders, lawyers, physicians, and businesspeople. Sometimes, this task is controversial. Religious leaders might increase public trust in the group.

Likewise, involving respected professionals leads to enhanced credibility. Finally, tapping local businesses for membership can sometimes gain financial assistance.

Relationship with the Sponsoring Agency. Some task groups are formed within an agency. For example, a task group for updating staff policies might best be composed of an agency's own staff members. However, other task groups might be more effective if they involve a cross section of various agency and community members.

For instance, consider a task group whose purpose is to reestablish funding of a special treatment program for adolescents with behavioral and emotional problems. The urban county that had previously supported the development and maintenance of the program slashed the program from its budget during a financial crisis. The most effective task group in this case might include agency personnel who had been providing the service, parents of children whose treatment had been cut off, and any other professional, religious, and business community leaders who support the program.

Diversity and Demographic Characteristics. At least three demographic variables are often important when assembling a task group: age, gender, and "socio-cultural factors" (Toseland & Rivas, 2012, p. 175).

The worker, of course, needs to use common sense regarding the extent to which such demographic characteristics are important. Sometimes potential members with diverse characteristics will not be available. Other times, such members will not want to join the group.

However, attending to both gender and ethnic/racial/cultural balance within a group is generally important for the worker. Task groups aimed at providing services to women should have appropriate representation of women in their membership. Likewise, task groups working on an issue involving some ethnic, racial, or cultural group should have substantial representation from the relevant group or groups in their membership.

Gender and sociocultural balance is especially important because of traditional oppressive power imbalances. In other words, for white males to make decisions about women or racial minorities is not acceptable. Members of oppressed groups must be fully involved in decisions that affect them.

Recruiting Task Group Members

Another crucial step involves the recruitment process for potential members (Toseland & Rivas, 2012). Task group members can be targeted using the variables described earlier. The worker can personally invite the individual to become a member of the group via a meeting, phone call, or letter. Additionally, the worker can publicize the need for members with certain areas of expertise or interests through fliers, notices in newsletters and newspapers, word of mouth, and even radio and television announcements.

Ongoing Group Assessment

We have established that assessment in groups is an ongoing process. A practitioner is responsible for monitoring the ongoing group climate. This climate includes the breadth of variables discussed in Chapter 3. One especially relevant area for assessment involves "communication and interaction patterns" (Toseland & Rivas, 2012, p. 244). This involves many of the concepts discussed in Chapter 3. The practitioner's responsibility as group leader is to monitor the openness of communication and the appropriateness of interactions. This responsibility involves encouraging participation of all group members, yet not allowing domination. It also concerns establishing and maintaining group structure so that progress can continuously be made toward accomplishing group goals.

Ongoing Assessment in Treatment Groups. Numerous ongoing assessment mechanisms have been developed for treatment groups (Toseland & Rivas, 2012). First, the individual self-rating questionnaires previously mentioned can be administered periodically to monitor progress in specific areas.

Second, clients may keep diaries or logs of daily events concerning the problems addressed in treatment. This approach helps clients focus on their problems and their progress toward solving them.

A third assessment mechanism involves charting the clients' improvement, which is discussed more thoroughly in Chapter 8. Simple charting might involve noting on a chart whenever a specified behavior occurs. For example, a client involved in an assertiveness training group might note on a chart each time she musters up enough confidence to contact another person by phone outside of the group.

Role playing within the group provides a fourth assessment mechanism. The group leader can ask group members to practice what they have learned in the group. The worker may then observe their progress, share his or her perceptions with the clients, and provide suggestions for improvement. After role playing, the worker can also solicit feedback from other group members. This information can be useful to both the role players and the individuals assessing them and articulating their feedback. Finally, the worker can involve outside observers. Observers can be used either in the group or to report clients' observed progress outside the group. An outsider observing the group, for instance, can note how frequently each group member speaks and for how long.

Another example concerns assessment feedback outside of a socialization group for children. The worker might contact the children's teachers to determine the extent to which they apply what they learn in the group to outside situations.

There are always ethical, reliability, and validity issues to consider when contemplating the use of outside sources of information. To the extent to which they are capable, clients have the right to determine whether you may contact others outside of the group. Clients should be fully informed about the involvement of family members, teachers, and others who will be asked to monitor their behaviors. Clients may be asked to suggest possible outside monitors in keeping with their right to self-determination. The information source must also be capable of providing a valid assessment of the client. People with their own biases or axes to grind may not provide accurate or consistent information, both of which are necessary.

ASSESSMENT IN MACRO PRACTICE

Micro practice, mezzo practice, and macro practice are all intimately intertwined. Any practice, of course, involves working with other people, necessitating the mastery of micro skills. Macro practice does not involve a focus on individuals or even on groups of individuals. Rather, as we have established in Chapter 4, macro practice focuses on making positive changes that affect large numbers of people. To implement these changes, generalist practitioners must work together with other individuals and groups. Thus, macro practice is both based upon and highly interactive with the other two practice modes. Hence, we have the generalist social work practitioner.

In the recent past and current eras of shrinking resources, the profession has become increasingly focused on the social environment and the context in which social workers practice. Generalist practitioners need to attend to the environment in which they work. The remainder of this chapter will focus on one example of macro-system assessment, namely, the assessment of a community's needs.

LO 5-9 Use Assessment Tools to Determine Community and Neighborhood Needs

Social workers often need to confront the environment in which they work. Necessary services may be unavailable. Public bureaucracies may be unresponsive to clients' needs. Archaic policies may significantly interfere with clients' lives.

Thus, the generalist practitioner may need to work to make changes within the clients' community. Focusing on community change instead of trying to change the client or something about how the client lives is difficult at first for many students. Nonetheless, combating inequities in the system can be a productive way to initiate changes for large groups of people.

When trying to assess clients' needs within a community, the first thing to do is to define what a community is. As we have discussed in Chapter 4, there are a number of ways of conceptualizing communities, including those focusing on geographical boundaries and those emphasizing groups of people with common interests and needs. For our purposes, the important thing is for generalist practitioners to clearly define the communities with which they work, regardless of the definition they choose to use.

Community needs assessment entails evaluation of a community's current and potential resources, existing problems, and barriers to solving problems. Needs assessments are designed to identify a community's needs and determine their relative priority. It is important to recognize that a need may involve something lacking in a community, such as adequate child care, or the existence of a problem, such as gang violence. In both cases, the community experiences discomfort with the situation and wants relief. The extent of a community's unhappiness about a situation serves as a motivating factor for identifying priorities and bringing about change.

There is no one best way of conducting a community needs assessment. Each situation and approach is unique, although there are some general variables that should be considered. These include such things as whether information about a situation is available, the existence of available resources to bring about change, and attitudes about the need or problem. (See Highlight 5.6.)

Employing Participatory Research in a Community Assessment

As discussed in Chapter 3, the participatory research model can be effective as a means of assessing a community using the assistance of those groups most at risk. For example, interviews of residents regarding problems with city services could be carried out by other residents affected by this perceived problem. Potential beneficiaries of change efforts that will follow the assessment may also be involved in identifying questions to be asked. One real benefit of participatory research is that it actively involves those community members who will benefit from change. This is one way that our knowledge of practice principles shapes and informs scientific inquiry.

Information. Before attempting a needs assessment, knowing what kind of information you are seeking is important. If you are working for a local agency, what information would be most relevant in terms of what that agency will be able to do? What are the best ways of obtaining the most useful information? How difficult will the information be to obtain? Will the information be accurate enough to make effective decisions?

Resources Available. A second variable to consider involves resources. On the one hand, you will need enough support and financial backing to conduct the assessment. On the other, how desperate is the community to have its needs met? In other words, are the needs extremely grave and meriting immediate

HIGHLIGHT 5.6

A Format for Analyzing a Community or Neighborhood

Understanding a community or neighborhood is an important ability for social work practitioners who work there. This often requires gathering information that helps paint a picture of the area's characteristics, its economic and political structures, communication systems, and quality of life. Following we have identified several categories of information that might be gathered in order to produce a complete community needs assessment.

- **Demographic factors:** These include factors such as the age, gender, ethnicity, and cultural backgrounds of residents.
- **Economic factors:** Included here are major sources of employment, income of residents, unemployment rates, quantity and quality of housing, costs of housing, and patterns of home ownership.
- **Communication systems:** In this category we want to know about the major avenues of communication among community members. This

includes newspapers, radio, television, and other media influences.
- **Social service organizations:** It is important to know the range and quality of social services available to community residents as well as how they are funded. This can range from counseling services to financial aid, welfare, and other public assistance programs. It may also include programs such as foster care.
- **Civic/service organizations:** These provide a wealth of functions for a community, including financial, community-building, socialization, and, sometimes, political functions.
- **Health and medical services:** Availability of medical care, prevention services, and long-term physical care is important to determine.

Gathering information on these areas should allow you to better understand the environment in which you live and work. It also will form a solid basis for efforts to intervene in the community.

---

attention? Will the potential reward of the assessment merit the time and expense it will take to conduct it?

Consideration of the current state of the community's resource system is also important. Are there other existing resources in the community that could potentially meet the community's needs at lesser costs? Would a needs assessment provide information useful for changing or improving the current state of the resource system?

Community Attitudes. Finally, community attitudes are important to consider prior to conducting a needs assessment. Will relevant community members be willing to provide information and participate in the assessment process? Does the community have the potential to respond positively to the implications of such an assessment? Will you find support in the community to carry out the assessment and implement recommendations? Will you encounter so much resistance that the process will seem like fighting on a battlefield?

An Example of a Community Assessment
In order to work with people in a community and understand their needs, being familiar with the culture, values, priorities, issues, and problems characterizing

the community is important. Several experts on the community have identified a variety of activities common to doing a community assessment (Homan, 2011; Netting, Kettner, McMurtry, & Thomas, 2012; Warren & Warren, 1984). The common elements typically involve a step-by-step process that helps identify characteristics that make each neighborhood or community unique. The steps in this process are delineated as follows.

Step 1: Exploring the Nature of the Neighborhood or Community. The first step in the investigatory process involves finding out how people in the neighborhood or community function. Before you *do* anything, you need enough background information to know *what* you are doing. How do people in the neighborhood or community solve their problems? What workable resources are available? Answers to these questions begin to provide you with information about the community's strengths and weaknesses. They can also help you determine the community's needs.

Local centers of government are good places to get information during this phase of your community assessment. A city hall, local courthouse, branch of social services, the chamber of commerce, and even a library all have useful information. There might be pamphlets available about the community. Notices about community events and services might be posted to inform the public (and you) about what generally goes on within the community.

Getting maps can be tremendously helpful because they can increase your confidence and agility in getting around the community. Maps also can give you information about how the community you are assessing fits in with surrounding communities or neighborhoods.

Telephone books also provide useful information. Not only can you find out where government offices are, but you can also find and explore the types of businesses in the community, the health care services available, and such other resources as churches and activity centers.

Newspapers provide a lot of information. Advertisements reflect what businesses are available and what appears to be significant in the local culture. News items reflect what the community feels is important. For instance, consider the fact that local cow prices are regularly posted on the front page of the small rural paper, the *Benjamin Key*. These postings imply that many community residents are rural farmers interested in this type of news.

Even if your job is oriented more toward micro or mezzo levels of social work practice, getting to know your clients' community is significant. Getting information and thinking about a community can prepare you much more effectively for working with its people.

Step 2: Getting to Know the Area and Its Residents. Getting a general impression of the community is probably the most useful thing to do at this point. Drive around the area and pay attention to what it is like. What are the buildings like? Are they well kept or in disrepair? Do some buildings look abandoned? Where do people seem to congregate? What businesses characterize the community? What are your general impressions of the community as a whole? Does it appear to be thriving or desolate, safe or unsafe, well managed or disorganized? As you continue to explore, establish the community's boundaries in your own mind. What areas in the community will be your chief concern? Are there geographical boundaries that characterize the community? For instance, is there a main street on which community members focus their attention? Do rivers, valleys, highways, or industrial sections cut the community in half or in sections?

Step 3: Identify the Community's Strengths. We have already established that in generalist social work practice, assessing strengths is just as important as evaluating problems or needs. Healthy businesses, homes kept in good repair, social clubs and organizations (e.g., Boy Scouts, bowling teams, or the Polish Nationalist Society), churches, and even friendly interaction with community residents all contribute to the community's strengths. The resources of a community come in many forms and can be used to help in the process of change.

Step 4: Talk to People in the Community. Identifying major community figures is critical. Talking with these people can give you substantial insight into the "fabric" and values of the community.

Obviously, there are many people you could talk to in order to obtain this information. One example would be elementary school principals. The person in this position is in regular contact with the core of community residents. The principal must work integrally with community families and understand their issues. You can obtain information about the economic situation, types of recreation people generally enjoy, religious affiliations, racial tensions, and other concerns.

Other individuals to contact include a range of community leaders. You should not try to contact every leader. Rather, identify those who you feel might have information most relevant for your needs. These might include local clergy, such public officials as city or county council members, the town board chairperson or the mayor, presidents of clubs and organizations (for instance, the Kiwanis Club or the Parent/Teacher Association), the heads of the homeowners' associations or Neighborhood Watch groups, prominent businesspeople, and other social workers in the area.

Sometimes, there are extremely vocal community members who others feel complain all the time. Talking to these people can be useful in targeting some of the community's hot spots. Often these people are relatively easy to talk to because they want to have their gripes heard.

Obtaining information about a broad cross section of the community is important. This information includes the wide range of age groups represented in the community. As we know, people's concerns vary according to their life's developmental stage. Additionally, finding out about all the primary ethnic and racial groups within the community is critical. You need to know about values and customs. You also need to know about conflicts between groups in order to examine how the community really functions.

Interviewing Persons in the Community. Warren and Warren (1984) make at least seven specific suggestions for things to say during your interviews with key community people. First, take time for small talk. The generalist practitioner utilizes micro practice skills even when pursuing a macro practice objective. In other words, establishing rapport with any new person you are interviewing is important. Warm, friendly, informal small talk about the weather, the place you are meeting, or the neighborhood itself is usually appropriate.

A second interviewing suggestion is to provide your interviewee with a clear definition of your purpose. Why are you there? Why should he or she take the time to talk to you? Your purpose might be to familiarize yourself with clients' community life because you have started a new job and will be working with them. Likewise, it might be that you are interested in initiating some new services within the community and would like to find out how to begin.

The third interviewing suggestion involves clearly explaining to your interviewee what community of people or neighborhood you are interested in. Is it a public school district (especially, if you are talking to a school principal)? Is it a geographical neighborhood delineated by specific streets marking off a certain number of city blocks? Is it an entire town? Regardless, avoiding misunderstandings and inaccuracies is important for you and your interviewee.

A fourth suggestion for interviewing involves asking your interviewee for suggestions about others you should talk to. Who might better be aware of other people most involved in and knowledgeable about the community than those who are already integrally involved with that community? Get names, telephone numbers, and addresses, if available. Make decisions about who might be most helpful to you and follow through on contacting them.

The fifth suggestion involves the art of interviewing. Your micro practice skills will come in handy here. You want your interviewees to feel comfortable with you, open up to you, and share what they know about the community. Sharing some information about yourself can be helpful. For instance, you might share how you lived in a similar neighborhood once, or you might contrast this neighborhood with the one in which you now live. Your intent is to find out information about a community, not to fill in blanks on an established questionnaire. Therefore, you want to give your interviewees opportunities to talk and raise new topics. Providing some relevant information about yourself can enhance the interviewees' comfort with the interview. It can also convey to the interviewees that such initiation of their own thoughts, ideas, and other topics is appropriate.

A sixth suggestion for interviewing concerns getting the specific information you need. One way of doing this is to ask your interviewee's opinion about what might happen if you pursued a particular direction in your contacts with others. For example, you might ask, "What if I contacted the person you suggested? Do you think she would be willing to take time and give me some information?" In another case, you might say, "I'm thinking about plans for the future. What if I initiated the program we were talking about? How cooperative do you think the community would be?"

The seventh suggestion involves closure of the interview. Becoming goal oriented and pressing methodically for the information you need is easy. However, encouraging your interviewee to share feelings about the information already given or about the interview itself is also important. You might simply ask if there is anything the person would like to add. In other words, make sure the interviewee has the opportunity to share opinions and to conclude the interview.

Step 5: Gather Other Information. Sometimes, the information you will need is not available locally. For example, what if you are interested in gathering comparative information about other communities or about programs that have been tried elsewhere that might work in your community? Much of this information can be found in databases, public libraries, and other venues. One easy way to gather this information is through the Internet. Potential information sources include the Economic Success Clearinghouse (ESC), which provides access to hundreds of organizations and thousands of electronic sources. The ESC gathers information regularly on other Web sites and provides data on policy issues, new state and local social programs, caseloads, characteristics of clients, and program designs. It also has available material on managing programs, assessment, and information on potential grants. Such information is helpful for macro assessment and also assists in planning, a topic addressed more thoroughly in Chapter 6. The Clearinghouse's online address is http://www.financeproject.org/index.cfm?page=24. Another ready source with over 6,000 pages of relevant information is The Community Tool Box at http://ctb.ku.edu. This site contains information on topics such as community organization and change, developing a community leadership corps, and increasing access for people with disabilities. Over time, you will learn to use these resources and to locate links to other sources that will expand your skills at assessment, planning, intervention, and evaluation.

Critical Thinking Questions 5.3

EP 2.1.3 Think about the community in which you have spent the most time in your life and consider the following questions.

- Can you identify five people by name whom you would consider key individuals to be interviewed in an assessment of the community?
- What strengths do you perceive this community as having?
- Based upon your own experience, what are the major challenges that the community faces?

ASSESSMENT, CLIENT EMPOWERMENT, AND STRENGTHS

It is sometimes easy to focus on gathering information for an assessment and lose sight of the purpose of this step in the planned change process. The information we gain is attained for the sole purpose of our collaborative work to help client systems resolve problems, expand their capacities, and use available resources more effectively. Assessment that focuses solely on the shortcomings of clients ignores their strengths and ability to participate fully in the change process. Client systems have a right and an obligation to be active partners in the change process. Similarly, as social workers we must continue to expect as much from our clients as from ourselves. We empower clients when we help them develop the ability to solve their own crises. Whether the client system is an individual, family, group, organization, or community, it is essential that we use the assessment process to recognize and build on client strengths and empower them to participate actively in the change effort.

Chapter Summary

The following summarizes this chapter's content as it relates to each learning objective (LO) presented at the beginning of the chapter. Chapter content helps prepare students to:

LO 5-1 Employ activities and skills needed for engagement with various-size systems.

Engagement is concerned with establishing a relationship between the social worker and client, the value of which is critical to the rest of the planned change process. Requisite components of building this relationship are a clear purpose, a commitment to meeting client needs, ethical standards of practice, the communication of warmth by the worker, genuineness, and empathy. Steps in the engagement process include greeting the client, demonstrating effective attending skills, discussing agency services and client expectations, deciding if the agency and worker can help, offering appropriate services, and orienting the client to the helping process. Finally, the worker must complete whatever paperwork or case recording the agency requires.

LO 5-2 Assess goals prior to intervention.

Assessment is the second step in the planned change process and is focused on defining the problem, identifying contributing factors, and recognizing what can be done to reduce or eliminate the problem. Assessment can be considered from at least three perspectives. One perspective is the individual and family, where the worker might be looking at transactions among members, family functioning, strengths, culture, and customs. We could also consider transactions between members and their environment. A second perspective for focus might be functioning at different points in the life cycle of family members, such as childhood, adolescence is, adulthood, or older adulthood. This may identify strengths, stressors, and resources that can be the focus of assessment.

A third perspective can be the specific problem that the client is experiencing. This might include depression, substance abuse, and behavioral problems, to name a few typically encountered problems.

The assessment methods and techniques used may vary depending on such factors as the knowledge and skill of the practitioner, cultural factors, the particular needs of the client, and client characteristics such as gender and age. Effective assessment looks at micro, mezzo, and macro aspects of the client situation and fully engages the client in the process. By its very nature, assessment involves making judgments, often with insufficient or incomplete information. The assessment must consider not only the identified problems but also the strengths and resources that characterize the client. Ideally, a clear definition of a problem is the goal, although this is not always possible. Assessment is a continuous activity and more information may come to light even after a preliminary goal has been established.

LO 5-3 Use practice behaviors such as defining and describing problems.

A clear understanding of the need, problem, or situation is a critical element of the assessment process. It requires defining the client system so that we know whether the focus of our work will be an individual, family, group, agency, organization, or community. You will need to ask yourself several potential questions. How is the client system's interactions with other systems? What information is missing, and where would I get it?

Types of problems might include interpersonal conflict, dissatisfaction in social relations, difficulty dealing with formal organizations, challenges in role performance, difficulty transitioning from one role to another, or psychological or behavioral problems. Additional problems might include lack of adequate resources, difficulty in decision making, and cultural or religious conflicts. Often we must deal with two or more problems, either sequentially or simultaneously. Ultimately, we (client and worker) must decide which problems seem to have higher priority.

LO 5-4   Assess client strengths and limitations.

We have emphasized the importance of client strengths in the helping process. Strengths can include such things as persistence, spiritual resources, motivation, intelligence, commitment to others, and experience grappling with the problem. Sources of strength might include family and friends, education and employment background, problem-solving and decision-making skills, personal qualities and characteristics, physical and financial resources, attitude and perspective, as well as others. Limitations are much more likely to be apparent because they are often reflected in the problem.

LO 5-5   Utilize micro-assessment tools such as the *Diagnostic and Statistical Manual (DSM-5)*, the Rathus Assertiveness Schedule, and an alcoholism test.

Assessment information can be gained from at least seven sources. These include information provided by clients when they first make contact with your agency. An example might be demographic information such as age and family size, employment data, and current family relationships. It may also include self-assessments completed by the client covering such areas as level of depression, parenting ability, and similar problem-oriented challenges.

A second source of information is that shared by the client during your time together. This may be in response to the questions you pose in order to better understand the client's situation. A third source will come from observations you make about time together. Does the client's nonverbal and verbal behavior match? Does the client evade certain areas or avoid talking about a specific situation?

A fourth source comes from your observations of the client's interactions with others. This might include how the client interacts with his or her significant other, spouse, children, or parents. These interactions can be useful in understanding issues related to interpersonal relationships.

Fifth, information may come from outside sources such as a client's friends and family, reports from other agencies, and data from physicians, psychologists, or other professionals. A sixth source may also be provided via psychological or other testing. The seventh source is based upon your own interactions with the client as you work together. For example, does the client's thinking process appear rational? Is the client hostile to your questions, or overly dependent on you or others? If you employed assessment instruments such as behavioral checklists or an assertiveness questionnaire, use this information to help inform your overall assessment of the client.

Although social workers typically use many of these sources of information for making their assessments, other professionals may employ different tools. One of these is the *Diagnostic and Statistical Manual (DSM)* produced by the American Psychiatric Association. The instrument lists criteria for identifying various mental disorders and is helpful in assessing individuals with problems that include clinical disorders (bipolar illness, posttraumatic stress disorder) personality disorders (antisocial personality, borderline personality disorder), physical conditions (infections, AIDS), environmental and psychosocial problems (stressors, loss of job), and overall level of functioning.

The *DSM* is useful to social workers as a means of communicating with those professionals who typically use it when completing their own client assessments. It provides a common language and can be helpful in defining or labeling a disorder. On the other hand, it can cause problems when we use *DSM* labels to pigeonhole clients and see them only as a label. The *DSM* also does not provide much help in identifying or designing interventions to help the client. Reliance on the *DSM* may focus attention only on the individual and ignore the environment that creates or maintains a problem. Finally, the *DSM* is a deficit-focused document and does not consider client strengths or resources.

LO 5-6   Decide to work with families following assessment.

Family assessment involves developing an understanding of a complex system composed of both adults and children. We are concerned with the individuals who comprise the family as well as the interactions among them. Based on our assessment, we may decide that only a part of the family needs assistance, such as the spouses or the children. Sometimes, we may focus on the family as a whole, one or more individual members, or on some external system that is contributing to the family's situation. When we are considering whether to work with a family, we must take into account who is affected by the problem, whether we have the time and resources to be of assistance, and the likelihood of success. We will take into account such factors as communication patterns, family structure, life-cycle challenges, impact of the social environment, and key areas of family conflict. Also, we may tools such as genograms or eco-maps to help us assess the family's situation.

LO 5-7   Effectively use home visits as an assessment mechanism.

Home visits can be an important source of information about families. The home is the family's natural setting and they may be more comfortable there. This may allow them to share more readily as well as allow the worker to observe them in a familiar environment. Home visits also allow the worker to view the family's living conditions and how members react to each other outside of the office. Home visits should be done at a time that is convenient for the family. Because the worker may encounter areas of the community that entail greater risk, it is important to use common sense and good judgment when deciding where and when to do a home visit.

LO 5-8   Assess both task and treatment groups.

Among the factors that must be considered when assessing task and treatment groups are such things as potential sponsorship and the extent to which your agency supports the worker's involvement in groups. In some cases such involvement may be part of the worker's job description or at least an expected activity. In others an agency may not be interested in the worker providing services to a group or serving as a member if it detracts from the worker's day-to-day work responsibilities.

A second assessment consideration is the group's membership. Who should be members of the group? The answer depends upon whether we are working with a treatment group or a task group. With the former, we take into account such things as a client's motivation to participate in a group, the purpose of the group, and the client's ability to communicate with others. We will also be gathering information on each potential treatment group member from a variety of sources.

With a task group, assessment is concerned with such things as the interests of potential members, their expertise in the area with which the group will be dealing, the degree of homogeneity or heterogeneity desired in the group, and other demographic characteristics such as age or gender. As with individual client assessment, the assessment process is never fully completed. We will continue to gather information and revise our assessment as the group evolves.

LO 5-9   Use assessment tools to determine community and neighborhood needs.

Common tools for use in communities and neighborhoods include a formal needs assessment, participatory research, and utilizing structured formats. Factors to take into account in such assessments include demographic factors, economic factors, range and quality of social service organizations, existence of civic or service organizations, and availability of health and medical services. Community attitudes may be important in considering whether to engage in a formal needs assessment, as much depends upon the willingness of members to provide information and participate in the process. A community assessment will take into account the nature and functioning of the neighborhood or community and gather information from a variety of formal and informal sources. The worker will gather impressions about such things as quality of housing, employment opportunities for residents, safety and security considerations, and community strengths, among others. Doing this will involve interviewing community residents, leaders, and influential community members, and putting this information together with data gathered from other sources.

Competency Notes

The following identifies where Educational Policy (EP) competencies and practice behaviors are discussed in the chapter.

EP 2.1.1c **Attend to professional roles and boundaries.** *(p. 165):* Maintaining appropriate documentation and record keeping is one component of the professional social worker's role.

EP 2.1.3 **Apply critical thinking to inform and communicate professional judgment,** *(pp. 171, 177, 179, 202):* Critical thinking is an important component of the engagement and assessment process.

EP 2.1.3c **Demonstrate effective oral and written communication in working with individuals, families, groups, organizations, communities, and colleagues.** *(p. 165):* Documentation required for social work demands good written communication skills.

EP 2.1.4 **Engage diversity and difference in practice.** *(p. 196):* When composing groups, both gender and sociocultural balance are important considerations because of traditional oppressive power imbalances. The goal is to fully involve members of oppressed groups in decisions that affect them.

EP 2.1.4a **Recognize the extent to which culture's structures and values may oppress, marginalize, alienate, or create/enhance privilege/power.** *(p. 166):* Part of the assessment process involves awareness of how cultural and other factors may have influenced the perspectives, behaviors, and attitudes of client systems.

EP 2.1.4b **Gain sufficient self-awareness to eliminate the influence of personal biases and values in working with diverse groups.** *(p. 166):* Workers need to consider how their own expectations, values, and biases might be affecting their judgments and attitudes toward clients. *(p. 187):* Workers' reactions to clients' life situations can affect their ability to accurately and fairly identify challenges and assess problems.

EP 2.1.5 **Advance human rights and social and economic justice.** *(p. 191):* Assessing the needs of groups will often result in the identification of those who have been denied human rights and justice. It is part of our responsibility as social workers to challenge these situations.

EP 2.1.6a **Use practice experience to inform scientific inquiry.** *(p. 199):* Social workers know that the potential beneficiaries of a change effort should be closely involved in deciding what goals to pursue and empowered to assist in the change process. This practice principle is employed when using participatory research in community assessment.

EP 2.1.7a **Utilize conceptual frameworks to guide the processes of assessment, intervention, and evaluation.** *(p. 183):* Conceptual frameworks are important when assessing the family within its environment.

EP 2.1.7b **Critique and apply knowledge to understand person and environment.** *(p. 183):* When attempting to assess client problems, it is often necessary to challenge existing conceptual frameworks when they don't help us accurately understand the situation.

EP 2.1.10 **Engage, assess, intervene, and evaluate with individuals, families, groups, organizations, and communities.** *(p. 162):* Engagement is the first step in the planned change process and is focused on establishing a professional relationship with all sizes of systems. *(p. 177):* Assessment is the second step in the planned change process and involves gathering data and evaluating problem situations within an environmental perspective. *(p. 182):* Assessing families is a major dimension of generalist social work practice. *(p. 199):* Assessing community needs is another activity of generalist practitioners.

EP 2.1.10b **Use empathy and other interpersonal skills.** *(p. 163):* Attending skills are among the interpersonal skills needed to assist clients.

EP 2.1.10c **Develop a mutually agreed-on focus of work and desired outcomes.** *(p. 177):* The client's perspective and priorities should be the major factor in deciding what problems or challenges to deal with first.

EP 2.1.10d **Collect, organize, and interpret client data.** *(p. 177):* There are multiple sources of information about our clients that we need to focus on in the assessment process.

EP 2.1.10e **Assess client strengths and limitations** *(pp. 168, 171, 174):* Assessment includes an analysis about the strengths that client systems possess and is as important as attending to identified problems.

EP 2.1.10f **Develop mutually agreed-on intervention goals and objectives.** *(pp. 177, 196):* Clients should be intimately involved in the process of selecting intervention goals and objectives.

EP 2.1.10h **Initiate actions to achieve organizational goals.** *(p. 191):* Social workers will be assisting to achieve organizational goals to the extent that their agency sanctions their interventions with various-size systems.

On the Internet

Visit the *Understanding Generalist Practice* CourseMate at **www.cengagebrain.com** for resources such as quizzes, glossaries and videos.

Planning in Generalist Practice

Jupiterimages/Stockbyte/Getty Images

Learning Objectives   *This chapter will help prepare students to:*

LO 6-1   Utilize an eight-step planning process in generalist practice integrating micro, mezzo, and macro approaches.

LO 6-2   Establish goals and objectives.

LO 6-3   Use contracts as part of the planning process.

LO 6-4   Engage in planning in mezzo practice.

LO 6-5   Engage in planning in macro practice.

HOW WOULD YOU PLAN TO WORK WITH THIS CASE? Robby, age 6, has cerebral palsy, a disability caused by brain damage occurring at or around the time of birth. The disorder affects muscle coordination and speech. Robby, who cannot walk and has difficulty controlling his hands, lives with both parents and three sisters. The family is poor, despite the fact that his father works two minimum-wage jobs. His mother is unable to work outside of the home because of the extensive care her children, especially Robby, need.

Here is one way to plan what to do:

1. Work closely with Robby and his parents. *They must believe in and be committed to the plan for it to succeed.*

2. Prioritize the problems. *Together with Robby's parents, you determine that Robby's physical disability is the top priority. Other prioritized problems and needs include, respectively: inadequate finances; father's low skill level; mother's inability to work outside the home; the need for day care; and poor housing.*

3. Translate the problems into needs. *Work with the top-priority problem first, Robby's disability. Robby needs a thorough evaluation to determine the extent of his disability. Depending on the findings, he may need such services as physical therapy, speech therapy, occupational therapy, or special education.*

4. Evaluate the level(s) of the intervention (micro, mezzo, or macro). *Will you initially plan to pursue a micro, mezzo, or macro approach to intervention? At this point, you select a micro intervention. You know that evaluation and therapeutic services are available and that Robby's family will qualify for financial aid to receive these services because of its low income level. Thus, you determine you do not need to address problems in agency policies or the social service system's delivery of services (some potential macro approaches). Robby and his needs become the focus of attention right now. Such mezzo aspects of intervention as family counseling or support groups might be options for the future, but you determine they are inappropriate at this point in the intervention process.*

5. Establish goals. *You and the family decide that your goal will be to have Robby's capabilities thoroughly evaluated so that you will know what services he will need.*

6. Specify objectives. *You will schedule an evaluation through your agency.*

7. Formalize a contract. *You and Robby's parents establish a verbal contract. You will initiate and set up the evaluation process within the next week. Within that time period you will contact the family about the details. They are committed to bringing Robby in as soon as the evaluation can be scheduled.*

Introduction

EP 2.1.10

The example of Robby and his family portrays one way that, as a generalist practitioner, you might formulate an intervention plan. This chapter concentrates on eight basic steps that form the core of planning in the Generalist Intervention Model (GIM). Planning involves establishing goals, specifying how goals will be achieved, and selecting the most appropriate courses of action.

In the planned change process, planning immediately follows assessment and precedes the actual intervention. Your plan is based on your assessment of the client's situation, problems, needs, and strengths. Subsequently, your plan serves to guide how you proceed to help your client.

LO 6-1 Utilize an Eight-Step Planning Process in Generalist Practice Integrating Micro, Mezzo, and Macro Approaches

The eight steps in the planning process are working with your client(s), prioritizing problems, translating problems into needs, evaluating the level of intervention (micro, mezzo, or macro), establishing goals, specifying objectives, setting action steps, and formulating a contract. These steps are illustrated in Figure 6.1.

STEP 1: WORK WITH YOUR CLIENT(S)

The importance of involving clients in every part of the intervention process cannot be emphasized enough. Clients are usually the best source of information in the assessment phase and must be fully involved in setting goals in the planning process. Although it sometimes is a temptation to think that you know what is best for the client, planning *with* the client is critical to the success of your efforts. At the same time, this is not always easy to do. Factors such as busy caseloads and other distractions sometimes tempt you to pressure clients to accept the plans you would like them to make without soliciting adequate input from them.

Critical Thinking Questions 6.1

EP 2.1.3

- What are some possible consequences of making decisions for clients instead of with them?
- Under what circumstances might a client be unable to actively participate in the assessment and goal-setting process?

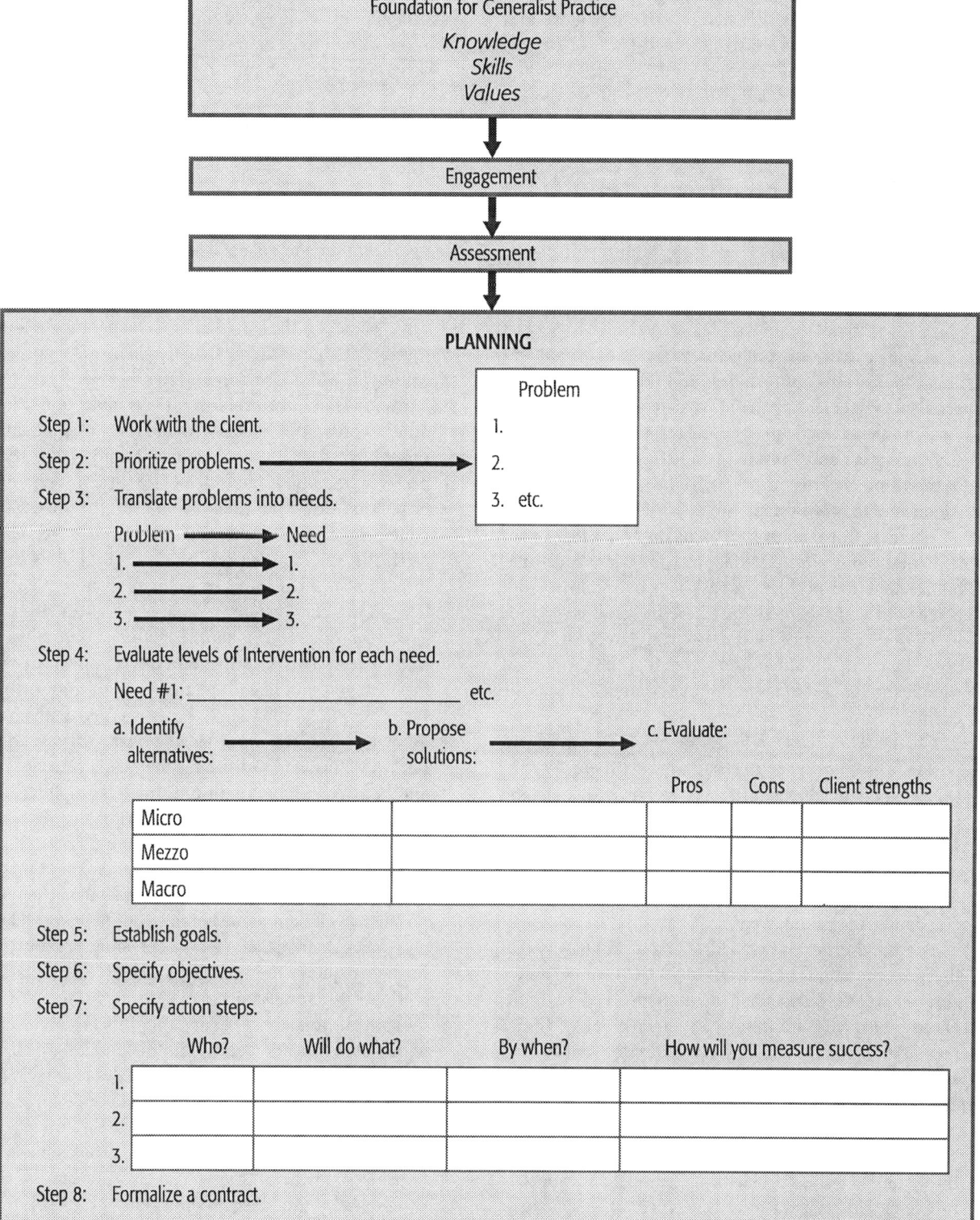

FIGURE 6.1 Planning in the Generalist Intervention Model (GIM)

Talking with clients and clarifying their needs and wishes takes time. Be courteous to your clients and demonstrate your interest in what they have to say. If clients do not feel included and, indeed, *own* the plan themselves, they will probably not be motivated to cooperate. Remember, empowering clients means enhancing their right to self-determination.

STEP 2: PRIORITIZE PROBLEMS—WHICH PROBLEM SHOULD YOU WORK ON FIRST?

Many clients will have multiple problems on multiple levels. In Chapter 5, we defined nine categories of problems: interpersonal conflict, dissatisfaction in social relations, problems with formal organizations, difficulties in role performance, problems in social transition, psychological and behavioral problems, inadequate resources, problems in decision making, and cultural conflicts. In view of the numerous categories of problems, how can you choose which one to work on?

The first thing to do is to focus on only those problems that fulfill three criteria. First, the client must recognize that the problem exists. You may or may not agree with your client about where the problem stands in a prioritized list of all the problems involved. However, the client should at least agree that the problem is significant enough to merit both your attention and the client's.

Clients who deny problems or fail to see their importance will not want to waste time on them. For instance, a client who denies his alcohol addiction will probably refuse to discuss the subject in an interview with you. However, you may be able to identify related problems, such as child abuse (while drinking) or lack of money (due to job loss because of the drinking), that are significant to the client.

A second criterion for addressing a problem is that the problem should be clearly defined in understandable terms. You and your client both need to know exactly what you are talking about in order to find a satisfactory solution. The importance of clarity and specificity in goal setting is an ongoing theme throughout this chapter.

A third criterion is that it must be realistically possible that you and your client will be able to do something about the problem. Fixating on hopeless problems is just a waste of time for both of you. For example, dwelling on the problem of a spouse who left home 3 years ago and has not been heard from since is

probably useless. Discussing problematic aspects of your client's situation as it stands right now might better merit your time. For instance, she might currently be very concerned about child care, finances, and housing.

Deciding which problem or problems to work on is critical. These become what we call the "target problem":

1. *Identify with the client the problems that are most significant to the client.* This list may be long or short. The important thing is to explore with clients all of their concerns. You will probably perceive some of the problems as being much less significant than others. Include them anyway because you will address them later.

2. *Explicitly state each problem in behavioral terms.* In other words, the precise nature of the problem should be clear in your mind. Additionally, the problem statement should include descriptions of behaviors that will later allow you to measure your progress and determine when you have succeeded in solving the problem. We will discuss the importance of behavioral specificity in more depth later in the chapter.

3. *Prioritize the problems in order of their importance to the client.* This prioritization alerts you to which problem you should address first, second, and so on. For example, a client may be concerned with the following problems in order of priority: paying the rent, her husband's drinking, her child's truancy, and her overweight condition, which is resulting in a number of health problems. Paying the rent is probably the problem you should address first.

Once again, this process is not as easy as it sounds. Frequently, how you rank the client's problems will be quite different from how your client ranks them. In such cases, it is up to you to further explore the problems with clients. You will need to establish a list of priorities satisfactory to both of you. Once again, this process involves good communication skills and making judgments. Throughout this process, the focus is on what the client believes he or she needs. Sometimes practitioners try to substitute their judgment for what the client needs and this is a bad omen in the relationship. However, the social worker can and should help the client define the problems by pointing out omissions in the client's thinking or identifying potential consequences. The purpose of this help is to arrive at a mutual understanding and agreement regarding the problems to be addressed. In the process the client may recognize other concerns that need attention and this recognition may alter client thinking about the intervention plan.

4. *Establish an initial agreement with the client regarding the problem you will attend to first.* This problem needs to be one in which the client is interested and that can be solved, even if it is not the very first one on your list. For instance, take a client who states the problem most critical to her is finding a job. She indicates her second most critical problem is that her landlord has turned off her heat in the middle of an icy winter. After exploring the matter, you determine that finding her a job is a more complicated task than it initially might seem. Your client is unskilled, has no high school diploma, and is responsible for several small children. Such issues as job training, transportation, and day care will require more effort to resolve.

However, you see the lack of heat problem as being more amenable to intervention than the unemployment problem. For one thing, for landlords to turn the heat off in apartment rentals in your state during winter is illegal. Therefore, calls to the landlord and, perhaps, the appropriate authorities have a good potential for resolving this problem. You can help your client explore potential solutions for both problems. Hopefully, you can come to an agreement to work on a problem that you feel can be solved in a relatively short period of time.

Sometimes you determine with the client that more than one problem can be addressed at the same time. For instance, consider the client mentioned previously. Her third problem might be that she does not have enough money to feed her children. You think she qualifies for assistance that she currently is not receiving. You can proceed to investigate the possibility of getting her these resources at approximately the same time you are working on the heat problem.

STEP 3: TRANSLATE PROBLEMS INTO NEEDS

Problems, of course, involve any source of perplexity or distress. Many times they are initiated by lack of resources. Clients will come to you because they have problems they need to solve. Helping them accomplish that is your job.

Needs, on the other hand, typically fall into three categories. The first is those items we depend upon for survival, including food, water, and shelter. These tend to be fairly universal in that all human beings have similar requirements. The second category is those items we require in order to maintain a sense of well-being. This includes things that keep us comfortable, healthy, or otherwise content and may well differ from individual to individual. For example, you might have a greater sense of well-being or happiness with a slab of medium-rare prime rib and a baked potato for dinner, and your friend might attain the same sense from a tofu burger with sprouts. Both will provide sustenance, but how content one feels tends to be idiosyncratic.

The third category is the items you require to achieve a sense of fulfillment in your life. This varies from person to person but might include having a satisfying job where you feel valued and appreciated and a relationship with someone who loves you. Needs may range from those that are social or psychological in nature to others that are economic and tangible. To figure out how to help your client, you must translate the client's problems into his or her needs.

Take, for instance, the lack of adequate resources—not having enough money. Dwelling on the problem does not help you figure out what to do about it. However, if you translate the problem into what the client *needs to solve it,* you can formulate ideas about what to do. The problem of lack of money means that the client *needs* better access to resources. The next logical step is to ask yourself the question, "Where might such resources be acquired?" Possible sources include public assistance, food stamps, paid employment, and charitable organizations, among many other resources. These ideas orient your thinking to possible goals for the client and strategies for achieving these goals. For example, you might then discuss with your client the possibility of applying for assistance or seeking job training. Figure 6.2 illustrates a variety of identified problems and their translation into related needs.

Problems, needs, and goals are all interrelated. Your goal will be to satisfy the need causing the problem. Simply translating problems into needs orients you toward establishing goals. It turns your thoughts from focusing on what is wrong to concentrating on how what is wrong can be remedied. Your major goal is usually to satisfy your client's needs.

Identified Problems	Related Needs
Alcohol addiction ⟶	Ongoing sobriety
Child abuse ⟶	Stop abuse, emotional control, child-management techniques
Unemployment ⟶	Employment
Homelessness ⟶	Place to live
Depression ⟶	Treatment for relief of depression
Grief at death of loved one ⟶	Grief management
Misbehavior of children ⟶	Improved parental control of children, child-management techniques
Poor performance in school ⟶	Improved school performance, motivation, family stability
Compulsive stealing ⟶	Treatment for compulsivity, access to adequate resources
Alzheimer's disease and loss of control ⟶	Placement in supportive setting

FIGURE 6.2 Examples of Related Needs Translated from Identified Problems

© Cengage Learning

STEP 4: EVALUATE LEVELS OF INTERVENTION—SELECTING A STRATEGY

Together with the client, you need to identify and assess various strategies with which to achieve the major goals related to the specified problems. In other words, your strategy is the route you and your clients will take to meet your client's needs. You can develop a strategy by doing the following:

1. Focus on the first need you and the client have selected to work on.
2. Review the need and consider identifying micro, mezzo, and macro alternative strategies to arrive at a solution.
3. Emphasize your client's strengths when establishing strategies.
4. Evaluate the pros and cons of each strategy you have considered with your client.
5. Select and pursue the strategy that appears to be most efficient and effective.

First, you and your client need to identify and review potential strategies that may involve micro, mezzo, or macro aspects of practice. You want to decide what your "unit of attention" will be; the unit of attention is the system you will focus on as a target of change. You should not just focus on the micro aspects of the client's problem situation, namely, what you and your client can do yourselves on your client's behalf. Perhaps your client's family needs to become involved. This inclusion, of course, involves a mezzo approach to

intervention. Perhaps your client could benefit from a treatment or self-help group. Take, for instance, a gambling-addicted client who could benefit from involvement in Gamblers Anonymous, a national self-help organization (similar in some ways to Alcoholics Anonymous) for people who have gambling problems.

Instead of micro or mezzo approaches, strategies involving macro skills might provide the most appropriate route for solving a particular problem. For instance, take a Hispanic client, Jorge Quiero, whose young children have not been allowed to enter a neighborhood school, despite the fact that the family has lived in that school's district for over a year. You feel that this entails blatant discrimination on the basis of culture and race. You might pursue advocating with the school system on behalf of your client. You might determine that educating school board members about the problem and collaborating with them to change policies is the most effective course of action. You might even decide that legal confrontation is necessary to effect change in the school system's policies.

In some cases, more than one strategy may be needed to attain a particular goal. In the case of the Quiero family, you and Mr. Quiero might conclude that he and his spouse could benefit from English lessons. They speak just enough English "to get along." They indicate that they have had difficulty expressing themselves adequately. Lessons could provide them with an enhanced ability to negotiate the difficult school system themselves. Note that this tactic would add a micro strategy (namely, the clients learning English) to the macro strategy already discussed (i.e., changing the school system's policy), although both are directed at the same goal. The goal, of course, is for the Quiero children to attain an education.

There will probably be many potential strategies to achieve any particular goal. You must depend on your professional judgment, expertise, and creativity to formulate the best possible strategy.

Sometimes brainstorming with clients helps generate ideas. Brainstorming is the process of generating as many options as possible. However, one should note that practitioners probably provide most of the resource information and technical help; clients would not need your help in the first place if they had all the answers.

Assessing Client Strengths

Emphasizing and incorporating your client's strengths when establishing strategies is useful in several ways. First, strengths provide blocks upon which to build intervention plans. Instead of focusing on problems, needs, and deficits, strengths provide you with something positive you can use to empower clients. Second, emphasizing clients' strengths allows you to give your clients positive feedback. You can talk about their strengths with them and build up their confidence. Emphasizing strengths can be used to convey your respect to clients. Third, incorporating clients' strengths into strategies allows you to work with and think about something concrete. To nonprofessionals, the intervention process (along with the professional jargon and fancy words involved) can appear vague and confusing. Highlight 6.1 elaborates upon nine areas you can explore with your clients to identify their strengths.

The following example illustrates how strengths can be incorporated into planned strategies. Harvey is a homeless Vietnam veteran with posttraumatic stress disorder. This disorder involves a psychological reaction to an event that is outside the range of normal human experience and typically continues well after the event has passed. In Harvey's case, this experience includes the horrors and massacres of brutal combat. Symptoms include such things as sleep disturbances, bad memories, hyper-awareness of things in your environment, emotional numbing, and trouble concentrating, among others. Harvey manifests virtually all of these symptoms. He has not been able to hold down a job or even remain in the same residence for more

than a month since the war ended. He has serious problems.

As a social worker, what can you do to help Harvey? First, translate his problems into needs. He needs therapy to deal with his stress disorder, emotional support from family and/or friends, a place to live, and a job. Because his disorder affects virtually every aspect of his life, you may easily be overwhelmed by his situation. However, elaborating upon his strengths provides inklings about what to do.

Harvey's strengths include: his status as a veteran (allowing him free access to help through Veterans' Administration [VA] hospitals and facilities), good physical health, a high school diploma, and an extremely supportive and concerned family. To figure out strategies to meet his needs (your ultimate goal), take his strengths and resources into consideration.

First, Harvey can be referred to the VA hospital for evaluation and therapy. The VA also has a program that provides temporary housing for veterans suffering from similar disorders. His family can be involved in his treatment to provide support in his continuation of it. His good physical health and high school diploma indicate that he is qualified for a number of blue-collar, physically oriented jobs. A related strength, we find out, is that when he was able to get and hold a job for a few weeks, it was usually in construction. He indicates that he enjoys this kind of work most when he is in better control of his disorder. Thus, perhaps a long-term goal is to involve him in this kind of work when he is ready.

Pros and Cons

In the process of planning strategies, you need to evaluate the pros and cons of each. You and your client will not be able to do everything at once. You will probably need to determine what the most efficient and potentially effective strategies would be. For example, take the case of the Quiero family. Major problems included enrolling their children in school and poor English-speaking skills. Consider the pros and cons of two of the possible strategies identified, as discussed next.

Macro Strategy 1. Advocate with the school system on behalf of your clients.

Pros

- The school system cannot legally deny children access on the basis of language, so the legal system is on the family's side. The system, therefore, might respond to additional pressure from the worker.

HIGHLIGHT 6.1

Potential Areas of Clients' Strengths

Sometimes clients do not recognize that they have any strengths because they have been struggling with their problems for some time. Part of your job is to explore with clients to identify and elaborate upon their strengths. Under each category is a series of questions. These are the types of questions you might consider asking your own clients.

1. *Special interests and activities.* Do you have special interests on which you would like to spend time? What skills and talents do you feel you have? Do you belong to any organizations or groups? If not, have you in the past? What types of activities do you participate in that make you feel good?
2. *Family and friends.* What family members are you particularly close to? Whom can you call on for support? Whom do you feel comfortable enough with to confide in? Do you have any close friends? Are you friends with any of your neighbors?
3. *Religion and values.* Is religion important and meaningful to you? If so, with what creed or denomination are you involved? Do you have a minister or priest you feel comfortable in going to for support or guidance? What values in life are especially important to you? Honesty? Being close to others? Supporting your children? Being dependable?
4. *Occupation and education.* What educational level have you achieved (as opposed to what level you have not achieved)? What work experience have you built up? What marketable skills do you have? Do you have any hobbies (e.g., woodworking) that might or do demonstrate special ability?
5. *Reaction to professional services.* What, if any, social services have you been involved with that you found helpful? How have you benefited from these services? Were there any particular professionals whom you especially liked or found exceptionally helpful?
6. *Emotional and mental health.* What things make you the happiest? During what times do you feel the strongest and most capable? What types of events or happenings help improve your mood? How do you usually go about making decisions or solving your problems?
7. *Physical condition.* What kinds of physical activities do you like most? What kinds of physical activity make you feel good? Which aspects of your health are especially good?
8. *Support system.* Where does most of your income come from? Do you have other assets you can rely on in needy times? Whom can you depend on to help you when you need it? What help can they provide?
9. *Other.* What strengths do you have other than the ones we have already covered?

- The worker knows the school's vice principal and two school board members. The school board, of course, has the greatest authority over what goes on in the school system. The worker feels there is good potential here to exercise influence in order to change the school's prior decision and overall policy.

Cons

- The school's principal and a number of other school board members are renowned for their conservative approach to changing policy. Thus, they might bristle and balk at additional pressure.
- Advocacy takes a lot of time. The worker's caseload is large, and there are numerous crises needing attention.

- The advocacy process is vague. The worker would need to sit down and develop a well-specified plan for whom to contact and how.
- The children might not be accepted into school for an inordinate period of time. Thus, their education could be seriously impeded.

Micro Strategy 2. Enroll parents in English classes so they may better advocate for themselves.

Pros

- This would enhance the Quieros' empowerment, ability to communicate, and prowess to fight for their own rights.
- The difficulties they experienced in dealing with a primarily English-speaking community would be decreased.

Cons

- No low-cost English classes are readily available in their area.
- Such classes are time consuming and require high motivation to continue with them over a substantial period of time.
- Although such education may be of some use to the Quieros in the long run, its usefulness in the current problem is questionable.
- There is some debate, especially in certain areas of the country with large Hispanic populations, about whether English must be the primary language. Is it fair or right to force English upon people already adept in Spanish?

The pros and cons noted in the preceding two examples of strategies are arbitrary. That is, there are many other approaches for you to consider. However, these examples convey the idea of what identifying, struggling with, and finally deciding on an actual course of action in real practice situations are like.

LO 6-2 Establish Goals and Objectives

STEP 5: ESTABLISH GOALS

 Several benefits occur from setting clear goals with clients. First, establishing goals helps ensure that clients and workers are in agreement about such matters as problem definition and the changes that must occur to produce a suitable outcome. Second, they validate the client's concerns and definition of the problem and facilitate client empowerment. Third, goals suggest the direction and nature of the intervention, which helps both client and social worker stay on course. Fourth, carefully defined goals lend themselves more easily to evaluation. Evaluation is, in turn, a critical component of the planned change process that allows both client and worker to know that progress has occurred. Progress is important because it is tied to the effectiveness of the interventions employed and often to reimbursement for service.

In summary, we establish goals to clarify the purpose of an intervention. A clearly stated goal allows you to determine whether or not your intervention has been successful. Goals are necessary whether your intervention strategy involves micro, mezzo, or macro practice. In micro practice, goals guide your work with individual clients. Mezzo-practice intervention may require goals involving each individual member and the entire group as a whole. Finally, in macro practice, a generalist practitioner might use goal setting to help a community or organization target what it wants to accomplish and how it will go about doing this.

Social workers set goals to help a client system identify and specify what it wants to achieve within the worker–client relationship. Worker and client must be moving in the same direction. They must clearly understand what they are trying to accomplish.

The importance of specifying goals should be emphasized regardless of whether you are participating in micro, mezzo, or macro interventions. You and your client system (be it individual, family, group, agency, or community) need to establish clearly and straightforwardly what you want to accomplish.

Examples of goals include:

- Get landlord to fix leaking plumbing.
- Improve parents' child-management skills.
- Participate for 6 months in support group for spouses of alcoholics.
- Change agency policy to include home visits for work with families.
- Develop program for rural homeless children.

Thus, your goal is a broad statement of what you and your clients want to achieve.

STEP 6: SPECIFY OBJECTIVES

Goals are usually so broadly stated that identifying how they will be achieved is virtually impossible. For instance, take the goal "get landlord to fix leaking plumbing." The goal statement gives no indication of how the goal can be accomplished or when the repair will take place. Will the client picket the landlord's office to demand attention? Will you call the Health Department to complain and demand that the landlord comply with housing codes that require maintaining plumbing in good working condition? Will the landlord suddenly see the error of his ways and get the pipes fixed?

Both you and your client know what needs to get done. The client needs plumbing that works adequately. The next step is to break that goal down into smaller objectives.

Objectives are behaviorally specific regarding what is to be achieved and how success will be measured. For example, take the goal "get client a job paying at least $300 a week." In order to attain this goal, you and the client would have to set objectives to help move her toward this end. If she has not completed high school, one objective might be to gain her high school equivalency certificate. A second objective might be to subsequently complete 6 months of job-skill training at a technical school.

Objectives can be further broken down as needed. For example, the client would need to apply for admission to the job-skill program and apply for financial aid to help pay for her schooling. Each of these are *action* steps on the way to achieving the objective of completing the job training program and meeting the goal of a job that pays at least $300 per week. Keep in mind that the purpose of goals and objectives is to keep you and your client on track so often it is helpful to set a deadline for completing a specific step.

Objectives Should Be Measurable

How will you know whether the goal has been achieved or whether you should continue striving to achieve it? For example, take an impoverished, single-parent client with three small children. Her *problem* is poverty. She *needs* money. Her *goal* is to get enough financial assistance to supply her family with food, shelter, and clothing. You and your client establish three specific *objectives* for helping her solve her problem. They include obtaining financial help from the local welfare office, becoming involved in a housing program,[1] and receiving food stamps.[2] Have your objectives been met when she begins receiving financial assistance and food stamps but remains on a long waiting list for housing assistance? Have your objectives been met when she receives $539 a month in financial assistance, $561 a month in food stamps, and $400 in rent subsidy, even if this total amount is inadequate for her to survive?

Instead, you could specify a more measurable objective. For example, you could establish the maximum amount she could possibly receive for each of these sources. If $1,500 is the maximum she is allowed to receive under current guidelines and you have specified that as your objective, then you have succeeded in reaching it. You then may need to establish a subsequent objective to gain additional resources so that she can feed and house her children adequately.

---

1. *Housing programs are* "publicly funded and monitored programs designed to provide suitable homes, especially for those unable to find or pay for homes themselves. In the United States, most of these programs are administered by the Department of Housing and Urban Development (DHUD). These programs include low-rent public housing, rent-subsidies, [and] home ownership assistance," among others (Barker, 2003, p. 202).

2. The food stamp program allows low-income people to purchase food with coupons or benefit cards. Eligibility is based on income and other resources. The program is federally financed.

Specifying goals and objectives, in addition to measuring their success, will be addressed more thoroughly later in the chapter. For example, setting objectives in micro practice involves determination of the specific performance required (what is the basic objective you are trying to achieve), the conditions under which this objective can be accomplished, and the standards by which its success can be measured. We will also address goals and objectives within the contexts of micro, mezzo, and macro practice. Emphasis will be placed on the importance of establishing clear, specific, and measurable statements, regardless of your practice area.

Sometimes Goals and Objectives Are Confusing

Sometimes the two terms become confusing because many people use *goals* and *objectives* synonymously. For our purposes, an objective should *always* be clear, specific, and measurable. A goal is often too complex to be measurable. Goals should still be stated as specifically as possible. Simple goals should be stated as if they were objectives. From here on, we will refer to objectives instead of goals in order to emphasize the importance of specificity.

Setting Objectives in Micro Practice

Many of the principles that apply to micro practice (e.g., the importance of being specific) apply to macro practice as well. In this section, we examine objectives within the context of work with individual clients. However, our emphasis on how objectives should be stated applies to mezzo and macro practice as well.

Throughout this discussion, we will be referring to objectives. However, remember that the principle of being clear and specific applies to both objectives and goals.

Establishing Objectives. Establish specific objectives with your clients. What does this statement mean? For one thing, the objective should indicate exactly how it can be met. It should be easy to tell when you have achieved your objective and when you have not. Consider the following examples:

- Objective: The client will become happier. How happy does the client have to be in order to have achieved this objective? Should he get very happy, or is just a little happy enough? Are we talking about one smile a day? Can the client be happy without smiling? What does "happy" mean anyway? How will we measure the change in level of happiness? There is obviously a broad range of subjective interpretations possible concerning this objective.

- It is not a good objective. The point about being specific is that you should have to expend as little thought and effort as possible to determine whether the objective has been met.
- Objective: The client's daughter (Sophia) will behave better. Does this statement mean that Sophia, age 6, will stop pinching her infant brother (which she does frequently throughout the day) and stop spitting at her mother when being reprimanded? Is the objective met if Sophia pinches her brother only 10 times during the day instead of her usual two dozen? What if she stops pinching but continues to spit? Has the objective been met? Is she behaving better enough? Is the objective even feasible if we have no way to determine the exact number of times that Sophia pinches her brother?

  Once again, interpreting the objective is difficult. Like the first example mentioned, this objective is subject to a wide range of interpretation. You would be put in the uncomfortable position of struggling to interpret whether you arbitrarily thought the objective had been met.

- Objective: The client (Mindy) will improve her communication skills. This time, the client is an 18-year-old woman with developmental disabilities. Although Mindy is capable of reading at a fourth-grade level, she is shy and rarely speaks to anyone. Will this objective be met if she speaks more frequently to her parents, with whom she lives? How much more frequently? Is two times a day enough? What if she only says one word each time? Should she speak to her parents two times each day for at least 5 minutes each time? Would the objective then be met? Should Mindy also be more adept at speaking to strangers she meets before the objective is met? What about the listening part of her communication skills? Must her capacity to listen and understand be improved before this objective is met? Does this objective involve her ability to carry on a full and meaningful conversation?

  Once again, establishing what is really meant by this objective is difficult. You would have to make a subjective decision regarding whether you were successful at meeting the objective or whether you needed to continue striving to achieve it.

What are your thoughts right now? Do you think we are being much too particular and absurd? The intent of these examples is not to frustrate or annoy you. In practice, you will be responsible for both formulating and achieving goals and objectives. What will you (or

your job, for that matter) be worth if you do not accomplish what you are supposed to? You will be accountable to your client, your supervisor, and your agency for achieving your intervention goals and objectives. Therefore, being able to cite clear, concrete, readily understandable objectives is much to your advantage. For any of the three objectives mentioned earlier, questions could easily be raised about whether you were achieving them or not. A clearly defined, specific objective helps us evaluate exactly what has been achieved.

Specifying objectives in the planning process is helpful. Ideal objectives are observable actions that are possible to measure in order to monitor progress. Our clients, supervisors, and colleagues should have a graphic, coherent picture in their minds of exactly what we mean.

Objectives should meet at least three criteria. First, they should be explicit or specific enough that anyone can tell that they have or have not been achieved. For practical purposes, this means they can be measured in some way. In other words, objectives should refer to something that can be seen and measured. For example, take one of our earlier "bad objective" examples regarding improving communication skills for Mindy, the young adult with developmental disabilities. In this case, what exactly should be improved? Should she be expected to speak in complete sentences and use correct grammar? Should she be expected to initiate conversations and ask questions in order to achieve "improved" communication skills? Think back to Chapter 2, which identified the many attending and interviewing skills used to enhance communication. Which of these should Mindy be expected to master in order to achieve the goal? The objectives leading up to the goal should specify exactly *what* behavior and *how much* of that behavior Mindy would need to learn in order to achieve the goal. In other words, improved communication would have to be carefully defined.

The second criterion is clarity. A clear objective is one that others can restate with precision. This includes everyone for whom the objective is relevant such as clients, family members, and other professionals. Regardless of who is doing the evaluating, all observers should see the same thing and be in agreement. In Mindy's case, anyone knowing what the objective is and observing Mindy's communication behavior should be able to determine whether the objective has been met or not.

Completeness, the last criterion, means that enough information should be given about how the objective can be attained. Once more, consider Mindy. The objective should specify the circumstances under which her communication should be improved. Should it involve interactions only with her parents and loved ones? Should it involve communication and interaction with others? Would it suffice to improve her communication with clerks at stores she visits? Would she also need to initiate communication with complete strangers in order to achieve the objective?

Ideal Objectives Can Be Measured. We have established that one of the major purposes of formulating objectives is to provide a means for measuring whether they have been attained or not. The point of having an objective is to reach it and know that you have done so. Three important components in a clear, well-written objective are behavior, condition, and performance level. Consider an objective used in a description of Superman's powers: "Leaps tall buildings with a single bound." This objective tells us the expected behavior, "leaping," the condition, "with a single bound," and a performance level, "tall buildings." If our superhero climbs the building stairs or takes the elevator, he is not engaging in the desired behavior. If he pole-vaults over a small shed, he is also not meeting the last two requirements, namely condition and performance level. Finally, if he bumps into the building and falls down, he may not be a superhero at all.

Performance involves what the client, worker, or other individual involved is to perform in order to attain the objective. The performance component in the context of changing a child's behavior illustrates exactly what you expect the child to do. What specific activity or behavior is involved in achieving the objective? Examples include "stands quietly in line," "says thank you when given a toy," or "buttons his own jacket."

The second component of a clear objective involves the conditions or circumstances under which the behaviors involved in achieving the objective are performed. What materials does the child need in order to finish the activity and subsequently achieve the objective? Must the child perform the activity alone or can someone help her? Is there a limited time frame within which she must complete the task? Examples of conditions include "given shoes with shoelaces," "within 2 minutes," "without prompting," or "for his parents in their kitchen after supper."

The standard of performance involves how well, how soon, or how often the performance, activity, or behavior should be done. Does the activity have to be done perfectly? Must it be done every single day? Is the objective still achieved if the child misses one day a week or mixes up two letters of the alphabet?

Highlight 6.2 applies this three-component basis for setting good objectives to situations typically found in social work. The importance of specificity continues to be a major theme (see Highlight 6.3).

STEP 7: SPECIFY ACTION STEPS

EP 2.1.10g

Establishing objectives requires specifying the action steps necessary in order to achieve those objectives. To achieve them, involved individuals will need to get things done. Action steps are important because they help identify appropriate intervention strategies. The basic formula for delegating responsibility is to specify *who* will do *what* by *when*. "Who" is the individual specified for accomplishing a task. "What" involves the tasks the individual has to complete in order to achieve the goal. Finally, "when" sets a time limit so that the task is not lost in some endless eternity. The following are examples of action steps:

- Ms. M (who) will call her mother about helping care for the children (what) by 3 p.m. next Monday (when).
- I (who) will contact my supervisor and establish a location for the group to meet (what) by Wednesday, November 23 (when).
- Mr. S. (who) will survey the agency's clientele to determine their primary needs and be ready to make a report (what) by the February staff meeting (when).

You might be asking yourself, "Why is it important to be so precise?" The answer is that if you are not explicit regarding who has the responsibility for accomplishing the task, it is likely that the task will not get done.

As a student you are probably very busy. You are not likely to have much time to do anything but the required coursework. Doing a lot of in-depth reading on topics that interest you would be nice. However, you probably assign these interests a relatively low priority. You do what you *have* to do first. It is the same with generalist practitioners in the field. As a social worker, you will probably have an abundance of clients and will constantly strive to prioritize what needs to get done first. If completing a task by a certain deadline is not your specifically identified responsibility, putting it off...and off...and off is easy. Such tasks rarely, if ever, get done.

HIGHLIGHT 6.2

Using the Concepts of Performance, Conditions, and Standards to Establish Goals and Objectives with Clients

For each of the following scenarios, a client will be described briefly. Subsequently, an arbitrary objective using the performance/conditions/standards formula will be presented. These scenarios illustrate an extension of the who-should-do-what-by-when formula for delegating responsibility and specifying objectives. For each scenario, the client is *who*. Likewise, the performance, conditions, and standards specify the *what* and by *when*.

Earl, age 83, resides in a large nursing home. He has arthritis, is gradually losing the use of his hands, and is slowly failing. The *objective* for this client is:

- *Performance:*   Earl will enhance and maintain eye–hand coordination

- *Conditions:*   by participating in a crafts activity hour offered four times each week

- *Standards:*   and attending them three out of four times each week (75 percent of the time).

Pearl, age 24, has been reported for physically abusing her two small children when they do not obey her demands. The *objective* for this client is:

- *Performance:*   Pearl will learn parent-effectiveness skills

- *Conditions:*   by attending Parent-Effectiveness Training Classes every Thursday evening at the local YMCA

- *Standards:*   and attending all six training sessions (100 percent of the time).

Johnny, age 15, is labeled by his parents as uncontrollable. He has been arrested for selling drugs twice, is frequently involved in gang-related fights, and often gets home after his curfew. The *objective* for this client is:

- *Performance:*   Johnny will arrive home by his curfew

- *Conditions:*   at 9 P.M. on weeknights and 11 P.M. on weekends

- *Standards:*   13 out of 14 nights every 2 weeks (93 percent of the time).

Ivy, age 21, has three small children and works a full-time first-shift job at a bakery. Ivy's own mother, who has been caring for Ivy's children, has recently become ill and can no longer babysit. Ivy does not want to lose her job. The *objective* for this client is:

- *Performance:*   Ivy will arrange for day care for her three children

- *Conditions:*   by calling five local day care agencies to determine cost and her children's eligibility

- *Standards:*   and reporting her findings to her social worker by next Thursday.

Storm, a 26-year-old adult with developmental disabilities, lives in a group home with other adults of similar ability levels. She moved in after the death of her mother, with whom she had lived her entire life. The *objective* for this client is:

- *Performance:*   Storm will complete specified daily living tasks

- *Conditions:*   and check off completed tasks on the clipboard holding her daily log of activities (e.g., making her bed, getting to work at the sheltered workshop on time, vacuuming the living room)

- *Standards:*   and complete 80 percent of all her required tasks each day.

Commentary

When these goals have been attained and when they have not can be clearly seen. If Storm, for example, only completes 78 percent of her required tasks, she has not met her objective. Likewise, if Johnny misses his curfew two times in 2 weeks, he has not accomplished his objective.

Clearly specifying how you will evaluate your objective will save many headaches in the long run. Specifying and agreeing upon goal expectations in advance will help you in avoiding potential arguments, having to make judgments about excuses, and even being the target of manipulation.

HIGHLIGHT 6.3

Clarifying Vague Goals and Objectives

Following is a case of a client with multiple problems. After the scenario is a series of vague statements that could be incorporated as possible objectives for the client portrayed. Unfortunately, these phrases are sometimes embodied in the goals proposed in real case records and reports.

For each vague goal statement:

1. Explain why the goal is vague. For example, which specific words are vague? How might their meanings be misinterpreted or interpreted in many different ways by different people?
2. Reformulate these objectives by using specific terminology and incorporating the performance/conditions/standards format illustrated in Highlight 6.2.

Sarah, age 24, has paraplegia. She broke her back in a car accident when she was 16. Afterward, she became clinically depressed, withdrawing from family and friends, and has isolated herself in her apartment for the past 3 years. She dresses slovenly, is generally lethargic, and remains unmotivated to get training for employment or improve her social life.

The low-rent apartment building in which she lives is being torn down. Sarah is panic-stricken and hostile to social workers and family members trying to help her and does not know what she will do.

Respond to the following potential goals for Sarah and answer the two questions previously posed for each. The first statement is followed by an example of how you might respond to the remaining goal statements.

- *Vague statement of objective (example):* Improve family communication. *Reason for vagueness: Improve* is a vague term. How can you measure family communication? How can you tell when the goal is achieved? Which aspects of family communication are being targeted? Those involving parents? Siblings? Grandparents? What aspects of the communication should change? What exactly does "communication" mean?
- *Improved restatement of an objective (performance, conditions, standards):* Three days each week, Sarah will call her mother on the phone and talk for at least 5 minutes.

Now, do the same thing for the following vague goal statements:

Vague Objective Statement	Reasons for Vagueness	Improved Restatement: Performance/Conditions/Standards
1. Enhance emotional health:		
2. Increase awareness of oneself:		
3. Find appropriate employment:		
4. Achieve a high level of family functioning:		
5. Accept physical disability:		
6. Dress better:		
7. Increase motivation:		
8. Demonstrate more interest:		
9. Respond appropriately:		
10. Try harder:		
11. Improve wife–husband relationship:		
12. Reduce hostile outbursts and tantrums:		

For example, you are at a staff meeting where you are discussing the progress of a client with a developmental disability. Other professionals at the meeting include your supervisor, a psychologist, a vocational counselor, a physician, a speech therapist, an occupational therapist, and a physical therapist. The purpose of the meeting is for each professional to report what progress has been made with this particular client to formulate plans and goals for the future. One of the goals established by the group is to "make a referral to another agency for intensive vocational testing." Such testing would determine your client's specific skills, abilities, and job interests. However, the task of making the referral has not been clearly specified and assigned.

Two months later, the same group meets again to reevaluate this client's progress. Your supervisor, who is leading the staff meeting, asks for a report on the vocational testing results. You gaze at the psychologist with a blank expression on your face. The psychologist looks at you. The occupational therapist looks at the vocational counselor. The vocational counselor looks at the psychologist, and so it goes. Each staff member assumed that some other staff member would make the referral. All were terribly busy with their own job responsibilities and had no time to do anything they did not absolutely have to do. As a result, no one "naturally" assumed responsibility for completing the task. Thus, the task did not get done. The client had lost 2 months of precious (and expensive) time.

One should note the phrase "get done." It is as if the task will magically do itself without any human intervention. In other words, this phrase is one to carefully scrutinize and avoid.

LO 6-3 Use Contracts as Part of the Planning Process

STEP 8: FORMALIZE A CONTRACT

Thus far, we have established seven steps in the planning phase of the planned change process: work with your client, prioritize problems, translate problems into needs, evaluate levels of intervention (micro, mezzo, and macro), establish goals, specify objectives, and specify action steps. The eighth and final step of the planning phase is to establish an intervention contract.

A contract is an agreement between a client and worker about what will occur in the intervention process. It can include goals, objectives, action steps, time frames, and responsibilities of people involved.

This definition can be broken down into four major components:

1. A contract specifies what will occur during the intervention process;
2. A contract is established by a worker and client making an agreement together;
3. A contract generally contains four types of information: goals, methods, timetables, and mutual obligations;
4. A contract's format can be written, oral, or implied.

The Purpose of a Contract

A contract represents the culmination of the planning step in the planned change process. It clarifies and summarizes exactly who is responsible for completing which tasks. Contracts achieve several objectives simultaneously. For example, they increase client motivation and investment in the change effort because the client has a large degree of control over the contract's contents. Although they are not legal documents in the typical sense, they help ensure the client's rights. They also specify each individual's role in the change process and who is responsible for doing what by when. Contracts clarify expectations of all parties and help serve as a monitoring and evaluation device for change. Contracts identify expectations and help avoid potential misunderstandings. The plan should be very clear to everyone involved.

Contracts can be used in any arena of practice. In micro practice, they can summarize specific responsibilities of client, worker, agency, and any involved others. In mezzo practice, contracts can specify individual and group goals and tasks. In macro practice, contracts can formalize any number of agreed-upon plans. A contract can, for instance, specify individual responsibilities of task group members advocating for a policy change concerning HIV-positive clients. This group's intent is to lobby for a change in state law that will prohibit insurance companies from canceling the policies of persons diagnosed as HIV-positive.

Another example of a contract in macro practice is *purchase-of-service agreements,* which are financial agreements involving at least two organizations. One organization agrees to pay another organization for providing service to a specific population. The agreement may specify a set payment for providing service for a specific number of people or identify a per-client payment based on the number of clients served. Purchase-of-service agreements allow the paying agency to offer services to its client base that the agency might otherwise not be able to provide. It also helps the service-providing agency by adding to its income.

A more specific example of a purchase-of-service contract is a rural county social services agency with children in foster care needing speech therapy services. The county was too small and had too few children needing such therapy to hire its own speech therapist. The county officials decided to purchase the needed speech therapy services from a private agency, Catholic Social Services (CSS). CSS was a statewide agency hiring a number of speech therapists to travel around the state and supply part-time speech therapy services to a number of counties in similar circumstances (i.e., needing speech therapy services for only a few clients).

Make Contracts with Clients

A contract summarizes what you as a worker and your client system agree to do during the intervention process. The emphasis is on the word *agree*. We continue to stress involving clients during every phase of the intervention process. The extensive involvement of clients in the development of intervention contracts is simply an extension of this theme.

The contract is not a legal contract as such. It has little to do with the contracts disputed in courts of law. It articulates a commitment valid only within the practitioner–client relationship. On the other hand, an intervention contract is flexible and subject to change by agreement between the worker and the client as new information or directions are identified. Thus, the ongoing involvement of the client system is critical.

There are several advantages to client involvement in establishing contracts. First, contracts can help motivate clients to work on their problems because they were active in establishing their own goals, objectives, and action steps. Second, client empowerment is enhanced as clients learn they can take charge and be major participants in the change effort. Third, clients who are "disorganized or forgetful" will benefit from a contract that reminds them of their agreements and responsibilities (Johnson & Yanca, 2010, p. 223). Finally, contracts provide a record of goals and plans that can assist in monitoring and evaluating the planned change effort.

That clients understand everything incorporated into a contract is important. All of the contract's terms should be clear to them. They should also be able to understand all of the words used.

Culturally Competent Contracting

The very nature of contracting presupposes willing agreement between two or more parties—a client and a social worker. However, contracting is sometimes problematic for people from different cultures. For example, some cultures may be more comfortable with the worker taking the lead and identifying what the clients must do to help solve their problems. This is in conflict with the idea of a mutually constructed document. Contracting itself may be confusing to clients whose native language is not English. In addition, those whose experiences with social agencies have been negative or hurtful are likely to be guarded and uncomfortable. Their willingness to enter into an agreement may be affected by this discomfort. Perceived or real power differentials between historically oppressed people of color and social workers can also produce unwillingness to enter into a contract. The social work value of self-determination is an important variable in culturally competent practice because clients must be confident that their choices have precedence in deciding whether and what to agree to. At the same time, the worker must be sensitive to the client's cultural expectations and work toward a satisfactory agreement.

The Format of a Contract

Contracts can be established in three different ways. First, they can be written and signed. Examples of this type will be given later. Second, they can involve a verbal agreement between client, worker, and any others involved. Third, they may be implicit or assumed.

The Written Contract. The written contract is the most formal type. It clearly and visually reflects what client, workers, and anyone involved have agreed upon. It should state specific objectives and follow the "who-will-do-what-by-when" format discussed earlier.

A primary advantage of a written contract is that it becomes a clear, virtually indisputable record. There can be no distortions of what earlier agreements involved. It can be reviewed by the worker and client at any time to refresh memories about what they agreed upon.

Another advantage is that participants sign the contract. A signature illustrates commitment and makes later questioning of who agreed to do what by when difficult.

Written contracts, however, have two disadvantages. First, they take time to draw up (Sheafor & Horejsi,

2012). A practitioner may be rushed, extremely busy, late, or overwhelmed. Second, clients may feel uncomfortable or pressured into signing a contract. Clients with a long history of having things done to them can feel they have no choice, despite any misgivings they may have.

Sheafor and Horejsi (2012) reflect on how to respond to some other extenuating circumstances:

It will be necessary to prepare the contract in the client's first language (e.g., Spanish) if he or she has a poor understanding of English. In cases where the client cannot read, the worker should consider preparing an audio recording of the agreement, in addition to preparing a written statement. (p. 235)

Finally, a copy of the written contract should always be placed in the client's file. It should be easily accessible at any time during the intervention process.

The Oral Contract. Oral contracts specify essentially the same thing as written contracts, although orally—the intent is to clearly identify all objectives and responsibilities in the planning process. Oral contracts should be just as clear as written contracts.

There are two advantages to an oral contract. First, it can be made swiftly and in a relatively easy fashion. Second, it can be a "help" when working with a "resistant or distrustful client" who refuses to sign a written document (Johnson & Yanca, 2010, p. 223). You can solicit agreement from such a client without trying to force a signature.

The client's record should still indicate that the oral contract was made along with a brief summary of what was involved; this summary should include:

- "who participated in the decision making;"
- "what decisions were made";
- "who has agreed to do what and when; and
- How the contract may be revised." (Kagle & Kopels, 2008, p. 72)

The major disadvantage of an oral contract is that forgetting the details of an agreement is easy unless they are written down. Jotting down informal notes to themselves so that they can remember exactly what transpired might be helpful for social workers.

Implicit Contracts. Implicit contracts are agreements that are implied or assumed but not actually articulated. Be wary about using them. It is easy to make two assumptions that can be false. First, you can mistakenly assume that your client has agreed when he or she really has not. Second, you can assume that your client understands all of the conditions and responsibilities of your perceived implicit contract when he or she does not. Always remember that implied contracts carry risks; whenever possible, use written or oral contracts.

In groups where the interpersonal process involved can be complex, there may be numerous assumed agreements. These might concern how individuals will perform and behave inside and outside of the group. There may be too many, and they may be too subtle to label openly. Such assumed agreements essentially compose an implicit contract. For instance, an implicit contract within a treatment group for alcoholic adults might be a prohibition of encouraging other group members to drink. Another term of the implicit contract for this particular group might be to behave in a socially appropriate manner. For instance, fingers should be kept out of noses, ears, and other orifices, and members should not swear at each other.

What to Include in Intervention Contracts

At the least, intervention contracts should include identifying information about the client and specified objectives and signatures of client and worker. Each type of information merits further discussion. Figure 6.3 depicts an example of an intervention contract.

Identifying Information. An intervention contract must always contain information that identifies the client. This information almost always includes the client's name. Sometimes, a case number is involved. At other times, there is a brief description of the problem included, as is illustrated in Figure 6.3. This description can help quickly orient a worker, who deals with many cases and many problems, to a particular case.

Contracts involving groups may include all members' names. The type of group may also be used as identifying information.

In contracts with other agencies, sometimes their names are specified as well. At other times, the contract will be identified by a project name.

Specified Objectives and Action Steps. The core of any intervention contract involves specification of objectives. Our previous discussion concerning the writing of objectives applies directly to writing them into contracts. They should be clear and easily understood by anyone reading them. They should indicate action steps, that is, who will do what by when, and they should be measurable.

Signatures. All written contracts should be signed. These signatures demonstrate that the participants are

Contract for Intervention Plan

Client Name:

1. Description of the Problem:

2. Primary Goals:

3. We, the undersigned, agree to the objectives in the following plan:

   A.

   B.

   C.

   D.

   E.

(Signature of Client)

(Signature of Worker)

(Date)

(Date)

FIGURE 6.3 An Example of a Written Contract Format

well informed about the plan, its objectives, and each participant's responsibilities. Additionally, a signature indicates commitment to the plan.

Contracts used in mezzo and macro practice may need room for a number of different signatures. All participants in the intervention plan should have a place to sign.

Dates. Finally, all intervention contracts should include the date the agreement was made. This date, which can usually be found directly underneath the participants' signatures, indicates the contract's currency. An old date might indicate that the contract's contents need to be reviewed.

Formats Vary. In reality, contract formats vary radically. For example, Kagle and Kopels indicate that a contract or service agreement might contain the following components: (1) Purpose of Service, (2) Goals, (3) Plans, (4) Indicators of Movement Toward Plan Completion, and (5) Agreements Regarding Termination of Services (2008, pp. 68–70).

Additionally, instructions for filling out the service agreement are included. Dates are also recorded a bit differently than those illustrated in Figure 6.3. They indicate the time that the contract covers—the date it was signed and the date it should be completed. The contract then ends with signature lines for both client and worker.

You should be prepared to find such different contract formats. Formats may depend on the agency's mission, client needs, and contract purpose. Regardless of the format your agency uses, the principles applying to writing good objectives still apply. Who is responsible for what tasks should be clear. Task completion dates should be specified. Finally, objectives should be measurable, so no question exists about whether or not they have been accomplished.

Contracts Often Change over Time. Contracts continue to change over time. Objectives are reached, new objectives are established, clients' situations change, and intervention plans must be adjusted to meet these changes. You should indicate such changes and the dates they were made either on the old contract or on a revised one.

Figure 6.4 illustrates a series of three monthly contracts used for residents in a halfway house for people recovering from alcohol and other types of drug abuse. Because the clients reside there, they receive daily supervision in addition to professional counseling. The goal is to help integrate them back into the com-

munity. Thus, the contracts focus on gaining employment and saving money.

Several differences are reflected in the three contracts. Some content changes as the months progress. Note six elements about the "First Month Contract." First, the contract starts with a basic commitment to follow the house rules. Second, it structures a statement committing the client to actively seek employment in a specified geographical area. Third, the contract requires that the client strive to put the specific amount of at least $100 in savings. Fourth, it structures the fact that a new contract will be established within 1 month. Fifth, it specifies that weekly counseling sessions are required. Sixth, blank spaces two through nine are left for the specification of individualized objectives.

Now view the "Second Month Contract" depicted in Figure 6.4. This contract is much less structured. The idea is that clients are gradually encouraged to make more decisions and accept greater responsibility for themselves. This contract omits the item about commitment to house rules. It allows the client to specify how much will be put into savings. Note that putting money into savings is still required. The contract assumes the client has already gotten a job. Likewise, weekly counseling sessions are still required. Additionally, blank spaces two through five are provided for establishing individualized objectives.

Finally, consider the "Third Month Contract." Once again, the client is required to place a set amount into savings but is again permitted to determine that amount. Next, a new goal is added, namely to work actively on the transition from a supervised living environment to living independently within the community. The contract then requires that the client continue evaluating individual goals and working with the counselor to develop new goals. This contract requires that the client attend group meetings instead of individual "weekly counseling sessions." Places for individualized objectives remain.

This series of contracts provides a good example of how objectives and the contracts that reflect them can change. The contracts go from making specific requirements to enhancing the client's independent decision-making capacity. Obviously, some of the objectives are highly structured—that clients must abide by some rules in order to continue in the program is the nature of this treatment program. The agency has found this structure to be the most effective means of treatment. Client participation in the treatment contract is encouraged as much as possible within this setting.

CEPHAS HALFWAY HOUSE

Lutheran Social Services

First Month Contract

In addition to following the House Rules, I, _____ , agree to the following terms in order to keep my residency at Cephas Halfway House.

I will look for employment in the Waukesha area every day until I find a job.

When I become employed, I will open a savings account and try to save at least one hundred dollars ($100).

Once this is done, I will approach my counselor to negotiate a second month contract, which will include goals that my agent and counselor want.

1. Weekly counseling sessions

2.   6.

3.   7.

4.   8.

5.   9.

(Staff)   (Date)

_____   _____
(Resident)

FIGURE 6.4 An Example of Progressively Changing Contracts
Source: This material has been adapted from contracts used by Cephas Halfway House, Waukesha, WI. Used with permission of Lutheran Social Services, 3200 W. Highland Blvd., Milwaukee, WI 53208.

LO 6-4 Engage in Planning in Mezzo Practice

Parts of the planning process for working with groups have been discussed in earlier chapters (specifically, Chapters 3 and 5). Namely, formulating group membership depends on a number of variables, including motivation of potential group members, group purpose, members' ability to communicate with each other, group size, group structure, and group duration.

The six-step planning process described in this section can be similarly applied to planning when working with groups. Of course, variations do exist because of

CEPHAS HALFWAY HOUSE

Lutheran Social Services

Second Month Contract

I, _____ , will agree to increase my savings account to_____ by the end of my second month. If there is any restitution, I will sit down with my agent and work out some arrangement and make out a schedule of payment in addition to the above.

My goals for the second month are as follows:

1. Weekly counseling sessions _____

2. _____

3. _____

4. _____

5. _____

(Staff)   (Date)

(Resident)

FIGURE 6.4 Continued

the increased complexity when more than one client is involved.

THE COMPLEXITY OF SETTING OBJECTIVES IN MEZZO PRACTICE

As we know, a *client system* can be an individual, family, group, or large organization. Your *client* is the individual or group you are helping. Working with families and other groups becomes more complicated than working with single individuals because you need to take all group members' needs into consideration. Nonetheless, the bottom line is to *work with* the client or clients. With task groups, treatment groups, and families, you need to make certain that each and every member is involved in the planning and goal-setting process.

Toseland and Rivas (2012) establish several points about formulating goals and objectives in groups.

CEPHAS HALFWAY HOUSE

Lutheran Social Services

Third Month Contract

I, _____ , agree to increase my savings account to _____ . In addition to this, I will work closely with my counselor in preparing for the transition from Cephas Halfway House to community living. Goal achievements will be looked at closely. I will continue to work on my goals previously set, in addition to what my counselor and I agree on in this third month. I will continue to attend my group meeting.

My goals for the third month are as follows:

1. _____

2. _____

3. _____

4. _____

5. _____

(Staff)   (Date)

(Resident)

© Cengage Learning

FIGURE 6.4 Continued

Clarifying Goals and Objectives

First, discussing and clarifying their goals and objectives takes substantially more time for members in groups. Much depends on the diversity of membership and the individuals' level of motivation. Even group members whose views diverge most strongly from the majority of other members must be satisfactorily integrated into the goal-setting process. Likewise, the least motivated group members must also be included for the group to succeed at its goals and objectives.

Input from Both Worker and Clients

Both the clients and the worker can propose, devise, and refine group goals and objectives. To be effective, the goal-setting process must meet the worker's needs as well as those of the group (Toseland & Rivas, 2012, pp. 213–220).

Workers' Perspective

Practitioners often propose goals and objectives reflecting their unique perspective:

> *As members of social service organizations, workers are aware of the aims and the limitations of the services they provide.... Workers' formulations of goals reflect what they believe can be accomplished with the support, resources, and limitations within the environment where the group operates. (Toseland & Rivas, 2012, p. 213)*

In treatment groups, practitioners:

> *...often have an opportunity to meet each member during the planning stage. Potential members are selected, in part, because of their compatibility with the purposes and goals developed for the group. Workers make preliminary assessments of members' needs and the capacities of each group member, as well as the tasks that face them. Goals are formulated on the basis of the assessment process. (Toseland & Rivas, 2012, p. 214)*

Likewise, in task groups, a practitioner can make assessments of the strengths, weaknesses, and areas of expertise demonstrated by individual group members. The practitioner can then help members develop goals and objectives that maximize their individual strengths. For instance, take a group whose task is to evaluate an agency's personnel policies and make recommendations for change to the upper-level administration. One member might be exceptionally oriented to minute detail and accuracy. That member might be the one to pursue the objective of evaluating the current agency policy manual for inconsistencies, which would help prepare for the primary goal of overhauling the entire policy manual.

You would not want such a task assigned to a group member who has little tolerance for detail. Accuracy, sometimes tedious accuracy, is necessary to complete this task adequately. The latter member, however, although poor in attending to detail, might be especially adept at developing new ideas and alternatives. This member's objective might be to survey personnel to develop a list of existing problems and suggested changes for the manual. Both members' individual strengths would then be put to their most effective use.

Group Members' Perspective

Individual group members establish goals and objectives on the basis of "their own perspective on the particular concerns, problems, and issues that affect them and their fellow group members" (Toseland & Rivas, 2012, p. 214).

When a group meets for the first time, members tend to formulate their goals based on five major variables. First, individual members' proposed goals and objectives are based on an evaluation of their own wants, lacks, and needs. What is the goal/objective that each member wants from the group? What does each member want the group to accomplish?

The second variable involves how effective each member has been in accomplishing such goals in the past. How likely is future success based on past experiences? How likely is failure?

The third variable involves other pressures and demands influencing group members. How much time and energy can each member afford to devote to the group and its goals in view of other personal and professional responsibilities?

The fourth variable concerns what each member feels capable of accomplishing. What skills, abilities, or competencies does the member bring to the group? What does the member feel capable and incapable of doing?

Finally, the fifth variable involves the member's prior involvement with the agency promoting the group and that member's faith in the agency's ability to accomplish goals effectively. Have past experiences been positive or negative? Does this member join the group with an optimistic or pessimistic attitude? Is his or her attitude more neutral? Ensuring that the group members' goal are incorporated in the change effort is critical to developing a mutually agreed-on focus of work, desired outcomes, and intervention goals and objectives.

Variations in Goals

Groups vary significantly in the degree to which they are capable of developing shared group goals and objectives. Sometimes, individual goals vary to such an extreme that finding common ground is difficult. At other times, group members have obviously similar needs that can lead to the establishment of common goals.

Consider, for example, a treatment group of agoraphobics (people who have extreme and irrational fears of open or crowded places). They often strive to avoid any location where they may feel uncomfortable. Extreme cases may feel safe and at ease only in their own homes. People subjected to such a desperate condition usually find their daily activities and lives seriously curtailed. Such individuals would probably be highly motivated to establish goals oriented to coping with and ridding themselves of this oppressive state.

In groups where members have unrelated needs and distinctly different perspectives, it will probably be much more difficult to work together and establish common goals. An example is a task group trying to establish a neighborhood recreational center. It is composed of members from a wide cross-section of the community. If one member joined the group primarily to create a job for himself, another to find potential dates, and still another to provide a centralized hub of activity for neighborhood adolescents, the group might find it extremely difficult to agree upon its goals.

Categories of Goals

Group goals and objectives can be classified into three major categories (Toseland & Rivas, 2012). First, there are goals that involve nourishing the group and keeping it going. These are "group-centered goals" (p. 215). For example, such a goal might be to enhance group members' ability to express their ideas and work out compromises. The second category of goals is made up of the "common group goals" referred to earlier (p. 215). These involve a goal arrived at and shared by all group members. For instance, all members of a task group might aim to decrease community taxes. A third type of goal is the "individual goal," which is where the individual member works to attain some specific goal for himself.

An example of the individual goal involves an eating disorders self-help (treatment) group. Eating disorders encompass a variety of psychological and physical problems involving eating behavior. One disorder, anorexia nervosa, is a condition where people, usually young women, experience a severe fear of gaining weight. This fear leads to extreme weight loss and sometimes starvation. A group member with this condition might formulate individual goals and objectives concerning her personal eating patterns. Additionally, she might establish a goal for a specific amount of weight gain. A young woman who is 5′11″ and 83 pounds might establish a weight goal for herself of 125 pounds.

CONTRACTS IN MEZZO PRACTICE

Toseland and Rivas (2012) identify five potential types of contracts involving groups. First, there may be a contract between the sponsoring agency and the group itself. This might cover what types of facilities will be provided and include group responsibilities regarding the facilities. A second contract is between the worker and the group. This type of contract usually covers such things as group procedures and goals. A third contract might exist between the group and an individual group

member. A fourth contract could be developed between the worker and a group member. Finally, two or more members of the group might enter into an agreement.

Critical Thinking Questions 6.2

- What might be included in a contract between a treatment group for compulsive liars and an individual group member?
- What might be included in a contract between two members of a treatment group for substance abusers?

LO 6-5 Engage in Planning in Macro Practice

Planning in macro practice follows the same basic steps as planning in micro and mezzo practice. As Chapter 4 describes, there are many avenues with which to practice on the macro level, such as social reform, social action, cause advocacy, and case advocacy. Likewise, there are many ways to change or initiate policies, programs, and organizations. Focusing more heavily on the micro and mezzo aspects of practice is easy for a beginning social worker. Working with people and helping them solve their individual problems is fascinating. Each person and problem is unique.

In order to demonstrate the significance and relevance of macro planning, we will provide one specific example here, namely, that of program development. Program development involves establishing a different or new service to clients. Sometimes, new programs are developed within existing agencies. At other times, they require starting up a whole new agency. Programs can entail virtually any type of service provision. Services can range from providing mental health counseling for veterans to residential treatment for delinquent adolescents to nursing home facilities for older adults.

The chances that you will be part of some program's development is likely; that you will be in a position to initiate some program yourself is also quite possible.

AN APPROACH TO PROGRAM PLANNING

Developing a program can be broken down into a number of specific procedures to follow. These often include:

1. Articulate the problem, and translate it into what clients need.

2. Marshal support for program development.
3. Identify a leadership group that will take responsibilities for the program. This may be an advisory group, a board of directors, or some other group.
4. Describe the purpose (or overall goal) of the proposed program.
5. Formulate clear subgoals or objectives.
6. Consider conducting a feasibility study to determine the need for, and potential success of, the program.
7. Solicit the financial resources you need to initiate the program.
8. Describe how the program will provide services.
9. Get the program going.
10. Establish how services will be effectively provided on an ongoing basis.

These procedures comply with our basic planning steps in the planned change process. The following discussion describes each of these procedures and integrates them within the planning model (see Figure 6.1).

Work with the Client

Working with the client system means that you need to work closely with those people who will be receiving the service. In macro practice, it also entails working with other professionals, organizations, and agencies that can help you complete your intervention. They can provide you with information about individual clients' needs and assist you in the actual intervention process. Working with the client system means that you remain open to feedback and responsive to the needs of others in the process.

Prioritize Problems

EP 2.1.10i

That problems have already been identified during the assessment phase of the planned change process has been assumed here. You are proceeding to develop a program. You are doing so because you have identified some specific problems. For example, there are no shelters for the homeless people in your area, or poor people are not getting access to the health care they need. Your intent is to identify the order in which you will address your specified problems. Your proposed program will take shape according to what problems you determine are most important to solve.

For instance, consider the problem of poor people not getting adequate access to health care. How you define and prioritize problems will have a significant impact on how your program will eventually work and what services it will provide. You might decide that the most significant problem is that there is no health delivery service in the targeted area. People are not getting health care because there is none. In this case, you may begin initiating an entire health program with facilities to be set up in the area where the care is needed. This is an example of a prevention intervention that can enhance clients' ability to help themselves reduce the chances of developing serious illness because routine care was not available. Highlight 6.4 provides an example of objectives.

On the other hand, you might decide that the primary problem is not that health care is unavailable. Rather, the problem is that poor people have neither money nor health insurance to pay for the health care provided in the community. In this situation, you might try to establish a program to provide poor people with funding for health care, or you could determine that funding is already potentially available. What is needed is a program to educate needy people regarding what is available and to assist them in applying for the funding.

The Glendale Apartment complex houses well over 800 residents, most of whom are refugees or immigrants from other countries such as Somalia, Sudan, Mexico, and Bosnia. Over 75 percent are non-native English speakers who participate in a variety of programs offered to residents of the complex. These include English-as-a-second-language classes, financial literacy, youth leadership, and many others. Volunteers from the local university and community residents contribute their time to assist the Glendale residents to learn to live in a environment vastly different than the ones with which they are familiar. Their needs include employment, transportation, and health care, among others. The present owners of the Glendale Apartments have been very cooperative in allowing agencies to use space at the facility to conduct various classes.

Recently, the Glendale Apartments were sold to a new owner who immediately began to raise the rent on tenants as their leases became due. These rent increases were substantial and may force many residents to move. Rather than have all of the recent immigrants and refugees located in one place with easy access to services, the move will result in families being dispersed across the city. Assume you are a new social worker assigned to the Glendale Apartments and respond to the following questions.

HIGHLIGHT 6.4

Planning a Health Clinic

Census data from Phoenix Township painted a bleak picture of health care. Over one-fourth of the 13,000 residents lacked affordable health care. Many lacked medical insurance but did not qualify for Medicaid or other governmental health care programs. A committee composed of health care professionals, social workers, and community residents develops a plan to address this problem. The goal of improving health care services for low-income Phoenix residents has several objectives.

1. The chair of the committee will make a formal request to the school board to donate space in the township high school for a free clinic. This request will be completed by June 1.
2. All committee members will solicit donations from area businesses and individuals to pay for the part-time medical staff that will staff the clinic. A total of $25,000 must be raised by August 15 to augment a pledge of $25,000 made by Phoenix Memorial Hospital.
3. The clinic will open its doors September 1 and will be staffed 9 hours per week by a nurse practitioner and 2 hours a week with a doctor. Initial staff will be drawn from members of the committee.

The committee establishes a number of other objectives. These objectives cover such areas as advertising the free clinic, soliciting referrals of low-income clients, evaluating the success of the clinic, and several others. As you can imagine, the success of this kind of macro-level undertaking requires careful attention to who will do what by when.

Critical Thinking Questions 6.3

EP 2.1.3

- Before meeting a single client, what problems do you anticipate that these residents are likely to face in the immediate future?
- Using the list of problems you have produced, prioritize these from highest to lowest.
- Taking the three highest-ranked problems, what needs would you identify?

Translate Problems into Needs

We have discussed how translating the problem into a need helps give you direction on fulfilling that need. It orients you away from dwelling on what is wrong to focusing on what can be done to solve the problem(s). This requires articulating the problem and translating it into what clients need. You have already established and prioritized problems. Now you need to translate them into needs that can be documented and clearly understood.

Identifying, verifying, and articulating an unmet need involves several steps. These include the following:

1. Get data and information to clarify exactly what the need is. Substantiating data can also be used to prove that the need is significant enough to merit intervention. You can obtain facts from statistical reports kept by public agencies. Census data often can be helpful. Public and private agencies often keep information on the requests for service that cannot be met. Research studies also sometimes document needs. Be creative. Think about what kinds of facts would be helpful to prove the need. Who else might be interested in the problem and need? Where might other interested parties make documentation available?

For instance, take the *problem* of many community teenagers being heavily involved in drugs. You determine that they *need* the establishment of a drug treatment program within the community. Where could you find facts and statistics to establish this need? One source might be police statistics. How many drug-related arrests have been made? Can the lack of treatment programs and referral sources be documented from their records? Another source might be local schools. What records are available regarding drug problems and seizures? Are research reports available, addressing similar adolescent populations that can support the need for drug rehabilitation programs in general?

2. A second step is to recognize and specify what other agencies or programs in the community are already addressing the identified need. If the need

is already being met somewhere else, why go through the effort needed to start a new program? Continue with our adolescent drug problem example. If a local hospital is already offering a program to address the treatment and rehabilitation need, further program development may not be necessary. Rather, your intervention approach might then be to educate teens and parents about the problem and program, in addition to facilitating their access to the already-existing program. On the other hand, establishing that no relevant programs exist only strengthens your position that a program is needed.

3. Talk to other professionals involved with clients. Find out how they perceive the problem and need. They might enhance your understanding of what is involved and give you ideas on how to proceed. Keep in mind that other professionals will likely have their own perspectives about a given problem that is affected by their professional identity and the organization with which they work.

4. The fourth step emphasizes involving clients. Talk to community residents and find out how they perceive the problem and need. For example, parent–teacher associations, church groups, and community businesspeople and professionals might provide further insight and support for your plans.

5. Consider doing a more formal needs assessment. This technique was addressed in Chapter 4. Such studies can document specific needs in a convincing manner and typically rely on sound data gathering methods.

Evaluate the Levels of Intervention

In essence, we have already chosen the macro approach as the target strategy in this discussion.

Establish Goals and Specify Objectives and Action Steps

The goal in program development, of course, is to define and develop a new program. To do so will require we will need to break the goal down into subgoals or objectives that are more easily measured. Then we must identify the specific steps needed to achieve these objectives.

Step 2 concerns marshaling support for program development. Initiating and establishing a new program or service completely by yourself is difficult, if not impossible. You need support from a variety of other sources. One especially useful means of soliciting a steady source of support is to establish an *action group*. This group helps acquire the resources and exerts the influence needed to achieve the ultimate goal, namely development of a program. The group will become an advocate and supporter of the program and help publicize the need for the program to other groups and decision makers in the community.

The committee referred to in Highlight 6.4 is one example of an action group. Action group members should be chosen very carefully. Chapter 3 examined task groups and their membership. You will want motivated individuals who are seriously interested in the proposed program. Additionally, you might solicit support by including influential community professionals, religious leaders, and businesspeople. They can provide you with credibility. Their views are generally listened to.

Finally, you might select action group members for their specific areas of expertise. For example, a certified alcohol and other drug abuse counselor could provide valuable input regarding how a drug rehabilitation program needs to be structured. Likewise, a lawyer whose practice targets juveniles or a police officer could contribute relevant information regarding the legal aspects of working with juvenile drug abusers.

From members of this action group, you might establish a more formalized governing body such as a board of directors. A board of directors is a group of individuals who have primary responsibility for setting the mission and goals of an organization and establishing operating policies. They also oversee the staff members who have day-to-day responsibility for implementing the board's policies. In social service agencies, board members are often drawn from influential community members who represent community values and perspectives. In other words, such a formalized group can lend support, credibility, and community influence.

Step 3 entails allocating responsibilities to this board or advisory council. The who-should-do-what-by-when formula clearly applies here. Board tasks can include establishing the basic direction of the program or agency, overseeing its operation by setting policy, engaging in planning, hiring competent leaders, providing or arranging for necessary resources, and a myriad of other tasks. The board is ultimately responsible for evaluating and ensuring the program's accountability, and representing the program to the general public.

Step 4 concerns describing the purpose (or overall goal) of the proposed program. A program's mission involves three facets. First, the unmet needs must be clearly defined and documented. Second, the clientele receiving the services must be clearly identified. Third, the services to be provided by the program must be plainly delineated. In other words, the purpose of the program should be well articulated so that everyone involved understands the program's structure and intentions.

Step 5 involves formulating clear objectives. As we have established, objectives must be very clear. This rule applies to micro, mezzo, and macro practice. Earlier, we discussed behavioral specificity within the context of micro practice. Objectives in macro practice should be just as clear and measurable as in any other type of intervention. Specifying the performance expected, the conditions under which that performance is to occur, and the standards by which success is measured in macro practice corresponds to doing the same thing in micro practice.

For example, return to the illustration of developing a program for adolescent drug abusers. A program objective might be to provide a 6-week inpatient treatment program (performance) for all identified drug-abusing teens within a specified geographic area (conditions) with at least 90 percent of clients remaining drug-free for 6 months after leaving the program (standards). Inpatient programs are those that require clients in treatment to live right in the facility both day and night.

Such an objective would also require a variety of action steps in order to be completed. What steps would need to be followed to develop this program? *Who* would need to do *what* by *when*? Macro practice, of course, involves more individuals and groups, in addition to agencies, policies, and organizations, than is common in micro practice. Therefore, you might anticipate having more action steps when working on the macro level than, for example, when working with a single individual. These might involve any number of individuals and groups before goals can be accomplished.

Step 6 of program development entails implementing a feasibility study. A feasibility study involves a careful evaluation of the resources needed to achieve a particular goal and the resources available to do so. To move in a new direction or to implement a new program, an organization must assess both what it will take to attain it, and whether the organization has or can acquire the resources needed to make it happen. In other words, you need to explore how realistic developing the program is. How much will staffing and facilities cost? What kind of backing can you expect from the community housing the program and from other community agencies?

Additionally, what other types of resources might be available? Common sources of funding include grants, assistance from local government, private donations by individuals and agencies, services and goods donated by other agencies, and the use of volunteers.

One especially beneficial resource for many agencies is the United Way. This agency is a national union of local organizations that coordinates fundraising and distribution of those funds to designated community social service agencies.

The main point is that you need to determine that you have enough resources to continue with your program development plan. If you cannot possibly afford to implement the program, you might as well halt the process at that point.

Soliciting the financial resources you need to initiate the program is step 7. Earlier, your feasibility study identified possible funding sources. This step involves actually *getting* the necessary funding to start the program. You need to transform the *potential* funding sources into *actual* funding sources. You need to work with these resources and convince the people controlling them that your proposed program does indeed merit their attention, support, and money. Additionally, you may want to instigate some fundraising efforts, a macro technique mentioned in Chapter 4.

Step 8 concerns describing how the program will provide services. How will the program actually work? For instance, what type of treatment techniques will the drug rehabilitation counselors be expected to use? What kind of training do they require in order to do their jobs well? Will there be an outpatient program in addition to inpatient? In outpatient treatment programs, clients receive health care by visiting the clinic or facility, not by staying overnight or receiving more extended ongoing care. How will the inpatient units be run? What types of treatment programs will clients have (e.g., group counseling, individual counseling, or job-seeking assistance)?

Specifying the details that describe how the program will be run is important. What specific kinds of services will the program deliver to clients? Exactly how will the program reach its specified objectives?

Actually getting the program going is step 9. Staff members with the necessary credentials need to be hired and scheduled. These staff members need to fully understand how the program is structured and run. All procedures should be stated clearly.

Sometimes, a trial run is helpful. Trying out the program with a few clients instead of having the program start out at full capacity can identify flaws. Such flaws can be addressed and remedied more easily when programs first begin. Precedents (i.e., established ways of doing things that guide how those things are done in the future) have not yet been set. Getting the new program to be responsive to needed changes and improvements is important.

Step 10 in program development concerns establishing how services will be provided on an ongoing basis. *How* services are delivered to clients is just as important as *what* services are delivered. Clients should be able to depend on any service being provided in a timely, predictable fashion. Appointments should be scheduled and meetings held according to clearly defined procedures. Staff members should have straightforward, accurate job descriptions. They should all know exactly the tasks for which they are responsible. Finally, billing should be organized and predictable.

Formalize a Contract

Contracts can be useful in program development on a variety of levels. They might be used to solidify the agreements made in action groups or by a board of directors.

The purchase-of-service contracts described earlier might be established with other agencies to provide services your program cannot. For instance, your agency might contract with another agency to provide vocational rehabilitation counseling. Your program might even use contracts with food suppliers and professional laundry facilities in order to take care of inpatient clients' daily needs.

Chapter Summary

The following summarizes this chapter's content as it relates to each learning objective (LO) presented at the beginning of the chapter. Chapter content helps prepare students to:

LO 6-1 Utilize an eight-step planning process in generalist practice integrating micro, mezzo, and macro approaches.

Steps in the planning process include working with your client, prioritizing problems, translating problems into needs, evaluating the level of intervention required (micro, mezzo, and/or macro), establishing goals, specifying objectives, setting action steps, and formulating a contract. Working with the client entails involving the client fully in each step in the planning process. It also requires the worker to recognize that the client is the best source of information about both problem and priorities.

A generalist perspective ensures that a client's problems are addressed at whatever levels are appropriate. Evaluating intervention levels really is about defining what strategy is most appropriate for helping the client resolve the problem. We might focus on the micro or individual level to deal with one challenge, deal with a mezzo (family or small-group) problem, or take on a macro-level situation. Depending upon the situation, we might employ all three strategies sequentially or simultaneously or select only a subset of the three levels. The client's strengths will be a factor in whatever level you engage. As you consider the possible strategies, you will need to consider the pros and cons of each approach.

In order to move to setting useful goals and objectives, we must prioritize the problems. This entails identifying what problems the client acknowledges, defining the problem in understandable terms, and deciding whether the problem can reasonably be addressed in your work together. Typically, clients help identify the problems of greatest concern to them.

Once prioritized, problems can be translated into needs, which may include survival needs, well-being needs, and fulfillment needs. Each is important and could be the basis for the goals and objectives to be selected next.

LO 6-2 Establish goals and objectives.

Establishing clear goals is essential because both worker and client must understand what they are hoping to accomplish. Goals also communicate the general purpose of your work together. Specifying objectives takes the goals established above to a much more explicit level. Objectives are behaviorally specific in that they suggest the steps that are needed to achieve each of them and they must be measureable enough so that we can know when they have been achieved.

Once objectives are specified the next step is listing action steps. Action steps indicate who will do what by when. They leave no room for someone saying later that he or she did not understand that a task was his or her responsibility.

LO 6-3 Use contracts as part of the planning process.

The final step in planning is to formalize a contract, either oral or written or implicit, that specifies what will occur during the intervention phase and identifies goals, methods, time tables, and mutual obligations of the client and worker.

LO 6-4 Engage in planning in mezzo practice.

Planning in mezzo practice depends a great deal on whether we are working with a task group or a treatment group. It is further complicated because the client system could be an individual group member, the entire group, and/or both. Group members must clarify their own goals and objectives, and the worker's perspective is an important consideration. Group members are likely to have individual goals and the group as a whole will have goals. Group goals can be focused on nourishing and maintaining the group, on common goals, or on goals of the individual members.

As with individual clients, workers may wish to employ contracts that are appropriate. These might be between the worker and the group, the worker and a group member, the group and a group member, between two or more members of the group, or between the sponsoring agency and the group.

LO 6-5 Engage in planning in macro practice.

Macro-practice planning follows the same basic steps as is the case in micro- and macro-practice situations. In macro practice, however, we are more likely to engage in program planning, which follows a set of procedures that are more detailed. They include articulating a problem, translating a problem into needs, marshalling support for program development, allocating responsibility to a group that will carry out the plan, describing the overall goal or purpose of the program, identifying clear objectives and action steps, implementing a feasibility study, soliciting needed financial resources, describing services to be provided, launching the program, and identifying how services will be provided for on an ongoing basis.

Competency Notes

The following identifies where Educational Policy (EP) competencies and practice behaviors are discussed in the chapter.

EP 2.1.3 Apply critical thinking to inform and communicate professional judgment. *(pp. 208, 230):* Critical thinking is needed in the planning process as we decide which interventions to employ and which objectives we will pursue. *(p. 232):* Designing contracts in mezzo practice requires critical thinking to ensure that the needs of the group are met.

EP 2.1.3b Analyze models of assessment, prevention, intervention, and evaluation. *(p. 213):* It is important to weigh the pros and cons of each intervention strategy being considered to increase the likelihood of success.

EP 2.1.4a Recognize the extent to which culture's structures and values may oppress, marginalize, alienate, or create/enhance privilege/power. *(p. 222):* Whatever type of contracting occurs between worker and client should be sensitive to the client's cultural background and experiences.

EP 2.1.10 Engage, assess, intervene, and evaluate with individuals, families, groups, organizations, and communities. *(p. 208):* Planning is a multistep process that precedes the intervention phase in the helping effort.

EP 2.1.10c Develop a mutually agreed-on focus of work and desired outcomes. *(pp. 210, 229):* It is critical to involve clients in the planning process to ensure that their needs are met and to increase their motivation level.

EP 2.1.10e Assess client strengths and limitations. *(p. 213):* Establishing intervention strategies should take into account client strengths.

EP 2.1.10f Develop mutually agreed-on intervention goals and objectives. *(pp. 210, 215, 229):* Clients should be intimately involved in the process of selecting intervention goals and objectives.

EP 2.1.10g Select appropriate intervention strategies. *(p. 218):* Action steps are a useful method of implementing intervention strategies.

EP 2.1.10i Implement prevention interventions that enhance client capabilities. *(p. 231):* Working to establish basic health care services for clients who lack access to such services helps enhance clients' capabilities to care for themselves and their families. It also prevents more serious illness by ensuring that minor and moderate illnesses or injuries are treated before they evolve into more serious challenges requiring emergency care.

On the Internet

Visit the *Understanding Generalist Practice* CourseMate at **www.cengagebrain.com** for resources such as quizzes, glossaries and videos.

CHAPTER

7

Implementation Applications

©istockphoto/Juanmonino

Learning Objectives   *This chapter will help prepare students to:*

LO 7-1	Recognize child maltreatment.
LO 7-2	Examine Child Protective Services.
LO 7-3	Apply the Generalist Intervention Model to practice in Child Protective Services.
LO 7-4	Examine and implement crisis intervention.
LO 7-5	Provide disaster relief and trauma counseling: Macro-level crisis intervention.
LO 7-6	Work with and empower older adults.
LO 7-7	Employ generalist practice in empowering immigrants.
LO 7-8	Address alcohol and other substance abuse.
LO 7-9	Appraise managed care and its effects on practice.

Introduction

Implementation in generalist practice deals with carrying out the intervention plan after initial engagement, assessment, and planning. It is the actual *doing* of social work. Figure 7.1 illustrates this process, which involves following, monitoring progress, revising as necessary, and completing the established plan. Intervention encompasses "'treatment' and other activities social workers use to solve or prevent problems or achieve goals" (Barker, 2003, p. 226). Thus, depending on the issues and client groups involved, special knowledge, skills, and techniques are useful when implementing an intervention plan. This chapter investigates several approaches generalist practitioners commonly use to address problems in designated practice areas. These areas are chosen for inclusion to reflect a broad range of practice issues and scenarios. They include child maltreatment, empowerment of older adults, crisis intervention, alcohol and other drug abuse (AODA), and dilemmas posed by managed care.

LO 7-1 Recognize Child Maltreatment

Social workers historically have been integrally involved in the detection, assessment, and treatment of child abuse and neglect (Wells, 2008). It is an area of practice many workers are likely to enter. Even workers addressing other issues and serving other populations must have a sound knowledge and skill base to assess maltreatment's occurrence and make appropriate referrals. This section first provides a profile of child maltreatment, relevant definitions, and the circumstances involved. Subsequent content will discuss Child Protective Services and how practitioners address child maltreatment by using the Generalist Intervention Model.

A PROFILE OF CHILD MALTREATMENT

There are a number of ways that children can be abused or neglected. The umbrella term that may be used to include all of them is *child maltreatment*.

Maltreatment includes "physical abuse, inadequate care and nourishment, deprivation of adequate medical care, insufficient encouragement to attend school consistently, exploitation by being forced to work too hard or too long, exposure to unwholesome or demoralizing circumstances," sexual abuse, and psychological abuse and neglect (Kadushin & Martin, 1988, p. 226; Miller-Perrin & Perrin, 2013; Wells, 2008). Definitions used by legal and social service agencies vary from locality to locality and state to state. Usually, however, all can be clustered under two headings: child abuse and child neglect.

Child maltreatment is a critical issue for social workers to understand. You need to know the clues that signify maltreatment. Even if you do not work directly in protective services, you need a basic understanding of child maltreatment in order to assess the possibility of occurrence in any families with which you work. You can then make appropriate referrals to resources that can help.

Physical Abuse

A general definition of *physical abuse* is the "nonaccidental injury inflicted on a child" usually by a caregiver, other adult, or, sometimes, an older child (Crosson-Tower, 2013, p. 180). Specific definitions of physical abuse vary, some focusing on whether the alleged abuser's purpose is to intentionally harm the child. Other definitions ignore the intent and, instead, emphasize the potential or actual harm done to the child.

A major issue involves the everyday fine line between physical abuse and parental discipline. When does discipline become abuse?

Crosson-Tower (2013) reflects on some of the issues concerning the cultural context of abuse versus parental discipline:

"Some cultures have customs or practices that child protection would consider abusive. For example, some Vietnamese families, in a ritual called cao gio, *rub their children with a coin heated to the point that it leaves burn marks. It is an intentional act but*

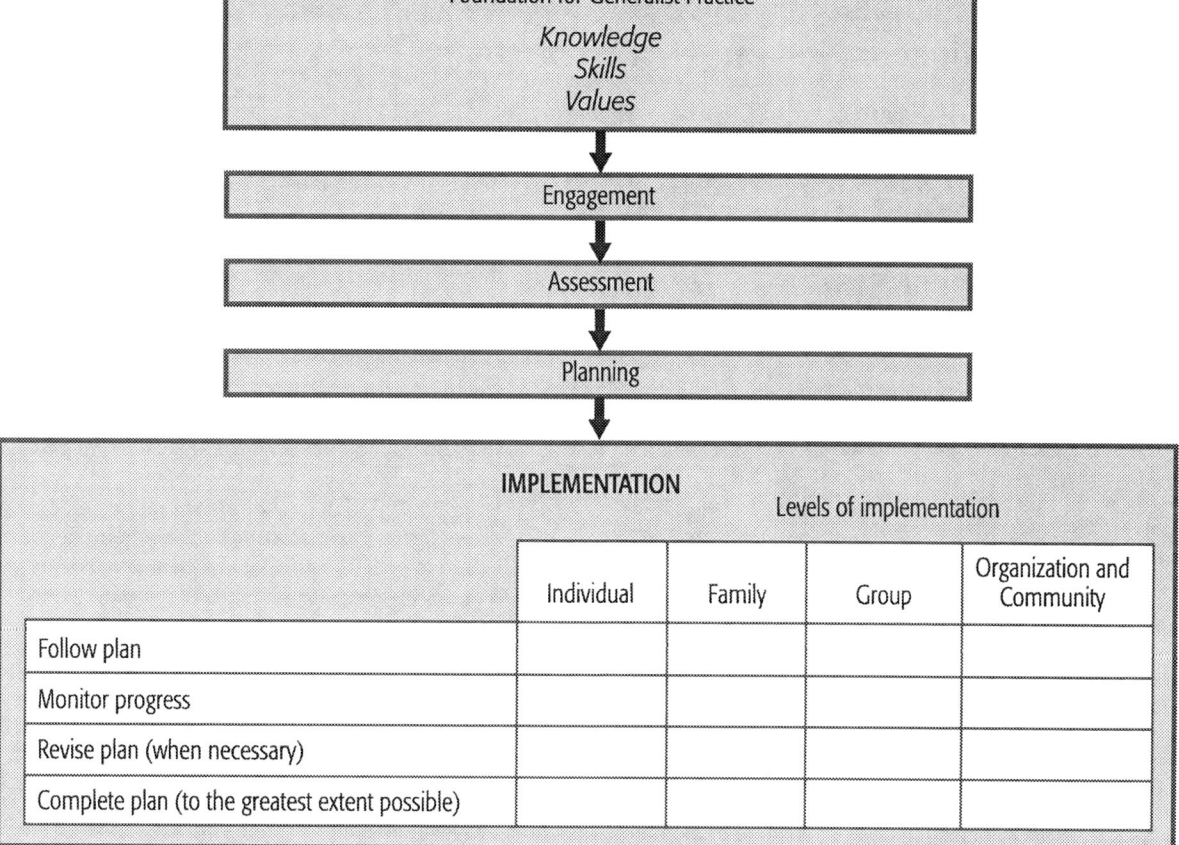

FIGURE 7.1 Implementation in the Generalist Intervention Model (GIM)

designed, in that culture, to cure a variety of ills. Do the good intentions of the parents exempt this practice from being considered abusive? Similarly, the use of corporal punishment is sanctioned in many Hispanic cultures, but is seen as abusive in this culture when it becomes excessive. Some child protection advocates adopt the "when in Rome do as the Romans do" attitude that says that minorities must abide by the laws of the culture in which they now reside. One Puerto Rican social worker, working in a predominantly Hispanic section of New York City, vehemently disagreed: "Yes, there are laws," he said, "but those laws were made by Anglos. Is it fair to deprive new immigrants of everything, including their customs? Maybe the laws should be changed?"

The reality is that, if a child is reported as being harmed for whatever reason, a child protection agency will usually investigate. If the reason is one of culture, this will be considered. Fontes (2008), in

speaking of Hispanic families using harsh discipline, suggests that understanding the cultural values and approaching the family in a nonblaming way will go a long way toward gaining cooperation." (p. 180)

Both physical and behavioral indicators provide clues that a child is being physically abused. Physical indicators can be broken down into six basic categories described in Highlight 7.1.

After considering the potential indicators of physical abuse described in Highlight 7.1, some of the major questions to ask yourself if you think a child may have been physically abused are:

• Does this child get hurt too often for someone his or her age?
• Does the child have multiple injuries?
• Do the injuries occur in patterns, assume recognizable shapes, or look like some of the injuries described here?

HIGHLIGHT 7.1

Physical Indicators of Physical Abuse

1. *Bruises.* Bruises on any infant should be suspect. Infants are not yet mobile; therefore, the chances that they can bruise themselves are not likely. Bruises in unusual places or forming unusual patterns may be indicators of physical abuse. Bruises that take on a recognizable shape, such as a hand mark or a belt mark, should be noted. Finally, bruises that display a variety of colors may portray abuse. This may be an indication that a series of bruises have been received over time. On lighter-skinned people, bruises usually progress from an initial bright red to blue to blackish-purple within the first day; they become shaded with a dark green color after 4 to 6 days, and finally turn pale green or yellow after 5 to 10 days have passed.

2. *Lacerations.* Cuts, scrapes, or scratches, especially if they occur frequently or their origin is poorly explained, may indicate physical abuse. Lacerations on the face and genitalia should be noted. Bite marks may also indicate abuse.

3. *Fractures.* Bone fractures and other skeletal injuries may indicate abuse. Strangely twisted fractures and multiple fractures are especially telltale signs. Infants' fractures may be the result of abuse. Additional indicators are joint dislocations and injuries where the periosteum, the thin membrane covering the bone, is detached.

4. *Burns.* Burns, especially ones that take odd forms or are in patterns, may indicate abuse. Children have been burned by cigarettes and ropes (from being tied up and confined). Burns that occur on normally inaccessible portions of the body, such as the stomach, genitals, or soles of the feet, are clues to abuse. Patterned burns may indicate that the child has been burned with some hot utensil. Sacklike burns result when a hand or foot has been submerged in a hot liquid. A doughnut-shaped burn will occur on the buttocks if a child has been immersed in very hot water. The central unburned area results from where the child's skin touched the bottom of the receptacle holding the water.

5. *Head injuries.* Head injuries that can indicate abuse include skull fractures, loss of hair due to vigorous pulling, and subdural hematomas (i.e., blood that has collected beneath the outer covering of the brain after strenuous shaking or hitting has occurred). Black eyes should be suspect. Retinas may detach or hemorrhage if a child is shaken vigorously.

6. *Internal injuries.* Children have received injuries to their spleen, kidneys, and intestines due to hitting and kicking. The vena cava, the large vein by which blood is brought from the lower extremities to the heart, may be ruptured. Peritonitis, where the lining of the abdominal cavity becomes inflamed, can be another indicator of abuse.

- Are the injuries such that they do not seem possible for a child at that stage of development?
- Do the explanations given for the injuries make sense?

If something does not seem right or logical to you, it may mean something is wrong. It might be called a "gut reaction." If a little voice way in the back of your mind is saying, "Uh-oh, that certainly is odd," perhaps you should pay attention. It might be a clue to abuse.

In addition to physical indicators, behavioral and emotional indicators provide another major dimension of clues to physical abuse. A physically abused child often tends to adopt behavioral extremes. Virtually all children display these extreme behaviors at one time or another. However, the frequency and severity of these behaviors in abused children are clearly notable. At least six categories of behavioral and psychological indicators have been established:

1. *Developmental lags* (Barnett, Miller-Perrin, & Perrin, 2011; Miller-Perrin & Perrin, 2013). Because abused children are forced to direct their attention and energy toward coping with their abusive situation, they will frequently show developmental delays. These may appear in the form of language delays, poorly developed social skills for their age level, or lags in motor development.

2. *Poor academic performance* (Barnett et al., 2011; Miller-Perrin & Perrin, 2013). Barnett and her colleagues (2011) reflect that "victims of [child physical abuse] . . . display poor school achievement and

adjustment, receive more special education services, score lower on reading and math tests, exhibit more learning disabilities, and are more likely to repeat a grade" (p. 159).

3. *Notably aggressive behaviors* and marked overt hostility toward others caused by rage and frustration at not getting needs met (Barnett et al., 2011; Crosson-Tower, 2010, 2013; Miller-Perrin & Perrin, 2013). Many physically abused children are so desperately in need of attention that they will try almost anything to get it. Even if they can provoke only negative attention from their parents and others, their aggressive behavior is reinforced.

4. *Extremely passive, accommodating, submissive behaviors* aimed at preserving a low profile and avoiding potential conflict with parents that might lead to abuse (Crosson-Tower, 2010, 2013). Abused children can be exceptionally calm and docile. They have learned this behavior in order to avoid any possible conflict with the abusive parents. If they are invisible, the parent may not be provoked. Many times abused children will even avoid playing because it draws too much attention to themselves. This behavioral pattern is sometimes called *hypervigilance.*

5. *Difficulties in peer interaction* (Miller-Perrin & Perrin, 2013). Physically abused children often have poorly developed social skills so they have problems making friends and interacting appropriately with peers.

6. *Psychological problems* (Barnett et al., 2011; Miller-Perrin & Perrin, 2013). Physically abused children frequently develop various psychiatric problems, including depression. They also tend to have low self-esteem and a sense of hopelessness.

Critical Thinking Questions 7.1

- Do parents have the right to spank their children?
- When does discipline become abuse?

Child Neglect

Child neglect is a caregiver's "failure to meet a child's basic needs" that may involve deprivation of physical, emotional, medical, mental health, or educational necessities (Erickson & Egeland, 2002; Miller-Perrin & Perrin, 2013; Shireman, 2003, p. 32). Whereas child abuse involves harming a child through actions, child neglect causes a child harm by *not* doing what is

necessary. Neglect occurs when children are not given what they need to survive and thrive. Highlight 7.2 describes 12 categories for general indicators of child neglect.

Emotional/Psychological Neglect and Abuse

Emotional/psychological neglect is a passive lack of attention to a child's needs that includes "inadequate nurturance, inadequate affection, refusal to provide adequate care, or knowingly allowing maladaptive behavior such as delinquency or drug use" (Crosson-Tower, 2010, p. 212). This neglect includes "parents who overlook their infants' cues and signals, particularly the children's cries and pleas for warmth and comfort" (Erickson & Egeland, 2002, p. 6). Neglectful parents may be extremely insensitive and unresponsive to their children's emotional needs and have little involvement with their children (p. 7).

Emotional/psychological abuse, like other abuse, is more aggressive and negative than emotional neglect. It includes "verbal and emotional assaults, threatened harm, or close confinement" (Crosson-Tower, 2010, p. 212). Emotional/psychological abuse involves purposefully "belittling, humiliating, rejecting, undermining a child's self-esteem, and generally not creating a positive atmosphere for a child" (Cohen, 1992, p. 175).

Emotional/psychological maltreatment encompasses both emotional/psychological neglect and emotional/psychological abuse. Often it is difficult to separate the abuse from the neglect; rather, this maltreatment involves a *pattern of psychically destructive behavior"* (Barnett et al., 2011; Crosson-Tower, 2010, p. 212). Emotional/psychological maltreatment can be classified into the following six types (Hart et al., 2011):

1. "SPURNING (hostile/rejecting/degrading) includes verbal and nonverbal caregiver acts that reject and degrade a child." Example: Freddy's father would scream at Freddy and call him vulgar names in front of everyone when he made mistakes during his baseball games.

2. "TERRORIZING includes caregiver behavior that threatens or is likely to physically hurt, kill, abandon, or place the child or child's loved ones/objects in recognizably dangerous situations." Example: Sydney's mother threatened to kill her dog if she didn't make her bed.

3. "ISOLATING includes caregiver acts that consistently deny the child opportunities to meet needs for interacting/communicating with peers or adults inside or outside the home." Example: Janelle's

HIGHLIGHT 7.2

Categories for General Indicators of Child Neglect

The following are categories for general indicators of child neglect (Barnett et al., 2011; Crosson-Tower, 2010, 2013; Erickson & Egeland, 2011; Miller-Perrin & Perrin, 2013):

1. *Physical health care.* Illnesses are not attended to, or proper dental care is not maintained.
2. *Mental health care.* Children's mental health problems are either ignored or left unattended. Sometimes caregivers refuse "to comply with recommended corrective or therapeutic procedures in cases in which a child is found to have a serious emotional or behavioral disorder" (Erickson & Egeland, 2002, p. 7).
3. *Educational neglect.* "[P]arents fail to comply with laws concerning school attendance" (Shireman, 2003, p. 33). Excessive truancy and tardiness without adequate or appropriate excuses may indicate neglect.
4. *Supervision.* Children often or almost always are left alone without adequate supervision. Examples of incidents reflective of this situation include when very young children or infants are left unattended. Another common situation is when very young children are left in the supervision of other children who themselves are too young to assume such responsibility. A third common situation occurs when unsupervised children get involved in activities in which they may harm themselves. For example, we periodically read in the newspaper how a young, unsupervised child plays with matches, starts a fire, burns down the house or apartment building, and usually dies in the fire. A fourth example involves children who do not receive adequate supervision to get them to school on time or at all.
5. *Abandonment and substitute child care.* The most blatant form of neglect is abandonment, where parents leave children alone and unattended. A related scenario involves parents who fail to return when they are supposed to, thereby leaving designated care providers in the lurch, not knowing what to do with the children.
6. *Housing hazards.* Housing may have inadequate heat, ventilation, or safety features. Dangerous substances such as drugs or weapons may be left in children's easy reach. Electrical fixtures may not be up to code and therefore dangerous.

7. *Household sanitation.* Food may be spoiled. The home may be filled with garbage or excrement. Plumbing might not work or be backed up.
8. *Personal hygiene.* Children's clothing may be ripped, filthy, and threadbare. Their hair might be unkempt and dirty. They might be unbathed and odorous.
9. *Nutrition.* Children who frequently complain that they are hungry and searching for food may be victims of neglect. Children receiving food that provides them with inadequate nutrition may be neglected. Significant delays in development resulting from malnutrition may also be a clue to neglect.
10. *Problems with social interaction and attachment issues.* Children may have problems interacting with parents and fail to maintain secure attachment relationships where they trust parents and respond positively and consistently to their parents' presence and interaction (Erickson & Egeland, 2002). Children may act "passive and withdrawn" with parents or the "parent exhibits low sensitivity to and involvement with [the] child" (Barnett, Miller-Perrin, & Perrin, 2005, p. 141). Children may also display problems in peer relationships including "socially withdrawn behavior, decreased prosocial behavior, greater conflict with friends, and fewer reciprocated friendships than nonneglected children" (Barnett et al., 2005, p. 142).
11. *"Cognitive and academic deficits"* (Barnett et al., 2011, p. 98). Children may exhibit language deficits, poor academic achievement, low grades, deficits in intelligence, decreased creativity, and difficulties in problem solving. Some research found that neglected children tend to experience greater cognitive and academic problems than physically abused children (Erickson & Egeland, 2011; Hildyard & Wolfe, 2002).
12. *"Emotional and behavioral problems"* (Barnett et al., 2013, p. 98). Neglected children may exhibit indifference, withdrawal and isolation, low self-esteem, "physical and verbal aggression," difficulties in paying attention, and psychiatric symptoms such as those characterizing anxiety or depression (Barnett et al., 2005, p. 141).

parents kept her locked up in her bedroom except to attend school.

4. "EXPLOITING/CORRUPTING includes caregiver acts that encourage the child to develop inappropriate behaviors (self-destructive, antisocial, criminal, deviant, or other maladaptive behaviors)." Example: Inga's parents encouraged her to have sex for money and then forced her to give the money to them.

5. "DENYING EMOTIONAL RESPONSIVENESS (ignoring) includes caregiver acts that ignore the child's attempts and needs to interact (failing to express affection, caring, and love for the child) and showing no emotion in interactions with the child." Example: Knute, age 8 months, would cry for hours. Although his mother fed him several times each day, changed his diapers, and bathed him, she would never talk to him, touch him unless she had to, or give him any other attention.

6. "MENTAL HEALTH, MEDICAL, AND EDUCATIONAL NEGLECT includes unwarranted caregiver acts that ignore, refuse to allow, or fail to provide the necessary treatment for the mental health, medical, and educational problems or needs for the child." Example: Wilhelm, age 8, went to school each day complaining of toothaches. His parents never instructed him to brush his teeth or took him to see a dentist. (pp. 127–128)

Emotional/psychological maltreatment can result in low self-esteem, aggressive and antisocial behavior, substance abuse, difficulty relating to others, learning deficits, and physical problems linked to lack of adequate health care (Hart et al., 2011).

Sexual Abuse

Sexual abuse is "*any* sexual interaction (including fondling, sexual kissing, and oral sex, as well as vaginal or anal penetration) between an adult and a prepubescent child. A broad definition also includes nonphysical contact, such as people exposing their genitals to children or having children pose nude or stimulate themselves while being filmed or photographed. It does not matter whether the child is perceived by the adult to be engaging in the sexual activity voluntarily. Because of the child's age, he or she cannot give informed consent; the activity can only be considered as self-serving to the adult" (Yarber et al., 2010, p. 594).

Incest, a form of sexual abuse is "sexual intercourse between people too closely related to legally marry (usually interpreted to mean father-daughter, mother-son, or brother-sister combinations). Sexual abuse in families can involve blood relatives, most commonly uncles and grandfathers, and step relatives, most often stepfathers and stepbrothers" (Yarber et al., 2010, p. 596). Four categories of symptoms indicate that sexual abuse may be occurring—physical problems, emotional indicators, increased or inappropriate sexual behavior, and difficulties in social relationships (Barnett et al., 2011; Yarber et al., 2010).

A variety of physical problems are indications of sexual abuse. For instance, a small child may become infected with a sexually transmitted disease. There may be pain, bleeding, or bruises in genital or anal areas. Pregnancy is still another indicator, especially if it occurs when a child is of an unusually young age to have sexual intercourse.

Emotional indicators provide the second category of symptoms. They include depression, anxiety, low self-esteem, and thoughts of suicide (Barnett et al., 2011; Yarber et al., 2010).

The third category of sexual abuse symptoms involves increased or inappropriate sexual behavior. Sexually abused children tend to manifest "behaviors such as overt sexual acting out toward adults or other children, compulsive masturbation, excessive sexual curiosity, sexual promiscuity, and precocious sexual play and knowledge. The sexual behaviors of sexually abused children are often associated with intercourse such as mimicking intercourse and inserting objects into the vagina or anus" (Barnett et al., 2011, p. 223; Miller-Perrin & Perrin, 2013). For example, one 8-year-old child's teacher expressed concern when she had to stop the child several times from mimicking sexual intercourse with another child (the term this teacher used was "humping") on the playground. Sexually abused children may also exhibit exceptionally intense interest in sexual topics or activity. Another teacher was alerted when one of her fifth-grade female students handed in 18 poems. The assignment had required only one. Each of the poems was saturated with sexual images and terminology.

Difficulties in social relationships make up the fourth category of sexual abuse symptoms. Sexually abused children are more likely to lack social skills and be less trusting of others (Berliner & Elliott, 2002; Miller-Perrin & Perrin, 2013). Other effects may include "difficulties at school, truancy, running away from home, and early marriages by abused adolescents" (Yarber et al., 2010, p. 598).

INCIDENCE OF CHILD MALTREATMENT

The actual number of child maltreatment cases is difficult to determine. Specific definitions for who can and cannot be included in specific categories vary dramatically. One thing, however, is certain. Any figures that are reported reflect a minimal number of actual cases. All indications are that vast numbers of cases remain unreported.

CHARACTERISTICS OF PERPETRATORS

The dynamics behind physical child abuse are complex and varied. However, general characteristics tend to fall within six major domains (Barnett et al., 2011; Crosson-Tower, 2010; Kolko, 2002; Miller-Perrin & Perrin, 2013). Although no one person may have all the problems mentioned, they will likely experience some.

First, they themselves most likely have serious *needs for support and nurturance* that remain unfulfilled from their own childhoods. Because their own needs were not met, they are unable to meet the needs of their children. They often invite rejection and hostility because they have little confidence in their own abilities. They do not know how to reach out for support. On the one hand, they often feel they are undeserving. On the other hand, they still have desperate needs for emotional support. Many perpetrators were abused as children themselves. Note, however, that "most abused children do not become abusive parents" (Kolko, 2002, p. 26; Widom, 1989).

A second problem characterizing abusers involves *social isolation.* Their own self-confidence is low. They feel that no one will like them, so they isolate themselves. They reject attention, even though they really need others for emotional support. They fear rejection so they do not try to reach out to others. As a result, when normal everyday stresses build up, they have no one to help them cope.

Communication and relationship difficulties make up a third dimension characterizing abusive parents. Relationships abusers do have with family, significant others, and others are often stormy. Communication may be difficult, hostile, and ineffective. Low self-esteem can also affect the relationship with a partner or significant other. Abusers may not know how to get their needs met. They may allow their disappointment and anger to build up because they do not know how to express these feelings more appropriately to others. They may feel isolated and alone even within a marriage or partnership. Children may become easy targets for parents who cannot communicate with each other. Children may provide a conduit for the expression of violence and anger really directed at a spouse.

A related problem is the fourth aspect characterizing abusive people—*not knowing how to raise children in a nurturing family environment.* Their own family environment of origin may have been hostile and abusive. They may never have observed nurturant behavior on the part of their own parents and caregivers. They could not learn what they were not taught. Additionally, their expectations for what constitutes inappropriate behavior at the various developmental levels may be lacking. For instance, their demands upon the child for behavioral submission and even perfection may be highly inappropriate.

A fifth common problem of abusers involves having *poor general coping skills.* Perpetrators may be unable to cope with stress, lashing out at their children instead. They may lack anger management skills. In addition to not knowing how to meet their own emotional needs, they may not have learned to separate their feelings and emotions from their behavior. Therefore, if they get mad, they do not talk about it; they hit.

Another unlearned facet of coping involves the appropriate delineation of responsibility. There is a tendency to blame others for their mistakes. For example, it is the child's fault he got hit and broke his arm because he was naughty.

They may also lack the decision-making or problem-solving skills involved in coping. Abusers tend to have little confidence in their own ability and so have little faith in their own judgment. They have difficulty articulating and evaluating the pros and cons of their alternatives and are indecisive.

One other coping skill abusers often fail to master is how to delay their own gratification. The here and now becomes all-important. If a child misbehaves, a kick will take care of it immediately. If their stress level is too high, they need immediate relief. They focus on the moment and have trouble looking at what the consequences of their behavior will be in the future.

A sixth factor often facing abusers concerns *extreme external stress and life crises.* Poverty is one thing that causes stress (Miller-Perrin & Perrin, 2013). The abuser, who may lack coping strategies anyway, may feel isolated and incompetent. Additional life crises such as losing a job, illness, a marital or family relationship dispute, or even a child's behavior problem may push people over the brink so that they cannot cope. They may take out their stress on the easiest, most available targets—their children.

Parents who neglect their children appear to have characteristics similar to physically abusive parents, although poverty can also contribute to the potential for neglect. "[I]n many families the lack of resources creates an environment of stress, a sense of demoralization, and often depression and a lack of hope. When these conditions occur, the child's opportunities for a positive living environment decrease" (Mather, Lager, & Harris, 2007, p. 93). Crosson-Tower (2010) explains that the "typical neglectful parent is an isolated individual who has difficulty forming relationships or carrying on the routine tasks of everyday life. Burdened with the anger and sadness over unmet childhood needs, this parent finds it impossible to consistently recognize and meet the needs of her or his children" (p. 81). This description, in some ways, resembles the description of the physically abusive parent. However, an abuser lashes out, whereas a neglectful parent tends to withdraw and fails to provide adequately for children.

Perpetrators of emotional/psychological maltreatment suffer similar emotional problems or deficits to those of other caregivers who physically abuse or neglect children. No clear-cut description characterizes people who sexually abuse children other than the majority are heterosexual males who often know the child, usually in a trusting relationship (Rosenthal, 2013). Establishing trust with the child gradually allows perpetrators to manipulate the child's behavior and involvement. Child sexual abusers tend to have deficient interpersonal skills and low self-esteem (Crooks & Baur, 2014; Hyde & DeLamater, 2011). "They are often more religious and conservative than average, and less knowledgeable about sexuality" (Crooks & Baur, 2014; Rosenthal, 2013, p. 419).

LO 7-2 Examine Child Protective Services

What would you, as a protective services worker, do when you receive a report that child maltreatment might be occurring? *Child Protective Services (CPS)* are those involving assessment and interventions by social workers and others in situations where children are deemed at risk of maltreatment. Protective services workers usually are employed by public departments of social services or law enforcement agencies and courts addressing the problem. The workers' major aim is to explore whether or not abuse is occurring, assess both strengths and risks involved in the family situation, make plans to ensure safety and minimize future risks, and implement plans to maintain healthier family functioning. The next sections will describe the family preservation philosophy that characterizes Child Protective Services and explore how the Generalist Intervention Model (GIM) can be applied in that work.

FAMILY PRESERVATION PHILOSOPHY: EMPOWERING FAMILIES

Philosophy involves the concepts and principles about how the world should, or actually does, function. Philosophy provides values and guidelines for what is considered important, which enables it to be used as a tool of intervention to help guide the intervention process. It emphasizes the aspects of a problem situation and the helping process that should be the focus of attention. Child maltreatment provides an example. A philosophy based on the medical model would orient your focus on the pathology of the child abuser. The medical model emphasizes how illnesses (or problems) should be cured (or solved). The focus is on "fixing" the individual. In the case of child abuse, intervention or treatment would be directed at the abuser.

A philosophy based on family systems, on the other hand, would emphasize the importance of the entire family's interaction with each other and the environment. Such a philosophy would guide intervention to involve all family members. It would not limit the intervention to the abuser alone.

One trend in protective services involves home-based services and an intensive family preservation philosophy and approach. This approach refers to "providing services to vulnerable families in order to prevent out-of-home-placement of children" (Child Welfare Information Gateway, 2003; Crosson-Tower, 2013; Maluccio, 1990, p. 18; Piccola & Tracy, 2008). A family preservation philosophy also involves concepts and principles about what's important for intervention in cases of child maltreatment. These concepts and principles provide guidelines for how practitioners should proceed with intervention. (Chapter 10 discusses family preservation more extensively.)

A significant principle concerns the importance of children remaining with their own families if at all possible. Another family intervention concept is that interventions are considered positive. People are considered capable of changing if they have help. Additionally, family preservation emphasizes the importance of positive intervention when crises occur, so that children need not be placed out of their own homes.

A philosophical perspective on family preservation emphasizes six points. First, the problem is seen as a social issue (Crosson-Tower, 2013). This involves "the idea that successful family life can take place only in concerned and supportive communities that have the resources to offer opportunity and hope to residents" (Shireman, 2003, p. 187). Child maltreatment occurs within the family, not because one or two parents intentionally decide to be mean to their children, but rather because of external stresses and pressures upon parents. The focus is on the environment and parents' interactions with that environment. Child maltreatment is more the fault of a difficult and unsupportive environment than the intentional deeds of particular parents.

The second principle indicates that workers should concentrate only on working constructively with the families "to ensure a partnership role" (Child Welfare Information Gateway, 2003; LeVine & Sallee, 1999, p. 366; Pecora, Whittaker, Maluccio, Bath, & DePanfilis, 2010). "Helpfulness" is the key word (Holder & Corey, 1991, p. 2). Punishing parents does not work. Instead, practitioners should *help* parents become stronger and more effective.

The third principle is that workers can help maltreating families by coordinating their intervention efforts with those of other professionals who can also be used to help the family (Crosson-Tower, 2010; Downs, Moore, & McFadden, 2009). One way of doing this coordination is through case management (the coordination of the work of all the professionals participating in the intervention). Chapter 15 addresses this activity in more depth. You, as the worker, do not have to do everything for the family yourself. Instead, you can be most useful by overseeing and integrating the work of others.

This philosophy is positive. The fourth principle dictates that maltreating child caregivers can improve their conduct with support and assistance (Child Welfare Information Gateway, 2003; Downs, Moore, McFadden, Michaud, & Costin 2004; Pecora et al., 2010). This view is different from approaching a difficult, abusive situation that you feel is hopeless. Instead, you review alternatives for helping the family until you find some that work. LeVine and Sallee (1999) explain that "[r]espect is shown for each family's strengths, potential, natural striving toward growth, and capacity for change. Each family is individualized, and its unique strengths and capacities are identified" (p. 366) and emphasized in the change process.

A fifth principle offers the guidance that keeping maltreated children within their own families, if at all possible, is best, as long as the children are safe (Downs

et al., 2009; Miller-Perrin & Perrin, 2013; Pecora et al., 2010). This principle relates to the idea that risk can be minimized and the children's safety maximized if internal and external pressures can be controlled and parents are taught coping strengths.

The sixth guiding principle is that clients should always be integrally involved in the intervention (Berry, 2005; Crosson-Tower, 2009; Pecora et al., 2010). We, as workers, do not go into their homes and mandate to them what they should do. This approach does not work. If you remember, this approach coincides with our consistent emphasis in generalist practice on client involvement.

A Cautionary Note Regarding Family Preservation

It is considered in children's best interest that they remain in their own homes with their own families. However, if it is determined that risk to children is too great, children may have to be removed in order to keep them safe and well cared for. The worker has responsibility for "identifying, considering, and weighing factors that affect the child's safety, permanency, and well-being" (Pecora et al., 2010, p. 157). Children's safety and their need for nurturance guide the actions of Child Protective Services workers. The other important related concept is that of *permanency planning*, the process of establishing a long-term placement plan (e.g., with relatives, foster parents, or adoptive parents) within a reasonable time frame in the event that placement with the family is deemed not possible. A later section will discuss risk assessment in the home.

LO 7-3 Apply the Generalist Intervention Model to Practice in Child Protective Services

As with other aspects of social work, protective service workers follow the planned change process proposed by the GIM. The seven steps in this process are discussed here and applied to generalist practice with respect to child maltreatment and Child Protective Services.

THE GENERALIST INTERVENTION MODEL: ENGAGEMENT

Engagement is especially critical in child maltreatment cases. When a social worker abruptly appears on a family's doorstep, feelings of "anxiety, discomfort, guilt, shame, defensiveness, as well as anger, resentment, resistance, and opposition" are likely aroused (Kadushin & Martin, 1988, p. 254). Defusing these negative reactions as much as possible is then up to the worker. The worker should attend to the child's and the entire family's emotional and psychological needs.

There are a number of suggestions for how to proceed (Kadushin & Martin, 1988). First, the worker should have a forthright and candid approach, making "a clear statement" on the agency's behalf "that it has learned that the child is in potential danger and that, representing the community, it would like to enlist the aid of the parents in determining what is happening" (1988, p. 253). The worker should emphasize that the process is a joint process where both worker and family are trying to address and resolve the problem. The worker should assume an approach of helper rather than authoritative investigator. The worker should reflect the agency's concern for the well-being of the entire family.

THE GENERALIST INTERVENTION MODEL: ASSESSMENT

During assessment the worker should interview and observe the behavior of the children and parents to identify clues that suggest child maltreatment. We have reviewed a range of indicators for various types of abuse and neglect. The practitioner should then assess the degree of risk to the child in the home. Approaches to risk assessment include interviewing the child, appraising the family system's dynamics, and evaluating the forces that contribute to risk.

Family Assessment: Interviewing the Child

There are several suggestions regarding talking to the child during both the engagement and assessment stages. First, you should be aware of how a child's perception might differ from that of adults in at least three dimensions (Crosson-Tower, 2010). Note that these differences may vary according to the child's developmental level and even from one child to another of the same age (Crosson-Tower, 2010; Sheafor & Horejsi, 2012). To begin with, children often use metaphors or stories representing what they want to say instead of using literal facts as adults do. Therefore, it is necessary for you to listen carefully in order to comprehend on many levels what the child means to say. Another difference between children and adults is perception of time. Specific numbers of days or weeks may have little meaning to children. However, referring to "milestones" such as "the time you got up" or "how long before Christmas" may provide better ways for the child to communicate about time (Crosson-Tower, 2010, p. 240). A third difference between children and adults is how a child's attention span is usually much more limited. Therefore, using activities such as role

playing, play therapy, or drawing may help a child attend longer and convey more information (Sheafor & Horejsi, 2012; Thompson & Rudolph, 2000). (*Play therapy* is a type of psychotherapy where the worker or other professional uses play, a natural means by which children express themselves, to facilitate communication [Thompson & Rudolph, 2000]. The child can use toys such as dolls to act out situations, address conflicts, and express emotions that are difficult to talk about [Barker, 2003]).

A second suggestion for interviewing children is to pay special attention to the interview setting (Crosson-Tower, 2010; Sheafor & Horejsi, 2012). Children are not accustomed to being interviewed or to being the center of adult attention during an interview's structured format. Selecting a familiar room where they feel comfortable, or at least someplace where there is some privacy, is helpful (Sheafor & Horejsi, 2012).

A third suggestion is to be especially sensitive to the child's emotional perspective in view of the turbulent context of abuse. Thompson and Rudolph (2000) explain:

"Abused children are not easy clients. They have learned not to trust themselves, other people, or their environment. The world and the people in it are inconsistent and hurt them. Withdrawal from this painful world is safer than chancing relationships. Building friendship and trust may be difficult." (p. 438)

Introducing yourself and informing the child about the purpose of the interview and your own role is the fourth suggestion (Crosson-Tower, 2010; Sheafor & Horejsi, 2012). This must be done carefully, however, so as not to frighten the child or imply blame. After introducing yourself, you might say something like, "My job is to help children who are having problems at home" (Sheafor & Horejsi, 2012, p. 357). To enhance your own credibility you then might say, "I've talked to many boys and girls who had this kind of problem" (Crosson-Tower, 2010, p. 243). Knowing more about why the worker is there may help to alleviate some of the child's anxiety. Please note that there is no formula for the perfect way to communicate with a child about maltreatment. It requires sensitivity and focused attention to respond to a child's unique emotional and developmental levels and perspectives about his or her family situation.

A fifth suggestion for interviewing a child is to use some initial small talk about the child's favorite toys, television shows, or what the child is wearing. This can soften the rigidity of the interview situation and enhance the engagement process (Sheafor & Horejsi, 2012).

Helping a child anticipate what will happen in the future is the sixth suggestion; there are several ways to accomplish this (Crosson-Tower, 2010). You might initiate the process by asking what the child "expects or wants to happen" (Crosson-Tower, 2010, p. 245). It is important that the child know that his or her desires may have little or nothing to do with what may actually occur. It should be clear that many variables are involved, and the child should not "be left with the feeling that they are to blame for the outcome" (Crosson-Tower, 2010, p. 246). To the extent possible, give details about the future process. If you will be interviewing the child again or meeting with the parents, you might say so. If a court appearance is ensuing, you might fill in some details about how the courtroom looks and what it is like to be part of the court process. The unknown is often scary, even for adults. The more a child knows about what to expect in the future, the more secure and less scared the child will probably be.

Family Assessment: Understanding the Family

In addition to soliciting information from the child, obtaining an accurate understanding of the family's circumstances is important (Crosson-Tower, 2010; Wells, 2008). Questions should focus on the forces of risk discussed later.

Details such as times, dates, and specific incidents can help the worker to discuss with the family why the worker, his or her agency, and the family should be concerned about the issues. For example, the parents arrived home at 1:30 a.m. on Sunday, October 25, and were very intoxicated. Their three children—2, 5, and 8 years old—had been alone the entire evening. When the parents arrived, the 2-year-old woke up and started to cry. The father screamed at her to "shut up" and slapped her twice across the face. A worker can use these details to discuss with the parents such issues as potential problems when children are unsupervised, loss of personal control after drinking, how to establish control of children's behavior, and maximizing children's well-being.

Risk Assessment

Another important task during initial assessment is to determine the degree of risk for children and the need to further involve the family with social services or law enforcement (Brissett-Chapman, 1995; Ragg, 2006). Risk assessment has become an important conceptual framework in deciding how likely the chances are that child maltreatment will occur in the family environment (Crosson-Tower, 2010; DePanfilis, 2011; Holder & Corey, 1991; Pecora et al., 2010). Numerous structured risk-assessment models have been developed or are under development that predict future child maltreatment incidents. (Risk assessment is future oriented in that its intent is to predict the potential for maltreatment at an upcoming time.)

Risk assessment has two primary purposes (Holder & Corey, 1991). One is to maximize children's safety within their environment. The other is to work to change and control those forces that act to increase risk within that environment. A child has greater safety when stresses impinging on the family are minimized and family members have been strengthened to better ward off such stresses in the future.

We have established that risk involves the likelihood that a child will be maltreated. Assessing how much at risk a child is for potential maltreatment is the protective services worker's responsibility. There are five forces that can either contribute to or diminish risk in a home: "maltreatment force," "child force," "parent force," "family force," and "intervention force" (Holder & Corey, 1991, p. 23).

Maltreatment Force. Maltreatment force involves the type and severity of maltreatment that is occurring in the home (Crosson-Tower, 2010; Downs et al., 2009; Pecora et al., 2010). Are children being neglected, burned, beaten, or sexually molested? It also focuses on the conditions under which maltreatment usually occurs. Is the abusive parent drunk, depressed, or explosive? Does the maltreatment occur randomly or only in times of crisis?

Child Force. Child force involves the maltreated child's personal characteristics (Crosson-Tower, 2010; Downs et al., 2009). Is the child extremely withdrawn, brashly aggressive, or exceptionally slow to respond? This force also involves the extent to which you, as the worker, perceive the child as being susceptible to maltreatment. For instance, very young children and children with physical disabilities are exceptionally vulnerable.

Parent Force. Parent force entails the characteristics of the parents in the family (Crosson-Tower, 2010; Downs et al., 2009; Pecora et al., 2010). How do they feel about themselves? Do they feel guilty after maltreatment occurs? How do they cope with external stresses?

A second aspect of parent force is the parents' child management skills. To what extent do the parents rely on physical punishment to control their children? How do they interact with the children? How responsive are they to the children's wants and demands?

The third facet of parent force concerns the parents' own upbringing and past experiences. How were they treated by their own parents? Do they have a prison record or record of legal convictions? Do they have health difficulties? The final component of parent force is the interactional patterns of the parents with others. How do they communicate with other people? Do they have friends or neighbors with whom they associate? To what extent are they isolated from others?

Family Force. Family force concerns three elements. First, what variables characterize the family in terms of demographics? Are one or both parents involved? How many children are there? Is the family a blended stepfamily? What levels of education, job training, and work experience do the parents have? What is their income level? Is unemployment a problem? What are their housing conditions?

The second facet of family force involves how the family can "function, interact, and communicate" (Crosson-Tower, 2010; Downs et al., 2009; Holder & Corey, 1991, p. 30). If the parents are married, how do they get along? How do they talk to each other? How would you describe their lifestyle? Are they prone to crises?

The third facet of family force is the overall support and nurturance the family receives from the surrounding social environment (Crosson-Tower, 2010; Wells, 2008). What relationships does the family have with extended family members? Do they have access to adequate transportation? Are they socially isolated?

Intervention Force. The fifth force that workers assess in risk management involves the intervention force. This force concerns your anticipation of how the family will react to intervention. Will the family members be angry, afraid, or wary? Intervention force also includes the outside pressures upon the family that might hinder the intervention process with the family. How large and manageable is your caseload? How frequently can you see the family? Are you readily available to them?

Assessing the Forces of Risk. Although various structured risk-assessment instruments are available, explaining them in detail is beyond the scope of this text. Hopefully, such structured and planned approaches will enhance workers' effectiveness, efficiency, and accountability when dealing with child maltreatment.

The idea behind risk-assessment systems is that maltreating families lie somewhere along a risk continuum. The more pressures the family is under and the less external support it has, the greater the risk of maltreatment for the children. As intervention progresses, the family is strengthened. As the family gains support and strength, the maltreatment risk to children decreases. Hopefully, the worker can eventually make the determination that the family has achieved its intervention goals and is strong enough to cope with external social stresses. Thus, when the maltreatment risk is significantly decreased, the case will be closed.

THE GENERALIST INTERVENTION MODEL: PLANNING

 As with any type of planning in generalist practice, objectives are specified, responsibilities assigned, and the who-will-do-what-by-when process is clearly established. Means of evaluating objectives are also determined. There are at least eight dimensions upon which goals are frequently based for families in risk management (Berry, 2005; Crosson-Tower, 2010; Holder & Corey, 1991, Appendix N, pp. 1–30):

1. *Self-sufficiency.* Parents and families frequently must enhance their ability to function independently. This dimension has to do with families being better able to fend for themselves and satisfy their own needs. Specific objectives often involve increasing self-esteem and confidence.
2. *Communication skills.* Goals focusing on improved communication skills among family members are common. Members may be encouraged to identify and express their feelings openly and honestly. Listening skills can be enhanced. Family members' ability to understand others' points of view can be improved.
3. *Parenting knowledge.* Parents may not know how to handle and control children. They may have been brought up in emotionally deprived environments themselves, and they may resort to force for controlling children's behavior because they have never been taught any other behavior management techniques. They can be taught not only to control, but also to play with and enjoy their children.

   Additionally, parents may need knowledge about normal development. They need to know what to expect in terms of normal behavior at each age level. Appropriate expectations may reduce the frustrations parents feel when children do not behave the way parents think they *should*.

4. *Stress management.* Parents can be taught to better manage their stress levels. They can be taught to release their feelings more appropriately, instead of allowing emotional pressure to build up and explode. Learning such specific stress management techniques as relaxation approaches can also help them cope with stress.

5. *Impulse control.* Many parents in families at risk have poor impulse control. They are under tremendous stress. They often need to learn how to direct their energies in more fruitful ways than violently lashing out at their children.

6. *Problem-solving skills.* Parents in high-risk families may be so frustrated and stressed that they feel they have little control over their lives and behavior. They can be taught how to analyze problems, translate these problems into needs, establish potential alternatives to meeting these needs, evaluate the pros and cons of alternatives, and, finally, select and pursue their most promising options.

7. *Interactive nurturing.* Many times, family members need to be taught how to both express their positive feelings and accept affection. They can be taught how to empathize with each other, verbalize their feelings, and reinforce their support and caring for each other.

8. *Resource enhancement.* A primary means of increasing the strength of families at risk is to increase their resources. Adequate employment, income, housing, food, and clothing all contribute to a family's well-being.

THE GENERALIST INTERVENTION MODEL: IMPLEMENTATION

The implementation approaches specified in the plan are carried out during this service-provision step. This step includes tasks for the CPS worker, the client family, and other professionals involved in the case. Other professionals may include those from medical, mental health, educational, and legal agencies. Services may include homemaker services, parent-aides, visiting nurses, special school programs, day care, emergency shelter and foster care, parent education programs, job-seeking and employment services, crisis nurseries and respite care to provide parents with breaks from child care, adequate housing, financial assistance, and transportation to and from programs. Any services that fortify a family's strengths may be part of the treatment

implementation. The chances that you, as a CPS worker, may function primarily as a case manager—the one who coordinates a range of services during this part of the intervention—are quite possible.

THE GENERALIST INTERVENTION MODEL: EVALUATION, TERMINATION, AND FOLLOW-UP

During the evaluation step, progress is documented, goals and objectives are reviewed, and intervention plans are amended to meet the current risk situation. Hopefully, the service provision during the intervention process has significantly decreased risk, increased safety, and generally strengthened the family unit.

The case is terminated when risk has been determined to no longer be present or has been significantly decreased so that the children are adequately safe. Goals and objectives that have been attained are specified and documented. A final risk assessment is likely to be concluded and recorded. Follow-up can be used to determine the risk conditions at some time in the future.

EMPOWERMENT, CHILD MALTREATMENT, AND PRACTICE WITH FAMILIES AND GROUPS

A generalist focus prepares workers for action with individuals, families, groups, organizations, and communities. As work addressing child maltreatment inherently focuses on the family, principles concerning how to work with groups are integrally involved. Other aspects of practice with groups that seek empowerment might include linking abusive parents with support or child-behavior-management groups. Support groups for survivors, both as children and adults, are other possibilities.

EMPOWERMENT, CHILD MALTREATMENT, AND PRACTICE WITH ORGANIZATIONS AND COMMUNITIES

There are numerous recommendations for changes in policy and practice at the macro level concerning the welfare of maltreated children. Social workers and other helping professionals are striving to find ever more effective and efficient means of improving the lives of children and their families. Enhanced service provision is also being pursued by local, state, and federal public units of government.

Such agency personnel are committed for both humanitarian reasons and fiscal accountability.

Practitioners should address child maltreatment by considering it as a continuum that includes prevention, reporting, and treatment. All aspects of intervention should focus on empowering children and families. Social workers must actively advocate for resources and positive change in these directions (Wells, 2008; for an idea of how these skills can be applied to older adults, see a later section of this chapter).

Workers might pursue improvements at the macro level in at least five areas (Schene, 1996). First, instead of emphasizing the reporting of child maltreatment, we should focus on providing services aimed at prevention. Second, a more supportive system geared toward improving resources and services for families in general is essential to maintain family strengths. Third, more resources should be directed at treatment instead of case finding. Fourth, we should focus on treatment outcomes and improvement rather than on treatment process. Fifth, more community and neighborhood supports should be located and developed.

Critical Thinking Questions 7.2

- What do you think could and should be done to address the problem of child maltreatment?
- What are your feelings about parents who maltreat their children?
- Is this an area in which you would feel comfortable working?

LO 7-4 Examine and Implement Crisis Intervention

The intervention strategy of crisis intervention is a brief and time-limited therapeutic intervention where a social worker or other mental health professional helps a client system in crisis recognize the precipitating problem and identify potential coping methods (Roberts, 2005b). In other words, crisis intervention helps people learn to cope with or adjust to extreme external pressures.

Kanel (2012) defines a crisis as a situation where:

(1) a precipitating event; (2) a perception of the event that causes subjective distress; and (3) the failure of a person's usual coping methods, which causes a person experiencing the precipitating event to function at a lower level than before the event. (p. 2)

Social workers use the term *crisis* in two ways. First, it can take the form of internal emotional distress on the part of an individual or family experiencing such incidents as the death of a loved one, job loss, or unwanted pregnancy. Second, it may be a social event in the macro environment causing disaster and major disruption of life for a large number of people (for example, a major earthquake, flood, drought, or terrorist attack).

Virtually any upsetting event can evoke a crisis. These include family and other interpersonal difficulties, financial problems, physical illnesses, accidents, problems related to age (such as those common in adolescence or old age), substance abuse, sexual assault, and involvement in the legal system (James & Gilliland, 2013; Kanel, 2012; Roberts, 2005b).

THE CRISIS PROCESS

Crises typically progress in the following manner (Eaton & Roberts, 2009; Echterling, Presbury, & McKee, 2005; Kanel, 2012). First, an individual is exposed to a heavy amount of stress over some period of time. Second, this stress acts to make the person exceptionally vulnerable to intimidation and assaults from outside. The usual emotional protection from worrisome and painful incidents is weaker than usual. The third aspect is some precipitating incident that served to trigger the client's crisis state, which is characterized by instability, ineffectiveness, and the inability to take action (Kanel, 2012). As the crisis continues, the individual perceives the precipitating factor and other stressors to which he or she is being exposed as increasingly serious threats. Finally, the person experiences surging anxiety and such accompanying troublesome emotions as depression or grief.

At this point, the individual will probably be most receptive to help. Normal defense mechanisms have been weakened. When people become more anxious and emotional, they typically become less objective and logical. Crises breed desperation. Desperation fosters panic and immobility. People in crisis can easily become frozen in their tracks. Your job is to get them moving again.

Crisis can happen to individuals, families, groups, communities, and organizations; however, regardless of level, the essential process of crisis buildup remains the same. Highlight 7.3 describes some of the major concepts involved.

HIGHLIGHT 7.3

Major Concepts in Crisis Intervention

EP 2.1.7a

There are many conceptual frameworks for crisis intervention. However, virtually all of them have the following themes in common:

1. *The primary goal of crisis intervention is to help the client return at least to the precrisis level of functioning* (Cournoyer, 2012; Kanel, 2012; Okun & Kantrowitz, 2008).

We have described the crisis process. A person is under a large amount of stress for some period of time. Subsequently, another upsetting event or series of events occurs. The person becomes emotionally shaken, usually loses an objective sense of self-direction, and becomes unable to proceed. Crisis intervention involves helping people in crisis return to the level of functioning they were at prior to the precipitating event. This means that crisis intervention goals are very specific and deal only with issues directly related to the crisis situation.

An example is a situation in which you, as the practitioner, receive a call from a client threatening suicide. Your primary goal would be to help that person return to her level of functioning prior to having suicidal thoughts and feelings. Crisis intervention would not seek to achieve more complicated, long-term goals. For example, you would not try to help the person to become more popular or improve her personality. These goals might be worked on in a longer-term counseling format.

This type of intervention does not mean that you should tell your clients to get worse again if they enhance their level of functioning above its precrisis level. If clients make greater improvements, that is wonderful. Your maximum goals with clients would be some improvement above their precrisis level of functioning. Goals in crisis intervention should be realistic and focus primarily on the individual's ability to cope with the *crisis*.

2. *Crisis intervention is relatively short term* (Cournoyer, 2012; Okun & Kantrowitz, 2008). Because the intent is to return the client to the precrisis level of functioning, crisis intervention progresses quickly. Your length of involvement will usually be shorter than your interventions in noncrisis situations. If, for example, you are working in a hospital emergency room, your contact would likely be for less than one day

(Boes & McDermott, 2005). In other settings, such as a mental health center, your length of intervention might last from four to six meetings (Kanel, 2012). Regardless, the crisis intervention process is significantly shorter than many other client relationships in practice.

3. *"Specific, current, observable difficulties are the target" of the intervention* (Kanel, 2012; Parsons & Wicks, 1994, p. 102).

Crisis intervention focuses purely on the crisis and those aspects of the client's life directly related to the crisis. Therefore, crisis intervention does little delving into clients' pasts. Only information about the past directly relevant to the crisis is gathered. You cannot afford to waste time on anything but resolving the immediate crisis.

4. *Crisis intervention strategies generally work better than other approaches when dealing with crises* (Eaton & Roberts, 2009; Kanel, 2012).

Crisis intervention is a well-defined, viable approach that is indeed the best approach to crisis situations. Crises are by nature severe. Their resolution merits the top priority in intervention. Other related stresses and problems can be dealt with later using other intervention methods.

5. *The practitioner in crisis intervention assumes an exceptionally active role, which may be more directive than that assumed in other approaches to generalist practice* (Aguilera & Messick, 1974, p. 15; James & Gilliland, 2013; Okun & Kantrowitz, 2008; Roberts, 2008).

Throughout this text, we emphasize the importance of client involvement. Integral client participation throughout the planned change process is essential. Clients should also be as involved *as possible* in the crisis intervention process. However, the key phrase here is "as possible." You might have to expend more pressure to get the client moving from his or her emotionally frozen position. With crises, you usually do not have the luxury of relaxed discussion time. Consider a bewildered, homeless client living with her family in her car when the wind chill factor is hitting 25 degrees below zero. You probably will not have time to discuss all possible options available in a leisurely fashion. Rather, you may need to strongly encourage her to take some direction you specify in order to keep her family from freezing.

STEPS IN CRISIS INTERVENTION

The following explores a clearly defined five-step crisis intervention model that coincides with the planned change process in generalist practice (Echterling et al., 2005; James & Gilliland, 2013; Kanel, 2012).

Step 1: Engagement

Kanel (2012) describes the importance of engaging the client in the worker–client relationship:

> *The foundation of crisis intervention is the development of **rapport**—a state of understanding and comfort—between client and counselor. As the client begins to feel rapport, trust and openness follow, allowing the interview to proceed. Before delving into the client's personal world, the [social worker]... must achieve this personal contact. The counseling relationship is unique in this regard; before any work can be done, the client must feel understood and accepted by the... [social worker. One way to put this might be,] "People don't care what you know, until they know that you care." (p. 46)*

Critical Thinking Question 7.3

- What skills have you learned in prior chapters that might help you engage a client in a beginning worker–client relationship?

Step 2: Assessment

The second step in crisis intervention is assessment. Engagement is assumed to be a part of this first step. The art in crisis intervention is to focus on the specific precipitating event that brought the client to you. Only clearly related aspects of the client's situation should be addressed. At least five specific areas of questioning should be pursued.

First, you must determine why the person called you or came in to see you on that particular day (Kanel 2012; Roberts, 2008). What precipitating event has occurred? The crisis usually occurs less than 2 weeks before a client seeks professional help. Often, the precipitating event has occurred within the prior 24 hours. For instance, one client was just told he has brain cancer, or another client just discovered that her husband is having an affair.

A typical first question to the client is something like, "What brings you in to see me today?" or "What has happened to make you so upset?" The intent is to identify and specify as soon as possible what the crisis is.

A second line of questioning should involve how your client views the crisis situation and precipitating event (Roberts, 2005b). How does he or she feel about the event? What impact does the client think it will have on his or her life now and in the future? You might ask yourself how objective your client appears to be about the situation.

The third relevant line of questioning involves whether your client has access to support from others (Echterling et al., 2005; Kanel, 2012). Is there anyone the client can talk to? Whom does he or she feel comfortable asking for help? The general guiding principle is, when necessary, crisis intervention may "involve collaboration and engagement with diverse others, including friends, relatives, neighbors, and both formal and informal groups and organizations throughout a community" (Cournoyer, 2012, p, 258). Crises are stressful. You have to act fast. The more support you can muster in helping your client return to the pre-crisis level of functioning, the better.

The fourth area of information to pursue concerns your client's history in solving similar problems (Okun & Kantrowitz, 2008; Roberts, 2005b). Has something like this crisis ever happened to him or her before? If so, how did it get resolved? How does your client usually cope with stressful events in general? Can any of these coping skills be applied to the current situation?

A fifth and very critical area of information to solicit involves the extent to which clients are in danger of harming either themselves or others (Eaton & Roberts, 2009; Roberts 2005a; Roberts & Yeager, 2005). If you determine that your client is seriously considering violently harming him- or herself or others, you may need to take more drastic steps. For example, immediate hospitalization or referral to a treatment program might be necessary.

Step 3: Planning

During this step, you must evaluate the extent to which the crisis has interfered with your client's ability to function. Which daily activities will the client be able to resume? Will he or she be able to return to a job, homemaking, parenting, education, or other activities? Additionally, how are others close to your client reacting to the crisis? Is your client receiving any support from them?

The second primary aspect of planning is to review potential alternatives, evaluate the pros and cons, and determine the course of action to pursue. Reviewing strategies that have worked in the past and deciding whether they might not be useful again is important during this phase.

Step 4: Implementation

Any of a variety of helping techniques can be used in crisis intervention. For example, workers addressing crisis situations vary in terms of the training they have had and in their practice settings. Regardless of background and setting, good interviewing and relationship-building skills are especially important. The crisis demands that you and your client move forward in a hurry.

The following are suggestions for what to address during the implementation phase of the process (Aguilera & Messick, 1974):

1. Help the client look at the crisis situation more objectively (James & Gilliland, 2013; Roberts, 2005b). People in crisis are in turmoil. When you are in emotional turmoil, it is difficult to think clearly and objectively. The worker's task is to help clients assess their situation rationally and begin to cut through the cloud of emotion that biases their rational thinking. Are they blowing the crisis and its related issues out of proportion? Are they failing to take into account other positive aspects of their lives? You can help clients evaluate their strengths and weaknesses more objectively and begin moving toward crisis resolution.

2. Help the client explore and express hidden feelings (Eaton & Roberts, 2009; Echterling et al., 2005; James & Gilliland, 2013; Roberts, 2005b). Stress frequently results in anxious discomfort and strong negative feelings. People trying to cope with stress will often desperately try to control these feelings, to hold them inside. They may fear the pain associated with anxiety, worry, grief, disappointment, and sadness. All such restrictive retention of feelings does is immobilize people. Before they can deal with their feelings and make logical choices regarding how to proceed, clients need to acknowledge that these feelings exist. Part of your role in crisis intervention is to help clients explore their emotional state. What blockages are preventing them from returning to their precrisis level of functioning? What feelings are making them "stuck"?

3. Identify and use coping approaches used in the past for resolving crises (James & Gilliland, 2013; Kanel, 2012; Okun & Kantrowitz, 2008; Roberts, 2005b, 2008). During assessment you should already have identified what mechanisms the client has used to cope with similar crises and issues in the past. Can these be applied to the current crisis? Additionally, what new methods of coping might you suggest your client try? Perhaps, in his or her emotional turmoil, the client is having difficulty seeing what alternatives exist.

   After the problem and precipitating factor for the crisis are clearly defined for the client, you, as the crisis intervention practitioner, can suggest potential alternatives to solve the problem. Part of the implementation process is to enable the client to make changes. Because crisis intervention is more directive than many other forms of intervention, "specific directions may be given as to what should be tried as tentative solutions" (Aguilera & Messick, 1974, p. 59). If you are in the position of meeting with the client again, you can later evaluate progress made and the effectiveness of the attempted alternatives. If the alternatives did not work, you can help your client to identify and assess the potential of new ones.

4. Reestablish old or develop new social support systems (Echterling et al., 2005; Halley et al., 1998). Such systems may include "family, friends, neighbors, church, organizations, work [and] recreation" (Halley et al., 1998, p. 447). If the crisis involved a loss such as a death or divorce, you can help the client identify people who can help them through the crisis. Likewise, you can help clients call upon those people closest to them in such crises as job loss or major health problems.

   People in crisis need as much social support and nurturance as possible. Identify and use the support that is already there. If such support is scanty or nonexistent, help the client open up new avenues of relationships. During the crisis intervention process you may choose to pursue any or all of these four options. There may be crisis cases where none readily applies. Determining the best way to proceed is up to your professional judgment.

Step 5: Planning for Future Crises

Planning for potential future crises helps clients prepare for any forthcoming traumatic events (Halley et al., 1998; Kanel, 2012). The final phase in crisis intervention focuses on articulating and summarizing what clients have learned during the crisis intervention process. What means have they developed to cope with stress? What have they learned from working through this crisis situation that they may be able to apply to stressful times in the future? One task of the worker is to help clients clearly identify and articulate coping behaviors so that these skills are more readily available when needed next.

In essence, the planning for the future phase of crisis intervention includes the evaluation and termination steps of the planned change process. Because of the fast-moving nature of crisis intervention, these phases are accomplished quickly. Often they are melded together. For instance, the summarizing involved in planning for future crises incorporates evaluation, as only effective coping mechanisms are included. Termination promptly follows.

Follow-up is the last phase of the planned change process. Because of the nature of crisis intervention, follow-up is not always possible. Practitioners often do not have time. Follow-up may not be part of their job responsibilities. Sometimes, agencies have alternative mechanisms for follow-up. Because referral is an integral part of the crisis intervention process, often the responsibility of follow-up rests on those providing the service for which the client has been referred.

A CASE EXAMPLE OF CRISIS INTERVENTION IN MICRO PRACTICE

The following is a case example of crisis intervention in micro practice. (Please note that items in italics reflect application of the substeps involved in the crisis intervention process.) Highlight 7.4 addresses the special crisis situation of coping with grief.

Mildred's husband, Marvin Murphy, was killed abruptly in a car accident 2 weeks earlier. Mildred, age 36, and Marvin, age 39, had been married for 17 years. They had two children: Monty, age 16, and Michael, age 14.

Mildred was distraught with grief. She did not know what to do next. She had lived with Marvin for almost half her life and just assumed he would always be there for her. They had their ups and downs, but generally she felt it had been a steady, fairly happy marriage (that was, of course, except for his one extramarital fling 15 years earlier). But even the fling had become ancient history to Mildred.

Marvin had been the family's primary breadwinner. He was an accountant who earned $66,743.67 a year.

Mildred had almost always worked outside of the home. However, it had consisted of doing nearly minimum-wage jobs on a part-time basis. They owned their midsized home in a suburb of Milwaukee. Rather, they owned about $24,000 in equity and made $1,300 monthly payments.

Mildred had spent the past 2 weeks coping with the immediate crises commonly caused by sudden tragic deaths. She had dealt with funeral arrangements, in addition to a multitude of insurance and legal issues to settle. This moment was the first time she really had time for the momentous impact of the event to hit her. What would she do now? She was lonely. She was acutely grief stricken. She was worried about her two children, both of whom were also seriously affected by their father's abrupt death. She could not afford to maintain the style of life to which the family had become accustomed. She panicked. She also had the wherewithal to seek help. She called the crisis intervention unit of the local community mental health center. The intake unit set up an appointment for her with Clark Kent, a social worker and crisis counselor. (A *community mental health center* is a local agency receiving some federal funding that offers various psychiatric and social services to community residents [Barker, 2003]. These include inpatient and outpatient services, counseling, emergency services such as crisis lines, and programs for people addressing a range of issues across the lifespan such as substance abuse, child behavior management, or coping with Alzheimer's disease.)

Step 1: Engagement

Mildred met with Clark early the next day. Clark began the meeting with cordial introductions. He displayed warmth, empathy, and genuineness. He used verbal and nonverbal attending skills. He gave her steady eye contact and assumed a facial expression of concern. He gently asked what brought Mildred in to see him. As Mildred began explaining, Clark leaned forward and nodded his encouragement to continue.

Step 2: Assessment

Clark and Mildred began the assessment process. Clark's intent was to crystallize the *problems affecting Mildred* and *how she felt* about them. After some discussion, they established the following list of prioritized problems: an immediate financial crisis, her extreme level of grief, worry about her children, worry about her future (specifically, her living arrangements), and her loneliness.

HIGHLIGHT 7.4

A Few Words About Helping People Cope with Grief and Loss

There are a number of suggestions for how you, as a professional, can help someone coping with death, a terminal disease, or virtually any type of extreme loss. Consider the following:

1. Encourage clients to talk about their loss, both with you and supportive others. Talking about grief eases loneliness and allows them to vent their feelings. Talking with close friends gives people a sense of security and brings them closer to others they love. Talking with people who have had similar losses helps put clients' problems in perspective. They will see that they are not the only ones with problems. Other people with similar crises may be able to give them positive suggestions about coping. Finally, clients may enhance their own self-esteem and sense of well-being when helping others.

2. Understand that many negative feelings may surface when a person is struggling to cope with a crisis. They might include anger, depression, or grief. Encourage expression of even these negative feelings so that clients might begin coping with them and moving forward.

3. Convey verbally and nonverbally that you are willing to talk about any concerns of the client. What you want to convey to clients is that you are emotionally ready to help them cope with their grief and to provide them with support. Remember, however, that clients may always choose not to share their feelings with you. You can encourage, but you cannot force them.

4. Do not discourage crying. Rather, people should be encouraged to cry as they feel the need. Crying releases tension that is part of grieving.

5. Answer questions as honestly as you can. Sometimes, this task is especially difficult. For instance, if you are dealing with a crisis where a client or someone close is dying or very ill, questions may be unpleasant. Answers may be awkward and even painful. Nonetheless, being as honest and straightforward as you possibly can is important. If you do not know an answer, seek out someone (e.g., a physician) who will accurately provide the requested information. Evasion or ambiguity in response to a dying person's questions will only increase his or her concerns. If there is a chance for recovery, this fact should be mentioned. Even a small margin of hope can be a comfort. The chances for recovery, however, should not be exaggerated.

6. If the crisis involves a dying person, help that person become the *star* of his or her own death. In other words, provide the person with requested information and help the person participate in decisions concerning death. Many people, when dying, reach a point where they want to tie up their loose ends. They want to consciously set their affairs in order, clarify their will, and discuss their wishes regarding their funeral. Avoiding such topics is easy for other people because of their own fears of death. Instead, many people feel more comfortable avoiding the painful topics and trying to remain unrealistically cheery. You, as a helping professional, can help your clients continue to appreciate their personal significance even when death is near. You can also urge your clients' loved ones to remain involved with your clients until the very end.

Critical Thinking Questions 7.4

EP 2.1.3

- Have you or someone you know well experienced grief due to the loss of a loved one, a terminal disease, a chronic debilitating injury, or some other extreme loss?
- If so, how did you or the identified person cope with the loss?
- What was or could have been done to provide support and assist in the coping process?

Clark continued by gently asking Mildred about her friends and family. He was investigating her *current access to support* from others. Had people generally been supportive to her during this time of great need? Were there any friends or family members in particular to whom she could turn for help? Did she and her sons have the ability to provide each other with support?

Clark empathized with Mildred concerning the depth of her grief. He emphasized that having an intimate partner of so many years plucked from her so hastily was indeed difficult. Searching for her innermost feelings, he indicated how losing her husband might be the most difficult loss with which she had ever had to deal. Mildred responded that it was. Only the death of her own mother 5 years ago reminded her of how she felt today. Clark then asked in a soft and warm manner how she had managed through the difficult times of coping with grief for her mother. He was seeking to *identify coping mechanisms Mildred had used in the past.* Mildred responded that her sister and one special old friend had both been exceptionally helpful to her at that time. She continued that she had not had much time to talk with either of them during the past 2 weeks.

Finally, Clark asked gently, yet straightforwardly, if Mildred was having any destructive thoughts about herself or others. He explained how easy it is for some people to turn their grief and anger at what had happened toward themselves or others close to them. Mildred indicated that she had not had such thoughts. Clark at this time was *evaluating the extent to which Mildred might be in danger of harming herself or others.*

Step 3: *Planning*

Clark *evaluated the extent to which the crisis interfered with the client's ability to function.* He determined that although this crisis situation had temporarily immobilized Mildred, she probably had the potential to carry on with her life if she was given adequate direction. Prior to her husband's death, Mildred had held her regular, although low-paying, receptionist position for the past 4 years. She reported having no major difficulties with her children other than what she termed "typical parent–adolescent spats." She was regularly involved with her own extended family members, many of whom lived in nearby areas. Thus, Mildred had a number of strengths upon which to base her plans.

Clark and Mildred *discussed alternative solutions* to some of her problems at this time. Her primary problem was that of financial crisis. He referred her to a financial planner right within his agency. The planner could help her determine the minimum amount of money she needed in order to live, review her total assets (e.g., current income, house equity, savings, insurance payments, and cash), and identify what alternatives she could pursue about her housing situation. Later on, Mildred might pursue with him the possibility of job training and financial resources to assist in solving her financial problems.

Mildred's second major problem involved her grief. Clark referred her to a support group[1] for survivors of the death of a loved one (held at another social services agency). He cited the specific time and place the group met. If they chose, her sons could also attend. Mildred indicated that she would pursue this idea.

Mildred's other problems involved worry about her future in general and her living arrangements in particular. Both of these were directly related to her financial decisions. Clark urged her to put off consideration of the two former problems until she had time to establish clearly the state of her financial affairs. Then she could review the options available to her.

They articulated specific objectives regarding who Mildred was to call by specified dates. Finally, they set up another appointment to meet 1 week from that day.

Step 4: *Implementation*

Altogether, Mildred met with Clark four times over 4 weeks. Mildred indicated that her meetings with the financial planner were going well. After including her husband's life insurance benefits, her assets were greater than she had anticipated. The planner was helping her develop short-term and long-term goals regarding living arrangements and employment.

Mildred and Clark talked about other realistic alternatives available to her. He helped her to start working through the emotional turmoil that was immobilizing her. She remained very sad. However, she began to understand that she would persevere through this very difficult time in her life. Clark's intent was to help her *gain a more realistic, objective perspective on her life* so that she could go on.

Additionally, during their meetings, Clark encouraged Mildred to stop desperately trying to contain her feelings. Rather, she should *express her hidden feelings and emotions* so that she could begin to deal with them and recover. Sometimes, she cried sorrowfully. Clark encouraged this as a natural expression of her grief.

Together, they continued to *explore and use coping mechanisms.* Clark encouraged Mildred to frequently contact her sister and her close friend, both of whom were so comforting to her after her mother's death. Additionally, Mildred and her sons did attend the

---

1. A *support group* is a treatment group consisting of participants who share common issues or problems and meet on an ongoing basis to cope with stress, give each other suggestions, provide encouragement, convey information, and furnish emotional support (Barker, 2003; Kirst-Ashman, 2013).

support group Clark had suggested, which she said was beneficial to her. She indicated that she was motivated to continue for the next few weeks and possibly even months.

In her discussion with Clark, Mildred recognized that she had much respect for the minister of her church. Although she had never discussed such personal matters with him before, she went to talk to him about her grief. Afterward, she told Clark that her pain was still raging. However, her minister had helped her gain some peace.

In terms of *reestablishing her social support network,* Mildred was not ready to entertain other people or enjoy herself regardless of the circumstance. However, she was able to return to work. She continued to attend her sons' sporting events, as both boys were actively involved in school sports. She spoke with her sister and good friend regularly.

Step 5: *Planning for Future Crises*

During Mildred's final session with Clark, they *summarized together the progress she had made* in so short a time. She was coping with her financial crisis by obtaining help from an expert. She and her sons discovered that groups can be beneficial. Additionally, Mildred worked on maintaining open communication with her sons so that they might support each other in their grief. Finally, she maintained strong and regular contact with those persons identified as being especially helpful to her in times of crisis—her sister, good friend, and minister.

Clark emphasized how well Mildred had pulled herself together. He commended her for having the strength to do so. He also *suggested how the coping methods she had discovered and were using might help her again in future times of need.* Clark wished Mildred the best. This case of crisis intervention was terminated.

CRISIS INTERVENTION WITH FAMILIES AND GROUPS

As we know, generalist practitioners are oriented to looking beyond the individual level; crisis intervention may also involve potential action with families, groups, communities, and organizations. For example, the crisis intervention example in micro practice portrayed earlier converges with mezzo practice. Mildred's two sons were also indirectly and integrally involved in the helping process, even though they did not actually meet with the crisis intervention practitioner.

Crisis intervention is relevant in practice with families. It can be used to help the entire family when one family member experiences a disturbing event or when the entire family system suffers a disruptive crisis. The planned change process should include assessing the family's and individual family members' strengths and weaknesses, their interest in and commitment to making positive changes, and their access to support, services, and resources. This is true regardless of which family member or members are most directly facing the problem and dealing with the crisis. A crisis affecting one or more members of a family affects the entire family. Likewise, intervention efforts directed at some member or part of a family will influence the entire family group. Crisis intervention can also be applicable within the context of small groups (Everly, Lating, & Mitchell, 2005). Groups can be used to help members avert more severe crises such as being hospitalized or institutionalized. They can help members deal with upcoming stressful events such as medical treatments or ensuing relocation. Additionally, they can help to work out issues concerning family disputes, struggles between parents and children, or marital difficulties.

CRISIS INTERVENTION WITH ORGANIZATIONS AND COMMUNITIES

Crisis intervention at the macro level is frequently used in response to crises involving major population groups suffering from natural disasters. Floods, earthquakes, droughts, and famines all require crisis intervention efforts on a massive scale. A macro perspective on crisis intervention could potentially involve countries, states, nations, and even continents, depending on the scope of the natural disaster. These other systems could contribute food, clothing, shelter, medical supplies, or funds to purchase what people in the crisis area need.

Crisis intervention at the macro level need not only involve natural disasters, but also other types of crises including wars, bombings, and terrorist attacks. Highlight 7.5 discusses social workers' integral involvement in crisis intervention and disaster relief, such as after the September 11, 2001, terrorist attacks on the World Trade Center and the Pentagon.

Crisis intervention in most macro situations requires a multidisciplinary approach. Many professionals and citizens are called upon to pool their efforts and address major crises. Social work practitioners may become one segment of the total intervention effort.

LO 7-5 Provide Disaster Relief and Trauma Counseling: Macro-Level Crisis Intervention

Disasters at the macro level are terrifying, devastating, and these days disturbingly anticipated. Disasters may be caused by nature, human error, or terrorists. Results may include shocking injuries and loss of human life, extensive destruction of property, and displacement of thousands. Think about superstorm Sandy slamming into the U.S. eastern seaboard in October 2012, killing dozens, misplacing thousands, and resulting in billions of dollars of property damage and business losses (CBSnews.com, 2012). Consider the terrorist attacks at the Boston Marathon and the allegedly accidental explosion at the fertilizer factory in West Texas, both occurring in the same week during April 2013 and resulting in death, serious injury, and devastation.

When Flights 11, 175, and 77 respectively smashed into the World Trade Center's twin towers and the Pentagon on September 11, 2001, the world changed forever for people in the United States. In quick response, thousands of social workers brought their own work and lives to an abrupt halt and responded to "the public's dire need for social services and mental health assistance" in the disaster's aftermath (O'Neill, 2001c, p. 1). Social workers "made up by far the largest professional group trained by the American Red Cross and ready to deliver crisis intervention" services (O'Neill, 2001b, p. 8).

Visualize the range of scenarios that occurred (O'Neill, 2001a, 2001b). Social workers helped people trying to find missing relatives cope with their terror and grief. They provided mental health counseling in walk-in clinics for family members of victims and for other staff addressing the disaster. They helped serve on crisis phone lines, talking with family members desperately seeking loved ones. They responded to community agencies requiring assistance and helped distribute clothing both to staff working at the sites and others in need.

Ilia Rivera-Sanchez, a native of Puerto Rico, provides an example of how social workers could help (O'Neill, 2001c). By 6:00 p.m. on September 11, she was at the Pentagon "providing water, food, iced towels and encouragement to fire fighters as they came down from ladders and to military personnel and other rescue workers. Once the fire was extinguished, she worked with military chaplains to help rescue workers as they sought to shore up the building so they could search

for victims. One night she was assigned to the morgue, to work with those bringing bodies out of the building" (O'Neill, 2001c, pp. 1, 8).

Kanel (2012) relates a story told by a former student of hers who was asked to help out after the September 11 attacks:

> He didn't know exactly what he would be doing, but he was ready to do anything. When he arrived, he went right up to the emergency workers, firefighters, and police, who were heaving heavy cement pieces from Ground Zero, searching for bodies. They were sweating, breathing heavily, and crying. He started helping them, until one of the workers told him to stop. The student said, "But I'm here to help." The worker looked at him and with tears in his eyes said, "This is our job. Your job is to take care of us. There are over 600 people in that building over there who need someone to talk to, share their feelings with, and we hope you can do this." The student walked over to the building and was met by hundreds of people that had been working day and night, survivors of the attacks, and people who had lost loved ones in the attacks. At this point, he certainly felt needed. (p. 175)

Disaster Relief Work versus Individual Crises

The third millennium has been plagued by horrifying catastrophic events and terrorist attacks. They have included vicious assaults, hurricanes, tornadoes, earthquakes, tsunamis, floods, landslides, and fires. During the aftermath, chaos, confusion, terrible grief, and struggle for survival often result. Roberts (2005a) describes the difference between the upheaval caused by individual crises and that by traumatic events affecting entire communities:

> For the most part, individuals function in their daily lives in a state of emotional balance. Occasionally, intensely stressful life events will stretch a person's sense of well-being and equilibrium. However, even stressful life events are frequently predictable within a person's ordinary routines, and he or she is able to mobilize effective coping methods to handle the stress. In sharp contrast, traumatic events lift people

(continued)

HIGHLIGHT 7.5 *(continued)*

out of their usual realm of equilibrium and make it difficult to reestablish a sense of balance or equilibrium. Trauma reactions are often precipitated by a sudden, random, and arbitrary traumatic event. . . . Traumatic events refer to overwhelming, unpredictable, and emotionally shocking experiences. (p. 161)

Disaster relief work primarily "involves teams that work directly on site and in the community with victims, survivors, and others associated with major catastrophes" (Okun & Kantrowitz, 2008, p. 265). Such teams may consist of various professionals, including social workers.

Assessment in Disaster Relief

EP 2.1.10d

"The first step in disaster intervention is *triage*, the quick assessment of severity and scope of need" (James & Gilliland, 2013; Okun & Kantrowitz, 2008, p. 265). Urgent health and medical needs should be evaluated. People's survival is paramount.

Survivors' psychological functioning in terms of their stability and decision-making ability should also be assessed. "During and shortly after an incident, nearly all of the direct victims experience overwhelming distress, grief, and anguish" (Echterling et al., 2005, p. 226). Data gathered should "include essential demographic information (name, address, phone number, e-mail address, etc.), perception of the magnitude of the traumatic event, coping methods, any presenting problems, safety issues, previous traumatic experiences, social support network, drug and alcohol use, preexisting psychiatric conditions, suicide risk, and homicide risk. . . . [P]sychological triage assessment refers to the immediate decision-making process in which the mental health worker determines lethality" (the extent of danger to life and health) and whether a referral to a hospital, out-patient treatment agency, social services agency, or support group is necessary (Roberts, 2005a, p. 151).

Okun and Kantrowitz (2008) comment on the initial response to a disaster:

Helper observations, feedback from others on site, and direct interactions facilitate decisions about what type of help is needed first. In some disasters, the pressing need is for food, water, and physical safety and deciding who is in need of what kind of

immediate services, who can wait, and who can be enlisted as a helping resource. (p. 265)

Intervention in Disaster Relief

EP 2.1.1d

EP 2.1.10g

After assessment, plans are made for how to proceed during the disaster relief process. The early intervention phase is usually described as occurring within the first month following the disaster (Kaul & Welzant, 2005). In addition to basic survival, other requirements "may include communication with family, friends, and community, the need for orientation to disaster services, and additional sources of social support. . . . Survivors and responders [to the emergency] are challenged by overwhelming and complex tasks, such as interacting with relief agencies, addressing insurance issues, rebuilding homes, and mourning losses" (Kaul & Welzant, 2005, p. 204). It is essential that information and referral services be provided so survivors can access the information and services they need.

First responders are those people initially responding to the physical safety and needs of survivors (Henry, 2005; Kaul & Welzant, 2005). They include emergency response teams, police, firefighters, medical staff, and others initially arriving at the scene. First responders also require support, encouragement, and a chance to vent their frustrations and horror at witnessing the disaster firsthand.

"[I]mmediate crisis counseling is the standard protocol for responding to community traumas" (Echterling et al., 2005, p. 230). Social workers can use their helping skills well in this capacity. Individual or group counseling can be provided. There are at least eight basic tasks practitioners should undertake while working with disaster survivors, the loved ones of victims, and others traumatized by the event (Behrman & Reid, 2005):

1. *Welcoming.* "This task involves building rapport, developing trust, and creating a psychologically safe environment in which to accomplish all the other tasks. The social worker communicates to others that he or she is emotionally and socially available and will perform his or her responsibilities with sensitivity, respect for diversity, and professional competence. . . . Welcoming can be accomplished through introductions, storytelling, ice-breakers, or expressions of care and concern for the client and community" (p. 293).

2. *Framing.* "This task entails framing the traumatic event in meaningful language that makes sense to individuals and the community. The goal is to understand what happened so that distorted information about the event can be reduced and the facts surrounding the event can be clearly communicated. This lowers the risk for rumors disconnecting people from each other" (Behrman & Reid, 2005, p. 295). What happened? Who was affected by the event? (Note that why the event happened should probably not be addressed at this stage, as this might solicit nonproductive blaming.)

3. *Educating.* This task involves providing information about the common effects of trauma, "such as numbness and fatigue, irritability, and fear" (Behrman & Reid, 2005, p. 295). The difference between stress and trauma should be emphasized. Coping strategies should be explained.

4. *Grieving.* Disaster involves loss. This task involves exploring what has been lost and what such loss means to the community and its residents. Feelings must be brought into the open so that they can be dealt with. Only then can discourse turn to identifying ways to deal with the loss and developing means to continue living.

5. *Integrating.* This task involves asking questions about the event and what it means to a survivor. How has this trauma affected a survivor's behavior, emotional well-being, and life in general? "Is it possible to be transformed by this experience, or is the only consequence tragedy and destruction? . . . The goal is to create new possibilities for transformative ways of living following the trauma" (Behrman & Reid, 2005, p. 299).

   Okun and Kantrowitz (2008) suggest a number of questions that can be asked to engage a survivor "in the process of understanding his/her emotional, cognitive, and behavioral reactions and in the development of adaptive strategies":
   What changes have occurred in your life recently, particularly in the past few days?
   Have you had any particular difficulties with people who are important to you, like a family member, boss, valued friend?
   What kinds of things have you already tried to do about this?

   Have you ever experienced these kinds of feelings before? If so, when, and what did you do about them?
   What do you think you need to have happen in order to get through this?
   Who in your life do you think might be most helpful to you at this time? (p. 267)

6. *Reflecting.* This task concerns exploring and identifying survivors' feelings about the community and what should be done to return it to health. What values are important to the community and its residents? What would make the community strong in residents' eyes? How do residents foresee a strong and vigorous future?

7. *Empowering.* "Empowering involves identifying from among these possibilities the most effective and efficient tasks that will facilitate the maintenance and enhancement of healthy outcomes following trauma. It also involves planning ways to obtain the resources necessary to successfully complete these tasks, deciding on the methods of task accomplishment, and considering obstacles that may interfere with task attainment" (Behrman & Reid, 2005, p. 299).

8. *Terminating and revisiting.* This task concerns summarizing what the individual or group counseling process has achieved. What have participants learned that will help them in the future? How might they remain empowered to live happy and productive lives?

Provision of Long-Term Help

Echterling and his colleagues (2005) discuss potential long-term consequences of a disaster:

> *Although the community trauma itself is terrifying and overwhelming for many members, it is just the beginning of a long series of problems. The survivors of a catastrophe have to cope with constant reminders, economic hardships, and losses that continue for years later. Dealing with the bureaucratic nightmare of disaster relief has been so maddeningly frustrating that many have labeled it "the second disaster" (Weaver, 1995, p. 73). In other words, community crises involve both acute and chronic stress and immediate and long-term challenges.*

> *For example, seven years after a flood, one man shared his long-term struggles with us. His account*

(continued)

HIGHLIGHT 7.5 *(continued)*

describes some of the financial stressors and emotional challenges that some survivors face:

> "We couldn't sell our house, so we had to remain here. We want to move. . . . I don't enjoy the river the way I used to. We weren't able to afford vacations. . . . Thanksgiving time has never meant the same since the flood. We don't decorate like we used to. Holidays are painful times now. All of our Christmas decorations were destroyed."

> The disaster itself may terrorize and horrify its victims for only a few moments, but if survivors do not achieve a positive resolution, they may feel disheartened and demoralized by its repercussions for years to come. (p. 227)

Communities often experience four phases following a disaster (Webster, 1995, pp. 767–768). First, there is the *heroism phase* (often coinciding with the early intervention phase), where helpers rally to respond to the crisis and help those in need. This phase is characterized by goodwill, caring, mutual aid, and "heightened feelings of community pride" (p. 767). Second, a *honeymoon phase* occurs, where people work together to begin rebuilding their community. This phase usually reflects a high level of hope and optimism about building a better future. (Note that the length of each phase varies depending on many variables.) The third stage is the *disillusionment phase,* where the burdens of accessing adequate resources and trying to rebuild become extremely difficult and frustrating. The fourth stage is *reconstruction,* where community residents take on the long-term, grueling task of rebuilding as best they can. Sometimes, new leaders surface, resources are found, and a strong new community is formulated. At other times, the reconstruction stage is less successful, the community flounders, and rebuilding seems far away. An example of a community experiencing a very difficult reconstruction phase is the lower ninth ward of New Orleans after Hurricane Katrina. Thomas, Darman, and Childress (2006) describe the scene:

> A year after the storm flooded New Orleans and killed more than a thousand people, the city has lost more than half its population. Water and electrical service are still out in some low-lying areas, garbage collection is spotty, many schools and hospitals are still closed, and the city buses don't run regularly or on time. Whole blocks still look as though they were bombed. On a sultry afternoon in late August, along Florida Avenue near the now

repaired Industrial Canal, gawkers stopped to photograph a house sitting on top of a car. The Gray Line bus company runs a Hurricane Katrina Tour, which charges tourists $35 a day to look at some of the worst-hit spots. (p. 31)

Social workers may work with disaster survivors for years after the disaster is over. They may continue to provide counseling and problem-solving assistance. They may also persist in linking survivors with needed resources.

Taking Care of Yourself in Disaster Relief

John Weaver, a social work expert on disaster mental health, declares that disaster work is not for everyone and cites tactics for coping with the resulting stress (Disaster Work, 2001, p. 14):

- Get information about the disaster's extent to understand the magnitude of the problem and emotionally prepare yourself to deal with it.
- "Tasks at hand should be the immediate and central focus, with the work broken up and small jobs done first."
- Use stress management techniques to maintain emotional control.
- Take care of yourself by acknowledging your own physical and emotional limitations, take rest breaks when needed, and attend to basic physical needs such as eating and sleeping.
- Seek out and use peer support to bolster your strength, vent your emotions, and share your distressing stories.

Social Work Role and Disaster Relief

Especially after the 9/11 terrorist attacks, there has been a call for more organized and extensive training of social workers in disaster relief crisis intervention (O'Neill, 2001a). Levy (2002) explains:

> Education of citizens along with coordination between agencies will help to combat that aim of terrorists to instill fear, vulnerability, and panic. Social workers with skills in crisis intervention and the ability to do effective group work, who know how to do debriefing, how to work with a multidisciplinary staff, and . . . how to take care of their own needs will be essential [in taking] control when needed most. (p. 6)

Practice Issues with Diverse Groups

 Working with diverse populations often requires special skills. We have talked about working on behalf of children when addressing child maltreatment. The following sections will focus on two other special populations—older adults and immigrants who may or may not have the rights of citizenship.

LO 7-6 Work with and Empower Older Adults

Practice with older adults can be multifaceted and challenging in view of the wide range of issues facing this population. Social workers may assume multiple roles to meet their diverse needs. Demographic trends indicate that practitioners will be working with increasing numbers of older people.

An empowerment orientation to practice can help older adults emphasize their strengths and use them for competent problem solving. Empowerment focuses on engaging older adults in actions to improve their lives and empower themselves. Empowerment rests on principles such as clients' integral involvement in the problem definition and planned change process, emphasizing and using clients' strengths, teaching needed skills, using support networks and collective action, and linking with necessary resources. Highlight 7.6 discusses older adults' spirituality and religion as potential sources of strength and empowerment.

TERMS USED FOR OLDER ADULTS

One of the issues in empowerment involves the terms used when referring to specific populations. A number of terms have historically been used to refer to people of advancing age. Often, the term "the elderly" has been used. However, the word *elderly* reflects a descriptive term like an adjective more than a noun. Huber and her colleagues aptly state that "no one wants to simply be a description!" (Huber, Nelson, Netting, & Borders, 2008, p. 9). Therefore, to emphasize respect for this wise and experienced population, you might use the terms *older adults, older persons,* or *older individuals* interchangeably. The word *senior* might occasionally be used as an adjective to refer respectfully to people with more years and greater experience.

POTENTIAL ASPECTS OF DECREASED POWER

 A focus on strengths and empowerment is especially important for older adults, as they may experience decreased power on several levels. The first aspect of decreased power involves how physical health tends to decline as people age (Morrow-Howell & Hasche, 2008). The most common health concerns for older adults include "arthritis, hypertension, and heart disease" (Naleppa & Reid, 2003, p. 10). However, McInnis-Dittrich (2014) reflects:

> *An overview of the demographics of aging shows a population of persons over the age of 65 that is growing and will continue to grow rapidly during the twenty-first century. Despite a higher incidence of chronic health problems, most older adults are not sick, not poor, and not living in nursing homes. The vast majority of older adults struggle with occasional health problems but continue to be active, involved, and productive members of society, defying the stereotypes of sick, isolated, and miserable old people. The economic picture, however, is bleakest for older adults of color, women, and the oldest of the old in the United States. If current trends continue, older adults will continue to live longer but not necessarily healthier lives unless chronic poverty and health-care inadequacies are addressed. (p. 7)*

A second aspect of decreased power is related to health concerns. It involves functional limitations and subsequent reliance on external support. Naleppa and Reid (2003) explain:

> *The term activities of daily living (ADL) refers to the ability to perform these basic personal care tasks. . . . Typically, ADLs include eating, dressing, toileting, bathing, and transferring (e.g., getting out of bed into a chair and vice versa). (p. 7)*

Although most older adults have no significant ADL limitations, the likelihood of experiencing them increases with age (Naleppa & Reid, 2003). Remaining in one's own home in contrast to placement in a residential facility is one vital aspect of independence. A major factor for seniors to remain living in their own home involves "the availability of family, friends, and agency services" (Kolb, 2003, p. 69). It is critical that older people receive the support they need to remain as independent as possible as long as possible. For example, McInnis-Dittrich (2014) explains how home health

HIGHLIGHT 7.6

Spirituality and Religion as Potential Sources of Strength for Older Adults

EP 2.1.4

EP 2.1.10e

Chapter 2 established that spirituality and religion may serve as important sources of strength for clients who embrace them. *Spirituality* is "the individual search for meaning, purpose, and values" that typically rises above everyday physical limitations and connects one to something greater than oneself (O'Neill, 1999, p. 3). Spirituality can provide hope, peace, and an introspective sense of life review for older adults. *Religion* involves people's spiritual beliefs concerning the origin, character, and reason for being, usually based on the existence of some higher power or powers. Religion implies membership in a spiritual organization with customs, traditions, and structure. Such involvement can afford access to emotional support and a wide range of tangible services. Naleppa and Reid (2003) explain:

Spirituality and religion play an important part in the life of many older adults, addressing important existential and emotional needs (Tobin, 1991). Religious groups should not be underestimated as a source of social support and friendship. Older adults are more likely to be members of churches and other religious groups than of any other type of community group. In addition to receiving support, individuals who actively participate in religious activities were found to be of better health than those only attending church or not being involved in religious activities at all (Rowe & Kahn, 1998). Prayer, meditation, and other spiritual activities provide a sense of grounding, peace of mind, and connectedness. Finally, it should be mentioned that many religious institutions are also involved in the delivery of formal services. All major religious institutions in this country maintain social pro-grams and agencies that provide services to older adults. (p. 34)

Social Work Assessment of Older Adults' Spirituality

Assessment of an older adult's spirituality starts with how these people describe their feelings about spirituality and religious affiliation; a number of questions might be posed (McInnis-Dittrich, 2014). What has been their experience with spirituality and religion as they were growing up and as they progressed through their lives? Are they or were they members of a church, synagogue, mosque, or other religious group? If so, which one? How involved in religious activities have they been? How supportive has religious involvement been to them in times of stress and crisis? How key and influential are spirituality and religion, generally, in their lives? To what extent does their spirituality provide them with personal strength, support, and hope?

Spirituality can provide a powerful source of peace and understanding for older adults. However, McInnis-Dittrich (2014) suggests that workers should use caution when addressing spirituality for three reasons. First, older adults may not have strong spiritual beliefs. They might find discussing such issues undesirable or intrusive. Practitioners should use care and listen carefully to clients concerning these clients' own values and beliefs. A second precaution is that practitioners should never proselytize to or try to convert older adult clients to the worker's own personal spiritual beliefs. This would be an unethical imposition on clients. The third precaution concerns involving spiritual issues with older adults or any clients experiencing a mental disorder or distorted thought processes. Such clients may find the exploration of their spirituality "highly disturbing" (p. 272).

care agencies can provide services and empower older adults:

Home health-care agencies, such as the Visiting Nurses Association, often have gerontological social workers [practitioners specializing in work with older adults] on staff as part of a team approach to providing services to older adults. Although the primary focus of home health care is to provide health-related services, such as checking blood pressure, changing dressings following surgery, or monitoring blood sugar levels for diabetic older adults, social workers can play an important role in addressing older adults' psychosocial needs. An older adult who has suffered a stroke may need medication and blood pressure monitoring from a health-care provider but may also need help with housekeeping, meal preparation, or transportation. The social worker can arrange for these support services and coordinate the total care plan. Older adults who are essentially homebound due to chronic health problems often experience intense isolation and may benefit from regular phone calls from an older adult call service or friendly visitor volunteer. Gerontological social workers who work in home health care often provide supportive or psychotherapeutic counseling services or arrange for those services from another agency in the community. (p. 9)

Critical Thinking Questions 7.5

- Do you know of an older adult who is dealing with health issues and potentially decreased independence?
- If so, how is that person coping with these issues?
- What types of support might enhance that individual's ability to remain as independent as possible as long as possible?

A third potential aspect of decreased power for older adults involves labor force participation. The number of older adults actively in the labor force has been increasing over the past decades; approximately 37 percent of people age 65 to 69 and 15 percent of people over age 70 continue to be employed (Federal Interagency Forum on Aging-Related Statistics, 2012). Mor-Barak and Wilson (2005) explain:

With improved health, increased life expectancy, and a general desire to continue working, the number of individuals age 55 and over in the workforce will continue to grow over the next few decades. However, although there are increasing numbers of older workers on the job and available for work, the work environment is changing in ways that are detrimental for this population. Most problematic are the systemic barriers that send conflicting and often negative messages to the older worker, clearly indicating a lack of enthusiasm to develop and fully use this human capital. In an examination of the current problems of older workers, multiple contradictions emerge:

- *Although demographic trends indicate a shrinking workforce because of diminishing cohorts of younger workers, there is still an expectation that older workers retire at the normative age or even earlier.*
- *Despite laws aimed at preventing age discrimination, overt and covert practices against hiring and*

retaining older adults are still prevalent in many organizations.

- *Although our social and economic well-being could benefit from the inclusion of older workers, legislation and public policies to enhance the employment opportunities of mature workers have been limited.*

These contradictions, coupled with young managers' myths and stereotypes of older workers, have led to the inevitable disenfranchisement of older workers." (p. 61)

A fourth potential aspect of decreased power involves economic status. The older adult population portrays a very diverse economic picture (Longino & Bradley, 2005; McInnis-Dittrich, 2014). About 6.2 percent of men age 65 and older and 10.7 percent of women in this age group live in poverty (National Women's Law Center, 2012). However, there is significant inequity among income levels in the senior population. Women and people of color in this population are more likely to be poor (U.S. Census Bureau, 2011; National Women's Law Center, 2012). People having low incomes throughout their lives are also more likely to be impoverished as older adults (McInnis-Dittrich, 2014). Note that if "all government support were removed from retirement income, however, including in-kind income (such as Medicare), half of the older households would dip below the poverty line" (Longino & Bradley, 2005, p. 27). (*In-kind benefits* are services [such as counseling or education] or supplies, "such as food stamps, housing assistance, and medical programs," instead of cash [Barusch, 2012, p. 126]. *Medicare* is "a form of social insurance financed by both employer and employee contributions based on earnings and other federal tax revenues" [Kirst-Ashman, 2013, p. 251].)

Critical Thinking Questions 7.6

- What do you think is the responsibility of society and government to provide services and financial support to older adults?
- What services and how much financial support should be provided?
- Who should pay for them?

ESSENTIAL CONCEPTS IN EMPOWERMENT

Four concepts are essential in empowering older adults: adaptation, competence, relatedness, and autonomy (Zuniga, 1995). First, workers should focus on *adaptation* to new experiences, issues, and even losses. An empowering approach emphasizes how people use their strengths to survive, adapt to new experiences, and learn to appreciate the positive aspects of these new experiences. A second concept is *competence.* Workers can help older adults focus on and emphasize what they *can* do instead of what they *cannot* do. Each individual should appreciate his or her own level of competence. *Relatedness,* the third concept, involves the sense of belonging and relating to other people. Hence, practitioners should work to strengthen older adults relationships with others, including friends, family members, and professional caregivers (such as visiting nurses or physical therapists). Support, activity, and educational groups are other mezzo options. *Autonomy,* the fourth concept, involves helping people to live as independently as possible. As they age, older adults must often adapt to lessened physical ability, illness, dependence on medication, and assistance from caregivers; it's important for workers to help clients accept their limitations, yet emphasize and reinforce the ways that older adults can remain autonomous (Zuniga, 1995).

STRATEGIES FOR WORKING WITH OLDER ADULTS

As a special diverse population that is particularly vulnerable, older adults require special sensitivity and understanding on the part of practitioners. There are at least five strategies for workers to increase their sensitivity to older adults and thus enhance their effectiveness (Toseland, 1995). First, practitioners should identify and face any preconceived notions and stereotypes they might harbor about older people. These judgments must be identified before they can be eliminated or changed. Second, workers should appreciate the different life situations experienced by people from different age groups within the senior population. For example, women seeking work in the 1930s will have experienced very different conditions than those employed in the 1940s (Toseland, 1995). Women in the 1930s probably had a very difficult time finding jobs during the Great Depression when unemployment was skyrocketing. However, women in the 1940s likely had a pick of many jobs when men were fighting World War II and industry was begging women to come to work.

The third strategy for increasing sensitivity toward older adults involves understanding that they are individuals with unique characteristics, experiences, and personalities just like anybody else. Consider one woman, Florence, 84 years old, whose life was filled with difficulties, including a decade of tuberculosis, the abrupt death from a heart attack of her husband at age 51 as he slept beside her, her caregiving responsibilities for 15 years for her own aging mother who suffered mental illness, and having to pinch pennies her entire life. Nonetheless, Florence remained cheerful, optimistic, and interested in the world around her throughout her life. One of her nieces took her to China, Disney World, New Orleans, and Europe after she turned 78 (not all in one trip, of course).

Contrast Florence with Carolle—also 84—Florence's maid of honor 65 years earlier. Carolle had a long, good life with a husband who adored her. He cooked and cleaned for her in addition to holding a lucrative engineering job. He died when she was 78. At that time Carolle remained financially stable. Carolle began experiencing health problems including hearing loss and diabetes at age 80. Complications from the diabetes forced her to enter a nursing home at age 83. Carolle's personality had always been persnickety. She demanded that she get her own way and usually got it, thanks to her devoted spouse. She was never interested in the world around her, despite the many innovations developed during her lifetime (television, a moon walk, personal computers, and so on). She was always a complainer; everything was always wrong.

Florence visited Carolle faithfully every Sunday for years and endured her endless whining and complaining. There could not be two more different people.

A fourth strategy for increasing sensitivity to older adults involves learning about how both gender and cultural background influence the aging experience (Richardson, 2009). Both older women and older people of color are more likely to be poor and to experience the effects of poverty (e.g., inadequate living conditions) (U.S. Census Bureau, 2011). Long-term experiences with discrimination can affect attitudes and expectations. Worker sensitivity to cultural differences in terms of communication, family relationships, and gender roles is critical. Chapter 12 discusses a range of cultural and ethnic differences more thoroughly.

The fifth suggestion for increasing sensitivity to older adults concerns understanding the developmental aspects of later life, such as people's physical, mental, living, and socioeconomic conditions. Highlight 7.7 identifies specific strategies for micro practice with older people.

HIGHLIGHT 7.7

Empowerment in Work with Individuals Who Are Older Adults

Six specific empowerment strategies are proposed for working with individuals who are older adults (Cox & Parsons, 1994):

1. Listen carefully to what clients are saying and work to understand what they mean (Richardson, 2009). "Engaging and drawing out the emotions" of older adults and "helping them frame their situations in view of past experiences and events are effective listening techniques" (Cox & Parsons, 1994, p. 112).
2. Help clients identify their coping skills and their abilities to implement planned change. Encouraging clients to talk about what is important to them, including their significant life experiences, is helpful. Explore how they have coped with their difficulties in the past.
3. Show clients recordings of other older adults talking about how they have learned to cope with similar issues. As with support group involvement, these sessions may help clients understand that they are not isolated and alone in their concerns.
4. Share newspaper articles, stories, or other informative materials with clients, especially those about older adults who have initiated service activities and political action. The Gray Panthers, an

advocacy organization for the rights and socio-economic needs of older adults, provides a good example of how people can work together for legislative and political change.
5. Connect clients with other older people to provide social support and combat social isolation. Groups might offer avenues of providing information, education, and pursuit of new interests and positive activities; groups may also address similar life issues with which group members may be struggling (Wilson & Rice, 2011). These include retirement, health challenges (e.g., Alzheimer disease), or losses of family members or friends.
6. Encourage clients to help others. For example, one social services agency gathered together a number of older adult clients and helped them assess their special competencies. They were then organized as volunteers to help each other. Those who could drive would transport others who could not for grocery shopping and medical appointments. People with good eyesight volunteered to read to those who could not see as well. People with exceptional organizational skills volunteered to organize and oversee the volunteer activities. Many people put their strengths to use and became productive members of the community.

EMPOWERMENT WITH OLDER ADULTS IN FAMILIES AND GROUPS

Social workers must look beyond the individual level when working with older adults. We have already mentioned the use of various support groups to help older adults. Family relationships should be nurtured and strengthened. Support groups for people providing care to older adults, especially those requiring much support, can help invigorate these caregivers and indirectly support older adult clients (Morrow-Howell & Hasche, 2008). *Respite care,* which involves the temporary relief and assumption of responsibilities by someone else, can also be provided to family members caring for older adult relatives.

EMPOWERMENT WITH OLDER ADULTS IN ORGANIZATIONS AND COMMUNITIES

Generalist practitioners can become politically involved in advocacy efforts. Issues include defending the rights of older adults, providing adequate choices in areas such as housing and health care, enhancing accessibility to services, promoting wellness, and providing culturally competent services (National Association of Social Workers [NASW], 2012). Keeping a careful eye on proposed legislation addressing older people's health care and social service needs is critical. For example, increasing the age at which older people can first begin receiving Social Security benefits has significant impact on older people's financial standing. Likewise, monitoring the availability of adequate health care for older adults is paramount. Legislative advocacy can effectively help establish an adequate quality of life for many older people.

Working to improve and develop community services for older adults provides other important macro-practice possibilities. For example, community-based adult day care services can be developed (Morrow-Howell & Hasche, 2008). Day care programs can provide a wide range of services related to social support and health, including counseling, group work, linkage to needed community resources, and long-term planning. Generalist practitioners are excellently situated and oriented to providing multiple supports and linkages with the community and community services. For example, Hooyman (2012) describes a community program providing a wide range of resources to empower older adults:

> Aging Your Way, *an asset-building approach in which social workers play central community organizing roles, is occurring in 12 diverse Seattle neighborhoods. Social workers have the competencies to promote the concept of living interdependently, and strategies to ensure social support and interpersonal connections are a core value of any living situation. With their person-environment perspective, social workers can also facilitate home modifications and the use of assistive technology, including computer-based options.... [Other services to help maintain older adults in their own homes include] meals on wheels, home repairs, and friendly visitors... [Additionally, a] growing number of communities are redefining senior centers to be community hubs for networks of social relationships and supports. (p. 540)*

Another example of a community-based program is one directed at helping older adults who are homeless and "sleeping on the streets at night" (Huber et al., 2008, p. 176). The shelter, initially oriented only to helping families, expanded its program to include more specialized service provision to single people over age 60. The shelter helped older adults "locate housing" and provided "a nutritious meals program for drop-ins" among various other services (p. 176). The shelter also established a solid working relationship with a local *senior center* (an organization providing facilities and opportunities for older people's socialization, recreation, and education) in order to facilitate access to services.

LO 7-7 Employ Generalist Practice in Empowering Immigrants

EP 2.1.4
EP 2.1.4a
EP 2.1.7b

Immigration involves the permanent movement from one country to another. *Immigration status,* another aspect of diversity, is a person's position in terms of legal rights and residency when entering and residing in a country that is not that person's legal country of origin. Social workers are often called upon to work with immigrants, so it's important to understand the terms and issues involved. Potocky-Tripodi (2002) defines many of the important concepts:

> *The fundamental distinction between immigrants and refugees is that immigrants leave their countries voluntarily (usually in search of better economic opportunities) whereas refugees are forced out of their countries because of human rights violations against them....*
>
> *Legally, anyone who is not a citizen of the United States is termed an alien. Aliens are further classified as immigrants and nonimmigrants, and as documented or undocumented (Loue, 1998). In this classification, an immigrant is a person who has been legally admitted into the United States and granted the privilege to be a permanent resident (a "green card" holder). A nonimmigrant is a foreign-born person who is in the United States temporarily, such as a tourist, a student or a journalist. Nonimmigrants also include temporary, or seasonal, workers, who come to the United States to work during certain periods of the year and return to their countries during the rest of the year. This typically refers to agricultural laborers.*
>
> *A documented alien is one who has been granted a legal right to be in the United States. This legal right is determined by admissions policy. The admissions policy details many categories of people who are eligible to be legally admitted. It also specifies how many people from each country may be legally admitted into the U.S. each year....*
>
> *An undocumented alien is one who does not have a legal right to be in the United States. These people are also sometimes referred to as illegal immigrants. They are also referred to as deportable aliens, because if discovered by immigration authorities, they are subject to deportation, or forcible return to their countries of origin. (pp. 4–5)*

In 2010, 1,043,000 people were granted legal permanent residence in the United States; it is estimated that 21,590,000 undocumented aliens entered the country in 2010 (U.S. Census Bureau, 2011). It is now estimated that about 4 percent of the population is undocumented aliens (Segal, U., 2010).

A concept closely related to immigration status is *national origin*. This involves individuals', their parents', or their ancestors' country of birth. National origin often is an important factor in people's cultural values and expectations. How you are raised, what you are taught, and how you learn to perceive the world around you varies dramatically from one corner of the world to another. Understanding values and customs derived from national origin helps social workers better understand their clients' perspectives and needs.

Many immigrants may need social services and help in adapting to their new lives. People of other national origins often find it difficult to integrate themselves into the mainstream culture. This is intensified when the use of different languages is a factor (Potocky, 2008). Finding employment, accessing adequate housing, and "fitting into" the social fabric of neighborhoods and communities can be difficult.

Hendricks (2009) reflects:

> The social work focus on "person-in-environment" takes on new meaning when working with immigrant populations. Social workers need to be skilled practitioners to work with diverse clients traumatized by poverty, discrimination, exploitation, war, famine, violence, genocide, and a range of physical and emotional problems related to leaving their homeland for a strange and all too often hostile environment. Social workers may recognize trauma in the lives of their diverse immigrant clients, but they need help to incorporate this knowledge into effective practice interventions.
>
> Special attention needs to be directed towards particular immigrant groups in U.S. society that are likely to require a range of human services because of differences in: (a) addressing health and mental health issues; (b) customs, traditions, beliefs and values; (c) family structures, child-rearing practices, and gender roles; (d) language and literacy; and (e) political ideology and oppressive experiences. (p. 66)

Note that when speaking about any racial, ethnic, or cultural group, it is important not to over generalize. Immigrants may embrace traditional cultural norms to various degrees. They may also experience *acculturation*, which we have defined as "the process wherein

the ethnic values, behaviors, and rituals clients hold from their traditional culture change over time and integrate with the values, behaviors, and rituals of the majority or host culture" (Lum, 2007, p. 310). This may include language, expectations, and beliefs. In other words, people from another country may gradually blend into and adopt the values and customs of the larger society. Therefore, when thinking about a racial, ethnic, or cultural group, it is important for social workers not to assume that all members comply with all cultural values or conform to the same extent. Being of German ethnic heritage does not automatically mean a person loves sauerkraut, liver sausage, bratwursts, and raw ground beef with onions on rye bread just because these are traditional ethnic foods.

Gushue and Sciarra (1995) address the difference in acculturation between first-generation and later-generation immigrants:

> As family members differentiate according to ability levels of the language of the dominant culture, distinct forms and levels of acculturation begin to emerge. Children, having gained a knowledge of the language and wanting to be accepted by their peers, take on the ways of the dominant culture. Parents, more isolated because of language and perhaps suspicious of the ways of the dominant culture, enter into conflict with their children. Issues of racial/cultural identity also emerge because children and parents feel differently about their cultural heritage. (p. 597)

Highlight 7.8 identifies a number of issues especially important for social workers helping immigrants and refugees.

LO 7-8 Address Alcohol and Other Substance Abuse

Generalist practitioners need a background in substance use and abuse, also referred to as alcohol and other drug abuse (AODA), for three basic reasons (Gray, 1995; Roffman, 1987; Straussner & Isralowitz, 2008). (See Highlight 7.9 for a discussion of concepts and definitions of terms.) First, social workers may be employed by agencies specializing in treatment for substance abuse.

Second, social workers with graduate degrees may serve as agency administrators, policy analysts and planners, consultants to planning groups, or legislative aides. These positions require knowledge of substance use and abuse even when not providing direct service to clients.

HIGHLIGHT 7.8

Critical Issues in Working with People Having Another National Origin

EP 2.1.4 b&c

EP 2.1.10 g&k

As you know, important social work principles and processes for working with any clients include pursuing the planned change process, emphasizing client strengths, and striving for cultural competency. In addition, the following are six special issues to address when working with people having other national origins.

1. *Cultural heritage.* A social work goal is to help immigrants and refugees "adapt to their new country without leaving behind their cultural customs and traditions" (Balgopal, 2000, p. 239; Hendricks, 2009; Potocky, 2008). Practitioners must strive to learn about the clients' culture. However, workers must also be sensitive to their own cultural values because these affect how workers perceive their clients and provide help. Workers should learn the appropriate etiquette and nonverbal behavior expected by people from other cultures and convey respect for these practices (Potocky-Tripodi, 2002). Chapter 12 discusses culturally competent social work practice more thoroughly.

2. *Maintaining ties with the country of origin.* Being uprooted from most of what is familiar and being thrust into a totally new environment can be frightening and intimidating. Nimmagadda and Balgopal (2000) maintain that it is very important, if at all possible, for immigrants and refugees to maintain contact with people they have left behind in their country of origin. They indicate that "[t]here are several routes by which these intimate ties are maintained, including visits to their home country, phone calls, e-mail, letters, newspapers, magazines, social and cultural events involving artists from their home country, movies, and visits from close relatives" (p. 53).

3. *Linkages with the ethnic community.* One means of maintaining cultural ties is participating in community activities and support systems with other immigrants and refugees from the same or similar national origins. For example, Delgado (1998) describes how Puerto Rican communities can provide natural support systems for older adult members. Such systems "are a network of individuals, with or without institutional affiliation (family/friends, religious groups, folk healers, and community institutions). They provide assistance . . . on an everyday basis, as well as in times of crisis, and represent a community's capacity to help itself. Natural support systems also serve as a mechanism for helping Puerto Ricans maintain their cultural heritage. . . . [B]eyond the provision of services, . . . [they] entail feelings of love, affection, respect, trust, loyalty, and mutuality" (p. 72). In addition to family, friends, religious organizations, and folk healers, such systems can also involve social clubs (Delgado, 1998).

Another example of community support and celebration involves the Labor Day Carnival held in Brooklyn by people from islands in the Caribbean (Francis, 2000). Originally a custom of Trinidad, the festival that includes "music, dance, food, and costumes" has evolved to include a range of West Indian populations and customs (e.g., reggae music from Jamaica). "Other American cities with large West Indian populations, such as Atlanta, Washington, and Baltimore, now hold their own Carnival activities" (p. 139).

4. *Language.* Because many refugees and immigrants do not speak English, social workers should "[t]ake responsibility for providing services in the language requested by the client" (Potocky-Tripodi, 2002, p. 630; 2009). Ideally, workers should speak the language, although this is often not possible. Practitioners should at least seek "access to bilingual and bicultural paraprofessionals" (Balgopal, 2000, p. 239). The important thing is to help clients make plans and get services. This can only be done by using language they understand.

Engel-Marder (2003) makes four suggestions for maximizing effectiveness when using interpreters. First, interpreters should be competent in both understanding professional terminology (e.g., planned change, intervention, specific service providers) and their "fluency or literacy in English and the target language (not all bilinguals can interpret standard usage)" (p. 22). Second, clear standards for confidentiality should be established. For example, a policy might involve both client and interpreter signing and receiving copies of a statement that the interpreter "will not repeat or discuss confidential information without the permission" of the client. Third, workers should strive to clarify information when interpreters make short summaries of prolonged communication. Interpreters may try to "'soften,' or render culturally appropriate, the manner in which a piece of information is delivered. Communication styles—and, therefore, perceptions of intent and character—vary from culture to culture" (p. 22). For example, consider "a lengthy Chinese or Farsi exchange, followed by a two-word rendition in English" by the interpreter (p. 22). The worker should then gently seek further clarification. Fourth, the social worker should always address the client (not the interpreter) directly and use culturally appropriate and respectful "nonverbal reinforcement such as body language, eye contact, and gestures" (p. 22).

5. *Learning about the U.S. system.* Newcomers to this country may know little about U.S. policies, services, politics, or the legal system (Nimmagadda & Dalgopal, 2000). Programs, benefits, and prerequisites for service may be radically different or nonexistent in their country of origin:

Sisneros (2002) provides some other specific suggestions:

> It is also good practice to offer "financial therapy," meaning helping clients understand the U.S. capitalistic system and basic concepts, such as how to balance a checkbook and U.S. currency values. Above all, immigrant clients should be alerted to the "merchants of misery," such as the fringe banking and lending industries and pawnshops that prey

on and profit from the undereducated poor. (p. 14)

6. *Advocacy.* Much more could be done to provide more responsive and adequate services to immigrants and refugees. People who migrate here illegally are especially susceptible to service deprivation because they fear deportation if "the system" finds out they are here. Social workers can advocate for improved policies to meet newcomers' needs.

Karger and Levine (2000) recommend a more responsive and "activist government" with more progressive policies and services, such as those in Israel. They explain:

> Under Israeli immigration policy, each immigrant family is entitled to an "absorption basket" containing time-limited (two years) subsidized housing; low-interest housing loans; a time-limited tax-exemption status on certain items such as furniture, appliances, and automobiles; job training; and subsidized language courses. When combined with services and other rights, this "basket" is intended to facilitate the economic and social absorption of new immigrants (Doron & Kramer, 1991).
>
> American immigration policy also should provide a "basket of immigration services" similar to that provided by Israel, to include temporary food assistance, job training and reeducation, health care, personal social services (including alcohol and substance abuse counseling), subsidized language courses, and policies that help immigrants buy and not simply rent housing. (p. 183)

The third reason for needing some background in substance use and abuse involves your role as referral agent. Even if you do not work in a specialized substance abuse setting, you will still probably have clients or family members of clients with alcohol and other drug problems. Thus, you must be capable of making appropriate referrals. (See Highlight 7.10, which identifies a range of resources, and Chapter 15, which discusses brokering services.)

Alcohol and other substance abuse is often masked by and interrelated to many other problems that generalist practitioners deal with. Consider that:

The addicted [drug dependent] person may seek help in a medical setting, a crisis clinic, a mental health

agency, a family service agency, or from a private practitioner or a public assistance agency. In the medical setting, the presenting problem may be pancreatitis, liver disease, traumatic injury, or broken bones. In the mental health setting, the person may present depression, suicidal feelings, self-destructive behavior, anxiety, psychotic symptoms, or problems associated with an organic brain syndrome. [Any of these conditions may result from the excessive consumption of alcohol or other drugs.] (Raskin & Daley, 1991, p. 25)

Thus, regardless of your practice setting, you will probably need to address substance use problems. Training you to be a substance abuse counselor is far

Important AODA Terms and Concepts

Familiarizing yourself with a number of terms commonly used in substance abuse intervention is useful. The jargon tends to revolve around the terms *alcohol, drug,* and *substance* (also referred to as *psychoactive substance*). In everyday usage, the term *alcohol* refers to any type of fermented or distilled liquor containing alcohol, such as whiskey or beer. *Drug* refers to a wide range of materials that alter mood or consciousness when ingested, including amphetamines, cannabis, stimulants (e.g. cocaine), and hallucinogens. *Substance* is commonly used to refer to mind-altering drugs, including alcohol (hence the term *alcohol and other substance abuse*). In the context of abuse, described here, the terms *substance* and *drugs* are often used interchangeably.

The *Diagnostic and Statistical Manual of Mental Disorders (DSM-5)*[a] published in 2013 by the American Psychiatric Association (APA) defines *substance use disorders* as "a cluster of cognitive, behavioral, and physiological symptoms" resulting from continued use of the substance even after experiencing notable resultant problems; the diagnosis of substance use disorder is made based upon "the pathological pattern of behaviors related to use of the substance" (p. 483). Such patterns are established by assessing symptoms and behavior in four general categories—"impaired control, social impairment, risky use, and pharmacological criteria" (p. 483).

Impaired control is characterized by the following symptoms:

1. The user uses greater quantities of the substance over a longer period of time than he or she meant to.
2. The user experiences repeated failures at trying to stop substance use.
3. The user expends significant time and energy getting the substance, using it, or recuperating from its aftermath.
4. The user experiences *craving,* an ongoing powerful desire to use the drug. Craving is more likely to occur in the same context as that of prior substance use (e.g., in certain places, at particular times, or when associating with certain people who may also be using the substance), although users may crave the substance at any time.

Social impairment is demonstrated by the following behavioral patterns or symptoms:

1. The user experiences repeated difficulties in assuming responsibilities and fulfilling

expectations in occupational, educational, or personal settings.
2. The user continues to use the substance despite the fact that the substance is causing or intensifying continued psychological and interpersonal difficulties.
3. The user curtails or avoids significant social, work, or recreational involvement due to substance use. For example, the user may frequently be late for or absent from work, or miss out on family events.

Risky use involves the following symptoms:

1. The user continues substance use even in settings where he or she is in physical danger (e.g., driving a car).
2. The user continues to use the substance despite being aware that the substance is causing or intensifying continued physical or psychological difficulties.

Pharmacological criteria involve the following conditions or symptoms:

1. The user experiences increased *tolerance* of the substance. This involves how the user requires increasingly more of the substance to reach the same level of mood alteration, or how the substance's effects diminish significantly with continued use.
2. The user suffers *withdrawal.* Here particular symptoms develop as a result of discontinued use of the substance and the user experiences the compulsion to use the substance to avert these symptoms. Despite discontinued use, the user still longs for the substance. Withdrawal symptoms may include severe abdominal pain, convulsions, anxiety attacks, depression, and uncontrollable trembling. Note that symptoms vary dramatically depending on the specific substance used.

Substance use disorders vary significantly in scope. They can be minor (mild) or extremely serious (severe). Generally speaking, manifestation of one or two of the aforementioned symptoms characterizes a *mild* disorder, four or five a *moderate* disorder, and six or more a *severe* disorder.

Other terms often used when referring to substance use disorders include *abuse, dependence, intoxication,* and *addiction.* (The terms *alcoholic* and *alcoholism* are discussed in another section of the chapter.) *Substance* or *drug abuse* refers to a pattern of substance or drug use that is harmful to the user and is considered medically unacceptable. *Substance* or *drug dependence* is the condition where a person has been exposed to enough of a substance over a sufficient period of time to require compulsive use of the substance; such use is necessary for the user to feel physically and/or psychologically "balanced" (Fetting, 2012, pp. 29–30). *Intoxication* is the development of a series of symptoms, often involving psychological or behavioral changes, related to intake of the substance; such symptoms are due to the substance's influence directly on the central nervous system. Specific symptoms may include inability to think clearly, distorted perception, temporary euphoria, and impaired motor functioning. *Addiction* is a term referring to the obsessive need for some substance; addiction is characterized by increased tolerance of the substance and, when the substance is not used, results in the physical effects of withdrawal (Lewis, Dana, & Blevins, 2011).

Professionals working with people who have substance use disorders may be referred to as substance abuse, AODA, or chemical dependency counselors. Practitioners counseling people who experience alcohol use disorders may be called *alcoholism* or *alcohol abuse counselors.*

Often, people have a substance of choice. That is, they prefer the type of mood alterations produced by one drug over that produced by another. For instance, one person may prefer beer over cocaine. Another person may feel just the opposite.

Being aware of the resources available to people with substance use disorders is important for social workers. A large-scale self-help organization is Alcoholics Anonymous (AA). Anyone who feels that he or she has encountered difficulties due to alcohol may join. Two alcoholics started the organization in 1935, which now has thousands of chapters throughout the country. More will be said about AA's approach and principles later in the chapter.

a. The *DSM-V* is the official authority for defining and explaining mental disorders and their accompanying symptoms. It is used to enhance accurate communication among social workers and other professionals regarding clients' conditions. It is also used to provide diagnoses for eligibility to receive third-party payments (e.g., Medicare or health insurance).

beyond the scope of this text. However, we will discuss some of the basic terms, individual and family dynamics, and treatment trends involved.

There are many similarities between alcohol abuse and other substance abuse in terms of biological, psychological, and interpersonal implications (APA, 2013). However, elaborating upon the effects of the numerous varieties of drugs available today is also beyond the scope of this book. Therefore, we will primarily focus on alcohol abuse.

PEOPLE WITH ALCOHOL PROBLEMS

One dictionary defines *alcoholism* as "a chronic disorder characterized by repeated excessive use of alcoholic beverages and the decreased ability to function socially and vocationally" (Nichols, 1999, p. 31). An *alcoholic* is a person suffering from this condition. Historically, the concept of alcoholism was based on the medical model (i.e., it was considered a disease with the cure being abstinent). However, more current thought views such alcohol use as a more complex problem that can be analyzed from a range of theoretical perspectives having their respective treatment approaches (APA, 2013; Doweiko, 2012; Fetting, 2012; Paylor, Measham, & Asher, 2012; Perkinson, 2012; Velleman, 2011).

Alcohol abuse is complex. People who use and abuse alcohol cannot be categorized at clearly established points on a continuum of alcohol use. However, the "end points of this continuum are total abstinence on one end through to the pathological or repetitive pattern of use that is the hallmark of addiction" on the other end (Doweiko, 2012, p. 10). Velleman (2011) suggests that a better term for alcoholism is *alcohol problem,* defined as follows: "If someone's drinking causes problems with his or her health, finances, the law, work, friends or relationships, then that drinking is problematic; if it causes problems for husbands, wives, children, parents, bosses, or subordinates, then that drinking is problematic" (p. 5).

Figure 7.2 reflects how people may fall anywhere on a continuum involving how much they drink and how many problems it causes them. Many people who drink alcohol do so on a social basis and consume socially acceptable amounts that do not result in drunkenness. Problems arise for those people who lose control of their consumption and become increasingly dependent on alcohol's effects. Each individual responds differently to alcohol dependence in terms of severity of physical and psychological effects and the length of time it takes to become dependent (Dziegielewski, 2005a).

HIGHLIGHT 7.10

Your Role as a Referral Agent

EP 2.1.1c

When you assess that alcohol or other substance abuse is a problem for a client, you need to know what resources are available to help them. We have indicated that Chapter 15 addresses brokering or referral skills in depth. Most resource agencies have similar goals in treating substance abusers. Their intent is to educate abusers and those close to them about the dynamics involved in abuse and help people to make positive changes. The following are some of the resources that are available (Abadinsky, 2011; Doweiko, 2012; Johnson, 2004; Lewis et al., 2011):

1. *Detoxification* "is short-term treatment designed to oversee the client's safe withdrawal from the substance to which he or she is addicted" (Lewis et al., 2011, p. 21). Clients may participate in an inpatient or outpatient program (both described following) over-seen by medical personnel and professional counselors (Doweiko, 2012; Lewis et al., 2011). The severity of withdrawal symptoms is one factor to consider when choosing the appropriate program.

2. *Outpatient treatment* is that received by participating in a program without staying overnight at a treatment facility. People who are drug dependent can remain in their own homes and still have services made available to them. Programs vary greatly regarding types of treatment involved (e.g., individual, group, or family therapy) and the extent of daily or weekly involvement.

3. *Inpatient treatment* is that received by remaining at the facility all day and night. It provides a comprehensive, structured environment that maximizes control of the treatment process.

4. *Therapeutic communities* are residential programs where clients remain for 1 to 3 years, although some require only a 6-month stay. Their intent is to immerse clients in an environment aimed at "a global change in lifestyle: abstinence from illicit substances, elimination of antisocial activity, development of employability, and prosocial attitudes" (DeLeon, 1994, p. 392; Doweiko, 2012; Johnson, 2004, p. 271).

5. *Halfway houses* are temporary residences to assist in the transition from an inpatient program to the real-life community. They provide support

and supervision that is less extensive to that given on a 24-hour institutional basis. Emphasis is on gradually increasing each resident's ability to handle responsibility at his or her own pace.

6. *Mutual self-help groups* are composed of nonprofessional members who voluntarily gather together to provide mutual support, talk about shared problems and concerns, and help each other to improve their lives. Specific programs include AA, Narcotics Anonymous (NA), and Cocaine Anonymous (CA). These groups provide exceptionally relevant treatment approaches in view of their established success. Support from peers in the process of recovery is especially critical (Abadinsky, 2011; Lewis et al., 2011).

In view of its prevalence, we will focus on AA here. This nationwide group provides support, information, and guidance necessary for many recovering alcoholics to maintain their recovery process. The organization's success rests upon several principles. First, other people who "really understand" are available to give the recovering dependent person friendship and warmth. Each new member is given a "sponsor," who can be called for support at any time during the day or night. Whenever the dependent person feels depressed or tempted, there is always the sponsor to turn to.

Additionally, AA provides the recovering alcoholic with a new social group with whom to talk and enjoy activities. Old friends with well-established drinking patterns usually become difficult to associate with. The recovering alcoholic can no longer participate in drinking activity. Often, social pressure is applied to drink again. AA provides a respite from such pressure and the opportunity to meet new people, if such an opportunity is needed.

AA bases its philosophy on the premise that "alcoholism" is a disease that the alcoholic cannot cure alone. He or she need no longer feel guilty about being an alcoholic. All that needs to be done is to stop drinking.

AA also encourages self-introspection. Members are encouraged to look inside themselves and face whatever they see. They are urged to acknowledge that they have flaws and will never be perfect. This perspective often helps people to stop fleeing from the pain of reality and hiding in alcohol and drugs. It helps them to redefine the expectations for themselves and to gain control. Within the context of this honesty, people often can also acknowledge their strengths. They learn that they do have some control over their own behavior and that they can accomplish things for themselves and others.

Organizations are also available to provide support for other family members and to give them information and suggestions. For example, Al-Anon is an organization for the families of alcoholics, and Alateen is designed specifically for teenagers within these families.

7. *Pharmacological adjuncts.* Some alcohol or other substance-dependent people need the help of prescribed medications (e.g., Antabuse, used to combat alcoholism) to help them begin the recovery process. This medication must be carefully monitored by medical staff.

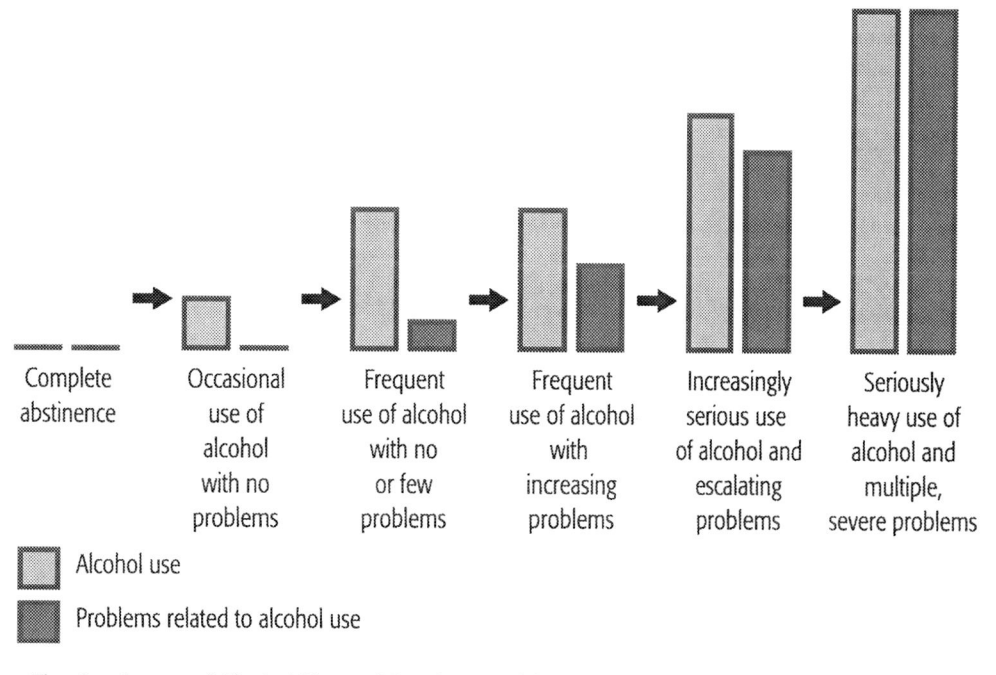

Complete abstinence

Occasional use of alcohol with no problems

Frequent use of alcohol with no or few problems

Frequent use of alcohol with increasing problems

Increasingly serious use of alcohol and escalating problems

Seriously heavy use of alcohol and multiple, severe problems

☐ Alcohol use

☐ Problems related to alcohol use

© Cengage Learning

FIGURE 7.2 The Continuum of Alcohol Use and Resulting Problems

People who abuse alcohol or other drugs typically adopt a series of defense mechanisms to protect themselves from having to deal with the problems caused by abuse. They include "minimization," "denial," and "rationalization" (Perkinson, 2012, p. 89). Each defense mechanism serves to avoid taking responsibility for one's own behavior.

Minimization means assigning little importance to drinking or its consequences. "When minimizing, the addict says, 'It's not so bad'" (Perkinson, 2012, p. 89). Here the person with an alcohol use disorder acknowledges that drinking is occurring but admits to very little and tries to make it unimportant. An alcoholic might fill a 10-ounce glass halfway with whiskey instead of

pouring it into a much smaller shot glass. This becomes "just one drink." Another person might say, "I really don't drink that much," while drinking three six-packs of beer a night.

Rationalization involves making excuses for the problems caused by the dependence on alcohol. For example, a person with an alcohol use disorder might say to him- or herself, "I really didn't flunk that exam because I had a hangover; the professor made the questions much harder than she said she would," or, "It's been a rotten day. I deserve a drink or two."

Denial, the most prevalent defense used by people with alcohol use disorders, involves insisting to oneself that nothing's wrong; there's no problem. Denial means distorting reality so that you just don't see the truth. An alcoholic who drinks a fifth of cheap vodka or a 12-pack of beer a day might say to him- or herself, "I don't really have to drink." Such an individual might totally ignore spousal complaints about spending money on booze or being verbally abusive when drunk. Out of sight, out of mind. If you don't think about it, it doesn't exist.

Numerous social and relationship problems result from alcohol and other substance abuse. They include marital and family difficulties, disruptions in friendships, trouble in work and school performance, accidents when operating vehicles, and being arrested for crimes committed while under the influence.

Alcohol or another substance of choice (i.e., the preferred substance) becomes the abuser's "best friend." It is something the abuser can always depend on. The effects are pleasantly predictable, and the abuser can escape from life's stresses whenever he or she wants. People can be disappointing or place pressure on you, but a drug always acts the same.

ALCOHOLISM AND FAMILY RELATIONSHIPS

Alcohol abuse and dependence are family systems problems (Doweiko, 2012; Fetting, 2012; Paylor et al., 2012; Perkinson, 2012). That is, the problem affects the entire family; what happens to one family member affects all others.

People living in families of alcoholics "live in a chaotic whirlwind" of stress and crisis (Perkinson, 2012, p. 215). Their lives focus on the abuser's alcohol-related behavior, whether it is coming home drunk and throwing up or hitting them, losing jobs and money, failing to carry through with any range of responsibilities, breaking solemn promises, or embarrassing them in front of friends and neighbors.

At least nine themes characterize the families of people who have alcohol use disorders. (Note that the family dynamics involved in families of other substance abusers resemble those with alcohol abuse.) First, the abuser's alcohol use becomes the "most important thing in the family's life" (Johnson, 2004; Wegscheider, 1981, p. 81). Because the abuser's top goal is getting enough alcohol, other family members must structure their own behavior around it.

Second, family members strive to keep the family together even when conditions are deteriorating due to the abuser's behavior (Johnson, 2004; Wegscheider, 1981). The unknown is scary. At least they know what the current conditions are, regardless of how bad.

Third, family members often act as *enablers* for the abuser's alcohol use (Doweiko, 2012; Perkinson, 2012; Wegscheider, 1981). Enablers assume increasing responsibility for maintaining family functioning and making excuses on the alcoholic's behalf (e.g., calling in sick for the abuser at work when the real problem is a terrible hangover). In essence, this role enables the alcoholic to continue drinking, yet assume less and less responsibility for the consequences of that behavior.

Fourth, "[f]amily members often feel incredible guilt. They think that they are at fault. The addicted person keeps denying responsibility, and someone must be held accountable, so the family members often take the blame. [For example,] [t]he spouse might feel that everything would be okay if he or she could just be the right kind of husband or wife or could just do the right thing" (Perkinson, 2012, p. 215).

Fifth, family members often feel out of control. "As more and more energy is expended in trying to control someone else, the family members lose contact with themselves. They become so involved in the addicted person that they lose who they are.... They do not know how they feel.... They cannot share how they feel. This leaves their interpersonal relationships empty, isolated, and alone. They cannot use their real feelings to solve problems. Therefore, their problems escalate out of control. They are on a treadmill, frantically trying to keep the family together" (Perkinson, 2012, p. 216).

Sixth, "family members do not know what they want. Their lives are centered on the addicted individual. They only know what the addict wants. That is the primary focus of attention. Most family members are trying to hold on to their sanity and to keep themselves, and the family, from going under. They have no time for the superficial wishes and wants of normal people. They only have vague hopes that everything can be better. They are so used to the broken promises that they do not listen anymore" (Perkinson, 2012, p. 217).

Seventh, "family members feel worthless. They feel as though no one cares for how they feel or for what they want. They feel profoundly inadequate and unlovable.... and somehow they feel as though...it is all their entire fault anyway. This would not be happening to them if they were better persons. This is all they deserve. This is the best they can get" (Perkinson, 2012, p. 217).

Eighth, family members do not trust others (Perkinson, 2008). They have been disappointed so many times by the dependent person's behavior that they cannot afford to dream about things getting better. They avoid discussing the problem with others inside or outside the family. They do not want to rock the boat.

Ninth, family members "have poor communication skills. They learned a long time ago the credo of the chemically dependent family: 'Don't talk, don't trust, and don't feel.' These individuals do not talk to their friends or other family members. They are cut off from everyone. They feel afraid of open communication. If they talked openly, then the truth might come out and the family would be destroyed" (Perkinson, 2012, p. 218).

The Effects of Alcoholic Parents on Their Children

Research indicates that children can often be deeply affected by parents who have alcohol use disorders (Doweiko, 2012; Dziegielewski, 2005b; Lewis et al., 2011). Lewis and her colleagues (2011) reflect:

Children of alcoholics need to cope with a great deal of stress but may have fewer physical, social, emotional, and mental resources than children living in more functional family systems. Their physical resources may be sapped because they are tired due to a lack of sleep, because they have internalized stress, or because they have been abused. (Of course, they may also be the victims of fetal alcohol syndrome, which causes developmental problems in the infants of alcoholic mothers.) Social resources may also be limited; hesitancy to bring other children into the home or to share information about the family may interfere with the development of intimate relationships. Emotional resources are affected by the pain, fear, and embarrassment that come with unstable living arrangements, financial difficulties, broken promises, accidents, and public intoxication. Even mental resources may be affected by a lack of parental help and by difficulties in maintaining regular school attendance. (p. 181)

Velleman (2011) warns that such children may risk experiencing problems in the following four areas:

[1] antisocial behavior and conduct disorder—delinquency, truancy, aggressive behavior, hyperactivity, temper tantrums; [2] school environment problems—learning difficulties, reading retardation, conduct and aggressive behavior, poor school performance, general loss of concentration; [3] emotional—general emotionally disturbed behavior, negative attitudes toward the problem-drinking parent, or toward the parents' marriage as a whole, psychosomatic complaints, self-blame; [and 4] adolescence—division between peer

relationships and home life; social isolation, attention-seeking behavior, leaving home early, early use of alcohol and other drugs. (p. 166)

Note that evidence indicates that children will not automatically experience such negative effects; variables such as family configuration, length of time the children are exposed to the alcoholism, and availability of a "parental surrogate" (such as an older sibling, close relative, or neighbor to provide alternative support can affect the consequences of alcoholism on children (Doweiko, 2012, p. 311). Not every child of an alcoholic is doomed to become a dysfunctional adult. However, the risks of experiencing difficulties in childhood, adolescence, and adulthood are increased, as with any other serious early encounters with trauma or deprivation.

Children of people with alcohol use disorders must be involved in the treatment process, including being the recipients of individual and/or group counseling. Such therapy "should concentrate on providing empathy and support and helping clients develop coping skills that can serve them effectively both in the current situation and in the future. Ideally, this process should help children deal with their uncertainties and, concurrently, prevent the development of chronic emotional problems.... The most useful approach with children may be to help them move to an active state. If they are isolated in their home environment, counseling should help them reach out to others. If they are afraid of their feelings, counseling should help them recognize and express their previously forbidden emotions. If they feel alone in their situation, counseling should convince them that others share their problems. Children of troubled parents need to know that they are not to blame for family difficulties and that their attempts to meet their own needs are in no way detrimental to other family members" (Lewis et al., 2011, pp. 181–182).

YOUR ROLE IN INTERVENTION WITH PEOPLE WHO HAVE ALCOHOL USE DISORDERS

We have already indicated that your career path may or may not lead you to become a specialized alcohol and other substance abuse counselor. However, your chief usefulness concerning these issues may be to maintain an awareness of the problems involved, include related information in the assessments you do regardless of your practice area, and make necessary referrals for treatment interventions elsewhere.

The following section will address treatment approaches for alcoholism. It will also discuss other issues including early screening for abuse and dependence and the problems of denial, relapses, and intoxicated clients.

TREATMENT APPROACHES FOR ALCOHOLISM

There are numerous treatment approaches to chemical dependency to help people resolve their problems. Highlight 7.10 identifies a range of programs and treatment contexts for referral.

At least four principles are important regardless of the treatment approach or program (Johnson, 2004). First, engagement "with the social worker in a trusting and open relationship" is essential for successful treatment; practitioners should "engage clients as partners in treatment, eliciting responses and actions that enhance motivation and promote willingness to take action on their own behalf" (p. 291). Second, a multiple-system approach should be used. That is, an individualized treatment plan should be developed to address the "client's unique needs, issues, and strengths"; the practitioner might "provide individual, group, or family treatment, engage the client's local community if needed, and provide access to specialty services such as vocational, recreational, or spiritual counseling when appropriate" (pp. 291–292). Third, follow-up care after primary treatment has ceased is critical to maintain progress. Fourth, "clients need help in developing a social network" of "people or groups to call upon for support, guidance, and recreation" (p. 292). These might include "twelve-step meetings, church groups, sober friends, family members, and other sources" (p. 292). Such a network helps them maintain control of their gains by providing "social and recreational outlets that replace key elements" in a lifestyle sustaining abuse or dependence (p. 292).

Two treatment models are described here—one based on the traditional abstinence approach to recovery and the other a strengths-based model focused on achieving greater control of drinking behavior (that may or may not include total abstinence).

A Four-Stage Recovery Model

One approach to alcoholism treatment maintains that dependency involves an entire lifestyle; therefore, to recover, one must abstain from drinking alcohol entirely in order to establish a healthier, substance-free way of life. The following four steps are involved (Johnson, 2004, pp. 286–290):

Stage 1: Abstinence. During this stage, that can persist for as long as 2 years, clients strive to maintain sobriety. A major focus is on avoidance of mind-altering substances. In essence, "the individual learns to get through most days without experiencing or giving in to overwhelming cravings or urges to use" (p. 286). Relapses are fairly common.

Stage 2: Confrontation. Lasting up to 5 years, during this stage "clients begin confronting and changing the personal, family, and social issues that contributed to their chemically dependent lifestyle. . . . They learn how to conduct adult relationships, assume responsibility for their actions, and explore lifestyles that do not include drugs and the people associated with their chemically dependent past" (p. 287). Clients are often "obsessed" with their abstinence and recovery, confronting people and experiences in their past on a daily basis, often with shame and guilt about what happened. For example, a recovering client was with new friends who knew little or nothing about her past. She abruptly ran into old friends who unabashedly talked about the "good old days" when they got "really high" together and would do "wild and crazy things" like running through the city streets naked. The client was mortified with shame.

Stage 3: Growth. Usually occurring after at least 5 years of abstinence, this phase reflects beginning a new lifestyle not involving alcohol use. New social networks are established and "daily life does not involve constant attention to maintaining abstinence and recovery" (p. 289).

Stage 4: Transformation. This stage marks a true change in life orientation from the former alcohol-using days. The client has established "social networks and personal skills" to live life and thrive. Alcohol no longer has a place in this new existence.

Note that although these stages are presented as if they occur in a "smooth and recognizable manner," in many—perhaps most—cases they do not follow such a smooth order (p. 290). People can move back and forth between stages and sometimes relapses occur. The latter "signals the need to discover which parts of the client's recovery foundation need work" (p. 290).

The Strengths Perspective on Alcohol Abuse and Dependence Treatment

We've established that it's important for practitioners to identify and emphasize clients' strengths and capabilities. They should not just focus on problems and issues. Recognition of strengths provides clues for how clients can make positive changes occur.

Van Wormer and Davis (2013) propose a strengths-based approach to treating alcohol and other substance abuse and dependence based on *harm reduction,* a treatment approach emphasizing means to reduce the "harm caused by the addiction" (p. 409). They explain:

[The idea is] to help people help themselves by moving from safer use, to managed use, to abstinence, if so desired. The labeling of clients, as is the custom in mental health circles ("He has an antisocial personality," "She is borderline") or in treatment circles (He's an alcoholic," "She has an eating disorder") is avoided; clients provide the definition of the situation as they see it. Clients who wish it are given advice on how to reduce the harm in drug use such as, "Don't drink on an empty stomach," or "Always make sure to use a clean needle." Most of the advice, however, is provided in a less direct fashion, such as, "Here are some options you might want to consider." Consistent with the strengths perspective, the counselor and client collaborate to consider a broad range of solutions to the client-defined problem; resources are gathered or located to meet the individual needs of the client. Above all, clients are viewed as amenable to change. (p. 34)

Van Wormer and Davis (2013) state that a more traditional disease model espoused by AA and described previously may experience success with "people who are highly vulnerable and clutching for support[,] something concrete, something more faith-based, to latch on to" (p. 28). However, a harm reduction approach provides more flexibility in terms of treatment planning and goals. It also stresses how clients have the strength to assume responsibility for changing their behavior. The emphasis is on what people can *do*, not the problems they have. Important variables indicating which approach might be more effective include clients' intensity of distress about their drug use and clients' motivation to alter their behavior (van Wormer & Davis, 2013).

A key component of a harm reduction approach is *choice* "about the goals of the helping relationship (harm reduction, including abstinence) . . . [This takes

into account both] informed choice about a variety of treatment contexts (same gender, group, individual, day treatment, outpatient, inpatient, mutual-help [self-help] groups) . . . and informed choice about treatment methods" (van Wormer & Davis, 2013, p. 406).

"Harm reduction strategies for alcohol misuse are based on the premise that alcohol use ranges across a continuum, starting with no consequences for use and ending with devastating consequences for use, with lots of states in between" (van Wormer & Davis, 2013, p. 416). A client may choose to establish a state of controlled consumption (e.g., limiting the amount drunk or times when drinking occurs) instead of seeking total abstinence. A plan might entail drinking only during weekends or special occasions and then limiting it to some designated amount. Drinking less is not as harmful as heavy, continuous, uncontrolled drinking.

The practitioner does not force clients to place labels on themselves. Rather, the practitioner assists clients in understanding the costs of drinking and exploring what options they have to gain greater control of their lives if that is what they desire. In essence, the practitioner focuses on the client's motivation to make positive changes. Highlight 7.11 presents some techniques that can be useful in the harm reduction approach.

Critical Thinking Questions 7.7

- Compare and contrast the traditional four-stage recovery model with the harm reduction approach.
- What are the strengths and weaknesses of each?
- Which do you believe is more effective and why?

OTHER ISSUES

This section of the chapter has provided a brief introduction to alcohol and other substance abuse treatment. Arbitrarily, we will address four additional issues—screening for substance use, denial of problem seriousness, relapses, and when a client arrives drunk.

Early Screening for Abuse and Dependence

One facet of early screening for abuse and dependence involves information concerning the pattern of alcohol use (Dziegielewski, 2005a). To what extent is the client experiencing problems as a result of alcohol or drug use? To what extent is a referral for further assessment

HIGHLIGHT 7.11

Helpful Techniques in the Harm Reduction Approach

EP 2.1.10b

Van Wormer and Davis (2013) identify the following five techniques for enhancing clients' motivation to change when using a harm reduction approach:

1. *Express empathy.* Be "warm, respectful, and accepting." Convey to clients that addressing problematic issues and making decisions is a normal part of life to work through. Clients are "stuck [in trying to deal with issues and problems resulting from drinking], not pathological" (p. 424).

2. *Develop discrepancy* (p. 424). Help clients define the discrepancies between what they are actually doing and what they would rather want to do. For instance, you might say, "On the one hand, you said that you go out for drinks after work several nights a week. But, you also said this results in frequent fighting with your wife when you get home, headaches at work the next day, and lots of sick days. Let's talk about this more."

   Discrepancies might also be pointed out between statements or perceptions voiced by a client. For example, consider a client who "define[s] him or herself as someone who cannot stop drinking, but tell[s] us about a time when he or she had stopped or controlled his or her drinking. This allows us to respond by asking, 'What was different in your life then?' or, 'How were

you able to do that at that time?'" (Velleman, 2011, p. 78).

3. *Avoid argumentation.* "[D]o not try to persuade, confront, or argue to clients that they are in deep trouble and would be much better off giving up their addiction" (van Wormer & Davis, 2013, p. 424). This turns many people off. This can be condescending and negative instead of helping them make choices about behavior they want to control.

4. *Roll with resistance.* "Compliance from the client is not a goal. Resistance can be redirected by the simple statement 'It's really up to you.' Reluctance and ambivalence are understood to be a natural stage of the change process. . . . New perspectives are invited, but not imposed. For example, 'What you do with this information is entirely up to you'" (p. 424).

5. *Support self-efficacy.* "If people have no hope for change, then regardless of how serious they believe the problem, they will not make an effort to change. The counselor can support people's confidence that they can change by removing the false idea that the counselor will change them, by showing them the success of others, and by inviting them to choose from alternative approaches to what they've already tried. A series of relapses or treatment 'failures' can be reframed as 'getting closer to their goal'" (p. 424).

---

necessary? The following provide examples of questions for seeking necessary information:

- "What drugs have been used?"
- "How old were you when you first started using?"
- "What was the last day that you used the drug?"
- "When do you usually use the drug? At what time of the week or day? How often during the day? Do you use every week or every day?"
- "How do you consume the drug?" (Obviously, you drink alcohol. However, other drugs can be injected, inhaled, smoked, or swallowed.)
- "Are you certain that the needles you used were clean? Do you ever use needles after they've been used by other people?" (If applicable)
- "Have you noticed any change in your drug tolerance level (that is, you need to take more or

less of the drug than before to achieve the same effect)?"

- "Do you suffer from any withdrawal symptoms (for example, physical symptoms like "the shakes" or nausea or psychological symptoms like radical mood swings) when you don't use the drug for a long period of time?"
- "Do you ever experience more serious consequences of your drug use? For example, have you ever overdosed? Do you ever experience blackouts?"
- "Have you ever received any citations for driving under the influence (DUI)? If so, what were the circumstances?"
- "Has drinking ever affected your performance at work or school? If so, in what ways?"

The Problem of Denial

What if a client denies the extent of the alcohol problem? Velleman (2011) reflects:

> Clients need to recognize—or to be aware at some level—that a problem exists [in order for them to come for help in the first place,] but the myth that counselors cannot start to work therapeutically with clients until the clients admit they are alcoholics has bedeviled the field for many years....
>
> Counseling is not about convincing clients. Counseling is about facilitating clients, about empowering them so they can go on to take control over their own lives. A good counselor does not try to force clients into admitting anything. (p. 146)

Taylor (2005) suggests that denial be addressed gradually. In a non-blaming manner, the practitioner should gently but straightforwardly confront the client with questions about the consequences of alcohol use. The client should then be encouraged to answer these questions "as honestly and as openly as possible" in order to make choices that result in more positive consequences (p. 50).

What If Your Client Has a Relapse?

Relapses are common. Three suggestions address how to reframe the experience into one that can be used for positive change (Jacobs, 1981). First, remain calm and be empathic. Do not scold. A client may be embarrassed or ashamed about a "slip." Second, treat the ordeal in as beneficial a light as possible. Emphasize what the client has learned from it and how the experience can be used to avoid similar situations in the future. Third, if the relapse was related to stress, address how to manage stress better in the future to avoid resorting to alcohol for relief.

What If Your Client Arrives Drunk?

Counseling cannot proceed effectively if a client comes to an interview drunk (Sheafor & Horejsi, 2009; Velleman, 2011). However, Velleman (2011) remarks:

> Now, this does not mean I ask the client to leave immediately, which might be very damaging to the counseling relationship. Instead, I might sit the client down, offer a cup of coffee, have a bit of a chat (during which time I will explain, if I have not already done so, that we are not having a 'proper' session because, in my estimation, it would not be helpful, due to the fact that they have had quite a bit to drink), and then move him or her on, perhaps

> having made an appointment for the next day, written it down, and put it in the client's pocket. It is sometimes surprising how many clients do return for appointments made while they are intoxicated. (p. 118)

A client may appear both drunk and verbally assaultive when coming for an interview. Your main goal should then be to minimize the disruption and send the client safely home (i.e., in a taxi or with a friend; your client of course should not drive his or her own car). You should never place yourself in physical jeopardy, so you should remain in an area where others are. Allow the client to vent feelings. To help diffuse tense circumstances, "comment on the situation rather than ignore it.... [You] should tell the client how ... [you] feel: 'I feel you are becoming angry with me. I don't want you to feel annoyed with me'" (Velleman, 2011, p. 116). Another approach involves adopting a "one-down" position: "I'm sorry if I've made you angry—what do I do?" (Velleman, 2011, p. 116). Other suggestions include: avoiding direct eye contact (that may be too confrontational); attempting not to appear frightened (e.g., by remaining as calm as possible and not fidgeting); trying to "divert the client's attention in a subtle way—'I really feel like a cup of coffee now; do you want one?'"; and avoiding any physical contact with the client (this may trigger an explosive episode) (Velleman, 2011, p. 117).

EMPOWERMENT AT THE MEZZO LEVEL

You will most likely fulfill one of two roles in mezzo-level practice when working with alcohol and other substance abusers. You will make assessments and subsequent referrals to self-help groups such as AA, and you will work with the abuser and his or her family.

Treatment of the family system focuses on family dynamics, communication, and change. Here "the goal of intervention is not just abstinence for the affected family member but also as improved functioning for the family unit as a whole" (Lewis et al., 2011, p. 171). Lewis and her colleagues (2011) reflect on the stages of family recovery:

> Families have distinctive needs at various stages of the recovery process. The goals of counseling differ according to whether substance abuse is active, whether the drug use behavior is in the process of alteration, or whether behavior change has been established.... Systems interventions are most effective

if they fit the family's stage of readiness. Of course, stages of family change differ in one important way from those of individual change: Not all family members reach points of readiness at the same time. The [social worker] . . . needs to be ready to help any family member who chooses to alter his or her part in the ongoing pattern of interaction. Growth and change can take place, whether or not the substance-abusing members takes part, as long as other family members make changes in their customary roles. (pp. 171–172)

EMPOWERMENT AT THE MACRO LEVEL

EP 2.1.8a

EP 2.1.10i

Implementation approaches at the macro level are those that go beyond the extent to which alcohol or other substance abusers and their families receive or do not receive treatment. Macro approaches concentrate on how abusers in general are treated and on what solutions to substance abuse problems society proposes.

Macro issues focus on at least three major areas. The first deals with the adequacy and effectiveness of treatment programs. Are adequate services available to all abusers and their families? Are our clients being served with the resources they need? An answer of no to either of these questions leads to the possibility of macro implementation. Do new programs need to be developed or old programs improved?

A second macro issue involves the accessibility of alcohol and other substances to abusers. In the case of illegal substances, is our legal system adequately regulating their distribution? Obviously, there are problems, or there would not be abusers. What should be done to address these problems? Should abusers, middleperson substance distributors, or major drug kingpins be the target for legal action and control? What policies and programs should be developed to curb substance abuse problems? (To understand policy and practice in a little more detail, see Highlight 7.12 for a discussion of managed care dilemmas.)

In the case of alcohol, an accessibility issue involves the degree to which social policies should be permissive concerning its use. This might involve placing age restrictions on the ability to purchase alcohol. It also might concern forbidding the purchase of alcohol in some or all geographical areas. Another serious issue involves the consequences for driving a motor vehicle while under the influence of alcohol.

A third macro issue concerns prevention of alcohol and other substance abuse. To what extent might the problem be solved by thwarting its development in the first place? Any programs aimed at prevention would require financial backing for facilities, staff, and materials. Finding financial support for any type of program is an ongoing controversial issue.

Critical Thinking Questions 7.8

EP 2.1.3

- To what extent should the purchase of alcohol be forbidden?
- What should be the minimal age to purchase alcohol (e.g., 18, 19, 21, 25)?
- Should restrictions differ for the purchase of beer, wine, and more potent hard liquor?
- What is a permissible blood alcohol level for driving?
- What consequences should drunk drivers receive?
- What might the best methods be to stop alcohol and other substance problems before abuse occurs?
- Should prevention focus on "early identification and treatment of alcohol-dependent individuals" or rather on "education . . . aimed at the entire citizenry"? (Anderson, 1987, p. 141)

Chapter Summary

The following summarizes this chapter's content as it relates to each learning objective (LO) presented at the beginning of the chapter. Chapter content helps prepare students to:

LO 7-1   Recognize child maltreatment.

Child maltreatment includes physical abuse, neglect, emotional/psychological neglect, emotional/psychological abuse, and sexual abuse. Physical abuse is the "nonaccidental injury inflicted on a child," usually by a caregiver, other adult, or, sometimes, an older child (Crosson-Tower, 2013, p. 180). Both physical and behavioral indicators characterize physical abuse. Child neglect causes children harm by caregivers not doing what is necessary for those children's well-being. Types of abuse and neglect are described. The dynamics behind child maltreatment are complex and varied.

LO 7-2   Examine Child Protective Services.

Child Protective Services (CPS) are those involving assessment and interventions by social workers and others in situations where children are deemed at risk of maltreatment. A family preservation philosophy typically characterizes CPS.

LO 7-9 Appraise Managed Care and Its Effects on Practice

EP 2.1.2
EP 2.1.2b&c
EP 2.1.8a
EP 2.1.9a&b
EP 2.1.10k

A chapter on implementing generalist social work intervention may seem an odd place for a highlight on managed care. However, the fact that practice can only occur within the overshadowing macro context of policy, regulations, and resource allocations must be stressed. For health care in the United States, managed care provides the framework for service provision. This is also true in the context of the Affordable Care Act passed in 2010, which represents a massive government expansion and legal renovation of the U.S. health care system. Managed care has been and probably will continue to be "the major form of administration and financing of health care in the United States" (Popple & Leighninger, 2011, p. 184). Managed care is "an integral aspect of social work practice in many settings," including health, mental health, family, child welfare, and a wide range of other public social service settings (Corcoran, 1997, p. 191). "Social workers play a variety of roles in managed care systems, including provider, gatekeeper [one who determines who may have access to services and who may not], planner, and advocate" (Popple & Leighninger, 2011, p. 203).

Managed care is the provision of medical care under an insurance plan, "which involves monitoring and controlling the decisions of health care providers" (Mooney et al., 2013, p. 45). These include determinations "about medical procedures, diagnostic tests, and other services that should be provided to patients" (Kendall, 2013, p. 235). An identified group or range of health and mental health care providers contracts with employers and governmental units to provide health care at a negotiated rate to large groups of individuals. This is in contrast to the historic approach of individuals and/or employers purchasing health insurance specifically for these individuals and their families. The original intent of managed care was to save agency administrations from the cost and inconvenience of providing employees with traditional health insurance. Managed care programs often do provide services beyond those typically prescribed by health insurance (e.g., prevention and family services).

Popple and Leighninger (2011) describe how managed care works:

First, most managed care programs refer to the people delivering health or mental health services, such as physicians, social workers, psychologists, and even

entire agencies, as "providers." Although you might think of "customers" as the people receiving the services, this term actually refers to the businesses or other bodies, such as state health or Medicaid departments, that contract with a managed care organization (sometimes abbreviated as MCO). These entities pay for the managed care plan through a system of capitation. In the traditional fee-for-service approach, the insurance plan pays health care professionals for each specific service they perform, such as a surgical procedure or an eye exam, that is covered in the plan. In capitation, the MCO pays a fixed, per-person amount to its providers for a given time period, regardless of the number of services rendered. The providers assume some or all of the risk in this arrangement. If they've figured correctly, the services they actually give to their clientele in a given month or year will balance the prepayment. The MCO has in turn been given a fixed amount by the customer (private employer or public entity) to arrange for care. Fewer services overall will mean an excess in payment, or profit for the MCO; more services, a monetary loss. (p. 187)

Two primary principles promoted by managed care include *retention of quality and access*, while *controlling cost.* That is, health and mental health services should be of high quality and readily accessible to clients, on the one hand. On the other hand, they should be cost-effective. However, Blau (2010) maintains that "managed care is not cheaper [than traditional health insurance], ... especially when the high administrative overhead of managed care is factored in" (p. 394). Many questions have also been raised about the quality of care and access to providers that patients choose, which will be discussed later in this highlight. At the time of this writing, it is unclear concerning how costs and service provision will be affected by the Affordable Care Act.

Managed Care and Social Work

"It seemed at first that managed care, which began with health services, would not affect social workers, but it was soon extended to mental health services, which employ tens of thousands of social workers" (Jansson, 2014, p. 259). (Note that it is important for all social workers, including those who do not work in mental health settings, to understand the impact of managed care. All clients in all settings are affected by health issues and their access to good health care.) Managed care "fundamentally transformed" traditional relationships between clients and workers in mental health settings (Lohmann,

(continued)

1997, p. 201). Historically, social workers established treatment plans in conjunction with clients, while stressing informed consent and confidentiality to comply with ethical standards. Managed care takes these decisions out of workers' and clients' hands and puts them into the hands of removed third-party decision makers. A managed care representative, often a utilization reviewer or case manager, then reviews documentation and regulates "the services that clients receive, especially what specific services will be provided and at what cost" (Corcoran, 1997, p. 194). This includes placing limits on the number of counseling sessions clients may receive regardless of the clients' needs (Popple & Leighninger, 2011). To Lohmann (1997), managed care "represents the complete . . . triumph of financial management concerns over virtually all other professional considerations" (p. 202).

As generalist practitioners, we must work within our employing agency setting. However, we are also responsible for maintaining ethical practices and for making sure that clients' needs are met. Several ethical issues may be raised concerning managed care. The first involves the potential conflict between "the gatekeeping role of some managed care organizations and client self-determination" (Corcoran, 1997, p. 196). When subject to managed care, clients experience significantly decreased choices in their service providers (Karger & Stoesz, 2013). Rather, the managed care utilization reviewer can make this determination.

Similarly, managed care may conflict with the ethical principle of informed consent:

Informed consent requires that the client know in advance the clinical procedures, the risk of those procedures, and the available alternative procedures. Managed care may destroy informed consent by restricting the available procedures to a limited number. For example, a managed care company may determine the preferred practice and the preferred providers, with little consideration or disclosure of alternative procedures. (Corcoran, 1997, p. 196)

Managed care also has the potential to violate client confidentiality (Popple & Leighninger, 2011). Social workers are bound by the *Code of Ethics* that emphasizes how "social workers should respect clients' right to privacy" and "should not solicit private information from clients unless it is essential to providing service" (NASW, 2008, §1.07a). However, if a managed care organization demands information before providing services, what should the worker do? What if the worker does not agree with the organization's expressed need for information and feels the regulations violate clients' right to privacy? Workers may be required to report

confidential information, whether they feel it is ethical or not. (Chapter 11 discusses the National Association of Social Workers *Code of Ethics* in depth.)

The point is not to get depressed about the managed care environment. Rather, practitioners must respond to the potential ethical dilemmas posed. Barusch (2012) explains:

Today's health-care system presents new challenges and opportunities for advocates, administrators, and practitioners. In a variety of settings and a variety of roles, social workers strive to ensure that vulnerable populations receive the care they need. At the state level, social workers battle against benefit cuts and monitor Medicaid managed care contracts. In clinics, hospitals, and other settings, social workers inform patients and their families of their rights and responsibilities and serve as intermediaries between members of minority groups and health-care institutions. In community agencies they work with nurses to educate low-income and immigrant families in the use of new and established medical technology. In Congress and state legislatures, social workers continue . . . investigating and reporting the needs and concerns of vulnerable Americans. (p. 201)

Popple and Leighninger (2008) emphasize the importance of advocating for "[l]aws protecting patients' rights in managed care." They explain:

Such legislation might include the right to information about a health plan's procedures and policies, the right of access to a medical specialist without approval of a primary care doctor, the right to an independent appeals process [for example, when patients disagree with gatekeepers' decisions], and the right to sue a health plan for damages when it improperly denies care. (p. 258)

Other aspects of improved legislation include the right to:

ensure patients' access to detailed information about coverage . . . [and] treatment options . . . ; require companies to cover emergency care without prior authorization . . . ; [and] make health plans comply with state and federal laws that protect the confidentiality of . . . health information. (Managed Care, 1998, p. 1)

On a final note, as of this writing we have established that no one really knows how the Affordable Care Act will play out in future years and affect the health care provision environment. Generalist practitioners must remain abreast of these issues as policies develop and changes occur.

LO 7-3 Apply the Generalist Intervention Model to Practice in Child Protective Services.

Protective service workers follow the planned change process proposed by the GIM. Engagement, assessment, planning, implementation, evaluation, and follow-up as described in the GIM are discussed. Assessment includes risk assessment for child maltreatment, which involves child, parent, family, and intervention forces. During intervention, perpetrators of maltreatment may be linked with support and educational groups. On the macro level, social workers should actively advocate for resources and positive change in prevention, reporting, and treatment.

LO 7-4 Examine and implement crisis intervention.

Crisis intervention is a brief and time-limited therapeutic intervention in which a social worker or other mental health professional helps a client system in crisis recognize the precipitating problem and identify potential coping mechanisms. Crises can happen to individuals, families, groups, communities, and organizations. The crisis process and major concepts in crisis intervention are described. Steps in crisis intervention include engagement, assessment, planning, implementation, and planning for future crises.

LO 7-5 Provide disaster relief and trauma counseling.

Social workers can provide help at the macro level in disaster relief and trauma counseling. Disasters may include vicious assaults, hurricanes, tornadoes, earthquakes, tsunamis, floods, landslides, and fires. An initial response to a disaster is triage. Survivors' psychological functioning should be assessed. Practitioners' basic tasks include welcoming, framing, educating, grieving, integrating, reflecting, and empowering, in addition to terminating and revisiting (Behrman & Reid, 2005). Long-term help should also be provided. Workers should take care of their own mental health.

LO 7-6 Work with and empower older adults.

Empowering practice with older adults emphasizes identification and use of their strengths. Aspects of decreased power may include physical health, functional limitations, labor force participation, and economic status. Important concepts in empowerment include adaptation, competence, relatedness, and autonomy (Zuniga, 1995). Spirituality and religion may serve as important sources of strength for clients who embrace them. Older adults may also be empowered at the family and group levels through nurturance of family relationships, provision of respite care, and involvement of support groups. Generalist practitioners can become involved in political advocacy for older adults at the organizational and community levels.

LO 7-7 Employ generalist practice in empowering immigrants.

Immigration status is a person's position in terms of legal rights and residency when entering and residing in a country that is not that person's legal country of origin. National origin concerns individuals', their parents', or their ancestors' country of birth. Many immigrants may need social services and help in adapting to their new lives. Issues concerning people having another national origin include cultural heritage, maintenance of ties with the country of origin, linkages with the ethnic community, language, learning about the U.S. system, and advocacy.

LO 7-8 Address alcohol and other substance abuse.

Criteria for diagnosing substance use disorders are described. *Alcohol, drug, substance, alcoholism, alcoholic, dependence, tolerance, withdrawal, abuse, intoxication,* and *addiction* are defined. People who use and abuse alcohol may fall anywhere on a continuum involving how much they drink and how many problems drinking causes them. Alcohol abuse causes various problems in family systems. Family members often strive to hide the abuse. Children may risk experiencing behavioral, school, emotional, and relationship problems (Velleman, 2011). Intervention approaches to alcohol use disorders include a traditional recovery model and one based on the strengths perspective. The traditional recovery model involves the respective stages of abstinence, confrontation, growth, and transformation. A strengths perspective on alcohol and other substance abuse treatment is based on harm reduction, which stresses decreasing the amount of harm resulting from use. Resources to address alcohol or other substance abuse include detoxification, outpatient treatment, inpatient treatment, therapeutic communities, halfway houses, mutual self-help groups, Alcoholics Anonymous, and pharmacological adjuncts.

Empowerment at the mezzo level may involve family participation in treatment and support groups. Issues at the macro level concern the adequacy of treatment programs, the accessibility of alcohol and other substances to abusers, and prevention of abuse in the first place.

LO 7-9 Appraise managed care and its effects on practice.

Managed care is "a generic label for a broad and constantly changing mix of health insurance, assistance, and payment programs that seek to retain quality and access while controlling the cost of physical and mental health services" (Lohmann, 1997, p. 200). Generalist practitioners must work within the employing agency setting, yet maintain ethical practices and make sure clients' needs are met. Ethical issues include gatekeeping with significantly decreased ability to choose service providers, informed consent, and client confidentiality. Practitioners should advocate for improved legislation concerning managed care.

Competency Notes

The following identifies where Educational Policy (EP) competencies and practice behaviors are discussed in the chapter.

EP 2.1.1c Attend to professional roles and boundaries. *(p. 274):* Social workers should understand their role as a referral agent in the area of substance abuse.

EP 2.1.1d Demonstrate professional demeanor in behavior, appearance, and communication. *(p. 253):* Social workers should demonstrate professional demeanor in terms of process and communication when undertaking crisis intervention. *(p. 254):* Practitioners should use professional, effective interviewing and relationship-building skills during the implementation phase of crisis intervention. *(p. 260):* During disaster relief intervention, generalist practitioners should manifest professional demeanor in terms of service provision and communication.

EP 2.1.2 Apply social work ethical principles to guide professional practice. *(p. 282):* Social workers should address potential ethical dilemmas such as those posed by managed care in order to engage in ethical professional practice.

EP 2.1.2b Make ethical decisions by applying standards of the NASW *Code of Ethics* and, as applicable, of the International Federation of Social Workers/International Association of Schools of Social Work *Ethics in Social Work, Statement of

Principles. *(p. 282):* Social workers should carefully consider the NASW *Code of Ethics*, especially concerning informed consent and confidentiality, when addressing ethical issues in managed care.

EP 2.1.2c Tolerate ambiguity in resolving ethical conflicts. *(p. 282):* Practitioners must tolerate conflicting needs and unclear direction when tackling ethical issues in managed care.

EP 2.1.3 Apply critical thinking to inform and communicate professional judgments. *(pp. 241, 251, 253, 256, 265, 265, 279, 284):* Critical thinking questions are posed.

EP 2.1.4 Engage diversity and difference in practice. *(p. 264):* Religion is a dimension of diversity. *(p. 268):* Immigration status is a dimension of diversity.

EP 2.1.4a Recognize the extent to which culture's structures and values may oppress, marginalize, alienate, or create or enhance privilege and power. *(p. 263):* Age and immigration status are dimensions of diversity. Because older adults and people without citizenship status are vulnerable populations, practitioners must understand their situations to practice effectively with them. *(p. 268):* Immigrants with customs and values that differ from those of the mainstream culture may experience oppression, alienation, and lack of power.

EP 2.1.4b Gain sufficient self-awareness to eliminate the influence of personal biases and values in working with diverse groups. *(p. 266):* Practitioners must work hard at self-awareness regarding any prejudices and stereotypes they may harbor toward older adults. *(p. 270):* As discussed under "Cultural Heritage," practitioners must become aware of their own cultural values to eliminate personal biases when working with people having other national origins.

EP 2.1.4c Recognize and communicate their understanding of the importance of difference in shaping life experiences. *(p. 270):* Social workers should appreciate that people having other national origins may require help in maintaining their customs, learning a new language, and gaining knowledge about a new system's policies and expectations.

EP 2.1.5a Understand the forms and mechanisms of oppression and discrimination. *(p. 263):* Social workers should understand the dynamics of older adults' potentially decreased power and the resulting potential oppression and discrimination.

EP 2.1.5b **Advocate for human rights and social and economic justice.** *(p. 267):* Generalist practitioners should advocate for improved legislation and community services to meet older adults' needs.

EP 2.1.7a **Utilize conceptual frameworks to guide the processes of assessment, intervention, and evaluation.** *(p. 248):* Risk assessment is a common conceptual framework aimed at assessing the amount of risk to which children are exposed in their home environments. *(p. 252):* Practitioners must understand the major themes characterizing crisis intervention conceptual frameworks as they assess problems, intervene with clients, and evaluate their work. *(p. 278):* Two contrasting conceptual frameworks for the treatment of alcoholism (a four-stage recovery model and a harm reduction approach) are discussed.

EP 2.1.7b **Critique and apply knowledge to understand person and environment.** *(p. 268):* Social workers must apply knowledge about immigration status and its effects on clients in their social environment.

EP 2.1.8a **Analyze, formulate, and advocate for policies that advance social well-being.** *(p. 250):* Social workers should advocate for policies in organizations and communities that enhance treatment provision and empower clients. *(p. 267):* Practitioners should advocate for improved legislative policies on behalf of older adults. *(p. 282):* Practitioners should advocate for substance abuse policies that advance social well-being. *(p. 283):* Generalist practitioners should advocate for policies that protect patients' rights and provide adequate access to health care.

EP 2.1.9a **Continuously discover, appraise, and attend to changing locales, populations, scientific and technological developments, and emerging societal trends to provide relevant services.** *(p. 282):* Social workers should pay close attention to the changing climate in the health care environment in order to advocate for policies and practices that meet their clients' health care needs.

EP 2.1.9b **Provide leadership in promoting sustainable changes in service delivery and practice to improve the quality of social services.** *(p. 282):* Generalist social workers can function as leaders in advocacy for adequate health care and services.

EP 2.1.10 **Engage, assess, intervene, and evaluate with individuals, families, groups, organizations, and** communities. *(p. 253):* Crisis intervention involves engagement, assessment, intervention, and evaluation in micro, mezzo, and macro practice.

EP 2.1.10a **Substantively and affectively prepare for action with individuals, families, groups, organizations, and communities.** *(p. 250):* Generalist practitioners can prepare for action with systems of all sizes when addressing child maltreatment. *(p. 258):* Social workers can prepare for crisis intervention action with systems of all sizes. Highlight 7.5 addresses crisis intervention with communities. *(p. 267):* It's important for practitioners to consider potential actions with families, groups, organizations, and communities in addition to working with the individual.

EP 2.1.10b **Use empathy and other interpersonal skills.** *(p. 280):* Practitioners should use empathy and other interpersonal skills when using a harm reduction approach.

EP 2.1.10c **Develop a mutually agreed-on focus of work and desired outcomes.** *(p. 245):* Clients should be integrally involved in developing goals and objectives when workers address child maltreatment to establish the focus of treatment and the results they would like to achieve. *(p. 279):* Collaboration with the client concerning the focus of work and desired outcomes is stressed in a harm reduction treatment approach.

EP 2.1.10d **Collect, organize, and interpret client data.** *(p. 249):* Practitioners must collect, organize, and interpret at least eight dimensions of data when establishing goals to end child maltreatment. *(p. 253):* Social workers conduct an assessment of client data when pursuing crisis intervention. *(p. 260):* Assessment of client data is an essential part of disaster relief.

EP 2.1.10e **Assess client strengths and limitations.** *(p. 263):* Because of decreased power, it's especially important to assess the strengths and limitations of older adults. *(p. 264):* Practitioners should explore the diversity dimensions of religion and spirituality as potential sources of strength. *(p. 279):* Social workers should focus on clients' strengths in addition to addressing limitations when using a harm reduction approach in substance abuse treatment.

EP 2.1.10f **Develop mutually agreed-on intervention goals and objectives.** *(p. 253):* Planning through the development of goals and objectives with clients is an integral part of crisis intervention. *(p. 279):* Clients are integrally involved in the determination of goals and objectives in the harm reduction approach to alcoholism.

EP 2.1.10g **Select appropriate intervention strategies.** *(p. 251):* Crisis intervention provides an appropriate intervention strategy that follows the planned change process and helps people experiencing severe stress and crises. *(p. 260):* Social workers must select appropriate intervention strategies when providing disaster relief. *(p. 270):* Special intervention strategies apply when working with people of other national origins. *(p. 278):* Agencies and practitioners should choose the conceptual approach that they determine is the most appropriate to treat alcoholism.

EP 2.1.10i **Implement prevention interventions that enhance client capacities.** *(p. 245):* Family preservation aims to prevent children's placement outside of their own homes. *(p. 284):* Social workers should explore and implement policies and practices that help to prevent alcoholism and the problems it causes.

EP 2.1.10j **Help clients resolve problems.** *(p. 254):* Practitioners help clients in crisis solve problems by implementing intervention plans. *(p. 278):* Numerous

intervention strategies and approaches are available to help people resolve their problem with alcoholism.

EP 2.1.10k **Negotiate, mediate, and advocate for clients.** *(p. 270):* As discussed under "Advocacy," practitioners should advocate on the behalf of people having other national origins so that they get the services they need. *(p. 282):* Generalist social workers have the responsibility of advocating on their clients' behalf for good health care.

EP 2.1.10m **Critically analyze, monitor, and evaluate interventions.** *(p. 250):* As part of the Generalist Intervention Model, social workers must evaluate the effectiveness of their interventions when addressing child maltreatment. *(p. 254):* Evaluating effective approaches in crisis intervention can help clients prepare to deal with such crises in the future.

On the Internet

Visit the *Understanding Generalist Practice* CourseMate at **www.cengagebrain.com** for resources such as quizzes, glossaries and videos.

Evaluation, Termination, and Follow-Up in Generalist Practice

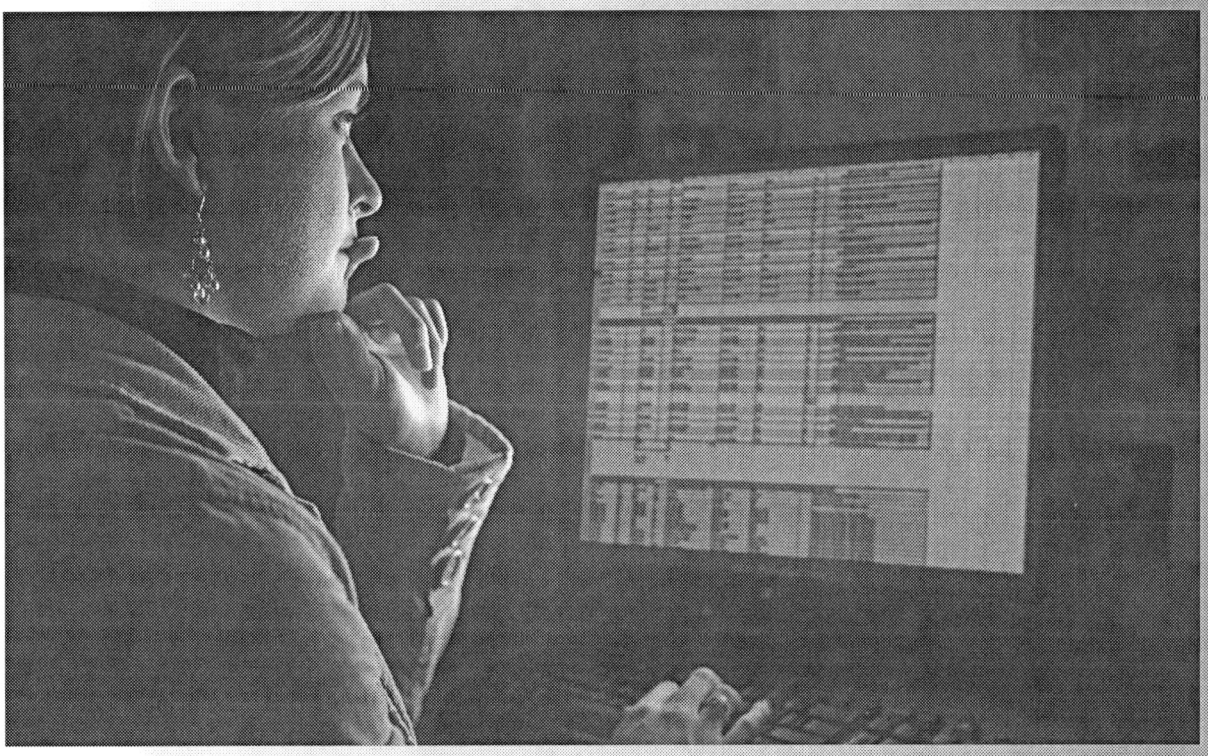

Image Source/Getty Images

Learning Objectives   *This chapter will help prepare students to:*

LO 8-1	Identify and use appropriate methods for evaluating practice.	**LO 8-6**	Practice personal reflection and self-correction regarding termination.
LO 8-2	Critically analyze concepts important to evaluation of practice.	**LO 8-7**	Help clients resolve problems concerning termination.
LO 8-3	Identify commonly used methods for program evaluation.	**LO 8-8**	Select appropriate termination strategies for client systems.
LO 8-4	Anticipate and deal with common practice evaluation problems.	**LO 8-9**	Implement prevention interventions to ensure maintenance of change.
LO 8-5	Facilitate transitions and endings (termination) for clients.	**LO 8-10**	Engage in follow-up activities with client systems.

AS A SOCIAL WORKER you may be confronted with any of the following tasks:

- Evaluating whether your efforts to help a juvenile delinquent stay out of the criminal justice system are working (In other words, has he remained out of jail and in the community?)
- Proving to county elected officials the effectiveness of a new parent nurturing program designed to reduce child abuse among at-risk low-income parents
- Determining whether your assertiveness training program is increasing group members' assertiveness (To what extent have group members increased their assertiveness without violating the rights of others?)
- Measuring the effectiveness of a foster parent recruitment program you have implemented (How many more foster

parents have you been able to recruit since the program began compared to the period before the program was instituted?)

- Helping a previously aggressive client in a group home for adolescents with behavioral disorders prepare to return to her home, school, old friends, and community
- Assisting a family (coping with a recent suicide attempt by its 14-year-old member) in the ending phase of a 6-week family bereavement program
- Easing the transition of a frightened yet strengthened mother leaving the safety of a battered women's shelter
- Following up on your chronically mentally ill adult client who has moved from a residential institution to a community-based program

Introduction

EP 2.1.10m

To be effective as a social worker, you must know whether the interventions you employ are working. This knowledge may seem simple enough in the abstract, but developing effective strategies to evaluate our practice is not always easy. Even when we have a clear plan for evaluating the outcomes of our practice or our programs, many things can challenge our conclusions about their effectiveness.

The evaluation process typically is ongoing in that we must always be alert to whether or not the goals we hoped to reach are being achieved (see Figure 8.1). Evaluation may also be thought of as an endpoint activity, often leading to the mutual client–worker decision to terminate the professional relationship. The last part of this chapter focuses on the knowledge and skills needed for effectively concluding professional social worker–client relationships.

LO 8-1 Identify and Use Appropriate Methods for Evaluating Practice

Evaluating Social Work Practice

EP 2.1.10m

EP 2.1.10h

Evaluation of social work practice has only recently been emphasized. It has been spurred by several factors, including demands for accountability, interest in improving social work practice, and the accreditation requirements of the Council on Social Work Education (CSWE).

Increased emphasis in social work and related literature on using "best practices" is also stressing the importance of evidence as a guiding factor in selecting interventions and designing programs. Evidenced-based practice (best practices) ensures that we use only knowledge that has been adequately tested using some degree of scientific rigor. It stands in opposition to authority-based practice, which relies on opinion and testimonials to support specific interventions. As Gambrill (1999) so correctly points out, none of us would want our physician to treat us based only on what she heard from a colleague nor would we want her to rely solely on the results of a single interesting study. Rather, we would want treatment based on carefully monitored trials with attention paid to scientific methods. This is one of the reasons why evaluation of our practice and programs is a critical, professional obligation of the generalist social worker.

DEFINITION AND PURPOSES OF EVALUATION

EP 2.1.6b

EP 2.1.10h

Evaluation "is a process of determining whether a given change effort was worthwhile" (Kirst-Ashman & Hull, 2012, p. 361). You would not make repeated visits to a lawyer who rarely was successful in defending her clients. Neither would you consult a physician who forgets what his diagnosis was 30 seconds after making it. We all engage in a certain degree of evaluation each time we use the services of a professional, organization, or business. We notice whether our expectations were met, whether the service we received was appropriate,

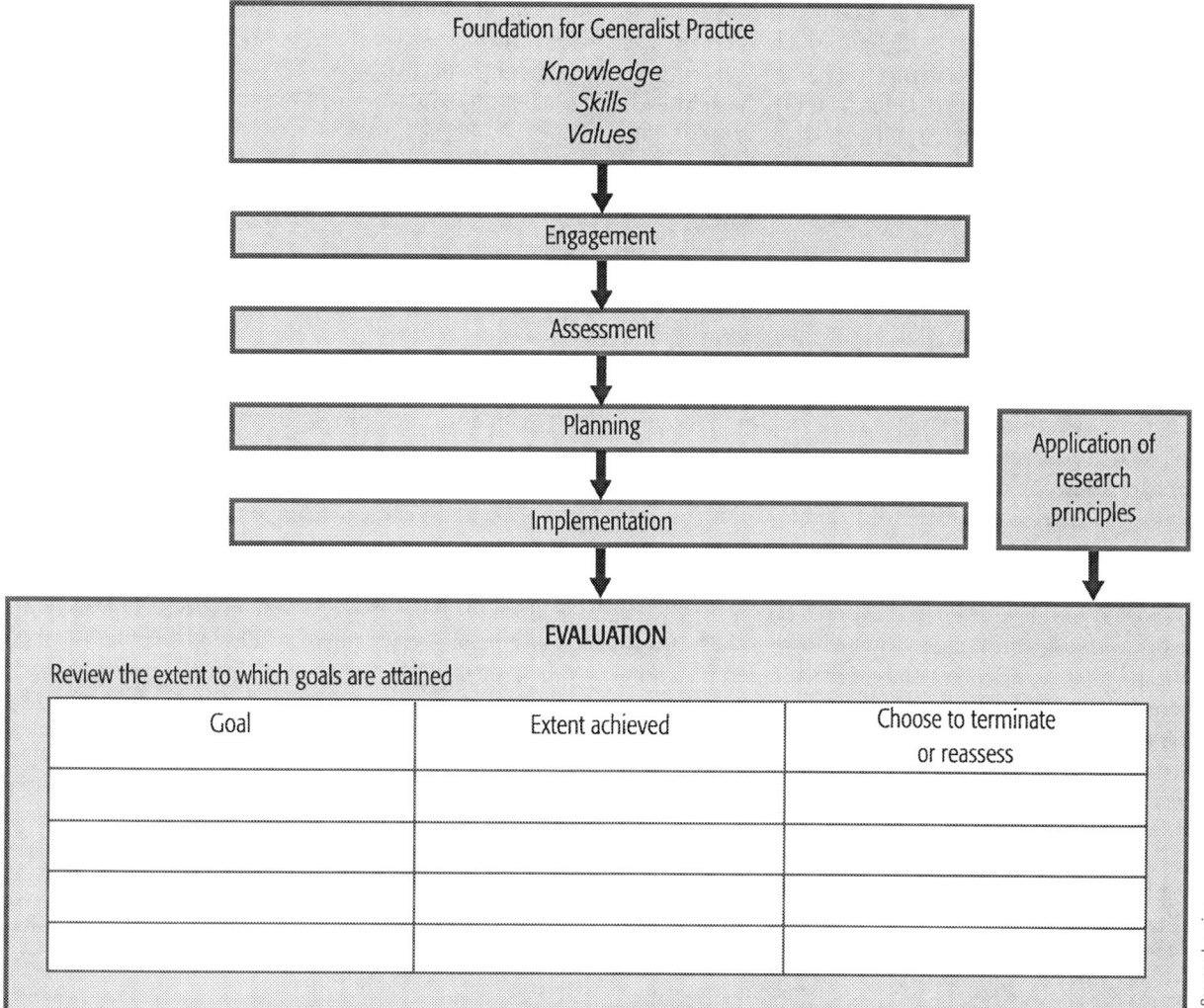

FIGURE 8.1 Evaluation in the Generalist Intervention Model (GIM)

and how well we were treated. When our evaluation concludes that the experience was negative, we do not patronize that person or service again.

At the micro level of practice, evaluation is designed to help us determine to what extent our work with a specific client was successful. We are concerned with whether the intervention goals were achieved and how satisfied clients were with the services provided. Evaluation aids in judging our competence as well as the methods, theories, and perspectives we use in generalist practice. Similarly, evaluation seeks to explain why a particular outcome occurred. Therefore, evaluation also focuses on process or determining how we got where we did.

At the mezzo level, we want to know if the treatment or educational group achieved its purposes. We are interested in whether group members reached the goals they set for themselves. In a task group, we need to decide whether or not the tasks were accomplished in a timely fashion. Because of the differential nature of the two group types, we are less concerned about whether task group members had their individual goals met.

Macro-practice evaluations are focused on whether entire programs accomplished their purpose. Also of concern is the relative cost of providing a program. Two programs providing similar services with nearly identical outcomes but at vastly different costs will not exist very long. Few of us would knowingly choose a service that was more costly but produced exactly the same result as a less expensive service.

As you can see, evaluation has a clear purpose at each level of generalist practice. Of course, there are many other reasons for undertaking evaluations. Evaluation is a normal step in the planned change process described in the Generalist Intervention Model (GIM) (see Chapter 1). It can no more be ignored than can assessment. As practitioners, we are interested in knowing whether what we are doing is working. This curiosity is natural. Our own interest is buttressed by the *Code of Ethics* of the National Association of Social Workers (NASW), which makes evaluation an ethical obligation of each social worker. Providing services that we know are ineffective is unethical. We also do evaluations because we must continually try to improve our professional skills and knowledge. To increase your own effectiveness as a worker requires feedback from others. We want to know how client systems experienced their work with us, which gives them a chance to be heard (a means to empowerment) and gives us important information. Finally, evaluation helps build the knowledge base of the profession. Both practice wisdom and published knowledge increase as we document the success of our efforts. Highlight 8.1 discusses other purposes for evaluating community programs.

EXTERNAL FACTORS IN EVALUATION

As sources of funding for social programs have become increasingly scarce during the last 25 years, the demands for evaluation of those programs have increased. Governmental and private funding sources wanted proof that their money was being put to good use. They demanded greater assurance that the money they allocated for programs was accomplishing the intended purposes. Although many agencies had been providing some kinds of evaluation, their emphasis was largely on output or measuring what the agency did. For example, the worth of an agency might be justified by noting that the agency staff provided 10,000 hours of one-on-one work with first offenders. Therefore, the implication is that the agency is productive. Still another agency might report that its caseload this year increased by 25 percent with no corresponding increase in staff. Thus, the agency implies its current staff is working harder. These types of measures provided some information about what agencies do. However, they did nothing to satisfy the basic questions. Did the agency accomplish its purpose, and was it actually successful in helping its clients?

Besides the economic importance of evaluation, political pressures played a role in demanding accountability from social programs. Elected state and federal officials called for increased emphasis on evaluation to justify the continued expenditure of funds, which was especially true for those skeptical of or opposed to social programs.

Simultaneously, a growing consumer movement was affecting human service programs across the country. It maintained that users of products or services had a right to know about their effectiveness. Consumers wanted some assurance that they were getting what they were paying for, whether the product was cornflakes, cars, or counseling.

The result of this confluence of political pressure, economic necessity, and consumer interest is a heightened awareness of the importance of accountability.

HIGHLIGHT 8.1

Evaluating Programs

Evaluation of either agency or community programs achieves several important purposes. These include:

1. Providing data that will assist current program improvement;
2. Helping agency administrators keep track of new programs still in the development stage;
3. Assisting agencies to determine which programs are most effective and should be continued;
4. Identifying programs with limited effectiveness to be considered for elimination;
5. Demonstrating to funding bodies that their money is being spent in accordance with their expectations; and
6. Proving to donors, legislators, and other organizational supporters that their support is justified.

Accountability in social work involves being responsible for and answerable to others for the quality and effectiveness of one's efforts. Those to whom we are accountable include clients, funding bodies, the community, and supervisors. We must be able to clearly articulate what it is that we do, how we do it, and that our work meets professional standards for competence. How can you, as a generalist practitioner, prove you are accomplishing what you say you are? In the following sections, we will look more closely at what evaluation means and the kinds of things that it achieves. We will also examine its relationship to accountability.

OBSTACLES TO EVALUATION

EP 2.1.6a
EP 2.1.10h

For workers to want to know the outcome of their efforts or to know that the program in which they work is effective may seem logical. Still, strangely enough, evaluation has not been an ongoing concern for many workers. One reason is that the very act of evaluating a practitioner's own work leaves the practitioner vulnerable. Workers might ask themselves, "What if I'm not successful with every client? What if some clients actually get worse? What if my caseload is so large that I don't have time to follow up on my clients' progress? What if my agency charges a lot of money for services I'm not sure really work?"

These are all legitimate concerns that have served as obstacles to workers evaluating their own practice. After all, evaluations make judgments about what was accomplished in the change process. These judgments might not always be favorable to the worker, especially if clients were worse off after receiving help.

A second reason for the lack of a routine system of evaluation is that workers are often too busy for any kind of formal evaluation. High caseloads and tight schedules often make finding time to evaluate results in more than a cursory, haphazard fashion difficult.

A third reason for the lack of effort focused on evaluation is that many agencies have not emphasized its importance. Simply counting cases seen or hours of service given was considered a satisfactory measure of an agency's effort. In addition, agencies did not have the money or time for extensive evaluation studies. Recording information and evaluating it is time-consuming and therefore expensive. You are paid for your time, so your time is worth money.

Another likely explanation was that many social workers lacked training in the use of evaluation approaches. Until the CSWE enacted standards requiring that social work education programs teach students specifically to evaluate their practice, most schools and universities neglected this content. Although students routinely took research classes as part of their work, these courses were generally not focused on evaluation of one's own practice. Rather, the primary goal was to produce a graduate who could read the professional journals and be an intelligent consumer of social work research. This is no longer the primary research goal of most social work education programs. Now, most students learn a variety of methods for evaluating their practice and for evaluating agency programs.

Typically, evaluations have one of two major thrusts. First, they can monitor the ongoing operation (effort) of an agency. Second, evaluations can assess the outcomes (effects) of a program or intervention. Monitoring and evaluation functions are complementary; monitoring looks at the process of giving service, and evaluation looks at the effectiveness of the service provided. The ultimate goal is to generate information that increases the effectiveness (and efficiency) of interventions. Effectiveness involves succeeding at what you set out to accomplish. Efficiency concerns doing it at a reasonable cost. In other words, evaluations can focus on effort or activity, outcome, adequacy of performance, or efficiency.

Evaluations can also focus on the process of giving help. Let us use an example to illustrate how this process might work. Assume you are a worker who has attempted to help a woman become more assertive.

Cloris described herself as always being "shy." She was terrified of meeting other people and had virtually no friends. Additionally, she found asserting herself at work difficult. As a result, she felt that her colleagues, all health care aides at a small nursing home, often took advantage of her.

As her worker, you cared whether or not Cloris became more assertive, which was the outcome she desired and the goal toward which you both worked for the past 6 months. Also, you probably wanted to know which of your interventions proved most helpful and which did not. You want to determine which techniques to continue using in the future and which to omit. Thus, you may be focusing on your *efforts* or *activities* on behalf of your client. When we decide to evaluate our own efforts and the results experienced by the client, we must use our practice experience to help us decide the appropriate type of evaluation. For example, because Cloris sought to become more assertive, our evaluation decisions must be based on this goal. If we attempted to measure changes in Cloris's assertiveness using a scale for depression, we would be way off the mark. Clearly, we must employ our practice knowledge to help inform our selection of appropriate evaluation tools.

Your agency, on the other hand, may be interested in different areas. For instance, the agency might want to evaluate the *adequacy of your performance*. For instance, the approach you were using with the client might not be as effective as others that are available. Similarly, the board of directors might be wondering whether this service is provided at the *lowest possible cost*. Their interest is in *efficiency* (the relationship between the resources used to effect change and the outcome of the change effort). If another agency provides similar results at lower cost, the board may decide that it cannot afford you or your program. You may be out of a job.

As you can see, this idea called evaluation has many facets. In the next section, we will look at the evaluation process itself, focusing on goals and some key concepts in performing evaluations.

LO 8-2 Critically Analyze Concepts Important to Evaluation of Practice

THE EVALUATION PROCESS

You will recall the emphasis we placed in earlier chapters on clearly identifying the objective of your work with client systems. The GIM approaches client systems with a clear plan for helping resolve problems, improve quality of life, and address broad client and human service needs. To accomplish this objective, in the planning stage we used data from the assessment stage to help clients frame goals and objectives that were specific, measurable, and clear. Without clear goals and objectives, knowing if we (client and worker) accomplished what we set out to do is difficult. As with other steps in the GIM, the success of succeeding stages depends upon the quality of effort that went into previous stages. Just as poor assessments lead to poor planning, vague or sloppy objectives set in the planning stage affect our ability to do later evaluations.

Evaluation of practice follows the same planned change approach used in the social work practice itself. For example, first we must define the problem to be evaluated. Once this definition is accomplished, the worker must consider the types of research approaches that might be appropriate (assessment). The best approach is then chosen (planning), and the research is carried out (implementation). Finally, the worker must examine and evaluate the results of the research effort.

As is evident, this approach mirrors almost exactly the way in which a worker deals with a problem involving any size system. Just as with our chapters on micro, mezzo, and macro practice, there are some key terms and ideas that are essential to understanding and conducting research on social work practice. These concepts include formative evaluation, summative evaluation, baseline, validity, reliability, data-gathering methods, independent variables, dependent variables, and generalizability.

Formative Evaluation

 We have indicated earlier that evaluations may be conducted for monitoring ongoing progress. Such *formative* evaluations assess the adequacy or amount of effort directed at solving a client system's problem and gathering data during the actual intervention.

Formative evaluations focus on the process of providing help instead of the end product of help giving. For example, Toseland and Rivas (2012) suggest that one can have group members complete a questionnaire following each individual group session. The questionnaire might ask the group members their opinions on what occurred in the group, perhaps focusing on what they learned. The results of the clients' evaluations would be used to help plan subsequent meetings. Formative evaluations help us assess whether or not the anticipated progress is achieved. For example, in educationally focused groups, the members may be given a pretest at the beginning of a session and a posttest after the session. These tests would help determine achievement of goals for that specific session. In other words, exactly how much did group members learn during that particular session? Similarly, the worker and client who periodically review progress made by the client over the past six meetings are engaging in a type of formative evaluation. The PERT chart we reviewed in Chapter 4 is also a kind of formative evaluation. As noted, a PERT chart provides a visual representation or diagram that includes program objectives, activities to be accomplished, timelines and sequences for achieving them, and identification of who is responsible for which objectives. At any point in the process, one can look at the chart and know what is to be done, by whom, and by what date. This chart allows us to know whether the process is proceeding as planned. It also enables us to make changes necessary to reach our goals.

Most students are familiar with one form of formative evaluation, namely, course or instructor evaluations.

These evaluations provide the instructor and the instructor's department with information to assess how well that teacher is conveying information to students. Although course evaluations occur at the end of a student's experience with an instructor, they are actually formative evaluations. These types of evaluations are used because they are intended to affect how the instructor teaches the course in the future.

Summative Evaluations

Frequently, we want to know whether or not the outcome we anticipated at the beginning of our planned change process has been achieved. This process requires that we conduct an evaluation after completing the planned change process. We call such evaluations *summative* because they occur at the end of the process. In one sense, end-of-semester examinations in a college course are summative evaluations. They help determine whether or not you have learned the material outlined in course objectives.

You may be a bit unclear about the distinction between summative and formative evaluations. The important thing to remember is that formative evaluations occur while a planned change process is continuing. Summative evaluations, on the other hand, occur at the conclusion of the planned change process, looking backward. Their goal is to summarize what has already occurred. Formative evaluations, on the other hand, are oriented toward the future. Their goal is to affect or influence what is yet to come.

Baseline

Another key concept is that of baseline. Baseline is a measure of the frequency, intensity, or duration of a behavior. *Baseline* is a term taken from behavioral research and is important in assessing the progress of some helping relationships. Take, for example, the case of Virginia Schwartz. Virginia went to a social worker for help because she and her daughter, Mary, fight furiously over Mary's boyfriend, Lonnie. Virginia says the fights occur "a lot, every day." Mary describes the frequency of fights by saying they occur "constantly." If the worker is to judge whether her efforts and those of the family are working, it will be important to learn whether the fights are decreasing or not. Without definitive information on the frequency of the fighting, it will be nearly impossible to know whether things are improving.

Before we can tell whether or not the behavior is changing, we must know how often it occurs. Thus, the worker might ask Virginia and Mary to record individually the number of fights they have in a week. This information would provide some basis for knowing whether the frequency of the fights is diminishing, increasing, or remaining the same.

In some situations, having several baselines might be important. Perhaps the fights going on between Mary and Virginia are affecting Mary's schoolwork. Mary's grades in certain subjects might be an additional measure to help determine whether the worker and clients are making progress.

Ideally, a baseline should be based on several observations. These should be made over a period of time prior to intervention. As you can see, baselines can be important in the helping process and are essential for conducting certain kinds of evaluations. We will discuss these types of evaluations later.

Validity

According to Marlow (2011, p. 187) *validity* refers to "the extent to which you are measuring what you think you are measuring." When we evaluate a practice situation, using appropriate measurements is important. Assume, for example, that you are a social worker in a deferred prosecution program. This program involves working with a group of first-time adult offenders (e.g., shoplifters or drunk drivers) referred to your program by the court system. If they successfully complete your program, they will have their records wiped clean. The assumption behind the existence of your program is that early intervention with first offenders will reduce the tendency toward recidivism (further contact with the criminal justice system).

A new coworker suggests that perhaps one measure of the success of your program is whether or not the participants feel positively about the experience. He suggests that you ask each member to rate the group experience on a scale of 1 to 10, with 10 being an extremely positive attitude toward the program.

What is the problem with such an approach? The primary problem is that the purpose of the group is to reduce recidivism among this group of first offenders. The measure suggested—that is, a client questionnaire focusing on feelings—has nothing to do with the real purpose of your program, namely, reducing actual recidivism. Such a measure is simply not a *valid* means of assessing the outcome of this group.

Validity is a significant concern in evaluation. It is entirely possible, for example, that the group members have enjoyed the group experience and still continue a life of crime. A client questionnaire asking group members to report any contacts with the criminal justice system would have greater validity than one that asked them to rate the group experience. An even more valid method of knowing whether or not the goals of the group were met would be to follow up on each group member at periodic points in time (6 months, 1 year, and so on) to see if there were any further arrests. Concluding that the intervention worked if only a small percentage of group members had subsequent arrests would be easier.

The matter of validity is a bit complicated, as there are really several types of validity. We can speak, for instance, of face validity. *Face validity* is simply a professional judgment about whether the measure actually measures what it is supposed to. Most of us would react strongly to a social work test containing questions unrelated to our course. If a statistics test asked us to reproduce Einstein's theorem, we would be angry. The test was supposed to measure our mastery of statistics, not the math involved in Einstein's theorem. In this case, the test questions do not have face validity. We would expect the final examination in a history of social welfare course to ask about the Elizabethan poor laws, Social Security amendments, Hull House, and the War on Poverty. As one might expect, achieving face validity is comparatively easy.

Another type of validity is concurrent validity. *Concurrent validity* exists when scores on one instrument correlate well with scores on another instrument that is already considered valid. Let us say we have a new test for depression that has not yet been determined valid. To test for concurrent validity, we might give the test to a group of patients who had previously been assessed as depressed using a valid depression scale. If the new test yields similar results, we can say it has concurrent validity. That is to say, the instrument has a clear relationship to the thing we hope to measure, namely, depression.

Predictive validity is another important form of validity. A measure has *predictive validity* when it can be used to predict future events. In theory at least, your performance in field placements should be predictive of how you will do in actual social work positions. Likewise, scores on the Scholastic Aptitude Test (SAT) and the American College Test (ACT) are used to predict how high school graduates will perform in a college or university academic environment. To the extent that an instrument accurately predicts later performance, behavior, or outcomes, it is said to have predictive validity.

Not all the types of validity have been included in this chapter. Your research course will likely provide much greater depth on this matter and further hone your skills as an evaluator of social work practice.

A new program has been established to address drug use among adolescents. The program provides after-school activities and both individual and group counseling. The following measures have been suggested as evaluation mechanisms:

1. Client satisfaction questionnaires to determine participants' feelings about the program.
2. Weekly urine tests to determine which, if any, participants are using drugs.
3. Pre- and posttests to measure participants' knowledge about drugs and drug abuse.
4. Monthly mailed surveys asking parents and school officials if they are aware of any current drug use by program participants.

Critical Thinking Questions 8.1

EP 2.1.3

- Rank from highest to lowest the preceding measures by the likelihood that they will be useful in evaluating the drug use of group members.
- What are potential disadvantages of each of the types of measurements listed?

Reliability

Most of us would probably object to the following situation: A three-credit course on interviewing is required for graduation. The total course grade is based on a one-time observation by one faculty member. That faculty member would be drawn at random from a pool of faculty, including those in psychology, sociology, and social work. The rater would thus be assigned to you by chance. Our objection would probably be based on the realization that each of the potential raters might have different criteria they would use to judge us. The person who rates us on our interview might think we did a good job. Another rater, however, might come to a different conclusion. Even if the whole pool of faculty came from the social work program, there would probably be some differences in their judgments. Although all might be competent to judge interviewing skills, there still might be little consistency in their grading. The very same interview might be given an A– by one and a C+ by another. Clearly, we want observers and instruments capable of making consistent judgments. This situation brings us to another concept of importance—reliability.

Reliability is "the extent to which an instrument measures the same phenomenon in the same way each time the measure is used" (Toseland & Rivas, 2012, p. 441). The key phrase here is *each time*. In the previous example, we might be more comfortable if each observer were using the same rating form with clearly defined criteria. If there is a high level of consistency among the raters, we have what is known as inter-rater reliability, a desirable characteristic.

Let us take a slightly different look at reliability. Assume we have an instrument that purports to measure assertiveness. A reliable instrument will produce similar results each time it is used. If a person scores low on the instrument one week and high the next, we would question if the measure is reliable. Reliable instruments produce consistent results over time. In theory at least, the only thing that should result in changing one's score on the assertiveness test is assertiveness training or some similar intervention.

There is also a clear relationship between reliability and validity. If an instrument (or rater) does not produce consistent results on subsequent trials, we cannot depend on its accuracy. However, for a measure to be reliable but not valid is possible. Let us take an obvious example. Your score on a written test of French vocabulary might be reliable in that it will always produce the same result, namely, a low score. If, however, the purpose of the test is to judge your ability to *speak* French, not *read* it, the written test is a much less valid measure of spoken vocabulary, as it does not really test this area at all.

Just as you would want to be evaluated in a manner that is both valid and reliable, so too should you want to evaluate your practice in a manner that is both valid and reliable. Sometimes, this goal is relatively easy to accomplish. If you wanted to know whether or not a depressed client was becoming less depressed, you might administer to that client one of the available depression scales. You could develop your own instrument, but it would likely prove costly, time-consuming, and less valid and reliable than existing methods. Using instruments where validity and reliability have been demonstrated is certainly an easier course to follow.

Whenever possible, we attempt to use multiple measures or indicators to help ensure that we are getting valid and reliable information. For example, a student doing field placement in a hospital outpatient setting used both weight loss and cholesterol levels as measures of whether clients were achieving the goals of a health improvement program.

If possible, getting independent verification of subjective items is also preferable. Although a client may accurately report a change in his or her behavior, having a report from other observers to substantiate the client's claims is sometimes better. A client may report improvement that is not observable to significant others. This claim, at least, raises a question about the accuracy of information the client provided.

Data-Gathering Methods

The choice of which or how many data-gathering methods to use is determined largely by the goals of the intervention. Social workers use many methods depending upon need. Commonly used methods include surveys, scores on instruments, interviews with significant others (parents, teachers, and so on), collected data (such as school attendance records and grades), and observations of the researcher and others involved in the change effort. Surveys or interviews may be structured (using a specific set of questions in a structured format) or unstructured (using open-ended questions in an informal discussion). Observations may be direct (person-to-person) or recorded in some way (e.g., videotaping). *Self-reports* (information provided by the client) are used when what must be measured is subjective. Feelings and beliefs of a client are examples of situations where self-reports are appropriate. Because you cannot "see" what the client believes, you must resort to asking the client to report on this area. Many instruments have been developed based on this premise. Methods frequently used to gather subjective data include depression scales, assertiveness schedules, and other devices. Highlight 8.2 refers to a number of such instruments.

Products, achievement of a specific task or change in behavior, are often used in the data-gathering process. A withdrawn child who talks to no one on the playground is exhibiting a specific behavior, that of silence. The worker can certainly assess change in that behavior by noting if the child begins to talk to other children. Likewise, a client who is trying to lose weight can easily measure progress by stepping on the scale.

Observational measures are those that rely on others to observe a change in the client's behavior. They are used when observing specific behavior in a situational context is relatively easy and appropriate. Consider, for example, evaluations of a student's interviewing technique. One of the more anxiety-producing parts of becoming a social worker is learning how to interview clients. Unlike other courses in college, this skill requires students to demonstrate that they can conduct

Finding Valid and Reliable Instruments

Locating a valid and reliable instrument to assist with your practice and evaluation efforts is sometimes quite easy. There are instruments to measure all of the following:

- Alcoholism (e.g., Alcohol Use Disorders Identification Test [AUDIT])
- Anger (e.g., The Clinical Anger Scale [CAS])
- Anxiety (e.g., Generalized Anxiety Disorder [GAD 2 and GAD 7])
- Assertiveness (e.g. Rathus Assertiveness Scale)
- Depression (e.g., Beck Depression Inventory [BDI])
- Fear (Fear Survey Schedule for Children–Revised)
- Marital happiness (Kansas Marital Satisfaction Scale [KMS])
- Parenting skills and knowledge (Family Activities Inventory)
- Peer relationships (Assessment of Peer Relations [APR])
- Self-esteem (Rosenberg Self-Esteem Scale [RSE])
- Sexual interaction (Sexual Interaction System Scale [SISS])
- Social skills (Social Skills Rating System [SSRS])

This list is only a small sample of the types of measures available. Existing measures such as these usually have information on validity and reliability as well as normative data so that comparisons with "normal" populations can be done.

There are a variety of sources for these instruments. A few of them are the following:

Fischer, J., & Corcoran, K. (2013). *Measures for clinical practice and research* (5th ed.). New York: Oxford.

McCubbin, H. I., & Thompson, A. I. (Eds.). (1991). *Family assessment inventories for research and practice*. Madison: University of Wisconsin Press.

Pietrzak, J., Ramler, M., Renner, T., Ford, L, & Gilbert, N. (1990). *Practical program evaluation*. Newbury Park, CA: Sage.

Rauch, J. B. (1993). *Assessment: A sourcebook for social work practice*. Milwaukee, WI: Families International.

Roberts, A. R., & Yeager, K. R. (2004). *Evidence-based practice manual: Research and outcome measures in health and human services*. New York: Oxford University Press.

Online Resources

Compendium of Assessment and Research Tools for Measuring Education and Youth Development Outcomes, http://cart.rmcdenver.com

Environmental Assessments, http://www.cdc.gov/ncipc/pub-res/pdf/YV/CDC_YV_SecIV.pdf

Screening Tests, http://pubs.niaaa.nih.gov/publications/arh28-2/78-79.htm

Center on Alcoholism, Substance Abuse, and Addictions, http://casaa.unm.edu/Instruments

---

an interview meeting prescribed standards. They can achieve this accomplishment by using audiotape, videotape, or actual live interviews. Faculty members then observe and rate the interview. Such a procedure provides a more valid indicator of interviewing skill than a pencil-and-paper test. The instructor is able to look for certain kinds of skills and judge whether or not the student has exhibited those skills in the interview. Ideally, the skills must be carefully defined and clearly known to both student and teacher. In addition, the observer must be competent to judge the presence or absence of the skill. In other words, the rating must be valid.

Independent and Dependent Variables

Two other concepts important in practice evaluation are independent variable and dependent variable. The *independent variable* is the factor we think is responsible for causing certain behaviors, reactions, or events. For example, taking a toy from a child may precipitate crying or a temper tantrum. Taking the toy away is the independent variable that leads to the child's behavior, which is the dependent variable. In a social work context, the helping process itself is considered the independent variable. We believe that our efforts to assist the client (the independent variable) will cause or contribute to changes in some aspects of the client's life (the dependent variable). Results (dependent variable) *depend* on our intervention effort (independent variable).

The *dependent variable* is the outcome or end product of the helping process. The assumption is that the outcome is dependent upon the helping efforts. Hence, it is called the dependent variable. If a client is part of a group working on increasing members' self-esteem, the level of self-esteem would be the dependent variable. In a new program designed to teach anger management to men who abuse their spouses, the ability to control their anger is the dependent variable.

In practice, we know that the independent variable (our helping) is not totally responsible for the outcome. Too many other intervening variables exist to make such a claim. For example, a client attempting to lose weight may join a weight-loss program that meets weekly. Although the weekly sessions are helpful in many ways, other factors affect the client's life. The reactions of other persons (spouse, children, friends) may have an enormous influence on the client. If significant others praise the client's willpower and acknowledge how much better he looks, the results of the group sessions will be enhanced. If, on the other hand, no one shows any recognition of the client's efforts or someone even belittles the effort, the outcome may be negatively affected. Remembering that many variables affect people's behavior is important. The worker's effort to help is simply one of these factors. We will discuss the importance of these alternate explanations for change later in this chapter.

Generalizability

Generalizability is the ability of a set of results in one situation to fit another circumstance or instance. Assume for a minute that we have been extremely successful in our efforts to help clients or that the program we are part of has had unusual success. Our feelings of success have been supported by the evaluation techniques we have used. Moreover, to begin thinking that these methods may prove useful to other similar groups is logical. We are now beginning to *generalize* the results of our research to other groups or populations.

Generalizability is a desirable characteristic of any successful program. However, the very limited size of our sample (a handful of individuals or groups) is too small to make generalizing appropriate. A substantial number of cases is necessary to establish that positive change has not come about simply by chance or other intervening factors.

In addition, for the results of a project to be generalized, we must have confidence that the members of the group are representative of (similar to) others who might benefit from this program. Without this assurance, any attempts to generalize from this group of clients to other clients are pure speculation. We shall refer to this matter again when we look at issues and problems in evaluation.

Generalization Across the Globe. Efforts to generalize from one population to another have resulted in numerous failures of practice and policy both in the United States and across the globe. For example, efforts to provide to other countries drugs that are effectively used in the United States often failed to recognize that cultural and economic differences can doom such programs. Some drugs, for example, depend upon the availability of health care practitioners to provide regular injections, a service not available worldwide. Other medications require refrigeration that may not be available in remote locations. Because a medical intervention is effective in one environment does not guarantee that it will work in another.

Likewise, attempts to encourage African women to use baby formula rather than breast-feed their infants ran into a variety of problems. These included the fact that breast milk was widely recognized as safer, healthier, and significantly cheaper. For example, lack of sufficient sanitary water to mix with formula and sterilize bottles is a major problem in many nations. Moreover, unlike formula milk, breast milk helps children develop immunity to various local diseases which tend to be greater health risks in developing countries. In addition, many people experience lactose intolerance to cows' milk, the main ingredient in most formulas. The attempt to generalize from the U.S. experience with the use of baby formula produced multiple negative consequences for many other countries and populations, underscoring the risks of overgeneralization.

The concepts we have discussed so far include formative and summative evaluation, baseline, validity (face validity, concurrent validity, predictive validity), and data-gathering methods. We also discussed reliability, independent and dependent variables, and generalizability. Each concept is important to the researcher, whether one is looking at one's own practice or attempting to evaluate an entire program. In the next section, we will be looking at several techniques the worker can use to evaluate his or her practice.

Critical Thinking Questions 8.2

- What is the relationship between validity and reliability?
- Can an instrument be valid but not reliable or reliable but not valid?
- How do formative evaluations differ from summative evaluations?

Evaluation Designs for Generalist Practice

EP 2.1.3a

Most of you will be involved in practice with client systems. Those client systems may be individuals, families, groups, organizations, or communities. The nature and level of your practice will be dependent upon your knowledge and skill, your level of education, the requirements of your agency, and the clientele served by your agency. Therefore, being familiar with a variety of techniques to valuate generalist practice is important. Among the most common are single-subject designs, goal-attainment scaling, task-achievement scaling, and client satisfaction questionnaires.

SINGLE-SUBJECT DESIGNS

Single-subject designs are research methods aimed at determining whether or not an intervention was successful. They derive their name from the fact that they are frequently used with a single case or client. Yegidis and Weinbach (2009) indicate that single-subject designs have had many names, including single N or N = 1 research, single-subject research, single-subject design, single-case-study design, single-system design, and time-series research or design. To complicate matters a bit more, the "single subject" may really be a family, a group, or a system of some other size. The structure of single-subject research is fairly simple. In its most basic form, we have a client with a problem, the problem is attacked through the intervention of the worker, and we have an outcome of that intervention. The outcome of the intervention is then compared to the state of affairs prior to intervention. Sometimes, this process is called the *AB design,* with A representing the pre-intervention state and B the intervention. Figure 8.2 shows an example of this design using a simple illustration.

The client here is in a halfway house for chemically dependent adults. The primary goal is helping the client find a job. The first objective is to encourage the client to engage in job-seeking efforts. The client applied for only one job per week prior to intervention. This information forms the baseline shown in Phase A. Phase B includes the period of time after the worker begins coaching the client in job-seeking skills. The solid vertical line represents the start of intervention. The dots show that the number of job applications increased following intervention and then stabilized at four per week.

Clearly, the client has made progress. He now makes significantly more job applications per week. This increase indicates that the intervention—namely, coaching the client in job-seeking skills—has been effective to some extent.

The steps in implementing the single-subject evaluation are straightforward. First, an easily measured goal is identified (e.g., one goal might be to get a nursing home resident out of her room from after breakfast until the noon meal). Then a baseline is done showing the frequency of the behavior prior to intervention, which is called Phase A. Finally, a record of the frequency of the behavior is kept during and following intervention. A graphical representation of the change can be prepared quite readily. Sometimes a baseline can be constructed using information from a case record. However, frequently this source of information is not

FIGURE 8.2 Single-Subject (AB) Design

possible. For example, consistent or easily measurable types of information might not have been recorded.

In the event that there is no opportunity to establish a baseline, the worker can still maintain a record of the behavior following intervention. This is the *B design*. Only the behavior occurring during and at the end of the intervention phase can be measured. The example shown in Figure 8.3 reflects an intervention with an adolescent who repeatedly violated his parents' curfew restrictions.

One should note that we consider results that occur in Phase B to be caused by the intervention. We know from our previous discussion that this notion is relatively simplistic. Many other variables may be at work helping to cause the changes seen following intervention.

There are other types of designs that fall into the single-subject design category. For example, we might have a situation where an *ABC design* is possible. A baseline is constructed (as might occur when we keep track of how long the client stayed out of her room in the nursing home between the hours of 8 a.m. and noon). The period prior to intervention is the A Phase. When the social worker begins to provide an intervention, we have the B Phase. Four weeks into the intervention, an additional treatment (C Phase) was prescribed (perhaps the client began to take medication). We now have an ABC design, where C represents the medication phase. Figure 8.4 is an example of this design.

Still another example concerns an *ABAB design*, which is where a baseline (A) is developed, and then the intervention (B) runs its course. Intervention (B) is then discontinued for a period of time (6 weeks, for example). Based on the measurement level when the last intervention stopped (A), the intervention (B) is begun again. An example of this design appears in Figure 8.5.

Although useful for testing the effectiveness of an intervention, the withdrawal of intervention can be ethically difficult to carry out. It can be used more easily when a worker must discontinue working with the client while the latter is on vacation. Deliberately discontinuing an intervention for the sole purpose of testing the effectiveness of that intervention raises ethical issues that cannot be addressed in this chapter.

Clearly, single-subject designs work well when there is an obvious behavior that can somehow be measured. A student used this method to chart arguments between two residents sharing a room in a nursing home. Both the residents and the nursing staff found the situation intolerable. The nursing staff maintained a record of when and how many arguments occurred, thus providing a baseline.

Efforts to increase or decrease the frequency of a given behavior are particularly appropriate for single-subject design. As was noted, this design can be used with client self-reports or where there is some sort of pre-and post-data-gathering device employed. That is, some specific instrument is used to measure a behavior prior to intervention and again after intervention. The Rathus Assertiveness Scale (Ünal, 2012) is an example. Scores on this instrument can be used to measure levels of assertiveness prior to and following intervention.

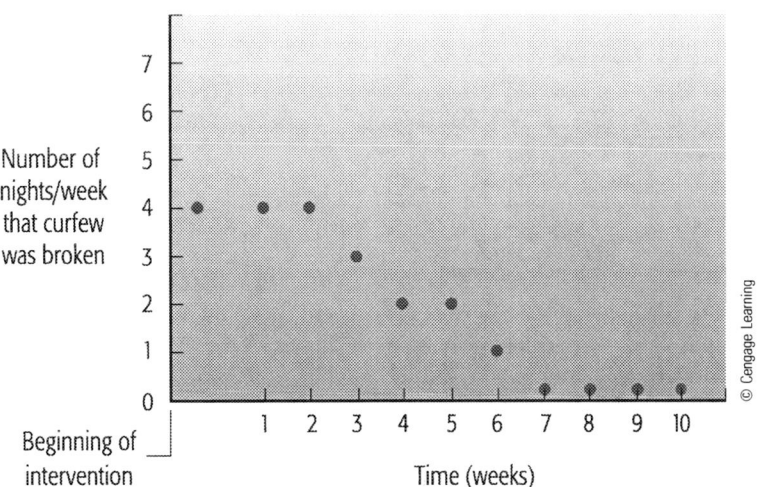

FIGURE 8.3 B Design without a Baseline

FIGURE 8.4 ABC Design

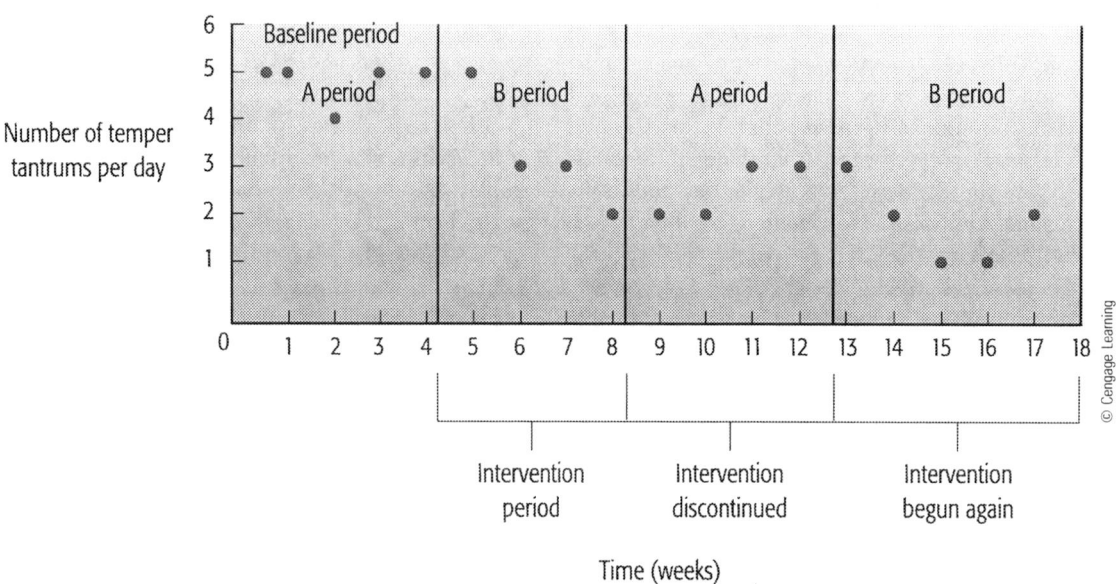

FIGURE 8.5 ABAB Design

Additional Perspectives on Single-Subject Designs

Looking over these various models, you may recognize other possibilities. Consider, for example, a family seeking help with their 13-year-old daughter, who is out of control. There is not sufficient time to do a baseline on either the daughter's or the parents' behavior. You begin the B Phase by providing counseling to the daughter separately. Parental complaints about broken curfews, school absences, and angry outbursts represent possible baselines. Although the parents reject the need for their involvement in family counseling, they agree to the worker's request that they keep a chart of how often these three behaviors occur. Thus, we have three items we could measure in some way: broken curfews, angry outbursts, and school absences. Multiple baselines are fairly common when dealing with complex problems.

FIGURE 8.6 BAB Design with Multiple Baselines

After four sessions leading to some improvement in the target behaviors, the family leaves for Christmas vacation. Shortly after returning from vacation the parents agree to additional help in the form of family counseling. Family counseling is really the introduction of a second intervention. Figure 8.6 shows this BAB design with multiple baselines.

One should note that single-subject designs can be adapted to other situations. For example, a group of adolescents learning about the risks and dangers of drug abuse might be tested at the first group session and again at the end. This testing would provide a measure of increased knowledge at the start and conclusion of the intervention period. Pre- and posttests of this sort are especially appropriate when the objective of intervention is increased knowledge.

GOAL-ATTAINMENT SCALING

Goal-attainment scaling is a method used when achievement of the goal is sufficiently important to be used as the primary outcome criterion. It is positive in its connotation because it focuses on a desired state (e.g., employment) rather than on a problem (e.g., being unemployed). It is also used when a goal does not lend itself to the kind of charting and evaluation needed for single-subject designs. Perhaps it is a situation where the client has multiple goals, many of which are related to one another. Perhaps the goals are not as easily measured by counting behaviors, as was the case in the nursing home situation mentioned earlier.

With goal-attainment scaling, various steps toward achieving a goal can be measured. Table 8.1 provides an example of these steps. The client is a mother of two children; all of them are living in a shelter for battered women. The client has three goals she wants to work on: (1) getting a temporary restraining order (TRO) from the court, which prevents her husband from contacting her; (2) finding a job, so she will be less dependent upon her husband for financial support; and (3) reestablishing her social support network (composed of family and friends). Although the client may not achieve the ultimate goal of leaving her husband, finding a good job, and developing many new friends, she may continue to make progress toward increasing her self-esteem and becoming more independent. This progress can be charted using goal-attainment scaling.

Timberlake and colleagues (Timberlake, Farber, & Sabatino, 2002) employ another type of goal-attainment scale using a point system. A slightly modified version of their goal-attainment scale is shown in Table 8.2. As you can see, the system is essentially similar to the one in Table 8.1. The difference is that the possibilities are arranged from the worst outcome (goal given up) to the best outcome (goal attained). This system can be easily modified and used with a wide variety of goals or client problems.

TASK-ACHIEVEMENT SCALING

Task-achievement scaling is a method of evaluating the degree to which an identified set of tasks has been accomplished. Many intervention activities carried out by social workers are very discrete, or task oriented. For example, brokering, advocacy, and service-coordination-type tasks cannot be as easily measured using single-subject designs or goal-attainment scaling. A good example is a hospital social worker doing discharge planning. Primary goals for a given client may consist of arranging home health care for a client being discharged or checking on financial arrangements needed for admission to a nursing home.

Task-achievement scaling allows us to measure the extent to which the worker and client have completed agreed-upon tasks, such as arranging transportation or filing an insurance claim. This model is especially

TABLE 8.1 Goal-Attainment Scaling

Levels of Predicted Outcomes	Objective 1[a]	Objective 2	Objective 3
Least favorable outcome	Client returns home to abuser, gives up goals	Client returns home to abuser, gives up goals	Client returns home to abuser, gives up goals
Less-than-expected outcome	Client contacts court about TRO	Client applies for one job	Client calls one old friend
Expected level of success	Client obtains TRO from court	Client applies for a few jobs	Client spends time with friend
More-than-expected level of success	Client's spouse does not contest TRO	Client offered a job, but turns it down	Client spends time with a few friends
Most favorable outcome	Spouse leaves home so client can live there	Client accepts good job	Client develops new friends

© Cengage Learning

[a]One might substitute the objective listing at the top with a brief description of the problem being addressed.

SOURCE: Lewis, V. J., Dell, L., & Matthews, L. R. (2013). Evaluating the feasibility of goal attainment scaling as a rehabilitation outcome measure for veterans. *Journal of Rehabilitation Medicine, 45*(4), 403–409.

TABLE 8.2 Modified Goal-Attainment Scaling

–3	–2	–1	0	+1	+2	+3
Goal given up	Much worse than at start	Little worse than at start	Starting point	Little better than at start	Much better than at start	Goal attained

© Cengage Learning

SOURCE: Timberlake, E., et al. (2002). *The general method of social work practice* (p. 260). Boston: Allyn & Bacon.

useful for situations in which there is limited contact between worker and client, as often happens in hospital discharge-planning units. It begins with the expectation that both client and worker agree on the tasks to be performed and who is to perform them. The focus is on results, not on effort. Typically, a five-point scale is used. Reid and Epstein (1977) use the following description of the points on the scale, ranging from 4 (completely achieved) to 0 (no opportunity to work on task).

A rating of 4 (completely achieved) applies to tasks that are fully accomplished (e.g., a job has been found, a homemaker secured, financial assistance obtained). It may also be used for tasks that are fully accomplished "for all practical purposes" (Reid & Epstein, 1977, p. 289). In the case of a couple whose goal was to reduce quarreling, a rating of 4 could be given if they reached a point where hostile interchanges occurred infrequently and no longer presented a problem and they saw no need for further work on the task.

A rating of 3 (substantially achieved) indicates that the task is largely accomplished, though further action

may be necessary before full accomplishment is realized. Thus, if the task is to improve work performance, significant improvement would merit a rating of 3 even though further improvement would be possible and desirable.

When a rating of 2 (partially achieved) is chosen, demonstrable progress has been made on the task, but considerable work remains to be done. For example, if the task is to obtain a job, a rating of 2 could be given if the client has actively been looking for work and found a job he could take (and might) but was reluctant to do so. This rating would be appropriate for a couple who had made some headway on a shared task of finding things of mutual interest to do together even though they and the caseworker were dissatisfied with their progress.

A rating of 1 (minimally achieved [or not achieved]) is used for tasks on which no progress has been made or on which progress has been insignificant or uncertain. If a client's task were to enroll in a suitable vocational training program, a rating of 1 would be given if

TABLE 8.3 Task-Achievement Scaling

Task	Degree of Achievement	Rating
1. Homemaker services arranged	Client on short waiting list for services. Services will begin in about 1 week.	3
2. Meals-on-Wheels services secured	Meals will begin the day client is discharged.	4
3. Hospital bed acquired	Hospital bed rented, will be delivered the day client is discharged.	4
4. Snow shoveling assistance secured	Have list of possible people who might provide service.	2
5. Contact son and daughter-in-law	No progress—family is out of town for 2 weeks.	1

SOURCE: Reid, W., & Epstein, L. (1972). *Task-centered casework.* New York: Columbia University Press.

© Cengage Learning

the client was unable to locate a program, even though much effort had gone into searching for one.

A 0 rating indicates no opportunity to work on the task. An example would be a client who cannot carry out a task in the classroom because school is closed due to a teachers' strike.

Table 8.3 shows one example of a task-achievement scale. Here, we are dealing with an older adult who will be confined to her home following a serious injury. She is physically able to care for herself but will need many services in order to remain at home and avoid moving to a nursing home. Five tasks were identified as important in keeping the woman in her own home. Two of the tasks, arranging for Meals-on-Wheels and locating a hospital bed, have been completely achieved. The client will receive homemaker services in about a week, although the original goal was to have these provided immediately. Snow shoveling services have not yet been acquired, but the client has a list of people who might provide this service. Finally, the son and daughter-in-law are out of town, making contacting them difficult.

As can be seen from the example in Table 8.3, one case may have many tasks that must be accomplished. In some situations, all tasks may be achieved. In other cases, fully completing only a portion of the tasks is possible. The task achievement scale allows for a rough assessment of the percentage of tasks accomplished.

Here is how progress illustrated in Table 8.3 might be calculated. There are a total of 5 goals, each with a maximum point rating of 4 (completely achieved). Multiplying the number of tasks (5 tasks) times the maximum points possible (4 points), we have a total of 20. Now if we add the number of actual points under the rating (3 + 4 + 4 + 2 + 1), we find we have a total of 14 points. If we divide that total (14 points) by the maximum points possible (20) we end up with a 70 percent achievement rating for all goals (14/20 = .70).

This is, of course, a very rough form of calculation. However, it does help us get some sense of how we are doing in achieving important tasks associated with a given case. It is a particularly useful method for task-oriented interventions (i.e., where specific tasks are identified to achieve specific goals).

CLIENT SATISFACTION QUESTIONNAIRES

In certain situations, knowing the client's reactions to our interventions is important. Businesses routinely use *client satisfaction questionnaires,* which are a series of questions designed to learn the reactions of the customer to various aspects of a product. For example, purchasers of automobiles are commonly surveyed about their level of satisfaction with recent acquisitions. They may be asked to identify any problems with the vehicle or to provide feedback about the person who sold them the car or the service department's performance. Similar activities are undertaken by restaurants and other service-oriented businesses.

Client satisfaction questionnaires may be used with a single case, a group of clients all served by the same worker, or all clients served by an agency. In this way, they can be used for both evaluation of generalist practice and evaluation of entire programs. One goal might be to help the agency identify service problems or areas where the service is insufficient. Sometimes, such questionnaires help identify unmet needs.

Client satisfaction questionnaires are designed to be used following an intervention. However, they may also prove useful for monitoring progress while service is being given. Toseland and Rivas (2012) suggest that there may be value in using client questionnaires during ongoing group meetings to gather information about the process. The method has been used routinely by some educational groups to help assess the effectiveness of each individual session. One advantage of this approach is that it can be used during intervention, immediately following termination of services, or at some later point in time.

Figure 8.7 shows one page from a client satisfaction questionnaire provided to clients seen by the admission staff of a nursing home.

Other questions on this questionnaire asked whether the social worker explained admission material clearly enough and whether the social service department helped to make the admission process as smooth as possible. There was also additional space for extended comments at the bottom of the questionnaire. This particular questionnaire was attempting to gather information both about the social service department itself as well as about the performance of a particular social worker. This figure shows the potential versatility of client satisfaction questionnaires.

Satisfaction surveys can also be used for other purposes. For example, an agency might use such a survey to gather opinions of employees on how well the organization is meeting its own goals. Questions might focus on communication between departments or work units, ability of supervisors to listen to workers' concerns, or willingness to accept disagreement or criticism from supervisees. Those surveyed can rank their level of satisfaction on a scale from extremely satisfied (5) to extremely unsatisfied (1).

One disadvantage of such questionnaires is their potential for misuse. Asking a cocaine-addicted client and drug dealer whether she benefited from an intervention aimed at keeping her out of the criminal justice system amounts to using the wrong tool for the job. Just as you would not use a screwdriver for driving a nail, you must carefully choose the tools you use in your evaluation efforts. Client satisfaction questionnaires should not be used in lieu of other methods that produce more valid conclusions about the intervention's effectiveness.

Please circle the number that corresponds to your chosen response.

1. How would you rate the overall quality of your admission process at the Center of Care?

1	2	3	4
Poor	Fair	Good	Excellent

Comments: _____

2. Did you get the kind of service you wanted?

1	2	3	4
No, definitely not	No, not really	Yes, generally	Yes, definitely

Comments: _____

3. To what extent has our social worker met your needs?

1	2	3	4
None of my needs has been met	Only a few of my needs have been met	Most of my needs have been met	Almost all of my needs have been met

Comments: _____

4. If a friend needed a similar nursing home, would you recommend this social service department to him or her?

1	2	3	4
No, definitely not	No, I don't think so	Yes, I think so	Yes, definitely

Comments: _____

© Cengage Learning

FIGURE 8.7 A Client Satisfaction Questionnaire

TABLE 8.4 Target-Problem Change Scale

Name of Rater: Teacher: Target Problem	Target-Problem Rating (Severity Scale)[a]			Target-Problem Rating (Degree of Change)[b]		Global Improvement Rating
	Start	Time 1	Time 2	Termination	Follow-Up	
Talks without raising hand	VS	S	NP	4	4	
Follows directions on assignments	ES	VS	NVS	3	5	4

[a]Degree of Severity Scale: NP (no problem), NVS (not very severe), S (severe), VS (very severe), ES (extremely severe).
[b]Improvement Scale: 1 (worse), 2 (no change), 3 (a little better), 4 (somewhat better), 5 (a lot better).

© Cengage Learning

TARGET-PROBLEM SCALING

Target-problem scaling is another method of evaluating changes over time. It is a process where a problem is identified, a plan is implemented, and changes in target problems are measured to determine if the problem has changed in severity or seriousness.

The original problems are rated by degree of severity. Subsequent ratings are completed using the scale shown in Table 8.4. This form was completed by the teacher based on the rating scale at the bottom of the table. The child was one of several children in a group led by a school social worker. Each child had been referred for problems related to classroom behavior. This chart reflects changes in one of the group members. The degree of change in each identified problem is also assessed following intervention and a month later. In the case noted in Table 8.4, improvement has occurred in both problems, hence the change in degree of severity ratings. The degree of change also is rated positively by the teacher. Finally, a global or average rating reflects an overall picture of the problems being addressed.

Other practice evaluation systems do exist. One is peer review, which involves an evaluation conducted by one's peers assessing the actions taken by an individual. The peers selected to perform this evaluation are considered to be particularly competent in a specific area, and their judgments are considered a valid measure. Unlike some of the methods previously described, peer review focuses almost exclusively on the process rather than the outcome of intervention. For example, an agency might adopt a system of evaluating monthly whether or not a worker's case files contain agreed-upon items such as a fact sheet, initial contact and assessment information, and written

intervention plan. Each month a different worker's files would be reviewed to determine if the worker was meeting the professional standards adopted by the agency.

LO 8-3 Identify Commonly Used Methods for Program Evaluation

Evaluation Designs for Programs

EP 2.1.3b

Up to this point, we have been talking primarily about evaluating our practice. The data-gathering mechanisms we have described are mostly useful for social workers wanting to evaluate what they do as individual professionals. Some of the approaches discussed also have potential value for evaluating the entire program with which the worker is associated. Program evaluation can help us determine whether or not one program is more effective or efficient than another. Program evaluation includes periodic as well as ongoing evaluation of the process and the outcomes.

Little and Estovald (2012) suggest that human service organizations are strengthened when they engage in evaluation because the results of such efforts leave the agency better prepared to cope with change. Agencies can use the data from such evaluations to revitalize existing services, recover from major setbacks, or even move in completely new directions, depending upon organizational need and environmental pressures.

In the following section, we will look very briefly at six program evaluation tools: needs assessments, evaluability assessments, process analysis, program outcome analysis, program monitoring, and continuous quality

TABLE 8.5 Evaluation Designs for Programs

Evaluation Designs	When Evaluation Is Conducted			Major Concepts	Major Questions Asked
	Before Intervention	During Intervention	After Intervention		
Needs Assessments	X			Meeting clients' needs	Are clients' needs being met? Do gaps in service exist?
Evaluability Assessments	X			Clarity of goals; adequacy of available information	Can this program be evaluated? Is the agency ready for evaluation?
Process Analysis		X		Adequacy of service provision	Are services adequate, effective, and efficient?
Program Outcome Analysis			X	Achievement of program goals	Are goals being accomplished?
Continuous Quality Assurance		X	X	Achievement of program goals	Is the program working? Evaluations: Are goals being accomplished?
Program Monitoring		X	X	Details of agency	Is agency activity effective operation and efficient? What is happening in the agency on a daily, weekly, monthly, and yearly basis?

© Cengage Learning

(Trevisan, 2007; Yegidis & Weinbach, 2009). Table 8.5 provides an overview of evaluation designs for programs.

NEEDS ASSESSMENTS

We discussed needs assessment in Chapter 4. *Needs assessments* are considered forms of front-end analysis. You may recall that they are systematic efforts to help an agency determine whether and to what extent a program is needed. They also can be used after a program has been in operation for a period of time to determine if unmet needs still exist. They may be useful for identifying gaps in service and helping an agency decide whether a need for a service still exists.

EVALUABILITY ASSESSMENTS

Evaluability assessments are methods designed primarily to answer the questions, "Can this program be evaluated? Is the agency evaluation ready?" (Pietrzak, Ramter, Renner, Ford, & Gilbert, 1990, p. 22). Although it might seem that any program can be evaluated, this is not always true. For example, if either the intervention or the goals are not defined with sufficient clarity, arriving at an assessment will be most difficult.

Sometimes outcomes cannot be readily measured because the program objectives or products are vague or undefined.

Other factors that might interfere with the ability to evaluate a program are lack of accurate identifying information about clients (which might preclude using client satisfaction questionnaires), high cost of conducting a particular type of evaluation, and poor program record keeping.

You can begin to see the importance of doing an "evaluability" assessment prior to launching into any evaluation of the program. Once an agency learns that it cannot adequately evaluate itself, it has two options. First, it can make changes that will allow future assessments. Second, it can continue on without change. The latter choice carries high risk because ultimately some sort of evaluation will be demanded of almost every agency.

PROCESS ANALYSIS

We briefly mentioned process evaluations (analysis) or formative evaluations earlier in this chapter. You will remember that they are designs used to evaluate the way interventions in the agency are carried out. Client satisfaction questionnaires can be used for this goal, as can peer reviews. Both of these have been previously described and will not be covered again. At its most basic level, *process analysis* might be concerned with numbers of clients served or the kinds of services provided. It might also be focused on productivity ratios, such as the actual per-child cost of a program screening infants for malnutrition. Process analysis can also help an agency improve service by looking at the ways in which service is provided. If clients are being transferred from one unit in an agency to another unit, are such transitions conducted smoothly? What could be done to make them better? Process analysis depends largely on gathering information from both the producers and consumers of the process, namely social workers and clients.

There are a variety of instruments available to assist in process assessment. Clearly, the instrument to be used will be affected by the information desired. Pietrzak et al. (1990) provide a fine review of process evaluation and examples of available instruments.

PROGRAM OUTCOME ANALYSIS

EP 2.1.10m

A *program outcome analysis* is an evaluation designed to tell us whether or not a program is working. It may also help us find out if a program is cost effective, that is, if the results merit the expense. There are multiple means of assessing program outcomes. If the program objectives have a consumer satisfaction component, then we might want to use the client satisfaction scales we discussed earlier.

Perhaps a program hopes to increase the client's knowledge, skills, or attitudes. Consider, for example, a group training program for prospective adoptive parents of hard-to-place children (e.g., children who have disabilities or are older). The goal was to help these applicants learn about the difficulties experienced by many of these hard-to-place children. The program began because many prospective adoptive parents did not have accurate information about the problems experienced by these children. In this example, the parents were given a pretest to determine their knowledge prior to intervention and a posttest at the conclusion of the group training. This information, along with a consumer satisfaction questionnaire, was used to assess the outcome of this program.

There are other questions for which we might like answers. Perhaps we want to know if the new family resource unit is accomplishing its purpose. Do clients in the nurturing program actually learn any new skills that they use at home? Are the short-term changes noted at termination continued over a 6-month period?

How often do group members served by our substance abuse team reach the goals they set at the onset of intervention? Are there problems or problem areas for which our interventions are not successful?

As you think about these questions, you might realize that an agency whose workers routinely evaluated their practice would be in a better position to respond. Let us say, for example, that goal-attainment scaling is completed on many or most of the agency clients. This would allow the agency to gather a rather sizable chunk of information useful for program outcome analysis. Similarly, single-subject designs routinely used with clients could produce a volume of information as part of an outcome assessment. One should understand by now that assessing some program outcomes is made easier if there is an ongoing attempt to assess the work of individual components (workers or units) in the agency. Pietrzak et al. (1990) provide excellent examples of outcome evaluation with a specific focus on child abuse programs.

CONTINUOUS QUALITY ASSURANCE EVALUATIONS

Continuous quality evaluations are focused on measuring attainment of previously identified program goals. The program goals are usually specific indicators that the agency has accepted as evidence of best practices. For example, one mental health agency used three indicators to assess quality service to clients. One indicator was the extent to which written assessments were completed within a 72-hour time frame following an initial client contact. The agency goal was to have 99 percent of all assessments completed in that period.

A second indicator was accuracy in social worker classification of clients. The goal was 100 percent accuracy, as correct classification directly affected whether the agency received reimbursement and payment for services provided to clients. Errors in classification cost the agency money.

The third indicator was client satisfaction, with a goal of 100 percent. This indicator was measured by using specific questions from a client satisfaction survey mailed to all clients following culmination of their work with the agency.

Continuous quality evaluation emphasizes determination of whether the agency is achieving its goals. It can be concerned not only with the outcomes of social workers' intervention with clients, but also with more mundane issues such as timely completion of paperwork. Although it is usually used to evaluate programs, it can clearly be used to assess aspects of the individual

TABLE 8.6 Continuous Quality Assurance Evaluation, for Strong Families (July 1, 2005–June 30, 2008), Northwest Center

Item	7/1/05 to 6/30/06	7/1/06 to 6/30/07	7/1/07 to 6/30/08
Required forms are completed and in file	73%	85%	94%
Initial intervention plan is appropriate	97%	95%	98%
Vocational rehabilitation needs are accurately assessed	89%	97%	100%
Discharge plans are documented	91%	98%	99%
Adequate follow-up is documented	80%	87%	95%
Total	**86%**	**92%**	**97%**

© Cengage Learning

worker's performance. For example, a pattern of worker performance characterized by inaccurate classifications or a failure to complete assessments within target deadlines could result in a worker receiving additional training, closer supervision, or more serious consequences such as suspension. Thus, this approach has implications for both program and practice evaluation. Table 8.6 shows the results of a family service agency's continuous quality evaluation. The average total of all items for a single year allows a rough assessment of the extent to which the agency is achieving a desired quality of service.

PROGRAM MONITORING

Program monitoring is an ongoing activity designed to provide information to the agency on all aspects of its operation. Data may be collected on presenting problems, client demographics, services provided, and outcomes achieved. Agencies develop information management systems so that they can routinely assess how various aspects of their programs are progressing. An agency might decide, for example, that it no longer has sufficient numbers of children placed for adoption to justify continued offering of adoption services. Another agency providing specialized services in the area of sexuality might notice that the type of client has changed over the years. Instead of working with mostly intact couples needing accurate information, they are now helping clients with very serious sexual dysfunctions.

From these examples you can see how important maintaining accurate and complete records is. An ongoing effort at program monitoring is essential to improve services within the agency or organization and to manage agency resources wisely.

LO 8-4 Anticipate and Deal with Common Practice Evaluation Problems

Issues and Problems in Evaluation

Any evaluation program, whether employed by the worker or the agency, has the potential to be misused or interpreted incorrectly. Part of this potential is due to the nature of the research tools available to us. Still other parts are inherent in any evaluation effort. For example, normally we are not able to randomly assign clients to treatment and control groups so that we will meet the high standards of the experimental model. Clients often need immediate help. Additionally, there are ethical concerns inherent in refusing clients an intervention because we wish to compare them with a group that is receiving service. We often must use quasi-experimental methods (i.e., experiments in natural social settings where some aspects of experimental design can be applied, albeit less rigorously than in a laboratory situation) rather than experimental methods. This is an inherent limitation with which we must live. In the next section, we will consider some of these issues.

PROBLEMS IN GENERALIZABILITY

As was mentioned earlier in this chapter, there is always a temptation to take evaluation results demonstrating a successful program and apply those results to other groups. We have also suggested that a program that is effective with a given group of clients may not work well with others. We often have no way of knowing if the clients we work with are representative of other clients. When we decide to evaluate our success with only a subset (sample) of the clients we have served, the potential for threats to generalizability to other client groups are obvious. Another potential challenge occurs when we attempt to generalize across different cultures. Highlight 8.3 provides recommendations for culturally competent research and evaluation.

One of the reasons that we attempt to obtain random samples when we survey people is that the mathematical characteristics of random samples allow us to infer from the sample to a larger population. A *random* *sample* is one in which all elements in a population have an equal probability of being included in the sample. An agency might wish to obtain a random sample of its clients. Staff can assign each client a different number and then use a table of random numbers to select those to be included in a sample. The idea is for the small subset of people being asked for information to resemble other people in the entire population as closely as possible.

HIGHLIGHT 8.3

Cultural Competence and Evaluation

Research and evaluation might seem like topics for which issues such as ethnic diversity and cultural competence have little relevance. However, an important role for evaluation and research is to help us capture the experiences of others and present a realistic picture of how things are as opposed to how we think they are. This reality can only be achieved when we respect and are aware of gender, cultural, racial, and ethnic differences. In the past, without this sensitivity, we have ended up with biased research. Biased research has led to assumptions about the life experiences of women based solely on the experiences of males. It has led to conclusions applied to members of all ethnic groups when the only subjects in the research study were Caucasians. It has fed stereotypes about many oppressed groups. The following are some ways in which cultural competence can be applied to our evaluation efforts (Marlow, 2011; Royce, Thyer, & Padgett, 2010; Yegidis & Weinbach, 2009):

1. Ensure that samples chosen for research accurately reflect the diversity and characteristics of the entire population. Men and women may have different experiences with our helping efforts and programs. Similarly, asking questions about respondents' sexual orientation may help us understand what impact programs have on gay and lesbian people.
2. Be sensitive to data-gathering approaches that may be less effective with some groups. Probing questions in interviews may be very threatening to individuals from cultures that prize privacy and saving face.
3. Recognize that language differences and lack of facility with English may place respondents from other cultures at a disadvantage in terms of understanding either written or oral interview questions.

4. Whenever possible, involve members of minority groups, people of color, women, and gay and lesbian people in the planning stages of research that affects them.
5. Recognize that questionnaires and other data sources that have worked well with men or white people may not work as well with women or people of color.
6. Use culturally sensitive language when developing instruments.
7. Where needed, use interpreters to ensure that respondents understand the question and the researcher understands the response. Minority interviewers may also be needed.
8. Avoid unnecessary emphasis on problems with oppressed populations. Focus on strengths to the extent possible.
9. Avoid generalizing findings to any other group than that represented in the study.
10. Look for differences among participants that may help explain differential outcomes. For example, do gender or ethnic differences affect the level of satisfaction with a particular program?
11. Ensure that all questions are gender neutral and not biased toward the life experiences of any particular group. For example, do not ask about employment unless you also leave an option for homemakers who are not employed outside the home.
12. When giving choices on questionnaires, make certain that you have not overlooked critical options such as ethnic group or forced choices that do not apply. For example, it may be better to allow respondents to check all cultural/racial groups with which they identify to avoid forced choices that are not truly relevant.

Sometimes, there are problems with this process. Let us say you wanted to know the views of all students majoring in social work. You decide to select a random sample of the majors and to use a questionnaire to gather their views. Although a random sample should result in a subset or group similar to all social work majors, you could end up with no males in the sample simply because males compose only about 12 percent of undergraduate social work majors. If you think that there may be a difference between males and females in the way they will answer the questionnaire, you might want to ensure that males will be proportionately represented in your sample. *Stratified random sampling* is a method of sampling that ensures some important subset or strata of a population (such as males) is not accidentally left out of a typical random sample. To create a stratified random sample, you must assign numbers to both male and female majors, and then, using a table of random numbers (located in most statistics texts, online [e.g., http://www.random.org], or generated using software such as Microsoft Excel), randomly select a proportionate number of males. If there are 100 social work majors and 88 percent are female, then 88 percent of your sample should also be female. There are a variety of other sampling methods that one may employ in the interests of ensuring that the sample is representative. A more detailed listing of these is included in Marlow (2011). Achieving a representative sample is essential if we hope to generalize the results of our evaluation.

WRONG CHOICES OF EVALUATION TOOLS

We have already noted that an evaluation instrument can be used inappropriately. Using a client satisfaction questionnaire to assess whether or not a program achieved its goal of reducing delinquent behavior is equivalent to hammering a screw into wood. The wrong tool is being used in both cases. The questionnaire is the wrong tool because the goal was to reduce delinquent behavior, not entertain adolescents. In this case, the most appropriate measure of success should include some means of assessing whether the level of delinquent behavior went up, down, or stayed the same. Asking the client if he liked the group home experience (client satisfaction questionnaire) is of little value. There is a possibility that he liked the group home very much because he learned some new techniques for burglarizing homes. Perhaps he has even become a more accomplished criminal as a result of this experience. As you might imagine, the use of inappropriate measurement systems is a potential

problem when agencies first begin to attempt evaluation of outcomes. A prime example of selecting the wrong evaluation tools involves attempts to prove the effectiveness of abstinence-only programs funded by both state and federal governments. These programs provide information to school-age children focused on encouraging them to refrain from sex but giving no instruction on other forms of prevention such as contraception. Contrary to the principle of using evidence-based programs, the policy to fund abstinence-only programs was chosen based on values promoted by various faith-based organizations and conservative political administrations. In an attempt to show that such programs work, the Bush administration decided that they would be evaluated based on factors such as teens' school attendance and their attitudes at the program's conclusion, neither of which are related to the question of whether abstinence-only programs are effective. Finally, when a study ordered by Congress was completed using outcomes such as abstinence from sex and similar factors, the results were disappointing. Findings indicate that

> programs had no statistically significant impact on eventual behavior. Based on data from the final follow-up survey, youth in the program group were no more likely to abstain from sex than their control group counterparts; among those who reported having had sex, program and control group youth had similar numbers of sexual partners and had initiated sex at the same mean age. Students who participated in these programs were just as likely to have sex as those who were not involved. Youth in the program group, however, were no more likely to have engaged in unprotected sex than their control group counterparts. Finally, there were no differences in potential consequences of teen sex, including pregnancies, births, and reported STDs. (Trenholm et al., 2007, p. 28)

An evidence-based approach would have saved federal and state governments hundreds of millions of dollars in wasted taxes.

FAILURE TO INVOLVE CLIENTS IN THE EVALUATION PROCESS

Ideally, clients should be involved in the evaluation process to the greatest extent possible. Doing research on clients without informing them is ethically wrong. Clients should be promised confidentiality. Only aggregate data omitting individual identification should be released. Clients' rights should be carefully protected. Moreover, client knowledge of the evaluation process may increase the effectiveness of the intervention and their level of satisfaction.

STAFF DISTRUST OF EVALUATION

We indicated earlier that many agencies do not routinely engage in evaluation of practice or programs. When a research effort is suggested, fear or distrust by those who will be evaluated is not uncommon. The agency's motives in asking for the evaluation may be questioned. Staff members may feel they are being criticized or condemned. Unless the agency can gain the trust of those being evaluated, the chances are likely that the process will be fraught with problems.

EVALUATION PROCESS INTERFERENCE WITH SERVICE PROVISION

Ideally, program evaluation should be accomplished in such a fashion that it does not interfere with providing service to clients. An effective management information system can make this process go more smoothly because much of the data needed can be computerized and retrieved with relative ease. If, on the other hand, clients must complete lengthy questionnaires after each session or maintain detailed logs between sessions, this evaluation may affect the intervention. Clients may find the process overly time-consuming or intrusive. They may cease coming or provide insufficient data to allow the purposes of the evaluation to be carried out. Similarly, data collection should be a manageable undertaking rather than overburdening the workers. If this situation happens, the evaluation process has begun to interfere with the service-provision process.

ALTERNATIVE EXPLANATIONS FOR PROGRAM OUTCOMES

When a client or program achieves the desired objectives, attributing the results to the intervention employed is tempting. The tendency to confuse two events, one following the other, with cause and effect is natural. This thinking implies that because one event precedes the other, it naturally caused the other—which is often not the case. Unfortunately, there are multiple explanations for the occurrence of any event. The outcomes of our interventions are no exception. Highlight 8.4 includes a partial list of such factors, many of which are also called threats to the interval validity of the study design. That is, they represent influences that can cloud or obscure the real reason that change occurred.

There are many other possible explanations for change that could confound the results of one's evaluation. Gibbs

(1991) and Yegidis and Weinbach (2009) have developed extensive lists and clear explanations of alternative or confounding causes. The important thing to remember is that multiple explanations may exist for changes that we observe following an intervention. These possible explanations should act as a caution to the worker evaluating the results of any intervention.

UNANTICIPATED CONSEQUENCES

Not infrequently, we discover that a program has had consequences or outcomes we did not envision. These may be categorized as either side effects or regressive effects. Further, some side effects may be classified as harmful to clients, and others may be neutral in their impact or beneficial. A person learning to be more assertive, for example, may adopt this new approach with an employer. The employer, unused to the employee's newfound assertiveness, reacts by firing the employee. This outcome might be viewed as a negative side effect of the client's assertiveness training. Another example involves a couple learning to communicate their needs more clearly to each other through a marriage enrichment program. They may discover that they really have incompatible goals in life. This leads them to a decision to divorce. This marriage enrichment program may then be seen as having an unintended impact on the couple's marriage.

Regressive effects, as the name implies, mean that a situation gets worse as a result of the intervention. An example or two should illustrate how regressive effects can happen. Mr. Jones was referred to a social worker by another social worker who was moving away. An assessment of Mr. Jones's situation had been made by the previous social worker and by the consulting psychiatrist. The primary symptom, as described in the record, was anxiety. During the first interview, the social worker noticed that the client was having trouble sleeping, had lost his appetite, and suffered from disinterest in his work. His relationship with his wife was also deteriorating. He was particularly anxious because his inability to concentrate at work was threatening his job. Mr. Jones had been receiving counseling about his anxiety and was taking tranquilizers prescribed by the psychiatrist. No one, it seemed, had recognized that Mr. Jones was suffering from depression. The medication prescribed for him was depressing him further. To make things even worse, he had been treated for the wrong problem.

Another example is drawn from the research on program effectiveness. The "scared straight" programs, in which juvenile delinquents are exposed to hardened

HIGHLIGHT 8.4

Alternate Explanations for Outcomes

Sometimes the outcomes we note in our evaluation have little or nothing to do with the intervention. These outcomes may be the result of other factors that we refer to as threats to validity. These include such things as history, maturation, mortality, creaming, regression toward the mean, and reactance, each of which are explained below.

- *History* is any event that occurs prior to the end of an intervention. Not infrequently, changes happening in the environment can affect the outcome of an intervention. For example, a 25 percent increase in the number of jobs in an area because of several companies expanding their workforce might explain why a job placement program was so successful. In the absence of these new jobs, the rate might have been quite different. There is also a possibility that the same number of unemployed people would have gotten jobs without the job placement program.

- *Maturation* is the process of aging. Sometimes, the results of an intervention can be attributed to changes being experienced by the subject. For example, most delinquent children reduce their delinquency as they age. A program that works with children from age 13 to 17 might be claiming success with its clients when the results may be more attributable to maturation.

- *Mortality* is the loss that occurs when some of the people in the sample begin to drop out. This explanation means that a select group is now being measured, and one cannot extrapolate from this group to the original population. Client self-selection is operating here in that clients themselves may have made the decision about whether or not to continue in a program. Ideally, a program ought to include as failures those who dropped out along the way rather than just those who stayed to the end without reaching their goals.

- *Creaming* is the tendency of some programs to take only the very best candidates for a program. One danger is that evaluating only the best may reflect significantly greater effectiveness than if all similar candidates in the population were included. Another danger is that perhaps these "best" candidates would have changed anyway. For example, many first-offender programs take those they consider good candidates for the program. Thus, they tend to bias the outcome. The selection of clients by the worker often creates a form of bias that can be quite powerful. Sometimes, workers are not aware they are selecting clients with specific characteristics.

- *Regression toward the mean* is the tendency for extreme scores to move toward the mean over time. This tendency occurs when those in the program were chosen because they varied greatly from the average. Take, for example, choosing all children with low scores on a self-esteem scale and exposing them to the treatment. This exposure will almost always result in their having higher scores the next time they are evaluated using the same scale. This is the result of a mathematical or statistical tendency for high scores to move toward the mean (or average) on subsequent testing. Scores far from a mean may be the result of statistical error, and a second testing would produce a score more in line with the expected mean.

- *Reactance* is the reaction or change of behavior that occurs simply because of a new situation or environment. Reactance occurs when people are merely reacting to something new. As soon as people get used to the situation, their reactions change, or they revert to former ways of behaving. Think about how you and your family interact when a stranger is present versus when you are alone together. Often one behaves differently because of the presence of an observer. Typically, the presence of a new treatment (or worker) may produce something of a honeymoon effect, where people begin to act naturally only after they are comfortable with the new situation. Evaluation results may be skewed (distorted) because people are acting unnaturally and will return to their old behavior after they get used to the presence of the worker or the treatment.

In program evaluation, one might be able to control some of these variables by comparing the results of the program with other situations where the program is not being used. This process is an attempt to create a control group of sorts and to use the experimental method of research. For example, the results of a first-offender diversion program in a city of 50,000 might be compared with the recidivism rate of first offenders in a city of comparable size that lacks such a program.

criminals at maximum-security prisons, have been extremely popular in the United States. The goal of these programs is to scare the delinquent youth into a law-abiding life. Adolescents are brought to a prison, and experienced criminals verbally threaten them and graphically suggest what their fate will be should they continue their delinquent behavior. Surely such a program would be effective, as it would bring delinquents face-to-face with the future consequences of their actions. Unfortunately, research on the scared straight program indicates that "controls" (i.e., delinquents who did not go through this program) committed fewer delinquencies than those who participated in the program (Petrosino, Turpin-Petrosino, Hollis-Peel, & Lavenberg, 2013). In addition, the offenses the controls committed were less serious than offenses committed by delinquents who had been "treated" in this program.

The important thing to keep in mind is that some of our efforts to help may have the opposite effect. Unintended consequences sometimes occur despite our best intentions. Finally, interventions that are effective for one client may not work as well with others. Gibbs (1991) has provided an excellent set of guidelines for practitioners tempted to use untested interventions or approaches that have limited research support.

Attempting to identify the factors that cause harmful side effects and modify the program accordingly is important. Offering clients help in overcoming negative experiences arising from prior agency contact is also important.

The completion of the evaluation phase leads to one of two conclusions. Either the client system has achieved the goals previously identified, or goals have not been reached. If the goals have not been attained, the worker needs to explore with the client whether or not continued intervention will be helpful. If both parties decide that continued work is needed, this decision may lead to a new process of planned change. If goals have been reached or there are other reasons for concluding the intervention, we then enter the termination phase of the helping process.

LO 8-5 Facilitate Transitions and Endings (Termination) for Clients

Termination and Follow-Up

EP 2.1.10I

Termination is the end of the professional social worker–client relationship. All relationships between social workers and clients must eventually come to an end. The ending may be scheduled or

unexpected, successful or unsuccessful. Despite the circumstances of the ending, the worker must be prepared to manage this phase of the planned change process. To do this phase effectively, social workers need knowledge and skill in two areas: termination and follow-up (see Figure 8.8). The tasks of termination are similar whether we are working with an individual, a family or group, a community, or an organization. This portion of the chapter focuses on the knowledge and skills needed for effectively concluding the professional social worker–client relationship.

ETHICAL PRACTICE AND CRITICAL THINKING ABOUT TERMINATION

The NASW *Code of Ethics* provides guidance about when social workers may terminate services to clients. The *Code of Ethics* is described in more detail in Chapter 11. Provisions of the *Code* require termination when services are no longer needed or serving a client's interests. Termination should not occur precipitously, and the worker should always arrange continued service through referral when this is indicated. Of course, termination, when it occurs, should be done for reasons relating to client needs and not based upon worker needs. The *Code* does allow termination of a client who fails to pay for services when payment is a clear condition of service and the consequences of ending the relationship have been thoroughly explored with the client.

Termination must be based upon clear evidence that the goals and objectives have been achieved. Gut-level feelings or impressions on the part of the worker do not represent a solid basis for such judgment. The worker is also obligated to use critical thinking skills at this stage of the planned change process. Assisting the client in considering if termination is appropriate given actual progress is helpful. For example, a client may feel immediately better in the early stages of work with a practitioner and come to believe that her problems are now manageable. The worker can help her analyze her reactions and challenge unwarranted assumptions. Consider a client victimized by her partner's battery. She might assume that her spouse's sudden change of heart and contrition are evidence that she no longer needs to be involved in a support group for domestic violence survivors. The worker can help her assess whether this assumption is grounded in fact or hope.

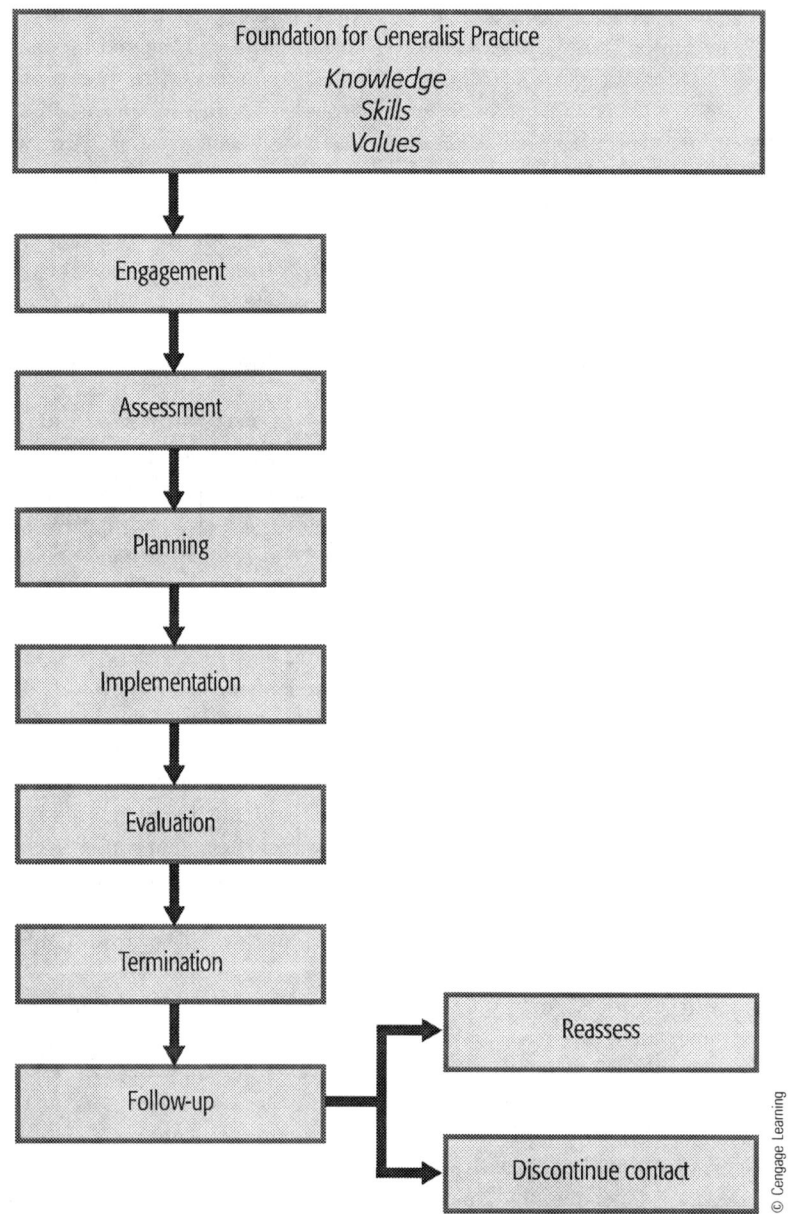

FIGURE 8.8 Planned Change Steps in the Generalist Intervention Model (GIM)

Critical Thinking Questions 8.3

Using the example of the client who has been the victim of a partner's battery (mentioned previously):

- What information might be presented to the client regarding her partner's change of heart and sudden contrition?

- Assuming you present this information and the client still elects to terminate, to what might you attribute her decision?

TERMINATING PROFESSIONAL RELATIONSHIPS

As stated previously, all professional relationships must terminate (end) at some point. When a client no longer needs service, the relationship will expectedly come to an end. However, not all terminations occur as one might hope. Sometimes, terminations occur unexpectedly and for reasons that the worker could not have predicted. Being aware of these possibilities and prepared to act professionally in any case is important for a social worker.

In this section we will look at several issues: the tasks of termination; timing and preparing for termination; reasons for termination; typical reactions to the termination phase; and making appropriate referrals.

TASKS OF TERMINATION

Termination of the closing phase of the planned change process involves a number of concrete steps. Hepworth, Rooney, Rooney, and Strom-Gottfried (2013) and Toseland and Rivas (2012) identify a similar set of tasks that the generalist worker and client system must undertake during the termination process. These tasks include the following:

1. *Deciding when to terminate the professional worker–client relationship.* Sometimes, we know from the onset exactly when the relationship between worker and client system will end. Members of an educational group designed to last for six sessions know precisely when the last meeting will be held. The hospital social worker helping a client being discharged tomorrow morning also knows exactly when their professional relationship will end. In other situations, the ending point will be determined depending on when the intervention's objectives have been achieved. Sometimes, the ending can be anticipated; other times it may not.

2. *Evaluating achievement of objectives.* One key task is evaluating whether or not the agreed-upon objectives have been achieved. Termination may occur when the desired outcomes have occurred or when further progress is no longer possible. An appropriate activity for the worker is summarizing achievements and helping the client system recognize growth.

3. *Maintaining and continuing progress.* The accomplishments that the worker and client system achieved in the helping process must be maintained following termination. The shy, introverted youth who became more outgoing in the group must maintain this assertiveness outside of the protected group environment. Similarly, the neighborhood association that successfully lobbied the police department for more foot patrols must continue its involvement and community-building activities. If it does not, things may begin to slip as other police priorities occur. Sometimes this is called generalizing or stabilizing the change effort.

4. *Resolving emotional reactions of the worker and client.* Reactions to termination can range from sorrow to relief or from a sense of loss to an antic-

ipation of increased freedom. Both worker and client may have emotional reactions that need to be recognized, discussed, and resolved.

5. *Making appropriate referrals.* When the termination process indicates that clients need additional help, the worker must make appropriate referrals. These referrals can be made to a specific individual such as a psychiatrist or to an agency providing the type of help clients need.

Ultimately, the goal at termination is to empower the client system. This empowerment means that clients will learn to use their own resources (instead of those of the social worker) to manage future difficulties they may encounter. Empowerment is the real importance of stabilizing the change effort. Later in this chapter we will discuss each component of termination. Evaluation has already been discussed.

As you can see, there is considerable agreement about the activities that must be undertaken as a relationship ends. One of the first steps, however, is to decide when to terminate. We will look at this topic next.

PLANNED TERMINATIONS

As has been suggested, one can easily predict that a worker–client relationship will eventually conclude. Thus, that the worker will consider the timing of the termination as an important part of the helping relationship is expected. Determining when to terminate is one of the most important tasks the worker must accomplish.

Frequently, an ending point is identified at the start of the professional relationship. For example, in task-centered practice situations, the sessions are expected to continue for some set time period and then conclude. Let us look at a family that contracts to see a social worker for six weekly sessions. The family (and the worker) expect that the professional relationship will end after the sixth week. Similarly, consider the situation of a school social worker who is helping to develop an individualized educational plan for a child with learning difficulties. She knows that the relationship will terminate following the end of the school year. The timing of the termination in each of these examples can reasonably be predicted in advance, and, by definition, these are planned terminations.

UNPLANNED TERMINATIONS

Unfortunately, not all terminations can be planned for, and many are unexpected. Terminations may also occur for reasons not under the control of either client or worker. Some terminations occur because no progress has been made or because problems are getting worse, not better. Lack of progress may be due to a misunderstanding between client and worker, incorrect or misinterpreted data, or an incorrect definition of the problem. Perhaps the wrong problem was selected for intervention, the goals selected were not attainable, or the alternative selected was inappropriate. Maybe the wrong intervention was made. In other situations, the expectations placed on the client by the worker–client contract are too demanding, too complicated, or too simple. Sometimes, unexpected negative consequences of a change effort require premature termination. Likewise, termination may be appropriate when there are relationship difficulties between client and worker.

Still other situations may bring about termination before either party would prefer. For instance, a school social worker may not continue seeing a client during the summer. Another example is a field practicum student who ends her placement while the client continues with the agency. Sometimes the worker must terminate with a client who is being referred to another worker or specialist. Additionally, a client may simply quit coming without notifying the worker. Sometimes when the area being probed is too sensitive and clients cannot tolerate opening the matter up, they may terminate early. Some clients end their sessions because the feelings associated with ending are too painful to discuss. (We will discuss some typical feelings about endings in a later section.) Others simply drop out because terminating their sessions appears to them to be a way of controlling the ending. In other words, by taking the first step of quitting, they avoid the pain and discomfort of dealing with the end of a relationship. This situation is a bit like a person who quits her job because she anticipates getting fired anyway. Finally, some clients drop out because they are dissatisfied or lack the resources to continue. Highlight 8.5 illustrates some reasons for unplanned terminations in groups.

OTHER POINTS ABOUT TERMINATION

Clearly, professional relationships can end for many reasons. Some of those reasons are under the control of the worker, and others are not. Some can be anticipated, and others cannot. What is most important is that the worker recognizes that unplanned terminations are fairly common. Whenever possible, the worker should plan for terminations and involve the client in that process.

If a client drops out prematurely (in the worker's opinion), attempting to discover reasons for the client's actions is appropriate for the worker. Perhaps this effort will result in the client returning, perhaps not. Still, it is part of one's professional responsibility to follow up on a client who has terminated early. Ultimately, the client's right to self-determination must guide the worker. That is, the bottom line is that clients have the right to quit if they want. Given the goal of helping the client become self-sufficient and less dependent upon the worker, it may even be a positive sign when clients decide they no longer need the worker's help.

REACTIONS AND FEELINGS IN TERMINATIONS

Feelings and reactions about termination are a somewhat controversial topic. Many authors spend a great

---

HIGHLIGHT 8.5

Unplanned Terminations in Groups

Group members may leave a group prematurely for any number of reasons. These may include any of the following factors:

1. Lack of motivation;
2. Changes in life that reduce interest in the group (such as moving, family death, and the like);
3. Problems with group meeting schedules;
4. Feeling out of place in the group;
5. Inability to form appropriate relationships with other group members;
6. Discomfort with strong feelings expressed in the group;
7. Insufficient orientation to therapy;
8. Feeling scapegoated in the group;
9. Problems arising from concurrent individual and group therapy;
10. Lack of financial resources to continue in the group; and
11. Satisfaction with current changes that have occurred.

deal of time declaring that clients experience a significant sense of loss when the relationship with the worker comes to an end. Other researchers have come to opposite conclusions. We shall try to include both perspectives here. Each is based on significant clinical and empirical research.

Extent and Range of Emotional Reactions

Several factors determine the extent to which clients experience given feelings about the termination process. For example, open-ended relationships in which the client and worker have had an extensive, ongoing professional association are more likely to result in stronger emotional reactions (Hepworth et al., 2013). Educationally focused groups likely experience weaker emotional reactions than is true for therapy groups. Task groups (such as committees) frequently experience endings as positive. Members may even feel relieved that their job is done.

Client reactions to terminations are affected by a variety of things. These include the nature of the problem, the duration and intensity of contact, whether the ending was natural or forced, client strengths and support systems, whether goals were achieved or not, and whether or not the termination ends service or results from the client being transferred to another worker. Generally, a client system's sense of loss is directly related to the extent to which the relationship focused on personal problems (such as depression, anxiety) as opposed to environmental issues (such as housing).

Amount of Contact

In some situations, the amount of contact between client and worker is so limited that even the concept of termination seems inappropriate. The hospital social worker who simply arranges for a client to get a hospital bed in her home while she recovers from a broken hip may terminate after only one or two short contacts with the client. There has often been such a limited degree of relationship building that perhaps the client's only reaction would be gratitude.

Size and Type of System

Similarly, the size and type of system one is working with will have some bearing on the reactions to termination. For example, remember the worker who helped the community of Clearwater described in Chapter 4. He had helped the community identify a number of major problems and come to consensus on those of greatest priority. He also left the community with several functioning task groups, each aimed at coping with an identified problem. Thus, he ended his work and moved on to other projects needing his help. The degree of dependency and level of self-disclosure in this relationship were quite low. The relationship had spanned a relatively short period of time. The issues dealt with were related to conditions in the community, not the personal lives of the clients. Reactions of those with whom he had worked were positive, and the amount of emotional content was limited.

Contrast the termination described in the preceding section to that found in the termination of a one-to-one relationship between a worker and a client recovering from depression. In the latter situation, the client and worker have been together for over 9 months. The client has talked with the worker about a variety of personal issues. Subsequently, he has gradually developed increased self-confidence and feelings of well-being. Because the nature of the relationship has become so intense from the client's perspective, ending it is likely to be emotionally charged. Table 8.7 summarizes factors affecting reactions to termination.

TABLE 8.7 Factors Affecting Reactions to Termination

Factors Likely to Produce More Intense Reactions	Factors Likely to Produce Less Intense Reactions
Open-ended relationships	Time-limited relationships
Frequent worker–client contact	Infrequent worker–client contact
Personal-problem-focused involvement	Environmental-problem-focused involvement
Absence of other client support systems	Presence of other client support systems
Individual or family client system	Organizational or community client system
High level of emotional content	Low level of emotional content
Treatment groups	Task groups

Mixed Feelings

Mixed feelings often characterize the conclusion of professional relationships. The ending of any relationship in which strong emotional sharing has occurred can be bittersweet. A sense of loss is common. Some clients also experience anger and feelings of rejection in these situations. Others feel pride, satisfaction, optimism, and a sense of achievement or mastery because of what they have accomplished. Some clients report that old problems, long since overcome, reappear. New problems sometimes develop. At other times, clients object to the relationship ending, claiming they are not ready yet. Still others will deny that the end is approaching or that they have any feelings about the upcoming event, distancing themselves from the inevitable. Some clients report feeling abandoned or rejected when the relationship comes to an end. Others feel sad or hurt or sometimes angry. These feelings may reflect such things as fear of the future or insecurity about whether the gains achieved can be maintained.

Roe, Dekel, Harel, Fennig, and Fennig (2006) found that many clients do not routinely experience negative feelings at termination. Reactions to even intense client–worker interaction are mixed, with some clients experiencing joy and pride while others had more negative feelings. Positive reactions were most often associated with looking forward to independence, practitioner openness to client returning if needed, positive growth that occurred in the client–worker relationship, and careful processing of the termination. Negative reactions of clients were more often associated with poor quality of the termination process, loss of a relationship with the practitioner, and/or feelings of disappointment, dissatisfaction, and failure. In summary, although there is potential for strong termination feelings to exist, the worker should not assume that all clients will experience the same reactions.

LO 8-6 Practice Personal Reflection and Self-Correction Regarding Termination

Worker Reactions to Termination

Interestingly, clients are not the only ones who have the potential to experience strong feelings at termination. Social workers themselves sometimes experience reactions to the end of a professional relationship. The extent and intensity of those feelings is likely to be controlled by the same set of factors previously described. In other words, workers are subject to the same potential feelings as clients, depending upon a variety of factors. Social workers need to be sufficiently self-reflective to recognize when these feelings occur and manage their reactions in a professional manner. Social workers may feel a sense of disappointment, loss, or guilt. Baum (2007) found that worker reactions could be quite strong and difficult, especially if it was the client who initiated the termination. Positive worker reactions to termination were more likely in the following situations:

- When terminations were gradual
- When workers felt a significant degree of control over the termination process
- When the worker–client relationship was important to both parties
- When change goals had been attained
- When the worker wanted the termination
- When workers felt they had control over termination

Sometimes it is helpful for workers to engage in a bit of self-disclosure around their own reactions to termination. Such sharing may free clients to address their own reactions to the termination. On the other hand, workers who are having trouble dealing with their own reactions ought to discuss this with a trusted supervisor or colleague. Seeking assistance in such instances is an appropriate use of supervision and can help the social worker engage in self-correction to better manage these emotional reactions. Inability to manage one's own reactions can interfere with the worker's ability to help the clients with this transition task.

LO 8-7 Help Clients Resolve Problems Concerning Termination

HELPING CLIENTS AT TERMINATION

One positive characteristic of termination is that it can always be anticipated. The exact timing of termination may vary but, like death and taxes, it will not go away. Usually, the worker can help clients at the termination point, and this section will look at a number of techniques for doing

Planning for Termination

Perhaps the most important way in which the worker can help a client at termination is to ensure that the topic of termination is addressed early in the relationship, preferably at the beginning. Planning for the termination and discussing it with the client will help reduce emotional attachment of the client to the worker and any resulting dependency. It also helps to temper the sense of loss we have already described. In time-limited interventions, termination is expected to occur at some specified point. A group that has planned to meet for seven sessions knows at the start when termination will occur. Residents of a halfway house may be told initially that they must move back into the community at the end of 9 months.

The worker can help this process along by reminding the client about the approaching date of termination. Ideally, this should occur several sessions before the last meeting. The worker should leave time in later sessions to talk about termination, especially when termination is occurring earlier than expected. This situation might happen when the worker moves out of the geographical area or the agency discontinues a particular program.

LO 8-8 Select Appropriate Termination Strategies for Client Systems

Addressing Feelings about Termination

As discussed earlier, terminations often produce feelings for both client and worker. One task for the worker is to help the client express any feelings associated with termination. The worker might say: "You've seemed a bit sadder the last two times we've met. I wonder what you're feeling." Another way to raise the issue is through what is known as the "generalized other." The worker might state: "Some of the other boys who have left here have said they felt good about leaving. Others said they thought it had been a waste of time. How about you?" Here, the worker lets the client know that other persons in the same situation have felt a certain way. He also invites the client to share his own reactions, which may or may not be similar.

Sometimes, sharing the worker's own feelings about the approaching termination can be helpful. For example, consider a practitioner who has been working with a 15-year-old adolescent. For a year, the boy has been living in a residential treatment center for adolescents with problems related to delinquency or behavior disorders. He was admitted to this center after a history of criminal behavior in his home community. Nearing the boy's release and the coinciding termination of the worker–client relationship, the worker might say, "You're going to be finishing the program at the center in another couple of weeks. I want you to know that I feel very good about how hard you've worked here.

I also want you to know that I'm going to miss you." In this way, the worker reminds the client of the upcoming termination and shares his own feelings about it. Frequently, this type of modeling by the worker is especially important for clients who have been socialized not to share feelings. It is through this kind of patient, sensitive work that the worker helps the client to address feelings about the ending process. Highlight 8.6 addresses termination feelings in groups and families.

Summarizing Progress

One of the important tasks of the termination phase is to recognize client accomplishments or achievements. Let us take the example of the boy mentioned in the previous paragraph. The worker might broach the topic of client growth by asking the client to summarize his progress over the time they have worked together. He might ask, "Can you remember back when you first came here? You wouldn't even talk to me. Now you've progressed from Step 1 all the way to Step 10, the highest level in the cottage. What's made the difference between the old Pat and the new?" This question helps the client begin to identify the areas of growth that have occurred. It focuses attention on positive experiences and helps to increase the client's sense of accomplishment.

The techniques of planning for termination, uncovering termination-related feelings, and summarizing progress are three primary activities of the termination phase. Equally important, however, is ensuring that changes occurring during an intervention will be sustained after the relationship ends. The stabilization of change process will be discussed next.

LO 8-9 Implement Prevention Interventions to Ensure Maintenance of Change

STABILIZATION OF CHANGE

There is sufficient evidence that changes that occur in the context of therapeutic relationships do not necessarily carry over into the other areas of a client's existence. Changes that have occurred in individual behavior, for example, may not generalize to other situations in a client's life. The young woman who stops using drugs while in a treatment program is going to find it much harder to maintain this drug-free state when she returns to her old friends. Ultimately, the goal is that change in one area carries over into all others.

HIGHLIGHT 8.6

Termination Feelings of Family and Group Members

Reactions to termination may vary in groups and families as well as among individual clients. For example, continuing members of a group may react to the departure of another member with guilt or anger. They may also raise questions about the value of the group, thereby challenging the leader.

Loss of several group members may ultimately result in the group ending because of an insufficient number of members. This situation is the ultimate threat to a group. Family members will still have each other to rely on after a family therapy session concludes. However, a group composed of unrelated adults from a large community is unlikely to offer members this degree of continuity. The latter may have lost a significant social support system. A family, on the other hand, continues to perform this supportive function. Members of contrived groups will have different reactions than members of family groups. However, recognizing that individual family members may each have their own reactions to the loss of an important worker–client relationship is important (Grant, 2000).

Toseland and Rivas (2012) suggest seven things that workers can do to help clients maintain and generalize changes:

1. *Helping clients select relevant and appropriate situations to work on.* This selection can be accomplished by helping the client select important problems or concerns to work on. For example, focusing on a client's job-seeking skills when the primary problem is unemployment would make sense. Although other issues (e.g., marital relationships, parenting skills, and so on) might be important, they are not as relevant to the basic problem of being out of work.

2. *Helping clients build confidence in their own abilities.* One of the ways the worker can assist is through helping clients review their work together. This review focuses on achievement of goals and sets the stage to talk about the future. Clients leaving a professional relationship often need reassurance. Discussing the client's progress can help to boost self-confidence.

3. *Using multiple situations and settings when helping members learn new behaviors.* Clients learning new skills and behaviors should be given multiple opportunities to use these. For example, people learning to be more assertive should be given the assignment to practice this with family, friends, coworkers, and strangers. The more situations in which the client can successfully employ a newfound skill, the greater the likelihood the skill will be used following termination.

4. *Using naturally occurring consequences rather than creating artificial ones.* Ultimately, clients will be confronted with the real world without the support of the social worker. To ensure that they are eventually prepared, clients need to be given every opportunity to practice their new behaviors in natural settings. For example, a client who is trying to improve his communication skills should eventually practice these skills in the real world. Away from the supportive environment of the worker or group, the client experiences the barriers encountered when people try to change their own behaviors. A client who can be assertive only in the assertiveness training group has benefited little from the group experience.

5. *Extending treatment through use of follow-up sessions.* Follow-up contacts between client and worker often serve as "boosters" to help clients maintain their changes over time. Whether the focus is on weight loss, learning new parenting skills, or becoming more assertive, follow-up sessions remind clients that others remain concerned about their progress. Seeing the worker or other group members may rekindle clients' dedication to their goals or reinforce efforts to maintain their growth.

6. *Reducing setbacks in other environments such as school, the workplace, or the home.* Sometimes clients' progress is undermined by other aspects of their environment. An example could be the student who is too easily influenced by his peers and gets into delinquent behavior when around them.

To help the client keep his distance from these "friends," the worker might enlist the help of parents or school officials. If multiple figures in the boy's life are working in concert to encourage and maintain positive behavior, the chances that the changes will last are more likely.

7. *Helping members confront future problems by teaching them a problem-solving process.* Finally, most clients must learn to live without the worker's regular support and encouragement. One way of reducing dependency is to teach clients the same planned change approach the worker uses. Once clients learn to confront problems from this framework, many seemingly insurmountable problems disappear. At the very least, the clients learn a system that can be used effectively in most areas of their lives. In essence, as the worker you are trying to put yourself out of business by teaching clients what you know. The goal is often to teach them practical planned change skills. Ideally, they will no longer need you and will be able to accomplish goals by themselves.

Stabilizing Change in Small Groups

Most of the approaches described earlier will work as well with small groups as with individuals. However, there are techniques that are especially effective with groups of various sizes. For example, many community-based programs take clients through a series of ever-increasing steps to independence. These steps finally culminate in the client's return to the community with a minimum of formal supervision. A shelter for battered women, for example, operates a halfway house in addition to the shelter itself. Many clients, after staying in the shelter for a period of time, are ready to move into a more independent living arrangement. At this point, the client may elect to move to the halfway house and remain there until she is able to make it on her own. The halfway house serves as a transition between the shelter and full return to the community. It also gradually reduces the role of the shelter staff so that clients do not become overly dependent on them for help.

There are still other effective strategies when working with client groups. One such technique involves varying the use of group activities. For example, in the early stages of a group, having members engage in activities that are group-building in nature (e.g., enhancing warmth and trust) is common. Thus, clients may be asked to do icebreaking activities such as having members interview each other and introduce the interviewee to the group. The icebreaker is designed to increase the "we" feeling of the group.

Conversely, group activities can be used to decrease this "we" feeling. For example, the leader may choose group activities that foster independence and reduce group cohesion. Take the members of an adolescent girls' group that has spent several weeks learning and practicing how to express their feelings to one another. In the last couple of sessions, the worker has asked the members to begin describing the ways their new communication skills are affecting relationships with parents and peers. By asking the members to focus their attention away from the group, the worker is helping to reconnect them with the larger environment in which they live.

Sometimes, groups plan ceremonies to help intensify the sense of ending and to acknowledge the client's progress in a program. Group homes for chemically dependent clients frequently have "graduation" ceremonies as clients prepare to leave the shelter of the group home environment.

Stabilizing Change in Large Systems

The guidelines previously described work well with individuals, families, and groups. However, additional approaches are needed when stabilizing change in communities and organizations. Timberlake, Zajicek-Farber, and Sabatino, (2008) suggest the importance of stabilization of change for work with large systems and provide some important suggestions, as discussed next.

Routinize Procedures and Processes. One of the goals when attempting to change large systems is to ensure that whatever is accomplished continues indefinitely. One way this goal is accomplished is for procedures and processes to become routine. For example, let us recall the case of the city of Algoma noted in Chapter 4. Algoma had no system for ensuring that neighbors would be notified when major zoning and land-use proposals affecting them came before the city council. The absence of a procedure for notifying residents about proposed changes in their neighborhood was a continual problem. The adoption of an ordinance (really, a policy) requiring notification by mail guaranteed residents the opportunity to be heard. This ordinance stabilized the desired change.

Clarification of Policies and Procedures. One way to help stabilize change in larger systems is to ensure that newly created policies and procedures are clear. Sometimes, individuals have "understandings" about what was decided or agreed upon. Later, no one can seem to recall exactly what was decided, or there is a major disagreement regarding what really transpired. To avoid this situation, you can follow the old bureaucratic adage and "put it in writing." Policies and procedures that are written down are less likely to be affected by faulty memories.

One approach is to use "memorandums of understanding." These are nothing more than memos or letters that restate in written form what has been agreed to verbally. Let us say the officer of an organization has verbally told you the organization will contribute $5,000 toward a new recreation program in your community. You could confirm this agreement by writing the person a letter reiterating what he has told you and thanking him for the organization's generosity. For example, you might simply state, "Thank you so much for your $5,000 pledge toward our new recreation program. Your generosity is very much appreciated." This "memorandum of understanding" is just a technique formalizing informal policies, agreements, or procedures. It helps prevent problems later on when people's memories become a bit ragged.

On the same note, if a new policy is agreed to, the sooner it is entered into the organization's policy manual, the better. Most social agencies have manuals containing their policies and operating procedures. These manuals are important documents because they control what workers can and cannot do. The same is true for most large organizations. Policies that are articulated in policy manuals are more likely to be followed than those that are unwritten.

Reducing the Influence of the Change Agent. There is another way to help maintain change and to increase the client system's opportunities to operate independently, namely, to reduce the worker's and agency's influence. This method is often accomplished by reducing the frequency and intensity of contact between the worker and client systems. The worker in Clearwater gradually reduced the frequency of his attendance at many of the ad hoc committee meetings. Eventually, local members of the community took leadership of the committees, and the worker's role became one of consultation. Finally, even this role was dropped as the indigenous leaders developed confidence and skill in leading their committees. The worker had deliberately reduced his level of involvement to facilitate the development of natural community leaders. In this way, positive changes would be maintained on an ongoing basis.

Addressing Ongoing Needs of Clients

The worker in the termination phase of the helping process must attend to the ongoing needs of the client system. We have already touched on the importance of discussing with the client resources for future needs. Letting the client know that the worker and agency remain available should future help be required might also be helpful. The worker should probably not offer to extend service without clearly knowing that a specific goal can be reached. This method prevents the client from becoming overly dependent upon the worker or agency. Still, keeping the door open for the client is important. If the termination is occurring prematurely, letting the client know of the worker's and agency's availability is especially important. The worker might say, "Denise, I know that you believe we have accomplished what you initially wanted to. I, too, feel we have come a long way. I think we were beginning to get into some other areas that don't seem so critical to you right now. I respect your right to bring this phase of our work together to a close. Still, I want you to know that I am available if you decide you would like additional help." The goal here is to ensure a continued good relationship between the agency and client. Thus, the client can return should she need to.

If necessary, referrals to other service organizations or persons may be made. Referrals should always be made to specific persons, if possible. In some situations, you may decide contacting the new agency while you and the client are together is best. This way there is no confusion about what was said. Be sure to check if the client can get to the new service provider and to give written directions if necessary. Because of the possibility of clients falling between the cracks, reminding clients to let you know if there are any problems receiving needed services from the new agency is usually helpful. Chapter 15 discusses the referral process in more detail.

Our effort to stabilize change in the client system is a prevention activity designed to forestall future problems. To the extent that we can strengthen the client's skills and capacity to manage challenges that lie ahead, we are helping to prevent the need for further assistance. At the same time, by offering assurances that the client can return as needed, we also demonstrate our willingness to intervene before the challenges become crises. This helps prevent or ameliorate future problems.

LO 8-10 Engage in Follow-Up Activities with Client Systems

Client Follow-Up

Social work research on the follow-up of clients who are no longer receiving intervention does not paint a positive picture. Too many clients do not maintain the changes that occurred during the intervention phase. There are several reasons for this outcome (Hepworth et al., 2013). One reason may be because going back to previous ways of doing things is easier than to continue the new behavior. Another reason is that the environment is not supportive of the new changes. Peers, friends, family, and the environment may all exert influences that undercut the new behaviors. Sometimes, failure occurs because the new behavior was not established long enough to become the norm. That clients who spend significant periods of time working on a problem are later unable to continue the gains they made is unfortunate. In this next section, we look at one method for dealing with this problem, namely, follow-up.

Follow-up is the act of acquiring information about a client following termination. It is usually focused on how the client is functioning in those areas that originally brought the client in for assistance. In other words, follow-up with a client involves learning how the client is doing after your mutual formal relationship has ended. Social workers frequently do not make efforts to follow up on their work with clients after the point of termination. This occurs because workers are too busy and often overloaded with other cases needing immediate attention.

There are, however, a number of reasons for doing follow-up. One involves finding out if the client is functioning without intervention. Another reason concerns offering whatever assistance is needed if the client is having difficulty. Generally the help workers can provide fall into the following scenarios listed in Highlight 8.7.

Follow-up can also help determine whether an intervention worked. Possible intervention outcomes that may be discovered during follow-up include:

1. The client may be functioning at the same level in follow-up as at termination. That is, there would be no clinically or statistically significant changes from termination to follow-up.
2. The client may have shown more improvement since termination. This may be attributable to an improvement trend that commenced before termination, a delayed intervention effort, or to other nonintervention factors that might have been responsible for improvement.
3. There may be a gradual deterioration that is a result of premature withdrawal of the intervention or of other unknown factors.
4. Rather than a gradual deterioration, there may be a complete relapse. An example is a recovered addict who is drug-free for a long period but relapses on one occasion and then resumes her former drug habit.

For some clients, the follow-up contact acts like a booster shot, increasing the effectiveness of the previous intervention. Contact by the worker reminds clients that others are interested in their success. The follow-up visit may help clients overcome a temporary hurdle or suggest the need for an additional intervention. In some types of interventions (e.g., task-centered), the follow-up is a planned part of the intervention. Both the worker and client are aware that the follow-up will occur.

Ideally, follow-up sessions should be discussed during the intervention. The inclusion of discussions about follow-up during the intervention itself may help explain the relatively high success rate for task-centered approaches. Follow-up becomes a normal part of the intervention and extends the amount of contact between client and worker.

DOING THE FOLLOW-UP

Agency protocol may establish a specific period at which follow-up contacts with clients are made as well as the process to follow. This protocol may include a letter asking the client to come in or a phone call from the worker. Reminding clients that a follow-up will occur is most helpful during the final sessions prior to termination. The purpose of follow-up, namely, checking on client progress, should be explained. Follow-up sessions are typically less formal than the ongoing sessions. They represent a time to catch up with the client's situation, to determine how things are going, and to glean additional insights into aspects of the professional relationship. For example, the client may be asked to identify worker actions or program activities that were more or less helpful in resolving the issues that brought the client in for assistance. Client suggestions and input following a few weeks or months of reflection may be more valuable than observations made in the termination process. Additional assistance may be provided for the client who indicates

HIGHLIGHT 8.7

Possible Tasks for the Worker at Follow-Up

1. *Advocate for and represent the client.* This representation may be necessary when a client is getting the runaround from an agency or organization. The worker may have to intervene personally (by phone or face-to-face) to ensure that the client receives reasonably timely assistance.

2. *Review and discuss problems.* Find out why the client is having trouble. Was the referral made to the wrong agency? Did the client present him- or herself in a manner that contributed to being denied assistance? Are these critical needs that are still not being met?

3. *Problem-solve to overcome difficulties.* Once the problems encountered by the client have been discussed, identifying means to overcome them may be possible. Perhaps the client was not eligible for a service or benefit and another resource can be found. Maybe the client made a mistake on the intake application that resulted in being declared ineligible.

   Often these matters can be straightened out with minimal assistance from the worker. At other times, intervening directly with the targeted agency will be necessary for the worker. There may even be situations where the worker must involve his or her supervisor. An example would be when Agency A refuses to qualify the client even though the worker's supervisor specifically suggested the client contact Agency A in the first place. Perhaps the worker's supervisor was incorrect about Agency A's being able to help. Often, the worker's supervisor will have to

contact his or her counterpart at Agency A to get that agency to reconsider its decision regarding the client.

   Another example involves a client's complaint to her worker that tenants in neighborhood rental units were parking cars on the front lawn of their duplex. She felt the parked cars were unsightly and contributed to the decline of the neighborhood. Seeing this mess during a home visit, the worker suggested to the client that she call the police and report the situation. The police told the client they were reluctant to enforce the ordinance. They hesitated to get involved in an area they considered to be the responsibility of the building inspector. The worker discussed the situation with his supervisor. The supervisor then telephoned the city manager with whom he had a good relationship. Within hours, the police department began enforcing the city ordinance. This is a good example of how involving relevant others and using good contacts can straighten out a perplexing difficulty.

4. *Prepare the consumer.* Perhaps clients will need to return to an agency or organization with which they have already had unpleasant experiences. What should clients expect on this visit? How will they respond to agency personnel? Will they be uncomfortable? It may be necessary to role-play with clients' future contacts with the agency. In this way, various scenarios can be anticipated.

---

that unresolved problems exist or who recognizes new issues. That assistance may be provided by the same worker or through referral to other practitioners or agencies.

OVERCOMING BARRIERS TO FOLLOW-UP

As we have noted earlier, a major barrier to doing follow-up is the heavy workload carried by many workers. Though this problem is real, there are ways to get around it. When a caseload is too high to follow up on every client, the worker can still sample randomly from the closed caseload. For example, selecting every fifth case closed last December rather than every single one is possibility. Alternatively, workers may choose

to follow up on only the clients they consider to have the highest risk of experiencing continuing problems. Follow-up can be by telephone or letter, although the first is preferable because it is more personal and less bureaucratic.

It is also possible to combine the follow-up phase with an evaluation. For example, one eating disorder clinic used a phone survey that both surveyed the client's current situation and looked at specific outcomes 1 year following termination of services. The survey also asked clients to identify the factors most important in assisting their recovery following discharge.

In addition to heavy workloads, another barrier to follow-up is the lack of agency policies or traditions that support this activity. Many agencies do not encourage workers to do follow-up. This reluctance may be due to concerns about worker caseload, philosophical objections to making clients too dependent on the worker, or for other reasons. Another barrier to follow-up may be the reluctance of the worker to intrude on the client following termination. This problem can be overcome by discussing follow-up during the intervention. This will prime the client to expect a follow-up contact, as it is considered part of the intervention.

Regardless of the method selected, follow-up should be viewed as part of your professional obligation to the client. Even if your agency does not require or encourage workers to follow up on clients after termination, doing so is your professional responsibility.

Chapter Summary

The following summarizes this chapter's content as it relates to each learning objective (LO) presented at the beginning of the chapter. Chapter content helps prepare students to:

LO 8-1 Identify and use appropriate methods for evaluating practice.

Evaluation is designed to determine whether a change effort was worthwhile. Evaluation of social work practice and programs is an ethical responsibility of social workers and is required by most funding agencies. Obstacles to evaluation include such things as fear of the results, lack of time by workers or lack of support by agencies, and insufficient familiarity with evaluation tools.

An important part of evaluating practice is gathering data that can be used to determine what changes have occurred as a result of our interventions. Data gathering can occur through the use of surveys or instruments, changes in behavior that can be measured (such as weight loss), or observations that rely on others to note changes in a client's behavior.

Social workers employ some commonly used evaluation designs for generalist practice, including single-subject designs, goal-attainment scaling, task-achievement scaling, client satisfaction questionnaires, and target-problem scaling. Each has strengths and drawbacks as an evaluation tool.

LO 8-2 Critically analyze concepts important to evaluation of practice.

Validity is the extent to which you are measuring what you think you are measuring. It is an important criterion in any evaluation effort. If you have selected, for example, an instrument to assess assertiveness, you want it to measure levels of assertiveness instead of anger management issues. A related, and equally important, concept is reliability. Reliability is the extent to which an instrument produces the same measurement every time it is used. Unreliable instruments will often give different results each time they are used, rendering the data useless.

Generalizability is the ability of a set of results in one situation to fit another circumstance or instance. In an ideal world we would like to be able to prove that the program we developed will likely be effective with similar clients or similar problems. In practice, it is often hard to generalize from one set of evaluation results because we cannot guarantee that different groups or situations are comparable.

Baseline is a measure of the frequency, intensity, or duration of a behavior. If we hope to reduce the incidence of child abuse or temper tantrums, we must have some idea how often these occur. Once established, a baseline then becomes the starting point against which we measure the success of our program or intervention.

Independent variables are those factors that we think are responsible for producing an outcome. Thus, our intervention with a child abuser is the independent variable in our goal of producing a reduction in child abuse or abusive behavior (dependent variable).

Evaluations may be formative or summative depending upon purpose and need. The former are designed to monitor progress, whereas summative evaluations are concerned about the outcome of the planned change process. They can be used separately or employed together in a complete system of monitoring and evaluating an intervention or program.

LO 8-3 Identify commonly used methods for program evaluation.

Evaluating programs often requires different instruments and methods than evaluating practice. Among the methods used are needs assessments, evaluability assessments, process analysis, program outcome analysis, continuous quality assurance evaluations, and program monitoring.

LO 8-4 Anticipate and deal with common practice evaluation problems.

Common problems associated with practice evaluations include problems in generalizability, choosing the wrong evaluation tools, failing to involve clients in the evaluation process, staff distrust of evaluation, evaluations that interfere with service giving, alternative explanations for program outcomes, and unanticipated consequences. Although we try to control or manage most of these problems by selecting valid and reliable instruments, keeping clients in the loop, and other methods, we may ultimately end up with consequences we did not expect.

LO 8-5 Facilitate transitions and endings (termination) for clients.

Terminating with clients is one step in the GIM model. Ending professional relationships is expected and can be planned for. The tasks of termination include deciding when to terminate, evaluating achievement of objectives, maintaining and continuing progress, managing emotional reactions of both worker and client, and making appropriate referrals when needed. Terminations may be planned or unplanned.

LO 8-6 Practice personal reflection and self-correction regarding termination.

To the extent to which social workers experience emotional reactions to termination, they are obligated to manage them. These feelings may involve a sense of loss, disappointment, or guilt, some of which may be appropriate to share with the client. If the feelings become too obtrusive, the worker should consult with a supervisor or colleague.

LO 8-7 Help clients resolve problems concerning termination.

Client reactions to termination may be characterized by mixed feelings or reactions similar to those felt by the social worker. The extent and range of these reactions will differ from client to client, and depending on whether the client is an individual, family, group, organization or community.

LO 8-8 Select appropriate termination strategies for client systems.

The first step to help the termination process along is to plan for it whenever possible. The second step is addressing feelings of the client system. The third step is to summarize the progress that has been made to highlight the changes that have occurred and the objectives that the client has met.

LO 8-9 Implement prevention interventions to ensure maintenance of change.

It is important to maintain changes that have occurred in your work with the client. This generally involves helping clients select relevant situations on which

they can work and assisting them to build self-confidence. It is essential to expand the number of situations where the client can learn and practice new behaviors. This helps clients prepare for the future.

It is also helpful to use naturally occurring consequences rather than contrived or artificial ones, as clients will face these in their everyday lives. When possible, use follow-up sessions to extend treatment and prevent relapses in behavior, and try to reduce setbacks in the client's environment. Finally, be sure to teach members how to utilize a problem-solving approach when they encounter future situations that challenge their ability to maintain their progress. In larger systems, stabilization of change will occur through routinization of processes and procedures, clarification and documentation of policies and procedures, reducing the influence of the change agent, and addressing ongoing needs of the client system.

LO 8-10 Engage in follow-up activities with client systems.

Follow-up is the act of acquiring information about a client following termination. It is an opportunity for the worker to represent the consumer, discuss problems, straighten out difficulties, and prepare the client to return to the agency if needed. If in-person follow-up is impractical for workload or other reasons, consider doing follow-up only on a subset of clients, or complete the follow-up by electronic communication or letter.

Competency Notes

The following identifies where Educational Policy (EP) competencies and practice behaviors are discussed in the chapter.

EP 2.1 **Use supervision and consultation.** *(p. 320):* If a social worker is struggling with his or her own reaction to termination, it is appropriate to seek consultation or supervision to assist in resolving these issues.

EP 2.1.1b **Practice personal reflection and self-correction to assure continual professional development.** *(p. 320):* Social workers must be aware of their own reactions to termination of the professional relationship with clients and manage these in ways that benefit the client–worker relationship.

EP 2.1.2b **Make ethical decisions by applying standards of the NASW *Code of Ethics* and, as applicable, of the International Federation of Social**

Workers/International Association of Schools of Social Work *Ethics in Social Work, Statement of Principles. (p. 292):* It is an ethical obligation of social workers to evaluate our practice to ensure that we are providing the most appropriate and effective services to our clients.

EP 2.1.3 Apply critical thinking to inform and communicate professional judgment. *(pp. 296, 299, 316):* Engaging in practice evaluation requires that social workers think critically about the specific methods and tools they will employ.

EP 2.1.3a Distinguish, appraise, and integrate multiple sources of knowledge, including research-based knowledge, and practice wisdom. *(p. 300):* Deciding on which designs are most appropriate for evaluating your practice requires familiarity with each approach, the ability to appraise the relative effectiveness of each, and sensitivity to the client population served by the agency.

EP 2.1.3b Analyze models of assessment, prevention, intervention, and evaluation. *(p. 307):* Evaluating social service programs requires that we carefully analyze and select the tools and evaluation models that are most likely to produce useful results.

EP 2.1.4a Recognize the extent to which culture's structures and values may oppress, marginalize, alienate, or create/enhance privilege/power. *(p. 311):* Cultural competence is just as important when evaluating our work as it is when we are engaged in assessment or intervention. Clients' past experiences can have a major influence on both the quality and quantity of data they are willing to provide during an evaluation.

EP 2.1.4c Recognize and communicate their understanding of the importance of difference in shaping life experiences. *(p. 311):* As in other areas of practice, evaluation must be sensitive to cultural differences and life experiences of others because their view of reality may be very different from that of the evaluator. For example, unfamiliarity with English may make it harder for respondents to answer questions on a survey. Likewise, probing questions may be viewed as intrusive by some individuals whose cultures prize privacy and saving face.

EP 2.1.6a Use practice experience to inform scientific inquiry. *(p. 293):* Designing evaluations to help measure the success of our change efforts should always be guided by practice experience. In this manner we select the right tools for the right job.

EP 2.1.6b Use research evidence to inform practice. *(p. 290):* To the extent possible, social workers should employ interventions that are supported by research (also referred to as evidence-based practice). *(p. 312):* Prior research findings can assist in identifying valid and reliable instruments that we can use in evaluating our own practice.

EP 2.1.7a Utilize conceptual frameworks to guide the processes of assessment, intervention, and evaluation. *(p. 294):* To be effective evaluators, social workers must be familiar with various research concepts and conceptual models.

EP 2.1.10h Initiate actions to achieve organizational goals. *(pp. 290, 292, 293):* Evaluating social work programs is a strategy that helps an agency achieve such organizational goals as accountability, effectiveness, and efficiency.

EP 2.1.10i Implement prevention interventions that enhance client capacities. *(p. 324):* One goal of stabilizing change is to prevent the recurrence of similar problems in the future. To the extent we are able to strengthen client capacities to overcome future challenges, we are helping prevent relapse and/or additional problems.

EP 2.1.10l Facilitate transitions and endings. *(p. 315):* Termination is an important part of the planned change process that has ethical implications and requires critical thinking skills.

EP 2.1.10m Critically analyze, monitor, and evaluate interventions. *(p. 290):* Evaluating the outcomes of our interventions is a key step in the planned change process for generalist social work practitioners. *(p. 290):* The Council on Social Work Education identifies analyzing, monitoring, and evaluating interventions as a competency expected of all social workers. *(p. 309):* Program monitoring is a useful way to gather data that we can use to evaluate the effectiveness or efficiency of a given program.

On the Internet

Visit the *Understanding Generalist Practice* CourseMate at **www.cengagebrain.com** for resources such as quizzes, glossaries and videos.

Understanding Families: Family Assessment

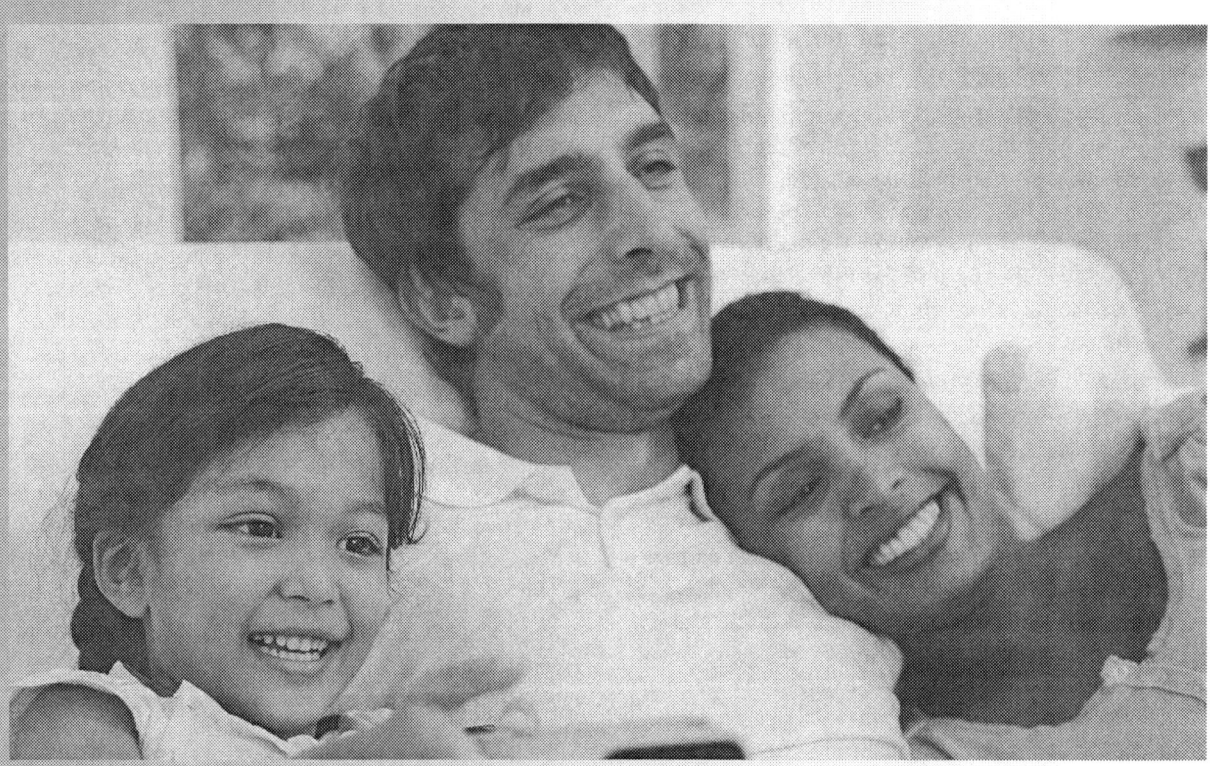

Masterfile

Learning Objectives   *This chapter will help prepare students to:*

LO 9-1   Assess families by using the Generalist Intervention Model (GIM).

LO 9-2   Examine verbal and nonverbal communication in families.

LO 9-3   Appraise family structure.

LO 9-4   Analyze family life-cycle adjustments.

LO 9-5   Appraise impacts of the impinging social environment.

LO 9-6   Analyze common family conflicts and problems.

LO 9-7   Examine variations in family structure.

LO 9-8   Demonstrate cultural competency in family assessment.

TELEVISION IMAGES OF FAMILIES HISTORICALLY have often reflected a version of real life that was somewhat idealized. Families, as displayed on *Leave It to Beaver* or *The Brady Bunch*, for example, were characterized by two heterosexual parents present in the home living a middle-class lifestyle. The family faced such typical life challenges as kids spending too much time on the phone and helping children learn to deal with successes and failures. Dad usually worked outside the home, and Mom stayed home to care for the kids. If Mom had to work, there always seemed to be a surrogate parent to help raise the kids, clean the house, and prepare meals. Life was sometimes stressful but always manageable.

Consider real-life families today. June and Ward Cleaver

> *. . . meet at the office (she's in marketing: he's in sales) and move in together after dating a couple of months. A year later June gets pregnant. What to do? Neither feels quite ready to make it legal and there's no pressure from parents, all of whom are divorced and remarried themselves. So little Wally is welcomed into the world with June's last name on the birth certificate. A few years later June gets pregnant again with the Beav. Ward is ambivalent about second-time fatherhood and moves out, but June decides to go ahead on her own. In her neighborhood, after all, single mother-hood is no big deal; the lesbians down the street adopted kids from South America and the soccer mom next door is divorced with a live-in boyfriend. (Kantrowitz & Wingert, 2001, pp. 46–48)*

Six months after the Beaver is born, June's company moves its operations to Mexico to reduce costs, and she is unemployed.

Ward married the daughter of the company's vice-president, moved to Texas, and no longer has any contact with his kids. Over the next few years, June uses up her unemployment insurance, goes on public assistance, gets a job at significantly less pay, and moves in with Hank, a man she met recently. As his drug abuse problem becomes more serious, Hank begins to abuse Wally and June. Wally's schoolteacher reports suspected abuse to the local protective services office, and the family receives services for the next year. Finally, June moves to a domestic violence shelter after realizing that Hank's abuse

is not going to stop. She gets a restraining order against him so that he is not allowed to have any contact with her or her kids. June and her boys are no longer at risk of abuse, but June discovers that she is pregnant again. After weighing her options and receiving counseling, June seeks an abortion. She tells no one about the abortion because it is against her religion. For years she has mixed feelings about her decision but has little time to worry about it because she has responsibility for raising two boys by herself. To make life harder, the Beav is diagnosed as hyperactive and having attention deficit disorder while Wally is coping with the reading disorder dyslexia. Though she has medical insurance through her employment, her HMO will not authorize a new medication that treats the Beav's disorder without the potential side effects of Ritalin. Sometimes, June thinks, "This is not the way I envisioned my life when I was 15. What went wrong?"

Of course, the Cleaver example only illustrates some of the changes in family life. For example, there are the changes in gender-role expectations with respect to earning a living. Then, there are the moral dilemmas now being faced concerning sexuality and intimacy. Also, there are the effects of advancing technology.

There are some changes in the basic nature of families that the Cleavers do not illustrate as well. The Cleavers are very white and very middle class. They do not reflect the increasing proportion of the population previously labeled as "minorities," in other words, people of nonwhite heritage. Nor do the Cleavers clearly demonstrate the increasing proportion of women and children who compose the poor and homeless.

Working with families, regardless of their specific individual circumstances, is a major facet of generalist social work practice. Practitioners need to understand the basic dynamics of today's family relationships and the problems these families face. The family needs to be viewed from several perspectives. These include the family system as an entity in itself, the individual people making up the family system, and the impacts of the social, political, and economic environment upon how the family functions. These issues are what this chapter is all about.

Introduction

Families continue to remain the foundation of most people's lives. They can provide the security, support, and intimacy people need. Social workers often encounter individual clients who initially appear to have individual problems. However, another way of looking at problems is from a family perspective. That is, you might view a problem not as belonging to the individual, but rather to the individual's entire family.

For example, consider a 24-year-old man who abuses alcohol. His alcoholism not only affects him, but also his wife whom he slaps around when he returns home from a drunken bout. It also affects his three children. His primary interactions with them involve hitting, screaming, and ignoring. Finally, it affects the man's parents and other family members when he typically bursts into fits of alcoholic rage at family gatherings.

An 87-year-old woman whose health is rapidly failing provides another example. Of course, her health is *her* problem. However, it is also the problem of her middle-aged son and daughter, both of whom live at least 75 miles from her home. Should one of them take her in and care for her? If so, which one? Both of their spouses hate the idea. The spouses see the older woman's presence as a terrible disruption of their own families' lives. So should her children put the older woman in a health care facility? Should they force her to go even if she hates that idea? If she does enter a facility, which one? How often should they visit? How can either of the older woman's children cope with their burden of guilt over not taking her in themselves?

Still another example involves an active 13-year-old boy who slips on the mud as he runs down to the river to swim. Although he has run down that same riverbank hundreds of times before, this time he slips and breaks his neck. What impact does his individual problem, namely that of being a quadriplegic, have on his parents, his siblings, his grandparents, and even other members of his extended family?

Thus, generalist social work practitioners will often be called upon to work with an entire family to solve a problem. This task does not mean that generalist practitioners are family therapists. The goal of family therapy is to change the communication and interaction patterns occurring within a family to improve relationships and overall family functioning.

Family therapists are specialized. Their focus of attention is the family unit. Family therapists help clients make changes in how they think, both about themselves and about other family members, in order to improve the family's interpersonal processes. Therapy typically takes place in the therapist's office and can be somewhat long term.

Generalist social workers, on the other hand, must address a broader variety of problems. As we have discussed, many of these problems involve outside systems. For example, a client may have lost her job. Part of a social worker's role then might be to help this client find other employment. Linking a client with employment agencies and other potential sources of jobs is one means of handling this case. Perhaps the worker might help the client get temporary financial help until she can once again support herself. Still another possibility is helping the client become involved in job training.

A second example of the broad range of problems addressed by generalist practitioners is homelessness. A generalist practitioner can help a homeless client find temporary shelter and resources. Subsequently, the worker might help the client find employment or become linked with other services and financial aid. Likewise, the client may require help in getting needed health care.

Still another example of a problem addressed by generalist practitioners involves helping the 13-year-old quadriplegic mentioned earlier. He will likely need help in a variety of ways. He may have difficulty coping with the reality of his disability. Likewise, the impacts of the accident on other family members may need attention. Generalist practitioners may help the quadriplegic and his family deal with these issues or refer them to someone else to do so. The options available to family members (such as pursuing resources) will probably need to be addressed. For instance, a generalist practitioner can work to help the 13-year-old get physical and occupational therapy and transportation services. A worker can find out what resources are available and help link him and his family with these resources. If services are not available, a generalist practitioner may advocate on the client's behalf so that the community and agencies within the community begin to respond to the client's needs.

Thus, generalist practitioners must adopt a broader view in helping individuals and families solve problems. They need a wide range of skills. They need to be able to tackle a variety of problems and try to solve them in whatever ethical manners they can figure out.

The family remains a significant force in people's lives. Family relationships are intimate and complex. In some ways, working with families in social work practice is different than working with individuals, other groups, or larger systems. Working with families is often considered to lie somewhere on a continuum between micro and mezzo practice. Therefore, social workers need a solid base of skills directly related to the planned change process with families.

LO 9-1 Assess Families by Using the Generalist Intervention Model (GIM)

EP 2.1.10a

Work with families follows the Generalist Intervention Model (GIM), just like any other type of social work intervention. A worker must engage a family, conduct an assessment, develop a plan, implement the plan while amending it as necessary, evaluate progress, terminate involvement with the family, and, finally, provide follow-up regarding subsequent status. This chapter and Chapter 10 will focus on these steps. Understanding family dynamics in order to conduct an assessment and proceed with intervention is critical for family treatment. The generalist practitioner must know what types of information to get and what issues to address in order to decide how best to intervene. Here the entire family itself will be viewed as the client system.

Therefore, this chapter will address assessment issues, emphasizing step 2 in the planned change process. Chapter 10 will focus on practice techniques and the remaining steps in the planned change process.

DEFINING FAMILIES

There are various ways to define *families*. One definition is "a primary group whose members assume certain obligations for each other and generally share common residences" (Barker, 2003, p. 154). Family structure may include "the nuclear family as well as alternatives to nuclear family which are adopted by persons in committed relationships and the people they consider to be 'family'" (Council on Social Work Education [CSWE], 2002). Persons within a family may be "related by ancestry, marriage, adoption, or choice" (Zinn, Eitzen, & Wells, 2011, p. 492). A family, then, can include two or more people who assume responsibility for each other's well-being over time (e.g., caring for children, providing economic support, or giving help and support during illness). Such a broad definition embraces many family configurations, including those involving female heads, parents with various sexual orientations, and family relationships that are not based on blood or the necessity of marriage. Once the family has been identified as your client system, there are a variety of dimensions in which the family's problems and interactions can be assessed. These include communication, family structure, life-cycle adjustments, and impacts of the impinging social environment.

LO 9-2 Examine Verbal and Nonverbal Communication in Families

EP 2.1.10d

How family members communicate with each other relates directly to how effectively the family flourishes as a system. Therefore, assessment of communication is essential in preparation for intervention. Several aspects of family communication will be discussed here. They include verbal and nonverbal communication in addition to the various avenues of communication.

VERBAL AND NONVERBAL COMMUNICATION

As we discussed in Chapter 2, regarding skills for working with individuals, communication involves transmitting information from one person to another. Both verbal and nonverbal communication are important in conveying meaning. That the *impact* on the receiver (what the receiver understands the sender to be saying) closely resembles the *intent* of the sender (what the sender means to say) is very important. As we know, inaccuracies or problems at any point in this process can stop the information from getting across to the receiver. At any point, distortion may interfere with the communication process.

Verbal communication patterns inside the family include who talks a lot and who talks only rarely. These patterns involve who talks to whom and who defers to whom. They also reflect the subtle and not so subtle aspects involved in family members' relationships. These qualities might involve hostility, pride, rejection, or over-involvement.

Nonverbal communication patterns are also important in families. Frequently, a receiver will attribute more value to the nonverbal aspects of the message than the verbal. Nonverbal communication can involve facial expressions, eye contact, and posture. It can also involve seemingly trifling behaviors. See Highlight 9.1 for an example of conflicting verbal and nonverbal communication.

The situation illustrated in Highlight 9.1 may seem a bit unrealistic, but it really did happen. It illustrates several points about family interaction and communication.

First, what one family member might say in words to another one may not be what that sender really means. Patti was not "fine," although she verbally stated she was. However, because of her anger and her feelings that Larry did not care about how she felt, she was not ready to express herself accurately with words.

Second, nonverbal behavior can provide important clues regarding what a sender really wants to convey. Patti did silly, although aggravating, things to convey to Larry that she was angry.

Third, critical nonverbal communication may involve any number of seemingly petty behaviors. Each of us has our "things" that, trivial as they may be, annoy us to no end. An annoyance may be how someone else puts the glasses into the dishwasher the wrong way

An Example of Conflict Between Verbal and Nonverbal Communication

Patti and Larry, a married couple, both work outside the home in professional careers. Because of their involvement in their respective jobs and the long hours they work, they see little of each other during the week. When Friday night rolls around, they typically relax together and enjoy talking about their work and future plans.

Patti made it a point to get home early one Friday and made Larry a relatively elegant beef stroganoff dinner—as elegant as it could get when it was started late Friday afternoon. The two, by the way, usually shared the cooking tasks.

Patti timed the dinner to be ready at 6:30 p.m., about the time Larry usually got home. Patti turned on the television and waited . . . and waited . . . and waited. Seven o'clock came and went. Seven-thirty rolled on by. Eight o'clock passed into oblivion. Time moved on from 9 and finally to 10 o'clock.

First, Patti took the dinner off of the stove and let it cool. An hour later she put it in the refrigerator so it would not spoil. Initially, Patti had been worried. What if Larry had been in a car wreck? But, no, the police would have called to let her know. Where was Larry? Why could he not call her to tell her why he wasn't home (although he had forgotten his cell phone)?

By 10 p.m., Patti had transcended far beyond her initial worry and even her anger. Her fury at Larry's inconsiderateness had escalated to immense proportions. As the evening had progressed, she had gone beyond turning the roll of toilet paper in the bathroom upside down, a behavior that really annoyed him. She usually only resorted to such nonverbal behavior to get her point across when it really mattered and verbal communication simply did not work. She not only vigorously squeezed the toothpaste down to the middle of the tube (another behavior that really aggravated Larry), but also squeezed it all the way down to the bottom.

He consistently and carefully liked to squeeze his toothpaste toward the top. Eventually, she had taken both the toilet paper roll and the toothpaste tube and thrown them in the garbage.

Patti then heard someone at the door. She, in addition, had also locked the door, another nonverbal means of displaying to Larry her serious disapproval. Someone out there was fidgeting with a key. There was scratching at the lock. Then, suddenly, the door burst open. There was Larry beaming a wide grin. He said with a somewhat drunken slur, "Well, hi ya, how're you doin'?"

Patti responded with a face of stone, her eyes black with rage, "I'm fine." She promptly left the room and went to bed.

Larry knew he was in the proverbial doghouse. Even after some unknown number of beers, he knew he should have called to tell Patti about Harvey's going-away party after work. He knew Patti was not "fine." He really knew how not "fine" she was when he discovered the missing toilet paper later that night and the phantom toothpaste the next morning.

Patti and Larry eventually talked the situation out. She told him how she thought he knew how she always looked forward to their Friday nights together. She told him how she had wanted to please him with dinner and how worried she had later become when he did not appear. She told him how she had felt he just did not care about her feelings. All he would have had to do was call her and tell her he would be late.

Larry apologized and said he would never do it again. Patti's nonverbal emphasis concerning the issue drove the point home. Later, verbal elaboration helped Larry understand the issue more clearly. However, to this day, Larry emphasizes how Patti "hates it when he has fun."

or forgets to turn out the hall light at night. It might be how someone close to us forgets to put a plastic garbage bag in the waste container before dumping chicken bones into it. It might be parking the car the wrong way in the driveway. Family members can use any of these things to communicate with each other.

A fourth point is that nonverbal behaviors often transcend trivial behaviors. They reflect feelings that the individual is unable or does not want to put into words. Emotions are strong among family members. Petty nonverbal behavior can wield formidable blows to those close to us.

There is a fifth point with respect to the story. Patti and Larry were able to unravel the problem themselves, despite the fact that Larry still feels Patti "hates it when he has fun." However, many times a generalist practitioner will be called upon to disentangle confused verbal and nonverbal communications. Helping communicators within the family to have their *intents* more closely match their *impacts* will be up to the worker.

The basic skills for micro practice clearly relate to working with families. In addition to understanding verbal and nonverbal communication, these skills include: being warm, empathic, and genuine; using interviewing techniques; and overcoming hurdles that often occur during the interviewing and problem-solving processes. Family interaction and communication are more complicated because more individuals are involved.

AVENUES OF COMMUNICATION

There are at least "five avenues of communication," any or all of which family members may use in a given day; they include "consonance, condemnation, submission, intellectualization, and indifference" (Collins, Jordan, & Coleman, 2013; Goldenberg & Goldenberg, 2013; Perez, 1979, p. 47). Evaluating how a family communicates using these avenues provides clear clues regarding where change is needed.

Consonance

Consonance refers to the extent to which the communication receiver accurately hears and understands the sender of the communication. In other words, to what extent does the sender's *intent* closely resemble the receiver's *impact*? Healthy families are likely to have high levels of consonance in their communications. That is, family members understand each other well. Unhealthy families, on the other hand, often have low levels of consonance. Members of these families do not communicate clearly with each other.

Condemnation

Condemnation involves family members severely criticizing, blaming, negatively judging, or nagging other family members. More than occurring only once or twice, condemnation involves a regular pattern of family interaction. This pattern may involve any number of the family members. In other words, one person may typically condemn another, or that one person may typically condemn all the others. Likewise, all other family members may condemn one in particular, or two or three members may condemn any one or more. Any configuration is possible.

People who form patterns of condemnation frequently do it to enhance their own self-esteem (Goldenberg & Goldenberg, 2013; Perez, 1979; Satir, 1972). Blaming or criticizing another person makes your own qualities and behaviors appear better or superior. For instance, take the 77-year-old woman who constantly condemned her husband of 55 years. He was 84. She regularly harped on how he was an alcoholic who could not keep a job. The strange thing, however, was that he had not touched a drop of liquor in over 40 years. Additionally, he had worked regularly as a carpenter for most of those years. However, when the woman dwelled on how bad her husband was, albeit for behavior that had occurred over 40 years ago, she made herself feel better. If he was so bad, then she looked good by comparison.

Submission

Submission involves feeling so downtrodden, guilt-ridden, or incapable that you succumb completely to another's will. You do not feel valuable or worthwhile enough to be assertive about your own rights and needs. Instead, you knuckle under the other person's will, submit, and obey. Situations involving submission may be summed up as follows:

> The submissive person, like the condemner, is difficult to live with. His [or her] feelings of ineptness and inadequacy put family members under constant pressure to support, to guide, to direct, to lead him. And again, when the dependency pressure becomes too demanding the family members may well respond via condemnation. (Perez, 1979, p. 49)

Intellectualization

Intellectualization is the process of staging all communication within a strictly logical, rational realm. The existence of any emotion is denied or suppressed. A person who intellectualizes likes to evaluate a problem rationally and establish a solution as soon as possible. This person does not want illogical emotions to interfere with the process of dealing with and controlling reality. The problem usually faced by the intellectualizer, however, is that everyone has emotions, even the intellectualizer. Emotions that are constantly suppressed may build up and explode uncontrollably at inopportune times. Explosions may even result in violence.

Another problem with intellectualization occurs when the intellectualizer is unable to meet the needs of other family members. A person who intellectualizes can seem very cold and unloving. Traditional gender-role stereotypes that direct men to be strong, unemotional decision makers encourage intellectualization. This gender role often becomes a problem in relationships for women, who traditionally have been raised to express emotions. A typical scenario involves a woman who seeks expressions of love and emotion from an intimate partner who instead intellectualizes.

Consider, for instance, one couple where the man states point-blank that he has no emotions; he says he is always happy. The woman responds with the question, "Well, then, what are you when you're yelling at me?"

The man replies hesitantly, "Then...I'm mad." At this the woman smiles silently to herself. She has made some progress by doubling her mate's emotional repertoire.

Indifference

Indifference involves remaining apparently unconcerned, not caring one way or the other, and appearing detachedly aloof. Two common ways indifference is manifested in families is through "silence" and "ignoring behaviors" (Perez, 1979, p. 51). One or more family members may not talk or respond to one or more other family members.

Indifference can be a very powerful and manipulative means of communicating. A mother who ignores her teenage daughter may convey a number of messages to her. Perhaps it makes the daughter feel her mother does not care enough about her to expend the energy, or maybe the mother is angry at her for some reason.

In addition to being disturbing, being ignored can be very painful. For instance, consider the newlywed wife who was very emotionally insecure. During the first few weeks of marriage, she would ask her husband a dozen times a day if he really loved her. At first, he would answer, "Yes, dear, I do." However, he soon tired of her constant need for reassurance. He began simply to turn her off and ignore her. She was devastated. She needed to learn that her constant questioning was not eliciting the response she desired. Instead of making herself feel more secure, she was driving her husband away from her. This served only to escalate her insecurity.

Critical Thinking Question 9.1

- How would you describe and assess the communication patterns in your own family of origin?

LO 9-3 Appraise Family Structure

EP 2.1.10d

Family structure refers to the organization of relationships and patterns of interaction occurring within the family. Family structure varies dramatically from one family to another. Some families involve blood relationships. Others do not. Cultural, ethnic, racial, sexual orientation, and age differences abound. Whatever their configuration, families should "exist both for the well-being of their members and for the well-being of society. Ideally, they offer predictability, structure, and safety as members mature and participate in the community. It is within families that children develop skills that prepare them for life outside the family, —first in school and friendships, and later in the workforce, and romantic partners. Through families, members meet basic human needs" (Collins et al., 2013, p. 28). Collins and his colleagues (2013) explain:

> *Contemporary family lifestyles and structures are fluid and evolving, necessitating that the...social worker adopt a broad definition of* family. *Judgments and decisions about family structures play an important role in deciding which resources and barriers a family will encounter in getting its needs met. Despite the difficulty of developing a clear and simple definition of* family, *most people can construct an unambiguous description to fit their own particular family, and working definitions of* family *can be established for most situations. The family, in its most basic conceptualization, is what a person in a family says it is. The experienced family reality, instead of reliance on a static, one-dimensional, and rigid definition, is crucial...and opens the mind for the work ahead. (pp. 35–36)*

Some of the variations in family structure will be discussed in more detail later in the chapter. Here we will examine five dimensions of family structure: the family as a system, family norms, family roles, the balance of power within the system, and intergenerational aspects. Communication might be included as an aspect of family structure. However, because of its significance, not only in assessment but throughout planned change, we have already discussed it as a separate issue.

EP 2.1.7a

THE FAMILY AS A SYSTEM

Families are systems. The concepts involved in the systems conceptual framework, which we discussed in Chapter 1, also apply to family systems. Family structure can be assessed by thinking of the family in systems theory terms. As Collins and his colleagues (2013) articulate:

> *According to family systems theory, all families are social systems, and it is this belief that guides understanding and work with families. Because family members are interdependent (rely on one another), behaviors do not exist in a vacuum. As such, family systems theory helps us see how problems spring from family relationships and transactions. In family work, the overall web of relationships within the family becomes the focus. Thus, one of the key beliefs of family systems theory is that problems that arise in families cannot usually be attributed to individual dysfunction or pathology. Rather, understanding family dynamics will help uncover family processes that seem to foster and maintain the presenting problem. Therefore, problems such as parent-child conflict, behavior problems, mental health issues, and so on, develop and continue within the family context.* (pp. 69–70)

Thinking of the family as a system is helpful when working with the family to help solve its problems. For instance, as in any system, all parts (family members) have relationships to all other parts (other family members). When assessing a family, you need to assess all of the relationships among individuals, even those that superficially appear subdued and less significant.

Additionally, systems theory prescribes that an event affecting one family member will actually have an effect on *all* family members. For example, take Kay, age 16. She met a boy at a Friday night high school dance, went out with him for pizza afterward, and later got in a serious car accident. Ironically, the accident happened at about midnight on Friday the 13th. Another car pulled out in front of the car in which Kay was a passenger. The driver in the other car tried to cut across the lane of his oncoming traffic to get to the other side of the boulevard. His car hit Kay's car head on. She was sitting in the middle front seat next to her new beau and was not wearing a seatbelt. Upon impact, her face was thrown down onto the radio in the dashboard. The result was a smashed right cheekbone, broken jaw, crushed nose, lost teeth, and several deep facial cuts.

In the 4 years following the accident, Kay went through a dozen plastic surgeries. Although the experience was painful, she later reflected that she had learned much from it. For instance, she quickly learned the old cliché that "beauty isn't everything." Her

accident helped her to put things of real value such as her religious beliefs and personal relationships into perspective. The insurance money and a 2-month trip to Europe were not so bad either. She eventually became a social worker.

Her immediate family members, however, were traumatized by the car accident. Kay's 12-year-old sister promptly fainted during her initial visit to Kay in the hospital with her ruined face. Her parents were distraught. Not only did the regular trips to the hospital regulate how they would structure their lives over the next few years, but also their worry over whether or not she would ever be able to live a normal life again because of her ugliness was devastating. Kay, now 39, reflects that her mother, Gloria, still maintains that Kay's accident was the worst thing that ever happened to her (meaning Gloria). Gloria stresses how it ruined her own life. Kay thinks this line of thinking is absurd because it was Kay's, not Gloria's, accident.

Boundaries and Subsystems

Two other systems theory concepts are exceptionally helpful when applied to family systems. They are boundaries and subsystems. A *boundary* is an invisible or symbolic "line of demarcation that separates an individual, a subsystem, or a system from outside surroundings" (Goldenberg & Goldenberg, 2013, p. 101). In a family system, boundaries determine who are members of that particular family system and who are not. Parents and children are within the boundaries of the family system. Close friends of the family are not.

Inside the family, "boundaries distinguish between subsystems, helping to define the separate subunits of the overall system" (Goldenberg & Goldenberg, 2013, p. 102). A *subsystem* is a secondary or subordinate system—a system within a system. The most obvious examples are the parental and sibling subsystems. Other more subtle subsystems may also exist depending on the boundaries established within the family system. A mother might form a subsystem with a daughter to whom she feels exceptionally close. Two siblings among four might form another subsystem because of their exceptionally close and unique relationship.

Each subsystem has its own specified membership. Either a family member is within the boundaries of the subsystem or he or she is not.

Boundaries between appropriate subsystems in families need to be maintained. For example, parents need to nurture and maintain their own subsystem as a marital couple. In an incestuous family, the marital subsystem boundaries may become blurred. The husband/father may form an intimate subsystem with one or more of his daughters. A family treatment perspective in this case might involve clarifying and strengthening the boundaries of the marital subsystem. Boundaries also need to be clearly delineated between the parental system and the children's subsystem.

FAMILY NORMS

Family norms are the rules that specify what is considered proper behavior within the family group. Many times, the most powerful rules are those that are not clearly and verbally stated. Rather, these are implicit rules or repeated family transactions that all family members understand but never discuss (e.g., see Highlight 9.2). Establishing norms that allow both the entire family and each individual member to function effectively and productively is important for families.

In families with problems, however, the family rules usually do not allow the family or the individual members to function effectively and productively. Ineffective norms need to be identified and changed. Positive, beneficial norms need to be developed and fostered.

The following is an example of a family in which there was an implicit, invalid, and ineffective norm

functioning. The norm was that no one in the family would smoke cigarettes. A husband, wife, four children, and two sets of grandparents composed this family. Although never discussed, the understanding was that no one had ever or would ever smoke. One day the husband found several cigarette butts in the ashtray of the car typically used by his wife. Because no one in the family smoked, he deduced that these butts must belong to someone else. He assumed that his wife was having an affair with another man, which devastated him. However, he said nothing about it and suffered in silence. His relationship with his wife began to deteriorate. He became sullen, and spats and conflicts became more frequent. Finally, in a heated conflict, he spit out his thoughts and feelings about the cigarette butts and her alleged affair. His wife expressed shocked disbelief. The reality was that it was she who smoked the cigarettes, but only when no one else was around. Her major time to be alone was when she was driving to and from work. She took advantage of this time to smoke but occasionally forgot to empty the ashtray. She told him the entire story, and he was tremendously relieved. Their relationship improved and prospered.

This example illustrates how an inappropriate norm almost ruined a family relationship. Of course, there

---

HIGHLIGHT 9.2

Family Norms Vary Dramatically from One Family to Another

Every family differs in its individual set of norms or rules. For example, Family A has a relatively conservative set of norms governing communication and interpersonal behavior. Although the norms allow frequent pleasant talk among family members, it is generally on a superficial level. The steaming hot summer weather or the status of the new variety of worms invading the cherry tree is fair game for conversation. However, nothing more personal is ever mentioned. Taboo subjects include anything to do with feelings, interpersonal relationships, or opinions about careers or jobs, let alone politics or moral issues. On one occasion, for example, a daughter-in-law asked the family matriarch what her son and other daughter-in-law would name their soon-to-be-born first baby. With a shocked expression on her face, the matriarch replied, "Oh, my heavens, I haven't asked. I don't want to interfere."

Family B, on the other hand, has a vastly different set of norms governing communication and behavior. Virtually everything is discussed and debated, not only among the nuclear family members but also among several generations. Personal methods of contraception, stances on abortion, opinions on capital punishment, and politics number among the emotionally heated issues discussed. Family members frequently talk about their personal relationships, including who is the favorite grandchild and who tends to fight all the time with rich old Aunt Harriet. The family is so open that price tags are left on Christmas gifts so each member knows what the other has spent.

The rules of behavior that govern Family B are very different from those of Family A. Yet, in each family, all the members consider their family's behavior to be normal and are comfortable with these rules. Members of each family may find it inconceivable that families could be any other way.

were other dynamics going on between the spouses involved. Relationships are complicated entities. However, such a simple thing as the wife being a "closet smoker" had the potential to tip the balance and destroy the marriage. In this instance, a simple correction in communication solved the problem. The interesting thing is that eventually the entire family learned of this incident. The wife still smokes but still insists on doing it privately. The family now functions effectively with an amended family rule that accepts but never mentions her smoking.

Social workers need to identify and understand family norms so that inappropriate, ineffective norms can be changed. At any point, a social worker can point out such an ineffective norm to family members, help them clarify alternative solutions and changes, and assist them in determining which solution is best to pursue.

FAMILY ROLES

Family roles are "individually prescribed patterns of behavior reinforced by the expectations and norms of the family" (Collins et al., 2013; Nichols, 2011; Ragg, 2006; Worden, 2003, p. 15). In families, these roles usually involve behaviors that work for the benefit of the family. For instance, the parental role prescribes behaviors helpful in supporting, directing, and raising children. Likewise, a parent might assume an employee role to earn financial sustenance for the family by being employed outside of the home. Children, on the other hand, might assume the roles of student in school and helping assistant in household tasks.

In addition to these more formal socially acceptable roles, family members may hold a variety of more informal roles, often related to individual personalities and interactional patterns among family members. For instance, such roles may include troublemaker, the oppressed one, the illustrious star, the one to blame for everything (scapegoat), Mr./Ms. Perfection, the old battle ax, or the family's black sheep.

There is a broad range of roles that can be assumed in families. One family comes to mind that has a "white sheep" within its flock. The nuclear family consists of two parents and three children, two females and one male, the latter of whom is also the youngest, although all the family members are adults. The family is not "bad," really—all members except for the youngest male like to drink, party, and do their share of swearing. None is involved in any organized religion. The youngest male, on the other hand, is a fundamentalist pastor. Hence, he has become the "white sheep" of the family.

Because each person and each family are unique, there is no ideal formula for what roles are best. Each family must be evaluated on how its unique configuration of roles functions to the family's advantage or disadvantage on the whole.

Social workers should assess the various roles family members play in order to better understand family functioning. Furthermore, practitioners should evaluate whether these roles are helping or hurting the family. During family assessment, consider asking the following questions:

- What specific roles does each family member occupy?
- Do the various roles played work well together for the family's benefit?
- Are any of the roles ambiguous, redundant, or left empty?
- Is there flexibility among family roles so that the family is better able to adjust to crisis situations?
- Do the family's roles conform with basic social norms (e.g., society does not condone a criminal role)?
- Do the family's roles function to enhance the family's feelings of self-worth and well-being or detract from these feelings? (Holman, 1983, p. 30)

Chapter 7 explained the chief enabler role and various norms commonly portrayed in families of alcohol abusers. These families are dysfunctional in that massive amounts of energy are wasted in trying to survive with an abuser in the family's midst.

BALANCE OF POWER WITHIN THE FAMILY SYSTEM

Power is the ability of prevailing family members to have authority and control over the perspectives or actions of other family members. Power is a vague concept that is difficult to specify clearly. It is usually related to holding a higher rank, having more prestige, being more respected, and having greater access to and control over resources than others in the system, in this case, the family system.

Power is relative. That is, one individual has more or less power than other individuals. It is irrelevant to one individual shipwrecked alone on a desert island.

Power is also complex and difficult to quantify. That is, different family members have more or less power over different matters. For instance, one parent who manages the checkbook and pays all the bills may have more influence over finances than the other parent. On the other hand, the other parent may have more control over family activities, such as what the family does from weekend to weekend. Influence varies depending on the issue.

Children, too, have power to various degrees. They can exert control over the behavior of parents and siblings. Take a 5-year-old boy who throws himself on the floor screaming whenever his single-parent mother takes him along to a supermarket. The child has power to the extent that he can force his mother to either leave the place or at least cut her shopping short.

Take another example: Christine and Jose, a married couple. Christine is very outgoing, assertive, and independent, whereas Jose is generally quiet, introspective, and not very socially oriented. Christine will make virtually all of their social plans with little or no input from Jose. Although Jose goes along with most of Christine's ideas, he has definite veto power. If he does not want to participate in a social activity, he simply says so. The activity is then either not planned at all or postponed. Hence, there is a balance of power in their relationship, at least concerning this particular issue.

Christine and Jose also illustrate how power relationships are often hidden or concealed. External appearances do not always accurately represent the reality of the balance of power. Although Christine outwardly appears to lead social activities in the relationship, she does so only with Jose's consent.

In assessing a family, the important question is whether or not the balance of power as perceived by each individual is adequate and fair. Situations where family members resent the balance of power may be ripe for planned change intervention. Take, for instance, an adolescent who feels hopelessly repressed and unable to express openly any opinions of her own. Consider one spouse who feels totally impotent and oppressed by the other spouse. Finally, consider a parent, either married or single, who feels he has no control over the children's behavior. Each of these families needs help.

ASSESSING INTERGENERATIONAL ASPECTS OF FAMILY SYSTEMS

Another important aspect of family structure is historical. What is the family's history? Under what conditions were the parents or the single parent in a family brought up? How did the parents' and the grandparents' early environments affect each generation's behavior and way of life? Has there been a history of alcoholism in the family? Has corporal punishment to the point of child abuse been considered a family norm?

Critical Thinking Questions 9.2

EP 2.1.3

- Focus on a family with which you feel you are quite familiar. Describe its structure as a system, norms, roles, balance of power, and inter-generational aspects.
- To what extent is this family functioning effectively?
- Where might improvements in family functioning be made?

LO 9-4 Analyze Family Life-Cycle Adjustments

EP 2.1.10d

In addition to family communication and structure, assessing life-cycle adjustments can give clear insights into a family's problems (Collins et al., 2013). As families mature and progress through time, they must successfully complete tasks appropriate to that stage of their development. Problems surface when these tasks cannot be completed.

Several decades ago, the family life cycle and the types of experiences family members had during specified phases of the cycle were much more predictable than today. This predictability is no longer the case. There is no "typical" cycle. McGoldrick, Carter, and Garcia-Preto (2011) explain:

Overall changes in family life cycle patterns have escalated dramatically, in recent decades owing especially to:

> *A lower birth rate*
> *Longer life expectancy*
> *The changing role of women*
> *The rise in unmarried motherhood*
> *The rise in unmarried couples*
> *Increasing single-parent adoptions*
> *Increasing LGBT[Q] gay and lesbian couples and families*
> *High divorce and remarriage rates*
> *Increasing two-paycheck marriages to the point where they are now the norm (p. 4)*

Historically, the traditional family life cycle was conceptualized as having six major phases (Carter & McGoldrick, 1980). Each phase focused on some emotional transition in terms of intimate relationships with other people and on changes of personal status.

Traditionally, the first stage involved an unattached young adult separating from his or her family of origin, establishing a personal identity, and developing new interpersonal relationships. Stage two concerned marrying and realigning life's joys and responsibilities within a couple's framework. Stage three entailed having children and meeting the children's needs. Stage four concerned dealing with adolescent children, whose needs and strivings for independence called for very different types of interaction than that appropriate for younger children. Stage four also often marked refocusing the couple's relationship and addressing the needs of their own aging parents. Stage five involved sending children forth into their own new relationships, addressing midlife career issues, and coping with the growing disabilities of their own parents. Finally, stage six entailed adjustments to aging themselves and addressing the inevitability of one's own death.

Today, no designated series of stages for a "typical" family life cycle is adequate or comprehensive enough. The complications, unpredictability, and vast range of different cultural and interpersonal contexts cause family life cycles to vary immensely. Many people no longer choose to marry or have children. Many others choose to delay doing so until much later in life. Divorce and remarriage are widespread, causing massive restructuring in family life. Additionally, "vast differences in family life cycle patterns are caused by oppressive social forces: racism, sexism, homophobia, classism, ageism, cultural prejudices of all kinds, poverty, and immigration" (McGoldrick et al., 2011, p. xxiv).

Poverty can pose immense consequences upon the life cycle of families. Socioeconomic class can determine what opportunities and resources are available to family members and how these, in turn, affect a family's ability to weather crises. Collins and his colleagues (2013) explain that families having insufficient resources frequently:

are politically powerless, socially disenfranchised, and likely to experience unemployment or job instability. Many also experience oppression by more powerful groups.... They live with little hope and struggle to get daily basic needs met. Social class is affected by factors such as culture, ethnicity, education, and gender.... Poverty decreases life span. It also collapses the time in which families experience life cycle stages, causes children to leave home earlier and set up their own families at younger ages, makes grandparenting occur earlier, decreases educational opportunities, and contributes to decreased employment opportunities. Economic conditions today are very different from those encountered by previous generations, making it more difficult for young adults to leave home, purchase their own homes, or even live independently when they are in their twenties. Young people who grow up in impoverished families risk dropping out of school early and encounter an elevated risk of unemployment. Early pregnancy among some teen girls means that they will start their life's journey on shaky ground. (p. 104)

In other words, social-class standing in the context of a family's surrounding community has huge implications regarding development of self-esteem and the ability to function effectively. It affects dreams of future accomplishments, basic opportunities, and what family members can realistically accomplish in the future.

Culture also affects the life cycle of families at every stage. Families radically differ regarding the emphasis placed on various life transitions, depending on their cultural background. Consider that

the Irish have always placed great emphasis on the wake, viewing death as the most important life cycle transition, which frees human beings from the suffering of this world and takes them ... to a happier afterlife. African-Americans, perhaps, as a result of similar life experiences with suffering, have also emphasized funerals. Both groups go to considerable expense and have traditionally delayed services until all family members can get there. Italian and Polish families have placed the greatest emphasis on weddings, often going to enormous expense ... [celebrating and] feasting for lengthy periods of time, reflecting the importance these groups place on continuation of the family into the next generation. Jewish families [stress the importance of] the bar mitzvah and bat mitzvah, a transition to adulthood for boys and girls, respectively, reflecting the value placed on intellectual development, a transition that most other Western groups do not mark at all. (Hines, Preto, McGoldrick, Almeida, & Weltman, 1999, p. 70)

Social workers must focus both on the individualized life transitions of clients and their dynamic interactions with the social systems enveloping them. Generalist practitioners are often called upon to help families when they are under their greatest stress. Being alert to the broad range of life's transitions and sensitive to families' needs as they progress through these phases can provide workers with significant clues for effective interventions.

LO 9-5 Appraise Impacts of the Impinging Social Environment

The social environment involves the conditions, circumstances, and human interactions that encompass human beings. A family-in-environment focus provides an important perspective for understanding how families interact with the many other systems surrounding them in the social environment. These systems may include other individuals, friends, families, work groups, social service organizations, political units, religious organizations, and educational systems. All affect how family systems and individual subsystems within the family can effectively go about their daily operations and daily lives. The other point to remember is that what happens to any individual family member ultimately affects the entire family system. Thus, macro systems impact entire families by affecting individual members.

The following is an example of how macro systems influence family systems. The family consists of two parents and three children aged 9, 13, and 16. Both parents work in a small sausage-processing plant in a rural community of about 12,000 people. Due to deteriorating external economic conditions, the plant is forced to close. Both parents are laid off. Although the parents desperately seek alternative employment, none is available. Unemployment in the community skyrockets. Competition for jobs is intense.

The family's involvement with the many other systems in the environment continues. The family's lack of resources stresses their ability to pay the bills. They get pressure from their landlord and the utility companies. Under such heavy stress, the parents begin to fight. Their children subsequently react to the stress, their parents' fighting, and their newly imposed poverty by starting to rebel. Their work in school suffers, and truancy becomes an increasing problem. The school then contacts the parents about these escalating problems, which, in turn, adds to the parents' stress. The parents' coping abilities are gradually eaten away.

This is just one of the multitude of examples that portray how family systems are integrally involved with the other systems in their environment. Families are not isolated units. Each member of a family system must constantly respond to surrounding environmental conditions. The next section discusses the importance of assessing a family's access to resources.

ASSESSING A FAMILY'S ACCESS TO RESOURCES

The previous example reflects the serious impact macro systems can have on families. Often, the systems involve the family's access to adequate resources. Limited resources can have a wide range of serious effects on a family's ability to function. Therefore, generalist practitioners must be acutely aware of any family's resource status.

There are numerous ways of examining how readily a particular family can obtain necessary, available resources. The Family Access to Basic Resources (FABR) format, illustrated in Figure 9.1, provides one useful means of accomplishing this (Vosler, 1990). "The . . . FABR assessment tool can enable professionals, families, and individual family members to determine the extent of stress and stress pileup caused by inadequate or unstable basic family resources. . . . The FABR outlines assessment areas for exploration with the family so that both the social worker and the family can begin to understand potential sources of chronic stress from the larger environment" (Vosler, 1990, p. 435).

When using the FABR, completing Parts 1 and 2 of the instrument before meeting with the family is best for the social worker. The FABR can provide the worker with some insights concerning a family's economic status before beginning work with the family.

Part 1 allows for a general estimation of what an average family (of the client family's size and composition) needs every month to function effectively. Such information can be obtained from a variety of sources. Public agencies may have these figures available as a result of their regular data collection procedures. Sometimes, census data can be helpful. If information is not readily available, "agencies or a local advocacy group could be called upon to develop estimates based on adequate resources needed for a *long-term decent standard of living* for various household sizes and family configurations" (Vosler, 1990, p. 438).

One should be aware that the poverty line established by the U.S. government is probably significantly lower than what a family actually needs to thrive. The *poverty line* or *poverty threshold* is a "yearly cash income . . . [minimum] (based on family size) set by the federal government to determine if an individual or household can be classified as poor" (Karger & Stoesz, 2010, p. 498).

Part 2 of the FABR focuses on what resources macro systems in the client family's social environment can potentially provide. What resources are actually

PART 1—Monthly Expenses for a Family of This Size and Composition

Work E		Health Care	
Transportation	$_____	Medical	$_____
Child Care	$_____	Dental	$_____
Taxes	$_____	Mental Health	$_____
Purchases for Basic Needs		Special Education (e.g., substance abuse)	$_____
Decent Housing	$_____	Family and Developmental	
Utilities	$_____	(Counseling) Services	$_____
Food	$_____	Procurement of Resources/Services	
Clothing	$_____	(e.g., transportation)	$_____
Personal Care	$_____		
Recreation	$_____	Monthly Total:	$_____

PART 2—Potential Monthly Family Resources

			YES	NO
Money Income		Clothing: Access to Used		
Wages (If parents' occupations are known, what are average monthly wages for these types of jobs?)	$_____	Clothing Store?	_____	_____
		Personal Care and Recreation		
Child Support (if applicable)	$_____	Access to Free Recreational		
Income Transfers (for those unemployed		Facilities?	_____	_____
or not expected to work)	$_____	Health Care		
Unemployment Insurance	$_____	Medicare?	_____	_____
Workmen's Compensation	$_____	Medicaid?	_____	_____
Social Security	$_____	Health Clinic?	_____	_____
Supplemental Security Income (SSI) . . .	$_____	Dental Clinic?	....	....
[Temporary Assistance to Needy Families (TANF)][a]	$_____	Mental Health Services?	_____	_____
Other (e.g., general relief, emergency assistance)	$_____	Special Services (e.g., drug		
Credits, Goods, and Services (free or sliding scale)	$_____	abuse treatment)?	_____	_____
		Education		
Housing		Public Education?	_____	_____
Section 8	$_____	Special Education?	_____	_____
Other Housing Assistance (e.g., public		Tutoring?	_____	_____
housing, shelter, hotel/motel)	$_____	General Equivalency		
Utilities Assistance	$_____	Diploma (GED)?	_____	_____
Food		Job Training?	_____	_____
Food Stamps	$_____	Family Developmental		
		(Counseling) Services		
		Family Services?	_____	_____
Women's, Infants', and Children's		Support Groups?	_____	_____
Supplementary Food Program (WIC)	$_____	Family Life Education?	_____	_____
Food Bank,[b] Food Pantry, and Other		Procurement		
Food Assistance	$_____	Transportation?	_____	_____
		Monthly Total:	$_____	

a. This form initially cited Aid to Families with Dependent Children (AFDC), which was replaced by TANF. AFDC was "a public assistance program . . . funded by the federal and state governments to provide financial aid for needy children who were deprived of parental support because of death, incapacitation, or absence" (Barker, 2003, pp. 13–14). The Personal Responsibility Act (PRA) passed by Congress in August 1996 abolished AFDC, "which had provided support for poor children and their mothers since its inception as Title IV of the 1935 Social Security Act"; AFDC was replaced by "block grants for Temporary Assistance to Needy Families (TANF)," which "put a cap on federal funds provided to the states" and allowed states greater discretion in benefit distribution (Abramovitz, 1997, pp. 311–312). The purpose of the FABR questionnaire is to determine resources regardless of their source. Therefore, you might include in this assessment with other new programs providing benefits to children and families.

(continued)

FIGURE 9.1 Family Access to Basic Resources (FABR)

Source: Nancy R. Vosler (1990). Assessing family access to basic resources: An essential component of social work practice, *Social Work, 35*(5), pp. 434–441. Copyright © 1990, National Association of Social Workers, Inc. Reprinted with permission from the NASW Press, Silver Spring, MD.

PART 3—Current Resources

A. Access to Resources Last Month
    Money Income
    Wages (use net pay; then subtract other work
      expenses from Part 1 above, including
      child care, transportation, etc.) $_____
    Child Support $_____
    Income Transfers[c] $_____

Credits, Goods, and Services

Housing	$_____
Food	$_____
Clothing	$_____
Personal Care and Recreation	$_____
Health Care	$_____
Education	$_____
Family and Developmental	
Services	$_____
Procurement	$_____
Monthly Total	$_____

B. Resource Stability

How stable was each resource over the past year (very stable, somewhat stable, somewhat unstable, very unstable)? Discuss for each type of resource.

Wages: Overall access to wages through employment? Types of jobs available? Part-time or full-time? Wage levels? Benefits? How would/do you deal with child care or supervision of youth? Quality of child care? Do you have choices? How would/do you deal with an ill child? How would/do you get to and from work? What education and training are needed for good jobs? What education and training opportunities are available? Have you been laid off or terminated or experienced a plant closing? Number of times unemployed? Length of time unemployed?

Child Support: How is this received? How was the amount decided? Are checks regular? Are payments up to date? Other problems?

Income Transfers: What experiences have you had in receiving benefits? What kinds of attitudes have you encountered? How adequate are benefits relative to your family's expenses? Has a check been cut? Has a check been delayed? Have you been dropped from benefits for reasons you didn't understand?

Housing: Rent or own? Choice? Maintenance a problem? Are utilities adequate? Have you been put on a waiting list or been dropped from Section 8 or other housing assistance? Have you had to move or been evicted because the landlord converted to higher rents, condominiums, etc.? Have you experienced homelessness?

Food: Quality? Variety? Have your Food Stamps or WIC been cut or delayed? If so, do you understand why? Has other food assistance been cut or changed?

Clothing: Variety for different roles?

Personal Care and Recreation: What kinds of recreation? Individual? Family?

Health Care: High quality? Choice? Available in crisis? Have you been dropped from health care coverage with an employer or from Medicaid? If so, why? Have you or another family member been put on a waiting list, for example, for medical or dental care, for counseling for a mental health problem, or for treatment for alcohol or drug abuse? If so, how long did the person have to wait for services?

Education: High quality? Available for all ages? For special needs? Choice? Have you participated in education or training paid for with loans? If so, how are you managing loan repayments?

Family and Developmental Services: High quality? Choice? Available in crisis? Have you or another family member been put on a waiting list, for example, for family counseling? If so, how long did the person have to wait for services?

Procurement: Bus? Car? What's within walking distance? How reliable is transportation (e.g., bus and/or car)? How close are bus lines to home, work, child care, shopping, etc.?

Other Comments and Reflections:

b. A *food bank* is a program that gathers surplus food from a wide range of sources, including grocery stores, restaurants, farmers, and individuals, and redistributes the food to various programs serving people in need (e. g., soup kitchens or homeless shelters).
c. An *income transfer* is cash that is collected from one segment of the population and distributed (or transferred) to another (e.g., Social Security or Medicare).

FIGURE 9.1 Continued

available to this family to help them reach the input level they need? What types of local, state, and national assistance can the family potentially use?

Part 3 of the FABR can be completed by the family itself during one of the worker's early meetings with the family. This portion identifies what resources the family actually has. Part 3 is divided into the family's "access to resources last month" and its "resource stability." The section on resource stability helps establish whether the resources obtained last month were abnormally high or low and whether or not the last month's input reflects that which is typical for the family.

A family's actual access to resources can be calculated by taking the family's total "access to resources last month" (Part 3A) and subtracting that from the total "monthly expenses for a [typical] family of this size and composition" (Part 1). The remaining amount refers to what the family needs to function but is not getting. Subsequently, Parts 2 and 3B help the worker identify specific problems in the family's access to resources.

Part 2 supplies clues for what resources the family is not getting but potentially could be. What services has the family not been aware of or taken advantage of in the past? How could the worker act as broker to link family members with the services they need?

Part 3B alerts the worker to problems in ongoing acquisition of resources. For instance, one question asks, "Have your Food Stamps[1] or WIC[2] [Special Supplementary Feeding Program for Women, Infants, and Children] been cut or delayed?" (Vosler, 1990, p. 437). Such questions can help the worker begin identifying problems in service delivery and exploring potential intervention approaches for positive change. What obstacles exist in impinging macro systems that prevent the family from getting needed resources? What macro systems are potential targets of change?

---

1. The *Food Stamp Program*, administered by the U.S. Department of Agriculture (USDA) and paid for by the federal government, was established in 1964 to supplement the ability of impoverished families to obtain food; if people meet a means test (i.e., if their income and assets fall below designated levels), they become eligible to receive coupons that can be used to purchase food (Karger & Stoesz, 2010). Note that the Personal Responsibility and Work Opportunity Reconciliation Act of 1996, which established TANF, also placed significant restrictions on Food Stamp accessibility.

2. *WIC*, the Special Supplementary Feeding Program for Women, Infants, and Children administered by the USDA, provides low-income women and their children at risk of insufficient nutrition with food subsidies.

On one level, the FABR indicates what the family needs in order to function adequately. It provides cues for how the worker should proceed. The worker can target where resources are lacking or not being used and establish plans to enhance the family's access to them.

On another level, the FABR indicates what resources impinging macro systems are failing to provide. By emphasizing the importance of the family's access to resources, it highlights the significance of the family's interactions with multiple macro systems. The FABR thus establishes links among micro, mezzo, and macro levels of practice. The FABR can provide documentation regarding where resources are lacking and where changes are needed in macro systems. When families have poor or no access to basic resources, interventions may need to involve "social planning, advocacy, and lobbying within larger social systems, including work at neighborhood, local, state, and national levels" (Logan, 2008; Vosler, 1990, p. 438).

Critical Thinking Questions 9.3

EP 2.1.3

- Fill out the FABR. How would you assess your own access to basic resources?
- What are your major strengths and weaknesses?

Highlight 9.3 discusses the potential difficulty of getting sensitive information from clients. Suggestions are provided for aiding this process.

LO 9-6 Analyze Common Family Conflicts and Problems

EP 2.1.10j

Conflict can be defined as "a struggle over ... resources, power and status, beliefs, and other preferences and desires" (Bisno, 1988, p. 13). Hostility, strife, disharmony, arguments, or disunity all can be involved. Conflicts are destined to occur in any group. As a matter of fact, many times conflicts are positive and desirable. Groups, including family groups, are made up of unique individuals, each with individual opinions and ideas. Conflict can represent the open sharing of these individual ideas. It can serve as a mechanism for improving communication, enhancing the closeness of relationships, and working out dissatisfactions.

Although each family is unique, conflicts and problems can occur in at least four categories. First, there

Difficulties in Soliciting Personal Information

One should note that soliciting such personal information from clients like much of what the FABR addresses may be difficult. People may be proud and feel uncomfortable talking about the public assistance they receive. There are several suggestions for helping them share information.

First, acknowledge the fact that solicitation may be difficult. Be conscious of how you phrase questions and how clients react to these questions. Second, use warmth, empathy, genuineness, an appropriate degree of self-disclosure, and other interpersonal skills to establish rapport. The more you can effectively engage clients and form a positive relationship with them, the more comfortable they will feel in answering questions. Third, you might start out with asking less-sensitive questions. Some informal chatting may soften the interviewing process. For example, soliciting information about children's names and their recreational interests might portray your interest and concern about the family's well-being. A fourth suggestion for soliciting

difficult information involves being tactful. Avoid criticizing clients or insensitively hurting their feelings.

A fifth suggestion concerns when clients refuse to provide information. Sheafor and Horejsi (2008) suggest that you:

> . . . follow up with an effort to engage the client in a discussion of general reasons why some topics might be hard for people to discuss and why people often want to withhold and protect certain information. These reasons might include feelings of shame and embarrassment, not knowing what words to use, not knowing how the social worker will react, not knowing if the worker would understand, fear that the worker might be judgmental, fear of a lack of confidentiality, fear that the information will be used to exploit the client, and so on. (p. 220)

Addressing these issues straightforwardly may enhance clients' trust in you and increase their comfort level in sharing personal information.

are relationship problems between primary partners who are, for example, spouses or significant others. Second, there are difficulties existing between parents and children. Third are the personal problems of individual family members. Finally, there are stresses imposed on the family by the external environment. Each will be discussed in more detail later.

Family problems do not necessarily fall neatly into one of these categories or another. Frequently, families experience more than one category of problems. Nor are these problem categories mutually exclusive. Many times one problem will be closely related to another. Take, for instance, a woman who is a wife, mother, legal librarian, and the primary breadwinner for her family. The law firm at which she has worked for the past 11 years suddenly decides to hire a lawyer to replace her. Despite massive efforts, she has not been able to find another job with similar responsibilities and salary. This situation can be considered a family problem caused by stresses in the environment. However, it is also a personal problem for the woman. Her sense of self-worth is seriously diminished as a result of her job loss and inability to find another position. As a result, she becomes cranky, short-tempered, and difficult to

live with. The environmental stress she is experiencing causes her to have difficulties relating to both children and spouse. The entire family system becomes disturbed.

PARTNER DIFFICULTIES

The first category of family problems involves difficulties between members of a couple. Couples may bring many issues to counseling, including disagreements about raising children, domestic violence, sexual problems, conflicts over money and recreational time, and unfaithfulness. Communication issues often surface as a primary concern (Collins et al., 2013; Worden, 2003). For instance, consider the following case scenario of communication problems within a marriage.

Case Scenario: An Example of Communication Problems Within a Marriage

Bill and Chantal, both in their mid-30s, have a communication problem. They have been married for 1 year. The marriage occurred after a lengthy dating period that was filled with strife. A primary source of stress was Chantal's desire for the permanent commitment of marriage and Bill's unwillingness to make such a commitment. In view of Chantal's threats to leave him, Bill finally decided to get married.

Prior to the marriage, a major source of difficulty concerned the time that Bill and Chantal spent together. They each owned their own condominiums, so they did not live together. Bill was very involved in a physical fitness program. He went to work out at a health club four nights each week, including Fridays. Bill also had numerous close friends at the club with whom he enjoyed spending his time. Chantal was infuriated that Bill restricted the time he spent with her to only some of the days when he did not work out at the club. Her major concern, however, remained Bill's inability to make a commitment. Chantal felt that things would change once they got married.

After marriage, things did not change much. Although Chantal and Bill now lived together, he still worked out at the club with his friends four nights a week. This schedule continued to infuriate Chantal.

In a discussion, the spouses expressed their feelings. Chantal said, "I hate all the time Bill spends at the club. I resent having him designate the time he thinks he can spend with me. I feel like he's putting my time into little boxes."

Bill responded, "My physical health is very important to me. I love to work out at the club. What should I do—stay home every night watching television and become a couch potato?"

One way of assessing this couple's communication is evaluating the *intent* (what the speaker wants to have communicated to the receiver) and the actual *impact* of the communication, that is, what the listener actually hears. Many times, the intent and impact of communication are different. A therapeutic goal is to improve the accuracy of communication, that is, the extent to which the intent of the speaker and the impact upon the listener resemble each other.

There were other difficulties within Bill and Chantal's relationship that are too lengthy to describe. Here we will limit our discussion to some of the issues involved in the simple communication addressed earlier. In a recent discussion, the following scenario developed. Chantal verbally stated that she hated seeing Bill go to the health club so often. The impact on Bill was that he felt Chantal was trying to control him and tell him what to do. He loved Chantal but was also very wary of losing his independence and what he viewed as his identity. When Chantal placed demands on him, he became even more protective of his time.

Chantal's intent in her communication was different than her impact; she felt that he thought the club and his friends were more important than she was. These feelings were related to her basic lack of self-esteem and self-confidence.

Bill's response to Chantal's statement also had serious discrepancies between its intent and impact. Bill was verbally stating that he loved to work out. The impact on Chantal, that is, what she heard Bill say, was that he liked the club and his friends more than he liked her. Bill's actual intent was to tell Chantal his physical health and appearance were very important to him. He also wanted to communicate to her that his sense of independence was important to him. He loved her and wanted to be committed to her, yet his long-term fear of commitment was related to his actual fear that he would lose his identity in someone else's. He was afraid of losing his right to make choices and decisions and of being told what to do.

Commentary on the Case Scenario

One frequent purpose in interventions involving couples and larger families is to enhance the congruence between intents and impacts as individuals communicate. A practitioner can help each partner communicate more effectively by giving suggestions about how to rephrase statements using words that reflect more clearly what the speakers really mean. Another suggestion is to encourage feedback, that is, to examine what happens when the receiver shares reactions about a message with the sender. For instance, instead of responding to Chantal's demands defensively, Bill might be encouraged to tell her, "I love you very much, Chantal. I need to keep in shape, and I need some time to myself. How can we work this out?"

Eventually, Bill and Chantal used a planned change approach to iron out their difficulties. The accuracy of their communication gradually improved through counseling. Each learned how to better communicate personal needs. Instead of their old standoff, they began to identify and evaluate alternatives. Their final solution involved several facets. First, Bill would continue to go to the club to work out three nights each week. However, Fridays would be spent with Chantal. It turned out that she was exceptionally annoyed at not being able to go out with Bill on Friday nights. Chantal, who also was an avid believer in physical fitness, would occasionally go with Bill to the health club to work out. This gave her the sense of freedom to join him when she chose. The important thing was that she no longer felt restricted. In reality, she rarely went with him to the club. Chantal also chose to take some postgraduate courses in her field on those evenings when Bill visited the club. She enjoyed such activities, and they enhanced her sense of professional competence. The personal issues of Bill's need to feel free and Chantal's lack of self-esteem demanded continued efforts on both spouses' parts. Enhanced communication skills helped them communicate their ongoing needs.

PARENT–CHILD RELATIONSHIP DIFFICULTIES

The second major type of family problems involves difficulties in the relationships between parents and children. Sometimes this entails the parents having trouble controlling children. Frequently, especially as children reach adolescence, this involves communication problems.

There are many perspectives on how best to manage children's behavior and improve parent–child communication. Approaches include applications of learning theory and communication techniques involving the use of active listening and the sending of "I-messages."

Practitioners can help parents improve their control of children by assessing the individual family situations and teaching parents some basic behavior modification techniques. *Behavior modification* involves the application of learning theory principles to real-life situations. For instance, getting into a punishment rut with a misbehaving child is easy for parents. Consider Shen, age 4, who spills the contents of drawers and cabinets in the kitchen area whenever he is unobserved. His parents have seen enough flour, honey, silverware, and plastic bags in heaps on the floor to last them several lifetimes. In their frustration, they typically respond by swatting Shen on the rump. He then cries a little bit until the next time he has the opportunity to be in the kitchen alone and start all over again.

In family counseling, Shen's parents were taught several new behavior management techniques (i.e., behavior modification techniques applied to specific child management situations). First, they were taught the value of *positive reinforcement*. These reinforcements are positive experiences or consequences that follow a behavior and increase the likelihood that it will recur. Instead of relying solely on punishment (i.e., rump swatting), the parents were taught to react more positively to Shen during those times when he was behaving well (i.e., playing appropriately and not emptying drawers). By closely examining Shen's behaviors and the circumstances surrounding him, his parents gradually learned to view Shen in a different way. They learned that he felt he was not getting enough attention in general. In order to get the attention he needed, he resorted to the destructive drawer-emptying behavior. Providing Shen with structured positive playing times

when they gave Shen their sole attention was much more effective. This technique, in addition to making positive comments about his good behavior, helped to diminish Shen's need for getting attention in inappropriate ways. Shen's parents also learned that their punishment was having the opposite effect of what they had intended. That is, instead of stopping his bad behavior, they were unwittingly encouraging it. Punishing Shen was actually a form of positive reinforcement because it gave him the attention he wanted. Thus, he continued his drawer-emptying behavior.

As an alternative to punishment, Shen's parents were taught the time-out technique. *Time-out* involves a procedure where reinforcement is withdrawn, resulting in a decrease in the occurrence of the behavior. Instead of swatting Shen when he emptied drawers, his parents were directed to place him in a corner with his eyes to the wall for 5 minutes. A few minutes should be the maximum duration of a time-out, as it loses its effectiveness after a very short length of time (Kazdin, 2008; Miltenberger, 2012; Spiegler & Guevremont, 2010). It was also important to administer the time-out to Shen immediately after his inappropriate behavior occurred. This quick response was necessary for him to relate the time-out directly to his misbehavior. Time-outs provided Shen's parents with a method to deprive Shen of attention without hurting him. Because attention was what Shen really wanted, this became a very effective behavioral control technique. It should be emphasized, however, that Shen needed continued attention and positive reinforcement for appropriate behavior. He would not have misbehaved in the first place had he not been trying to let his parents know about an important need, namely, his desire for attention.

Two other suggestions concerning communication between parents and children are relevant here—using active listening and sending "I-messages" (Collins et al., 2013; Gordon, 1975; Sheafor & Horejsi, 2012). *Active listening* resembles the intent–impact communication approach described earlier when discussing couples' communication. It involves two basic steps. First, the receiver of the message tries earnestly to understand the sender's feelings and messages. Another way of explaining this process is that the receiver tries to understand the actual intent of the sender. In the second step, the receiver puts this "understanding into [his/her] own words . . . and feeds it back for the sender's verification" (Gordon, 1975, p. 53).

For instance, 13-year-old Tyrone says to his mother, "Dances are boring. I'm not going to that boring old dance on Friday."

His mother works hard at active listening and tries to see the situation from Tyrone's perspective. She replies, "You mean you'd really like to go but you don't think you can dance very well."

Tyron responds, "Yep." His mother had accurately heard his real concerns.

A second technique useful in parent–child communication is the use of *I-messages*. These involve responding to another person's verbal or nonverbal behavior by clearly stating your feelings and reactions to that behavior. Instead of using a blaming "you-message" (e.g., Don't *you* ever take money out of my purse without asking again!), structure your verbal response to use an "I-message" (e.g., *I* felt really disappointed when you took money out of my purse without asking. *I* would like to be able to trust you). Such messages do not blame the other person but rather convey to him or her how his or her behavior affected you. This leaves the responsibility for changing the behavior squarely on the person receiving the "I-message."

PERSONAL PROBLEMS OF INDIVIDUAL FAMILY MEMBERS

Sometimes, a family will come to a practitioner for help and identify one family member as causing the trouble, the third category of family problems. A basic principle of family therapy is that the entire family owns the problem (Goldenberg & Goldenberg, 2013; Worden, 2003). In other words, sometimes one family member becomes the scapegoat for malfunctioning within the entire family system. *Scapegoating* is the "process of identifying one member as the problem"; "[f]amilies and children develop scapegoating stories as a way to keep the family's attention from other issues they may not want to deal with, for example, marital conflict" (Hull & Mather, 2006, p. 64). The practitioner is then responsible for helping the family define the problem as a family group, rather than an individual problem. Treatment goals will then most likely involve the restructuring of various family relationships.

For instance, a family of five came in for treatment. The family consisted of a 48-year-old husband and father, a 45-year-old wife and mother, and three children: Rob, 19; Ralph, 16; and Rachel, 13. The family came from a rural Wisconsin town of 8,000 people. The father was a successful businessman who was involved in town politics. The mother was a homemaker who did not work outside of the home. Rob was a freshman at the University of Wisconsin at Madison. The identified problem was Ralph. For the past year,

Ralph had been stealing neighbors' cars whenever he had the chance and running down people's mailboxes. To say the least, this activity became annoying to the local townspeople. The family came to counseling as their last resort to try controlling the problem.

After several sessions of family members pointing blaming fingers at Ralph, Rachel quietly commented to her parents, "Well, you never say anything about *his* problem," and proceeded to point at Rob. Suddenly, as if a floodgate had been opened, the entire family situation came pouring out. Rachel had been referring to her parents' difficulties in accepting Rob's recent announcement that he was gay. Rob was going through a difficult period as he was "coming out," in terms of making lifestyle decisions and relating to old friends and family members. The father was terrified that the local townspeople, who had extremely negative and irrational fears of gay people *(homophobia)*, would find out. The father feared that he would lose precious social status and that it would damage his political career. The mother turned out to be a serious alcoholic, a secret that the entire family had worked hard to keep. The mother and father had not had a sexual relationship for 10 years; they slept in separate bedrooms. The father was a harsh, stern man who felt it necessary to maintain what he considered absolute control over family members, including the mother. He was very critical of them all and never risked sharing his own feelings. Finally, Rachel was having serious problems both with her grades and attendance in school. She was also sexually active with a variety of young men. Both she and her parents lived in constant fear of her becoming pregnant.

As it turned out, Ralph was one of the better-adjusted individuals in the family. He attended school regularly, got straight B's, and was active in high school sports (before being suspended for his car-stealing, mailbox-crushing behavior). This family provides a good illustration of a family-owned problem. The entire family system was showing disturbances. Ralph was the scapegoat, the identified problem. All Ralph was doing was calling attention to the family's many, more global problems.

EXTERNAL ENVIRONMENTAL STRESSES: THE IMPACT OF SOCIAL AND ECONOMIC FORCES

EP 2.1.4 a&c

The fourth category of problems frequently found in families includes those caused by factors outside of the family in the external environment. These problems can include inadequate income, unemployment, poor housing conditions, poor access to means of transportation and places for recreation, and inadequate job opportunities. Included in the multitude of other potential problems are poor health conditions, inadequate schools, and dangerous neighborhoods.

To begin addressing these problems, practitioners need sharp brokering skills. That is, they need to know what services are available and how to make a connection with families in need of these services.

Many times appropriate services will be unavailable or nonexistent. Practitioners will need to advocate for clients. That is, they will need to plead actively the cause of their clients, often far beyond what is minimally required. Sometimes, services will need to be developed. Other times, unresponsive agency administrations will need to be confronted. Legal assistance may be necessary. There are no easy solutions to solving nationwide problems for families such as poverty and its related issues. This is a constant, ongoing process. Political involvement will be necessary. Many external environmental stresses are difficult to change and diminish. However, such environmental stresses pose serious problems for families that practitioners will not be able to ignore.

Critical Thinking Questions 9.4

- Focus on your own family or a family with whom you are familiar. Does this family experience conflict between partners, difficulties between parents and children, individual problems, or stresses imposed by the external environment?
- To what extent does this family system successfully resolve its conflicts?
- What, if any, strategies for resolution are effective?

LO 9-7 Examine Variations in Family Structure

Changing values, issues, economic support, and technology have had an awesome impact on family life over the past decades. Generalist practitioners cannot assume that the families on their caseloads will consist primarily of intact, two-parent families with two to four relatively well-adjusted, blood-related siblings. Practitioners today will address a wide variety of family structures and issues. Thus, being aware of the broad range of dynamics that can operate within these various structures is important. Here, we will consider two of these variations—single-parent families and blended families.

SINGLE-PARENT FAMILIES

The traditional family configuration (two parents, one a mother who remains in the home to provide full-time care) is becoming less and less common, demonstrated by the following facts (U.S. Census Bureau, 2011):

- Approximately 30 percent of U.S. families with dependent children are supported by single parents.
- A substantial majority (almost 87 percent) of single parents are women.
- Over 63 percent of single women and over 61 percent of married women age 16 or older work outside the home. Almost 68 percent of single mothers with children under age 6 are employed.
- Although 74 percent of white families with children under age 18 have both parents living within the home, only about 41 percent of African-American families and 66 percent of Hispanic families have both parents living there.
- Whereas 13.5 percent of all white females are living below the poverty level (compared to 11.2 percent of white males), 27.5 percent of African-American females and 27.4 percent of Hispanic females live below the poverty level.
- The median income for all married-couple families is $71,830. In contrast, the median income for female family heads with no husband present is about 45.4 percent of that (or $32,597). This compares with a median income of $48,084 for male family heads with no wife present.
- Women earn about 80.5 percent of what men earn, African-American women earn about 69.6 percent of what white men earn, and Hispanic/Latina women only about 59.8 percent (U.S. Bureau of Labor Statistics, 2011).
- Almost 41 percent of babies are born to unmarried women in the United States (U.S. Census Bureau, 2011).

These statistics have at least two clear-cut implications for generalist social workers. First, social workers must be flexible regarding what is considered a "typical" or "normal" family. Second, poverty and lack of resources are characterizing a growing number of American women and children.

As in two-parent families, such issues as effective communication among family members and satisfactory child management are vitally important. Likewise, a focus on the family's relationships with other systems in the environment is important. However, two aspects should be highlighted for single-parent families. First, there are often greater pressures brought to bear on a single parent to assume virtually all of the parental responsibilities by him- or (more frequently) herself. Chapter 13, which addresses gender-sensitive social work practice, discusses some of the special issues women face.

The second aspect to emphasize in single-parent families is their even greater likelihood of impoverishment. At one level, linking families with needed resources is critically important. Chapter 15, on brokering, addresses this in greater depth. On another level, advocacy on the behalf of children and their families is often called for. Chapter 14 further describes this likeliness of impoverishment.

Single Teenage Parents

A group of single parents deserving special attention is that of single teenage parents. The rate of teen pregnancy has declined since its peak in 1991, but it is still the highest such rate among Western industrialized countries (Crooks & Baur, 2014). Pregnancy rates for African-American and Hispanic teens are higher than for their white counterparts, although white teens who live in poverty also have higher pregnancy rates (Yarber, Sayad, & Strong, 2010).

Mooney, Knox, and Schacht (2011) reflect on some of the reasons for teen pregnancy:

Low academic achievement is both a contributing factor and a potential outcome of teenage parenthood. Teenage females who do poorly in school may have little hope of success and achievement in pursuing educational and occupational goals, and they may think that their only remaining option for a meaningful role in life is to become a parent. . . .

Teens from low socioeconomic backgrounds are more likely than those from higher socioeconomic backgrounds to become teenage parents. Although many teen mothers experience poverty before becoming pregnant, teenage childbearing tends to exacerbate the problems that these disadvantaged young women already face. Most teenagers who become parents are not married and have no means of economic support or have limited earning capacity. Teen mothers often rely on the support of their own parents or rely on public assistance. Having a child at a young age makes it difficult for the teen parent to attain academic credentials, compete in the job market, and break out of what for many is a cycle of poverty that includes their children. (p. 180)

Weatherley and Cartoof (1988) propose a series of suggestions for working with single adolescent parents; they focus on "a continuum of services thought to be appro-

priate at various stages of adolescent pregnancy and parenthood" (p. 39), discussed in the following subsections.

 Preventing Pregnancy. Primary pregnancy prevention refers to preventing the problem altogether, assuming that the pregnancy is a problem. To attempt prevention, adolescents need both information and ready access to contraception so that they can make responsible decisions. Research indicates that sound sex education programs can delay first intercourse, and reduce pregnancy and sexually transmitted infections; additionally, those including "content on contraception and communication skills have been found to delay the onset of sexual intercourse or reduce the frequency of sexual intercourse, reduce the number of sexual partners, and increase the use of contraception" (Carroll, 2013, p. 201).

Effective sex education programs:

1. focus on risk reduction;
2. are grounded in social learning theories;
3. focus on activities that address media and social influences; and
4. teach and allow for practice in communication and negotiation skills. (Hyde & DeLamater, 2011, pp. 514–515)

Ready access to contraception also seems to be important (Crooks & Baur, 2014; Hyde & DeLamater, 2011). Renzetti, Curran, and Maier (2012) maintain that sex education is not enough and that "tutoring, SAT preparation, job skills, medical and dental care, sports, and creative arts—that is, programs that provide educational, employment, and personal enrichment opportunities" are most effective in decreasing teen pregnancy (p. 181).

Promotion of chastity has been proposed as a means of pregnancy prevention. However, research has not established that this approach works (Carroll, 2013; Hyde & DeLamater, 2011). "Just say no" is easy to say but hard to do. Several pictures come to mind. One possible scenario involves just saying no to a hot fudge sundae if you absolutely adore hot fudge but are desperately trying to stay on your liquid protein diet. Another is just saying no to a friend offering you a cigarette when you are out at a party where everyone in the world seems to be smoking and you just quit this morning. One final scene involves one of those hot, passionate, decision-making moments when you are madly in love and you are simply certain it will last forever (again). Just saying no is not always so easy.

Help During Pregnancy. Providing support during pregnancy can be important. Becoming depressed and isolated during that time is easy. Physical changes may have impacts, especially in view of the great emphasis placed on physical appearance, attractiveness, and popularity during adolescence. One junior high teacher once said that talking about the responsibility of pregnancy and teen parenthood had absolutely no effect on her students. However, the young women sat up with serious faces and widened eyes when told that once you have a baby, you often have stretch marks on your abdomen for the rest of your life. To these young women, stretch marks were serious consequences.

Pregnant adolescents may need help relating to friends and family members, which involves maintaining good communication with and emotional support from others around them. Many times a social worker may need to do active outreach to the pregnant teen. Home visits may be especially useful. Counseling can be provided either individually or in a group.

Pregnant teens most often need counseling about good nutrition and the impacts of lifestyle upon the fetus. For instance, they need to be well informed about the results of alcohol and drug use during pregnancy. Teens also may need help in determining what to do about the pregnancy and other future plans involving living conditions, day care, education, and employment.

Helping Adolescent Fathers. Not forgetting that babies born to adolescent mothers also have fathers is important. Despite myths to the contrary, most teen fathers are significantly affected by their child's birth and are involved to various degrees in the child's early life (Yarber et al., 2010).

An adolescent father may need help in expressing his feelings, defining his role, and contributing where he can in taking over responsibilities for his child. Many adolescent fathers have psychological repercussions as a result of the pregnancy; they tend to do less well educationally and economically (Yarber et al., 2010). Therefore, they may need help and encouragement in pursuing educational and vocational goals.

Helping Mothers After the Pregnancy. Keeping the continuum of service in mind is important. The mother's needs do not suddenly stop after the baby is born. The case is not automatically closed. There are three major areas where adolescent mothers may need ongoing help (Weatherley & Cartoof, 1988):

1. They may need help in learning about positive parenting and child management skills. Several aspects have been found to enhance this training. For one thing, training should be "flexible, informal, and individualized" (p. 49).
2. Adolescent mothers often need help in avoiding more pregnancies. Pregnancy is no guarantee that they have an adequate knowledge of decreasing the chances of conception or of birth control methodology. Both information and ready access to contraception are necessary.
3. Young mothers often need assistance in their future life planning. Issues include continuing their education, gaining employment, finding day care for the child, and determining where and how they will live.

Assessment and Personal Values

 A few comments about personal values are warranted here. Clarifying their own personal values and prohibiting these values from interfering with assessment and other aspects of practice is critically important for workers (Dolgoff, Harrington, & Loewenberg, 2012; NASW, 2008). Personal values have the potential to affect many aspects of the helping process including treatment approaches chosen, goals set, means of evaluating treatment effectiveness, and communication with clients (Corey, Corey, & Callanan, 2011; Reamer, 2008). However, "if clients are encouraged to change the direction of their values without being aware of what they are doing, they are being deprived of self-determination" (Corey et al., 2011, p. 79).

Working with pregnant adolescents provides a useful example of how personal values may be in direct conflict with clients' values. Strong opinions are involved. You may personally feel that a 13-year-old female is unable to care adequately for an infant. You may think that for this 13-year-old's mother to assume primary responsibility for the infant's care is unfair. You may strongly favor or reject the concept of abortion. Regardless of your personal values regarding an individual case, helping a client assess all available alternatives is still important for you. Only she can evaluate which course is best for her. Chapter 11 discusses values and ethics in much greater depth.

REMARRIAGE AND BLENDED FAMILIES

"A *blended family* is any nontraditional configuration of people who live together, are committed to each other, and perform functions traditionally assumed by families. Such relationships may not involve biological or legal linkages. The important thing is that such groups *function* as families" (Zastrow & Kirst-Ashman, 2013, p. 168). In the context of remarriage, the blended family involves the newlywed couple who may bring children to the family from prior relationships or may have children together, resulting in a combination of "his, hers, and theirs." Such blended families are also often referred to as stepfamilies.

Blended families differ from intact nuclear families in that they are more likely to experience certain problems (Visher & Visher, 1988). Because of the increased prevalence of such reconstituted families, being aware of their special issues and needs is important for generalist practitioners. For one thing, loyalty conflicts may arise. Which parent of the divorced or separated couple should the children be loyal to? How does a newly married stepparent fit into the family's scheme of things? Should a remarried parent devote more attention to his or her new spouse or to children from the prior marriage?

Defense of territoriality is often another major issue in blended families. How is power and authority reestablished and changed when new parts of family systems are melded together? Many questions arise in newly blended families. Will the stepchildren resent the new stepmother assuming the same parental authority as their biological father and, for that matter, their biological mother? How will the new spouse get along with the stepchildren's other biological parent? Because of old interactional patterns, how difficult will it be for a new stepparent to adjust to all the firmly established interactional patterns of the old family system? How will stepchildren adjust to new stepparental rule?

The "basic struggle for a blended family is the search for its identity as a family unit" (Visher & Visher, 1988, p. 224); these researchers go on to identify at least seven aspects characterizing blended families that are stepfamilies. Each merits the worker's attention when working with such families.

The first area needing attention is that of "changes" on the one hand, and "losses" on the other (Goldenberg & Goldenberg, 2013, p. 435; Visher & Visher, 1988). Members of blended families are subject to massive changes. Place of residence or schools may change. Daily family procedures may be altered. When and what the family eats may be modified by the new stepparent's wishes. Children may have to modify their bedroom sleeping arrangements to incorporate new stepbrothers and sisters. Where the family traditionally spends Thanksgiving, Christmas Eve, Hanukkah, or birthdays may change. Members of stepfamilies are forced to make a broad variety of adjustments. These range from major alterations in basic living conditions to minor adjustments in everyday habits.

Additionally, a blended family suffers losses. Sometimes it loses regular contact with the `absent parent.

Other times, it loses friends or possessions. Perhaps the children never see their grandparents on one side of the family anymore.

The point is that attending to the vast array of changes, including losses, that confront stepfamily members is especially important for practitioners. These changes may provide clear clues regarding what direction interventions need to take.

A second aspect of blended family life important for workers to address is the idea of "unrealistic belief systems" (Visher & Visher, 1988, p. 227). Modeling our idea of the perfect family on the intact nuclear family is easy. There may be pressure for parents in newly blended families to try to make these new families conform to old rules that may no longer be appropriate. For example, there is the idea that stepbrothers and stepsisters should become emotionally close and get along almost immediately, like an instant family. This idea is unrealistic. Relationships take time to develop. Positive feelings take time to be nurtured and grow. The practitioner may need to help the family set more realistic expectations for its interaction. However, some individual family members may never come to like each other.

A third important issue to address with blended families is that of "insiders versus outsiders" (Visher & Visher, 1988, p. 228). Outsiders may include "a stepparent without children who joins a parent with children, a fourteen-year-old girl who comes to live with her father and stepmother after they have been married for five years, or a mother and her two children who move into her new husband's former home" (1988, p. 228). Practitioners need to watch out for family members placed in outsider roles. Feeling like an outsider in what is supposed to be one's own home inevitably causes problems. The social worker may need to help the family define ways to make all members become insiders and feel "at home." (See Highlight 9.4.)

The fourth important aspect operating within blended families is that of "power" (Visher & Visher, 1988, p. 229). Power is a complicated concept that is difficult to define concisely. It involves who controls or influences whom within the stepfamily. It concerns the hierarchy of command. In other words, who will be paid attention to before someone else? Power also involves the amount of respect various stepfamily members have for each other. Usually, the ranking system places the biological parent living with the children first, the biological parent not living with the children second, the stepparent living with the children third, and the stepparent not living with the children last.

HIGHLIGHT 9.4

An Example of Life Within a Blended Family

One stepmother, Cathy, after 1 1/2 years of marriage, made some wise comments about blended family life. Cathy married for the first time in her mid-30s to someone a few years older than herself. He was divorced and had two teenage daughters.

Both of these daughters lived with Cathy and her new husband. Cathy spoke of how she naively entered the marriage and blended family life, never anticipating the struggles that were about to occur.

Cathy described her stepdaughters as beautiful but spoiled. She, by the way, was a social worker by profession. Discrepancies in values between stepmother and stepdaughters were huge. Problematic issues in stepfamily life were ominous. Cathy's stepdaughters would associate only with "upper-class" people (meaning people who had a lot of money) and people of their same race. Neither daughter liked poor people very much. Additionally, one daughter kept things fastidiously clean, and the other maintained a disorganized mess. Cathy's own approach to housework was somewhere in between. The daughter who emphasized cleanliness was also anorexic. This made family meals and eating in general a continual struggle. For instance, Cathy confided that sometimes she would bake muffins for her anorexic stepdaughter, which the latter loved. On the outside these looked like ordinary muffins high in fiber content and low in calories. On the inside, however, they were packed with a special, highly caloric substance made for people who needed additional nutrition. Hence, the muffin appeared to be 80 calories by looking at the outside, but in reality it exceeded 800. Her anorexic stepdaughter

would eagerly eat two or three muffins at a sitting. In this way, Cathy could trick the anorexic into getting her needed nutrition. Cathy said the anorexic daughter probably "would've fainted dead away" had she had any inkling regarding how many calories there really were in what she considered a "diet" muffin.

Cathy also commented on how difficult feeling automatic love toward her stepdaughters was. She did not have the loving, nurturing childhood years (at least, these years should be such theoretically) to develop a strong relationship with them. The common daily struggles and annoyances of teenagers versus parents in addition to the major differences in values made it very difficult for positive feelings to bloom.

A positive aspect about the family was that Cathy and her husband maintained a good relationship between them. Her husband worked hard at not taking sides against her on behalf of his daughters.

Due to the conflicts and the anorexia, the entire family entered family counseling. Cathy expressed profuse relief at being able to step out of her social work role and say how she really felt as "the wicked stepmother." She felt the sessions were very helpful to the family as communication began to improve. Although the family did not become blissfully happy, at least it could function and accomplish its daily activities. Cathy continued to work at her marriage. Cathy also recognized that the daily living problems with her stepdaughters would gradually decrease as the girls matured and moved into their own living arrangements for good. She was willing to bide her time.

More complex custody arrangements such as joint custody may complicate the power hierarchy even more.

Problems arise when people feel powerless in blended families. A problem can easily develop when stepparents feel stepchildren do not listen to them. A situation can be difficult for a child who feels divided between two stepfamilies and unable to control his or her own life. Likewise, a noncustodial parent refusing to follow the terms of the custodial agreement and collecting or returning children unpredictably can be problematic.

At any rate, when power is an issue, the worker needs to help the family clarify to the extent possible

who has what power and *what that power involves.* That all family members feel they are valuable family participants and not simply helpless pawns is important.

Power conflicts may also result from differences in parenting styles among households. Children in blended families frequently trek from one household to another, depending on parental involvement, custodial agreements, and visitation arrangements. Frequently, each household will have different rules, expectations, and parenting styles (Goldenberg & Goldenberg, 2013). Cooperative parenting should be stressed, which involves maintaining open communication and consistency between households where children reside at different times (Goldenberg & Goldenberg, 2013).

The following is an example of a power conflict where cooperative parenting could be improved. Becca, who is 8 years old, lives with her biological father; biological brother Daniel, 10; stepmother; and stepsister. Becca and Daniel spend every other weekend and designated holidays with their biological mother. On visitation weekends, Becca's mother dresses Becca in tight, seductive clothing and encourages her to paint her nails. When Becca returns to her biological father's home, he forbids her to wear such clothing at home or school. He also forbids her from using nail polish because she has spilled it on the carpet several times. This situation is only one of numerous conflicts in childrearing practices. Becca's biological parents detest each other, never having recovered from a bitter divorce. Unfortunately, their differences in child treatment give Becca numerous double messages. Who is right? Whom should she believe?

"Loyalty conflicts" involve the fifth problem commonly found in blended families (Goldenberg & Goldenberg, 2013, p. 435; Visher & Visher, 1988). Children may feel pulled between two divorced parents. A parent may feel torn between loyalty to a new spouse and loyalty to children from a prior marriage. Because of the new mixing of people and the more complicated structures involved in blended families, such loyalty conflicts are understandably common occurrences.

A social worker faced with these issues needs to help make the family understand that people do not have limited quantities of love that must be divided between some finite number of people. Rather, love can be shared and expressed in many ways. It might be the task of the practitioner to help family members establish ways of displaying love and affection differently and more effectively than they have in the past.

"Boundary problems" make up the sixth area important to monitor in blended families (Goldenberg & Goldenberg, 2013; Nichols, 2011; Visher & Visher, 1988, p. 232). As we have discussed, appropriate boundaries are important to maintain in any family. For instance, the spouse system needs to maintain its special, unique status. However, in blended families boundaries may easily become vague or confused because of the complex nature of relationships.

The seventh potential problem area in blended families involves "discrepant life cycles" (Visher & Visher, 1988, p. 232). When two 25-year-olds marry and start out together, their life cycles are synchronized. They are progressing through their life stages at the same pace and are experiencing major life events more or less coincidentally. However, when remarriage is involved, other variables often come into play. There may be a substantial age difference between spouses. One's children may be preschoolers while the other's are in high school. One may not have children at all.

An issue that commonly surfaces is that of whether or not to have children together in this new family. There is no ideal decision to make about this issue. Each individual couple needs to examine the pros and cons of each choice, including how strongly each feels about the issue. As with other issues addressed in families, generalist practitioners can facilitate family members in making such decisions.

Intervention with blended families is similar to that with intact families. Of course, some attention needs to be directed to the special issues we have described in addition to problems common in intact families. However, many of the same techniques can be used in blended families to achieve similar ends.

Critical Thinking Questions 9.5

EP 2.1.3

- Picture a blended family with whom you are familiar. To what extent does this family experience the seven potential problem areas of change versus loss, unrealistic beliefs, insiders versus outsiders, power issues, loyalty conflicts, boundary problems, or discrepant lifestyles?
- How do you think the family might address these issues?

LO 9-8 Demonstrate Cultural Competency in Family Assessment

EP 2.1.4

Cultural and ethnic diversity are essential aspects of family life. Although Chapter 12 discusses ethnicity in greater depth, it is so basic to family assessment and understanding that several concepts will be discussed here specifically with respect to diverse families.

First, four relevant issues—immigration history, acculturation, school adjustment, and employment—will be discussed. Second, specific questions will be posed to use when assessing families from diverse cultures. Third, nine principles for working with families from diverse cultures will be proposed. Finally, Highlight 9.5 will discuss four "personal competencies" important when working with people from diverse cultures (Hogan, 2013, p. 65).

HIGHLIGHT 9.5

Personal Competencies for Working with People from Diverse Cultures

EP 2.1.1e
EP 2.1.2a
EP 2.1.4b&d

Hogan (2013) cites at least four "personal competencies" that are important to develop when working with people from diverse cultures (p. 65):

- **"Pay attention to thoughts and feelings.** Take your own thoughts and feelings seriously. Become aware of concern, anticipation, and all the feelings that come up in an interaction. Keep in touch with your interior reactions to the people with whom you verbally interact. If you remain alert to your interior responses, you can more easily frame your verbal and nonverbal responses in effective ways." (p. 66)
- **"Assume complexity.** Recognize in an ongoing way that in a culturally challenging situation, diverse perspectives and outcomes remain multiple in nature. Administrative assistant Mike Rodriguez, a monolingual English speaker, is routinely asked to translate Spanish words and phrases into English for his coworkers throughout the company. They assume, because of his Spanish surname, that he understands Spanish. Paradoxically, Mary Johnson, fluent in English and Spanish, routinely employs her linguistic skill in assisting bilingual clients but finds herself rebuffed or ignored by them because she has blond hair, blue eyes, and white skin. To some native Spanish speakers, she is an outsider." (p. 67)
- **"Tolerate the stress of uncertainty.** Avoid showing irritation or annoyance with the ambiguity of the culturally diverse situation. . . . The powerful emotions of fear, anger, anxiety, and frustration,

when they present themselves, demand serious attention during culturally diverse encounters. For example, Vietnamese emigrant Ba That, upon arrival at L.A. International Airport, becomes appalled at the spectacle of the people who surround her, hugging and kissing, upon their reunion with family and loved ones. 'What are they doing?' she asks, aghast, as she explains to her sponsor that she had never witnessed such personal and physical displays of affection in her native land." (p. 67)
- **"Keep a sense of humor.** Cultivate an active awareness of the absurdity that often arises when cultural differences converge. Avoid taking things so seriously that you lose your perspective and are unable to laugh at yourself. Learn to laugh with others, never at others. Find humor in the irony of life. For example, a manager in an assembly plant with mostly first-generation Vietnamese employees gestured 'good luck' to them at the end of [a] team meeting. Later, he was aghast when he learned the gesture was the 'dirty finger signal' in their home country. When he heard that many of the Vietnamese American employees realized the mistake and thought the interaction was hilarious, the manager laughed as well, especially as he recalled the surprised look on many of their faces." (p. 68)

Enhancing self-awareness and demonstrating cultural competency are ongoing, career-long processes. Being open to new unknown situations and to learning your clients' cultures from the clients themselves is essential for effective practice.

ISSUES TO ADDRESS WHEN WORKING WITH FAMILIES FROM DIVERSE CULTURES

Lum (2004) cites at least four important issues to address when working with people from diverse cultures:

1. *Immigration history—the family's transition from the culture of origin to American society*
2. *Acculturation—the adjustment, change, and maintenance of culture in the family*
3. *School adjustment, which is crucial in children's survival performance*

4. *Employment, which is critical for adults' self-esteem and respect in the ethnic community (p. 227)*

Immigration and Acculturation

Immigration and acculturation were introduced in earlier chapters. Immigration history affects a family's perspective on its current living situation and problems. The following four factors can seriously affect a practitioner's ability to establish a relationship and solicit assessment information: "(1) how long ago newcomers arrived; (2) the circumstances of their arrival; (3) the support system they found upon arrival; and (4) the degree of acceptance they found here" (Goldenberg & Goldenberg, 2013, p. 81). A Hispanic family illegally immigrating to the United States from Mexico would logically be wary of contact with social workers or other representatives of "the system." In order to understand family functioning, social workers must be sensitive to such people's vulnerability, potential emotional turmoil, and possible traumatic experiences.

The extent of acculturation of each family member affects the internal operation of the family and each member's adjustment in the surrounding community. A third-generation Vietnamese family may be more assimilated into the mainstream culture than one immigrating 6 months ago. Language poses an additional factor. Recent immigrants may have had less chance to learn English and thus face a greater communication barrier.

School Adjustment

Lum (2004) comments on the importance of conducting a school assessment in diverse families concerning the children's experience in school:

> School adjustment is an important determinant of academic and social functioning. The worker should gain a sense of the school environment. Is it a safe, pleasant place conducive to learning, or is it a violent-prone, conflicting, racist environment that detracts from learning and social growth? Ethnic students tend to be objects of white students' hostility or to act out negative behavior as a response to an unfriendly environment. Fights, drug use, property damage, and early sexual involvement are expressions of behavioral reaction to a social situation. (p. 230)

A worker who determines that children are experiencing problems in school should contact school personnel to bring issues to the school's attention. Both educational and interpersonal relationship concerns are important to address.

Employment

Assessment of family members' employment experiences is also essential. Lum (2004) explains:

> It is important to assess the family's work history. To what extent do family members have stable employment? Given the state of the economy and a tight market for hiring, many adults are without jobs. For immigrants and refugees, language problems and educational requirements may limit employment opportunities.

> Many new arrivals are in English-as-a-second-language classes or job-training programs. Some are low-skilled service workers or seasonal workers in agriculture. Others have given up, remain on welfare assistance, and are caring for children at home.

> The single most important factor for family stability is the placement of an adult in a reliable, steady job. Many Southeast Asian refugees have pooled their resources to open restaurants, croissant and donut shops, and related business ventures; they are able to use their practical skills and create business opportunities.

> Many (First Nations Peoples) are now employed in gambling casinos that have opened on reservations across the country. African-Americans have taken out small business loans to start small enterprises in the inner city and have employed African-American service and construction workers. Latino Americans are often agricultural and construction workers. (pp. 231–232)

QUESTIONS FOR ASSESSING CULTURALLY DIVERSE FAMILIES

The following are questions you might ask about a family to enhance your understanding of its cultural perspective and enlighten you about its "needs and concerns":

1. *Where did this family come from?*
2. *When did they come to this country?*
3. *What were the circumstances that brought them to this country?*
4. *What is important to this family?*
5. *Who are the current members of this family?*
6. *What kind of people would they describe themselves as?*
7. *How do family members describe themselves racially?*
8. *How . . . [does each member define him- or herself]?*
9. *What good and bad things have happened to them over time?*
10. *What were or are the group's experiences with oppression?*
11. *What lessons have they learned from their experiences?*
12. *What are the ways in which pride and shame issues are shown in this family?*

> These questions examine the family experiences both within the family and through the members' larger group and community experiences and biases. Knowledge and understanding of the family's collective story of how they have been coping with life

events and how they have responded to pain and troubles can emerge. The practitioner hears the context of the family concerns, and meaning becomes clearer. (DeMaria, Weeks, & Hoff, 1999; Thomlison, 2010, p. 49)

Critical Thinking Question 9.6

- How would you answer the preceding questions posed about your own family?

PRINCIPLES FOR THE ASSESSMENT OF DIVERSE FAMILIES

Understanding cultural values can help practitioners emphasize a family system's "strengths and resiliency" rather than "the families' presumed deficiencies or weaknesses" (Proctor, Davis, & Vosler, 1995, p. 944). Thomlison (2010) proposes the application of the following nine principles when working with families from diverse cultures:

1. *Acknowledge the role that culture plays in shaping behaviors, values, and view of the society.*
2. *Respect the unique, culturally defined needs of various populations.*
3. *For families who are not fluent in English, avoid using the family's bilingual children as translators: this is embarrassing to parents because it makes them partially dependent on their children, and the children may have limited vocabulary.*
4. *Recognize that primary sources of support for minority populations are natural helping systems such as churches, community leaders, extended family members, healers, and others.*
5. *Acknowledge differences in the concepts of* family *and* community *among various cultures and even subgroups within cultures.*
6. *Remember that minority populations are usually best served by people who are part of that culture.*
7. *When working with minority families, know that process is as important as outcome. [How you undertake your work with the family is just as important as what you accomplish.]*
8. *Understand and recognize when values of minority families are in conflict with dominant society values.*
9. *Practice with the knowledge that some behaviors are adjustments to being different. (p. 48)*

Recognition of cultural differences and sensitivity to how such variations influence work with clients is critical. Each worker/client/family interaction may be quite different. Thomlison (2010) explains and provides examples:

Latino children may have caretakers whom they refer to as "Mom" and "Dad" who may not legally be guardians. Native-American mothers may leave younger children in care of older children as a commonly accepted practice in their communities. In African-American families, a man may not be an official part of the household even though he is an integral part of the family system. Furthermore, time concepts may be different, and formal appointments may not be accepted or understood. Work hours, spiritual practices, or family obligations may conflict with traditional practices of agencies and organizations for home-visit appointments. Each of these situations could be interpreted as weakness or family maladaptation if the practitioner is not sensitive to cultural behaviors of the family. Determining what is normative in the context of the family's culture is necessary for accurate assessment information. (pp. 48–49)

Chapter Summary

The following summarizes this chapter's content as it relates to each learning objective (LO) presented at the beginning of the chapter. Chapter content helps prepare students to:

LO 9-1 Assess families by using the Generalist Intervention Model (GIM).

The GIM can be readily applied to planned change with families. This chapter addresses assessment in the planned change process.

LO 9-2 Examine verbal and nonverbal communication in families.

Assessment of communication skills is essential in preparation for intervention with families. Verbal and nonverbal patterns of communication are significant. Avenues of communication include consonance, condemnation, submission, intellectualization, and indifference.

LO 9-3 Appraise family structure.

Family structure refers to the organization of relationships and patterns of interaction occurring within the family. Families are systems with boundaries and sub-systems. Family norms are the rules that specify what is considered proper behavior within the family group. Family roles are "individually prescribed patterns of behavior reinforced by the expectations and norms of the family" (Worden, 2003, p. 15). Balance of power and intergenerational aspects are other aspects of family systems to address.

LO 9-4 Analyze family life-cycle adjustments.

Assessing life-cycle adjustments can give clear insights into a family's problems. The traditional family life cycle has six major phases. Today, this is considered an overly simplistic view because of numerous complications and differences among families.

LO 9-5 Appraise impacts of the impinging social environment.

The social environment involves the conditions, circumstances, and human interactions that encompass human beings. Practitioners must assess the multiple systems with which a family system interacts. It's important to assess a family's access to basic resources, as such access seriously impacts a family's ability to function effectively.

LO 9-6 Analyze common family conflicts and problems.

Family conflicts include partner difficulties, parent–child relationship difficulties, personal problems of individual family members, and external environment stresses.

LO 9-7 Examine variations in family structure.

Changing values, issues, economic support, and technology have had an awesome impact on family life over the past decades. Variations from the traditional intact family (consisting of two parents and their biological children living together) include single-parent families and blended families. Single teenage parents deserve special attention.

LO 9-8 Demonstrate cultural competency in family assessment.

Cultural and ethnic diversity are essential aspects of family life. Four important issues to assess are immigration history, acculturation, school adjustment, and employment (Lum, 2004). Questions for assessing diverse families are suggested. Principles for the assessment of diverse families are provided. "Personal competencies" for working with people from diverse cultures are discussed (Hogan, 2013, p. 65).

Competency Notes

The following identifies where Educational Policy (EP) competencies and practice behaviors are discussed in the chapter.

EP 2.1.1e **Engage in career-long learning.** *(p. 356):* Enhancing cultural competency is a career-long process.

EP 2.1.2a **Recognize and manage personal values in a way that allows professional values to guide practice.** *(p. 352):* Assessment of personal values is critical in preventing them from interfering with client self-determination. *(p. 356):* Developing cultural competency involves becoming aware of your personal values so that these don't interfere with effective practice.

EP 2.1.3 **Apply critical thinking to inform and communicate professional judgments.** *(pp. 336, 340, 345, 350, 355, 358):* Critical thinking questions are posed.

EP 2.1.4 **Engage diversity and difference in practice.** *(p. 355):* Cultural and ethnic diversity issues, including immigration, acculturation, school adjustment, and employment, are essential aspects of family life.

EP 2.1.4a **Recognize the extent to which a culture's structures and values may oppress, marginalize, alienate, or create or enhance privilege and power.** *(p. 349):* Practitioners should recognize that external environmental structures and pressures such as poverty may oppress and marginalize people. *(p. 358):* These assessment principles stress how a culture's structures and values may affect the status and lives of families from diverse cultures.

EP 2.1.4b **Gain sufficient self-awareness to eliminate the influence of personal biases and values in working with diverse groups.** *(p. 356):* Developing cultural competency involves becoming aware of your personal values so that these don't interfere with effective practice.

EP 2.1.4c **Recognize and communicate their understanding of the importance of difference in shaping life experiences.** *(p. 349):* Workers should recognize that external environment stresses such as poverty result in dramatically different life experiences. *(p. 350):* Variations in family structure result in very different life experiences for family members. *(p. 358):* These assessment principles emphasize how cultural differences shape life experiences.

EP 2.1.4d **View themselves as learners and engage those with whom they work as informants.** *(p. 356):* It's very important to learn about your clients' cultural values and expectations from your clients.

EP 2.1.7a **Utilize conceptual frameworks to guide the processes of assessment, intervention, and evaluation.** *(p. 336):* The systems conceptual framework is useful in understanding families.

EP 2.1.7b **Critique and apply knowledge to understand person and environment.** *(p. 342):* A family-in-environment focus is important to understand how families function in the social environment.

EP 2.1.10a **Substantively and affectively prepare for action with individuals, families, groups, organizations, and communities.** *(p. 332):* This chapter's key thrust is assessment of families in preparation for action.

EP 2.1.10d **Collect, organize, and interpret client data.** *(pp. 333, 336, 340, 342):* The assessment of family communication, family structure, life-cycle adjustments, and access to resources are important aspects of collecting client data when working with families.

EP 2.1.10i **Implement prevention interventions that enhance client capacities.** *(p. 351):* By providing information and contraception, unwanted pregnancies can be avoided.

EP 2.1.10j **Help clients resolve problems.** *(p. 345):* Generalist practitioners help families resolve conflicts and problems.

On the Internet

Visit the *Understanding Generalist Practice* CourseMate at **www.cengagebrain.com** for resources such as quizzes, glossaries and videos.

Working with Families

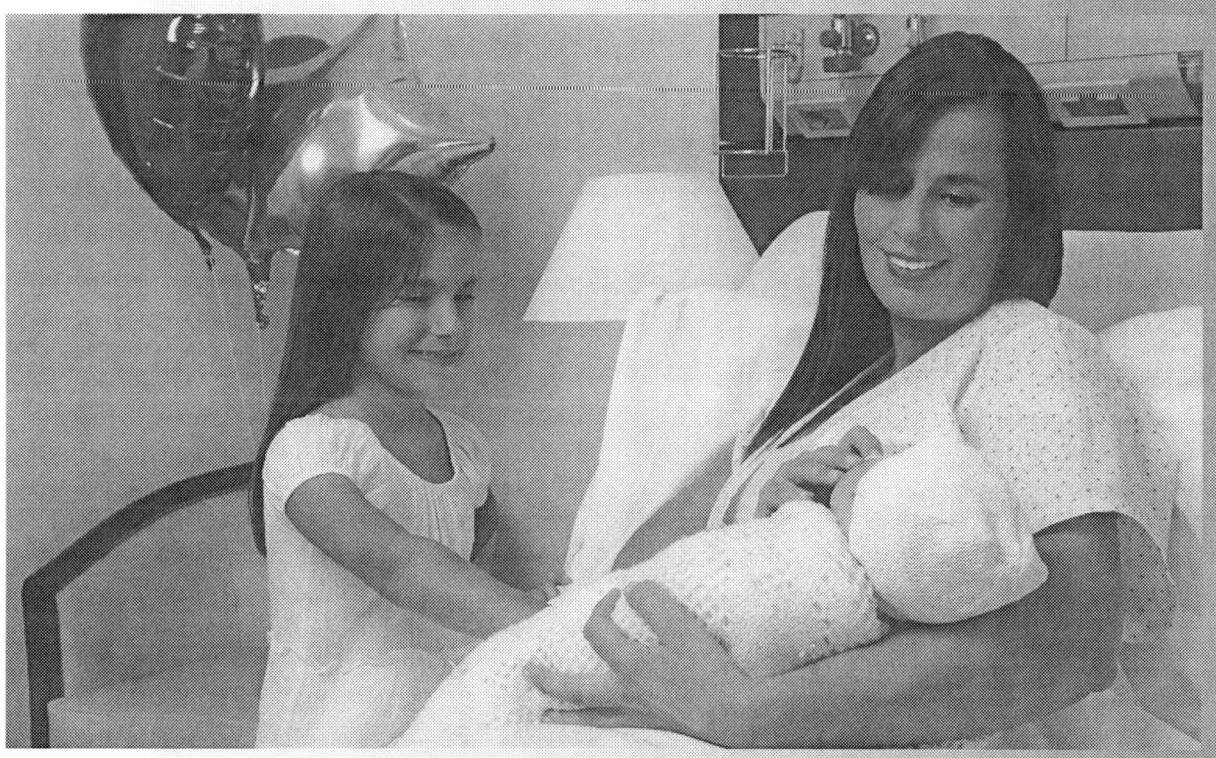

Glow Wellness/Getty Images

Learning Objectives *This chapter will help prepare students to:*

LO 10-1 Use generalist practice skills with families.

LO 10-2 Assess and emphasize family strengths.

LO 10-3 Engage, assess, and plan with families.

LO 10-4 Employ various approaches to implementing family intervention.

LO 10-5 Evaluate, terminate, and follow-up with families.

LO 10-6 Address family issues and provide relevant services.

LO 10-7 Enhance cultural competency in working with families.

LO 10-8 Explore the current status of family services.

LO 10-9 Engage in macro practice with families by promoting social and economic justice.

DONNA DID NOT KNOW WHAT TO DO. She was 36 years old and divorced. She had a 5-year-old son from her prior marriage. An attractive woman with fiery red hair and penetrating bright blue eyes, she was tremendously proud of being a junior in college. She had worked hard raising her son with no child support payments from his father, who was pretty much out of the picture. Donna's grades were excellent, and she looked forward to a bright professional future.

All of these things had little or nothing to do with the problem upon which she was so intently focused. After dating a number of men steadily and some not so steadily, she had finally found a man with whom she would like to spend the remainder of her life. Thanh, age 40, was also divorced. Donna and he were deeply in love and were planning to marry within a few months.

Thanh also had a child from his prior marriage. His daughter Josie had just turned 18. Here was the problem: Josie had become pregnant when she was 17 and single. Her daughter, Dawn, was born just 2 weeks after Josie turned 18. Josie, therefore, was considered an adult who was supposed to be a responsible guardian for Dawn. The alleged father denied his paternity and wanted nothing to do with either of them.

However, Josie had a number of problems that interfered with her ability to be the responsible adult she was supposed to be. For one thing, Josie was a crack addict. For another, she experienced radical swings in her feelings toward Dawn. One minute Josie would hold Dawn lovingly, and the next, she'd throw her down on the couch, run out the door, and leave Dawn alone screaming wildly in their tiny, sparsely furnished apartment.

Once, Josie got so frustrated that she screamed she could not "stand it" anymore ("it" being the burdensome responsibility of parenthood, Dawn's crying, and the infant's constant demands for attention). She then picked Dawn up, ran down the hall of her apartment building, stopped at the first door from which she heard music emanating, and knocked. She had no idea who the apartment's residents were. Nonetheless, she almost threw Dawn at the woman who answered and brashly ordered the woman to take care of her baby. Josie said she had something she must do and would be right back. Josie did not return to the apartment to pick up Dawn for a full 2 full days.

Donna was terribly worried about Dawn and soon would become Dawn's stepgrandmother. Donna would be an integral part of the family and would thus be one of the owners of the problem. Donna did not think Josie really wanted to keep Dawn, yet Josie was terrified of giving Dawn up.

Donna felt Josie was abusing and neglecting Dawn. What should Donna do? Should she call Child Protective Services and explain what has been happening? What would Josie think of Donna then? Dawn is now 2 months old. How much longer can she stay in such an environment with Josie and not be seriously damaged? Should Dawn be placed in foster care? But even then, how could Donna be certain that the foster care placement would be a good one?

Donna did have an idea. She had an aunt who lived 2,000 miles away. Her aunt was 38 years old, married, and infertile. Donna felt her aunt would give virtually anything to have a baby of her own. Her aunt had difficulties applying for an adoptive child for a number of reasons, including being in her late 30s. On the other hand, Donna's aunt was doing well in the business she and her husband owned. They were financially well off.

Donna wondered if she should call her aunt and tell her about Dawn. Would her aunt be interested? What if her aunt would pay Josie, perhaps, $20,000 to cover "adoption costs"? Josie was broke and would really like the cash.

But what were the legal ramifications? Was such an adoption possible? Would Josie go for it? If Donna called her aunt, would she just be raising her aunt's hopes for nothing? What if Josie bluntly refused any such idea? Then, there is still Dawn, poor, precious Dawn, crying all the time.

Donna did not know what to do.

Introduction

The preceding story illustrates some of the infinite issues and problems that can confront families. Working with families can be phenomenally complex, monumentally frustrating, and yet fantastically fascinating. When the story left off, Donna was in the process of contacting a social worker to help her with some of her issues and questions. The problem obviously is difficult. Yet those with the worst problems can use the most help.

This chapter will examine how to work with families in generalist social work practice. Based on the content in Chapter 9, this chapter will explore specific approaches and techniques for helping families address their problems and issues.

LO 10-1 Use Generalist Practice Skills with Families

EP 2.1.10a

Many of the same skills that apply to any other type of intervention in social work practice also apply to families. Working with families is built upon understanding the relationship-building and interviewing skills discussed in Chapter 2 that are necessary for generalist micro practice. Families are made up of individuals who communicate with each other. Planned change is based on communication. Therefore, many of the same skills are used when working with families. These include: monitoring your own and clients' verbal and nonverbal behavior; maximizing warmth, empathy, and genuineness; using verbal responses and initiators such as classification, interpretation, and summarization as part of the planned change process; and overcoming issues and hurdles such as clients who insist on not saying anything or on voicing extreme hostility.

Working with families also requires the skills discussed in Chapter 3, which we refer to as mezzo skills. These involve working with groups. Because a family is a special kind of group, these skills also apply. Group dynamics, decision-making strategies, and roles are concepts that also apply to families. Making assessments, formulating plans, and leading people through the intervention process occurs in families much as it takes place in other types of groups.

Finally, working with families often requires those skills discussed in Chapter 4, which emphasizes working in and with agencies and systems. Policies regarding how families are treated may be unfair. Families may not have access to the resources they desperately need.

Additionally, there are a number of more specific techniques that apply primarily or only to families. The main focus of this chapter is the special approaches for working with families in view of the issues confronting them. As with any other generalist intervention, we will apply a planned change approach.

FAMILY TREATMENT AND THE PLANNED CHANGE PROCESS

Working with or treating families follows the Generalist Intervention Model (GIM), just as any other type of social work intervention would. First, the worker must engage the family—that is, establish a professional relationship between him- or herself and the family system. Second, the practitioner must assess the family's needs from micro, mezzo, and macro perspectives. (Chapters 5 and 9 explore various family assessment approaches and issues.) Next, just as in any other type of intervention, a plan needs to be formulated. Some of the family's micro, mezzo, and macro aspects will be targeted for change. The next stage involves the implementation or actual carrying out of the plan. Following this process, the intervention needs to be evaluated to determine its effectiveness. Finally, termination and follow-up should occur.

It is important to stress that throughout the planned change process, workers should focus on and use family strengths. Highlight 10.1 discusses the traditional problem-solving versus strengths-based approaches and suggests some strengths-based techniques.

STRATEGIZING FOR FAMILY INTERVENTION: DO YOU ALWAYS HAVE TO SEE THE ENTIRE FAMILY?

EP 3.1.10g

As we know, a family is a system. Every single part of a system is important because what affects any *part* of the system affects the *whole* system. Therefore, because each family member is an important part of the family system, as many family members as possible should be involved in the intervention process (Collins, Jordan, & Coleman, 2013). Ideally, all family members should be included. The term *conjoint* family treatment refers to meetings involving at least two family members; it also refers to treatment of spouses or partners for an identified problem.

There are at least three advantages to seeing the entire family together. First, being able to observe the entire family in interaction can give great insight to understanding its dynamics (Janzen, Harris, Jordan, & Franklin, 2006; Worden, 2003). When family members are missing, part of the family's interactional patterns are also lacking. For example, a single-parent mother and her 12-year-old daughter might consistently complain together about the 16-year-old son/brother in the family. They say he's "no good." He fights with them all the time, lies, steals, and is generally impossible to live with. Without being able to observe the mother's and daughter's interaction with this boy, the worker does not really know what is going on in the family. The worker can see neither the boy's behavior nor the family's problems from the boy's perspective. Perhaps the mother clearly favors her daughter and regularly

HIGHLIGHT 10.1

LO 10-2 Assess and Emphasize Family Strengths

Use of a strengths perspective is very important when working with families (Benard & Truebridge, 2013; Early & Glenmaye, 2000; Poulin, 2010). We have established that a strengths perspective emphasizes that people have strengths, capabilities, coping potential, knowledge, and resources that only need be identified and tapped to help clients address their issues and needs. This approach emphasizes that people have the ability to grow, change, and enhance their own well-being. Families have the right to care for their members and receive caregiving and help when they need it (Benard, 2006).

Traditional Problem-Solving versus Strengths-Based Approaches

The traditional problem-solving approach assumes that problems are a naturally occurring part of people's lives. Social workers then work with clients to develop plans to solve the identified problems. This perspective emphasizes different features of the planned change process and differs from a strengths approach in at least two major ways (Early & GlenMaye, 2000). First, traditional problem solving emphasizes problem assessment. Workers expend much time and pay a great deal of attention to exploring the dynamics and details

involved in the problem. Practitioners using a strengths approach, on the other hand, "will spend little time trying to understand what caused the problem or trying to name it. Instead, the social worker will focus on identifying or uncovering strengths, recognizing that a problem—or deficit—focus may create a mindset that is an obstacle to looking at positives and assets of client functioning" (p. 123). During assessment, workers using this approach will instead emphasize the family's "vision and hopes for the future" (p. 124). Problems are not ignored but "serve a minor role as a catalyst, in that families seek social work services when they have problems or difficulties" (p. 123).

The following figure enclosed in this highlight reflects this difference by portraying the process, "identify problems," in large, boldface, all-caps type for the traditional problem-solving approach and in smaller, regular type for the strengths-based approach.

A second difference between the approaches involves how a strengths approach always focuses on identifying and using clients' strengths and resources to address issues and make plans. Workers using a traditional problem-solving perspective may identify strengths and try to "reframe things in a positive way. . . . However, the strengths approach is more than positive reframing and identifying strengths. It is a consistent focus on identifying client strengths and resources and mobilizing resources that directly or indirectly improve the problem situation" (p. 123).

The accompanying figure also illustrates this difference by providing arrows to the words "Possible use of 'positive reframing' and strength identification" as only a potential, not absolute, part of the problem-solving process. In the diagram illustrating a strengths-based approach, the words "Identify client strengths and resources" are provided in large, boldface, all-caps type to emphasize the fundamental role this plays in a strengths-oriented process.

Finally, both the traditional problem-solving and strengths-based approaches illustrated in the diagram focus on getting results. The words "Find solutions" demonstrate this for traditional problem-solving approach, and the diagram utilizes the words "Use resources to improve the problematic circumstances" for the strengths-based approach. Once again, a strengths-based perspective stresses the positive use of resources to improve conditions.

Strengths-Based Strategies for Working with Families

Early and GlenMaye (2000) suggest at least six practice strategies utilizing a strengths perspective when working with families:

1. Build on the family's strengths and inherent desire to "meet needs and reach goals.... Strengths include survivor's pride, hope for the future, the ability to understand another's needs and perspectives, and the ability to identify and make choices about individual and family goals" (p. 124).
2. Work "collaboratively" with families who "are experts on their lives, their strengths, resources, and capacities" (p. 124). The worker should focus on what family members are already doing right for themselves and encourage them to strengthen and develop these tactics.
3. Help the family formulate "a vision of how life will be when they no longer 'have' the problem" (p. 125).

   "A strengths assessment asks the question, What kind of life does the client want? And focuses on the client's capabilities and aspirations in all areas of life functioning" (p. 124).
4. Boost "family participation and involvement.... Activities with families should support family and child coping efforts, through such mechanisms

as acknowledging existing coping skills to build better survival skills" (p. 125).
5. Utilize "environmental modification" that "may take the form of educating other people in the client's environment. It might also take the form of helping clients develop self-advocacy, living, or coping skills" (p. 120).
6. Model "high expectations" for family participation, change, and achievement (p. 125). Think optimistically and believe in the family's ability to change positively.

A Case Example

Early and GlenMaye (2000, pp. 125–127) provide an example of a social worker using a strengths-based perspective while working with a family. It involves a mother, Deanna, and her son Andy, age 10. Andy exhibited severe temper tantrums and an inability to follow rules. Deanna was also stressed by poverty, unemployment, and a general sense of despair. Andy's behavior deteriorated to the point where he required residential treatment at a center for children with severe emotional and behavior problems.

The center's social worker assumed a strengths-based approach to the case. First, she explored "with Andy and Deanna their vision of how they wanted their family life to be. They talked of their mutual wish to be together and for Andy to be able to manage his anger" (p. 126). The social worker also investigated their inherent strengths. These included their desire to reunite successfully as a family and "the ability to make choices about their personal and family goals.... Individual strengths included Deanna's prior work experience and her ability to provide a comforting home environment, as well as Andy's artistic ability (drawing) and sense of humor" (p. 126).

Together the worker and family collaborated to develop a plan targeting resources Deanna required and anger management skills Andy needed to learn. Implementing the plan included the worker providing information about resources and behavior, participating in role playing addressing Deanna's and Andy's interaction, and assisting Andy in practicing new, more appropriate behaviors. The worker also modeled "high expectations of what the family could accomplish ... to reflect her appreciation of the family's strengths" (p. 126).

One specific goal involved increasing and improving family interaction. The worker explored with Deanna "various potential sources of social support such as extended family and friends" (p. 126). She discovered that

(continued)

HIGHLIGHT 10.1 *(continued)*

Deanna had a brother close by who had spent time with Andy in the past, but with whom Deanna had lost contact. Deanna chose to contact her brother, who indicated he was happy to resume his contact with Andy. This provided Andy with opportunities for enjoyable activities (e.g., fishing) and positive interaction.

The worker and family also helped to develop a point system to reinforce Andy's improved behavior and enhance his anger management skills. While exploring Deanna's own history, the worker discovered a hidden strength, namely, that Deanna had been a nurse in the past. Deanna's certification had lapsed years before, so she thought nursing was no longer an option for her. The worker helped her develop a plan to get recertified, including taking a refresher course. She eventually gained part-time employment as a nurse that significantly increased her standard of living.

A year later Andy had returned home and attended regular school. Deanna "felt much more in control of her life and her son's life" (p. 127). She attended individualized educational program (IEP) conferences aimed at developing a plan for Andy. She advocated for him to have an extensive assessment of academic skills; be allowed to participate in drawing each day, an activity he much enjoyed; and be provided the additional academic help he needed. In essence, "Deanna was empowered to take over much of the function that the social worker had provided" (p. 127).

Source: Other than the material cited by Benard (2006), material in this highlight is based on the article "Valuing Families: Social Work Practice with Families from a Strengths Perspective" by T. J. Early and L. F. GlenMaye (2000) in *Social Work, 45*(2), pp. 118–130.

---

criticizes her son. Maybe his acting out is his way of expressing his anger at the situation and demanding attention.

This line of reasoning leads us to the second advantage of seeing the whole family together. It enhances the worker's ability to be fair and objective. In other words, the worker is better able to assess and understand the problem from the perspective of all family members. The worker is thus less likely to take sides on the part of one person or the other or assume any one person is the spokesperson for the entire family.

A third advantage to seeing the entire family involves the opportunity to see communication patterns. Janzen (2006) and his colleagues explain:

The family is seen as a living system that maintains a relationship with the environment through communication, which involves the sending and receiving of messages and a feedback process. As a result, family relationships are products of communication. Family members establish rules that regulate the ways they relate to each other and to the outside world. Once these rules are established, the family seeks to maintain the status quo. In other words, the family is viewed as a rule-governed, complex, interactive system, with communication patterns playing a primary role in family functioning. Communication is defined as all verbal and nonverbal behavior within a social context. This speaks to the complexity of the process

of communication. We can readily imagine a simultaneous sending and receiving of messages by gesture, manner of dress, tone of voice, family expression, body posture, and so on. (p. 39)

Assessing what you can observe right in front of you is much easier than hearing about it secondhand. The difference between how family members think they communicate and how they really do communicate is often a major part of the family's problem.

However, stipulating that the entire family must be present during problem-solving sessions often presents problems. Sometimes, there are family members who refuse to participate. At other times, questions may be raised regarding the need for everyone to be there. For example, if the parents are having sexual difficulties, is it appropriate for their four children, ranging in age from 8 to 18, to be present during the meetings? At other times, scheduling everyone together may be impossible or nearly impossible. For instance, parents may work opposite shifts and are only available on weekends when you are not scheduled to work. Sometimes, family members live out of town. Finally, is it really necessary to solving the designated problems that all family members expend the time and energy to be present all the time?

Family treatment involves any practice interventions that serve to change a family. The important thing is to help solve the family's problems. Although family treatment means that the end result should benefit the entire family unit, this result is accomplished in many different ways. On the one hand, seeing one or two individuals may be more advantageous. On the other, working with the entire family in order to effect needed changes may be necessary. The critical thing is that the family benefits from the change effort.

Perhaps the best guideline is to see the entire family together at least once if the task is at all possible. From there, arbitrarily determine which subsystems are needed to work on which problems. If getting everyone together is not possible, then do the best you can. Get as many together as is possible and reasonable. Even seeing family members individually is better than not seeing them at all. As we have emphasized many times, social workers must be flexible. They need to do the best they can with what they have. Situations are rarely ideal. The important thing is to help effect change and solve problems.

For example, a "family therapist," who incidentally is not a social worker by profession, is beginning treatment with a family consisting of a mother, a father, a 16-year-old daughter, and a 19-year-old son. The identified problem (i.e., the reason the family members stated they came in for treatment) is the son, who is extremely depressed. The real problem is something quite different.

This therapist is of the school of thought that the entire family must be present in order for the therapeutic process to do any good. He believes treatment is useless unless all family members are involved.

As the interview progresses, a discovery surfaces that the son is gay. He is having a terrible time coping with the ramifications of the fact, which include the homophobic responses of other people and the realities of living outside of the heterosexual mainstream. He also has difficulties accepting himself for what he is, namely, a worthwhile human being.

The young man's father states adamantly that homosexuality is "bad and wrong." The father refuses to discuss his feelings during this interview or at any time in the future. He states that he will not attend any more therapy sessions until the son stops being gay. This, of course, devastates his son, who, teary-eyed, is pleading for his father's acceptance.

After going around and around on the issue, the therapist responds that if the whole family does not attend therapy sessions, he will not continue therapy. That is that. This declaration is despite the fact that both mother and daughter express serious concern for their son/brother and commitment to the therapeutic process.

Perhaps the therapist is trying to force the father into participating in the treatment sessions. Maybe the therapist sincerely believes working with the incomplete family system is useless and that nothing can be achieved under such conditions. At any rate, the young man hangs himself the following week.

Critical Thinking Questions 10.1

- As a generalist practitioner, what would you have done with this family and the troubled, suicidal son?
- What other alternatives might have been available?

The therapist involved with this case assumed a unilateral approach. He considered no other options. As a generalist practitioner in this situation, you might have considered seeing only those family members who were available and doing what you could within those limitations. Another possibility would be to refer the young man to someone who could work with him individually. Referral to a gay support network or group would be yet another option.

That the young man killed himself was not the therapist's fault. We are all ultimately responsible for our own lives. However, the problem can be attributed to the lack of options presented to the clients. The family was cut off because of one member's unwillingness to comply with the therapist's rules. The young man may have killed himself anyway. No one will ever know. However, perhaps a more compassionate approach would have helped. Maybe providing him with some other options would have made the young man feel as though someone cared.

LO 10-3 Engage, Assess, and Plan with Families

As social workers engage, assess, and plan with families, there are three primary goals when beginning the intervention process (Council on Social Work Education [CSWE], 2008; Janzen et al., 2006). First, the worker needs to get a clear picture of the family's interaction, the problem itself, and how the family's interaction serves to maintain the problem. Second, the worker must gain the family's consent to begin treatment and commitment to participate. This task may not be easily achieved. Some or all family members may deny that the problem even exists. They may insist that a certain family member or members are really to blame for the problem and, therefore, really should be the target of intervention. They may not even feel that anyone but the person with the identified problem should participate in treatment. The third initial goal when beginning an intervention with families is "to set procedures for change in motion. Family members should be able to leave with beginning confidence that they have been understood, that something new is being offered, and that something positive can happen as a result of agency contact" (2006, p. 74).

There are at least five phases to beginning treatment (Collins et al., 2013; Janzen et al., 2006). These phases are examined in the following sections.

PHASE 1: ALLEVIATE OR AT LEAST MINIMIZE EARLY APPREHENSION

The purpose of this phase is "to acknowledge the family members and make them somewhat comfortable in the office before moving on to the task at hand" (Nichols, 2010; Worden, 2003, p. 27). A warm, cordial greeting and introduction is a pleasant way of initiating the worker–family system relationship. The practitioner might comment about how pleasant meeting the family is. Some agreeable small talk can soften the meeting and enhance comfort levels. For example, the practitioner might say, "Did you have any trouble finding the place?" or "I hope you haven't been waiting long." Other pleasantries might include comments about the weather, traffic, or family members' general health and well-being.

The social worker might then complete family introductions by saying something like, "Let me make sure I have your names right. You must be Matilda. I'm glad you could come. You're 17, correct? What school do you attend? Don't you live in the Smartbrain District?" Of course, the worker does not want to blast family members with one question after another, but rather demonstrate interest in individual family members.

The worker can also clarify relationships during this phase. For instance, the worker might say, "Bob, you're Amelia's son by birth, and, Harvey, you're Bob's stepdad? Am I right?" Including children in all these processes as well as adults is important.

The practitioner may relate a brief history of contacts with the family and what information about the family is at his or her disposal. The worker may also establish the "ground rules for working together" (Helton & Jackson, 1997, p. 50). These rules may include emphasizing the following: how all family members' input is valuable; how members are expected to demonstrate respect for each other verbally and nonverbally; how members should refrain from interrupting each other; and how the practitioner's job is to share perceptions and recommendations about family interaction and communication and answer any questions the family might have (Nichols, 2010, 2011; Worden, 2003).

The intent of providing information is to help fill in the scary unknown with concrete information. The better family members understand the social worker and the helping process, the more comfortable they are likely to feel. Thinking of how clients might be reacting as they enter this likely unfamiliar situation is important. Will this social worker ask personal questions in front of everybody else? Will he or she cut me down to nothing? Will everyone have to lie down on couches? Do they still perform lobotomies? Therefore, alleviating unsubstantiated fears and beginning discussion about the realities of family intervention is crucial.

Another technique for calming anxiety is asking each person to describe his or her thoughts and feelings about being there. Specific questions you might ask include:

- "What kinds of things did you expect when you first walked in? Is this anything like you thought it would be?"
- "Did you have a chance to discuss our meeting beforehand? If so, what kinds of things did you talk about?"
- "I know this is a new experience for you. How do you feel about being here?"

Many of the introductory techniques resemble those described in Chapter 2 on micro practice. However, there are two major differences between initial individual and initial family interviews. First, as the worker you have more than one person to interact with and observe. Second, you need to make certain that each individual has the opportunity to voice opinions. Each individual needs to feel that he or she is important right from the beginning.

PHASE 2: ASK FAMILY MEMBERS TO EXPLAIN WHAT IS WRONG

The second phase in initial family intervention involves asking each family member to specify what he or she thinks the problem involves. There will likely be a wide variety of different perceptions. Asking for individual viewpoints also allows the worker to observe each member's reactions to the rest of the family's definitions. One should note that this phase is not the right time to start solving the problem—it is a time for observation. The problem must be clearly understood before the change process begins.

Frequently, family members will point their fingers at one person and blame that individual for the problem. Confronting this blaming behavior and starting discussion about how the problem belongs to the entire family may be tempting. However, allowing the family to act as naturally as possible at this point is important. The worker wants to set the groundwork for change. The important thing here is to observe interactions, understand the problems, and target the most appropriate things for change.

Other issues may emerge. For instance, some family members may find restraining themselves from talking and waiting their turn difficult. They may burst in and interrupt. For example, parents may find it a challenge to be patient and allow their teenage daughter, the identified problem in their eyes, a chance to tell her side of the story. Old interactional patterns may kick in. The parents may immediately think how they have heard their daughter's side before and turn themselves off to it. In this case, the worker needs to establish one of the rules for the sessions. Namely, family members must not interrupt each other. All family members must feel their opinions are important. However, in this example, noting the interaction between parents and child is relevant for the worker. It probably dramatizes what typically occurs in their daily living situations.

At other times, there may be family members who will not say anything. The worker may then attempt to draw them out. For instance, the worker might say, "You're being awfully quiet right now. What are your feelings about the problem?" The important thing is to let the quiet person know that his or her feelings are also valued. For example, the worker might say, "Your ideas are important. I'd really like to hear them whenever you're ready." Clients should know that their input will be welcomed when they feel comfortable enough to give it.

PHASE 3: ESTABLISH AGREEMENT ABOUT WHAT IS WRONG

EP 2.1.10c

After problem definitions have been elicited from all family members, the trick is to come to some agreement about what problem or problems should be worked on. Problems are usually complex. It may be difficult to determine the "real" problem. In any family, having a clear, concisely agreed-upon definition of the problem would be nice.

Note that any problem that surfaces is probably "real" to someone in the family. However, to try to seek out a single problem that is the clearest, purest concern for all family members is pretty much impossible. In other words, there is probably no crystal clear, absolute problem that all family members will agree upon equally.

Perhaps a more useful perspective is to think of most stated problems in terms of their "representativeness" (Reid, 1985, p. 31). Many families will verbalize superficial issues that are related to underlying problems. For example, a teenage son will state that his mother nags him about "everything all the time." His mother, on the other hand, says the problem is that her son will neither clean up his room like he is supposed to nor obey her curfew limitations concerning when he gets in at night. These perceptions are significant and important in the pair's day-to-day lives. However, a more pertinent issue involves the struggle for control between mother and son. The stated issues are really symptoms of the difficulties in the overall interaction.

Instead of concentrating on solving specific problems, work with families often involves changing the way family members communicate with each other, interact, and cope with interpersonal stress. The end result is teaching them different means of problem solving than those they have used unsuccessfully in the past. Changing family processes enables the family to solve a wide range of problems, instead of the relatively limited ones they initially verbalize.

Let us return briefly to the example of mother and son cited earlier. The son probably will not agree that he is to blame for the real problem because he neither cleans up his room nor gets in on time. Nor will the mother probably agree that the real problem is her fault, namely, that she criticizes and badgers her son excessively. However, a worker might get them to agree that the conflict occurring regularly between the two is a problem for both of them.

There are several techniques for engineering a problem consensus (Reid, 1985). The initial two summarize much of what we have already discussed. First, attempt to focus on a problem or some aspect of a problem over which the family will concur. Second, reframe "problems expressed in individual terms as problems of interactions between family members or as problems of the family as a whole" (1985, p. 35).

Third, help the family to articulate problems you observe in their interaction during the interview, problems that they are not able to express verbally themselves. For instance, consider a family where each member actively criticizes each other family member during the interview. However, they do not define the problem as involving excessive criticism. Rather, each family member states that the real problem is the behavior of other family members. For example, verbalized problems might include drinking excessively, running away, not being able to hold a job, or poor housekeeping. Each problem is expressed as being someone else's fault. The worker might assume a totally different perspective. Intervention may focus on defining the family's hostile confrontational communication instead.

There is a fourth technique for establishing agreement about a problem. If several problems have surfaced, present them to the family in the order you consider them important. Ask each family member to rank the problems in the order he or she feels they are important. Then compare and contrast the results (Hanna, 2007). Generally, problems that are considered more important by the most family members would be given higher priority. If there seems to be a tie between problems for top places, you can choose the problem you feel is the easiest to solve. Achieving some success in its treatment as soon as possible is important for the family.

The fifth technique for gaining problem consensus within a family must be used especially carefully. It involves preventing family members from pointing their fingers at some individual and making that person the family scapegoat, at least during the process of coming to a consensus. (A *scapegoat* is a family or group member who is the object of blame or criticism concerning an issue or problem that is really someone else's fault or responsibility.) Preventing scapegoating behavior might be done by labeling the scapegoating as it occurs. Such feedback can help family members begin to identify their behavior and patterns of interaction. Another subsequent approach is to ask family members to stop the scapegoating in order to continue their progress toward a problem consensus.

Note that at other times during the planned change process, scapegoating might be temporarily allowed. For example, at some time during assessment, the practitioner will probably want to observe the family's genuine interaction in order to plan for effective changes. Practitioners must first observe problem behaviors before targeting them for change.

Practitioners may also ask scapegoats to share their perspectives of the family problems. Likewise, scapegoats can be asked how they feel about being targets of blame. Soliciting scapegoats' feelings can serve to enhance empathy among family members. Additionally, such encouragement serves to tell scapegoats that their feelings are important, too. No one should be made to feel the lonely target of blame. Finally, encouraging such participation demonstrates how each family member's input is important. The practitioner can emphasize how the problem is owned by the family and concerns all family members.

There are two additional suggestions for targeting the family's problems (Reid, 1985). The first is to limit the initial list of problems to three. The list can always be changed and modified at a later time. The second suggestion is that even a vague problem about which the family has a consensus is better than a list of minor, specific complaints. For instance, "improving family communication," although vague and global, would be more desirable than a list like "talks on the phone too long," "wears the same socks for 5 days in a row," and "is sarcastic whenever asked a question," where there is no consensus.

PHASE 4: CONCENTRATE ON HOW FAMILY MEMBERS RELATE TO EACH OTHER

Focusing on how family members relate to and communicate with each other is the fourth phase in beginning family treatment. This phase follows establishment of a problem consensus with the family. Typically, during this step the worker orchestrates discussion of the problem by family members. There are three structured ways of doing this.

The first way involves communication between the worker and individual family members. The worker directs questions to members that further explore the problem. Four major aspects of the target problem can be explored (Reid, 1985): how long the problem has existed and major events related to the problem since it began; the problem's intensity and incidence for the week or two prior to the interview; what family members have done to try to solve the problem in the past; and what barriers have been operating both inside and outside the family, which have prevented the problem's solution until now. Highlight 10.2 provides an example of how a target problem can be explored.

Hearing how each family member talks about the problem provides the worker with much information. She can find out how the problem evolved and how it has been intertwined in the family's interpersonal dynamics.

A second way the worker can structure how family members talk about a problem is through a discussion in which all family members participate. The worker instructs the family members to talk to each other

HIGHLIGHT 10.2

Four Ways of Exploring a Target Problem

The Situation

Rosie, age 58, works part-time as a salesperson at a small shoe store. She is married to Bob, age 61, a retired luggage department manager for Sears. Their three children, Sean, Shane, and Sher, are married and live in other states. The problem is Bob's mother, Yetta, age 87, whose health has seriously declined. She has difficulty walking, her sight is failing, and she is becoming increasingly forgetful. Yetta has been living in the same urban flat since her husband died 40 years ago. Rosie and Bob live in another area of the same city. Yetta has one other son who lives in another state and who rarely comes to visit her.

Yetta receives Meals-on-Wheels every day. This supportive service delivers daily noon meals to older adults in their own homes for relatively reasonable fees. One day, the delivery person finds Yetta disoriented and babbling. Yetta mumbles that she fell and hit her head.

The Meals-on-Wheels delivery person calls for an ambulance, and Yetta is taken to the hospital. She remains in the hospital for several days to evaluate her condition. Medical staff members raise questions regarding whether Yetta is capable of living alone in her own home anymore. The case is referred to the hospital social worker.

Exploration of the Problem

The hospital social worker arranges a meeting with Bob, Rosie, and Yetta to discuss Yetta's situation. Yetta is no longer disoriented, so is able to share her feelings. The worker proceeds to explore the problem by pursuing four major dimensions involving the following questions; she receives the information that is recorded after each:

1. *How long has the problem existed, and what were the major events related to the problem since it began?* Yetta's health has been gradually failing over the past 3 years. However, she has fallen only once before this, which was about a month ago. Until now she has never really hurt herself.

2. *How intense has the problem become in the past 2 weeks?* Yetta admits that she has fallen several times during the past 2 weeks. However, she emphasizes that she has never really gotten hurt until now. Bob and Rosie were unaware of any of the other falls.

3. *What have family members done to solve the problem in the past?* Bob has tried to talk to Rosie about the possibility of Yetta moving in with them several times since Yetta's health began to fail. Rosie, however, has consistently refused to talk about it. She would typically "cut Bob off" and state that they should just "leave well enough alone." Yetta has never raised the issue of moving to either of them.

4. *What barriers have been operating both inside and outside the family that have prevented the problem's solution until now?* Yetta has adamantly maintained that she does not want to move from her home. She is determined not to enter a nursing home.

Rosie has never gotten along very well with Yetta. Rosie feels Yetta is stubborn and overly talkative. She feels she has been good to Yetta and cares about her well-being. However, Rosie has consistently avoided discussing the possibility of letting Yetta live with her and Bob. Rosie has been enjoying her time and relative freedom since her children have left. She dreads having to give these up to care for Yetta. Rosie does not feel that becoming a "full-time nurse" at her age is fair.

Bob worries intensely about his mother. Whenever he has tried to talk to Rosie about his concerns, she has abruptly refused. He feels Yetta should leave her flat and come to live with him and Rosie. He feels he has a responsibility to take care of his mother, and he wishes Rosie felt the same way. However, he also worries about how Rosie and Yetta would get along. He does not want to live on a battlefield.

The family has no information about the nursing homes in the city. Nor do they know how to go about getting it.

Several external supports have been working to maintain Yetta in her own home. Thus, the problem of Yetta's failing health has not been addressed. First, Meals-on-Wheels has provided one hot meal a day, so Yetta has been getting adequate nutrition. Second, Alice, a concerned friend from Yetta's church, looks in on Yetta almost every other day. Additionally, Alice, who is 20 years Yetta's junior, takes her to church activities when Yetta feels up to it. Yetta's minister also visits her regularly. Finally, Bob and Rosie call Yetta at least twice a week, frequently take her on outings, invite her for dinner, and help her with laundry and shopping.

(continued)

HIGHLIGHT 10.2 (continued)

Summary

The intent of this brief vignette involving Yetta and her family is to provide an example of how a social worker might begin to explore at least four dimensions of a target problem. This problem situation has many other facets that are beyond the scope of this abbreviated description. In real life, many other questions could be asked and other issues examined.

So What Happens?

We will not take the time here to explain how all of the specific steps in the Generalist Intervention Model are applied. However, we will tell you what happens.

Because Yetta remains insistent upon staying in her own home, she does so, at least temporarily. The social worker obtains some additional supportive equipment for her. This includes a walker that Yetta can lean on for balance as she walks and a "beeper" worn around her neck that will notify the hospital immediately if pressed when she has trouble and needs help.

For 4 months Yetta continues to receive support from family, friends, her minister, and Meals-on-Wheels. However, she eventually falls again and breaks her arm. She, together with Bob and Rosie, then makes the decision that she will move in with them. Rosie does her best to take care of Yetta. One year later, Yetta becomes extremely disoriented. Several times she wanders out of the house for no apparent reason and gets lost. Finally, she can no longer control her bladder.

Bob and Rosie go to the County Department of Social Services and ask how to go about finding a "good" nursing home placement for Yetta. There they are referred to the appropriate social worker. They explore a variety of nursing homes, evaluate the respective pros and cons of each, and eventually place Yetta in the one they consider best for her.

Problems do not always have one best solution. Often, there are a number of possible solutions. Sometimes, as in Yetta's case, the solutions are progressive.

about the problem. At the same time, the family is instructed not to direct any communication to the worker. In this way, the worker can observe how family members participate in problem solving together and what some of the obstructions in communication are.

Janzen and Harris (1997) note some of the communication difficulties that can be observed in families:

> Communications may be unclear; topics may be changed before issues are resolved, statements interrupted, blame affixed, [and] support offered. Statements may be addressed to nobody in particular, and some individuals may attempt to speak for others. (pp. 118–119)

Additionally, family members may vie for power, initiate conflicts, form liaisons, or give support to each other. These are the interactions that the worker can observe and later use to help the family target ineffective interactions for change.

The third way a worker can structure a family's discussion of problems is to instruct only two family members to talk about how to solve the problem with each other. At any point the worker can establish parameters about how communication will occur (Janzen et al., 2006). For example, the worker can spec-

ify that one person may not interrupt another, discussion should not stray far from the targeted topic, and that speakers will take responsibility for their own feelings and avoid speaking for other people.

Any of these three approaches provides the worker with a small sample of the family's real-life interaction. In effect, a small laboratory is created. Working with families is difficult because there are so many dimensions and nuances involved. Sometimes, a worker can find out a lot about a family early on. At other times, learning about the family takes much longer. At the very least, however, structuring such communication at the beginning of family treatment shows the family the types of things that can go on in family intervention and prepares them somewhat for future work.

PHASE 5: ESTABLISH A COMMITMENT TO A PLAN OF ACTION

EP 2.1.10f

Establishing an agreement or contract regarding what is to be done and who is to do it is an important aspect of planning (Collins et al., 2013; Janzen et al., 2006). The information in Chapter 6 on planning in the Generalist Intervention Model relates to contracting with families just as it relates to contracting with individuals, groups, organizations, and communities. The contract becomes both a map or guide for the implementation process and a seal of commitment of both family and worker.

Implementation of Family Intervention

Social workers address a wide range of family problems and issues. Thus, the techniques and approaches used vary dramatically. It is challenging to determine the most effective research-informed intervention approach with a particular family experiencing its distinctive problems. During the implementation phase, a practitioner tries to "help the family with issues and/or problems that are preventing optimal functioning" by carrying out goals established during the planning phase (Helton & Jackson, 1997, pp. 55–56). Implementation can involve a range of treatment approaches. Specific techniques can emphasize the family's strengths. Other methods include reframing, teaching families problem-solving techniques, training parents in child management methods, and offering support (Collins et al., 2013; Proctor, Davis, & Vosler, 1995). Additional techniques that you may find useful in practice include role playing, digital recording, and homework assignments.

LO 10-4 Employ Various Approaches to Implementing Family Intervention

There are numerous approaches to implementing family intervention. Generalist practitioners should select treatment approaches and techniques that have been found effective in designated practice situations. Approaches discussed here include empowerment by emphasizing family strengths, reframing, teaching problem-solving techniques, teaching child management methods, offering families support, role playing, digital recording, and homework assignments.

EMPOWERMENT BY EMPHASIZING FAMILY STRENGTHS

Reinforcing and reaffirming the positive qualities, strengths, and resources of a family should be an ongoing theme in work with families.

Hanna (2007) makes the following five specific suggestions:

- *Emphasize positive statements reported by family members (e.g., My mother listens to me when I have*

a problem). Observing behaviors that reflect sensitivity, appreciation, or cooperation between family members is also important.

- *Encourage family members to share stories about themselves. Spend extra time discussing those aspects of their stories that reveal how the family has coped successfully with problems.*

- *Note family interactions that reflect strength and competency (e.g., I like the way you help your daughter find her own answers to the problem). Underscoring positive family interactions helps the interviewer to identify other strengths and competencies.*

- *Investigate times that family members enjoy together. What are they doing? What makes these experiences enjoyable? These questions offer opportunities to discuss strengths and capabilities....*

- *Emphasize what families do well. All families have areas of strength (such as patience, certain skills, and coping behavior). By asking questions, the ... [practitioner] can learn how families utilize these strengths to solve problems (e.g., What works best with your child? Tell me about the times you were able to get him to ____. What did you do? How were you able to get him to ____? What does that say about your ability to get him to do that in the future?). (pp. 92–93)*

REFRAMING

Reframing is a strategy that helps family members view a problem or issue with a different outlook or understand it in a different way. It "consists of changing the conceptual or emotional viewpoint so as to change the meaning of the problem without changing the facts—in other words, the situation doesn't change, but the interpretation does" (Hanna, 2007, p. 93). It usually means helping one or more family members change negative thinking about another family member to a new, more positive perspective (Nichols, 2011; Nichols & Schwartz, 2004). Reframing usually provides still another means of empowering a family by emphasizing that family's strengths. It often helps one person better empathize with another person or understand content more clearly from that person's perspective.

The following are some examples of a client's statement followed by a worker's reframing of the client's thought:

- Client's statement: *"Johnny hates me. All he does is scream at me. I don't even want to go near him anymore."*

- Worker's reframing: *"You sound upset and hurt at how Johnny yells at you so much. Maybe he's upset and hurt, too. Maybe he feels you're avoiding him. If he didn't care about you, he probably wouldn't expend so much energy yelling at you and trying to get your attention."*
- Client's statement: *"My dad says I'm much too close to my grandmother. He says it's a sick relationship, that all she does is manipulate me."*
- Worker's reframing: *"It's interesting that he's so concerned about that relationship. Maybe he's jealous that you two are so close. Maybe he'd like to feel closer to you, too. After all, you visit your grandmother whenever you have the chance. Yet, you never visit him. Also, you've told me how he resents his own mother and how she tried to manipulate him when he was small. Maybe that has something to do with it."*
- Client's statement: *"All my parents do is try to control me. They're like two little dictators. They ask me who I'm going out with every second I'm gone. They tell me I'm supposed to have a 10 p.m. curfew. If I'm a few seconds late, they're waiting for me at the door to ask me where I've been. They're driving me crazy."*
- Worker's reframing: *"You sound as though you're feeling suffocated by your parents. It sounds to me like they're very concerned about you. If they didn't really care what happened to you, they wouldn't be interested in what you did. Maybe they don't see their behavior as controlling. Maybe they see it as being good parents and trying to keep you out of trouble."*

TEACHING FAMILIES PROBLEM-SOLVING TECHNIQUES

EP 2.1.10j

Problem solving "focuses on how the family experienced differences as well as on its methods for solving difficulties. For example, did the parents fight, or did they hide their problems from the children? What about problems between parents and children; how are they resolved? In this exploration, you are trying to determine how problems were raised and then resolved in the family" (Ragg, 2006, pp. 138–139). We have established that planned change and problem solving can be used interchangeably. You can teach a family many of the same steps and substeps involved in the Generalist Intervention Model's seven-step process. Just as you can use many of them in practice, so can a

family learn to use many in its daily life. For example, consider goal setting, a major aspect of planning. A family can adopt the same who-will-do-what-by-when action step format for goals that you use in practice with individuals. The technique simply provides a means for getting things done. For example, a family might follow the plan that Mom and Dad will make an appointment to talk with the Humdrum School social worker about special testing by next Tuesday.

Remember, however, that families with problems usually require help in improving communication among members before they can master other problem-solving skills. Only when members can work together by using effective communication can a family plan and implement positive changes.

TEACHING CHILD MANAGEMENT METHODS

EP 2.1.6b

Teaching parents how to improve their children's behavior is a common goal in family treatment. Substantial research supports parents' potential effectiveness in increasing children's positive behavior and decreasing maladaptive behavior by applying child management skills (Kazdin, 2001, 2008; Miltenberger, 2012; Sundel & Sundel, 2005). Chapter 9 introduced two techniques used for this purpose, I-language and active listening.

Behavioral approaches to child management have been found especially effective (Degangi & Kendall, 2008; Kazdin, 2001, 2008; Sundel & Sundel, 2005). Such evidence-based approaches have successfully addressed many problems, including anxiety, depression, eating disorders, enuresis (unintentional emission of urine), and oppositional behavior (e.g., "losing one's temper, arguing with parents or teachers, refusing to follow rules, being mean or seeking revenge, deliberately annoying people, being angry and resentful, blaming others for one's own mistakes, and persistently being stubborn and unwilling to compromise"; American Psychological Association, 2010a). "Behavioral therapy's treatment goal is to increase infrequent appropriate behaviors or eliminate excessive inappropriate ones" (Orton, 1997, p. 339). It is far beyond the scope of this book to teach behavioral techniques, but basic principles include the following:

1. *Positive reinforcement* is a procedure or consequence that increases the frequency of the behavior immediately preceding it. For example, a mother gives her daughter a warm hug every time the daughter gets an A on a test. Such hugging is positive

reinforcement if it increases the child's studying behavior that results in getting A's on tests.

2. *Negative reinforcement* is the removal of a negative or aversive event or consequence that serves to increase the frequency of a particular behavior. For example, consider the alarm clock buzzer waking a child up in the morning. It is negative reinforcement when turning the buzzer off increases the child's behavior of getting up immediately.

3. *Punishment* is the presentation of an aversive event or the removal of a positive event that results in the decreased frequency of a particular behavior. For example, a father sharply criticizes his daughter when she slurps her soup. This criticism is punishment— the presentation of an aversive event—if it decreases her soup-slurping behavior. Likewise, the father might inform his daughter that she will not get dessert if she chews with her mouth open. This threat is punishment—the removal of a positive event (dessert)—if it inhibits her from chewing with her mouth open.

4. *Modeling* is the learning of behavior by observing another individual engage in that behavior. For instance, parents often teach their children how to tie shoes by showing them how. The children watch how to do it and learn how themselves. The parents have thus used modeling to teach behavior.

OFFERING FAMILIES SUPPORT

Providing support does not necessarily coincide with traditional, specialized family therapy where a family attends regular appointments in a therapist's comfortable office. However, it is also important to marshal support from other external sources in the family's social environment, especially when working with families who are poor and isolated. Support can take the form of public assistance, school and educational services, job skills training, employment-seeking services, housing, help from religious institutions, health care, food, participation in formal support groups, or involvement with informal support systems "such as other families with similar problems, naturally formed support groups, extended family networks, close friends, and understanding co-workers" (Helton & Jackson, 1997, p. 56). A prime directive for social workers is to assess client systems' access to resources and advocate for resources when those available are inadequate, inaccessible, or nonexistent. Later in this chapter, Highlight 10.5 discusses a number of policy areas social workers might address for macro-level change.

ROLE PLAYING

Role playing refers to having a person assume a different role or part than the one he or she would normally assume. It usually involves one of two scenarios. First, within the family treatment context, the worker directs one family member to assume the role or character of another. The major requirement is that the role player attempts to act and feel the way he or she thinks the other person does in real life. Role playing allows family members to understand more clearly how other family members feel from their own unique perspectives. Frequently, a technique called *role reversal* is used, where two family members are asked to exchange and act out each other's roles. The intent is usually to help people see how they each perceive each other.

An example concerns a father and his "uncontrollable" 14-year-old daughter who are asked to reverse roles. The father portrays his daughter by walking around in a huff, swearing at his role-play "father," and threatening to break things. On the other hand, the daughter acts out her father by screaming at her role-play "daughter," telling her she's grounded, and savagely raising her fist as if ready to strike.

The practitioner would then help the clients to begin talking about how each perceived the situation and how each felt. One intent of such discussion is to enhance their empathy toward each other.

The 14-year-old then describes to her father how she feels about her situation and how her feelings were demonstrated by her role-play actions. She does not have a very positive self-concept. She feels making friends is difficult for her, so she hangs out with those who will accept her. She does not care if they shave their heads and have dozens of piercings on multiple body parts. She is caught in a no-win situation when her father tells her she cannot associate with them anymore. She feels she has no choice. If she does not associate with the friends she has, she will have no one.

Her father also explains his feelings and why he acted the way he did. In reality, he stresses, he feels worried and frustrated. He feels his daughter will not listen to him as children "should" respond to their parents. To him she looks like "a mental case" by the way she dresses. He is feeling like a failure as a parent because nothing he tries helps him get control over the situation. He is desperately worried that belonging to such a "wrong crowd" will only result in drug use, sex, and who knows what else.

Having these two people reverse roles and interact with each other may provide some interesting insights into their own behavior. When the father walks around in a huff, swears at the daughter, and threatens to break things, the daughter sees how she looks to other people. On the other hand, when the daughter screams at the father, telling him he is grounded, and raises her hand to strike him, the father may get some insight into his own actions. He may never have had any idea regarding how his behavior looked to anyone else.

Of course, family members will probably not get instantaneous revelations and have their problems miraculously cured by doing role reversal. However, there is potential for them to increase their empathy for others, broaden their view of problem situations, and become aware of alternatives never thought of before.

The second kind of role playing involves having people remain themselves but act differently than they normally would in some defined situation. This technique allows them to try out and practice new ways of behaving in fabricated situations, without taking the risks those new behaviors might pose in real life.

For instance, consider a woman who is afraid to share her true feelings with her husband. She feels he is a domineering man and would not listen to her anyway. Via role playing, she can practice what to say and how to say it before ever really confronting him, which allows her to gain confidence in how to act. It also lets her think through ahead of time how she might respond to a variety of his possible reactions.

The bad thing about role playing is that an obviously unreal situation can feel "fake" to participants. However, the very good thing is that it allows people to think about and address situations in advance.

DIGITAL RECORDING

"I hate watching myself on a recording" is a frequent comment of students who are forced to digitally record themselves for their social work practice courses. They do not like the grating tone or the soft mumbling of their voices. They hate to see how they jiggle their feet or slump in their chairs. They think they look too fat or too lanky.

What recording does is make people observe themselves as others see them. It makes them confront the effectiveness and appropriateness of their various verbal and nonverbal behaviors. So it also is with families.

When viewing recordings of their interaction, family members can be made to see themselves as others see them. When a mother tells her delinquent son, "I love you," she can see the scowl on her face and hear the angry, harsh tone of her voice. Recording can be useful for pointing out double messages such as this.

The mother was saying one thing verbally but communicating quite another thing nonverbally.

Recording can be used to demonstrate family alliances. For example, a mother may observe herself sitting next to her young daughter and patting her daughter's arm lovingly and frequently during an earlier interview. Recording can also dramatize conflicts. For instance, two partners who live together can watch themselves both talking at the same time, trying to cut each other off, and struggling to be heard.

There is one note of caution, however. Workers should use discretion regarding how much of a family session to play back. Time, of course, is valuable. Segments of family interviews should be selected to illustrate specific points related to target problems.

One other point to keep in mind is the fact that some families may initially feel uncomfortable or self-conscious when recorded. This, however, usually passes with time. Most become accustomed to the equipment being there and essentially forget about it. Recording should never be used without each family member's clearly expressed permission.

HOMEWORK ASSIGNMENTS

Homework assignments are tasks given to clients to be completed at home outside of the interview. They can be given to individuals or entire families, depending on the assignment. The important thing is that they are clearly specified. They should incorporate at least one of the following elements:

1. Directions regarding specifically what is to be done (e.g., talk about a specified issue, study a handout, or rehearse a specified activity);
2. Specification regarding frequency or amount of times the homework should be done (e.g., do the homework two times each day or during three evenings next week);
3. Specification of how the homework is to be counted or kept track of (e.g., each time the specified homework is done, mark it down on a progress sheet);
4. Directions regarding what is to be brought to the next interview or meeting (e.g., bring your behavioral chart or a list of your partner's strengths);
5. Indications of what will happen under specified circumstance (e.g., you will earn 30 minutes of free time, gain one additional point, or place one dollar in the treatment account each time you participate in the specified behavior). (Rosenthal, 2000; Sheafor & Horejsi, 2012)

In other words, homework assignments should follow our general guidelines for specificity. Family members should understand the assignment's purpose. They should know who will do what and how by when. Finally, they should clearly understand the results of these actions.

Social workers are not required to give homework assignments to families. Sometimes, there are none that are appropriate. At other times, families are not willing to cooperate. However, such assignments do provide a viable option for enhancing family treatment time. That is, time to work on problem solving is expanded because some of it occurs outside of the session. Assignments also provide opportunities for families to apply new behaviors and skills they have learned in treatment sessions to what they do in their real lives outside of treatment.

LO 10-5 Evaluate, Terminate, and Follow-Up with Families

EP 2.1.10 l & m

As we know, evaluation, termination, and follow-up are important phases of the planned change process in generalist practice. This is as much the case with families as with any other client system.

EVALUATION OF FAMILY INTERVENTION

Evaluating progress and goal achievement is vital when working with families. One facet of evaluation is determining when longer-term goals have been met in preparation for termination. Goals should be as clear as possible so that a worker can easily measure their accomplishment. Another facet of evaluation is the ongoing measurement of progress. For instance, a worker might ask at the beginning of a family session how things went since the last meeting. Were family members able to follow through on recommendations and plans? Did any events occur to interfere with progress? Did family members accomplish homework assignments? What were the results?

Chapter 8 discusses various concepts and approaches used in the evaluation process. Many of these may be applied to family intervention.

TERMINATION OF FAMILY INTERVENTION

As in termination with any client system, preparing the family for the end of contact with the worker and the agency is important for the worker. Practice with families occurs in various contexts including, child welfare (e.g., adoption and foster care, protective services, and juvenile court services), mental health counseling, services for people with disabilities, resources for older adults, and many others. Sometimes clients are voluntary and other times they are involuntary. Some clients may resist the intervention process or decide to terminate the process on their own, for whatever reason (Collins et al., 2013).

Bitter (2009) suggests that termination of family intervention should be "based on effectively reaching a state in which problems have improved or have been eliminated" (p. 203). There should also be indications that the family is stable enough to continue its improved functioning in the future (Collins et al., 2013). Hepworth, Rooney, Rooney, and Strom-Gottfried (2013) add that terminations can take place "when clients make a transition to other services" and "when time-limited services are concluded" (p. 595).

In those instances where you as the practitioner can plan for termination with a family, consider the following suggestions:

1. When possible, talk about the ultimate termination of the intervention early in the service provision process. Nichols (2011) suggests introducing the concept of termination at the beginning of service provision. Talking about termination well before it occurs is important in order to prepare the family to part with the worker and the worker's help. The generalist practitioner typically has only temporary involvement as a helper with the family. When the family solves its problems or improves its functioning adequately, it's time for the worker to move on. Ideally, the family should be prepared to continue on its own, using what family members have learned during the intervention process. The family should not become dependent on the worker. Rather, family members should be aware of the impending termination and be prepared to make choices and plans independently when the worker is no longer involved.

2. Evaluate the extent to which goals have been achieved or progress made (Nichols, 2011). Is termination appropriate or should new or revised goals be established? "Do minor recurrences of problems reflect lack of resolution of some underlying dynamic or merely that the family has to readjust to function without the [worker]...?" (Nichols, 2011, p. 38). Are changes in the family such that you should refer the family to other resources that may now be appropriate?

3. Determine how well the family understands the dynamics involved in whatever the problem was and how service provision proceeded (Nichols, 2011). Ask family members to comment on their reactions to the intervention and to articulate what they've learned (Collins et al., 2013). If they can specify exactly what happened during the intervention, what positive changes were made, and what they've learned, such positive changes are probably more likely to continue.

4. Provide feedback to family members concerning their comments and thoughts about the intervention process and termination (Collins et al., 2013). Help clarify those areas that are vague or not clearly understood. Also, positively reinforce what family members have done well and how hard they've worked to address issues and solve problems. Family members who feel positive about themselves and their progress may have greater confidence to maintain these gains in the future (Collins et al., 2013).

5. Discuss with family members how they will handle issues and problems encountered in the future (Collins et al., 2013). Help family members to consider termination as a "transition," not a final conclusion or endpoint (Collins et al., 2013, p. 449). Assist family members in being able to view themselves as people capable of coping and problem solving in the future without the help of a worker. Also, make certain that family members are aware of the formal and informal support systems available to them in the community. Make them aware that services remain available should significant problems re-emerge (Collins et al., 2013).

FOLLOW-UP WITH FAMILIES

Follow-up is also important for families. It "can be done with a letter, phone call, or brief follow-up" meeting (Nichols, 2011, p. 38). There is a significant relationship between follow-up and other aspects of the intervention process. We've established that you can't adequately evaluate progress with a family or terminate the intervention process without talking about and looking toward the future.

One aspect of follow-up is to make certain the family can identify resources to address any issues that may have arisen and to continue maintenance of the family's homeostasis. Such resources include both what the family has learned throughout the intervention process and external supports they enjoy as a result of the process (such as support from schools, public agencies, or health care organizations). Another aspect of follow-up concerns contacting the family to review its status and maintenance of achieved goals. If old problems have resurfaced or new ones have developed, making a new referral may be necessary.

LO 10-6 Address Family Issues and Provide Relevant Services

Many other issues and services concerning families are important to address. Two discussed here are multiproblem families and family preservation.

MULTIPROBLEM FAMILIES

Many families that come to you for help will be overwhelmed with a hoard of mammoth problems. For instance, one family of five may have the following problems affecting one or more of its members: poverty, physical disability, delinquency, alcoholism, developmental disability, marital or partner discord, inadequate housing, and unemployment. Families will often come to you because they have nowhere else to turn. They will probably be desperate. A state of crisis is likely. (Crisis intervention is discussed in Chapter 7.)

What will you do? Where will you start? How will you begin to sort out the problems and plan strategies to solve them? "[O]ne of the most successful approaches to helping the multiproblem family is a problem-solving model that enables the family to untangle the web of problems it confronts to establish specific goals to be achieved, and develop the skills needed to solve their problems" (Thorman, 1982, p. 112)

When you work with problems having such multiple levels, there are five primary points to remember:

1. *Do not get overwhelmed yourself.* Stay calm. Try to remain objective. Avoid getting emotionally involved with a series of small crises. You can be of no help to the family unless you retain your professional objectivity and judgment.

2. *Follow the planned change process as you would with any other problem situation in micro, mezzo, or macro practice.* Keep on track. Engage, assess, plan, implement, evaluate, terminate, and follow up. Clarify for yourself where you are in the planned change process at all times.

3. *Partialize and prioritize the problems involved.* Partialize or divide the problems up. Define what each problem involves and specify the family member(s) it most affects. Next, prioritize the problems as you

would prioritize them for any other case situation. Which are felt to be most important by all family members? Which are most critical? For which do you have a good potential for achieving solutions?

4. *Determine which, if any, problems you can work on yourself.* Part of planning for implementation involves translating client problems into needs. The next logical step is to review what services are available to satisfy these needs. What intervention possibilities fall within your own skill level and job description? Which are services that your agency readily provides? Which are possible to accomplish within your caseload responsibilities and time constraints? Meeting all the needs evident in a multiproblem family is usually humanly impossible for one practitioner.

5. *Identify and use relevant community resources.* Which client needs demand resources and services that can best be supplied by your agency's staff other than yourself or by other agencies entirely? Making this decision necessitates your need to know about the resources available in your community. Chapter 15 stresses and explains the importance of brokering and case management for a wide range of interventions, including those targeting multiproblem families.

FAMILY PRESERVATION

 Family preservation involves providing intensive intervention services over a relatively brief time period that are tailored to the family's unique needs and are often provided in the client's home (Downs, Moore, & McFadden, 2009; Piccola & Tracy, 2008; Tracy, 1995). The concept of family preservation has become a major thrust in agencies throughout the country. It involves doing everything possible to keep the child in the home and provide treatment for the family. A related approach, *family-based services,* reflects most of the same principles involved in family preservation, but services are not quite as intense—that is, they may involve longer time frames and larger caseloads (Pecora, Whittaker, Maluccio, Barth, & Plotnick, 2000) or be crisis oriented (Piccola & Tracy, 2008).

Six goals of family preservation services are: "(1) to protect children, (2) to maintain and strengthen family bonds, (3) to stabilize the crisis situation, (4) to increase the family's skills and competencies, (5) to facilitate the family's use of a variety of formal and informal helping resources, and (6) to prevent unnecessary out-of-home placement of children" (Berry 2005;

Crosson-Tower, 2013; Tracy, 1995; Tracy, Haapala, Kinney, & Pecora, 1991, p. 1).

In past decades, working with families usually involved focusing on protecting the child. This protection, in turn, often meant removing the child from the home. Services were then provided in a segmented manner by a variety of workers. For example, consider an alleged case of child abuse. One protective services intake worker would gather the intake data when the child was initially referred. Another outreach protective services worker might provide services to the family. Still another would work with the foster family if the child had been placed there.

Family preservation, on the other hand, emphasizes service provision to the family unit in a more coordinated fashion. For instance, one worker might do the majority of the engagement, assessment, planning, intervention, evaluation, termination, and follow-up process. The child would likely remain in the home during the entire process. All services would be provided or coordinated by a designated worker with the intent of helping the intact family solve its range of problems. Under this coordinator's direction, services could be "provided by a treatment team," proceeding with a coordinated and unified effort (often made up of case manager, worker/therapist, and such support staff as the parent educator, homemaker, and so on) (Berg, 1994, p. 5).

Major Themes in Family Preservation

 Eleven concepts characterize family preservation programs (Berry, 2005; Crosson-Tower, 2013; Downs et al., 2009; Hull & Mather, 2006; Maluccio, 1990; Piccola & Tracy, 2008):

1. *Crisis orientation.* Family preservation is based on intervention when a crisis is taking place within the home. Workers can then take advantage of the family's motivation to alleviate the stress it is experiencing.

2. *Focus on family.* The family is all important. The family is considered the optimum place for children to remain. All intervention emphasis is directed toward keeping the family together and strengthening its members.

3. *Home-based services.* Services are provided in the home whenever possible. The ongoing thrust is improving the home environment.

4. *Time limits.* Because family preservation workers intervene during times of crisis, they work quickly.

Intervention usually lasts from one to several months (Piccola & Tracy, 2008). Setting time limits helps workers and their clients evaluate progress regularly.

5. *Limited, focused objectives.* All intervention objectives are clearly specified. The primary goal is to alleviate the crisis situation and strengthen the family unit so that a crisis is less likely to erupt again.

6. *Intensive, comprehensive services.* Workers' time and attention is concentrated on the families and their progress. Caseloads may involve only one or two families at a time who each spend between 4 and 20 hours a week with the worker (Crosson-Tower, 2009). Services include providing direct services such as problem-solving counseling and parenting skills education, in addition to arranging for and coordinating other resources.

7. *Emphasis on education and skill building.* The family preservation approach is a positive one. The assumption is that people can improve if they are provided with the appropriate information and support. The focus is on family strengths and resiliency.

8. *Coordination.* Because intervention is intensive and numerous resources often are involved, coordination is important, often involving case management.

9. *Flexibility.* Each family is different, having varying problems and needs. Flexibility enables practitioners to match a wide range of services and resources with the individual family's needs.

10. *Accessibility.* Workers in family preservation must be readily accessible to families in crisis. Their work is intensive and time-limited. Workers' caseloads typically are small so that they can concentrate their efforts.

11. *Accountability.* Accountability, the obligation to accept responsibility for your actions and practice, is considered important. The emphasis on focused objectives and time-limited interventions enhances workers' ability to evaluate their effectiveness.

Family Preservation and Planned Change

EP 2.1.6b

Families that are candidates for family preservation generally are threatened with their children's removal from the home, or are seeking to get back children who have already been removed (Crosson-Tower, 2013). Typical risk factors tend to characterize these families. Berry (2005) explains:

The parent or associated adult has usually been found to have physically abused or neglected [his or her] . . . child. Often, the family is headed by a single parent (usually the mother), who has multiple children younger than school age, who are therefore in need of all-day attention. She is usually young, often less than 30 years old, and has little education beyond high school. The parenting problems center around inconsistent attention to, or discipline of, the children; low patience or tolerance of frustration; and inappropriate knowledge or expectations of children's behavior. . . .

Given their history of neglect and/or abuse, the children are likely to have behavior problems. Due to poor access to health care in poor communities, they are also likely to have medical, physical, developmental, or learning disabilities that have often gone undetected by the medical community. Because the children are likely to be less than 6 years old, they require constant and diligent attention, which overwhelmed mothers or fathers can seldom sustain. . . .

Environmentally, the family is often living in substandard housing and communities with poor resources. (p. 325)

The following sections discuss each step of the planned change process as it applies to family preservation.

EP 2.1.1d

Engagement. During engagement, the practitioner works to establish a positive, trusting relationship with family members. The worker should use active listening and a nonjudgmental tone of voice when attempting to engage the family in treatment and listen to family members' perspectives. What do they really want and need? The worker can talk with the family about agency roles, responsibilities, and goals. Frequently, the worker looks for some concrete way to help the family, such as making a referral or providing a service to meet an immediate need (Piccola & Tracy, 2008).

Assessment. Assessment seeks information about the total family's functioning. Special emphasis is placed on safety issues for children and others in the family in addition to the family's access to necessary resources (including food, shelter, transportation, medical care, and child care) (Piccola & Tracy, 2008). The worker also assesses parents' ability to manage children's behavior, administer appropriate discipline, control anger, and communicate with children. Practitioners can assess family members' concern about issues by observing clients' emotional reactions, verbal and nonverbal cues, expressed desire to work on issues, and level of hopefulness about improvement (Berg, 1994). Throughout assessment, emphasizing clients' strengths is critical (Crosson-Tower, 2013). Berg (1994) gives the example of a 22-year-old single mother of a 5-year-old child. A worker should focus on the fact that this mother was able to work through the difficulties and responsibilities of motherhood while she herself was still a child. This woman "had to solve hundreds of the large and small problems of daily living at a young age. This reframes her as being a competent woman, rather than an irresponsible, ... [single] teenage mother" (p. 40).

Planning. Planning for family preservation intervention involves goal setting and contracting just like intervention in other generalist practice scenarios. Common goals for individual families might be to obtain adequate resources for family functioning (e.g., housing or other essentials such as food) from available service providers; to improve parenting, communication, or coping skills; and to participate in substance abuse treatment (Crosson-Tower, 2013; Downs et al., 2009).

There are five suggestions for goal formulation (Berg, 1994). First, the client must feel that goals are significant. Goals cannot be one-sided on the worker's part. Clients must be committed to working on them. Second, goals should emphasize social interaction both among family members and between them and others in the social environment. The focus of the change process is on the whole family within its own social and economic context, not a particular individual (Crosson-Tower, 2013). Third, goals should be "small, simple, and realistically achievable" (emphasis omitted) (Berg, 1994, p. 70). Like any goals established during planned change, they should be clear and behaviorally specific.

Fourth, goals should be viewed in terms of what can be done positively instead of focusing on problems. For example, consider a situation where a worker focuses on a problem and asks a mother, "When Enrique pokes his finger in his little brother Herman's ear, what do you do?" The mother responds, "Well, I scream at the top of my lungs for him to stop or he'll break Herman's eardrum." The worker could rephrase the question to focus on positive rather than negative behavior by asking the mother, "How do you think you can get Enrique to keep his fingers to himself and play more appropriately with Herman?" The mother might then respond, "Maybe I could give him some activity projects and praise him for staying on task."

A fifth suggestion for goal formulation is to emphasize that goals are difficult to achieve. In reality, even small goals may be difficult for clients when they involve changing well-established behaviors. If the client fails to achieve a goal as well as could be, you can blame the problem's difficulty, not the client, for failure. Similarly, the client who achieves a difficult goal can take pride in the achievement.

Implementation. Implementation of a plan can involve a broad range of service provision. Some implementations emphasize "soft" services that entail providing education and building skills. These include "direct intervention aimed at improving self-esteem, improving communication between family members, teaching anger control, teaching stress management, increasing frustration tolerance, and increasing the caregiver's repertoire of parenting skills" (Quinn, 1993, p. 32). Other services are "concrete" or "hard." These include "advocacy, information and referral, case management, respite care, and homemaker services" (Quinn, 1993, p. 32). Housing or financial benefits are also examples of concrete services.

Evaluation. Evaluation in family preservation on one level involves determination of whether or not individual family goals were met during the intervention process. On a programmatic level, evaluation concerns how effective family preservation programs are "in keeping families together and reducing service costs" (Rzepnicki, Schuerman, & Littell, 1991, p. 71). It's not only important to determine *whether* a program worked, but also *how* it worked. Ongoing research is necessary to determine what approaches best work with what families to establish a stronger foundation of evidence-based practice (Berry, 2005; Piccola & Tracy, 2008).

Termination. In view of family preservation's time-limited approach, termination is actually introduced during the first family visit when the date is set (Tracy, 1995). The whole service provision process is focused on accomplishing goals and completing itself. There are two dimensions to termination (1995). First, termination establishes the extent to which service goals were achieved for the family. Second, termination should involve linking families to ongoing resources. Family preservation does not intend to cure families of all their ills. Rather, it aims to provide families with necessary skills and connect them to continuing resources in order to keep the family unit intact.

Follow-Up. Follow-up usually occurs at established intervals following termination (such as 3 months, 6 months, or a year; Tracy, 1995). Agencies and workers can gather information about family functioning, including whether or not the family has remained together. Practitioners can also establish the extent to which families have maintained progress made during the planned change process. Finally, follow-up can provide feedback regarding various aspects of workers' performance and the service provision process.

LO 10-7 Enhance Cultural Competency in Working with Families

EP 2.1.4

No two families are alike. We have been discussing some of the general techniques that can be applied in a broad range of work with families. Now we will discuss two subgroups of the total pie of diverse families—lesbian and gay families, and African-American families.

LESBIAN AND GAY FAMILIES

Many of the issues faced in families where parents are gay or lesbian closely resemble those addressed in families with heterosexual parents. However, generalists should be aware of some special issues affecting lesbian and gay families. Six issues addressed here are the impacts of homophobia, coming out, lesbians and gay men as parents, parents coming out to children, special environmental issues in gay relationships, and empowerment of lesbian and gay people. Note that people who are *bisexual* (those sexually and emotionally attracted to both genders) and *transgender* (those whose behavior and appearance do not conform to traditional gender roles) may experience similar issues.

Homophobia

EP 2.1.5a

Homophobia is extreme and irrational fear and hatred of lesbian and gay people. It and the behavior resulting from it can victimize, intimidate, oppress, and injure people who have a sexual orientation toward people of their same gender. *Sexual orientation* is "a person's erotic and romantic attraction to one or both sexes" (McAnulty & Burnette, 2003, p. 490).

The Roman Catholic Church has decried homosexual behavior as sinful. In many Protestant churches (although not all denominations), lesbian and gay people are not allowed to join the clergy. Lesbian and gay people have been denied or lost jobs and housing purely on the basis of their sexual orientation. Violence against lesbian and gay people continues.

Generalist practitioners need to examine homophobia from two perspectives. First, they need to explore and cope with their own homophobia. Second, they must be aware of the oppressive impacts homophobia wreaks on the families of lesbian and gay clients.

Confronting your own homophobia may be very difficult (see Highlight 10.3). It may involve serious soul-searching to identify and evaluate your own personal values. A possible consequence may be making some hard distinctions between your own personal opinions and professional values. Some people have expressed serious religious convictions that condemn homosexuality. On the other hand, the professional social work *Code of Ethics* of the National Association of Social Workers (NASW) emphasizes individual clients' rights to make choices about their own lives. As a professional social worker, assisting people in solving their problems is your job. Professionally and ethically, you cannot tell clients what to do or how to act.

Critical Thinking Questions 10.2

EP 2.1.3

- What are your feelings and perceptions about people who have a sexual orientation other than your own?
- Do you foresee any potential difficulties in working with such people? If so, what are they?
- What might enhance your empathy for and understanding of people with a sexual orientation other than your own?

The second perspective concerning homophobia involves the oppression lesbian and gay people and their families suffer. We have already noted some aspects of discrimination. Gay people may be denied access to certain jobs and residences. They may be ostracized socially. They may live in constant fear that they will be fired from their jobs if found out. You may need to address the additional problems generated by homophobia just as any other problems your clients may have.

Coming Out to Oneself and Others

Coming out is the process of "acknowledging to oneself, and then to others, that one is gay or lesbian" (Hyde & DeLamater, 2011, p. 318). Regardless of an individual's situation, there are three basic steps in the coming-out process—"self-acknowledgement," "self-acceptance,"

HIGHLIGHT 10.3

Confronting Homophobia

 EP 2.1.4a Lesbian and gay people live in a heterosexual world. To help understand what being gay or lesbian is like, viewing the world from their perspective is useful. Assuming that you are heterosexual, what would living in a world where mainstream society was gay be like? Consider the following questions:

1. What do you think caused your heterosexuality?
2. Have you ever been attracted to someone of your same gender?
3. Do your parents know that you are heterosexual?
4. Are you not worried that your children may also turn out to be heterosexual?
5. Do you ever suffer any discrimination because of your heterosexuality?
6. Why do you not try homosexuality? You might like it.
7. Would you not rather fit in with everybody else in our homosexual society?
8. In view of the fact that there is such a high divorce rate even among persons of the same gender, would not sharing a life with someone of the opposite gender be even more difficult?

and "disclosure" (Crooks & Baur, 2014, pp. 269–271). Crooks and Baur (2011) explain:

> The initial step in coming out is usually a person's realization that she or he feels different from the mainstream heterosexual model (Meyer & Schwitzer, 1999). Some people report knowing that they were attracted to the same sex when they were small children. Many realize during adolescence that something is missing in their heterosexual involvements and that they find same-sex peers sexually attractive (Cloud, 2005). Some may feel uncertain of their sexual orientation: One study found that 2% of youth ages 12 to 25 reported being "unsure" of their sexual orientation (Ott et al., 2011).
>
> Once individuals recognize . . . feelings [toward the same gender], they must usually confront their own internalized homophobia as they deal with the reality that they belong to a stigmatized minority group (Herek et al., 2009). Some lesbian, gay, and bisexual individuals attempt to conceal or suppress their sexual orientation, even from their own awareness. These people actively seek sexual encounters with members of the other sex, and it is not uncommon for them to marry in an attempt to convince themselves of their "normalcy" and avoid openly confronting their sexual orientation (Hudson et al., 2007; Malcolm, 2008). . . . [The more a society stigmatizes homosexuality, the more likely gay and lesbian people are to enter into heterosexual marriages.] For example, although prejudice against homosexuality has lessened slightly in China, nearly 80% of men who identify themselves as homosexual either are married or intend to marry (Cui, 2006). . . .
>
> Accepting one's homosexuality is the next important step after realizing it. Self-acceptance is often difficult, because it involves overcoming the internalized negative and homophobic societal view of homosexuality . . . [It's as if society is saying that being gay is bad. It then follows that if a person is gay, this implies that the person is bad.] . . .
>
> Following acknowledgment and self-acceptance is the decision to be secretive or open. Occasionally, a gay man, lesbian, or bisexual individual will find others abruptly opening the closet door for him or her. [Being in the closet refers to concealment of a non-heterosexual orientation.] Outing is the term for the public disclosure of someone's secret homosexual orientation by someone else. Otherwise, being homosexual usually requires ongoing decisions about whether to be in or out of the closet as new relationships and situations unfold. (pp. 269–271)

"Studies clearly indicate that disclosing one's gay or lesbian identity increases self-esteem, self-worth, and overall psychological adjustment" (Barret & Logan, 2002, p. 38). However, coming out can be a difficult process in view of the potentially severe homophobic reactions of others. Coming out to one's family may "be even more difficult than disclosing it to others" because of the importance of these relationships (Crooks & Baur, 2014, p. 272). It may be especially tough for adolescents who are trying to develop many dimensions of their own identities, while trying to fit into a heterosexual world. Upon coming out, they may be faced with "shock," "denial," "guilt," or "acceptance" (Barret & Logan, 2002, p. 41).

Hunter and Hickerson (2003) discuss how practitioners can assist in the coming-out process:

One of the aspects of disclosures that practitioners can help clients realistically assess is whether they can handle the repercussions in their interpersonal lives. One way to do this is to ask clients to envision the reactions of others through questions such as: If you make disclosures, how would your mother/father; best friend/girlfriend/ boyfriend; wife or husband; children; religious leader, and/or employer react and how would you respond? Which friends would be supportive? (p. 251)

Barret and Logan (2003) suggest that practitioners ask a client who is coming out a number of questions:

Who? *Determine to whom the client is planning on coming out. Explore the ramifications, potential outcomes, and pitfalls.*

What? *Help the client decide what to say when he or she comes out. For example, prepare a written statement or role play various scenarios.*

Why? *Before disclosing, encourage the client to explore why he/she is disclosing at this particular time. Prepare your client for potential questions he/ she might be asked:*

- *Are you sure you're gay?*
- *How long have you been gay?*
- *Have you tried to change?*
- *Have you tried to be involved with a person of the opposite sex? Did something go wrong?*
- *Do you think you'll always be gay?*
- *What is your gay life like?*
- *Don't you want children?*
- *Do you hate men or women?*

Where? *Help your client decide where he or she will disclose, whether it's in a letter, over the phone, or, preferably, in a quiet, private place.*

When? *Encourage your client not to disclose during an event or holiday. [Coming out is] [a]n important occasion, let it have the full attention it deserves." (p. 39; Berzon, 1988)*

Note that referrals can also be made at the group, organizational, and community levels to help people who are coming out. Support groups can "decrease emotional and social isolation . . . and . . . provide a safe environment" (Hunter & Hickerson, 2003, p. 332). Many large urban communities also have newspapers, activity groups, and referral services for gay and lesbian people (Hunter & Hickerson, 2003).

Lesbians and Gay Men as Parents

Many lesbian and gay people have children (Carroll, 2013; Hunter & Hickerson, 2003; Mallon, 2008). However, giving an exact number is impossible because sexual orientation is a complex matter and no accurate studies exist of how many people are gay (Mallon, 2008). Estimates for the number of people who are gay or lesbian generally range from 2 to 4 percent up to more than 10 percent of all males, and 1 to 3 percent of all females (Carroll, 2013). It is thought that 1 to 9 million children are raised by lesbian and gay parents in the United States (Mallon, 2008). Realizing that myths prevail about gay and lesbian parents with respect to their children is important. For example, one involves the idea that gay people will goad their children into being gay. This belief is not the case. Children raised by gay or lesbian parents are no more likely to "become gay" than children raised by heterosexual parents (Hyde & DeLamater, 2011; Rosenthall, 2013). Perhaps children with gay parents are raised and influenced to be more aware and acceptant of individual human differences in general (Woodman, 1995). Sexual orientation is only one of many ways in which human beings differ from one another.

Parents Coming Out to Children

Coming out to their children is an issue that many gay and lesbian parents must address. Gay and lesbian people are recommended to come out to their children at the earliest opportune time when their children "are old enough to understand and ask questions" (Hunter & Hickerson, 2003, p. 178; Moses & Hawkins, 1982). It is important to be candid, genuine, open, and receptive in addition to using language that children can readily comprehend (Morales, 1995). A trusting atmosphere between parent and child may encourage children to express their thoughts and feelings more openly.

There are at least four reasons for coming out to children early (Moses & Hawkins, 1982). First, hiding one's homosexuality creates an atmosphere of secrecy. It can give children the impression that sexuality is something to be ashamed of. Second, evading the issue hinders positive, straightforward communication between parents and children. Children may get the idea that they cannot talk to their parents openly about other issues in the same way they cannot talk about their parents' relationships and sexuality. Third, avoidance of the issue runs the risk that children may be informed about their parents' homosexuality from others. Such information may be conveyed in a negative and critical manner. This "information" may only validate for children the homophobic idea that being gay or lesbian is bad. Fourth, the effort of maintaining such secrecy may put pressure on family relationships. Problems such as resentment, anger, rebelliousness, or communication lapses may result.

Social workers may be placed in the position of helping gay and lesbian parents come out to their children. There are a number of ways social workers can help parents do this (Barret & Logan, 2002; Moses & Hawkins, 1982). First, gay and lesbian parents need to be comfortable with the fact that they are gay or lesbian. The more secure gay parents are in their identity as gay people, the more likely the experience of telling their children will be positive (Morales, 1995). The parent may initially express resistance and voice concern about coming out to children. In this case, the social worker can help the parent explore reasons for these feelings. Are these reasons valid? Is the parent painting an exceptionally dark picture? The parent needs to understand that the children eventually will find out anyway. A social worker can help parents evaluate the possible results and repercussions if they tell the children themselves versus if the children find out from some other source. A social worker can help gay and lesbian parents explore the contrast between explaining their sexual orientation as a positive aspect of life as opposed to finding out about it as a surprise in a possibly negative way.

Second, gay and lesbian parents need to plan exactly what to tell their children about sexual orientation (Morales, 1995). A social worker can help them think through what they want to say and how they want to say it, in addition to assisting them in role playing the scenario before it actually occurs. Parents can also be helped to prepare themselves for the potential negative responses of their children. As a social worker, you can suggest ways that parents can react to and cope with such less-than-desirable reactions. Thinking through the entire situation ahead of time can decrease parents' anxiety and help them to feel they are in greater control.

The third suggestion for helping gay and lesbian parents come out to their children involves timing. If possible, coming out to children who are young is probably least difficult. Becoming familiar and comfortable with an environment in which differences in sexual orientation are considered "normal" helps children incorporate the concept as just another part of life. Sexual orientation then becomes nothing out of the ordinary with which they need to become concerned.

One should note that very young children may not be able to hide the fact of sexual orientation from others very well. They may not be able to discriminate between when sharing this information is appropriate and inappropriate. Children are not sophisticated enough to analyze the effects of telling someone they have parents who are gay or lesbian. Therefore, gay and lesbian parents who come out to very young children need to be prepared to come out to everyone, even if they would choose not to.

An example comes to mind. Take Tabitha, the 6-year-old daughter of a lesbian mother living with her lifetime lover and partner. Tabitha's teacher was talking to Tabitha's first-grade class about the upcoming parent–teacher conferences. Her teacher was saying that she hoped both mothers and fathers would be able to attend. Tabitha raised her hand and, when called upon, blurted out, "I don't have a dad, but both my moms are coming. They sleep together." One's response might be, "So much for subtlety."

Also consider that children with gay or lesbian parents may experience "various expressions of homophobia, such as bullying, name-calling in school, or being forbidden by friends' parents to visit those friends at home (Signorile, 2011; van Gelderen et al., 2012). Research has found that attending schools with curricula that include discussions of homosexuality and socializing with other lesbian families helped to lessen the impact of the homophobic stigma the children encountered (Bos, van Balen, Gartrell, Peyser, & Sandfort, 2008).... As acceptance of homosexuality increases, the well-being of gay and lesbian parents will benefit from a favorable legal climate, gay-friendliness of the neighborhood, and support in the workplace and from friends and families (Goldberg & Smith, 2011)" (Crooks & Baur, 2014, p. 276).

One idea is to teach children contextual alertness. In other words, teach children to evaluate each situation and the potential reactions of specific individuals involved. They can learn to formulate questions in their heads. For example, does this person seem like one who might be open to homosexuality? What might the negative results be if this person were told? On the other hand, what might the positive results be? Might simply remaining silent be best?

Social and Economic Oppression of Lesbian and Gay People

There are a number of special environmental circumstances characterizing gay relationships. Social workers need to be aware of these distinctive conditions in order to help gay and lesbian families cope with them. The first issue involves the right to marry. A hot debate over same-gender marriages has been raging, spurred by socially conservative activists who seek their prohibition.

Although same-gender marriage is legal in Canada, as of this writing it is legal in only sixteen states and the District of Columbia (CNN Library, 2013). The remaining states (except for New Mexico) ban or do not allow gay marriage (CNN Library, 2013). Significant advances for gay rights occurred in June 2013 with 2 U. S. Supreme Court rulings. First, the Court struck down portions of the federal Defense of Marriage Act (DOMA), which defines marriage as a legal union between one man and one woman and declares that states need not recognize same-gender marriages established in other states. One result is "that married same-sex couples are entitled to federal benefits" (Liptak, 2013). Second, the Court declined to address a California case, effectively allowing same-sex marriages there to resume (CNN Library, 2013). However, these rulings do not affect laws in states that prohibit same-sex marriage (Liptak, 2013).

An alternative option to marriage is a civil union. A *civil union* conveys legal status to a unification of two people of the same gender and has many, but not all, of the same rights and responsibilities as marriage. Legal arenas in which civil unions may treat lesbian or gay couples the same as straight couples may include "child custody, probate court, workers' compensation, and family leave benefits" (American Association of Sex Educators, Counselors, and Therapists [AASECT], April 2000, p. 6; States that Allow, 2013b). However, legal experts indicate that other states will probably not accept such unions as legal.

Yet another alternative to marriage is a *domestic partnership,* which is a less formal alliance that may offer some specific legal rights that vary from state to state (States that Allow, 2013a). Domestic partnerships may involve either same-gender or heterosexual relationships. They are not necessarily initiated by a formal contract or ceremony. Depending on the state, legal rights may range from employment benefits or other limited legal rights to a status nearing that of marriage (States that Allow, 2013a).

A recent Gallup poll found that 53 percent of people felt that same-gender marriage should be legalized and that partners should have the same legal rights as partners in heterosexual marriages (Gallup, 2013).

Critical Thinking Questions 10.3

- What is your opinion of same-gender marriage and why?
- To what extent does your opinion comply with the social work value of self-determination?

Heterosexual unions tend to be characterized by much celebration and legal support. Families and friends hold wedding showers, give gifts, and make the wedding itself a major social event. Gay people, however, at this time do not have this legal alternative in the large majority of states, which forbid same-gender marriage. "Partners" often cannot be included in employment benefit policies. Nor can partners file joint tax returns.

The unmarried partner of a gay or lesbian person who becomes critically ill and needs hospitalization may be denied visiting privileges (Hunter & Hickerson, 2003). Gay lovers and unmarried partners have no legal rights because they do not fall under the legal definition of family. Gay and lesbian couples are encouraged, therefore, to draw up a legal document involving the medical power of attorney; these may address "visitation rights, the right to be consulted and to give or withhold consent about medical decisions, and in case of death, the right to personal effects and the right to dispose of the body" (Schwaber, 1985, p. 92).

Wills and the exercising of their instructions are another source of difficulty for many gay and lesbian couples (Berger & Kelly, 1995; Hunter & Hickerson, 2003; Tully, 1995). Unmarried gay partners have no rights at all to any inheritance if there is no will. All inheritance will be given to legal family members. Therefore, gay people are strongly encouraged to have a will made. Wills may clearly specify what possessions will go to which people.

However, relatives may still challenge a will under the concept of "undue influence" (Peters, 1982, p. 24). This principle implies that unfair manipulation has occurred on the part of the gay partner to influence the dictates of a will. Gay people are therefore encouraged to update the contents of the will from time to time. Each time they should ascertain that the will accurately reflects their current assets and that all is well documented.

Being sensitive to the unfairness and oppression suffered by gay and lesbian people is important for social workers. Plans and interventions can target not only improving an individual gay or lesbian person's situation, but also changing larger systems. At the macro level, practitioners can advocate for new laws that forbid discrimination on the basis of sexual orientation. Likewise, workers can exert pressure for the dissolution of old laws and policies that oppress gay and lesbian people.

Highlight 10.4 provides some additional tips for empowering lesbian and gay people.

WORKING WITH AFRICAN-AMERICAN FAMILIES

Understanding the cultural expectations, economic conditions, and social realities of the various ethnically and culturally diverse groups that generalist social work practitioners work with is a necessity. Lum (2004) maintains that "every population has color, language, and behavioral characteristics that distinguish it as a unique group in a multiracial society" (p. 11).

We have established that it is a social worker's responsibility to recognize the importance of difference, including that of color, race, and culture, when working with diverse populations. Such differences directly affect life experiences and access to resources and power. This section examines some aspects of practice with African-American families. Chapter 12 addresses ethnically and racially sensitive practice more thoroughly with a variety of ethnic groups.

The Many Strengths of African-American Families

McRoy (2003) asserts that "[u]sing a strengths approach, the worker is able to form a client-worker partnership, and jointly the client and worker examine the client's knowledge and experience. This allows the worker to understand and embrace the client's behavioral styles, belief systems, and coping patterns" (p. 235). This is equally true within the family context.

One strength of African-American families involves the strong kinship system and support network developed beyond the simple nuclear family (Jones, 2005; Diller, 2011; Evans, 2013; Sudarkasa, 2007; Zinn, Eitzen, & Wells, 2011). Viewing this family structure as inferior and inadequate is easy for workers coming from a white mainstream orientation.

HIGHLIGHT 10.4

Empowerment of Lesbian and Gay People

The following are suggestions for empowering lesbian and gay people at the micro level:

1. Don't assume that all people are heterosexual (Tully, 2000).
2. Be sensitive to the language and terminology you use. Instead of using the terms *husband* or *wife*, you might use *partner* or *significant other* (Barrett & Logan, 2002). Explore with clients what terms they prefer.
3. Have a work environment that's friendly to gay and lesbian people. Do you have books about homosexuality on your office shelves or lesbian and gay magazines in the waiting room? (Barrett & Logan, 2002).
4. Become more knowledgeable about lesbian and gay life, issues, and culture (Barrett & Logan, 2002).
5. Be aware of the wide range of diversity within the lesbian and gay communities, just as there is diversity within the heterosexual community (Barrett & Logan, 2002).
6. "Develop a list of local resources for gay and lesbian clients" (Barrett & Logan, 2002, p. 19).

Empowerment at the macro level is also critical, as the following suggests (Tully, 2000):

1. "Understand the many legal issues associated with lesbians and gays;
2. Confront institutional homophobia at the state and federal levels;
3. Become an expert in the field of gay and lesbian issues;
4. Join and support pro lesbian and gay organizations" (p. 111);
5. Support political candidates who have pro-lesbian and pro-gay agendas;
6. Become politically active on the behalf of lesbian and gay rights by building gay-friendly support networks, coalitions, and constituencies.

For instance, one practitioner worked for a day treatment center that offered both special education and therapy for adolescents with behavioral and emotional problems. A 12-year-old African-American client at the center was the source of unending frustration to the social worker and the other staff. The boy seemed to change his place of residence on a weekly or biweekly basis, which required repeated updating of the bus route responsible for picking him up every day. Additionally, it made working with the boy's family difficult for the boy's social worker. For one thing, knowing who the primary caregivers were was challenging because there were so many people involved. For another thing, that kind of extended family structure simply did not fit into the family counseling model to which the worker was accustomed. The worker was white and middle class. She had been trained to work within the context of a nuclear family where the child's two parents were supposed to take total responsibility for the child's welfare.

In this case, the worker could have assumed a more appropriate and effective perspective. She could have looked at the substantial extended family network as a strength rather than a deficit. There were many caring, involved resources and role models available to this boy instead of the one or two provided by parents.

A second strength often available to African-American families is the flexibility of family roles (McAdoo, 1997; Diller, 2011; Sudarkasa, 2007; Zinn et al., 2011). Contrary to traditional gender stereotypes, both men and women can assume either emotionally expressive or economically supportive roles. This versatility in roles allows greater flexibility in terms of improving family functioning. It follows that in a family where both parents are present, a worker should not assume a matriarchal structure just because the mother/spouse makes her points strongly. Marital relationships in African-American families tend to be egalitarian by nature.

A third strength often inherent in African-American families is their dedication to spirituality and serious involvement in their churches (Diller, 2011; Evans, 2013; Moore 2008; Pipes, 2007). African-American churches provide a massive resource for hope and spiritual growth, social support, and a range of services to meet members' needs. Such services may include "senior citizen activities, child care, educational groups, parenting groups, and housing development" (Ho, 1987, p. 182).

Social Work Practice with African-American Families

There are at least three major roles for social workers to assume when helping African-American families

(Jones, 2005; McAdoo, 1987). First, the worker needs to develop empathy for the cultural context saturated with oppression in which African-American families must live. Second, the worker must maximize the use of practice skills and available resources to improve the social and economic conditions of African-American families. Third, the practitioner must advocate on behalf of African-American families to change the policies, regulations, and expectations that act to discriminate against African Americans (Evans, 2013).

There are at least four major approaches that are useful when working with African-American families: (1) engaging the client or family, (2) assessing the family in the past and present, (3) setting mutual goals, and (4) identifying the target system for change (Ho, 1987; Jones, 2005). The following sections discuss each concept.

 Engage the Client/Family. Regardless of race, empathizing with a family and its situation is important. The referral process may have been tedious or confusing. Family members may have had bad experiences with agencies in the past, which can eat away at trust.

Understanding the initial silence and apparent lack of communication often posed by African-American family members is also important. This silence may convey their lack of faith and confidence either in your ability to help them while in the role of worker or in the agency's commitment in and ability to do so. Family members may be experiencing their own anger at how they have been treated by white society. Their resentment may indirectly be projected onto you.

Reasons for communication blocks need to be addressed just like any other issues raised in the problem-solving process. If you are not African American and especially if you are white, you may want to discuss straightforwardly any racial tensions you may perceive. Do not be defensive if family members express anger. It is logical for them, if they have negative feelings, to vent them at you just because you are there. These feelings must be addressed and placed within perspective before the problem-solving process can proceed.

On the one hand, be understanding. However, on the other, also be strong and assertive. Most African-American families will expect the worker to competently and straightforwardly lead the intervention process.

Finally, realize that most African-American families will react most positively to an intervention process with clearly identified goals and with constraints on how long it will take to get results. In other words, telling an African-American family that the change process will take an indeterminable amount of time will probably not be well received.

Assess the Family in Past and Present. Understanding dynamics in African-American families is as critical as it is in other families. Most African-American families are more interested in what is going on in the present than in the past. Therefore, the reasons for soliciting information about more historical issues (e.g., how parents themselves were raised by grandparents or what family incidents occurred several years ago that had serious impact on the family) need clear explanation regarding why they are important.

Set Mutual Goals. Mutual goal setting is just as important when working with African-American families as with any other families. The chances are likely that the African-American family will be plagued by a number of concurrent problems. Therefore, the worker must both be problem-oriented and maintain a focus on how circumstances outside of the family fuel the problem. An African-American family might well think that solving an economically related problem (such as unemployment) is much more important than resolving interpersonal conflicts (e.g., a disagreement between partners). The family's top priorities need to be addressed first. Additionally, the faster a problem can be solved, the more cooperative family members will probably become.

Identify the Target System for Change. As with any other family, the worker needs to identify the systems in need of change. This identification should be done in a prioritized order. Sometimes, the problem can best be solved by targeting some external system, such as the schools or the health care system. At still other times, interpersonal changes are needed within the African-American family system.

LO 10-8 Explore the Current Status of Family Services

Family services are those provided by human service agencies that focus on the needs of families and couples. In other words, a broad array of agencies can provide services to families as long as these agencies clearly state that families are to be the primary recipients of service. Primary concerns of families include poverty, unemployment, health insurance, housing, domestic violence, mental health issues, and substance abuse. Various programs address these issues, including those providing counseling, treatment, education, financial assistance, various benefits (e.g., food stamps), and political advocacy. Highlight 10.5 discusses six important policy areas.

The types of family services available in any particular community depend on what the community needs, on the one hand, and what it can afford to pay for, on the other. Thus, the services available to families vary drastically from one area to another.

Most family service agencies provide services directly to individuals, groups of individuals facing similar problems, and the families themselves. For example, they might provide individual counseling for depressed family members, support groups for battered women, or family counseling for entire families.

However, there is also a definite macro-practice aspect to the family service agency. It typically addresses problems held by a number of people in the community. In the event that services are not available, the generalist practitioner may need to assess the community's needs. For instance, the worker may determine that substance abuse treatment services are inadequate to meet the needs of families within the community. That worker may then proceed to gather data to document that the need truly exists and subsequently to advocate for the expansion of current programs.

In another situation, the worker may discover that substance abuse services are available but are not getting to the people who really need them. In this case, the worker may investigate what is causing this blockage and try to remedy the problem. For instance, are available treatment programs not being publicized adequately? Is the red tape so thick that cutting through it and getting service is difficult for people? For some reason, are agency policies making the neediest people ineligible?

Whatever the reason, family service agencies can provide effective and flexible resources to help satisfy community families' real needs. Generalist social workers may be called upon not only to serve individuals, families, and groups, but also to advocate for changes in agency policies, governmental legislation regarding how resources are distributed, and expansion of services that are already there.

The United States is not the only nation facing crises in its system of service provision to families. This is an international issue. Globally, nations are struggling to meet the escalating needs of children and families in the face of swelling populations and shrinking resources.

HIGHLIGHT 10.5

Families, Macro Practice, and the Integration of Policy and Practice

EP 2.1.8a
EP 2.1.9a

Because of the major focus on resources and their availability to families, the importance of macro practice is easily stressed. Needed resources are only available if agencies and organizations provide them. These agencies offer them only if their policies and procedures allow them to do so. Sometimes, agency and social policies restrict resources. At other times, policies simply deny that such potential resources exist. Hence, as a generalist social work practitioner, you may have to advocate and work for changes in organizational and social policies so that resources are made available to the people who need them.

There are a number of policy areas that critically affect the well-being of families (Jansson, 2014; Karger & Stoesz, 2013; Popple & Leighninger, 2011). The policies existing in these areas merit careful attention and scrutiny. Each policy issue has dramatic and direct effects upon your clients, including both families and individuals. They include employment, direct provision of income or substitutes for income, health care, homelessness, and day care.

1. Employment

How family members can work to gain income is dictated by policy. World and national policies determine where jobs will be located and what kind they will be. For example, if the cost of running a farm continues to escalate and small U.S. farmers cannot compete with others in the world, small U.S. farmers may go bankrupt. However, the government can subsidize these farmers. Another example concerns the government can (and does) formulate policies to help farmers pay their farming costs. Other policies can add charges to imported farm produce so that U.S. farmers can compete with foreign prices. Such policies significantly decrease the farmer's potential for bankruptcy.

Another illustration involves providing money for job training. Programs can be developed to pay for training certain segments of the population for jobs that need to be filled. Training takes money. If poor people in an urban ghetto or a rural enclave cannot afford training, they will not get it. Thus, they will not get the jobs. However, if training is provided and paid for in another way, these same people will get jobs.

Critical Thinking Questions 10.4

EP 2.1.3

- What if the unemployment rate in your clients' community is more than 50 percent, as is the case for many young people in urban ghettos? (Note that those who are employed receive minimum wages and no benefits such as sick leave or vacation.)
- What can you do to help your clients gain adequate employment under such circumstances if no programs and policies exist to help you?

This book is neither an economics nor a policy text. You probably guessed that. However, the book does intend to depict clearly how policy at various system levels has direct impact on clients and what they are able to do. It also affects what *you* can *do* for clients.

2. Direct Provision of Income or Substitutes for Income

How income is provided or not provided to designated groups of people is a policy matter. How much money is provided to a family without resources varies drastically from one state to another. This money directly affects the family's quality of life. States vary in the amount of public assistance given. A family in a state with more assistance has a greater potential for a better standard of living than a family in a state with a lower level of assistance.

Substitutes for income, otherwise referred to as "in-kind income transfers," can also provide resources to families. Food stamps, which can be exchanged only for groceries, are a good example. Criteria for who is eligible to get food stamps and how many they can get vary drastically from state to state.

Critical Thinking Questions 10.5

- What might you do when your clients are not eligible for enough cash and in-kind income transfers to survive?
- What might you do if policies neglect clients who are slowly starving to death?

3. Health Care

Policies determine who is eligible to receive what types of health care, how much care will cost, and who will pay for it. At the time of this writing, many questions have been raised regarding how health care will operate at a national level in the United States. Some predict premiums and costs will escalate for individuals and employers. Some warn that access to adequate care will shrink. Some envisage a much fairer, adequate system that will be available to all who need help. Regardless, because access to health care significantly affects clients to such a great degree, it's crucial that social workers keep abreast of whatever characterizes the current health care scenario.

Critical Thinking Questions 10.6

- How should health care be financed? Should taxes be increased? If so, whose taxes? Should other programs and services be reduced so that money can be reallocated to finance health care? If so, which programs and services? Where else might financing be found?
- Should health care costs be controlled? If so, how?
- What are the reasons for your opinions?

4. Homelessness

More and more families, especially those including only women and children, are homeless. Rents are escalating. Affordable housing is becoming increasingly difficult to find throughout the nation.

Critical Thinking Questions 10.7

- What should you as a social worker do if there are no programs with policies to provide your clients temporary shelter, food, and longer-term housing?
- What should you do if families are literally living on the streets?

5. Day Care

Most women work. More specifically, most women with children work. Adequate day care for their children is difficult, if not impossible, to find. It is also expensive, and the quality is highly variable.

Critical Thinking Questions 10.8

- Should the federal, state, and/or local governments establish policies to provide resources for day care so that parents can work?
- Are you and others willing to pay taxes to finance these services?
- What if your client is a single parent who receives public assistance payments barely allowing her to subsist below the poverty level?
- What if she wants to go out, get a job, and support herself, but is unable to because she cannot afford the available day care?
- What policy changes might help her?

The problems evident in all five policy issues are difficult to solve. The questions raised are hard to answer. However, these are questions and issues that generalist practitioners must face every day. What provides the direction is the social worker's ethical perspective of seeking the best route for the common good. Many times, advocacy on behalf of clients is paramount. Searching and working for policy change may be critical.

LO 10-9 Engage in Macro Practice with Families by Promoting Social and Economic Justice

EP 2.1.5b

Unavailability of health care, lack of supportive day care services for the children of parents who work, and a dearth of strategies to train workers for skilled vocations where jobs are available are among the multitude of problems confronting America's families.

Generalist practitioners in agency positions often feel frustrated and overwhelmed at the concept of changing the system because it is not working right. They often feel they have enough to do with their daily micro- and mezzo-practice concerns. However, the roots of clients' problems should always be kept in mind. Sometimes there might be an opportunity to amend an agency policy, even a relatively minor one, so that clients are better served. A worker may be able to assist in a political campaign to elect people who are more sensitive to families and their needs. A worker might be able to advocate for clients to prove the need for some service and to succeed in making that service available to people who really need it.

The Generalist Intervention Model emphasizes constant awareness of the impact of macro systems. The potential to make improvements in agencies, organizations, and systems should never be forgotten as one means of effecting positive change for clients.

Poverty is a major stumbling block obstructing the progress of multitudes of American children, and, in effect, their families; a different configuration of services could be made available to American families if policies geared toward family were improved (Jansson, 2014; Karger & Stoesz, 2013). Generalist practitioners should keep these concepts in mind when considering intervention alternatives. Sometimes, macro-level changes may be possible. Improved family service policies would follow the seven principles discussed next.

First, all families should have access to the services they need regardless of their income bracket. Second, services should be distributed along neither racial nor economic lines. In other words, the same quality of services should be available to everyone. Agencies providing family services should have a mixture of races and economic levels characterizing their clientele. Third, services should be convenient for everyone. All families should have access to coordinating referral and appointment centers that they can contact. Fourth, families should have as many options as possible so that they can select the service of their preference. Fifth, parents should be given significant input into the agencies and their policies serving families. Sixth, more volunteers and paraprofessionals should be used to aid in service delivery. Using such people to perform less specialized tasks would minimize the cost of expensive specialists. Finally, seventh, more resources should be devoted to preventing problems before they occur rather than applying Band-Aids after the problems already exist. A more superficial view sees prevention as an extravagance that is not absolutely necessary. Therefore, the programs and services that could prevent and minimize problems often rest at the bottom of priority lists. When money runs out, programs aimed at prevention are frequently among those first cut.

Chapter Summary

The following summarizes this chapter's content as it relates to each learning objective (LO) presented at the beginning of the chapter. Chapter content helps prepare students to:

LO 10-1 Use generalist practice skills with families.

Working with or treating families follows the planned change process proposed by the Generalist Intervention Model. One issue in family treatment involves deter-mining whether the entire family or just some of its members must be involved in the intervention process.

LO 10-2 Assess and emphasize family strengths.

The strengths perspective emphasizes identifying family strengths and resources to improve problematic circumstances. It stresses identifying and building upon assets, which is a more positive focus than the traditional focus on problems. Strengths-based strategies include using strengths to establish goals and a view of a better life, emphasizing current positives, working collaboratively with families, increasing family interaction and coping skills, and developing high expectations for change.

LO 10-3 Engage, assess, and plan with families.

Working with families follows the planned change process. The five phases of beginning treatment are minimizing early apprehension, asking each family member to explain the problem, establishing agreement about problems, focusing on family relationships and interaction, and establishing a commitment to a plan of action.

LO 10-4 Employ various approaches to implementing family intervention.

Techniques and approaches used during implementation vary dramatically due to each family's distinctive problems. Such approaches include emphasizing family strengths, reframing, teaching families problem-solving techniques, teaching child management methods, offering families support, role playing, digital recording, and homework assignments.

LO 10-5 Evaluate, terminate, and follow-up with families.

Evaluation of progress and goal achievement is important. Termination concerns preparing the family for the end of contact. Follow-up involves examining the family's resources and reviewing the status of achieved goals.

LO 10-6 Address family issues and provide relevant services.

Techniques for helping multiproblem families include staying calm, following the planned change process, partializing and prioritizing problems, determining which problems to work on and which to refer elsewhere, and identifying and using relevant community resources.

Family preservation involves providing intensive intervention over a relatively brief time period, tailored to the family's unique needs and often provided in the client's home. Major themes include a crisis orientation; a focus on family; home-based services; time limits; limited, focused objectives; intensive, comprehensive services; emphasis on education and skill building; coordination; flexibility; accessibility; and accountability. Family preservation follows the planned change process.

LO 10-7 Enhance cultural competency in working with families.

Many of the issues faced in families where parents are gay, lesbian, bisexual, or transgender closely resemble those addressed in families with heterosexual parents. However, special issues affecting these families include homophobia, coming out to their children and others, and social and economic oppression. Suggestions for the empowerment of gay and lesbian people are provided.

Understanding the cultural expectations, economic conditions, and social realities of African-American families is crucial. These families often have many strengths, including a strong kinship system, flexibility of family roles, and dedication to spirituality. Social work roles and practice with African-American families are discussed.

LO 10-8 Explore the current status of family services.

At least five policy areas critically affect the well-being of families: employment, direct provision of income or substitutes for income, health care, homelessness, and day care. These can be the target of advocacy for social and economic justice.

LO 10-9 Engage in macro practice with families by promoting social and economic justice.

Generalist social workers should engage in macro practice when possible to promote social and economic justice. All families should have access to the resources and services they need.

Competency Notes

The following identifies where Educational Policy (EP) competencies and practice behaviors are discussed in the chapter.

EP 2.1.1d Demonstrate professional demeanor in behavior, appearance, and communication. *(p. 368):* Social workers should exhibit appropriate

professional behavior when engaging family members and initiating family treatment. *(p. 380):* In family preservation practice, social workers should demonstrate a professional demeanor. *(p. 388):* Social workers should demonstrate a professional demeanor when working with African-American families.

EP 2.1.3 Apply critical thinking to inform and communicate professional judgments. *(pp. 367, 382, 386, 390):* Critical thinking questions are posed.

EP 2.1.3a Distinguish, appraise, and integrate multiple sources of knowledge, including research-based knowledge, and practice wisdom. *(p. 373):* Generalist practitioners must draw from their extensive knowledge base to select intervention strategies that address specific family problems.

EP 2.1.4 Engage diversity and difference in practice. *(p. 382):* Lesbian and gay families and African-American families are members of diverse groups.

EP 2.1.4a Recognize the extent to which culture's structures and values may oppress, marginalize, alienate, or create or enhance privilege or power. *(p. 383):* Self-awareness about the experience of lesbian and gay people, many times due to homophobia, is an important aspect of engaging diversity in practice.

EP 2.1.5a Understand the forms and mechanisms of oppression and discrimination. *(p. 382):* Homophobia can cause oppression and discrimination. *(p. 386):* Gay and lesbian people suffer from social and economic oppression.

EP 2.1.5b Advocate for human rights and social and economic justice. *(p. 391):* Practitioners should advocate for social and economic justice on the behalf of families.

EP 2.1.5c Engage in practices that advance social and economic justice. *(p. 387):* Social workers should seek to empower lesbian and gay people at the micro, mezzo, and macro levels.

EP 2.1.6b Use research evidence to inform practice. *(p. 374):* Practitioners should choose child management techniques that have been proven effective. *(p. 380):* Research has established that certain risk factors typically characterize families who are candidates for family preservation. Practitioners should be aware of these factors and take them into consideration during family intervention. *(p. 381):* Ongoing research is necessary to determine the most effective approaches in family preservation work.

EP 2.1.8a **Analyze, formulate, and advocate for policies that advance social well-being.** *(p. 390):* Social workers should analyze, formulate, and advocate for policies that advance the well-being of families. These include policies concerning employment, income provision, health care, homelessness, and day care.

EP 2.1.9a **Continuously discover, appraise, and attend to changing locales, populations, scientific and technological developments, and emerging societal trends to provide relevant services.** *(p. 390):* Social workers should keep abreast of the ever-changing macro environment and its effects on the families served.

EP 2.1.10 **Engage, assess, intervene, and evaluate with individuals, families, groups, organizations, and communities.** *(p. 367):* Social workers engage, assess, and plan when working with families. *(p. 381):* Family preservation follows the planned change process, including engaging, assessing, intervening, and evaluating with families.

EP 2.1.10a **Substantively and affectively prepare for action with individuals, families, groups, organizations, and communities.** *(p. 363):* Generalist practitioners should prepare for action with families by using generalist practice skills.

EP 2.1.10c **Develop a mutually agreed-on focus of work and desired outcomes.** *(p. 369):* It is critical for practitioners to establish a mutually acceptable agreement with family members about plans and goals.

EP 2.1.10e **Assess clients' strengths and limitations.** *(p. 364):* Practitioners should assess and use clients' strengths when working with families. *(p. 373):* Emphasizing strengths should be an ongoing theme in family intervention. *(p. 379):* Family preservation stresses family strengths. *(p. 387):* It is important to emphasize the many strengths manifested by African-American families.

EP 2.1.10f **Develop mutually agreed-on intervention goals and objectives.** *(p. 372):* Working with family members to establish a contract develops mutually agreed-on goals and objectives. *(p. 389):* Just as with any other family, practitioners should engage in mutual goal setting when working with African-American families.

EP 2.1.10g **Select appropriate intervention strategies.** *(p. 363):* A practitioner's intervention strategy might involve seeing the entire family or only some family members. *(p. 373):* It is important to select techniques and approaches for working with families that are effective.

EP 2.1.10i **Implement prevention interventions that enhance client capacities.** *(p. 379):* One intent of family preservation is to prevent the removal of children from their own homes.

EP 2.1.10j **Help clients resolve problems.** *(p. 374):* Family problem solving involves recognizing both differences among family members and ways to address problems.

EP 2.1.10l **Facilitate transitions and endings.** *(p. 377):* Appropriate termination approaches are part of generalist practice with families.

EP 2.1.10m **Critically analyze, monitor, and evaluate interventions.** *(p. 377):* Evaluation of progress is an important part of family intervention.

On the Internet

Visit the *Understanding Generalist Practice* CourseMate at **www.cengagebrain.com** for resources such as quizzes, glossaries and videos.

Values, Ethics, and the Resolution of Ethical Dilemmas

© Wavebreakmedia/Shutterstock.com

Learning Objectives   *This chapter will help prepare students to:*

LO 11-1   Examine and apply the National Association of Social Workers (NASW) *Code of Ethics.*

LO 11-2   Recognize the Canadian Association of Social Workers *Code of Ethics.*

LO 11-3   Examine international ethical principles.

LO 11-4   Identify ethical dilemmas.

LO 11-5   Conceptualize and apply a decision-making strategy to address ethical dilemmas.

LO 11-6   Rank ethical principles.

LO 11-7   Discuss and resolve ethical dilemmas in generalist practice contexts.

LO 11-8   Demonstrate ethical communication and "Netiquette" on the Internet.

LO 11-9   Examine self-determination and people with disabilities: An empowerment approach.

LO 11-10 Appraise personal and professional values.

TWO SISTERS, SHELBY, 5, and Mary Ann, 7 months, are placed in a temporary foster home when both parents are killed in a violent car crash. Tina, their social worker, must decide whether they should be placed for adoption separately or together. The problem is that placing infants is much easier than older children. Mary Ann's chances of adoption are excellent if placed alone. The chances of placing both Shelby and Mary Ann together are much slimmer. However, Tina feels strongly that there are many positive reasons to keep the sisters together. What should she recommend?[1]

Denny's kidneys are failing. At age 31, he is extremely sick from regular renal dialysis. His health is rapidly deteriorating, and he has become extremely depressed. Chances of receiving a kidney transplant are slim due to his rare tissue type and poor general health. Denny knows he cannot live like this much longer. He begs his hospital social worker, Tony, to help him pull the plug and discontinue his treatments. Denny is in such excruciating pain. He cannot stand it anymore.

Denny's parents are mortified about his wish to "commit suicide," which is how they see his request. They sincerely love their son and want to hold on to him as long as possible. They desperately cling to the hope of a kidney transplant and vehemently disagree with Denny's request, beseeching Tony to tell Denny it is ridiculous. What should Tony do? Who is right?

Bernie, 17, tells his school social worker Cyndi that he intends to steal his father's car and any money he can get hold of and take off for San Francisco. For the past several weeks, Cyndi has been seeing Bernie, who has a case of mild depression and family problems. She knows if she reports Bernie's plan, he will never talk to her again. On the other hand, if she pretends she does not know about the plan, she fears what will happen if he really does take off. What will happen to him? To his parents? To her? What should she do?

Andra is a social worker providing substance abuse counseling at a community center. The agency primarily serves low-income clients and relies heavily on grants to keep it going. Suddenly, one of its primary grant-funding agencies demands that it requires access to client records to monitor the appropriate use of funds. On her clients' behalf, Andra is outraged. Clients use the center and its services with the understanding that their involvement will be kept confidential. Many clients have much to lose if private information became public. For example, a number of clients are HIV-positive. They are terrified of losing jobs and any health insurance they do have. If this funding stops, the number of clients the agency serves will be cut by approximately one-third. However, if the funding agency gets access to client records, the results are repercussions to clients and violation of their right to confidentiality. What should Andra do?

These examples are just a few of the many ethical dilemmas social workers frequently encounter in practice. How can practitioners evaluate these scenarios? What guidelines can help them decide what to do? Values and ethics provide a major foundation of practice. This chapter addresses such issues.

Introduction

EP 2.1.2

Chapter 1 introduced the concepts of values and ethics. Along with knowledge and skills, professional values comprise the third basis for the foundation of generalist social work practice. *Values* involve what you consider important and what you do not. They concern what is considered having worth and what is not. They also involve making judgments or decisions about relative worth, that is, what is more valuable and what is less valuable. Common social work values include promotion of client well-being and individual dignity, self-determination, the right to have basic needs met, the right to actualize one's full potential, client empowerment, human diversity, and the promotion of social and economic justice (Council on Social Work Education [CSWE], 2008; Reamer, 2006).

Ethics involve principles that specify what is good and bad. They clarify what should and should not be done. As you know, social workers are guided by the specific *Code of Ethics* of the National Association of Social Workers (NASW) that is based on professional values (NASW, 2008). Ethics and values are clearly related, although they are not the same thing. Dolgoff, Harrington, and Loewenberg (2012) state that "ethics are deduced from values and must be in consonance with them. The difference between them is that values are concerned with what is *good* and *desirable,* while ethics deal with what is *right* and *correct*" (p. 25). Values, then, deal with what beliefs are appropriate. Ethics address what to *do* with or how to *apply* those beliefs.

---

1. The basic ideas for this and the second vignette are taken from J. C. Rothman (1998), *From the front lines: Student cases in social work ethics.* Boston: Allyn & Bacon.

Cournoyer (2011) clearly summarizes the momentous importance of social work ethics:

We must consider every aspect of practice, every decision, every assessment, every intervention, and virtually every action we undertake as social workers from the perspective of our professional ethics and obligations. This dimension supersedes all others. Ethical responsibilities take precedence over theoretical knowledge, research findings, practice wisdom, agency policies, and, of course, your own personal values, preferences, and beliefs. (p. 126)

From a superficial perspective, professional judgments may look like a simple matter of common sense. However, in real-life decisions values and ethical principles conflict constantly. These conflicts can result in *ethical dilemmas,* namely, problematic situations whose possible solutions all offer imperfect and unsatisfactory answers. For example, your client informs you of an activity such as dealing drugs that you are required to report. How can you maintain confidentiality and report at the same time? Perhaps you find that your agency's eligibility requirements cut off services to some clients who are in dire need. You are ethically responsible for serving these clients effectively, yet you are also professionally committed to your employer as its agent.

This chapter deals with making ethical decisions within a wide range of generalist practice contexts. It focuses on those decisions you must make when there is no absolutely clear *right* thing to do.

LO 11-1 Examine and Apply the National Association of Social Workers (NASW) *Code of Ethics*

EP 2.1.2b&c

EP 2.1.5c

We have established the importance of ethics in guiding professional behavior. Because of its significance, we will examine the NASW *Code of Ethics* (2008) section by section. (The *Code* can be accessed at http://www.socialworkers .org/pubs/code/code.asp). It is divided into four primary facets. First, there is a preamble that summarizes social work's mission and identifies its core values. The mission "is to enhance human well-being and help meet the basic human needs of all people, with particular attention to the needs and empowerment of people who are vulnerable, oppressed,

and living in poverty." The six core values are as follows:

1. *Service:* Social workers should provide help, resources, and benefits so that people may achieve their maximum potential. Workers should place effective service provision above their own convenience and advantage. They should also take opportunities to volunteer their services when possible and appropriate.

2. *Social justice:* Social workers should pursue social justice, the idea that in a perfect world all citizens would possess equal fundamental "rights, protection, opportunities, obligations, and social benefits," regardless of their backgrounds and membership in diverse groups (Barker, 2003, pp. 404–405). Seeking social justice includes combating oppression, seeking fair and equal treatment for all, providing people with opportunities for growth and improvement, and advocating for significant involvement and input by people in decisions affecting their lives.

3. *Dignity and worth of the person:* Social workers should hold people in high esteem and appreciate individual value. They should treat people with respect, support people's ability to make their own responsible decisions, and encourage opportunities for people to enhance their own well-being.

4. *Importance of human relationships:* Social workers should value the significance of supportive interpersonal interaction and effective communication to achieve people's optimal well-being. Workers should establish collaborative relationships with clients and seek positive change that enriches the human condition. This may involve working with systems of any size, including individuals, families, groups, organizations, or communities.

5. *Integrity:* Social workers should be responsible, honest, and reliable. They should remain knowledgeable and vigilant about professional values and ethics and take care that their practice and behavior complies with these values and ethics. Workers should monitor and support principled policies and procedures in the agencies where they practice.

6. *Competence:* Social workers should possess the necessary skills and abilities to perform work with clients effectively. They should persistently try to improve their professional practice by engaging in learning new knowledge and skills throughout their careers. Whenever possible, workers should strive to add to the foundation of knowledge and learned experience underpinning the field of social work.

The second major facet in the *Code*, "Purpose of NASW *Code of Ethics*," identifies the *Code*'s six major aims. These are:

1. identifying primary social work values;
2. summarizing broad ethical principles as guidelines for practice;
3. helping determine relevant considerations when addressing an ethical dilemma;
4. providing broad ethical standards for the public in general to which it may hold the profession accountable;
5. socializing new practitioners to the mission, goals, and ethics inherent in the profession; and
6. articulating specific standards that the profession may use to judge its members' conduct.

Additionally, this section "emphasizes various resources social workers should consider when faced with difficult ethical decisions," which include "ethical theory and decision-making, social work practice theory and research, laws, regulations, agency policies, and other relevant codes of ethics" (Reamer, 2006, p. 9). Of particular note is how the *Code* emphasizes the complexity of ethical dilemmas. A *dilemma* is a situation where one must make a difficult choice among two or more alternatives. *Ethical dilemmas* in social work practice involve problematic situations where possible solutions all offer imperfect and unsatisfactory answers in terms of what ethically should be done.

Many ethical dilemmas are quite complex and difficult to solve. It is important for generalist practitioners to tolerate ambiguity as they resolve ethical conflicts. *Ambiguity* involves the state of being indistinct or of having the potential to be viewed from different perspectives. Ethical dilemmas are often ambiguous in that solutions are unclear or no perfect answers exist.

The *Code* provides no cookbook formulas for resolution. Rather, it stresses that ethical dilemmas may be viewed from a range of perspectives. It also emphasizes that each social worker should strive to resolve ethical issues using these ethical standards and professional judgment to the best of his or her ability.

The *Code*'s third facet, "Ethical Principles," is based on the six core values described earlier and sets forth standards to which all practitioners should strive. For example, the ethical principle relative to the value of *social justice* states that "social workers challenge social injustice." Likewise, the principle based on *integrity* states that "social workers [should] behave in a trustworthy manner."

The final facet of the *Code*, "Ethical Standards," is by far the most extensive. It encompasses 155 specific principles clustered under six major categories. These principles include social workers' ethical responsibilities to clients and colleagues, in practice settings, as professionals, to the social work profession, and to the broader society. Highlight 11.1 summarizes the major concepts that are subsequently explained more thoroughly. The *Code* is published in its entirety at the Web address given earlier.

SOCIAL WORKERS' ETHICAL RESPONSIBILITIES TO CLIENTS

The first category of ethical standards identifies social workers' ethical responsibilities to clients. How should practitioners behave with respect to clients? What aspects of worker–client interaction are most significant within an ethical context? Ethical responsibilities to clients involve 16 specific concepts, each of which is identified in this section. In order to offer some depth to the concept and to help you understand some of its ramifications, practice examples will be provided for each concept. Some examples demonstrate compliance with the ethical standard involved. Others portray a worker's violation of the standard. Still other examples raise a question for you to determine in your own mind the ethical thing to do.

1.01 Commitment to Clients

Commitment to clients involves the importance of a worker's dedication to clients' well-being and the primacy of their interests. However, the *Code* cautions that there will be times when other obligations, such as those "to the larger society or specific legal obligations," will supersede loyalty to clients. In such cases, the *Code* instructs social workers to inform the clients about what they intend to do.

Example of Compliance. A 21-year-old single mother, Nerene, confides in her public assistance worker, Horace, that she is planning to shoot her boyfriend. Horace must report Nerene's intentions to the proper authorities because the potential harm to Nerene's boyfriend supersedes Horace's commitment to Nerene. Horace explains his serious concerns and informs Nerene that he is required by law to inform authorities of her threats. Horace then informs the designated authorities and warns Nerene's boyfriend.

1.02 Self-Determination

Practitioners should nurture and support client self-determination. *Self-determination* is each individual's right to make his or her own decisions. Applied to social work this means that practitioners are responsible

HIGHLIGHT 11.1

A Summary of Ethical Standards in the NASW *Code of Ethics*

1. Social Workers' Ethical Responsibilities to Clients

   1.01 Commitment to Clients
   1.02 Self-Determination
   1.03 Informed Consent
   1.04 Competence
   1.05 Cultural Competence and Social Diversity
   1.06 Conflicts of Interest
   1.07 Privacy and Confidentiality
   1.08 Access to Records
   1.09 Sexual Relationships
   1.10 Physical Contact
   1.11 Sexual Harassment
   1.12 Derogatory Language
   1.13 Payment for Services
   1.14 Clients Who Lack Decision-Making Capacity
   1.15 Interruption of Services
   1.16 Termination of Services

2. Social Workers' Ethical Responsibilities to Colleagues

   2.01 Respect
   2.02 Confidentiality
   2.03 Interdisciplinary Collaboration
   2.04 Disputes Involving Colleagues
   2.05 Consultation
   2.06 Referral for Services
   2.07 Sexual Relationships
   2.08 Sexual Harassment
   2.09 Impairment of Colleagues
   2.10 Incompetence of Colleagues
   2.11 Unethical Conduct of Colleagues

3. Social Workers' Ethical Responsibilities in Practice Settings

   3.01 Supervision and Consultation
   3.02 Education and Training
   3.03 Performance Evaluation
   3.04 Client Records
   3.05 Billing
   3.06 Client Transfer
   3.07 Administration
   3.08 Continuing Education and Staff Development
   3.09 Commitments to Employers
   3.10 Labor–Management Disputes

4. Social Workers' Ethical Responsibilities as Professionals

   4.01 Competence
   4.02 Discrimination
   4.03 Private Conduct
   4.04 Dishonesty, Fraud, and Deception
   4.05 Impairment
   4.06 Misrepresentation
   4.07 Solicitations
   4.08 Acknowledging Credit

5. Social Workers' Ethical Responsibilities to the Social Work Profession

   5.01 Integrity of the Profession
   5.02 Evaluation and Research

6. Social Workers' Ethical Responsibilities to the Broader Society

   6.01 Social Welfare
   6.02 Public Participation
   6.03 Public Emergencies
   6.04 Social and Political Action

Source: National Association of Social Workers, Inc. Copyright © 1996, National Association of Social Workers, Inc., NASW *Code of Ethics*. Reprinted with permission.

for: (1) informing clients about available resources, (2) helping them define and articulate their alternatives, and (3) assisting them in evaluating the consequences of each option. The point is to assist clients in making the best, most informed choices possible.

Example of a Violation. Lulabelle is a job coach for a county social services department. Stella, age 19, is one of Lulabelle's clients. Stella emphasizes how she would like to get a clerical job such as being a secretary or administrative assistant. She says she is generally shy with people and would like a job where she could work in a more solitary manner. She also states she has always been good at typing. Lulabelle knows that Stella never graduated from high school and cannot believe that Stella's typing or writing skills are anywhere near adequate for such a position. Therefore, Lulabelle decides not to inform Stella about available clerical alternatives. Rather, she steers Stella to think about becoming a sales clerk.

Critical Thinking Question 11.1

- What could Lulabelle have done in her work with Stella that would have been more ethical and placed her in compliance with the standard on self-determination?

1.03 Informed Consent

Workers should provide clients with informed consent. *Informed consent* is the condition where clients grant permission for the worker to undertake the intervention process after the worker clearly informs clients of all the facts, risks, and alternatives involved.

Example of Compliance. Paige Turner is a case manager for people with severe physical disabilities. A case manager typically assesses the needs of the client and the client's family, when appropriate, and arranges, coordinates, monitors, evaluates, and advocates for a package of multiple services to meet the specific client's complex needs. Usually, one individual is designated case manager for specific cases and serves to coordinate a range of services, often provided by a variety of workers from different agencies. The intent is to make total service provision as effective and efficient as possible.

Paige often coordinates services provided by group homes, in-home support services, Meals-on-Wheels,[2] medical centers, physical therapists, speech therapists, occupational therapists, and others, depending on the client's needs. Paige always makes it a point to work the service plan out with clients and obtains their permission to proceed. She reviews with clients the pros and cons of each prescribed service. She works hard to make certain clients understand what each service involves and what expectations they must fulfill. For example, physical therapy might involve a designated number of weekly sessions, physical work, and possibly pain. On the other hand, positive results may include significantly increased agility, flexibility, strength, and speed. Clients then can make informed decisions about whether to proceed with receiving that service or not.

---

2. *Meals-on-Wheels* is a social service program in which prepared meals are delivered directly to the homes of people in need. Such programs may be sponsored by a range of organizations, including public or private social service agencies and health care, senior, or community centers.

1.04 Competence

Social workers should be competent. Competence involves having the qualifications, ability, and skill to conduct social work practice effectively with the particular clients and problems involved.

Example of a Violation. Herb is an Adult Protective Services worker for an urban county. His clients are older adults who may be victims of physical or psychological maltreatment. Living arrangements vary from staying with relatives to being homeless. Services Herb's unit provides include assessments, linkage with health and mental health services, assistance with living arrangements either in the home or in a residential facility, referral to legal resources, transportation, and other resources clients might need (Brownell & Otto, 2008). A typical issue involves addressing the legal complications of moving a client into a more supportive setting such as assisted living or a nursing home.

Herb has begun working with one case that especially interests him. Louise, 82, lives with her daughter, Grizelda, 57, who appears to have a serious alcohol abuse problem. Herb feels this problem is directly related to her alleged abuse of her mother. Herb has no training in alcohol and other substance abuse. However, he thinks to himself, "How hard can it really be?" He proceeds to "counsel" Grizelda regarding her alcohol abuse.

Critical Thinking Question 11.2

- What might Herb do to be in compliance with the ethical standard on competence?

1.05 Cultural Competence and Social Diversity

Workers should pursue the understanding and ongoing application of cultural competence and social diversity. The *Code* defines *cultural competence* as: (1) understanding the concept of culture, (2) appreciating the strengths inherent in all diverse cultures, (3) acquiring a continuously growing knowledge base about clients' cultures that can be applied to practice, (4) being sensitive to and appreciative of cultural differences, and (5) seeking to understand the nature of oppression and social diversity as they apply to various groups. *Social diversity* is the configuration of elements characterizing various groups of people. Social workers must be especially concerned with people at risk of oppression due to the elements of "race, ethnicity, national origin, color, sex, sexual orientation, gender identity or expression, age, marital status, political belief, religion, immigration status, and mental or physical disability" (CSWE, 2008, EP 2.1.4; NASW, 2008, §1.05).

Example of Compliance. Gschu, a counselor at a homeless shelter, is seeing an increasing number of Haitian immigrants enter the shelter. She determines that she must enhance her knowledge of their cultural values in order to work with them more effectively. She gradually begins to understand their difficult past experiences with economic and political oppression. Gschu discovers that a local organization exists primarily to assist immigrants of Caribbean origin socially, economically, and politically. Some of the organization's goals include improving the community through development of businesses and affordable housing, in addition to matching residents with jobs. Seeking information about Haitian immigrants from this organization enhances both Gschu's understanding of their culture and her ability to communicate with her clients. It also makes her aware of a whole new orb of resources potentially available to clients.

1.06 Conflicts of Interest

Workers should avoid conflicts of interest such as those between a worker's personal interests and his or her professional responsibility. Conflicts of interest may also occur when a worker is responsible to two or more clients whose interests are in conflict with each other.

Example of a Violation. Lucinea, a hospital social worker, is married to Wilbur, a counselor at AIDS Alert, a clinic that serves HIV-positive people. Wilbur counsels people with HIV/AIDS, runs support groups, provides family counseling, and makes appropriate referrals to other medical, financial, and support services. Wilbur's clinic is primarily supported by public funds and private insurance payments. As such, AIDS Alert can use as much financial help as possible in order to adequately pay Wilbur and other personnel. Lucinea is well aware of the financial strains on AIDS Alert and, as a result, on Wilbur and her. She begins searching out people with HIV/AIDS, especially those with private insurance, and strongly urges them to seek service provision from AIDS Alert.

Critical Thinking Question 11.3

- In what ways is Lucinea violating the ethical standard on conflicts of interest?

1.07 Privacy and Confidentiality

Practitioners should uphold client privacy and confidentiality. *Privacy* is the condition of being free from unauthorized observation or intrusion. *Confidentiality* is the ethical principle that workers should not share information provided by a client or about a client unless that worker has the client's explicit permission to do so.

There is much more to confidentiality than is superficially apparent. Maintaining confidentiality requires workers not to solicit unnecessary information; to inform clients about the limitations of confidentiality with respect to agency policy, interagency work, legal requirements, and funding requirements; and to expend substantial effort in safe-keeping confidential information.

Example of a Violation. Mutt and Jeff are social work counselors at a group home for adolescent boys with emotional and behavioral problems. They and their significant others occasionally have dinner with a mutual friend, Jerry, a county social services worker, along with his significant other. The three workers regularly compare "battle stories" about their most difficult cases, despite the fact that their caseloads are all different and their significant others are present. Sometimes, after a few cocktails, voices elevate, and other diners can overhear.

Critical Thinking Question 11.4

- In what ways are Mutt and Jeff violating the ethical standard of privacy and confidentiality?

1.08 Access to Records

Workers should provide clients with "reasonable" access to records. Access should be limited "only in exceptional circumstances when there is compelling evidence that such access would cause serious harm to the client" (NASW, 2008, §1.08). A worker should clearly document in the clients' files any client requests to see records and reasons for declining such requests.

What Is the Ethical Thing to Do? Yvonne is a Child Protective Services (CPS) worker. "CPS agencies and workers carry out their responsibility of protecting children in four ways: (a) by investigating reports of maltreatment, (b) by providing treatment services, (c) by coordinating the services offered by other agencies in the community to child victims and their families, and (d) by implementing preventive services" (Miller-Perrin & Perrin, 2013, p. 264). After receiving a referral, Yvonne or other assigned workers will begin their investigation and service provision process.

Yvonne has a 4-year-old client, Lolita, who was allegedly abused by both parents. Lolita currently resides with her mother Reza, who is receiving counseling and other services, including job training. Bill, Lolita's father, no longer lives in the home but has told Yvonne he would like to seek custody of Lolita. Bill calls Yvonne to complain about Reza's treatment of Lolita. He states that Lolita often wets her bed at night and Reza simply ignores it by allowing Lolita to sleep in her wet bed. Then, Reza does not change the dirtied sheets for Lolita. Yvonne notes carefully what Bill tells her in Lolita's case record.

The next day Reza calls Yvonne in a panic. She cries that Bill is threatening to take Lolita away from her. Reza says Bill told her he called Yvonne to complain about Reza's treatment of Lolita. Reza, stressing that she does not want to lose her little girl, demands to see Lolita's records. Should Yvonne show Reza the incriminating records or not?

Critical Thinking Questions 11.5

- What issues are involved in Yvonne's situation that relate to the access-to-records ethical standard?
- What are Yvonne's various choices and the pros and cons of each?

1.09 Sexual Relationships

Simply put, social workers should not have sexual relationships with current clients, clients' relatives or others personally involved with clients, or former clients. If a social worker pursues this type of relationship, under "extraordinary circumstances, it is social workers—not their clients—who assume the full burden of demonstrating that the former client has not been exploited, coerced, or manipulated, intentionally or unintentionally" (NASW, 2008, §1.09). Also, social workers should not provide clinical services to clients with whom they were formerly sexual partners.

The *Code* uses powerful language to emphasize that workers should not have sex with clients under any circumstances. Cox, Erlich, Rothman, and Tropman (1987) comment:

> *Great damage has been done to clients who have been exploited by trusted physicians, therapists and other "helping persons," and to the professions (especially in the mental health field) which have seen public confidence in their motives, competence, and integrity steadily eroded. (p. 426)*

Example of a Violation. Sheila, age 24, is a counselor at a community-based halfway house for men on parole who are also recovering substance abusers.[3] Most of the clients are in their 20s and early 30s. Sheila finds herself physically attracted to Biff, a good-looking, charming, 26-year-old parolee who resides in the house. She fights her feelings but finally gives in. When he asks her for a date, she assents and begins an intimate relationship with Biff "on the sly." Agency policy clearly forbids any such relationships with current clients or anyone who has been a client within the past 6 months.

Critical Thinking Question 11.6

- What are the potential negative consequences of having sexual relationships with clients?

1.10 Physical Contact

Social workers should not engage in any physical contact with clients when there is the potential of inflicting psychological harm on the clients.

What Is the Ethical Thing to Do? Herman, 37, a substance abuse counselor, is currently seeing Anne, a 37-year-old alcoholic client. Herman views Anne as a timid, needy woman who is working on increasing her self-esteem, problem-solving skills, and assertiveness in the context of addressing her alcoholism problem. Treatment is going exceptionally well. Anne has not been drinking for months and has been attending

---

3. *Parole* is the "conditional release of a prisoner serving an indeterminate or unexpired sentence," usually for good behavior or the promise of good behavior, under the supervision of a designated parole officer (Mish, 2008, p. 902).

Alcoholics Anonymous meetings regularly. Anne is grateful to Herman for all she feels he has done for her. One day at the end of the counseling session, Anne walks up to Herman and says, "I really need a hug!" What should Herman do? On the one hand, Anne is needy of approval and affection. She wishes to convey her gratitude to Herman. On the other, he does not want to convey inappropriate feelings that do not exist. Should he allow her to hug him or not?

Critical Thinking Questions 11.7

- What are the pros and cons of having physical contact (such as a hug) with Anne?
- What might Anne's reactions be if Herman hugs her or not?
- What might be an appropriate thing for Herman to say to avoid a hug?

1.11 Sexual Harassment

Social workers should not sexually harass clients. Sexual harassment includes sexual advances, sexual solicitation, requests for sexual favors, and other verbal or physical conduct of a sexual nature. (NASW, 2008, §1.11)

Example of a Violation. Aaron is a probation officer with a caseload of young men and women.[4] He is helping Brenda, a 19-year-old-client, find a job. Aaron finds he really enjoys Brenda and respects her gumption in view of many negative life experiences. One day he invites her to lunch. This makes her a bit uncomfortable, but she goes along with it. In the car he places his hand on her knee and tells her what a "mountain of a woman" she is. At lunch Brenda tries to maintain appropriate conversation and chitchat. Seemingly out of the blue, Aaron comments, "What a little seductress you are, aren't you?" Brenda does not know what to do because Aaron has a lot of control over her life.

Critical Thinking Question 11.8

- How might Brenda respond to Aaron? (Chapter 13 discusses the issue of sexual harassment and provides some suggestions for addressing it.)

---

4. *Probation* is the condition of suspending imprisonment for an offender convicted of a lesser crime and placing the offender under the supervision of a probation officer (G. F. Allen, 1995).

1.12 Derogatory Language

Workers should be respectful in both written and verbal communication about clients, avoiding any use of derogatory terms.

Example of a Violation. Carmen is a counselor at a domestic violence shelter. She attends a case staffing where counselors discuss current residents, their plans, and their progress. Daffodil is a client with three children who has left her extremely abusive husband and fled to the shelter four different times. After each time, she returned to her abusive partner. She is wavering once again in her determination to leave her abusive home situation. She says she really loves her husband and feels her children need a father, even one who is abusive. During the staff meeting, Carmen states, "Daffodil is such a wuss. She just doesn't have the guts to leave that jerk and get on with her life!"

Critical Thinking Question 11.9

- In what ways might Carmen's derogatory language be harmful to the client, Carmen herself, or the agency?

1.13 Payment for Services

Practitioners should set fair fees when appropriate for services performed. Receiving goods for services instead of financial payment should be avoided in view of potential conflicts of interests and inequities. Workers should not solicit private fees from clients when services are available through their employer or agency.

What Is the Ethical Thing to Do? Sue married Jim 2 years after the biological father of her daughter Andrea seemingly disappeared from the face of the earth. They have now been married for 7 years. Andrea, 8, and Jim have become very close. Jim feels just as if Andrea is his biological daughter. Jim and Sue pursue the possibility of Jim adopting Andrea. Mary Ellen is the adoptions worker assigned to the case. She helps with the relatively complex process of having the biological father relinquish his parental rights for Andrea when he is nowhere to be found. Mary Ellen has completed a number of stepparent adoptions and has become quite competent in their successful completion. Jim and Sue, wanting to show their gratitude, give Mary Ellen a $50 gift certificate to a popular local restaurant. Is this gift appropriate or not? Should Mary Ellen keep the gift or return it? What is the ethical and tactful thing to do?

Critical Thinking Question 11.10

- What are the pros and cons of accepting gifts from clients?

1.14 Clients Who Lack Decision-Making Capacity

Workers should "take reasonable steps to safeguard the interests and rights of those clients" who are unable to make informed decisions (NASW, 2008, §1.14).

When a client is determined "legally incompetent," the social worker should do everything possible to make certain that the client's rights are not violated. When someone else has been designated to act on the client's behalf, the social worker should keep the client's rights and well-being in mind at all times. Social workers should never participate in any activities that infringe upon their clients' constitutional rights.

What Is the Ethical Thing to Do? Lloyd is a social worker at a group home for people who have intellectual disabilities.[5] Ellie, 35, has been a resident at the group home for 8 years. She has relatively high adaptive functioning in terms of daily living skills, can read at the fourth-grade level, and has successfully worked at a sheltered workshop since entering the group home. She has no known relatives. The court has designated a lawyer as her *guardian ad litem* (i.e., court appointee whose responsibility is to protect and oversee the affairs of another individual who is considered incapable of doing so him or herself, especially when court actions are involved).

Without warning, Ellie cheerfully approaches Lloyd one day and informs him that she has saved enough money to go to Disney World, her dream of a lifetime. She chatters on about getting the tickets and taking her first airplane ride. Lloyd is familiar with Ellie's capabilities and strongly feels this endeavor is far beyond her capacities.

---

5. *Intellectual disability* is the newer alternative term referring to mental retardation. *Mental retardation* is a condition occurring before age 18 where an individual has intellectual functioning that is significantly below average, in addition to experiencing difficulties in adaptive functioning in at least two of the following domains: communication skills, ability to care for self, self-direction, functioning at home, social interaction and interpersonal skills, ability to function academically, use of community resources, work environment, recreation, health, and safety (American Psychiatric Association, 2000). Many professionals feel that referring to such individuals as having an intellectual disability is far more positive than using the term *mentally retarded*.

Critical Thinking Questions 11.11

- What should Lloyd do?
- What might he say to Ellie?

1.15 Interruption of Services

Practitioners "should make reasonable efforts to ensure continuity of services" for clients when such "services are interrupted by factors such as unavailability, relocation, illness, disability, or death" (NASW, 2008, §1.15).

Example of a Violation. Greta, a worker for a community diagnostic and treatment center for children with multiple disabilities, is changing to a different job. At the center, her responsibilities include providing family counseling, using brokering skills to refer clients to other resources, running support groups, and helping interpret complicated medical findings to clients. Greta is 3 months behind on her case progress notes. If they are not updated, a new worker will have to start from scratch for most cases, not knowing which clients were currently being seen or what has been done.

Greta does not like her supervisor Barb. She feels that Barb has treated her unfairly and denied her deserved raises. She has also developed a grudge against the agency and does not want to do it any favors. Thus, Greta decides killing herself to update progress notes is not worth the effort. She gives the agency 2 weeks' notice, deciding not to work too hard. She takes excessively long lunch breaks, avoids updating her notes, and leaves.

Critical Thinking Questions 11.12

- How is Greta's behavior harmful?
- Who might suffer its effects?

1.16 Termination of Services

Social workers should terminate services to clients when goals have been achieved or such services are no longer necessary. A practitioner should make all efforts to continue needed services elsewhere if for some reason the relationship with that practitioner should end and services are still required. Workers should notify clients of any ensuing termination as promptly as possible and inform them of other viable service options. Social workers should not terminate services for their own personal gain (such as beginning an intimate relationship with a client).

What Is the Ethical Thing to Do? Ricardo is a social services worker specializing in teaching parents effective child management skills. Over the past 6 months, he has worked with Irma, a former crack user, to gain control of her four children's behavior. Although trusting Ricardo was very difficult at first for Irma, they now have established a trusting relationship where Irma feels free to discuss difficult issues with Ricardo. Ideally, Ricardo would like to continue work with Irma for the next several months. However, he has been transferred to another unit's position with a higher salary. Irma has achieved many of the major goals but still could make significant improvements in how she treats her children. Ricardo feels becoming accustomed to and working with another worker would be difficult for Irma. What should he do?

Critical Thinking Question 11.13

- What are Ricardo's alternatives and the pros and cons of each?

SOCIAL WORKERS' ETHICAL RESPONSIBILITIES TO COLLEAGUES

The NASW *Code of Ethics* specifies 11 areas in which practitioners have ethical responsibilities to colleagues. These include respect, confidentiality, interdisciplinary collaboration, disputes involving colleagues, consultation, referral for services, sexual relationships, sexual harassment, impairment of colleagues, colleagues' incompetence, and colleagues' unethical conduct. As in the preceding section of social workers' ethical responsibilities to clients, examples will be provided regarding compliance with, violation of, or questions raised concerning the *Code's* application.

2.01 Respect

Social workers should respect and work cooperatively with colleagues. They should avoid unfounded criticism of colleagues, including that directed at personal characteristics unrelated to professional performance.

Example of a Violation. Wenonah, a foster care worker, intensely dislikes her colleague Ralph, a worker

in the same unit. She feels he is lazy, knows little, and fails to take his job seriously. She takes every opportunity to criticize him to other workers behind his back by focusing on the fact that he has a single eyebrow that flows across his Neanderthal-like forehead.

Critical Thinking Question 11.14

- What are the potential negative consequences of behavior such as Wenonah's?

2.02 Confidentiality

Social workers should hold confidential information conveyed by colleagues about practice situations. Workers should also make certain colleagues understand obligations to respect confidentiality.

Example of Compliance. Viveca, a case manager for people with serious physical disabilities, makes a point to stop colleagues whenever they start talking about cases she has nothing to do with. She feels that although such information at times can be "juicy," it violates a professional's responsibility to maintain confidentiality among colleagues.

2.03 Interdisciplinary Collaboration

When working with teams involving other disciplines, social workers should make contributions based on professional social work knowledge, skills, and values to the best of their ability in the clients' best interests. Should an ethical issue arise, a social worker should follow the appropriate channels for resolution. In the event an issue cannot be resolved, the worker should pursue alternatives reflecting the clients' best interests.

What Is the Ethical Thing to Do? Nick is a counselor for teenagers with severe emotional and behavioral problems who reside in a residential treatment center. He sees himself as a shy person who finds confronting issues in conflictual situations difficult. As a member of an interdisciplinary team, he attends a staff meeting for one of his clients where progress is reviewed and future plans are established.[6] Dr. Schmaltz, the psychiatrist attending the meeting, is a powerful, authoritarian man who makes strong points completely in opposition to what Nick is proposing for the client being reviewed.

---

6. An *interdisciplinary team* involves members of various professions all working on behalf of a designated client system.

Dr. Schmaltz commands much authority and respect among other staff. What should Nick do?

Critical Thinking Question 11.15

- What might Nick say that respects both Dr. Schmaltz's views and his own views?

2.04 Disputes Involving Colleagues

Social workers should not use disputes between other colleagues and their employer for personal gain. Nor should practitioners exploit clients by involving them in discussions about interstaff or interagency conflicts.

Example of a Violation. Harry, a social worker at a day care center, is angry with the administration. He feels the administration is unfair to the center's workers and is not treating clients the way they should be treated. He calls parents to complain to them about the agency's other workers and administrators.

Critical Thinking Questions 11.16

- How is Harry's behavior harmful and to whom?
- What alternatives might Harry have to address his issues?

2.05 Consultation

When necessary, social workers should consult with colleagues in order to provide their clients with the most effective service possible. Practitioners should remain well informed about colleagues' areas of expertise in order to seek appropriate consultation. Finally, when seeking help, social workers should disclose only that information about cases that is absolutely necessary, in order to protect client confidentiality.

When facing an overly problematic situation concerning a client, a supervisor or colleague can be helpful. Getting help when overwhelmed by some problem is a worker's ethical responsibility. Adopting an "out of sight, out of mind" approach is inappropriate. Rather, a worker's responsibility is to tackle the problem to the best of his or her ability, including the solicitation of help where appropriate.

Example of Compliance. Paula, a substance abuse counselor, takes her work seriously. She is working with Reba, an alcoholic. As they address issues, Paula discovers that Reba abuses her children when she is drinking. Paula does not consider herself an expert in the area of child abuse and neglect. Paula talks with other agency colleagues regularly, trying to keep track of their areas of interest and professional development. Paula's supervisor Robin urges her staff to share their expertise with one another. Paula knows that Robin has substantial experience working with child abuse cases, so she takes talking with Robin about Reba upon herself.

2.06 Referral for Services

Social workers should refer clients to other professionals when these others have knowledge and skills necessary for making effective progress with clients. Practitioners should make such referrals as smoothly as possible, conveying vital information to the new service provider. Workers should receive no personal payment or gain from such referrals.

Example of Compliance. Rich is a housing worker for a county social services department that helps "disadvantaged populations who need assistance in obtaining quality and affordable housing in the housing market" (Gibelman, 1995, pp. 298–299). One of Rich's clients, Kendra, has significant physical disabilities, including advancing arthritis and declining eyesight. Rich determines that housing is only one of Kendra's needs. Her health requirements are also critically significant. Rich acknowledges that he knows little about the health services that Kendra needs. He thus refers her to another agency worker with expertise in that area. Meanwhile, Rich continues working to fulfill her housing needs.

2.07 Sexual Relationships

Social workers who are supervisors or educators should not involve themselves in sexual liaisons with supervisees. Likewise, practitioners should avoid forming sexual relationships with colleagues whenever "there is a potential for conflict of interest" (NASW, 2008, §2.07b).

Example of a Violation. Clint is a counselor in an employee assistance program (EAP) in a large corporation. EAPs "are services provided by organizations that focus on workers' mental health and on adjustment problems that interfere with their work performance" (Kirst-Ashman, 2013, p. 403). Examples of personal problems are substance abuse or mental health issues such as depression.

Clint supervises Sherry, a social work intern. Clint finds Sherry a delightful, attractive young woman with whom he feels he has much in common. He knows he really is not supposed to do it, but he asks her out on a date. He rationalizes the behavior, telling himself that she will get an A in her practicum anyway and that he has rarely found a woman to whom he is so drawn.

Critical Thinking Question 11.17

- What are the potential negative consequences of forming sexual relationships with supervisors, supervisees, or colleagues?

2.08 Sexual Harassment

"Social workers should not sexually harass supervisees, students, trainees, or colleagues" (NASW, 2008, §2.08). We have defined sexual harassment as involving unwanted sexual overtures and verbal or physical conduct of a sexual nature.

Example of a Violation. Duncan, a social worker, watches late-night television just so he can tell the dirtiest jokes at work the next day. He thinks he is ever so clever. He enjoys the guffaws of some of his fellow coworkers, most of whom are men. He ignores the scornful scowls he sometimes gets from coworkers Serena and Anne after telling some of his best ones. Duncan passes these latter responses off. He thinks to himself, "What's wrong with those old women? Don't they have a sense of humor?"

Critical Thinking Question 11.18

- How might Duncan's inappropriate behavior be addressed?

2.09 Impairment of Colleagues

Social workers who are aware of a colleague's impairment "due to personal problems, psychosocial distress, substance abuse, or mental health difficulties and that interferes with practice effectiveness should consult with that colleague when feasible and assist the colleague in taking remedial action" (2008, §2.09a). In the event that this assistance does not help, social workers should proceed through the "appropriate channels established by employers, agencies, NASW, licensing and regulatory bodies, and other professional organizations" to make sure the problem is addressed and clients are not harmed (2008, §2.10).

Example of Compliance. Karen and Madeline are both workers for a rural social services agency. They also have been personal friends for a long time. At work both are pressured by lack of resources, multigenerational family farm closures, and clients' oppressive poverty. Karen notices that Madeline often sucks on intensively minty breath lozenges. They almost smell like alcohol. Karen also notices that, on several occasions, Madeline slurred her words when first coming to work. Finally, on three occasions, Karen drops in on Madeline and finds her quickly shoving something in her desk drawer. All three times Karen thinks she smells alcohol. Karen has often prided herself on an exceptional sense of smell (for better or for worse). Oddly enough, Karen notices that Madeline's office door is frequently closed these days. Karen wonders if Madeline could possibly have an alcohol problem. She knows Madeline is a social drinker. On the one hand, Karen worries how a confrontation might affect their personal relationship, which she really values. On the other, Karen worries about how alcohol might be influencing Madeline's practice and harming her clients. Karen decides that, difficult as approaching will be, she must confront Madeline about her possible drinking.

2.10 Incompetence of Colleagues

Social workers who determine that a colleague is practicing ineffectively or incompetently should discuss the issues with that colleague when possible and help the colleague to make improvements. In the event that improvements are not made, the social worker should pursue the appropriate channels to address the issue and prevent harm to clients.

Example of Compliance. Yaba is a family planning counselor at a Planned Parenthood clinic. She helps clients choose contraceptive methodology and make reproductive decisions. Gretchen is a new worker who just transferred in from a small satellite clinic that had to be closed because of budget cuts. Yaba has several opportunities to talk with Gretchen about the clinic's services. Gretchen makes several comments to Yaba, but her facts are blatantly in error. Yaba wonders what kind of information Gretchen is giving clients. Yaba asks Gretchen to lunch so that she might informally talk to Gretchen about her concerns. During this meeting Yaba identifies some reading materials and a series of inservices Gretchen might pursue to improve her effectiveness.

2.11 Unethical Conduct of Colleagues

"Social workers should take adequate measures to discourage, prevent, expose, and correct the unethical conduct of colleagues" (2008, §2.11a). Furthermore, practitioners should familiarize themselves with available policies and procedures for addressing unethical behavior via agency, local, state, and national channels. When finding evidence of unethical conduct, social workers should try to address their concerns with the colleague to help resolve them. If this approach does not work, the practitioner should seek resolution through established channels. Finally, social workers should help innocent colleagues who are unfairly accused of unethical practice.

What Is the Ethical Thing to Do? Chuck is a youth counselor at an urban YMCA.[7] He is in his early 20s, good at sports, familiar with young people's jargon, and, thus, extremely popular with his teenage clientele. Emilio is another youth counselor at the same agency. One night after work, Emilio accidentally observes Chuck smoking a joint with two of his clients in the shadows of an alley. After serious thought the next day, Emilio confronts Chuck about his behavior. Chuck responds that he only smoked marijuana and that it provided a way for him to "join with" and be accepted by some of his clients. He rationalizes that smoking joints prevents many young people from using harder, more dangerous drugs. He further implies that Emilio is just jealous of Chuck's good rapport with the clientele. What should Emilio do now?

Critical Thinking Question 11.19

- What are Emilio's alternatives at this point and the potential pros and cons of each?

SOCIAL WORKERS' ETHICAL RESPONSIBILITIES IN PRACTICE SETTINGS

Social workers' ethical responsibilities in practice settings involve 10 major areas. This book introduces you to generalist practice and emphasizes micro practice as a building block for mezzo and macro levels of practice. Many of the ethical issues addressed in the Code's next section reflect performance in macro contexts such as supervision, administration, and

management. Therefore, content will focus on summarizing major ethical principles without elaborating via extensive examples of compliance or violation as in earlier sections.

3.01 Supervision and Consultation

Social work supervisors should be competent to provide the supervision and information their supervisees need. Supervisors should establish clear boundaries for the supervisor–supervisee relationship. They "should not engage in any dual or multiple relationships with supervisees in which there is a risk of exploitation of or potential harm to the supervisee" (2008, §3.01c). Dual relationships include sexual and business relationships with the potential to hurt the supervisee or undermine the professional supervisor–supervisee relationship. Last, supervisors should evaluate their supervisees' work in a fair and respectful manner.

3.02 Education and Training

Social workers assuming the educator role, including that of field instructor, should be knowledgeable in the area of instruction. Social workers evaluating students should do so in a "fair and respectful" manner (2008, §3.02b). Such workers should inform clients when services are being provided by students whenever reasonable. Dual or mutual relationships with students should be avoided.

3.03 Performance Evaluation

Social workers who are in the position of evaluating others' performance should do so "in a fair and considerate manner and on the basis of clearly stated criteria" (2008, §3.03).

3.04 Client Records

Social workers should record information as accurately and adequately as possible in a timely manner. They should protect clients' privacy and include in the record only information directly related to the worker's service delivery. Records should be maintained and stored for a reasonable amount of time to allow for future access.

3.05 Billing

Social workers should establish billing procedures, when appropriate, that accurately reflect the nature of services and who is to provide them.

3.06 Client Transfer

Social workers should carefully consider client needs when new clients transfer into agencies. To the greatest

---

7. *YMCA* refers to the Young Men's Christian Association, an international organization dedicated to the "spiritual, intellectual, social, and physical" well-being of young men (Mish, 2008, p. 1453). Note that, in some areas, membership is no longer restricted to Christians, youth, or males.

extent possible, workers should discuss with clients the pros and cons of change in order to facilitate the transition and maximize service effectiveness. Workers should also discuss with transfer clients "whether consultation with the previous service provider is in the client's best interest" (2008, §3.06).

3.07 Administration

Social work administrators should advocate both for adequate resources to meet clients' needs and for fair, equitable resource allocation procedures. Additionally, they should maintain reasonable staff supervision to the greatest extent possible and oversee the working environment so that it remains consistent with the *Code of Ethics.*

3.08 Continuing Education and Staff Development

Social work supervisors and administrators should provide staff with reasonable access to continuing education and training to improve staff performance.

3.09 Commitments to Employers

"Social workers generally should adhere to commitments made to employers and employing organizations" (2008, §3.09a). They should take responsibility to make certain that agency policies and procedures reflect effective service delivery, that employers are aware of their ethical obligations according to the *Code of Ethics,* and that their organizations comply with such standards. Social workers should work to rid an organization of discrimination in "work assignments and in its employment policies and practices" (2008, §3.09e). Social workers should accept jobs or place social work interns only in those organizations with fair personnel policies. Finally, social workers should strive to work efficiently and conserve funds whenever possible, never using available funding for other than its intended purposes.

3.10 Labor–Management Disputes

"Social workers may engage in organized action, including the formation of and participation in labor unions, to improve services to clients and working conditions" (2008, §3.10a). When so doing, actions should be guided by professional ethical principles. Impact on client well-being should be carefully examined.

SOCIAL WORKERS' ETHICAL RESPONSIBILITIES AS PROFESSIONALS

Social workers' ethical responsibilities as professionals include broad dimensions by which they should judge their behavior and responsibility. They include: competence; discrimination; private conduct; dishonesty, fraud, and deception; impairment; misrepresentation; solicitations; and acknowledging credit.

4.01 Competence

 Succinctly put, social workers should accept only responsibilities for which they are competent. They should strive to remain current in their knowledge of practice by keeping up with professional readings and participating in continuing education. Practitioners should base all practice decisions on social work knowledge, research, and ethics.

Upon face value, this standard sounds good, and of course, the intent is good. However, it may not always be that easy to follow. For example, suppose you joyfully embrace the first professional social work job offer you get following graduation. What if you find that you really do not feel qualified to do the job the way it should be done? What if you lack necessary skills even though you are technically qualified for the job?

Competence involves a number of issues. First, you should never mislead employers about your credentials. This issue adheres to the principle of professional honesty discussed earlier. The bottom line is that you get a job on the basis of honest and accurate qualifications.

If you find out a job requires skills you do not currently have, the second issue concerns how you should plan to acquire needed skills if at all possible. If you require more advanced counseling skills, can you enroll in an educational program to enhance and extend your credentials in that area? Can you attend continuing education seminars, in-service training, or professional conferences to develop needed skills? Many states require that professional social workers undertake an ongoing program of postgraduate training for a designated number of hours every 1 to 3 years. For example, you might seek out additional training in assessing child abuse, running groups for domestic violence perpetrators, or working with managed care. You can also continue your professional education by reading up on knowledge and skills you need. You may want to audit a course at a local university. Finally, you can seek out help from your supervisor and others at your agency.

Assimilating and using knowledge is an endless process. Professional readings should include *Social Work* (a journal available to all NASW members). Additionally, practitioners often subscribe to journals more specifically directed at their own clientele or arena of practice. *Public Welfare, Affilia: Journal of Women and Social Work, Families in Society,* the *Journal of Community Practice,* and *Social Work with Groups* are among the many journals available. Books provide another important source of knowledge.

4.02 Discrimination

 Social workers should never "practice, condone, facilitate, or collaborate with any form of discrimination on the basis of race, ethnicity, national origin, color, sex, sexual orientation, gender identity or expression, age, marital status, political belief, religion, immigration status or mental or physical disability" (2008, §4.02).

Actively thwarting any cruelty, unfairness, or discrimination workers observe is their responsibility. This standard really places the ultimate responsibility upon the individual worker to make certain that service is provided fairly and people are treated justly, which does not relinquish the responsibility of agency administrators. However, individual professional social workers also have responsibility to advocate for and pursue positive change.

4.03 Private Conduct

Social workers should not allow their private behavior and voicing of opinions to intrude on fulfillment of professional responsibility.

4.04 Dishonesty, Fraud, and Deception

"Social workers should not participate in, condone, or be associated with dishonesty, fraud, or deception" (2008, §4.04).

4.05 Impairment

Social workers should not allow personal problems to interfere with professional practice or clients' best interests. When personal problems begin to interfere with competent professional performance, social workers should seek appropriate consultation and help.

Everyone has problems, as we know all too well. This fact includes professional social workers. One study found that "social work students are more likely than a comparison group to report having grown up in families where there was psychosocial trauma," including alcohol or drug addiction and child maltreatment (Rompf & Royse, 1994, p. 169). What do we as professionals do with our own dysfunctions, especially when they become serious?

The answer involves expending effort to maintain awareness of our own mental health and performance.

It also involves honesty. As difficult as the situation may be, if you honestly feel that personal problems are interfering with work, then do something about them. Get professional help for yourself. If problems are so severe that you cannot function adequately, then you should get into an inpatient treatment program, take a leave of absence, or quit. Your professional work and your clients' interests come first.

4.06 Misrepresentation

Social workers should clearly distinguish between personal statements and opinions and the social work profession's standards and values. When representing a professional organization, social workers should ascertain that what they say clearly and accurately reflects the organization's positions. Practitioners should accurately report their own credentials and claim only those credentials they really possess.

4.07 Solicitations

"Social workers should not engage in uninvited solicitation of potential clients who, because of their circumstances, are vulnerable to undue influence, manipulation, or coercion" (NASW, 2008, §4.07a). Social workers should not solicit testimonials from current or past clients "who, because of their particular circumstances, are vulnerable to undue influence" (2008, §4.07b).

4.08 Acknowledging Credit

Social workers should only take credit for work they actually did, while honestly acknowledging the work of others. This responsibility includes prohibitions against plagiarism.

SOCIAL WORKERS' ETHICAL RESPONSIBILITIES TO THE SOCIAL WORK PROFESSION

Ethical responsibilities to the social work profession focus on integrity in addition to evaluation and research.

5.01 Integrity of the Profession

 Integrity refers to social workers' promotion of high practice standards. Social workers should strive to maintain and enhance professional knowledge, values, and ethics. They should also participate in activities aimed at professional contributions such as "teaching, research, consultation, service, legislative testimony, presentations in the community, and participation in their professional organizations" (NASW, 2008, §5.01c) and contribute to the social work knowledge base. Finally, social workers should work to prevent and eliminate unqualified and unauthorized practice.

For one thing, you should not talk about social work disparagingly. Talk about your chosen field with due respect. So often when asked about their major or field of study, students say something like, "I'm in social work. I know I won't make as much money as in business, but I like it." Do not do that. This is an apology. Social work is an honorable profession with a solid knowledge, skill, and value base. Social work values involve serious concern for the well-being of other people. What more virtuous value exists than that? Additionally, social workers, as do many other types of professionals, can carve out excellent careers for themselves by expanding their knowledge and skills in a wide range of areas.

5.02 Evaluation and Research

Social workers should encourage research and evaluation of practice effectiveness, monitor practice policies and interventions to ensure effectiveness, and maintain current knowledge of evaluation approaches. Research for enhancing practice effectiveness should reflect practice experience and practice needs. When conducting research, social workers should follow professional guidelines (such as those established by institutional review boards) and obtain voluntary, informed consent of participants. Social workers should protect research participants from physical or mental distress and provide access to supportive services when necessary. Social workers engaged in research should discuss results only for professional reasons and maintain participant anonymity. Researchers should inform participants concerning the limits of confidentiality. All research findings should be reported accurately. Conflicts of interest and dual relationships with participants should be avoided. Social workers should strive to inform themselves, students, and others involved in research regarding responsible research practices.

Two themes that surface when reading over these ethical standards are concern for the rights and needs of others and a commitment to honesty and fairness. You should undertake any research endeavors only while holding the well-being of others, especially your research subjects, as your highest priority. Additionally, you should be honest with all involved regarding what you plan to do while conducting the research, who will have access to any information and findings gained, and who deserves credit for any findings obtained.

SOCIAL WORKERS' ETHICAL RESPONSIBILITIES TO THE BROADER SOCIETY

Ethical responsibilities to the broader society reflect the basic core of social work, namely, to advocate and work for people's general welfare. This responsibility surpasses those merely listed in most job descriptions. The four categories involved are social welfare, public participation, public emergencies, and social and political action.

6.01 Social Welfare

Social workers should promote the general welfare of society, from local to global levels, and the development of people, their communities, and their environments. Social workers should advocate for living conditions conducive to the fulfillment of basic human needs and should promote social, economic, political, and cultural values and institutions that are compatible with the realization of social justice. (NASW, 2008, §6.01)

6.02 Public Participation

Social workers should encourage and assist public involvement in formulating social policies.

6.03 Public Emergencies

When emergencies arise, social workers should provide professional services to the best of their ability. When people suffer extreme circumstances, you are ethically committed to help them. Several examples of disasters come to mind where help was desperately needed. Two involve the horribly destructive 2010 earthquakes in Haiti and Chile. Others concern the 2012 superstorm Sandy slamming into the U.S. eastern seaboard and Hurricane Katrina devastating New Orleans in 2005. Yet others involve the terrorist attacks at the Boston Marathon and the allegedly accidental explosion at the fertilizer factory in West, Texas. Both occurred during the same week in April 2013 and both resulted in death, serious injury, and devastation. Whenever social workers are even peripherally involved, they are obligated to do whatever they can to help people in desperate need. Chapter 7 discussed crisis intervention and disaster relief in greater depth.

6.04 Social and Political Action

As part of their professional responsibility, social workers should work with colleagues and clients to pursue social and political action seeking fair and equal access to resources and opportunities. They should actively support policies to improve the human condition and promote social justice for all. Practitioners should particularly work to enhance opportunities especially for "vulnerable, disadvantaged, oppressed, and exploited people and groups" (NASW, 2008, §6.04b). Social workers should support conditions and policies that respect cultural diversity. Similarly, they should work to prevent and eliminate conditions and policies discriminating against or exploiting people, especially vulnerable populations.

Being an active participant and leader in the national and state NASW is one means of affecting social policies. Contributing financially to supportive funds such as the NASW Political Action for Candidate Election (PACE) fund is another means of promoting the profession. PACE organizes people and resources to elect politicians supporting social work values and services. You might also become directly involved in the election campaigns of political candidates supporting social work values. Even writing legislators concerning your opinions on a range of issues critical to social work and clients can have substantial impact on social policy development. You might even participate in an organized network of social workers, already established in some states, who contact each other when political pressure is needed to sway elected officials' decisions and votes.

Ethical Responsibilities to the Broader Society on a Global Basis

One aspect of responsibility to the broader society concerns ethical responsibility on a global basis. It is our obligation to work to expand choice for all persons and to promote conditions that reflect respect for cultural and social diversity throughout the world. Social workers are responsible for assuming a global perspective and for recognizing "global interconnections of oppression" (CSWE, 2008, EP 2.1.5). The next sections discuss social work ethical principles from an international perspective, first focusing on the Canadian Association of Social Workers *Code of Ethics* and then on globally established ethical principles.

LO 11-2 Recognize the Canadian Association of Social Workers *Code of Ethics*

Basic principles in the Canadian Association of Social Workers (CASW) *Code of Ethics* (2005) resemble those in the NASW *Code*. (Highlight 11.2 relates the CASW *Code*.) Similarities between the codes include the following:

- *greater emphasis on the social justice mission of social work*

- *core principles of respect for dignity and worth of individuals, pursuit of social justice, service to humanity, integrity in professional practice, competence in professional practice, confidentiality in professional practice, client collaboration to bring about best interests of the client*
- *guidelines on confidentiality, informed consent, and disclosure, as well as expanded guidelines for private practice and research*
- *reference to values and principles (CASW, 2013)*

Highlight 11.2 describes the CASW *Code*'s six core values. Note that the *Code* in its entirety also elaborates on the principles upon which each core value is based. Additionally, the CASW presents extensive guidelines for ethical practice. All of this information is available at http://casw-acts.ca/sites/default/files/attachements/CASW_Code%20of%20Ethics.pdf.

LO 11-3 Examine International Ethical Principles

Chapter 1 introduced the International Federation of Social Workers (IFSW) and the International Association of Schools of Social Work (IASSW). The IFSW (2013) is "a global organisation striving for social justice, human rights and social development through the promotion of social work, best practice models and the facilitation of international cooperation." The IASSW is an association of schools of social work, social work educators, and supportive organizations. Its purpose is to encourage and support high quality social work education, promote communication and the sharing of ideas on an international level, sponsor "forums for sharing social work research and scholarship," and promote "human rights and social development through policy and advocacy activities" (IASSW, 2013a).[8] Together, the IFSW and IASSW developed an *Ethics in Social Work, Statement of Principles* (IASSW, 2013b).[9] The *Statement of Principles* is divided into five sections: "Preface," "Definition of Social Work," "International Conventions" (international documents and declarations that are "particularly relevant to social work

---

8. The IFSW's and IASSW's Web sites are http://ifsw.org/ and http://www.iassw-aiets.org/, respectively.

9. The *Ethics in Social Work, Statement of Principles* can be accessed at http://www.iassw-aiets.org/uploads/file/20130506_Ethics%20in%20Social%20Work,%20Statement,%20IFSW,%20IASSW,%202004.pdf.

HIGHLIGHT 11.2

Canadian Association of Social Workers *Code of Ethics* Core Values

"Value 1: Respect for the Inherent Dignity and Worth of Persons"

Social work is founded on a long-standing commitment to respect the inherent dignity and individual worth of all persons. When required by law to override a client's wishes, social workers take care to use the minimum coercion required. Social workers recognize and respect the diversity of Canadian society, taking into account the breadth of differences that exist among individuals, families, groups and communities. Social workers uphold the human rights of individuals and groups as expressed in The *Canadian Charter of Rights and Freedoms* (1982) and the United Nations *Universal Declaration of Human Rights* (1948). . . .

"Value 2: Pursuit of Social Justice"

Social workers believe in the obligation of people, individually and collectively, to provide resources, services . . . and opportunities for the overall benefit of humanity and to afford them protection from harm. Social workers promote social fairness and the equitable distribution of resources, and act to reduce barriers and expand choice for all persons, with special regard for those who are marginalized, disadvantaged, vulnerable, and/or have exceptional needs. Social workers oppose prejudice and discrimination against any person or group of persons, on any grounds, and specifically challenge views and actions that stereotype particular persons or groups. . . .

"Value 3: Service to Humanity"

The social work profession upholds service in the interests of others, consistent with social justice, as a core professional objective. In professional practice, social workers balance individual needs, and rights and freedoms with collective interests in the service of humanity. When acting in a professional capacity, social workers place professional service before personal goals or advantage, and use their power and authority in disciplined and responsible ways that serve society. The social work profession contributes to knowledge and skills that assist in the management of conflicts and the wide-ranging consequences of conflict. . . .

"Value 4: Integrity in Professional Practice"

Social workers demonstrate respect for the profession's purpose, values . . . and ethical principles relevant to their field of practice. Social workers maintain a high level of professional conduct by acting honestly and responsibly, and promoting the values of the profession. Social workers strive for impartiality in their professional practice, and refrain from imposing their personal values, views, . . . and preferences on clients. It is the responsibility of social workers to establish the tenor of their professional relationship with clients, and others to whom they have a professional duty, and to maintain professional boundaries. As individuals, social workers take care in their actions to not bring the reputation of the profession into disrepute. An essential element of integrity in professional practice is ethical accountability based on this *Code of Ethics,* the IFSW *International Declaration of Ethical Principles of Social Work,* and other relevant provincial/territorial standards and guidelines. Where conflicts exist with respect to these sources of ethical guidance, social workers are encouraged to seek advice, including consultation with their regulatory body. . . .

"Value 5: Confidentiality in Professional Practice"

A cornerstone of professional social work relationships is confidentiality with respect to all matters associated with professional services to clients. Social workers demonstrate respect for the trust and confidence placed in them by clients, communities and other professionals by protecting the privacy of client information and respecting the client's right to control when or whether this information will be shared with third parties. Social workers only disclose confidential information to other parties (including family members) with the informed consent of clients, clients' legally authorized representatives or when required by law or court order. The general expectation that social workers will keep information confidential does not apply when disclosure is necessary to prevent serious, foreseeable and imminent harm to a client or others. In all instances, social workers disclose the least amount of confidential information necessary to achieve the desired purpose. . . .

"Value 6: Competence in Professional Practice"

Social workers respect a client's right to competent social worker services. Social workers analyze the nature

(continued)

of social needs and problems, and encourage innovative, effective strategies and techniques to meet both new and existing needs and, where possible, contribute to the knowledge base of the profession. Social workers have a responsibility to maintain professional proficiency, to continually strive to increase their professional knowledge and skills, and to apply new knowledge in practice commensurate with their level of professional education, skill and competency,

seeking consultation and supervision as appropriate. (CASW, 2005, pp. 4–8)

Source: This Social Work Code of Ethics, adopted by the Board of Directors of the Canadian Association of Social Workers (CASW) is effective March, 2005 and replaces the CASW Code of Ethics (1994). The *Code* is reprinted here with the permission of CASW. The copyright in the document has been registered with Canadian Intellectual Property Office, registration No. 1030330.

practice and action"), "Principles," and "Professional Conduct" (IASSW, 2013b).

The NASW *Code of Ethics* calls upon social workers to "promote the general welfare of society, from local to global levels" (NASW, 2008, 6.01). Practitioners are also expected to apply standards proposed in the international *Statement of Principles* "as applicable" regarding their practice and ethical concerns on a global level (CSWE, 2008, EP 2.1.2b). Although it is beyond the scope of this book to review the *Statement of Principles* in detail, we will address the two primary and related principles the *Statement* stresses—"human rights and social justice" (IASSW, 2013b).

HUMAN RIGHTS AND SOCIAL JUSTICE

Social workers are responsible for extending their "social justice values within the context of global human rights" (NASW, 2012, p. 205). *Human rights* involve the premise that all people, regardless of race, culture, or national origin, are entitled to basic rights and treatment. We have established that *social justice* is "an ideal condition" in which all members of society have "the same basic rights, protection, opportunities, obligations, and social benefits" (Barker, 2003, pp. 404–405). Human rights are entitlements to which people should automatically have access. Social justice involves the protection and preservation of human rights politically and legally.

In response to the atrocities of World War II, the General Assembly of the United Nations adopted a Universal Declaration of Human Rights (UNDR) in December 1948 (United Nations [UN], 1948). Mapp (2008) elaborates:

Within the UNDR, there are three areas of rights: [1] political and civil rights, [2] social, economic, and

cultural rights, and [3] collective rights. Political and civil rights are often referred to as "negative freedoms" as they require a government to refrain from an overuse of its power against individuals. Included in this are rights such as freedom of speech and the right to a fair trial. The second grouping of rights— social, economic, and cultural rights—are referred to as "positive freedoms" as they require a government to take action for them to be realized for individuals. They include such rights as medical care, the right to an education, and the right to a fair wage. The last group, collective rights, are rights for groups of people and include the rights to religion, peace, and development." (pp. 17–18)

NASW policy statements maintain that the struggle for human rights continues; this is demonstrated by "events such as wars, genocide, and ethnic cleansing; discrimination and social exclusion based on race, ethnicity, caste, or religious identity; gender inequality, battering, rape, and the sale of women; child abuse; sweatshops, child labor, and slavery" (NASW, 2012, p. 205). NASW calls for social workers to advocate for human rights on a global basis; for example, practitioners should "work for the eradication of modern-day slavery and growing incidence of human trafficking" and "advocate for the elimination of the practice of torture" (NASW, 2012, p. 207).

LO 11-4 Identify Ethical Dilemmas

EP 2.1.2c

Throughout a career in social work practice, one encounters a wide range of ethical dilemmas. We have already established that a *dilemma* is a situation where one must make a difficult choice among two or more alternatives. We've also defined *ethical dilemmas* in social work practice as problematic situations whose possible solutions all offer imperfect and unsatisfactory answers in terms of what ethically should be done. In other words, ethical principles conflict with each other. There is no one perfect answer that can conform to all of the ethical principles in the professional codes. Some level of ambiguity and uncertainty exists. *Ambiguity* has been defined as the state of being indistinct or of having the potential to be viewed from different perspectives. You are stuck with deciding what to do.

Thankfully, social workers have established professional values to help guide them through the difficult decision-making process when solving an ethical dilemma. Rarely, if ever, does an ethical dilemma involve being faced with bad alternatives that are exactly equal. Rather, we can use values to carefully examine and weigh the pros and cons of each alternative to determine the best course of action.

An ethical dilemma involves being faced with a situation where a decision must be made under circumstances where ethical principles are in conflict. For example, perhaps you cannot abide by the social work ethic of confidentiality and save a suicidal person's life at the same time. However, because we have professional values, we can formulate some guidelines for making tough choices. We can establish a hierarchy to decide what aspect of any particular ethical dilemma is more important than another and then act on that decision. The following sections will first establish a process for conceptualizing an ethical dilemma, review a procedure for ethical decision making, and then examine a range of ethical dilemmas common in social work practice.

LO 11-5 Conceptualize and Apply a Decision-Making Strategy to Address Ethical Dilemmas

EP 2.1.2d

The first step in determining what to do about an ethical dilemma is to establish the fact that one actually exists. There is a series of variables to consider as you first conceptualize the potential problem. Figure 11.1 illustrates eight steps in the decision-making process.

STEP 1: RECOGNIZE THE PROBLEM

EP 2.1.1b

The first step in confronting a potential ethical dilemma is to begin recognizing the problem (Corey, Corey, & Callanan, 2011). The seed might be a gut reaction, that is, an unarticulated emotional feeling

that something is not right. Something does not fit together or make any sense. You must determine that an ethical dilemma exists before going any further.

Case Scenario

To illustrate how to proceed when you first become aware of an ethical dilemma's possibility, we will take you through an example by following the proposed step-by-step conceptualization process. The scenario's intent, however, is not to provide you with a recipe for how to approach ethical dilemmas. In reality, each dilemma is different. Each worker may perceive the dilemma differently, focus upon different variables, and eventually make a different choice. This scenario only depicts one worker's situation and thought process. There is not necessarily one uniquely best solution.

The dilemma involves Carla, a secondary school social worker who runs a series of support groups for troubled teens. One of her 16-year-old clients, Tom, faithfully attends a support group for young people suffering from depression. Through no fault of his own, Tom has had a turbulent history, having lived in eight different foster homes. His biological parents were tragically killed in a car accident when he was only 4. As there were no relatives available to take Tom and his siblings in, they were shifted from foster home to foster home. Sometimes, some of them were placed together; more often than not they were separated. Tom was virtually never to blame for his displacement. For instance, one foster father developed cancer and could no longer care for foster children. Another foster family moved out of state when the parents got new and better jobs. Yet another foster mother became pregnant with triplets, and the couple decided they could no longer adequately care for foster kids.

Tom struggles with many issues. Although a bright, good-looking young man, he thinks very little of himself. He has limited self-confidence and is shy. Without good reason, he tends to blame himself for having such a troubled history. He has had thoughts of harming himself and "getting it over with" many times.

Tom currently resides with his 21-year-old sister Beth, her 6-month-old daughter Ally, and her 24-year-old boyfriend Michael. Tom is extremely grateful for this haven, finally feels somewhat settled, and wants to remain there.

One day after group sessions, Tom lingers in Carla's office pretending to look at some algebra homework. After the other group members leave, he asks Carla if he could talk to her a minute. She replies that of course

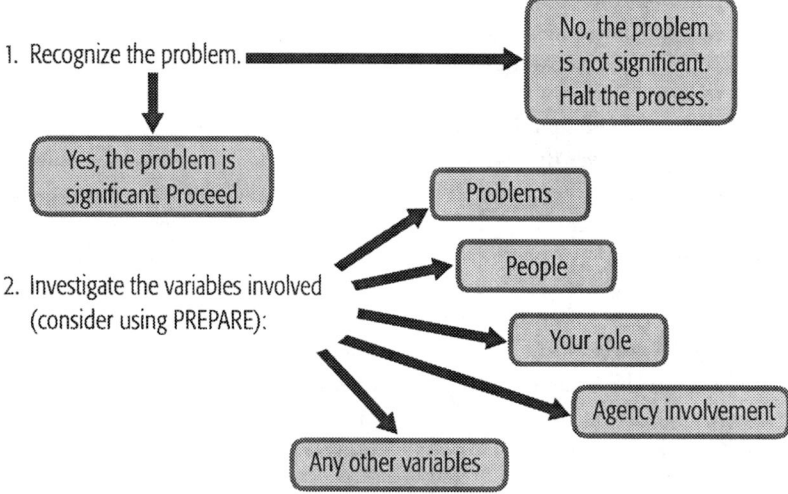

1. Recognize the problem.

No, the problem is not significant. Halt the process.

Yes, the problem is significant. Proceed.

2. Investigate the variables involved (consider using PREPARE):

Problems

People

Your role

Agency involvement

Any other variables

3. Get feedback from others.

4. Appraise what values and ethical standards apply to the dilemma.

5. Evaluate the dilemma on the basis of established ethical principles.

6. Identify and think about possible alternatives to pursue:

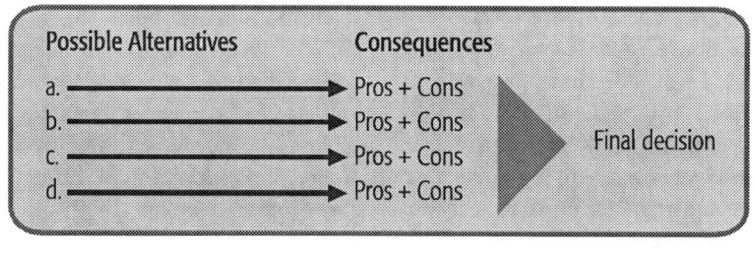

Possible Alternatives	Consequences	
a.	Pros + Cons	
b.	Pros + Cons	
c.	Pros + Cons	Final decision
d.	Pros + Cons	

7. Weigh the pros and cons of each alternative.

8. Make your decision.

© Cengage Learning

FIGURE 11.1 Conceptualizing an Ethical Dilemma

he could, and Tom begins his story. It turns out that his sister Beth and her boyfriend Michael fight a lot. Sometimes, after arguments, Michael stomps out on his own to go drinking, leaving Beth to stew in unresolved anger. At such times, Beth has little patience. When Ally cries, Beth can become infuriated. She takes out her frustration by putting Ally's head under the faucet and dousing it with either very cold or very hot water. Tom is greatly worried about his niece. Thus, Carla *recognizes that a serious problem exists.*

STEP 2: INVESTIGATE THE VARIABLES INVOLVED

The second step in the conceptualization process concerns investigating the complex matrix of variables that encompass the dilemma (Corey et al., 2011; Dolgoff et al., 2012). What problems are involved? What is your agency's involvement? Roll the dilemma around in your mind. Think deeply about what it is and why it exists. What other variables are concerned that might provide you with clues to a workable solution?

Case Scenario

Consider how you might apply this step to the case vignette concerning Carla and Tom. Carla needs more information, so she *investigates the variables involved.* She urges Tom to proceed with his explanation of his home environment. Tom emphasizes his dilemma: If he causes any trouble, Michael has warned that he will kick Tom out. Where would Tom go then? He has nowhere to go. If Beth and Michael find out

Tom told someone, Tom is certain they will get rid of him. Yet if nothing's done, he is terrified that Ally will be seriously hurt.

Carla knows that Tom has a foster care worker, Peter, who monitors Tom's placement with Beth. Tom feels that if he tells Peter about the abuse, the same thing will happen—he will lose his home.

Carla also knows that reporting any suspected abuse or neglect is mandatory for social workers in her state. Tom also knows this law. Carla told Tom's support group members during their first group session what types of information she is required to report and, thus, be unable to keep confidential.

STEP 3: GET FEEDBACK FROM OTHERS

If at all possible, talk to other people about your concerns (Corey et al., 2011; Sinclair, 1993). Bounce your ideas off of them to more firmly establish your objectivity. Brainstorm with them, looking for different ways of viewing and eventually handling the dilemma. A trusted supervisor or colleagues familiar with the dilemma's context would be helpful.

Case Scenario

Carla *gets feedback from others.* She talks with her supervisor about Tom's situation. She also solicits ideas from a trusted coworker who has worked for the school system for 20 years.

STEP 4: APPRAISE WHAT VALUES AND ETHICAL STANDARDS APPLY TO THE DILEMMA

Assess and choose what values and ethical standards might best apply to the dilemma (Corey et al., 2011; Dolgoff, Harrington, & Loewenberg, 2012). What specific ethical aspects of the NASW *Code of Ethics* do you feel are being violated? You may discover that there is really no ethical *dilemma,* only a more straightforward ethical *problem.* A problem can have some clear solution, whereas a dilemma, by definition, has competing, imperfect solutions. If the *Code* provides you with a clear answer, then use the *Code's* directives to follow steps toward the problem's resolution.

Case Scenario

Carla *determines that a number of professional values and ethical standards apply to the dilemma.* Values include service, dignity and worth of the person, importance of human relationships, and integrity. Carla's responsibility is to serve both Tom and Ally as people who are in great need. She must also consider the dignity of both. She respects Tom's right to make his own choices. She also respects the value of Ally's health and well-being. Carla knows her relationship with Tom is important. To some extent, he depends on her to help him work on his self-confidence and his ability to look more objectively at himself and his life. Carla also realizes that Tom's relationship with his sister is critical. If at all possible, she would certainly choose to strengthen rather than weaken their bonds. Finally, Carla must maintain her integrity. She must make an ethical decision to produce the least harm and enhance people's well-being to the best of her ability.

Ethical standards involved in this case include commitment to clients, self-determination, confidentiality, and commitment to social welfare (NASW, 2008, §§1.01, 1.02, 1.07, 6.01). Carla must maintain her commitment to her client Tom and his well-being. Yet, she also must be concerned with Ally's welfare. Child abuse is certainly at odds with society's and the individual's social welfare. Carla must respect Tom's privacy and confidentiality as much as possible. Likewise, to the greatest extent possible, Tom should be able to make his own decisions about what he will do.

STEP 5: EVALUATE THE DILEMMA ON THE BASIS OF ESTABLISHED ETHICAL PRINCIPLES

Making conscious decisions about what values are more important than others is possible. You can establish a hierarchy of principles based on values that can guide you through the process of confronting an ethical dilemma. Remember that ethical dilemmas always involve situations with imperfect solutions. Each dilemma involves some conflict among ethical principles so that abiding by them all is impossible for you. For example, you might determine that staying alive is more important than telling the truth. Telling the truth is the ethical thing to do. However, what if you are in a situation where telling the truth and keeping someone (perhaps yourself) alive at the same time is impossible? Your arbitrarily best course of action might then be not to tell the truth.

Case Scenario

Carla *evaluates the dilemma on the basis of established ethical principles.* This process is getting difficult to discuss because a suggested hierarchy of principles for ethical decision making will not be explained until the next section. Suffice it to say that the ethical principle assuming the highest priority involves the sanctity of human life. Ethical choices must be made to allow people to survive and thrive, existing with their basic needs met. Other principles in order of their priority include fair and equal treatment, free choice and freedom, least harm, good quality of life, confidentiality, and access to information. In this hierarchy, confidentiality is significantly less critical than the right to life or even the right to protection from harm.

STEP 6: IDENTIFY AND THINK ABOUT POSSIBLE ALTERNATIVES TO PURSUE

 What can you do in your job to solve the dilemma? What creative ideas can you come up with? What other people might help you with their consultation, support, or action to solve the problem?

Case Scenario

Carla *identifies a number of alternative plans of action.* First, she could simply report the abuse, and repercussions would result as they may. Second, Carla could ignore the fact that Tom shared the information with her and go on with her own business. Third, Carla could work with Tom to determine a way to alert authorities to the problem more indirectly.

STEP 7: WEIGH THE PROS AND CONS OF EACH ALTERNATIVE

Weighing the pros and cons of each alternative is a common perspective in various aspects of social work practice. This approach is also useful in resolving ethical dilemmas (Corey et al., 2011). What course of action is best for the client? What alternative is most likely to succeed? How might you best proceed?

Case Scenario

Carla *weighs the pros and cons of each alternative.* Her first option is to call the authorities and report the abuse. Tom would have to suffer whatever consequences descend upon him. It is likely that Ally would be removed from the home. Beth and Michael might evict Tom from their home. Tom would then need someplace else to go. A major question concerns how this eviction would affect his depression, overall mental health, and his relationship with Carla.

Carla's second alternative is to ignore the situation entirely. This alternative is irresponsible in that she then fails to help Ally, who is in great danger of harm. This choice is also illegal because her state requires reporting of alleged abuse.

Carla's third option is to figure out another way of informing authorities without directly implicating Tom. This would both protect Tom and address Ally's situation.

STEP 8: MAKE YOUR DECISION

Finally, make a decision regarding what is the best route for you to take. The main thing when confronting an ethical dilemma is to do some serious thinking about it.

Case Scenario

Carla *makes a decision.* She works on her third option, namely notifying authorities while protecting Tom. She talks with Tom about this possibility. They decide to contact Tom's foster care worker Peter and discuss the problem with him. Together they determine that a viable option would be to keep Tom's report of the abuse anonymous. His name would not enter into the issue at all. Anonymous reports can originate from neighbors, concerned friends, or other family members. Peter, as a foster care worker, is responsible for Tom's well-being while residing in the foster placement. Any suspected abuse might also involve Tom as a victim. Thus, Peter can legitimately involve himself in the situation and work with a protective services worker. Peter can help to protect Tom, yet focus on the real problem, the abuse.

LO 11-6 Rank Ethical Principles

 There are various ways of addressing ethical dilemmas and making decisions regarding how to proceed. The following section will focus on one prominent method, Dolgoff and his colleagues' "Ethical Principles Screen" (2012, pp. 80–82). This approach proposes a hierarchy of ethical principles with which to evaluate the potential courses of action possible for any ethical dilemma. A hierarchy is a ranked order in which a principle takes precedence over the principles below it. In other words, abiding by the first principle is more important than abiding by principles 2 through 7, the second principle than principles 3 through 7, and so on. Thus, the "Ethical Principles Screen" is a prioritized list of seven ethical principles summarized in Figure 11.2 (2012, pp. 80–82). The acronym ETHICS for U is used to assist in remembering the principles' order.

PRINCIPLE 1: PEOPLE HAVE THE RIGHT TO EXIST WITH THEIR BASIC NEEDS MET

This principle stresses that people have a basic right to life. Therefore, social workers should abide by this principle before any other ethical principle. When an

Principle		Ethical Right—People Have the Right to:
1	**E**	**E**xist with their basic needs met.
2	**T**	**T**reatment that is fair and equal.
3	**H**	**H**ave free choice and freedom.
4	**I**	**I**njury that is minimal or nonexistent.
5	**C**	**C**ultivate a good quality of life.
6	**S**	**S**ecure their privacy and confidentiality.
	for	
7	**U**	**U**nderstand the truth and all available information.

© Cengage Learning

FIGURE 11.2 A Hierarchy of Ethical Rights: ETHICS for U

ethical dilemma involves a life-or-death variable, choose an action to save the life, even if this means breaking confidentiality with a client or suppressing the rights of others. Sustaining life takes precedence.

PRINCIPLE 2: PEOPLE HAVE THE RIGHT TO TREATMENT THAT IS FAIR AND EQUAL

The second ethical principle guarantees fair and equal treatment. Social workers should make decisions to abide by this principle except in those cases where life or death is involved. Ethical principle 1 is the only condition that takes precedence.

PRINCIPLE 3: PEOPLE HAVE THE RIGHT TO HAVE FREE CHOICE AND FREEDOM

Ethical principle 3 maintains that people's right to be free is the third priority in addressing an ethical dilemma. We all know the value that social work places on the principle of self-determination. Making their own decisions is people's basic right. The "Ethical Principles Screen" indicates that only people's right to survival or their right to equal treatment takes precedence over their freedom.

PRINCIPLE 4: PEOPLE HAVE THE RIGHT TO EXPERIENCE INJURY THAT IS MINIMAL OR NONEXISTENT

This principle states that people have the basic right to be protected from injury. In the event of potential harm, people have the right to experience the least initial injury possible, the least lasting harm or injury, and, finally, "the most easily reversible harm" (Dolgoff et al., 2012, p. 82). However, this is so only if the earlier principles of having the right to free choice and fair treatment are satisfied.

PRINCIPLE 5: PEOPLE HAVE THE RIGHT TO CULTIVATE A GOOD QUALITY OF LIFE

People have the right to seek and attain a "better quality of life" than they currently have (Dolgoff et al., 2012, p. 82). This principle applies to individuals, groups, neighborhoods, communities, states, and nations. Only principles 1 through 4 take precedence over this right.

PRINCIPLE 6: PEOPLE HAVE THE RIGHT TO SECURE THEIR PRIVACY AND CONFIDENTIALITY

Social workers should strive to secure people's privacy and confidentiality. People have the right not to have their private information made public. We have established that confidentiality is the ethical principle that workers should not share information provided by a client or about a client unless the worker has the client's explicit permission to do so. Such information might include basic data about clients, what they say, professional beliefs and findings, and anything else written about the clients (Barker, 2003).

Confidentiality is a principle strongly stressed in social work practice. Why, then, is it number six of seven in the Ethical Principles Screen's list? Maintaining confidentiality assumes less precedence than the principle of having the right to cultivate a good quality of life. Later portions of the chapter focusing on ethical dilemmas will discuss this issue more thoroughly.

PRINCIPLE 7: PEOPLE HAVE THE RIGHT TO UNDERSTAND THE TRUTH AND ALL AVAILABLE INFORMATION

Ethical principle 7 states that people have the right to know and understand the truth. They have the right to accurate information. However, as the last principle in the hierarchy, it has even less precedence than the right to confidentiality.

Having the truth and nothing but the truth unveiled to you all of the time would be nice. When possible, this axiom is important for social workers to follow. However, if you are legally forbidden to disclose information to clients, what do you do? Should you be forced to tell them everything you think about them, even when your thoughts and ideas are negative? Must you always show people all your notes about them and the issues concerning them?

POSTSCRIPT

You may or may not personally agree with the ethical guidelines proposed by Dolgoff and his colleagues. They provide one example of an ethical guide to decision making in practice. The guidelines are solidly founded on the NASW *Code of Ethics*. Regardless of what ethical guidelines you use in practice, you will continue to be responsible for your own behavior and decisions.

LO 11-7 Discuss and Resolve Ethical Dilemmas in Generalist Practice Contexts

EP 2.1.2c

This text can't address the endless array of potential ethical dilemmas encountered in generalist practice. However, we will discuss some of the most significant ones. It's important for social workers to think critically about ethical dilemmas, tolerate whatever level of ambiguity is involved, and determine the best solution. Ethical dilemmas examined here include confidentiality and privileged communication; self-determination and paternalism; dual relationships; truth telling; laws, policies, and regulations; whistle-blowing; and the distribution of limited resources (Reamer, 1995, pp. 897–989; 2002, pp. 65–67; 2006; 2009).

CONFIDENTIALITY AND PRIVILEGED COMMUNICATION

Confidential information includes personal details about the client's identity, records of verbal statements made by the client, professional reports or professed opinions concerning the client, and content from other records (e.g., employment, health, or educational). The *Code of Ethics* clearly states:

> *Social workers should respect clients' right to privacy. Social workers should not solicit private information from clients unless it is essential to providing service or conducting social work evaluation or research. Once private information is shared, standards of confidentiality apply. (2008, §1.07a)*

This principle sounds simple enough, but what if a client tells you that he is sexually abusing his 5-year-old child, that he cannot control himself, and that he does not want anyone to know about it? What if a client tells you that she made $3,500 last week in her cocaine dealings? What if a married client tells you he is really gay, has had numerous unprotected sexual encounters with other men over the past 15 years, worries about having contracted AIDS, but absolutely does not want to tell his wife about his fears?

Confidentiality is not a simple concept. Actually, two dimensions are involved: relative confidentiality and privilege. Confidentiality, often referred to as *relative confidentiality*, is a more global concept intended to protect clients' privacy, yet permit some degree of disclosure, particularly to other agency staff who may need information to perform their part in the planned change process. Relative confidentiality involves the professional's ethical responsibility to keep information as confidential as possible.

Privilege, on the other hand, refers to legal rights (Gambrill, 1997, 2006). Privilege means that what has transpired between the worker and client is protected by law and cannot be revealed without that client's expressed permission (Corey et al., 2011; Gothard, 1995). However, in most, if not all, states, even legal privilege is vulnerable. (Note that states vary considerably regarding their policies on privilege and privacy.) Circumstances usually exist where workers must disclose privileged communication. For example, consider child or older adult maltreatment cases or situations where clients threaten to hurt themselves or others. In such instances, laws often maintain that protecting victims takes precedence over worker–client privilege (Hepworth, Rooney, Rooney, & Strom-Gottfried, 2013). There are numerous incidents in which privilege might be waived. This includes "during legal proceedings, such as malpractice or personal injury lawsuits, divorce cases, termination-of-parental-rights proceedings, and criminal court hearings" (Reamer, 2009, p. 55). Other specific incidents when privilege might be waived include when "a minor is involved in criminal activity," "a client is using certain types of drugs," "the court orders a professional examination," "a professional needs to collect fees for services rendered," or "the client dies" (Gambrill, 2006, p. 49).

A landmark California court decision, *Tarasoff v. The Regents of the University of California* (1976), was the first "to recognize the duty of a psychotherapist to protect a third party from the foreseeable harm of a client" (Polowy & Gorenberg, 1997, p. 182). The case involved a student who told his therapist at a university outpatient clinic that he planned to murder his former girlfriend, who had dropped him. The therapist notified the campus police of the threat but failed to contact the young woman or her parents. As a result, the police apprehended the man but let him go shortly because he "appeared rational" and promised not to hurt her (p. 182). About 2 months later he killed her. Subsequently, the woman's parents sued the therapist for failing to warn her of the potential danger. The California Supreme Court determined that the client–therapist relationship was "special" (p. 182). Therefore, the therapist was responsible for taking "protective action by releasing confidential information about the client to those who are capable of preventing the threatened harm"; such responsibility "can include warning an outpatient's caregiver or family, involving the police, warning the potential victim, or involuntarily committing the client" (p. 182). This case clearly accentuates social workers' responsibility to notify potential victims of ensuing harm.

With so many restrictions, relative confidentiality is much more common than privilege. However, note that in a 1996 decision, the U.S. Supreme Court "ruled in *Jaffe v. Redmond* that clinical social workers and their clients have the right to privileged communication" (Alexander, 1997, p. 387). Licensed *clinical* social workers or psychotherapists make up only one portion of the social work practitioners' pie. Additionally, *Jaffe v. Redmond* concerns only "federal issues"; "state laws do not provide absolute confidentiality to psychotherapists and differ in their exceptions for privileged communication" (p. 390). Further implications of the ruling are currently being investigated.

Despite confidentiality's complexity, in practice you must comply with its basic principles to the best of your ability. Thankfully, the NASW *Code of Ethics* provides a number of specific suggestions.

For one thing, the *Code* states that "social workers may disclose confidential information when appropriate with valid consent from a client or a person legally authorized to consent on behalf of a client" (NASW, 2008, §1.07b). This suggestion refers to the concept of *informed consent*. In the event that information must be disclosed, a worker should inform the client of this fact and solicit from the client written permission to do so. If the client refuses permission, the worker had best seek legal counsel about what to do.

When workers are legally required to break confidentiality and are unable to gain the client's consent, they "should inform clients to the extent possible about the disclosure of confidential information and the potential consequences, when feasible before the disclosure is made" (NASW, 2008, §1.07d). This suggestion, at least, allows clients to prepare for the disclosure's potential repercussions.

When disclosure is required with or without consent, "in all instances, social workers should disclose the least amount of confidential information necessary to achieve the desired purpose" (NASW, 2008, §1.07c). In other words, say no more than is absolutely necessary to fulfill the disclosure requirement.

Even before situations arise that require disclosure of confidential information, social workers should inform clients about their limitations concerning confidentiality (NASW, 2008, §1.07e). For example, you might inform a minor as soon as possible in the intervention process that you must report any statement she makes concerning using drugs or violating other state laws. Additionally, mandatory reporting includes clients' reports of intention to harm themselves or others. Making these limitations early in the interviewing and intervention process places the responsibility on the client for maintaining confidentiality. They let clients know that they should not tell you specific types of information that they do not want reported.

Workers should also discuss with clients limitations on confidentiality within the agency setting. Clients should be aware that records may be viewed by secretaries who have access to records, supervisors for consultation, administrators for monitoring practice, other colleagues involved with the case, or students in field internships.

Workers should take great care in handling records (NASW, 2008, §1.07l). To the greatest extent possible, you should store hard copies of records where unauthorized persons are least likely to secure access. Highlight 11.3 addresses the issue of ethics and confidentiality on the Internet.

HIGHLIGHT 11.3

LO 11-8 Demonstrate Ethical Communication and "Netiquette" on the Internet

EP 2.1.3c

Numerous issues have arisen with the "evolution and proliferation of information technologies" and the resulting expanded "ways in which social workers provide services to clients, administer agencies, educate practitioners, and conduct research and evaluation" (NASW, 2012, p. 333). The *Code of Ethics* encourages practitioners to "take precautions to ensure and maintain the confidentiality of information transmitted to other parties through the use of computers, electronic mail, facsimile machines, telephones and telephone answering machines and other electronic and computer technology" (NASW, 2008, §1.07m).

Password Protection in E-Mail and Other Accounts

Protecting your password by adhering to the following suggestions is a major precaution in guarding clients' confidentiality:

1. "Do not share a password with anyone." This should be agency policy for all staff.
2. "Never invoke a password with someone present in your office or in the room." That is too much like discussing clients' situations loudly in a public place.
3. "Never use a password that can be found in any database." Avoid writing passwords down by memorizing them instead. You might also use a combination of letters, numbers, and other characters to make the password more difficult for others to identify and remember.
4. "Change your password at least once every three months." (Marson, 2000, p. 20)

Social workers should be knowledgeable about technology and seek additional training when needed (NASW, 2012). They might also follow these additional suggestions for general etiquette on the Internet ("netiquette"):

- *Do not use harsh or offensive language.*
- *Be willing to share expert opinions.*
- *Respect others' privacy.*
- *Be forgiving of grammar and spelling slips (first drafts are commonly transmitted). (Marson & Brackin, 2000, p. 32)*

Precautions About Using E-Mail and Other Social Media

"Communications over the Internet are notoriously subject to interception" (Gingerich, 2002, p. 83). Who

might possibly see the facsimile you sent? How easy is it for other staff to access confidential client records? The National Association of Social Workers (2012) policy manual indicates that "information technology use is becoming increasingly frequent for practitioners, which raises ethical issues surrounding their use, such as document loss or interception and lack of privacy"; the NASW policy statement also supports "policies that ensure that technology does no harm to people" (pp. 334–335).

Conroy (2012) cautions social work students about the use of electronic communication during their internships:

> With regard to e-mail and other social media, a student needs to know the guidelines of the agency, academic school, or program, and the ethics of the profession. Not all agencies have specific policies for the use of e-mail, but in general one should remember that once an e-mail message is sent, it may end up in the in-boxes of many different people—sometimes in error. . . . [T]his . . . means that e-mails about the client should contain no information that makes the client identifiable by anyone who does not have a role in the case. The student should review the contents of all electronic communications and determine this: If the message was erroneously sent to a distribution list of 50 people, would recipients know who was being discussed? Case numbers and other identifiers that can be used by other people working with the client are acceptable, but names, addresses, and extensive details about the client should never be transmitted via e-mail. . . . Students should refrain from contacting clients or other stakeholders from their personal, private e-mail accounts and should not supply e-mail for personal correspondence or sharing jokes, inspirational stories, photographs, or anything else not related to business. All electronic communications that a student sends via the placement agency's e-mail system may be subject to archiving and electronic discovery should the agency be party to any type of lawsuit. (p. 95)

Healy and Mulholland (2012) comment on the potential problems with texting in the context of a social work agency:

> Firstly, it is hard to encrypt [texting] so that it is available only to the proper readers . . . Not only this, but

it is vulnerable to fake messages, and this can be serious in a social work situation. For example, a relative who has access to a person's mobile phone could send a false message which appears to come from a client to his or her social worker, and could interfere with or even attempt to close the client and social worker relationship. Also, as with emails, your intended reader can easily pass on your message to others without your knowledge or consent. Other problems specific to texting include:

1. It may be done hastily and without due care.
2. It may not be taken seriously because of its haste and errors.
3. A text is not easily recorded and so may escape its place in case notes and action files, and so on. So a social worker needs to find a systematic and efficient way to transfer all work from texting to [a] more secure and storable form [of recordkeeping].
4. Clients may not record what is in the message, so, for example, a meeting date may not be diarized or heeded. (p. 55)

Vigilant care should also be taken with the use of other social media such as Facebook and Twitter (Conroy, 2012; Healy & Mulholland, 2012). Conroy (2012) cautions students in their field internships:

While many agencies do not have detailed policies regarding e-mail, even fewer have policies about the use of social media. Students should be exceedingly alert to maintaining professional standards while discussing their experiences in field placements on social media platforms like Facebook or Twitter. Best practices include never mentioning the names of one's field placement agency in social media and public forums and never speaking about case specifics or client names. The concerns here are multiple. First, the student does not want to violate client confidentiality or discuss the client in a way that would be detrimental to the client if he/she or his or her family members or friends were to see what was written. Second, the student will damage his or her own professional reputation with potential employers and colleagues if they find that the student posted material that was unflattering to a field a field placement agency on the Internet. . . . Finally, a student's glib or negative comment about fieldwork, in a blog, for example, written spontaneously after a frustrating day, could also reflect poorly on the student's school or academic program if readers were to interpret the remark as evidence of a less-than-serious and empathic approach to clients or social work practice. (pp. 95–96)

Although many of these comments were made in the context of a student's field placement, they also apply directly to appropriate behavior in a professional social work job. The primary point is to be very careful about what is said in electronic formats, how and where it appears, and who might have access to reading it.

Note that Chapter 16 provides more information about using the Internet, including e-mail composition and confidentiality.

Social workers should also exercise extreme caution concerning talking about clients in both professional and personal settings (NASW, 2008, §1.07l). A worker should not talk about a case around colleagues unless there is some specific reasons for doing so. Likewise, workers should not informally share information about clients with friends or family or in public places where others might overhear. Consider the information serious and avoid using it as juicy tidbits in social conversation.

In summary, a generalist practitioner should make every effort to keep information about the client confidential. However, the worker should also be aware that, depending on the particular situation, there are many constraints about what really can and cannot be kept secret. Constraints include those imposed by the agency and other legal restrictions regarding what must be shared. Therefore, the worker should clarify to the client what these constraints are in order to maximize client understanding and control.

The following case provides an example of an ethical dilemma concerning confidentiality. Both the steps for conceptualizing an ethical dilemma and ETHICS for U will be applied.

Case Vignette

Ursula, a 12-year-old, develops a life-threatening bronchial infection. As a result, she is rushed to the hospital and remains there for several days to recuperate. Ursula's condition gradually improves. On several occasions, nurses observe her curling up into a fetal position and crying softly to herself. They ask her what is wrong, but she refuses to answer. She shakes her head when asked if something physically related to her illness is bothering her. To find out what's going on, the nurses refer Ursula to Joy, the hospital social worker, who visits Ursula. At first, Ursula barely utters a word, but gradually she warms to Joy. Ursula hesitantly confesses that she is 2½ months pregnant. Hence, Joy *recognizes the problem* and *begins investigating the variables involved* (steps one and two in conceptualizing an ethical dilemma). Ursula desperately pleads with Joy not to tell her parents but to help her make plans so she can have and keep the baby.

At this point, several ethical dilemmas confront Joy. First, considering to keep the baby without her parents knowing is unrealistic for Ursula. Second, the potential negative social, emotional, and physical ramifications for Ursula are huge if she has and keeps the baby. Third, questions must be raised about Ursula's competence concerning making such a mammoth decision. To what extent is Ursula capable of understanding the consequences? Finally, Joy must question the extent to which she can influence Ursula one way or another. She surely has no right to pressure Ursula to have an abortion.

Joy *appraises values that apply to these dilemmas* (step four in conceptualizing an ethical dilemma). Joy is unable to pursue step three, *getting feedback from others,* because of her stringent time constraints. The NASW *Code of Ethics* does not address this specific dilemma. Applying the values of service, social justice, dignity and worth of the person, the importance of human relationships, integrity, and competency is difficult. Clients have the right to self-determination. However, to what extent does Ursula have adequate decision-making capacity? What are her parents' rights and responsibilities?

Joy proceeds to *evaluate the dilemma on the basis of established ethical principles* (step five in conceptualizing an ethical dilemma). Consideration of such a situation involves several facets (Dolgoff et al., 2012). Ethical principle 6 in ETHICS for U emphasizes the client's right to privacy and confidentiality. Ethical principle 3 focuses on one's right to have free choice and freedom. Both principles underscore Ursula's right to make her own decisions and follow her directive of not contacting her parents. However, principle 1 emphasizes people's right to life and having their basic needs fulfilled. Joy carefully considers Ursula's well-being, including the physical variable related to her health and the risks assumed in bearing a child at such an early age.

Joy *identifies possible alternatives* and *weighs the pros and cons of each* (steps six and seven in conceptualizing an ethical dilemma). One choice is to ignore the pregnancy revelation and pretend Ursula never informed her. Pros might include avoiding the worrisome issue. On the other hand, cons include failing to assume professional responsibility in looking after her client's welfare.

Another alternative is to inform Ursula's parents about the pregnancy. Cons include breaking Ursula's confidentiality and probably losing her trust. Pros include looking out for Ursula's well-being and involving her guardians in the decision-making process.

Joy decides that ethical principle 1, looking out for what Joy determines is Ursula's best interest, must take precedence. Joy *makes her decision* (step eight in conceptualizing an ethical dilemma) and, after informing Ursula of her plans, immediately calls Ursula's parents.

SELF-DETERMINATION AND PATERNALISM

The NASW *Code of Ethics* requires that "[s]ocial workers respect and promote the right of clients to self-determination and assist clients in their efforts to identify and clarify their goals" (2008, §1.02). We have established that *self-determination* is an ethical principle in social work that acknowledges people's right to make their own decisions and determine their own course of action. Maintaining a commitment to client self-determination may enhance a positive relationship between worker and client.

Maximizing client self-determination to whatever extent possible is the practitioner's responsibility. For example, Abramson (1988) found that, to varying degrees, self-determination is possible for older adult patients in their own discharge planning from acute care hospitals. Most patients "participated actively in their own discharge planning process, and many controlled the discharge decisions" (p. 446). Those with the poorest levels of mental and physical functioning participated the least. People with moderate to severe, although not mild, dementia[10] found determining courses of action more difficult. Abramson (1988) concludes:

Social workers should assess the capacity of each individual and provide choices at whatever level the patient can respond to them. For example, encouraging someone to pick the hour for discharge (a task within the capacity of many demented individuals), or the clothing or other possessions to bring to a new setting, might have significant effects on

---

10. *Dementia* is a condition of seriously impaired mental ability, including loss of memory, diminished judgment, inability to think abstractly, alterations in personality, and, often, disturbed behavior.

postdischarge outcome. Although such strategies do not provide true client self-determination, they do enhance individual perceived control, which in itself has been found to be beneficial. (p. 446)

Paternalism is deliberate action on behalf of a client or decision making about what is best for a client with "the intentional overriding" of what the client wants to do or how the client prefers to be treated (Csikai & Chaitin, 2006, p. 19). Examples include preventing clients from harming themselves, providing necessary services that clients do not want, failing to provide information to clients, or providing clients with censored, inaccurate, or altered information (Reamer, 1995). The worker's underlying motive consistently concerns making a decision that supersedes the client's wishes on behalf of the client's well-being. Highlight 11.4 addresses ethical issues concerning self-determination and paternalism when working with people who have physical disabilities.

Ethical dilemmas involving self-determination and paternalism often focus on two other concepts: informed consent and clients' decision-making capacity (Csikai & Chaitin, 2006; Reamer, 1995). *Informed consent* means that workers should clearly inform clients about the purposes, risks, limitations, possible costs, alternatives, right of refusal, and time frames concerning the services provided (NASW, 2008, §1.03). A potential problem is that a client may be unable to make an informed decision. For example, lacking maturity and experience, a child client may not be capable of making an informed decision (NASW, 2008, §1.02). Likewise, a client who lacks mental competence (e.g., an individual with serious intellectual impairment or mental disability) may be unable to grasp the implications of a decision (NASW, 2008, §1.02).

Client's decision-making capacity can also induce ethical dilemmas. The NASW *Code of Ethics* states that "social workers may limit clients' right to self-determination when, in the social workers' professional judgment, clients' actions or potential actions pose a serious, foreseeable, and imminent risk to themselves or others" (2008, §1.02). It also urges workers to "act on behalf of clients who lack the capacity to make informed decisions" and pursue courses of action that safeguard such clients (2008, §1.14).

Examples of such dilemmas abound. A pregnant 13-year-old whose parents are deceased and who is living in a foster home insists that she will keep the baby and bring it up by herself. A man in his 50s with an incapacitating, progressive, and severely painful disease

explores ways to commit suicide. A senior woman with increasing forgetfulness and lack of mental clarity demands that she remain alone in her own home, despite the fact that she has already started two minor fires by forgetting to turn off her stove burners. A young man with AIDS boasts about having numerous sexual conquests without informing partners about their potential infection.

The variations regarding the concepts of informed consent and clients' decision-making capacity and their involvement in ethical dilemmas are endless. The following two cases provide examples. For the first case, steps conceptualizing an ethical dilemma and ETHICS for U will be applied (note that steps are printed in italics). The second case begins by taking you through the steps for conceptualizing an ethical dilemma and then allows you to establish your own conclusion.

Case Example 1

Enid is a social worker for a homeless shelter in a northern inner-city neighborhood. Her job involves counseling residents regarding future plans, job training, employment possibilities, resource acquisition, empowerment, and self-confidence issues. She also does some outreach to homeless people in the community, offering them the shelter's services.

One January day Enid is walking through the shelter's neighborhood, which has many deserted buildings often frequented by homeless people. She sees a woman dressed in rags and hauling a large green garbage bag filled with some kind of stuffing. Enid calls out to the woman, but the woman scurries away around the corner of a building. Although Enid tries to follow her, the woman abruptly disappears from view. Enid *recognizes that there is a problem:* This woman appears alone and homeless on a cold winter day. Yet, she flees from Enid's overtures. Enid decides to *investigate the variables involved* and *gets feedback from others.*

Enid talks to other neighborhood and shelter residents about the woman. She finds out that the woman is a 27-year-old named Beth who has an intellectual disability (mental retardation), has been diagnosed with schizophrenia,[11] and is homeless. She discovers that Beth has refused help from shelter employees, police officers, and others on numerous occasions.

---

11. *Schizophrenia* is "a disturbance that lasts for at least six months and includes at least one month of active-phase symptoms (i.e., two [or more] of the following: delusions, hallucinations, disorganized speech, grossly disorganized or catatonic behavior, negative symptoms)"(American Psychiatric Association, 2000, p. 298).

HIGHLIGHT 11.4

LO 11-9 Examine Self-Determination and People with Physical Disabilities: An Empowerment Approach

 The concept of self-determination has special ethical implications for adults having physical disabilities. Disability is one important "dimension of diversity" (CSWE, 2008, EP 2.1.4). "Client self-determination is closely linked with the concept of autonomy," a person's ability to function independently (Major, 2000, p. 9). Depending on the type and degree of the disabilities, people with physical disabilities often experience greater difficulties maintaining autonomy than do able-bodied people. For example, a person with a serious visual impairment may have great difficulty getting around in an unfamiliar neighborhood without assistance.

Gilson, Bricout, and Baskind (1998) interviewed six people with physical disabilities who felt social workers tended to focus more on their health status and limitations than on themselves as unique individuals. Ethical concerns included stereotyping people based on the disability label and clearly visible disabilities, ignoring strengths, accessing personal information without receiving client permission, and not consulting clients as expert resources for information about their disabilities and issues. Although limited in scope due to small sample size, this study and its implications of paternalism raise serious ethical questions regarding social workers maximizing self-determination. It apparently is easy for social workers to make assumptions about people with disabilities that emphasize weakness instead of strength.

The following are recommendations for improving service provision to this population-at-risk.

Adopt a Consumer-Oriented Approach (Mackelprang & Salsgiver, 2009; Major, 2000; Pfeiffer, 2005; Rothman, 2003)

 Treating people as consumers involves assuming that they are knowledgeable about their own needs and are capable of making intelligent decisions about services. This approach contrasts sharply with that of making decisions about what's best for clients without their input, recommendations, and consent.

Three facets are especially important. First, listen very carefully to what the client is saying instead of jumping to conclusions based on the disability label.

Second, ask the client to clarify when you do not understand. Third, carefully scrutinize any possible assumptions you may be making about your client and his or her disability. Face your stereotypes and work to get rid of them.

Learn About Services and Resources (Beckett & Maynard, 2005; Mackelprang & Salsgiver, 2009; Major, 2000; Rothman, 2003)

 People with physical disabilities have the same needs and wants as able-bodied people. They just have more obstacles in the way of getting what they need. Services include rehabilitation, employment, and health, residential, recreational, and personal care. Financial resources include various sources of public funding, such as disability insurance, workers' compensation, Supplemental Security Income (SSI), and other forms of public assistance.

One aspect of linking people to resources requires social workers "to pass on their knowledge of how to access resources to consumers and to help them develop personal brokering skills. They can teach consumers how to make phone calls, write letters, and participate in meetings with bureaucrats. Consumers may also need to learn how to connect the services of various agencies and how to organize others with disabilities." (Mackelprang & Salsgiver, 2009, p. 445)

Advocate for Clients with Disabilities Whenever Possible (Jansson, 2011; Mackelprang & Salsgiver, 2009; Major, 2000)

 Clients may need expanded services or additional resources. Work with your clients to determine their needs. Strive to make changes in agency policy and laws governing resources to benefit people with physical disabilities.

Sometimes, political advocacy is necessary. The Americans with Disabilities Act of 1990 (ADA) is a good example of positive legislation on the behalf of people with disabilities. As Karger and Stoesz (2013) reflect:

The ADA extends to . . . people [with disabilities] civil rights similar to those made available on the basis of race, sex, color, national origin, and religion through the Civil Rights Act of 1964. For example, the ADA

> *prohibits discrimination on the basis of disability in private sector employment; in state and local government activities; and in public accommodations and services, including transportation provided by both public and private entities. (pp. 83–84)*

The ADA "has legitimized the idea that the fundamental problems facing people are less medical than social and structural" (Renz-Beaulaurier, 1998, p. 81). It redefines problems as belonging to the *community*, not to people with disabilities living in the community. For example, "the problem of how to get up the steps (problem with the individual) changes to how to get a ramp installed (problem outside the individual)" (p. 80).

However, the need for continued advocacy continues. Karger and Stoesz (2013) maintain:

> *Despite the ADA and other federal laws, discrimination is still widespread against people with disabilities. For instance, most buildings still do not meet the needs of [people with physical disabilities] . . . in term of access, exits, restrooms, parking lots, warning systems, and so forth. Many apartment complexes and stores continue to be built without allowing for the needs of people with disabilities. The struggle for full social, political, and economic integration [for people with disabilities] . . . remains an ongoing battle. (pp. 84–85)*

Enid *considers the values that apply to this dilemma.* Her duty is to serve people in need. Additionally, Beth deserves to maintain dignity and worth, which is very difficult when homeless. Beth deserves to receive supportive help and services. Beth also has the right to self-determination and to control her own path in life. Finally, there is the question regarding whether or not Beth is competent to make decisions in her best interest.

Enid proceeds to *evaluate the dilemma on the basis of established ethical principles.* Ethical principle 3 relates to Beth's right to choose how she will live, which takes precedence over ethical principle 4, the right to experience the least harm possible. Beth would be safer, warmer, and better fed if she would accept services. Principle 3 also takes precedence over ethical principle 5, a person's right to attain a good quality of life. Beth has the right to choose her life path, even if it is not the one providing the best quality of life she might have possible. However, Enid decides that ethical principle 1 is the key. People have the right to have their basic needs met. Scurrying from one empty, dilapidated, unheated building to another between biting, snowy gales poses too great a risk to Beth's survival. Enid also considers Beth's ability to make competent decisions in view of her mental and emotional disabilities.

Enid *identifies the possible alternatives to pursue* and *weighs their respective pros and cons.* First, she can forget about Beth and allow her to lead whatever life she chooses. A pro of this is that Enid may then stop worrying about the dilemma and invest her energies elsewhere in other productive ways. A con of this alternative is that Beth may likely suffer severe consequences, including frostbite, starvation, and possible death.

Enid's second alternative is to call Adult Protective Services and inform the agency about Beth. Such social services include "social, medical, legal, residential, and custodial care" provided for adults who are unable to take adequate care of themselves and have no significant other who might provide necessary care (Barker, 2003, p. 10). In Enid's city, Adult Protective Services can pick up people like Beth and take them to a facility for assessment and treatment.

Enid *makes her decision.* She calls Adult Protective Services and explains to them about Beth.

Critical Thinking Questions 11.20

- In the example presented here, do you agree with Enid's decision? Why or why not?
- If you did not agree, what would you have done in her place?

Case Example 2

Edgar is a 42-year-old who is HIV-positive. He is suffering from more frequent and more serious bouts of a variety of painful infections. Allen, one of Edgar's social workers, works for an agency that provides supportive services for eligible older adults and sick people. Allen helps clients accomplish daily activities and make decisions so that they might remain in their homes as long as possible. Allen usually visits Edgar three times a week, although more when necessary. During one visit, Edgar bluntly announces to Allen that he intends to kill himself. Allen quickly *recognizes that a problem exists.*

Allen further *investigates the variables involved* and explores Edgar's perceptions and feelings. Edgar, responding in a monotone to Allen's probing questions, explains that because he has been too sick he has not been able to go to his accounting job for quite some time. As a result, his savings are almost depleted. Within days he will lose his condo and home of 13 years. He does not want to leave his home and move into whatever public housing assistance might provide. Edgar hates the hospital and only goes when absolutely necessary. He is in continuous excruciating pain and has become extremely depressed.

When Allen leaves Edgar, he *gets feedback from others.* He talks to his supervisor, who refers him to the local AIDS Support Project. A physician there informs Allen that there is a new mixture or "cocktail" of drugs available that has helped many other HIV-positive patients. The physician urges Allen to encourage Edgar to try them.

Allen thanks the physician and once again visits Edgar with some rays of hope. Edgar thanks Allen for his efforts but declares they are of no use. He has made up his mind—to him life is no longer worth living.

Critical Thinking Questions 11.21

- What social work values might apply to Edgar's dilemma?
- How might Allen evaluate this dilemma using the ETHICS for U principles?
- What possible alternatives might Allen pursue?
- What are the pros and cons of each?
- Finally, what should Allen do?

DUAL RELATIONSHIPS

Dual relationships "occur when professionals assume two or more roles at the same time or sequentially with a client" (Corey et al., 2011, p. 268). In other words, such relationships occur when social workers assume more than one role either concurrently or consecutively than that of professional practitioner in practice, work, or educational settings. Such roles might include "friend, employer, teacher, business associate, or sex partner" in addition to professional worker (Kagle & Giebelhausen, 1994, p. 213). Another term for dual relationships is *multiple relationships,* as many types of such associations can occur, including those where a worker assumes more than two roles at one time (Corey et al., 2011; NASW, 2008).

Dual relationships involve *boundary issues.* In this context, boundaries are invisible barriers that separate various roles and limit the types of interaction expected and considered ethically appropriate for each role. For example, a social worker and his client might attend the same church. Here the social worker assumes roles of both professional practitioner and congregational member with respect to this client.

There is an almost endless configuration of dual relationships that workers might assume in practice and in life. Our discussion here focuses on some of those between social workers and clients, educators and students, and supervisors and supervisees.

Social Workers' Dual Relationships with Clients

The *Code of Ethics* standard 1.06(c) (2008) states that "social workers should not engage in dual or multiple relationships with clients or former clients in which there is a risk of exploitation or potential harm to the client." Strom-Gottfried (2003) "examined 894 of the 901 ethics cases filed with NASW between July 1, 1986, and December 31, 1997" (p. 86). She found that "147 cases (55 percent of all those in which there were findings) resulted in conclusions of some form of boundary violation.... Sexual activities accounted for 107 violations" and other dual relationships for 77 (Strom-Gottfried, 2000, p. 253; 2003).

One way of looking at relationships involves various degrees of intimacy. Sexual relationships might be considered the most extreme. The *Code* clearly states that "[s]ocial workers should under no circumstances engage in sexual activities or sexual contact with current clients" (1.09a) or "with former clients because of the potential for harm to the client" (1.09c). Such involvement is clearly unethical behavior. The fact that the most ethics violations filed with the NASW concerned sexual activities probably results from the fact that people are imperfect and have multiple needs, whether they are professionals or not. Suggestions for avoiding such behavior will be discussed later.

Less clear are other types of relationships and scenarios. Congress (1999) comments that "while most social workers believe that sexual relationships with current clients are unethical, they are much more divided when it comes to social, occupational, or educational relationships with current clients" (Congress, 1996, p. 110). Reamer (2006) comments:

> *Dual or multiple relationships can assume many forms, not all of which are ethically problematic. At one extreme are dual and multiple relationships that*

are not typically problematic, for example, when a social worker and client coincidentally attend the same play and have adjacent seats. The boundary issues are temporary and, most likely, manageable. There may be awkward moments, particularly when the client meets the social worker's spouse or partner during intermission, but this kind of unanticipated boundary issue may not unleash complex issues in the therapeutic relationship. This is not to say that an unanticipated social contact should be ignored—it may be useful to address the client's feelings about the encounter. However, in the long run this is not the kind of dual relationship that is likely to have harmful, long-standing consequences. (p. 48)

One scenario comes to mind. Kathy, a social work therapist at a day treatment center for adolescents with behavioral and emotional problems, attended the Fourth of July fireworks, a colossal annual display shot off over Lake Michigan in downtown Milwaukee. She was with 23 other people, including her parents, siblings and their spouses, nieces, nephew, aunt, uncle, grandmother, and neighbor's family of six. Suddenly, Brad, 16, one of her clients, popped into view with a huge grin on his face. This setting was very different than where their typical interactions took place in her office, his classroom, or the halls of the treatment center. Kathy was happy to see him, returned a big smile, and said a welcoming hello. Three seconds of silence followed. Then Brad said, "Well, aren't you going to introduce me to everyone?" Kathy, taken aback, nonetheless began the complicated introductions of who each person was. It took about 15 minutes.

This is the kind of impromptu interaction that might happen to any social worker. It was important to Brad to be treated respectfully and warmly. There was really no harm in the simple interaction, even though it peripherally involved Kathy's roles in her personal life. Other scenarios unlikely to be problematic include living in the same neighborhood as a client, participating in the same community activities, taking continuing education classes with a client's parent, or attending the same fitness center as do clients (Reamer, 2006).

Three examples illustrate gray areas where solutions are a bit less clear (Reamer, 2006). One involves Fernando, a substance abuse counselor who had been working with his client Trixie for several years. Trixie attributes much of her success in maintaining sobriety to Fernando's help and efforts. Fernando receives an invitation to Trixie's wedding with a note saying how much it would mean to Trixie for him to attend.

Another example involves Kasinda, a hospice social worker. She visits her 72-year-old hospice client Leona weekly to provide supportive counseling and link her with needed resources. One week Leona invites Kasinda to have lunch with her.

One other example concerns Darwin, a private practitioner in a rural area, who provides counseling on a range of issues. Gilbert, his client for 2 years, addressed serious self-esteem issues during the course of counseling. Partially as a result of the counseling, Gilbert went back to school and earned a BSW and MSW. Six years after his counseling ended, Gilbert approaches Darwin and asks him to provide clinical supervision. Gilbert expresses how much he respects Darwin and how no other MSWs are available in the area.

Social workers express significant disagreement about what is ethically appropriate in social relationships with clients (Congress, 1999; Dolgoff et al., 2012). Jayaratne, Croston, and Mattison (1997) surveyed a sample of NASW members in Michigan and found that 21 percent of respondents felt that it was appropriate to "develop a friendship with a former client"; 39.3 percent to "touch a client as a regular part of the therapy process"; 30.2 percent to "participate in recreational or social activities with clients"; and 57.3 percent to "provide your home telephone number to clients" (p. 192).

Kagle and Giebelhausen (1994) maintain that:

dual relationships [including nonsexual] are potentially exploitive, crossing the boundaries of ethical practice, satisfying the practitioner's needs, and impairing his or her judgment. . . . They cross the line between the therapeutic relationship and a second relationship, undermining the distinctive nature of the therapeutic relationship, blurring the roles of practitioner and client, and permitting the abuse of power. (pp. 213, 217)

Robison and Reeser (2000) make an interesting analogy:

A physician who giggled when examining you would be acting unprofessionally, no matter how funny you might look. A social worker who made friends with clients would have crossed the same sort of boundary. These boundaries can be difficult to draw or maintain, but both parties to the relationship have obligations that come from being in a professional relationship. (p. 92)

Any type of dual relationship requires serious scrutiny and thought. The following are suggestions for reflecting on, avoiding, or handling potential dual-relationship problems with clients:

1. Think about boundary issues and establish clear professional boundaries from the beginning of involvement with a client (Corey et al., 2011).
2. Consult with supervisors and professional colleagues about how to deal with potentially problematic dual relationships. You need to carefully consider the potential consequences of your actions upon clients and your professional relationship with them.
3. Carefully scrutinize your own motivations, wants, and needs (Reamer, 2006). It is critical always to keep in mind that you are there for the client, not the other way around.
4. In the event that dual relationships occur involuntarily, discuss these issues frankly with clients, identify risks, and consider how to deal with such occurrences in the future (Corey et al., 2011; Reamer, 2006).

5. If you feel attracted to a client and tempted to get sexually involved, address your feelings as early as possible. The ethical guideline is simply to *not* do it. Talk the issue over with your supervisor or get counseling help. Face and evaluate the serious negative consequences for both you and the client. If you can no longer control your sexual feelings toward a client, terminate the professional relationship (Corey et al., 2011). However, make sure the client is referred to another practitioner so that services to that client will continue.

   A related issue concerns getting sexually involved with former clients or relatives of clients. In either case, it is the social worker's responsibility to evaluate the potential effects on the client, on others involved, and on the treatment process. The social worker assumes all risk and the substantial burden of any negative consequences (Reamer, 2006).
6. Distribute fliers on client rights and professional ethics to clients to educate them about these issues (Kagle & Giebelhausen, 1994).

Social Work Educators' Dual Relationships with Students

The *Code of Ethics* (2008) states that:

Social workers who function as educators or field instructors for students should not engage in any dual or multiple relationships with students in which there is a risk of exploitation or potential harm to the student. Social work educators and field instructors are responsible for setting clear, appropriate, and culturally sensitive boundaries. (3.02d)

Dual relationships between educators and current or former students include educator as "sexual partner," "friend," "therapist," and "employer" (Congress, 1996, p. 333). As with dual relationships with clients, dual relationships concerning educators and students must be carefully evaluated. The issue becomes more complicated concerning former students.

Having *sexual relationships* with students is serious. Consider the following scenario:

A male social work student presented a dozen red roses to his female field instructor on the last day of supervision, and one month later they were engaged. At the risk of being unromantic, one can question the quality of her social work supervision throughout the year if there had been a growing personal relationship. (Congress, 1996, p. 334)

Critical Thinking Question 11.25

- In this example, to what extent could this supervisor evaluate the student's "performance in a manner that is fair and respectful"? (NASW, 2008, §3.02b).

Another example involves a male professor who dated students for years, one student at a time. Sometimes, they were taking the course he was teaching, sometimes not. Eventually, he married one of them.

Critical Thinking Question 11.26

- To what extent is it ethical for an instructor to date a current student?

Another male professor in his mid-50s had been in social work education for over two decades. He had lost his wife, whom he dearly loved and to whom he had been earnestly devoted, to cancer 10 years earlier. Since then he had dated occasionally but found no one whom he felt was right for him. A returning student of about his age entered his social work program and took a course he taught. They immediately hit it off, being quite attracted to each other. As soon as the course was over, they began discreetly dating. They were married shortly after she graduated from the program.

Critical Thinking Question 11.27

- To what extent is it ethical for an instructor to marry a former student?

Educators being *friends* with students is a second type of dual relationship. These relationships also require careful consideration, especially because the social work education environment has become relatively informal and flexible (Congress, 1996). We all know it is important for educators to evaluate a student's performance fairly and grade in an equitable, unbiased manner. It is difficult to be objective with friends. The situation becomes yet more difficult when friendships predate the academic relationship (Congress, 1996). On the other hand, Congress (1996) maintains that caution does not mean educators "should avoid participation in a social activity with a student" (p. 334).

One Social Work Club holds annual banquets for its members and invites faculty, who usually attend. Often, faculty and students meet in the bar for cocktails and Cokes before the banquet begins. Conversations are informal and mildly personal in terms of focusing on nonacademic topics.

Critical Thinking Questions 11.28

- To what extent is it ethical for faculty to participate in such informal events?
- To what extent can and should faculty use such informal occasions to interact with their students? Explain your reasons.

What about relationships with former students? Petula, a female professor, was Burt's advisor throughout his 4 years of college in addition to being his instructor for several courses. Upon meeting they immediately developed a good rapport. They came from the same town and both had a straightforward, "tell it like it is" personal communication style. Throughout his college career, they addressed various academic issues in addition to discussing some personal problems. He had cerebral palsy, which sometimes limited his ready access to campus resources and made dating more difficult because of discrimination. He graduated with his BSW and immediately went on for his MSW. Upon completion Burt called Petula and volunteered to serve as a speaker in one of her courses. She invited him, and he did a nice job. Afterward, she invited him to lunch, which she did with all her speakers. Over the next 10 years, Petula invited him to speak each semester. Over time they became good friends, comfortable in discussing many topics ranging from family problems to vacation plans to financial worries to professional issues.

Critical Thinking Questions 11.29

- To what extent is the development of this friendship ethical?
- To what extent does such a relationship serve to enhance or impair the lives of people involved?

Dual relationships can also involve educators assuming a *therapist* role. Educators often serve as academic advisers who help students with academic concerns and career path development. Personal factors integrally intertwined with a person's present and future often surface with respect to these other concerns. For example, how does one distinctly separate getting a job after graduation, deciding whether or not to get married, and coordinating career plans with a possible spouse?

Students may initiate counseling with an educator when facing a crisis. An educator might help a student address an acute problematic situation during one meeting, or even two or three. However, any long-term issues are better addressed by referral to the university's counseling center or an outside therapist (Congress, 1996).

At other times, students begin feeling close to instructors or advisors after working with them for some time and talking to them about various issues. When a trusting relationship is established, students sometimes seek help concerning nonacademic problems. For example, Alicia, 32, originally from Ecuador, was bilingual. She consistently expressed feelings of inferiority and felt her peers were exceptionally critical of her due to her accent. Chantrell, one of her instructors, met several times with Alicia over the course of the semester at Alicia's request, focusing on Alicia's many strengths and helping her develop ways to deal with her classmates.

Critical Thinking Question 11.30

- To what extent is Chantrell and Alicia's relationship ethically sound?

Another possible dual role for educators is that of *employer*. For example, an educator might hire a student as a research assistant or babysitter. What if the student's employment responsibilities interfere with the student's ability to complete work on time or study adequately for an exam? To what extent does the student feel free to refuse employment assignments without fearing negative repercussions from the educator/employer?

Six questions should be asked when determining the appropriateness of a dual relationship between educator and student (Congress, 1996). First, what type of dual role is involved—sexual partner, friend, therapist, or employer—and what will its effects be on the relationship between educator and student? Second, to what extent will the dual relationship potentially hurt or exploit the student? Third, to what extent does the dual relationship "take undue advantage of the educator's greater power in the relationship" (p. 336)? Fourth, what are the potential effects on other students? Fifth, does the dual relationship involve a present or past student (in that less potential harm probably lies with former students)? Sixth, "[h]ow do other colleagues view the dual relationship" (p. 336)?

Highlight 11.5 explores the issue of dual relationships between supervisors and supervisees.

TELLING THE TRUTH

Do clients always have the right to know all available information? Should they always have access to their records? Do instances exist when having information withheld is in the client's best interests?

The NASW *Code of Ethics* states that "social workers should not participate in, condone, or be associated with dishonesty, fraud, or deception" (2008, §4.04). The *Code* also states that "social workers should provide clients with reasonable access to records concerning the clients" (2008, §1.08). However, the *Code* continues that "social workers should limit clients' access to their records, or portions of their records, only in exceptional circumstances when there is compelling evidence that such access would cause serious harm to the client" (2008, §1.08).

Reamer (2006) elaborates:

Practitioners have come to recognize that clients have a right to know what social workers record about their life circumstances, mental health symptoms, treatment plans, and progress. Earlier in the profession's history, relatively few social workers believed that clients should have the right to examine their own records, and records were typically viewed as agency property. More recently, this thinking has evolved: Social workers now understand why clients may want or need to see their records and that such disclosure can be therapeutically beneficial if handled properly. . . .

At times social workers may be concerned that clients' access to their records could be harmful or cause serious misunderstanding. This may occur because, in the social worker's judgment, the client is too fragile emotionally to handle reading the social worker's notes about the clinical situation, or the client is likely to misunderstand what the social worker has written. With few exceptions, even in these circumstances—when there is compelling evidence that a client's access to the records would cause serious harm—should social workers withhold records (or portions of records). This could occur, for example, when a social worker has evidence that a client is suicidal or homicidal and that providing the client with access to specific information in the case record would likely lead to serious harm. In such exceptional circumstances, both the client's request to see the record and the social worker's rationale for withholding some or all of it should be documented. Consultation with colleagues, supervisors, and legal

HIGHLIGHT 11.5

Dual Relationships Between Supervisors and Supervisees

Supervisors have substantial power over supervisees, including what discretion supervisees have in making decisions, what responsibilities they must assume, how they must accomplish their assigned tasks, what vacation times they take, and what merit they earn. Therefore, the potential for the abuse of power is significant when a supervisor assumes a dual relationship. Any kind of exploitation of a person with less power is unethical (Dolgoff et al., 2012). Of course, sexual relationships are obviously unethical, but what about other types of dual relationships?

Consider Earl, a county social services supervisor, who took his supervisee Carla, a relatively new MSW with 1 year of experience, under his wing. Earl genuinely liked Carla, her enthusiasm, and her serious desire to do the best job possible. He took her on home visits to provide a role model for how these should be done. At her request, he helped her develop counseling techniques and write efficient, effective reports. In some ways, he assumed the role of friend with her. For example, when he held a party for all his supervisees and coworkers, he asked her to help him with the arrangements, which she gladly did. Carla respected and admired Earl. At one point, she felt she was even falling in love with him, although Earl never felt any reciprocal romantic feelings toward her (they were both single). Eventually, Earl left the agency for another position. Twenty-five years later Carla still thinks fondly of Earl and appreciates all he taught her. Carla, by the way, is happily married to somebody else.

Critical Thinking Questions 11.31

- To what extent was Earl and Carla's relationship a dual relationship?
- To what extent was it ethical? Why or why not?

Congress (1999) makes the following suggestions for determining whether a potential dual relationship is appropriate or ethical:

1. *Clearly define the nature of the dual relationship involved.*
2. *Examine carefully the risk of exploitation and harm to the most vulnerable person.*
3. *Anticipate possible consequences, positive and negative, of proceeding with a dual relationship.*
4. *Discuss with colleagues and...[others] the advisability of developing a dual relationship.*
5. *Ascertain which other part of the code, in addition to the section on dual relationships, might help determine whether a dual relationship is inappropriate.*
6. *Affirm the responsibility of the professional social worker to avoid even the possibility of exploiting the most vulnerable [persons involved].* (p. 115)

---

counsel may be important in these situations, because there is widespread presumption that clients should have access to their records. Clients who are denied access to their records may have grounds for a lawsuit or ethics complaint. (pp. 77–78)

Depending on the situation, ethical decision making may help you determine the most positive course of action. The following two case examples portray truth-telling dilemmas. How might you handle each one?

Case Example 1

Willie Lee is a 23-year-old resident in a center for people who have intellectual disabilities. Willie Lee can eat by himself and take care of most of his daily hygiene needs. His vocabulary is small, but he usually under-

stands much more than he can express. He is a friendly person who socializes well with peers, is generally respectful of staff, and looks forward to his father's rare visits, which come only once or twice a year. His mother died at his birth.

Willie Lee's father, Horace, has recently remarried and is moving across the continent. He has hired an attorney and wants to terminate his guardianship and responsibility for Willie Lee. Horace has always found Willie Lee a burden and has been embarrassed by Willie Lee's disability. Horace feels this move is his chance to abandon the whole problem and not think about it anymore. Although Willie Lee is always happy when Horace visits, he never asks about him, which may be partially due to Willie Lee's communication difficulties.

Horace succeeds in terminating his rights and moves away. He informs the center that he plans on having no further contact with Willie Lee.

Critical Thinking Questions 11.32

- In this case example, should the center social worker inform Willie Lee of his father's leaving and termination of rights?
- Does Willie Lee have the right to know about his father's status?

How might you apply the steps for conceptualizing an ethical dilemma is this case? What principles in ETHICS for U apply and in what ways?

Case Example 2

Ling is an 86-year-old bedridden resident in a nursing home. Although she has numerous physical difficulties, she has maintained fairly strong mental faculties. She enjoys the company of her two daughters who visit regularly. Ling's physician has just discovered that Ling has developed a lethal form of intestinal cancer and has only weeks, possibly a few months, to live. Ling's daughters beg the nursing home social worker not to tell Ling of her condition. They plan to visit Ling daily and want her to enjoy her time as best she can. They feel informing her about the cancer would only ruin her last days.

Critical Thinking Questions 11.33

- In this case example, what should the social worker do?
- Should she inform Ling of her condition?
- What are the pros and cons of informing or not informing?
- How might you apply the steps for conceptualizing an ethical dilemma and ETHICS for U to this example?

LAWS, POLICIES, AND REGULATIONS

Many social workers believe they should carefully obey laws and comply with agency policies and regulations. However, such rules may not always coincide with professional social work values. What does a practitioner do in such instances? The following cases are examples of potential ethical dilemmas regarding laws, policies, and regulations that may confront you in practice.

Case Example 1

You are a financial assistance worker. Agency policy requires you to report any extra income clients may earn. The exact amount of such income is then deducted from their financial assistance checks. An excited client with four children bursts out, "I'm so happy! My neighbor is going to pay me to take care of her two children while she works. This will do wonders for my grocery bill."

Critical Thinking Questions 11.34

- In this case, as this client's social worker, what should you do?
- Should you report the additional income and thereby decrease her financial assistance check?
- If so, will you tell her what you plan to do?
- What do you think her reaction might be?
- Should you keep her statement confidential, thereby disobeying agency policy?
- What is the ethical thing to do?

Case Example 2

You work for a social services agency serving almost all Hispanic and African-American clients. All the social workers and administrators are white. None of the professional staff speaks Spanish.[12]

Critical Thinking Questions 11.35

- In this agency, how might clients be better served?
- What are the agency's needs?
- What options might you consider pursuing?
- What is the ethical thing to do?

Case Example 3

You are a social worker at a shelter and treatment center for runaways. The center typically uses volunteers to serve many of its functions, including counseling youth and families. Although volunteers receive 20 hours of training, you feel this does not make them competent to counsel young people and their families.

---

12. This vignette is adapted from one presented in B. Cournoyer (2011). *The social work skills workbook* (3rd ed.). Pacific Grove, CA: Brooks/Cole, p. 162.

Critical Thinking Questions 11.36

 EP 2.1.3

- What, if anything, is wrong with this agency's volunteer policy?
- What might you do to make changes?
- What might those changes be?
- What is the ethical thing to do?

WHISTLE-BLOWING

Whistle-blowing is the act of informing on another or making public an individual's, group's, or organization's corrupt, wrong, illegal, wasteful, or dangerous behavior. Within an organizational context, it can involve inefficient or unethical policies. Whistle-blowing can occur within an organization when an employee reports a problem to higher levels of administration. It can also happen when an employee informs entities outside of the organization, such as a regulatory agency or the general public, about an internal problem. Of course, someone entirely outside of an organization can also whistle-blow to internal administration, outside agencies, or the public.

Some organizations, such as the federal government, provide established means for whistle-blowing to occur, while maintaining the anonymity of the person reporting the problem. Likewise, laws do exist to protect the whistle-blower from retaliation of supervisory and administrative personnel whose positions are threatened by the whistle-blower's unappealing revelations.

However, despite the fact that sometimes there is some protection, whistle-blowing is usually risky. Whistle-blowing carries a degree of risk that varies in direct proportion to the seriousness of the allegations, which only makes sense. Going over the head of someone in your own agency and informing those with greater power about bad, inappropriate, or unethical behavior can anger and intimidate the person in question. Similarly, airing "dirty laundry" outside of an agency can be threatening to people who run the agency. All agencies have problems of one sort or another, just as all individual people have problems. However, people responsible for agency activity do not like the negative aspects of this activity to be obtrusively displayed for all to see. Such exposure reflects badly on those who run the agency. The implication, perhaps rightly so, is that the administration is at fault. As a result, whistle-blowers have been fired, reassigned to insignificant responsibilities at remote locations, and harassed into quitting. In short, administrators and other people in power can make a whistle-blower's life extremely miserable.

Whistle-blowing can have many consequences that affect the whistle-blower. Those in the organizational administration or others who resent the allegations can attack them personally. Others can seek to pinpoint and emphasize the whistle-blower's faults. We know that *everyone* has faults. Colleagues may ostracize whistle-blowers, thus making them feel tremendously isolated and alone. They may receive threats to themselves or loved ones. They may even lose their jobs. Perhaps, worse yet, they may be blacklisted as troublemakers in the professional community. Thus, they may discover that finding new employment—unless they undertake a major relocation—is virtually impossible.

Yet, sometimes whistle-blowing is necessary, especially after other less extreme measures (such as working through the agency administration) have already been tried and failed. Sometimes, whistle-blowing is an ethical imperative "when the violations of policy or law seriously threaten the welfare of others" (Reamer, 1990, p. 219).

Consider the choice of whether to blow the whistle or not:

> *The choice must be based upon the seriousness and the consequences of the organization's failing; the relationship of the failing to the organization's obligations to others; and the relationship and responsibility of the social worker to both. Whistle-blowing is not always justifiable, but is often necessary in the interest of fairness and justice, and in the interest of institutional responsibility. Whatever it is that the social worker may offer in justification of the act after the fact—for example, in an adjudication of a complaint or a grievance brought under the Code of Ethics of the social work profession—the social worker should carefully consider before the act. (Levy, 1982, p. 57)*

Most cases involving potential whistle-blowing are ambiguous; there is frequently a fine line between *breaking* the rules and only *bending* them (Reamer, 1990). Therefore, we continue to stress that the decision to act be an extremely serious one. Before blowing the whistle on an agency or colleagues, consider four questions (Reamer, 1990, pp. 219–223):

1. How great is the threat to the potential victims? Is it life or death? Or is it only a minor infraction of the rules? Is it worth the time, energy, and risk to blow the whistle?
2. What type and quality of proof are available that the wrongdoing has occurred or is going on? How solid is your evidence? Do you have written

documentation? Do you have witnesses? Or do you only have some ideas based on minor informal observations and hearsay?

3. Are there less severe alternative measures you might take to remedy the problem? Are there established agency channels through which you can work? How difficult would navigating through these channels be? How much resistance do you anticipate encountering? Can you confront the abuser personally before trying other, more severe measures? Can you solicit support from colleagues? Will your supervisor help?

4. Can you assume the burden of risk? How much do you really have to lose? Is it worth the risk? Is whistle-blowing really the only way you can attack the ethical problem? Or are there other, less risky alternatives you can pursue?

The decision to blow the whistle, whether it be to higher levels of administration beyond your immediate supervisor or to someone outside the agency, is a tough one. Depending on your own individual situation, it requires weighing numerous pros and cons. If the ethical dilemma concerns literally life and death, you ethically must attack the problem in some way. However, what way would you choose? There are many courses of action available to you. Whistle-blowing is probably only one of them.

If you do choose to blow the whistle because you see no other choice, there are several recommendations to follow. First, be certain that you clearly define the variables and issues involved. What, specifically, is the problem? What documentation can you employ as proof of your allegations? What ethical standards or rules are being violated? Exactly in what ways are these standards and rules being breached?

The second suggestion for blowing the whistle involves knowing what your rights are. Do you work for a public agency whose policy sanctions employees' right to free speech? On the other hand, is it part of agency policy to address procedural issues internally and internally only? Is there an available grievance or complaint procedure that you could utilize? How easy is it for your agency to fire you? Do you belong to a union on which you could depend for help? Is the union strong in actuality or is it relatively weak?

The third recommendation for whistle-blowing entails being prepared for the consequences. What is the worst thing that could happen to you? Might it be that your supervisor would put a note of reprimand in your permanent file, barring you from future promotions? Would such a note work against your potential

for a positive letter of recommendation? Might you be fired as a result of your actions? Would blowing the whistle ruin your reputation in the professional community, thereby branding you as a troublemaker no other agency wants to hire? In the event that the worst would happen to you, what would you be prepared to do?

The fourth suggestion for whistle-blowing concerns following the chain of command. Going over your supervisor's head almost always puts you at risk of his or her resentment and wrath. By doing so, you appear to negate his or her authority and competence, which usually threatens supervisors. It probably would be threatening to you, too, were you in their same position. At any rate, if at all possible, before pursuing the whistle-blowing option, try to follow the agency's predetermined, sanctioned chain of command. If that route does not work, then you might consider more extreme options such as whistle-blowing.

Finally, the fifth recommendation for blowing the whistle involves establishing a clearly defined plan of action. Whom do you plan to tell about the problem? In what order will you tell people? What will you do if they react positively? How will you proceed if they respond negatively? Whom can you solicit as allies? Are other workers and administrators willing to support you? Are there external organizations, such as NASW or licensing bodies, that would aid you or even advocate on your cause's behalf? Can you beseech experts to support your case? What specific goals do you hope to attain? What is your time frame for achieving them?

In summary, considering the whistle-blowing alternative carefully is extremely important. Weigh potential gains against risks and negative consequences. There is no crystal ball. All you can do is act as your conscience dictates and do the best you can.

DISTRIBUTION OF LIMITED RESOURCES

EP 2.1.5c

A consistent ethical problem in social work is the distribution of resources that are always in a limited supply (Beckett & Maynard, 2005). Workers must often make hard decisions regarding what is more and less necessary. For example, large numbers of Latino migrant workers and their families have historically come to work on farms in a midwestern agricultural state during the summer months. Over time, large corporations have overtaken and consumed smaller family farms and now use expensive machinery for tasks formerly accomplished by migrants. The migrants continue to depend on such work for subsistence, despite the existence of a shrinking number of jobs available. Migrant families come to the state in the summer and find themselves unemployed and impoverished. They desperately need resources to survive. The state, however, with its limited resources and services, can barely support its own poor citizens. Some must go without. The question concerns who should receive the limited resources. Who should be left to starve?

The former example reflects how limited resources might be allocated among competing groups. On another level, a larger pool of resources might be allocated for different purposes, serving distinctly different populations. For example, substantial public resources have been allocated to drug prevention programs for teens and relatively little to helping the homeless.

Generally, decisions to provide or shift limited resources lie within the macro realm of practice. What rules, policies, and laws apply to the resources? How might administrators and decision makers reallocate resources so that the most critical needs, such as that of survival, are met? However, advocating for people in need and seeking political change is also each individual professional's responsibility at the micro level (NASW, 2008, §6.04). How might you, as a social work practitioner, address such issues?

There are a number of variables to consider when distributing limited resources (Reamer, 1995). First, think about *equality*. Can resources be divided equitably, or, at least, can all involved be given the chance to vie for some access to resources? A second variable for disbursing resources is *need*. Those in greatest need would then be given priority for receiving resources rather than focusing on equal amounts or equal opportunity. A third variable to determine resource allocation is the participants' ability to repay what is given or potentially *contribute* to the resource pool at some time to come. Those most likely to provide some kind of payback would receive precedence in resource allocation. Should not people who contribute more to a resource delivery system get more from that system than people who contribute less? Consider, for example, Social Security. There are no easy answers.

LO 11-10 Appraise Personal and Professional Values

EP 2.1.2a

"*Values* involve what you do and do not consider important and worthwhile. They also involve judgments and decisions about relative worth—that is, about what is more valuable and what is less valuable"

(Kirst-Ashman, 2013, p. 33). We all have the right to our personal values. We have ideas about how we personally feel things should be. We have personal opinions about the death penalty, capital punishment, and abortion. We have personal values and beliefs concerning spirituality, state and federal tax rates, and whether women should change their last names to that of their spouses upon marriage.

What if our personal values conflict with professional values? Welfel (2013) discusses the issue of personal versus professional values:

No one enters [social work]…practice as a blank slate. All professionals have values and beliefs that have served as major influences on the way they have lived their lives and the choices they have made. Some of these values are rooted in a religious identity, while others derive from upbringing or educational experiences. Some are quite admirable, such as devotion to helping others or a commitment to be a responsible citizen in a democracy, and other[s] are not, such as the belief that all people are self-interested and will take advantage of anyone who lets them. Many admirable beliefs and values are highly consistent with the values of the [social work profession]…and integrating those values into one's identity as a professional happens smoothly. Other personal values may be at odds with professional values. For example, one professional's personal belief may be that he or she has a duty to share the message of [his or her]…religion with others or someone may believe that no one has a right to make any decision that would hasten death. These beliefs conflict with the stance of the profession that endorses the principle of respect for autonomy; no practitioner has the right to proselytize or work to convince someone that [his or her]…belief that it is morally acceptable to hasten death is wrong. Similarly, a trainee may have a deeply held conviction that homosexual activity is morally wrong. When these conflicts occur, they can be a source of substantial stress for the new professional. What is most important for the professional is to confront the conflict honestly and openly and to seek multiple sources of consultation and education. Such a process takes time and patience. In rare cases a novice may decide that the conflict is so great that this career is impossible. Most of the time, however, a way forward is found to make a commitment to professional values that does not negate personal beliefs. What is unacceptable and unethical is to feign agreement with professional values and continue in the work with the aim of imposing personal beliefs on [clients]. (p. 23)

Conflicts between personal and professional values frequently pose ethical dilemmas for workers:

1. Your personal value might be that abortions, although legal in your state, are morally wrong. However, you have an adult client who asks you to help her seek one.
2. You have an adult client with a life-threatening disease who desperately needs surgery to ensure survival. However, the client refuses such medical help because it conflicts with his strong religious beliefs. You personally feel this perspective is stupid.
3. You believe strongly in the equality of men and women and in their right to equal choices and chances. You work with a family who culturally maintains a patriarchal perspective where female family members are given much less respect, allowed less input, and generally have significantly less power than male members.

At this point in your social work education, you should be regularly addressing the concept of personal values and how they must stand apart from professional values. Each dilemma requires workers to consider carefully the contending needs and rights of the client, the agency, the social work profession, and society to make the most useful and effective decision. For each client and each case, workers must conduct an ongoing evaluation of personal values and how these might affect their ability to intervene effectively.

Barsky (2010) makes the following suggestions "to ensure that you are aware of your attitudes and remain open to other perspectives based on a full analysis of facts and other points of view":

- *Identify attitudes that may be affecting your thought processes.*
- *Assess the strength of each attitude in relation to extremity [How extreme or radical is your point of view compared to others' perspectives?], certainty [How sure are you that you are correct and accurate?], and centrality [What is society's general point of view, if there is one, on the issue?]. Identify the source of each attitude (e.g., personal or professional experience, professional education, family role models, media, or religious upbringing).*
- *Remind yourself to be open to hearing facts, opinions, and perspectives that may conflict with [your]...own attitudes and beliefs.*
- *Make use of supervision or consultation to help you assess how your attitudes might be impairing your ethical decision making and to help you strategize how to deal with these issues. (p. 59)*

Chapter Summary

The following summarizes this chapter's content as it relates to each learning objective (LO) presented at the beginning of the chapter. Chapter content helps prepare students to:

LO 11-1 Examine and apply the National Association of Social Workers (NASW) *Code of Ethics.*

The six core values in the NASW *Code of Ethics* are "service," "social justice," "dignity and worth of the person," "the importance of human relationships," "integrity," and "competence" (2008). The *Code* addresses social workers' ethical responsibilities to clients, to colleagues, in practice settings, as professionals, to the social work profession, and to the broader society.

An example of compliance with or violation of professional ethical standards, or an unresolved ethical dilemma, is provided for each of the social worker's ethical responsibilities to clients and to colleagues. Critical thinking questions are posed for each example of a violation or unresolved dilemma.

LO 11-2 Recognize the Canadian Association of Social Workers *Code of Ethics.*

The CASW *Code of Ethics* core values are "Respect for the Inherent Dignity and Worth of Persons," the "Pursuit of Social Justice," "Service to Humanity," "Integrity in Professional Practice," "Confidentiality in Professional Practice," and "Competence in Professional Practice" (2005).

LO 11-3 Examine international ethical principles.

The International Federation of Social Workers (IFSW) and the International Association of Schools of Social Work (IASSW) have developed ethical guidelines entitled *Ethics in Social Work, Statement of Principles.* The document is divided into five sections: The "Preface," "Definition of Social Work," "International Conventions" (international documents and declarations that are "particularly relevant to social work practice and action"), "Principles," and "Professional Conduct" (IASSW, 2013b). Two of its primary principles include "human rights" and "social justice."

LO 11-4 Identify ethical dilemmas.

Ethical dilemmas in social work practice are problematic situations in which possible solutions all offer imperfect and unsatisfactory answers in terms of what ethically should be done. In other words, ethical principles conflict with each other. Some level of ambiguity and uncertainty exists regarding the most appropriate and effective way to proceed.

LO 11-5 Conceptualize and apply a decision-making strategy to address ethical dilemmas.

Conceptualizing and addressing an ethical dilemma involves eight decision-making steps: (1) recognize the problem; (2) investigate the variables involved; (3) get feedback from others; (4) appraise what values and ethical standards apply to the dilemma; (5) evaluate the dilemma on the basis of established ethical principles; (6) identify and think about possible alternatives to pursue; (7) weigh the pros and cons of each alternative; and (8) make your decision.

LO 11-6 Rank ethical principles.

Dolgoff et al.'s "Ethical Principles Screen" (reflected in "ETHICS for U") involves a ranking of seven principles and suggests which principles should take precedence over others (2012, pp. 80–82).

LO 11-7 Discuss and resolve ethical dilemmas in generalist practice contexts.

Ambiguity, the state of being indistinct or of having the potential to be viewed from different perspectives, characterizes ethical dilemmas. Numerous ethical dilemmas involving the NASW *Code*'s ethical responsibilities with clients and to colleagues are provided that require solutions. Complex ethical issues are discussed, including confidentiality and privileged communication; self-determination and paternalism; dual relationships; truth telling; laws, policies, and regulations; whistle-blowing; and distributing limited resources.

LO 11-8 Demonstrate ethical communication and "Netiquette" on the Internet.

Practitioners should use the Internet carefully and conscientiously. They should be knowledgeable about technology and strive to maintain confidentiality. Exceptional care should be taken when using e-mail and other social media such as Facebook and Twitter.

LO 11-9 Examine self-determination and people with disabilities.

Practitioners must be sensitive to the special needs of people with disabilities. They should adopt a consumer-oriented approach, learn about services and resources, and advocate when necessary.

LO 11-10 Appraise personal and professional values.

"Values involve what you do and do not consider important and worthwhile. They also involve judgments and decisions about relative worth" (Kirst-Ashman, 2013, p. 33). Personal values may conflict with professional values, resulting in ethical dilemmas. Each dilemma requires workers to consider carefully the contending needs and rights of the client, the agency, the social work profession, and society to make the most useful and effective decision.

Competency Notes

The following identifies where Educational Policy (EP) competencies and practice behaviors are discussed in the chapter.

EP 2.1.1b Practice personal reflection and self-correction to assure continual professional development. *(p. 415):* Self-reflection and serious consideration of issues is often required to identify and understand ethical dilemmas. *(p. 426):* Practitioners should practice self-reflection to understand the perspectives of people with disabilities in order to provide effective service.

EP 2.1.1c Attend to professional roles and boundaries. *(p. 402):* Social workers should maintain the boundaries between personal and professional relationships. *(p. 428):* Practitioners should carefully monitor potential dual and multiple relationships in order to maintain appropriate professional roles and boundaries.

EP 2.1.1d Demonstrate professional demeanor in behavior, appearance, and communication. *(p. 400):* One aspect of professional demeanor is competence. *(p. 410):* Social workers should maintain professional integrity and promote high practice standards.

EP 2.1.1e Engage in career-long learning. *(p. 409):* To remain competent and current, social workers should participate in ongoing learning experiences.

EP 2.1.1f Use supervision and consultation. *(p. 406):* Social workers should use consultation when needed. *(p. 408):* Social work supervisors should be competent in providing supervision to supervisees.

EP 2.1.2 Apply social work ethical principles to guide professional practice. *(p. 396):* Social workers must be knowledgeable about the value base of the profession. They also must engage in decision making based on ethical principles. This entire chapter addresses these issues.

EP 2.1.2a Recognize and manage personal values in a way that allows professional values to guide practice. *(p. 437):* Personal values must stand apart from professional values so that they do not interfere with ethical practice.

EP 2.1.2b Make ethical decisions by applying standards of the National Association of Social Workers (NASW) *Code of Ethics* **and, as applicable, of the International Federation of Social Workers/International Association of Schools of Social Work** *Ethics in Social Work, Statement of Principles.* *(p. 397):* Social workers make ethical decisions by applying the NASW *Code of Ethics.* *(p. 412):* When applicable, generalist practitioners should make ethical decisions by applying the IFSW/IASSW *Ethics in Social Work, Statement of Principles.*

EP 2.1.2c Tolerate ambiguity in resolving ethical conflicts. *(p. 397):* Numerous examples of ethical dilemmas and critical thinking questions are presented in the subsequent sections that involve compliance with and violations of ethical principles, in addition to unresolved dilemmas. The intent is to give students the opportunity to consider dilemmas in some depth and learn to tolerate ambiguity. *(p. 414):* Ethical dilemmas by nature involve ambiguity. *(p. 418):* Students are encouraged to identify and evaluate various alternatives when addressing an ethical dilemma. Often such evaluation involves significant ambiguity. *(p. 420):* Several common ethical dilemmas are examined from various perspectives where ambiguous issues are discussed.

EP 2.1.2d Apply strategies of ethical reasoning to arrive at principled decisions. *(p. 415):* A procedure is provided for conceptualizing and making decisions about ethical dilemmas. *(p. 418):* A system for ranking ethical principles is described.

EP 2.1.3 Apply critical thinking to inform and communicate professional judgments. *(p. 400):* Critical thinking questions are posed. *NOTE:* Because of the large number of critical thinking questions occurring in this chapter, only the first is called out by a helping hands icon.

EP 2.1.3a Distinguish, appraise, and integrate multiple sources of knowledge, including research-based knowledge, and practice wisdom. *(p. 427):* Comprehensive discussion accompanies a number of critical thinking questions involving common ethical dilemmas faced in practice.

EP 2.1.3c Demonstrate effective oral and written communication in working with individuals, families, groups, organizations, communities, and colleagues. *(p. 408):* Social workers should record client information accurately and efficiently. *(p. 422):* Effective communication on the Internet is as important as other professional oral and written communication.

EP 2.1.4 Engage diversity and difference in practice. *(p. 400):* The *Code* emphasizes the importance of recognizing the extent of oppression experienced by diverse groups and of ongoing learning about different cultures. *(p. 426):* Disability is one important aspect of human diversity.

EP 2.1.4a Recognize the extent to which culture's structures and values may oppress, marginalize, alienate, or create or enhance privilege and power. *(p. 410):* Practitioners must understand the dynamics of discrimination in order to fight it.

EP 2.1.5 Advance human rights and social and economic justice. *(p. 412):* Social workers should recognize the global connections of oppression as they apply strategies to promote human and civil rights.

EP 2.1.5a Understand the forms and mechanisms of oppression and discrimination. *(p. 426):* Generalist practitioners must understand the conditions and issues that tend to oppress people with disabilities in order to fight discrimination and help them get what they need.

EP 2.1.5b Advocate for human rights and social and economic justice. *(p. 412):* Both the *Ethics in Social Work, Statement of Principles* and the *CASW Code of Ethics* stress advocacy for social justice. *(p. 426):* Social workers should advocate for clients with disabilities so that their needs will be met.

EP 2.1.5c Engage in practices that advance social and economic justice. *(p. 397):* Seeking social justice is a core value for professional social workers. *(p. 411):* Participation in political action can pursue social and economic justice. *(p. 436):* Generalist practitioners should pursue distribution of resources as fairly, equitably, and adequately as possible.

EP 2.1.6a Use practice experience to inform scientific inquiry. *(p. 411):* Social workers should participate in and conduct research that enhances practice effectiveness.

EP 2.1.8b **Collaborate with colleagues and clients for effective policy action.** *(p. 411):* Social workers should collaborate with colleagues and clients to pursue social and political action.

EP 2.1.9b **Provide leadership in promoting sustainable changes in service delivery and practice to improve the quality of social services.** *(p. 411):* Active leadership in the NASW provides one mechanism to improve conditions for service delivery and quality.

EP 2.1.10h **Initiate actions to achieve organizational goals.** *(p. 412):* Joining and participating in international organizations such as IFSW or IASSW can help achieve organizational goals such as the enhancement of human rights and social justice.

EP 2.1.10l **Facilitate transitions and endings.** *(p. 404):* Practitioners are responsible for facilitating transitions and termination with clients.

On the Internet

Visit the *Understanding Generalist Practice* CourseMate at **www.cengagebrain.com** for resources such as quizzes, glossaries and videos.

Culturally Competent Social Work Practice

© Dmitry Berkut/Shutterstock.com

Learning Objectives   *This chapter will help prepare students to:*

LO 12-1   Recognize how cultural structures and values may oppress, alienate, or produce privilege/power.

LO 12-2   Enhance self-awareness to eliminate personal biases/values in work with diverse groups.

LO 12-3   Demonstrate understanding of how differences shape life experiences.

LO 12-4   View themselves as learners and clients as teachers regarding cultural and other differences.

JANIS ENGLAND WAS MYSTIFIED. Talking with Lana Black Bear, the mother of a family on her caseload, she learned that Mr. Black Bear's two nephews were coming to live with the family for a while. The Black Bear family already had great trouble getting by on their meager income from the sawmill. How could they afford to care for two more children? In addition, Lana Black Bear had serious medical problems stemming from a car accident 2 years ago. Why would she want to take on this extra burden on top of raising her own three children? "It seems crazy," Janis thought to herself. "I guess I'll have to talk to the Black Bears about this."

John Martin, social worker for the Dinh Phuc Van family, had just walked into the waiting room of the human services department. This meeting was to be his first with the family,

which had been recently referred to him by the Salvation Army social worker. The Dinh Phuc Vans were recent Vietnamese refugees and had just arrived in the city. "Hello, Dinh, how are you today?" He smiled and shook Dinh Phuc Van's hand. He greeted the wife similarly, shaking her hand and motioning them both toward his office.

Although John expected the family to be somewhat hesitant in asking for help, he was very surprised when the couple seemed both distant and uncommunicative. During the brief interview, John learned nothing that would help him decide how to help the family. The interview concluded when the husband apologized for bothering John and said they had to leave.

Introduction

The United States is a pluralistic nation composed of, except for Native Americans, immigrants or the descendants of immigrants. With a total population of over 300 million, the United States is an extremely diverse society. About 40 million people are of African-American heritage, 14.6 million are from Asian-American or Pacific Islander backgrounds, and 48.4 million are of Hispanic or Latino extraction. An additional 4.9 million are First Nations Peoples (U.S. Census Bureau, 2012a).

The white population is a similarly diverse amalgam of peoples from Western and Eastern Europe, sometimes representing cultures with long histories of enmity and conflict. The traditional American view of this amalgam was that the differences and animosities that many people from many countries felt toward each other became submerged in what we liked to call the melting pot. The melting pot idea has been used repeatedly to suggest that all peoples who come to America get figuratively stirred into a giant pot and come out looking, thinking, and acting alike. As a concept, it was an attractive way for a nation to see itself—a country where all people could go and become as one.

Yet the reality of America is vastly different from the image of the melting pot, as we will discuss in this chapter. For example, we will look at the two cases that opened this chapter, identifying problems caused by social workers who lacked cultural competency.

LO 12-1 Recognize How Cultural Structures and Values May Oppress, Alienate, or Produce Privilege/Power

Diversity in the United States

In the following subsections, we cover race and ethnicity, disabilities, and historic and current discrimination as aspects of diversity in the United States.

RACE AND ETHNICITY

In the introduction to this chapter, we noted that the United States is an enormously diverse society. Over 25 percent of our current population is descended from people who did not come from the European backgrounds that characterized immigrants in the eighteenth, nineteenth, and first half of the twentieth centuries. The U.S. Bureau of the Census (2012b) projects that by 2060 about 56 percent of the U.S. population will be composed of blacks, Asians/Pacific Islanders, First Nations People, and Hispanics. The melting pot concept is not applicable to the experiences of these people of color. It does not even adequately address the history of white immigrants to America, who often maintained their values, beliefs, traditions, and behavior through successive generations, and ignores enormous diversity within Anglo (white) culture. Worse, it completely fails to address the experiences of people of color. Unfortunately, it has been a popular notion and still has vestiges of support. This support compounds the difficulties already experienced by racial and ethnic groups in our society.

Even the terminology we use to discuss diversity is fraught with problems. For example, the term *minority* is offensive to many who believe it connotes inferiority and reflects racism. Others point out that the term is meaningless because throughout the world, those traditionally labeled minorities (e.g., people of color) compose the majority of the population. The term is sometimes used to convey subordinate social, political, or economic status, at which point it can apply to women, children, gays and lesbians, and others experiencing social and economic injustice. Using this definition, any group oppressed by another could be considered a minority even if numerically superior in numbers. This situation was the case in South Africa under apartheid, where power was held by a relatively small group of whites over vast numbers of South Africans, and in Iraq, where Sunni Muslims held power over more numerous Shiite Muslims.

Similar concern is raised about the term *race.* Although *race* is used routinely in our legal system, the concept is more social than biological in importance. Geneticist James King recognizes this viewpoint in his book *The Biology of Race* (1981, pp. 156–157) when he notes that cultural factors determine both race and racial differences. Issues such as "history, tradition, and personal training and experiences" are what individuals use to designate themselves as members of particular groups (p. 156). He concludes that "there are no objective boundaries to set off one subspecies from another" (p. 197). Similar conclusions are echoed by Smedley and Smedley (2005) and Morning (2011).

The increase in populations involving mixed ancestry, mixed race, intermarriage, and recognition of multiracial heritage confounds attempts to categorize or pigeonhole people. The potential of this change is enormous (see Highlight 12.1). The U.S. Bureau of the Census uses the familiar categories of race but is now faced with finding ways to accommodate the millions of individuals who recognize and celebrate their mixed racial heritage. Laws, rules, and regulations exist prohibiting discrimination based on race and asking individuals to select a single group to which they belong. The changes these accommodations would evoke in everything from preschool applications to official government documents are fascinating to consider.

Whenever possible, this chapter will use the term *multicultural group* to replace common but sometimes

objectionable terms such as minority group, diverse groups, ethnic group, and similar phrases. Customary racial groups will be discussed when needed to convey conceptual approaches to understanding individual and group differences as well as the consequences of oppression and social and economic injustice. However, we will try to emphasize that differences within individual groups often are greater than those between groups. We also caution in advance that individuals and families from mixed racial backgrounds may share all, some, or none of the characteristics, values, and beliefs commonly attributed to the groups with which they identify.

DISABILITIES

About 57 million people suffer from disabilities (U.S. Census Bureau, 2012c). This includes people with motor impairments, visual or hearing deficits, psychological disorders, cognitive disabilities, and many others. The Census Bureau reports the following:

- 8% of children under 15 have disabilities
- 21% of people 15 and older have disabilities
- 17% of people 21 to 64 have disabilities
- 50% of adults 65 and older have disabilities
- 8 million people 15 and older have a hearing difficulty
- 8 million over 15 have vision difficulties
- 31 million have difficulty walking or climbing stairs
- 4 million use a wheelchair for mobility, and 12 million use a cane or walker

The Americans with Disabilities Act (ADA) defines disability as a "physical or mental impairment that substantially limits one or more of the major life events of such an individual" (Equal Employment Opportunity Commission [EEOC], 1991, p. 1-25). It also includes individuals who have a record of impairments as well as those who are considered by others to have such an impairment. The ADA goes on to define physical or mental impairment to include "any physiological disorder or condition, cosmetic disfigurement, or anatomical loss affecting one or more of the following body systems: neurological, musculoskeletal, special sense organs, respiratory (including speech organs), cardiovascular, reproductive, digestive, genitourinary, hemic and lymphatic, skin, and endocrine; or any mental or psychological disorder such as mental retardation, organic brain syndrome, emotional or mental illness, and specific learning disabilities" (EEOC, 1991, p. 1-26). Major life events include

HIGHLIGHT 12.1

Common Terminology

Ableism

Ableism is the belief that people with disabilities are inferior to nondisabled people because of their differences. It "devalues people with disabilities and results in segregation, social isolation, and social policies that limit their opportunities for full societal participation." (Mackelprang & Salsgiver, 2009, p. 9).

Cultural Competence

Culture competence is the ability to apply knowledge and skills to social work practice with diverse groups. Cultural competence includes specific knowledge about individual cultures, valuing of and sensitivity to cultural differences, awareness of the patterns of oppression experienced by those cultures, and the skill to utilize culturally appropriate interventions (Lum, 2011; NASW, 2007).

Ethnocentrism

Ethnocentrism is the belief that one's own racial, ethnicity, or cultural group is superior to all others. This belief, epitomized in Hitler's idea of a "master race," led to the extermination of millions of Jews during and prior to World War II. It is also characteristic of apartheid in South Africa and of the extremist views of such groups as the Ku Klux Klan.

Individual Racism

"Racism is the cognitive belief that one ethnic group is superior to and dominant over another inferior and sub-

jugated group, supposedly because of genetic composition, intelligence, skin color, character, or related rationale" (Lum, 2011, p. 58). Results of racism include violence and exclusion. Individual racism is often supported by institutionalized racism.

Institutional Racism

Institutional racism is reflected in actions, policies, and procedures built into organizations and bureaucracies that oppress groups based on their race or ethnicity. For example, college admission standards that admit only students receiving extremely high scores on the Scholastic Aptitude Test (SAT) or other similar tests systematically exclude many minorities who, as a group, may not do as well on such tests.

Minority

Minority is a term referring to any group or person lacking power or resources when compared to the dominant majority in a community or society.

People of Color

People of color are those whose skin color differs from that of the community's predominant group. Typically, this group includes Native Americans, Asian Americans, African Americans, and some other groups.

"caring for oneself, performing manual tasks, walking, seeing, hearing, speaking, breathing, learning, and working" (EEOC, 1991, p. 1-27). It is important to recognize that the definition used by the EEOC is broader than that used by the Social Security Administration (SSA). The SSA (2013) only pays benefits for total disability, which the SSA defines as having three components:

- You cannot do work that you did before,
- You cannot adjust to other work because of your medical conditions, and
- Your disability has lasted or is expected to last for at least 1 year or to result in death.

As is obvious, this is a much more restrictive definition than that contained in the EEOC documents.

Congress passed the ADA in 1990 to combat significant and continuous discrimination faced by those with disabilities. The act defined disability and required employers and others to provide reasonable accommodations to assist those with disabilities to attain and maintain employment. Reasonable accommodations might include changes in recruitment and application procedures, increasing the accessibility of a building or work area, providing special equipment or interpreters, and restructuring a particular job. The ADA, coupled with previous laws, was intended to guarantee the same civil rights to persons with disabilities as those enjoyed by the rest of the population. The reasons for these laws will become apparent in following sections.

This chapter approaches the topic of culturally competent social work practice assuming that most of the readers are not people of color and relatively few have experience with disabilities or people of color. Thus, an adequate background of knowledge is a requisite for culturally competent practice.

HISTORIC AND CURRENT DISCRIMINATION
Discrimination Based on Culture

 That there are major difficulties experienced by multicultural groups is evident. From historic accounts of inhumane treatment of Native Americans, African Americans, and Asian Americans to current reports of police brutality toward certain populations, there is substantial evidence of systematic discrimination in our society. Most multicultural groups in the United States have encountered some level of prejudice and discrimination in dealing with various societal institutions, including social service agencies.

Moreover, the United States has historically discriminated against multicultural groups. Europeans who colonized this country brought racism with them, which was evident in the wholesale genocide practiced on the indigenous First Nations population. Although our government is predicated upon the primacy of dignity, freedom, equality, and human rights, our economy before the Civil War depended heavily upon slavery. The period between the Civil War and World War II saw many examples of racist behavior toward Native Americans, Asians, and Hispanics. Institutional racism within education was the law of the land until 1954, when the U.S. Supreme Court overturned supposedly separate-but-equal educational systems. Despite this ruling, de facto (actual) segregation of school systems still exists in hundreds of school districts throughout the United States.

In the 1960s, multicultural groups won expanded rights both to attend colleges and universities and to vote without harassment. Of course, these were rights that many white Americans had enjoyed for almost two centuries. Actually, they were rights enjoyed specifically (and only) by males until 1920, when women gained the right to vote. The right to vote was not extended to Native Americans until passage of the Indian Citizenship Act of 1924.

In the 1960s, 1970s, and 1980s, continued efforts were made to improve economic opportunities for people of color (Garvin & Cox, 2001). In the 1980s, a conservative, antigovernment series of political administrations systematically eliminated or reduced the role of the federal government in helping assure equality and economic justice to multicultural groups.

The picture for people of color in the first decade of the millennium remains problematic. African-American families continue to be more likely to fall below the poverty level. Inner-city multicultural groups experience high levels of gang- and drug-related violence. Medical and health problems affect these group members disproportionately. Economic disadvantage affects almost all people of color.

The level of disadvantage, combined with reduced federal and state social service programs and a corresponding increase in the poverty level, makes ignoring the link between governmental policy and economic deprivation difficult. Institutional racism remains a fact of life for a large portion of the multicultural population in the United States.

People of color must deal with experiences that many white families do not confront, such as educational and employment discrimination. In addition, they must help their children understand and cope with racism and its negative effects on self-image.

Most multicultural groups have been victims of discrimination at the hands of almost every major social institution in our society, including schools, the justice system, health care providers, even the social welfare system. Homma-True, Greene, Lopez, and Trimble (1993), after a thorough review of the mental health literature, found that major differences in diagnosis and treatment were made based on the race of the client. Patients of color were more likely to be given group rather than individual therapy and diagnosed with schizophrenia instead of less serious illnesses. Both medication and restraints were used with greater frequency, and people of color were more likely to be admitted involuntarily to mental health facilities. Similar findings of ethnic bias in diagnosing personality disorders were noted by Iwamasa, Larrabee, and Merrit (1995). A study by the U.S. Surgeon General's office (2001) concluded that "Ethnic minorities collectively experience a greater disability burden from mental illness than do whites. The higher level of burden stems from minorities receiving less care and poorer quality of care, rather than from their illnesses being more severe or more prevalent in the community" (p. 168). An Institute of Medicine 2002 report on this topic also concluded that "minorities have less access to mental health services and are less likely to receive needed services, that minorities in treatment often receive a poorer quality of mental healthcare, and that minorities are underrepresented in mental health research" (p. 611). Thus, bias can intrude even in the mental health arena. As a consequence, multicultural group members may be more likely to view such institutions with distrust and suspicion. Unfortunately, social work itself has too long focused on blaming-the-victim psychological change strategies. These strategies assume that the victims have brought upon themselves the problems they experience. For example, assuming that an unemployed father is simply lazy or chooses not to work is easier than understanding the role of racism and cyclical unemployment in a capitalist economic system. Thus, multicultural groups' doubt about whether social workers have the skill or motivation to help solve basic institutional problems is not unusual. Many of the problems of these clients are, in fact, intertwined with the behavior of the oppressive institutions with which they interface.

Discrimination Based on Ability

As mentioned earlier, one of the primary reasons for the creation of the Americans with Disabilities Act was the pervasive and serious discrimination experienced by those with disabilities. This discrimination was evident throughout society, from inaccessible housing, to denial of employment and educational opportunities, to a blatant lack of available transportation. Every major institution in society contributed in some way to limiting opportunity for people with disabilities. They were stereotyped as being unemployable, difficult to train, and in need of segregation from the rest of society. Reactions toward those with disabilities ranged from fear to pity. Some were avoided, and others were viewed as children, needing continued care. Most were simply considered incompetent. Others attributed the disability to a curse or gift from God. Only the creation of a series of laws opened up the possibility that persons with disabilities could lead normal, satisfying lives with dignity. Mackelprang and Salsgiver (2009) briefly describe these laws and the problems they were designed to combat.

The first major laws began with concern about soldiers who received disabilities in wartime. The National Defense Act of 1916 was created to help disabled soldiers find employment when they returned to civilian life. Four years later, the National Rehabilitation Act provided funds so that ordinary citizens could get job training and other forms of employment assistance, in addition to necessary prosthetics. It also shifted some of the cost for these services to the states.

The 1935 Social Security Act provided public funds for blind persons and for children with disabilities. Subsequent changes to the law in 1956 expanded coverage to anyone with a disability. However, there were important restrictions on this coverage, which resulted in

many people not receiving assistance. The Supplemental Security Income (SSI) program, enacted in 1974, guaranteed a basic income for people with disabilities. Federal funds were available to those who had medical disabilities, were unemployed, or were employed with very low wages. One of the ancillary benefits of SSI is that recipients qualify for Medicaid, which covers doctor, hospital, and other medical services.

The 1973 Rehabilitation Act expanded the rights and services available to those with disabilities. It ensured that most individuals with disabilities received priority services and required creation of an individual rehabilitation program. Perhaps equally important, it began a process of eliminating physical barriers in public buildings. Subsequent amendments to the act expanded the responsibilities of federal service providers to create affirmative action plans for those with disabilities and prohibited discrimination against persons with disabilities by any employer who contracts with the federal government.

In 1975, the Equal Education for All Handicapped Children Act was passed. The original act, plus later revisions, covered children between 3 and 21 years of age and mandated that education be provided in the least restrictive or most normal environment. The law also required that parents and the child play a major role in creating an individualized educational plan (IEP) for the child and advocated for services that would not stigmatize or discriminate against the child with disabilities.

Finally, in 1990, the Americans with Disabilities Act was passed. We have described this law earlier and its promise of expanded civil rights and opportunities for those with disabilities. However, the full impact of this and other laws has not been evidenced by greatly higher levels of employment among those with disabilities. There are many possible reasons for this, including the tendency for those doing the hiring to offer employment to those with whom they are comfortable, excluding the disabled (G. Nerrode, personal communication, May 1, 2000). The Bureau of Labor Statistics reports that in 2012, about 18 percent of people with a disability were employed compared to 64 percent for those without a disability. As is often the case, intersectionality also appears to make a difference. For example, blacks and Hispanics with a disability were more likely to be unemployed. The following chart reflects the influence of disability on employment.

Persons with a disability who had completed higher levels of education generally have lower unemployment rates than those with less education. At all levels of education, persons with a disability had higher unemployment rates than their counterparts with no disability.

Unemployment rate by selected characteristics of those without and with a disability, 2012 annual averages

Persons without a disability

- Hispanic or Latino ethnicity: 10.1
- Asian: 5.8
- Black or African American: 13.6
- White: 7
- Women: 7.7
- Men: 8
- Total: 7.9

Persons with a disability

- Hispanic or Latino ethnicity: 19
- Asian: 11.8
- Black or African American: 20.8
- White: 12.3
- Women: 13.7
- Men: 13.2
- Total: 13.4

Percent

Source: U.S. Bureau of Labor Statistics

The largest groups of workers with disabilities are found in the executive and administrative, machine operator, food preparation, and service and sales workers categories, where about 25 percent are employed. This declines to less than 1 percent for the combined areas of computer programmers, librarians, counselors, pharmacists, lawyers, judges, physicians, dentists, and firefighters.

Clearly, the impact of the ADA has not been as strongly felt as is desirable. Those with disabilities still face major obstacles to gainful employment, exacerbated by continued stereotyping and discrimination.

LO 12-2 Enhance Self-Awareness to Eliminate Personal Biases/Values in Work with Diverse Groups

Barriers to Culturally Competent Social Work

Being an effective social worker in a multicultural society requires that we be aware of the many barriers that impede our ability to function. For example, continued acceptance of the myth of the melting pot is a barrier. It uses an inappropriate and inadequate theory that often blames people of color for failing to "melt." Another barrier is the assumption that all who come to our country will be overjoyed to be here. Some may be; others may be depressed or unhappy over leaving their homeland, loss of family members and loved ones, and the enormous burden of surviving in a strange land. Some may be anxious and fear the unknown. Expecting every new immigrant to be delighted is unrealistic.

A third barrier is the tendency to explain people's behavior by reference to their culture or disability. Certainly, many people of the same culture share life experiences. Yet this shared experience does not explain all or even most of a person's behavior. Instead, it ignores the enormous diversity that always exists within a given culture. All multicultural and disability groups are heterogeneous. They are as different individually as any group.

Similarly, lumping all people of any one group together would be a mistake. For example, despite their enormous poverty and multiple problems as a group, most adult African Americans are employed, not receiving public assistance, and not involved in the criminal justice system.

A fourth barrier is an attempt to be color-blind. Color-blindness occurs when a person decides to "treat everybody alike" and pretends that culture and experience have no role in determining behavior. As with the third barrier, this is an extreme position and equally troublesome.

A fifth barrier is our tendency to assume that words mean the same thing to everyone. A client who talks of going home to her "man" may or may not be referring to her husband. Another client who says she "whips" her children may not be admitting child abuse. Language differences can be a source of confusion to social workers and other helpers. This may be particularly problematic to people for whom English is not the primary language.

A sixth barrier is assuming that clients think as you do. Two people can look at the same situation and come to totally different conclusions about what happened, who was at fault, and what should be done. Even eyewitnesses to events do not report similar enough accounts to be trusted in court. We tend to see life experiences in relation to our frame of reference. Expect that clients may think differently than you do. Take the case of a youngster sent to the principal because he was talking in class and got out of his seat. According to the teacher, his behavior was inappropriate to an academic setting and shows he was not paying attention. According to the child, he did not hear what the teacher said and, wanting to understand the assignment, got up to ask a friend in the next row.

A seventh barrier is expecting that clients will understand the social worker's role. The chances are just as likely that some clients will make erroneous conclusions about you based on their experience with other social workers they may have encountered. Clients may need to be told about confidentiality, what is expected of them, and what occurs in a social worker–client relationship. These explanations will be especially important with cultures that are hesitant to share personal information with nonfamily members. For example, in many Asian cultures, admitting a problem to someone outside the family is to lose face and brings shame upon oneself and one's family.

An eighth barrier is insufficient self-awareness. By this we mean a lack of understanding of your own culture (including ethnic heritage, values, beliefs, expectations, and behavior). We may also lack sensitivity to our own biases. All of us grow up exposed to a variety of beliefs about other groups and interpretations of what is "good" or "right." These beliefs are part of what makes us a product of our culture. They are also what often makes us ethnocentric. We may conclude that things are "crazy," "odd," or "different" because they are not what we are used to. Thus, we tend to see life through a set of cultural sunglasses that color all we experience, personally and professionally.

A ninth barrier is the absence of a repertoire of effective, multicultural intervention techniques. This barrier includes both those that are likely to be effective across various groups and those specific to a single group. Much of the remainder of this chapter will address such intervention skills.

A tenth barrier is lack of knowledge of the culture and experiences of specific groups with whom you are likely

to work Practically speaking, the chances that you will become an expert in working with every racial, ethnic, or disability group is small. Rather, you are expected to take the additional time to learn about the cultural and life experiences of those unique groups that comprise your caseload or that live in your geographical area.

Critical Thinking Questions 12.1

 Consider your own cultural heritage and life experience in responding to the following questions.

- With which nationality, ethnic, or cultural group do you most closely identify?
- What practices or activities are most closely associated with your group? To what extent do you engage in these?
- What values of this group do you consider to be most important to you?

LO 12-3 Demonstrate Understanding of How Differences Shape Life Experiences

Integrating Cultural Competence in the Generalist Intervention Model

The various steps in the Generalist Intervention Model (GIM)—engagement through follow-up—are influenced by the worker's knowledge of diversity. Culturally competent practitioners will utilize their knowledge and skills differently within each of the stages of the planned change process. In the sections that follow, we will identify issues, concerns, and topics that can influence worker behavior in the engagement, assessment, planning, implementation, evaluation, termination, and follow-up stages. These sections are intended to be only brief introductions to the influence of diversity on various steps of the helping process.

ENGAGEMENT

Generalist practitioners must learn to approach clients from multicultural groups with a clear understanding of their own view of the world and how it differs from that of others (Fulcher, 2012). For example, individuals who have routinely experienced discrimination and oppression from people in authority may well approach the engagement process with trepidation, anger, and distrust. Workers should be prepared should these feelings be evident in the engagement phase. Additionally, recent immigrants unfamiliar with American norms and expectations may need to be approached differently. For example, common actions such as pointing your finger at an adult Hmong or crossing your arms when talking will both be perceived as insulting, as is direct eye contact (Carteret, 2012; Pitter, 1992). Become familiar with the particular communication patterns and nonverbal issues associated with the groups with whom you will be interacting. When language and cultural differences appear to be a major barrier, consider the sensitive use of interpreters.

The stigma associated with mental health problems may be a barrier in the engagement process and later. Having this understanding may necessitate a more indirect route to discussing sensitive family or individual problems.

Taking a greater amount of time to develop the worker–client relationship when working with multicultural groups is not uncommon. The goal is to create an informal, comfortable communication tone that sets a warm atmosphere for building a relationship.

The eye contact so dear to the hearts of social workers may also be problematic. As we shall see later, some multicultural groups find maintaining eye contact uncomfortable, rude, or disrespectful. Thus, a recent immigrant from Nigeria may well avert his eyes as a sign of respect. The worker might interpret this action as deception without knowing the particular meaning that eye contact holds for different groups. Even the physical distance between worker and client may be an issue. Some groups, for example, may use a distance of less than 15 inches for conversation, whereas the norm for the worker may be 2 feet. Without knowing this differential use of space, the worker may find the proximity uncomfortable or even threatening.

ASSESSMENT

Clients from multicultural groups often live in two cultures, the dominant one and the one associated with their ethnic or racial background. This poses a special challenge because the client must operate in these dual and possibly incongruent environments. That is, a behavior or action effective in one of these cultures may be ineffective or counterproductive in the other. The example of sharing one's meager food or resources with friends or relatives that opened this chapter is a case in point. The worker could not understand why anyone with such limited resources would make the problem worse by sharing with others.

Effective assessment requires recognizing client system strengths. Many groups have multiple strengths that may be overlooked by an insensitive worker or one who focuses on client problems rather than challenges. Consider such areas as spirituality, mutual support, respect for elders, and a willingness to share with others as strengths upon which to build. For example, Kadushin and Kadushin (2013) and Gilbert (2000) suggest the value of practitioners exploring spirituality with clients. This includes assessing the spiritual aspects of clients' lives, considering these as potential resources, and encouraging discussion of spiritual issues individually and with groups. In some cases, practitioners may find it helpful to work with a client's spiritual or religious leader when such efforts are approved by the client and beneficial to the outcome. Another potential source of strength may come from the client's culture. This may include belief systems and cultural values along with resources that may prove useful for planning and intervention. Also look for resources outside the family as possible strengths. Churches and social organizations may be resources that are especially salient for some multicultural groups, especially African Americans, Hispanics, and Asian Americans.

Recognizing that different approaches to understanding and treating physical or emotional illness reflect group traditions and may enhance, and in some cases replace, typical health care interventions is also important. Workers must be open to this possibility.

Our ways of thinking about a client's situation can also affect our assessment. For example, if we think of a family as dysfunctional or multiproblem, are we really focusing on pathology and weakness? Compare these terms to *overwhelmed, multi-stressed,* or *overly stressed,* all of which have a more positive connotation than either *dysfunctional* or *multiproblem.* At times in almost anyone's life it is possible to be overwhelmed or to be facing too many stressors at one time. Using these terms in both your thinking and talking with clients can help normalize the challenges they face without pathologizing, blaming, or judging them. It also focuses attention on identifying the factors that overwhelm individuals and families.

Assessment is also concerned with the client's cultural or racial identity. The extent to which a client identifies with, accepts, and practices traditional values, norms, and beliefs can be an important variable to consider. For example, two First Nations clients may have vastly different identification with their heritage. Assuming that the heritage is equally important to each of them would be a mistake. Assessment should explore the importance of the identity.

Many people from multicultural groups see themselves as "individuals within a collective." One example of this is the fact that in times of family hardship, African-American grandparents are nearly twice as likely to become caretakers of their own grandchildren than are white grandparents (U.S. Census Bureau, 2009). The sense of being part of a collective means that these grandparents are more likely to see themselves as natural resources in critical times. Like other multicultural groups, their relationships with family members, community, their own cultural or racial history, and the larger world are critical to their sense of well-being. That sense of interdependence differs greatly from the typical Anglo-American view of the individual. Without awareness of the importance of the larger picture, assessment decisions are likely to be in error.

Assessing the responsiveness of agencies to the needs of multicultural groups is also important. Consider an agency where workers and administrators do not know the actual demographics of their own service area, lack linkages with agencies that serve multicultural groups, and are unconcerned about having a culturally and racially diverse staff. This agency is contributing to the oppression of multicultural groups. As such, it presents a logical target of change for the generalist social worker.

PLANNING

In the previous example, the unresponsive agency might benefit from a plan that would focus increased attention on building relationships and developing resources with the community. Training of all personnel in order to create an agency truly characterized by culturally competent services is another logical goal.

Planning undertaken to confront community social problems can also be influenced by differences among multicultural groups. For example, North and Smith (1994) report on significant differences among white and nonwhite homeless populations. Homeless white men were more likely to suffer from alcohol problems, whereas nonwhite men reported histories of drug abuse that contributed to their being homeless. Despite equal levels of education and higher rates of employment for nonwhite homeless men, their total incomes were lower than those of whites. White women who were homeless experienced greater rates of interpersonal and intrapersonal difficulties, whereas their nonwhite counterparts suffered primarily from socioeconomic problems. Teruya and her colleagues (2010) also found disparities in health care needs of homeless women from different ethnic groups. As you can see, ending homelessness for each group will require planning for different strategies.

With micro-level interventions, cultural competence may involve knowing "when it is appropriate to reinforce the client's culturally patterned behavior or

problem-solving method and when to encourage adoption of culturally different solutions" (Chau, 1990, p. 126). If the client's culturally sanctioned approach to resolving an issue appears to show some promise, the worker should encourage the client in its use. At the same time, the goal may be to help clients learn additional mainstream behaviors that will help them to surmount the obstacles they face (Chau, 1990).

Another influence on planning is the decision to consider the family as the client instead of the individual when working with Asian clients. Whereas Anglo-Americans focus on the individual, the Asian culture typically places higher value on the family unit. The importance of extended families within Asian and other cultures makes it wise to consider including all family members in development of the case plan. Similarly, within both Hispanic and Asian families, including the elderly in the planning process is important. Their experience and perspectives are respected by family members and should be considered.

IMPLEMENTATION

Implementations that are focused on the individual or family must also be sensitive to the differences among and within multicultural groups. For example, the use of short stories, anecdotes, and analogies may be an effective means of approaching a topic indirectly or symbolically. This approach has been suggested for both Hispanics and Asians to help the client system consider difficult-to-approach issues without feeling threatened. An example might be a client suffering from depression who is not taking her medication regularly. In discussion with the worker, the client admits she is ashamed and embarrassed about having to take drugs every day to cope with what she considers an emotional problem. She thinks she should be able to get over the depression if she just had enough willpower. Rather than reminding the client how important it is to take her medicine daily, the worker addresses the topic indirectly by drawing an analogy. She observes that the client's daughter takes medicine for her diabetes, a biochemical disorder caused by the body's inability to produce insulin. She explains that depression is also a biochemical illness requiring medicine to help the body function as it was designed. She comments that neither mother nor daughter can control biochemical problems through willpower.

Within Asian cultures, the worker will need to be very conscious of nonverbal communication that may have greater importance than spoken words. A professional helping relationship may slowly change to more of a mentor–mentee relationship as the implementation period continues, a difference the worker must consider as more appropriate. Rather than be considered the "expert," a role common at the start of a relationship, the worker will become more of a wise elder. This change in roles increases clients' sense of empowerment and reduces the distance between client and worker. Similarly, the worker may need to self-disclose more than usual, another step to reducing distance. Providing more suggestions and advice than is common is also recommended.

Interventions such as family preservation, some models of which have the social worker as a partner and part of the family available at all times, would likely be considered inappropriate by many Asian families (Fong & Peralta, 1994). A goal of empowering the family may well provoke conflicts with the "clan or larger community" (p. 5). Nor will first-generation Asian males necessarily readily accept a female social worker. First-generation Asians perceive the male as the authority figure and the family system as hierarchical. Social workers would not be perceived as partners either by male or female family members under these circumstances. The role is simply not supported by the culture. Thus, adaptations of the family preservation model clearly would be needed if this approach to implementation is selected.

EVALUATION

There are at least two ways in which evaluation and research are influenced by diversity. First, the use we make of research findings appearing in our professional literature must be tempered by the realization that the results may not apply to multicultural groups. Generalist practitioners need to recognize that much of the research reported in the literature has limited generalizability. This limitation occurs in part because people from multicultural groups are underrepresented or nonexistent among the groups studied. Thus, the study results cannot necessarily be used as a basis for working with diverse clients without determining if the findings are culturally relevant. When examining studies reported in social work journals or at professional conferences, ask yourself if multicultural groups are represented in the research. This process will at least sensitize you to the potential limitations of some research.

The second influence of diversity is on the evaluation of your own practice and the research you undertake as a practitioner. To increase your cultural sensitivity, one of the most important recommendations is to involve the client directly in the evaluation process. Not only is this inclusion empowering, but it also helps reduce clients' feelings that they are being looked at under a microscope.

When deciding what evaluation approach is appropriate to use, you also must consider whether or not the method needs to be adapted to multicultural groups. For example, asking questions in a face-to-face interview may be more effective than giving clients a questionnaire to complete (Marlow, 2011). If you are using existing instruments such as checklists, rapid assessment instruments, and similar items, determining whether or not these items have been validated with multicultural groups would be wise. Look the instrument over carefully to see if there is anything that might be inappropriate for diverse groups. Perhaps a questionnaire on family decision making lists only a mother and father as principal decision makers when the intended audience typically seeks the advice of the clan, extended family members, or others.

Similarly, instruments that were normed on Anglo-Americans cannot be used with equal validity on other groups. What is typical for white college-educated males is not necessarily characteristic of women, non-whites, or those with less education.

When using such devices as client satisfaction surveys, asking whether or not the ethnicity or race of the worker was significant to the client may be helpful, particularly when client and worker are from different groups. Asking the client to address how the worker might have been more helpful can allow the client freedom to address this issue. Contacting those who dropped out of the client–worker relationship to see if diversity issues played a role in their decision is also important.

TERMINATION AND FOLLOW-UP

Diversity issues exist in the termination and follow-up stages as well as the other areas of the planned change process. For example, if racial issues were dealt with (as might happen in multicultural groups or in community interventions), taking time to discuss these topics during termination is important. This process is especially true if the issues were difficult and emotionally charged.

Premature termination may occur when the worker is perceived as culturally incompetent or insensitive to clients from different ethnic or racial groups. This perception could occur because the worker has probed too far too fast or demonstrated lack of respect for the client. Offering clients the opportunity to come back at any time can leave the door open for a subsequent contact. It also communicates worker interest in the client's continued welfare. Periodic follow-up can also achieve the same end.

As you can see, diversity can and does influence each phase in the GIM. Generalist practitioners must be alert to how a client's race, ethnicity, gender, or sexual orientation impacts on the helping process. This alertness is helpful as you seek to become a culturally competent social worker.

Practice Knowledge and Skills

The intent of this section is not to make you an expert on working with multicultural groups. Instead, you should begin to develop an understanding of the experiences of many group members. We also intend for you to learn specific skills that are generally effective with specific groups. The last portion of this section will focus on some principles that are useful across multiple groups.

Please remember that just because an individual is a member of one of these ethnic and multicultural groups does not mean that he or she adheres to all the values and customs described. For example, Chapter 9 discusses how people may become *acculturated*. Acculturation "involves the adjustment and adaptation of the individual from the culture of origin to the dominant culture" (Lum, 2011, p. 55). Clients with various ethnic heritages may embrace aspects of their traditional culture, or they may not. Similarly, they may adhere to traditional customs and values to varying degrees. Each individual is unique. Highlight 12.3 discusses this issue further. The important thing is for you to be as knowledgeable as possible and sensitive to the possibility that these values and issues apply. Keep in mind that the knowledge you have regarding a specific group will be only a starting point when working with diverse groups. Your knowledge of human behavior and the social environment makes you aware that a client's life experiences will profoundly shape his or her perspectives. Thus, two clients from the same cultural background may well differ significantly with respect to their adherence to cultural norms and practices. You will learn a great deal more about clients' cultures and about diversity if you encourage clients to provide this information. If you consider yourself a learner and your clients as potential teachers, it will further your education about diversity.

NATIVE AMERICANS/FIRST NATIONS PEOPLES

Intervening effectively with First Nations Peoples requires understanding the unique history of this culture in North and South America. Unlike all the other groups that eventually populated these regions, Native Americans were here first. To reflect this reality, many authors refer to this group as *First Nations Peoples*. The terminology is also important because it reinforces the fact that Native Americans were an intact nation prior to the arrival of the Europeans. First Nations cultures ranged from highly sophisticated social systems (such as the Aztecs, Mayas, and Incas) to more simple organizations (such as the Paiute). Most were farmers and fishermen living in villages and communities. Though they numbered in the millions, they were no match for the military societies of Europe. Slowly, inexorably driven off their land, they were murdered and subjected to all manners of individual and institutional racism. At various times, exterminating, erasing, or otherwise ridding the continent of First Nations Peoples was federal government policy. Military force was used to destroy tribal communities that refused to obey federal orders to move from their homeland. Tribal leaders were killed by white soldiers or by other First Nations Peoples working for the U.S. Army. Using the melting pot myth, later efforts attempted to assimilate or acculturate Indians with the ultimate goal of destroying forever the group's culture.

In the century just past, the federal government attempted to eliminate tribes by disposing of the reservations where they lived. Massive efforts were undertaken to teach First Nations youth the "white man's way." By removing children from their reservation homes and sending them to Bureau of Indian Affairs boarding schools, the federal government managed to destroy the family lives of millions of First Nations Peoples. In addition, it prevented many children from learning the traditional (and usually nonpunitive) child-rearing approaches used by First Nations Peoples. Rather, the Bureau's actions exposed them to the indifferent (and often brutal) discipline used at the boarding schools. Child abuse among First Nations Peoples was relatively unknown until recently because corporal punishment (administering physical pain such as spanking) was rare. Boarding school personnel used beatings, head shavings, and other indignities to punish First Nations children for such crimes as speaking their native language, observing their religion, or running away from the boarding school. Many of the poor parenting skills noted among some First Nations adults can be traced to these experiences.

Traditional cultural styles of First Nations Peoples are significantly different from those of most European cultures. Knowing these differences is often important for social workers. Applying culturally irrelevant or inappropriate interventions can be prevented with a basic knowledge of the culture of the client with whom we are working. Let us look at a few areas where First Nations cultural values and approaches can influence social work effectiveness.

The Value of Time

Compared to First Nations cultures, white Americans are often said to be in a hurry. Most of us maintain calendars to keep track of our busy schedules. We frequently violate speed limits as we hurry to get to our destinations. We talk of not wasting time or of ways to "save time," although no one has yet found a way to accumulate the time we have saved and use it later.

Traditional First Nations Peoples do not share this near obsession with time. Instead, they have several values that supersede time—values like spending time with people or of not intruding on the life space of others. Practically speaking, this means that they are not married to the clock. Their approach to time is more flexible and relaxed. Consequently, they are less rigid when it comes to the starting time for meetings or being on time for appointments. For example, let us say you have an appointment at 10 a.m. with a First Nations client. If a friend stops by to chat with your client just before your appointment, spending time with that friend may well take precedence over getting to the appointment on time.

Similarly, we frequently advocate that meetings start on time and that latecomers simply experience the consequences of their untimely arrival. First Nations Peoples are much more likely to wait until all the important people are present, even if this means others must wait. The lack of a time focus is really part of a people-focused perspective on the world. Thus, expecting longer periods to develop relationships and to settle on mutually agreeable goals is advisable. Reaching those goals will also take longer. The idea of focusing on people instead of other issues is compatible with the values of the social work profession.

First Nations Noninterference

We mentioned that First Nations Peoples object to intruding in the lives of others. First Nations noninterference could be considered a logical extension of social work's value of client self-determination. Within the culture, resenting workers who try to rush into the interview or rush into contacting is typical for First Nations Peoples. These clients need time to get to know (and trust) the worker and to become comfortable in the social worker-client relationship. This value also means that intrusive, aggressive styles of probing for information are likely to be ineffective. Participatory, self-directed relationships have greater value.

In group settings, the value of noninterference may manifest itself in other ways. Silence and lack of peer pressure are common. Peer pressure is just another way of intruding on others and is unacceptable. In task group situations, this value is apt to mean that decision making will emerge from consensus instead of majority rule. Group decisions are also more likely to take precedence over individual decisions. This means that the will of the group may overrule individual preferences of group members. Members thus defer to the decision of the group. When designing programs to benefit an entire community, maximum involvement of the people to be affected is important. Participatory decision making is critical.

Communication Patterns

We have mentioned the quietness of First Nations Peoples. Indian communication usually is considered to be more nonverbal than in white culture. It is not a loud culture. First Nations children who are quiet in school may be viewed as problems by teachers. Such teachers may be ignorant of the value this culture places on deference to authority and individual dignity (Morgan, 2009).

Native Americans also do not self-disclose readily (Diller, 2007), nor do they share information that might discredit their family members. Family loyalty is important to them. Children are less likely to brag about their accomplishments, a behavior that would seem to place them above others. Conversely, not praising them in front of others is important. Praise that might be viewed positively by others may embarrass First Nations Peoples.

Fatalism

Other Indian values are also important to social work practice. For example, First Nations Peoples show greater acceptance of fatalism (a trait they share with Hispanics). *Fatalism* is the attitude that one has relatively little control over events in one's life and that attempting to change is fruitless because such efforts cannot alter predetermined outcomes. The attitude that "what will be, will be" is anathema to social workers taught to believe that things in life can be changed. Taken to an extreme, Native Americans are sometimes criticized as "lazy." This criticism occurs when those ignorant of First Nations culture misinterpret this more relaxed, laid-back behavior as being negative. Fatalism may well be a logical reaction for any group whose ideas, values, and perspectives are repeatedly ignored, overridden, or devalued by more dominant groups in society. It may reflect a healthy adaptation to overwhelming efforts by dominant groups to subjugate those with less power.

Sharing and Acquiring

A corollary is that many First Nations Peoples do not possess the white value of acquisition for acquisition's sake (Morgan, 2009). In Indian culture, sharing is more important than acquiring for oneself. This aspect often means that First Nations Peoples will share their home, food, and resources with others though it places a strain on their own lives. If you think back to the case that opened this chapter, you will recall the upset social worker wondering how the Black Bear family would take on responsibility for children of relatives when their own situation was so tenuous. Caring for and sharing with others, especially family, is more important than hoarding your own resources. One should realize that this value of sharing is not universal within First Nations culture. For example, it is more important to the Sioux culture than in the Chippewa. However, the value of generosity transcends tribal culture.

Voss, Douville, Little Soldier, and White Hat (1999) provide another lesson on the role of First Nations sharing and the importance of understanding this cultural value. A Lakota child was being discharged from the hospital into the custody of his extended family. "The plan was for the child to live in a tent in the backyard. This was considered inadequate by state social services, who challenged the discharge plan, failing to recognize that it is not uncommon for Lakota children to share close space in the family or relative's home." It was also commonplace for many children from the extended family to "share a small space in the family dwelling or outbuildings or tents" during the summer. The practice "affirms the Lakota value of close kinship bonds and enjoyment of children" (p. 83).

Attending Skills

Attending skills may have to be modified when working with First Nations Peoples. For example, we frequently exhibit the nonverbal behavior of leaning forward toward the client and maintaining eye contact in order to demonstrate our attentiveness. However, both behaviors are inappropriate. Leaning forward may be seen as intruding into the life space of another.

Likewise, First Nations children who do not make eye contact with the teacher, or look away when the teacher looks at them, sometimes give the impression they are not paying attention. These children adopt such behavior because sustained eye contact is considered rude in First Nations culture. As a social worker, you will need to adjust your attending behavior to avoid violating these cultural taboos.

Intervention Styles

Adapting one's intervention style to the culture of the client is a challenge for the social worker. Sometimes a portion of the approaches we normally use will work well. For example, techniques such as restatement, clarification, summarization, reflection, and empathy can be useful with First Nations clients. Similarly, clients' confidence in you as the social worker will increase to the extent that they believe in your ability, trust you, and know you understand their culture. See Highlight 12.2.

Brammer (2012) suggests that person-centered strategies are less likely to work with First Nations Peoples, who may appear more passive. He believes that more directive approaches will be effective. Thus, considering using elements of both approaches may be appropriate. For example, the positive regard, honesty, authenticity, and sensitivity to feelings that characterize

---

HIGHLIGHT 12.2

Online Resources

 EP 2.1.1e

For the generalist social worker practicing with First Nations Peoples, there are several excellent online sources of information. These include:

- Inndianz.com (http://www.indianz.com/). This site provides current news reports covering First Nations issues in the United States.

- National Indian Child Welfare Association (http://www.nicwa.org). This site is a comprehensive source of information on First Nations child welfare.
- WWW Virtual Library—American Indians (http://www.hanksville.org/NAresources/). This site offers the opportunity to search for a variety of resources on First Nations history, culture, and other topics.

the client-centered approach might be used along with behavioral or cognitive-behavioral interventions. This combines the low-key, nonintrusive benefits of the first approach with the confidence-inspiring characteristics of the latter.

Brammer (2012, p. 194) recommends "restorative or healing interventions" instead of focusing only on problems. Flexibility is important on the part of the social worker both in terms of willingness to merge elements of traditional approaches and in scheduling of sessions. Showing respect for the client's culture and individual dignity are important.

One way of increasing client trust in you is through your involvement in other aspects of the client's life. Home visits, participation in tribal activities such as pow-wows (community social gatherings), and an evident appreciation for the culture are useful. Additionally, your office should contain some evidence of your interest in First Nations life. This interest might include paintings, decorations, or books related to First Nations culture.

A Cautionary Note

There are over 560 federally recognized First Nations tribes in the United States (Bureau of Indian Affairs, 2013). Though almost all have experienced varying degrees of institutionalized and individual racism and discrimination, their histories and tribal experiences are often quite different. The result is that individual clients may be different in perceptions, expectations, and behavior. You cannot expect to be an expert on every group. There is no shame in admitting ignorance of aspects of a culture or of a specific meaning or event in a client's life. Sensitivity to cultural influences and a willingness to learn about clients' experiences are essential to work with First Nations and other cultures.

Williams and Ellison (1996) suggest that considering First Nations Peoples on a continuum of lifestyles ranging from traditional to marginal, middle class, and Pan-Indian may be helpful. For example, they suggest that *traditionalists* abide by traditional customs, are more likely to use natural healers for health care, and value inclusion of the family in attempts to help.

Marginal First Nations Peoples are in the middle between their traditional roots and the Anglo lifestyle, which is a stressful position because neither group may accept them. *Middle-class First Nations Peoples* are much more likely to have adopted Anglo lifestyles, including using health care facilities and social workers. They are likely to have more education, less contact with the reservation, fewer family members in their network, and previous experience with Anglo health care.

Pan-Indians have a multitribe perspective and adopt lifestyles that are in concert with traditional First Nations values, though not those necessarily of a particular tribal group. They are in essence mixing a variety of First Nations traditions and are less likely to use Anglo health services or mental health organizations. Recognizing that First Nations Peoples may fall anywhere along this continuum, the generalist practitioner should not assume that all members of this group share similar values, beliefs, and practices.

LATINOS/HISPANICS

Hispanics are one of the fastest growing multicultural groups in the United States. Hispanic culture is often an amalgam of European, Indian, and African traditions and values. Even the term *Hispanic* covers such a wide group of nations as to be somewhat overbroad. For example, *Hispanic* covers people from at least 26 countries, including Puerto Rico, Cuba, Mexico, and Central and South America (Lum, 2011). As Furman et al. (2009) point out: "The cultural and ethnic backgrounds of Latinos are also diverse and include Spanish, Aztec, Mayan, Incan, and Caribbean. Latinos may be of Native American, white, and African American racial or ethnic background" (p. 168). Although the term *Hispanic* is used frequently, *Latino* is preferred by many others. *Chicano,* a term used on the West Coast, refers to Mexican Americans and persons of Mexican lineage born in the United States. Note that *Latina* and *Chicana* are the feminine forms of *Latino* and *Chicano,* respectively.

Most of the groups covered by the term *Hispanic* came to the United States as immigrants. Yet many Mexican Americans can trace their lineage to ancestors who were residents of Texas, New Mexico, California, or Arizona when those territories were annexed by the United States. Consequently, they are not direct descendants of immigrants and share the same claim to birth rights as First Nations Peoples. Like First Nations Peoples, they also share a legacy of institutionalized racism and discrimination focused on genocide and acquisition of their territory (Lum, 2011). Institutional racism, you may recall, systematically produces unequal outcomes for multicultural groups. The history of the United States reflects a consistent devaluing of these groups. This pattern has implications for our current efforts to understand and work with all groups, including Hispanics.

Hispanic culture, like that of First Nations Peoples, has vastly different values, beliefs, and practices from Anglo culture. The term *Anglo* refers to U.S. citizens of non-Latin extraction. In the following sections, we will look at the impact some of these differences have on social work practice.

Family Centering

The typical Anglo value of individualism is at odds with the Hispanic family-centered cultural approach. The Hispanic family represents the one solid refuge from a difficult world (Brammer, 2012). The "family" (*familismo*) may really be a combination of both nuclear and extended relatives and other networks, such as friends and neighbors.

The family is central to Hispanic culture and is hierarchical in structure. That is, the father may be the primary authority figure but the women hold the family together (Brammer, 2012). Children owe respect to the parents but especially to their father. Thus remaining in the home until they marry is not uncommon for children. This tradition occurs in part because children owe a debt to the family that they can never repay. Contrast this belief with the common Anglo idea that parents should do everything possible to help their children.

The closeness of the Hispanic family may be seen as problematic by those assessing the family using typical Anglo approaches. For example, the interdependence expected of, and seen among, family members may be viewed as enmeshment. Enmeshed families inhibit independent functioning of members through patterns of confused or unclear role boundaries. In other words, the family may be viewed as much too close. This type of family structure does not, however, mean that the Hispanics believe individualism is bad; instead, individualism must occur within the context of the family and traditional Hispanic values (Furman et al., 2009). Consequently, efforts to increase the independence (or reduce the dependency) of individual family members may be culturally inappropriate. As such, familismo emphasizes interdependence and collectiveness rather than independence. "Latinos/as draw their strengths, celebrate, mourn, derive their values, create their dreams, and define their sense of self" (Brammer, 2012, p. 117).

Parental Roles

Many Hispanic fathers appear somewhat aloof from the family, especially the children. Commonly, the father is less likely to express emotional support. The father's role is to pursue instrumental roles such as earning a living; thus he may appear more distant. He may not consult the mother in making decisions, yet he expects to be obeyed. The mother's role typically is to balance the father's (Demo, Allen, & Fine, 2000). Mothers receive help in fulfilling this role from other members of the extended family. When intervening in Hispanic families, including other family members who play crucial roles in the family constellation may be necessary.

Similarly, even when the problem seems restricted to a single family member, encouraging other family involvement whenever possible is often wise. Illness, for example, may be viewed as a family affair requiring family intervention. Even if the client does not mention family members, asking about them is appropriate. This interest shows an awareness of the importance of family members to the client. Sometimes, these casual questions will lead to disclosures of problem areas or strengths and can set the stage for further interventions. For example, asking about a daughter may elicit parental concern that she is becoming "too independent" of their control. Asking for further clarification from the parents will help the worker know whether the situation reflects normal parent–child tension associated with adolescent independence, potential delinquent behavior, or other problems needing help.

Communication Patterns

Like First Nations Peoples, Hispanic communication patterns have a strong nonverbal tradition. Thus, the worker must be alert to facial expressions that often provide more clues to feelings than verbal comments. Verbal expressions of feelings are much less common than among white clients. Therefore, you should expect to spend more time in building a relationship and in assessing the situation than would normally be the case. That the client becomes comfortable with you and trusts your skills as a worker is essential.

Interviews should typically begin with a period of small talk reflecting the informality valued by Hispanics. Jumping right in would be considered rude. Like First Nations Peoples, Hispanics dislike being singled out and are apt to avoid competition. Hispanic culture emphasizes being personal and informal in contrast to the Anglo focus on efficiency and impersonality. Thus, Hispanics may appear passive and inappropriately nonaggressive when compared to the Anglo emphasis on competitiveness and quest for achievement.

Fatalism

As with First Nations Peoples, fatalism plays a major role in the Hispanic outlook on the future. Consequently, Hispanics may disregard ideas that seem out of their control. Future-oriented approaches may be of less importance than concrete services offered right now. Thus, helping the family work on a current problem and demonstrating that you and they do have the ability to effect change may be more important. This approach might mean arranging temporary day care for an elderly family member with Alzheimer's disease, while postponing discussion of a son's future college degree. The parents may not believe that they have much control over the latter.

Bilingualism

Learning to speak Spanish clearly facilitates the efforts of a social worker serving large numbers of Hispanic clients. Social work students with ability in language might seriously consider learning Spanish. The shortage of bilingual workers will continue to stymie efforts to serve large groups of Hispanic clients. For example, there are continual problems in getting Hispanics to use community mental health facilities. Bilingual social workers could help confront this problem.

At the same time, the efforts of Hispanic children to learn two languages (English and Spanish) may be a source of stress for them. Learning Spanish at home and English at school may subtly communicate that their native language is not highly valued.

One way that social workers can help negate this message is to stress the importance and value of being bilingual in a rapidly changing population. Not being fluent in English frequently causes difficulties when attempting to access needed social service programs. These programs may not have applications written in Spanish and might not have interpreters readily available. Bilingualism is a valuable skill for eliminating these kinds of challenges.

Intervention Styles

Being bilingual, however, will not help if the worker continues to use interventions that are appropriate primarily for Anglos. Fortunately, the usual approaches associated with good interpersonal interventions will be effective with many Hispanic clients. In other words, empathy, genuineness, warmth, and positive regard toward the client will be helpful. Hispanics value respect and dignity of the person. They may appear submissive when first seen because of their emphasis on not being rude. Attempting to teach skills such as assertiveness may be somewhat difficult, especially for Hispanic women, in view of the patriarchal nature of the culture. Teaching such women to be more assertive and recognize that others' needs do not always have to come first may be appropriate. Workers should remember, however, that teaching assertiveness may place the client at odds with her own culture.

A more directive approach using fewer reflective techniques may be useful when combined with the characteristics described in the previous paragraph. For example, the worker may need to suggest specific actions that the client may wish to take to manage a particular problem. These suggestions can be given in such a way that the worker is seen as providing direct consultation or advice, which the client is free to follow. As always, giving advice to clients carries some risk.

Using group and family interventions may also be appropriate because of the strong sense of connectedness in Hispanic families. Such approaches are often more effective with multicultural groups because of their focus on interdependence.

It is generally recommended that practitioners working with Hispanic clients find out the family's cultural background, country of origin or nationality. Because of the degree of diversity within this culture it is also helpful to inquire whether the client is a member of some ethnic group within a given nationality. If you are not already familiar with a particular group's history or its migration history, ask. Whenever possible, look for formal and information service providers who specialize in meeting the needs of the client's group. Among the list of such providers are civic or spiritual/religious organization, and any other public and private agencies.

A Cautionary Note

We have described how the term *Hispanic* applies to people whose heritage derives from any of several countries. Each of these countries has its own history, which influences how citizens experience the world. Knowing something about this history can help with individual clients. However, even immigrants from the same country are likely to have differences in expectations, social class, and life experiences. Each of these factors has implications for individual adjustment.

In addition, ethnicity is not immutable. People can select aspects or elements of their ethnicity that they wish to observe. Despite the enormous influence culture has on most people, none of us are automatically programmed to accept all the values and beliefs of our culture, whether it be Anglo or Hispanic. We may choose to value certain aspects of our cultural heritage and deemphasize others. Never assume that a Hispanic client (or any other client, for that matter) is controlled by cultural, ethnic, or racial experience. Human beings continue to confound those who would predict and control their behavior.

AFRICAN AMERICANS

Of all the other ethnic and racial groups that comprise the United States, only one, African Americans, came here as slaves. That background and an almost continuous history of maltreatment have combined to produce one of the saddest stories in U.S. history.

African Americans have been the victims of both institutional and individual racism in ways that have left almost indelible imprints on every man, woman, and child. By all the usual outcome measures (economic, educational, and occupational) African Americans have suffered at the hands of a predominantly white nation. African Americans have a substantially lower per-capita income, despite their level of education. Almost 26 percent of African-American families live in poverty, according to the U.S. Census Bureau (2013). As a group they are much less likely to attain the educational qualifications needed for advancement in a technologically oriented society. The jobs that are open to them are more likely to be lower paying and offer the least opportunity for advancement. They experience discrimination in employment, housing, health care, and education. In addition, they experience higher rates of disability than all groups except for First Nations Peoples/Alaskan Natives (U.S. Census Bureau, 2011).

Moreover, African Americans have a higher prevalence of mental disorders, "are under-represented in some private outpatient populations, over-represented in inpatient populations, and more likely than whites to use the emergency room for mental health treatment" (Coridan & Connell, 2003, p. 2). They are also more likely to enter treatment later and drop out of treatment sooner than whites. At the same time, they receive incorrect diagnoses more frequently and when diagnosed are more likely to be labeled as having a severe mental illness than are white clients.

As a nation, we have had great difficulty confronting the multiple problems experienced by African Americans. Even well-intentioned programs that grew out of the 1960s War on Poverty (e.g., Job Corps, Head Start, VISTA) were seriously underfunded and opposed by those who benefited from the status quo. In recent decades, conservative political administrations have systematically dismantled programs benefiting the poor (African Americans included), producing dramatic results. Instead of having fewer people in poverty, a trend that began in the 1960s and continued into the 1970s, we have stagnated. In 2011 we had a larger percentage of people in poverty (15 percent) than was true in 1973 (11.1 percent) (U.S. Census Bureau, 2012d). The homeless population has about doubled since 1980 although the trend from 2008 to 2013 has been downward (National Alliance to End Homelessness, 2013a). Of the homeless population, about 18 percent can be classed as severely mentally ill (National Alliance to End Homelessness, 2013b). This government indifference and neglect has disproportionately affected African Americans. Conservative attempts to gut affirmative action programs (programs designed by employers to encourage hiring of underrepresented workers) have similarly hurt African Americans and other minorities.

Even our attempts to describe African Americans have been problematic. The term *colored people* gave way to *negro,* which was supplanted in turn by *black.* Although some would argue that the words we use are unimportant, words do convey a variety of messages. The term *black,* for instance, is simply a variant of *negro. (Negro* is from the Latin word *niger,* which means black.) Historically, the color black has been associated with ignorance, evil, and darkness. White is associated with light, goodness, and purity, all positive connotations. Although the term *black* may have had value during the 1960s and 1970s (primarily through its association with Black Power), it still has significant limitations. We have given up references to Asians as *yellow* and do not speak about the *red man.* Using terms that lack negative connotations and are consistent with the primary geographical origins of most African Americans (namely, Africa) makes more sense.

Communication Patterns

 You may hear frequent references to the terms *African-American English, Ebonics,* or *Black English.* Often, these terms are an attempt to describe a pattern of word usage and sentence structure used by many African Americans. The connotation, of course, is that Black English is a substandard variant of ordinary English. Actually, the language patterns of many African Americans follow a set of rules as complex and understandable as those of standard English (Horton-Ikard, 2009). Accepting this language and focusing our efforts on understanding African-American clients is far more appropriate than to worry about whether or not the words they use are correct according to Anglo standards. If you do not understand what a word used by the client means, ask. This suggestion does not mean you must adopt language with which you are uncomfortable. To do so may come across as fake or insincere. Proctor and Davis (1996) give a wonderful example of why pretending or assuming you understand what a client has said can be problematic:

Client: Like I was saying, Fred, I miss my main squeeze very much, even though I've got so many hammers after me.
Worker: Well, Joe, it sounds like you're in good spirits. I am surprised in light of the fact that last week you were unhappy over your wife leaving you. Are you feeling better because of the woodworking you're doing?

By not being familiar with some of the words, the worker does not understand that the client still misses his wife a great deal even though several women are interested in him. Asking would have been wiser. Fear of losing credibility should not stand in the way of achieving clarity.

More important than *how* African-American clients communicate is *what* they communicate. Clients may be reluctant to reveal personal weaknesses because they do not know how the social worker will react. Consequently, clients can appear suspicious of or reserved toward persons in positions of power or authority. A possible area to explore in assessment is how past interactions with other social systems have reinforced or extinguished certain behaviors. How have they influenced the person's self-esteem? For example, has the client experienced racism or discrimination that has left him or her feeling angry, inferior, or put down? Recognize that experiences with discrimination may lead to feelings of powerlessness and despair, manifest in nonverbal, resistive, or even hostile, defensive behavior. Sensitivity to the possible influence of these experiences may help you understand the communication patterns of African-American clients.

Family Experiences

Religion plays an important role in the family lives of most African Americans and other people of color. The church serves as a source of inspiration and support as well as a meeting place. African-American churches have played an important part in the history of the civil rights movement. Thus, when working with African-American families, assessing the significance of religious values and experiences for family members is important. Figuring out whether or not the church is a resource for the family is also important. For example, the church should be considered a "significant other" (e.g., like a family member, loved one, or otherwise important person) when determining family strengths and problems. As with First Nations Peoples,

attention should be paid to extended family members who may play an important role in family decisions. Even single-parent households may have others who are playing one or more significant roles in the accomplishment of family tasks. These individuals could be related by blood, marriage, or friendship. Demo et al. (2000) note that African-American families have a rich tradition of kinship care in which members of the extended family provide temporary caregiving for children of relatives. When the possibility of placing a child outside the home is being considered, they recommend inclusion of all family members in the decision-making process. This method can be considered an effective step to preserving the African-American family as well as empowering all family members. Understanding and using these resources can be helpful in the assessment and intervention stages.

Intervention Styles

EP 2.1.5a

We have discussed before the importance of showing respect for clients by using their formal names and titles. This advice remains salient for African-American clients. Do not use nicknames, first names, or other signs of informality unless invited to do so. In other words, use Mr. or Ms. to convey respect. You might ask a client if she prefers Mrs. or Miss, and if she does, use it. Although many consider it a sexist term, being referred to as she pleases is the client's right. This respect also will help ensure that the client knows you are seeking a relationship based on mutual respect and sharing of information, instead of the superior–inferior hierarchy that characterizes many professional–client relationships (such as doctor–patient or lawyer–client). We must communicate respect by recognizing and building upon clients' strengths.

We have also discussed the importance of learning about the cultures with which you will be working. For example, it may be wise to study African-American literature and music to get a sense of how life experiences affect how the world is perceived. For example, many African-American writers and poets paint a portrait in words of what it is like to be a person of color in a white society. Through their eyes you may become aware of events and behaviors that are perceived as negative (e.g., how celebrating Columbus's arrival is not perceived positively by many First Nations Peoples). Similarly, reading African-American newspapers is helpful. These typically reflect the interests and perspectives of group members and give additional insight into their world. As Proctor and Davis (1996) note, the clients may well wonder whether you can help them if you lack knowledge of their culture. Increasing your understanding of the culture can help raise their confidence in you.

In some situations, there may be value in acknowledging the differences in culture and experiences between you and your clients. This acknowledgment is especially true if these differences appear to be problematic. For example, clients who raise questions about whether you can understand their situation should be answered frankly. Most of us do not have to be hit with a brick to know it will hurt. Yet, some clients doubt whether you can understand their feelings if you have not gone through the same experience. Discussing these differences openly and honestly is likely to lead to a more productive relationship with your client.

Clients often expect those in power to be reluctant or hesitant to act on their behalf. With African Americans, there is genuine value in moving aggressively to confront the environmental obstacles with which they may be struggling. Providing concrete services and connecting clients to these services through brokering are important. Avoid vague discussions about what might be done and concentrate on achievements that show your commitment to helping solve the client's problems. To the greatest extent possible, our interventions should be based on a goal of empowering our clients. Empowerment, you may recall, is "the process of increasing personal, interpersonal, or political power so that individuals can take action to improve their life situations" (Gutierrez, 2001, p. 210). Thus, you need to be seen as a peer who helps people develop confidence in their ability to cause change in their lives. The social worker becomes a resource instead of an expert in this process.

Lum (2011) has suggested that one emerging paradigm in social work practice is Afrocentricity. This model includes the cultural values of those of African descent that have significant import for generalist practitioners. For example, social workers frequently use theories that focus on helping clients recognize that their thoughts are the "cause" of many of the specific feelings they are experiencing. These approaches are based on cognitive theory and are concerned with rational thought processes. According to this theory, if the client can just be taught to think more rationally, improvement in the form of fewer negative emotions, less depression, and greater satisfaction with life will result. Other interventions are concerned with helping the client get in touch with feelings, identify them, and work through troublesome emotions. In contrast, the Afrocentric perspective does not consider either thoughts or feelings as occurring independently. Rather, they are coequal, with neither being more important than the other. Rationality and emotionality are two sides of the same coin. As a consequence, practitioners who focus on feelings or thoughts as independent entities will likely be perceived as lacking understanding of the client. A concern with objectivity is also inconsistent with Afrocentricity. The client expects a worker to show positive feelings and avoid the professional aloofness that maintains a distance between helper and helpee.

We also need to assess whether race or ethnicity is a factor within the institutional or organizational environment in which the client must operate. For example, some clients will blame themselves for situations that arise from subtle racism in work or school environments. Although not all problems can be traced to macro-system or environmental causes, the possibility should be considered whenever dealing with people of color. This consideration is especially true when the client is having trouble with other social systems, such as being denied service, given the runaround, or otherwise mistreated.

Macro-Level Approaches to Intervention

Finally, we must look at our own agencies and environments to decide if they are sensitive and responsive to the situations of African Americans and other groups. Does our agency provide outreach services, or do we wait for multicultural clients to come to us? Do we recruit and hire people of color to work directly with clients or only for clerical and less powerful roles? Does the agency's environment reflect the cultural diversity of society? Do we contribute to clients' unhappiness with the system? Are we part of the problem or part of the solution?

A Cautionary Note

Remember that people's behaviors or problems cannot be explained solely by their ethnicity or culture. Be as cognizant of this idea with African-American clients as you will be with other people of color.

ASIAN AMERICANS AND PACIFIC ISLANDERS

Despite the fact that they have been called a "model minority," there is enormous variation within Asian culture (Brammer, 2012). Among these groups are Japanese, Filipinos, Koreans, Burmese, Indonesians, Guamanians, Hmong, Samoans, South Vietnamese, and Thais, to name only a few. Contrary to popular belief,

Asians and Pacific Islanders are not homogeneous. Each group has its own language, history, religion, and culture. The groups differ in terms of group cohesion, socioeconomic status, and level of education. For example, the level of education and socio-economic status of Japanese Americans approaches that of the dominant white majority, whereas for Samoan Americans, both are lower.

In addition, we have both differences between groups as well as differences within each group. Wong, Kim, Lim, and Morishima (1983) and others describe possible factors capable of producing differences within a single group. These factors appear in Highlight 12.3.

As you can see from Highlight 12.3, there are many factors that can affect the Asian-American or Pacific Islander client and produce differences even within peoples from the same national background. Yet, similarities do exist. In particular, *filial piety* and respect for authority are common to all these groups. Filial piety means a devotion to and compliance with parental and familial authority, to the point of sacrificing individual desires and ambitions. Listening to and obeying their parents is the duty of Asian children. Because of this

respect for and obedience to the family, Asians generally seek to enhance the family name. This goal may be accomplished, for example, through occupational or academic success. On the other hand, they are apt to experience a sense of guilt or shame in seeking social services. They may believe that having personal or social problems reflects negatively on their family.

Another important concept among Asian Americans and Pacific Islanders is "losing face" (Ho, Fu, Wai, & Ng, 2004; Shi, 2006). Generally speaking, losing face is equated with being embarrassed, challenged, contradicted, or made to look bad in public. Using protocols such as treating those in authority with respect and seeking to involve these individuals in assessment, planning, and implementation are keys to helping clients maintain face.

Family Centering

Devotion to the family also means that clients are reluctant to discuss personal or psychological problems with nonfamily members. To do so is to bring shame on themselves and their families. The stigma of accepting service arises from the value placed on pride and dignity and the desire to keep difficulties within the

---

HIGHLIGHT 12.3

Enhancing Cultural Competency: Understanding Within-Group Differences

Within-group differences include those factors that produce different expectations, experiences, aspirations, and reactions of immigrant groups of similar national origin. For example, any of these factors might help explain why two people of Vietnamese descent are so different culturally. Although the emotions in various groups may differ little, the life experiences, sense of priorities, and intensity of reactions may vary dramatically. Wong et al. (1983) and Porter and Haslam (2005) have identified some of the factors that can produce within-group differences:

- migrational experiences (degree of difficulty, losses suffered, and so on);
- location of residence;
- generational status (first generation frequently holds to traditional patterns more than subsequent generations);
- degree of assimilation/acculturation (some individuals and groups adapt more readily to a

new culture, whereas others observe "the old ways");
- degree of fluency with one's native language;
- degree of fluency with English;
- extent of identification with one's country or region of origin;
- level and location of education (in one's former country or in the new one);
- age;
- gender;
- composition and degree of intactness of one's family;
- level of integration into formal and informal networks (such as churches, clubs, family associations, and so on);
- religious/spiritual beliefs and values;
- financial resources; and
- whether both of one's parents are from the same nation.

home. There is an expectation that the family should take care of its own needs.

The father's role is that of head of the family. Individual achievement of family members is encouraged when it brings recognition to the family. Whenever possible, you should attempt to work through the father when planning interventions involving the family or other family members.

In addition, family experiences may be different depending upon whether we are working with people who have been in the United States for extended periods (50 or more years), are recent arrivals, or were born here. For example, recent and older immigrants may request specific services, such as advocacy or brokering. American-born Asians are more likely to accept counseling and interpersonal interventions. In addition, the experiences of refugees who left their homeland, suffering enormously in the process, will be quite different from those of other Asian immigrants. Services needed may vary as well.

Clients seen in family settings may appear uncaring or cold to outsiders. This coldness is because Asian Americans and Pacific Islanders are less likely to show much feeling in interactions with their children, especially in the presence of strangers.

Communication Patterns

We have mentioned that many cultures employ nonverbal communication to a much greater extent than verbal communication. This fact is also true in Asian-American cultures. Looks and gestures may convey more than words can ever tell. Therefore, you must be alert to this form of communication. In addition, some gestures may be confusing to the novice. For example, a Japanese person may nod his head to show he is following your conversation. The uninitiated may notice this gesture and mistakenly conclude the client is agreeing with the worker.

As when working with Native Americans, confusing respect for authority with passiveness or refusal to express feelings is easy. Tactfully encouraging clients to self-disclose may help them become more comfortable with the expectations of the social work experience. For example, saying to a mother and father that "it must be very difficult to raise children to respect the old ways" acknowledges how such influences as peer pressure, drugs, or violence in neighborhood schools and urban gangs can undercut the best efforts of the parents.

Showing respect by learning the client's name is also important. For example, in Vietnamese, a person typically has a three-word name. The first word is the family name, the second is the middle name, and the third is a given name. Because formalities are observed, a stranger would call Dinh Phuc Van, "Mr. Van." A close friend would call him "Van." If you recall, the social worker in the vignette at the start of this chapter called the client "Dinh," as if it were an American first name. Not only did he use the wrong name as if he were on a first-name basis, but he did not use the "Mr.," which is a title of respect.

Attending Skills

Attending skills are just as important when working with Asian Americans and Pacific Islanders as with other groups. As with Native Americans, avoidance of eye contact is typical among some Asians. For example, the Vietnamese find eye contact more problematic than do whites. There is also a protocol to the introductions of many Asian Americans. For example, handshakes are generally a part of our lifestyle. We extend our hands to almost everyone. Within traditional Vietnamese culture, however, it is an insult for an adult male to shake the hand of, or touch, adult females. Similarly, avoiding being in a closed room with females over 12 years of age is important. You may remember that John Martin, the social worker greeting the family of Dinh Phuc Van, shook Ms. Van's hand. The combination of failing to show respect by proper use of the man's name, failing to use the term "Mr.," and touching Ms. Van helped contribute to the premature end of this interview.

As newly arrived immigrants, the Vans are more likely to observe traditional customs, a point that the worker ignored. With time, the Vans may adopt such typical American customs as shaking hands in greeting and using first names. As with any such group, the degree of adaptation to the new culture will differ from one generation to another and over time within the same generation. Those who have been here for longer periods are more likely to adopt many of the same norms as native-born Americans. This adaptation is a pattern that has been observed for almost every ethnic group coming to the United States. Thus, the generalist practitioner would be wise to consider this factor when working with immigrants.

Intervention Skills

That clients have confidence in you is important. You should attempt to project a calm, dignified image and have a clear sense of where you are going with the relationship. If you look like you are floundering, clients will lose confidence in you. Thus, a more direct, goal-oriented approach is often preferable. Counselors are expected to be directive, like other authority figures, including teachers. Similarly, you should strive to be reliable and dependable. Both are virtues in the Asian culture.

Self-disclosure may be useful to a degree if it helps engender trust in the worker. But, as always, the purpose of self-disclosure is to help the client, not address the needs of the social worker. This suggestion means that disclosing some of your own experiences is appropriate when it relates directly to what clients are saying and when doing so will help show clients that you understand their experience. It should not be done simply because you feel like sharing information or because you want to talk about your experience.

Paraphrasing is a skill that probably should be used less than in most practice situations because it may seem unnatural to the client. That is, clients may perceive that you do not have confidence in (or that you doubt) what they have said.

Questioning should be used carefully and sparingly. Overwhelming clients or appearing to be bombarding them is easy. Questioning often gives the impression that when all the answers are provided, the worker will give the client a decision or recommendation. Sometimes, the client does not need a "solution" but a forum to talk about ideas and discover his or her own individual solution. Also, asking specific questions about topics such as illnesses or sexual behavior may be considered extremely rude or intrusive. When a client considers some problems private, asking about them may make the social worker appear pushy. Overcoming this hesitancy takes time and patience.

Speaking of time, some Asian-American and Pacific Islander groups (for instance, the Vietnamese) have values about time similar to those of Native Americans. They view time as elastic, not static. Specific limited units of time are unimportant. They are often more patient and relaxed about time, and awareness of this value can make understanding some Vietnamese behavior and viewing it within a cultural context easier.

Community-based services are more likely to be accepted and used in the Asian-American community, which is especially true of those located physically close to the population to be served. These agencies are more likely to develop close ties to the community, enhancing their utility to the clients.

Asian Americans and Pacific Islanders tend to have an orientation that focuses on the group rather than the self (Lum, 2011). Despite this fact, some group situations can be difficult for Asian Americans, especially if they must open up in front of strangers. In group situations, avoiding use of confrontational tactics with Asian-American clients is important. Conflict is generally considered disharmonious. The loss of face that confrontation produces can undermine anything previously accomplished. Yet, assertiveness and considerable structure are appropriate, especially in the early phases of group interventions. Also in group situations, do not expect Asian Americans to compete with one another. Mutual aid and reciprocity are more valued than competition.

Individual approaches that are more useful with Asian Americans and Pacific Islanders include giving suggestions, warning clients about the consequences of particular courses of action, and adapting a more authoritative and direct style (Diller, 2007; Brammer, 2012). For example, with an Asian-American client who is thinking about dropping out of college in mid-semester, you might say: "Dropping out of school before the end of the semester is likely to affect your financial aid, your ability to remain in the dormitory, and your ability to take classes next semester." Clients need to be completely aware of possible consequences to make an informed decision about their options.

The value of cognitive approaches stems from the fact that Asian Americans and Pacific Islanders are often unwilling or unable to talk about their feelings. Cognitive approaches such as appeals to logic and clarifying the client's thinking may be acceptable alternatives to discussing feelings. Another useful technique involves reframing identified problems within the appropriate cultural context. For example, with clients from cultures that explain problems in terms of spiritual issues, the social worker might acknowledge the role that spiritual factors play in the client's life. Likewise, support is an important approach to use with Asian-American clients. This may include supporting traditional family or cultural values or roles that the client may see as threatened or undervalued (Brammer, 2012). Focusing on willpower and self-control approaches also fits in nicely with the Asian culture's belief system. For example, you might stress to the Asian-American client previously described that she is the one who decides whether or not she achieves her goals and that she must make the decision to stay in school. This approach emphasizes the client's responsibility for her actions and her control over her future. Additionally, you may teach clients assertiveness skills, but you must do this carefully. A skill useful for navigating American society may be problematic in an Asian culture. For example, a traditional Asian-American wife who suddenly becomes more assertive with her husband can provoke marital problems that did not previously exist.

Like many other cultures, Asian Americans and Pacific Islanders are more likely to recognize the value of indigenous healing approaches. The use of acupuncture, massage, natural medications, and herbs should not be discouraged simply because the worker does not recognize or use these treatments. Use of these approaches typically stems from cultural explanations of mental or physical problems. Problems are thought to be caused by the mystical (supernatural) or to be punishment for failing to abide by cultural norms. In some instances, the problem also may be attributed to bad luck. Often, convincing the client both to use these natural approaches and to consult a physician is possible. You can thus assure the benefits of both cultures' wisdom.

Empowerment is a goal to which we should strive with all groups that have been historically exposed to or are presently experiencing discrimination and prejudice. However, as Patel (2007) has noted, this concept must be adapted with Asian Americans. Clients who are trying to live between two cultures, often with conflicting values, may experience social or emotional problems. Coming to the United States was a major culture shock for many Southeast Asians. For example, problems with low self-respect may be common to groups that, after coming to America, have to accept welfare or low-status employment. They need help to understand and negotiate the systems that are causing or contributing to the problems.

Another way of showing respect for clients whose native language is other than English is through the skillful use of interpreters. However, children should never be used as translators for adults. Such juxtaposing of family roles causes embarrassment for both child and parent. When an interpreter is used, it should be another adult, preferably one already trusted by the client. You should address your questions to the client by looking at the client, instead of talking to the interpreter. Some videotaped interviews look as if the client is invisible because the worker talks only to the interpreter, which is a mistake.

Finally, focusing efforts on providing concrete services such as referrals, housing resources, and economic assistance in an atmosphere of respect for the client and his or her values is appropriate. Concrete services show the efficacy of the social worker and the ability to help the client meet identified needs. They also, in turn, increase the client's confidence in the

worker and can open the way to the client seeking help in additional areas.

A Cautionary Note

Clearly, there are both similarities and dissimilarities among the various cultural groups with which you may come in contact. Asian Americans and Pacific Islanders are extremely diverse groups. Aiming to adopt strategies that will work with all the groups subsumed under this title is logical, nut to do so would likely be a mistake. In a later section, we will look at some techniques that generally can be used with a wide range of Asians and other people of color. However, alert social workers must constantly guard against generalizations that do not apply to the particular clients with whom they are working.

Critical Thinking Question 12.2

 Based upon your current knowledge of each of the following groups, identify one or two traits, values, or behaviors you believe are common to traditional members of the group.

- African Americans
- Hispanics/Latinos
- Asian Americans
- First Nations Peoples

PEOPLE WITH DISABILITIES

As with people from different ethnic and cultural groups, people with disabilities share similarities and many differences. In this section, we will identify some of the ways in which social workers can become more effective in meeting the needs of those with disabilities.

Language and Communication

Improving our ability to communicate with people with disabilities requires a rethinking of some of the language we habitually use. Often we speak without thinking about how others might construe its meaning. The language we use can perpetuate stereotypes and diminish the worth and dignity of those with whom we work. The Coalition (1994), Brammer (2012), and Lum (2011) provide some excellent guidelines on the use of language, as noted in Highlight 12.4.

Social Work Roles

Social workers can adopt a number of roles when working with various populations having disabilities.

HIGHLIGHT 12.4

Talking About Disabilities—Some Dos and Don'ts

Do

- Refer to a person's disability only when it is relevant to do so.
- Use the word *disabled* instead of *handicapped.*
- Become familiar with specialized services dedicated to meeting the needs of people with disabilities.
- Encourage clients to avail themselves of such services that address specific needs.
- Refer to the person first and then the disability when this is needed (e.g., a woman with a cognitive disability rather than a mentally disabled woman). Remember that the client is a person first and foremost and is not defined by the disability. As mentioned earlier, an exception to this guideline may be needed with certain clients with hearing impairments.
- Ask a person with a disability before trying to help him or her.
- Follow the walking or talking pace of the person with the disability.
- Assume that a person with disabilities has other strengths and abilities.
- When meeting a person with a visual impairment, introduce yourself and anyone else who is present.
- Recognize that human beings are more than just physical bodies.
- Continue to use terms such as *see, walk,* or *hear.* Avoiding these terms is awkward and overemphasizes the disability.
- Use the term *accessible* to describe bathrooms and parking spaces.

Don't

- Use terms such as *crippled* or *defective* when referring to people.
- Refer to people with disabilities as "the disabled," "the mentally ill," or "the blind."
- Employ terms that are unnecessarily derogatory, such as *Mongoloid* or *spastic.*
- Use terms such as *invalid, victim of,* or *suffers from,* which are negative in application.
- Refer to the able-bodied population as "normal."
- Use terms such as *wheelchair bound* or *confined to a wheelchair.*
- Assume that people with a communication disorder such as a speech impediment, hearing loss, or motor impairment have cognitive disabilities as well.
- Suggest that those with disabilities are special, heroes, or in some way out of the ordinary because they cope with their disability.
- Use the term *handicapped.*
- Lean on a wheelchair when talking; it is someone else's personal space.
- Use terms such as *dwarf or midget* to refer to people of small or short stature.

The following are suggestions for working with people who have hearing impairments and people with psychiatric disabilities.

People with Hearing Impairments. Like intellectual or mental disabilities, hearing impairments often appear to be such an invisible disability that it is easy for social workers to ignore them. People with this disability may have minor or more serious degrees of impairment and, contrary to popular opinion, hearing aids often do not correct hearing in the same way that glasses improve vision. Unclear, fuzzy, or overly loud background noises may result in jumbled messages. Frustration with the device's limitations frequently results in a decision not to wear the hearing aid. In addition, not all deaf people use American Sign Language to communicate. Communicating with those having a hearing impairment requires greater patience. The challenges and experiences faced by those with a hearing impairment have helped result in the creation of pride groups that affirm their status. As Lum (2011) points out, deaf persons often use different language to refer to the term "deaf." The hearing impairment is referred to with a small "d," whereas the Deaf culture is expressed with a capital D. This has led many to develop pride in belonging to the Deaf culture. They also prefer to refer to persons with a hearing impairment as a "deaf person" rather than "a person with deafness."

Recommendations for behaviors that are sensitive to those with hearing impairments include such things as speaking clearly and a bit more slowly, leaving pauses between words as needed to ensure comprehension. Facing the individual and maintaining good eye contact are also appropriate. Although a louder tone may be needed, it is not necessary to yell—think about how you feel when you are yelled at. Avoid speaking into someone's ear, as the absence of visual cues may inhibit your message. Avoid placing your hands in front of your mouth or any other gesture that reduces the client's ability to see your face.

It is also important to find other ways of communicating when needed. Change your wording or rephrase a question if the client does not understand it. Use drawings or pictures as needed to convey topics where words would be confusing. Many social workers have learned sign language to help them communicate with their clients who understand American Sign Language (ASL). Advocate for persons with a disability when they are not receiving appropriate services. Be aware of a variety of coping devices available for those with hearing disabilities. These include telephone devices for the deaf (TTD) and flashing light systems that operate when the doorbell is rung, an alarm clock goes off, a baby monitor picks up sound, or a smoke alarm rings. There are also closed-caption devices on television and similar devices at the movies to assist those with hearing deficits. Finally, hearing dogs are used in a manner similar to seeing-eye dogs. They alert owners to sounds such as telephones, doorbells, and smoke alarms.

Agencies can also become more sensitive to those with hearing impairments. Phone calls where the client asks for information to be repeated may be a sign of this disability. Carpeted floors tend to facilitate conversation, whereas solid surfaces provide acoustical problems. Adequate lighting can also ensure that the client can see the worker's face and more easily read lips or recognize other visual clues. In settings with large numbers of people with hearing disabilities (such as nursing homes), social workers should be familiar with such things as proper placement of the hearing aid, battery replacement, and how to turn them on and off. Family members can also be helped to understand the problems experienced by the person with the impairment.

People with Psychiatric Disabilities. Persons with mental or psychiatric disabilities often struggle not only with their own impairment but with societal negative attitudes toward mental illness. Many such disabilities are overcome, managed, or controlled by various therapies, alone or in combination with medication. Nevertheless, the stigma often remains well after the individual has overcome the disability. The serious and chronic nature of some mental illnesses often places a tremendous burden on family members coping with a troubled child, parent, sibling, or other relative. This includes veterans returning from war coping with posttraumatic stress disorder (PTSD) and combat-related brain injuries. Mosher-Ashley, Bogen, Ates, and Franklin (1996) and Sheafor and Horejsi (2012) recommend that when working with clients having psychiatric disabilities, you should be alert to the potential for burnout among family caregivers. This means spending time talking to the caregivers to assess the need for respite care or alternative placement. Helping caregivers learn to anticipate and manage behavioral problems common to chronic mental illness can strengthen their capacity to continue in their role. Educate yourself about self-help organizations that exist solely to help those with mental disabilities. Most larger communities have one or more such groups. These organizations provide a sense of community as well as therapeutic value for the client. Many (such as the National Alliance for the Mentally Ill [NAMI]) also serve as advocacy bodies for their members.

It is also important to encourage clients to stay on their medication, remain in therapy, continue with their group, and so on and to give specific reasons for this. It is critical that the social worker remain upbeat and confident that clients can manage with their disabilities. You may be the only person who has faith in their ability to survive.

General Intervention Principles

Mackelprang and Salsgiver (2009) provide a set of general guidelines that will be helpful for social work intervention with people experiencing disabilities. The first principle is that social workers should always assume people are "capable or potentially capable" (p. 436). It is part of our responsibility to help them use their capability or to develop it more fully. Though limited in one dimension, such as ability to hear, the client is able to think, write, and act. We should always recognize the other parts that comprise the whole individual.

The second principle is to refuse to accept interventions or approaches that target the problem as being the individual who in turn must be "fixed." Many of the problems experienced by those with disabilities are the result of stereotyping, prejudice, discrimination, and the outright refusal of individuals, agencies, organizations, communities, and others to make appropriate accommodations.

The third principle is that, at least at one level, intervention is a political activity that recognizes how the access to societal rewards and benefits affects persons with disabilities. If societies had already taken all needed steps to provide reasonable accommodations, we would likely view children with disabilities the same way we view our own children. That is, with the right combination of appropriate education, training, and opportunities, they will become adult members of society. On the other hand, if opportunities for our children are blocked or nonexistent and/or education and training are substandard, the chances increase that we will recognize our children as a social problem. Thus, disability is a "social construct" that must be viewed in the context of the society in which it exists.

The fourth principle is that disability has both a history and a culture. Persons with disabilities often share a history of "oppression, containment, and isolation" (Mackelprang & Salsgiver, 2009, p. 437). You also need to know the political process and how it contributes to the well-being of those with disabilities.

Despite discrimination, there is also the possibility of joy to be found in disability. This assumes that most people with disabilities can and do lead satisfying lives. We contribute to this possibility when we recognize that having a disability is another characteristic like ethnicity, gender, or sexual orientation that helps make this a diverse and fascinating world.

Finally, people with disabilities have the right to manage their own lives. They have the same right to accept or reject services as those without disabilities. They also have the right to live as independently as possible with "the same rights and opportunities as nondisabled persons" (Mackelprang & Salsgiver, 2009, p. 438). Helping them achieve that is a primary role for the generalist social worker.

Developing Culturally Competent Interventions

EP 2.1.4b

Culturally competent social work requires skills in several areas: attending, assessment, and intervention. Highlight 12.5 provides several recommendations important in cross-cultural assessment.

Lum (2011) and Green (1999) discuss the attributes of a culturally responsive social worker. They recommend that workers should think about clients in terms of both group strengths and limitations in addition to individual problems. In other words, you should be able to use knowledge about clients' racial or ethnic group in the assessment process (see Table 12.1). Simultaneously, you must remember that membership in a particular ethnic group does not automatically explain a person's behavior.

Other characteristics of a culturally responsive social worker include recognizing one's own cultural limitations and appreciating cultural differences. Our own biases and anxieties when working with multicultural groups can become a problem. Anxiety or guilt can get in the way of being empathic. Moreover, we may tend to transfer our reactions to situations to clients, assuming they will react, feel, and think as we do. A willingness and eagerness to learn about a client's culture will go a long way toward building better cross-cultural relationships.

LO 12-4 View Themselves as Learners and Clients as Teachers Regarding Cultural and Other Differences

Dillard (1983) has summarized his recommendations for effective cross-cultural interventions, focusing largely on interpersonal dimensions and attending skills. Practitioners should:

1. Maintain awareness that nonverbal communication probably constitutes more of the communication in a counseling relationship with people of color than does the verbal component.
2. Recognize that eye contact can be a problem for many ethnic groups.
3. Use both open-ended and closed-ended questions. They are almost universally acceptable.
4. Remember that reflection of feelings works with many cultures but not with all (in many cultures, reaching for feelings should be used carefully and slowly).
5. Recall that paraphrasing generally is an acceptable technique in most cultures.
6. Utilize self-disclosure judiciously.
7. Give interpretations and advice in cultures expecting a directive helper.
8. Summarize from time to time.
9. Use confrontation appropriately and carefully with certain racial groups.
10. Remember that openness, authenticity, and genuineness are respected in all cultures.

HIGHLIGHT 12.5

Strategies for Cultural Competence

1. Consider clients first as individuals, then as members of a multicultural group, and finally as members of a specific group. This method avoids overgeneralizing.

2. Do not assume that ethnic identity tells you anything about a person's values or behavior. Within-culture differences are substantial, and two clients from the same culture may have vastly different life experiences.

3. Treat "facts" you have learned about cultural values and traits as hypotheses and subject them to testing with each new client.

4. Remember that multicultural groups are at least bicultural. That is, they all live in at least two cultures, their own and the majority culture. The percentage may be 90 to 10 in either direction, and the values systems may well be in conflict.

5. Allow clients to tell you which portions of their cultural history, values, and lifestyle are relevant to your work with them.

6. Identify strengths in the client's cultural orientation that you can build upon. Help the client identify areas that create social or psychological conflict related to biculturalism and work to reduce dissonance in those areas. Also, help the client adopt some Anglo behaviors in settings where such behaviors are important. Like tools, they do not need to be used in every situation.

7. Be aware of your own attitude about cultural pluralism. Know whether you tend to promote assimilation into the dominant society or you stress the maintenance of traditional cultural beliefs and practices. Your own biases and perspectives are important and can affect your work with clients.

8. Engage your client actively in the process of learning what cultural content should be considered by asking clearly about the client's experiences, beliefs, and values.

9. Keep in mind that there are no substitutes for good clinical skills, empathy, caring, and a sense of humor.

10. Demonstrate interest in a client's traditions and customs.

11. Consult traditional healers and spiritual leaders.

12. Recall that respect and courtesy are always culturally appropriate.

Sources: Lum, D. (2011). *Culturally competent practice.* Belmont, CA: Brooks/Cole; Williams, E. E., & Ellison, F. (1996). Culturally informed social work practice with American Indian clients: Guidelines for non-Indian social workers. *Social Work, 47*(2); Proctor, E. K., & Davis, L. E. (1996). The challenge of racial difference: Skills for clinical practice. In P. L. Ewalt, E. M. Freeman, S. A. Kirk, & D. L. Poole (Eds.), *Multicultural Issues in Social Work.* Washington, DC: NASW Press.

Dillard (1983) concludes that using approaches that are not culturally sensitive is a form of ethnocentrism, a perpetuation of racism, and an imposition of one group's ideas on another.

Whenever we work with clients from different culture groups, it is important to explore how clients and their respective reference group see a particular problem. The way a person defines or views a problem is often affected by that person's culture. It is often useful to find out the views of important members of the client's family, including extended family members and nonmembers who have family status, such as godparents.

Whenever possible, we should focus on the specific problems for which the client sought help before getting into areas where the client has not yet seen a problem. For example, that a client is showing signs of

serious problems in his marriage may be clear to us from an initial session. However, the client has sought help for problems with his oldest son. Thus, we should first focus our attention on this area.

As a corollary, you should use the client's definition of a successful intervention, not just your own. Sometimes, the client defines a problem as "solved" although the social worker will recognize additional areas where work could still be done. Self-determination is especially important in work with multicultural groups. Likewise, demonstrating respect for the client's worth and dignity will be effective in all cultures.

Openness to the use of indigenous (natural) helpers is also recommended. For example, many cultures value natural helpers (such as *curanderos,* medicine men) and other paraprofessionals. When clients have faith in the work of these auxiliary helpers, we should

TABLE 12.1 A Brief Summary of Cross-Cultural Differences

	Family Versus Individual Orientation	Respect for Elders	Concern with Shame and Loss of Face	Approach to Time	Fatalism	Importance of Spirituality/ Religion
African American	Family	High	No	Flexible	No	High
Asian American	Family	High	Yes	Depends on group	Some groups	High
First Nations Peoples	Family	High	No	Flexible	Yes	High
Hispanic American	Family	High	Yes	Flexible	Yes	High
Anglo-American	Individual	Low	No	Rigid	No	Low

not discourage their utilization. Using both clients' cultural resources and those of their community are appropriate helping activities.

In some situations, there really is no easy or simple solution to be found. For example, clients have realistic problems such as getting along on a public assistance budget. No amount of counseling will eliminate this problem. Providing empathy and helping clients find creative ways to stretch their budgets have their place but also their limits. Ultimately, political stances strongly supporting adequate resources for human service programs are more helpful. Those stances include writing and calling your political representatives, lobbying for increased budgets, and working with the NASW and other organizations. In addition, social workers must become active in the political process, which is the only way to ensure that elected officials at the school board, city council, legislature, Congress, governor's office, and White House are sensitive to diversity and the specific needs of multicultural groups.

Moreover, social workers need to continue to focus efforts on political and social action to create changes that benefit those who have been historic victims of discrimination. For example, health care should be available to all citizens and not be dependent solely on the beneficence of an employer. Recently, too many companies and businesses have strived to hire part-time employees to avoid paying the health and other benefits available to full-time employees. Such policies affect multicultural groups and women adversely and disproportionately.

In addition, we need to encourage research that tests various approaches to understanding and intervening in problems experienced by various groups. We should know which interventions work best with which groups and why. Our level of understanding in this area remains rudimentary at best.

Critical Thinking Questions 12.3

EP 2.1.3

Based upon information contained in this chapter, consider the following:

- Give two examples of between-group differences and within-group differences. Why are these differences important?
- Identify two indigenous or natural helpers whom clients might utilize. Why might a client trust these resources over more modern ones?

Chapter Summary

The following summarizes this chapter's content as it relates to each learning objective (LO) presented at the beginning of the chapter. Chapter content helps prepare students to:

LO 12-1 Recognize how cultural structures and values may oppress, alienate, or produce privilege/power.

An enormous diversity within the populations of the United States is both a source of pride and a strength for this country. At the same time, those who are different from the majority have faced long and continued discrimination, oppression, and marginalization. Many have endured social and economic injustice simply because of the ways in which they differ from the mainstream culture. A multitude of examples highlight the ways in which various groups have been oppressed. From the enslavement of African Americans to policies of extermination of First Nations Peoples, the early history of our country is replete with policies and practices that justified mistreatment of others. In more modern times, cultural values that sanctioned discrimination against people with disabilities were finally challenged by the Americans with Disabilities Act. However, even this law and others fail to address the extent and depth of discrimination experienced by those with disabilities. In addition, the current animosity and resentment expressed toward immigrants and refugees reflects an ongoing struggle within our culture to humanely deal with differences.

Ten years into the 21st century, evidence abounds of the ways in which our culture's structures and values harm others. People of color are more likely to be poor, homeless, unemployed, incarcerated, and/or victims of inadequate treatment in all realms of society. Race remains a basis for some, but certainly not all, discrimination. Social workers need to remain observant and sensitive to their own actions as well as the policies and practices of organizations, communities, and other institutions that have the power to oppress others.

LO 12-2 Enhance self-awareness to eliminate personal biases/values in work with diverse groups.

Effective cross-cultural social work practice demands that social workers recognize the extent to which their own values, beliefs, and biases impact on their thinking about diverse groups. It requires acknowledging that we all have a culture that has influenced us profoundly in ways we have often not considered. Social work practitioners also need to gain exposure to the values and experiences of other groups that may differ from us by virtue of their skin color, ethnicity, disability, gender, or sexual orientation. Learning as much as possible about the groups with which we work can help a great deal in this regard.

LO 12-3 Demonstrate understanding of how differences shape life experiences.

Using the knowledge we have of human behavior and the social environment, values, and diversity, we can demonstrate our awareness of the challenges faced by clients whose life experiences differ from ours. We can show in each step of the Generalist Intervention Model (engagement, assessment, planning, intervention, evaluation, termination, and follow-up) that we recognize that people's lives have been influenced significantly by a variety of factors. To this understanding, social workers also can bring a repertoire of culturally sensitive practice skills that are most effective with specific groups.

LO 12-4 View themselves as learners and clients as teachers regarding cultural and other differences.

Recognizing that no social worker can know all that needs to be known about other groups, it behooves us to learn from our clients. If we approach clients with an openness to learning about their lives, values, beliefs, and customs, we demonstrate receptivity and a genuine interest in them. Regardless of the individual's culture, however, we should always consider ourselves as students of others. This also means viewing clients as teachers who can help us be come more effective social workers.

Competency Notes

The following identifies where Educational Policy (EP) competencies and practice behaviors are discussed in the chapter.

EP 2.1.1e Engage in career-long learning. *(p. 455):* One of the foremost reasons for career-long learning is the need to learn about the culture and experiences of other groups in society, especially those that have experienced discrimination and oppression.

EP 2.1.2a Recognize and manage personal values in a way that allows professional values to guide practice. *(p. 448):* Social workers need to be aware of their values and how they can be a barrier to cultural competence. Professional values must take precedence over one's personal values.

EP 2.1.3 Apply critical thinking to inform and communicate professional judgment. *(pp. 465, 470):* Thinking critically about our knowledge of different diverse groups can help us avoid mistakes that perpetuate stereotypes.

EP 2.1.4a Recognize the extent to which culture's structures and values may oppress, marginalize, alienate, or create/enhance privilege/power. *(p. 443):* The experiences of many groups exemplify the ways that the larger culture can oppress, marginalize, and alienate subordinate populations on the basis of race, sexual orientation, and religion. *(p. 446):* People of color often must prepare their children to understand and cope with racism and its negative effects on self-image. *(p. 448):* The melting pot myth was a convenient way of blaming people of color for not fitting in with the majority society. *(p. 446):* The past history of groups such as First Nations Peoples has been characterized by official government efforts to exterminate, erase, or otherwise eliminate them.

EP 2.1.4b Gain sufficient self-awareness to eliminate the influence of personal biases and values in working with diverse groups. *(p. 449):* Workers must recognize that the knowledge they have about the experiences of diverse groups is limited and guard against making unwarranted assumptions. *(p. 468):* Considering one's own cultural heritage and life experience can help the social worker develop greater self-awareness.

EP 2.1.4c **Recognize and communicate their understanding of the importance of difference in shaping life experiences.** *(p. 453):* It is important for social workers to convey their awareness and acceptance of the fact that a client's life experience can profoundly influence their perspectives, worldviews, and expectations. Life experiences can foster a positive outlook on life or lead one to view the world from a negative perspective.

EP 2.1.4d **View themselves as learners and engage those with whom they work as informants.** *(p. 450):* Understanding the salience of a client's culture or racial identity requires that we encourage and allow the person to share this information with us while avoiding preconceived judgments. *(p. 453):* Take every opportunity to learn from clients regarding their life experiences.

EP 2.1.5a **Understand the forms and mechanisms of oppression and discrimination.** *(p. 447):* Laws such as the Americans with Disabilities Act were designed to help ensure that people will not face discrimination because of their disability. Discrimination against those with disabilities prevented them from gaining employment and limited their educational opportunities. *(p. 459):* What African-American clients are able and willing to communicate with social workers may well be affected by such things as past patterns of discrimination and feelings of powerlessness, and despair. In some cases, these experiences may be manifested via nonverbal, resistive, or defensive behavior. *(p. 460):* Race and ethnicity can be factors within institutional or organizational environments in which clients must operate. Subtle racism can cause clients to blame themselves for their misfortune when the environment may share part of the responsibility.

EP 2.1.6b **Use research evidence to inform practice.** *(p. 451):* When trying to identify ways to help homeless populations, it is important to be familiar with research that suggests that no single solution to homelessness will work with everyone. Many homeless individuals experience vastly different challenges because of such factors as their skin color or gender. *(p 452):* Before accepting research findings as legitimate and possibly generalizing the results, it is necessary to determine whether multicultural groups or individuals were represented in a particular study. Generalizing from one group to another carries significant risk.

EP 2.1.10e **Assess client strengths and limitations.** *(p. 450):* One source of strength that must be considered is the cultural values of a particular group.

On the Internet

Visit the *Understanding Generalist Practice* CourseMate at **www.cengagebrain.com** for resources such as quizzes, glossaries and videos.

Gender-Sensitive
Social Work Practice

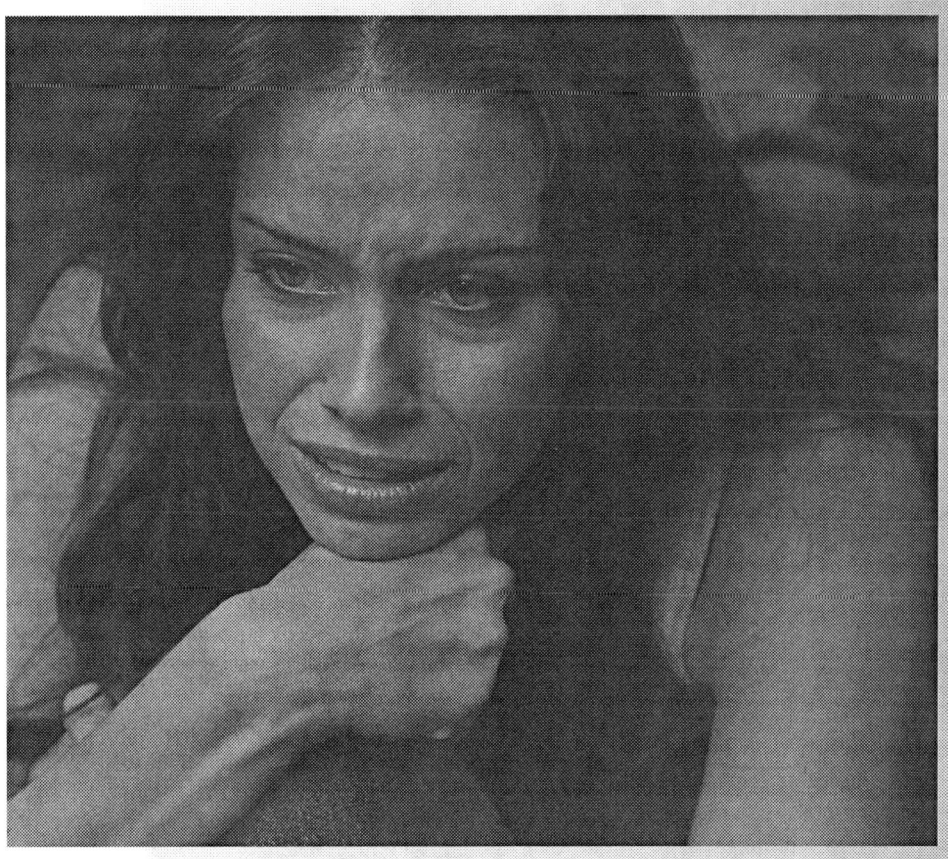

© iStockphoto.com/Stock Shop Photography LLC

Learning Objectives   *This chapter will help prepare students to:*

LO 13-1   Develop self-awareness about gender sensitivity.

LO 13-2   Work with women using the Generalist Intervention Model.

LO 13-3   Examine feminist perspectives on generalist practice.

LO 13-4   Empower women as individuals.

LO 13-5   Provide assistance to women as survivors of sexual assault.

LO 13-6   Intervene with battered women.

LO 13-7   Examine the feminization of poverty.

JULIA, AGE 23, and her four young children are homeless. All the shelters are filled.

Married at age 17, she never worked outside of the home. She and her children had always been poor, her husband jumping from one low-paying job to another. Last month, her husband told her he was sick of her and all his responsibility and abruptly left without telling her where he was going. Julia has no money and desperately needs food and clothing for her family. She has no relatives or other personal support systems to turn to for help. Also, to remove herself from her homeless situation permanently, she needs job training along with concurrent day care.

Jeannette, age 29, was raped 14 months ago and just discovered she has AIDS. Her health has deteriorated rapidly. She desperately needs health care, including expensive drugs that could help her keep at least some of the more severe infections at bay. She had been a secretary, but her health problems no longer allow her to work. Her savings are completely depleted.

Danielle, age 15, has been on the streets for 2 years and is addicted to cocaine and alcohol. She ran away from home because her stepfather had been sexually abusing her since she was 11, and she could not stand it anymore. She needs both a home and an expensive rehabilitation program to survive.

Gertie, age 37, is violently assaulted by her spouse on a regular basis. The beatings are getting worse. She does not know how long she literally can live in her environment. She is only one of about 150 battered women identified in her small midwestern town. Counseling, day care, legal aid, and a place of respite for these women are badly needed. However, a minimum of $45,000 is required to keep the shelter for them open for another 3 months.

Ruth, age 57, has been divorced for 23 months. Her ex-husband, a businessman 2 years her senior, left her to run off with a 26-year-old woman. He got an expensive lawyer and manipulated most of their assets so that they were unavailable to her. She received half of the money from their house and $430 a month in alimony for 2 years. Their house was beautiful, but their equity in it was relatively small. As a result, Ruth now has almost no money left, and her alimony is about to stop. Her ex-husband has spent 35 years establishing a career for himself. He is well off. Ruth, however, has spent her life taking care of his home, entertaining his associates, and doing charity work for her community. She has no experience working outside of the home other than the minimum-wage job she has managed to get at a local frozen yogurt store. Her cash is almost gone. What she earns now will barely pay for her rent, let alone for her food, health care, and other needs. She has no idea what she will do.

Introduction

All of the preceding situations involve women. All portray situations and conditions either unique to women or more likely to characterize women than men. The core issues for most of the examples are poverty and violence, two widespread problems that plague multitudes of women in this country and around the world. This chapter explores the specific approaches to intervention with women and their special environmental circumstances. These circumstances are different from those that characterize the world of men.

LO 13-1 Develop Self-Awareness About Gender Sensitivity

EP 2.1.2a
EP 2.1.4a&b
EP 2.1.5a

As we begin to explore the special sphere of women, being familiar with a number of terms is important. These terms relate to subjugation and power.

- *Sexism:* "Prejudice or discrimination based on sex, especially discrimination against women" that involves "behavior, conditions, or attitudes that foster stereotypes of social roles based on sex" (Mish, 2008, p. 1141).

- *Gender- (or sex-) role stereotypes:* Expectations about how people should behave based upon their gender. Gender stereotypes reflect the expectations for behavior and expression characterizing the "opposite sexes; men are aggressive, whereas women are passive; men embody instrumentality [being problem-solvers] and are task-oriented, whereas women embody expressiveness and are emotion-oriented; men are rational, whereas women are irrational; men want sex, whereas women want love; and so on" (emphasis omitted) (Yarber, Sayad, & Strong, 2010, p. 130).

- *Oppression:* The act and result of putting extreme limitations and constraints on some person, group, or larger system because the involved targets fit into some common category or have some common set of characteristics (Kirst-Ashman, 2013, 2014). Typically, oppression involves unfair treatment and denial of rights.

- *Sex discrimination:* Differential treatment of people based solely on their gender. Examples include paying males more than females for the same or comparable jobs or hiring only women for certain jobs.

Many people are initially "turned off" by the concept of sexism. They find it difficult to consciously recognize and accept the possibility that the world is imperfect, sexist. They think things are supposed to be fair, and they should not have to waste their time and energy battling such problems as sexism. For many women, adopting an "out of sight, out of mind" philosophy is easier. In other words, if one does not think about a problem, then it does not really exist. Why make up and dwell on problems that are nonexistent or insignificant?

Note that it's important for generalist practitioners to "gain sufficient self-awareness to eliminate the influence of personal biases and values in working with diverse groups" (Council on Social Work Education [CSWE], 2008, EP 2.1.4b). Everyone has personal biases about someone or something. The important thing for social workers is to continuously assess personal values when working with clients. It's an ongoing process to analyze personal values and make sure they don't bias practice decisions. This is true when working with women or any other diverse group (e.g., cultural, racial, etc.).

Now consider the following facts:

- *Approximately 58.6 percent of all women age 16 and over work outside of the home (U.S. Census Bureau, 2011). About 72 percent of single mothers and 69.8 percent of married mothers are employed outside of the home (U.S. Census Bureau, 2011).*
- *On the average, women's full-time, year-round median[1] weekly earnings are approximately 80.5 percent of men's (U.S. Census Bureau, 2011).*
- *For all races, women earn significantly less than men do at every educational level (Kirk & Okazawa-Rey, 2013; Renzetti, Curran, & Maier, 2012; U.S. Census Bureau, 2011).*
- *"More women than men make up the working poor, and women of color are more than twice as likely to be poor than white women" (Kirk & Okazawa-Rey, 2013, p. 316).*
- *"Even with a college education . . . and equivalent work experience and skills, professional women are far less likely than men to get to the top of their*

professions or corporations. They are halted by unseen structural barriers, such as men's negative attitudes to senior women and perceptions of their leadership abilities and styles, their motivation, training, and skills" (Hyde, 2008; Kirk & Okazawa-Rey, 2013, p. 316).

- *Women are clustered in low-paying supportive occupations, such as clerical workers, teachers, and service workers, whereas men tend to assume higher-paying occupations such as high-level managers, professionals, and construction workers (Shaw & Lee, 2012; U.S. Census Bureau, 2011).*
- *A "sexual assault [including rape] occurs about every two minutes" (Shaw & Lee, 2012, p. 504).*
- *Only a small percentage of all rapes is ever reported (Carroll, 2013; Crooks & Baur, 2014; Shaw & Lee, 2012).*
- *According to various studies, women have between a 15 and 25 percent chance of being raped sometime in their lives (Hyde & Else-Quest, 2013). It is "estimated that one in four U.S. college women was a victim of rape or attempted rape" (Kirk & Okazawa-Rey, 2013, p. 264).*
- *"Nearly one in four women in the United States reported experiencing violence by a current or former spouse or boyfriend at some point in her life, and U.S. women experience some two million injuries from intimate partner violence each year. Abuse-related injuries include bruises, cuts, burns and scalds, concussion, broken bones, penetrating injuries from knives, miscarriages, permanent injuries such as damage to joints, partial loss of hearing or vision, and physical disfigurement" (Kirk & Okazawa-Rey, 2013, p. 262).*

LO 13-2 Work with Women Using the Generalist Intervention Model

We have established that social workers must be sensitive to and knowledgeable about various aspects of human diversity, including gender, to practice effectively (NASW, 2008). As a generalist practitioner, you will be called upon to work with women. Women are more likely than men to be poor. They are more likely to be primary caretakers of children and older adults than men. Additionally, women are victimized by specific kinds of violence not suffered by men. This chapter will review a range of practice issues based on common circumstances

---

1. A *median* is a value in the exact middle of an ordered listing of values—half of the values fall above it and half of the values fall below it.

facing women. Throughout the planned change process, understanding the world from a woman's perspective is critical. As we will see, she often experiences different options, strengths, and barriers than those encountered by men.

For example, consider Erline, age 25, a single mother with three children. Billy, her partner and the father of her two youngest children, abruptly deserted her for parts unknown. As a construction worker with some specialized skills, he could get work almost anywhere and yet be hard for her to track down. They were not married. Hiring a lawyer, finding Billy, and getting him to furnish some child support would take much more money than Erline had ever seen. While they were together, Erline worked as a part-time checker at a local Superduper Saver Mart. Without Billy's financial support, Erline could not afford the rent and was evicted. She was forced to quit her job and take her children to a homeless shelter in a neighborhood renowned for its high crime levels. Erline had no close relatives or friends to whom she could turn. Billy had abused her regularly both physically and emotionally. He had forced her to cut off any friendships she did have.

Amy, the shelter's social worker, began the planned change process prescribed by the Generalist Intervention Model (GIM). During *engagement,* Amy found Erline to be quite shy and unassertive, different from most male clients with whom she worked. Erline had little confidence in her own abilities, including that of supporting her family financially. Erline had been raised to assume roles of mother and wife, not that of breadwinner, to which many men aspire. Amy gently encouraged Erline to share her concerns. She worked to establish an egalitarian relationship with Erline, a goal of feminist practice, where they would work together to help Erline and her family (Featherstone & Morris, 2012; Rabin, 2005; Vasquez, 2003). This role differs from the more formal historical and patriarchal perspective where a clinician with superior knowledge helps a client who assumes an inferior position (Hyde & Else-Quest, 2013).

During *assessment,* Amy emphasized the concept of empowerment for Erline. She worked with Erline to reframe her perception of herself and her position. According to traditional patriarchal standards, Erline felt she did not measure up. She had no economic resources, and she had failed in her relationship with Billy. Homeless men residing at the shelter rarely had children unless their wives were with them. Erline, on the other hand, was a responsible caretaker of her three

children. Amy stressed the skills and parental competence that keeping a family together under such adverse circumstances required. Amy worked with Erline to identify her many other strengths, including intelligence, organization skills, job skills (Erline was dependable, responsible, and took employment very seriously), family commitment, and desire to improve her life circumstances.

Planning concentrated on consciousness raising, the process by which people examine their lives, increase awareness of issues affecting them, and begin thinking of ways to change their conditions. Amy helped Erline to assume a new perspective on power, namely that a woman's homelessness is not simply and purely her fault. Rather, homelessness is interrelated with oppression based on racial, class, and gender variables.

Amy worked with Erline to identify and evaluate options available to her, including some she had never thought of before. Amy informed Erline that a nearby community college had a program to help women just like her get back into the labor force. First, interests and abilities were evaluated, and then training was provided for minimal cost. Grants and loans were available. Although a new concept to Erline, the thought of establishing a career for herself looked better and better as she made this a primary goal. A related goal was getting low-cost housing when she could afford it.

Another aspect of planning involved Erline's communication and assertiveness skills, dimensions often addressed in feminist counseling (Hyde, 2008; Hyde & Else-Quest, 2013; Van Den Bergh & Cooper, 1986). Erline felt guilty for failing in her relationship. She felt the abuse Billy administered was really her fault. Amy worked with Erline to stop blaming herself for causing problems, traditionally a common issue for women (Chaplin, 1988; Lum, 2004; Matlin, 2012). Goals involved increasing assertiveness, enhancing communication skills, and evaluating personal potential.

During *implementation,* Amy and Erline discussed the logic and fairness of being forced to abide by traditional gender-role stereotypes and expectations, regardless of the individual's strengths and needs. These expectations involve how the female partner should automatically fulfill the couple's socio-emotional needs and how the male partner should assume the active behavioral role of getting things done. Erline began to look more objectively at herself, her competence, and her options.

Erline also pursued her plan of getting vocational assessment and training. Amy helped Erline involve herself with a cooperative day care program sponsored by the shelter so she could attend school and later look for a job. Amy assisted Erline in getting her name on a waiting list for local low-cost housing.

Evaluation 6 months later indicated that Erline had made progress toward or achieved many of her goals. She had completed vocational testing and training and gotten a job as a receptionist at a health care facility. Although she would never be a millionaire, she managed to make enough to meet her family's needs. She found some temporary housing at a boarding house. Although inadequate, she knew it was only until she could get into a larger, better, low-cost housing unit. She continued to participate in the shelter's cooperative day care program.

Amy *terminated* her involvement with Erline when the latter left the shelter. However, because of day care program involvement, Amy often briefly saw Erline.

Follow-up 6 months later revealed that Erline had maintained most of her progress. Her job was going well, she continued to improve her assertiveness and communication skills, and she persisted in waiting for better housing. However, the world is not perfect. She was seeing a man who struck her in anger several weeks after they began dating. She was struggling with what to do about the relationship.

LO 13-3 Examine Feminist Perspectives on Generalist Practice

Before we review specific intervention techniques for working with women, we need to set the stage. You must understand the basis for why working with women is different from working with men. A brief discussion of feminist social work practice will help to achieve this.

A basic definition of *feminism* is the philosophy of legal, social, educational, and economic equality between women and men. Superficially, this definition may seem quite clear. However, in reality the issues are complicated (see Highlight 13.1).

In many ways, feminist social work conforms well with the principles and values of traditional social work practice. For example, both stress the importance of individuals' interactions with their surrounding environments and communities. Additionally, both emphasize the significance of being concerned with "human dignity and the rights of self-determination" (Figueira-McDonough, 2008; Hyde, 2008; Van Den Bergh & Cooper, 1986, p. 3).

A feminist perspective on practice with women as individuals (micro practice) targets women's inner feelings and access to personal power. For instance, some research indicates that women tend to have slightly

---

HIGHLIGHT 13.1

Are You a Feminist?

- Do you believe that women should have the same rights as men?
- Do you believe that women should be able to have the same access to jobs and social status as men?
- Do you believe that women should *not* be discriminated against or *denied* opportunities and choices on the basis of their gender?
- Do you believe that ideally people's attitudes and behavior should reflect the equal treatment of women?
- Do you think that many people need to become more educated about women's issues?
- Would you be willing to advocate on behalf of women (e.g., for poor women or women who have been raped)?

- Do you believe that both men and women have the right to their own individual differences (i.e., of course, differences that do not harm other people)?
- Do you think that our society is generally structured legally, socially, and economically by and for men instead of women? (This last question is probably the most difficult and perhaps the most painful to answer.)

If you have answered "yes" to all or most of these questions, according to our definition, which will be discussed later, there is a good chance that you are a feminist.

lower levels of self-esteem and self-confidence than men, at least in some instances (Hyde & Else-Quest, 2013).Women also tend to be less aggressive than men; this fact is true essentially for all types of aggression, including both physical and verbal (Greenberg, Bruess, & Conklin, 2011; Hyde & DeLamater, 2011). This lack of aggressiveness can also cause problems for women who do not appropriately stand up for their own rights. Self-esteem may be related to aggression in that women who do not value themselves may not feel capable of asserting themselves.

Later in the chapter, we will discuss the continuum of aggression, assertiveness, and passivity. We will also provide some intervention suggestions for helping women become more appropriately assertive.

A feminist perspective on practice with families and groups (mezzo practice) focuses on women's relationships with others around them. This perspective involves both personal relationships and interactions in their world of work. If women tend to have lower levels of self-esteem and aggression, how does this affect their relationships? These situations again may involve having difficulty in feeling good enough about themselves to be appropriately assertive.

The micro and mezzo levels of a feminist practice perspective are intimately intertwined. Classifying which aspect of working with women falls clearly within micro practice and which falls within mezzo practice is difficult. Likewise, the feminist practice perspective concerning organizations and communities (macro practice) is intimately related to what occurs in women's personal, interpersonal, and work lives.

We have already presented some facts that reflect how women are oppressed. On the one hand, many women need to enhance their own self-esteem to better advocate for themselves. On the other hand, there are obvious impediments and hazards women must endure that have little or no impact on men's lives. For example, what structural barriers confront women in our society that lead them to earn significantly less than men? Why is there the likelihood that one in four women will be sexually assaulted at some time in their lives? How does this fact restrict women's behavior? Should they not go to the library at night to study because walking home is dangerous? How does it affect their ability to compete with men who have no such fears and restrictions? In other words, feminists view our world as being one primarily built by and for men. The special needs of women frequently remain unmet.

A feminist perspective on macro practice then looks at the social policies and political structures that hamper women in leading free and productive lives. As a generalist practitioner, you must be aware of oppression and willing to advocate for and sometimes fight on behalf of oppressed people. This chapter assumes a feminist perspective for generalist social work practice.

A DEFINITION OF FEMINISM FOR PRACTITIONERS

Feminism is related to social work practice in that it emphasizes an obligation to changing and improving how people conduct their personal and public lives. Both feminism and generalist social work practice seek an end to domination and oppression.

Some people have extremely negative reactions to the word *feminism.* The emotional barriers they forge and the resulting resistance they foster make approaching the concept with them difficult. Others consider feminism a radical ideology that emphasizes separatism and fanaticism. In other words, they think feminism involves the philosophy adopted by women who spurn men, resent past inequities, and strive violently to overthrow male supremacists. Still others think of feminism as an outmoded tradition that is no longer relevant.

The definition of feminism presented here is designed to relate to basic concepts involving the daily lives of people like you (Kirst-Ashman, 1991). Many people have failed to develop a sensitivity to the sexist barriers surrounding them. For one thing, acknowledging such unfairness is painful. For another, it is easy to assume that "that's the way things are" simply because people have not thought about better ways of doing things.

For our purposes here, feminism is defined as the *philosophy of equality* between women and men that involves *both attitudes and actions,* that infiltrates virtually *all aspects of life,* that often necessitates providing *education and advocacy* on behalf of women, and that appreciates the existence of *individual differences* and personal accomplishments regardless of gender. There are five major components within this definition that relate directly to the core of professional social work practice.

The first component is equality. Equality does not mean that women are trying to shed their female identities and become clones of men. Nor does it mean that women should seek to adopt behaviors that are typically "masculine." Feminism does involve equal or identical rights to opportunities and choices. It relates to women's and men's rights not to be discriminated against nor denied opportunities and choices on the basis of gender.

The second major component inherent in feminism is the fact that it embodies both attitudes and actions. Attitudes concern how we look at the world and perceive other people. Feminism involves viewing other people from a fair and objective perspective and avoiding stereotypes.

For example, consider a social services supervisor who firmly states she is a feminist. However, she ignores one of her male supervisees, who consistently makes sexist comments about his female colleagues. The worker frequently tells sexist jokes about breast size. He also likes to tell his colleagues how women just get too emotionally involved with their clients and are not able to be objective enough to formulate effective intervention plans. This man's behavior is a form of sexual harassment. His supervisor is legally responsible to see that such obtrusive behavior does not occur in the work environment. The point is that although this supervisor may be a feminist in terms of attitude, she is not a feminist in terms of action. A feminist supervisor would confront her supervisee about his specific inappropriate, sexist remarks. Feminism involves acting on one's beliefs on behalf of gender equality.

The third critical component of feminism is the idea that it concerns all aspects of life (Hyde, 2008). Equality does not only apply to an equal unhindered chance at getting a specific job or promotion. It also involves the right to have personal opinions about political issues and the right to make decisions within personal relationships. It entails a woman's right to make a decision about what to do on a Friday night date, as well as her right to choose whether or not to have a sexual encounter. Essentially, this step includes the acknowledgment that our social, legal, and political structure is oriented toward men, not women.

A fourth important aspect of feminism is the frequent need to provide education and advocacy on behalf of women (Hyde, 2008). We have established that feminism involves values. Values provide the basis for decisions about how a person behaves. If a person sees things occurring that are contrary to her values, in this case to feminist values, actions may be necessary to help remedy the situation. Many times, people need information about women's issues. The male worker mentioned earlier who is sexually harassing female colleagues may need information about what sexual harassment is and how it negatively affects women. He may be ignorant of these effects. A feminist will share and provide information to others to initiate positive changes in their attitudes and behavior.

Sometimes, there will be a need for even greater effort, and advocacy may be called for. *Advocacy* is defending and actively representing others, with one of its goals being client empowerment. This process often involves initiating change or going out of one's way to provide help. Feminism focuses on helping women achieve greater equality and opportunity. Feminist advocacy involves speaking out for others who need help. A natural part of advocacy is helping those with less power and opportunity.

The fifth major concept involved in the definition of feminism is the appreciation of individual differences (Hyde & Else-Quest, 2013; Lum, 2004; Van Den Bergh, 1995). The feminist perspective lauds the concept of empowering women by emphasizing individual strengths and qualities. Feminism stresses freedom and the right to make life choices. See Highlight 13.2 for a discussion of feminist principles.

Micro Practice with Women: Common Problems

It's important that practitioners recognize the importance of gender differences when working with clients; they then must communicate this understanding to clients. Workers' grasp of women's concerns often forms the basis for intervention with women. The issues women often bring to counseling situations are related to traditional gender roles and to the situations in which women often find themselves. This fact does not suggest that men never suffer from any of these needs, but rather that women are more likely to have these needs because of their gender-role socialization. These problems are clustered in two major categories—stressful life events, and lack of self-esteem and a sense of powerlessness.

STRESSFUL LIFE EVENTS

At least two groups of events can be stressful to women. The first group involves happenings in women's personal lives, such as separation and divorce. For many women, the natural aging process can also cause undue stress. Accepting the inevitable fact that one will lose both youth and beauty can be difficult, especially in a society that stresses their importance, particularly for women. Accepting the death of someone close can also be difficult. Finally, many women are forced to move from familiar surroundings to new, unknown environments due to a job change or out of economic necessity. Such changes and forced readjustments can be stressful.

HIGHLIGHT 13.2

Principles of Feminist Counseling

EP 2.1.10 c&f

At least seven principles of feminist intervention provide lenses with which to view women and their problems (Figueira-McDonowgh, 2008; Hannam, 2012; Herlihy & Corey, 2005; Hyde, 2008; Hyde & Else-Quest, 2013; Lum, 2004; Van Den Bergh & Cooper, 1986; Vasquez, 2003). They involve assumptions about the causes of many problems. Therefore, they are like molds with which social workers can shape their interventions, thereby providing clues and guidelines for how to proceed:

1. A client's problems should be viewed from a social and political perspective. These problems are often rooted in a sexist social and political structure and cannot be considered simply personal or individual. Another way of making this statement is that for women, the "personal is political" (Hyde, 2008, p. 218; Van Den Bergh & Cooper, 1986, p. 613; Vasquez, 2003, p. 558).

2. Clients need encouragement to free themselves from traditional gender role bonds. They need encouragement to make free choices and pursue the tasks and achievements they choose. Tasks and goals should not be limited to those allocated primarily to women. They should include those traditionally offered primarily to men.

3. Intervention should focus on the identification and enhancement of clients' strengths rather than on pathologies. Strengths provide a foundation upon which to build. Women need to be empowered so they can enhance their control over their environment and their lives to meet their essential needs.

4. Women should be encouraged to develop an autonomous identity that is not a reflection of or reaction to their relationships with other people. Women's identities should not be determined by whom they are married to or whom they are dating. Rather, their identity should be solidly based on their own strengths, achievements, and individuality.

5. Other women are considered valuable and important. In a society that devalues women in general, seeing other women as being insignificant is easy even for women (who, of course, are also part of that society). Feminist intervention urges clients to reevaluate their relationships with other women. This principle of feminist intervention emphasizes how valuable other women can be to clients. It is related to the concept of networking, that is, strengthening and seeking linkages between the client and relevant family members and friends. Other women can serve as effective resources in helping to achieve the client's goals. They can share their experiences and solutions they have found to similar problems. Additionally, they can provide nurturance and emotional support.

6. Feminist intervention emphasizes finding a balance between work and personal relationships. A corollary of this balance is that men and women are encouraged to share in both the nurturing aspects of their lives and in providing economic resources.

7. Generalist practitioners should work with their female clients in a relationship that's as equal as possible. Feminist practitioners don't perceive themselves as experts directing their clients regarding what to do. Rather, feminist practitioners work together with clients to help clients identify their needs and establish their goals, with the result of client empowerment.

Feminist intervention fits well with our generalist planned change model. It emphasizes focusing on clients' strengths and is oriented toward viewing the individual as a dynamic micro system interacting with the many mezzo and macro systems in her environment. Emphasizing the significance of the environment in which people live easily sets the stage for advocacy and macro-practice change. You need to focus your attention on "the system" to find out what is wrong with it and then structure your interventions so that they work for positive change.

EP 2.1.3

Critical Thinking Question 13.1

- To what extent do you agree or disagree with the principles of feminist counseling? Explain.

The other group of events that can cause women substantial stress concerns work and financial status. Women may have low self-esteem and worry about the adequacy of their job performance. They may be overburdened with employment, home, and child care responsibilities. With or without jobs, women have a high likelihood of being poor and experiencing the resultant stresses and strains.

Finally, women may suffer from blatant sex discrimination at work. For instance, consider a woman who is hired at the same time as a man for identical jobs. Both have similar levels of education, experience, and skills. The woman, however, is hired at 80 percent of the man's salary. Women are unfairly socialized to blame themselves. The woman in this example is likely to feel that there is something wrong with *her,* which results in her lower salary. She is likely to accept the situation as it stands (after all, it must be her fault), instead of fighting for what she rightly deserves.

LACK OF SELF-ESTEEM AND A SENSE OF POWERLESSNESS

 Women who have been taught to be deferent and dependent often do not feel they can take control of their lives (GlenMaye, 1998; Lum, 2004; Vasquez, 2003). They feel no matter what they do, their taking control will not change anything. Because of lack of practice in being assertive and making decisions, they do not feel they have the potential to do so.

Because of being herded down certain gender role–related paths, women do not often see the variety of alternatives that may be open to them. For instance, establishing a career for herself may not even occur to a divorced woman who has never worked outside the home. A battered woman may be so cowed by her perpetrator that she might not even think leaving him is an option.

Women who come to counseling may not have the words to clearly express what they mean; additionally, they may not feel that they have the right to say what they think (GlenMaye, 1998). Opportunities to discriminate between nonassertion, aggression, and appropriate assertion may never have been available to them.

Women who have devoted themselves to nurturing and caring for others may feel their own identity is lost (Collier, 1982; Lum, 2004). They may be searching for who they are and what they can do for themselves.

They may have sacrificed so much for others that they no longer know what they as independent individuals need or want. Your tasks as a social worker may include focusing on a woman's inner emotional needs, helping her establish a clear sense of who she is, and aiding her in defining what she needs and wants for herself (GlenMaye, 1998; Herlihy & Corey, 2005; Hyde & Else-Quest, 2013; Matlin, 2012).

If a woman has low self-esteem and, for a variety of reasons, little experience in independent action, she may have difficulty trusting her own judgment (Herlihy & Corey, 2005). Consider, for example, a professional woman in her early 40s who has no children and is recently divorced. She is taking on herself the responsibility to build her house. It is a custom-built contemporary home with steeply descending areas of roof and bold lines. Whenever asked about the house, her statements seem to end with question marks. For instance, she might say, "It certainly is contemporary. I wonder if it's too drastic," or "I'm finishing the cabinets myself; I hope they're not too light-colored and the coating isn't too rough."

No one should criticize her. Building a home and making the hundreds of choices required ranging from what color the living room rug should be to where to place the electrical outlets is quite a task. However, noting how "insecure" she appears, to try to assure herself that she has made an adequate choice is easy. A social worker might slip into "nurturance mode" and say things like, "Why, it's beautiful; I'm sure you'll love it when it's done." A more helpful response would be, "I think you can trust your own decisions. You've given each one a lot of thought and done the best you can. That took talent and courage!" More than likely, a man would not react in the same insecure way that the woman has. But then traditional male stereotypes dictate that men are supposed to be decisive and never expose any sign of emotion or self-doubt.

LO 13-4 Empower Women as Individuals

 As a social worker, you can help a woman client regain her sense of power and control over her own life. It's important to select appropriate intervention strategies. The "personal traits that have clearly been shown to relate positively to measures of self-esteem or subjective well-being are the same for women as for men; and include assertiveness, independence, self-responsibility, and efficacy...characteristics that are typically associated with men" (Lott, 1994, pp. 306–307). The following sections propose strategies for helping women: enhance self-esteem; increase assertiveness; expand options; change rules and expectations; and work together for macro change.

ENHANCE SELF-ESTEEM

Self-confidence and self-esteem are essential for empowerment. There are at least six tactics you can use to address this issue. First, help your client *explore* how she feels about herself. Ask her for positive and negative adjectives that she feels best describe her. Have her describe her strengths and weaknesses. Then help her to summarize how she perceives her self-esteem. Does she feel good about herself, or does she criticize herself every chance she gets?

Second, give your client *feedback* about her responses. Is thinking of strengths difficult for her? You can share with her your perceptions about her strengths. Emphasizing strengths is illustrated throughout this text. Strengths may include virtually anything— for example, personal qualities such as being a hard worker, being motivated for change, and being caring or articulate.

Third, help your client look more realistically at those areas where she is experiencing *guilt* (GlenMaye, 1998). There is some tendency for women with low self-esteem to blame themselves for everything that is wrong. The battered woman typically blames herself for being battered. She had supper on the table 1½ minutes too late. Perhaps your client blames herself for any unhappiness other family members experience. She feels she could have been more supportive or should have anticipated the problem. You can help your client distinguish between the point at which her responsibility ends and other individuals' begins.

Fourth, help your client accept the fact that most aspects of life have both *positive* and *negative* sides. Categorizing themselves as essentially bad in comparison to other people who are essentially good is easy for people with low self-esteem. Looking realistically at themselves and the world around them is important for clients. A good approach is to view the world in terms of having both strengths and weaknesses, highs and lows, times of happiness and times of sadness. Acknowledging the negatives does not mean you have to dwell on them. However, admitting to yourself that they exist can save a lot of energy that would be spent

in trying to hide or fight them. Even winning $20,000,000 in the lottery might have its disadvantages. How many of your friends and relatives will expect you to dole out money to them? What is the matter with you? Can you not share? Might some criminal kidnap your child or baby sister or mother in order to get a big ransom? Then, there is always the next tax audit to worry about.

The other side of this strength/weakness coin is acknowledging, appreciating, and using strengths. Help your clients appreciate the positive, while acknowledging the negative. For example, a single mother of five children may hate having to receive public assistance. Yet, a strength in this situation is that she is able to care for her children full-time. That is, it is a strength until the public assistance system forces her to work outside the home and she can't find adequate day care.

The fifth thing you can do to enhance self-esteem is help clients target those areas in which they want to see *improvements.* You can assist them to pinpoint where they are exceptionally self-critical or on what aspect they want to work at feeling better about themselves. You can help them identify and examine what qualities people with higher self-esteem have and then help them work out how they might apply those characteristics to themselves.

Sixth, encourage a female client to *take care of herself* (Herlihy & Corey, 2005; Hyde & Else-Quest, 2013; Vasquez, 2003). The qualities that she likes about herself can be nurtured. A woman can learn that she has the right to have time for herself and to participate in activities she enjoys.

INCREASE ASSERTIVENESS

Social workers can teach women about assertiveness and how to develop assertiveness skills. They can provide practice situations and guide their female clients through more effective ways of handling difficult or uncomfortable situations. Assertiveness improves personal interactions, which in turn builds confidence.

Assertiveness involves verbal or nonverbal behavior that is straightforward but not offensive. Assertiveness involves taking into account both your own rights and the rights of others.

It sounds simple, but for many people, appropriate assertiveness is difficult to master. For instance, consider the situation where you are patiently waiting in line at the grocery store. A man hurriedly steps in front of you, slams his six-pack of beer on the counter, and throws a $10 bill at the clerk. He is big, threatening, and obviously rude. Do you shyly allow him to continue because you will be glad to see him leave as soon as possible? Do you brashly step in front of him and shout, "You turkey, I was in line first!" Do you calmly and straightforwardly say to the clerk, "Excuse me, I was in line first. Here are my groceries."

Many times, looking at a situation objectively and taking the feelings and needs of all concerned into account is difficult. It is often especially difficult for women who have been taught to be sensitive to others' needs, are frequently critical of themselves because of low self-esteem, and are not accustomed to assuming a strong leadership role.

Assertiveness involves specific skills that can be taught with assertiveness training. Here we will discuss in more depth the meaning of assertiveness and some concepts involved in assertiveness training.

The Meaning of Assertiveness

Do you have trouble telling someone when you are annoyed? Do you hate arguments and avoid them at all cost? Do you feel uncomfortable asking people for favors even when you are in desperate situations? Do you feel that your views are not quite as important as the next person's? If you answer "yes" to any of these questions, you may be having difficulty being assertive enough.

Note that women are not the only people who sometimes have trouble with assertiveness. However, as we have discussed, traditional gender role stereotypes and expectations may make developing assertiveness skills harder for many women. Many of your female clients will have difficulty being appropriately assertive. They will come to you with problems involving poverty, jobs, domestic violence, relationships, or sexual assault. Many of them would benefit greatly by developing assertiveness skills to address their respective problematic situations.

Assertiveness can be perceived as the center of a continuum ranging from aggression to passivity. Alberti and Emmons describe typical behavior evident in each of these three styles:

In the nonassertive style, you are likely to hesitate, speak softly, look away, avoid the issue, agree regardless of your own feelings, not express opinions, value yourself "below" others, and hurt yourself to avoid any chance of hurting others.

In the aggressive style, you typically answer before the other person is through talking, speak loudly and abusively, glare at the other person, speak "past" the issue (accusing, blaming, demeaning), vehemently expound your feelings and opinions, value yourself "above" others, and hurt others to avoid hurting yourself.

In the assertive style, you will answer spontaneously; speak with a conversational tone and volume, and look at the other person, speak to the issue, openly express your personal feelings and opinions (anger, love, disagreement, sorrow), value yourself equally to others, and hurt neither yourself nor others. (1974, p. 24; 2008)

These three styles might be characterized respectively as the "martyr," the "persecutor," and the "balancer" (Apgar & Callahan, 1980, pp. 43–44). A martyr is a nonassertive, passive person whose primary aim is to keep others happy. She will put aside her own needs and wants in deference to the wants of others because she does not think of herself as important.

The persecutor, on the other hand, thinks of only herself as being important. Other people do not really matter. The persecutor will insist upon getting her own way. She is aggressive. She "gets what she wants by dominating, manipulating, and humiliating others" (Apgar & Callahan, 1980, p. 43). Frequently, she is hostile in her interactions or ignores other people altogether.

The balancer does just that. She balances both her needs and the needs of others. Appropriate assertiveness involves consideration of both yourself and others.

Consider a situation where you are involved in a deep conversation with a good friend. Another mutual acquaintance walks up, rudely interrupts, and begins to talk about how he recently received the highest grade in the class on his last exam. The following illustrates possible responses:

- *The unassertive martyr says and does nothing.*
- *The aggressive persecutor loudly screams, "Shut up, you lowlife dirtball! Can't you see we were talking? Go away."*
- *The assertive balancer calmly states, "Excuse me. You interrupted an important conversation. Maybe we can talk later."*

Assertiveness Training

Assertiveness training helps people distinguish among assertive, aggressive, and nonassertive responses. It gradually helps people to shape their behavior so that they become consciously more assertive. It helps them gain control of their emotions and their lives.

As we know, social work is practical. Therefore, you can use the suggestions provided to enhance both your client's assertiveness and your own. Alberti and

Emmons (1974, 2008) developed the following steps to help establish assertive behavior:

1. Help your client scrutinize her own actions. How does she behave in situations requiring assertiveness? Does she tend to be nonassertive, assertive, or aggressive in most of her communications?

2. Ask your client to make a record of those situations where she feels she lacked assertiveness or was overly aggressive. How could she have behaved more effectively, either more assertively or less aggressively?

3. Help your client select and focus on some specific instance where she feels she could have been more assertive. Encourage her to visualize the specific details. What exactly did she say? How did she feel?

4. Help your client analyze how she reacted. Examine closely her verbal and nonverbal behavior. Alberti and Emmons cite the following seven aspects of behavior that are important to monitor during assertiveness training:

   a. *Eye contact.* Did your client look the person in the eye? Or, were her eyes downcast? Did she find herself avoiding eye contact when she was uncomfortable?

   b. *Body posture.* Was she standing up straight or was she slouching? Was she sheepishly leaning away from the person? Was she holding her head high as she looked the person in the eye?

   c. *Gestures.* Were her hand gestures fitting for the situation? Did she feel at ease? Was she tapping her foot or cracking her knuckles?

   d. *Facial expressions.* Did she have a serious expression on her face? Was she smiling or giggling uncomfortably, thereby giving the impression that she was not really serious?

   e. *Voice tone, inflection, and volume.* Did she speak in a normal voice tone? Did she whisper timidly? Did she raise her voice to the point of stressful screeching? Did she sound as if she were whining?

   f. *Timing.* Making an appropriate assertive response right after a remark is made or an incident happens is best. Considering whether or not a particular situation really requires assertiveness is also important. At times, remaining silent and "letting it go" might be best. For example, telling a prospective employer that he has horrendously offensive breath during a job interview might not be best.

   g. *Content.* What she says in her assertive response is obviously important. Did she choose her words carefully? Did her response have the impact she wanted it to have? Why or why not? (1974, pp. 31–32)

5. Help your client identify a role model and examine how that person handled a situation requiring assertiveness. What exactly happened during the incident? What words did the role model use that were particularly effective? What aspects of her nonverbal behavior helped to get her points across?

6. Assist your client in identifying a range of other new responses for situations where she lacks assertiveness. In the future, what other words could she use? What nonverbal behaviors might be more effective?

7. Ask your client to picture herself in the identified problematic situation. Having her close her eyes and concentrate often helps. Step by step, tell her to imagine how she could handle the situation more assertively.

8. Help your client practice the way she has envisioned herself being more assertive. Ask her to target a real-life situation that remains unresolved. For example, perhaps the person she lives with always leaves dirty socks lying around the living room or drinks all her soda and forgets to tell her when the refrigerator is empty. You can also help your client role play the situation. Role playing provides effective mechanisms for practicing responses before clients have to use them spontaneously in real life.

9. Once again, review her new assertive responses. Help her emphasize her strong points and remedy her flaws.

10. Continue practicing steps 7, 8, and 9 until her newly developed assertive approach feels comfortable and natural to her.

11. Direct your client to try out her new assertiveness approach in a real-life situation.

12. Encourage your client to continue to expand her assertiveness repertoire until such behavior becomes part of her personal interactive style. She can review the earlier steps and try them out with an increasingly wider range of problematic situations.

13. Reinforce your client for her achievements in becoming more assertive. Changing long-standing patterns of behavior is not easy. Encourage her to focus on and revel in the good feelings she experiences as a result of her successes (see Highlight 13.3).

HIGHLIGHT 13.3

Each of Us Has Certain Assertive Rights

Part of becoming assertive involves clearly figuring out and believing that we are valuable and worthwhile people. Criticizing ourselves for our mistakes and imperfections is easy. Holding our feelings in because we are afraid that we will hurt someone else's feelings or that someone will reject us is also easy. Sometimes, feelings that are held in too long will burst out in an aggressive tirade. These situations apply to any of us, including our clients.

For example, let us say some close friends from a distant state come to visit with their 16-month-old baby, Robert. They obviously adore Robert. They also feel that Robert "has a mind of his own" and allow Robert to do more or less exactly what he wants. First, he plays with all your magazines and casually throws them all over the floor. You find this mildly annoying, but do not get too upset because you rarely get to see your friends. What harm can Robert do to magazines anyway? They then feed Robert some crackers and later some sticky candy. Robert smears the food all over himself, the furniture, and the rug. His parents do not seem to notice. You find this annoying but think that the furniture, the rug, and probably Robert can all be cleaned up later.

Robert then spies your prized collection of DVDs and heads directly for them. His mother calmly remarks, "Oh, look, Robert's found the DVDs. It's funny he hadn't noticed them before this." She smiles lovingly at him as he pulls the first one out of the case. This, you think, is too much, and try to calmly say, "Let's go into the kitchen and round up some lunch." Finally, back in the living room, Robert breaks a lamp. His parents say they're sorry. By this time all you're beginning to focus on is your anger. You muster up the stamina and say, "Oh, that's all right. It was an old lamp anyway." You retreat to the kitchen to take several deep breaths and regain control. You return to the living room with some drinks. Robert's father comes up to you and timidly says, "Well, Robert really ruined your picture." Earlier you had shown your friends a picture of your family

given you by your grandmother. It was sentimentally invaluable to you and also irreplaceable.

The picture was the last straw. The room turns red. Your blood feels like it is boiling in your veins. You turn to your friends and say, "Get out! Get out! Take that devil-monster with you and never come back!"

This final calamity could have been avoided if early on in the process you had acknowledged that you, too, had rights.

The following are eight of your and your clients' assertive rights.

1. You have the right to express your ideas and opinions openly and honestly.
2. You have the right to be wrong. Everyone makes mistakes.
3. You have the right to direct and govern your own life. In other words, you have the right to be responsible for yourself.
4. You have the right to stand up for yourself without unwarranted anxiety and make choices that are good for you.
5. You have the right *not* to be liked by everyone. (Do you like *everyone* you know?)
6. You have the right, on the one hand, to make requests and, on the other hand, to refuse them without feeling guilty.
7. You have the right to ask for information if you need it.
8. Finally, you have the right to decide not to exercise your assertive rights. In other words, you can choose not to be assertive if you do not want to.

Sources: Most of these rights have been adapted from those identified in L. Z. Bloom, K. Coburn, and J. Perlman (1976), *The New Assertive Woman*, New York: Dell; and in K. Apgar and B. N. Callahan (1980), *Four One-Day Workshops*, Boston: Resource Communications Inc. and Family Service Association of Greater Boston.

These suggestions concerning enhancing self-esteem and increasing assertiveness are related to each other. Each one strengthens the accomplishments of the others. Becoming more assertive enhances one's sense of control. An increased sense of control improves self-esteem. Greater self-esteem increases one's confidence in being assertive. The overall intent is to establish a confident, competent sense of self, which is every person's right.

Critical Thinking Questions 13.2

- To what extent do you see yourself as being an assertive person?
- Are there situations in which you think you are either too unassertive or too aggressive?
- If so, how might you change your behavior in that situation?

EXPAND OPTIONS

Help women recognize the various alternatives available to them and evaluate the pros and cons of each. In other words, teach them how to make decisions and solve problems. Success at using such skills breeds more success. Once women have learned the process of making their own decisions and solving their own problems, they can apply these skills to more decisions and more problems. These alternatives can help to build their feelings of being in control.

CHANGE OLD RULES AND EXPECTATIONS

Female clients often not only need to change how they view themselves and the world, but also their expectations for what is appropriate, effective behavior. This includes both their own actions and those of others. For instance, perhaps in the past a client felt she should be agreeable with and obedient to her spouse regardless of the issue. In view of her enhanced self-esteem and increased assertiveness, she no longer assumes this consistently deferent approach. Rather, she assertively shares her own feelings about issues and aims to get her own needs met in addition to those of her spouse. In other words, as part of the micro intervention process, clients will integrate what they have learned about themselves, and their values about how things "should be" will change.

HELP WOMEN WORK TOGETHER FOR MACRO-LEVEL EMPOWERMENT

EP 2.1.5c

Encourage women to work together to advocate for positive change and achieve equality. GlenMaye (1998) reflects:

> Though empowerment for women is fundamentally related to autonomy and self-determination, women must also work together to change themselves and society. Rather than work merely for individual solutions to individual problems, practitioners must find ways to bring women together and to work with women clients toward social change. (p. 50)

Common Circumstances Facing Women

EP 2.1.9a

Understanding the special, internal dynamics of women at the micro level before proceeding to the mezzo and macro levels of intervention is important. Here we will arbitrarily examine three common circumstances facing women. They are sexual assault, domestic violence, and poverty.

For each, background information will first be provided so that you better understand the issue. Next, intervention strategies at the micro and mezzo levels will be proposed. Frequently, clearly separating out the micro level from the mezzo level of intervention is difficult because the personal and the interpersonal are so integrally related. Thus, we will discuss these strategies together. Finally, we will examine the macro aspects of each issue and propose macro methods of intervention (see Highlight 13.4).

LO 13-5 Provide Assistance to Women as Survivors of Sexual Assault

In 2010, 269,700 sexual assaults, including rapes, were committed, attempted, or threatened (Planty, Langston, Krebs, Berzofsky, & Smiley-McDonald, 2013). Because rape is often not reported, the actual number of rapes is likely much higher (Carroll, 2013; Crooks & Baur, 2014). It is estimated that one in four U.S. college students has been victimized by rape or attempted rape (Kirk & Okazawa-Rey, 2013). Hence, sexual assaults upon women are very common. How can this be? Why are women in our society so terribly vulnerable?

This section will examine the feminist perspective on sexual assault, typical reactions of rape survivors, and suggestions for counseling. Finally, a macro-practice perspective on the problem will be explored.

First, we need to define our terms. The most intimate violation of a person's privacy and dignity is sexual assault. *Sexual assaults* are any unwanted sexual contact where verbal or physical force is used. Although legal definitions of *rape* vary, they commonly include "three elements: penetration of the vagina, mouth, or anus; force or threat of force; and nonconsent of the victim" (McCammon & Knox, 2007, p. 526). Now we need to explore why sexual assault is such a major problem.

THE FEMINIST PERSPECTIVE ON SEXUAL ASSAULT

EP 2.1.7a

The feminist perspective emphasizes that rape is the logical reaction of men who are socialized to dominate women. Rape is seen as a manifestation of men's need to aggressively maintain power over women. It has little to do with sexuality. Sexuality

HIGHLIGHT 13.4

A Feminist Approach to Macro Practice: Seeking Social and Economic Justice

EP 2.1.5c

EP 2.1.8b

We have established that, in many ways, a feminist perspective corresponds well with the basic principles of generalist practice. At least four aspects of the feminist approach can be applied to macro practice in terms of policymaking, community change, and administration (Brandwein, 1987; Hyde, 2005; Weil, 2001).

First, feminist macro practice values the process of how things are accomplished as much as the final result of the process. For example, policies are important. However, a feminist perspective emphasizes that how well a policy is implemented is just as important as what the policy says. Consider an agency policy stating that both men and women should be treated equally in terms of receiving annual raises in salary. The policy is clearly stated on the books. However, if women typically receive significantly fewer raises than men, then the policy is not working. Feminist macro practice then focuses in an ongoing manner on how well things are accomplished.

Second, feminist macro practice adopts a "win-win" rather than a "win-lose" philosophy (Brandwein, 1987, p. 889). A feminist view of power does not reflect trying to get power over others, but rather empowering oneself. In feminist macro practice, you do not have to crush the enemy. Rather, you work things out with those in disagreement. Power is not something available only in limited, finite quantities to be doled out to a select few. It can be shared, and compromises can be made. Feminist macro practice espouses a collaborative style of decision making in which a group of equals comes together and works toward a mutually satisfactory decision. There is no strict hierarchy where each participant has a quantifiable amount of power, either more or less than every other participant.

A third principle of feminist macro practice emphasizes the importance of interpersonal relationships. A nonfeminist approach might stress forming relationships temporarily to complete some specified task. Feminist practice, on the other hand, values the establishment of relationships on an ongoing basis. Tasks to achieve goals must be completed. However, a primary focus is on how all participants in the system continue working together. Feminists strive collectively to establish a unified force with other women in order to "make progressive changes in their communities, in policies, and in their own lives" (Alzate, Andharia, Chowa, Weil, & Doernberg, 2013, p. 653).

The fourth principle is the high value placed on human diversity. Differences are applauded and appreciated rather than denied. All participants in a process are considered equal. There is no concept of one person being better than another for some reason.

So how do all these principles apply to the actual practice of generalist social work? First, the emphasis on diversity helps to sensitize feminist practitioners to the existence of inequality and oppression. Feminist practitioners then are more likely to turn to macro interventions to change the systems that cause the oppression.

Second, the high value placed on the process of how things are accomplished orients practitioners to focus on policy. Policies provide the rules for what you as a social worker can and cannot do. Feminist practitioners are concerned with policies because policies control the ongoing process of how things are done.

The third application to macro practice involves community change. The feminist's concern with equality and collaborative decision making fits well with the idea of getting as many community people involved as possible. The emphasis on equality frames each participant's view as important.

A fourth application of feminist macro practice concerns administration. Feminists emphasize the value of employee input. Because employees are seen as significant participants, development of their skills is important. Attention is given both to how things are accomplished and to how people get along with each other during the work process. The result should be better outcomes and improved interpersonal interaction.

only provides a clear-cut means for exercising power. Rape is seen as a consequence of attitudes toward women that are intimately intertwined throughout the culture. The feminist perspective views rape as both a societal problem and an individual one.

A prevalent *rape myth* ("the attitudes and beliefs that are generally false but are widely and persistently held, and that serve to deny and justify male sexual aggression against women") is that sexual aggression is a part of normal human behavior (McCammon &

Knox, 2007, p. 528). If perpetrators (batterers) and victims are brought up to believe sexual aggression is natural, it makes sense that survivors tend to blame themselves for the assault (Crooks & Baur, 2014; Hyde & Else-Quest, 2013). The rationale is that they should have expected to be raped and should have been prepared or have done something to prevent it.

An analogous situation concerning self-blame is the example of a woman who has her purse snatched while shopping on a Saturday afternoon. If the self-blame concept were applied, it would follow that the woman would blame herself for the incident. She would chastise herself by saying it was her fault. She never should have taken her purse with her to shop in the first place. Maybe she should shop only by catalog from now on. Of course, taking that course of action would be absurd. The woman was not at fault. The one who should be held responsible was the purse snatcher, who broke the law.

Blaming oneself for being raped is equally inappropriate. The feminist view holds that society is wrong for socializing people to assume that male sexual aggression is natural. Socializing women to consider themselves weak and nurturing also contributes to the problem. Developing a victim mentality helps, that is, an expectation that for women to be victims is natural. The feminist perspective emphasizes that these attitudes need to be changed. Only then can rape as a social problem disappear.

The term *victim* implies weakness and powerlessness. From here on, therefore, we will use the term rape *survivor* instead. Survivor implies strength and is oriented toward the future. It coincides with the suggestions for counseling that emphasize helping rape survivors regain confidence and control of their lives.

REACTIONS TO RAPE

One study of rape survivors found that women can experience serious psychological effects that can persist for a half year or more following a rape; they call these emotional changes the *rape trauma syndrome,* currently considered an aspect of *posttraumatic stress disorder (PTSD)* (Burgess & Holmstrom, 1974; Carroll, 2013; Crooks & Baur, 2014; Hyde & DeLamater, 2011). "Posttraumatic stress disorder is an official diagnosis that was originally developed to describe the long-term psychological distress suffered by war veterans, most of whom are men. Symptoms can include persistently re-experiencing the traumatic event (flashbacks, nightmares), . . . avoiding certain locations or activities [associated with the rape,] . . . sleep difficulties,

difficulties concentrating [and] irritability" (Hyde & DeLamater, 2011, p. 367). The syndrome has two basic phases. The first is the acute phase, which involves the woman's emotional reactions immediately following the rape and up to several weeks thereafter. The second involves a long-term reorganization phase.

The Acute Phase

Immediately following a rape, the survivor usually reacts in one of two ways (Masters, Johnson, & Kolodney, 1995). She may show her emotions by crying, expressing anger, or demonstrating fear. On the other hand, she may try to control these intense emotions and hide them from view. Emotions experienced during the acute phase range from humiliation and guilt to shock, anger, and desire for revenge (Lott, 1994).

Additionally, during this phase women will often experience physical problems including difficulties related directly to the rape (Crooks & Baur, 2014; Hyde & DeLamater, 2011). For instance, a woman may suffer irritation of the genitals or rectal bleeding from an anal rape. Physical problems also include stress-related discomforts such as headaches, stomach difficulties, or inability to sleep.

The two primary emotions experienced during the acute phase are fear and self-blame. Fear results from the violence of the experience. Many rape survivors report that during the attack they felt their life had come to an end. They had no control over what the attacker would do to them and were terrified. Such fear can linger. Often survivors are afraid that rape can easily happen again. The second emotion, self-blame, results from society's tendency to blame the survivor instead of the perpetrator (i.e., the rapist) for the crime.

Women fail to report being raped for many reasons. Survivors whose bodies have been brutally violated often desperately want to forget that the horror ever happened. To report the rape means dwelling on the details and going over the event again and again in their minds. Other survivors fear retribution from the rapist. If they call public attention to him, he might do it again to punish them. No police officer will be available all of the time for protection. Other victims feel that people around them will think less of them because they have been raped. They may feel as if a part of themselves has been spoiled, a part that they would prefer to hide from other people. Rape is an ugly crisis that takes a great amount of courage to face.

A social work instructor describes her experience with a young female student that illustrates some of these points:

A student, age 22, entered my office and sat down. She had a stern look on her face. She could have been there for any number of reasons. Perhaps she needed feedback on her research assignment or wanted me to double check that she had fulfilled all her requirements for her upcoming graduation. I asked her what she needed. Spontaneously, she began to cry almost uncontrollably. She said she had been at a party the past Saturday night (it was now Tuesday afternoon). The party was held at the home of a young lawyer who was a mutual friend of a group of her best friends. She described the party as being "typical," meaning a big crowd, lots of beer, some drugs, and loud music. She said that she found herself sitting on a bed with the young lawyer who lived in the apartment. (To me the scene resembled a common pre-dating ritual where a couple meets and decides if there is some "spark" there.) Suddenly, he got up, closed the bedroom door, locked it, threw her down on the bed, and raped her. She was stunned. How could this be? He was a good friend of her friends. He was a lawyer!

So, we returned to the present. It turned out that her primary fear was that her friends would find out about the rape. We talked about how it was the rapist's fault, not her fault. We discussed how he had taken total control from her by virtue of a surprise attack. She never would have suspected that a lawyer would commit such a crime. I also commended her for surviving. In a crisis situation like that, a woman can have no idea what a perpetrator will do. He could kill her, for all she knew.

Finally, we discussed her friends. What true friends would condone such violence? She began to look at the experience more objectively. She started to get in touch with her intense anger at the lawyer for what he had done to her. She started to regain some of her sense of self-confidence. We also talked about pregnancy, but she felt the risk was minimal since she was taking birth control pills. Health issues such as sexually transmitted infections also required attention. We spoke of the alternatives available to her. I called a local rape crisis center and made a referral that she said she would follow up on. We talked about reporting the rapist. It was too late to prosecute successfully. However, she could report his name to the local authorities and said she wanted to do so.

Finally, she said she was going to tell her friends about the whole experience. She felt they needed to know what this man was really like.

In summary, we could not erase the horror. The incident had happened. However, the young woman was able to begin dealing with her feelings and gaining control.

Techniques for helping rape survivors will be discussed more thoroughly in a later section of this chapter.

The Long-Term Reorganization Phase

The second stage of the rape trauma syndrome is the long-term reorganization and recovery phase; the emotional changes and reactions of this phase may linger on for years (Carroll, 2013; Yarber et al., 2010). Reported reactions included fear of being alone, depression, sleeplessness, and, most frequently, an attitude of suspicion toward other people. Other long-term changes that sometimes occur include avoiding involvement with men and suffering various sexual dysfunctions such as lack of sexual desire or aversion to sexual contact (Carroll, 2013; Yarber et al., 2010).

Dealing with even the most negative feelings and getting on with their lives is important for survivors of rape. In some ways, rape might be compared to accepting the death of a loved one. The fact that either has occurred cannot be changed. Survivors must learn to cope. Life continues.

COUNSELING SURVIVORS OF SEXUAL ASSAULTS

EP 2.1.10j

Research has established that individual or group counseling can alleviate some of the suffering caused by rape and strengthen survivors' ability to cope; frequently "the process of reviewing the event allows them to gain control over their painful feelings and to begin the process of healing" (Crooks & Baur, 2014, p. 521). Greenberg and his colleagues explain:

Many survivors of sexual assault do heal and do just fine in their lives. They probably do not forget, but they do move on. There is a great deal of hope today for such survivors. (2011, p. 527)

Three basic issues are involved in working with a woman who has survived a rape. First, she is most likely in a state of emotional upheaval. Her self-concept is probably seriously shaken. Various suggestions for helping a rape survivor in such a traumatic emotional state will be provided. Second, the rape survivor must decide whether or not to call the police and press charges. Third, the rape survivor must assess her medical status following the rape, including injuries, disease, or potential pregnancy.

Emotional Issues

Helping women who have been sexually assaulted involves three major stages (Collier, 1982). First, as a social worker you need to provide the rape survivor with immediate warmth and support (Crooks & Baur, 2014). The survivor must feel safe and free to talk. She needs to ventilate and acknowledge her feelings before she can begin to deal with them. To the greatest extent possible, help the survivor to know she is now in control of her situation. Do not pressure her to talk. Rather, encourage her to share her feelings, even the worst ones, with you.

Although talking freely is important to the survivor, that she not be grilled with intimate, detailed questions is also important. She will have enough of those to deal with if she chooses to report the assault to the police.

Frequently, the survivor will dwell on what she could or should have done (Crooks & Baur, 2014; Yarber et al., 2010). Emphasizing what she did right is helpful. After all, she is alive, safe, and not severely physically harmed. She managed to survive a terrifying and dangerous experience. Talking about how she reacted normally, as anyone else in her situation would most probably have reacted, is also helpful. This suggestion does not mean minimizing the incident; rather, one should talk objectively about how traumatizing and potentially dangerous the incident was. One other useful suggestion for dealing with a rape survivor is to help her place the blame where it belongs, namely on the rapist. He chose to rape her. It was not her doing.

The second stage of counseling involves eliciting support from others (Collier, 1982; Crooks & Baur, 2014; Hyde & DeLamater, 2011). This support may include that of professional resources such as a local rape crisis center as well as support from people who are emotionally close to the survivor. Sometimes, you will need to educate those close to the survivor. They must find out that what the survivor needs is warmth and support and to feel loved. Avoid questions that emphasize her feelings of self-blame, such as why she did not fight back or why she was wearing a low-cut blouse.

A female social work instructor describes an anecdote illustrating the importance of educating people close to the survivor:

I was sitting in my office late one afternoon finishing up some extremely dull paperwork. The university halls were empty and desolate as they get in late afternoons. I suddenly heard a knock at my door and looked up. There stood an extremely tall, red-headed, handsome young man of about 24 or 25. I knew at once that he did not look familiar. He then asked if I was so-and-so who had just been quoted in the university newspaper about some information on sexual assault. I replied that I was. Meanwhile, I thought to myself, "Now this guy could not have been raped... although you never know." I also became aware of how big he was and how alone I was.

At any rate, he sat down and told me his story. His girlfriend had recently shared with him how she had been brutally raped by one of their mutual acquaintances last year. He said he loved this young woman dearly and planned to marry her. However, he could not bear even to think about the horrible incident. He said she had been trying to talk to him about it because it still disturbed her, but each time she tried, he'd cut her off. His anger at the rapist was so overwhelming he feared he couldn't control it.

We sat for over two hours and discussed his situation and his options. We talked about the emotions survivors of sexual assault typically experience. What were the consequences of not allowing her to talk to him about the assault? Perhaps she would feel that he was blaming her for some part in the assault. Maybe she would feel dirty or permanently violated. Or, at the very least, he was probably communicating to her that she would be unable to talk to him about things such as this which were critically important to her.

On the other hand, what if he could acknowledge and gain control of his anger? What would he be communicating to her if he encouraged her to talk to him about something as painful as this? He came to realize that taking this route would probably communicate to her how much he loved her. She would see that he truly cared how she felt and was trying desperately to understand. It would also probably destroy any feelings she had that he felt she was damaged or to blame. Finally, it would communicate to the young woman that she would be able to share virtually anything with him, even something this difficult. He decided that he definitely needed to listen to his girlfriend and break through his own defenses and help her as much as he could.

The young man left my office with a number of handouts supplying information similar to that presented here. Although I never heard from him again, I sincerely hope that he was able to help his girlfriend work through the aftermath of that nightmarish experience. I also romantically like to think of them still living happily together.

The third stage of counseling involves rebuilding the survivor's trust in herself, in the environment around her, and in her other personal relationships. Rape weakens a woman. It destroys her trust in herself and in others. During this stage of counseling, you need to focus on the survivor's objective evaluation of herself and her situation. You need to clarify and emphasize her strong points so that she may gain confidence in herself.

The survivor also needs to look objectively at her surrounding environment. She cannot remain cooped up in her apartment for the rest of her life. She can take precautions against being raped but needs to continue living a normal life.

Finally, you can help the survivor assess her other personal relationships objectively. Just because she was intimately violated by one aggressor, this event has nothing to do with the other people in her life. She needs to concentrate on the positive aspects of her other relationships. She must not allow the fear and terror she experienced during that one terrible incident to taint other interactions. She must clearly distinguish the rape and rapist from her other relationships.

A woman who has been raped may initially want to talk with another woman. However, talking to men, including those close to her, might also be important. That not all men are rapists is important for the survivor to realize. Sometimes there is a male partner, and his willingness to let the victim express her feelings and, in return, offer support and empathy is important (Hyde & DeLamater, 2011; Masters et al., 1995).

Reporting to the Police

The initial reaction to being raped might logically be to call the police and report the incident. However, many survivors choose not to follow through with this action. There are numerous reasons why people do not report the rape, including fear that the rapist will try to get revenge, fear of public embarrassment and derogation, an attitude that it will not matter anyway because most rapists get off free, and fear of the legal process (Hyde & Else-Quest, 2013; Kirk & Okazawa-Rey, 2013; Masters et al., 1995). Taking a rape case to court can be financially expensive and is emotionally draining.

In some cases, improvements have been made in police investigation and legal handling of rape cases. Greenberg and his colleagues (2011) explain:

Changes have . . . been made in relation to law enforcement personnel. Training has been designed to help them become more sensitive to the problem of sexual assault. More female officers are used, and there is improved cooperation between law enforcement personnel and medical and support personnel. Guidelines for handling survivors of sexual assault have also been established. (p. 529)

Despite the potential difficulties in reporting a rape, the fact remains that if the survivor does not report it, the rapist will not be held responsible for his actions. A rape survivor needs to think through her various alternatives and weigh the respective positive and negative consequences in order to come to this often difficult decision.

In the event that a survivor decides to report, she should not take a shower. Washing will remove vital evidence. However, survivors often feel defiled and dirty. Trying to cleanse themselves and forgetting that the incident ever occurred is a logical initial reaction. You must emphasize to a client who has been raped that she should not wash, despite how much she would like to do so.

Reporting a rape should be done as soon as possible after the assault. The sooner the rape is reported and the evidence gathered, the better the chance of being able to get a conviction.

Medical Status of the Survivor

In addition to emotional issues and the decision whether or not to report the incident, a third major issue, medical status, merits attention (Hyde & DeLamater, 2011). At some point, the survivor must attend to the possibility of pregnancy. She should be asked about this issue at an appropriate time and in a gentle manner. She should be encouraged to seek medical help both for this possibility and for screening sexually transmitted infections, including HIV. The negative possibilities should not be emphasized, but the survivor needs to attend to these issues at some point. Of course, you should also urge the survivor to seek immediate medical care if she has any physical injury.

MACRO ISSUES CONCERNING SEXUAL ASSAULT

EP 2.1.10

We have been primarily discussing the micro and mezzo aspects of intervention with survivors of sexual assault. The micro aspects focus attention on a woman's inner sense of self. The mezzo facets involve the survivor's relationships with others around her. The macro perspective on sexual assault is just as significant. It involves the way society perceives rape survivors, how they are treated, and what services are available to them. Three macro issues concerning sexual assault discussed here are sexual assault prevention programs, legislation, and service provision.

Sexual Assault Prevention Programs

EP 2.1.9b

Feminists emphasize that sexual assault prevention should not be the responsibility of women alone. The general population should be educated regarding the dynamics involved in sexual assault.

How society views rape survivors is critically important to what services are made available. Resources are generally scarce. Therefore, decisions must be made about what is important enough to use them for and what is not. People involved in the justice system, those who work in emergency rooms, and even the friends and family of survivors should understand that rape survivors should not be blamed for sexual assaults. To the extent that society and the general population consider rape to be a woman's own fault, they are less likely to support her with resources and services. Bergen and Maier (2011) report:

> Victims continue to be revictimized by the medical, criminal justice, and legal systems as well as by members of their community. Revictimization refers to the blame and stigmatizing responses to victims by police or others and the trauma that victims experience following the rape itself. More specifically, the term has been used to refer to the distress, alienation, and blame that victims may experience after the assault at the hands of the criminal justice and medical systems . . .
>
> Victims may face revictimization partly because of the persistence of rape myths or false and prejudicial beliefs about rape, rape victims, and rapists. Rape myths have been defined as attitudes and beliefs that are generally false but are widely and persistently held and serve to deny and justify male sexual aggression against women. (p. 233)

Education about sexual assault may rebuff the following myths and replace them with facts (Carroll, 2013):

- [Myth 1:] Only "bad" women get raped.
- [Myth 2:] Women make false reports of rape.
- [Myth 3:] Women fantasize about rape.
- [Myth 4:] Men can't be raped.
- [Myth 5:] You can tell a rapist by the way he looks.
- [Myth 6:] No woman or man can be raped against his or her will.
- [Myth 7:] A man can't rape his wife.
- [Myth 8:] Rape only happens to young, attractive women.
- [Myth 9:] Most rapists rape only once.
- [Myth 10:] False reporting of rape is common. (p. 464)

Hyde and Else-Quest (2013, pp. 291–292) identify several types of rape prevention programs that have been developed and studied:

1. Awareness-based programs *aim to create community change by raising people's awareness of the prevalence of sexual assault.*
2. *Empathy-based programs seek to increase the audience's understanding of the consequences for victims, thereby increasing empathy.*
3. Social norms-based programs *encourage individuals to question the gendered norms that support violence against women.*
4. *Skills-based programs teach people, especially women, skills that will decrease their risk of being the objects of sexual violence (e.g., avoid excessive drinking).*
5. *Bystander intervention programs encourage people to intervene actively if they see violence occurring. (Gidycz et al., 2011)*

Hyde and Else-Quest (2013) reflect on the success of such programs:

> A key characteristic of effective programs involves having the participants actively practice skills (Gidycz et al., 2011). Passive programs with an expert lecturing to a class are less effective. Peer-led programs that focus on a single gender in a small group (e.g., an athletic team), and [continue] for multiple sessions seem to be most effective. (p. 292)

One potential goal, then, of macro practice is to educate both the general public and, more specifically, those most likely to deal directly with rape survivors. This education might involve using your macro-practice skills to disseminate information, set up educational task forces, or mobilize community groups.

Legislation

EP 2.1.8a

EP 2.1.9a

Adoption of improved sexual assault legislation "has been a piecemeal process and also varies from state to state" (Kirk & Okazawa-Rey, 2013, p. 271). However, Greenberg and his colleagues (2011) reflect on positive developments in many states' legislation regarding sexual assault:

There have . . . been major changes in laws related to rape in the past few decades. Many of the newer rape laws (1) establish "degrees" of rape to describe types of sexual assault more accurately; (2) are gender neutral and do not apply only to attacks by men on women; (3) eliminate requirements that victims prove they resisted by "fighting back" and that corroborating evidence be presented; (4) shield victims from inquiries into past sexual experience; and (5) allow a husband to be charged with raping his wife. In fact, in many states the term forced sex *or* sexual assault *has replaced the word* rape. *The convicted rapist can often be sentenced to life in prison. (p. 529)*

Kirk and Okazawa-Rey (2013) continue:

On the federal level, the Violence Against Women Act (VAWA) was signed into law as part of the Violent Crime and Law Enforcement Act of 1994. It authorized funds for battered women's shelters and community initiatives, training for judges and court personnel, improvements in arrest policies, and legal advocacy programs for victims. (p. 271)

When legislation is lacking or inadequate, it is the responsibility of generalist practitioners to advocate for improvements. Social workers should continuously appraise the environmental context and conditions for clients so that they may seek to provide needed and effective services.

Service Provision

Recent decades have shown an increase and expansion of resources and services for survivors of sexual assault; although the number of rape crisis centers has increased over the years, such programs still face serious challenges (Bergen & Maier, 2011). Bergen and Maier (2011) discuss the current condition of rape crisis centers in addition to providing examples of community coalitions to support the survivors of sexual assault:

For some centers, lack of funding is the single most important challenge they face and has resulted in reduction of services to survivors and contributed to

problems recruiting and retaining staff. . . . Because of limited funds, staff members fill multiple roles, which often leads to stress and burnout. (p. 229)

Decades ago most centers were founded on the basis of feminist principles, including the necessity of advocacy on women's behalf; funding issues have forced many centers to cut back on this advocacy practice (Bergen & Maier, 2011). This makes it all the more important for social workers to advocate on the behalf of survivors for rights and services.

An example of a positive initiative is the establishment of Sexual Assault Nurse Examiner (SANE) programs that "provide immediate, compassionate, culturally sensitive, and comprehensive forensic evaluation and treatment by trained nurses" (p. 232). Such SANE programs often operate in conjunction with Sexual Assault Response Teams (SARTs), described as follows:

SARTs typically involve a coordinated effort among community members including victim advocates, law enforcement, the prosecutor's office, and the SANE, with the goal of assisting a survivor of sexual violence through the medical and legal systems. . . . These programs began in the early 1990s, in an effort to achieve a "more coordinated and consistent response to sexual assault" (Pennsylvania Coalition Against Rape, 2002). Two important components of SART are to provide better evidence collection and greater support for survivors. . . . SARTs can play an important role in recognizing the diverse needs of survivors of sexual assault and increasing communication among team members to minimize trauma, meet the survivor's needs, and increase participation in the legal process. (p. 233)

LO 13-6 Intervene with Battered Women

Intervention with battered women is the second issue we will address from the micro-, mezzo-, and macro-level intervention perspectives. Terms associated with *wife beating* include *domestic violence, family violence, spouse abuse,* and *battered women. Battering* is a catch-all term that includes, but is not limited to, slapping, punching, knocking down, choking, kicking, hitting with objects, threatening with weapons, stabbing, and shooting. The battered woman syndrome implies the systematic and repeated use of one or more of these practices against a woman by her husband or partner.

Although we use the term *wife* throughout the next few sections, the principles involved apply to all women in intimate relationships characterized by battery, regardless of marital status.

Some of the myths about battered women include the following:

- *Battered women are not really hurt that badly.*
- *Beatings and other abuses just happen; they are not a regular occurrence.*
- *Women who stay in such homes must really enjoy the beatings they get, otherwise they would leave.*
- *Wife battering only occurs in lower-class families.*

A PROFILE OF BATTERED WOMEN

Shaw and Lee (2012) describe the incidence of battery against women:

Although women are less likely than men to be victims of violent of crimes overall, women are 5 to 8 times more likely to be victimized by an intimate partner. Intimate partner violence is primarily a crime against women and all races are equally vulnerable. . . . [In a recent year] the Bureau of Justice reported that 96 percent of women experiencing nonfatal partner violence were victimized by a male and about 85 percent of all victims were female. According to FBI statistics, every day about four women (approximately 1,400 a year) die in the United States as a result of domestic violence. Although about half a million reports of physical assault by intimates officially reach federal officials each year, it is estimated that 2 to 4 million women are battered each year; about one every 20 seconds or so. Women of all races and classes are battered, although rates are 5 times higher among families below poverty levels, and severe spouse abuse is twice as likely to be committed by unemployed men as by those working full time. These differences reflect economic vulnerability and lack of resources, as well as the ways these families have more contact with authorities like social services that increases opportunities for reporting. Women who are pregnant are especially at risk of violence. Approximately 17 percent of pregnant women report having been battered, and the results include miscarriages, stillbirths, and a two- to fourfold greater likelihood of bearing a low birth weight baby. . . .

Women who are physically abused are also always emotionally abused because they experience emotional abuse by virtue of being physically terrorized. . . . Emotional abuse, however, does not always involve physical abuse. A man, for example, *who constantly tells his partner that she is worthless, stupid, or ugly can emotionally abuse without being physically abusive. Sometimes the scars of emotional abuse take longer to heal than physical abuse and help explain why women might stay with abusive partners. (pp. 516–517)*

Kirk and Okazawa-Rey (2013) indicate that injuries resulting from physical abuse may consist of "bruises, cuts, burns and scalds, concussion, broken bones, penetrating injuries from knives, miscarriages, permanent injuries such as damage to joints, partial loss of hearing or vision, and physical disfigurement. There are also serious mental health effects of isolation, humiliation, and ongoing threats of violence" (p. 262).

Battered women do not like to be beaten. They may initially experience "shock, disbelief, and denial, followed by terror, then attempts to reestablish the level of safety previously believed to have existed, followed by depression with intermittent inner-directed rage and outbursts of anger" (Harway, 1993, p. 38). They do not enjoy the pain and suffering, but, for reasons that will be discussed later, they tolerate it.

The following sections will introduce a strengths perspective on battery, describe common characteristics of abusive partners, explain the battering cycle, and explore why so many battered women opt to remain in abusive environments. Counseling strategies will be suggested to help a woman address her situation from the micro and mezzo perspectives. Finally, implications for macro-practice intervention on the part of battered women will be discussed.

SURVIVORS VERSUS VICTIMS: A STRENGTHS PERSPECTIVE

As with survivors of sexual assault, we will refer to people who have survived domestic violence as *survivors* instead of *victims*. Once again, instead of focusing on a woman's weakness, which the word *victim* implies, we will use the term *survivor* to emphasize her survival strengths and attempts to get out of her abusive environment.

THE ABUSIVE PERPETRATOR

Men who batter come from all walks of life and income groups. Batterers tend to adhere to common masculine gender-role stereotypes such as failing to display emotion or sensitivity to others because they perceive these as reflecting weakness (Shaw & Lee, 2012). Such men likely feel it is important to maintain male dominance in society and keep women under control (Papalia,

Olds, & Feldman, 2009). "Many call on cultural norms about male passions and female weaknesses to describe their actions as normal and even nonviolent" (Anderson & Umberson, 2001; Sapiro, 2003, p. 392; Shaw & Lee, 2012). "Some men rationalize their violent acts as having been provoked by their wives or partners" (Papalia et al., 2007, p. 532; Umberson, Anderson, Williams, & Chen, 2003).

CULTURAL INFLUENCES AND BATTERED WOMEN

Kail and Cavanaugh (2013) reflect on the influence of culture on battering:

> *Culture is also an important contextual factor in understanding partner abuse.*
>
> *In particular, violence against women worldwide reflects cultural traditions, beliefs, and values of patriarchal societies; this can be seen in the commonplace violent practices against women, which include sexual slavery, female genital cutting, intimate partner violence, and honor killing (Parrot & Cummings, 2006). For example, cultures that emphasize honor, that portray females as passive, nurturing supporters of men's activities, and that emphasize loyalty and sacrifice for the family may also contribute to tolerating abuse.*
>
> *Vandello (2000) reported two studies—of Latino Americans, European Americans who live in the southern part of the United States, and European Americans who live in the northern part of the United States—that examined these ideas. Latino Americans and European Americans who lived in the southern part of the United States placed more value on honor. These groups rated a woman in an abusive relationship more positively if she stayed with the man; they also communicated less disapproval of a woman whom they witnessed being shoved and restrained if she portrayed herself as contrite and self-blaming than did European Americans who lived in the northern part of the United States, who rated the woman more positively if she left the man. Research on Mexican women who were victims of partner abuse confirm[s] that, even when they are willing to seek help, they nevertheless still follow cultural dictates to cope (Vargas, 2007).*
>
> *Chinese Americans are more likely to define domestic violence in terms of physical and sexual aggression and do not include psychological forms of abuse (Yick, 2000). And South Asian immigrants to the United States report the use of social isolation (e.g., not being able to interact with family, friends,*

or coworkers) as a very painful form of abuse that is often tied to being financially dependent on the husband and traditional cultural roles (Abraham, 2000).

> *Additionally, international data indicate that rates of abuse are higher in cultures that emphasize female purity, male status, and family honor. For example, a common cause of women's murders in Arab countries is brothers or other male relatives killing the victim because she violated the family's honor (Kulwicki, 2002). Intimate partner violence is prevalent in China (43% lifetime risk in one study) and has strong associations with male patriarchal values and conflict resolutions (Xu et al., 2005). (pp. 392–393)*

Ivey, Kramer, and Yoshioka (2005) discuss cultural considerations concerning female immigrants in the United States who come from various cultures. They recommend that "[a]lthough care should be taken to approach the issue in a culturally sensitive manner, it is important that every woman be given the opportunity to have private time with an appropriate interpreter away from family members in order to fully assess her risks and inform her of her options for receiving care, support services, and asylum" (p. 278). They continue:

> *If the [social worker] . . . establishes that a patient has a history of victimization, concern should be evidenced for the [client] . . . and the [client] . . . reassured that help is available. Safety needs should be addressed first, including the safety of dependents such as children. In the context of the immigrant woman, it is important to identify those resources in the community that are likely to have language interpretation skills available. In addition, the need for family-centered treatment should be determined because it may be more acceptable to immigrant women from cultures in which the family is supreme. In the United States, the patient should be told that protection exists under current law, even if she is a recent or undocumented immigrant. Laws that mandate reporting of injuries from domestic violence vary from state to state in the United States and certainly cannot be expected to be the same across countries. [Social workers] . . . should be familiar with the laws on domestic violence in their states and respective countries (Hyman, Schillinger, & Lo, 1995).*
>
> *Finally, working with women from other cultural contexts will require [social workers] . . . to reexamine their convictions about the need for culturally competent practices and feminist principles that call for*

the end of patriarchal structures that oppress women. There is a dilemma inherent in the work that raises difficult questions about what constitutes ethical practice that each of us must answer individually. It is also an area of collective concern that [practitioners] ... and researchers must begin to discuss. (pp. 278–279)

Critical Thinking Questions 13.3

- To what extent should culture be used as a rationale to perpetuate the battering of women?
- How can social workers advocate for battered women and still respect diverse cultural expectations?

THE BATTERING CYCLE

Three basic phases tend to characterize battery in an intimate relationship (Mooney, Knox, & Schacht, 2011; Shaw & Lee, 2012; Walker, 1979a, 2009). The first phase involves the building up of stress and tension. The wife tries to "make things OK" and avoid confrontations. There may be a few minor abusive incidents, but this phase is primarily characterized by the buildup of excessive tension.

The second phase in the battering cycle is the explosion. This point is where the tension breaks, the batterer loses control, and the battering occurs. Although this phase is the shortest of the three phases, it may last for a few hours to several days.

The third phase involves making up and being in love again. Because his tension has been released, the batterer now adamantly states that he is truly sorry for what he has done and swears he will never do it again. The battered woman relents and believes him. He is forgiven, and all seems well—that is, until the cycle of violence begins again.

WHY DOES SHE STAY?

Many people wonder why the battered woman remains in the home and in the relationship. There are many reasons why women stay in the battering environment (Mooney et al., 2011; Papalia et al., 2009; Shaw & Lee, 2012). Research suggests that women tend to attempt leaving the abusive relationship and return five to seven times before they leave permanently (Shaw & Lee, 2012). Many women who seek help from shelters and even those who initiate separation through the courts eventually return to their abusive home situations. The reasons they remain or return include economic

dependence, lack of self-confidence, lack of power, fear of the abuser, adherence to traditional beliefs, guilt, feeling isolated with nowhere to go, fear for their children, and love.

Economic Dependence

Many battered women are afraid to leave the perpetrator for economic reasons (Mooney et al., 2011; Shaw & Lee, 2012). Many are financially dependent on the abuser as the primary wage earner for both themselves and their children. Although battering of women occurs at all socioeconomic levels, it is more likely to happen in families with fewer resources. Three economic factors related to increased wife abuse include poverty, underemployment, and unemployment. When children are involved, there is the additional problem of who would care for them if their mother had to increase the amount of time she spent outside of the home in order to earn a living.

Lack of Self-Confidence

Domestic violence involves not only physical abuse, but also sexual and psychological abuse (Mooney et al., 2011; Papalia et al., 2009). Psychological abuse may entail regular tirades by battering men who criticize and blast survivors with derogatory remarks. Bit by bit, such treatment eats away at the women's self-esteem and shrinks their self-confidence. Perpetrators tend to emphasize how their female partners could not possibly survive without them, and after an extended period of time, these women start to believe them. In some ways, psychological abuse is similar to the brainwashing of prisoners of war (Davis, 1995).

Mustering the self-confidence to leave a painful situation and strike out for the unknown takes great initiative and courage. The unknown is frightening. If the domestic violence survivor remains in the home, at least she knows she has a place to stay.

Lack of Power

A battered woman views herself as having significantly less power in her relationship with the abuser than does a woman with a partner who is nonviolent (Forte, Franks, Forte, & Rigsby, 1996; Shaw & Lee, 2012). Battered women see their relationships as almost completely dominated by the perpetrator. Batterers' systematic regimen of intimidation, criticism, and violence places women in a vulnerable and difficult position.

However, one should note that even in the face of such adversity, indeed "daily surveillance and torture," these women utilize their strengths; Burstow (1992) explains:

> They are not simply submitting, even where submission is key and even though submission is expectable and blameless. They are also making active and critical decisions about how to cope and survive on a moment-to-moment basis. They are deciding to hide certain things. They are deciding to duck. They are deciding not to duck. Each in her own way is resisting. Actively and passively, survivors resist violation, whether that resistance takes the form of numbing themselves so that they will not feel the pain, finding ways of avoiding the abuser's ire, or saying no. (p. 153)

Fear of the Abuser

Fearing brutal retaliation by the perpetrator if she leaves him is logical for a battered woman (Papalia et al., 2009; Shaw & Lee, 2012). A person who has dealt with stress by physical brutality before might do so again when it is initiated by the stress of his female partner leaving him. The battered woman might even fear being murdered by an abandoned male partner.

One myth is that battered women stay in the relationship because they like being beaten, which is not true. For reasons discussed here, they tolerate their circumstances in order to survive.

Guilt

Many battered women feel that being abused is their own fault (Mooney et al., 2011; Papalia et al., 2009; Shaw & Lee, 2012). They tend to believe in men being the dominant decision makers and leaders of the family and that women should be submissive and obedient. To some extent, this guilt may be due to their husbands telling them that they are to blame for causing trouble. Perhaps because of their low levels of self-esteem, being critical of themselves is easy for survivors. Their beliefs in traditional gender-role stereotypes may cause them to wonder how they have failed in their submissive, nurturing role of wife.

Feeling Isolated with Nowhere to Go

Battered women often try to keep the facts of their battery a secret. They may feel and be isolated from friends and family by the time their battery reaches such crisis proportions (Papalia et al., 2009; Shaw & Lee, 2012). Frequently, the perpetrator strongly discourages his female partner's interactions with friends and family. He criticizes them. He makes communicating with them as difficult as possible for her. He gradually gets her to cut others off. Then he can have her all to himself. When the abuser becomes everything to the survivor, losing him means that she would be all alone.

Fear for Her Children

A battered woman who is a mother usually fears for her children's safety (Shaw & Lee, 2012). First, she might be worried about her ability to support them financially without her male partner. Second, she may firmly adhere to the traditional belief that children need a father. She may think that a father who abuses his wife is better than no father at all. Third, she may even fear losing the custody of her children. The abuser may threaten to take them away from her. She may have little knowledge of the complicated legal system and may believe that he can and will do it.

Love

Many battered women still love their abusive husbands (Mooney et al., 2011). Many who seek help would prefer to remain in their relationships if the battering would stop. Walker (1979b) cites one senior woman's reactions to her husband's death. The woman, a university professor, had been married for 53 years to a man who battered her throughout their relationship. The woman states, "We did everything together.... I loved him; you know, even when he was brutal and mean.... I'm sorry he's dead, although there were days when I wished he would die.... He was my best friend.... He beat me right up to the end.... It was a good life and I really do miss him."

EMPOWERING BATTERED WOMEN THROUGH SERVICE PROVISION

Despite the difficulties in dealing with domestic violence, there are definite intervention strategies that can be undertaken. They involve shelters, crisis intervention hotlines, individual and group counseling, public education, legal advocacy, and batterers' intervention programs. Specific counseling approaches to empower battered women are also discussed.

Shelters for Battered Women

The most immediate need of a woman who has been seriously battered is a place to go. For this purpose, shelters have been developed around the country. This occurrence is relatively recent. The first American shelters for battered women, Rainbow Retreat in Phoenix and Transition House in Boston, opened in 1973 (Barusch, 2012).

Shelters provide safe places of refuge for battered women and their children. Most shelters allow survivors of domestic violence to stay for several months while receiving other services and becoming empowered to take care of themselves and their families (MassResources.org, 2013). Residential facilities may include those funded by public Department of Social Services or by nonprofit organizations; sometimes community residents provide "safe houses" (MassResources.org, 2013). Shelters often provide a range of other services, including crisis intervention hotlines, individual counseling and support groups, public education, legal advocacy, batterers' intervention programs, and many other innovative services geared to meeting battered women's needs (Wisconsin Department of Health & Human Services [DHHS], 2010).

Crisis Intervention Hotlines

Shelters have crisis hotlines where women can call for help on a 24-hour basis for a range of information and referral possibilities (MassResources.org, 2013; Wisconsin DHHS, 2010). All information is strictly confidential to protect callers' identities and whereabouts. Clients can acquire information about the dynamics involved in battering, counseling, and advocacy concerning social services, legal involvement, and health care needs. Hotline counselors refer callers to applicable services offered by the shelter and other agencies. Note that it is important to have bilingual staff receiving hotline calls in areas with populations whose primary language is not English (MassResources.org, 2013).

Individual Counseling and Support Groups

A shelter may offer individual counseling and support groups for survivors of domestic violence. Issues addressed include "safety, self-esteem, assertiveness, self-sufficiency, and life without violence" (Wisconsin DHHS, 2010). Groups can provide information on topics including financial management, goal planning, and job-finding, in addition to improved communication and child management skills. Individual and group counseling may also focus on longer lasting psychological consequences of domestic abuse, including emotional difficulties, depression, and anger.

Public Education

Shelter staff can provide public education on a variety of issues, including the dynamics of domestic abuse, prevention, community resources, effects of abuse on children, and how to help battered women. Staff can make educational presentations before virtually any organization or group in the community, including those in workplaces, churches, service clubs, schools, and universities.

Legal Advocacy

Shelter staff can help battered women by providing them both with support and with information about legal issues and court proceedings. Staff can guide survivors through the processes of obtaining restraining orders, negotiating divorce proceedings, and settling custody disputes (Wisconsin DHHS, 2010). This includes accompanying clients during court hearings to provide support, offer another layer of safety, and help the clients work through the legal process.

Batterers' Intervention Programs

Group counseling may provide perpetrators with information concerning the dynamics and cycle of abuse. Such groups can focus on developing insight into personal motivation and interpersonal dynamics. Additionally, they can teach anger management skills and means of controlling abusive behaviors.

Critical Thinking Question 13.4

- To what extent do you think resources should be funneled to help perpetrators rather than the battered women themselves? What are your reasons?

COUNSELING STRATEGIES

The following are some basic suggestions, gathered from a range of sources, regarding how social workers and counselors can help battered women.

Offer Support

A battered woman has probably been weakened both physically and emotionally. She needs someone to empathize with her and express genuine concern. She needs some time to sit back, experience some relief, and think.

Emphasize Strengths

The most important aspect of helping a battery survivor is to clarify and emphasize her strengths. She has been weakened and hurt both physically and psychologically. Cowger (1997) gives the following suggestions for emphasizing strengths during the assessment process:

1. *Believe the client.* A central concept in the strengths perspective is that clients are trustworthy and will tell the truth. A battery survivor may require assistance

in looking at herself and her situation objectively, identifying alternatives she had not thought of before, and emphasizing strengths she does not yet appreciate. However, a client's perception of her reality is real. It should be taken seriously and addressed.

2. *Discover what the client wants.* This suggestion involves two facets: what the client expects you to do for her and how the client wants her situation improved. Does she want the perpetrator to enter a treatment program so she can go home again? Does she want to disappear with her children so that she can be safe? Is she still unclear about what she realistically wants? You can help her articulate her concerns, identify possibilities, and evaluate her choices. You can also clarify what you can do to help. For example, you may be able to provide her with a safe place to stay, but not put the perpetrator in jail. You can help her think through her alternatives, but not make her decisions.

3. *Move the assessment toward personal and environmental strengths.* Help your client think about a wide range of strengths. Personal strengths may include the fact that she is bright, a terrific mother, a hard worker, or that she has established some excellent coping skills in the past. You might stress how well she communicates, has been able to protect her children under harrowing circumstances, has accomplished educational or training goals, or has developed exceptional organizational skills to hold her family together. Environmental strengths might include access to resources, including finances, transportation, housing, family, friends, religious support, or available social services. (p. 64)

Review Alternatives

A battered woman may feel trapped and be so overwhelmed that alternatives may not even have occurred to her. Her alternatives may include returning to the marriage, getting counseling for both herself and her husband, temporarily separating from her husband, establishing other means of financial support and independent living conditions for herself, finding good child care, or filing for divorce.

Furnish Information

Most survivors probably do not have much information about how they can be helped. Information about available legal, medical, and social services may open up alternatives to better enable them to help themselves.

Advocate

An advocate can seek out information for a survivor of domestic violence and provide her with encouragement. An advocate can also help the survivor get in touch with legal, medical, and social service resources and help the survivor find her way through bureaucratic processes. Advocacy involves expending extra energy, "going that extra mile," on the survivor's behalf.

Perhaps an even more critical aspect of advocacy involves changing legal macro systems:

> *Effective intervention requires some fundamental changes in current police and court practices. In many communities, advocates for battered women pushed for pro-arrest policies, a more aggressive approach to prosecution and sentences geared towards victim safety. Advocates promote civil processes that complemented the criminal court response and pushed for a coordination of civil and criminal approaches to ensure the maximum protection for victims.* (Duprey, McDonnell, Paymar, Regan, & Soderber, 1996, p. 10)

The following are specific suggestions regarding the initial interview, the range of the victim's emotional reactions, and specific counseling techniques.

The Initial Interview

A battered woman will probably be filled with anxiety during her initial meeting with a social worker. She may be worried about what to say to you. Therefore, you should try to make the woman as comfortable as possible and emphasize that she does not have to talk about anything if she does not want to.

The battered woman may also anticipate that you will be judgmental and critical of her. It is important to put personal feelings aside and not pressure the battered woman into any particular course of action. This suggestion may be especially difficult when you have some strong personal feelings that the woman should leave the abusive situation. A basic principle is that what the woman will choose to do is her decision. In those cases where the battered woman chooses to return home, the counselor should help the woman clarify the reasons behind this decision.

Confidentiality may also be an issue for the battered woman. She may be especially fearful of the abuser finding out she is seeking help and of his possible retaliation. You need to assure her that no information will be given to anyone unless she wants it to. In the event that she does need a place to go, make her understand that the shelter is available.

The woman may show some embarrassment at being a "battered woman." The label may make her feel uncomfortable. Therefore, you should make efforts to dispel any embarrassment by emphasizing that she is not the perpetrator. The abuser is to blame for his own violent behavior. This problem has nothing to do with her character or with her intrinsic human value.

Emotional Reactions

Many battered women will display a range of emotional reactions, which include helplessness, fear, anger, guilt, embarrassment, and even doubts about their sanity. You need to encourage the battered woman to get all of these emotions out in the open because only then will she be able to deal with them. You now can help her look objectively at various aspects of her situation and help get control of her own life.

Specific Counseling Techniques

The foundation of good counseling is good listening ability. The battered woman needs to know that she can talk freely to you and that what she says will have meaning.

A battered woman is often overwhelmed and confused. One of the most helpful things you can do is to help her sort through her various issues by using problem-solving skills. She cannot do everything at once, but she can begin getting control of her life by addressing one issue at a time and making step-by-step decisions.

One other important counseling technique is helping the woman establish a "safety plan" (Dziegielewski, Resnick, & Krause, 1996, p. 166). This involves clarifying exactly how she should react in the event she has contact with the abuser. It should be clear to her what she should do in a variety of different circumstances. "The plan should focus on how the victim can escape, where she can go, and who can help her. This should be laid out in terms of very specific behaviors, including such items as which phone she would use and where she could keep some clothes, an extra set of car keys, and the like" (Dziegielewski et al., 1996, p. 166).

In summary, battered women need to strengthen their self-esteem and define more objectively the alternatives available to them. They need a chance to vent their feelings and to have someone there to listen to them. They need to have a place of refuge until they can think through their situations and make decisive future plans of action.

SUGGESTIONS FOR MACRO PRACTICE ON BEHALF OF BATTERED WOMEN

Strengthening legislation and service provision for battered women at the local, state, and national levels is critically important. Passage of the Violence Against Women Act (VAWA) in 1994 demonstrates some progress, as this legislation calls for: increased funding of shelters and programs; tougher treatment of offenders; establishment of a national hotline; education of judges, other court staff, and youth in general about domestic violence; and "a provision that makes crossing state lines in pursuit of a fleeing partner a federal offense" (Renzetti et al., 2012, p. 208). "The impact of the law continues to be assessed, but the hope is that it will help turn the tables on batterers who historically have been afforded more legal protection in our society than those they victimize" (Renzetti et al., 2012, pp. 208–209). Highlight 13.5 addresses some dimensions of the international picture of domestic violence.

One avenue of macro intervention is to continue lobbying actively for stronger legislation at the state and national levels. Another aspect of macro practice is to advocate for the establishment of services within your community. Once again, informing the community of the need and organizing potentially interested community groups to help in the task is a possibility. Services should be coordinated and comprehensive as agencies and colleagues work together to combat domestic violence. Agency administration can provide staff with educational opportunities to explore issues and intervention concerning domestic violence. Staff can inform clients about their legal rights. Practitioners can offer a range of counseling options to families involved in domestic violence and remain informed about community options to make appropriate referrals.

LO 13-7 Examine the Feminization of Poverty

The term *feminization of poverty* has been coined to reflect the fact that women as a group are more likely to be poor than are men. Earlier this chapter established that most women, even those with very young children, work outside of the home. On the average, women's full-time, year-round median weekly earnings are approximately 80.5 percent of men's (U.S. Census

HIGHLIGHT 13.5

An International Perspective on Domestic Violence

EP 2.1.5

"Canada has similar programs [to that of VAWA] . . . [for helping] battered women. Efforts to protect women and eliminate gender-based violence also are under way in various European and Latin American countries. In England and Brazil, police are being trained to understand gender-based violence and to help women feel comfortable in reporting it" (Papalia, Olds, & Feldman, 2004, p. 511; Walker, 1999).

Yoshihama (2002) conducted "the first study in Japan to use face-to-face interviews with a community-based sample of battered women" and reported on the status of service provision and treatment there (p. 391). Although prior studies found less domestic violence in Japan than in the United States, this may have been due to traditional values about the issue. There are "prevailing attitudes among public officials and the general public that domestic violence is largely a private, personal matter, as opposed to a social problem or crime. Studies have documented a high degree of tolerance for domestic violence in Japan" (p. 390). Additionally, as Japanese law mandates reconciliation if one member of a couple rejects divorce, women may be forced to remain in abusive relationships. Therefore, Yoshihama (2002) suggests that much abuse is hidden. Similar to statistics in the United States, one-third of women murdered in Japan are "killed by their male intimate partners" (p. 390).

Yoshihama (2002) used "focus groups— semi-structured interviews in a group setting" to explore participants' observations and experiences (p. 390). She found that the nature of violence varied significantly among participants, "ranging from slapping, punching, kicking, dragging, and strangling. Household items, furniture, knives, and guns were used as weapons, often inflicting grave injuries. Alcohol may or may not have been involved at the time of the

violent incidents. Some women were forced to have sex, which was often accompanied by physical violence. Many women reported that they were physically abused when they refused to have sex. One woman suffered from multiple unwanted pregnancies because of her partner's refusal to use contraception. Violence during pregnancy threatened the health of the woman and her fetus. Verbal put-downs were common and included, 'idiot,' 'lazy,' 'female pig,' 'useless,' and derogatory terms referring to feces" (p. 393).

Domestic violence "began to be recognized as a significant social problem" in Japan only since the early 1990s (Yoshihama, 2002, p. 397). "The first battered women's shelter opened in 1993 in Tokyo, and currently there are more than 30 shelters nationwide" (p. 391). In 2001, the first law was passed that advanced "social policies and services" specifically to deal with domestic violence (p. 390). Yoshihama (2002) stresses the "central role grassroots women's organizations have played in increasing institutional responses to domestic violence" both in Japan and in the United States, although "almost 20 years apart" (p. 391). She calls for the continued need for social workers in both countries to advocate for improved legislation that protects survivors and provides needed services.

Walker (2009) summarizes a central issue concerning domestic violence at the international level:

As long as patriarchal values prevail and sex roles are assigned by the culture, women are treated as less important than men. In some countries, like India, the discrimination starts with paying midwives less who deliver female babies while others are more sophisticated but still discriminate against women. As the world organizations have declared, women must be treated as equals with men before violence against them by men will stop. (p. 310)

Bureau, 2011). Women are significantly more likely to be poor within their lifetimes. "The two poorest groups in the United States are women raising children alone and women over sixty-five living alone" (Kirk & Okazawa-Rey, 2013, p. 319). Families with children under age 18 that are maintained by women comprise over 21 percent of all white families, 54 percent of all African-American families, and 30 percent of all Hispanic families (U.S. Census Bureau, 2011).

Census figures reflect how female-headed families are especially at risk of falling below the *poverty threshold* (the quantity of money established by the government that is necessary to maintain a minimal subsistence level of living). Figure 13.1 depicts how people living in families headed by single women are much more likely to live in poverty regardless of race (U.S. Census Bureau, 2011). African-American and Hispanic female-headed families experience the

	White Alone	African-American	Hispanic	Asian
Single Female Household Head	27.3%	36.7%	38.8%	16.9%
Single Male Household Head	15.0%	25.0%	23.0%	12.6%
Married Couple Household Heads	5.4%	8.6%	16.0%	7.9%

© Cengage Learning

FIGURE 13.1 Percentage of People Living in Poverty: Comparisons by Family Structure and Race

greatest risk, with over 36 percent of all people living in such families being poor. Note that people living in families headed by a married couple are significantly less likely to be poor than those living in female-headed families, with white married-couple families experiencing the least risk of poverty. With the exception of Hispanics, people living in families headed by a single male are somewhat more likely to be poor than those living in families headed by a married couple. However, the risk of poverty for people living in female-headed families is almost double or more that of their male-headed family counterparts.

As Figure 13.1 reflects, with the exception of Asian women, women of color suffer even greater risks of living in poverty than do white women. The average median weekly earnings of African-American women are less than 88.7 percent of what non-Hispanic white women earn, and Hispanic women only 73.9 percent (U.S. Census Bureau, 2011).

Women are generally clustered in low-paying, supportive occupations (U.S. Census Bureau, 2011). For instance, women tend to be dental assistants instead of dentists or engineering technicians instead of engineers. Occupations pursued primarily by women include nurses, elementary and middle school teachers, paralegals, maids, child care workers, receptionists, and administrative assistants. Men, on the other hand, are more likely to pursue better-paying occupations such as doctor, lawyer, engineer, architect, or dentist. Perhaps an even more striking finding is that women earn significantly less than men in every major occupation category when comparing their median incomes (U.S. Census Bureau, 2011). See Table 13.1. See Highlight 13.6 for how women's salaries have compared to men's in social work.

Critical Thinking Question 13.5

EP 2.1.3

- What do you think should be done to make the earnings of women and men more equitable?

MICRO AND MEZZO PERSPECTIVES ON WOMEN AND POVERTY

Much attention has been given to the widening gap between the rich and the poor in the United States. Job losses, lack of salary increases, housing expense, decreased property values, loss of private pension accounts, escalating expense of higher education, lack of access to adequate educational opportunities, soaring educational debt, little family wealth, disability, age, race, gender, and a range of other variables affect

TABLE 13.1 Comparison of Women's and Men's Median Earnings in Major Occupation Categories*

Occupation	Percentage of Full-Time, Year-Round Women's Median Earnings Compared to Men's
Management, business, and financial occupations	72.7
Professional and related occupations	73.6
Service occupations	75.3
Sales and office occupations	75.1
Natural resource construction and maintenance	75.5
Production, transportation, and material moving occupations	69.0
Armed forces**	Data unavailable**

© Cengage Learning

*This information was taken from "Table 650. Workers with Earnings by Occupation of Longest Held Job and Sex: 2009" in the *U.S. Census Bureau's Statistical Abstract of the United States: 2012* (Washington, DC: U.S. Census Bureau, 2011).

**Data is unavailable for comparison because the number of women employed did not meet the minimum for inclusion in the information.

what people are able to achieve. As they say, the playing field is not level. People do not have *equal* opportunities and support.

How does education in the inner cities compare with that in the much richer suburbs? How well are people in lower classes prepared educationally to compete for college entrance, vocational training programs, or jobs, compared with more fortunate people? Where will they get the money in order to attend? In terms of prioritizing need, where will a poor, single mother find enough additional money to pay for day care for her children, transportation to and from work, and appropriate clothing to get and keep a job? Her main concern is to keep her family solvent from day to day with enough food and shelter to live. The point is that the same options are simply not available to poor people that are to middle- and upper-class people.

For example, one social worker describes her experience:

I will never forget a client who taught me about the futility encompassing poverty. She was a 15-year-old female client named Marcia. Her mother had never been married and had given birth to Marcia when she was just 16.

Marcia attended a day treatment facility where she received special education and therapy, yet still returned to her home each evening. She had a lengthy history of self-abuse including drug abuse, truancy, running away, and sexual activity with older men. Marcia was assigned to my social work case-load for counseling.

Marcia was obviously bright. She grasped ideas quickly and articulated her thoughts well. At times, she showed interest in areas such as photography and nature, which contrasted starkly with what was available in her home environment. Although she

HIGHLIGHT 13.6

Women's Salaries in Social Work

Unfortunately, the same dreary picture has prevailed in social work as in other professions in terms of salary and gender inequity (Brandwein, 2008; Malai, 2013; NASW Center for Workforce Studies, 2011; Pace, 2010). Research conducted since 1961 reflects a significant, consistent wage differential between men and women in social work (Gibelman, 2003). One study found that female social workers earned a median salary that was less than 83 percent of male social workers' salaries (Pace, 2010). Salary differences were evident even when controlling such factors as degree level, years of experience, age, actual number of weekly hours worked, field of practice (e.g., child welfare, mental health, older adults), and type of practice (e.g., direct practice versus administration); female social workers made 86 percent of what male social workers earned (NASW Center for Workforce Studies, 2011). When looking at the total picture, female social workers are significantly overrepresented in the lower-earning category (89 percent) versus males (11 percent) (NASW Center for Workforce Studies, 2011). Generally speaking, social workers who are male, are older, and have more education earn higher salaries (NASW Center for Workforce Studies, 2011; Pace, 2010).

was still behind in school, she was making significant strides and demonstrated excellent potential for being a good student.

At one point, I asked Marcia if she had ever considered going to college. She looked at me as if I had just developed hundreds of huge purple spots all over my body. "Where would somebody like me ever get the money to go to college? Are you nuts?" she asked.

The interesting thing was that I could not think of a rational response. "Yep," I thought to myself, "where would she get the money?" She would not get it from a scholarship because she essentially had no grade point at her special therapeutic school. Her mother and everyone else she knew except for staff at the treatment center were devastatingly poor.

Working her way through college would be difficult because any job she would be able to get would barely cover the cost of food, clothing, and rent. Worse yet, where would she get the confidence to go on to college, assuming that she could even obtain her high school equivalency through our program? Where would she find out how to apply to schools? Where would she learn how to act and how to study? She was used to the streets and special treatment programs. Nobody she knew at home ever went to college. In fact, few even completed high school. There was no one to serve as a model or to encourage her. My involvement with her would only last a few months. Then what?

The hurdles this young woman would have to overcome were awesome. Her realistic alternatives were severely limited. I certainly had no magic answers.

Several years later, long after I left my job, I ran into another staff member. We began talking about old times, and Marcia's name came up. I found out she had gotten pregnant when she was 17, quit school, and lived with a series of men after that.

Marcia's environment was restrictive. Her resources were limited, and she simply was not prepared to compete in a middle-class world. That is why when we talk about women and poverty, we will emphasize the macro approaches for change. The "system" as it exists provides her with few, restricted options, and it, rather than Marcia, needs to be changed.

Of course, some individuals can fight against amazing odds and eventually get a good job or receive vocational training or even a college degree. But the chances of success for the vast majority of these individuals are slim.

At the micro and mezzo levels of intervention, you can essentially do four things to enhance your client's strengths. First, you can work to increase your client's self-confidence. Second, you can help your client to define and evaluate the realistic opportunities available to her. Third, you can educate her regarding the resources that are available and help her get involved with them. Fourth, you can actively reach out into the community and your client's homes, asking questions, educating them about how to deal with the system, and going far beyond your call of duty in helping them to do so.

MACRO PERSPECTIVES ON WOMEN AND POVERTY

 EP 2.1.5b

You already know about macro practice and how making even minor changes in mammoth bureaucratic systems can be difficult. However, this issue is so crucial that evaluating the possibility of macro changes whenever you can is important as a generalist practitioner. We will discuss three potential approaches: reforming society's ideas about women's life experiences involving employment and family responsibilities, bettering conditions and resources in the workplace, and improving legislation providing for equality. The first two are closely related to changes in legislation, as incentives for such changes are essential.

Reforming Society's Perspective

Society's perspective on women's family and work responsibilities is a significant problem. On the one hand, society has traditionally viewed a woman in terms of her family role, and she is considered the nurturing, giving maintainer of the home whose primary responsibility is to keep her family healthy and together (Kirk & Okazawa-Rey, 2013; Shaw & Lee, 2012).

Women who are married have poor odds of being able to fulfill this primary role without assuming economic responsibility for their family. Women have only a "50:50 chance of remaining married for life" (Kail & Cavanaugh, 2013, p. 409). Women may experience significant difficulty receiving child support payments from fathers (Shaw & Lee, 2012). Mooney and her colleagues (2011) reflect on the economic consequences of divorce:

Following divorce, there tends to be a dramatic drop in women's income and a slight drop in men's income (Gadalla, 2009). Compared to married individuals, divorced individuals have a lower standard of living, have less wealth, and experience greater economic hardship, although this difference is considerably greater for women than for men (Amato, 2003). The economic costs of divorce are greater for women and children because women tend to earn less than men ... and because mothers devote substantially more time to household and child-care tasks than fathers do. The time women invest in this unpaid labor restricts their educational and job opportunities as well as their income. Men are less likely than women to be economically disadvantaged after divorce because they continue to profit from earlier investments in education and career. (p. 172)

There are millions of female-headed families living in poverty in this country. Those headed by women of color are even more likely to be poor. It is a significant problem. Many women have primary responsibility both for their family's caregiving and for its economic support.

Kirk and Okazawa-Rey (2013) maintain that society should adopt a more supportive perspective where families can:

- *care for family members emotionally and materially;*
- *promote egalitarian relationships among the adults, who should not abuse their power over children;*
- *share parenting between women and men so that it is not the province of either gender;*
- *do away with a gendered division of labor;*
- *teach children nonsexist, antiracist, and anticlassist attitudes and behavior and the values of caring and connectedness to others; and*
- *pass on cultural heritage. (p. 320)*

Society is telling women that they must assume responsibility for their children, both as primary caregivers and as economic providers, but it does not provide the minimal essential resources to do so. The link between women's family responsibilities, poverty, and their access to adequate working opportunities is becoming clearer. If we expect women to both care for their families and support themselves, more resources must be made available. Women need to have greater accessibility to adequate jobs. Their work environment needs to be more supportive, and supplementary resources for their children such as high-quality day care must be made more obtainable. The final sections of this chapter address these issues.

Improving Conditions in the Workplace

As a generalist practitioner, you need to be aware of intimidating conditions for women in the workplace so that you may use your macro skills to alleviate them. At least five conditions make performing effectively in the workplace particularly difficult for women: multiple roles, job segregation by gender, lack of female leadership in powerful positions, discrimination, and sexual harassment.

Multiple Roles. The first factor making performance in the workplace more difficult for women involves the numerous family responsibilities and the multiple roles women are expected to perform in their work and personal worlds. Additionally, employed women who are in relationships with men still maintain primary responsibility for most of the in-home work. Although the amount of housework women perform has decreased from several decades ago and the amount done by men has increased, consider two facts. First, married women currently still do about two-thirds of all housework in the home (Shaw & Lee, 2012). Note that the amount of time women spend performing household duties may indeed be underreported. Women more than men tend to do multiple tasks at one time (multitasking); they also tend to assume the "kin keeping" responsibilities (e.g., "remembering birthdays, sending cards, preparing for holidays, organizing vacations, keeping in touch with relatives, and providing 'spousal career support' by entertaining, volunteering, and networking") (Shaw & Lee, 2012, pp. 395–396). Such "kin keeping" tasks are difficult to quantify.

The second fact concerning gender differences in housework is that the types of housework women tend to do differ from the tasks men complete around the home (Shaw & Lee, 2012). Women are likely to complete the daily, necessary, monotonous tasks necessary to maintain the home and family on a regular basis. For example, women do significantly more cleaning, laundry, and clean-up following meals. Men, on the other hand, are more likely to do "less repetitive or seasonal tasks"; examples include paying bills, making household repairs, and completing outdoor upkeep (p. 397).

As a generalist practitioner what can you do about these problems? You can work to influence employers to provide assistance to working women. At least three strategies are possible. First, child care could be provided (Kirk & Okazawa-Rey, 2013; Malai, 2013). It could be considered one of a series of possible benefits from which employees might choose. For instance, if one spouse has medical coverage at her full-time job, the other might opt for child care at his full-time job instead of duplicating health care coverage.

A second thing you can advocate for employers to do is to offer flexible working hours. The strictly enforced 9-to-5 working day is not carved in stone. Arranging for alternative day care or being home when the children arrive from school may be easier if a parent is allowed to work from 7 a.m. to 3 p.m. instead. Flexible working hours may be facilitated by doing work electronically at home.

The final suggestion for employers is to provide adequate mandatory parental child care leaves at full or partial salary. Return to the same job should be guaranteed, and a woman's seniority should not be sacrificed because of her leave.

Job Segregation by Gender. In addition to multiple roles, a second condition confronting women in the workplace is that jobs are segregated by gender. Attending to this issue involves encouraging women to pursue fields and careers traditionally sought primarily by men. Examples include math, science, engineering, and skilled trades such as carpentry. Similarly, it means encouraging men to seek jobs traditionally held by women, such as child care work, teaching, and nursing. Employers can be pressured to recruit women into nontraditional fields more actively.

Lack of Female Leadership in Powerful Positions. A third problem women may encounter in the workplace involves lack of female leadership in powerful positions. For example, as of this writing, 20 of the 100 (or 20 percent) U.S. senators and 78 of the 435 (or 17.9 percent) U.S. Representatives are women; 5 of the 50 state governors are women (Center for American Women and Politics, 2013).

What can you do to encourage women's participation both in elected office and in other important leadership positions? For one thing, be sensitive to the composition of any particular group. Is there gender balance? If women are lacking, encourage their inclusion. Evaluate political candidates concerning their views on women and women's issues. Strongly support female candidates whose views coincide with yours. Educate other people to become more gender sensitive. When you see things in the media that you find gender insensitive or offensive, write and complain. Encourage and support women to assume important positions. If you are a woman, consider aiming for important positions yourself.

Discrimination. A fourth barrier to women in the workplace concerns discrimination (Hyde & Else-Quest, 2013; Rotella, 2001). We have already explained that women earn significantly less than men even when performing the same jobs. Rotella (2001) explains:

Discrimination can take a number of different forms. When women are paid less than equally productive men, they are being discriminated against. When women are excluded from some jobs or training so that they must work in jobs in which their productivity is not as high as it might be, their earnings are lowered due to discrimination. (p. 392)

Making employment decisions based on stereotypes about women and their ability to perform rather than on individual qualities and strengths is discrimination. Such discrimination might occur in the hiring process or in supporting promotions (Hyde & Else-Quest, 2013). For example, consider employers who choose to hire a male job applicant over an equally qualified female applicant because they think women, for some reason, are less competent, are ineffective leaders, or are more likely to prioritize their responsibilities at home over those at work. Some research indicates that male and female managers are more likely to select men over women for important assignments (Hyde & Else-Quest, 2013). When asked why, they say things like, "My own experience with customers is that many of them prefer to deal with men"; male managers have also explained, "Males project trust and believability" (Trentham & Larwood, 1998, pp. 16–17).

Another aspect of discrimination is the *glass ceiling,* the phenomenon where women proceed smoothly in organizational advancement until they reach some barrier that prevents them from rising any further in the power structure (Hyde & Else-Quest, 2013; Shaw & Lee, 2012). Shaw and Lee (2012) explain:

While women are increasingly moving into middle management positions, 2010 data show their relative absence in top leadership positions. Only 12 Fortune 500 companies (slightly over 2 percent) have women CEOs or presidents and another 14 women CEOs are in the Fortune 1000 (approximately 1.5 percent). Finally, although women make up more than 60 percent of the nonprofit workplace, they still lack access to top management positions, share of foundation dollars, and board positions. Women of color are relatively absent in the higher echelons of corporate power in all sectors. (p. 410)

Elaborating on the extensive research in support of such inequities is beyond the scope of this text. Nevertheless, you as a generalist practitioner are encouraged to be aware of such potential discrimination and combat it where it exists.

Establishing labor unions is one method to confront and change inequitable practices (Kirk & Okazawa-Rey, 2013; Shaw & Lee, 2012). A strong union with numerous members can exert substantial pressure on an employer. Women must have significant clout within a union's membership for it to work on their behalf. A variety of macro skills for organizing could be useful here.

Sexual Harassment. A fifth factor working against employed women at their jobs is sexual harassment. According to federal Equal Employment Opportunity Commission (EEOC) guidelines, *sexual harassment* involves unwelcome sexual advances, requests for sexual favors, and other verbal or physical conduct of a sexual nature and has the following three components (Shaw & Lee, 2012; U.S. Equal Opportunity Commission [EEOC], 2013a): First, submission to such conduct is required as a condition of employment or education. Second, submission to such conduct is used as a basis for decisions that affect an individual's employment or academic achievement. Third, such conduct results in a hostile, intimidating, or anxiety-producing work or educational environment.

Sexual harassment includes not only sexual solicitations and physical attacks, but also any type of behavior that makes a work setting uncomfortable, unproductive, or hostile. Harassment also includes gender-biased remarks, crude sexist jokes, and unfair treatment on the basis of gender that occur repeatedly over time.

An accurate, specific profile of when, where, how, and to whom sexual harassment occurs does not exist. However, it is quite prevalent in a variety of settings (Hyde & DeLamater, 2011; Morgan & Gruber, 2011). To gain some insight on how to combat sexual harassment, see Highlight 13.7.

Improving Legislation for Equality

EP 2.1.5b
EP 2.1.8a

Chapter 4 discussed specific skills for influencing decision makers. Those same skills apply here regarding the improvement of pro-equality legislation. We will therefore discuss three of the issues that demand legislative attention: pressing for antidiscrimination legislation and initiating lawsuits when unfairness surfaces, bolstering affirmative action activities, and actively supporting the comparable-worth movement.

Antidiscrimination Legislation. Numerous bills have been passed since 1963 that prohibit discrimination on the basis of gender. Thus, some legislative progress has been made. For example Title VII of the Civil Rights Act of 1964 prohibits discrimination in initial hiring of employees, provision of benefits (such as sick leave, health benefits, or vacation time), or other personnel determinations (e.g. decisions about promotions) on the basis of an individual's "race, color, religion, sex, or national origin" (EEOC, 2013b). This applies to employing organizations with at least 15 employees. However, this policy does not apply to smaller employing organizations.

Another example of positive legislation is the Equal Pay Act of 1963, which "requires that men and women be given equal pay for equal work in the same establishment. The jobs need not be identical, but they must be substantially equal. It is job content, not job titles, that determines whether jobs are substantially equal" (Society for Human Resource Management, 2013). Yet looming problems and issues still remain. Interpretation of these laws may not serve in the favor of women's equal treatment. For instance, Renzetti and her colleagues (2012) note the following regarding the Equal Pay Act:

> *Pay need not be equal if the difference is based on employee's relative seniority, merit, the quantity or quality of their production, or any other factor other than sex such as the profitability of their work....*
> *Thus, for example, the Equal Pay Act may not prevent wage discrimination for women in leadership or managerial positions (Eisenberg, 2010, p. 19). Female CEOs in private firms earn 46 percent less than males even when controlling for age and education (Cole & Mehran, 2008). Since the Equal Pay Act requires that jobs require equal skill, effort, and responsibility, it is challenging for women in high positions to prove they are not receiving pay equal to that of their male counterparts, since these positions tend to be less standardized (Eisenberg, 2010). (p. 252)*

Even with the progress some legislation has made, the overriding problem of job segregation based on gender and the resulting significant wage discrepancies remains. Much work still needs to be done. Legislative progress can be made on women's behalf. Generalist practitioners can be vigilant in their pursuit of gender-fair policies and positive legislative change. Affirmative action and comparable-worth policies discussed briefly in the next section provide examples of legislative issues to address.

HIGHLIGHT 13.7

Confronting Sexual Harassment

Victims of sexual harassment have several alternatives available to them. Each has its own potential positive and negative consequences. Alternatives include ignoring the harassing behavior, avoiding the harasser, or confronting the harasser and asking him to stop. One major classic study found that ignoring the behavior had virtually no effect (U.S. Merit Systems Protection Board [MSPB], 1981). Asking the harasser to stop, however, effectively terminated the harassment in half of the cases.

Avoiding the harasser is another option. A severe shortcoming of this approach is that the victim is the one who must expend the effort in avoidance behavior. The ultimate avoidance is actually quitting the job or dropping the class in order to avoid contact with a sexual harasser. This route is the least fair (and potentially most damaging) alternative for the victim.

There are, however, several other suggestions to help victims confront sexual harassment. In many cases using these strategies will stop harassment. First, a victim needs to know her or his rights. A call to the Equal Employment Opportunity Commission (EEOC), the federal agency designated to address the issue of sexual harassment, can be helpful. Many women can obtain necessary information about their rights and the appropriate procedures to follow for filing a formal complaint.

Sexual harassment is illegal at the national level. Many states also have laws that specify what can be done to combat it and often have agencies or offices that victims may call for help and information. For example, Wisconsin has the Wisconsin Equal Rights Division to address such issues. Additionally, organizations and agencies have specific policies against sexual harassment. Filing a formal complaint through established procedures is often a viable option.

Many victims, however, choose not to pursue the formal complaint route because they fear reprisal or retaliation. Others do not want to be labeled "troublemakers." Still others choose not to expend the time and effort necessary to carry out a formal process. Most victims simply want the harassment to end so that they can do their work peacefully and productively.

In addition to knowing your rights, the following suggestions can be applied to most situations where sexual harassment is occurring:

1. *Confront your harasser* (Feminist Majority Foundation, 2013; Northwestern University, 2010). Tell the harasser which specific behaviors are unwanted and unacceptable. If you feel you cannot handle a direct confrontation, write the harasser a letter. Criticizing the harasser's behavior rather than the harasser as a person is helpful. The intent is to stop the harassment and maintain a pleasant, productive work environment. There is also the chance that the harasser was not aware that his or her behavior was offensive. In these cases, giving specific feedback is frequently effective.

2. *Be assertive.* When giving the harasser feedback, look him or her directly in the eye and assume an assertive stance. Do not smile or giggle even though you may be uncomfortable. Stand up straight, adopt a serious expression, and calmly state, "Please stop touching me by putting your arms around me and rubbing my neck. I don't like it." This situation is serious, and you need to get your point across.

3. *Document your situation.* Record every incident that occurs. Note when, where, who, what was said or done, what you were wearing, and any available witnesses. Be as accurate as possible. Documentation does not have to be elaborate or fancy. Simple handwritten notes including the facts will suffice. Keeping copies of your notes in another location is also a good idea.

4. *Talk to other people about the problem.* Get support from friends and colleagues. Sexual harassment often erodes self-confidence. Victims do not feel they are in control of the situation. Emotional support from others can bolster self-confidence and give victims the strength needed to confront sexual harassment. Frequently, sharing these problems with others will also allow victims to discover they are not alone. Corroboration with other victims will not only provide emotional support, but it will also strengthen a formal complaint if that option needs to be taken sometime in the future.

5. *Get witnesses.* Look around when the sexual harassment is occurring and note who else can observe it. Talk to these people and solicit their support. Try to make arrangements for others to be around you when you anticipate that sexual harassment is likely to occur.

Affirmative Action. Affirmative action involves "steps taken by an organization to remedy imbalances in the employment of people of color and women, promotions, and other opportunities" (Barker, 2003, p. 11). You can use affirmative action to pursue three positive thrusts on the behalf of women (Gottlieb, 1987). First, affirmative action can be used to monitor the proportion of women in any particular job category. Employment of women in an agency or organization should approach that proportion. For example, if 14 percent of all skilled bricklayers in the country are women, then logically about 14 percent of the bricklayers employed by a given construction company should be women.

A second manner in which affirmative action can be used involves "identifying areas in which women are poorly represented, setting goals for improvement, and monitoring those goals" (Gottlieb, 1987, p. 565). Affirmative action provides a rationale and mechanism for addressing these inequities.

The third way in which affirmative action can be helpful involves wiping out discriminatory policies and practices. For example, advertising a job position for a social worker who must be a male violates affirmative action principles.

Comparable Worth. We have established several facts. First, most women work outside of the home. Second, women tend to be clustered in small number of relatively low-paying occupations. Third, women have significantly less political power in terms of the actual number of political offices they hold.

The principle of *comparable worth* (sometimes referred to as *pay equity*) may be defined as calling for equal pay for comparable work that requires similar skills, knowledge, and responsibilities, and that is conducted under similar working conditions. Comparable worth does not refer to jobs that are identical but rather that are similar or comparable (Kirk & Okazawa-Rey, 2013; Renzetti et al., 2012). For example, a male janitor might receive a substantially higher salary than a female secretary, even though both jobs might require similar *levels,* not types, of training and experience.

The underlying principle, of course, is that women's work has been traditionally undervalued in the paid workplace. Women are often compensated less for doing work comparable to that done by men.

Although there is no federal legislation on comparable worth, several states have implemented legal policies for some of their working populations such as public employees (USLegal.com, 2013). Other countries, including Canada, Australia, and Great Britain,

have embraced the concept to a greater extent (Renzetti et al., 2012).

There are two basic suggestions for how the doctrine of comparable worth might be attained. First, a system of "job evaluation" must be developed. Job evaluation would involve evaluating each job in an organization on the basis of "skill requirements, effort, responsibility, and working conditions" (Schwab, 1984, p. 86; USLegal.com, 2013). A system would have to be worked out whereby these job aspects could be analyzed, compared, and rated on a certain scale. The end result would be *comparable* job classifications with *comparable* salaries.

The second recommendation for implementing the doctrine of comparable worth would be to establish legislation to mandate compliance. Laws need to be created to require both governmental and private business organizations to abide by comparable-worth principles. These laws would require the development of job evaluation systems. They would also necessitate careful monitoring of organizations to make certain that the organizations comply with or obey the rules.

Critical Thinking Questions 13.6

EP 2.1.3

- What are your opinions about antidiscrimination legislation, affirmative action, and comparable worth?
- What kinds of legislation concerning these issues, if any, do you think should be drafted and passed?

The Need for Ongoing Learning

EP 2.1.1e

EP 2.1.4d

This chapter has discussed many issues and practice approaches relevant to women. Interventions with women, just as in other areas of human diversity, require ongoing learning in terms of improved understanding of issues, updating of information, and enhanced practice effectiveness.

Sources of learning are many. You can read about research and study books on feminist practice or women's issues. You can attend professional conferences on these topics. You can talk with colleagues and supervisors about ways to improve your ability to work with and help female clients. Very important, you can learn from the clients themselves. How do they view the world? What are their chief concerns? What help and resources do they think they need?

Learning new skills and techniques to improve effectiveness in generalist practice is a continuous process. This is true for any area of practice in which you choose to work.

Chapter Summary

The following summarizes this chapter's content as it relates to each learning objective (LO) presented at the beginning of the chapter. Chapter content helps prepare students to:

LO 13-1 Develop self-awareness about gender sensitivity.

Women can experience sexism, gender-role stereotypes, oppression, and sex discrimination. Facts indicate a range of areas where they suffer more hardship than men.

LO 13-2 Work with women using the Generalist Intervention Model.

The Generalist Intervention Model and planned change process can readily be applied to women from a feminist perspective.

LO 13-3 Examine feminist perspectives on generalist practice.

Feminism for practitioners is defined as the philosophy of equality between women and men that involves both attitudes and actions, that infiltrates virtually all aspects of life, that often necessitates providing education and advocacy on behalf of women, and that appreciates the existence of individual differences and personal accomplishments regardless of gender.

Problems commonly experienced by women in greater magnitude than men include certain stressful life events, and a lack of self-esteem with a resulting sense of powerlessness.

LO 13-4 Empower women as individuals.

Practitioners can empower women by enhancing women's self-esteem through a number of counseling strategies. Assertiveness is another intervention approach. Assertiveness means taking into account both your own rights and the rights of others. Assertiveness training involves a series of steps to identify and evaluate assertive behavior. All individuals have assertive rights. Helping women expand their options, change old rules and expectations, and work together for macro-level empowerment are other intervention approaches.

LO 13-5 Provide assistance to women as survivors of sexual assault.

Sexual assault of women is a major problem today. The feminist perspective emphasizes that rape is the logical reaction of men who are socialized to dominate women. Women's reactions to rape include both acute and long-term reorganization phases. Counseling survivors involves emotional issues, reporting to the police, and medical status. The macro perspective on sexual assault can involve sexual assault prevention programs, improved legislation, and support of service provision.

LO 13-6 Intervene with battered women.

The battered woman syndrome implies the systematic and repeated use of violence and emotional manipulation against a woman. The abusive perpetrator tends to adhere to common masculine gender-role stereotypes. Cultural influences can affect how battering is generally viewed. The battering cycle involves a buildup of tension, the explosion, and making up. Women stay in battering relationships due to economic dependence, lack of self-confidence, lack of power, fear of the abuser, guilt, feeling isolated with nowhere to go, fear for their children, and love.

Community empowerment of battered women includes provision of shelters, crisis hotlines, counseling and support groups, public education, legal advocacy, and batterers' intervention programs. Various counseling strategies are available to help battered women. Strengthening legislation and service provision for battered women at the local, state, and national levels is critically important. An international perspective on domestic violence is introduced.

LO 13-7 Examine the feminization of poverty.

The term *feminization of poverty* means that women as a group are more likely to be poor than are men. On the average, women's full-time, year-round median weekly earnings are approximately 80.5 percent of men's (U.S. Census Bureau, 2011).

Potential macro approaches for addressing the feminization of poverty include reforming society's ideas about women's life experiences involving employment and family responsibilities, bettering conditions and resources in the workplace, and improving legislation providing for equality. Five conditions that make effective performance particularly difficult for women in the workplace are assuming multiple roles, job segregation by gender, lack of female leadership in powerful positions, discrimination, and sexual harassment. Means of confronting sexual harassment are proposed. Suggestions for improving legislation focus on antidiscrimination laws, affirmative action, and comparable worth. Generalist practitioners should engage in ongoing learning to improve their understanding of issues, keep updated, and enhance practice effectiveness.

Competency Notes

The following identifies where Educational Policy (EP) competencies and practice behaviors are discussed in the chapter.

EP 2.1.1e Engage in career-long learning. *(p. 509):* Generalist social workers should continue to learn about women's concerns and issues throughout their careers.

EP 2.1.2a Recognize and manage personal values in a way that allows professional values to guide practice. *(p. 474):* It is important to recognize personal values about women's concerns and issues so that these values do not interfere with effective practice.

EP 2.1.3 Apply critical thinking to inform and communicate professional judgments. *(pp. 480, 485, 496, 498, 502, 509):* Critical thinking questions are posed.

EP 2.1.4 Engage diversity and difference in practice. *(p. 475):* It is important for practitioners to be sensitive to women's issues as they proceed with the planned change process.

EP 2.1.4a Recognize the extent to which culture's structures and values may oppress, marginalize, alienate, or create or enhance privilege or power. *(p. 474):* Women can be subjected to oppression and decreased power. This entire chapter concerns the special circumstances and issues affecting women. *(p. 495):* Cultural values and norms can affect how battering is viewed and can even encourage battering.

EP 2.1.4b Gain sufficient self-awareness to eliminate the influence of personal biases and values in working with diverse groups. *(p. 474):* Self-awareness of personal biases, including those concerning women, is important so they don't interfere with effective practice. *(p. 477):* Questions are raised to enhance self-awareness about women and their situations.

EP 2.1.4c Recognize and communicate their understanding of the importance of difference in shaping life experiences. *(p. 479):* Interventions with women often are based on issues more likely experienced by women. Workers must understand and convey empathy in order to select appropriate intervention strategies.

EP 2.1.4d View themselves as learners and engage those with whom they work as informants. *(p. 509):* Generalist practitioners should view themselves as learners who can learn from their female clients.

EP 2.1.5 Advance human rights and social and economic justice. *(p. 501):* Domestic violence involves oppression of women. It is important to recognize the global interconnections of oppression in order to develop strategies promoting human and civil rights.

EP 2.1.5a Understand the forms and mechanisms of oppression and discrimination. *(p. 474):* Concepts related to sexism and oppression and discrimination based on gender are defined. *(p. 500):* The feminization of poverty is a complex condition that oppresses women.

EP 2.1.5b Advocate for human rights and social and economic justice. *(p. 499):* Generalist practitioners should advocate for women's rights and macro-level changes on their behalf. *(p. 500):* Practitioners should advocate for social and economic justice on the behalf of battered women. *(p. 504):* Advocating for women in poverty should be done at the macro level to achieve social and economic justice. *(p. 507):* One means of advocating for human rights and social and economic justice involves seeking improved policies in the legal arena.

EP 2.1.5c Engage in practices that advance social and economic justice. *(p. 486):* Women can work together in the macro context to achieve social and economic justice. *(p. 487):* Feminist macro practice ultimately seeks social and economic justice.

EP 2.1.7a Utilize conceptual frameworks to guide the processes of assessment, intervention, and evaluation. *(p. 477):* A feminist conceptual framework is useful for understanding women and guiding the intervention process. *(p. 486):* A feminist conceptual framework is exceptionally useful for understanding the dynamics of sexual assault and helping survivors.

EP 2.1.8a Analyze, formulate, and advocate for policies that advance social well-being. *(p. 493):* Generalist practitioners have the responsibility of advocating for improved legislation concerning sexual assault survivors. *(p. 507):* Social workers should understand, formulate, and advocate for improved legislative policies to improve women's status in the workplace.

EP 2.1.8b **Collaborate with colleagues and clients for effective policy action.** *(p. 487):* A feminist perspective on macro practice on the behalf of women emphasizes collaboration and cooperation with others to achieve goals. *(p. 500):* Cooperation among agencies and colleagues can help pursue effective policy action concerning domestic violence.

EP 2.1.9a **Continuously discover, appraise, and attend to changing locales, populations, scientific and technological developments, and emerging societal trends to provide relevant services.** *(p. 486):* Social workers should keep abreast of the current legislative scene in order to advocate for and provide relevant services. *(p. 493):* Generalist practitioners must keep abreast of the ever-changing problems and issues facing women (including sexual assault, domestic violence against women, and poverty) in order to provide effective services.

EP 2.1.9b **Provide leadership in promoting sustainable changes in service delivery and practice to improve the quality of social service.** *(p. 492):* Generalist practitioners may provide leadership in educating the public concerning sexual assault and advocating for survivors.

EP 2.1.10 **Engage, assess, intervene, and evaluate with individuals, families, groups, organizations, and communities.** *(p. 475):* Planned change steps including engagement, assessment, intervention, and evaluation are used when working with women, as is demonstrated by the subsequent case example. *(p. 492):* Dealing with and changing organizational and community perceptions in addition to improving social policies provide avenues for helping survivors of sexual assault other than micro and mezzo interventions.

EP 2.1.10a **Substantively and affectively prepare for action with individuals, families, groups, organizations, and communities.** *(p. 500):* Addressing domestic violence against women should also be done at the macro level through organizational, community, and policy change.

EP 2.1.10b **Use empathy and other interpersonal skills.** *(p. 498):* Social workers must use empathy and other interpersonal skills when counseling battered women.

EP 2.1.10c **Develop a mutually agreed-on focus of work and desired outcomes.** *(p. 480):* A principle of feminist counseling emphasizes working together with the client.

EP 2.1.10e **Assess clients' strengths and limitations.** *(p. 482):* Practitioners should identify and focus on female clients' strengths.

EP 2.1.10f **Develop mutually agreed-on intervention goals and objectives.** *(p. 480):* A principle of feminist counseling emphasizes working together with the client.

EP 2.1.10g **Select appropriate intervention strategies.** *(p. 481):* Some intervention strategies discussed here are particularly appropriate for many women. *(p. 497):* Generalist social workers must be knowledgeable about the various service alternatives available to battered women in order to select appropriate intervention strategies.

EP 2.1.10j **Help clients resolve problems.** *(p. 481):* Generalist practitioners can help women address deference and dependency by enhancing their sense of self-esteem. *(p. 489):* Specific approaches have been found effective when counseling survivors of sexual assault and helping them resolve their problems.

On the Internet

Visit the *Understanding Generalist Practice* CourseMate at **www.cengagebrain.com** for resources such as quizzes, glossaries and videos.

Advocacy

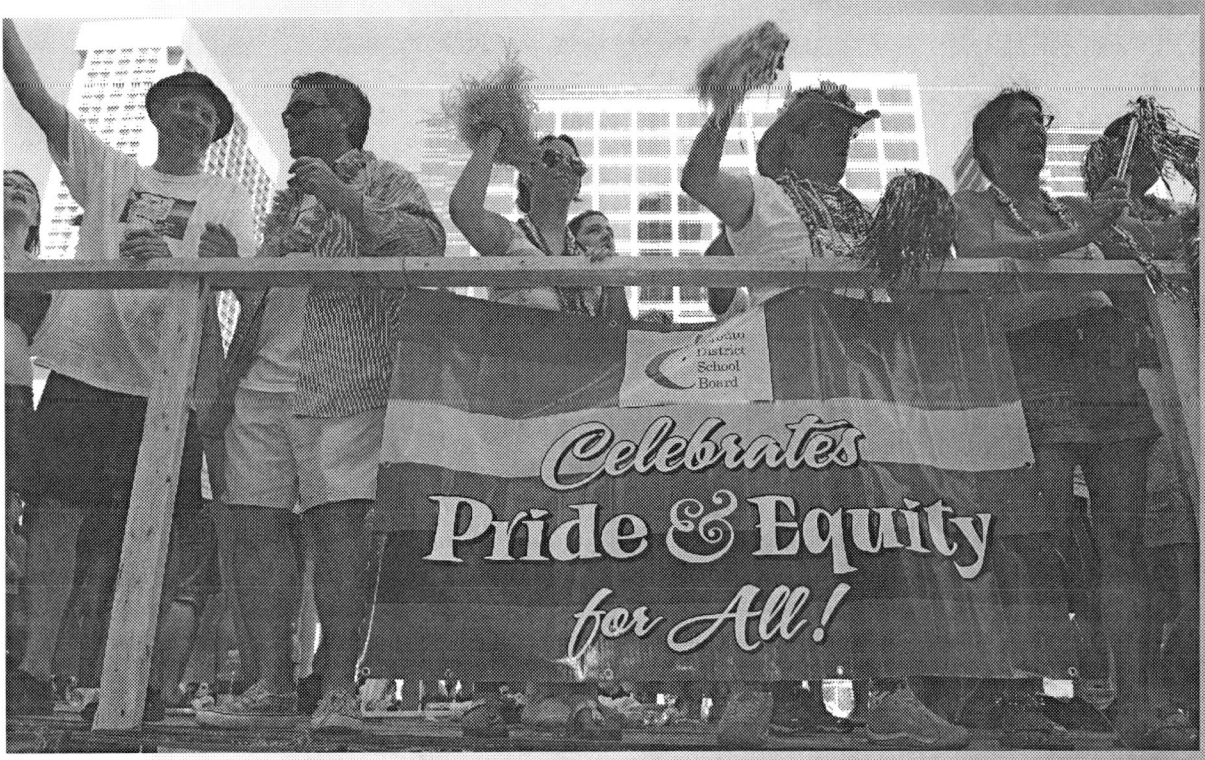

© Zoran Karapancev/Shutterstock.com

Learning Objectives

This chapter will help prepare students to:

LO 14-1 Advocate for clients in the context of generalist practice.

LO 14-2 Implement the professional role of advocate.

LO 14-3 Utilize conceptual frameworks related to advocacy.

LO 14-4 Employ specific knowledge and skills in advocacy.

LO 14-5 Engage in legislative advocacy to advance social and economic justice.

SHARON MCMANUS RAN INTO A BRICK WALL. Trying desperately to find housing for her homeless client, she finally located a house that met the family's needs. The house was large enough to accommodate Mr. Vue and his four children, eliminating the need for the family to continue sleeping in their car. (Mr. Vue was a Hmong who had immigrated from Vietnam with his family.) The only problem was that the house had to be approved by the Indian Falls City Housing Authority if Mr. Vue were to receive a housing subsidy. The subsidy was a monthly payment from the housing authority that would help Mr. Vue pay the rent on this house.

When Sharon called the housing authority requesting approval of the house, she learned that it would be several weeks before the home could be inspected and certified for inclusion in the housing subsidy program. Sharon knew that Mr. Vue did not have several weeks. His children were not in school, he lacked food, and the family could not be expected to continue living out

of his car. Frustrated, Sharon decided it was time to try a different approach. Assuming the advocate role, Sharon contacted Barbara Soderholm, her representative on the Indian Falls City Council. She explained the situation to Councilwoman Soderholm and asked if there was anything she could do to speed up the process. Within the day, Sharon received a call from the housing authority. Councilwoman Soderholm had called an official she knew at the housing authority and exercised her influence to speed up the process. The housing authority representative would inspect the house the following day.

Sharon was elated. She arranged for the house to be cleaned before the visit by the housing authority and notified Mr. Vue of the good news. Following the visit, the house passed inspection, and the Vue family finally had a home. Sharon then helped Mr. Vue enroll his children in school. She followed up with him for the next few months to ensure that his transition to his new home was proceeding satisfactorily.

Defining Advocacy

EP 2.1.1a
EP 2.1.10k

One of the most important objectives of social work is to help people obtain needed resources. Often this objective occurs through the brokering role discussed briefly in Chapter 1 and in detail in Chapter 15. The broker role requires that the social worker help clients by connecting them to appropriate agencies or services. Sometimes the worker must act as a mediator between the client and a resource. This role might be required, for example, when a client has been refused service of benefits through a misunderstanding or confusion about whether or not the client was eligible for the service.

In other situations, the worker must assume another role—namely, that of advocate. *Advocacy* is defending, representing, and championing the rights of individuals, groups, or communities using direct action, empowerment, or other means designed to achieve desired outcomes. It is an obligation of all social workers and acknowledged as so in the National Association of Social Workers (NASW) *Code of Ethics* (2008).

Briar (1967) was one of the first to argue that case advocacy should be considered a natural part of the professional social work role. He noted that the advocate is the client's supporter, advisor, champion, and representative in "dealings with the court, the police,

the social agency, and other organizations" (p. 28). Social workers use their position and professional skills to bring about services and policies that are needed by individuals, groups, and communities. As part of the social work profession's obligation to serve the most vulnerable populations, we must expect that many clients will need our assistance. Isolated clients, those with disabilities, deinstitutionalized clients, and children are examples of situations where advocacy may be essential. Many organizations exist specifically to advocate for certain issues or categories of clients. Examples include Mothers Against Drunk Driving (MADD), the National Alliance for the Mentally 111, and the Gray Panthers.

Advocacy has long been employed by the legal system to describe the attorney's role as a representative or partisan who champions the interests of clients. As advocates, social workers work for a client's benefit even when that involves taking stands against their own agencies' policies and practices. Advocacy entails bargaining, speaking out, and negotiating to achieve social and economic justice. Advocacy is a core activity of social work, setting social workers apart from other helping professions, and grows out of social work's emphasis on understanding people within their environment. It is also rooted in the profession's awareness of how that environment can influence clients' well-being.

LO 14-1 Advocate for Clients in the Context of Generalist Practice

ADVOCACY AND THE GENERALIST INTERVENTION MODEL

Advocacy is an implementation strategy in the Generalist Intervention Model (GIM). It is the means the worker chooses as the most effective way of bringing about change. Because it is more complex and potentially more problematic than other approaches, advocacy must be carefully considered during the assessment and planning phases. We have included some general thoughts to consider as you contemplate a situation where advocacy may be required.

CASE ADVOCACY

Case advocacy, as the name implies, refers to activity on behalf of a single case. It is usually employed in situations where the individual is in conflict with an organization, perhaps over benefits that have been denied. As we described in Chapter 4, the "case" may be an individual, a family, or a small group. The example that opened this chapter shows how case advocacy can be employed to meet the needs of an individual or family. In some situations, changes brought about as a result of advocacy on behalf of an individual or family will also result in long-term benefits to others in similar straits.

Effective case advocacy requires several types of knowledge:

- knowledge of the agency's policies, regulations, and administrative structure;
- knowledge of the agency's appeal procedures;
- knowledge of ethical principles impacting advocacy;
- knowledge of available legal remedies;
- knowledge of the agency's formal and informal power structure;
- knowledge of external forces that the organization responds to; and
- knowledge of the consequences (for the client, others, and yourself) of escalating issues (Hepworth, Rooney, Rooney, & Strom-Gottfried, 2013; Sheafor & Horejsi 2012; Shulman, 2012).

You may be wondering at what point case advocacy becomes cause or class advocacy. The line between advocating for a single client and engaging in macro practice (working on behalf of whole groups or populations of clients) can become somewhat blurry. For example,

a successful appeal of an adversary's decision in the case of a single client may result in a new interpretation of old rules benefiting all clients in similar situations. Yet, a discouraging reality of case advocacy is that although the advocate may successfully challenge the agency on behalf of a specific client, no long-term change in agency policy is guaranteed. Consequently, other clients may face the same hurdles in their interactions with the agency.

Although there are similarities between the two approaches, case advocacy generally involves strategies and tactics different from those employed for cause advocacy. These differences are especially true when we look at legislative advocacy, a form of cause advocacy discussed later in the chapter.

CAUSE ADVOCACY

Cause advocacy involves social workers' efforts to address an issue of overriding importance to some client group. The emphasis on *cause* means that this type of advocacy affects multiple groups of clients or potential clients. It is also sometimes called class advocacy.

For example, early social workers were active in efforts to develop kindergartens, to create laws prohibiting child labor, and to require education for persons with physical disabilities. The beneficiaries of these efforts were not individual clients but entire categories of people. A more current example might involve a social worker advocating to serve a category of clients more effectively within his or her own agency. Perhaps the location and office hours of an agency make using the agency's services difficult for low-income clients. A worker might attempt to get the agency to open an office in a different, more accessible location or to extend agency office hours further into the evening.

Let us reexamine the case involving a social worker named Glen, described in Chapter 4. You may recall that Glen's supervisor wanted prospective foster parents to come in during the day for their appointments, even if it meant taking time off from their work. In this case, Glen used cause advocacy. He advocated for all prospective foster parents as a large group and tried to convince his supervisor that the agency should be more flexible. He argued that the agency should expand its hours in the evening so more foster parent candidates could have access to its services.

The need for class advocacy may become more obvious after repeated cases arise having similar characteristics. You may notice patterns in case records or observe striking similarities in the types of problems clients are having.

At the agency level, individual social workers may conduct cause advocacy working alone. Beyond the agency level, advocates are much more likely to involve themselves in coalitions with other workers and agencies because some forms of advocacy require major effort. Consider a state law that requires community agencies to serve formerly institutionalized clients but does not provide any funding for such services. Because the problem is at a level far above the individual agency, advocacy will require many groups working in concert to change the law or ensure funding is provided. Coalitions tend to increase the effectiveness of advocacy efforts because they allow for "additional staff time and funding, as well as a broader range of ideas and contacts" (Hoefer, 2005, p. 223). Hoefer's research also suggests that evidence-based advocacy requires a recognition that approaches effective at the state level may not be of equal efficacy on a national level. In fact, tactics that work well in one state may not work as well in others. Factors such as the amount of resources devoted to advocacy, collaborative versus confrontational strategies, relationships with decision makers, use of coalitions, and the existence of government officials sympathetic to one's cause are all variables that can influence whether cause advocacy efforts will be effective. *One size fits all* is no more appropriate for advocacy than it is for shoes.

Cause advocacy often involves resistance because it requires significant change in the status quo. You may have to use tactics involving conflict to overcome this resistance. We have established that people in power usually do not want to give it up.

In Glen's case, pressuring his agency to expand its hours has implications and repercussions. More hours require spending more money to staff the agency longer. Agency administrators may resent being pressured to dig up more funding or to allow workers to accrue compensatory time. They might resist any change in the status quo. People in administration also tend to resist being told or pressured regarding what to do, which is especially the case when it involves employees theoretically under their control.

Some cause advocacy has resulted in lawsuits challenging official regulations and governmental inaction. Much social change in areas that include mental health, civil rights, and individual freedom are the result of legal action challenging existing laws. The 2013 Supreme Court decisions on the Defense of Marriage Act (DOMA) and California Proposition 8 are two examples of using legal action to overturn a federal law that discriminated against gay marriage. In both of these cases, the NASW filed *amicus curiae* ("friend of the court") briefs supporting overturning both of these laws. In addition, the organization has joined similar lawsuits designed to achieve social and economic justice for specific groups. Lawsuits can be extremely threatening to an agency's or organization's administration. They usually involve potentially significant conflict. Lawsuits make problems public and are expensive. For both reasons, administrators will frequently avoid them like the plague.

Cause advocacy often involves risks, both to the agency and to the worker initiating it. These risks are why advocacy requires such sensitivity, tact, and skill. As an advocate, you want to facilitate change for the well-being of your clients. However, you probably do not want to get fired.

Critical Thinking Questions 14.1

 Case advocacy and cause advocacy are both activities in which social workers may become engaged. For each of the activities shown in the following list, identify which are examples of case advocacy and which are examples of cause advocacy. Provide a brief explanation for your decision.

- Advocating for a client being evicted from her home
- Advocating for apartment tenants who are facing an infestation of rats and other vermin
- Testifying to a legislative committee about the need for increased funds for children's health insurance
- Talking to parents about becoming more flexible in their expectations of their teenage daughter
- Marching in a rally supporting increased immigration quotas for refugees from Iraq
- Advocating for admission of a gifted minority student into an elite preparatory school that has historically discriminated against people of color

LO 14-2 Implement the Professional Role of Advocate

USING SKILLS IN ADVOCACY

The effective advocate will need to know how to use government documents and other data sources. Often documenting the existence of a problem will be necessary. You may need to know where to get facts, information, and official statistics.

Comfort with and ability to use the political process are also important. Most of the rules, regulations, and funding for human service programs are derived from state or federal laws. Changing laws require that you know how the political process works and can use this process to achieve social work goals.

Whether the target is an agency supervisor, a board of directors, or a legislative committee, the advocate must be comfortable speaking in public. For example, you may find yourself needing to present arguments or ideas to groups such as legislators or members of an agency board of directors. Public speaking skills will make advocating easier.

A level of tolerance for conflict is also important. Change is often difficult for others, and resistance is common. You must be comfortable in situations where people disagree with you or your ideas.

IDENTIFYING THE GOALS OF ADVOCACY

The advocate (either alone or in consort with others) is attempting to influence others to take positions or make decisions that they would not normally have done. We have emphasized throughout this text the planned change framework that is used by social workers. Advocacy is simply a more radical approach to planned change. One purpose of advocacy is to help clients attain services or benefits to which they are entitled but cannot obtain. The nature of this task is such that advocacy is more likely to involve confrontation than are most other interventions.

Making a distinction between two aspects of advocacy is important. On the one hand, advocacy involves making certain that clients have *access to existing rights and entitlements*. On the other hand, advocacy also concerns *social action to secure new rights and entitlements*. We have discussed social action in previous chapters and will revisit the topic again later in this chapter. Essentially, the advocate is working to help clients reach goals they have defined as desirable. Those goals usually require some action on the part of a decision maker. That decision maker may have to change a previous decision, reinterpret rules, or modify procedures to benefit the client. On the other hand, you may be asking an organization to abide by and enforce existing rules or regulations. In the case opening this chapter, the goal was to influence the decision maker (representative from the housing authority) to act immediately in a crisis rather than following the usual procedures.

ENGAGING IN ADVOCACY AND EMPOWERMENT

Often the process of engaging in advocacy has the effect of empowering clients. This can occur as they participate in advocating for themselves as well as when they acquire new rights and opportunities. For example, Linhorst, Eckert, and Hamilton (2005) found that efforts to increase the involvement of clients with severe mental illness in the human service organizations that served them was empowering. Clients who served on agency committees, consumer councils, boards of directors, or other organizational bodies were able to persuade agencies to increase funding for specific programs, modify problematic internal policies, improve facilities, and otherwise benefit clients with serious emotional disorders.

TARGETS OF ADVOCACY

Targets of advocacy may include individuals, groups or organizations, elected or appointed officials, public and private human service agencies, legislative bodies, court systems, or governmental entities (such as the housing authority). Any of these persons or organizations may impede client access to services or treat clients inhumanely. By doing so, they become potential targets of advocacy because, as social workers, we adhere to several principles.

First, we work to increase accessibility of social services to clients. Not only should needed services exist, but clients should also be able to use them without undue difficulty. For example, clients for whom English is not their primary language will have difficulty completing lengthy forms written in that language. If they cannot complete the forms, they will not receive the services.

Sometimes, the services themselves are satisfactory, but other problems prevent clients from using them. For example, services may be available only during the day when clients work, or there may be long waiting periods before services can be received. Another problem entails services offered at locations that are inaccessible to clients, such as when a building is not accessible to people with disabilities or when services are offered at sites far from clients' homes.

A second principle is that advocates promote service delivery that does not detract from clients' dignity. In other words, clients should not be put in humiliating or embarrassing situations in order to receive services. For instance, consider a situation where clients must wait in a filthy, crowded waiting room for hours to receive needed public assistance. Advocating that such conditions be changed because they are an affront to clients' dignity is appropriate.

Sometimes, services are provided in a fashion that is demeaning to clients. For example, one large county social services agency provided workers with desks located within a giant facility that resembled a remodeled warehouse. There were no walls or partitions between workers' desks. Thus, anyone within sight or hearing of the desks could easily find out what the client and the worker were talking about. Privacy was almost nonexistent.

A third principle to guide advocates involves working to assure equal access to all who are eligible. For example, service delivery that is more accessible to white clients than to African-American or Hispanic clients is unacceptable.

Hepworth et al. (2013) provide additional examples in Highlight 14.1 of situations where advocacy may be appropriate. As you will see from the examples, the targets of advocacy may vary depending upon the individual situation.

RECOGNIZING THE HISTORY OF ADVOCACY IN SOCIAL WORK

The social work profession's advocating for clients has a strong but uneven history, as Haynes and Mickelson (2010) point out. They note that the period from 1895 to 1915 is considered a progressive era in social work because of the supposed high level of social action and advocacy carried out by social workers. However, they note that "many social workers honored advocacy more with rhetoric than with practice" (p. 37). They point out that social workers of this era were more likely to act as brokers or facilitators than advocates. They note that the Charily Organization Society movement saw individual clients as dysfunctional and tried to change the clients. Meanwhile, the social settlement house workers tried to "reform the social environment that made people losers" (p. 38) The era saw both case advocacy (advocating for individual clients, families, or groups) and class or cause advocacy (advocating for large groups of people sharing common characteristics or advocating for social legislation).

Unfortunately, even the limited progressiveness of this era did not continue in the following years. Instead, social work practice has experienced what appears to be cycles of advocacy. Following the earlier progressive era came a period in which social workers paid more attention to becoming professionals and adopting psychological treatment approaches than to solving client problems.

Later, a resurgence of advocacy occurred during the Great Depression. Then, social workers participated in many programs designed to combat the unemployment and malaise of the 1930s. The period of the 1940s and 1950s appears in retrospect to mark another decline in social work focus on advocacy. The 1960s marked a

---

HIGHLIGHT 14.1

Indications for Advocacy

Advocacy is likely to be the role of choice in any of the following situations:

- when organizational barriers to services are created by agency policies or procedures;
- when clients are refused legally entitled benefits or services;
- when existing services are inadequate to meet identified needs of individual clients or groups of clients;
- when services provided to clients are inhumane or dehumanizing;
- when agencies or staff discriminate against clients because of gender, race, religion, sexual orientation, or for other reasons;
- when services or benefits are not provided to clients in a manner consistent with the immediacy of their need (e.g., refusing to provide timely services in crisis situations);

- when multiple clients clearly have the same need for which no services or benefits yet exist;
- when clients cannot adequately protect their own interests or act on their own behalf;
- when existing services or benefits make the situation worse;
- when clients are denied civil rights or other legal protections;
- when clients are denied a voice in the planning for or creation of services;
- when social workers can help clients mobilize in their own interest to obtain services or benefits routinely available to those with more resources; and
- when social workers can help achieve social and economic justice for individual or groups of clients.

Source: D. H. Hepworth et al. (2013), *Direct Social Work Practice*, Belmont, CA: Brooks/Cole, p. 452.

resurgence of interest in advocating for both individual clients and for classes of people. Social workers contributed to many efforts to change organizations and institutions and make them more responsive to clients and oppressed groups. Advocates represented clients against urban renewal, expansion of universities into low income housing neighborhoods, and the location of roads and highways that ignored the needs of local residents. On the downswing, the 1970s and 1980s showed less advocacy for oppressed groups as the nation experienced a period of conservative political leadership. The early 1990s saw the growth of advocacy-oriented, self-help groups dedicated to bringing better treatment and conditions to their members and increased advocacy to combat attacks on social service programming.

Clearly, advocacy today is an important role for social workers as they help clients negotiate the social environment. The political climate of the past 20 years has eroded services and benefits for some of our most vulnerable populations. Simultaneously, there is renewed interest in using the political process to create changes needed by these populations. Social workers today must use knowledge and a variety of skills to help clients. As mentioned earlier, it is also a period of increased use of legal action to achieve social and economic justice. In the sections that follow, we will look carefully at advocacy in social work practice.

Observations About Advocacy

The social worker playing the advocate role is operating under a different set of circumstances than is true in roles such as broker or facilitator. These observations represent a starting point in understanding how change takes place, the influence of advocates and clients in the planned change process, and the role of power in advocacy situations. As such, they help guide the advocate in interactions with client systems, organizations, and other targets of advocacy. They also reflect a belief that change in large systems is possible. The observations cover three areas:

- *observations about power*
- *observations about organizations*
- *observations about clients*

OBSERVATIONS ABOUT POWER

Five observations about power are helpful in understanding advocacy:

1. Those who hold power are generally reluctant to give up that power.

2. Those who hold power generally have greater access to resources than people with less power. For instance, those with more money have more access to legal services, education, and health care.
3. Resources in general, including power, are not distributed equally. Some people simply have significantly more power than others.
4. Conflict between people and between people and institutions is inevitable, especially when those in power treat those with less power unfairly. People do not want or like to be underdogs. Too often, large institutions in society dominate more vulnerable societal groups and exacerbate struggles between minority and majority groups.
5. You must have power in order to change existing organizations and institutions. Otherwise, large systems are resistant to change. Change takes effort and work. Systems tend to cling to the stable state they are used to, whether or not that state is effective. Thus, having access to sufficient power to influence the outcome of the change effort is necessary for the advocate. Later in this chapter we will discuss ways in which workers can garner power to enhance their advocacy.

OBSERVATIONS ABOUT ORGANIZATIONS

We have established that advocacy involves thinking about and manipulating power. Advocacy also entails working with organizations and their policies. Understanding organizations can help us to target them and their policies more effectively. Within the advocacy context, we have four major observations about organizations:

1. There are many reasons why organizations and institutions fail to meet client needs. Sometimes, the system does not recognize a problem or chooses not to address it. Other times, agencies and organizations serve their own needs rather than their clients' needs. Organizations may be experiencing a budget crisis. Top administrators may be more concerned about their own reputations than about serving clients' needs, or caseloads may be so great that clients cannot be served adequately.
2. Agencies and organizations, just like people, *do* have potential to change. Advocacy grows out of a philosophy that people have the same rights to tax-supported social services and benefits as they do to such things as public education and city streets. It is a fact of life that benefits and services are not distributed equally in any society. Some individuals and groups receive a greater share because of a variety

of circumstances, ranging from luck to political, social, or economic power. The advocate's role is to help right the imbalance by working on behalf of those with less luck or power. Social workers believe that agencies and organizations can change to meet client needs. Influencing the organization to change requires that the worker mobilize resources on behalf of less-powerful clients. Of course, accomplishing this is often not a simple task.

3. Many agency leaders would prefer that workers not advocate for changes in their organization. Agency board members and administrators usually find that maintaining the status quo is easier if you do not have people urging you to change or expand services and resources. Therefore, attempts at change may be met with resistance. For example, the workers in a county human services agency wanted to provide each public assistance recipient with a booklet describing their rights and the benefits to which they were legally entitled. The booklets, developed by a client advocacy group, contained factually correct information that encouraged clients to get the benefits they needed. A request to include these booklets in the regular monthly mailing of benefit checks was denied by the agency administrator. The administrator feared that clients might assert rights that the agency was unwilling to recognize, which would inevitably cost the agency more money. This increase, in turn, would raise the wrath of the county board. The administrator wanted to avoid this scenario at all costs. He adamantly refused to have anyone think he supported giving benefits to clients, other than those the agency was forced to provide.

4. Not only can agencies refuse to be helpful, but they may also subvert the rules or try to be secretive. Advocacy is needed because some human service agencies and institutions are insensitive to client needs or deny clients needed services. Additionally, agencies and organizations can fail to follow rules or hide how their workers and supervisors are really performing. Similarly, they can keep clients ignorant of their rights. Sometimes the clients are too discouraged or powerless to stand up for themselves. Sometimes clients receive inappropriate treatment or mistreatment by the very agencies charged with responsibility to help them. Ultimately, the social worker must understand the dynamics of organizations and institutions. That understanding will be helpful at the point of assessing and planning for change.

OBSERVATIONS ABOUT CLIENTS

One of the most important observations about clients is derived from the social work conceptualization of the client in the environment. In this model, clients are never seen as existing separately from their environment. That is, clients both influence and are influenced by their environment. Whatever problems exist occur because of the dynamic interaction between the two.

In the past, the emphasis was on how people deserved what they got. When applied to clients, this assumption meant that the clients' problems were their own fault. We now refer to this approach as "blaming the victim" and see that it is often the environment and how that environment influences clients that are really to blame for problems.

The second observation concerning advocacy is that clients should be helped to help themselves. This assumption means that workers should not act as advocates for clients when they can advocate for themselves. People tend to become dependent when we do things for them that they can do without us. Often, we can help people be advocates for themselves by teaching them to be assertive and modeling this ourselves.

A third observation of advocacy is that it should never be carried out without the full knowledge and consent of the client. We will discuss the reasons for this caveat in the section on assessment in advocacy situations.

Knowledge Required by Advocates

Workers acting as advocates need to know many things. They need to know the rights of clients and the avenues of redress available to clients. They must know the resources that can be mobilized on behalf of the client. Finally, they must master strategies and tactics that are most likely to be effective.

KNOWING THE RIGHTS OF CLIENTS

The effective client advocate must know the rights and entitlements of clients. Rights are those things to which individuals and society at large have a just claim. Rights are rooted in both legal and moral grounds. There are two types of rights: individual rights and societal rights. Individual rights are those that you as an individual are guaranteed. Examples include the right to an education and freedom of speech. Societal rights, on the other hand, are the collective rights of the people as a whole that are considered more important than individual rights. For instance, members of society have the right not to be murdered by another individual.

Sometimes, individual and societal rights are in conflict. For example, owning land along a river and using that land as you see fit (individual rights) are possible for you. The river itself, however, cannot be modified by the landowner. You cannot forbid people to use the river, nor can you alter the riverbank without permission (societal rights).

Another example of rights in conflict involves freedom of speech (an individual right). Saying whatever you want, however, does not allow you to shout "fire" in a theater when there really is no fire. Such exercising of freedom would threaten the safely of others (a societal right).

As you can see, there are limits even to the most basic rights we have as citizens. Understanding both the rights and the limitations of those rights is important. In view of societal rights, we cannot make unreasonable or illegal demands on agencies no matter how much clients want us to pursue their individual rights.

IDENTIFYING AVENUES OF APPEAL

Challenging the actions of agency administrators or employees requires a thorough knowledge of the avenues of redress or appeal open to the client. For example, consider a decision that has been made by a line worker in the agency. To whom can this decision be appealed? Is the worker's supervisor the next step in the chain of command? Does the agency have an ombudsman (an individual designated to investigate charges and complaints) to whom complaints can be directed? Does the law provide for a fair hearing process in which clients can appeal decisions with which they disagree?

Entitlements are benefits to which a person is guaranteed access either by law or by other agreements. For example, Social Security is a program to which people are entitled because they have contributed to creation of the fund through payroll taxes. The nature of the entitlement may dictate the avenues of appeal available. Entitlements may arise from several sources. First are those that are established or defined by law or regulation. These include federal, state, and local laws and regulations. Because laws or regulations are not always clear, a second category of entitlements is those based upon an interpretation of law or regulation. A third category is those based upon an organization's own policies. Finally, because policies can be just as confusing and debatable as laws, a fourth category of entitlements is based upon interpretation of organizational policy.

Knowing the source of the entitlement may help us decide what form our advocacy will take. For example, most entitlements guaranteed by law have specific appeal procedures built into the law. Agencies may or may not have identified appeal procedures for those who disagree with agency policy.

Frequently, appeal procedures appear in agency handbooks or regulations. Whenever possible, the established appeal procedures should be followed before considering other options. If you and the client have not exhausted the appeal system, brushing off your complaint is easy for the agency. The agency can always say you have not followed proper procedures, which is why knowing specifically how to appeal different kinds of decisions is important.

IDENTIFYING AVAILABLE RESOURCES

Often, social workers will seek the help of other resources in carrying out the role of advocate. Resources include both people and agencies and organizations that may help you and the client. One of the most important resources is assistance with legal questions. Although knowing everything about every client's rights may not be possible, having access to those who do know is possible and advisable. Attorneys are important sources of information about certain kinds of rights, such as those written into existing laws or guaranteed by the Constitution.

In addition, some organizations work actively to protect the rights of the individual citizen. For example, the American Civil Liberties Union exists to help ensure that individual rights are not abridged or limited, particularly by those elements of our society that are the most powerful (government and business). This organization may prove helpful to workers unsure about the legal rights of a client.

Legal Aid is another organization providing pro bono (free) legal services. Sometimes, the worker will know an attorney who will provide free service or help at a nominal cost. Perhaps an organization like the National Alliance for the Mentally ill will be available to help. In the assessment section of this chapter, we will discuss other possible resources.

Another resource to pursue change is through federal and state agencies responsible for overseeing compliance with various laws and regulations. For example, the federal Office of Civil Rights may undertake an investigation of violations of civil rights laws. One university hospital was the target of such an investigation for allegedly failing to provide interpretive services for non-English-speaking patients as is required by federal guidelines. Those rules require that such services be provided free to patients and apply to facilities receiving federal funding.

In some cases, the NASW Legal Defense Fund (LDF) can provide assistance to social workers whose rights have been violated by employers or who are being punished for engaging in advocacy on behalf of vulnerable populations. The LDF has also filed legal briefs in more than 300 cases related to social work's commitment to the underserved, poor, and groups discriminated against by institutions, governments, and other organizations.

Critical Thinking Questions 14.2

 As a student in a social work education program, you have certain rights and obligations. What steps would you need to take if you believed that your rights in the following situations were not being recognized?

- An instructor gave you a failing grade on an assignment allegedly because you verbally disagreed with her viewpoint expressed in class.
- Another student asked to see an early draft of your paper, copied portions of it, and turned it in to the instructor first. The instructor now thinks that your paper was plagiarized.
- The student newspaper interviewed you for an article on your social work program. When the article appeared, you were misquoted and portrayed as an angry student who disparaged your own program.

THINKING STRATEGICALLY ABOUT INTERVENTION

The worker will need to be familiar with a variety of techniques and approaches useful in advocacy situations. Some of these strategies and tactics resemble those used in other social work roles. Others are unique to the role of advocate. Much of the remainder of this chapter will be devoted to discussing strategies and tactics.

The successful advocate requires two types of skills. Required first are the generalist practice skills useful in virtually any type of intervention. These skills include such things as empathy, confrontation, active listening, nonverbal communication, interviewing, observing, being supportive, and understanding resistance. Advocates also need to understand the group process, decision making in groups, and both formal and informal structures and procedures. The ability to gather and present data is also important.

The second category of skills required by advocates includes those needed specifically for particular

situations. For example, political or legislative advocacy requires skills somewhat different from those needed in advocating for an individual client. We will discuss these skills later in this chapter.

Assessing Advocacy Situations

 As in any assessment, there are several considerations an advocate needs to take into account. On the one hand, examining your own position and potential ability to advocate is important. On the other hand, you need to assess aspects of the potential advocacy situation outside yourself. These aspects include the clients' resources and strengths, characteristics of the adversary (i.e., the person, organization, agency, or policy that needs to change), and the resources, strategies, and tactics available to cause change.

SELF-ASSESSMENT

One of the first questions to address is the source of the advocate's sanction. In other words, who or what gives you the right to advocate? Does your job description include serving as an advocate for clients? Does the sanction come from the clients' clearly stated legal rights that are not being observed? Perhaps the primary source of sanction is the ethics of the social work profession as described in the NASW *Code of Ethics.*

There are many barriers to successful advocacy, such as internal agency policies and external obstacles. For example, sometimes you will experience a lack of support from colleagues and superiors. Placing client interests above those of your own agency may cause conflict with peers and others. The combination of barriers can make your job stressful. Workers must realistically assess their own vulnerability. What risks exist in serving as an advocate? Are the risks minor or great? What is the source of the risk? What means exist to counter the risk? Are the likely gains worth the risk? Do the tactics considered increase or decrease the risk?

Another factor is the worker's ability to devote the necessary time to the change effort. Advocacy often takes more time because problems are more intractable.

In addition, workers must deal with their own discomfort about being advocates. When dealing with people in power, the worker is in the uncomfortable position of asking for help instead of giving it. Often, the people targeted for change by the advocate have great experience in avoiding the issue. Because such people are frustrating to deal with, the worker may have to risk appearing aggressive or antagonistic to get anything done. The worker should be aware of and prepared for this possibility.

LO 14-3 Utilize Conceptual Frameworks Related to Advocacy

IDENTIFYING YOUR SOURCES OF POWER

What sources and kinds of power do advocates have available to cause change? There are several different types of power, according to Raven (1993). *Legitimate power* exists when person A believes person B has the right to influence him or her. The right often derives from a person's authority based on one's position in an organization. For example, supervisors usually are perceived as having a legitimate right to direct the behavior of subordinates. Similarly, you usually step on the brake and pull over when you notice the police car with flashing red and blue lights in your rearview mirror. This action rests on your perception that the police have a legitimate right to direct you to stop (although you may argue with the officer for doing so).

Reward power is the ability to provide positive reinforcement to another person. Examples of rewards are salary increases, praise, promotions, and other things perceived by the receiver to be beneficial. Reward power may be lodged in any number of persons (e.g., parents, spouses, employers, and friends).

Coercive power is the ability of someone to punish or use negative reinforcement on another individual. Here there is the real or potential threat that something bad will happen or something good will be taken away if you do not cooperate. In addition to their legitimate power, police officers have a certain amount of coercive power they can employ. The threat of a speeding ticket is supposed to coerce you to obey the speed limit.

What is experienced as coercive depends a great deal on the person being coerced. Because individuals vary so greatly, something considered coercive or unpleasant by one person may not be seen as bad by another. For example, sitting in a smoke-filled bar with extremely loud music playing might be a delight to one person and a noxious nightmare to another.

Referent power exists when one person is influenced by another person because of admiration for that individual. If you look up to others, admire their values or ideas, or otherwise would like to emulate them, you have accorded them referent power. Conversely, someone you find repulsive or unpleasant is not likely to have any referent power over you.

The final type of power is *expert power*. Expert power is available to those we consider to be authorities or especially proficient in some area. We generally accord physicians expert authority because we believe they know more than we do about the field of medicine.

Not infrequently, multiple sources of power exist in the same person or organization. For example, job supervisors may have legitimate power, coercive power, and reward power. Ideally, the advocate should attempt to marshal as many types of power as possible. If the adversary is vulnerable because he or she has broken the law, using legitimate power to cause change is possible. You may recall the case of the landlord who refused to fix up his slum apartments in violation of city law. Remember also in this case that tenants contacted the news media, which held the landlord up to public condemnation and ridicule, a coercive power.

OTHER ASSESSMENT CONSIDERATIONS

Three dimensions are important in assessment when contemplating advocacy. First is the nature of the problem situation. The second concerns the strengths, rights, and resources of the client. The third entails the characteristics of the adversary.

Determining the Nature of the Problem Situation

Before beginning to advocate, you certainly need to understand the nature of the problem situation itself. For example, will the change effort take place at the level of the decision maker, or does it require change in agency policy, administrative procedures or regulations, or social policy? Is the problem occurring because the client has a special need that is not being addressed? Is it because there is a bad relationship between the target system and the client?

You will remember that the target system is the individual, group, or community to be changed in order to accomplish our goals. Is there a deficiency of some sort in the target system (either structural or in personnel)? Is the problem a bad or ineffective social or agency policy? Is the target system a worker, administrator, policymaker, or legislator who is not functioning the way you think she or he should? Is the target system external to or part of the worker's own agency? What types of relationships exist between the advocate and the target system? The answers to these questions suggest different strategies and tactics.

Keeping an open mind about the situation and the target system is also important, at least at first. For example, do not automatically presume that people or groups acting as barriers are malicious, deliberate, or mean-spirited. Often target system actions may be inadvertent or result from different perceptions of the situation. Initially assuming the worst may create a self-fulfilling prophecy. Highlight 14.2 shows an example of a problem in which several alternative hypotheses are possible.

Sometimes problems occur because of staff ignorance of client cultural values and beliefs because the staff has not taken enough time to develop rapport with clients. Perhaps the client has not understood the necessity for certain information or misunderstood what was asked. Even the application forms clients must complete for specific entitlement programs (e.g., Medicaid) may cause problems. Questions may be vague or call for answers the client does not have. One can wonder whether the use of confusing application forms exists to discourage clients from applying for help or simply reflects an agency's lack of sensitivity.

Before advocating, you need to address a number of questions. First, is the goal to acquire new resources or improve existing ones? How long has the problem existed? How serious is it? How many people are affected by it? Is there any history of advocacy efforts that would add information to the current assessment? If past efforts failed, what were the reasons for these failures? Has anything changed that would make the decision to advocate more likely to succeed?

The answers to all of these questions should lead you to believe you can influence the decision maker. Your assessment should make you certain that you can persuade or coerce the target system into acting as you wish. Otherwise, you are probably wasting your time and should consider other intervention options.

HIGHLIGHT 14.2

When the System Is Not Working

Nathan Washington and Ramon Vallejo owned a duplex together in the midsized college town of Fort Druid. They had lived there for almost 17 years and were happy in their quiet, residential neighborhood.

One morning, they were suddenly awakened by the eager rap, rap, rap of pounding hammers coming from the house immediately next door. The noise annoyed them. However, this noise was nothing compared to their annoyance and displeasure when they found the structure was being converted to tiny units of inexpensive student housing. They were infuriated. All they could envision was loud, pulsing music in wee morning hours and cases of empty beer cans strewn around the yard. Neither Nathan nor Ramon had been notified about this pending change.

It so happened that the city ordinance in Fort Druid is quite clear regarding such structural changes. Any time there is a major change proposed in the use of a building or in its structure, residents within 300 feet are to be notified. The city is required to send a letter describing the proposed action. For example, a request by a property owner to convert a single-family home into an apartment must have the approval of the city planning commission. The commission must hold an open hearing (a meeting where anyone who wishes to come and speak can do so) and allow neighbors to present their views. The ordinance calls for notification of neighbors because changes in their neighborhood can have economic and quality-of-life significance for them.

If you were advocating on behalf of Nathan and Ramon, three issues would confront you. First, the owners of the house may not have obeyed the law by seeking permission to modify their building. Second, if they had sought proper approval, the failure to notify residents as required by law may make the actions of the planning commission illegal. Therefore, their approval of the house conversion may be invalid. Third, there is the question of why the problem occurred in the first place. Were the neighbors not notified because the required open meeting had never been held? Had they failed to read the notice when it was mailed to their home? Was it a mistake by an individual staff person in city hall who simply forgot to mail the notice? Was it an attempt to keep the neighbors from exercising their legal rights to present their objections to the planning commission? Were the notices lost in the mail?

What actions an advocate might take are clearly dependent on the problem's cause. Assessment is critical to identify these numerous potential causes, explore their substance, and target the one that appears to be real.

Assessing the Client

Clients must be closely involved in the decision to select advocacy strategies. You need to assess their motivation to participate and their ability to do so. There are at least five reasons for this involvement. First, the chance for success is greatest if clients participate in planning the intervention. Second, clients are more likely to use and value resources they had a hand in developing. Third, resources are more likely to be appropriate when clients have helped develop or create them. Fourth, clients gain an important sense of efficacy when they participate in actions designed to reach their goals. Fifth, working with others helps produce a sense of participation and involvement that may be important for clients lacking self-esteem and a support network.

You might ask yourself a number of questions. For instance, how important is the issue to the client? Is it an emergency or less pressing? Does the client have any ability to compromise, or is the issue too basic? Will this effort cause problems for the client at some later point? What resources does the client have (e.g., verbal skills, determination, leadership ability, social skills, intelligence)? Does the client have any other sources of power?

The answers to such questions will help you plan more carefully and wisely. For example, you can decide how quickly you need to act. You will also know if compromises are possible and what role the client may play.

There are also ethical issues involved in the process of assessing the client's involvement in advocacy. Acting on behalf of a client without his or her full awareness of the potential consequences is simply unethical. If clients may suffer repercussions as a result of advocacy, they should be aware of this. The risk is theirs to take. The social worker cannot make this choice for them. Attempts to bring about change on behalf of others without their complete investment in the process is dangerous on both the local and global level. For example, recent military interventions by the United States ostensibly to benefit the populations of other countries have proven disastrous for the intended beneficiaries.

Assessing the Adversary

Understanding the adversary or target system well is critical. For example, you will want to know the structure and communication channels of the adversary system. Information about how decisions are made and what rules or regulations govern the system are also important.

What are the adversaries like? What do we know about their jobs, titles, motivation, and capabilities?

Perhaps the first question to address is how *open to change* is the adversary or target system? Additionally, to what degree do you and the target system share the same views about client needs? You must know whether or not the target system (adversary) will be receptive to change. The target may be resistant, sympathetic, or indifferent to our efforts. Receptivity may be a function of the type of objective pursued. For example, if the objective is to increase access to already-existing resources, the target system might be more open to change. If, on the other hand, you are seeking changes in the basic policies or procedures of an agency, expect more resistance.

You also want to know the *degree of vulnerability* of the adversary. Is the person violating agency policy (which is somewhat minor) or violating a law (which is much more serious)? Is the action taken permitted within the discretion normally granted the decision maker, or has the person exceeded that authority?

Knowing how this adversary *handled complaints or challenges in the past* may be important. For example, does the person respond best to face-to-face meetings, or are all decisions made by reviewing written materials? Does the person usually make quick decisions or need time to think about requests? Does the person consult others before deciding?

Finally, knowing the *values* of the adversary would be helpful. What are the person's goals? Is this person likely to be more sympathetic to the client's viewpoint or to the worker's? Substantial differences in values and goals decrease the probability of quick solutions. The greater the divergence between the values and goals of the client and adversary, the more power is required to change the situation. Determining the availability and potency of power is an important part of the assessment process.

Planning in Advocacy Situations

Planning in advocacy situations requires considering the knowledge gained from the assessment steps previously identified and selecting the most appropriate interventions. The first step in planning is to consider the resources, strategies, and tactics that you will employ to bring about change. *Resources* may include money, power, prestige, authority, commitment, and any other means you can muster to help reach your goal. You as an advocate, your client, or some aspect of the environment may be tapped for resources.

Outcomes depend partly on the resources of the change agent and the receptivity of the target system. The most effective advocates use this information and adopt a variety of resources and techniques.

Strategy concerns broad issues and your plan for approaching advocacy. For example, a strategy might entail the amount of conflict you plan to use in an advocacy effort. What strategies make the most sense given the available resources? As in the planning phase of the planned change model, you must select a strategy based on the problem, the objectives, your sanctions, and characteristics of the change agent and target systems.

Tactics represent the specifics of your plan, such as how conflict is used and when. For example, confronting the adversary immediately with an overwhelming show of support for your ideas might be important. Recall the case mentioned in Chapter 4, where the city council was intent on supporting a bypass highway around the city. By quickly confronting the city council with a petition signed by almost every business owner on the highway, the proposed bypass was rejected immediately.

One of the most important factors in the decision to advocate is the resources available to use in the intervention effort. Are there others who will join in to work on the problem? From whom can you expect support? Do you have some influence with the decision maker? Is some amount of money or power available to you?

LO 14-4 Employ Specific Knowledge and Skills in Advocacy

MAKING THE ULTIMATE DECISION

Ultimately, the social worker must make a decision about when and when not to advocate. This decision is sometimes difficult. Fruitless efforts to change target systems are demoralizing to clients and workers. When the assessment phase points to the eventual failure of the intervention, stopping before committing further resources to the endeavor is better for everyone concerned.

Engaging in Intervention: Advocacy Strategies and Tactics

Following assessment and planning, the worker and client must decide the appropriate strategy and tactics to use for a given advocacy situation. In this section, we will look closely at the techniques that advocates often employ (see Highlight 14.3). They

include persuasion, fair hearings and legal appeals, political and community pressure, using the media, and petitioning. Some of these were discussed in Chapter 4 and will only be addressed briefly here.

PERSUADING

Persuading others to take certain actions can be simple or extremely difficult. It depends on several factors, including the nature of the problem, the degree of resistance experienced, the client's wishes, and the capabilities of the worker.

Because advocacy work usually involves challenging the status quo, resistance will occur. We often select a strategy based on our perception of how difficult influencing the adversary will be. Adversaries who share your views will probably require little persuasion. You may then need only to define the issue clearly and present your evidence that a problem exists that the adversary can resolve. In other words, persuasion is more likely to work when the target system understands the client's needs and values, accepts the worker's perspective, and shares the values of the worker. In these cases, collaborative strategies are possible and recommended. Collaborative strategies are synergistic. That is, working together gets more accomplished with less effort than people working alone. Collaboration involves giving and clarifying information. In a sense, advocates can then educate their adversaries. Jointly planned change is possible, and both parties can begin working together on a solution.

Effective persuasion of adversaries is a challenge. Social workers are recommended to approach this challenge by using the following steps:

1. Clearly state the issue of concern (i.e., a policy, procedure, decision, or process) that you believe is a problem.
2. Allow adequate time for discussing the issue and answering questions. Do not attempt to hurry the process. People who feel pressured are more likely to say no just to get rid of the pressure.
3. Identify exactly what you want done. Do you want a policy or rule changed, a different decision, or an exception made?
4. As the discussion unfolds, summarize areas of agreement between you and the adversary. This summarization helps build a bridge of understanding and reduces the feeling of distance between your respective positions.
5. Attempt to find a common ground whenever possible. Seek areas where you have similar interests with the adversary.

HIGHLIGHT 14.3

Guidelines for Advocacy

The following guidelines for advocacy are useful in almost all situations where you may serve as a client's advocate and where persuasion, fair hearings, appeals, petitioning, and more-confrontational strategies are used:

1. Serve as an advocate only with clear permission of your client. Clients have a right to decide if they wish you to undertake advocacy on their behalf.
2. Acknowledge to the client and yourself that acting as an advocate can affect your relationships with other people and organizations. This impact can be positive or negative.
3. Advocacy is appropriate only to help the client, not to pursue your personal agenda.
4. Get the facts first. Your credibility is influenced by having accurate information, such as dates, times, actions, statistics, and other hard data. Do not go into a situation unprepared.
5. Always enter an advocacy situation with a clear list of concerns and questions. Know exactly what you want and be prepared to assertively ask the target to meet your request.
6. Look at issues from both sides. Put yourself in the shoes of the adversary. Can you employ your empathy and other practice skills to see how things look to them? Being able to convey this

understanding, while demonstrating respect for your opponent, leaves the door open for that person to give in. No one appreciates being put down, misunderstood, or treated badly.
7. Keep a record of things that are said in meetings that relate to your goal. If you are told something is true, check it out. If you are getting different messages from different people, determine which are true or whether the facts lie somewhere else.
8. Always find out who makes decisions at the next higher level. Learn the chain of command. If you are turned down at one level, knowing the next line of appeal is important. Inform your opponent that you intend to take the matter to his or her supervisor or governing board, depending on which is most appropriate.
9. Record all steps you take to resolve an issue. Note details such as time, place, date, decisions, and decision makers. Be prepared for taking the next step.

Sources: B. W. Sheafor and C. R. Horejsi (2012), *Techniques and Guidelines for Social Work Practice* (9th ed.), Boston, MA: Allyn & Bacon; and B. R. Compton, B. Galaway, and B. R. Cournoyer (2005), *Social Work Processes* (7th ed.), Belmont, CA: Thomson Brooks/Cole.

6. Avoid vague statements and always make your positions, requests, and points clear to the opponent.
7. Be candid about what you will do if the problem is not remedied. This straightforwardness is not done in the form of a threat but only as a matter-of-fact statement of intent. If you intend to appeal a decision or assume a more conflictual stance, let the opponent know it. In some cases, using this method may get the opponent to reconsider his or her position.
8. Convey your sincerity and determination to resolve the matter.
9. Maintain eye contact and avoid any gestures (such as looking down) that might undercut your firmness.
10. Approach the adversary as if you both have a desire to resolve things. Do not start by suggesting that the opponent is not willing to hear your position.

11. Do not filibuster or monopolize the conversation. Listen empathetically and allow the other person a chance to be heard.
12. Do not lose your cool. Getting angry is a mistake. Those who blow up emotionally lose power in these situations.

In other situations, you may choose different tactics. For example, you may try negotiating with the adversary, bargaining, or offering compromises to achieve as much of your goal as possible. This posture assumes that the matter of concern is one where compromise is possible and is sanctioned (supported) by the client.

When Persuasion Does Not Work

Sometimes, you may need to consider using confrontation and more conflictual approaches. These approaches are usually used when the advocate has little influence over the decision maker. This lack of influence suggests the need to take more drastic steps.

Confrontational approaches involve three dimensions. First, you can threaten to disclose the adversary's failure to follow law or policy. Second, you can actually disclose the information and allow the natural consequences to occur. Finally, you can appeal through administrative hearings or the courts.

The latter option is not employed routinely because of the cost involved. It may be appropriate only when other alternatives fail. Administrative appeals occur much more frequently because they are often the only way to cause changes in rules and regulations or decisions based on those rules and regulations.

USING FAIR HEARINGS AND LEGAL APPEALS

"Fair hearings and grievances are administrative procedures designed to ensure that clients or client groups who have been denied benefits or rights to which they are entitled get equitable treatment" (Kirst-Ashman & Hull, 2012, p. 409). Normally, the clients notify the agency that they wish to have a fair hearing concerning the adversary's decision, which means that an outside person (usually a state employee) will be appointed to hear both sides of the argument. The fair hearing examiner may find the adversary has violated state or federal policies. Then the examiner may direct the adversary to comply with the rules and award the client his or her rightful benefits. Sometimes just the threat of using the formal appeal process will be enough to change an adversary's earlier decision. Other times, the agency may have no policy for a fair hearing or appeal and other confrontational tactics can be employed. For example, seeking advice and assistance from an attorney is often possible. Not infrequently, an attorney's letter presenting the possibility of legal action is sufficient to cause adversaries to change their position.

EMPLOYING POLITICAL AND COMMUNITY PRESSURE

Consider the case discussed earlier regarding finding housing for a Hmong client. The worker used an elected official (a city council member) to pressure a city agency to act in a responsive and timely fashion. Many political figures proudly tell their constituents of their efforts to combat bureaucracies at all levels on their constituents' behalf. For example, most members of the U.S. House of Representatives and Senate provide such help to constituents. The latter usually have expressed unhappiness about decisions or lack of action taken by the Social Security Administration and other federal agencies.

Do not ignore state representatives and senators either. Workers at one agency, faced with laying off almost a dozen staff members because of a proposed change in how the state contracted with providers of family services, wrote a persuasive letter to their state representative. The letter, outlining the concerns and problems, asked the legislator to meet with agency representatives to discuss the matter. Shortly thereafter the state agency backed down on its proposal (J. Campbell, personal communication, May 26, 1999).

In other situations, pressure may be brought through community groups such as the Alliance for the Mentally ill. Advocacy organizations exist to work for their members. They will often intervene to help their members cope with uncooperative systems. Organizational pressures of this type depend on the existence and availability of such supportive associations.

Another means of creating community pressure is using door-to-door solicitation—speaking to residents, handing out flyers, and gathering signatures on petitions designed to convince decision makers. It is also possible to hold community meetings designed to address issues that affect residents such as changes in laws, policies, or other regulations. Social workers have been involved in all of these activities in pursuit of their commitment to social justice.

USING THE MEDIA

Advocates may be able to use the media as a confrontational tactic to cause change. For example, some television stations conduct public service programs that respond to viewers' written complaints about agencies or organizations. A reporter will investigate the situation and discuss it on the evening news. Often this type of pressure will result in a favorable change for the client.

One should note that the problem does not have to involve a government bureaucracy. Clients who have received unsatisfactory responses from businesses have used these television programs to publicize their complaints.

Advocates can also use the media to publicize wrongdoing. This tactic, you may recall, was used by the apartment residents to embarrass the landlord. The landlord was unresponsive to both his own tenants and to the city's feeble enforcement efforts until the television stations reported the situation on the evening news. This is really a combination of using the media and employing community pressure. A similar approach was used by All Together, an agency advocating for the rights of people with physical disabilities. The agency's clients complained that transportation services they needed were being denied or so restricted that they were hampered in their efforts to maintain employment and lead productive lives. Prior attempts at letter writing had been unsuccessful, and some clients felt they had been victims of retaliation for voicing their concerns. To demonstrate their unhappiness, the clients and staff of All Together picketed a fundraising event for the transportation agency. Clients, many in wheelchairs, carried picket signs and chanted their concerns. The event, which was being attended by the news media, quickly focused attention on the transportation needs of clients with physical disabilities. It also caused community residents and transportation service board members to look more closely at the way the agency was meeting client needs. Within a short time afterward, the Board of Directors asked the transportation services director to step down and began a wholesale revamping of the services provided to clients with disabilities.

Chapter 4 offers a more detailed discussion on using the media.

PETITIONING

Another tactic you can employ as an advocate involves circulating petitions. We discussed this approach earlier, in Chapter 4. As you may recall, petitioning is the collecting of signatures on a piece of paper requesting some type of action. You might collect neighborhood signatures asking for stoplights at a dangerous intersection. Petitions can be effective. However, many people will sign petitions without real commitment to the cause. Because signatures on petitions are generally easy to get, many officials discount their importance. Therefore, you should carefully consider their potential effectiveness before using them.

SELECTING A STRATEGY FOR ADVOCACY

Whenever possible, select the advocacy approach that requires the least effort and stress to achieve your desired goals. Nonconfrontational approaches should be used before confrontational ones. For example, collaborative strategies should be applied before conflictual ones, if possible. Confrontation can wear on you. It can siphon your energy away from your other job tasks.

Consider three conditions before deciding to exert pressure and cause a confrontation:

1. You have already tried less confrontational ways of instituting change. For example, you have tried unsuccessfully to persuade your adversary.
2. You have enough proof that clients have been treated unfairly and are absolutely certain that your grievance is consequential.

3. You determine that you have a good chance at succeeding by exerting pressure and initiating a confrontation. You do not want to waste your energy if the cause is hopeless.

Whistle-Blowing

Whistle-blowing is the act of pointing out wrongdoing or practices that are illegal, dangerous, or otherwise problematic within an organization or entity. Often the person doing the whistle-blowing is employed by the organization and became aware of the problem as a result of that employment. Usually, the whistle-blower raises the concerns to the media, government oversight bodies, or other groups or individuals who have the capacity to do something about the alleged problem. Whistle-blowers can point out health or safely violations, threats to the public interest, and wasteful policies or violations of organizational policies. Some organizations, such as those in the federal government, provide means for whistle-blowing to occur while maintaining the anonymity of the person reporting the problem. There are even laws designed to protect the whistle-blower from retaliation by supervisory and administrative personnel whose positions are threatened by the revelations. These laws notwithstanding, whistle-blowing carries a degree of risk that varies in direct proportion to the seriousness of the allegations. Whistle-blowers have been fired, have been reassigned to insignificant responsibilities at remote locations, and have been harassed into quitting.

The purpose of providing this caveat is not to discourage social workers from advocating for clients with their own agencies or with others who are not acting in an appropriate manner. Rather, it is to assure that the decision to advocate is an informed one that has taken into consideration the risks involved.

LO 14-5 Engage in Legislative Advocacy to Advance Social and Economic Justice

Pursuing Legislative Advocacy

Earlier in this chapter we discussed case advocacy and cause advocacy. In this section, we will discuss a third type of advocacy called legislative advocacy. *Legislative advocacy* is similar to cause advocacy in that the social worker is working for a broad category of clients or citizens. Legislative advocacy specifically entails efforts to change legislation to benefit some category of clients. In many cases, creation of new legislation is the most effective means of addressing the human service needs of large groups of clients. The Americans with Disabilities Act (ADA) discussed in Chapter 12 is a strong advocacy tool enabling people with disabilities to achieve social and economic justice previously denied to a huge minority group.

Legislative advocacy also may embody efforts to defeat bills considered harmful in some way. For example, a proposed reduction in funding for the Head Start program would mean limiting or cutting off Head Start services previously available to clients. Head Start is a federal program established in 1965 to provide disadvantaged minority preschool children with education to compensate for previous social deprivation.

Another example of harmful legislation is a proposed bill to restrict access to reproductive health services such as Planned Parenthood. This agency provides information, contraception, counseling, and physical examinations, all directed at helping people (usually women) gain control over their own reproduction. Services are usually provided on a sliding-fee scale. This means that fees are based on how much people can pay. Poorer people pay less than richer people.

Legislation limiting access might incorporate requirements such as forcing women under age 18 to provide written parental permission before they can receive any services. Another inhibiting proposal might involve denying state or federal funding if agency staff members discuss abortion as a possible alternative to unwanted pregnancy. Both of these examples limit available services. The first places restrictions on the basis of age. The second limits the potential for informing clients of the options available to them.

Responsibility for legislative advocacy is part of being a social worker. So many decisions affecting social work programs, social workers, and clients are made in the legislative arena that *not* to be concerned about and involved in legislative advocacy is impossible.

Some social workers may feel a bit awed at the prospect of trying to get laws passed and programs funded. Fortunately, legislative advocacy has one unique feature that makes this effort less difficult than it seems. The primary rule of legislative advocacy is that getting elected and reelected is the most important activity of most legislators (Haynes & Mickelson, 2010). Consequently, this "rule" means that most legislators like to know what their constituents want and are susceptible to their constituents' influence.

In addition, most legislators must make decisions about any particular proposed bill based on limited information. Many bills are complex, which increases the likelihood that the legislator will need to depend on others for information. As a consequence, legislators may very well be influenced by a small number of advocates or by a particularly persuasive argument about a given bill. In other words, you are encouraged to tell your state and federal senators and representatives what you think should be done about bills and issues (see Highlight 14.4). You can also mobilize other workers or clients to write or call in what they think. This tactic is one means of gaining at least some power over which laws are passed or defeated in the political process. Comparing your views on various legislative issues with those of your elected representatives is possible by consulting the World Wide Web. For example, Project Vote Smart, a not-for-profit and nonpartisan research organization, has compiled ratings from almost 100 interest groups. You can look up your U.S. senator's or representative's voting records on any number of issues. The Web address is http://www.vote-smart.org. You can also express your opinions at http://www.congress.org

Of course, there are realistic barriers that reduce the likelihood of getting new legislation passed. First, there is the fact that most bills are not actually passed. Only about as few as 15 percent of proposed bills eventually receive legislative approval and are signed by the governor or president to become law. Moreover, most legislative sessions are somewhat short, lasting only a matter of months. The legislature might not even get to the bill in which you are interested. Therefore, desired legislation may have to be reintroduced the following year, which often involves starting the whole process of influence again from scratch.

Additionally, legislative bodies are unpredictable. Turnover in membership from session to session after elections, changes in control from Republican to Democratic leadership, or economic news (e.g., lower-than-expected tax revenues resulting in less money available) can make the entire legislative process more complicated. People in power also make unpredictable decisions that affect legislation. For example, in one race for governor, the incumbent ran for reelection based on his success in increasing the economic growth and well-being of the state. He emphasized how well the state was doing financially because of his wonderful work and effort. Three weeks after winning the election, he announced that the state was experiencing a multimillion dollar shortfall in revenue because of

HIGHLIGHT 14.4

Writing Elected Officials

Social workers often have reason for writing to elected officials. It is important to use the correct form and address for such letters. Some common addresses and the accompanying salutations are shown here.

Letters to the President

The President
The White House
1600 Pennsylvania Ave. NW
Washington, DC 20500
http://www.whitehouse.gov

Salutation

Dear Mr./Ms. President:

Letters to U.S. Senators

The Honorable (insert full name)
United States Senate
Washington, DC 20510
http://www.senate.gov/contacting/index.cfm

Salutation

Dear Senator (insert last name):

Letters to Members of the House of Representatives

The Honorable (insert full name)
U.S. House of Representatives
Washington, DC 20515
http://www.house.gov/house/MemberWWW.html

Salutation

Dear Representative (insert last name):

Letters to Cabinet Secretaries

The Honorable (insert full name)
Secretary of (insert name of department)
Washington, DC (insert correct zip code)
http://www.whitehouse.gov/government/cabinet-secretaries.html

Salutation

Dear Secretary (insert last name):

Here are several additional guidelines for writing to elected officials:

- Write using your own words rather than sending a form letter. The latter carries less weight.
- Keep your letter brief and polite. Threats or impolite letters are likely to be ignored.
- Identify yourself as an informed constituent who is concerned about a specific, timely issue.
- Identify the specific action you would like, such as "vote for AB 297."
- Give clear reasons for your request, supported with facts and figures.
- Send a follow-up thank-you letter if your representative acts in accordance with your request.

Lists of your elected representatives can be acquired from the public library or by contacting your city hall. In addition, some states publish very detailed books listing all state officials. These lists may be found in your public library and often can be obtained free from your state legislator. You might also go on the Internet and check the Democrats' site (http://www.democrats.org/) and the Republicans' site (http://www.rnc.org/).

---

economic conditions. In other words, the state had millions of dollars less than it had been expected to have. This required a freeze on hiring and a reduction in budgets for all state agencies, including social services. As a result, many social workers who had supported that governor felt betrayed. Thus, the unpredictability of the legislative process means that the advocate must remain flexible and ready to change strategies as needed.

Legislative advocates soon realize that a bill may not be passed just because it is a good bill. Even

documented evidence strongly supporting a bill will not guarantee passage if other factors intervene. These factors include economic conditions, political positions, lawmakers' personal values or life experiences, and legislative precedent. Each of these aspects may override logic and compelling arguments. Besides, even when legislators support a bill, it may be buried or defeated in a committee composed of a smaller group of legislators who evaluate the bill and prepare it for presentation to the entire legislature. Once on the floor of the legislature, a bill may be defeated or returned to committee. Finally, governors may veto bills for their own idiosyncratic reasons.

RECOGNIZING FACTORS AFFECTING LEGISLATIVE ADVOCACY

Being successful as a legislative advocate requires that you understand some factors influencing whether or not a bill will be passed. For example, the fiscal consequences of a bill are extremely important to its chances for success. The cost of a proposed piece of legislation is perhaps the most important factor affecting its likelihood of becoming law. Logic might dictate that a bill's merit or usefulness is the most important aspect in making it pass, but this reasoning is not true in practice. Generally speaking, bills that ultimately require spending less money are more likely to pass.

The popularity of a bill also has some bearing on its potential success. The more popular a bill is, that is, the more support it has among constituents and legislators, the more likely it is to become law. Such bills are usually those that have little impact on social change and require little or nothing from the public. In other words, bills that are popular and do not affect most people directly are more likely to pass. A bill to increase the penalty for selling drugs is a good example. It is likely to be popular with the general public because its impact will only be on a relatively small group of people, and it supports commonly held values about selling drugs.

STEPS IN LEGISLATIVE ADVOCACY

Legislatures follow a series of steps to pass new legislation; likewise, there are coinciding steps a social worker can take to advocate for the passage of a new bill (Haynes & Mickelson, 2010). The steps for legislative advocacy include the following: developing a draft of the bill; figuring out who else will help you in support of the bill; getting specific legislators to sponsor the bill; asking your legislative sponsors to introduce the bill; educating the general public about the bill's worth and usefulness; trying to positively influence any legislative subcommittee members responsible for decision making about the bill; and trying to influence other legislators who will be voting on the bill's passage.

Step 1: Developing and Revising the Draft Bill

Formulating an original piece of legislation can be a formidable task. It requires both knowledge of the law and familiarity with existing regulations, policies, and programs related to the proposed bill. Consequently, most proposals are sent to an already-established unit (sometimes called a legislative reference bureau), which is responsible for writing the first draft of a bill. This body is usually an arm of the legislature. Its staff members often prepare a summary of the bill to help legislators understand its intent. Once in draft form, the bill needs to be refined. Often, clarifications and changes need to be made so that the bill reflects its supporters' intentions.

Step 2: Identifying, Obtaining, and Maintaining the Bill's Supporters

Initially, identifying those who are natural supporters of a bill is important, that is, who is naturally interested in the bill's topic or will obviously benefit from the bill. Predicting who will be neutral or opposed to a bill is equally important. If you hope to see this bill become law, you will need to know who is likely to dislike the bill. Knowing those who are initially neutral may give you a basis for later persuading them to support the bill. These people may include legislators, their staffs, external groups (e.g., the NASW), governmental agencies (e.g., the Department of Health and Human Services), and social service providers. Ironing out differences between factions supporting the bill is important. For example, people support a bill for many different reasons. Each supporter may have ideas about how to improve the bill. One group may dislike a particular word or section in the bill. These differing perspectives must be reconciled if you are to reach an agreement on the final bill. Keeping supporters on board is important, and modifying the bill may be one cost of achieving this consensus.

Arranging face-to-face meetings and providing copies of the draft bill to potential allies and adversaries may be necessary. Such tactics will allow these individuals a chance to explain their support (or opposition) and give you a chance to convince them to support the bill. This process also may result in changes in the bill as neutral or opposing groups come on board.

Attempt to get support from the governor and official state agencies affected by the bill. For example, a bill affecting who can be placed on probation would likely be of interest to the state bureau of corrections. State agencies are more likely to get bills they support through the legislature. Such agencies' opposition can be fatal to a bill because they are part of the arm of state government designed to administer bills passed by the legislature. Thus, they are considered to be experts on legislation affecting their respective areas of responsibility.

Step 3: Arranging for Sponsorship of the Bill

Finding legislators who are willing to introduce and work for a bill is a crucial step. Supporters who will do nothing to help a bill pass are not useful except to stay out of the way. If you are trying to get a bill passed, involve legislative staff members in discussions about the bill. Frequently, these staff members (those who work for the legislator) have the greatest influence with the legislator. Making changes in the bill to gain their support can be especially important. For instance, they may be more likely to support a bill after you have made some compromises honoring their needs and wishes.

Past track records of legislators can be important as guides to how they will vote on any given bill. Have they supported similar bills in the past? Have they made public statements supporting the bill's intent? Have they been critical of issues the bill addresses?

The "safety" of the legislator's seat also will be a factor. Those reelected by large margins or without opposition are often in stronger positions than legislators worrying that each vote may cost them the next election. Stronger positions may allow legislators to take greater risks. For instance, they may be more likely to support a bill that will require spending money if they believe in the merits of the bill.

Similarly, keeping away from legislative extremists who will never compromise is important. Compromise is the currency of politics. Unwillingness to compromise on a bill is likely to lead to its defeat.

If possible, obtain support of legislators in the majority party. Gaining support from members of both parties (bipartisan support) is even better. Obtain as many sponsors as possible for a bill because it will increase your support and the likelihood that the bill will pass.

Step 4: Introducing the Bill

Ask the legislative sponsors of your bill to introduce it before the legislative session or as early in the session as possible. Doing so leaves more time for lobbying and modifying the bill to satisfy additional supporters. Bills introduced late in a session often do not become law because of time constraints. Lobbying is seeking to influence laws or policies through direct contact with legislators or other policymakers. It can take the form of such things as face-to-face meetings with the legislator or a legislative staff person, letter writing, and/or arranging for others to communicate with elected officials or policymakers in order to convince them to take a particular course of action.

Step 5: Working with Interest Groups to Broaden Support for the Bill

Every bill has many potential supporters, some of whom never participate in the legislative process. Often, potential supporters simply do not know that a bill has been introduced, or they may not believe they can have much influence on the bill. Try to get as many potential supporters behind your bill as possible.

Step 6: Educating the Public

Educating the public is often difficult because frequently bills do not appear to be of interest to many people. One example of public education occurred in a state where the NASW was attempting to pass a law for certifying social workers. Articles appeared in newspapers around the state describing situations where unethical social workers continued to practice without licensing. Social workers and others sent letters to and wrote articles for newspapers stressing the importance of protecting the public from incompetent and unethical professionals. Such articles and letters served to educate the public about the issues and benefits of licensing social workers.

Step 7: Influencing Legislative Committee Consideration

All bills introduced in a legislature are referred or assigned to one or more committees prior to being considered by the entire body. Legislatures thrive on committees. Committees are formed of smaller groups of legislators charged with analyzing, refining, and making recommendations about proposed legislation. Committees typically have jurisdiction over matters on a particular topic. For example, there may be a committee on agriculture, health, and human services, another on judiciary and consumer affairs, one on education, and so on. Legislators usually express an interest in serving on a particular committee. Committee appointments are normally made by the leadership of the respective legislative body. Thus, the Speaker of the House or the Senate president will have major influence over who gets on what committee.

In addition, subcommittees are formed within committees to investigate an even more narrowly defined area. For instance, the agriculture, health, and human service committee previously mentioned would probably have separate subcommittees on each of the three areas: agriculture, health, and human services.

Every bill must go through one (or more) committee or subcommittee. Committees can allow a bill to die by not acting on it and also can refuse to pass a bill that the sponsor will not agree to modify. Ultimately, if a bill is to go to the legislative body for a vote, it must have been approved by the respective committee to which it was assigned. Advocates must lobby committee members, ask for public hearings on a bill where a broad range of people can voice their views, and arrange for expert testimony at those hearings. Hearings increase the likelihood that a bill will pass and provide opportunities for further lobbying. They also offer chances to make compromises with opponents that will make the bill more satisfactory to a larger number of people.

Testimony at public hearings should be carefully planned to include who will speak, in what order, and what they will say. People who testify should provide a written copy of any testimony to the committee members before speaking. Not everyone who testifies needs to be an expert on a topic. The purpose of a hearing is to listen to all who wish to speak on the bill under consideration. Thus, both experts and interested parties are welcome to participate. There are a number of suggestions about how testimony should be structured and presented. These suggestions can apply to your own testimony or that of others you are helping to prepare for testimony.

First, the written statement should be able to stand on its own (i.e., it should not need any additional verbal clarification). Additionally, it should be worded so that it is clear, straightforward, and readily understandable by most adults. Jargon should be omitted. The statement should specifically explain why this law is important and what particular benefits it will have. Argue the case on its merits and never preach. Use factual material and cite its source (e.g., census data, specific government studies or publications). Potential online sources for information include the following:

- http://www.cdfactioncouncil.org
- http://www.urbaninstitute.org

Using case examples to illustrate the impact of a specific bill is also permissible. However, use humor carefully because being perceived as a serious professional person is important.

Avoid hostility and focus testimony on the proposed legislation. Be brief, show respect for committee members, and be ready to answer questions, including hostile ones. Finally, when you are finished, thank the committee for the opportunity to speak.

Step 8: Influencing Action on the Floor

Bills may be amended or modified by legislators making motions from the floor. The advocate needs to anticipate this possibility and be ready to compromise in ways that will not destroy the bill. When a bill is on the legislative floor, only legislators can participate in what is done with it.

Outside of the actual legislative floor, you as a supporter can help by contacting uncommitted legislators and communicating your point of view. You can also help by seeking media coverage of the bill. Phone calls can be made to legislators within the 48 hours before voting commences. This time schedule helps ensure the legislator will remember the call when the bill is ready to be voted on.

Keep track of supporters and opponents. Advocates for legislation should contact both those who support a bill and those who oppose it. All who will vote on the bill need to know constituents are supporting it. Lobbying cannot be restricted to those already predisposed to the bill's passage.

Seek media coverage of the bill to reach and interest large numbers of constituents. You should plan to attend and be present for the debate on a bill. Doing so will help you understand any opposition to the bill, and you can then suggest to the legislator or his or her staff amendments or changes that might keep the bill on track. When contacting legislators or the media, you must be current regarding all the issues. Being present for the debate will help you in this regard.

You should not be discouraged by the amending process. Amended bills get through the legislature with much greater frequency than those without amendments.

Once a bill has received favorable action in one house of the legislature, the same eight steps are repeated in the other house. Generally, a bill may be introduced in either house first, although some state constitutions require that certain types of bills must originate in one house or the other. One hopes to see the legislative process end with the governor signing the bill into law.

One other aspect of legislative advocacy involves helping good legislators get elected. By "good," we mean people with values similar to our professional values. Helping a candidate win an election is an exhilarating experience. Because political campaigns require so many varied skills, finding a role in a campaign is always possible. Possibilities include campaigning door to door; distributing flyers door to door (called mail drops) or on campus; telephoning potential voters; soliciting or contributing money; transporting voters to the polls; putting up yard signs; placing a sign on your car; folding, stuffing, and sealing letters; and typing. The value of this work is clear. Elected officials remember who helped them and will be most sensitive to their helpers' views.

The NASW founded Political Action for Candidate Election (PACE) to help elect candidates favorable to social work positions on issues. PACE is active in both state and national elections and provides financial support and other assistance to a wide range of campaigns. Becoming involved in PACE gives you yet another way to become politically active.

Chapter Summary

The following summarizes this chapter's content as it relates to each learning objective (LO) presented at the beginning of the chapter. Chapter content helps prepare students to:

LO 14-1 Advocate for clients in the context of generalist practice.

Advocacy is an implementation strategy in the Generalist Intervention Model. The advocate works on behalf of a client, negotiating, bargaining, speaking, and arguing for the client's interests. Advocacy can be on behalf of a single case (case advocacy) or address an issue that affects multiple groups of people (cause advocacy). Cause advocates can work alone or in coalitions with like-minded professionals, clients, or ordinary citizens.

LO 14-2 Implement the professional role of advocate.

The role of advocate is just one of several professional roles played by social workers. It differs from others in its goal of attempting to influence others to take positions or make decisions they would not normally have done. The social worker can be advocating for clients to have access to existing entitlements as well as using social action to secure new rights and entitlements. Advocacy can also empower clients as they participate in the process of pursuing change.

The target of advocacy can be individuals, groups, or organizations. In addition, elected or appointed officials, public and private human service agencies, courts, legislative bodies, and other governmental entities can be targeted for change.

LO 14-3 Utilize conceptual frameworks related to advocacy.

One concept important to advocates is power. Power, as you may recall, is the ability to get someone to do something they likely would not do on their own.

Often, those we are attempting to influence hold power of their own. It is important to remember that those who hold power are generally reluctant to give it up. Those with power are also likely to have greater access to resources than those who are less powerful. This underscores the reality that power is not distributed equally and that some people have more power than others.

This unequal distribution of resources and power is likely to make some degree of conflict inevitable. Advocacy identifies with those with less power and those who have been denied social and economic justice. Remedying this imbalance requires the acquisition of sufficient power to overcome the resistance to change that is inherent in power imbalances.

A second concept to better understand is that of organizations. Organizations and institutions fail to meet client needs for many reasons—failure to recognize a problem, a decision not to address a problem, a desire to serve their own needs instead of those of their clients, or inadequate resources to deal with a problem.

Just like people, organizations and institutions do have the capacity and potential to change. Creating conditions for that change to take place requires mobilizing sufficient resources on behalf of the client system. At the same time, most agencies would prefer that their workers not advocate for change within their own organization. Consequently, pursuing change within one's own agency is likely to be met with resistance.

A third concept to understand is that of the person in the environment. Social workers recognize that clients are profoundly affected by their environments and that the environment can contribute to many of the challenges facing the client. In addition, advocacy must emphasize helping clients to help themselves instead of doing things for them. Moreover, social workers should not advocate for clients without the full knowledge and consent of the clients.

LO 14-4 Employ specific knowledge and skills in advocacy.

Advocacy requires both knowledge and skills to be effective. The first area of knowledge required is the rights and entitlements of clients. Rights are typically rooted in both legal and moral grounds. Two types of rights are common, individual rights and societal rights. Individual rights are guaranteed to the individual, such as freedom of religion or freedom of speech. Societal rights are the collective rights of people as a whole. Sometimes the two types of rights are in conflict. For example, the individual right of free speech allows you to say what you want, but if you lie to the police you can be charged with a crime because society has take the position that those responsible for social control (i.e., the police) must be told the truth.

A second knowledge area is the avenues of appeal that are available to the client who feels unfairly treated by an organization. The appeal avenues may be incorporated in laws, regulations, agency policies, or in the interpretation of those items.

A third area of knowledge involves the resources available for advocacy. Resources can be people, agencies, or organizations that might be helpful in advocating for change.

A final knowledge area covers the tactics and strategies that may be useful for advocacy situations. This includes both generalist practice skills and skills useful for advocacy.

LO 14-5 Engage in legislative advocacy to advance social and economic justice.

Assessment in advocacy situations involves doing a self-assessment as to your source of sanction, barriers you foresee encountering, adequacy of time to devote to the change effort, and your own comfort level in the advocate role. Further, you must assess the kinds of power that are available. These can include legitimate power, reward power, coercive power, referent power, and expert power. In addition, other assessment considerations include the nature of the problem situation, the motivation and capacities of your client, and the motivations and capabilities of the adversary.

Planning in advocacy situations involves identifying resources that can be brought to bear on the situation, the strategies you might employ, and the specific tactics that would be most likely to help.

Intervention in advocacy situations involves such things as the use of persuasion, fair hearings and legal appeals, use of the media, and petitioning. Generally, we recommend using the tactic that requires the least effort and stress to achieve your goal. Use nonconfrontational approaches before confrontational ones.

Legislative lobbying is another intervention approach to use in the effort to create, change, or eliminate laws or regulations. Legislative lobbying can take the form of direct contact with elected officials, letter writing, or using steps in the legislative process to accomplish your goals. These steps include developing and revising a draft bill; identifying, obtaining, and maintaining bill sponsors; arranging sponsorship; introducing a bill; working with interest groups to broaden support; educating the public; influencing legislative committees; and action on the floor to ensure passage.

Competency Notes

The following identifies where Educational Policy (EP) competencies and practice behaviors are discussed in the chapter.

EP 2.1.1a **Advocate for client access to the services of social work.** *(p. 514):* Advocacy is designed to ensure that clients receive services they need including those provided by social workers and social agencies.

EP 2.1.1d **Demonstrate professional demeanor in behavior, appearance, and communication.** *(p. 533):* Testifying at public and legislative hearings requires that the social worker demonstrate professional demeanor in behavior, appearance, and communication.

EP 2.1.3 **Apply critical thinking to inform and communicate professional judgment.** *(pp. 516, 522):* Social workers use critical thinking skills when considering whether to engage in case advocacy or cause advocacy in a given situation.

EP 2.1.3b **Analyze models of assessment, prevention, intervention, and evaluation.** *(p. 526):* Social workers must carefully decide whether advocacy is an appropriate intervention in a given situation and what methods of advocacy are most likely to be useful.

EP 2.1.3c **Demonstrate effective oral and written communication in working with individuals, families, groups, organizations, communities, and colleagues.** *(p. 531):* Writing to elected officials requires that social workers use good written communication skills.

EP 2.1.5b **Advocate for human rights and social and economic justice.** *(p. 518):* Advocacy is indicated in any number of situations, ranging from organizational barriers to service caused by agency policies or procedures to denial of civil rights to client groups.

EP 2.1.5c **Engage in practices that advance social and economic justice.** *(p. 518):* Advocacy is one means of advancing social and economic justice for clients and for the larger society.

EP 2.1.7b **Critique and apply knowledge to understand person and environment.** *(p. 529):* The profession of social work has long emphasized the influence of the environment on the individual's well-being.

EP 2.1.8a **Analyze, formulate, and advocate for policies that advance social well-being.** *(p. 529):*

Advocating for changes in laws and social policy is a logical method of advancing social well-being.

EP 2.1.10d **Collect, organize, and interpret client data.** *(p. 522):* Assessment in advocacy situations involve such things as a self-assessment of the advocate and assessment of potential sources of power, the nature of the problem situation, the client's strengths and limitations, and the characteristics of the adversary.

EP 2.1.10e **Assess client strengths and limitations.** *(p. 522):* Client strengths and limitations are an important factor in advocacy assessment.

EP 2.1.10g **Select appropriate intervention strategies.** *(p. 525):* Part of the planning step in the planned change model is considering what resources, strategies, and tactics are available to use in the intervention phase. *(p. 526):* Advocacy might include such things as the use of persuasion, fair hearings, political or community pressure, the media, and petitioning. *(p. 529).* Other approaches to advocacy are whistleblowing and legislative advocacy.

EP 2.1.10h **Initiate actions to achieve organizational goals.** *(p. 533):* Oftentimes agency representatives will testify in favor of a bill because it furthers their own organizational goals of service to a specific group of clients.

EP 2.1.10k **Negotiate, mediate, and advocate for clients.** *(p. 514):* Advocacy is an important social work activity dedicated to representing others and championing the rights of client systems.

On the Internet

Visit the *Understanding Generalist Practice* CourseMate at **www.cengagebrain.com** for resources such as quizzes, glossaries and videos.

CHAPTER

15 Brokering and Case Management

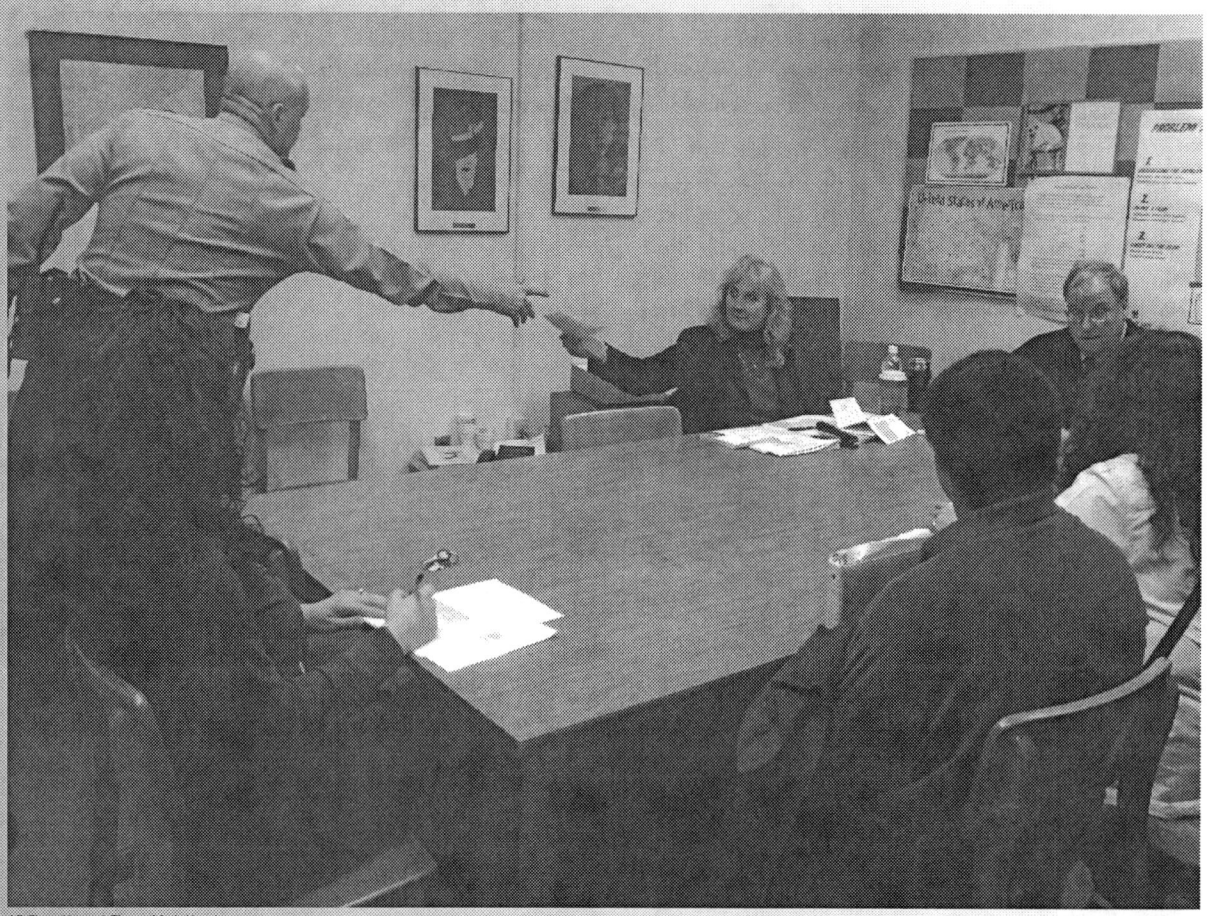

AP Photo/Journal Times, Mark Hertzberg

Learning Objectives   *This chapter will help prepare students to:*

LO 15-1   Employ the professional role of broker.

LO 15-2   Employ the professional role of case manager.

LO 15-3   Engage in practices that advance social and economic justice.

LO 15-4   Use research evidence to inform practice.

"**MARY ANN GIBBONS,** please call the E.R." As she heard the hospital loudspeaker page her, Mary Ann tensed slightly. She knew that emergency room pages were always serious. Because she was already on the first floor, Mary Ann walked briskly to the hospital's trauma center. The nurse on duty quickly explained the situation: Mr. B. Darwin arrived at the trauma center after suffering a heart attack on a nearby highway. Attempts to revive him failed, and the emergency room physician was about to talk to his wife. The Darwins, both in their late 60s, had apparently been traveling through the state on the way to visit relatives.

Mary Ann accompanied the doctor to the trauma center waiting room where they met Mrs. Darwin. A petite woman, Mrs. Darwin looked very weary. The crumpled handkerchief in her hand was damp from tears. The doctor introduced herself and Mary Ann. Mary Ann then sat next to Mrs. Darwin.

"Is he dead?" Mrs. Darwin asked quietly. The doctor slowly nodded her head and responded, "Yes, he is."

Mrs. Darwin put her head in her hands and cried softly for a minute. She raised her head and asked, "What am I going to do now?"

Mary Ann said that she knew this must be a terrible time for Mrs. Darwin. She offered to do everything she could to help Mrs. Darwin and invited her to come to the social work office. As the doctor departed, Mary Ann reached out her hand and helped Mrs. Darwin to her feet. Together they took the elevator to Mary Ann's office.

Mary Ann again expressed her sensitivity to Mrs. Darwin's situation and offered to help in any way she could. Slowly, Mrs. Darwin described the events of the day that preceded the death of her husband. In a few minutes, Mary Ann discovered the following information.

The Darwins, who were residents of Wisconsin, were traveling through Minnesota to visit relatives in Iowa. They had car trouble about 15 miles from the hospital. When Mr. Darwin got out to check on the car, he fell to the ground. A passing trucker radioed a nearby highway patrol officer, and together they attempted cardiopulmonary resuscitation. An ambulance arrived shortly and transported Mr. Darwin to the hospital. The highway patrol officer brought Mrs. Darwin to the hospital with their pet, a small dog. Mrs. Darwin said the car was still on the side of the highway and contained a large load of frozen meat in the trunk that was to be a gift to her daughter in Iowa. As they talked, Mary Ann began to make mental notes of the tasks ahead. She also learned some information about Mrs. Darwin that would prove helpful as they worked together to resolve the woman's concerns. Future tasks included:

1. Mrs. Darwin needed to notify her daughter and son about the death of her husband.
2. Mrs. Darwin needed a place to stay for the evening (a place that would allow dogs).
3. The disabled car would have to be towed into town.
4. The frozen meat in the trunk would need to be cared for before it spoiled.
5. Mrs. Darwin would need to find transportation back to her home.
6. Mrs. Darwin would need to arrange the funeral and transportation of Mr. Darwin's body.

Mary Ann also tactfully asked if this situation had created any critical financial problems for Mrs. Darwin. Did Mrs. Darwin have enough money to pay for lodging and meals? Could she depend on her daughter and son to be supportive in this time of grief? Did she know anyone in this area of the state?

Which of the problems or tasks could Mrs. Darwin handle herself and which would need Mary Ann's intervention? As Mary Ann and Mrs. Darwin continued talking, the answers to each of these questions became clear. By the end of the day, each problem, in addition to several others, had been resolved.

Introduction

Place yourself in Mary Ann's position. Would you know how to resolve each of these problems? In what order would you tackle them? Would you know what community resources might be appropriate to help Mrs. Darwin as she copes with this crisis? This example is only a small sample of the many challenges facing a social worker. The ability to provide service to a client often requires knowing what resources are available. Brokering is the subject of the first portion of this chapter.

Case management is the focus of the second portion of the chapter. Case management goes beyond brokering and involves coordinating the provision of a network of services.

LO 15-1 Employ the Professional Role of Broker

A Definition of Brokering

Brokering is the linking of client systems to needed resources. Such resources can target a broad range of client needs. Brokering might include helping a client get needed financial, legal, or medical assistance. It might involve helping a client find quality day care for children. Similarly, it might focus on helping to place a family member in a nursing home or a group home for people with developmental disabilities.

By itself, the idea of brokering seems somewhat simple. A client has a particular problem, and the worker tells the client about a resource that matches the client's problem. Of course, this explanation is an oversimplification of what really occurs in generalist social work practice. It is oversimplified because it assumes client needs can be met through existing services and resources. As discussed in earlier chapters, sometimes resources do not exist and must be created. These situations call for other social work roles, including advocacy, a topic discussed in Chapter 14.

The role of the broker in social work has appeared in social work literature for over 70 years (Hamilton, 1939). Social workers have long used directories of community resources to help clients. That social workers must know about community resources and services has been taken for granted. After assessing clients' needs, the worker is then expected to connect the client to available resources.

THE IMPORTANCE OF THE BROKERING ROLE IN GENERALIST PRACTICE

Sometimes, a social worker's only role is that of broker. Often, the broker role is combined with others, depending on client need. For example, in addition to being a broker, the generalist social worker also might need to be an advocate for clients denied access to existing resources. For instance, a homeless person by definition has no address. An agency policy might require that an address is necessary in order for that person to receive financial aid. A worker might first have to advocate on behalf of the client to change the policy before helping the client to actually receive the resources.

Additionally, the worker may play any of the roles described in previous chapters (e.g., mediator or educator) either simultaneously or sequentially. Most simply, the generalist social worker plays the broker role by helping clients assess their needs and locating appropriate resources to meet those needs. Once a resource is identified, the worker connects the client to that resource through a referral. Finally, the worker evaluates with the client the effectiveness of the resource in meeting the client's needs. First, we will discuss the importance of being familiar with various types of resources.

The Effective Broker

Becoming effective in the role of broker requires more than simply memorizing the names of available agencies. First, it requires knowledge of agency eligibility criteria (such as income or age limits). Second, it necessitates familiarity with many different kinds of resource systems (e.g., emergency housing, food pantries, general assistance, Temporary Assistance to Needy Families [TANF]). Third, it requires that the worker develop a network of contact people to whom clients may be referred. In other words, you need to know specifically whom to call. You must also know who can and will give your client the most help.

Maintaining familiarity with eligibility criteria is perhaps the most difficult of the tasks facing the worker because such criteria are constantly changing. New regulations, legislation, and evolving agency policies and procedures all affect eligibility criteria and complicate the job of the worker.

THE IMPORTANCE OF KNOWING RESOURCES

One of the most challenging aspects of beginning your professional life as a social worker is becoming familiar with the community or area in which you practice. Even social workers who grew up in a community may not know the myriad of agencies, services, and programs available in that area. The difficulty compounds if you have just moved and have little knowledge of your new community. New workers often develop their own resource lists that include information on each new agency or service they encounter. However, this method is not very systematic because the list contains only resources the new worker comes upon in a given period. Later in the chapter, we will discuss more thoroughly this matter of identifying resources.

Eligibility Criteria of Resource Agencies

It is unrealistic to believe that every social worker is going to become intimately familiar with all criteria for each program, agency, or resource available in a community. A familiarity would require an extraordinary memory for detail. Even if you could remember it all, the information quickly becomes dated as criteria change. However, for you to become familiar with the broad categories of programs and to know generally the types of needs a program addresses is appropriate.

For example, you might refer a family with no food to a free pantry (operated by churches, hospitals, or other groups), to the Salvation Army, or to the local public assistance agency where the family could qualify for food stamps. Similarly, you might most appropriately refer a battered woman to a domestic violence shelter. In each case, you need to know what types of resources are available and be able to discriminate which clients qualify for which programs.

Conversely, you must be capable of determining which resources are inappropriate. For instance, you would not refer a sexual assault victim to a treatment group for sex offenders.

Because eligibility criteria do change, the worker will find remaining knowledgeable about specifics of each program difficult. This problem can be alleviated somewhat by creating a homemade database. The database could be computerized, on alphabetized note cards, or any other system fitting your organizational style. The database should contain information such as types of problems for which referral is appropriate, names of contact persons, addresses and telephone numbers, and notes about eligibility criteria. For example, knowing that a given agency provides help only to those having incomes falling below a certain level is helpful. Although this level may change periodically, at least you would know there is such a level and have some idea about where the cutoff line has been. Finally, if you have an ongoing system of agency contacts, you can simply call the likely contact person to figure out whether a client fits agency criteria.

Characteristics of Resource Agencies

Besides the criteria used by an agency in determining eligibility, you should be aware of a variety of agency characteristics. Such characteristics affect how well services are delivered to your particular client. For example, is this agency extremely formal and rule bound, or does it have a flexible attitude toward solving client problems? What are the goals of the agency and the level of available resources? Does the agency provide assistance with fuel costs in the winter, and, if so, what form does that assistance take? Will the food pantry allow a person to come every week, or are there specified limits regarding the number of weeks that food will be made available? How accessible is the building? Are ramps or elevators available to those with disabilities? Are there waiting periods before assistance can be given? Is there a long waiting list for certain kinds of service? What hours is the agency open? Is the service provided only seasonally (e.g., at Christmas time)?

Such information helps the client and worker decide about the appropriateness of a given referral. It also can prevent clients from being referred to an agency that cannot meet their needs. When inappropriate referrals occur, clients may become discouraged and withdraw entirely from the helping process. Besides knowing the broad criteria and characteristics of various agencies, the worker should develop a network of contact persons within each agency. The reasons for this network will be discussed in the next section.

Contact Persons in Resource Agencies

In larger communities, you cannot be expected to learn the names of each person in every agency. We are, however, capable of remembering the names of an extraordinary number of people. A person can easily remember the names of well over 100 people. If you doubt this fact, begin by writing down all the people in your family, nuclear and extended, and add to the list all your friends, people in your class, faculty members, and teachers. Add university staff, doctors, dentists, storekeepers, bartenders, and so on. As you can see, the list gets longer and longer. With the names of agency contact people, the task is easier because you will be listing these people in your database of resource agencies.

When arriving in a new community, spending some time visiting various agencies to become familiar with their programs and staff is helpful. Learning the names of staff members who handle intake, as they may be the first people with whom your client will come in contact, is especially important. Whenever you phone an agency, make a point to jot down the names of the people you talked with and their areas of responsibility.

An advantage of having more than one contact person at an agency is that you can give a client other alternatives. This information is helpful if the first person is not in when the client contacts the agency. Having alternative contacts increases the likelihood that the client will receive the desired service.

Finally, make a point to become involved in your community. Join a service club, participate in community meetings, sit in on city council meetings, or attend major community events (pancake day, fireman's chicken dinner, Fourth of July celebrations, and so on). These activities will increase your knowledge of community resources and enlarge the circle of people you can call upon in times of need. The smaller the community, the more important it is that you involve yourself in its life.

TYPES OF RESOURCES

Internet Resources

The Internet can also provide useful information about resources. For example, locating suicide centers and mental health or substance abuse counselors or treatment facilities by zip code is now possible (http://www.samhsa.gov). It is also possible to fine-tune one's search to look for providers or services targeted to specific topics, such as detoxification, or using certain approaches (e.g., methadone). Information is also available on topics of interest to gay, lesbian, bisexual, transgendered, and questioning (GLBTQ) clients, such as at http://www.gay.com. Many sites have links to other resources, including service providers, merchants, and products aimed at the gay and lesbian population. States and counties also operate their own directories of human services. For example, Arizona offers this information online at http://www.cir.org, and others use the 211 designation to link residents to their information and referral services, as is the case with Fairfield County, Ohio (http://fairfieldcounty211.org/).

Other organizations are using the Web to facilitate finding information on service providers and to provide general information. Private foundations and government organizations are providing results of their research as well as sources of data on particular issues. For example, the Annie E. Casey Foundation (http://www.aecf.org) has important information on advocacy; the U.S. Census Bureau site provides data on such topics as education, poverty, and ethnicity; and http://www.FreeTranslation.com helps translate text written in a foreign language. Information about the homeless can be accessed at the National Law Center on Homelessness and Poverty (http://www.nlchp.org). Clients needing help selecting an appropriate nursing home can consult http://www.medicare.gov. Similarly, specialized resources can be located for people with specific disabilities. A list of some of these sites along with online addresses is shown in Table 15.1.

The variety of resources in a community is almost limitless. One resource directory for three (mostly rural) Wisconsin counties turned up almost 400 different agencies. The challenge is to use the many available sources of information.

Community Resource Directories

One commonly used source of information about community resources is directories listing social or human services. These booklets are often put together by information and referral agencies, social service agencies, volunteer groups, or educational institutions. Ideally, the directory should contain both an alphabetical index of agencies and services and a problem-focused index. You should be able to look up not only the agency's name but also the type of problem you need to address. Highlight 15.1 is an example from a typical directory listing legal services, nursing homes, and nursing services. Under each topic is a list of specific agencies providing services that address these needs and the problems involved.

The listing for each agency in a directory should contain certain common items of information, such as:

- *name of the organization;*
- *address, telephone number, and Web address;*
- *office hours;*
- *executive director or contact person;*
- *services provided;*
- *eligibility guidelines;*
- *accessibility for the handicapped;*
- *geographical boundaries of services; and*
- *source of funds.*

Each directory should contain listings for various categories of services. These listings may include sources of emergency food, lodging, or clothing; financial help; and job and employment assistance. The directory should also list marital counseling or therapy; abortion and adoption agencies; services for

TABLE 15.1 Online Resources for People with Disabilities

AccessAbility, Inc.	Not-for-profit rehabilitation agency	http://www.accessability.org
Brain Actuated Technologies	Allows hands-free control of computers and other electrical items	http://www.brainfingers.com
DisabilityInfo.gov	Links to government resources on disabilities.	https://www.disability.gov
National Council on Disability	Independent agency that makes recommendations to Congress and the president about issues affecting individuals with disabilities	http://www.ncd.gov
Health & Disability Advocates	National advocacy organization committed to the rights of children, people with disabilities, and low-income older adults.	http://www.hdadvocates.org

© Cengage Learning

HIGHLIGHT 15.1

Community Resource Directory Index

categories of people such as the elderly, children, those with physical disabilities, and the chemically dependent; child care services; correctional services; hospitals; educational and recreational services; and volunteer organizations. Highlight 15.2 shows a sample listing for two such agencies.

Telephone Books

Of course, resource directories are not the only source of information about community services. Most telephone books have listings for a variety of human services. Typically, these listings appear in the Yellow Pages under a range of headings, such as the following:

- *Alcoholism Information and Treatment Centers*
- *Associations*
- *Attorney Referral Service*
- *Career and Vocational Counseling*
- *Crisis Intervention Service*
- *Drug Abuse and Addiction Information and Treatment*
- *Hot Line and Helping Lines*
- *Human Service Organizations*
- *Marriage, Family, Child, and Individual Counselors*
- *Mental Health Services*
- *Psychologists*
- *Rehabilitation Services*
- *Social Service Organizations*
- *Social Workers*
- *Stress Management Services*
- *Suicide Prevention Service*

These listings include not only formal social service agencies, but also organizations and associations that may provide assistance for particular kinds of activities or events. Examples include the following:

- *American Red Cross*
- *Boy Scouts*
- *Camp Fire, Inc.*
- *Epilepsy Center*
- *Girl Scouts*
- *New Concepts for the Handicapped Foundation, Inc.*
- *Special Olympics*
- *YMCA/YWCA*

HIGHLIGHT 15.2

Resource Directory Listing

Attorney General's Office of Consumer Protection

750 W. Lincoln Avenue
Room 370
P.O. Box 7000
Madison, WI 54707
(608) 277-1962
(800) 355-8203 (toll free)

MILWAUKEE
714 E. Elm St.
Room 900
(414) 299-1234

Office Hours

Madison: 7:45 AM–4:45 PM
Milwaukee: 8:00 AM-5:00 PM

Services

Investigates consumer complaints; enforces Wisconsin consumer fraud laws; seeks injunctions to stop businesses or individuals from engaging in fraud and deception; can order restitution; uses computer data bank to analyze consumer problems; may enjoin public nuisance; provides consumer information/ education materials upon request.

Serves

Wisconsin consumers

Accessibility to Handicapped

Office located on mezzanine; reach by stairs and elevators from West Lincoln Ave. entrance—no stairs from side entrance, Hauser St.

Area Served

State of Wisconsin

Source of Funds

State tax supported

Benevolent Group Home

222 Haynes
P.O. Box 178
Janesville, WI 53547
(608) 943-8211

Office Hours

Twenty-four hours a day, seven days a week

Director

Walter Mitty

Services

Counseling for individuals and family crisis counseling, vocation exploration, instructive and corrective experiential living, educational planning, adventure-based recreation, and behavior modification resident program.

Serves

Status and delinquent youth ages 13 to 17

Accessibility to Handicapped

Yes—ramp

Area Served

Roan County and surrounding counties

Sources of Funds

Roan County Department of Social Services and grants

Information and Referral Services

Consulting established information and referral agencies or services provides another useful source of information about community resources. Public libraries and human service agencies often provide such a resource. One of your first steps as a new worker should be to find out which agency provides information and referral services for your community. Often, a phone call or an Internet search is all you need to locate a particular service or resource.

Service Organizations and Clubs

Communities of every size have service clubs or organizations that offer a variety of resources. Examples of such organizations include the following:

- *American Legion*
- *Eagles Club*
- *Elks*
- *Exchange Club*
- *JCs*

- *Kiwanis*
- *Knights of Columbus*
- *League of Women Voters*
- *Lions*
- *Masonic Lodge*
- *Moose*
- *Rotary International*
- *Shriners*
- *United Way*
- *Veterans of Foreign Wars (VFW)*

Most of these organizations provide specific services to their communities, such as money to pay for special projects (e.g., neighborhood parks, equipment for people with disabilities, or medical treatment for specific handicaps). Others provide the labor needed to undertake and complete community projects. The Kiwanis, for example, donates money to help many community causes benefiting individuals, groups, and the community as a whole. Its members also donate hours of work for such projects as community beautification and building projects. The Lions have a particular interest in vision and eye-related problems. The Shriners operate a specialized hospital that treats burn victims.

Unless you know of such groups and understand what each sees as its mission in the community, you might miss an important resource. One social worker successfully approached two service organizations to fund a year of college for her client. For another client with serious respiratory problems, the same worker successfully approached a local service club and convinced members to donate a much-needed air conditioner.

You can usually request listings of community organizations and service clubs from the local chamber of commerce or from the United Way. Once you receive a listing, you can make a point to learn more about these organizations. As your knowledge of these groups increases, they become yet another important resource for clients.

Other Informal Natural Resource Systems

As a generalist practitioner, you can use limitless creativity in identifying and brokering resources. Your supervisor and other workers may be additional resources for information. They may know of services or be able to suggest alternatives you have not considered. Again, the Internet may be helpful in obtaining data or services. In addition, you may often identify and use informal or natural resource systems. Sometimes, they may ultimately have more importance in the lives of your clients than more formal structured resources. Informal natural resource systems include groups or individuals with which clients are naturally

involved (e.g., relatives, friends, neighbors, or clergy). We sometimes call such systems social networks. We will refer to more informal types of resources periodically throughout the rest of the chapter.

Critical Thinking Questions 15.1

- Which community service organizations might provide assistance to children with medical problems?
- Where might you find information for a client who has a physical disability and believes employers have discriminated against him based on his disability?

THE PLANNED CHANGE PROCESS IN BROKERING

We have discussed the planned change process in greater depth in earlier chapters. This section will review briefly how that process applies to the role of broker, focusing primarily on the intervention phase.

Identifying and Assessing Client Needs

When clients come to us or are brought to our attention, gaining breadth and depth in understanding their needs is important. As part of the assessment process, we have the obligation to assess the urgency and priority of client needs. Cultural characteristics and group identification also play roles in how clients request and accept help for specific needs. The client's attitude and reaction toward accepting help may be a barrier to providing that help. For example, a Tongan client may be reluctant to accept help because doing so violates cultural expectations that one should rely on family in times of need. Accepting help may also imply that clients cannot manage their own affairs, which is also looked down on within the Tongan culture.

Social Work Values

Social work values play a clear role in the identification-of-need process. For example, the decision about which resource to use is always ultimately the client's. Client self-determination plays an important role in the assessment of needs. The social worker may believe that certain problems should have greater priority. Still, if the client will not acknowledge those problems or thinks them less important, there is little the worker can do. As a worker, you can provide your client with alternatives. You can help your client identify the pros and cons of each. However, making the final choice about what to do or accept is your client's right and responsibility.

It is essential that the worker and client be absolutely clear about the client's needs. Without this clarity, evaluating the extent to which the resource system has helped will be impossible. Once the needs are clarified, the worker is in a much better position to identify potential resource systems. Chapter 5 addressed the process of assessing client needs in detail. Thus, this chapter will not elaborate further on the process except to note that assessment is essentially the same in most planned change situations.

Identifying and Assessing Potential Resource Systems

As the client's needs become clearer, the worker as broker begins to consider which of the available resources will be of most assistance in the particular situation. Perhaps there are informal resources the client has overlooked. These sources might include family, friends, coworkers, and others with whom the client has existing relationships. On the other hand, such relationships may be unavailable or inappropriate, and then the worker needs to help the client explore other options. At this point, a community resource directory can be of inestimable value.

As we have discussed, even if such a document is not available, the worker should have his or her own list of resource systems. As the worker, you should know the services provided by various agencies and have a rough knowledge of their eligibility requirements and other pertinent information. For example, you should know if the agency charges a fee for service and if financial help is available. You can share this information with the client, along with any other likely problems or obstacles the client may encounter. If clients are likely to be placed on a waiting list for service, you should alert them to this. Only when clients are knowledgeable about available options can they make informed choices. You are obliged to help clients make decisions based upon the best information available.

Helping the Client Select the Best Resource System

Many clients know little about existing agencies or services. Other clients will have rudimentary information but do not understand certain aspects of the service network. Still other clients will be experienced users of available services. By talking to the client, you can figure out the client's understanding of potential resources. If this understanding is inaccurate, you can help the client

develop a more factual perspective. Helping the client make a choice is also your responsibility, which can be done by answering client questions. If appropriate, you can recommend a specific service based on your knowledge of its effectiveness.

Although a wealth of options may seem positive, there is a possibility that the multitude of agencies, organizations, and services will only confuse the client. Also, what is clear to the worker may appear unduly complex to clients not accustomed to formal resource systems. Therefore, you need to make certain the client clearly understands what is involved.

Within the broker role, there are essentially at least four ways of connecting clients and resource systems. First, a simple approach is to refer the client to an existing service. This option presumes that the client now has sufficient information about different agencies to make an informed decision.

A second option is to provide the resource yourself. This option is appropriate when the expertise needed is within your capacity as a helper and is sanctioned by your agency.

The third choice comes into play when existing services or resources do not meet the client's needs and the worker must be creative in finding or developing a resource. In this situation, the worker has a couple of options. One involves tapping the potentially most helpful resource, knowing full well that it will probably not solve the entire problem. This alternative is perhaps the least desirable and should never be chosen without the client understanding that the outcome is likely to be somewhat unsatisfactory.

The fourth choice is to create a resource. The worker who sought and received assistance from a service club for a client's college tuition pursued this option. No existing service organization provided the kind of financial assistance needed. Nevertheless, the worker targeted an organization whose interests closely matched those of the client. She then convinced the organization's members to stretch their criteria to meet the client's needs. The worker's ingenuity and imaginativeness helped create a resource that had not previously existed.

Frequently, clients have multiple needs requiring the resources of more than one agency or organization. In these situations, the responsibility of the worker is coordination of existing resources. The goal is to oversee the timely and efficient distribution of resources to the client. Because this last option relates to the concept of case management, we will discuss it later in this chapter's section on case management.

Making the Referral

Making an appropriate referral requires more than simply giving a client the name and address of an agency. There are several actions you can take that will enhance the success of the referral. In the interest of client self-determination, offering clients as many resources as possible is better. Sometimes this method is not feasible, as only one agency provides the needed services. When a client makes a decision about a particular agency, you can facilitate the transition by writing out the necessary information about the agency and giving it to the client. These methods can include the agency's name and address, telephone number, names of contact persons, and even a brief description of what to expect. For frequently used agencies, you can prepare this information in advance.

Another valuable technique is to send the new agency a written description or referral outlining the client's needs. Sometimes this information is helpful because clients will not have to repeat all the information they already told you. Meeting with the worker or professional from the other agency to discuss the case and go over any written records may also be appropriate for you.

You can set the actual appointment time for the client before he or she leaves your office. For example, you or the client can call the new resource and establish the appointment time right then and there.

A final possibility is to accompany the client to the new agency. This technique occurs less frequently because it is time consuming. Still, this option makes sense when clients are hesitant to go and no one else is available to accompany them. This step may be particularly important when the client is under great stress or is undergoing a medical procedure, such as an abortion.

How much you do for the client should depend upon the client's ability. Clients suffering from serious mental impairment, for example, are more likely to rely on the worker. A general guideline is not to do things for clients that they can do for themselves. Creating unnecessary dependency in clients is undesirable.

In addition, you should avoid giving clients a falsely positive impression about what the new resource will or can do. Optimism is appropriate, but painting an unrealistic portrait of the helping agency is not. Clients will only become disappointed and disillusioned.

Helping the Client Use Resource Systems

Obviously, part of helping clients use resource systems involves giving them encouragement to do so. For a variety of reasons, clients may be reluctant to approach yet another agency. Many clients find the experience of having to discuss their problems quite traumatic. Verbalizing problems may conjure up images of accepting charily or having failed in a particular role (breadwinner, mother, and so on) or may simply be embarrassing. Other clients will be uncomfortable with anything that suggests accepting "welfare." An example involves an elderly client who feared placement in a nursing home. Her primary worry was that the cost of the nursing home placement would be paid for, in her words, by the "county." For her, this understanding meant she would be going "on welfare," which had a distinctly negative connotation for her. The worker reminded the client that she and her husband had spent their entire working life paying taxes to build roads, maintain schools, provide for needy families, and pay for social service staff. The client had been paying all these years for some services that she was just now getting a chance to use. When put in this context, the client became more comfortable about the impending nursing home placement. She believed she had already paid her fair share.

When clients have to explain their situation to more than one agency, you can help them in several ways. First, you can provide a written referral to the new agency, or you can explain the basic details to a staff person in the new agency. You can also brief clients about the actual procedures used by the new agency and barriers that they might encounter. As mentioned earlier, clients should be given the names of more than one contact person in case the first person is absent when the client contacts the agency. You can also call clients right before their appointments to see if they have any last-minute concerns or problems. Such calls can act as boosters to encourage clients to keep appointments.

Follow-Up and Evaluation of Resource Systems

The most important measure of the success of a referral is whether it met the client's needs. To know the outcome, you must learn the result of the referral. This means either that you contact the client or that you ask the client to call you back after the referral. You can also schedule an appointment with the client following the referral visit. Such appointments can be set before clients visit the new agencies. In this way, you remind clients that you will be following up on the referral, thus providing another form of encouragement. Of course, if you accompany the client to the new agency, follow-up occurs on the spot.

If the client will be having several sessions at the new agency, you could choose to meet the client after each session. This method provides for direct follow-up and may be desirable to reinforce the client's participation. On the other hand, the client whose needs are met by the new agency may not want to continue meeting with you anymore because you are not providing service. Ultimately, respecting the client's rights is important. Following up on referral is part of your responsibility as a professional social worker to evaluate your practice. You need to know if the client encountered barriers or if the referral itself was inappropriate. Perhaps the services were not available in a timely fashion, or perhaps the agency did not operate according to your or your client's expectations.

Maybe the agency denied services to which the client was entitled. If so, you may need to assume the role of advocate to help cut through the red tape and bureaucratic subterfuge. Perhaps a higher degree of coordination is necessary if multiple resource systems have been involved. The worker needs this type of information if a realistic evaluation of the referral is to take place.

Workers may discover that a given agency is inadvertently creating problems for clients. Part of the worker's obligation to the client is to provide this knowledge to the agency as a way to help improve the functioning of that resource system.

A referral's success is evaluated according to whether the client's identified needs have been fulfilled. If the client was referred for job training, was the training provided? Was the job the client trained for appropriate? Did the client ultimately get a job in that field? Sometimes, a client satisfaction questionnaire will provide sufficient information to conclude that the referral was successful. Chapter 8 describes several evaluation tools that can be used to assess goal achievement. Many of these can be employed to evaluate the success of the worker acting in the broker role. Choosing the correct one requires experience and good judgment.

LO 15-2 Employ the Professional Role of Case Manager

CASE MANAGEMENT

The role of case management is not new to the profession of social work. Case management has existed since the 19th century but has received more attention recently (NASW, 2013). One reason for this attention is that case management services are now required for specific categories of clients by both federal and state laws and regulations. In 1984, the National Association of Social Workers published standards for case management services to functionally impaired client populations. In 1992, a set of 10 standards for social work case management was created, and in 2013, a new detailed set of 12 standards was adopted.

WHAT IS CASE MANAGEMENT?

According to the NASW (2013), social work *case management* is a process to plan, seek, advocate for, and monitor services from different social services or health care organizations and staff on behalf of a client. The process enables social workers in an organization, or in different organizations, to coordinate their efforts to serve a given clients through professional teamwork, thus expanding the range of needed services offered (p. 13). Services are considered coordinated when providers are in agreement about the services to be provided and are committed to the same end.

For example, consider Edward McShane, age 32, who suffers both from a chronic mental illness and from kidney disease. He was institutionalized at a state mental hospital at age 19 and is now being returned to his home community. Ed has no living family members and no place to live. He needs regular monitoring to ensure that he takes his prescribed medication. Ed needs a variety of services, including housing in the community, medical and mental health services, employment opportunities, and possibly financial aid. All of these services must be coordinated so that they are working toward the same goal: keeping Ed out of an institution and functioning as independently as possible in the community.

Case management is the intervention of choice for clients like Ed who have multiple ongoing needs. The principles of case management have been articulated by Gerhart (1990, p. 216), Ellison and Dunn (2006), and Woodside and McClam (2013):

- *Individualization of services. Services are developed or designed specifically to meet the identified needs of the client.*
- *Comprehensiveness of services. Comprehensive services encompass all areas of the client's life, including housing, recreation, employment, social, financial, medical care, mental health care, and so on. This principle helps ensure that no need will go unfulfilled and that services will be integrated.*

- *Parsimonious services.* The meaning of parsimonious services is that duplication of services will be discouraged and that costs for services will be controlled. Uncoordinated services may result in some needs being met by duplicate agencies, while other needs go unmet.
- *Fostering autonomy and empowerment.* A major focus of case management is on helping clients become as self-sufficient and empowered as possible. It also means providing maximum client self-determination so clients make as many decisions regarding their own care as is possible.
- *Continuity of care.* Continuity of care means that as the client moves through life, requiring inpatient services and help in the community, case management services will ensure continued monitoring of needs. There is an expectation that most of the clients will require assistance throughout their lives because the conditions that they suffer from are chronic and not subject to quick recovery. Such expectations are especially true in the cases of clients with chronic mental illnesses and those with significant developmental disabilities.

Essentially, case management uses the same planned change process described throughout this text. The problems are typically multiple ones and need the interventions of many agencies and organizations. As in any worker–client relationship, the client's active involvement in the helping process is expected. Moreover, the chances are likely that the worker serving as case manager may have to advocate for clients in certain situations. If services or resources that the client is entitled to are not provided, the worker may take necessary steps to correct the problem. Existing resources are used to the maximum extent possible. If services or resources to meet client needs do not exist, the worker has an obligation to work toward the development of such resources.

As you can see, the case manager plays several roles, including broker, advocate, counselor, teacher, community organizer, or planner. Client needs determine the worker's role. Most important, however, case managers provide the link between clients and the human services system. Case managers know the comprehensive needs of clients, connect them to appropriate services, and ensure that those services are provided effectively. This method requires the case manager to encourage clients to use services and to give them the emotional support they need to survive day to day. As might be expected, high-quality case management services involve frequent and intense client–case manager contact.

Although case managers play a variety of roles, including that of broker, it is important to underscore that the concepts of broker and case manager are not synonymous. The role of case manager goes well beyond that of broker (see Highlight 15.3). The broker may refer clients to one or more specific services. The case manager has the broader task of ensuring that a wide spectrum of clients' needs is met in an efficient and effective manner. Both brokers and case managers require knowledge of community resources and where such information can be found. Both require good working relationships with service providers and organizations that may be used by clients. Ultimately, the case manager is responsible for coordinating, monitoring, and evaluating the service provided to clients, which are activities beyond the routine duties of a broker (Hepworth, Rooney, Rooney, & Strom-Gottfried, 2013).

The breadth of the case manager role parallels that of social workers providing services directly to clients. In reality, the case manager typically is directly involved in the care of some clients to an extensive degree. Hepworth et al. (2013) point out that the case manager has great responsibility for ensuring that the client receives services to meet a variety of needs.

One other important responsibility of the case manager involves integrating the formal support system (agencies and services) with that of the informal support system (e.g., family, friends, and others directly involved with the client). The case manager strives to help the client function independently by facilitating interpersonal relationships. This may involve negotiations between formal and informal support systems. For example, family members may be reluctant to work with an agency, or they may be unwilling to allow the client the independence needed to function in the community. Perhaps relationships between the client and family members are strained. In either case, the interpersonal problems prevent the client's needs from being met. In such situations the case manager is both an enabler and a facilitator whose primary responsibility is to help clients function independently.

THE IMPORTANCE OF CASE MANAGEMENT FOR GENERALIST PRACTICE

 EP 2.2.10h Within this country, most states now either require or recommend case management services for certain categories of clients. Moreover, several federal laws have specifically identified case management as a desired form of service to offer clients (Woodside & McClam, 2013). Within the field of

HIGHLIGHT 15.3

An Overview of Case Management

1. Definition of case management: A process to plan, seek, advocate for, and monitor services from different social services or health care organizations and staff on behalf of a client. The process enables social workers in an organization, or in different organizations, to coordinate their efforts to serve a given client through professional teamwork, thus expanding the range of needed services offered. (NASW, 2013)

2. Purpose of case management:
   a. Promoting the skills and capability of the client in using social services and social supports.
   b. Developing the abilities of social networks and relevant service providers to further the functioning of the client.
   c. Promoting effective and efficient service delivery.

3. Focus of case management: Formulating a client support network that integrates client skill development, involvement of social networks, and involvement of multiple providers.

4. Tasks of case managers:
   a. Assessing client needs, social network capabilities, and abilities of social service providers.
   b. Developing a comprehensive service plan that includes multidisciplinary professional involvement and maximum client involvement.
   c. Intervention directly with clients to strengthen skills and capacities for self-care and/or indirectly with systems impinging on the client.
   d. Monitoring of service plan implementation and tracking of client status, service delivery, and involvement of social network members.
   e. Evaluation of service plan effectiveness and its impact on client functioning, on social network's capacity to support client, and on the ability of the social service professional to work with the client.

social work, case management has been recognized as a major social work function.

Increasingly, major companies are using case managers to help employees get appropriate rehabilitative care for job-related injuries and to reduce costs of that care. Interest in case management has spread so rapidly in recent years that private case management firms are now commonplace. They are helping clients receive homemaker services, alternative housing, day care, transportation services, chore services, and in-home meals.

The Developmental Disabilities Assistance and Bill of Rights Act (Public Law 95–602) specifically lists case management as a priority service. Case management is being used extensively in the developmental disability field, with those suffering from chronic mental impairment, and in the field of child welfare (Mather & Hull, 2009).

Of particular importance for the social work profession is the fact that case management is an approach consistent with social work's emphasis on the client's rights. As should be evident, the goals of social work and the goals of case management are similar (see Figure 15.1). Both aim to help people increase their problem-solving and coping skills, obtain resources, make organizations responsive to their needs, and facilitate interactions between clients and their environment. Contrary to the implications of the term, the *clients* are not being managed, but the *services* are. Case managers need the skill to intervene with individuals, families, agencies, and the larger community. These same skills are needed by generalist social workers regardless of their practice settings. Case managers are currently being used by hospitals and health maintenance organizations, with social workers and nurses being the primary professions charged with this responsibility.

Several factors are operating to increase the importance of case management for social workers, such as:

1. Increased emphasis on maintaining clients in the least restrictive environment;
2. The goal of keeping people out of institutions;
3. The objective of maintaining the elderly in their homes as long as possible;
4. Efforts to reduce or contain costs of providing health and other forms of care to clients;

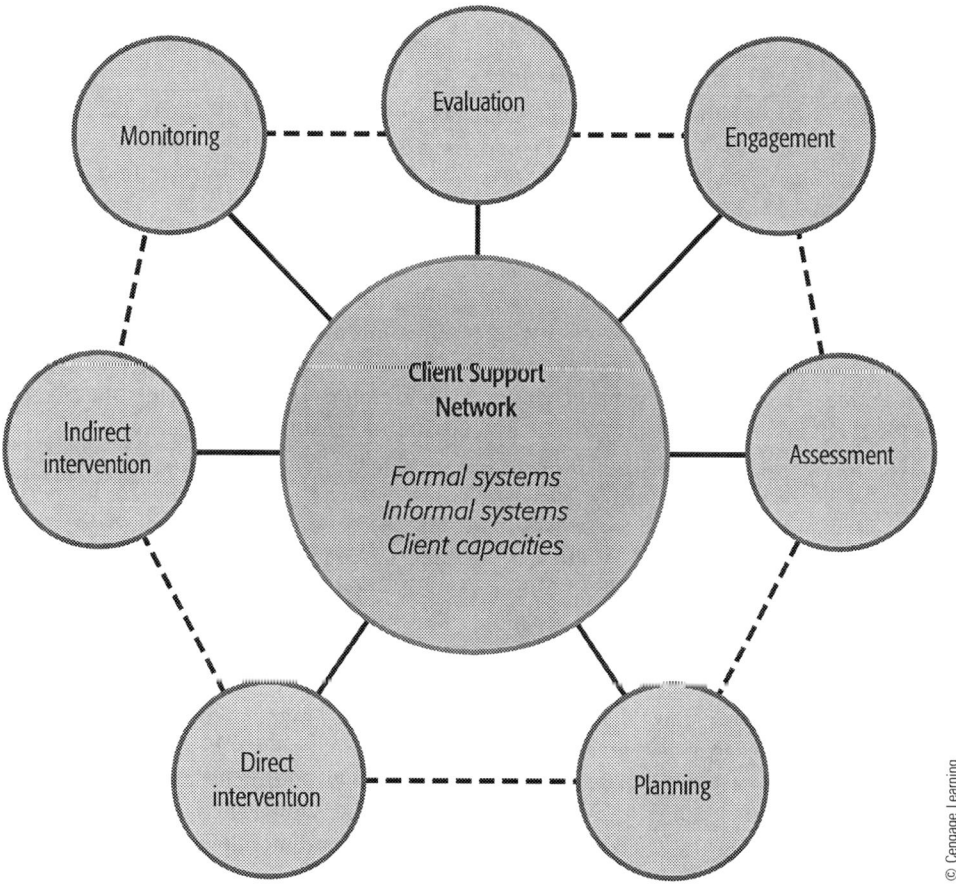

© Cengage Learning

FIGURE 15.1 Worker Responsibilities in Case Management

5. Increased attention to rights of clients who often lack awareness of available resources;

6. Awareness that some clients cannot follow through on the ordinary referral because of their limited capacities (e.g., mental impairment);

7. Increased focus on how the environment contributes to client problems;

8. Decreased focus on the medical model of practice (the medical model tends to view clients' problems as "diseases"; hence, the client should be "cured");

9. Expansion of human service programs and increased complexity and fragmentation of services (i.e., greater specialization, with no program taking overall responsibility for client service) (Ellison & Dunn, 2006); and

10. Inclusion of case management services in federal legislation.

ASSESSMENT

EP 2.1.10e

Assessment is the part of the planned change process where the case manager learns the current and future needs and problems of the client. Because so many clients have long-term needs, future needs have perhaps a higher priority than is true in other areas of social work. The assessment must cover medical, psychological, recreational, social, educational, and vocational areas.

Consider, for example, a client with a physical disability. Here several issues are involved. First, a problem may be caused directly by the disability itself. An example would be absence of mobility caused by paralysis of both legs. Second, a need may have no relationship at all to the disability. A client who lacks clothing or adequate shelter may have had the same problem even without the disability (e.g., if his company laid off many workers who then could not locate other employment).

A third source of problems could be caused by the client's informal support system. For example, a parent's attempts to protect a young adult who has a developmental disability may prevent that person from learning skills that would help him to become more independent.

Fourth, problems may occur in the formal resource systems designed to help clients. For instance, an agency may refuse to provide a service to which the client is entitled. The agency's policies may be inappropriately applied. Perhaps the person denying the client service dislikes the client or feels he is taking advantage of the agency. There is also a chance that the resource system simply lacks the ability to deliver a specific service. The budget may be inadequate, or maybe a specific resource cannot be located. An example of the latter is an agency that has been unable to hire a bilingual social worker to serve as an interpreter for the agency's Hispanic clients.

There are obviously a variety of explanations that can exist for a given need discovered in the assessment process. These explanations mean that the assessment must concern itself with at least three areas, as discussed in the following sections.

Assessing the Client's Ability to Meet Environmental Challenges

Environmental challenges include a client's self-care ability (e.g., to take care of hygiene, dressing, money management, and so on). In this process you need to find out what clients need from their informal and formal resource systems. A need can be anything that you and your client view as necessary for a positive quality of life. The first thing is to determine which needs can be met with little or no outside help. The focus is on the client's strengths and capabilities, not on deficits or shortcomings. You also need to determine which available services or resources the client can use. In assessment it is important not to make clients excessively dependent upon others, nor to assume they can do more for themselves than is really the case. A simple example is a babysitter who carried a 1-year-old baby all around the house because she just assumed that the child could not walk. She was astounded upon her arrival one evening to find the baby toddling after his parents. Thus, you will assess client skills that need to be maintained and those that will need to be enhanced.

Finding out why the client has sought assistance at this particular time may also be important. Does the request for help coincide with important changes in the client's personal resources (e.g., loss of job, eviction), changes in the client's primary support group (e.g., aging parents), or the recent availability of formal resources (e.g., a newly created program)? As in any assessment, you will want to find out something about the history of the problem as understood by the client or the client's family. For example, is it a problem for which other interventions have failed, or is it something the client is only now willing to admit? Will the client need ongoing service or only in times of stress? Does the client have effective relationships with informal resource systems? What is the client's involvement within formal resource systems?

Finally, as with any assessment, the case manager may have a role in determining if the client is eligible for service. This decision will largely be based on the information gathered previously.

A good example of this assessment process is the situation involving Latisha, who is a 35-year-old divorced woman with a long history of schizophrenia, a serious form of psychosis characterized by disturbances in thoughts, mood, and behavior. She has been in and out of hospitals over the past 10 years, mainly when she has gone off her medication and begun to wander the streets. Each time, she has become stabilized for a period of several months to years but then has quit taking her "crazy pills," as she calls them. She survives financially on a small trust fund left by her deceased parents. She has just been referred to a new community program designed to help people with chronic mental health problems. Noel, a social worker with the new program, has just received the referral. Over the next several days, he will assess Latisha's strengths, challenges, and resources and develop a service plan appropriate for her situation. One of the first things Noel does is focus on Latisha's ability to meet environmental challenges.

Noel talks with a worker from the referring agency who has worked with Latisha. He also interviews Latisha and her sister and brother-in-law. From this information, Latisha seems to be able to care for herself (such as hygiene, dressing, and so on), and to manage her money when she is on her medication. She also can hold a job, although she has very few skills and no formal training past high school. That medication and support together are usually sufficient to keep Latisha from relapsing is also plain. The absence of either one apparently triggers her downfall. Noel concludes that Latisha has many strengths. She is employable, responds to medication and support for her condition, and can take care of herself in most situations. This step is the first in assessing her ability to meet environmental challenges.

Assessing the Caretaking Ability of the Client's Informal Support Group

How capable are the client's family and friends to meet identified needs? These needs may include basic items such as food or shelter or more abstract things such as social or emotional support. You will want to determine both immediate and extended family members and their relationships with the client. Are there others who serve as informal resources for the client? These resources might include friends, coworkers, neighbors, storekeepers, members from the same church or club, and schoolmates (Frankel & Gelman, 2012). What kinds of assistance can the primary support group give? How do members of the primary support group interact with the client? How well does this resource system interact with formal resource systems?

From Noel's discussions with Latisha and her sister, the constant monitoring of Latisha appears to be hard on the family. Although the sister and her husband are willing to have Latisha live with them, they sometimes get overburdened themselves. Latisha can be argumentative, boisterous, and difficult at times. The family feels as though they can never leave her alone for even a few days because they do not know if she will stay on her medication. The caretaker role is taxing both husband and wife. Latisha has no real friends. Her major love in life is bingo, which she plays every Thursday night down at the Hully Gully Church of the Doomed. She has a couple of acquaintances who play bingo the same night.

Noel concludes that the family is a potential resource for caretaking if additional support can be generated externally. The family cannot care for Latisha without outside help.

Assessing the Resources of Formal Support Systems

The focus here is on the capability of formal resource systems to meet client needs. As we have seen, the formal system may not have the capacity to meet a client's needs (e.g., due to a lack of money). Perhaps it denies the client services to which he is otherwise entitled. This may occur, for instance, because of confusion over eligibility or because of inappropriately applied policies.

As we assess each of these areas, we must focus on the availability, adequacy, appropriateness, acceptability,

and accessibility of the resources. The *availability* of a service is simply whether or not it exists. Absent services are not available. Sometimes resources are available to fill a need but remain unused because no one knows they exist (Hepworth et al., 2012). In other instances, a client's needs are not known because the client is isolated or protected by family members or because of the absence of a prior needs assessment.

There is also the possibility that a client has not shared a need with anyone. For persons with disabilities that are not visible to others (e.g., learning disabilities where they are unable to read), keeping their "secret" from all but a handful of friends is not unusual. Some may not share the information with anyone. Often, only an in-depth assessment will disclose the problem.

The *adequacy* and *appropriateness* of a resource system must also be considered. For example, a resource may be inadequate for a client in that it meets only a portion of the person's needs. Despite a resource's inadequacy, it may still be appropriate because at least a portion of the client's needs can be met. Ideally, a resource would be both adequate and appropriate.

In other situations, the *acceptability* of a resource may be low. Maybe the client refuses to accept help from a specific source. Perhaps the client is too proud to ask for help from a particular agency because of past bad experiences or the negative reputation of the agency. Perhaps the client believes there is a stigma in accepting help from the agency. Any of these factors may reduce the acceptability of the resource, even if it meets all the other criteria.

Accessibility of a resource becomes a problem when the client lacks transportation, mobility, or other means to access the resource. Much of the available housing in this country is not accessible to people with physical disabilities because of stairs, narrow doorways, or equipment that cannot be reached by clients in wheelchairs.

Of course, accessibility may be blocked by other factors. Perhaps the client does not have enough money to use the resource. Maybe the client does not qualify for a service because he or she has too much income. A program or service may be inaccessible because a health insurance program will not pay for a needed service. As you can see, many things can block access to a resource.

Assessment also may help us to understand the factors that cause or contribute to a particular problem. It is not sufficient simply to know that a child is being abused because we lack information that would assist us with the intervention. Here we know what the problem is but not necessarily what is causing it. Intervention needs to target the cause. Child abuse can result from lack of parenting ability, involve traditions of family interpersonal violence or be related to acute stresses being experienced in the family unit. Without knowing the cause, any particular intervention is likely to be wrong. A parent abusing her child as a result of a serious mental illness is not likely to benefit right now from parenting classes.

The process of gathering information needed for assessment for case management is similar to other assessments. For example, the case manager reviews pertinent records (agency, school, and so on), interviews appropriate people (client, family, friends, and so on), and refers the client to specialists who can provide other kinds of data. This data may include psychological testing, vocational or educational assessment, medical examinations, and similar evaluations. Assessment in case management has several facets. For example it is:

1. *Need-related.* This means we focus specifically on client needs.
2. *Comprehensive.* This means we attempt to assess clients' needs in all areas, instead of just a few. We will concern ourselves with needs covering income, shelter, work, education, physical and mental health, social and other relationships, recreation and leisure time, transportation, legal, and so on.
3. *Cross-disciplinary.* This suggests the importance of using the expertise of various disciplines to understand clients' needs. Examples include physicians, social workers, psychologists, speech pathologists, occupational therapists, physical therapists, and others.
4. *Client Participatory.* The client is fully involved in assessing his or her own needs and maintains maximum self-determination.
5. *Ongoing.* This concerns a simple recognition that assessment is an ongoing, changing, progressive type of interaction.
6. *Systematic.* This ensures that each area of potential need is explored in sufficient depth and breadth.
7. *An Outcome.* When completed, the assessment should be in written form. It should be a product that guides planning and intervention. For example, Noel must next assess the formal support system that may be available to help Latisha. His agency

provides a clubhouse near the downtown area, where people with conditions similar to hers can interact with friends, relax, watch television, and talk with social work staff. Noel thinks that this program might be helpful to Latisha. It is located on the bus line, so transportation is available. It is also focused on developing friendships and mutual support groups for persons with chronic mental illness. Equally important, the clubhouse has four rooms that are available for temporary lodging for its members. These rooms are used for members when their caregivers need a respite. Noel is aware of the toll that caring for a person with chronic mental illness can exact on a family. Perhaps if the family can periodically take vacations or just get away from their responsibilities for a while, they can carry their burden longer. Noel also knows that having Latisha visit the clubhouse daily will bring her into contact with others struggling with their own illnesses (and taking their medication each day). Seeing them maintain themselves may have something of a modeling effect on her. The primary challenge is to determine if Latisha is interested in receiving service from the clubhouse program.

Table 15.2 provides an overview of case management assessment that emphasizes two perspectives. The first is a focus on identification of client needs. The second involves the assessment of the capacities of the client (self-care), informal support systems (mutual care), and formal support systems (professional care). It also contains a brief description of the assessment process.

In summary, the assessment process in case management and that described in Chapter 5 are essentially identical. Each must consider the capacities of the client, clients' informal support systems, and formal support systems.

PLANNING

Planning in case management is a process of finding and securing needed services. These services may include those required for assessment of the client situation, planning, or intervention. The services used should match client needs to the greatest extent possible. The case manager is responsible for monitoring and evaluating the adequacy of services. The client must be involved to the maximum degree possible in the planning process and is always free to reject a given service.

TABLE 15.2 The Structure of Case Management

Characteristic of Assessment: Organizing Concepts	Identification of Client Needs: Unmet Needs	Assessment of Self-Care: Client Functioning	Assessment of Mutual Care: Social Network, Social Support	Assessment of Professional Care: Formal Human Services
Basic Units of Assessment	Income Housing/shelter Employment/vocational training Health Mental health Social/interpersonal Recreation/leisure Activities of daily living Transportation Legal Education	Physical functioning Cognitive functioning Emotional functioning Behavioral functioning	Social network structure Social network interaction Emotional support Instrumental support Material support	Resource inventory Availability Adequacy Appropriateness Acceptability Accessibility
Process of Assessment	Review with client, others, and professionals the needs of client in key areas of daily living	Match needs with client functional areas to assess whether client can fulfill own needs	Match needs with mutual care resources to assess whether social network can fulfill client needs	Match needs with professional care resources to assess whether formal service can fulfill client needs

© Cengage Learning

Service Plans

In planning, the case manager creates a service plan that incorporates six dimensions:

1. Client needs are prioritized.
2. Goals and objectives of service are established.
3. Resource systems that will be involved are identified.
4. Time frames are identified within which services will be delivered and goals achieved.
5. Outcome measures are formulated that will be used to evaluate achievement of case plans.
6. Specific tasks are assigned to individuals and groups so that it is clear who is responsible for what.

Impact Goals

EP 2.1.10f

Planning in case management often involves setting impact goals. Impact goals include goals that result in changing some major aspects of the client's life and are the expected results of our intervention. One such goal might involve resolving the transportation needs of a young man who uses a wheelchair. Arranging for the acquisition of a vehicle that would accommodate the client's chair would be an impact

goal with major consequences for several areas of the client's life. For example, it would provide transportation to work, give increased access to other community resources, and improve recreational opportunities. Another example would be providing for in-home medical care for a client, which would enable the client to remain at home rather than being placed in a nursing home.

Service Objectives

Service objectives should be differentiated from impact goals. They describe steps that must be undertaken to achieve an impact goal. For example, let us assume you have a client who lives in a home that is not accessible to someone in a wheelchair. The client is suffering from a condition that restricts her to a wheelchair indefinitely. Service objectives might include identifying the changes needed in the client's house to make it accessible to her and locating someone competent to make the changes. Making the home accessible is the impact goal, and service objectives help achieve the impact goal.

Noel's service plan for Latisha is shown in Figure 15.2. Because of the importance of client involvement in the assessment and planning process, Latisha must sign off on the service plan. As you can

Client: Latisha Denver   Case manager: Noel Valtierra

Impact goal: Develop supportive services designed to maintain Ms. Denver's stability
Priority: #1

Service Objectives	Responsibility	Target Date	Actual Date of Accomplishment	Notes
Latisha visits downtown clubhouse	Noel/Latisha	3-13-14		
Latisha participates in weekly activities at clubhouse	Latisha	4-01-14		
Latisha uses clubhouse as temporary lodging while sister's family is on respite	Latisha	As needed		
Latisha's sister's family notifies Noel when respite is needed	Sister	As needed		
Explore having other clubhouse members attend bingo with Latisha	Noel	4-15-14		

Client's signature _____ Date: _____

Case manager's signature _____ Date: _____

© Cengage Learning

FIGURE 15.2 Case Management Plan

see, the service plan has both impact goals and service objectives and indicates who will do what by when. It does not show the dates of accomplishment yet. These will be entered along with any notes as the case service plan progresses.

Another slightly different type of case plan is shown in Table 15.3. It describes the impact goal (expected results) and details what the intervention plan will be. It also shows who will do what and sets a date when the impact goal is to be achieved. The interventions described here are essentially a list of service objectives (e.g., apply for Medicaid, undergo eye exam). The plan is developed in cooperation with the client or client's family, if the client is a child. As you can see, the case manager must have substantial familiarity with available formal resource systems and a working relationship with many different professionals. Following completion of the service plan, the implementation phase begins.

INTERVENTION

EP 2.1.10g

The intervention phase can be regarded as having two parts. One concerns the direct services provided by the case manager. The other involves indirect services provided by other resource systems. Some argue that the case manager should not provide direct services but simply arrange for others to do so. They reason that the time and effort needed to provide direct services may detract from more needed indirect-service facilitation. Still, most writers agree that the case manager will provide some direct services to clients.

Direct Services

The case manager may be called upon to provide several direct services to clients. Although these services may not involve counseling or therapy, they will still be important to clients. Direct services may include crisis intervention (e.g., locating temporary housing

TABLE 15.3 A Complete Service Plan

	Problem Expected Results	Intervention/Strategy	Time Line
1	Child has appropriate day care.	Client will go to Craven County Child Development Center. Parent will first visit center and make application. Center will provide structured program to enhance developmental skills of client.	9-27-13
2	Family receives food stamps until they are employed and can afford adequate food.	Speak with food stamp worker about emergency stamps. Establish an appointment.	5-20-13
2	The client's parents are employed.	Refer parents to job service. Give job suggestions to parents.	5-20-13
2	Client has medical coverage.	Check eligibility requirements for Medicaid. Refer family to make application with Medicaid. Client will be eligible since spend-down was met in March 1992.	5-30-13
3	Family knows if child has normal vision in both eyes.	Client will visit Dr. Jones for an eye exam.	5-30-13

Source: *Social Work Cases, March 12, 2000.*

for desperate, homeless people), supporting clients making difficult decisions, helping to modify clients' environments (e.g., arranging for transportation within the community), and helping clients overcome emotional reactions to their crisis situations.

Other case managers may serve in the role of teacher. For instance, they might instruct clients in money management or personal hygiene. Sometimes, case managers share professional knowledge and judgment with a client or provide important information to clients trying to make decisions. Clients may need to be taught important job-seeking skills before gaining employment. Some teaching techniques available to social workers were described in Chapter 3.

Sometimes, case managers will need to motivate clients, especially when clients have experienced past failures in attempting to make positive changes in their lives or when they have experienced disappointments in getting the resources they needed. Simple discouragement can make clients doubt that anything could ever possibly be different. Frequently, you will need to continue motivating the client throughout the assessment and planning processes. Highlight 15.4 provides some suggestions for motivating clients.

Workers also will have to support clients through periods of change and help them survive and prosper in their environment. One way of providing this support is to give clients useful information. Another is to praise client changes and growth. As a case manager, you will be working both to help the client change and to assist informal networks in aiding the client. Clients will encounter multiple service and aid programs that

are confusing and complex. Eligibility criteria may be unintelligible. Regulations may appear arbitrary. The worker will be providing direct service by helping clients negotiate formal resource systems.

Indirect Services

Indirect services provided by the case manager are largely limited to two roles. The first involves linking clients with needed resource systems. These systems may be formal in that they are existing social agencies. However, they also may include mutual care systems, such as associates from various sectors of the client's life (school, church, work). Self-help groups such as Alcoholics Anonymous, Parents Anonymous, Parents Without Partners, and the National Alliance for the Mentally ill can also be used to provide mutual care services.

Perhaps contacting other service-providing agencies either in person or in writing will be necessary for the case manager. In such instances, the advantage of knowing staff members in other agencies is critical. Respecting and valuing the contributions of the other caregivers is also important for case managers. Whether the needed care is given by you or some other resource system, remember that the ultimate goal is to help clients help themselves.

A second indirect service role involves advocating with various systems on behalf of clients. Much of a case manager's indirect service addresses this latter task. Changing the system to help the client is more difficult than asking the client to change. The case manager may have to develop new resources (often in

HIGHLIGHT 15.4

Motivating Techniques

The following techniques can be used to motivate disgusted, disheartened, or discouraged clients:

1. Encourage client autonomy by asking clients about their own plans. These might include completing school, learning a trade, living independently, getting along better with family members, or establishing an intimate relationship.
2. Demonstrate empathy and acceptance about client resistance. Most people don't accept change easily and it is helpful to identify the specific reasons for a client's resistance. If possible, recognize resistance as a positive effort toward self-protection.
3. Relabel, reframe, and redefine problems as opportunities to grow.
4. Contribute realistic suggestions aimed at enhancing the client's life and forestalling relapses. For example, tell the client exactly what to expect when approaching a new agency for help. Suggest ways the client might respond to a negative decision by the agency.
5. Deal with persistent refusal to consider change by identifying the consequences and likely outcomes of existing behavior patterns. Essentially, this leaves the client to decide whether to change or to accept responsibility for the decision to maintain the status quo.

6. Discuss points of disagreement between worker and client and work out realistic compromises. For instance, identify options that satisfy both you and the client.
7. Develop a contract with the client specifying mutual goals.
8. Identify the steps that must be taken and the service providers that can help the client to reach agreed goals.
9. Provide the client with data about service providers. Such information might include eligibility requirements, location, transportation, the nature of services, or the length of service.
10. Discuss any of the obstacles the client can foresee in using the proposed services. For example, suggest the client bring certain forms of identification along when applying for a specific service, which might eliminate typical delays in qualifying for assistance.
11. Review what the responsibilities of each party will be in completing the linkage with a particular service provider. For instance, ask the client if he or she understands what you, as the case manager, will do and what the client is responsible for doing (Frankel & Gelman, 2012; Hepworth et al., 2012; Summers, 2006).

---

collaboration with others) or improve access to existing resources. Sometimes such actions mean advocating and intervening with clients' informal resource systems (family and friends). At other times, the worker must coordinate services so that clients get only those they need. Technical assistance and consultation to resource systems may be required as they attempt to deliver needed services to the client. As needed, the case manager meets with the client and agency representatives to facilitate referrals and service provision. Meetings also may be held to negotiate problems that exist between the informal system and formal resource systems.

As in other areas of generalist social work practice, the case manager's responsibilities and activities are determined largely by clients' needs. Those needs change over time and require the case manager to provide an ever-changing pattern of direct and indirect service. As the client becomes more involved with

existing resource systems (formal and informal), the worker's role shifts to the next phase of the process—monitoring.

Monitoring

 EP 2.1.10m

Monitoring is one of the primary tasks during the intervention phase. During the monitoring process, the case manager continues to communicate with service providers. This process involves two tasks. The first concerns determining if the service plan is being completed. The second focuses on whether or not the original goals are being accomplished.

During the monitoring stage, rewriting the case plan may be necessary. The case manager maintains necessary records and documentation. Managers look for gaps in service and fill them. If clients fail to appear for scheduled appointments, the case manager follows up to see what happened. If the client is receiving medication, the case manager will help assess whether the client is under- or overmedicated. If expected outcomes are not being achieved, the case manager will use assessment skills to figure out the cause. Are new needs emerging? Is the original process being followed, or have changes occurred? What can be done to improve service delivery and effectiveness?

Case managers continue to advocate for the client when the need arises. A case manager also serves as the contact person for the case. Thus, the manager represents the client to resource systems (both formal and informal) and represents those agencies and people in contact with the client. Monitoring also helps ensure that clients do not use the system inappropriately. For instance, a client might receive duplicate services or similar benefits from two or more resource systems. Appropriate coordination of services usually can prevent such problems from happening. The monitoring function occurs through the use of formal communications, formal and informal meetings, phone contacts, case recording, and formal evaluation devices (e.g., instruments, test results). The primary focus is on how services are provided. Though there is heed paid to the outcomes attained, primary attention to this matter occurs in the evaluation phase.

Additional Roles

The nature of case management is such that the worker provides a vast variety of services or roles. The absence of natural or informal support systems (families, friends) may put the worker in a position of having to help the client develop such a resource. Other clients may infrequently use available services. Thus, the case manager may engage in outreach, namely, reaching out to potential clients who need and qualify for the service. This task might include public education about the availability of a service and what the referral process involves. It may also involve advocating with an agency to provide services in a different location or during different time frames to fit potential clients not previously served.

EVALUATION IN CASE MANAGEMENT

The importance of evaluating the outcomes of case management services is critical. Although some studies show that case management is cost-effective (i.e., receiving adequate or better services for the amount they cost), others do not (Rothman, 2009a; Walsh, 2009). There is clearly more research needed to assess the effectiveness of case management.

As we have discussed, some evaluation occurs during the intervention phase. There we were concerned with whether or not the original case management plan and goals remained appropriate.

During the evaluation phase, we want to determine if impact goals have been achieved. Perhaps the first task is to decide how data will be collected. Do we use existing case records? Are external assessments of the client's progress necessary, such as your own observations or calls to other agencies?

Another thing we need to do is look carefully at outcomes. Did the client get and keep a job? Has the major health problem that brought the client to our attention been alleviated? Does the client have a reliable form of transportation, thus allowing participation in the sheltered workshop program? Is the client taking the medication as prescribed? Has the client quit talking to walls and doors? Is the home now fully accessible to a person in a wheelchair?

Achievement of many of these goals can be easily assessed because the case manager, significant others, and the client can simply observe results. Other goals are not as observable and require more subjective judgments.

Sometimes we want to know if the case management services themselves were helpful and in what ways. What was the impact of service delivery upon the client? Was the client satisfied with the service? Depending upon the ability of the client, client satisfaction questionnaires and surveys might be used. Similar instruments might be created to gather impressions from others involved with the case (e.g., family, friends, or formal resources systems).

Other targets of evaluation include the resource systems that served the client. Can these networks provide continued service to the client? Will they need to be augmented (increased or improved) in some way? Were there problems that have been overcome? What barriers remain?

These evaluations require more subjective judgments and are less easily measured. Yet they remain important questions. The answers may determine the continued effectiveness of the helping agencies.

TERMINATION IN CASE MANAGEMENT

Discussing the termination of case management services is more difficult than in other short-term interventions. Many clients receiving case management services have chronic, debilitating conditions. Some case management services continue throughout the client's life. In these situations, the only terminations will occur when the worker leaves or the client dies or moves away. When any of these situations happen, the termination issues described in Chapter 9 remain relevant. When case management services end, closure with the individual or family and with those resource systems that have provided service are involved. As with any termination, the worker, client, and any others involved will experience a variety of potential feelings that must be dealt with. In addition, the client may need further referral to new and different services. Finally, the case record must be closed. Chapter 16 addresses this issue.

FOLLOW-UP IN CASE MANAGEMENT

Follow-up of clients receiving case management services is critical. Because of the extreme nature of the problems facing these clients (e.g., developmental disabilities, chronic mental illness, or serious physical disabilities), they remain at risk throughout their lives. Rothman (2009a) reminds us that follow-up can help prevent reversion to previous problems and other potential catastrophes. The case manager can attempt to contact clients by phone, letter, or home visit as necessary.

Gibelman (1982) provides an excellent example of the type of client frequently needing case management services and the ongoing nature of some cases. See Highlight 15.5, which describes how the case of a client with mental disabilities was managed.

FACTORS INFLUENCING CASE MANAGEMENT SERVICE DELIVERY

The amount of research on the effectiveness of case management is limited, but growing. However, there is some evidence that smaller caseloads influence service delivery. When caseloads become too large, the managers have time to respond only to crises. Similarly, there is a corresponding deterioration in the case manager's relationship with clients (Knight, Broome, Simpson, & Flynn, 2008). As a general rule, caseload size is inversely correlated with number and frequency of contacts with client, personal nature of contacts with clients, and proactiveness of the case manager (King, Meadows, & Le Bas, 2004). In large rural service areas, 30 cases may be much too great because of the additional travel time needed to see clients and access resources. However, caseload size alone may not always be a factor in quality of service delivered. For example, the intensive nature of some client situations may also limit the case manager's capacity to handle additional cases. Recognizing this, attempts have been made to identify formulas or caseload management systems that will more accurately manage the number and types of cases that a case manager can handle.

Chinman, Allende, Bailey, Maust, and Davidson (1999) found that a major factor in case manager effectiveness was their persistence and their determination to ensure client needs were met.

Another factor that may influence service delivery is the extent to which the case manager's responsibilities are clearly delineated. Typically, case managers with vaguely defined responsibilities end up largely providing direct services to the client instead of focusing on the diversity of services needed.

The quality of supervision that supervisors provide to case managers also can have a bearing on the manager's performance. Although supervisors can be of great assistance to case managers, this requires that the supervisor know exactly what the case managers are doing. This lack of knowledge reduces the effectiveness of the supervisor as a source of support.

Stress and burnout of case managers is also a factor influencing service to clients. The relatively high demands on individual case managers has prompted suggestions that the burnout might be prevented by assigning a team of workers to serve as case managers for specific clients. Presumably, the team would share responsibility for the client's well-being, reducing the burden on any single case manager.

Critical Thinking Questions 15.2

EP 2.1.3

- Assume your supervisor asked you to explain what case management is to a group of community leaders visiting your agency. Identity six to eight bullet points that you would want to cover.
- Articulate how case management is related to generalist practice.

General Observations About Both Brokering and Case Management

Because social workers engaging in brokering and case management often perform similar or overlapping functions, it is important to point out some areas that apply to both roles. In both brokering and case management, the key to effectively intervening is to correctly identify client needs and locate resources that can directly respond to the needs. In brokering, an effective referral may be critical to the client receiving

Case Management for a Client Who Has Mental Disabilities

The police brought Oliver to the county crisis unit after he had caused a disturbance in a bank. The Crisis Unit staff had often seen Oliver before. Fifty-six years old, with organic brain syndrome caused by paresis, syphilis, and chronic alcoholism, he had been deteriorating mentally for the last several years. Because he was incoherent and threatening, he was placed in the inpatient unit at Marin General Hospital.

Henja got involved in the case after hospital staff decided that Oliver's crisis had passed. They determined, however, that he needed long-term treatment in a skilled psychiatric nursing facility. But no local facility would accept him for a variety of reasons, including the fact that they had no vacancies, they lacked the proper security, and the patient was dangerous or unmanageable. Henja was asked to find a psychiatric nursing facility in a neighboring county.

She did so, but the process was not simple. The work included:

- consulting with Marin General Hospital's inpatient staff, the patient's family, and the Transitional Services staff;
- reviewing Oliver's medical, psychiatric, and social history;
- clarifying his legal status;
- interviewing him to assess his current mental status and potential for violence;
- arranging funding through Supplemental Security Income (SSI) and MediCal, the state's medical benefit plan (similar to other states' Medicaid);
- presenting the information, including the potential for violence, to the facility's intake worker and convincing the facility to accept Oliver;
- asking MediCal to authorize treatment; and
- arranging transportation to the facility.

The case was not over, though. Oliver got worse. He started assaulting other patients and injured a staff member. Henja got a telephone call: Take Oliver away from here. When he returned to the Crisis Unit, a treatment conference determined that he needed to go to Napa State Hospital. But the hospital would not accept him. The director of admissions argued that the hospital was short of beds and that Oliver's prognosis was so poor that he would never be discharged.

Henja got on the phone and, at the request of a country mental health supervisor, she spoke to the director at Napa. Because Henja is a state employee who had worked at the hospital and knows the staff, she was in a position to influence the situation. "I worked out an agreement with the director," she recalls. "If he would assure me that the hospital would evaluate Oliver's condition and develop a treatment plan for him, I would promise to place him in a county facility as soon as he was ready."

Henja kept in weekly contact with Oliver and the hospital treatment team. Fortunately, Oliver responded to the lithium and therapy that were prescribed and became generally friendly and cooperative. But he retained symptoms of his organic brain syndrome and refused to acknowledge either his illness or his alcoholism. He said his plans for the future were to go back to work, continue drinking, and keep "fooling around with the ladies." Over 4 months, Henja and the hospital team developed a plan that would allow Oliver to be transferred to a locked skilled nursing facility, where he could continue treatment but also get passes out. With Henja's considerable trepidation, the transfer took place. Because Oliver has continued on lithium and has stopped drinking, the placement has worked well, and Oliver may soon be transferred to a less restrictive facility. In getting Oliver out of the state hospital, Henja kept her promise to the admissions director.

appropriate services. In case management, an effective intervention may well involve multiple roles, responding to client long-term needs, and monitoring to ensure that the needs are met. In addition, both roles involve the responsibility to engage in practices that advance social and economic justice and using research evidence to inform our practice. Both apply equally well to social work practice in these key roles and are discussed briefly in the following section.

LO 15-3 Engage in Practices That Advance Social and Economic Justice

Both brokering and case management help clients receive resources that they badly need to overcome challenges. In some instances, the case manager will advocate for the client to receive services that have previously been denied. Identifying services and resources that will help clients achieve social and economic justice is a function performed by both brokers and case managers. All of the tactics of advocacy described in Chapter 14 may be utilized when clients are deprived of rights, due process, and subjected to social or economic injustice. It is entirely possible that an agency that a broker or case manager has depended upon to assist a client refuses to do. Perhaps it is an issue of policy, or procedure, or a personal dislike of a client. In any case, the social worker will need to expend additional effort to ensure that clients, needs are met in a timely fashion.

In some cases, resources may not exist but could be created with adequate funding or changes in policies or procedures. Social workers may need to advocate for establishment of services that meet the needs of multiple clients, particularly when the needs have been repeatedly demonstrated. This underscores the fact that social workers often perform multiple roles simultaneously or consecutively, depending upon the circumstances.

LO 15-4 Use Research Evidence to Inform Practice

We have described previously in this chapter and in others the importance of using research evidence to improve practice. This includes knowing when a service or practice is less effective or not effective at all. Clients should not be sent to agencies providing services or interventions that are viewed in the profession as unethical, ineffective, or of unproven merit. Too often, agencies or individual providers offer services of questionable quality or using approaches that are considered inappropriate. For example, some practitioners offer so-called reparative or conversion therapies purported to help gay and lesbian individuals become straight. These therapies are offered despite the nearly complete lack of evidence supporting them and the opposition of most reputable professional organizations including the NASW and the American Psychological Association. Others offer approaches to curb oppositional defiance disorder using techniques that have been denounced as ineffective and potentially dangerous. Other troubling problems encountered by families including autism, attention deficit hyperactivity disorder (ADHD), reactive attachment disorder, cancer, and dyslexia have given rise to a host of questionable psychological and other treatments.

Social workers have an obligation to clients to refer them to services that will meet their needs and to not knowingly expose them to harm. Clients have a right to know whether the service to which you are referring them offers effective help. They should also be informed about whether a given intervention is simply untested, identified as ineffective, or considered potentially harmful to their well-being.

Chapter Summary

The following summarizes this chapter's content as it relates to each learning objective (LO) presented at the beginning of the chapter. Chapter content helps prepare students to:

LO 15-1 Employ the professional role of broker.

Brokering is the linking of client systems to needed resources. It is a major professional role for social workers and may be the only service provided to a client or combined with other roles. When the social worker engages in one or more professional roles, these may be performed consecutively or concurrently. The effective broker knows community resources well and must be aware of such things as eligibility criteria of resource agencies, agency characteristics, and names of contacts within the resource agency. Potential sources of information on appropriate agency resources are community resource directories, telephone books, information and referral services, service organizations and clubs, and the Internet.

The planned change process in brokering involves identifying and assessing client needs, identifying and assessing potential resource systems, helping the client select the best resource, making the referral, helping the client use the resource system, and evaluating the adequacy of the resource system's help for the client.

LO 15-2 Employ the professional role of case manager.

Case management is a method of providing services whereby a professional social worker assesses the needs of the client and the client's family, when appropriate, and arranges, coordinates, monitors, evaluates, and advocates for a package of multiple services to meet the specific client's complex needs. The principles of case management include individualization of services, comprehensiveness of services, parsimonious services, fostering autonomy, and continuity of care. Case managers may be called upon to plan multiple roles, including broker, advocate, counselor, and so on. The planned change process in case management is more or less the same as in generalist practice. This includes assessment, in which the worker assesses the client's ability to meet environmental challenges, the caretaking ability of the client's informal support group, and the resources of formal support systems. Planning includes creating a service plan that includes impact goals and service objectives. Intervention includes both the direct services provided to the client by the case manager as well as the indirect services provided by other organizations.

Evaluation of case management involves determining whether impact goals have been achieved and deciding with the client whether other services are needed. Because so many clients receiving case management services have chronic, long-term challenges, termination may not always follow the evaluation phase. In many cases, clients will need services for the same or unrelated problems and the case manager may have a long-term professional relationship with the client.

LO 15-3 Engage in practices that advance social and economic justice.

Both brokering and case management help clients receive resources that they badly need to overcome challenges. In some instances, the case manager will advocate for the client to receive services that have previously been denied. Identifying services and resources that will help clients achieve social and economic justice is a function performed by both brokers and case managers.

LO 15-4 Use research evidence to inform practice.

Previous research on the effectiveness of case management shows mixed results. Many studies report that these services meet the critical needs of clients in a cost-effective manner. Other studies show less positive outcomes. Overall, the value of case management is recognized by the many organizations and agencies providing this service.

Competency Notes

The following identifies where Educational Policy (EP) competencies and practice behaviors are discussed in the chapter.

EP 2.1.1c Attend to professional roles and boundaries. *(p. 540):* Brokering is one of the most common roles in social work practice. *(p. 548):* Case managers are likely to play several roles, including broker, advocate, counselor, teacher, community organizer, or planner.

**EP 2.1.2b Make ethical decisions by applying standards of the NASW *Code of Ethics* and, as applicable, of the International Federation of Social Workers/International Association of Schools of Social Work *Ethics in Social Work, Statement of Principles.* *(p. 545):* Client self-determination plays a large role in deciding which problems should have priority and which interventions should be undertaken.

EP 2.1.3 Apply critical thinking to inform and communicate professional judgment. *(p. 545):* Social workers use critical thinking skills to help them decide which community resources are most likely to assist a client with a specific problem. *(p. 560):* Critical thinking is involved when you must decide the best way to communicate a difficult or complicated topic.

EP 2.1.10e Assess client strengths and limitations. *(p. 551):* Case managers engage in assessing the current and future needs of clients along with their strengths and limitations.

EP 2.1.10f Develop mutually agreed-on intervention goals and objectives. *(p. 555):* Case managers work with clients to identify impact goals that will result in changing some major aspect of the client's life. They must also decide what service objectives will help achieve the impact goal.

EP 2.1.10g Select appropriate intervention strategies. *(p. 545):* The social worker must decide whether brokering alone is sufficient to help the client or whether other implementation roles are needed. *(p. 556):* Interventions may include both direct services provided by the case manager as well as indirect services provided by other resource systems.

EP 2.1.10h Initiate actions to achieve organizational goals. *(p. 549):* Social workers doing case management in employee assistance programs are helping achieve organizational goals such as assisting employees to recover faster and reducing costs to the employer.

EP 2.1.10i **Facilitate transitions and endings.** *(p. 559):* Termination in case management may not occur until a client dies in the case of clients with chronic, debilitating conditions.

EP 2.1.10m **Critically analyze, monitor, and evaluate interventions.** *(p. 558):* Monitoring is one of the primary tasks in case management and helps determine whether the interventions are achieving their purpose. *(p. 559):* Evaluation in case management is intended to determine if the impact goals have been achieved.

On the Internet

Visit the *Understanding Generalist Practice* CourseMate at **www.cengagebrain.com** for resources such as quizzes, glossaries and videos.

Recording in Generalist Social Work Practice

© kurhan/Shutterstock.com

Learning Objectives

This chapter will help prepare students to:

LO 16-1   Recognize the significance of recording in social work.

LO 16-2   Identify content contained in records.

LO 16-3   Employ a range of recording formats.

LO 16-4   Attend to technological advances in record keeping.

LO 16-5   Strive for confidentiality in electronic record keeping.

LO 16-6   Employ good writing skills in recording.

LO 16-7   Examine privacy principles with respect to recording.

1. The client is a very sick individual.
2. He looked like a derelict.
3. She was perfectly average.
4. Petey has mongoloid features.
5. The house was filthy.
6. We solved all their problems.
7. I'm sure she will have a wonderful life.
8. They should lock him up and throw away the key.

WHAT IS WRONG OR POTENTIALLY WRONG WITH THE PRECEDING STATEMENTS? Let us examine them one by one:

1. The client is a very sick individual. *What does "very sick" mean? Does it refer to physical or mental illness? Does the client have diabetes, brain cancer, or paranoid schizophrenia? Read by itself, the statement is difficult to understand. It provides great potential for inaccuracy and misinterpretation. It could even resemble a value judgment declared in anger when a person brazenly steps in front of you in a long line at a store.*

2. He looked like a derelict. *"Derelict" is not a flattering term. It labels someone in a derogatory manner. It lacks specificity regarding a person's behavior and appearance. Finally, it is missing any empathy regarding understanding and examining an individual's situation.*

3. She was perfectly average. *What does "average" mean? Are you average? Is your best friend average, or your Uncle Donald? Does it mean you are all alike or just somewhat alike? Is "perfectly average" better than just plain-old "average"? The point is that terms such as average or normal are vague. To each of us, they elicit a different picture. Thus, this statement read alone can conjure up a wide variety of meanings. There is also a strong possibility of miscommunication.*

4. Petey has mongoloid features. *Mongolism or Down syndrome is "a congenital condition characterized by moderate to severe mental retardation, slanting eyes, a broad short skull, broad hands with short fingers, and trisomy of the human chromosome numbered 21" (Mish, 2008, p. 377). The main point about the accuracy of this statement is whether or not Petey has been formally diagnosed as having mongolism. The statement should only be made if the fact has been medically established.*

   This particular example is rooted in fact. As a very young, naïve, and inexperienced graduate student, my field supervisor assigned me the task of writing my first complete assessment of my first client, Petey. I made the mistake of stating in my report that he had "mongoloid features," an archaic term that is now considered offensive but was in common usage at that time. Unfortunately for me, Petey had not been diagnosed as having mongolism at all. He simply looked "kind of mongoloid" to me. My field supervisor ranted and raved about what horrible repercussions could occur by writing such a thing in a formal record. Petey could be labeled "mongoloid" with all of its ramifications for life. I will never forget that mistake. In actuality, Petey could have been mongoloid because he had a wide variety of developmental disabilities. However, it was not my place to make up a fact.

5. The house was filthy. *What is "filthy"? To some people, this term might mean a week's worth of dust on the bookcase. To others, it could mean mounds of dirty dishes in the sink, animal feces on the floor, and greasy grime on the walls. This kind of statement can have major implications for people if made in a formal record. It might be used against a parent in a custody debate or in an alleged child neglect case. The point is that such a statement needs clarification and more detailed description. It should be clearly stated whether what we are talking about is dust or feces, for example.*

6. We solved all their problems. *This statement read by itself is simply too general and vague. What were the problems? How did you establish that all of them were solved? How were the solutions evaluated? Can people ever have all of their problems solved?*

7. I'm sure she will have a wonderful life. *Inexperienced students easily make this or similar statements when completing their first written assessment or social history. This statement has two primary errors in it. First, how can you ever be absolutely certain about anything in the future? Are you sure that tomorrow will be rainy or that you will get an A in your generalist practice course? There are other ways of stating strong impressions or opinions. For instance, "It is my strong feeling that . . . " or "It is my impression that. . . . "*

   The second error in the statement involves the "wonderful life" part. What is a "wonderful life"? Does it mean one completely free of problems? What if this person gets divorced or must have a mastectomy? When does a life switch from being "wonderful" to "not so wonderful"? Especially when first beginning in social work, overlooking problems is easy. People become adept at concealing and disguising those problems that are most troublesome to them. The real question involves what is hidden behind the "wonderful" part. No one's life is absolutely trouble free.

8. They should lock him up and throw away the key. *This sentence makes a strong statement about this person's future. It implies no hope for rehabilitation. Such a statement in a report made to the court could have serious consequences if it influences a judge's decision regarding prescribed punishment. What factors influenced the social worker to make such a strong statement? By itself the statement gives no clue.*

Introduction

The point of the preceding discussion is to emphasize how important it is to carefully choose the words you use in social work recording. This chapter will explore social work recording in much greater depth. Most of the principles and issues discussed will apply regardless of whether the practice setting involves work with individuals, families, groups, organizations, or communities. Any setting is unique in terms of the specific types of records it requires you to keep.

LO 16-1 Recognize the Significance of Recording in Social Work

Why is what you write so important in social work? The answer is simply that often you *are* what you write either electronically or in hard copy. In other words, often you will not be there to testify about a client's problems or accomplishments. Others must rely on what you have written to communicate what both you and your client have done. The effective use of writing in professional communication offers one means of demonstrating professional conduct in social work. Studies and the professional literature have established that writing and recording skills are extremely important for social work practitioners on a daily basis (Healy & Mulholland, 2012; Sidell, 2011; Simon, 2012). There are at least 10 specific reasons, each of which is discussed next, why social work records are important (Healy & Mulholland, 2012; Kagle, 2008; Kagle & Kopels, 2008, pp. 11–18; Sidell, 2011).

1. IDENTIFYING THE CLIENT AND THE NEED

Recording information about your clients provides the basis upon which you continue to work. You identify who your clients are and specifically what problems they bring to you. It helps you establish that your clients are indeed eligible for services and that your job involves intervention with them. Recording their existence and situations makes them part of your caseload. A *caseload* is the total number of clients a social worker is accountable for at any given time.

Recording information helps you explore the nature of your clients' strengths, needs, and problems. It helps you plan and structure how you will proceed with your intervention. It assists you in monitoring your clients' progress. Finally, it allows your agency to oversee how well all of its clients are being served.

2. DOCUMENTING SERVICES

Recording your work with a client simply provides proof that such work has been done. If a colleague or your supervisor asks what you do, you can refer to your documentation to describe your assessments, plans, interventions, evaluations, terminations, and follow-ups. Documentation proves that you have accomplished what you say you have accomplished. It makes you accountable for what you have done.

Sometimes your client will be involved with the courts. Consider, for example, clients on probation or those having child custody disputes. In these cases, your documentation of what occurred in the clients' situations can have significant impact on their lives.

3. MAINTAINING CASE CONTINUITY

Client problems often change their focus over time. For instance, an unmarried pregnant teen will need different services before and after her baby is born, often requiring the involvement of other agencies. Recording information about the client, the client's situation, and progress made prevents having to invent the wheel all over again. In other words, having access to what has been done in the past is much more efficient than starting from scratch.

Workers (including you) come and go as they move on in their careers. Accurate recording allows clients to be transferred with minimal interruption in their service. Having documented who the client is and what has been done allows for new workers and other professionals working with the client to begin where the last intervention left off rather than starting over from the beginning.

4. ASSISTING IN INTERPROFESSIONAL COMMUNICATION

We have established that many times clients are involved with numerous agencies and workers. Frequently, clients have multiple problems addressed by multiple agencies. These involvements necessitate accurate communication between social workers and other professionals working with the client, such as psychologists, medical staff, occupational therapists, speech therapists, physical therapists, or psychiatrists.

Recording information about the client allows for many professionals to share this data. Some might say that actual meetings with professionals are most effective. During such a meeting, a group of professionals can dynamically share information, discuss potential alternatives, and develop intervention strategies. These meetings, often called case or treatment conferences, encourage the development of creative new ideas that might not occur to individuals working by themselves. Nonetheless, such meetings are time consuming and expensive due to the involvement of numerous staff. Therefore, recording information and sharing it in writing provides an efficient and effective means of communicating with others involved with the client.

5. SHARING INFORMATION WITH THE CLIENT

EP 2.1.10 c&f

Sometimes, sharing recorded information with the client is helpful. For instance, if you are doing a behavioral assessment, showing a client a chart of progress can provide a rich incentive for continuing that progress. At other times, sharing with clients what you have stated about them can clarify for them their strengths, problems, plans, or achievements.

However, you should be aware that laws concerning client confidentiality and agency policies about such sharing with clients and involved others may restrict or prohibit such sharing. You also should be sensitive to how your client might react to the written record. For example, you record on paper that you think your client is a cocaine addict. If the client reads this when you have not discussed this supposition with her and she is still in a state of denial over the problem, do not expect a pleasant or cooperative reaction on her part. Confidentiality issues will be discussed more thoroughly in a later section of this chapter.

6. FACILITATING SUPERVISION, CONSULTATION, AND PEER REVIEW

EP 2.1.1f

Recording your perceptions and your progress will provide a means for you to get direction, feedback, and help from other professionals. Recording your perceptions, for example, can provide a supervisor with a means of evaluating your work. A good supervisor will provide you with constructive criticism, making specific suggestions for how you might be more effective with any particular case. Sometimes you will be at an impasse with some new problem and simply will not know how to proceed. During these situations, a written record can be helpful when consulting others for new ideas and suggestions. What you think and what you have done can be clearly presented to them in writing. This written presentation provides an opportunity for giving specific feedback.

7. MONITORING THE PROCESS AND IMPACT OF SERVICE

EP 2.1.10m

Throughout this text, we have emphasized the importance of monitoring the effectiveness of your plans and interventions. It helps you to organize your thinking about how to proceed with the client. Recording information about clients' progress or lack thereof provides you with clear-cut descriptions of your clients' situations at any particular point in time. Comparing past records with present ones allows you to measure how much progress has been made.

8. EDUCATING STUDENTS AND OTHER PROFESSIONALS

EP 2.1.1e

Social work records can provide an excellent means for educating both students and practitioners already in the field about effective interventions. They can help formulate answers to many questions. What are the most important facets of a case to assess? How can clients' strengths best be described? How do other practitioners formulate plans? What types of intervention have worked most effectively in the past with a particular type of problem? What often happens after such cases are terminated?

9. SUPPLYING INFORMATION FOR ADMINISTRATIVE TASKS

EP 2.1.10h

Both large and small social service agencies must keep track of the services they provide and how effective these services are. Just like individuals, agencies must be accountable for their work. They need to justify their existence. Additionally, administrative personnel must attend to issues in service delivery, including "service patterns, workload management, personnel performance, and allocation of resources" (Kagle, 1991, p. 4; 1996; Kagle & Kopels, 2008).

10. PROVIDING DATA FOR RESEARCH-INFORMED PRACTICE

EP 2.1.6

EP 2.1.6a&b

In order to improve their effectiveness, agencies and organizations must evaluate the extent to which they are achieving their stated goals. Recording information about large numbers of clients can contribute to a database that is very useful for research. For instance, an agency can develop a typical client profile, or an organization can evaluate the effectiveness of a number of intervention models. What approaches work best with specific types of clients and problems? Research, for instance, can prove that 95 percent of adoptive placements are successful or that only 14 percent of clients have to return for services after a 1-year period.

LO 16-2 Identify Content Contained in Records

Seven major types of information typically incorporated in agency records are subsequently identified and discussed in this section (Halley, Kopp, & Austin, 1998; Sormanti, 2012).

1. THE DATE OF YOUR INTERACTION WITH THE CLIENT

This information can be recorded simply and quickly. For example, you might jot down "6/5/15" in the left-hand margin of a page. You should include the year to eliminate confusion in the future.

2. BASIC INFORMATION ABOUT THE CLIENT

This information is also referred to as identifying information. Frequently, an agency will consistently use a *face sheet,* which is a page of information, usually placed at the front of a client's file or in the beginning of a record. It can also be called "a demographic sheet" or "an information summary sheet" (Sidell, 2011, p. 73). A face sheet provides basic identifying information about the client, including name, address, phone number, gender, income, names of other family members, and fundamental information about the reasons for referral. Other information requested will vary somewhat according to agency needs. Questions on forms depend on the types of clients the agency serves and the services the agency provides. For instance, a Planned Parenthood agency that focuses on contraceptive choices and reproductive health will probably seek more information pertaining to the client's health record. Generally speaking, not only face sheets, but virtually all social work records vary dramatically from one agency to another in structure and content.

An example of a face sheet is given in Figure 16.1. This sheet provides basic information about an adult potentially in need of services. *Adult services* or *adult social services* is a broad term that may include a wide range of services and assistance provided to people after they reach age 18; "these are governed and admin-

istered by different laws and agencies and are not generally considered to be an entitlement [a guaranteed service to which all such people are automatically entitled], but rather are made available based on need and resource availability" (Family Center on Technology and Disability, 2013). Examples of adult services include Adult Protective Services that seek to protect vulnerable older adults from neglect, abuse, or exploitation; substance abuse assessment and treatment; and case management for people with mental health problems.

Additionally, note that records may be kept in an electronic, handwritten, or typed format. Examples such as Figure 16.1 are included here only to give you an idea about what to expect in social work practice. A number of examples will be included in this chapter. Some will be blank forms actually used by individual agencies. Others will be completed examples depicting what has been recorded about specific clients and cases. The ones you will encounter when you get a job will resemble the examples here in that they will have an established format and will require you to include specific information. However, your chances are about as unlikely as your winning a state lottery that you will use these identical forms in real social work practice.

3. REASON FOR CLIENT CONTACT

What is the client's problem and situation? Why is the client coming to you and your agency for help? This information can be a brief account of the primary problems described by the client and spelled out by the worker. The following examples are a few of the many that you may encounter:

- *School referred Arlo to Opportunity Enterprises for evaluation services in order to assess vocational strengths and limitations and to assist in occupational planning.*
- *Mr. C. called Crisis Line and threatened suicide. He said he was depressed and requested counseling.*
- *The juvenile court referred Blake and her family for counseling following her numerous truancies and recent apprehension for selling illegal drugs.*

4. MORE DETAILED INFORMATION ABOUT THE CLIENT'S PROBLEM AND SITUATION

Here you must choose which information is most relevant to the client's problem, including his or her strengths, and which is least significant.

Agencies vary in the amount and type of information they solicit during the intake process. *Intake* involves the established procedures for an agency's

Adult Services Face Sheet

Name of Client: _____ Date of Intake: _____

Case Number: _____ Social Security Number: _____

Address: _____

E-mail: _____ Date of Birth: _____ Age: _____

Telephone Number (Work): _____ (Home): _____ (Cell): _____

Gender: ❏ Male ❏ Female   Race: _____

Marital Status: _____ Religion: _____

Occupation: _____ Education: _____

Insurance Information: _____

Contact Type: ❏ Phone Contact   ❏ Office Contact   ❏ Home Contact   ❏ Other Location

Referral Source: Self _____   Other (Please Specify) _____

Address of Referral Source (If Other): _____

Telephone Number of Referral Source: _____

Client's Involvement in Referral:

❏ Client Present and Involved   ❏ Client Present but Uninvolved   ❏ Client Absent but Concurs with Referral

❏ Client Absent but Aware of Referral   ❏ Client Unaware of Referral   ❏ Client Wishes Not Known

Presenting Problem(s) as Described by Referral Source(s): _____

_____

_____

_____

Additional Pertinent History: _____

_____

_____

Nature of Assistance Sought by Referral Source: _____

_____

Other Persons in Household:

Full Name	Relationship to Client	Age
_____	_____	_____
_____	_____	_____
_____	_____	_____
_____	_____	_____
_____	_____	_____

Signature of Intake Social Worker: _____

FIGURE 16.1 An Example of a Face Sheet

initial contact with a client. Such procedures might include telling clients about agency programs, service requirements, and costs. They also include obtaining necessary information about the client, making an initial determination about the client's problem and motivation for service, and designating a specific worker to provide service.

An example of an intake form is presented in Figure 16.2. Note that an agency can determine what kind of information it initially needs for a particular service provision program, how to structure a form for gathering this information, and how such a form will be labeled. Figure 16.2 is labeled "Initial Client Assessment—Individual Risk and Needs Assessment." This is an intake form for a program that serves pregnant women who are deciding what to do about their lives and their pregnancies. This form seeks out relevant information, including health information, pregnancy history, adoption and parenting assessments, services needed, and history of domestic violence.

Depending on why the information is needed and at what point in the intervention process it is gathered, the record can be detailed or relatively brief and straightforward. The following is an example of a narrative information summary that details the situation where Calum, an adult with intellectual disabilities (formerly referred to as mental retardation), is referred to an agency for vocational evaluation and placement. All of the summary's content is related to the vocational planning goal.

Calum, age 52, lives with his brother and family in Omro. Education consists of a high school diploma earned through special educational programming in 1984. Calum reported that he most enjoyed reading classes and least enjoyed arithmetic during his school years. Work history consists of 30 years as a farm laborer. Duties included washing cows, carrying milk, cleaning barns, haying, and driving tractors to haul wagons. Wages were $200 per month plus room and board. Calum also worked at a local theater on weekends as an usher for 6 years. Disability is listed as Borderline Intellectual Functioning DSMIV-TR V62.89. Full-scale IQ is reported at 73. Academic skills are at the third-grade level. Medical history involves no record of recent hospitalization. Calum did state that 7 years ago he had a farm accident that resulted in a compound fracture of the right arm. Strenuous heavy lifting sometimes bothers him. Leisure activities include fishing and collecting stamps. Calum stated he would like to work at Vocational Enterprises.

Social Histories

 Frequently, more extensive information is gathered in a "social assessment report" (Sheafor & Horejsi, 2012). This type of document is often referred to as a *social history* (Kagle & Kopels, 2008; Sheafor & Horejsi, 2012). Specifically, a social history is a comprehensive portrayal of a client's current situation and past, developed by gathering information about the client's development, family, interpersonal relationships, education, and socioeconomic status. It provides an important means of collecting, organizing, and interpreting client data. A social history can be organized topic by topic (e.g., "employment history" and "extended family"). It can also be written in a chronological, narrative format. Narrative formats refer to those that are written paragraph by paragraph in story-like form. Regardless of format, in addition to information about the client and problem, most social histories include specific recommendations for how to begin the implementation process. Figure 16.3 on page 578 illustrates an outline of a social history format oriented toward a child.

Note that social histories vary significantly in emphasis and content depending on the age of the client and type of service provision (Andrews, 2007). Social histories oriented toward very young children age 0 to 5 years would stress detail about achievement of developmental milestones such as "smiling, rolling over, crawling, talking, walking, [and] writing" in addition to issues such as toilet-training conditions and ages (p. 134). A social history of a child age 6 through 11 would focus on specific "academic strengths and weaknesses," "peer relationships," "[s]kills, achievement, extracurricular activities," and "education about sexuality" (p. 135). A social history of a 12- to 17-year-old would stress aspects such as "[e]ducational participation and performance (attendance, academic strengths and weaknesses, behavioral problems, parental involvement in school on behalf of the child)," "peer relationships (Who? Quality of these relationships?)," "afterschool activities," "employment history," "romantic relationships," and "development of sexual identity" (pp. 135–136).

Social histories of adults would place greater emphasis on variables such as "social relations," "intimate relationships," "family relations" and dynamics, "employment/education," "military service," "contributions to community," "daily living" habits and activities, "spirituality and religion," "alcohol or other drug

Region: _____ Case Manager: _____ Estimated Due Date: _____

Initial Client Assessment- Individual Risk and Needs Assessment

Please Print Legibly and Complete ALL Sections of This Form

Today's Date: _____

Client Name: _____

| First | Middle | Last | (Maiden) |

DOB: _____ Medical (DCN#): _____

Address: _____

City: _____ County: _____ State: _____ Zip: _____

Telephone Number: _____ Mobile #: _____

Marital Status: ❑ Single ❑ Divorced ❑ Widowed ❑ Married ❑ Separated

SSN#: _____

Do You Have: ❑ Private Insurance ❑ Uninsured ❑ Medicaid

Name of MC+ Provider: _____

Race: ❑ White ❑ African American ❑ Amer. Indian/Alaskan Native ❑ Asian/Pacific Islander ❑ Other

Ethnic Background: ❑ Hispanic ❑ Non-Hispanic

Father of the Baby   ❑ Unknown   ❑ Refuse to Give

Name: _____ DOB: _____

SSN#: _____ Employed? _____ Student? _____ Race: _____

Number of School Years Completed: _____

Emergency Contact

Name: _____ Relationship to Client: _____

Address: _____

City: _____ County: _____ State: _____ Zip: _____

Telephone Number: _____

Do You Have Family Support? Y N   Referred to Agency by: _____

Enrolled in Prenatal Care? Y N   Date Entered Prenatal Care: _____/_____/ _____

Number of School Years Completed: _____   Are You Currently a Student? Y N

GED? Y N   Language Spoken at Home: _____

Able to Read? Y N   Able to Write? Y N

English as a Second Language? Y N

FIGURE 16.2 An Example of an Intake Form
Source: This material is reprinted with permission of Family and Children's Services of Missouri, 8631 Delmar Boulevard, St. Louis, MO 63124.

Living Arrangements – *Where they are living (house, apartment) and who they are living with (children, parents, friend, etc.)* _____

_____

Cultural/Religious Beliefs: _____

Are you working with any other social service agencies? If yes, please list. _____

Are you currently employed?   Y   N   *(Please attach proof of income)*

Income (Not Including Food Stamps) _____ Weekly _____ Monthly _____ Annually

Number of People Supported by Income: _____ **(INCLUDE UNBORN CHILD)**

Individual Risk and Needs Assessment

I am seeking these services due to: (check all that apply)

☐ Financial Hardship	☐ Lack of Family Support	☐ Previos Abortion	☐ Unplanned Pregnancy
☐ Encouragement of Others	☐ Desire to Finish School	☐ Age	☐ Emotional Stress

Others options that I have considered include: ☐ Adoption   ☐ Abortion

ON A TYPICAL DAY:

Do you smoke? Y   N   What do you smoke? _____

Are you, or have you been in a relationship where someone hit, slapped, kicked you or abused you in any way?

_____

Have you been feeling down or blue recently?

☐ None of the Time   ☐ A Little of the Time   ☐ Some of the Time   ☐ Good Part of the Time   ☐ Most of the Time

PSI–Parental Stress Indicator. Score 1-5 with 5 being the most stressed.   **Score**: _____

BEFORE GETTING PREGNANT DID YOU:

Use Alcohol _____ Use Street Drugs _____ Use Over the Counter Drugs _____

Type of Drug, Amount, and Date of Last Used _____

Allergies: _____

Medications (Name & Dosages): _____

FIGURE 16.2 Continued

	Yes	No	Past	Present			Yes	No	Past	Present
1. Cardiovascular disease	☐	☐	☐	☐		5. Hematologic	☐	☐	☐	☐
(hypertension, blood clots, migraine, varicose veins)						*(anemia, sickle cell, Rh)*				
2. Metabolic	☐	☐	☐	☐		6. Genitourinary	☐	☐	☐	☐
(diabetes, thyroid disease, gallbladder, hepatitis)						*(STD's, vaginal infections)*				
3. Cancer	☐	☐	☐	☐		7. Breasts	☐	☐	☐	☐
(breast, genital, DES exposure)						*(lump, cysts)*				
4. Neurological	☐	☐	☐	☐		8. Respiratory	☐	☐	☐	☐
(depression, epilepsy, nervousness)						*(T.B., asthma, other chronic respiratory disease)*				

Additional Comments: _____

_____

Pregnancy History

	Length of Pregnancy in weeks	Termination or Delivery Date	Type of Delivery	Prenatal Complications	Sex	Weight	Length (in.)
#1							
#2							
#3							
#4							
#5							
#6							
#7							

Labor and delivery complications:

_____

_____

FIGURE 16.2 Continued

Staff Comments:

_____

_____

Identified Strengths:

_____

_____

Concerns of Client:

_____

_____

Adoption Assessment

Previous Exposure with Adoption? _____

Would you like more information regarding adoption? _____ If no, go to Parenting Assessment

4- High   3- Medium   2- Low   1- None

Openness to Adoption Information: _____

Knowledge on Adoption Process: _____

Birth Father Support for Adoption: _____

Extended Family Adoption Support: _____

Adoption Plan Being Considered for This Child? _____

Reasons for Considering Adoption? _____

Parenting Assessment

First Time Parent? _____   Single Parent? _____

4- High   3- Medium   2- Low   1- None

Family Support for Parenting _____

Birth Father Support for Parenting: _____

Client Anxiety Regarding Parenting newborn _____

Client's Frustrations w/Current Parenting Responsibilities _____

FIGURE 16.2 Continued

Services Needed

Describe:

☐ Prenatal Care _____

☐ Ultrasound Services _____

☐ Housing _____

☐ Utilities _____

☐ Education _____

☐ Job Training & Placement _____

☐ Established Paternity/Father Involment _____

☐ Adoption Issues _____

☐ Help in Quitting Drugs/Alcohol Use _____

☐ Help in Quitting Smoking _____

☐ Domestic Abuse Protection/Partner Violence _____

☐ Medical Care _____

☐ Newborn or Infant Care _____

☐ Child Care _____

☐ Mental Health Care _____

☐ Parenting Skills _____

☐ Transportation _____

☐ Clothing _____

☐ Food _____

☐ Supplies _____

☐ Other Services _____

FIGURE 16.2 Continued

Domestic Violence Assessment
Initial Client Assessment

Client Name: _____

DOB: _____

SSN: _____

Please check all that are true:

Adult Domestic Violence:

☐ Have you ever been emotionally or physically abused by your partner or someone important to you?

☐ Within the last year, have you been hit, slapped, kicked or otherwise physically hurt by someone?

☐ Since you've been pregnant, were you hit, slapped, kicked or otherwise physically hurt by someone?

☐ Within the last year, has anyone forced you to have sexual activity?

Child Abuse/Sexual Violence:

☐ As a child, have you been emotionally or physically abused?

☐ As a child, were you ever hit, slapped, kicked or otherwise physically hurt by someone?

☐ As a child, did anyone force you to have sexual activity?

☐ As a child, I have never experienced any of the above.

FIGURE 16.2 Continued

---

abuse," "mental health," "health condition" and issues, "criminal activity," and "self-perceptions" (Andrews, 2007, pp. 143–146). Social history content for an older adult anticipating residential care placement would minimize or omit the early developmental history of childhood and focus on such dimensions as current social and emotional functioning, health issues, ability level, self-care skills, and financial situation, in addition to family and social support systems (McInnis-Dittrich, 2014).

Social history formats also vary from agency to agency depending on their purpose and the agency's orientation. For example, some might emphasize "legal system history," "traumatic events," or "ethnic/cultural community" (Andrews, 2007, pp. 139–141).

Critical Thinking Question 16.1

EP 2.1.3

- If you were to do a social history on yourself, what aspects would you emphasize as being most important and why?

5. ASPECTS OF THE IMPLEMENTATION PROCESS

This information includes your impressions concerning assessment of the client-in-situation, your specific plans for intervention, contacts you have had with clients and others involved in the case, progress made, and information about how the case was terminated. Each agency is unique in the specific records it requires

Name: _____ (d.o.b.)[date of birth]: _____

Address: _____

Telephone: _____

School and Grade: _____

Place of Birth: _____

OUTLINE FOR SOCIAL HISTORY

    I. **FAMILY COMPOSITION**
      (Note if any parent or sibling is deceased and date)

      Natural Father: d.o.b.:
      Address:
      Occupation:
      Religion:

      Stepfather: (If appropriate)   d.o.b.:
      Address:
      Occupation:
      Religion:

      Natural Mother: d.o.b.:
      Address:
      Occupation:
      Religion:

      Stepmother: (If appropriate)   d.o.b.:
      Address:
      Occupation:
      Religion:

      Siblings:
      Name, date of birth, school, and grade. List all siblings, including those out of home and current situation. If client or siblings are living with others, state names, addresses, and relationship.

FIGURE 16.3 An Example of a Social History Format
Source: Adapted from form "Outline for Social History." Used with permission of the Community Human Services Department, Waukesha County, 500 Riverview Ave., Waukesha, WI 53188.

Name: _____ (d.o.b.): _____

II. CHILD UNDER CONSIDERATION

Describe personality and physical characteristics.

III. REASON FOR REFERRAL

Short statement about immediate concern, current situation, and by whom referred. Parent and child's attitude about possible placement outside the home.

IV. FAMILY BACKGROUND

A. Mother

1. Relationship to each of mother's parents; relationship between mother's parents; evidence of emotional disturbance in family.

2. Mother's educational and vocational history.

3. Medical history if pertinent.

4. Previous marriages, with significant details.

5. History of mother's courting and marriage, including feelings about marriage and children.

B. Father

1. Relationship to each of father's parents; relationship between father's parents; evidence of emotional disturbance in family.

FIGURE 16.3 Continued

Name: _____ (d.o.b.): _____

   2. Father's educational and vocational history.

   3. Medical history if pertinent.

   4. Previous marriages, with significant details.

   5. History of father's courting and marriage, including feelings about marriage and children.

C. Family Development

   1. Describe parental relationships, who disciplines whom and how, nature and reasons for conflicts, family attitude toward current situation, family's financial situation and community involvement, family involvement with law enforcement and mental health agencies. What do you see happening in the family and why? This section should contain a historical perspective and comment on the past as well as the present.

   2. Sibling Relationships

      Describe child's relationship with each sibling, to whom the child is closest and from whom most alienated, reaction to birth of next youngest sibling, and any specific problems or emotional difficulties siblings in family have or have had in the past and how handled by parents.

   3. Other Significant Adults

      Grandparents, aunts, uncles, neighbors, and teachers. Indicate who, type of relationship, and when it began.

   4. Environment

      Significance of neighborhoods family has lived in and their dwellings.

FIGURE 16.3 Continued

Name: _____   (d.o.b.): _____

V. PERSONAL HISTORY OF CHILD

A. Developmental Data

1. From pregnancy to current parental relationship during pregnancy, reaction to pregnancy, preferred sex, mother's health (signs of miscarriage, emotional state, significant use or abuse of drugs or alcohol).

2. Birth
Delivery, premature or full term, spontaneous, physical condition of mother and child, length of hospital stay.

3. Early Months
Note any changes in mother's physical or emotional health. Any difficulties in adjusting to the home; was it stable at this time? Did child have colic or other problems? Was child breast- or bottle-fed; any feeding difficulties? Note changes in any caretakers and significant losses.

4. Later Months and Toddler Stage
Note ages at which child walked, talked, and was toilet trained. Note any difficulties with sleeping and eating patterns.

5. Coordination and Motor Pattern
A general statement as well as noting any hyperactivity, sluggishness, head or body rocking, or random or unorganized activity.

6. Parent's feelings regarding above and how they attempted to handle any difficulties.

FIGURE 16.3 Continued

Name: _____ (d.o.b.): _____

B. Personality and Social Growth

1. Responsiveness

   Did child like to be held, or did he or she withdraw from people? Did he or she play with adults and/or children? Did he or she play in group or prefer to play alone?

2. Relationships

   Describe relationship with each parent as related by both parents and child; explore any differences. What about relationships with siblings?

3. Separations from either or both parents

   When, why, how long; note also parental and child response toward separating to attend school.

4. Describe child's outstanding traits and fears, if any; e.g., is child happy, sullen, stubborn, dependent, independent; does he or she have any persistent fears, phobias, or compulsions?

5. Discipline

   How and by whom? How have parents and child reacted to it?

6. Sexual Development

   Amount of sex education, provided by whom; unusual behavior or preoccupations; kinds of questions or curiosity displayed; masturbation, parental response.

FIGURE 16.3 Continued

Name: _____ (d.o.b.): _____

C. Medical History

1. Any illness or disease suffered; injuries, falls, high fevers, convulsions, fainting or other spells; allergies or other somatic disturbances; child and parent reactions. Also any hospitalization history. Touch on any previous treatment for current problems, previous psychiatric treatment. Type and extent of drug usage, if any.

2. Birth disfigurements, speech defects, enuresis, handicaps.

3. Present health.

D. Educational Experiences

1. Schools and years attended, achievement, testing dates done by schools, M-Team Reports, interpersonal relationships of child; parent's relationship with school systems, extracurricular activities.

2. Psychological and psychiatric evaluations; previous referrals, contacts, treatment, and progress.

E. Employment Experience

VI. PREVIOUS TREATMENT

1. Prior placements and services, successful completion of or failure of services and/or placements.

FIGURE 16.3 Continued

Name: _____   (d.o.b.): _____

2. Substantiate care and services that would permit the child to remain at home that have been investigated and considered and are not available or likely to become available within a reasonable time to meet the needs of the child.

   a. What alternatives to the plan are available?

   b. What alternatives have been explored?

   c. Why aren't the explored alternatives appropriate?

   d. Discuss objectives of rehabilitation, treatment, and care.

VII. REFERENCE SOURCES

Label and date interviews, reports, and letters used to complete the social history.

Date: _____

Prepared by: _____
                   (Social Worker)

Approved by: _____
                 (Supervisor)

SS-153 (Rev. '82)

FIGURE 16.3 Continued

workers to keep. As we will discuss in more depth later on, some agencies primarily use reporting formats where you simply fill in the blanks. Other agencies require formatting, which has more of a narrative quality whether information is recorded on paper or electronically.

Frequently, workers will record a brief entry for each contact with the client and others involved chronologically throughout the intervention process. This entry includes phone calls made concerning the case. Such notes need not be lengthy; brief phrases will suffice. Dates should always be noted. Even in those few agencies that do not require this type of recording, keeping your own notes is often wise. Note that the agency may have a format for progress notes for you to follow.

The following are examples of brief progress notes:

- *3/14/15 Marah's probation officer called. She missed last appointment with him. If that happens once more, he will refer M. back to court. I will call M.'s mother to arrange for a home visit.*
- *5/20/15 Wrote Dr. Morrison that staff noticed Josh's continued odor problems—even the day after Monday's bath.*
- *8/4/15 Held progress review today. Refer to Report for details.*
- *10/8/15 Met with Mr. Petrie. Discussed current job situation. He will follow through on my five referrals and call me back regarding progress by 10/13/15.*

Due to their significance, subsequent sections will provide additional examples of progress note formats.

6. FOLLOW-UP INFORMATION

Is there a plan for follow-up? If so, specifically, who will do what by when?

For instance, a worker might record:

- *8/5/15 Terminated with Kelly. Summarized progress. I will call within 4 weeks to determine if alcohol abuse has stopped and if she continues involvement with AA [Alcoholics Anonymous].*
- *9/2/15 Called Kelly. She states she has stopped abuse and continues AA involvement. I will call once more in mid-November to determine her progress.*

7. COMMENTS AND QUESTIONS TO DISCUSS WITH A SUPERVISOR OR ANOTHER WORKER

Your own notions and impressions about a case in addition to questions you would like to have answered are also appropriate for agency records. Noting these on paper when you think of them can remind you to refer to them during your next meeting with a supervisor.

For example, you might note questions like: "Are services available in her community for domestic violence?"; "Ms. U. seems detached; is schizophrenia resurfacing?"; or "What are major symptoms of her disease?".

LO 16-3 Employ a Range of Recording Formats

Social workers use a wide range of recording formats for many purposes. These formats include process recording, digital recording; progress notes, narrative recording, summaries of treatment conferences, problem-oriented recording, recording progress in groups, letters, e-mails, memos, and meeting agendas and minutes. Because process recording and recording interactions with clients via digital recording are typically employed to train social work students, we will discuss them first.

PROCESS RECORDING

Wilson (1980) describes *process recording* as:

> *... a specialized and highly detailed form of recording. Everything that takes place in an interview is recorded using an "I said then [s]he said" style. In effect, the social worker writes down everything that would have been heard or observed had a [digital] ... recorder ... been monitoring the interview. Most process recording uses direct quotes. (p. 18)*

Additionally, the worker's or student's impressions and comments are noted in a special column right next to what has just been said. Figure 16.4 illustrates an example of a process recording.

In summary, process recording requires that the recorder must:

1. *Reconstruct the interview.*
2. *Describe the words they spoke and actions they took.*

3. *Reflect on the way in which they used themselves in the interview.*
4. *Assess their practice; and, in some examples.*
5. *Name the specific skill they were using at the time."* (Conroy, 2012, p. 88)

As you can see, Figure 16.4 records word for word what the worker and client say to each other. The worker then comments on her own feelings and impressions about what transpired between herself and her client. Note that you do not have to write a comment concerning each statement. Record one only when you feel it is appropriate and relevant.

Process recording is time consuming. Time is precious, and doing this type of recording prevents you from doing other job tasks. Therefore, this type of recording is used primarily for students in their internships. It allows you as a student to analyze in detail your interactions with clients. It also allows your supervisor to give you specific feedback even though he or she was not present when the interaction occurred.

		Comments
Worker:	Good morning, Ms. Wonderbread. How are you feeling today?	I was worried about her adjustment as this was her third day here.
Client:	Oh, not very well, I'm afraid. My feet hurt, and I sure do miss my own home.	It made me nervous when she complained like this. I didn't know what to say.
Worker:	I know you do, Ms. Wonderbread. It was a very difficult thing for you to do. Leave that house and come here, I mean.	I was trying to show empathy and let her know I really cared.
Client:	Can't I please go home? Please? I promise that I'll eat the way I should.	This made me uncomfortable.
Worker:	You know we worked to keep you at home as long as we could. But you lost 40 pounds and fell four times. We were really worried about you.	I tried to review the facts.
Client:	Oh, I know I fell, but I promise I won't anymore. Please let me go home. Please! I hate it here!	
Worker:	You know I wish I could say all right. But you agreed that your health just wouldn't allow you to take care of yourself there anymore.	
Client:	My son, that traitor. He doesn't care about me. Nobody cares about me.	She was expressing her anger.
Worker:	You know I care about you, Ms. Wonderbread. And I hate hearing you so unhappy. Do you have some time to come out and visit the garden? I'd like to show you the roses. I know how you love flowers.	I think there are things here at the home that she'll learn to enjoy. I'll try to get her more involved.
Client:	Well, I guess so. I do love roses.	

FIGURE 16.4 Portion of a Process Recording with a Client Who Has Just Entered a Nursing Home

© Cengage Learning

USING DIGITAL RECORDING

EP 2.1.1b&f

Recording your sessions with clients can be tremendously useful. For one thing, recording can supply you with general feedback about yourself. You may not like to see or hear yourself. Your voice may sound too scratchy to you, or you may not like the way you slouch your back. However, viewing or listening to recordings of yourself can furnish you with invaluable information about how your clients perceive you. It provides you with a clear picture of your own unique style of communication and interaction (Ivey, Ivey, & Zalaquett, 2010). You may decide to try to change some things. For instance, you may determine that you do not speak loudly enough for others to understand you clearly and easily. You may notice other habits for the first time, such as rolling your eyes and staring deeply into space when concentrating intensively, tapping your feet loudly and rhythmically, or drumming the table with your fingers.

Recording your sessions with clients can also be used to gain specific feedback about your interviewing and problem-solving styles. A supervisor viewing or listening to a recording can furnish you with specific suggestions for what you might have said or how you might have proceeded at any particular part of the session. In this way, you can get ideas about alternative and possibly more effective strategies.

There is a possibility that digital recording will be used in your student field placement or in your social work practice courses because of their educational value. Although they can be valuable in the real work setting, they, like process recording, are time consuming and thus expensive.

There are six steps for using recording technology (Kagle, 1996). First, you must get the client's explicit permission to conduct such recording (Ivey et al., 2010). *Never* record an interview without the client's knowledge. It violates the client's right to confidentiality and self-determination. Some agencies have established permission forms for such activities.

Although the client (and, perhaps, you) may feel uncomfortable initially during recording, this feeling will probably pass soon. People usually get involved in the ongoing discussion and forget that recording is occurring, which is especially true after the first time.

One creative way of recording the session entails having your supervisor observe you during the session from behind a one-way mirror. This is possible only if the equipment and setting are readily available. As your supervisor observes, he or she may record comments into a digital recorder. Later on, you can review both recordings together, getting your supervisor's feedback as you are actually watching yourself proceed with the interview. The supervisor need not be present.

The second step in the recording process is actually doing the recording. The third step involves writing out what transpired during the recording word by word. This task resembles a process recording, although you may or may not include your subjective impressions and concerns. Because this process is so time consuming, this step is optional.

The fourth step involves writing a summary of the recorded session, which may be unstructured in that you summarize what happened during the entire session. You might organize an unstructured summary according to the most important things that happened chronologically, or you might structure the report by prioritizing what occurred in the interview in order of importance. Either approach involves determining what was most significant in the interview and what amounted to unnecessary detail. Summarizing is one of the most difficult tasks to learn about recording. Accurate discrimination between what is important and what is not generally improves with experience. The more you think about your interviews and make decisions, the easier this task is the next time.

Your summary report may also follow a more structured format. In other words, it may respond to a series of questions, directions, or both. For instance, one format directs you to respond to or answer the following:

1. Briefly summarize chronologically the most significant critical points that occurred during the interview.
2. What specific problems, needs, and strengths surfaced during your meeting?
3. What specific methods did you use during the interview? For each method, describe the extent to which you felt it was effective or not effective.
4. Where during the interview do you feel you could have used more effective techniques? Describe your recommended techniques.
5. What are your recommendations for your next meeting with the client?

The fifth step in the recording process involves reviewing your recording, the summary, and, perhaps, the verbatim record with your supervisor. Your supervisor can give you feedback regarding both your intervention approaches and your report writing.

The sixth step involves adapting what you have learned during this discussion and writing a report that complies with the conventional format your agency uses.

Critical Thinking Questions 16.2

- Have you ever had the opportunity to view a digital recording of yourself engaging in a role play or other activity? If so, what did you notice about your appearance, including your verbal and nonverbal behavior?
- In what ways were your communication skills effective and why?
- In what ways could your communication skills, including your verbal and nonverbal behavior, have been improved and why?

PROGRESS NOTES

Progress notes or *case notes* are commonly used during the planned change process to summarize what occurs during service provision, describe case progress, and articulate future plans and goals (Sheafor & Horejsi, 2012; Sidell, 2011; Sormanti, 2012). They are used for many purposes, including documenting new information affecting service provision; making changes in treatment planning or direction; formulating termination plans; evaluating the effectiveness of treatment approaches; maintaining accountability; documenting that the worker is adhering to prescribed treatment procedures; providing data necessary for supervision or consultation; and furnishing required information to administration for decision-making purposes (Kagle, 1991, 1996; Kagle & Kopels, 2008; Sidell, 2011). Thus, in addition to case progress and goals, progress notes may include a wide range of information including dates of meetings, names of people involved, significant facts clients provide, information given to clients about agency policy, and changes in clients' life circumstances. As do other types of agency records, progress notes may have very different formats depending upon the agency and the services provided. Subsequent sections of this chapter will describe some formats that are more formally structured and others that assume a more narrative approach.

Progress notes can vary in length depending on their purpose. When a client reports numerous specific facts or important details, the progress note may be quite lengthy. For example, the client might be "supplying specific factual data that will be difficult to remember accurately without a reminder" such as "names of family members, addresses, dates of birth, exact amounts of income," and other detailed information (Wilson, 1980, p. 7). Longer notes might also be necessary to explain a situation with legal ramifications. For instance, a client might report extensive details involved in child sexual abuse or a drug deal. In such cases, accuracy and thoroughness are critical.

Other progress notes may be brief, depending on their purpose. The note might simply indicate the date a client was seen and the major purpose of the interview. Nothing significant or new might have occurred; for example, "9/17/15—Mr. Simpson discussed job search plans."

Progress notes may include full, grammatically correct sentences or short phrases, once again depending on their intent and the format used. An example involving a note with short phrases is "1/25/15—Client angry. No progress made."

Sidell (2011) proposes some basic tactics to keep in mind regardless of what progress note format is used:

- The meeting date including year should always be placed at the beginning of the note.
- The worker's name should always be legibly cited. Note that some agencies allow the worker's initials. The important thing is that the recorder responsible for writing the note is clearly identified.
- Use "specific dates and times" rather than general terms (p. 111). For example, a worker might state that the client will achieve a specific goal by "January 30" rather than "within a month."
- Being as concise as possible is essential. The reader shouldn't have to wade through a lot of words to figure out what the main points are. The most significant aspects of the case and case progress should be clearly evident.
- Avoid repetition of what has already been said unless something has changed.
- Wording should be objective and situations described specifically and behaviorally. For example, a worker might state that the client's "clothing look disheveled and dirty with splatters of mud on the shirt and pants" instead of the client "looked like a slob."

We've noted that progress notes can assume a wide range of formats. Figure 16.5 provides an example of a basic, relatively brief progress note format. Workers record the date of contact. They then refer to a specific problem among a potential list of problems that had been addressed with the client. (During intake, problems

Client Name: _____   Case ID/MA #: _____

Date Mo/Day/Yr	Problem Number	Progress Note	Initials

FIGURE 16.5 An Example of a Progress Note Format
Source: Adapted from form HSD-004 (3/89) entitled "Waukesha County Community Services Department Progress Notes." Used with permission of the Community Human Services Department, Waukesha County, 500 Riverview Ave., Waukesha, WI 53188.

are sometimes listed and assigned numbers. This is to facilitate the note-taking process, as it's faster to refer to a number than to write out the entire problem once again.) Workers then briefly note what progress has been made, what changes have occurred, or other significant information. Finally, workers initial the note so that it is clear who had the contact with the client and entered the observation.

Another section of this chapter describes one other formally structured format for progress notes, which is broken down into four parts: subjective information (S), objective information (O), assessments (A), and plans (P) (SOAP). SOAP is described within the context of problem-oriented recording.

TAKING NOTES DURING THE INTERVIEW

Recording notes about what has occurred during an interview is very important so that progress can be made over time and redundancy avoided. Kagle and Kopels (2008) explain:

Key words and phrases are often sufficient to help the worker remember essential information. The habit of brief note-taking can be effective in helping the practitioner prepare accurate and specific records, especially when record-keeping takes place more than a day or two after the service encounter. Experienced workers find that note-taking helps them retain complex observations and re-create in detail the sequence of events in complicated cases. Students and new workers find that notes form the foundation for building skills in observation and assessment as well as recordkeeping. In general, note-taking strengthens the content of the record and aids in the recording process. (p. 177)

Ivey and his colleagues (2010) discuss whether or not to take notes during the interview with a client:

A frequently asked question is whether one should take notes during an interview. As might be expected, the answer is dependent on you, the client, and the situation. If you personally are relaxed about note taking, it will seldom become an issue in the interview. If you are worried about taking notes, it likely will be a problem. When working with a new client, obtain permission early in the session. We find it useful to say something like the following, according to your own natural style:

"I'd like to take a few notes while you talk. Would that be OK? It often helps us refer back to important thoughts. I also like to write down your exact words for the important points. . . ."

Clearly, detailed note taking where the writing takes precedence over listening is to be avoided. Beyond that one major warning, you and your client can usually work out an arrangement suitable for both of you. . . .

There is nothing wrong with not taking notes in the session, but it is essential to have a comprehensive and accurate summary afterward. Most [workers] . . . probably write their notes after the session, but in doing so they may miss key items, as no one's recall is perfect. In-session note taking is often most helpful in the initial portions of interviewing and counseling and will become less important as you get to know the client better. (pp. 224–225)

Critical Thinking Questions 16.3

- What is your opinion of taking notes during interviews with clients?
- What are the pros and cons of taking such notes?

NARRATIVE RECORDING

Narrative recordings are reports that summarize the main issues addressed, plans developed, and results achieved with a client during the intervention process; they are written in a narrative format, that is, including written paragraphs using correct grammar to describe the case's progress (Kagle & Kopels, 2008; Sidell, 2011). Although they are time consuming, an advantage is that narrative recordings are flexible and a worker can choose the type and amount of detail to provide about a case. Often, their content is divided under several headings, such as "Referral," "Background," and "Service Information" (Kagle, 1991, 1996, p. 96). Data may include the "nature of the client-need-situation," the "purpose of service," "decisions and actions affecting services," the "process of service," and the "impact of services on the client-need-situation" (Kagle & Kopels, 2008, p. 125).

The following is an example of a partial narrative report by a hospital social worker that involves Joey, age 3, whose father took him to the emergency room because of burns allegedly from a bath that was too hot (Kagle & Kopels, 2008). Upon admission, staff noted that Joey also had numerous bruises on various places on his body. Joey had five siblings also living with both parents. The following reflects the "Service Information" section:

The physician filed an abuse report on 9/24/15 stating that Joey's burns were from scalding bath water and that the bruises indicate Joey's attempts to resist and pull himself from the tub. Dr. P and I immediately informed the parents of the abuse report; she explained that all suspicious injuries must be reported. The Smiths threatened to remove Joey from the hospital but were persuaded that he should stay. I asked them to bring their other five children to the hospital for checkups the following day (9/25). All were evaluated and, although some of the children had health problems that needed treatment, none showed signs of abuse.

We have coordinated services with the Child Welfare Department, which investigated and found evidence of abuse. Although the Smiths have been encouraged to visit Joey daily, they have visited only briefly once or twice a week during Joey's two-week hospitalization. Upon discharge, Joey will return home, under department supervision. On 10/21 he is to be evaluated for the Early Childhood Education Program. (p. 130)

Summary Narrative Recordings

Narrative recordings can also be used to summarize progress over a period of time. Such summaries may reflect the culmination of progress notes recorded over weeks or even months. Notes may be organized chronologically and kept in one place, such as an electronic file or loose-leaf notebook.

Focusing on Strengths

It is important to emphasize strengths whenever possible with any type of record, including narrative recording. Consider the case of Doug, age 38, who had suffered from a seizure disorder for 20 years after a head injury (Weick & Chamberlain, 2002). He indicated to his case manager that he was extremely depressed because he could not work. Other problems included limited education, not being able to drive because of the seizure disorder, and an extensive record of substance abuse. Instead of avoiding the job issue, focusing on Doug's depression, and urging him to lower his expectations, the case manager listened to what Doug said was important to him, namely, finding a job, and proceeded to help him do it. The following reflects a strengths-based narrative summary recording concerning Doug's long-term progress:

[I] was able to locate a grocery store near his boarding home that was willing to hire people with disabilities. However, because of his seizures, Doug was unable to climb ladders, making it impossible to

stock shelves or handle cutters to open cartons. Because of his brain damage, he was unable to operate a cash register. The only reasonable safe job was janitorial work and even that required that he wear a helmet while cleaning rest rooms because of the danger presented by the possibility of falling against porcelain.

Doug was thrilled to have a job. His mood rapidly improved, and over time, his seizures became less frequent. Doug became a valued employee, and, after three years of demonstrating reliability and competence, he began training as a butcher. Through his stable income, he was able to buy a modest house. When asked to characterize these changes in his situation, Doug summed up his success by saying, "life is good." (pp. 98–99)

SUMMARIES OF TREATMENT CONFERENCES

A special type of summary recording involves *treatment conferences,* also called *case conferences.* A treatment conference is a meeting where various professionals, often from diverse disciplines, come together to discuss clients' problems, progress, and plans (Bogg, 2012; Toseland & Rivas, 2012). Participants may include the client's social worker, the social work supervisor, other professionals working directly with the client (e.g., medical staff, occupational therapists, psychologists), experts who can provide useful information and recommendations for treatment, and the client's relatives or significant others who might furnish relevant information about progress and potential resources.

Thus, a treatment conference may involve a meeting of social workers, professionals in other disciplines, clients, and others involved with clients. As a social worker, you are likely to assume the role of conference leader. You may be the case manager, which involves coordinating virtually all of the services provided to one or more clients. Chapter 15 discussed the case management role in depth. Sometimes, depending on the agency, treatment conferences are also referred to as *staffings, multidisciplinary team conferences,* or *interdisciplinary team meetings.*

A treatment conference may have four purposes (Halley et al., 1998). First, it helps to assess and clearly describe the client's problem. Second, it enhances the involved professional's grasp of the client's behavior and situation. Third, it provides an arena in which intervention plans may be formulated and ongoing goals reevaluated. Fourth, it affords a medium for coordinating resources and services. Treatment conference summaries can provide an effective means to prepare for action with individuals and families.

Your own presentation at a treatment conference should involve the following:

1. *A statement of the [client's] . . . problem;*
2. *Your observations of the [client] . . . ;*
3. *How you have been working with the [client] . . . the service plan to date;*
4. *A summary of the results of any [intervention] . . . used or service delivered;*
5. *The reasons this particular information is being shared with other workers and specific questions highlighting the problem areas that other workers can help you answer. (Halley et al., 1998, p. 394)*

Such summaries may be done either orally or in writing. Frequently, agencies require that the written report be added to the client's ongoing record.

You will also likely assume responsibility for summarizing the final findings and conclusions of the entire treatment conference. Such summaries should follow a similar format to include the preceding information. The specific format of a treatment conference summary may vary somewhat from agency to agency. One important thing to remember, however, is to clearly specify plans and goals, as discussed in Chapter 6.

PROBLEM-ORIENTED RECORDING

Problem-oriented recording (POR) involves using a specified format to list problems and another related format to note progress made toward their solutions. POR has four primary components: a database, list of problems, implementation plans, and progress in implementing the plans (Kagle & Kopels, 2008; Sidell, 2011).

Database

A *database* is "a collection of information stored electronically so that it is accessible by computer and digitally searchable" (Guffey & Loewy, 2013, p. 285). "Regarding a specific client, social workers might include in a database such items as demographic characteristics, a social history, intake information, treatment plans, and progress notes. These data can be readily retrieved to track the progress of the client or merged with data from other clients to prepare a report. Database programs also can be used to schedule appointments, manage 'to do' lists, and otherwise reduce paperwork" (Sheafor & Horejsi, 2012, p. 132). Agencies can use a database to evaluate treatment programs, monitor trends in service provision, and plan for future needs.

Problem List

Problems can include any that the client is concerned about, in addition to those identified by client and worker during the assessment process. Both client and worker must agree on which problems the implementation will focus on in addition to their priority. In other words, in what order should they work on the problems? Developing this list helps workers clarify problems and set goals.

The respective problems should be numbered (Kagle & Kopels, 2008; Sheafor & Horejsi, 2012). Concisely stated problems can provide you with an easily scanned checklist that prevents you from focusing on only one problem. Additionally, when a problem is solved or no longer relevant, simply delete it from the list. An example of a format for prioritizing problems is presented in Figure 16.6. Note that the second portion of the figure also has a section for identifying strengths. Such strengths often provide the basis for determining solutions.

Consider the following problem list of a single mother who has two small children and is living on public assistance:

1. Inadequate food
2. Extremely poor living conditions
3. No job
4. No day care for the children
5. No social support system

If you help your client find employment, you can simply delete problem number three from the list. Yet, you still maintain a perspective on how problems are prioritized and how much has been accomplished.

Initial Implementation Plans

Planning in generalist practice was explored in Chapter 6. As you recall, plans can involve implementation at the micro, mezzo, or macro levels. Plans should be numbered to correspond to the respective problems they address (Kagle & Kopels, 2008) and should be updated periodically to respond to changing client problems and needs.

Progress in Plan Implementation

We have established that progress notes do just what their name implies—they reflect any new developments and progress you and your client have made with the case. A frequently used format for problem-oriented

PROBLEM AREAS OF MAJOR CONCERN

Please describe below problems or things about you or your situation that you would like to see change as a result of counseling/treatment.

For each major problem that you list, please describe one or two specific examples of the behavior or feeling about which you are most concerned, telling how often the behavior occurs (e.g., four times per day, three times per week, twice per month, or whatever).

Problem or Concern No. 1:

_____

_____

_____

Problem or Concern No. 2:

_____

_____

_____

Problem or Concern No. 3:

_____

_____

_____

Problem or Concern No. 4:

_____

_____

_____

Problem or Concern No. 5:

_____

_____

_____

_____

_____
Signature
_____
Date

Please continue to "Things I Like Most about Myself and/or My Situation."

FIGURE 16.6 An Example of a Format for Prioritizing Problems
Source: Reprinted with permission of Lutheran Social Services, 3200 W. Highland Blvd., Milwaukee, WI 53208.

THINGS I LIKE MOST ABOUT MYSELF AND/OR MY SITUATION

Positive or Strength No. 1:

_____
_____
_____

Positive or Strength No. 2:

_____
_____
_____

Positive or Strength No. 3:

_____
_____
_____

Positive or Strength No. 4:

_____
_____
_____

Positive or Strength No. 5:

_____
_____
_____

FIGURE 16.6 Continued

recording that includes progress notes is referred to as SOAP, discussed in the next section.

SOAP

SOAP is an acronym for the following components: subjective information, objective information, assessments, and plans (Burack-Weiss, 2012; Kagle & Kopels, 2008; Sheafor & Horejsi, 2012; Sidel, 2011).

Subjective Information. This aspect involves recording the client's perception of the problem and situation. It entails individual perceptions and opinions instead of established fact. For example, you might state: "Mr. G indicated that his apartment is in a shabby, rundown condition." Or you might record: "The client perceives the problem as being very severe." Subjective information might also be provided by family members or other people involved in the case.

Objective Information. This aspect includes the facts and observations you believe are relevant to record. For instance, have any tests been administered to the client? Are the results of such tests relevant to the client's problem and situation? Additionally, objective information involves your professional observations during a meeting or interview. For example, you might state after an interview with a 16-year-old male on probation: "When I asked about his mother, he scowled, opened his jacket, and showed me the handle of a gun held in an inside pocket." (At some subsequent point, you would probably add that this behavior resulted in revocation of his probation and eventually incarceration.)

In other words, any objective information involves facts. Perhaps you want to record the fact that your client made a particular statement. In that event, you state verbatim what the client said. A fact might be that you called an agency to make a referral for your client. A fact also might be that your client arrived 30 minutes late.

Assessments. Chapter 5 dealt with assessments in generalist practice. In progress notes, assessments involve your impressions about how much progress has been or not been made. What is your client's current condition or state? How has the problem situation changed or not changed?

Sometimes the distinction between subjective impressions and objective information is not perfectly clear. For example, consider a client who meets you with a blank look on her face, dilated pupils, and slurred speech. These specific observations are facts. Therefore, they are included in the objective information section. However, your impression that your client

has taken an illegal drug is a subjective judgment. In your mind, you are absolutely certain that this judgment is correct, but your perception may or may not be fact. Perhaps your client is having a reaction to having taken some prescribed medication for an illness such as diabetes. On the other hand, the fact may be that she did just shoot up some heroin.

The important point here is to remain aware of the distinction between subjective and objective information. Sometimes, you will make mistakes, as everyone does. You can only try to do your best.

Plans. Chapter 6 addressed planning in generalist practice. In progress notes, a plan needs to be concise and accurate. What is your next step? What have you and your client committed yourselves to doing? Recording plans is an ongoing process. As situations change and problems are solved, plans change.

Figure 16.7 presents an example of a format for SOAP progress notes. Highlight 16.1 provides a case example of problem-oriented recording using a SOAP progress note format.

Advantages of Problem-Oriented Recording

There are a number of advantages of problem-oriented recording (Sheafor & Horejsi, 2006). First, it allows others involved with the case to understand how the worker approached the client's problems. Second, although problem-oriented recording depicts how a number of problems are interrelated, it still allows the worker to focus on one problem at a time. Third, it allows for good communication among team members because problems are clearly specified. Fourth, even when one worker leaves the agency, problem-oriented recording allows continuity of service because of clearly specified plans. Fifth, it provides a useful tool for follow-up. The client's problem status and progress are clearly specified at any point in time, including termination. Sixth, it promotes clear, concise records because of its structured format and brevity.

Disadvantages of Problem-Oriented Recording

A major disadvantage of the traditional problem-oriented record is that there is no specified place to identify and focus upon strengths. As Chapters 5 and 6 discuss, strengths can provide invaluable keys to solving problems. Plans utilizing existing strengths increase the potential for success.

A second disadvantage to the problem-oriented record involves its focus on problems without explicit identification of needs. Simply expanding the problem portion to include needs will remedy this.

Case Progress Notes

Entry No. _____ BGC No. _____ Interview Date: _____ Length of Contact: _____

Counselor: _____ People Involved: _____

S: _____

O: _____

A: _____

P: _____

Entry No. _____ BGC No. _____ Interview Date: _____ Length of Contact: _____

Counselor: _____ People Involved: _____

S: _____

O: _____

A: _____

P: _____

Entry No. _____ BGC No. _____ Interview Date: _____ Length of Contact: _____

Counselor: _____ People Involved: _____

S: _____

O: _____

A: _____

P: _____

© Cengage Learning

FIGURE 16.7 An Example of a Format for SOAP Progress Notes
Source: Reprinted with permission of Lutheran Social Services, 3200 Highland Blvd., Milwaukee, WI 53208.

HIGHLIGHT 16.1

An Amended Case Example of Problem-Oriented Recording: A Focus on Strengths

The following is an example of problem-oriented recording. The client is an adult with an intellectual (or cognitive) disability who was referred to a multiservice agency for evaluation, vocational training, social activities, job placement services, in-home supervision, and group home placement.

This example is amended somewhat to help overcome the disadvantages mentioned earlier. Specifically, the problem list has been expanded to include both problems and needs. Second, an additional section has been added that lists strengths. Third, a macro orientation has been applied in the last progress note.

Client: Freddie Weaver
Date of Birth: January 13, 1989

1. Database

Freddie was referred by County Social Services on 6/27/15 for a multiple-level evaluation and subsequent placement in job and living arrangements. He had been living with his much older mother, who died on 6/15/15. Freddie's brother and his brother's wife have been in regular contact with Social Services and express serious concern over his well-being and future placement. Freddie is residing with them until further plans can be made.

Freddie graduated from high school, having taken primarily special education courses. He reports difficulty with math and spelling. Achievement grade levels are: reading, 3.4; math, 3.8; and spelling, 3.0. He was employed at a local cheese factory from the time of his high school graduation until 2 years ago when he was laid off.

His daily activities have included caring for his mother who was bed-bound, shopping for groceries, and watching television. He reports having no friends.

Freddie's sister-in-law has been regularly involved in Freddie's and his mother's care. Living 40 miles away, she has made weekly visits to help with paying bills, cleaning, washing, and other household tasks. She has indicated that he will not be able to continue living with her and her husband because of the brothers' inability to get along.

Freddie appears to be a pleasant individual with a good sense of humor. He speaks slowly and is difficult to understand. He stated that he would like to find both a job and a place to live independently. He indicated that he did not want to continue living with his brother.

2. List of Problems and Needs

Problem	Date Becomes Active:	Inactive/ Resolved:
1. Needs evaluation of intellectual, social, and vocational capacities	7/5/15	
2. Needs permanent place to live	7/5/15	
3. Needs employment	7/5/15	
4. Lack of social support system	7/5/15	
5. Poor relationship with brother	7/5/15	7/10/15

3. Strengths

1. Willingness to cooperate
2. Prior job experience
3. Supportive sister-in-law
4. Pleasant personality
5. Daily living skills developed while caring for his mother

4. Initial Intervention Plans

No. 1: Needs evaluation of intellectual, social, and vocational capacities

- I will refer Freddie to Evaluation Unit by 7/9/15

No. 2: Needs permanent place to live

- Wait until receive evaluation results and discuss alternatives with family.

No. 5: Poor relationship with brother

- I will meet with Freddie, his brother, and his sister-in-law within 2 weeks to discuss living alternatives.

5. Progress Notes

7/3/15
No. 1: Needs evaluation

S: Freddie appeared nervous. He states he's anxious to get the testing over with.
O: Accompanied Freddie to Evaluation Unit. Will receive results by 7/9/12.
P: Will discuss evaluation results with Freddie and family as soon as possible.—B.A.

(continued)

7/10/15

No. 1: Needs evaluation

S: F.'s very close to his sister-in-law. Relationship with brother not as negative as first appeared.

O: Met with F., brother, and wife to discuss eval. results.

No. 2: Needs permanent place to live

S: F. seems anxious to move out of brother's home.

O: Test results indicate high level of adaptive functioning in all three areas tested.

A: F. capable of living alone in apartment with some staff supervision.

P: Within 2 days I will consult with Living Arrangements supervisor to explore alternative locations.

No. 4: Lack of social support system

S: F. seems personable and lonely.

O: Activities for socialization here appropriate for F. include baseball team, dance group, and bingo.

A: Good potential to fulfill F.'s social needs here.

P: I will discuss available activities with F. during our next meeting on Thurs, and encourage him to attend. If necessary, I'll accompany him the first time.

No. 5: Poor relationship with brother

A: Relationship may improve when F. moves out. They communicate to some extent.

P: Inactive unless further problems.—B.A.

7/14/15

No. 2: Needs permanent place to live

S: F. eager to move out.

O: There is no reasonable housing available within close proximity to the agency.

A: Housing needs to be made available. Other clients have similar needs.

P: I will consult supervisor tomorrow to explore ways of locating or developing housing resources.—B.A.

Some Comments About This Particular Record

As we have already indicated, a section on client and situation strengths has been added. Strengths provide clues for how to proceed with planning. For example, a willingness to cooperate implies that plans can be made and acted upon relatively quickly with minimal resistance. This willingness to cooperate, in addition to Freddie's pleasant personality, implies that his social needs have a good chance of being met by the agency. Uncooperative or hostile clients would not readily fit into established social groups.

You might note that the problems and strengths are numbered. This is done arbitrarily to minimize confusion. Additionally, because strengths are difficult to measure and prioritize, they may be listed in any order. For instance, it would be difficult to prioritize whether Freddie's willingness to cooperate or his supportive sister-in-law would ultimately be the most valuable to him. The important thing is that a list of strengths is readily available to you to draw from creatively in your planning.

Also consider that the exact formats for problem-oriented recording and subjective information, objective information, assessments, and plans (SOAP) structure differ from agency to agency. For example, the date of the progress note entry may be placed on either the right or the left side of the page. Some agencies have an entirely separate page to list problems, which allows enough room to continue adding and omitting problems in one spot without interfering with the ongoing flow of progress notes. It also allows you to locate and read the problem list quickly.

Including dates both in the active and inactive portions of your problem list and for each of your progress notes is important. Otherwise, with a busy workload, losing your perception of how much time has passed is very easy. You might wonder, for instance, whether 2 weeks or 5 weeks have passed since you last contacted that particular client.

Additionally, we suggest that you record the year along with the month and day. This addition is especially important for follow-up and for re-referrals. Years later, figuring out when an intervention occurred is difficult or impossible if the date is not clearly specified.

You might also note that abbreviations are sometimes used in this problem-oriented recording. For example, "F." replaces "Freddie" as the report continues. In real situations, workers will frequently use abbreviations to make their work easier and less time-consuming.

Problem No. 1 is another example of using abbreviation. After being used several times, it is abbreviated from "Needs evaluation of intellectual, social, and vocational capacities" to "Needs evaluation" because the types of evaluation needed were already firmly established within the report. The time it took to write out the additional words was no longer needed. The important thing is that a person reading the report for the first time can understand clearly what is being said.

This particular record used the word "I" frequently, which clearly indicates those tasks for which the worker had responsibility. Sometimes, progress notes will omit the "I." For instance, instead of writing, "I will call F.'s sister-in-law tomorrow," the record might state, "Will call F.'s sister-in-law tomorrow." Once again, this is done on behalf of brevity.

As the worker, you must be extremely clear who wrote the note, which may be done using a variety of formats. The one illustrated in this highlight has the worker's initials "B.A." noted after each progress note entry for a specified date. Different agencies require different notations. For example, another one might require the worker to sign her first initial and full last name (e.g., B. Aardvark) right after the date at the beginning of the progress note.

Not all of the problems are addressed in the Initial Intervention Plans section because the worker plans to address them later. The worker has determined that Freddie's employment status and social support system can only be addressed after his other evaluations are completed. Thereafter, more information will be available to help with developing alternatives and making decisions.

Nor are *all* the problems necessarily addressed under any particular daily entry in the progress notes.

Only include the ones upon which some action has been taken. For example, Problems 1, 2, 4, and 5 are recognized on 7/1/15. The worker did not address Problem No. 3, "Needs employment," because No. 3 was placed on the back burner to look at in the future. Other aspects of Freddie's situation needed to be settled before he could adjust properly to a job.

Only *portions* of the SOAP structure might be included under any particular problem in the progress notes. For example, no "A" is included in the 7/3/15 progress note entry because the worker decided that an adequate *assessment* could not be made until tests were completed and results examined.

One of the problems, No. 5, "Poor relationship with brother," was noted as going from an active status to inactive on 7/10/15; the worker determined that the brothers' relationship problem would subside when they no longer had to live together on a daily basis.

Finally, consider that at times progress made involves more than one problem. For example, the worker sat down and talked with Freddie and his family to discuss both his evaluation results and his living situation. Instead of writing a similar SOAP under both progress notes, the worker can decide which problem was more significant and note SOAP only once. Writing essentially the same thing twice is a waste of time.

A third disadvantage is the traditional orientation to micro and, to some extent, mezzo practice, thus ignoring macro practice. This disadvantage can be overcome, however, by making certain that macro aspects of the client situation are examined and, where viable, integrated into the intervention plan.

RECORDING PROGRESS IN GROUPS

You might find yourself in the position of running groups and having to record plans and progress. There are many reasons for recording in mezzo practice. They include:

- initially assessing a group's functioning, including members' needs, interpersonal dynamics, and communication;
- evaluating the effectiveness of specific intervention approaches;
- assessing the progress of individual members and the entire group toward achieving goals;
- rendering accountability to funding sources concerning a group's usefulness and effectiveness;

- providing feedback to group leaders so that they might improve their skills; and
- providing a means for group members to express satisfaction or dissatisfaction with the group and its process. (Toseland & Rivas, 2012)

Addressing the many facets of recording in mezzo practice is beyond the scope of this book. Thus, our discussion will be limited to two suggestions where recording might be helpful.

First, a group leader should monitor a group to determine if its goals are being met (Hepworth, Rooney, Rooney, & Strom-Gottfried, 2013; Toseland & Rivas, 2012). Depending on the type of group, the leader must initially determine what sort of information is needed and subsequently how to collect it. Consider the example of a treatment group aimed at developing communication, interpersonal, and social skills for individual members. Just as records should be kept for recording the "functional and dysfunctional responses" of individual group members, so should a similar type of system be used for recording the "patterns" of "functional and dysfunctional" behavior evident in the group as a whole (Hepworth et al., 2013, pp. 311, 313). This system can be created by developing a form where you focus on such issues as the formation of subgroups and affiliations, who holds power within the group, how the group proceeds to make decisions, what norms develop within the group, and how the group progresses toward achieving group goals. Figure 16.8 provides an example of a form developed to monitor such group processes.

A second suggestion for recording in groups involves using *sociograms*, which are diagrams reflecting how people relate to each other in a group at a particular point in time. A sociogram illustrates group dynamics by using figures such as circles to represent individuals and lines between these figures to represent various forms of interaction. Chapter 5 explains sociograms more thoroughly.

WRITING LETTERS

EP 2.1.1d
EP 2.1.3c

There are many reasons for writing letters within an agency setting. "A quick e-mail cannot convey the same level of formality and seriousness that can be conveyed by a letter printed on [agency]... letterhead" (Cram, 2007, p. 148; Guffey & Loewy, 2013). For example, you may need to communicate something in writing to a specific client or to write a legislator to advocate that an unmet community need be addressed.

There are at least 12 points to remember when writing letters (Clark & Clark, 2007; Cram, 2007; Guffey & Seefer, 2014; Sheafor & Horejsi, 2012):

1. Think carefully about and plan what you want to say in a letter, even if the letter is brief. People's impressions of you as a professional are formed when they read what you write.
2. Reread letters to modify them and make improvements. Always proofread a letter before sending it out.
3. Create model letters or portions of letters (e.g., introductions or closings) that concern issues frequently addressed in your work setting. Use them to start out when writing new letters.
4. You should format a professional letter to include at least the following elements (see Figure 16.9 for an example of a letter):

   - *Letterhead...*
   - *Dateline...*
   - *Inside address...*
   - *Salutation [a letter greeting such as "Dear Ms.:" Or "Dear Mr.:" followed by a colon]...*

   - *Body...*
   - *Complimentary close [e.g., "Sincerely," or "Best wishes"]...*
   - *Signature block [space for your signature beneath the complimentary close with your printed name and title below that]*
   - *Your department should also be included underneath your title as part of the signature block if the department is not clearly specified in the letterhead. (Guffey & Seefer, 2014, pp. 406–409)*

Other aspects of structuring a letter's format concern including enclosures or attachments and sending copies to others. When you send an enclosure with a letter or a memo (the latter is discussed in the next section), indicate so at the bottom of the page beginning at the left-hand margin. One enclosure may be cited as "Enclosure" or "Attachment" that may be abbreviated to "Enc." or "Att.," respectively (Guffey & Seefer, 2014, p. 410). If there is more than one enclosure, "Enc:" or "Att:" should be followed by a colon and the number of enclosures. You may also cite the name of the enclosure or enclosures following the colon. See Figure 16.9 for an illustration of an enclosure citation in the second-to-last line on the page.

When you are sending a copy of the letter (or memo) to other than the designated recipient, you can also indicate this at the bottom far left of the letter (below any enclosures or attachments followed by one blank line for separation). Copies may be indicated by "c:" (for "copy") or "cc:" (for "courtesy copy") (Guffey & Seefer, 2014, p. 410) followed by the names of the individuals receiving copies (Newman & Ober, 2013, p. 506). You might just cite the name of the person receiving a copy or also include his or her title and possibly full address. Figure 16.9 provides an example of a copy citation at the bottom of the letter.

You can also send *blind* copies to designated individuals, which means sending copies of the letter to people other than the identified recipient without indicating on the letter that you are doing so (Clark & Clark, 2007). However, you should send blind copies only for some clearly identified reason or purpose.

5. At times you will need to write letters in which you are complaining, criticizing, making objections, challenging, or insisting. Be assertive when writing your letter by striking an appropriate balance between being overly pushy or aggressive and

GROUP PROCESS NOTES

Title of Group: ——————————————————————————

Type of Group: ——————————————————————————

Name of Group Leader: ————————————————————

Date of Group Meeting: ————————————————————

Group Members in Attendance:

Group Members Absent:

Group Purpose:

Designated Goals for This Meeting:

Group Process:

     Subgroups:

     Power Issues:

     Decision Making::

     Group Norms:

Commentary on Progress toward Achieving Group Goals:

Recommendations for the Future:

FIGURE 16.8 An Example of a Recording Form for a Group Process

Source: This form is loosely adapted from an example provided by R. W. Toseland and R. F. Rivas (2012), *An Introduction to Group Work Practice* (7th ed.), Boston, MA: Allyn & Bacon, p. 601.

Marengo County Department of Human Services
1800 North Fireside Drive
Northeast Overshoe, Vermont 09123
512 745-9000

November 18, 2015

Juniper Holt, M.S.W.
Southeast Vermont Office on Aging
791 Park Street West
Majestic Prince, VT 09124

Dear Ms. Holt:

Enclosed are two copies of the final report for our Rural Aging Outreach Program. As you know, the success of the program has been most gratifying. The program served nearly twice as many citizens as originally planned and still came in under budget. We appreciate greatly your willingness to extend the program funding for an additional year until Marengo County can absorb the program into its ongoing service system. At a recent conference, I spoke about the program to colleagues from across the country. The interest in developing similar initiatives in other rural communities was significant. I believe this project could easily become a model for other counties and states interested in meeting the needs of older adults living outside metropolitan areas.

Thank you again for your support. If you have any questions about the accompanying report, please give me a call.

Sincerely,

Rudi Marshaum

Rudensa Marshaum, B.S.W.
Social Worker II
Older Adult Services Division

Enc.

cc: John Dillinger, Assistant Director

© Cengage Learning

FIGURE 16.9 An Example of a Letter

ineffectively timid and apologetic. Make your points, keeping both your and the other person's rights and feelings in mind. Chapter 13 explores in much greater depth how to become appropriately assertive. Guffey and Loewy (2013) make the following additional suggestions:

- *Begin with a compliment, point of agreement, statement of the problem, or brief review of action you have taken to resolve the problem....*
- *Prove that your claim is valid; explain why the receiver is responsible.*
- *Enclose document copies supporting your claim [if available or appropriate].*
- *Appeal to the receiver's fairness, [and] ethical and legal responsibilities.*
- *Describe your feelings and disappointment.*
- *Avoid sounding angry, emotional, or irrational.*
- *Close by telling exactly what you want done.* (p. 217)

6. Think of the person you are writing to as a real person. Communicate straightforwardly, yet do not appear cold, aloof, and totally unemotional. The person you are contacting is not a machine.

 Think about how you would speak to the individual if you were interacting face to face. If appropriate, you might thank the individual for already having done something for you. At the very least, you might say something like: "Thank you for your time and consideration." You might comment that you look forward to hearing from the person soon. The point is to display a consideration for the other person's feelings (Guffey & Loewy, 2013).

7. On the other hand, do not be overly friendly, especially when writing formal letters to people in prominent, influential positions. Some degree of politeness and formality conveys to them your respect.

8. Be cautious about using the word "I" too often. It may be appropriate two or three times in one letter. However, be sensitive to how it has the potential to convey the impression that you are an egotistical person.

9. Address people by using appropriate titles. For instance, "Mr.," "Ms.," or "Dr." (if you know the latter is the case) is respectful.

10. Be conscious of who might read the letter after it is sent. For instance, do not include private information about a client that another family member might read.

11. When writing to clients, use words that they can clearly understand. Be sensitive to their level of education and potential comprehension. Do not use long, technical, theoretically impressive words for clients who have little formal education. On the other hand, do not be condescending.

12. *Never* send out a letter without keeping a copy. This copy provides an ongoing record of communication and progress for a client or an agency. Otherwise, remembering what transpired and when is too difficult.

Besides including the various parts (discussed in point 4), structuring the overall letter's format is another concern. Two commonly used approaches to formatting letters include full block and modified block styles (Guffey & Seefer, 2014; Newman & Ober, 2013). In the *full block* format, "the easiest to use", "[y]ou start every line at the left margin and do not need to worry about setting tabs or indenting paragraphs. With the *modified block* format, you indent the first line of every paragraph" one tab; additionally, "you indent the date and the closing so they start from the center point of the page" (Cram, 2007, p. 160) (emphasis added). Some use the modified block format by indenting the date and the closing from the center of the page, but not indenting the first line of each paragraph, which remain starting at the left margin (Clark & Clark, 2007). "Which letter format you use depends on your own preferences and those of the organization where you work" (Cram, 2007, p. 160).

Figure 16.9 provides an example of a letter using a full block format with items aligned evenly at the left-hand margin. The information at the top beginning with "Marengo County..." is the letterhead. In your professional role, you will most likely be using paper printed with your agency's letterhead, that is, agency name, address, and phone number. Note that many times the letterhead will not reflect your individualized agency unit. Therefore, this letter states that Rudensa is part of the "Older Adult Services Division" cited after his professional title "Social Worker II" at the bottom of the letter. This information is included so that any material sent to Rudensa would get to him as quickly as possible.

The letter illustrated in Figure 16.9 states facts in a relatively concise, organized, and clear manner (Berger, 1993). Likewise, statements are phrased positively and in an active rather than passive voice (Berger, 1993).

E-MAILS AND MEMOS

When working in an agency you must choose the most effective type of communication to use in any particular situation. Two types of written communication are e-mails and memos. *E-mail* (electronic mail) is an electronic mailbox to which messages can be sent via phone, computer, and Internet connection on an immediate basis. A *memo* (memorandum) is "a written message sent [via hard copy] to someone within (or internal to) an organization" (Newman & Ober, 2013, p. 533). Guffey and Loewy (2013) suggest that you use e-mail "when you need feedback but not immediately. [Consider that] [l]ack of security makes it problematic for personal, emotional, or private messages" (p. 40). They continue that you should use a memo "when you want a written record to clearly explain policies, discuss procedures, or collect information within an organization" (p. 40). Guffey and Loewy (2013) reflect about using e-mails or memos:

> *E-mail is appropriate for short, informal messages that request information and respond to inquiries. It is especially effective for messages to multiple receivers and messages that must be archived (saved). An e-mail is also appropriate as a cover document when sending longer attachments.*
>
> *E-mail, however, is not a substitute for face-to-face conversations, telephone calls, or letters. Face-to-face conversations or telephone calls are better channel choices if your goal is to convey enthusiasm or warmth, explain a complex situation, present a persuasive argument, or smooth over disagreements....*
>
> *Although e-mail is more often used today, memos are still useful for important internal messages that require a permanent record or formality. For example, organizations use memos to deliver changes in procedures, official instructions, reports, and long internal documents. (p. 107)*

E-Mails

E-mails have eight structural elements (Guffey & Seefer, 2014, pp. 404–405). First, e-mails begin with lines labeled "*To*" (recipient's address) and "*From*" (sender's address). The next line indicates "*Cc*" ("carbon copy or courtesy copy") or "*Bcc*" ("blind carbon copy"). "Some writers use *bcc* to send a copy of the message without the addressee's knowledge. Writers also use the *bcc* line for mailing lists. When a message is sent to a number of people and their e-mail addresses should not be revealed, the *bcc* line works well to conceal the names and addresses of all receivers." The "*subject*" line then follows. You should "[i]dentify the subject of the e-mail with a brief but descriptive summary of the topic." Letters of primary words in the subject line should be capitalized.

As in a letter, the "*salutation*" is the greeting in the body of the e-mail. Often, it is less formal than that used in letters. For example, it might read something like "Hi, Grafton" or "Greetings." You might identify and adhere to your agency's expectations for how to phrase salutations (Newman & Ober, 2013). The body of the e-mail contains the "*message*." This message should be brief, concise, and concerning only one major topic. The "*closing*" may resemble that used in a letter (e.g., "Best wishes,"). "*Attachments*" may also be added to the e-mail. Such additions are usually referred to in the body of the e-mail.

Reasons for Using E-Mail. Although it is easy to zip off an e-mail message without much thought, it is important to give careful consideration to what is said in each message sent in a professional context. Guffey and Loewy (2011) suggest asking yourself the following questions before sending an e-mail:

- ***Do I really need to write this e-mail...?*** *A phone call or a quick visit to a nearby coworker might solve the problem—and save the time and expense of a written message. On the other hand, some written messages are needed to provide a permanent record or to show a well-conceived plan.*
- ***Why am I writing?*** *Know why you are writing and what you hope to achieve. This will help you recognize what the important points are and where to place them.*
- ***How will the reader react?*** *Visualize the reader and the effect your message will have. In preparing written messages, imagine that you are sitting and talking with your reader. Avoid speaking bluntly, failing to explain, or ignoring your reader's needs. Consider ways to shape the message to benefit the reader. Also remember that your message may very well be forwarded to someone else....*
- ***How can I save my reader's time?*** *Think of ways that you can make your message easier to comprehend at a glance. Use bullets, asterisks, lists, headings, and white space...to improve readability. (p. 221)*

Composing an E-Mail Message. The following are suggestions for e-mail message composition:

Make an outline of the points you wish to cover. For short messages jot down notes on the document you are answering or make a scratch list at your computer.... As you compose your message, avoid amassing huge blocks of text. No one wants to read endless lines of type. Instead, group related information into paragraphs, preferably short ones. Paragraphs separated by white space look inviting. Be sure each paragraph begins with the main point and is backed up by details. If you bury your main point in the middle of a paragraph, the reader may miss it. (Guffey & Loewy, 2011, p. 221)

How to state the subject of an e-mail is important because it "summarizes the central idea, thus providing quick identification for reading and for filing. Busy readers glance at a subject line and decide when and whether to read the message. Those without subject lines are often automatically deleted" (Guffey & Loewy, 2011, p. 191; Lehman & DuFrene, 2011; Newman & Ober, 2013).

A strong introduction is also important (Levitt & Craig, 2006). An e-mail should "reveal the main idea immediately. Even though the purpose of the memo or e-mail is summarized in the subject line, that purpose should be restated—and amplified—in the first sentence" (Guffey & Loewy, 2011, p. 191). This serves to seize the reader's attention and focus him or her on the issue being discussed. Guffey and Loewy (2011) continue:

What does it take to get your message read? For one thing, stay away from meaningless or dangerous words. A sure way to get you message deleted or ignored is to use a one-word heading such as Issue, Problem, Important, *or* Help. *Including a word such as* Free *is dangerous because it may trigger spam filters. Try to make your subject line "talk" by including a verb. Explain the purpose of the message and how it relates to the reader ... (* Staff Meeting Rescheduled for May 12 *rather than ...* Staff meeting*). (p. 191)*

"The body [of an e-mail] provides more information about the reason for writing. It explains and discusses the subject logically. Good e-mail messages and memos generally discuss only one topic. Limiting the topic helps the receiver act on the subject and file it appropriately" (Guffey & Loewy, 2013, p. 108; Lehman &

DuFrene, 2011). Additionally, make your e-mail message as short and concise as possible (Clark & Clark, 2007; Guffey & Loewy, 2013, 2014). Keep paragraphs short "to improve readability" (Newman & Ober, 2013, p. 117). You neither want to waste the reader's time nor discourage the reader from reading the entire e-mail.

The closing of an e-mail should be purposeful and generally include one of three things (Guffey & Loewy, 2011, 2013). First, it can indicate what action is needed. It might involve a deadline for getting something done or a statement about what you plan to do. Second, the closing can summarize the communication to help the reader clarify it in his or her own mind and remember it. Third, you might end an e-mail with a concluding reflection "(*I'm glad to answer your questions* or *This sounds like a useful project*).... [If you don't end with one of the other two types of conclusions mentioned earlier,] some closing thought is often necessary to prevent sounding abrupt. Closings can show gratitude or encourage feedback with remarks such as *I sincerely appreciate your help* or *What are your ideas on the proposal?* Other closings look forward to what's next, such as *How would you like to proceed?* Avoid closing with overused expressions such as *Please let me know if I may be of further assistance.* This ending sounds mechanical and insincere" (Guffey & Loewy, 2013, p. 109).

The Importance of Proofreading. Because it's so easy to zip off an e-mail immediately and speedily, it's easy to make mistakes. The importance of proofreading your e-mails can't be stressed enough (Lehman & DuFrene, 2011). Newman and Ober (2013) advise that you carefully screen your e-mails for accuracy in at least the following three areas:

- *Content Errors: First, read through your message quickly, checking for content errors. Was any material omitted unintentionally? As you revise, you may move, delete, or duplicate text. Check to be sure that you r message makes sense.*
- *Typographical Errors: Next, read through your message slowly, checking for typographical errors. Look carefully for hard-to-spot errors:*
  - *Misused words that spellcheckers won't flag—for example, "I took the date form last month's report."*
  - *Repeated or omitted words, such as articles (the, a, an).*
  - *Proper names and numbers.*
  - *Titles and headings....*

- *Formatting Errors: Visually inspect the message for appropriate format. Are all the parts included and in the correct position? Does the message look attractive? (p. 124)*

Responses to E-Mail. Levitt and Craig (2006) propose the following guidelines for responding to e-mail messages:

1. *Answer promptly. If you can't respond completely, reply indicating when you can.*
2. *Read the entire message first. Some writers bury important information.*
3. *Answer all questions completely.*
4. *Comment directly in the sender's message. Use a different font type or color to comment or respond to content or questions in the body of the sender's e-mail. This helps senders match your response to their message. (p. 82)*

Additional Suggestions for Using E-Mail: Netiquette. *Netiquette* is the term for "polite online interaction" (Guffey and Loewy, 2013, p. 113). The following are suggestions for using netiquette when sending e-mail messages:

1. "Avoid using a series of all capital letters in the body of your message. Besides hindering readability, all capital letters are considered the e-mail equivalent of shouting and may be construed as rude" (Clark & Clark, 2007, p. 334; Guffey & Loewy, 2013).
2. Be cautious about using both humor and sarcasm in e-mail (Levitt & Craig, 2006). When you are speaking face to face with another person, you can communicate much information by your nonverbal behavior and tone of voice. You can also receive significant information about how the receiver is reacting to the communication. E-mail has no nonverbal dimension. Therefore, there is a much greater chance of causing offense or experiencing a misunderstanding when using e-mail.
3. If you send an e-mail to a mailing list, be brief and to the point. Long, tedious messages may only annoy readers.
4. If you mistakenly receive an e-mail meant for someone else, inform the sender about the mistake or forward the e-mail to the intended recipient if you are aware of the address. It is impolite to read other people's e-mail without their permission.
5. Always remember that any e-mail you send to one person may be forwarded to other people. Guffey and Seefer (2014) warn:

Don't send anything you wouldn't want published. Because e-mail seems like a telephone call or a person-to-person conversation, writers sometimes send sensitive, confidential, inflammatory, or potentially embarrassing messages. Beware! E-mail creates a permanent record that often does not go away even when deleted. . . . Don't write anything that you wouldn't want your boss, your family, or a judge to read. (p. 244)

6. Never respond to an e-mail when you're angry (Guffey & Loewy, 2013, 2014; Lehman & DuFrene, 2011). Always allow some time to cool off before shooting off a response to an upsetting message. Sleeping on it may help. You are likely to be much calmer and more rational the next day. You often come up with different and better alternatives after thinking about what was said. If you allow emotion to take over when writing a response, people are likely to focus on the emotional component instead of the points you are trying to get across. It may be best to iron out intense differences in person.

Critical Thinking Questions 16.4

- How careful are you about the formatting and content of your e-mails?
- After reading the suggestions made here, are there any ways you might improve the quality and structure of your e-mails? If so, what are they?

Memos

Although formats vary somewhat, memos are usually entitled "Memorandum" at the top (Cram, 2007). In an overflowing heap of paper on a desk, this identifies what they are. Additionally, the intended recipient(s) of the memo, the name and position of its sender, the date the memo was written, and a general summary of its content are usually all included right at the beginning (Cram, 2007). The general format used is as follows (Clark & Clark, 2007; Newman & Ober, 2013):

To:
From:
Date:
Subject:

Some people use "Re:" (for "Regarding:") as an alternative for "Subject:." Figure 16.10 is an example of a memo.

MEMORANDUM

To: All Social Work Staff
From: Tom Blackwell, Supervisor
Date: Oct. 19, 2015
Subject: Recording

Recently, we received another memo from the state concerning accountability and uniformity relating to record-keeping. Through no one's fault, there is little consistency from one worker to another regarding writing regular progress notes for clients.

From now on there will be an individual progress sheet for each of your clients on your individual billing clipboards. Please make a brief entry including date and progress summary each time you see a client. We will discuss format and content further at our next group supervisory meeting.

Please feel free to see me if you have any questions. Thank you for your help and cooperation.

FIGURE 16.10 An Example of a Memo

Suggestions for Writing Memos. Suggestions for writing memos resemble many of those for writing e-mails. They include:

1. As with e-mails, plan carefully what you want to say in the memo. The rationale for sending it should be clearly articulated in your mind.
2. State the purpose of your memo right at the beginning. Readers need to orient themselves to why they are receiving the memo in the first place. Why do they need to spend valuable time reading it? What might the memo tell them to do? What information does the memo contain that is important for them to know?
3. Make the memo as short and to the point as possible. You don't want to waste the reader's time trying to wade through prolific verbosity to get to the point.
4. Memos should be sent out early enough to allow plenty of time for the recipient to respond or comply with your wishes. In other words, do not send a memo requesting a colleague to finish a 30-page report by tomorrow.
5. As with e-mails, address only one topic per memo. If more than one important item is included, topics can easily get lost. For example, where will you file a single copy of a memo that addresses the needs of two different clients? Filing copies of the memo in two different client files violates their respective confidentiality.
6. As with e-mails, avoid writing a memo when you're angry. Allow some time to cool off and think about the best, most effective way to address the issue.
7. Memos can be used for documentation purposes. A memo can clarify and document proposed plans.

For example, consider the situation where you establish several specific plans over the phone with a colleague involved with the same client case. Sending a brief memo to that colleague that clearly summarizes the plans (who will do what by when) documents the fact that the phone conversation took place and who is responsible for which tasks.

A memo can also be used to document for the record your own performance. For instance, you might want to formally notify your supervisor that you had followed through on his or her specific instructions concerning a case. You might also include the results of your intervention. This documentation provides a clear record of your work for supervisory purposes or for the evaluation of your own on-the-job performance.

8. Always proofread your memo carefully before sending it.

RECORDING IN MEETINGS

Organizing meetings and recording what occurs are other primary responsibilities of many social workers. Two types of documents you must understand are agendas and minutes.

An *agenda* is a list of topics to be addressed at a meeting in a prioritized order. Figure 16.11 provides an example of an agenda for a meeting held by a social work student club. Agendas frequently begin with a "call to order" and end with "adjournment," although not always. Sometimes, these aspects of meetings are simply assumed.

Agenda items are usually from one to a few words alerting group members to what topics will be discussed at the meeting. The agenda should be sent out in advance, noting the time and place of the meeting. The list of topics is usually brief and concise.

AGENDA
Social Work Student Club
November 24, 2015
Pitchfork Hall, Room 219
4:00 PM

1. Call to Order

2. Approval of Minutes—Meeting of November 10, 2015

3. Treasurer's Report—Willie Patterson, Treasurer

4. Executive Committee Report—Adah Hull, Chairperson

   A. Adopt-a-Highway Cleanup Project

   B. Sweatshirt Sale

5. Activities Committee Report—Florzell Hawkins, Chairperson

   A. Speakers for Upcoming Meetings

   B. Job Search Seminar

6. Old Business

7. New Business

8. Announcements

9. Adjournment

FIGURE 16.11 An Example of an Agenda

Sometimes, group leaders develop the agenda. At other times, group members are asked to contribute items. Agendas help a group stick to the topics it is supposed to address and not waste time on extraneous issues.

An agenda may suggest to members that they should bring along some materials to the meeting. For example, the item "possible speakers for upcoming meetings" indicates to members that they should bring suggestions, including names, titles, and phone numbers, to the meeting.

Usually, the most important items are listed first to make certain they are addressed if the meeting takes longer than expected. In ongoing groups, approval of the prior meeting's minutes (record of what occurred) is done first. Minutes should be distributed along with the agenda. "Old business" and "new business" are common agenda items, allowing group members to bring up old or new items about which they are concerned or have news. Announcements are usually placed either at the end or at the beginning of the agenda. If they are significant or relate to other agenda items, they should be made earlier. If announcements are not significant, they may be placed near the agenda's end. Then, if the meeting time runs short, they may always be noted in the minutes.

The agenda shown in Figure 16.11 also notes who is responsible for initiating a report. For example, Florzell Hawkins is responsible for discussing upcoming activities. Some agendas indicate who placed the item on the agenda so that members know who is responsible for initiating the topic. Members then have the opportunity of contacting that person with questions or comments before the meeting.

Clark and Clark (2007) define a meeting's minutes and describe typical contents:

Minutes *are compiled to provide a written record of announcements, reports, significant discussions, and decisions that have taken place during a meeting [emphasis added]. Although the degree of formality and extent of coverage may vary, the specific information contained in the meeting minutes usually includes the following:*

1. *Name of group and meeting*
2. *Date, place, and time meeting was called to order, time of adjournment*
3. *Names of persons present (if applicable, names of persons absent)*
4. *Approval of (or additions to) the agenda*

5. *Disposition [for example, making a motion to pass] of any previous minutes*
6. *Announcements*
7. *Summaries of reports*
8. *Motions presented and actions taken on motions*
9. *Summaries of significant discussions*
10. *Name and signature of person compiling minutes.* (p. 436)

Note that the "organization and format of formal minutes do not follow precise criteria" (Clark & Clark, 2007, p. 436). Figure 16.12 provides an example of more formal minutes that use a structured approach and reflect most of the content described previously. Note that topic headings are in boldface type to help to organize content.

Minutes should reflect "the precise wording of motions" and indicate the results of votes on motions (Guffey & Loewy, 2013, p. 261). Generally speaking, such structure helps ensure participants' right to speak and controls conflict. People proposing the motion and "seconding" the motion should be identified.

The group's secretary or a volunteer usually records minutes and should sign his or her name at the end of the minutes as indicated (Guffey & Loewy, 2013). The "complimentary closing" before the secretary's name is usually "Respectfully submitted," (Clark & Clark, 2007, p. 438).

The amount of detail included under any particular topic will vary depending on the purpose of the meeting and the minutes. Some minutes reflect only formal motions, seconds, and votes according to strict parliamentary procedure (discussed in Chapter 3). In contrast, the minutes in Figure 16.12 include more detail concerning discussion so that members might use the information to determine future meeting agendas.

Figure 16.13 provides an alternative example of a meeting's minutes that is less structured in terms of format.

OTHER TYPES OF RECORDING FORMATS

There are many other ways of recording information. Chapter 8 addresses some, including single-subject design, goal-attainment scaling, and task-achievement scaling. We have established that agencies often vary widely regarding the type of information they need and how they record that information. Recording should always be done for a clearly specified purpose and be as easy to decipher as possible.

Wisconsin Association of Social Work Educators
Biannual Conference
Heavenly Haven, Wisconsin Dells
April 1–2, 2015
Business Meeting Minutes

Present: Jack Penney, Fredric Marchingham, Carol Cuskegee, Dorothy Dandelion, Darilyn Dunroe, Won Penney, Berry Pomo, Jacyline Balance, Roberta Ding, Petra Pool, Beth Jamakowski, Susan Pielman, Andrea Rollinger, Rhett Rutler, Michael Walloman, Brittany Michelly, Lucas James, Laura Tirsk, Rebecca Lynskow, Margaret Patney, Dan Markellabor, Frank Binatra, Carol Cing, George Klumy, Barbara Bushowsko, James Butterknife, Cheryl Barrel.

Call to Order/Approval of the 10–10–14 minutes

The meeting commenced at 1:00 PM Patney/Walloman moved that the 10–10–14 minutes be approved. Motion passed.

Announcements

Members are urged to encourage students to join NASW-WI.
Anyone interested in committee membership should contact Pielman.

Treasurer's Report

Patney circulated the Treasurer's Report, which has a 4–2-15 balance of $8,290.31. James/Rollinger moved approval of the report. Motion passed.

WASWE Constitution

Tirsk circulated and explained proposed revisions of the WASWE Constitution. Members should e-mail her any suggestions they have. Voting on it should be placed on the fall 2015 agenda.

WASWE History

Penney circulated his historic summary of WASWE from 1973–2014 and identified missing information.
It was suggested that the Secretary be responsible for keeping the archives, including Penney's historical information and ongoing Executive Committee and Business Meeting minutes.

Midwest Conferences

Rutler reported on the spring 2015 conference. He met with participants from other Midwest states and discussed the historical development of Midwest conferences and future plans. Rutler will e-mail schools in the Midwest states to determine whether they have social work education organizations and, if so, whom to contact.
He indicated that future regional conferences will be held in the following states: 2016 Iowa; 2018 Illinois; 2020 Wisconsin; 2022 Indiana; 2024 Nebraska.

FIGURE 16.12 An Example of a Meeting's Formal Minutes

Discussion focused on what would happen if a state did not want to host the conference during its allotted year. It was determined that the next state in line would host the conference. Rutler stressed the importance of soliciting input about Midwest conferences from all involved states. He emphasized the importance of considering geography and travel issues when planning these meetings to encourage participation and attendance.

Fall 2015 Meeting

It was agreed that WASWE should have a fall meeting on Oct. 7–8, 2015, preferably at Heavenly Haven. (A second choice date is Oct. 14–15, 2015.)

The following are ideas presented for topics:

- Very Smart presenting her paper on the international declaration of human rights and national codes of ethics. It was suggested that packaging it so that it would fulfill the requirement for ethics. Continuing Education Hours would be helpful. Pielman will contact her.
- Student portfolios.
- Markellabor's dissertation work concerning TANF recipients.

Adjournment

Michelly/Lynskow moved adjournment. Motion passed. The meeting was adjourned at 5:15 PM.

Respectfully submitted,

Darilyn Dunroe

Darilyn Dunroe
Secretary

© Cengage Learning

FIGURE 16.12 Continued

LO 16-4 Attend to Technological Advances in Record Keeping

EP 2.1.9a

Technology will continue advancing. It's important for social workers to continuously keep abreast of new approaches and methodology. Although it is beyond the scope of this chapter to describe these skills in greater detail, it is recommended that you develop some degree of proficiency in the following areas

- *"Installing and maintaining software,"* such as *"downloading and installing software from the Internet"*
- *"Virus protection,"* including *updating antivirus programs and using them consistently*

- *"File protection,"* such as *"knowing how to set protection on your data files so others cannot view them"*
- Negotiating the *"World Wide Web,"* including *"learning the different abilities of various search engines, directories, meta-sites and databases"*
- Learning to use *"graphics and presentation software"* to enhance your ability to convey information and ideas
- Developing and using *"Web pages"* for such purposes as providing the public with information about your agency *(Smith, 2001, pp. 24–25)*

One other issue important to stress when navigating the electronic environment is the importance of client confidentiality because of the numerous new ways available to violate it. Highlight 16.2 proposes a number of

Association of Baccalaureate Social Work Program Directors

Board of Directors Meeting
September 20, 2015
New Orleans, LA

The Board of Directors met at 12 noon in the Hotel Monteleone. Those in attendance included Alvin Sallee, Anita Curry Jackson, Jack Sellars, Anita Cowan, Kay Hoffman, and Grafton Hull. Non-Board members present included Forrest Swall, Barbara Shank, and Ken Kazmerski.

A brief report was provided on the conference evaluation form, and then the discussion turned to the CSWE Strategic Plan. The consensus was that BPD should take a position on the Plan, but there was insufficient time to allow a thorough review at this Board meeting. As a consequence, no position was articulated or voted upon. The topic will be taken up by the Board at its January meeting.

Forrest Swall provided a concept statement on the social action network, which had been suggested at the previous meeting of the Board. The focus of the network would be on eliminating or reducing poverty. Questions were raised as to whether this organization would duplicate or overlap with NASW and ELAN, and it was suggested that the interests of NASW and the network may not coincide. ELAN does not operate in every state, which further underscores the need for a separate organization. Concerns remained about whether this network would further splinter the social work profession. It was suggested that an article in *Update* to be written by Carol Schulke might help clarify the intent and purpose of the network.

The consensus seemed to be in favor of supporting the network as long as it worked in conjunction with NASW whenever possible. There was hesitance expressed about whether BPD, as a nonprofit organization, could actively be involved in such an effort. Finally, Cowan moved and Hoffman seconded a motion to allocate up to $500 for activities of the network with a clear understanding that the concerns expressed by the Board would be taken into account as the network becomes more fully developed. The motion also supports the preliminary plan that was presented by Forrest Swall. Motion passed.

It was announced that Mary Cunningham will write an article for *Update* on stipends for BSW students through grants from such organizations as NIMH.

Anita Cowan, Treasurer, provided copies of our Incorporation papers. After some discussion, Anita was directed to invest $5,000 of our reserve funds in a 90-day Certificate of Deposit.

The meeting adjourned at 1:50 PM.

Respectfully submitted,

Grafton H. Hull, Jr.

Grafton H. Hull, Jr., Secretary

FIGURE 16.13 An Example of Minutes for a Meeting

LO 16-5 Strive for Confidentiality in Electronic Record Keeping

EP 2.1.2b

EP 2.1.9a

The potential for violation of confidentiality is soaring in the electronic record-keeping environment, an issue introduced in Chapter 11. Historically, social workers managed information by filing hard copies of reports about clients in some designated agency location. Although such systems had their own confidentiality issues, potential problems characterizing today's electronic record-keeping environment can also be severe. Healy and Mulholland (2012) elaborate:

> *Many social workers access information databases, such as client information databases, in their everyday practice. . . . [T]he term "information and communication technologies" (ICTs) is used to "cover all the digital methods by which information is created, stored, manipulated and shared. This includes computer hardware and peripherals of all kinds and the software and the networks they use to store, process and communicate information [Hill & Shaw, 2011, p. 21]. . . .*
>
> *A key effect of ICTs as data management tools is that social workers have much quicker and more complete access to client information than previously. In many organizations, any worker with the appropriate security clearance can gain access to large amounts of client data in the course of [his or her] . . . work. This means that a worker can have immediate access to information about prior assessment and intervention. . . .*
>
> *[However,] there are concerns about the privacy implications of ICTs. Social workers are particularly committed to the confidentiality of client information, but with the advent of networked computer systems and centralized client databases, information is no longer stored only on the individual social worker's computer or filing system (Hill and Shaw, 2011). While this practice has always characterized social work practice, especially in large bureaucracies, the advent of centralized electronic client databases has deepened the privacy problem in information management. This is because contemporary data storage systems potentially allow a great deal more information storage and also promote easier access to client information within human service organizations. For example, any organizational member with client*

> *database access rights may have the capacity to access client data on-line, regardless of his or her geographical context or relationship to the client. (pp. 28–29)*

Consider the following examples of unethical practices in a range of settings (Gelman, Pollack, & Weiner, 1999, pp. 245–246):

- County administrators illegally made public the personal records of 400 patients when seeking a private operator to take over a county hospital. Information included the patients' names, type of treatment, and costs (Morley, 1997).
- Two thousand "patient records from a pharmacy in Arizona were still on a computer purchased at an Internet auction" (Markoff, 1997).
- "A Maryland banker who served on a state health commission accessed a list of every cancer patient in his area and checked it against the names of customers at his bank. He rescinded the mortgages of his customers who had a cancer diagnosis (Breitenstein & Nagel, 1997)."
- The *New York Times* ran a special report stating that "electronic dossiers have become the common currency of computer-age sleuths, and a semi-underground information market offers . . . private telephone records, credit card bills, airline travel records, and even medical treatment histories (Bernstein, 1997, pp. A1, A20)."

In order to minimize the potential for breaches in confidentiality, consider the following practices (Rock & Congress, 1999):

1. Be aware of current legislation concerning confidentiality in addition to recent court determinations. For example, the Federal Privacy Act of 1974 provides an exemplary model for protecting personal privacy (Gelman et al., 1999). It identifies precautions for protecting personal information and safer access methods. A relevant court case is that of *Jaffe v. Redmond*, where the court ruled that "clinical social workers and their clients have the right to privileged communication" (Alexander, 1997, p. 387). However, note that this applies only to licensed clinical social workers and concerns only "federal issues," as state laws vary concerning how they treat the issue.

(continued)

One other piece of legislation about which you should be aware is the Health Information Privacy Portability and Accountability Act of 1996 (HIPAA). You probably have noticed that any time you go to a health care facility for help, the receptionist promptly gives you a form to sign allowing release of your health care information to relevant insurance providers, among others. HIPAA sets standards for protecting individuals' health care information. A primary intent "is to ensure that individuals' health information is properly protected while allowing the flow of health information needed to provide and promote high quality health care and to protect the public's health and well being" (Department of Health & Human Services [DHHS], n. d.). Care recipients "must be provided a consent form detailing how information will be used" (Boyle, Hull, Mather, Smith, & Farley, 2009, p. 53). Forms vary fairly dramatically regarding format, wording, and specific information provided and required (Repa, 2010). An example of a form might include authorization (who is to receive information about whom), length of time for the authorization, what type of health information may be released, other statements about patients' rights, and, of course, the patient's signature. Ethical questions have been raised about how HIPAA may potentially limit access of information for caregivers (such as close relatives) who must make decisions when the patient can't do so or for some reason the form has not been signed (Repa, 2010). Other ethical questions involve who might have easy or incidental access to confidential information stored electronically.

2. When possible, look to the *Code of Ethics* of the National Association of Social Workers (NASW) for guidance. Note that it specifically indicates that workers should be vigilant regarding protecting clients' "electronic records and other sensitive information" (NASW, 2008, 1.07[l]).

3. "Assess the level of confidentiality that is needed" (Rock & Congress, 1999, p. 260). For example, consider a woman who "is the victim of severe and persistent battering by her husband, who has threatened her with death repeatedly if she were to leave him or reveal the battering" (p. 258). After an especially brutal beating, she goes to a hospital emergency room and then to a shelter where she can be safe. It is of paramount

importance that confidentiality be maintained. This woman's husband should not be allowed access to information about her whereabouts, as it is a life-and-death situation.

On the other hand, consider a hospital social worker who "is planning the discharge to a nursing home a patient who has had a stroke. The social worker records the assessment, plan, and outcome into the hospital computerized medical record" (Rock & Congress, 1999, p. 259). The level of confidentiality necessary here is not nearly as great in view of the potential harm an infraction could cause. For instance, if another staff member accidentally accesses the information, potential harm to the patient would probably be negligible.

4. Find out what protections for confidentiality are offered by your agency and other agencies with which your clients are involved. Policy manuals should provide a good source of such information.

5. As the *Code of Ethics* instructs, clarify to clients the limits of confidentiality. Explain who else might have access to their personal information and under what circumstances.

6. Cooperate with staff, administrators, clients, and workers at other agencies to develop collaborative plans that maximize confidentiality. "Agency-based and private practice practitioners can build coalitions with professionals within managed care organizations to monitor and protect necessary confidentiality in a technological environment" (Rock & Congress, 1999, p. 260).

7. "Educate professionals, [care] providers, and students about confidentiality with advanced technology" (Rock & Congress, 1999, p. 260). Practitioners must be aware of and sensitive to the issues involved in order to safeguard clients' privacy to the greatest extent possible.

Three additional suggestions for maximizing confidentiality in the electronic environment include the following:

8. Carefully evaluate how a computer system is used in your agency and search for possible ways that confidentiality may be breached.

9. Monitor and control who may have access to records.

10. Establish clearly defined procedures for how data should be processed and records kept, which, of course, should be done whether records are kept on disk or in filing cabinets.

methods to minimize breaches in confidentiality when using electronic record-keeping systems.

LO 16-6 Employ Good Writing Skills in Recording

EP 2.1.1d
EP 2.1.3c

This text does not try to teach basic writing skills, even though good grammar and excellent spelling are absolute necessities. The following summarizes the importance of such skills:

> If deficits in writing ability make it impossible for the worker or student to communicate the fact that he is doing effective social work, situations will arise in which it really won't matter whether his skills are any good or not.... Thus if a worker's supervisor, professional colleagues, quality control reviewers, and others see only poor, unclear written communication as a reflection of his skills, it will be *difficult to convince them that the individual is actually a highly skilled professional. (Wilson, 1980, p. 117)*

Writing skills usually improve with practice. In other words, you tend to become more accustomed to writing memos and selecting certain types of words to use.

Using colleagues and supervisors as models is also helpful. Who in the agency has a reputation for clear communication and exceptional reports? You can identify what formats and phrases these people use and incorporate them into your own writing style. Targeting people working with similar client populations and having similar jobs to yours is especially helpful. Typically, they will focus on similar issues and use the same professional jargon that is relevant to you.

Highlight 16.3 summarizes some basic writing suggestions. Additionally, please have a dictionary and thesaurus on hand. These resources are useful for any

HIGHLIGHT 16.3

Some Basic Good Writing Suggestions

- Choose your words carefully. Write exactly what you mean. Every word should be there for a good reason.
- Avoid slang. It is unprofessional. Use "young men" or "boys" instead of "guys." Use "mother" instead of "mom." Instead of a term like "fizzled out," use "didn't succeed" or something similar.
- Avoid words such as "always," "average," "perfect," or "all." These words can be unclear and misleading.
- Avoid sexist language. Use "Ms." instead of "Mrs." Use "woman" instead of "lady." Use "homemaker" or "woman who does not work outside of the home" instead of "housewife." Do not call adult women "girls."
- Avoid labeling people with terms such as "sleazy," "strange," "punks," "slobs," or "low class."
- Do not abbreviate. Some people may not understand abbreviations. You can spell the term out the first time and put the abbreviation in parenthesis right after it. Thereafter, you can just use the abbreviation. For example, "The National Association of Social Workers (NASW) is the major professional organization for social work practitioners. NASW provides members with a journal and newspaper focusing on current practice issues."

- Be concise. Determine if a sentence could use fewer words. Consider dividing long sentences into two or more smaller ones.
- Use paragraphs to divide content into different topics, points, or issues. A solid page of text without paragraph breaks is hard to read. Each paragraph should have a unifying theme. Avoid using one-sentence paragraphs.
- Distinguish between verified facts and your impression of the facts. Examples of ways to phrase your impressions include "My impression is . . . ," "It appears that . . . ," or "It seems that. . . . "
- Proofread your written products before they go out (Lehman & DuFrene, 2011). Failure to do so can ruin the impact of your message. Consider the social worker whose letter to another professional raised the problem of "drive-by-shooings" and the need for her adolescent client to "absent himself from sex." Clearly, this letter was not proofread before it went out.

Source: These suggestions were taken from those presented in K. K. Kirst-Ashman, C. Zastrow, & V. Vogel (2001), *Student Manual of Classroom Exercises and Study Guide for Understanding Human Behavior and the Social Environment* (5th ed.), Belmont, CA: Wadsworth, pp. 19–20.

type of writing. Finally, a manual of style can be helpful. How often do you forget if a comma should be used or not, or how a reference should be listed? One commonly used manual is the *Publication Manual of the American Psychological Association* (2010b). There are a number of others, any of which you can use to make your style consistent.

LO 16-7 Examine Privacy Principles with Respect to Recording

EP 2.1.2b

When information is formally recorded about clients, several ethical issues emerge. Although Chapter 11 discusses this more thoroughly, we will briefly approach it here. We have established that privacy and confidentiality are important ethical principles in social work practice (NASW, 2008, 1.07).

Kagle (2008) identifies five "privacy principles" that relate to what should be recorded about clients and who should have access to this information: "confidentiality, abridgment, access, anonymity, and security" (2008, p. 224).

Confidentiality is the ethical principle that workers should not share information provided by a client or about a client unless the client has given explicit permission to do so. Chapter 11 establishes that, superficially, the issue may seem simple. What you write about a client should remain confidential, right? But should the client have the right to see what you have written? What if you have recorded some negative things about the client? Should your supervisor be allowed to read what you have written to provide direction and oversee agency operations? What about the information you share at treatment conferences? How confidential does it remain then? What if a client tells you he is sexually abusing his 9-year-old daughter but specifies that you are not to tell anyone else? What happens in states (e.g., Wisconsin) where professionals are legally *required* to report even *suspicions* of such abuse? Highlight 16.2 discussed confidentiality within the context of electronic record keeping.

In situations such as these, the other four privacy principles come into play. *Abridgment* refers to restricting the type of information that is put into the record and the period of time over which the record can be retained. Agency policies and legal restrictions vary drastically from state to state regarding these two issues. Thus, no clear-cut generalization regarding what you should do can be made here. However, you can note that abridgment serves to enhance a client's

privacy. For example, only information pertinent to the services the client is receiving may be recorded. Highly personal information not relating to services received may be omitted. Likewise, agencies or laws may specify how long such records may be kept. For instance, an agency might require that the record be disposed of 6 months following case termination. This requirement protects clients' privacy to some extent by not allowing access to their records indefinitely.

Access refers to the client's right to see what and how information is being recorded. As with abridgment, client access to records varies widely from state to state and agency to agency. Why might you not feel free to share with your clients everything you write about them? Does not such sharing enhance client trust and client–worker communication? One issue involves the concern that clients may see information provided confidentially by others that is included in the record. Another matter involves how clients reading their records might have difficulty comprehending or may resent what is said.

Anonymity refers to using recorded information about clients but omitting identifying data. For example, an agency can evaluate its effectiveness of service provision by analyzing information gathered anonymously on all its clientele. No particular case need be identified as a specific individual or family. Or when educating staff or students, specific identifying information such as names and addresses can simply be blocked out in the record. Such cases can still be used as examples and as training cases. In these instances, names are irrelevant.

"*Security* protects privacy through a system of administrative policies and procedures, and physical and technical safeguards, that prevent unwarranted access to records and unauthorized release of or tampering with the personal information they contain. In fact, efforts to protect privacy via confidentiality, abridgment, access, and anonymity are useless if records and their contents are not kept secure. Due to continuing advances in technology and ongoing threats to records security, agency policies, procedures, and practices need continual review and revision" (Kagle & Kopels, 2008, p. 226).

Kagle (1991) summarizes the essence of the dilemma by stating that "the goal of social work should be to maximize client privacy while meeting the necessary demands of accountability" (p. 180). Accountability refers to being answerable to the community and to your clients for the competent, effective provision of the services you say you are providing. In order to be

LUTHERAN FAMILY AND CHILDREN'S SEVICES OF MISSOURI

RELEASE OF CONFIDENTIAL CLIENT INFORMATION

I,_____, authorize and request Lutheran Family and Children's Services
(Client, Parent, Guardian)
of Missouri and its authorized employees, agents, and/or representatives to release information concerning

me and/or_____

to: _____
(Name, Address)
and/or authorize and request _____ to release
information to LFCS and its authorized employees. *(Name, Address)*

The purpose of this information is: _____ Medical _____ Legal _____ Social _____ Continuity of Care _____ Other

_____

The specific information to be disclosed is:

_____ Evaluation _____ Social/Educational _____ Medical _____ Psychotherapy Progress Notes/Summary _____ All other

_____

My signature, below, acknowledges my understanding and authorization for the following:

1. This consent to release information is subject to revocation by me, at any time, by giving LFCS and

    _____ written notification that my consent is formally revoked.
    Any actions taken before revocation will not be affected.

2. This consent to release information is for:

    _____ *One time, only--(Not to exceed 90 days from signature date)*

    _____ *Time-limited period--beginning _____ and ending _____.*
    (Not to exceed 1 year from signature date)

3. I hereby release any person, firm, physician, clinic, hospital, or agency, public or private, from any liability
    for information furnished pursuant to this authorization.

4. I understand that LFCS will not re-release any information received as a result of this Authorization without
    my written permission.

5. I understand that if the recipient of this information is not a health care provider or health plan under the
    Federal Privacy Rule, my personal health information used or disclosed as described above may not be
    covered under the Privacy Act and may be re-disclosed without my permission.

6. I understand that I have the right to receive a copy of this authorization.

_____   _____
(Client's Signature)   *(Date)*

_____   _____
(Address)   *(City & State)*   *(Zip)*

_____   _____
(Signature of Parent or Legal Guardian)   *(Date)*

_____   _____
(Witness)   *(Date)*

Please send information requested by this release to_____ at the LFCS address checked below:
(Name of Worker)

_____ **Elm Point Early Childhood Center**	_____ **LFCS–Southeast Missouri Office**	_____ **LFCS–Mid-Missouri Office**
3601 Mueller Road	3178 Blattner	401 West Blvd., North
St. Charles, MO 63301	**Cape Girardeau,** MO 63703	**Columbia,** MO 65203
_____ **Hilltop Day Care**	_____ **LFCS–Southwest Missouri Office**	_____ **LFCS–St. Louis Office**
6155 West Florissant	2130 N. Glenstone	8631 Delmar Blvd.,
St. Louis, MO 63136	**Springfield,** MO 65803	**St. Louis,** MO 63124

Information, including _____, released by _____ on _____.

© Cengage Learning

FIGURE 16.14 An Example of a Release-of-Information Form
Source: This form is reprinted with permission of Lutheran Family and Children's Services of Missouri, 8631 Delmar Boulevard, St. Louis, MO 63124.

accountable, you must record some aspects of the intervention process. As we have discussed, the specific aspects vary widely. Legal and agency policies differ drastically regarding what they require to have recorded and how that information should be shared with others. You need to be well informed regarding these rules and restrictions. You then need to make professional decisions regarding how to fulfill your responsibilities for being accountable and yet maximize your clients' right to privacy.

Kagle (1991, 1996) makes several suggestions for achieving this. First, you should seriously consider what information should and should not be kept in the record. What information is necessary to document provision of service and benefit the intervention process? Agency policies that clearly specify what is and is not appropriate can greatly assist workers in making these sometimes difficult decisions.

A second suggestion for enhancing confidentiality of records involves establishing strict policies for access to clients' electronic records and keeping hard-copy files and sources of information "physically safe-guarded from unwarranted access" (Kagle, 1991, p. 181; 1996). Computerized databases need additional safeguards, such as passwords, for limited access. Hard copies of client records may be kept in locked files or rooms or be placed in areas to which only appropriate staff persons have ready access. Regardless of record type, agency staff should be instructed to strictly abide by rules of confidentiality.

A third suggestion for maintaining client confidentiality involves having clearly specified release-of-information forms and procedures. In general, information should only be released when clients are informed and they or their guardians have given their signed consent. Additionally, clients should sign separate release forms for each recipient of the information. An example of a release form is provided in Figure 16.14.

A fourth suggestion for enhancing client confidentiality involves advocating on your clients' behalf, which entails making certain that established client rights are not violated and reporting such breaches when they occur. It also concerns becoming knowledgeable about legal and agency constraints and evaluating their effectiveness in maximizing the protection of your clients' privacy.

Chapter Summary

The following summarizes this chapter's content as it relates to each learning objective (LO) presented at the beginning of the chapter. Chapter content helps prepare students to:

LO 16-1   Recognize the significance of recording in social work.

Social workers use writing for many purposes, including identifying the client and need, documenting services, maintaining case continuity, assisting in interprofessional communication, sharing information with the client, facilitating supervision, monitoring service, educating students, supplying information needed by administration, and providing data for research-informed practice.

LO 16-2   Identify content contained in records.

Information contained in records includes dates of interactions, basic client information, reasons for client contact, details about the problem, aspects of the implementation process, follow-up information, and comments and questions to discuss with a supervisor or other workers.

LO 16-3   Employ a range of recording formats.

Common recording formats include social histories, process recording, use of digital recording, progress notes, narrative recording, summaries of treatment conferences, the problem-oriented record, SOAP, recording progress in groups, letters, e-mails, memos, and meeting agendas and minutes.

LO 16-4   Attend to technological advances in record keeping.

Practitioners should continue updating their knowledge about computer and Internet use. The use of e-mail is examined, including its structure, reasons for use, e-mail composition, the importance of proofreading, and responses to e-mail. Suggestions are provided for how workers can use "netiquette," the term for "polite online interaction" (Guffey & Loewy, 2013, p. 113).

LO 16-5   Strive for confidentiality in electronic record keeping.

The importance of confidentiality in electronic record keeping is stressed. Suggestions for minimizing potential breaches in confidentiality are provided.

LO 16-6   Employ good writing skills in recording.

Good grammar and spelling are essential. Using colleagues and supervisors as models is also helpful. Words used in recording should be chosen carefully. Other suggestions for good writing are offered.

LO 16-7 Examine privacy principles with respect to recording.

"Privacy principles" include "confidentiality, abridgment, access, anonymity, and security" (Kagle, 2008, p. 224). Practitioners should "maximize client privacy while meeting the necessary demands of accountability" (Kagle, 1991, p. 180). Workers should be vigilant concerning confidentiality both with hard-copy records and computerized databases.

Competency Notes

The following identifies where Educational Policy (EP) competencies and practice behaviors are discussed in the chapter.

EP 2.1.1b Practice personal reflection and self-correction to assure continual professional development. *(p. 585):* Process recording provides a means to get feedback from others in order to improve performance. *(p. 587):* Recording sessions digitally or on tape with clients can be used to gain feedback about interpersonal, interviewing, and problem-solving styles.

EP 2.1.1d Demonstrate professional demeanor in behavior, appearance, and communication. *(p. 567):* Professional demeanor can be demonstrated through communication in writing. *(p. 600):* Generalist practitioners should demonstrate professional demeanor when writing professional letters. *(p. 604):* Social workers should demonstrate professional demeanor when communicating with e-mails and memos. *(p. 608):* Practitioners should demonstrate professional behavior and communication when developing agendas and recording meeting minutes. *(p. 615):* Demonstration of good writing skills is an important aspect of professional demeanor and communication.

EP 2.1.1e Engage in career-long learning. *(p. 568):* Social work records can provide an effective means of educating practitioners throughout their careers.

EP 2.1.1f Use supervision and consultation. *(p. 568):* Sharing your records with supervisors, consultants, and others can provide an effective means of getting feedback. *(p. 585):* Practitioners can record questions or issues in records to discuss during supervision or consultation. *(p. 585):* Process recording provides a means for supervisors and others to answer questions and give feedback about a worker's or student's perceptions. *(p. 587):* Supervisors and others can readily provide feedback when viewing or listening to recordings of worker–client interactions.

**EP 2.1.2b Make ethical decisions by applying standards of the NASW *Code of Ethics* and, as applicable, of the International Federation of Social Workers/International Association of Schools of Social Work *Ethics in Social Work, Statement of Principles.* *(p. 613):* In electronic record keeping, social workers should seek to maximize client confidentiality, which is emphasized in the NASW *Code of Ethics,* section 1.07. *(p. 616):* According to the NASW *Code of Ethics,* section 1.07, practitioners should maintain client privacy to the greatest extent possible.

EP 2.1.3 Apply critical thinking to inform and communicate professional judgments. *(pp. 577, 588, 590, 606):* Critical thinking questions are posed.

EP 2.1.3c Demonstrate effective oral and written communication in working with individuals, families, groups, organizations, communities, and colleagues. *(p. 567):* Developing competence in recording skills allows social workers to demonstrate effective written communication in working with individuals, families, groups, organizations, communities, and colleagues. *(p. 567):* Recording provides a written means of communication with colleagues and other professionals. *(p. 600):* Practitioners should write effective professional letters. *(p. 604):* E-mails and memos written by generalist social workers should be effective. *(p. 608):* Workers should accurately and effectively develop agendas and write minutes when recording in meetings. *(p. 615):* Social workers should develop good writing skills to demonstrate effective written communication.

EP 2.1.6 Engage in research-informed practice and practice-informed research. *(p. 568):* Various recording formats are used to collect practice-informed research to apply in research-informed practice.

EP 2.1.6a Use practice experience to inform scientific inquiry. *(p. 568):* Keeping records of service provision can provide guidance for what types of research would be useful to improve practice effectiveness.

EP 2.1.6b Use research evidence to inform practice. *(p. 568):* Keeping records of service provision can provide guidance for what types of research would be useful to improve practice effectiveness.

EP 2.1.9a Continuously discover, appraise, and attend to changing locales, populations, scientific and technological developments, and emerging societal trends to provide relevant services. *(p. 611):*

Practitioners must keep abreast of technological developments to communicate and work effectively. *(p. 613):* Social workers should keep abreast of current legislation concerning confidentiality to protect their clients and serve them most effectively.

EP 2.1.10 Engage, assess, intervene, and evaluate with individuals, families, groups, organizations, and communities. *(p. 588):* Progress notes can assist workers as they assess, intervene, and evaluate with client systems. *(p. 599):* Recording progress in groups can help practitioners engage, assess, intervene, and evaluate with groups and their individual members.

EP 2.1.10a Substantively and affectively prepare for action with individuals, families, groups, organizations, and communities. *(p. 569):* Recording client contact dates, basic client demographic information, reasons for client contacts, and detailed information about clients' problems helps workers prepare for action with clients. *(p. 591):* Treatment conference summaries provide ones means of preparing for action with individuals and families.

EP 2.1.10c Develop a mutually agreed-on focus of work and desired outcomes. *(p. 568):* Sharing records with clients can assist workers in developing a mutually agreed-on focus of work and desired outcomes.

EP 2.1.10d Collect, organize, and interpret client data. *(p. 567):* Recording in social work provides a means of collecting, organizing, and interpreting client data. *(p. 571):* Social histories provide an effective mechanism for collecting, organizing, and interpreting data. *(p. 588):* Progress notes can assist workers in collecting, organizing, and interpreting client data. *(p. 599):* Recording progress in groups can help practitioners collect, organize, and interpret group data.

EP 2.1.10e Assess clients' strengths and limitations. *(p. 591):* Social work records should emphasize the assessment of client strengths whenever possible. *(p. 597):* The proposed problem-oriented recording format includes assessment of both clients' limitations and strengths.

EP 2.1.10f Develop mutually agreed-on intervention goals and objectives. *(p. 568):* Sharing records with clients can facilitate the establishment of mutually agreed-on intervention goals and objectives.

EP 2.1.10g Select appropriate intervention strategies. *(p. 588):* Progress notes can assist workers in understanding clients, monitoring goals, and choosing effective interventions. *(p. 599):* Recording progress in groups can help practitioners select appropriate intervention strategies.

EP 2.1.10h Initiate action to achieve organizational goals. *(p. 568):* Keeping records of service provision and effectiveness can help agencies monitor progress on and achievement of goals.

EP 2.1.10l Facilitate transitions and ending. *(p. 567):* Recording can facilitate transitions as clients require different services or are transferred to different workers.

EP 2.1.10m Critically analyze, monitor, and evaluate interventions. *(p. 568):* Recording information about client progress provides a mechanism for critically analyzing, monitoring, and evaluating interventions. *(p. 588):* Progress notes provide one means of helping practitioners analyze, monitor, and evaluate interventions. *(p. 599):* Recording progress in groups can assist workers in analyzing, monitoring, and evaluating group interventions.

On the Internet

Visit the Understanding Generalist Practice CourseMate at **www.cengagebrain.com** for resources such as web quizzing, glossary, and videos.

Bibliography

Abadinsky, H. (2011). *Drug use and abuse: A comprehensive introduction* (7th ed.). Belmont, CA: Wadsworth.

Abraham, M. (2000). Isolation as a form of marital violence: The South Asian immigrant experience. *Journal of Social Distress and the Homeless, 9,* 221–236.

Abramovitz, M. (2010). Ideological perspectives and conflicts. In J. Blau with M. Abramovitz, *The dynamics of social welfare policy* (3rd ed., pp. 131–188). New York: Oxford.

Abramson, J. (1988). Participation of elderly patients in discharge planning: Is self-determination a reality? *Social Work, 33*(5), 443–448.

Aguilara, D. C., & Messick, J. M. (1974). *Crisis intervention: Theory and methodology* (2nd ed.). St. Louis, MO: C. V. Mosby.

Ai, A. L., Evans-Campbell, T., Aisenberg, G., & Cascio, T. (2006). Diverse sociopolitical reactions to the 9/11 attack and associations with religious coping. *Journal of Religion and Spirituality in Social Work, 25*(2), 19–42.

Alberti, R., & Emmons, M. (2008). *Your perfect right* (9th ed.). Atascadero, CA: Impact.

Alberti, R. E., & Emmons, M. L. (1974). *Your perfect right* (2nd ed.) Atascadero, CA: Impact.

Alexander, G. (2004). Project homeless. In R. F. Rivas & G. H. H., Jr. (Eds.), *Case studies in generalist practice* (3rd ed., pp. 135–141). Belmont, CA: Brooks/Cole.

Alexander, R., Jr. (1997). Social workers and privileged communication in the federal legal system. *Social Work, 42*(4), 387–391.

Allen, G. F. (1995). Probation and parole. In *Encyclopedia of social work* (19th ed., Vol. 3, pp. 1910–1916). Washington, DC: NASW Press.

Alzate, M. M., Andharia, J., Chowa, G. A. N., Weil, M., & Doernberg, A. (2013). Women and leadership in development, planning, organizing, and social change. In M. Weil (Ed.), *The handbook of community practice* (2nd ed., pp. 653–681). Thousand Oaks, CA: Sage.

Amato, P. (2003). The consequences of divorce for adults and children. In A. S. Skolnick & J. H. Skolnick (Eds.), *Family in transition* (12th ed., pp. 190–213). Boston: Allyn & Bacon.

American Association of Sex Educators, Counselors, and Therapists (AASECT). (2000, April). Quick hits: Sex in the news. *Contemporary Sexuality, 34*(4), 6–9.

American Psychiatric Association. (2000). *Diagnostic and statistical manual of mental disorders* (4th ed., text revision) *[DSM-IV-TR]*. Washington, DC: Author.

American Psychiatric Association. (2013). *Diagnostic and statistical manual of mental disorders* (5th ed.) *[DSM-5]*. Washington, DC: Author.

American Psychological Association. (2010a). A guide to beneficial psychotherapy. Division 12, Society of Clinical Psychology. Retrieved from http://www.apa.org/divisions/div12/cppi.html

American Psychological Association. (2010b). *Publication manual of the American Psychological Association* (6th ed.). Washington, DC: Author.

Anderson, K. L., & Umberson, D. (2001). Gendering violence: Masculinity and power in men's accounts of domestic violence. *Gender and Society, 15*(3), 358–380.

Anderson, S. C. (1987). Alcohol use and addiction. In A. Minihan (Editor-in-chief), *Encyclopedia of social work* (18th ed., Vol. 1, pp. 132–192). Silver Spring, MD: National Association of Social Workers.

Anderson-Butcher, D., Khairallah, A. O., & Race-Bigelow, J. (2004). Mutual support groups for long-term recipients of TANF. *Social Work, 49*(1), 131–140.

Andrews, A. B. (2007). *Social history assessment.* Thousand Oaks, CA: Sage.

Apgar, K., & Callahan, B. N. (1980). *Four one-day workshops.* Boston: Resource Communications, Inc.

Atkins-Burnett, S. (2010). Children with disabilities. In P. Allen-Meares (Ed.), *Social work in schools* (6th ed., pp. 157–190). Boston: Allyn & Bacon.

Balgopal, P. R. (2000). Conclusion. In P. R. Balgopal (Ed.), *Social work practice with immigrants and refugees* (pp. 229–240). New York: Columbia.

Bandura, A. (1986). *Social foundations of thought and action: A social cognitive theory.* Englewood Cliffs, NJ: Prentice Hall.

Bandura, A. (2004). Swimming against the mainstream: The early years from chilly tributary to transformative mainstream. *Behaviour Research & Therapy, 42*(6), 613–631.

Bandura, A. (2006). Toward a psychology of human agency. *Perspectives on Psychological Science, 1*(2), 164–180.

Barak, Z., Klein, B., & Proudfoot, J. G. (2009). Defining Internet-supported therapeutic interventions. *Annals of Behavioral Medicine, 38*(1), 4–17.

Barker, R. L. (2003). *The social work dictionary.* Washington, DC: NASW Press.

Barnett, O., Miller-Perrin, C. L., & Perrin, R. C. (2005). *Family violence across the lifespan: An introduction* (2nd ed.). Thousand Oaks, CA: Sage.

Barnett, O. W., Miller-Perrin, C. L., & Perrin, R. D. (2011). *Family violence across the lifespan: An introduction* (3rd ed.). Thousand Oaks, CA: Sage.

Barret, B., & Logan, C. (2002). *Counseling gay men and lesbians: A practice primer.* Pacific Grove, CA: Brooks/Cole.

Barsky, A. E. (2010). *Ethics and values in social work: An integrated approach for a comprehensive curriculum.* New York: Oxford.

Barusch, A. S. (2012). *Foundations of social policy: Social justice in human perspective* (4th ed.). Belmont, CA: Brooks/Cole.

Baum, N. (2007). Therapists' responses to treatment termination: An inquiry into the variables that contribute to therapists' experiences. *Clinical Social Work Journal, 35*(2), 97–106.

Beckett, C., & Maynard, A. (2005). *Values & ethics in social work: An introduction.* Thousand Oaks, CA: Sage.

Behrman, G., & Reid, W. J. (2005) Posttrauma intervention: Basic tasks. In A. R. Roberts (Ed.), *Crisis intervention handbook* (3rd ed., pp. 291–302). New York: Oxford.

Benard, B. (2006). Using strengths-based practice to tap the resilience of families. In D. Saleebey (Ed.), *The strengths perspective in social work practice* (4th ed., pp. 197–220). Boston: Allyn & Bacon.

Berg, I. K. (1994). *Family based services: A solution-focused approach.* New York: Norton.

Berge, J. M., Law, D. D., Johnson, J., & Wells, M.W. (2010). Effectiveness of a psychoeducational parenting group on child, parent, and family behavior: A pilot study in a family practice clinic with an underserved population. *Families, Systems & Health, 28*(3), 224–235.

Bergen, R. K., & Maier, S. L. (2011). Sexual assault services. In C. M. Renzetti, J. L. Edleson, & R. K. Bergen (Eds.), *Sourcebook on violence against women* (2nd ed., pp. 227–244). Thousand Oaks, CA: Sage.

Berger, A. A. (1993). *Improving writing skills: Memos, letters, reports, and proposals.* Newbury Park, CA: Sage.

Berger, R. M., & Kelly, J. J. (1995). Gay men overview. In *Encyclopedia of social work* (19th ed., Vol. 2, pp. 1064–1075). Washington, DC: NASW Press.

Berliner, L., & Elliott, D. M. (2002). Sexual abuse of children. In J. E. B. Myers, L. Berliner, J. Briere, C. T. Hendrix, C. Jenny, & T. A. Reid (Eds.), *The APSAC handbook on child maltreatment* (2nd ed., pp. 55–78). Thousand Oaks, CA: Sage.

Bernstein, N. (1997, June 12). Personal files via computer offer money and pose threat. *New York Times,* pp. A1, B14, B15.

Berry, M. (2005). Overview of family preservation. In G. P. Mallon & P. M. Hess (Eds.), *Child welfare for the 21st century: A handbook of practices, policies, and programs* (pp. 319–334). New York: Columbia.

Bertolino, B. (2010). *Strengths-based engagement and practice.* Boston: Allyn & Bacon.

Berzon, B. (1988). *Permanent partners: Building gay and lesbian relationships that last.* New York: Plume.

Bisno, H. (1988). *Managing conflict.* Newbury Park, CA: Sage.

Bickel, W. K., & Christensen, D. R., & Marsch, L. A. (2011). A review of computer-based interventions used in the assessment, treatment, and research on drug addiction. *Substance Use and Misuse, 46*(1), 4–9.

Bisno, H. (1988). *Managing conflict.* Newbury Park, CA: Sage.

Bitter, J. R. (2009). *Theory and practice of family therapy and counseling.* Belmont, CA: Brooks/Cole.

Blair, T., & Minkler, M. (2009). Participatory action research with older adults: Key principles in practice. *Gerontologist, 49*(5), 651–662.

Blank, B. T. (2005). Safety first: Playing heed to, and preventing, professional risks. *The New Social Worker, 12*(3), 20–23.

Blau, J., with Abramovitz, M.. (2010). *The dynamics of social welfare policy* (3rd ed.). New York: Oxford. Bloom, L. Z., Coburn, K., & Perlman, J. (1976). *The new assertive woman.* New York: Dell.

Bloom, L. Z., Coburn, K., & Perlman, J. (1976). *The new assertive woman.* New York: Dell.

Blundo, R. (2008). Strengths-based framework. In T. Mizrahi & L. E. Davis (Eds.), *Encyclopedia of social work* (20th ed., Vol. 4, pp. 173–177). Washington, DC: NASW Press.

Boes, M., & McDermott, V. (2005). Crisis intervention in the hospital emergency room. In A. R. Roberts (Ed.), *Crisis intervention handbook* (3rd ed., pp. 543–565). New York: Oxford.

Bogg, D. (2012). *Report writing.* Berkshire, England: Open University Press.

Bonner, B. L. (2004). Expertise in group problem solving: Recognition, social combination, and performance. *Group Dynamics: Theory, Research, and Practice, 8*(4), 277–290.

Bos, H., van Balen, F., Gartrell, N., Peyser, H., & Sandfort, T. (2008). Children in planned lesbian families: A cross-cultural comparison between the United States and the Netherlands. *American Journal of Orthopsychiatry, 78,* 211–219.

Boyle, S. W., Hull, G. H., Jr., Mather, J. H., Smith, L. L., & Farley, O. W. (2009). *Direct practice in social work* (2nd ed.). Boston: Allyn & Bacon.

Bragadóttir, H. (2008). Computer-mediated support group intervention for parents. *Journal of Nursing Scholarship, 40*(1), 32–38.

Brammer, R. (2004). *Diversity in counseling.* Belmont, CA: Thomson Brooks/Cole.

Brandwein, R. A. (1987). Women in macro practice. In *Encyclopedia of social work* (18th ed., Vol. 2, pp. 881–892). Silver Spring, MD: National Association of Social Workers.

Brandwein, R. A. (2008). Women: Overview. In T. Mizrahi & L. E. Davis (Eds.), *Encyclopedia of social work* (20th ed., Vol. 4, pp. 290–298). Washington, DC: NASW Press.

Bransford, C. L. (2006). The exercise of authority by social workers in a managed mental health care organization: A critical ethnography. *Journal of Progressive Human Services, 17*(2), 63–85.

Breitenstein, A. G., & Nagel, D. M. (1997, September 1). Medical "privacy" bill is misnomer. *Record,* p. A18.

Briar, S. (1967). *The current crisis in social casework in social work practice.* New York: Columbia University Press.

Brissett-Chapman, S. (1995). Child abuse and neglect: Direct practice. In *Encyclopedia of social work* (19th ed., Vol. 1, pp. 353–366). Washington, DC: NASW Press.

Brody, R. (2005). *Effectively managing human service organizations* (3rd ed.). Thousand Oaks, CA: Sage.

Brown, D., Reyes, S., Brown, B., & Gonzenbach, M. (2012). The effectiveness of group treatment for female adult incest survivors. *Journal of Child Sexual Abuse, 22*(2), 143–152.

Brown, S. (2013, March 28). Supreme Court reviews gay marriage. The Daily Tar Heel. Retrieved from http://www.dailytarheel.com/article/2013/03/gay-marriage-reviewed#print

Brownstein, A.L. (2003). Biased predecision processing. *Psychological Bulletin, 129*(4), 545–568.

Burack-Weiss, A. (2012). Writing in the field of aging. In W. Green & B. L. Simon (Eds.), *The Columbia guide to social work writing* (pp. 276–291). New York: Columbia University Press.

Bureau of Indian Affairs. (2013). FAQs. Retrieved from http://www.bia.gov/FAQs/index.htm

Burgess, A. W., & Holmstrom, L. L. (1974). *Rape: Victims of crisis.* Bowie, MD: Robert J. Brady.

Burstow, B. (1992). *Radical feminist therapy: Working in the context of violence.* Newbury Park, CA: Sage.

Byrnes, M., Lichtenberg, P.A., & Lysack, C. (2006). Environmental press,, aging in place, and residential satisfaction or urban older adults. *Journal of Applied Sociology/Sociological Practice, 23*(2), 50-77.

Callahan, A., & Inckle, K. (2012). Cybertherapy or psychobabble? A mixed methods study of online emotional support. *British Journal of Guidance and Counseling, 40*(3), 261–278.

Canadian Association of Social Workers. (2005). Code of ethics. Retrieved from http://www.casw-acts.ca

Canda, E. R. (1997). Spirituality. In R. L. Edwards (Ed.), *Encyclopedia of social work, 19th edition supplement* (pp. 299–309). Washington, DC: National Association of Social Workers.

Carroll, J. L. (2013). *Sexuality now: Embracing diversity* (4th ed.). Belmont, CA: Wadsworth.

Carroll, M. M. (1997). Spirituality and clinical social work: Implications of past and current perspectives. *Arete, 22*(1), 25–34.

Carter, E. A., & McGoldrick, M. (1980). *The family life cycle: A framework for family therapy.* New York: Gardner Press.

Carteret, M. (2012). Providing healthcare to Hmong patients and families. *Dimensions of Culture.* Retrieved from http://www.dimensionsofculture.com/2012/01/providing-healthcare-to-hmong-patients-and-families/

CBSnews.com. (2012). Superstorm Sandy slams East Coast, leaving floods, millions without power. Retrieved from http://www.cbsnews.com/8301-201_162-57542332/superstorm-sandy-slams-east-coast-leaving-floods-millions-without-power/

Center for Women in Politics. (2013). Current number of women officeholders. Retrieved from http://www.cawp.rutgers.edu/fast_facts/levels_of_office/Current_Numbers.php

Chang, V., Scott, S, & Decker, C. (2013). *Developing helping skills: A step-by-step approach to competency* (2nd ed.). Belmont, CA: Brooks/Cole.

Chaplin, J. (1988). Never married, single, adolescent parents. In C. Chilman, E. Nunnally, & F. Cox (Eds.), *Variant family forms* (pp. 17–38). Newbury Park, CA: Sage.

Chau, K. L. (1990). A model for teaching cross-cultural practice in social work. *Journal of Social Work Education, 26*(2), 124–133.

Chien, W., Norman, I., & Thompson, D. R. (2006). Perceived benefits and difficulties experienced in a mutual support group for family carers of people with schizophrenia. *Qualitative Health Research, 16*(7), 962–981.

Child Welfare Information Gateway. (2003). Child Protective Services: A guide for caseworkers. Retrieved from https://www.childwelfare.gov/pubs/usermanuals/cps/

Chinman, M., Allende, M., Bailey, P., Maust, J., & Davidson, L. (1999). Therapeutic agents of assertive community treatment. *Psychiatric Quarterly, 70*, 137–162.

Chirewa, B. (2012). Development of a practical toolkit using participatory action research to address health inequalities through NGOs in the UK: Challenges and lessons learned. *Perspectives in Public Health, 132*(5), 228–234.

Clark, E. J., (2013, March). From the chief executive officer: A resilient profession. *NASW News,* p. 3.

Clark, J. L., & Clark, L. (2007). *A handbook for office professionals: How 11.* Mason, OH: South-Western.

Cloud, J. (2005, October 10). The battle over gay teens. *Time,* 43–51.

CNN Library. Same sex marriage fast facts. (2013, October 22). Retrieved on November 3, 2013 from http://www.cnn.com/2013/05/28/us/same-sex-marriage-fast-facts

CNN Library. (2013, November 29). Same sex marriage fast facts. Retrieved on December 2, 2013 from http://www.cnn.com/2013/05/28/us/same-sex-marriage-fast-facts

Coalition (1994). *Talking about disabilities: A guide to using appropriate language.* Nashville, TN: COALITION for Tennesseans with Disabilities.

Cohen, N. A. (1992). The continuum of child welfare services. In N. A. Cohen (Ed.), *Child welfare: A multicultural approach* (pp. 39–83). Boston: Allyn & Bacon.

Cole, R., & Mehran, H. (2008). *What can we learn from privately held firms about executive compensation?* MRPA Paper, #4710. University Library of Munich, Germany. Retrieved from http://www.mpra.ub.uni-muenchen.de/4710/1/MPRA_paper_4710.pf

Collier, H. V. (1982). *Counseling women: A guide for therapists.* New York: Free Press.

Collins, D., Jordan, C., & Coleman, H. (2013). *An introduction to family social work* (4th ed.). Belmont, CA: Brooks/Cole.

Compton, B. R., Galaway, B., & Cournoyer, B. R. (2005). *Social work processes* (7th ed.). Belmont, CA: Brooks/Cole.

Congress, E. P. (1996). Dual relationships in academia: Dilemmas for social work educators. *Journal of Social Work Education, 32*(3), 329–338.

Congress, E. P. (1999). *Social work values and ethics: Identifying and resolving professional dilemmas.* Chicago: Nelson-Hall.

Connaway, R. S., & Gentry, M. E. (1988). *Social work practice.* Englewood Cliffs, NJ: Prentice Hall.

Conroy, K. (2012). Student writing in field education. In W. Green & B. L. Simon (Eds.), *The Columbia guide to social work writing* (pp. 85–97). New York: Columbia University Press.

Corcoran, J. (2008). Direct practice. In T. Mizrahi & L. E. Davis (Eds.), *Encyclopedia of social work* (20th ed., Vol. 2, pp. 31–36). Washington, DC: NASW Press.

Corcoran, K. (1997). Managed care: Implications for social work practice. In *Encyclopedia of social work 1997 supplement* (pp. 191–200). Washington, DC: NASW Press.

Corey, G. (2012). *Theory and practice of group counseling* (8th ed.). Belmont, CA: Brooks/Cole.

Corey, G. (2013). *Theory and practice of counseling and psychotherapy* (9th ed.). Belmont, CA: Brooks/Cole.

Corey, G., Corey, M. S., & Callanan, P. (2011). *Issues and ethics in the helping professions* (8th ed.). Belmont, CA: Brooks/Cole.

Coridan, C., & Connell, C. (2003). *Meeting the challenge: Ending treatment disparities for women of color.* Washington, DC: National Mental Health Association.

Cormier, S., & Hackney, H. (2008). *Counseling strategies and interventions* (7th ed.). Boston: Allyn & Bacon.

Cormier, S., & Nurius, P. S. (2003). *Interviewing and change strategies for helpers: Fundamental skills and cognitive behavioral interventions* (5th ed.). Belmont, CA: Brooks/Cole.

Cormier, S., Nurius, P. S., & Osborn, C. J. (2013). *Interviewing and change strategies for helpers* (7th ed.). Belmont, CA: Brooks/Cole.

Council on Social Work Education (CSWE). (2002). Glossary. In CSWE (Ed.), *Educational policy and accreditation standards.* Alexandria, VA: Author.

Council on Social Work Education (CSWE). (2008). *Educational policy and accreditation standards.* Alexandria, VA: Author.

Cournoyer, B. R. (2011). *The social work skills workbook* (6th ed.). Belmont, CA: Brooks/Cole.

Cournoyer, B. R. (2012). Crisis intervention. In M. Gray, J. Midgley, & S. A. Webb (Eds.), *The SAGE handbook of social work* (pp. 248–263). Thousand Oaks, CA: Sage.

Couture, L. (2012). Loneliness linked to serious health problems and death among elderly. *Activities, Adaptation, & Aging, 36*(3), 266–268.

Cowger, C. (1997). Assessing client strengths: Assessment for client empowerment. In D. Saleeby (Ed.), *The strengths perspective in social work practice* (2nd ed., pp. 59–73). White Plains, NY: Longman.

Cowger, C. D. (1994). Assessing client strengths: Clinical assessment for client empowerment. *Social Work, 39*(3), 262–268.

Cox, E. O., & Parsons, R. J. (1994). *Empowerment-oriented social work practice with the elderly.* Pacific Grove, CA: Brooks/Cole.

Cox, F. M., Erlich, J. L., Rothman, J., & Tropman, J. E. (1987). *Strategies of community organization.* Itasca, IL: Peacock.

Cram, C. M. (2007). *Communicating in business with technology.* Mason, OH: South-Western.

Crooks, R., & Baur, K. (2011). *Our sexuality* (11th ed.). Belmont, CA: Wadsworth.

Crooks, R., & Baur, K. (2014). *Our sexuality* (12th ed.). Belmont, CA: Wadsworth.

Crosson-Tower, C. (2009). *Exploring child welfare: A practice perspective* (5th ed.). Boston: Allyn & Bacon.

Crosson-Tower, C. (2010). *Understanding child abuse and neglect* (8th ed.). Boston: Allyn & Bacon.

Crosson-Tower, C. (2013). *Exploring child welfare: A practice perspective* (6th ed.). Boston: Pearson.

Csikai, E. L., & Chaitin, E. (2006). *Ethics in end-of-life decisions in social work practice.* Chicago: Lyceum.

Cui, J. (2006, May/June). China's cracked closet. *Foreign Policy,* 90–92.

Daft, R. L. (2013). *Organization theory and design* (11th ed.). Mason, OH: South-Western.

Davis, L. V. (1995). Domestic violence. In *Encyclopedia of social work* (19th ed., Vol. 1. pp. 780–789). Washington, DC: NASW Press.

Degangi, G. A., & Kendall, A. (2008). *Effective parenting for the hard-to-manage child: A skills-based book.* New York: Routledge.

DeLeon, G. (1994). Therapeutic communities. In M. Galanter & H. D. Kleber (Eds.), *Textbook of substance abuse treatment.* Washington, DC: American Psychiatric Press.

Delgado, M. (1998). *Social services in Latino communities.* Binghamton, NY: Haworth Press.

DeMaria, R., Weeks, G., & Hoff, L. (1999). *Focused genograms: Intergenerational assessment of individuals, couples, and families.* Philadelphia, PA: Brunner/Mazel.

DeMaria, R. M. (1999). Family therapy and child welfare. In C. W. LeCroy (Ed.), *Case studies in social work practice* (2nd ed., pp. 59–63). Pacific Grove, CA: Brooks-Cole.

Demo, D. H., Allen, K. R., & Fine, M. A. (2000). *Handbook of family diversity.* New York: Oxford University Press.

DePanfilis, D. (2011). Child protection system. In J. E. B. Myers (Ed.), *The APSAC handbook on child maltreatment* (3rd ed., pp. 39–66). Thousand Oaks, CA: Sage.

Derezotes, D. S. (2006). *Spiritually oriented social work practice.* Boston: Allyn & Bacon.

DeRosa, D. M., Smith, C. L., & Hantula, D. A. (2007). The medium matters: Mining the long-promised merit of group interaction in creative idea generation tasks in a meta-analysis of the electronic group brainstorming literature. *Computers in Human Behavior, 23*(3) 1549–1581.

Devore, W., & Schlesinger, E. G. (1999). *Ethnic-sensitive social work practice* (5th ed.). Boston: Allyn & Bacon.

Dietrich, F., Shipherd, A. M., Gershgoren, L., Filho, E. M., & Basevitch, I. (2012). Sport psychology group consultation using social networking web sites. *Psychological Services, 9*(3), 323–324.

Dillard, J. M. (1983). *Multicultural counseling.* Chicago: Nelson-Hall.

Diller, J. V. (2007). *Cultural diversity* (3rd ed.). Belmont, CA: Brooks/Cole.

Diller, J. V. (2011). *Cultural diversity: A primer for the human services* (4th ed.). Belmont, CA: Brooks/Cole.

Disaster work not for everyone. (2001, November). *NASW News,* p. 14.

Dolgoff, R., Harrington, D., & Loewenberg, F. M. (2012). *Ethical decisions for social work practice.* Belmont, CA: Brooks/Cole.

Doron, A., & Kramer, R. (1991). *The welfare state in Israel.* Boulder, CO: Westview Press.

Doweiko, H. E. (2012). *Concepts of chemical dependency* (8th ed.). Belmont, CA: Brooks/Cole.

Downs, S. W., Moore, E., & McFadden, E. J. (2009). *Child welfare and family services: Policies and practice* (8th ed.). Boston: Allyn & Bacon.

Downs, S. W., Moore, E., McFadden, E. J., Michaud, S. M., & Costin, L. B. (2004). *Child welfare and family services: Policies and practice* (7th ed.). Boston: Allyn & Bacon.

Dudley, J. R. (2005). *Research methods for social work.* Boston: Allyn & Bacon.

Dudley, J. R., & Stone, G. (2001). *Fathering at risk: Helping nonresidential fathers.* New York: Springer.

Duffany, A., & Panos, P. T. (2009. Outcome evaluation of a group treatment of sexually abused and reactive children. *Research on Social Work Practice, 9*(3), 291–303.

Duprey, M., McDonnell, C., Paymar, M., Regan, K., & Soderberg, J. (Eds.). (1996). *Coordinated community response to domestic assault cases: A guide for policy development.* Duluth, MN: Domestic Abuse Intervention Project.

Dziegielewski, S. F. (2005a). An introduction to formal diagnostic assessment and documentation. In S. F. Dziegielewski (Ed.), *Understanding substance addictions: Assessment and intervention* (pp. 15–52). Chicago: Lyceum.

Dziegielewski, S. F. (2005b). Understanding substance addictions: An overview. In S. F. Dziegielewski (Ed.), *Understanding substance addictions: Assessment and intervention* (pp. 1–14). Chicago: Lyceum.

Dziegielewski, S. F., Resnick, C., & Krause, N. B. (1996). Shelter-based crisis intervention with battered women. In A. R. Roberts (Ed.), *Helping battered women: New perspectives and remedies* (pp. 159–171). New York: Oxford University Press.

Early, T. J., & GlenMaye, L. F. (2000). Valuing families: Social work practice with families from a strengths perspective. *Social Work, 45*(2), 118–130.

Eaton, Y. M., & Roberts, A. R. (2009). Front line crisis intervention. In A. R. Roberts (Editor-in-chief), *The social workers' desk reference* (2nd ed., pp. 207–215). New York: Oxford.

eBiz/MBA. (2013). Top 15 most popular social networking sites, March 2013. Retrieved from http://www.ebizmba.com/articles/social-networking-websites

Echterling, L. G., Presbury, J. H., & McKee, J. E. (2005). *Crisis intervention: Promoting resilience and resolution in troubled times.* Upper Saddle River, NJ: Pearson.

Egan, G. (2014). *The skilled helper* (10th ed.). Belmont, CA: Brooks/Cole.

Eisenberg, D. T. (2010). Shattering the Equal Pay Act's glass ceiling. *Southern Methodist University Law Review, 63,* 2–64.

Ellison, M. L., & Dunn, E. C. (2006). Empowering and demedicalizing case management practice: Perspectives of mental health consumer leaders and professionals. *Journal of Social Work in Disability and Rehabilitation, 5*(2), 11–17.

Emery, R., Sbarra, D., & Grover, T. (2005). Divorce mediation: Research and reflections. *Family Court Review, 43,* 22–37.

Emmelkamp, P.M. (2011). Effectiveness of cybertherapy in mental health: A critical appraisal. *Studies in Health Technology and Informatics, 167,* 3–8.

Engel-Marder, C. (2003). Breaking the language barrier: A guide to interpreter use. *Social Work Today, 3*(4), 20–22.

Epstein, I. (1981). Advocates on advocacy: An exploratory study. *Social Work Research and Abstracts, 17*(2), 5–12.

Erickson, M. F., & Egeland, B. (2002). Child neglect. In J. E. B. Myers, L. Berliner, J. Briere, C. T. Hendrix, C. Jenny, & T. A. Reid (Eds.), *The APSAC handbook on children maltreatment* (2nd ed., pp. 3–20). Thousand Oaks, CA: Sage.

Evans, D. R., Hearn, M. T., Uhlemann, M. R., & Ivey, A. E. (2008). *Essential interviewing* (7th ed.). Belmont, CA: Brooks/Cole.

Evans, K. M. (2013). Culturally alert counseling with African Americans. In G. McAuliffe & Associates (Eds.), *Culturally alert counseling: A comprehensive introduction* (2nd ed., pp. 125–155). Thousand Oaks, CA: Sage.

Everly, G. S., Jr., Lating, J. M., & Mitchell, J. T. (2005). Innovations in group crisis intervention. In A. R. Roberts (Ed.), *Crisis intervention handbook: Assessment, treatment, and research* (3rd ed., pp. 221–245). New York: Oxford.

Family Center on Technology and Disability (FCTD). (2013). FCTD AT fact sheet series: Assistive technology glossary. Retrieved from http://www.fctd.info/show/glossary

Farone, D. W. (2006). Schizophrenia, community integration, and recovery: Implications for social work practice. *Social Work in Mental Health, 4*(4), 21–36.

Featherstone, B., & Morris, K. (2012). Feminist ethics of care. In M. Gray, J. Midgley, & S. A. Webb (Eds.), *The SAGE handbook of social work* (pp. 341–354). Thousand Oaks, CA: Sage.

Federal Interagency Forum on Aging-Related Statistics. (2012). Older Americans 2012: Key indicators of well-being. Retrieved from http://www.agingstats.gov/agingstatsdotnet/Main_Site/Data/2012_Documents/Docs/EntireChartbook.pdf

Feminist Majority Foundation. (2013). Sexual harassment fact sheet. Retrieved from http://www.eeoc.gov/laws/types/sexual_harassment.cfm

Fetting, M. (2012). *Perspectives on addiction: An integrative treatment model with clinical case studies.* Thousand Oaks, CA: Sage.

Figueira-McDonough, J. (2008). Women: Practice interventions. In T. Mizrahi & L. E. Davis (Eds.), *Encyclopedia of social work* (20th ed., Vol. 4, pp. 290–298). Washington, DC: NASW Press.

Fong, R., & Peralta, F. (1994, March). Family preservation values and services: Cultural sensitivity toward Asian and Hispanic families. Paper presented at the Council on Social Work Education Annual Program Meeting, Atlanta, GA.

Fontes, L. A. (2008). *Child abuse and culture.* New York: Guilford.

Forte, J. A., Franks, D. D., Forte, J. A., & Rigsby, D. (1996). Asymmetrical role-taking: Comparing battered and nonbattered women. *Social Work, 41*(1), 59–73.

Fortune, A. E. (1995). Termination in direct practice. In *Encyclopedia of social work* (19th ed., Vol. 3, pp. 2398–2404). Washington, DC: NASW Press.

Frame, M. W. (2003). *Integrating religion and spirituality into counseling: A comprehensive approach.* Pacific Grove, CA: Brooks/Cole.

Francis, E. A. (2000). Social work practice with African-descent immigrants. In P. R. Balgopal (Ed.), *Social work practice with immigrants and refugees* (pp. 127–166). New York: Columbia.

Frankel, A. J., & Gelman, S. R. (2012). *Case management* (3rd. ed). Chicago: Lyceum.

Fulcher, L. C. (2012). Culturally responsive work with indigenous children and youth. *Reclaiming Children and Youth, 21*(3), 53–57.

Furman, R., & Negi, N. (2010). *Social work practice with Latinos: Key issues and emerging themes.* Chicago: Lyceum.

Furman, R., Negi, N. J., Iwamoto, D. K., Rowan, D., Shukraft, A, & Gragg, J. (2009). Social work practice with Latinos: Key issues for social workers. *Social Work, 54*(2), 167–174.

Gadalla, T. M. (2009). Impact of marital dissolution on men's and women's income: A longitudinal study. *Journal of Divorce & Remarriage, 50*(1), 55–65.

Gallup. (2013). Marriage. Retrieved from http://www.gallup.com/poll/117328/marriage.aspx

Gambrill, E. (1997). *Social work practice: A critical thinker's guide.* New York: Oxford University Press.

Gambrill, E. (1999). Evidenced-based practice: An alternative to authority-based practice. *Families in Society, 80*(4), 341–350.

Gambrill, E. (2006). *Social work practice: A critical thinker's guide* (2nd ed.). New York: Oxford.

Gambrill, E. & Gibbs, L. (2009). *Critical thinking for helping professionals: A skills-related workbook* (3rd ed.). New York: Oxford.

Garvin, C. D., & Cox, F. M. (2001). A history of community organizing since the Civil War with special reference to oppressed communities. In J. Rothman, J. E. Erlich, & J. Tropman (Eds.), *Strategies of community intervention* (6th ed., pp. 65–100). Itasca, IL: Peacock.

Gelman, S. R., Pollack, D., & Weiner, A. (1999). Confidentiality of social work records in the computer age. *Social Work, 44*(3), 243–252.

Gerhart, U. C. (1990). *Caring for the chronic mentally ill.* Itasca, IL: Peacock.

Gibbs, L. (1991). *Scientific reasoning for social workers.* New York: Macmillan.

Gibbs, L., Gambrill, E., Blakemore, J., Begun, A., Keniston, A., Peden, B., & Lefcowitz, J. (1994). A measure of critical thinking about practice. Unpublished paper presented at the fall Conference of the Wisconsin Council on Social Work Education, Stevens Point, WI.

Gibelman, M. (1982). Finding the least restrictive environment. *Practice Digest, 4*(4), 15–17.

Gibelman, M. (1995). *What social workers do.* Washington, DC: NASW Press.

Gibelman, M. (2003). So how far have we come? Pestilent and persistent gender gap in pay. *Social Work, 48*(1), 22–32.

Gidycz, C. A., et al., (2011). Primary prevention of sexual violence. In J. White et al. (Eds.), *Violence against women and children* (Vol. 2, pp. 159–180). Washington, DC: American Psychological Association.

Gilbert, M. C. (2000). Spirituality in social work groups: Practitioners speak out. *Social Work with Groups, 22*(4), 67–84.

Gilbert, M. J. (2008). Transgender people. In T. Mizrahi & L. E. Davis (Editors-in-chief), *Encyclopedia of Social Work* (Vol. 4, pp. 238–241). Washington, DC: NASW Press.

Gilson, S. F., Bricout, J. C., & Baskind, F. R. (1998). Listening to the voices of people with disabilities. *Families in Society: The Journal of Contemporary Human Services, 79*(2), 188–202.

Gingerich, W. J. (2002). Online social work. In A. R. Roberts & G. J. Greene (Eds.), *Social workers' desk reference* (pp. 81–85). New York: Oxford.

Gitlin, L. N., & Lyons, K. J. (2008). *Successful grant writing.* New York: Springer.

GlenMaye, L. (1998). Empowerment of women. In L. M. Gutierrez, R. J. Parsons, & E. O. Cox (Eds.), *Empowerment in social work practice: A sourcebook.* Pacific Grove, CA: Brooks/Cole, 29–51.

Glicken, M. D. (2006). *Learning from resilient people: Lessons we can apply to counseling and psychology.* Thousand Oaks, CA: Sage.

Goldberg, A., & Smith, J. (2011). Stigma, social context and mental health: Lesbian and gay couples across the transition to adoptive parenthood. *Journal of Counseling Psychology, 58,* 139–150.

Goldenberg, H., & Goldenberg, I. (2013). *Family therapy: An overview* (8th ed.). Belmont, CA: Brooks/Cole.

Gordon, T. (1975). *P.E.T. parent effectiveness training.* New York: New American Library.

Gothard, S. (1995). Legal issues: Confidentiality and privileged communication. In *Encyclopedia of social work* (19th ed., Vol. 2, pp. 1579–1584). Washington, DC: NASW Press.

Gotterer, R. (2001). The spiritual dimension in clinical social work practice: A client perspective. *Families in Society, 82*(2), 187–193.

Gottlieb, N. (1987). Sex discrimination and inequality. In *Encyclopedia of social work* (18th ed., Vol. 1, pp. 561–569). Silver Spring, MD: National Association of Social Workers.

Graefe, A., & Armstrong, J. S. (2011). Comparing face-to-face meetings, nominal groups, Delphi and prediction markets on an estimation task. *International Journal of Forecasting, 27*(1), 183–195.

Grant, H. B. (2000). Termination: How families experience the end of family therapy. *Dissertation Abstracts International Section A: Humanities and Social Sciences, 60*(11-A), 4196.

Gray, M. (1995). African Americans. In J. Philleo & F. L. Brisbane (Eds.), *Cultural competence for social workers: A guide for alcohol and other drug abuse prevention professionals working with ethnic/racial communities* (pp. 69–101) Washington, DC: U. S. Department of Health and Human Services.

Gray, M., & Coates, J. (2013). Changing values and valuing change: Toward an ecospiritual perspective in social work. *International Social Work, 56*(3), 356–368.

Green, J. W. (1999). *Cultural awareness in the human services: A multi-ethnic approach* (3rd ed.). Boston: Allyn & Bacon.

Greenberg, J. S., Bruess, C. E., & Conklin, S. C. (2011). *Exploring the dimensions of human sexuality* (4th ed.). Sudbury, MA: Jones and Bartlett.

Greene, R. R., & Conrad, A. P. (2012). Resilience: Basic assumptions and terms. In R. R. Greene (Ed.), *Resiliency: An integrated approach to practice, policy, and research* (2nd ed., pp. 29–62). Washington, DC: NASW Press.

Greene, R. R., & Livingston, N. C. (2002). A social construct. In R. R. Greene (Ed.), *Resiliency: An integrated approach to practice, policy, and research* (pp. 63–93). Washington, DC: NASW Press.

Guffey, M. E., & Loewy, D. (2011). *Business communication: Process & product* (7th ed.). Mason, OH: South-Western.

Guffey, M. E., & Loewy, D. (2013). *Essentials of business communication* (9th ed.). Mason, OH: South-Western.

Guffey, M. E., & Seefer, C. M. (2014). *Business English* (11th ed.). Mason, OH: South-Western.

Gushue, G. V., & Sciarra, D. T. (1995). Culture and families: A multidimensional approach. In J. G. Ponterotto, J. M. Casas, L. A. Suzuki, & C. M. Alexander (Eds.), *Handbook of multicultural counseling* (2nd ed., pp. 586–606). Thousand Oaks, CA: Sage.

Gutierrez, L. M. (2001). Working with women of color: An empowerment perspective. In J. Rothman, J. L. Erlich, & J. E. Tropman (Eds.), *Strategies of community intervention* (6th ed., pp. 209–217). Itasca, IL: Peacock.

Gutiérrez, L. M., Parsons, R. J., & Cox, E. O. (2003). *Empowerment in social work practice.* Mason, OH: Cengage.

Halley, A. A., Kopp, J., & Austin, M. J. (1998). *Delivering human services: A learning approach to practice* (4th ed.). New York: Longman.

Hamilton, G. (1939). Basic concepts in social case work. In Fern Lowry (Ed.), *Readings in social case work, 1920–1938* (pp. 155–171). New York: Columbia University Press.

Hanna, S. M. (2007). *The practice of family therapy: Key elements across models* (4th ed.). Belmont, CA: Brooks/Cole.

Hannam, J. (2012). *Feminism*. Great Britain: Pearson Education Limited.

Hardina, D. (2000). Models and tactics taught in community organization courses: Findings from a survey of practice instructors. *Journal of Community Practice, 7*(1), 5–18.

Harris-Robinson, M. (2006). The use of spiritual-focused caring among working-class black women. *Journal of Religion and Spirituality in Social Work, 25*(2), 77–90.

Hart, S. N., Brassard, M. R., Davidson, H. A., Rivelis, E., Diaz, V., & Binggeli, N. J. (2011). Psychological maltreatment. In J. E. B. Myers (Ed.), *The APSAC handbook on child maltreatment* (3rd ed., pp. 125–144). Thousand Oaks, CA: Sage.

Hartman, A. (1970). To think about the unthinkable. *Social Casework, 51*(8), 467–474.

Hartman, A. (1978). Diagrammatic assessment of family relationships. *Social Casework, 59*, 465–476.

Harway, M. (1993). Battered women: Characteristics and causes. In M. Hansen & M. Harway (Eds.), *Battering and family therapy: A feminist perspective* (pp. 29–41). Newbury Park, CA: Sage.

Haynes, K. S., & Mickelson, J. S. (2010). *Affecting change*. Boston: Allyn & Bacon.

Healy, K., & Mulholland, J. (2012). *Writing skills for social workers* (2nd ed.). Thousand Oaks, CA: Sage.

Helton, L. R., & Jackson, M. (1997). *Social work practice with families: A diversity model*. Boston: Allyn & Bacon.

Hendricks, C. O. (2009). Culturally competent social work practice with immigrant populations. In F. Chang-Muy & E. P. Congress (Eds.), *Social work with immigrants and refugees: Legal issues, clinical skills, and advocacy* (pp. 65–78). New York: Springer.

Henry, V. E. (2005). Crisis intervention and first responders to events involving terrorism and weapons of mass destruction. In A. R. Roberts (Ed.), *Crisis intervention handbook* (3rd ed., pp. 171–199). New York: Oxford.

Hepworth, D. H., Rooney, R. H., Rooney, G. D., & Strom-Gottfried, G. D. (2013). *Direct social work practice: Theory and skills* (9th ed.). Belmont, CA: Brooks/Cole.

Herek, G., Gillis, R., & Gogan, J. (2009). Internalized stigma among sexual minority adults: Insights from a social psychological perspective. *Journal of Counseling Psychology, 56*, 32–43.

Herlihy, B., & Corey, G. (2005). Feminist therapy. In G. Corey (Ed.), *Theory and practice of counseling & psychotherapy* (7th ed., pp. 338–381). Belmont, CA: Brooks/Cole.

Hernandez, V. R. (2008). Generalist and advanced generalist social practice. In T. Mizrahi & L. E. Davis (Eds.), *Encyclopedia of social work* (20th ed., Vol. 2, pp. 260–268). Washington, DC: NASW Press.

Herrick, J. M. (2008). Social policy: Overview. In T. Mizrahi & L. E. Davis (Eds.), *Encyclopedia of social work* (20th ed., Vol. 4, pp. 61–66). Washington, DC: NASW Press.

Hester, R. K., Delaney, H. D., & Campbell, W. (2012). The college drinker's check-up: Outcomes of two randomized clinical trials of a computer-delivered intervention. *Psychology of Addictive Behaviors, 26*(1), 1–12.

Hildyard, K. L., & Wolfe, D. A. (2002). Child neglect: Developmental issues and outcomes. *Child Abuse & Neglect, 2*(3/4), 679–695.

Hill, A., & Shaw, I. (2011). *Social work and ICT*. London: Sage.

Hines, P. M., Preto, N. G., McGoldrick, M., Almeida, R., & Weltman, S. (1999). Culture and the family life cycle. In B. Carter & M. McGoldrick (Eds.), *The expanded family life cycle: Individual, family, and social perspectives* (3rd ed., pp. 69–87). Boston: Allyn & Bacon.

Ho, D. Y., Fu, W., & Ng, S. M. (2004). Guilt, shame and embarrassment: Revelations of face and self. *Culture and Psychology, 10*(1), 64–84.

Ho, M. K. (1987). *Family therapy with ethnic minorities*. Newbury Park, CA: Sage.

Hodge, D. R. (2005). Developing a spiritual assessment toolbase: A discussion of the strengths and limitations of five different assessment methods. *Health and Social Work, 30*(44), 314–323.

Hoefer, R. (2005). Altering state policy: Interest group effectiveness among state-level advocacy groups. *Social Work, 50*(3), 219–227.

Hogan, M. (2013). *Four skills of cultural diversity competence: A process for understanding and practice* (4th ed.). Belmont, CA: Brooks/Cole.

Holder, W., & Corey, M. K. (1991). *Child protective services risk management: A decision making handbook.* Charlotte, NC: Action for Child Protection.

Holman, A. M. (1983). *Family assessment: Tools for understanding and intervention.* Beverly Hills, CA: Sage.

Homan, M. S. (2011). *Promoting community change: Making it happen in the real world* (5th ed.). Belmont, CA: Brooks/Cole.

Homma-True, R., Greene, B., Lopez, S., & Trimble, J. E. (1993). Ethnocultural diversity in clinical psychology. *Clinical Psychologist, 46,* 50–63.

Hooyman, N. (2012). Older people. In M. Gray, J. Midgley, & S. A. Webb (Eds.), *The SAGE handbook of social work* (pp. 531–546). Thousand Oaks, CA: Sage.

Hooyman, N., & Kiyak, A. (1999). *Social gerontology* (5th ed.). Boston: Allyn & Bacon.

Horton-Ikard, R. (2009). Cohesive adequacy in the narrative samples of school-age children who use African American English. *Language, Speech, & Hearing Services in Schools, 40*(4), 393–402.

Huber, R., Nelson, H. W., Netting, F. E., & Borders, K. W. (2008). *Elder advocacy: Essential knowledge & skills across settings.* Belmont, CA: Brooks/Cole.

Hudson, J., Prestage, G., & Weerakoon, G. (2007). The married men have sex with men study: An outline of findings. Paper presented at the 18th Congress of the World Association for Sexual Health, Sydney, Australia, April 15–19.

Hull, G. H., Jr., & Mather, J. (2006). *Understanding generalist practice with families.* Belmont, CA: Brooks/Cole. Hull, G. H., Ray, J., Rogers, J., & Smith, M. (1992). BPD outcome study report of phase I. *The BPD Forum,* 54–62.

Hunter, S., & Hickerson, J. C. (2003). *Affirmative practice: Understanding and working with lesbian, gay, bisexual, and transgender persons.* Washington, DC: NASW Press.

Hurdle, D. E. (2001). Social support: A critical factor in women's health and health promotion. *Health and Social Work, 26*(2), 72–80.

Hyde, C. (2005). Feminist community practice. In M. Weil (Ed.), *The handbook of community practice* (pp. 360–386). Thousand Oaks, CA: Sage.

Hyde, C. A. (2008). Feminist social work practice. In T. Mizrahi & L. E. Davis (Eds.), *Encyclopedia of social work* (20th ed., Vol. 2, pp. 216–221). Washington, DC: NASW Press.

Hyde, J. S., & DeLamater, J. D. (2011). *Understanding human sexuality* (11th ed.). New York: McGraw-Hill.

Hyde, J. S., & Else-Quest, N. (2013). *Half the human experience: The psychology of women* (8th ed.). Belmont, CA: Brooks/Cole.

Hyman, A., Schillinger, D., & Lo, B. (1995). Laws mandating reporting of domestic violence. Do they promote patient well-being? *Journal of the American Medical Association, 273*(22), 1781–1787.

Iatridis, D. S. (2008). Policy practice. In T. Mizrahi & L. E. Davis (Eds.), *Encyclopedia of social work* (20th ed., Vol. 3, pp. 362–368). Washington, DC: NASW Press.

Institute of Medicine. (2002). *Unequal Treatment: Confronting racial and ethnic disparities in health care.* Washington, DC: Author.

International Association of Schools of Social Work (IASSW). (2013a). About IASSW: Overview. Retrieved from http://www.iassw-aiets.org/about-iassw

International Association of Schools of Social Work (IASSW). (2013b). Ethics in social work: Statement of principles. Retrieved from http://www.iassw-aiets .org/ethics-in-social-work-statement-of-principles

International Federation of Social Workers (IFSW). (2013). Home. Retrieved on May 17, 2013 from http://ifsw.org/

Ivanoff, A., Blythe, B. J., & Tripodi, T. (1994). *Involuntary clients in social work practice: A research-based approach.* New York: Aldine de Gruyter.

Ivey, A. E., & Ivey, M. B. (2008). *Essentials of intentional interviewing: Counseling in a multicultural world.* Belmont, CA: Brooks/Cole.

Ivey, A. E., Ivey, M. B., & Zalaquett, C. P. (2010). *Intentional interviewing & counseling: Facilitating client development in a multicultural society* (7th ed.). Belmont, CA: Brooks/Cole.

Ivey, A. E., Ivey, M. B., & Zalaquett, C. P., with Quirk, K. (2012). *Essentials of intentional interviewing: Counseling in a multicultural world* (2nd ed.). Belmont, CA: Brooks/Cole.

Ivey, S. L., Kramer, E., & Yoshioka, A. M. (2005). Violence against women in the family: Immigrant women and the U.S. health care system. In C. L. Rabin (Ed.), *Understanding gender and culture in the helping process: Practitioners' narratives from global perspectives* (pp. 267–282). Belmont, CA: Brooks/Cole.

Iwamasa, G. Y., Larrabee, A. L., & Merritt, R. D. (1995, August). Are personality disorders ethnically and gender biased? Poster presented at the annual meeting of the American Psychological Association, New York.

Jacobs, M. R. (1981). *Problems presented by alcoholic clients.* Toronto, Ontario, Canada: Addiction Research Foundation.

Jaffee v. Redmond, WL 315 841 (U.S. 1996).

James, R. K., & Gilliland, B. E. (2013). *Crisis intervention strategies* (7th ed.). Belmont, CA: Brooks/Cole.

Janis, I. L. (1982). *Groupthink: Psychological studies of policy decisions and fiascoes* (2nd ed.). New York: Houghton Mifflin.

Jansson, B. S. (2011). *Becoming an effective policy advocate: From policy practice to social justice* (6th ed.). Belmont, CA: Brooks/Cole.

Jansson, B. S. (2014). *Becoming an effective policy advocate: From policy to practice to social justice* (7th ed.). Belmont, CA: Brooks/Cole.

Janzen, C., & Harris, O. (1997). *Family treatment in social work practice* (3rd ed.). Itasca, IL: F. E. Peacock.

Janzen, C., Harris, O., Jordan, C., & Franklin, C. (2006). *Family treatment: Evidence-based practice with populations at risk* (4th ed.). Belmont, CA. Brooks/Cole.

Jayaratne, S., Croxton, T., & Mattison, D. (1997, March). Social work professional standards: An exploratory study. *Social Work, 42*(2), 187–199.

Johnson, D. W. (2009). *Reaching out: Interpersonal effectiveness and self-actualization* (10th ed.). Upper Saddle River, NJ: Merrill.

Johnson, J. L. (2004). *Fundamentals of substance abuse practice.* Pacific Grove, CA: Brooks/Cole.

Johnson, L. C., & Yanca, S. J. (2010). *Social work practice* (10th ed.). Boston: Allyn & Bacon.

Johnston, S. K., Bettenhausen, K., & Gibbons, E. (2009). Realities of working in virtual teams: Affective and attitudinal outcomes of using computer-mediated communication. *Small Group Research, 40*(6), 623–649.

Jones, T. C. (2005). Social work practice with African Americans. In D. Lum (Ed.), *Cultural competence, practice stages, and client systems: A case study approach* (pp. 59–87). Belmont, CA: Brooks/Cole.

Kadushin, A., & Harkness, D. (2002). *Supervision in social work.* New York: Columbia.

Kadushin, A., & Kadushin, G. (1997). *The social work interview: A guide for human service professionals.* New York: Columbia University Press.

Kadushin, A., & Kadushin, G. (2013). *The social work interview* (5th ed.). New York: Columbia University Press.

Kadushin, A., & Martin, J. A. (1988). *Child welfare services* (4th ed.) New York: Macmillan.

Kagle, J. (1991) *Social work records.* Belmont, CA: Wadsworth.

Kagle, J. (1996) *Social work records* (2nd ed.). Prospect Heights, IL: Waveland.

Kagle, J. D. (2008). Recording. In T. Mizrahi & L. E. Davis (Eds.), *Encyclopedia of social work* (20th ed., Vol. 3, pp. 497–498). Washington, DC: NASW Press.

Kagle, J. D., & Giebelhausen, P. N. (1994, March). Dual relationships and professional boundaries. *Social Work, 39*(2), 213–220.

Kagle, J. D., & Kopels, S. (2008). *Social work records* (3rd ed.). Long Grove, IL: Waveland.

Kail, R. V., & Cavanaugh, J. C. (2013). *Human development: A life-span view* (6th ed.). Belmont, CA: Wadsworth.

Kanel, K. (2012). *A guide to crisis intervention* (4th ed.). Belmont, CA: Brooks/Cole.

Kantrowicz, B., & Wingert, P. (2001, May). Unmarried with children. *Newsweek,* pp. 46–48.

Karger, H. J., & Levine, J. (2000). Social work practice with European immigrants. In P. R. Balgopal (Ed.), *Social work practice with immigrants and refugees* (pp. 167–197). New York: Columbia.

Karger, H. J., & Stoesz, D. (2010). *American social welfare policy: A pluralist approach* (6th ed.). Boston: Allyn & Bacon.

Karger, H. J., & Stoesz, D. (2013). *American social welfare policy: A pluralist approach* (Brief ed.). Boston: Pearson.

Karls, J. M., & O'Keefe, M. E. (2009). Person-in-environment system. In A. R. Roberts (Ed.), *The social workers' desk reference* (2nd ed., pp. 371–376). New York: Oxford University Press.

Kaul, R. E., & Welzant, V. (2005). Disaster mental health: A discussion of best practices as applied after the Pentagon attack. In A. R. Roberts (Ed.), *Crisis intervention handbook* (3rd ed., pp. 200–220). New York: Oxford.

Kavanagh, P. S., Robins, S. C., & Ellis, B. J. (2010). The mating sociometer: A regulatory mechanism for mating aspirations. *Journal of Personality and Social Psychology, 99*(1), 120–132.

Kazdin, A. E. (2001). *Behavior modification in applied settings* (6th ed.). Belmont, CA: Wadsworth.

Kazdin, A. E. (2008). *The KAZDIN METHOD for parenting the defiant child.* Boston: Mariner.

Keefe, T., & Maypole, D. E. (1983). *Relationships in social service practice.* Pacific Grove, CA: Brooks/Cole.

Kelly, G. F. (2006). *Sexuality today: The human perspective* (8th ed.). Boston: McGraw-Hill.

Kendall, D. (2013). *Social problems in a diverse society* (6th ed.). Boston: Pearson.

Kim, J. S. (2008). Strengths perspective. In T. Mizrahi & L. E. Davis (Eds.), *Encyclopedia of social work* (20th ed., Vol. 4, pp. 177–181). Washington, DC: NASW Press.

King, J. C. (1981). *The biology of race.* Berkeley: University of California Press.

King, R., Meadows, G., & Le Bas, J. (2004). Compiling a caseload index for mental health case management. *Australian and New Zealand Journal of Psychiatry, 38,* 455–462.

Kirk, G., & Okazawa-Rey, M. (2013). *Women's lives: Multicultural perspectives* (6th ed.). New York: McGraw-Hill.

Kirst-Ashman, K. (1991, March). Feminist values and social work: A model for educating non-feminists. Paper presented at the Council on Social Work Annual Program Meeting, New Orleans, LA.

Kirst-Ashman, K. K. (2011). *Human behavior in the macro social environment: An empowerment approach to understanding communities, organizations, and groups* (3rd ed.). Belmont, CA: Brooks/Cole.

Kirst-Ashman, K. K. (2013). *Introduction to social work and social welfare: Critical thinking perspectives* (4th ed.). Belmont, CA: Brooks/Cole.

Kirst-Ashman, K. K. (2014). *Human behavior in the macro social environment: An empowerment approach to understanding communities, organizations, and groups* (4th ed.). Belmont, CA: Brooks/Cole.

Kirst-Ashman, K. K., & Hull, G. H., Jr. (2012). *Generalist practice with organizations and communities* (5th ed.). Belmont, CA: Brooks/Cole.

Knight, D. K., Broome, K. M., Simpson, D. D., & Flynn, P. M. (2008). Program structure and counselor-client contact in outpatient substance abuse treatment. *Human Services Research, 43*(2), 616–634.

Knox, K. S., & Roberts, A. R. (2009). The social worker in a police department. In A. R. Roberts (Editor-in-chief), *The social workers' desk reference* (2nd ed., pp. 85–94). New York: Oxford.

Kolb, P. J. (2003). *Caring for our elders: Multicultural experiences with nursing home placement.* New York: Columbia.

Kolko, D. J. (2002). Child physical abuse. In J. E. B. Myers, L. Berliner, J. Briere, C. T. Hendrix, C. Jenny, & T. A. Reid (Eds.), *The APSAC handbook on child maltreatment* (2nd ed., pp. 21–54). Thousand Oaks, CA: Sage.

Kondrat, M. E. (2008). Person-in-environment. In T. Mizrahi & L. E. Davis (Eds.), *Encyclopedia of social work* (20th ed., Vol. 3, pp. 348–354). Washington, DC: NASW Press.

Krysik, J. L., & Finn, J. (2007). *Research for effective social work practice.* New York: McGraw-Hill.

Kulwicki, A. D. (2002). The practice of honor crimes: A glimpse of domestic violence in the Arab world. *Issues in Mental Health Nursing, 23,* 77–87.

Lad Lake. (2007). Outreach. From http://www.ladlake .org/programs/outreach.php

Lally, E. M., & Haynes, H. A. (1995). Alaska natives. In *Encyclopedia of social work* (19th ed., Vol. 1, pp. 194–203). Washington, DC: NASW Press.

Landon, P. S. (1995). Generalist and advanced generalist practice. In *Encyclopedia of social work* (19th ed., Vol. 2, pp. 1101–1108). Washington, DC: NASW Press.

Lefley, H. P. (2010). Treating difficult cases in a psychoeducational family support group for serious mental illness. *Journal of Family Psychotherapy, 21*(4), 253–268.

Lehman, C. M., & DuFrene, D. D. (2011). *Business communication* (16th ed.). Mason, OH: South-Western.

Leigh, J. W. (1998). *Communicating for cultural competence.* Boston: Allyn & Bacon.

Levesque, D. A., Ciavatta, M. M., Castle, P. H., Prochaska, J. M., & Prochaska, J. O. (2012). Evaluation of a stage-based computer-tailored adjunct to usual care for domestic violence offenders. *Psychology of Violence, 2*(4), 368–384.

LeVine, E. A., & Sallee, A. L. (1999). *Child welfare: Clinical theory and practice.* Dubuque, IA: Eddie Bowers.

Levitt, J. G., & Craig, J. (2006). *Power tools for business writing.* Mason, OH: South-Western.

Levy, C. S. (1982). *Guide to ethical decisions and actions for social service administrators: A handbook for managerial personnel.* New York: Haworth.

Levy, P. (2002, May 11). Terrorism and social work practice: Memories of terrorism in Israel. Retrieved from http://bpdupdateonline.bizland.com/ bpdupdateonline spring2002/id1.html

Lewis, J. A., Dana, R. Q., & Blevins, G. A. (2011). *Substance abuse counseling* (4th ed.). Belmont, CA: Brooks/Cole.

Lewis, V. J., Dell, L., & Matthews, L. R. (2013). Evaluating the feasibility of goal attainment scaling as a rehabilitation outcome measure for veterans. *Journal of Rehabilitation Medicine, 45*(4), 403–409.

Linhorst, D. M., Eckert, A., & Hamilton, G. (2005). Promoting participation in organizational decision making by clients with severe mental illness. *Social Work, 50*(1), 21–30.

Liptak, A. (2013, June 27). Rulings advance gay marriage. *Milwaukee Journal Sentinel*, 1A.

Little, M., & Estovald, T. (2012). Return on investment: The evaluation of costs and benefits of evidence-based programs. *Psychosocial Intervention, 21*(2), 215–221.

Logan, S. L. M. (2008). Family: Overview. In T. Mizrahi & L. E. Davis (Eds.), *Encyclopedia of social work* (20th ed., Vol. 2, pp. 175–182). Washington, DC: NASW Press.

Lohmann, R. A. (1997). Managed care: A review of recent research. In *Encyclopedia of social work 1997 supplement* (pp. 200–213). Washington, DC: NASW Press.

Long, C. G., Fulton, B., Dolley, O., & Hollin, C. R. (2011). Dealing with feelings: The effectiveness of cognitive behavioural group treatment for women in secure settings. *Behavioural & Cognitive Psychotherapy, 39*(2), 243–247.

Longino, C. F., Jr., & Bradley, D. E. (2005). The demography of productive aging. In L. W. Kaye (Ed.), *Perspectives on productive aging: Social work with the new aged* (pp. 19–36). Washington, DC: NASW Press.

Lott, B. (1994). *Women's lives: Themes and variations in gender learning* (2nd ed.). Pacific Grove, CA: Brooks/Cole.

Lou, V. W. Q., & Zhang, Y. (2006). Evaluating the effectiveness of a participatory empowerment group for Chinese type 2 diabetes patients. *Research on Social Work Practice, 16*(5), 491.

Loue, S. (1998). Defining the immigrant. In S. Loue (Ed.), *Handbook of immigrant health* (pp. 19–36). New York: Plenum Press.

Lum, D. (1999). *Culturally competent practice: A framework for growth and action*. Pacific Grove, CA: Brooks/Cole.

Lum, D. (2004). *Social work practice and people of color: A process-stage approach* (5th ed.). Belmont, CA: Brooks/Cole.

Lum, D. (2007). *Culturally competent practice: A framework for understanding diverse groups and justice issues* (3rd ed.). Belmont, CA: Brooks/Cole.

Lum, D. (2011). *Culturally competent practice: A framework for understanding diverse groups and justice issues* (4th ed.). Belmont, CA: Brooks/Cole.

Macionis, J. J. (2013). *Social problems* (5th ed.). Upper Saddle River, NJ: Pearson.

Mackelprang, R. W., & Salsgiver, R. O. (2009). *Disability: A diversity model approach in human service practice* (2nd ed.). Chicago: Lyceum.

Major, E. (2000, Winter). Self-determination and the disabled adult. *The New Social Worker, 7*(1), 9–16.

Malai, R. (2013, May). NASW forum examines women and poverty. *NASW News, 58*(5), 1, 5.

Malcolm, J. (2008). Heterosexually married men who have sex with men: Marital separation and psychological adjustment. *Journal of Sex Research, 45*, 350–357.

Maluccio, A. N. (1990). Family preservation: An overview. In *Family preservation: Papers from the Institute for Social Work Educators 1990* (pp. 17–28). Riverdale, IL: National Association for Family-Based Services.

Mallon, G. P. (2008). Gay families and parenting. In T. Mizrahi & L. E. Davis (Eds.), *Encyclopedia of social work* (20th ed., Vol. 2, pp. 241–247). Washington, DC: NASW Press.

Managed care curbs backed: Would establish reviews of payment denials. (1998, January). *NASW News*, pp. 1, 10.

Mapp, S. (2008). *Human rights and social justice in a global perspective: An introduction to international social work*. New York: Oxford.

Marett, K., & George, J. F. (2013). Barriers to deceiving other group members in virtual settings. *Group Decision and Negotiation, 22*(1), 89–115.

Markoff, J. (1997, April 4). Patient files turn up in used computer. *New York Times*, p. A14.

Marlow, C. (2011). *Research methods for generalist social work* (5th ed.). Belmont, CA: Brooks/Cole.

Marson, S. M. (2000). Internet ethics for social workers. *The New Social Worker, 7*(3), 19–20.

Marson, S. M., & Brackin, S. B. (2000). Ethical interaction in cyberspace for social work practice. *Advances in Social Work, 1*(1), 27–42.

Martínez-Moreno, E., Zornoza, A., González-Navarro, P., & Thompson, L. F. (2012). Investigating face-to-face and virtual teamwork over time: When does early task conflict trigger relationship conflict? *Group Dynamics: Theory, Research, and Practice, 16*(3), 159–171.

MassResources.Org. (2013). Resources for victims/survivors of domestic violence and sexual assault in Massachusetts. Retrieved from http://www.massresources.org/domestic-violence.html

Masters, W. H., Johnson, V. E., & Kolodney, R. C. (1995). *Human sexuality* (6th ed.). New York: HarperCollins.

Mather, J., & Hull, G. H. (2009). Case management and child welfare. In A. R Roberts (Ed.), *The social workers' desk reference* (2nd ed., p. 765–769). New York: Oxford University Press.

Mather, J., Lager, P. B., & Harris, N. J. (2007). *Child welfare: Policies and best practices* (2nd ed.). Belmont, CA: Brooks/Cole.

Matlin, M. W. (2012). *The psychology of women* (7th ed.). Belmont, CA: Wadsworth.

Mattison, D., Jayaratne, S., & Croxton, T. (2000, Spring). Social workers' religiosity and its impact on religious practice behaviors. *Advances in Social Work, 1*(1), 43–59.

McAdoo, H. (1987). Blacks. In *Encyclopedia of social work* (18th ed., Vol. 1, pp. 194–206). Silver Spring, MD: National Association of Social Workers.

McAnulty, R. D., & Burnette, M. M. (2003). *Fundamentals of human sexuality: Making healthy decisions.* Boston: Allyn & Bacon.

McCammon, S., & Knox, D. (2007). *Choices in sexuality* (3rd ed.). Belmont, CA: Thomson.

McGoldrick, M., Carter, B., & Garcia-Preto, N. (2011). *The expanded family life cycle* (4th ed.). Boston: Allyn & Bacon.

McInnis, K. M. (1990). The Hmong family. In K. M. McInnis, H. E. Petracchi, & M. Morgenbesser (Eds.), *The Hmong in America: Providing ethnic-sensitive health, education, and human services.* Dubuque, IA: Kendall-Hunt.

McInnis-Dittrich, K. (2014). *Social work with older adults* (4th ed.). Boston: Pearson.

McRoy, R. G. (2003). Cultural competence with African Americans. In D. Lum (Ed.), *Culturally competent practice: A framework for understanding diverse groups and justice issues* (2nd ed., pp. 217–237). Pacific Grove, CA: Brooks/Cole.

Meyer, C. H. (1995). Assessment. In *Encyclopedia of social work* (19th ed., Vol. 1, pp. 260–270). Washington, DC: NASW Press.

Meyer, S., & Schwitzer, A. (1999). Stages of identity development among college students with minority sexual orientations. *Journal of College Student Psychotherapy, 13,* 41–65.

Mezey, S. G. (2001). Law and equality: The continuing struggle for women's rights. In S. Ruth (Ed.), *Issues in feminism: An introduction to women's studies* (5th ed., pp. 408–423). Mountain View, CA: Mayfield.

Miley, K. K., O'Melia, M., & DuBois, B. (2011). *Generalist social work practice* (6th ed.). Boston: Allyn & Bacon.

Miller-Perrin, C. L., & Perrin, R. D. (2013). *Child maltreatment: An introduction* (3rd ed.). Thousand Oaks, CA: Sage.

Miltenberger, R. G. (2012). *Behavior modification: Principles & procedures* (5th ed.). Belmont, CA: Wadsworth.

Mish, F. C. (2008). *Merriam-Webster's collegiate dictionary* (11th ed.). Springfield, MA: Merriam-Webster.

Mishna, F., Michalski, J., & Cummings, R. (2001). Camps as social work interventions: Returning to our roots. *Social Work with Groups, 24*(3/4), 153.

Mooney, L. A., Knox, D., & Schacht, C. (2011). *Understanding social problems* (7th ed.). Belmont, CA: Brooks/Cole.

Moore, S. E. (2008). African Americans: Practice interventions. In T. Mizrahi & L. E. Davis (Eds.), *Encyclopedia of social work* (20th ed., Vol. 1, pp. 81–85). Washington, DC: NASW Press.

Morales, J. (1995). Gay men: Parenting. In *Encyclopedia of social work* (Vol. 2, pp. 1085–1095). Washington, DC: NASW Press.

Mor-Barak, M. E., & Wilson, S. (2005). Labor force participation of older adults: Benefits, barriers, and social work interactions. In L. W. Kaye (Ed.), *Perspectives on productive aging: Social work with the new aged* (pp. 61–82). Washington, DC: NASW Press.

Morell, H. E. R, & Myers, M. G. (2009). Group therapy for substance abuse. In L. M. Cohen, F. L. Collins, Jr., A. M. Young, D. E. McChargue, T. R. Lefingwell, and K. L. Cook (Eds.), *Pharmacology and treatment of substance abuse: Evidence- and outcome-based perspectives* (pp. 179–196). New York: Routledge.

Morgan, H. (2009, Summer). Teaching Native American students. *Multicultural Education, 16,* 10–12.

Morgan, P., & Gruber, J. E. (2011). Sexual harassment: Violence against women at work and in schools. In C. M. Renzetti, J. L. Edleson, & R. K. Bergen (Eds.), *Sourcebook on violence against women* (2nd ed., pp. 75–94). Thousand Oaks, CA: Sage.

Morley, H. R. (1997, August 28). Pines patients' records made public. *Record,* p. A1.

Morning, A. (2011). *The nature of race: How scientists think and teach about human difference.* Berkeley, CA: University of California Press.

Morrongiello, B. A., Schwebel, D. C., Bell, M., Stewart, J., & Davis, A. L. (2012). An evaluation of The Great Escape: Can an interactive computer game improve young children's fire safety knowledge and behavior? *Health Psychology, 31*(4), 496–502.

Morrow-Howell, N., & Hasche, L. (2008). Aging: Services. In T. Mizrahi & L. E. Davis (Eds.), *Encyclopedia of social work* (20th ed., Vol. 1, pp. 110–119). Washington, DC: NASW Press.

Moses, A. E., & Hawkins, R. O. (1982). *Counseling lesbian women and gay men: A life-issues approach.* St. Louis, MO: Mosby-Year Book.

Mosher-Ashley, P. M., Bogen, H., Ates, E. F., & Franklin, G. (1996). Placing elderly persons with psychiatric impairments in residential care homes. *Adult Residential Care Journal, 10*(1), 38–53.

Murase, K. (1995). Asian Americans: Japanese. In R. L. Edwards (Editor-in-chief), *Encyclopedia of social work* (Vol. I, pp. 241–249). Washington, DC: NASW Press.

Murphy, Y., Hunt, V., Zajicek, A. M., Norris, A. N., & Hamilton, L. (2009). *Incorporating intersectionality in social work practice, research, policy, and education.* Washington, DC: NASW Press.

Nagata, D. K. (1991). Transgenerational impact of the Japanese American internment: Clinical issues in working with children of former internees. *Psychotherapy, 28*(1), 121–128.

Naleppa, M. J., & Reid, W. J. (2003). *Gerontological social work: A task-centered approach.* New York: Columbia.

NASW Center for Workforce Studies & Social Work Practice. (2011). Social work salaries by gender: Occupational profile. Retrieved from http://workforce.socialworkers.org/studies/profiles/Gender.pdf

National Alliance to End Homelessness. (2013a). The state of homelessness in America 2013. Retrieved from http://www.endhomelessness.org/library/entry/the-state-of-homelessness-2013

National Alliance to End Homelessness. (2013b). Homelessness and mental health: Moving past stereotypes. Retrieved from http://www.endhomelessness.org/blog/entry/homelessness-and-mental-health-moving-past-stereotypes#.UdYZcMrnaM9

National Association of Social Workers (NASW). (2008). *Code of ethics.* Washington, DC: Author.

National Association of Social Workers. (2007). Indicators for the achievement of the NASW standards for cultural competence in social work practice. Washington, DC: Author.

National Association of Social Workers (NASW). (2012). *Social work speaks: National Association of Social Workers policy statements 2012–2014* (9th ed.). Washington, DC: NASW Press.

National Association of Social Workers (NASW). (2013). *NASW standards for social work case management.* Washington, DC: Author.

National Institute on Alcohol Abuse and Alcoholism. (2013). *NIAA recognizes alcohol awareness month.* Washington, DC: National Institute of Health.

National Women's Law Center. (2012). Insecure & unequal: Poverty and income among women and families 2000–2011. Retrieved from http://www.nwlc.org/sites/default/files/pdfs/nwlc_2012_povertyreport.pdf Nelson-Becker, H. B., Nakashima, M., & Canda, E. R. (2003). Spiritual assessment with older adults. Paper presented at the National Gerontological Social Work Conference. Atlanta, GA.

Netting, F. E., Kettner, P. M., McMurtry, S. L. & Thomas, M. L. (2012). *Social work macro practice* (5th ed.). Boston: Allyn & Bacon.

Newman, A., & Ober, S. (2013). *Business communication in person, in print, online* (8th ed.). Mason, OH: South-Western.

Nichols, M. P. (2010). *Family therapy. Concepts and methods* (9th ed.). Belmont, CA: Brooks/Cole.

Nichols, M. P. (2011). *The essentials of family therapy* (5th ed.). Boston: Allyn & Bacon.

Nichols, M. P., & Schwartz, R. C. (2004). *Family therapy: Concepts and methods.* Boston: Allyn & Bacon.

Nichols, W. R. (Ed.). (1999). *Random House Webster's college dictionary.* New York: Random House.

Nimmagadda, J., & Balgopal, P. R. (2000). Social work practice with Asian immigrants. In P. R. Balgopal (Ed.), *Social work practice with immigrants and refugees* (pp. 30–64). New York: Columbia.

Norman, E. (2000). Introduction: The strengths perspective and resiliency enhancement—A natural partnership. In E. Norman (Ed.), *Resiliency enhancement: Putting the strengths perspective into social work practice* (pp. 1–16). New York: Columbia.

North, C. S., & Smith, E. M. (1994). Comparison of white and nonwhite homeless men and women. *Social Work, 39*(6), 639–647.

Northwestern University. (2010). Suggestions for confronting sexual harassment. Retrieved from http://www.northwestern.edu/sexual-harassment/confronting_harassment.pdf

Okun, B. F., & Kantrowitz, R. E. (2008). *Effective helping: Interviewing and counseling techniques* (7th ed.). Belmont, CA: Brooks/Cole.

Okun, B. F., & Suyemoto, K. L. (2013). *Conceptualization and treatment planning for effective helping.* Belmont, CA: Brooks/Cole.

Olesen, S.C., Butterworth, P., Leach, L. S., Kelaher, M. & Pirkis, J. (2013). Mental health affects future employment as job loss affects mental health: Findings from a longitudinal population study. *BMC Psychiatry, 13,* 144.

O'Neill, J. W. (1999, September). Social work turns back to the spiritual. *NASW News,* p. 3.

O'Neill, J. W. (2001a, October). NASW responds to terror attacks. *NASW News,* pp. 1, 10.

O'Neill, J. W. (2001b, November). Red Cross, NASW have pact. *NASW News,* p. 8.

O'Neill, J. W. (2001c, November). Social workers heed call after the attacks. *NASW News,* pp. 1, 8, 10.

Orton, G. L. (1997). *Strategies for counseling with children and their parents.* Pacific Grove, CA: Brooks/ Cole.

Ott, M., et al. (2011). Stability and change in self-reported sexual orientation identity in young people. *Archives of Sexual Behavior, 40,* 519–532.

Pace, P. R. (2010, June). Salary survey released. *NASW News,* 55 (6), 8.

Padgett, D. (2008). Qualitative research. In T. Mizrahi & L. E. Davis (Eds.), *Encyclopedia of social work* (20th ed., Vol. 3, pp. 485–489). Washington, DC: NASW Press.

Papalia, D. E., Olds, S. W., & Feldman, R. D. (2004). *Human development* (9th ed.). Boston: McGraw-Hill.

Papalia, D. E., Olds, S. W., & Feldman, R. D. (2009). *Human development* (11th ed.). Boston: McGraw-Hill.

Parrot, A., & Cummings, N. (2006). *Forsaken females: The global brutalization of women.* Lanham, MD: Rowman & Littlefield.

Parsons, R. J. (2008). Empowerment practice. In T. Mizrahi & L. E. Davis (Eds.), *Encyclopedia of social work* (20th ed., Vol. 2, pp. 123–126). Washington, DC: NASW Press.

Parsons, R. J., & Wicks, R. D. (1994). *Counseling strategies and intervention techniques for the human services* (4th ed.). Boston: Allyn & Bacon.

Patel, N. R. (2007). The construction of South-Asian-American womanhood. *Women and Therapy, 30*(3), 51–61.

Patti, R. J., & Resnick, H. (1980). Changing the agency from within. In H. Resnick & R. J. Patti (Eds.), *Change from within: Humanizing social welfare organizations* (pp. 217–230). Philadelphia: Temple University Press.

Paylor, I., Measham, F., & Asher, H. (2012). *Social work and drug use.* New York: McGraw-Hill.

Peckover, C. A., Vasquez, M. L., Van Housen, S. L., Saunders, J. A., & Allen, L. (2013). Preparing school social work for the future: An update of school social workers' tasks in Iowa. *Children Schools, 35*(1), 9–17.

Pecora, P. J., Whittaker, J. K., Maluccio, A. N., Barth, R. P., & DePanfilis, D., with Plotnick, R. D. (2010). *The child welfare challenge: Policy, practice, and research* (3rd ed.). New Brunswick, NJ: Transaction Publishers.

Pecora, P. J., Whittaker, J. K., Maluccio, A. N., Barth, R. P., & Plotnick, R. D. (2000). *The child welfare challenge: Policy, practice, and research* (2nd ed.). New York: Aldine de Gruyter.

Perez, J. E. (1979). *Family counseling theory and practice.* New York: Van Nostrand Reinhold.

Perkinson, R. R. (2012). *Chemical dependency counseling: A practical guide* (4th ed.). Thousand Oaks, CA: Sage.

Peters, H. (1982). The legal rights of gays. In A. E. Moses & R. O. Hawkins (Eds.), *Counseling lesbian women and gay men: A life issues approach* (pp. 21–26). St. Louis, MO: Mosby-Year Book.

Petrosino, A., Turpin-Petrosino, C., Hollis-Peel, M. E., & Lavenberg, J. G. (2013). "Scared Straight" and other juvenile awareness programs for preventing juvenile delinquency. *Cochrane Database of Systematic Reviews,* 3.

Pfeiffer, D. (2005). The conceptualization of disability. In G. E. May & M. B. Raske (Eds.), *Ending disability discrimination: Strategies for social workers* (pp. 25–44). Boston: Allyn & Bacon.

Piccola, T. D., & Tracy, E. M. (2008). Family preservation and home-based services. In T. Mizrahi & L. E. Davis (Eds.), *Encyclopedia of social work* (20th ed., Vol. 2, pp. 200–206). Washington, DC: NASW Press.

Pietrzak, J., Ramler, M., Renner, T., Ford, L., & Gilbert, N. (1990). *Practical program evaluation.* Newbury Park, CA: Sage.

Pincus, A., & Minahan, A. (1973). *Social work practice: Model and method.* Itasca, IL: Peacock.

Pipes, W. H. (2007). Old-time religion. In H. P. McAdoo (Ed.), *Black families* (4th ed., pp. 101–124). Thousand Oaks, CA: Sage.

Pitter, G. E. (1992, September). Policing cultural celebrations. *FBI Law Enforcement Bulletin, 61*(9), 10–14.

Planty, M., Langston, L., Krebs, C., Berzofsky, M., & Smiley-McDonald, H. (2013, March). Female victims of sexual violence, 1994–2010. Retrieved from http://bjs.gov/content/pub/pdf/fvsv9410.pdf

Polowy, C. I., & Gorenberg, C. (1997). Legal issues: Recent developments in confidentiality and privilege. In *Encyclopedia of social work 1997 supplement* (pp. 179–190). Washington, DC: NASW Press.

Popple, P. R., & Leighninger, L. (2008). *The policy-based profession: An introduction to social welfare policy analysis for social workers* (4th ed.). Boston: Allyn & Bacon.

Popple, P. R., & Leighninger, L. (2011). *The policy-based profession: An introduction to social welfare policy analysis for social workers* (5th ed.). Boston: Allyn & Bacon.

Porter, M., & Haslam, N. (2005). Predisplacement and postdisplacement factors associated with mental health of refugees and internally displaced persons: A meta-analysis. *Journal of the American Medical Association, 294*(5), 602–612.

Postmes, T., Spears, R., & Cihangir, S. (2001). Quality of decision making and group norms. *Journal of Personality and Social Psychology, 80*(6), 918–930.

Potocky, M. (2008). Immigrants and refugees. In T. Mizrahi & L. E. Davis (Eds.), *Encyclopedia of social work* (20th ed., Vol. 2, pp. 441–445). Washington, DC: NASW Press.

Potocky-Tripodi, M. (2002). Effective practice with refugees and immigrants. In A. R. Roberts & G. J. Greene (Eds.), *Social workers' desk reference* (pp. 628–631). New York: Oxford University Press.

Poulin, J. (with Contributors). (2010). *Strengths-based generalist practice: A collaborative approach* (3rd ed.). Belmont, CA: Wadsworth.

Proctor, E. K., & Davis, L. E. (1996). The challenge of racial difference: Skills for clinical practice. In P. L. Ewalt, E. M. Freeman, S. A. Kirk, & D. L. Poole (Eds.), *Multicultural issues in social work.* Washington, DC: NASW Press.

Proctor, E. K., Davis, L. E., & Vosler, N. R. (1995). Families: Direct practice. In *Encyclopedia of social work* (19th ed., Vol. 2, pp. 941–950). Washington, DC: NASW Press.

Quinn, A. E. (1993). Child protective services and intensive family preservation: A primary relationship. In E. S. Morton & R. K. Grigsby (Eds.), *Advancing family preservation practice.* Newbury Park, CA: Sage.

Rabin, C. L. (2005). Gender and culture in the helping process: A professional journey. In C. L. Rabin (Ed.), *Understanding gender and culture in the helping process: Practitioners' narratives from global perspectives* (pp. 9–30). Belmont, CA: Brooks/Cole.

Rabinowitz, P. (2013). Ethical issues in community interventions. *The Community Tool Box.* Retrieved from http://ctb.ku.edu/en/tablecontents/sub_section_main_1165.aspx

Ragg, D. M. (2006). *Building family practice skills: Methods, strategies, and tools.* Belmont, CA: Brooks/Cole.

Raskin, M. S., & Daley, D. C. (1991). Assessment of addiction problems. In M. S. Raskin and D. C. Daley (Eds.), *Treating the chemically dependent and their families* (pp. 22–56). Newbury Park, CA: Sage.

Raven, B. H. (1993). The bases of power: Origins and recent developments, *Journal of Social Issues, 49*(4), 227–251.

Reamer, F. G. (1987). Values and ethics. In *Encyclopedia of social work* (18th ed., Vol. 2, pp. 801–809). Silver Spring, MD: National Association of Social Workers.

Reamer, F. G. (1990). *Ethical dilemmas in social service* (2nd ed.). New York: Columbia University Press.

Reamer, F. G. (1995). Ethics and values. In *Encyclopedia of social work* (19th ed., Vol. 1, pp. 893–902). Washington, DC: NASW Press.

Reamer, F. G. (2006). *Ethical standards in social work: A review of the NASW code of ethics.* Washington, DC: NASW Press.

Reamer, F. G. (2008). Ethics and values. In T. Mizrahi & L. E. Davis (Eds.), *Encyclopedia of social work* (20th ed., Vol. 2, pp. 143–151). Washington, DC: NASW Press.

Reamer, F. G. (2009). *The social work ethics casebook: Cases and commentary.* Washington, DC: NASW Press.

Reid, W., & Epstein, L. (1972). *Task centered casework.* New York: Columbia University Press.

Reid, W., & Epstein, L. (1977). *Task centered practice.* New York: Columbia University Press.

Reid, W. J. (1985). *Family problem solving.* New York: Columbia University Press.

Reisch, M., & Lowe, J. I. (2000). Of means and ends revisited: Teaching ethical community organizing in an unethical society. *Journal of Community Practice, 7*(1), 19–38.

Renz-Beaulaurier, R. (1998). Empowering people with disabilities: The role of choice. In L. M. Gutierrez, R. J. Parsons, & E. O. Cox (Eds.), *Empowerment in social work practice: A sourcebook* (pp. 73–84). Pacific Grove, CA: Brooks/Cole.

Renzetti, C. M., Curran, D. J., & Maier, S. L. (2012). *Women, men, and society* (6th ed.). Boston: Pearson.

Repa, B. K. (2010). FAQ: How can I get a free HIPAA release form? Retrieved from http://www.caring .com/questions/hipaa-release-form

Richardson, V. E. (2009). Clinical social work with older adults. In A. R. Roberts (Editor-in-chief), *The social workers' desk reference* (2nd ed., pp. 939–943). New York: Oxford.

Rietzschel, E. F., Nijstad, B. A., & Storebe, W. (2006). Productivity is not enough: A comparison of interactive and nominal brainstorming groups on idea generation and selection. *Journal of Experimental Social Psychology, 42*(2), 244–251.

Robert, H. M. & others. (2000). *Robert's Rules of Order newly revised* (10th ed.). Cambridge, MA: Perseus Publishing.

Roberts, A. R. (2005a). The ACT model: Assessment, crisis intervention, and trauma treatment in the aftermath of community disaster and terrorism attacks. In A. R. Roberts (Ed.), *Crisis intervention handbook: Assessment, treatment, and research* (3rd ed., pp. 143–170). New York: Oxford.

Roberts, A. R. (2005b). Bridging the past and present to the future of crisis intervention and crisis management. In A. R. Roberts (Ed.), *Crisis intervention handbook* (3rd ed., pp. 3–34). New York: Oxford.

Roberts, A. R. (2008). Crisis intervention. In T. Mizrahi & L. E. Davis (Eds.), *Encyclopedia of social work* (20th ed., Vol. 1, pp. 484–487). Washington, DC: NASW Press.

Roberts, A. R., & Yeager, K. R. (2005). Lethality assessment and crisis intervention with persons presenting with suicidal ideation. In A. R. Roberts (Ed.), *Crisis intervention handbook* (3rd ed., pp. 35–63). New York: Oxford.

Robison, W., & Reeser, L. C. (2000). *Ethical decision making in social work.* Boston: Allyn & Bacon.

Rock, B., & Congress, E. (1999). The new confidentiality for the 21st century in a managed care environment. *Social Work, 44*(3), 253–262.

Roe, D., Dekel, R., Harel, G., Fennig, S., & Fennig, S. (2006). Clients' feelings during termination of psychodynamically oriented psychotherapy. *Bulletin of the Menninger Clinic, 70*(1), 68–81.

Roeder, K. R. (2002, Fall). Practicing with honorable spirit: The use and non-use of spirituality in social work practice. *The New Social Worker,* 11–12.

Roffman, R. A. (1987). Drug use and abuse. In *Encyclopedia of social work* (18th ed., Vol. 1, pp. 477–487). Silver Spring, MD: National Association of Social Workers.

Rompf, E. L., & Royse, D. (1994). Choice of social work as a career: Possible influences. *Journal of Social Work Education, 30*(2), 163–171.

Rosenthal, H. (2000). *Favorite counseling and therapy homework assignments.* Philadelphia: Brunner-Routlege.

Rosenthal, M. S. (2013). *Human sexuality: From cells to society.* Belmont, CA: Wadsworth.

Rotella, E. J. (2001). Women and the American economy. In S. Ruth (Ed.), *Issues in feminism: An introduction to women's studies* (5th ed., pp. 383–397). Mountain View, CA: Mayfield.

Rothman, J. (2007). Multi modes of intervention at the macro level. *Journal of Community Practice, 15*(4), 11–40.

Rothman, J. (2009). An overview of case management. In A. R. Roberts (Ed.), *The social workers' desk reference* (2nd ed., pp. 751–755). New York: Oxford University Press.

Rothman, J. C. (2003). *Social work practice across disability.* Boston: Allyn & Bacon.

Rowe, J. W., & Kahn, R. L. (1998). *Successful aging.* New York: Random House.

Royce, D., Thyer, B. A., & Padgett, D. K. (2010). *Program evaluation* (5th ed.). Belmont, CA: Wadsworth.

Rubin, A., & Babbie, E. (2011). *Research methods for social work* (7th ed.). Belmont, CA: Wadsworth.

Rubin, A., & Babbie, E. (2013). *Essential research methods for social work* (3rd ed.). Belmont, CA: Brooks/Cole.

Rubin, H. J., & Rubin, I. S. (2008). *Community organizing and development.* Boston: Allyn & Bacon.

Ruscio, J. (2006). *Critical thinking in psychology: Separating sense from nonsense* (2nd ed.). Belmont, CA: Wadsworth.

Rzepnicki, T. L., Schuerman, J. R., & Littell, J. H. (1991). Issues in evaluating intensive family preservation services. In E. M. Tracy, D. A. Haapala, J. M. Kinney, & P. J. Pecora (Eds.), *Intensive family preservation services: An instructional sourcebook* (pp. 71–93). Cleveland, OH: Case Western Reserve University.

Saleebey, D. (2013). *The strengths perspective in social work practice* (6th ed.). Boston: Pearson.

Sapiro, V. (2003). *Women in American society: An introduction to women's studies* (5th ed.). Boston: McGraw-Hill.

Satir, V. M. (1972). *Peoplemaking.* Palo Alto, CA: Science and Behavior Books.

Schene, P. (1996). Child abuse and neglect policy: History, models, and future directions. In J. Briere et al. (Eds.), *The APSAC handbook on child maltreatment* (pp. 385–397). Thousand Oaks, CA: Sage.

Schwab, D. P. (1984, June 6–7). Using job evaluation to obtain pay equity. In *Comparable worth: Issue for the 80's: A consultation for the U.S. Commission on Civil Rights, 1,* 83–92. Washington, DC: U.S. Government Printing Office.

Schwaber, F. H. (1985). Some legal issues related to outside institutions. In H. Hidalgo et al. (Eds.), *Lesbian and gay issues: A resource manual for social workers* (pp. 92–99). Silver Spring, MD: National Association of Social Workers.

Segal, U. (2010). United States: The changing face of the United States of America. In U. A. Segal, D. Elliott, & N. S. Mayadas (Eds.), *Immigration worldwide: Policies, practices, and trends* (pp. 29–46). New York: Oxford.

Shaw, S. M., & Lee, J. (2012). *Women's voices: Feminist visions* (5th ed.). New York: McGraw-Hill.

Sheafor, B. W., & Horejsi, C. R. (2006). *Techniques and guidelines for social work practice* (7th ed.). Boston: Allyn & Bacon.

Sheafor, B. W., & Horejsi, C. J. (2012). *Techniques and guidelines for social work practice* (9th ed.). Boston: Allyn & Bacon.

Shebib, B. (2003). *Choices: Counseling skills for social workers and other professionals.* Boston: Allyn & Bacon.

Sheets, J., Wittenstrom, K., Fong, R., James, J., Tecci, M., Baumann, D. J., & Rodriguez, C. (2009). Evidence-based practice in family group decision-making for Anglo, African American and Hispanic families. *Children and Youth Services Review, 31*(11), 1187–1191.

Shi, L. (2006). The successors to Confucianism or a new generation? A questionnaire study of Chinese students' culture of learning English. *Language, Culture and Curriculum, 19*(1), 122–147.

Shireman, J. (2003). *Critical issues in child welfare.* New York: Columbia.

Shulman, L. (2012). *The skills of helping individuals, families, groups, and communities* (7th ed.). Belmont, CA: Brooks/Cole.

Siberski, J. (2003). Home visit safety assessment. *Social Work Today, 3*(14), 18–20.

Sibony, O. (2012). Collaborative strategic planning: Three observations. *McKinsey Quarterly, 2,* 94–97.

Sidell, N. L. (2011). *Social work documentation: A guide to strengthening your case recording.* Washington, DC: NASW Press.

Signorile, M. (2011, January). The bully pulpit. *Advocate,* 22–23.

Simon, B. (1994). *The empowerment tradition in American social work.* New York: Columbia University Press.

Simon, B. L. (2012). Writing in social work in the United States: 1880s to the present. In *The Columbia guide to social work writing* (pp. 3–24). New York: Columbia University Press.

Siporin, M. (1975). *Introduction to social work practice.* New York: Macmillan.

Sisneros, J., Stakeman, C., Joyner, M. C., & Schmitz, C. L. (2008). *Critical multicultural social work.* Chicago: Lyceum.

Sisneros, J. A. (2002). Social work practice with Mexican immigrants: Steps to understanding. *Social Work Today, 2*(18), 13–15.

Smedley, A., & Smedley, B. D. (2005). Race as biology is fiction, racism as a social problem is real: Anthropological and historical perspectives on the social construction of race. *American Psychologist, 60*(1), 16–26.

Social Security Administration. (2013). Disability planner: What we mean by disability. Retrieved from http://www.ssa.gov/dibplan/dqualify4.htm

Society for Human Resource Management. (2013). Equal Pay Act of 1963. Retrieved from http://www.shrm.org/LegalIssues/FederalResources/FederalStatutesRegulationsandGuidanc/Pages/EqualPayActof1963.aspx

Sormanti, M. (2012). Writing for and about clinical practice. In *The Columbia guide to social work writing* (pp. 114–132). New York: Columbia University Press.

Spiegler, M. D., & Guevremont, D. C. (2010). *Contemporary behavior therapy* (5th ed.). Belmont, CA: Wadsworth.

States That Allow Gay Marriage. (2013a). Domestic partnerships. Retrieved from http://statesthatallowgaymarriage.com/

States That Allow Gay Marriage. (2013b). Civil union vs. marriage. Retrieved from http://statesthatallowgaymarriage.com/civil-union-vs-marriage/

Straussner, S. L. A., & Isralowitz, R. (2008). Alcohol and drug problems: Overview. In T. Mizrahi & L. E. Davis (Eds.), *Encyclopedia of social work* (20th ed., Vol. 1, pp. 121–130). Washington, DC: NASW Press.

Strom-Gottfried, K. (2000, May). Ensuring ethical practice: An examination of NASW code violations, 1986–97. *Social Work, 45*(3), 251–261.

Strozier, A. L. (2012). The effectiveness of support groups in increasing social support for kinship caregivers. *Children and Youth Services Review, 34*(5), 876-881.

Sudarkasa, N. (2007). African American female-headed households: Some neglected dimensions. In H. P. McAdoo (Ed.), *Black families* (4th ed., pp. 157–171). Thousand Oaks, CA: Sage.

Summers, N. (2006). *Fundamentals of case management practice*. Belmont, CA: Brooks/Cole.

Sundel, M., & Sundel, S. S. (2005). *Behavior change in the human services: Behavioral and cognitive principles and applications* (5th ed.). Thousand Oaks, CA: Sage.

Tangenberg, K. M. (2005). Faith-based human services initiatives: Considerations for social work practice and theory. *Social Work, 50*(3), 197–206.

Tarasoff v. Board of Regents of the University of California, 17 Cal. 3d 425, 551 (1976).

Taylor, P. (2005). *Diagnosis & treatment of substance-related disorders: The DECLARE model.* Boston: Pearson.

Teruya, C., Longshore, D., Andersen, R. M., Arangua, L., Nyamathi, A., Leake, B., & Gelberg, L. (2010). Health and health care disparities among homeless women. *Women & Health, 50*(8), 719–736.

Texas Workforce Commission. (2004, May 10). Charitable choice bulletin board: Frequently asked questions. Retrieved from http://www.twc.state.tx.us/svcs/charchoice/ccfaq.html

Thomas, E., Darman, J., & Childress, S. (2006, September 4). New Orleans blues. *Newsweek,* 22–36.

Thomas, M. (2004). *Personal village: How to have people in your life by choice, not chance.* Seattle, WA: Milestone Books.

Thomlison, B. (2010). *Family assessment handbook: An introduction and practical guide to family assessment* (3rd ed.). Belmont, CA: Brooks/Cole.

Thompson, C. L., & Rudolph, L. B., (2000). *Counseling children* (5th ed.). Pacific Grove, CA: Brooks/Cole.

Thorman, G. (1982). *Helping troubled families: A social work perspective.* New York: Aldine.

Thornton, S., & Garrett, K. J. (1995). Ethnography as a bridge to multicultural practice. *Journal of Social Work Education, 31*(1), 67–74.

Timberlake, E. M., Farber, M. Z., & Sabatino, C. A. (2002). *The general method of social work practice* (4th ed.). Boston: Allyn & Bacon.

Timberlake, E. M., Farber, M. Z., & Sabatino, C. A. (2008). *The general method of social work practice* (5th ed.). Boston: Allyn & Bacon.

Tobin, S. S. (1991). *Personhood in advanced old age.* New York: Springer.

Toseland, R. W. (1995). Aging: Direct practice. In *Encyclopedia of social work* (19th ed., Vol. 1, pp. 153–159). Washington, DC: NASW Press.

Toseland, R. W., & Rivas, R. F. (2012). *An introduction to group work practice* (7th ed.). Boston: Allyn & Bacon.

Tracy, E. M. (1995). Family preservation and home-based services. In *Encyclopedia of social work* (19th ed., Vol. 2, pp. 973–983). Washington, DC: NASW Press.

Tracy, E. M., Haapala, D. A., Kinney, J. M., & Pecora, P. J. (1991). Intensive family preservation services: A strategic response to families in crisis. In E. M. Tracy, D. A. Haapala, J. M. Kinney, & P. J. Pecora (Eds.), *Intensive family preservation services: An instructional sourcebook* (pp. 1–13). Cleveland, OH: Case Western Reserve University.

Trenholm, C., Devaney, B., Fortson, K., Quay L., Wheeler, J., & Clark, M. (2007). *Impacts of four Title V, Section 510 abstinence education programs: Final report, April 2007.* Princeton, NJ: Mathematica Policy Research, Inc.

Trentham, S., & Larwood, L. (1998). Gender discrimination and the workplace: An examination of rational bias theory. *Sex Roles, 38,* 1–28.

Trevisan, M. S. (2007). Evaluability assessment from 1986–2006. *American Journal of Evaluation, 23*(3), 290–303.

Tripodi, T., & Lalayants, M. (2008). Research: Overview. In T. Mizrahi & L. E. Davis (Eds.), *Encyclopedia of social work* (20th ed., Vol. 3, pp. 512–520). Washington, DC: NASW Press.

Trotter, C. (2006). *Working with involuntary clients: A guide to practice* (2nd ed.). Thousand Oaks, CA: Sage.

Tully, C. T. (1995). Lesbians overview. *Encyclopedia of social work* (19th ed., Vol. 2, pp. 1591–1596). Washington, DC: NASW Press.

Umberson, D., Anderson, K. L., Williams, K., & Chen, M. D. (2003). Relationship dynamics, emotion state, and domestic violence. *Journal of Marriage and Family, 65,* 233–247.

Ünal, S. (2012). Evaluating the effect of self-awareness and communication techniques on nurses' assertiveness and self-esteem. *Contemporary Nurse, 43*(1), 90–98.

United Nations (UN). (1948). Universal declaration of human rights. Adopted December 10, 1948. GA Res. 217 AIII (UN Doc. A/810). Retrieved from http://www.un.org/Overview/rights.html

U.S. Bureau of Labor Statistics. (2013). Persons with a disability: Labor force characteristics—2012. Retrieved from http://www.bls.gov/news.release/disabl.nr0.htm

U.S. Bureau of Labor Statistics. (2011). Highlights of women's earnings in 2010. Retrieved from http://www.bls.gov/cps/cpswom2010.pdf

U.S. Census Bureau. (2009). Facts for features. Retrieved from http://www.census.gov/PressRelease/www/releases/archives/facts_for_features_special_editions/013739.html

U.S. Census Bureau. (2011a). *Statistical abstract of the United States: 2012.* Washington, DC: Author.

U.S. Census Bureau. (2011b). Disability characteristics. 2011 American Community Survey 1-year estimates. Retrieved from http://factfinder2.census.gov/faces/tableservices/jsf/pages/productview.xhtml?pid=ACS_11_1YR_S1810&prodType=table

U.S. Census Bureau. (2012a). *Statistical abstract of the United States: 2012.* Washington, DC: Author.

U.S. Census Bureau. (2012b). *2012 National populations projections: Summary tables.* Washington, DC: Author.

U.S. Census Bureau. (2012c). Factors for features: Anniversary of Americans with Disabilities Act, July 26. Retrieved from http://www.census.gov/newsroom/releases/archives/facts_for_features_special_editions/cb12-ff16.html

U.S. Census Bureau. (2012d). Poverty. Retrieved from http://www.census.gov/hhes/www/poverty/about/overview/index.html

U.S. Census Bureau. (2013). *Poverty rates for selected detailed race and Hispanic groups by state and place: 2007–2011.* Washington, DC: Author.

U.S. Department of Health and Human Services. (2001). *Mental health: Culture, race, and ethnicity—a supplement to Mental Health: A Report of the Surgeon General.* Rockville, MD: U.S. Department of Health and Human Services, Substance Abuse and Mental Health Services Administration, Center for Mental Health Services.

U.S. Equal Employment Opportunity Commission (EEOC) and the U.S. Department of Justice. (1991). *Americans with Disabilities Act Handbook.* Washington, DC: U.S. Government Printing Office.

U.S. Equal Employment Opportunity Commission (EEOC) and the U.S. Department of Justice Civil Rights Division. (2008). *The Americans with Disabilities Act: Questions and answers.* Retrieved from http://www.ada.gov/qandaeng.htm

U.S. Equal Employment Opportunity Commission (EEOC). (2013a). Sexual harassment. Retrieved from http://www.eeoc.gov/laws/types/sexual_harassment.cfm

U.S. Equal Employment Opportunity Commission (EEOC). (2013b). Title VII of the Civil Rights Act of 1964. Retrieved from http://www.eeoc.gov/laws/statutes/titlevii.cfm

U.S. Merit Systems Protection Board (MSPB). (1981). *Sexual harassment in the work place: Is it a problem?* Washington, DC: U.S. Government Printing Office.

USLegal.com. (2013). Comparable worth law and legal definition. Retrieved from http://definitions.uslegal.com/c/comparable-worth/

Van Den Bergh, N. (1995). Feminist social work practice: Where have we been … Where are we going? In N. Van Den Bergh (Ed.), *Feminist practice in the 21st century* (pp. xi–xxxix). Washington, DC: NASW Press.

Van Den Bergh, N., & Cooper, L. B. (Eds.). (1986). *Feminist visions for social work.* Washington, DC: NASW Press.

van Gelderen, L., et al. (2012). Stigmatization associated with growing up in a lesbian-parented family: What do adolescents experience and how do they deal with it? Children and Youth Services Review, doi: 10.1016/j.childyouth.2012.01.048. Retrieved from http://www.nllfs.org/images/uploads/pdf/nllfs-stigmatization.pdf

van Wormer, K., & Davis, D. R. (2013). *Addiction treatment: A strengths perspective* (3rd ed.). Belmont, CA: Brooks/Cole.

Vandello, J. A. (2000). Domestic violence in cultural context: Male honor, female fidelity, and loyalty. *Dissertation Abstracts International: Section B: The Sciences and Engineering, 61*(5-B), 2821.

Vargas, M. G. (2007). An existential approach to Mexican women's ways of coping with domestic violence: An exploratory study. *Dissertation Abstracts International. Section A: Humanities and Social Sciences, 67*(7-A), 2782.

Vasquez, M. J. T. (2003). Ethical responsibilities in therapy: A feminist perspective. In M. Kopala & M. A. Keitel (Eds.), *Handbook of counseling women* (pp. 557–573). Thousand Oaks, CA: Sage.

Velleman, R. (2011). *Counseling for alcohol problems* (3rd ed.). Thousand Oaks, CA: Sage.

Visher, E. B., & Visher, J. S. (1988). Treating families with problems associated with remarriage and step relationships. In C. S. Chilman, E. W. Nunnally, & F. M. Cox (Eds.), *Variant family forms* (pp. 222–244). Newbury Park, CA: Sage.

Vosler, N. K. (1990). Assessing family access to basic resources: An essential component of social work practice. *Social Work, 37*(5), 434–441.

Voss, R. W., Douville, V., Little Soldier, A., & White Hat, A. (1999). Wo'Lakol Kiciyapi: Traditional philosophies of helping and healing among the Lakotas: Toward a Lakota-centric practice of social work. *Journal of Multicultural Social work, 7*(1/2), 73–93.

Walker, L. E. (1979a). *The battered woman.* New York: Harper & Row.

Walker, L. E. (1979b). The battered woman syndrome. In G. T. Holteling, D. Finkelhor, J. T. Kirkpatrick, & M. A. Straus (Eds.), *Family abuse and its consequences.* Newbury Park: Sage.

Walker, L. E. (1999). Psychology and domestic violence around the world. *American Psychologist, 54,* 21–29.

Walker, L. E. (2009). *The battered woman* (3rd ed.). New York: Springer.

Walsh, J. (2009). Clinical case management. In A. R. Roberts (Editor-in-chief), *The social workers' desk reference* (2nd ed., pp. 755–758). New York: Oxford.

Warheit, G. J., Bell, R. A., & Schwab, J. J. (1977). *Planning for change: Needs assessment approaches.* Washington, DC: National Institute of Mental Health Warren, R. B., & Warren, D. E. (1984). How to diagnose a neighborhood. In F. Cox, J. L. Erlich, J. Rothman, & J. E. Tropman (Eds.), *Tactics and techniques of community practice* (2nd ed., pp. 27–40). Itasca, IL: Peacock.

Weaver, J. D. (1995). *Disasters: Mental health interventions.* Sarasota, FL: Professional Resource Press.

Webster, S. A. (1995). Disasters and disaster aid. In R. L. Edwards (Ed.), *Encyclopedia of social work* (19th ed., Vol. 1, pp. 761–771). Washington, DC: NASW Press.

Wegscheider, S. (1981). *Another chance: Hope and health for the alcoholic family.* Palo Alto, CA: Science Behavior Books.

Weick, A., & Chamberlain, R. (2002). Putting problems in their place: Further explorations in the strengths perspective. In D. Saleeby (Ed.), *The strengths perspective in social work practice* (3rd ed., pp. 95–105). Boston: Allyn & Bacon.

Weil, M. (2001). Women, community, and organizing. In J. E. Tropman, J. L. Ehrlich, & J. Rothman (Eds.), *Tactics & techniques of community intervention* (4th ed., pp. 204–220). Belmont, CA: Brooks/Cole.

Weinbach, R. W. (2005). *Evaluating social work services and programs.* Boston: Allyn & Bacon.

Welfel, E. R. (2013). *Ethics in counseling & psychotherapy: Standards, research, and emerging issues* (5th ed.). Belmont, CA: Brooks/Cole.

Wells, S. J. (2008). Child abuse and neglect. In T. Mizrahi & L. E. Davis (Eds.), *Encyclopedia of social work* (20th ed., Vol. 1, pp. 236–240). Washington, DC: NASW Press.

Whitehill, J. M., Webster, D. W., & Vernick, J. S. (2013). Street conflict mediation to prevent youth violence: Conflict characteristics and outcomes. *Injury Prevention, 19*(3), 204–209.

Widom, C. S. (1989). Does violence beget violence? A critical examination of the literature. *Psychological Bulletin, 106,* 3–28.

Williams, E. E., & Ellison, F. (1996). Culturally informed social work practice with American Indian clients: Guidelines for non-Indian social workers. *Social Work, 41*(2), 147–151.

Williams, J. B. W. (2009). Using the *Diagnostic and Statistical Manual of Mental Health Disorders,* fourth edition, text revision. In A. R. Roberts (Ed.), *The social workers' desk reference* (2nd ed., pp. 325–334). New York: Oxford University Press.

Williams, N. R. (2002) Surviving violence: Resiliency in action at the micro level. In R. R. Greene (Ed.), *Resiliency: An integrated approach to practice, policy, and research* (pp. 195–215). Washington, DC: NASW Press.

Williams, N. R., Lindsey, E., Kurtz, P. D., & Jarvis, S. (2001). From trauma to resilience: Lessons from formerly runaway and homeless youth. *Journal of Youth Studies, 4,* 233–253.

Wilson, S., & Rice, S. (2011). Group work with older adults. In G. L. Greif & P. H. Ephross (Eds.), *Group work with populations at risk* (3rd ed., pp. 115–135). New York: Oxford.

Wilson, S. J. (1980). *Recording guidelines for social workers.* New York: Free Press.

Wisconsin Department of Health and Human Services (DHHS). (2010). Association for the Prevention of Family Violence (APFV). Retrieved from http://www.co.walworth.wi.us/Health%20and%20Human%20Services/Intervention/apfv.aspx

Wolf, R., & Johnson, K. (2013, March 26). Supreme Court justices question gay marriage bans. *USA Today.* Retrieved from http://www.usatoday.com/story/news/politics/2013/03/26/supreme-court-same-sex-gays-lesbians-marriage-california-proposition-8/2017597/

Wong, H. Z., Kim, L. I., Lim, D. T., & Morishima, J. K. (1983). The training of psychologists for Asian and Pacific American communities. In J. C. Chunn, P. J. Dunston, & F. Ross-Sheriff (Eds.), *Mental health and people of color* (pp. 23–41).

Wood, D. P., Wiederhold, M. D., Spira, J., School, D., Pyne, J., & Wiederhold, B. K. (2010). Cybertherapy for combat related posttraumatic stress disorder, pain management and physical rehabilitation following stroke. In B. K. Wiederhold (Ed.) *Coping with posttraumatic stress disorder in returning troops: Wounds of war II.* Amsterdam, Netherlands: IOS Press.

Woodman, N. J. (1995). Lesbians: Direct practice. In R. L. Edwards (Editor-in-chief), *Encyclopedia of social work* (19th ed., Vol. 2, pp. 1597–1604). Washington, DC: NASW Press.

Woodside, M., & McClam, T. (2013). *Generalist case management* (4th ed.). Belmont, CA: Brooks/Cole.

Worden, M. (2003). *Family therapy basics* (3rd ed.). Pacific Grove, CA: Brooks/Cole.

Xu, X., Zhu, F., O'Campo, P., Koenig, M. A., Mock, V., & Campbell, J. (2005). Prevalence of and risk factors for intimate partner violence in China. *American Journal of Public Health, 95,* 78–85.

Yarber, W. L., Sayad, B. W., & Strong, B. (2010). *Human sexuality: Diversity in contemporary America* (7th ed.). New York: McGraw-Hill.

Yegidis, B. L., & Weinbach, R. W. (2009). *Research methods for social workers*. Boston: Allyn & Bacon.

Yessian, M. R., & Broskowski, A. (1983). Generalists in human service systems: Their problems and prospects. In R. M. Kramer & H. Specht (Eds.), *Readings in community organization practice* (pp. 180–198). Englewood Cliffs, NJ: Prentice Hall.

Yick, A. G. (2000). Domestic violence beliefs and attitudes in the Chinese American community. *Journal of Social Service Research, 27,* 29–51.

Yoon, D. P. (2006). Factors affecting subject well-being for rural elderly individuals: The importance of spirituality, religiousness, and social support. *Journal of Religion and Spirituality in Social Work, 25*(2), 59–75.

Yoshihama, M. (2002). Breaking the web of abuse and silence: Voice of battered women in Japan. *Social Work, 47*(4), 389–400.

Zastrow, C. H., & Kirst-Ashman, K. K. (2013). *Understanding human behavior and the social environment* (9th ed.). Belmont, CA: Brooks/Cole.

Zhang, W. (2012). Use with care: Culturally incorrect attending can be rude. In A. E. Ivey, M. B. Ivey, & C. P. Zalaquett with K. Quirk (Eds.), *Essentials of intentional interviewing* (p. 76). Belmont, CA: Brooks/Cole.

Zinn, M. B., Eitzen, D. S., & Wells, B. (2011). *Diversity in families* (9th ed.). Boston: Allyn & Bacon.

Zuniga, M. E. (1995). Aging: Social work practice. In *Encyclopedia of social work* (19th ed., Vol. 1, pp. 173–183). Washington, DC: NASW Press.

Name Index

Subject Index

AA (Alcoholics Anonymous), 273, 274
AB design, 300
ABAB design, 301, 302
Abandonment, 242
ABC design, 301, 302
Ableism, 445
Ability, discrimination based on, 447-448
Aboriginal Australians, 56
Abridgment, 616
Absorption basket, 271
Abstinence-only program, 312
Abstinence stage, 278
Abuse. *See* Child maltreatment
Academic deficits, 241, 242
Acceptability of resources, 553
Access, 614, 616
    to clients' records, 401-402
Accessibility, 380, 553
Accountability, 292-293, 616-617
    in family preservation, 380
Accreditation, 6
Acculturation, 77, 269, 356-357, 453
Action group, 233
Action plan, 372-373
Action steps
    definition of, 45
    specifying, 45, 218, 223, 233-235
Action system, 13, 147
Actions, and feminism, 479
Active listening, 348-349
Activities of daily living (ADL), 263-265
Acute phase, 488-489
ADA (Americans with Disabilities Act of
    1990), 426-427, 444-445, 447-448, 530
Adaptation, 14
    concept in empowerment, 266
Addiction, 273
Adequacy and appropriateness of resource,
    553
Ad hoc committees, 97, 114
ADL (Activities of daily living), 263-265
Administration
    ethical responsibilities for, 409
    providing data for, 568
Adult day care, 268
Adult Protective Services, 569
Adult services, 569
Adversaries, assessing, 525

Advocacy, 8, 29
    for African American families, 388
    assessment in, 522-525
    barriers to successful, 522
    for battered women, 498, 499
    case, 134-135, 515, 518
    cause, 133-134, 515-516, 518
    class, 134, 515, 518
    for clients with disabilities, 426-427, 467
    conceptual frameworks related to,
        523-526
    definition of, 4, 29, 129, 133, 479, 514
    dimensions to consider, 523-525
    and empowerment, 517
    evidence-based, 516
    for families, 350
    and feminism, 479
    during follow-up, 326
    and the Generalist Intervention Model,
        515-516
    goals of, 517
    guidelines for, 527
    history of, 518-519
    for human rights and social justice, 29,
        100
    for immigrants, 271
    indicators for, 518
    interventions for, 522
    knowledge required for, 526-529
    legal, 498
    legislative, 268, 529-535. *See also*
        Legislative advocacy
    managed care, 284
    observations about, 284
    for older adults, 267
    for other national origins, 271
    planning in, 525-526
    political, 426-427
    resources for, 521-522, 525-526
    skills in, 516-517, 526-529
    social, 133
    for social and economic justice, 562
    strategies and tactics, 526-529
    targets of, 517-518
Advocate role, 31, 90, 350, 516-517, 540, 549
    in organizational and community change,
        154
    knowledge required by, 520-522

AFDC (Aid to Families with Dependent
    Children), 343
Affilia: Journal of Women and Social Work,
    409-410
Affirmative Action, 459, 509
Affordable Care Act, 111, 283
African-American English, 459
African Americans
    Afrocentricity, 461
    and assessment, 174
    communication patterns, 459
    demographics, 443
    employment, 357
    engaging the family, 388-389
    experiences of, 460-461
    and extended family importance, 460, 470
    families, 387-389
    family experiences, 460
    grandparents as caretakers, 450-451
    importance of churches in, 450, 460
    institutional/individual racism, 459
    intervention, 460-461
    and life cycle adjustments, 341
    macro-level intervention, 461
    mutual goal setting, 389
    past and present assessment, 389, 460
    and poverty, 446, 459, 501, 502
    respect for elders, 470
    social work practice with, 388-389
    and spirituality/church, 388, 470
    strengths of, 387-388
    terms to describe, 459
    working with, 387-389, 459-461
African women, 299
Afrocentricity, 460
Age composition in groups, 108
Age discrimination, 265
Ageism, 28, 42
Agencies
    and advocacy, 519
    characteristics of, 541
    contact persons in, 541
    eligibility criteria for, 540-541
    when part of the problem is the, 130
Agency policies, 17, 130
Agency services, 164, 165
Agendas, 114, 124, 608-609
    example of, 608

653